# COMPANY DIRECTORS

# COMPANY DIRECTORS

## Duties, Liabilities, and Remedies

*Edited by*

SIMON MORTIMORE QC

OXFORD

UNIVERSITY PRESS

# OXFORD
UNIVERSITY PRESS

Great Clarendon Street, Oxford OX2 6DP

Oxford University Press is a department of the University of Oxford.
It furthers the University's objective of excellence in research, scholarship,
and education by publishing worldwide in

Oxford New York

Auckland  Cape Town  Dar es Salaam  Hong Kong  Karachi
Kuala Lumpur  Madrid  Melbourne  Mexico City  Nairobi
New Delhi  Shanghai  Taipei  Toronto

With offices in

Argentina  Austria  Brazil  Chile  Czech Republic  France  Greece
Guatemala  Hungary  Italy  Japan  Poland  Portugal  Singapore
South Korea  Switzerland  Thailand  Turkey  Ukraine  Vietnam

Oxford is a registered trade mark of Oxford University Press
in the UK and in certain other countries

Published in the United States
by Oxford University Press Inc., New York

British Library Cataloguing in Publication Data

Data available

Library of Congress Cataloging in Publication Data

Data available

Typeset by Cepha Imaging Private Ltd, Bangalore, India
Printed in Great Britain
on acid-free paper by
CPI Antony Rowe

ISBN 978–0–19–921778–6

1 3 5 7 9 10 8 6 4 2

# FOREWORD

I first met Simon Mortimore when we were on the same side in a long running saga called *Babanaft International Co SA v Bassatne*, in which he showed a deep knowledge of all matters relating to companies, including their directors, receivership and liquidation. He was in no small degree responsible for the development of the worldwide *Mareva* injunction (now, of course, freezing order) and of what became known as the *Babanaft* proviso.

This book is by any standards a *magnum opus*, running as it does to over 1,100 pages of text, not counting indexes and appendices. It was conceived in the light of the Company Law Reform Bill, now of course the Companies Act 2006, which those much more knowledgeable than me (including Simon) tell me has put company law in a much better state than before. A notable feature of company law is that litigation and case law tend to concentrate on (1) management by directors, breach of directors' duties and remedies for breach, (2) struggle for control of companies and (3) companies' reorganizations. Litigation in the latter two areas invariably results from disagreements about or failings in management by directors. The new Act gives considerable prominence to the functions and duties of directors, including their codification. What better moment for a book about directors?

A glance at the contents shows that even someone as clever and knowledgeable as Simon could not have done it on his own. He has therefore assembled a team of experts, not only from his Chambers at 3–4 South Square, but from specialist barristers in other chambers, solicitors and academics. The result is a comprehensive analysis of the legal principles affecting directors which will be of inestimable value both to directors themselves and their companies and to the army of lawyers, accountants, insolvency practitioners, and academics whose professional lives involve giving advice about corporate matters of every kind.

I predict that, as the years go by *Company Directors* will be as much cited and relied upon in the courts and valued by the judges as, say, *Buckley* or *Gower*. Speaking entirely for myself, as they say in the Court of Appeal, I am confident that this is the first of what will be many editions.

Sir Anthony Clarke MR
Royal Courts of Justice
December 2008

# PREFACE

This book, conceived shortly before the Company Law Reform Bill was presented to Parliament, was intended to be completed at about the time when the new law came into force. The Government's origin full implementation date for the Companies Act 2006, as the Bill became, was 1 October 2008. That was delayed until 1 October 2009, but 1 October 2008 was retained as a feasible and desirable target date for completing this book. It was a desirable date, because by then all the provisions of the Companies Act of most concern to directors would be in force and the subordinate legislation, would either have been made or, at least, published in draft.

In the event 1 October 2008 occurred at a time of unprecedented upheaval in the commercial life of the United Kingdom for reasons far more profound than the coming into force of provisions of Companies Act. On 15 September 2008 Lehman Brothers entered insolvency proceedings in the United States and England. The already fragile confidence in banks and capital markets evaporated. In the days after 1 October the global banking system appeared to be on the verge of collapse. Governments had to take urgent steps to recapitalize banks to restore confidence, but the impact of the banking crisis has spread deeply into the wider economy. It is inevitable that these circumstances will expose improper conduct by directors and improvident corporate transactions. The new provisions of the Companies Act concerning directors' duties will be put to the test as a multitude of claims are made to recover losses.

This book would not have been possible without the efforts of a large team of skilled and experienced contributors supported by expert reviewers. I have been fortunate in being able to call on fifteen of my colleagues at 3–4 South Square to undertake the bulk of the writing. In spite of their heavy professional commitments they performed their tasks with skill, diligence, and enthusiasm. I hope they will forgive me for not mentioning them by name. I am particularly indebted to my other contributors who have provided their specialist expertise: Martin Griffiths QC and Edward Brown of Essex Court Chambers (employment), Stuart Hill and Cary Kochberg, partners at Lovells LLP (insurance), Henry Legge of 5 Stone Buildings (pensions), and Clare Sibson of Matrix Chambers (white collar crime). I was also able to call on the support of distinguished academics. Professor Sarah Worthington, who is an academic member of 3–4 South Square, contributed to Chapters 6, 7 and 8. Professor John Birds gave the benefit of his knowledge and expertise in reviewing Chapters 3, 4, 5, 23 and 24. Lucy Fergusson, a corporate partner at Linklaters LLP and Steven Turnbull (then a corporate partner at Linklaters LLP and now a partner at the London office of Shepherd and Wedderburn) were kind enough to review Chapters 3 to 8 and 23 to 25. Raymond Jeffers, a partner and head of the employment group at Linklaters LLP, reviewed Chapters 6 to 8. I and my contributors are greatly indebted to our reviewers for giving us the benefit of their practical experience and knowledge of the areas of company law covered in these chapters.

Finally I would like to thank my family, Fiona, Laura and Edward, for their support and tolerance of 'the book' which intruded over too many weekends and holidays.

This book attempts to state the law at 1 October 2008. It also describes the new provisions of the Companies Act that will come into force on 1 October 2009.

Simon Mortimore QC
Christmas Eve 2008

# LIST OF CONTRIBUTORS

**Adam Al-Attar**   *Chapter 28 (section D(1)–(4))*
BA (Oxon), BCL; practices at 3–4 South Square, Gray's Inn; specializes in insolvency and company law, banking and financial law and the law of trusts.

**Mark Arnold**   *Chapters 9, 11 (section E), 13, and 14 (section D)*
MA (Cantab) (Downing College), called to the Bar (Middle Temple) 1988; practices at 3–4 South Square, Gray's Inn; specializes in insolvency and reconstruction law, company law, commercial and financial law.

**Edward Brown**   *Chapters 7 and 8 (co-author)*
BA (Cantab), LLM (LSE), MA (Siena); called to the Bar (Lincoln's Inn) 2002; practices at Essex Court Chambers; specializes in employment and commercial law.

**Glen Davis**   *Chapter 28 (sections A–C and section D(5)–(6))*
MA (Oxon), Dip. Law (City), called to the Bar (Middle Temple) 1992; practices at 3–4 South Square, Gray's Inn; specializes in insolvency and reconstruction law, company law, commercial and financial law; called for specific cases to the Gibraltar Bar; Member, Insolvency Rules Committee; Member, Insolvency and Companies Court Users Committee.

**Adam Goodison**   *Chapters 3 and 4*
Called to the Bar (Middle Temple) 1990; practices at 3–4 South Square, Gray's Inn; specializes in insolvency and reconstruction law, company law and commercial law; member of the Bar Council.

**Martin Griffiths QC**   *Chapter 6 (co-author)*
QC, MA (Oxon), Dip. Law (City), called to the Bar (Inner Temple) 1986, QC 2006; practices at Essex Court Chambers, 24 Lincoln's Inn Fields London WC2A 3EG; specializes in employment and commercial law. Member, Bar Council. Committee Member, Employment Law Bar Association.

**Marcus Haywood**   *Chapters 10, 11 (sections A–D), 12, 14 (sections A–C, E, and F), and 15*
Marcus Haywood is a barrister practicing at 3–4 South Square, Gray's Inn. He specializes in all aspects of company law with a particular emphasis on corporate insolvency. He was called to the Bar by Lincoln's Inn in 2002.

**Stuart Hill**   *Chapter 20 (co-author)*
MA (Cantab); solicitor (1993), solicitor advocate (2001); since 2002, Partner in Lovells LLP specializing in insurance and reinsurance litigation.

**Lexa Hilliard**   *Chapter 27*
LLB (LSE), called to the Bar (Middle Temple) 1987; practices at 3–4 South Square, Gray's Inn; specializes in insolvency and reconstruction law, company law, commercial and financial law.

**Barry Isaacs**   *Chapter 29*
Barry Isaacs is a graduate of Oxford and Harvard Universities and is an Associate of the Society of Actuaries. He was called to the Bar of England and Wales in 1994 and the Bar of Bermuda in 1999. He practices at 3–4 South Square, Gray's Inn, specializing in insolvency, company and commercial law.

**Cary Kochberg**   *Chapter 20 (co-author)*
BA (University of Toronto); LLB (Osgoode Hall, Toronto), qualified Canada (1986) and England (1992), Partner in Lovells LLP since 1994 specializing in corporate, commercial, fraud and insolvency litigation.

**Blair Leahy**   *Chapter 19 (co-author)*
BA (York), Dip. Law (City), called to the Bar (Inner Temple) 2001; practices at 3–4 South Square, Gray's Inn; specializes in insolvency, company and commercial law.

**Henry Legge**   *Chapter 26*
BA (Oxon) Dip. Law (City) called to the Bar (Middle Temple) 1993 and for specific cases to the Cayman Bar; practices from 5 Stone Buildings, Lincoln's Inn, specializing in trust and pensions law.

**Simon Mortimore QC**   *Consultant editor, contributor to Chapters 1, 2, 19 (co-author), 21(sections E and F (co-author)), and 22 (co-author)*
LLB (Exon), called to the Bar (Inner Temple) 1972, QC 1991; practices at 3–4 South Square, Gray's Inn; specializes in insolvency and reconstruction law, company law, commercial and financial law; called to the BVI Bar, 1991; accredited CEDR mediator.

**Georgina Peters**   *Chapter 21 (sections A–D; E and F (co-author))*
MA (Cantab) History (Christ's College, Cambridge), called to the Bar (Lincoln's Inn) 2005; practices at 3–4 South Square, Gray's Inn; specializes in international and domestic insolvency and reconstruction law, company law, commercial and chancery law.

**Stephen Robins**   *Chapters 23 and 24*
BA Hons (Oxon), called to the Bar (Lincoln's Inn) 2001; practices at 3–4 South Square, Gray's Inn; specializes in insolvency law, company law and commercial litigation.

**Clare Sibson**   *Chapter 30*
MA (Cantab) (Foundation Scholar, Corpus Christi) called to the Bar 1997; practices at Matrix Chambers; specializes in criminal law.

**Adam Silver**   *Chapter 20 (assistant co-author)*
BA (Oxon); solicitor (2002); senior associate at Lovells LLP, specializing in corporate, commercial, fraud and insolvency litigation.

**Tom Smith**   *Chapters 25 and 31*
MA, LLM (Cantab), called to the Bar (Middle Temple) 1999; practices at 3–4 South Square, Gray's Inn; specializes in banking law, insolvency and reconstruction law, company law, commercial and financial law.

**Lloyd Tamlyn**   *Chapters 17 and 18*
BA (Cantab), called to the Bar (Gray's Inn) 1991; practices at 3–4 South Square, Gray's Inn; specializes in insolvency and reconstruction law, company law, commercial and financial law.

**Hannah Thornley**   *Chapter 22 (co-author)*
MA (Cantab), BCL (Oxon), called to the Bar (Middle Temple) 2003; practices at 3–4 South Square, Gray's Inn primarily in the fields of commercial litigation, corporate and personal insolvency and company law.

**William Willson**   *Chapter 5*
MA (Oxon), CPE (City), called to the Bar (Lincoln's Inn) 2006; practices at 3–4 South Square, Gray's Inn; specializes in commercial law, financial law, company law, and insolvency and reconstruction law.

**Sarah Worthington**   *Chapters 6, 7, and 8 (co-author)*
BSc (ANU), LLB (Qld), LLM (Melb), PhD (Cantab), called to the Bar (Middle Temple) 2005, Professor of Law, LSE and academic member of 3–4 South Square, Gray's Inn; specializes in company law, personal property and commercial equity.

**Antony Zacaroli QC**   *Chapter 16*
BA, BCL (Oxon), called to the Bar (Middle Temple) 1987, QC 2006; practices at 3–4 South Square, Gray's Inn, specializing in insolvency and reconstruction, company, commercial, banking and financial law; called to the BVI Bar, 2004.

# CONTENTS—SUMMARY

## IV DIRECTORS' PARTICULAR FUNCTIONS AND DUTIES

# CONTENTS

## I INTRODUCTION

## II THE OFFICE OF DIRECTOR

### 3. Directors and Other Officers; Requirement and Definitions

### 4. Directors' Powers and Responsibilities

## III THE GENERAL DUTIES OF DIRECTORS

# Contents

## IV DIRECTORS' PARTICULAR FUNCTIONS AND DUTIES

## 22. Decision-Making by Members

## V OTHER LIABILITIES OF DIRECTORS

# VI DIRECTORS OF FOREIGN COMPANIES

# TABLE OF CASES

# TABLE OF LEGISLATION

## PRACTICE DIRECTIONS

## TABLE OF INTERNATIONAL
## TREATIES AND CONVENTIONS

# GLOSSARY

The following table sets out the abbreviations used in this work. Reference should also be made to the Companies Act 2006, Schedule 8[1] which is an index of expressions defined in that Act. In addition the Insolvency Act 1986,[2] the Company Directors Disqualification Act 1986,[3] and the Financial Services and Management Act 2000[4] contain interpretation sections.

| Expression | Meaning |
| --- | --- |
| 1844 Act | The Act for the Registration, Incorporation, and Regulation of Joint Stock Companies (7&8 Vic, c 110) |
| 1844 Winding Up Act | The Act for facilitating the winding up of the Affairs of Joint Stock Companies unable to meet their pecuniary Engagements (7&8 Vic, c 111) |
| 1856 Act | The Joint Stock Companies Act 1856 |
| 1862 Act | The Companies Act 1862 |
| 1908 Act | The Companies (Consolidation) Act 1908 |
| 1929 Act | The Companies Act 1929 |
| 1948 Act | The Companies Act 1948 |
| 1967 Act | The Companies Act 1967 |
| 1980 Act | The Companies Act 1980 |
| 1981 Act | The Companies Act 1981 |
| 1985 Act | The Companies Act 1985 |
| 1989 Act | The Companies Act 1989 |
| 2006 Act | The Companies Act 2006, also called the Companies Act |
| 2006 Act Commencement Order No 1 | The Companies Act 2006 (Commencement No 1, Transitional Provisions and Savings) Order 2006 (SI 2006/3428) |

---

[1] Introduced by s 1174.

[2] Sections 247–251 for the first group of Parts, concerning company insolvency and companies' winding up, and ss 435–436A which are of general application.

[3] s 22.

[4] ss 102A–103 which contain interpretative provisions for Part VI concerning official listing and s 417 which contains definitions used in FSMA.

| Expression | Meaning |
|---|---|
| 2006 Act Commencement Order No 2 | The Companies Act 2006 (Commencement No 2, Consequential Amendments, Transitional Provisions and Savings) Order 2007 (SI 2007/1093) |
| 2006 Act Commencement Order No 3 | The Companies Act 2006 (Commencement No 3, Consequential Amendments, Transitional Provisions and Savings) Order 2007 (SI 2007/2194) |
| 2006 Act Commencement Order No 4 | The Companies Act 2006 (Commencement No 4 and Commencement No 3 (Amendment)) Order 2007 (SI 2007/2607) |
| 2006 Act Commencement Order No 5 | The Companies Act 2006 (Commencement No 5, Transitional Provisions and Savings) Order 2007 (SI 2007/3495) |
| 2006 Act Commencement Order No 6 | The Companies Act 2006 (Commencement No 6, Saving and Commencement Nos 3 and 5 (Amendment)) Order 2008 (SI 2008/674) |
| 2006 Act Commencement Order No 7 | The Companies Act 2006 (Commencement No 7 and Transitional Provisions) Order 2008 (SI 2008/1886) |
| 2006 Act Commencement Order No 8 | The Companies Act 2006 (Commencement No 8, Transitional Provisions and Savings) Order 2008 (SI 2008/2860) |
| AGM | Annual General Meeting |
| AIM | Alternative Investment Market of the London Stock Exchange |
| Bankruptcy Act | The Bankruptcy Act 1914 |
| BERR | Department of Business, Enterprise, and Regulatory Reform |
| Cadbury Committee | The Committee on the Financial Aspects of Corporate Governance, chaired by Sir Adrian Cadbury, which reported in June 1992 |
| C(AICE) Act 2004 | The Companies (Audit, Investigations and Community Enterprise) Act 2004 |
| CDDA | Company Directors Disqualification Act 1986 |
| CIB | Companies Investigation Branch of BERR |
| CJA | Criminal Justice Act 1987 |
| CLR | The Company Law Review set up by the Secretary of State for Trade and Industry on 4 March 1998 under the auspices of the Company Law and Reporting Commission and/or The Company Law Review Steering Group |

| Expression | Meaning |
|---|---|
| CLR: *The Strategic Framework* | Modern Company Law For a Competitive Economy, The Strategic Framework, a Consultation Document published by the Company Law Review Steering Group in February 1999 (URN 99/654) |
| CLR: *Developing the Framework* | Modern Company Law For a Competitive Economy, Developing the Framework, a Consultation Document published by the Company Law Review Steering Group in March 2000 (URN 00/656) |
| CLR: *Completing the Structure* | Modern Company Law For a Competitive Economy, Completing the Structure, a Consultation Document published by the Company Law Review Steering Group in March 2000 (URN 00/1335) |
| CLR: *Final Report* | Modern Company Law For a Competitive Economy, Final Report published by the Company Law Review Steering Group in July 2001 (URN 01/942, 943) |
| Cohen Committee | The Committee on Company Law Amendment under the chairmanship of Cohen J, whose report was presented to Parliament in June 1945 (Cmd 6659) |
| Cork Committee | The Committee on Insolvency Law and Practice under the chairmanship of Sir Kenneth Cork, whose report was presented to Parliament in June 1982 (Cmnd 8558) |
| Combined Code | The Principles of Good Governance and Code of Best Practice, prepared by the Hampel Committee and published in June 1998, amended and updated in July 2003, June 2006, and June 2008 |
| COMI | Centre of Main Interests |
| Companies Act | Companies Act 2006, also called the 2006 Act |
| CPR | Civil Procedure Rules 1998 applicable to proceedings in the High Court and the County Courts |
| CVA | Company voluntary arrangement |
| D&O Insurance | Directors and officers liability insurance |
| Davey Committee | The Committee on Company Law Amendment under the chairmanship of Lord Davey, whose report was presented to Parliament in 1895 (C 7779) |
| DTI | Department of Trade and Industry |
| EC | European Community |

| Expression | Meaning |
|---|---|
| ECHR | European Convention on Human Rights |
| EEA | European Economic Area |
| EEC | European Economic Community |
| EEIG | European Economic Interest Grouping |
| EGM | Extraordinary General Meeting |
| ERA | Employment Rights Act 1996 |
| EU | European Union |
| | |
| Former Companies Acts | The Companies Acts 1862–1985 |
| FRRP | Financial Reporting Review Panel |
| FSA | Financial Services Authority |
| FSMA | Financial Services and Markets Act 2000 |
| | |
| GC100 | The Association for the General Counsel and Company Secretaries of FTSE100 Companies |
| Greenbury Committee | The Study Group on Directors' Remuneration, chaired by Sir Richard Greenbury, which reported in June 1995 |
| Greene Committee | The Committee on Company Law Amendment under the chairmanship of Sir Wilfred Greene KC, whose report was presented to Parliament in 1926 (Cmd 2657) |
| Hampel Committee | The Committee on Corporate Governance, chaired by Sir Ronald Hampel |
| Higgs Report | Report on the Effectiveness of Non-executive Directors of a committee chaired by Sir Derek Higgs |
| IAS | International Accounting Standards |
| Insolvency Act | Insolvency Act 1986 |
| Insolvency Rules | Insolvency Rules 1986 |
| Jenkins Committee | The Company Law Committee under the chairmanship of Lord Jenkins, whose report was presented to Parliament in June 1962 (Cmnd 1749) |
| Listing Rules | The rules made by the FSA as UK Listing Authority governing admission to listing, the continuing obligations of issuers, the enforcement of those obligations, and suspension and cancellation of listing |

| Expression | Meaning |
| --- | --- |
| Loreburn Committee | The Committee on Company Law Amendment under the original chairmanship of Sir Robert Reid KC (later Lord Loreburn), whose report was presented to Parliament in 1906 (cd 3052) |
| MFR | Minimum funding requirement (concerning pensions) |
| Model Articles Regulations | The Companies (Model Articles) Regulations 2008 (SI 2008) |
| Model Articles (pclg) | Model articles for private companies limited by guarantee, prescribed by the Model Articles Regulations |
| Model Articles (pcls) | Model articles for private companies limited by shares, prescribed by the Model Articles Regulations |
| Model Articles (plc) | Model articles for public companies, prescribed by the Model Articles Regulations |
| NED | Non-executive Director |
| OFR | Operating and Financial Review |
| OFT | Office of Fair Trading |
| PACE | Police and Criminal Evidence Act 1984 |
| Panel | Panel on Takeovers and Mergers |
| PILON | Payment in lieu of notice |
| PPER Act | Political Parties, Elections and Referendums Act 2000 |
| POS Regulations | Public Offers of Securities Regulations |
| Registrar | The Registrar of Companies for England and Wales |
| SCE | European Co-operative Society |
| SE | Societas Europaea (a European Company) |
| SFO | Serious Fraud Office (concerning crime) |
| SFO | Statutory Funding Objective (concerning pensions) |
| Table A | Table A, regulations for the management of a company limited by shares, prescribed by the Companies (Tables A to F) Regulations 1985 (SI 1985/805) |
| Tables A to F Amendment Regulations 2007 and 2008 | The Companies (Tables A to F) (Amendment) Regulations 2007 (SI 2007/2541), The Companies (Tables A to F) (Amendment) (No 2) Regulations 2007 (SI 2007/2826) and The Companies (Tables A to F) (Amendment) Regulations 2008 (SI 2008/739) |

| Expression | Meaning |
|---|---|
| Takeover Code | City Code on Takeovers and Mergers, published by the Panel |
| UKLA | United Kingdom Listing Authority |
| White Paper: Modernising Company Law | White Paper, Modernising Company Law, presented to Parliament by the Secretary of State for Trade and Industry, July 2002 (CM 5553-1) |
| White Paper: Company Law Reform | White Paper, Company Law Reform, presented to Parliament by the Secretary of State for Trade and Industry, March 2005 (CM 6456) |

# PART I

## INTRODUCTION

# 1

# THE CURRENT LEGAL FRAMEWORK RELATING TO DIRECTORS

## A. Introduction

The focus of this book is on the office of directors and the general and specific duties **1.01** and liabilities of directors, both civil and criminal. The legal framework affecting these matters is largely made up of provisions in the company's constitution and in the Companies Acts, but common law rules and equitable principles have always had an important part to play. Some statutory provisions codify, with or without modification, common law rules and equitable principles (eg directors' duties and the prohibition on making distributions out of capital). In other cases statute has left the common law rules and equitable principles unaffected (eg rules requiring directors to take account of the interests of creditors or which prevent the company from ratifying acts or omissions of directors which prejudice creditors and the rule recognizing that members may bind the company by their unanimous but informal assent).

The Companies Act 2006 begins with two definition sections. Section 1 explains **1.02** the meaning of 'company' in the Companies Acts and s 2 explains the meaning of the 'Companies Acts'. These expressions are discussed in Sections B and C of this chapter. Section D discusses the reforms made by the Companies Act 2006, its implementation, and approaches to its interpretation.

**1.03** This work attempts to state the law of England and Wales relating to directors of companies as at 1 October 2008.[1] At that date most of the provisions of the 2006 Act, particularly those of most immediate concern to directors, were in force, but many other provisions, including those relating to the fundamental features of a company and its capital, do not come into force until 1 October 2009. Where the provisions of the 2006 Act are not in force, the corresponding provisions of the Companies Act 1985 remain in effect. The provisions of the Companies Act 2006 extend to the whole of the United Kingdom, including Northern Ireland, unless the context otherwise requires.[2] In contrast the Companies Act 1985, to the extent that it is still in force, does not extend to Northern Ireland or apply to companies registered or incorporated in Northern Ireland or outside Great Britain, except where expressly provided.[3]

## B. Definitions: Company, Body Corporate, and Corporation

**1.04** Immediately preceding this chapter is a Glossary of expressions used in this work, which includes definitions in the 2006 Act, s 1174 and Schedule 8.[4]

**1.05** In a book about directors of companies it is essential to understand the meanings of 'company' and 'director'. Whereas the word 'company' has a precise meaning, as discussed in the following paragraphs, 'director' does not. In the Companies Acts 'director' is given an inclusive meaning: a director is any person occupying the position of director, by whatever name called.[5] Chapter 3 discusses the meaning of 'director' and the different types of director.

*Company*

**1.06** Under the Companies Acts 1985 and 2006, 'company' means a company formed and registered under those Acts or an existing company which was formed and

---

[1] It does not consider limited liability partnerships, open-ended investment companies, industrial and provident societies, friendly societies, European Economic Interest Groupings, or European Public Limited Liability Companies.

[2] 2006 Act, ss 1284–1287, 1299.

[3] 1985 Act, s 745. Express provision is made for overseas companies by Part XXIII, ss 690A–703R, which will be replaced by 2006 Act, Part 34, ss 1044–1059 on 1 October 2009. Under the regime preceding the 2006 Act special provision is made for Northern Ireland by the Companies (Northern Ireland) Order 1986 (SI 1986/1032 (NI 6)), the Companies Consolidation (Consequential Provisions) (Northern Ireland) Order 1986 (SI 1986/1035 (NI 9)), and Part 3 of the Companies (Audit, Investigations and Community Enterprise) Order 2005 (SI 2005/1967 (NI 17)).

[4] Definitions used in the 1985 Act are contained in Part XXVI, ss 735–744 and s 744A is an index of defined expressions used in the 1985 Act.

[5] 2006 Act, s 250.

registered under the former Companies Acts.[6] The types of companies that may be formed under the 2006 Act are:

(1) limited or unlimited companies; limited companies being limited by shares or by guarantee, but a company cannot be limited by guarantee with a share capital;[7]

(2) private and public companies;[8] the two main differences being that a private company is prohibited from making a public offer, and a public company must have a minimum share capital of £50,000 or the euro equivalent.[9]

For certain provisions of the 2006 Act it is necessary to identify particular types of company.  **1.07**

(1) Sometimes the reason is to identify the relationship between companies: holding company, subsidiary company, and wholly-owned subsidiary.[10] A company is a subsidiary of another company, its holding company, if the latter company (a) holds a majority of voting rights in it, or (b) is a member of it and has the right to appoint or remove a majority of its board of directors, or (c) is a member of it and controls alone, pursuant to an agreement with other members, a majority of the voting rights in it. A company is also a subsidiary of another company, its holding company, if it is a subsidiary of a company which is a subsidiary of another company.

(2) Accounting and reporting requirements vary, depending on whether the company is a small company, so as to qualify for the small companies regime,[11] a quoted or unquoted company,[12] or an unquoted company.[13] A quoted company is one whose equity share capital (a) has been included in the official list in accordance with FSMA, Part 6, (b) is officially listed in an EEA State, or (c) is admitted to dealing on the New York Stock Exchange or the Nasdaq exchange.

---

[6] On 1 October 2009 the 2006 Act, s 1 replaces the 1985 Act, s 735(1)(a)(b) and (4) without material change. By subs 1(2) and Parts 33 and 34, ss 1040–1059 certain provisions of that Act may also extend to companies authorized to register under the 2006 Act, unregistered companies incorporated in and having a principal place of business in the United Kingdom, and overseas companies.

[7] 2006 Act, ss 3, and 5 which replaces 1985 Act, ss 1(2)(a)–(c), without change on 1 October 2009.

[8] 2006 Act, s 4, which replaces 1985 Act, s 1(3) without change on 1 October 2009.

[9] 2006 Act, Part 20, ss 755(1) and (2), 756, and 760 (which replace 1985 Act ss 58(3), 81(1) and (3), and s 742A, ss 755(3)(4)) and 2006 Act, ss 757–759 are new. 2006 Act, ss 761–764 and 767 replace 1985 Act, ss 117 and 118 with changes and new provisions on 1 October 2009. 2006 Act, ss 765 and 766 are new.

[10] 2006 Act, s 1159 and Schedule 6, which replace 1985 Act, ss 736 and 736A without change. This definition may be amended by regulations: s 1160.

[11] 2006 Act, ss 381–384. For eligibility for the small companies regime, see Chapter 23, paragraphs 23.03–23.06.

[12] 2006 Act, ss 361, 385(2), and 531, which definition may be amended or replaced by regulations (s 385(4)–(6)).

[13] 2006 Act, s 385, which contains new provisions, but the core definition of 'quoted company' is taken from 1985 Act, s 262.

Also in relation to accounts and reports, which derive from the Seventh Company Law Directive 83/349/EEC, it is necessary to identify 'parent company', 'parent undertaking', and 'subsidiary undertaking'.[14]

(3) The definition of 'quoted company' also applies to Part 13 (resolutions and meetings), where there are special rules for polls of meetings of quoted companies.[15] However, the new provisions in the 2006 Act, Part 9, as to the enjoyment of information rights by persons nominated by the registered member, apply to companies whose shares are admitted to trading on a regulated market.[16]

(4) There are special rules for distributions by investment companies, by which they may make distributions out of accumulated revenue profits.[17] For this purpose an investment company is one which had notified the Registrar of its intention to carry on business as an investment company and which (a) invests its funds mainly in securities, with the aim of spreading risk and giving members of the company the benefit of the results of the management of its funds, (b) complies with the 2006 Act, s 834 in that none of its holdings in companies (other than other investment companies) represents more than 15% by value of the company's investments, (c) is prohibited by its articles from distributing capital profits, and (d) does not retain more than 15% of the income it derives from securities.

(5) Finally, the reason for the distinction may be geographical. There are special provisions for overseas companies, being companies incorporated outside the United Kingdom.[18] There are also distinctions depending on where the company was incorporated within the United Kingdom.[19]

**1.08** The activity of a company may determine whether particular provisions of the Companies Acts apply to it and whether it is subject to other forms of regulation:

(1) banks and banking companies,[20] insurance companies,[21] and open-ended investment companies,[22] which are regulated by the FSA;

---

[14] 2006 Act, ss 1162, 1173(1), and Schedule 7, which replace 1985 Act, ss 258, 742(1), and Schedule 10A without change.

[15] 2006 Act, ss 341–351 and 361. By s 531, the definition applies for the purpose of identifying quoted companies in respect of which members may raise voting concerns at accounts meetings under Part 16, Chapter 5, ss 527–531.

[16] 2006 Act, s 146(1). By s 1173(1) 'regulated market' has the same meaning as in Directive 2004/39/EC, Art 4.1(14), unless the relevant State has not implemented that Directive; in which case 'regulated market' has the same meaning as in Council Directive 93/22/EEC.

[17] 2006 Act, ss 832–835, which replaced 1985 Act, ss 265–267 on 6 April 2008: 2006 Commencement Order No 5, art 3(1)(k).

[18] 2006 Act, s 1044.

[19] 2006 Act, s 88 (Welsh company), ss 861(5) and 879(6) in relation to registration of company charges, and s 1158 (UK-registered company).

[20] 2006 Act, s 1164, which replaces 1985 Act, s 742B, and FSMA, Schedule 4.

[21] 2006 Act, s 1165, which replaces 1985 Act, s 742C, and FSMA, Schedule 4.

[22] FSMA, Part XVII (collective investment schemes) and in particular ss 236, 262, and 263; the Open-Ended Investment Companies Regulations 2001 (SI 2001/1228); the Open-Ended

(2) charitable companies, for which there are modifications to the Companies Act, including modifications in relation to constitutional limitations, directors' duties, and transactions with directors,[23] and which are subject to oversight by the Charity Commissioners;

(3) community interest companies, which are subject to the Companies (Audit, Investigations and Community Enterprise) Act 2004 (C(AICE) Act 2004), Part 2.[24]

Some organizations have similarities to companies, but are not companies unless they exercise statutory powers to convert into companies.　**1.09**

(1) Building societies are regulated by the Building Societies Acts 1986 and 1997 and supervised by the FSA.[25] They are not companies, but are managed by directors and can convert into public companies.[26]

(2) Cooperatives (such as consumer, agricultural, or housing cooperatives) and credit unions may be organized as companies, subject to the Companies Acts, but are more frequently organized as industrial and provident societies and registered under the Industrial and Provident Societies Acts 1965–2002. They are regulated by the FSA. An industrial and provident society may convert to a company.[27]

(3) Friendly Societies (such as workmen's clubs) could not be companies until the Friendly Societies Act 1992 enabled them to establish as, or convert to, companies.

### *'Body corporate' and 'corporation'*

By the new provisions of the 2006 Act, s 1173(1), the expressions 'body corporate' and 'corporation' include 'a body incorporated outside the United Kingdom, but do not include (a) a corporation sole,[28] or (b) a partnership that, whether or not　**1.10**

---

Investment Companies (Amendment) Regulations 2005 (SI 2005/923). Open-ended investment companies can buy back their shares free of the restrictions that apply to ordinary companies. The FSA refers to them as 'investment companies with variable capital'.

[23] 2006 Act, s 42 (which derives from Charities Act 1993, s 65, and replaces it on 1 October 2009) and s 181; Charities Act 1993, s 66 as substituted by 2006 Act, s 226.

[24] By 2006 Act, s 6, a company may be formed as a community interest company. Also see the Community Interest Company Regulations 2005 (SI 2005/1788).

[25] As to supervision by the FSA, which includes the Building Societies Commission, see Building Societies Act 1986, Part VI (as amended).

[26] See in particular Building Societies Act 1986, Part VII, and Building Societies Act 1997, Part III.

[27] Industrial and Provident Societies Act 1965, ss 52, 53, as amended by the Industrial and Provident Societies Act 2002. Unless it converts into a company, it is not a company for the purposes of the Insolvency Act (in the absence of a contrary statutory intention): *Re Devon and Somerset Farmers Ltd* [1994] Ch 57.

[28] An individual constitutes a corporation sole by virtue of holding a particular office (the Sovereign, an Archbishop, or the Public Trustee), so the property of the office passes to the successive holders of the office by virtue of appointment or succession without the need for conveyance: Law Commission, *The Execution of Deeds and Documents by or on Behalf of Bodies* (1998, No 253) at para 4.23; *Halsbury's Laws of England* (4th edn reissue, 2006) Vol 9(2), para 1111.

a legal person, is not regarded as a body corporate under the law by which it is governed'. A 'body corporate' in the 2006 Act is a corporation aggregate; ie 'a body of persons which is recognised by the law as having personality which is distinct from the separate personalities of the members of the body or the personality of the individual holder of the office in question for the time being'.[29]

**1.11** The expressions 'body corporate' and 'corporation' may include:

(1) a company incorporated under the Companies Acts 1985 and 2006 and former Companies Acts;[30]

(2) a company incorporated in the United Kingdom otherwise than under those Acts (ie by royal charter,[31] private or local Act of Parliament,[32] or special public Act of Parliament[33]) to which the 1985 and 2006 Acts apply either because it is entitled to and does register under those Acts,[34] or because their provisions apply to it as an unregistered company;[35]

(3) limited liability partnerships under the Limited Liability Partnerships Act 2000, since such partnerships are bodies corporate with unlimited capacity;[36]

(4) companies incorporated outside the United Kingdom, to which the 2006 Act, Part 34 may apply;[37]

---

[29] Law Commission, *The Execution of Deeds and Documents by or on Behalf of Bodies* (1998, No 253) at para 4.1; *Halsbury's Laws of England* (4th edn reissue, 2006) Vol 9(2), para 1109.

[30] This is made explicit by 2006 Act, s 16(2) and (3).

[31] At common law these companies, unlike others incorporated by Act of Parliament, have unlimited capacity: *Sutton's Hospital Case* (1612) 10 Co Re 1a, 23a, 30b; *Baroness Wenlock v River Dee Co* (1883) 36 Ch D 675, 685, per Bowen LJ (upheld on appeal at (1885) 10 AC 354). Examples of companies incorporated by Royal Charter are the Institute of Chartered Accountants and the Institute of Chartered Secretaries and Administrators, incorporated in 1880 and 1902 respectively.

[32] These were usually incorporated to undertake public utilities and few remain in existence.

[33] These were usually formed for public sector activity, but few of them remain after the Government's privatization programme, beginning with the Telecommunications Act 1984.

[34] 1985 Act, ss 680–683, which are replaced without change by 2006 Act, ss 1040–1042 on 1 October 2009. The Non-Companies Acts Companies Authorised to Register Regulations (SI 2008/) (draft) were intended to come into effect on 1 October 2008.

[35] 2006 Act, s 1043 which came into effect on 6 April 2007 and replaced 1985 Act, s 718 with changes. The Companies Acts (Unregistered Companies) Regulations (SI 2007/318) and the Companies (Unregistered Companies) Regulations 2008 (SI 2008/) (draft) apply most of the provisions of the 2006 Act that have been brought into force to unregistered companies (including those relating to directors). CLR recommended that most provisions of the main companies legislation should apply to unregistered companies CLR: *Final Report* at paras 11.34–11.38.

[36] Limited Partnerships Act 2000, s 1. The Limited Liability Partnerships Regulations 2001 (SI 2001/1090), as amended by the Limited Liability Partnerships (Amendment) Regulations 2007 (SI 2007/2073) and the Markets in Financial Instruments Directive (Consequential Amendments) Regulations 2007 (SI 2007/2932), apply many of the provisions of the 1985 Act to LLPs. The Limited Liability Partnerships (Accounts and Audit) (Application of the Companies Act 2006) Regulations 2008 (SI 2008/1911), apply provisions in 2006 Act, Parts 15 and 16 (accounts, reports, and audit) to limited liability partnerships with effect from 1 October 2008. Other provisions of the 2006 Act will be applied to limited liability partnerships with effect from 1 October 2009.

[37] Part 34, ss 1044–1059 come into force on 1 October 2009 and provide a new regime for overseas companies replacing 1985 Act, ss 690A–703R, as discussed in Chapter 31 of this work.

(5) European Economic Interest Groupings (EEIG), which if registered in Great Britain are bodies corporate;[38]

(6) European companies or Societas Europaea (SE), intended to facilitate cross-border mergers, which may be set up within the Community in the form of a European public limited-liability company with legal personality;[39]

(7) European Co-operative Societies (SCE) which have separate legal personality and may be formed to further members' economic and social activities.[40]

Whereas 'corporation' is only used in connection with the representation of a **1.12** corporation at a company meeting,[41] the expression 'body corporate' is used in many varied instances. It is used to enable provisions of the Companies Acts to reach corporations other than companies as defined above; eg corporate bodies that may be subject to a petition by the Secretary of State on the ground of unfair prejudice to members,[42] overseas companies carrying on business in Great Britain which may be subject to investigation by the Secretary of State or inspectors appointed by him,[43] companies which may commit offences,[44] and companies subject to the company communications provisions.[45] It is also used to identify the bodies corporate in respect of which members do not have to approve transactions with directors.[46] More often it is used so that the provision may apply to a corporate entity with dealings or connections with a company as:

(1) a member,[47] holding company,[48] associated body corporate,[49] subsidiary undertaking or company,[50] or a person interested in shares in a company;[51]

---

[38] Council Regulation (EEC) No 2137/85; European Economic Interest Grouping Regulations 1989 (SI 1989/638); the European Economic Interest Grouping (Fees) Regulations 2004 (SI 2004/2407). An EEIG may be formed with legal personality (Art 1(3) and reg 3) by existing firms or undertakings in Member States to provide cross-border non-profit-making ancillary services for its members on the basis of unlimited liability (Art 24). An EEIG may be wound up under the Insolvency Act as an unregistered company (regs 7 and 8) and, if wound up, the CDDA applies (reg 20).

[39] Council Regulation 2157/2001; Directive 2001/86; the European Public Limited Company Regulations 2004 (SI 2004/2326); the European Public Limited Company (Fees) Regulations 2004 (SI 2004/2407). These came into force in 2004. An SE may be wound up under the Insolvency Act if its registered office is in Great Britain (Art 63).

[40] Council Regulation 1435/2003; Directive 2003/72. These came into force on 18 August 2006. An SCE may be wound up under the Insolvency Act if it is registered.

[41] 2006 Act, ss 318 and 323.

[42] 2006 Act, s 55.

[43] 1985 Act, Parts XIV and XV, as amended by 2006 Act, ss 1035–1039, in particular 1985 Act, s 453.

[44] 2006 Act, ss 949(3), 1123, and 1127.

[45] 2006 Act, s 1148, applying to ss 1144–1148 and Schedules 4 and 5.

[46] 2006 Act, ss 188(6), s 190(4), 198(6), 200(6), 201(6), 203(5), 217(4), 218(4), s 226 (substituting the Charities Act 1993, s 66A).

[47] 2006 Act, ss 136(1)(a), 137(1), 148(3)(b), 384(2)(b), 467(2)(b).

[48] 2006 Act, ss 251(3) (shadow director), 1159.

[49] 2006 Act, ss 176(2), 203(1), 208(1) and (2), 220(2), 256.

[50] 2006 Act, ss 499(2)(a), 500(1), 532(4), 1159, 1161.

[51] 2006 Act, ss 823(1) and (2).

(2) a director, secretary, or person authorized to certificate share transfers on behalf of the company;[52]

(3) an entity in which a director is interested,[53] with which a director is connected,[54] or which is controlled by a director;[55]

(4) a person associated for the purposes of independence requirements;[56]

(5) an organization in relation to the provisions about political donations and expenditure;[57]

(6) an entity with whom the company is proposing to merge or enter into an arrangement to allot shares.[58]

## C. The Companies Acts and Other Statutes Affecting Directors

**1.13** The Companies Act 2006 consists of 47 Parts and 1,300 sections. It also has 16 Schedules and is supplemented by a number of statutory instruments, which are identified in Appendix 1 to this work (some of the intended statutory instruments are still in draft). Subsection 2(1) defines the Companies Acts as:[59]

(1) the company law provisions of the 2006 Act, being Parts 1–39, ss 1–1181, and the provisions of Parts 45–47, ss 1284–1300, as they apply for the purposes of those parts, with Schedules 1–9 and 16;[60]

(2) the Companies (Audit, Investigations and Community Enterprise) Act 2004, Part 2, ss 26–67, concerning community interest companies;[61]

(3) the provisions of the Companies Act 1985, which remain in force, namely Parts XIV and XV, ss 431–457 (investigation of companies and their affairs;

---

[52] 2006 Act, ss 164, 165(6), 278(1), 775(4)(b).

[53] 2006 Act, s 185(2), (3).

[54] 2006 Act, ss 252(2), 254, 255.

[55] 2006 Act, ss 255, 412(b).

[56] 2006 Act, ss 345(2)(b), 937(2), (3) and (4), 1150, 1152.

[57] 2006 Act, s 379(1).

[58] 2006 Act, ss 93(6), 594(6), 595, 616.

[59] Section 2 came into force on 6 April 2007. Under 1985 Act, s 744 'the Companies Acts' meant the 1985 Act, Criminal Justice Act 1993, Part V (insider dealing), and the Companies Consolidation (Consequential Provisions) Act 1985.

[60] The Parts of the 2006 Act that are not company law provisions are: Part 40, ss 1182–1191 (Company Directors: Foreign Disqualification etc); Part 41, ss 1192–1208 (Business Names); Part 42, ss 1209–1264 (Statutory Auditors); Part 43, ss 1265–1273 (Transparency Obligations and Related Matters); Part 44, ss 1274–1283 (Miscellaneous Provisions); the related Schedules 10–15. Parts 45–47 (ss 1284–1300) contain extensions of the Companies Acts and other enactments to Northern Ireland, general supplementary and final provisions.

[61] The provisions about community interest companies in the C(AICE) Act 2004 form a complete code, which is additional to company law. 2006 Act, s 1295 and Schedule 16 repeals C(AICE) Act 2004, Part 1, ss 1–10, 11(1), 12, 13, 19, and 20.

requisition of documents; and orders imposing restrictions on shares under the 1985 Act, s 445[62]), as amended by the 2006 Act, Part 32, ss 1035–1039;[63] and

(4) the provisions of the Companies Consolidation (Consequential Provisions) Act 1985, which remain in force, concerning old public companies, as defined by s 1, and miscellaneous savings and amendments relating to the 1985 Act.

Those provisions are considered to be core provisions of company law in that they are concerned with the way companies are formed and run. As described below, the 2006 Act is not yet fully in force and certain provisions of the 1985 Act, in addition to the provisions in paragraph (3) above, have not yet been repealed and remain in force (these as yet unrepealed provisions mainly concern constitutional matters and capital).

Other statutes of direct relevance to directors are considered to be on the fringe of **1.14** core company law. These are statutory provisions, including those formerly included in the 1985 Act, about:

(1) the issue of securities (the Financial Services and Markets Act 2000, Part VI, including amendments made by the 2006 Act, Part 43[64]), which are considered in Chapter 27 of this work in so far as they expose directors to the risk of liability to third parties;

(2) disqualification of directors (the Company Directors Disqualification Act 1986 and the 2006 Act, Part 40 concerning foreign disqualification orders[65]), which are considered in Chapter 28 of this work;

(3) insolvency (the Insolvency Act 1986), the provisions of which of particular concern to directors are considered in Chapter 29 of this work.

# D. The Companies Act 2006

## (1) The reforms

Apart from changes in style and structure to make the 2006 Act more accessible **1.15** (eg by clearly differentiating the provisions that apply to private and public companies), the Act makes a number of changes of substance which are of particular importance to directors.

---

[62] These provisions were not included in the 2006 Act, because they can go beyond companies and apply to other types of organization.

[63] The other provisions of the 1985 Act are repealed by 2006 Act, s 1295 and Schedule 16.

[64] These came into force on the Royal Assent, 8 November 2006 (s 1300(1)(a)).

[65] The provisions about foreign disqualification orders are to come into force on 1 October 2009.

*Parts 1–7: The fundamentals of a company*

**1.16**  These provisions concern types of company (paragraph 1.06 above), company formation, a company's constitution, its capacity to act, its name, its registered office, and change of status.[66]

**1.17**  The new provisions, which simplify the procedure for forming a company and its constitution (Parts 2 and 3), do not come into force until 1 October 2009. Until then a company will be formed under the 1985 Act, but amendments have been made to Tables A–F to reflect changes made by the 2006 Act and already in force.[67]

**1.18**  When the 2006 Act, Part 2, s 7 comes into force a single person may form a private or public company.[68] By s 9,[69] to form a company there must be delivered to the Registrar (a) the memorandum of association, stating that the subscribers wish to form a company under the Act and agree to become members and, in the case of a company that is to have a share capital, to take at least one share each,[70] (b) an application for registration containing prescribed information about the company, including particulars of its proposed share capital (if any) and its first directors and secretaries, with consents to act,[71] (c) a copy of the proposed articles unless the applicable Model Article is to apply,[72] and (d) a statement of compliance in accordance with s 13.

**1.19**  The main change from the procedure under the 1985 Act is that under the 2006 Act the memorandum is a simple document which provides a historical record evidencing the intention of the founder members to form the company and become members. It therefore underpins the statutory contract between members and

---

[66]  As Sir John Vinelott put it in 'Individual Insolvency—The Insolvency Acts 1985 and 1986' (1987) 40 *Current Legal Problems* 1, 11: 'A company, like a good soldier has a name, a number and a place.'

[67]  The Companies (Tables A to F) (Amendment) (No 2) Regulations 2007 (SI 2007/2541) and the Companies (Tables A to F) (Amendment) (No 2) Regulations 2007 (SI 2007/2826), which apply to companies incorporated between 1 October 2007 and 1 October 2009. The Companies (Tables A to F) (Amendment) Regulations 2008 (SI 2008/739) made amendments to Tables C and E with effect from 6 April 2008.

[68]  Under 1985 Act, s 1(3A), inserted by the Companies (Single Member Private Limited Companies) Regulations 1992 (SI 1992/1699) with effect from 15 July 1992, a single person may form a private company. The reforms in relation to formation largely adopt the recommendations of the CLR *Final Report* at paras 9.2 and 9.4.

[69]  See also the Companies (Registration) Regulations 2008 (SI 2008/3014), made pursuant to ss 8(2), 10(3), and 11(2), and the Companies (Shares, Share Capital and Authorised Minimum) Regulations 2008 (draft), to be made pursuant to ss 10(2) and 32(2).

[70]  2006 Act, s 8.

[71]  2006 Act, ss 9–12. For public companies the statement about the company's share capital is linked to Article 2 of the Second Company Law Directive (77/91/EC).

[72]  Pursuant to 2006 Act, s 19, the Companies (Model Articles) Regulations 2008 (SI 2008/3229) prescribe default model articles for private companies limited by shares pcls, private companies limited by guarantee pclg, and public companies plc.

the company.[73] It cannot be changed or updated, but there is no need to do so. The memorandum does not state the company's objects and much of the information that used to be contained in it is now contained in the application for registration.

There are also changes to a company's constitution. The 1985 Act does not refer **1.20** to a company's constitution as such, but it included the memorandum, which states the company's objects, and the articles of association, which prescribe its regulations, both of which could be altered by special resolution.[74] Under the 2006 Act, s 17 a company's constitution includes its articles, which may be the Model Articles[75] and also any resolutions or agreements, described in s 29,[76] which affect its constitution. The constitution may now include entrenched provisions, which can only be amended or repealed by procedures more restrictive than a special resolution.[77] Another change is that a company's objects are unrestricted, giving it the same plenary capacity as an individual, unless specifically restricted by its articles.[78] The provisions of the constitution 'bind the company and its members to the same extent as if there were covenants on the part of the company and each member to observe those provisions'.[79]

There are new rules about choice of name and trading disclosures, most of which **1.21** do not come into force until 1 October 2009 (Part 5). These provisions should be considered with the supporting regulations[80] and Part 41, which contains new provisions about business names and provisions derived from the Business Names Act 1985, with changes. One matter of particular significance to directors is that they are no longer personally liable if the company's name is not correctly stated

---

[73] 2006 Act, s 33(1), replacing 1985 Act, s 14(1).

[74] 1985 Act, ss 4–9, 378, 380. For further discussion about resolutions, see Chapter 2, paragraphs 2.28–2.30, and Chapter 22. Note that 1985 Act, s 35A, inserted by the 1989 Act, s 108, refers to limitations under the company's constitution in an inclusive way.

[75] 2006 Act, ss 18–20.

[76] An informal agreement of the type considered in *Cane v Jones* [1980] 1 WLR 1451 would be part of the constitution and subject to the rules about forwarding to the Registrar (s 30) and being provided to members (s 32).

[77] 2006 Act, s 22 and for alteration of articles: ss 21–27.

[78] 2006 Act, ss 31 and 39. For charitable companies, see s 42.

[79] 2006 Act, s 33(1), replacing 1985 Act, s 14(1). Unlike its predecessor, s 33 expressly refers to the company. For cases on former provisions, see *Welton v Saffery* [1897] AC 299, 315 and *Hickman v Romney Marsh Sheep-Breeders Association* [1915] 1 Ch 881. Section 33 (like 1985 Act, s 14) is excepted from the general principle set out in Contracts (Rights of Third Parties) Act 1999, s 1 and so the provisions of a company's constitution will not confer any rights on persons other than the company and its members.

[80] The supporting regulations are or will be The Non-Companies Acts Companies Authorised to Register Regulations 2008 (draft), the Company Names Adjudicator Rules 2008 (SI 2008/1738), the Companies (Trading Disclosures) Regulations 2008 (SI 2008/495), the Companies (Unregistered Companies) Regs 2008 (draft), the Company and Business Names (Miscellaneous Provisions) Regulations 2008 (draft), and the Companies (Trading Disclosures) (Amendment) Regulations 2008 (laid in draft before Parliament).

on its contracts and bills, because the 1985 Act, s 349, was repealed with effect from 1 October 2008.[81]

*Part 9: Exercise of members' rights*

**1.22**  In recognition of the fact that shares are often held through nominees, there are new provisions, which came into force on 1 October 2007, enabling the registered member to nominate another person to exercise members' rights where the company's articles so provide,[82] or to nominate another person to enjoy information rights where the company is a traded company.[83]

*Part 10: A company's directors*

**1.23**  Part 10, concerning directors, contains a number of significant reforms, all of which are in force, except for provisions about the register of directors, disclosure of directors' residential addresses, and the power to make provision for employees on cessation of business.[84] Every company must have one natural director, who cannot be under the age of 16, but there are no upper age limits.[85] These matters are discussed in Chapter 6 of this work.

**1.24**  There is a statutory statement of directors' general duties and independent directors are given power to authorize a director to have a conflict of interest or take the benefit of a corporate opportunity.[86] These provisions are discussed in Chapters 9–16 of this work.

**1.25**  There are changes to the rules about directors declaring their interests in existing transactions and about transactions with directors requiring approval of members.[87] These matters are discussed in Chapters 17 and 18 of this work. Certain restrictions on transactions with directors, formerly contained in the 1985 Act, Part X (enforcement of fair dealing by directors), have been repealed and not replaced by provisions in the 2006 Act.[88]

---

[81]  2006 Act Commencement Order No 5, Art 8(b) and Schedule 3.

[82]  2006 Act, s 145.

[83]  2006 Act, ss 146–153. The reforms in Part 9 were recommended by the CLR in its *Final Report* at Chapter 7. These matters are referred to in Chapter 22 at paragraph 22.92.

[84]  2006 Act, ss 162–167, 240–247, supported by the Companies (Fees for Inspection of Company Records) Regulations 2008 (SI 2008/3007), made pursuant to s 162(5)(b), and the Companies (Disclosure of Address) Regulations 2008 (laid before Parliament), made pursuant to s 243(3)–(6), which also come into force on 1 October 2009. In the meantime the corresponding provisions of the 1985 Act remain in force: ss 288, 289, 719, 723B–723E, and Schedule 24.

[85]  2006 Act, Part 10, Chapter 1, ss 154–169.

[86]  2006 Act, Part 10, Chapter 2, ss 170–181.

[87]  2006 Act, Part 10, Chapters 3–6, ss 182–231.

[88]  The provisions of 1985 Act, Part 10, concerning transactions with directors, that have been repealed and not replaced are s 311 (prohibition on tax-free payments to directors), ss 323 and 327 (prohibition on directors dealing in share options), ss 324–326, 328, 329, and Schedule 13, Parts 2–4 (register of directors' interests), s 342 (criminal liability for loans to directors), and ss 343 and

There are new provisions about qualifying pension scheme indemnity provision **1.26** in respect of directors' liabilities and ratification of a director's wrongful conduct by independent members,[89] which are discussed in Chapter 19 of this work.

Finally, there are new restrictions on the disclosure of directors' residential **1.27** addresses, which are not yet in force (discussed in Chapter 6 of this work).[90]

### Part 11: Derivative claims

There is a new statutory procedure for derivative claims by members arising from **1.28** a breach of duty by directors,[91] which came into force on 1 October 2007 (discussed in Chapter 21 of this work).

### Part 12: Company secretaries

There is no need for private companies to have a secretary. The provisions of Part **1.29** 12 are in force except for ss 275–279 concerning the register of secretaries.[92]

### Part 13: Resolutions and meetings

The way in which companies pass resolutions is simplified. The reforms, which **1.30** are in force, include the following: (a) there are now only ordinary and special resolutions (extraordinary resolutions have been abolished),[93] (b) written resolutions are the normal procedure for private companies,[94] (c) all company meetings are convened on 14 days' notice, except public company AGMs which require 21 days,[95] (d) communications in relation to company meetings may be sent electronically,[96] (e) private companies are no longer obliged to hold AGMs,[97] and (f) there are new provisions for polls for quoted companies.[98]

---

344 (special procedure for disclosure by banks). These repeals reflected the recommendations of the Law Commission. The Government repealed the provisions about the register of directors' interests because the FSA requires disclosure by companies whose shares are traded on a regulated market to comply with the EU Market Abuse Directive and the Government did not wish to extend those requirements to other companies. Since 2006 Act, s 413 makes special provision for disclosure requirements by banking companies, the provisions of 1985 Act, ss 343 and 344 were no longer required.

[89] 2006 Act, Part 10, Chapter 7, ss 232–239.

[90] 2006 Act, Part 10, Chapter 8, ss 240–246. In the meantime the provisions of 1985 Act, ss 723B–723E remain in force.

[91] 2006 Act, Part 11, ss 260–264 (claims in England and Wales or Northern Ireland).

[92] 2006 Act, Part 12, ss 270–280. The Companies (Fees for Inspection of Company Records) Regulations 2008 (SI 2008/3007) are made pursuant to s 275(5)(b) and come into force on 1 October 2009. Company secretaries are discussed in Chapter 3, Section E of this work.

[93] 2006 Act, ss 281–283.

[94] 2006 Act, ss 288–300.

[95] 2006 Act, s 307.

[96] 2006 Act, s 333.

[97] The provisions about AGMs for public companies are in 2006 Act, ss 336–340.

[98] 2006 Act, ss 341–354 (written resolutions).

*Parts 15 and 16: Accounts, reports, and audit*

**1.31**   The provisions of the 2006 Act concerning accounts, reports, and audit are all in force.[99] Chapter 23 of this work discusses directors' functions and duties in respect of these matters.

**1.32**   In relation to accounts and reports (Part 15), directors are under a new duty not to approve accounts unless they give a true and fair view.[100] There are new requirements for a company's annual accounts to disclose information about directors' benefits and for a business review in the directors' report for all companies other than those subject to the small companies regime.[101] The annual accounts of quoted companies must be published on their website.[102] The time for filing accounts and reports with the Registrar is reduced from ten months after the end of the relevant accounting reference period to nine months for private companies and six months for public companies.[103] There is a new provision making a director liable to compensate the company for any loss suffered by it as a result of an untrue or misleading statement in, or omission from the directors' report, the directors' remuneration report, or any summary financial statement derived from them.[104]

**1.33**   Part 16, concerning audit, contains new provisions to improve the accountability of auditors, including (a) new provisions relating to the appointment of auditors of private companies and the disclosure of the terms of an auditor's appointment;[105] (b) a requirement that an auditor's report given by a firm must be signed by an individual as senior statutory auditor;[106] (c) new provisions about offences relating to the audit report;[107] (d) obligations of the auditor and the company to notify the appropriate audit authority if the auditor ceases to hold office;[108] (e) a new right of shareholders in a quoted company to raise audit concerns at an accounts meeting of a quoted company;[109] and (f) new provisions relating to indemnity and limitation of auditors' liability.[110]

---

[99]   These parts are supported by regulations noted in nn 128 and 129 to paragraph 1.45 below and in the Table in Appendix 1 under Parts 15 and 16.

[100]   2006 Act, s 393.

[101]   2006 Act, ss 412, 413, 417.

[102]   2006 Act, s 430.

[103]   2006 Act, s 442.

[104]   2006 Act, s 463.

[105]   2006 Act, ss 485(2)–(5), 487, 488, 493, and 514.

[106]   2006 Act, ss 503, 504, and 506.

[107]   2006 Act, ss 507 and 508.

[108]   2006 Act, ss 522–525.

[109]   2006 Act, ss 527–531.

[110]   2006 Act, ss 532–538.

*Parts 17 and 18: A company's share capital and acquisition by a limited company of its own shares*

Most of the provisions in the 2006 Act concerning a company's capital replace **1.34** provisions in the 1985 Act without change and come into force on 1 October 2009 (Chapter 24 of this work discusses directors' functions and duties in respect of capital). There are two relaxations in the capital maintenance rules for private companies which came into force on 1 October 2008. First, a private company may reduce its capital without a court order, provided that the directors make a solvency statement.[111] Secondly, the prohibition on giving financial assistance in the purchase of its own shares no longer applies to a private company (and the 'whitewash' provisions no longer apply to them).[112]

Other new provisions, which come into force on 1 October 2009, provide that **1.35** (a) companies no longer have an authorized capital, but shares must have a nominal value and cannot be in the form of stock,[113] (b) directors of a private company with only one class of shares may allot shares without prior approval of members (as required by the 1985 Act, s 80) unless prohibited by the company's articles,[114] and (c) a company may redenominate the currency of its share capital.[115]

*Part 21: Certification and transfer of securities*

These provisions are in force. They include a new provision, s 771 (to be read with **1.36** s 851), which makes clear the directors' duties when a transfer of shares in or debentures of a company is lodged.[116] As soon as reasonably practicable and in any event within two months after the date of lodgement the company must either

---

[111] 2006 Act, ss 641(1)(a) and (2)–(6), 642–644, 652(1) and (3), and 654, which were brought into force by 2006 Act Commencement Order No 7, Arts 2(a)–(c). See also the Companies (Reduction of Share Capital) Order 2008 (SI 2008/1915), which prescribes the form of solvency statement and provides for the treatment of reserves as distributable profits, unless, where the court confirms the reduction, it orders that it is not distributable. This reform was recommended by the CLR: *Completing the Structure* at paras 7.9 and 7.10 and CLR: *Final Report* at para 10.6.

[112] 2006 Act CLR: Commencement Order No 5, arts 5(2) and 8(b) and Schedule 3 repeal 1985 Act, ss 151–153 and 155–158 as regards private companies. The CLR recommended the dis-application of these provisions in CLR: *Completing the Structure* at para 7.12 and CLR: *Final Report* at para 10.6. Paragraph 52 of Schedule 4 to that Commencement Order makes it clear that the repeal could not have the effect that a case of financial assistance given by a private company might be impugned under the rule of law derived from *Trevor v Whitworth* (1887) 12 App Cas 409, HL (see commentary in para 7 of the Explanatory Memorandum to Commencement Order No 5). The provisions of the 2006 Act concerning financial assistance, ss 677–683 expressly apply only to public companies.

[113] 2006 Act, ss 540(2) and (3), 542, 545, and 546. The abolition of authorized capital was recommended by the CLR: *Completing the Structure* at para 7.7 and CLR: *Final Report* at para 10.6.

[114] 2006 Act, s 550. This reform was recommended by the CLR: *Final Report* para 4.5. The directors' power of allotment is of course subject to any pre-emption rights of existing shareholders, which in the case of a private company may be excluded by the articles or disapplied by the articles or special resolution (ss 567 and 569).

[115] 2006 Act, ss 622–628.

[116] 2006 Act, s 771 replaces 1985 Act, s 183(5), as recommended by the CLR: *Final Report* at paras 7.44 and 7.45. See further Chapter 24, paragraph 24.215 of this work.

register the transfer or give the transferee notice of refusal with reasons. The requirement for reasons is new. If the section is not complied with the company and every officer in default commits an offence.

*Part 23: Distributions*

**1.37** The 2006 Act, s 845, which is in force, provides a solution to a problem in making an inter-group transfer of a non-cash asset at book value, which was thought to be caused by the decision in *Aveling Barford Ltd v Perion Ltd*.[117] The new section enables a company, which has distributable profits, to sell or transfer a non-cash asset to a member of its group at book value without being treated as having made a distribution.

*Part 31: Dissolution and restoration to the register*

**1.38** There are new provisions, which come into effect on 1 October 2009, for restoring a dissolved company to the register, either administratively by the Registrar on the application of a former director or member if certain conditions are met, or by the court on the application of a former director and others, provided that the application is made within six years of dissolution (unless the application is for the purpose of bringing a claim against the company for damages for personal injury).[118] Under the 1985 Act a former director does not have standing to apply to restore a dissolved company to the register. The powers of directors in relation to dissolution and restoration to the register are discussed in Chapter 4, Section A(4) of this work.

## (2) Implementation

**1.39** When the Companies Act obtained the Royal Assent on 8 November 2006 Parts 46 and 47 (general supplementary and final provisions, except repeals in s 1295) came into force, including the continuity of law provision in s 1297, as did the non-company law provisions of Parts 43 and 44. Part 43, concerned with transparency obligations, makes amendments to FSMA, Part 6, which are discussed in Chapter 27 of this work.

**1.40** Since then the 2006 Act has been implemented in stages; so far by seven Commencement Orders, each of which contains relevant repeals and transitional provisions. In its approach to implementing the Act the Government has had

---

[117] [1989] BCLC 626. In that case a transfer of property by an insolvent company to its parent at book value, which was known to be below market value was set aside as a disguised and unlawful distribution. The CLR recommended that there should be provision enabling solvent companies to make inter-group transfers at book value: CLR: *Capital Maintenance: Other Issues* (URN 00/880) at paras 24–43 and CLR: *Completing the Structure* at para 7.21. Directors' functions and duties in relation to distributions are discussed in Chapter 24 of this work.

[118] 2006 Act, ss 1024–1032. The CLR recommended administrative restoration to the register in *Final Report* at paras 11.17–11.20.

three main objectives: (i) the new law should apply in the same way to existing companies and companies formed under the 2006 Act; (ii) existing bargains should not be overridden; and (iii) it should be as easy as possible for existing companies to take advantage of the new freedoms in the 2006 Act.[119]

As at 1 October 2008 more than half the company law provisions[120] are in force, and **1.41** the corresponding provisions of the 1985 Act are repealed. The provisions of Parts 36–38, ss 1121–1174 (offences, supplementary provisions, and interpretation) come into force with the provisions to which they relate.[121] Appendix 1 to this work contains a Table showing the progress of implementation of the 2006 Act and the making of supporting regulations and orders. The Table identifies when and how the provisions of the 2006 Act in force on 1 October 2008 came into force and the remaining provisions which will come into force on 1 October 2009.

The reasons for the delay in implementation have been the need for time to put in **1.42** place the necessary secondary legislation (eg the statutory instrument prescribing the Model Articles), to enable companies and their advisers to familiarize themselves with the new legislation, and to enable Companies House to change its regulatory systems and processes. In fact, the time needed to implement changes at Companies House meant that final implementation of all provisions had to be postponed from 1 October 2008 to 1 October 2009.[122]

*Commencement Orders Nos 1 and 2: effective 1 January, 20 January,*
*and 6 April 2007*

The first two Commencement Orders were concerned in the main to give effect **1.43** to EC Directives.

---

[119] *Implementation of the Companies Act 2006*, a DTI Consultative Document (February 2007) at para 4.6. The Government's approach is supported by the leading authorities: *Yew Bon Tew v Kenderaan Bas Mara* [1983] 1 AC 553, 562, 563, PC, per Lord Brightman; *Secretary of State for Social Security v Tunnicliffe* [1991] 2 All ER 712, 724, CA, per Staughton LJ; *L'Office Cherifien des Phosphates v Yamashita-Shinnihon Steamship Co Ltd* [1994] 1 AC 486, 524, 525, HL, per Lord Mustill; *R v Field* [2003] 1 WLR 882, CA at paras 60, 61; *Wilson v First County Trust Ltd (No 2)* [2004] 1 AC 816, HL at paras 18 and 19, per Lord Nicholls; para 98, per Lord Hope; paras 153 and 154, per Lord Scott; and paras 186–202, per Lord Rodger.

[120] Those in Parts 1–39, 45–47.

[121] The Companies (Company Records) Regulations 2008 (SI 2008/3006), made pursuant to ss 1136, 1137, and 1292(1)(a), and the Companies (Fees for Inspection of Company Records) Regulations 2008 (SI 2008/3007), made pursuant to ss 162(5)(b), 275(5)(b), 877(4)(b), 892(4)(b), 1137, 1167, and 1292(1)(c), come into force on 1 October 2009.

[122] The original final implementation date was 1 October 2008 (written statements of the Minister of State for Industry and the Regions (Margaret Hodge) on 2 November 2006 and 28 February 2007), but on 7 November 2007 the Minister for Competitiveness (Stephen Timms) announced in the House of Commons (confirmed in a written statement dated 13 December 2007) that final implementation would be postponed to 1 October 2009, because Companies House could not confirm that it would be able to implement the necessary changes to its systems and processes by 1 October 2008.

(1) On 1 January 2007: Part 35 relating to changes to the First Company Law Directive, designed to ensure increased facilities for e-communications with the Registrar;[123]

(2) On 20 January 2007: the company communication provisions in Parts 13 and 37, providing for communications between a company and its share-holders and others, including provisions facilitating electronic communication, and Part 22 concerning a public company's right to investigate who has an interest in shares (both linked to implementation of the Transparency Obligations Directive[124]); also s 463, which sets out a statutory basis of directors' liability to the company in relation to the directors' report (including business review) and the directors' remuneration report;

(3) On 6 April 2007: Part 28 about takeovers, giving effect to the Directive on Takeover Bids;[125] also repeal of the 1985 Act, s 41 (authentication of documents), ss 293, 294 (provisions relating to directors aged 70 and over in public companies or private companies which are subsidiaries of public companies), certain sections in Part 10,[126] and s 438, which gave power to the Secretary of State to bring civil proceedings on behalf of a company.

*Commencement Orders Nos 3 and 4: effective 1 October 2007*

**1.44**  On 1 October 2007 there came into force a number of important provisions concerning directors and the management of companies, including the new provisions in Part 9 about the exercise of members' rights, most of the provisions in Part 10 about directors, the new provisions in Part 11 about derivative claims, and new provisions in Part 13 about resolutions and meetings.[127]

---

[123]  Directive 2003/58/EC of the European Parliament and of the Council amended the First Company Law Directive, Council Directive 68/151/EEC.

[124]  Directive 2004/109/EC of the European Parliament and of the Council on the harmonisation of transparency requirements in relation to information about issuers whose securities are admitted to trading on a regulated market and amending Directive 2001/34/EC.

[125]  In order to give effect to Directive 2004/25/EC of the European Parliament and Council on Takeover Bids, which had been due to be implemented into national law by 20 May 2006. Because of the delay in passing the 2006 Act, as a temporary measure the Takeovers Directive was implemented by the Takeovers Directive (Interim Implementation) Regulations 2006 (SI 2006/1183) made under European Communities Act 1972, s 2(2). The Companies Acts (Unregistered Companies) Regulations 2007 (SI 2007/318) apply Part 28 (Takeovers etc) and certain ancillary provisions to unregistered companies.

[126]  The repealed sections in Part 10 were s 311(prohibitions on tax-free payments to directors), ss 323 and 327 (prohibition on directors dealing in share options), ss 324–326, 328, 329, and Schedule 13, Parts 2–4 (register of directors' interests) and ss 343 and 344 (special procedure for disclosure by banks).

[127]  Most of these provisions were brought into force by the 2006 Act Commencement Order No 3, but the 2006 Act Commencement Order No 4 brought into effect regulations about fees for inspecting company records and corrected an error in the previous Commencement Order.

*Commencement Orders Nos 5–7: effective 6 April and 1 October 2008*

The provisions brought into effect on 6 April 2008 included new provisions in **1.45** Part 12 about company secretaries, all the remaining provisions in Parts 15 (accounts and reports[128]), 16 (audit[129]), 19 (debentures), 20 (private and public companies), 21 (certification of transfers of securities), 23 (distributions), 26 (arrangements and reconstructions), and 27 (mergers and divisions of public companies).

On 1 October 2008 provisions in Part 5 about a company's name and trading **1.46** disclosures came into force,[130] as did the remaining provisions in Part 10 about directors, apart from those about disclosure of directors' residential addresses. In relation to a company's share capital the new provisions enabling a private company to reduce its share capital without the need for a court order came into force,[131] as did the repeal of the restrictions under the 1985 Act, ss 151–153, and 155–158 on the giving by a private company of financial assistance for acquisition of its own shares, including the 'whitewash' procedure.[132]

*Commencement Order No 8: effective 1 October 2009*

The provisions of the 2006 Act that will come into force on 1 October 2009 **1.47** mainly concern the new provisions about incorporation, a company's constitution (including the Model Articles), records kept by the Registrar, and share capital.[133] These are all provisions supported by secondary legislation, some of which have been published in draft as indicated in the Table in Appendix 1.

---

[128] These provisions are supported by the following regulations, which came into force on 6 April 2008: The Companies (Revision of Defective Accounts and Reports) Regulations 2008 (SI 2008/373); The Companies (Summary Financial Statement) Regulations 2008 (SI 2008/374); The Companies Act 2006 (Amendment) (Accounts and Reports) Regulations 2008 (SI 2008/393); The Small Companies and Groups (Accounts and Directors' Report) Regulations 2008 (SI 2008/409); The Large and Medium-sized Companies and Groups (Accounts and Reports) Regulations 2008 (SI 2008/410).

[129] These provisions are supported by the Companies (Disclosure of Auditor Remuneration and Liability Limitation Agreements) Regulations 2008 (SI 2008/489).

[130] The provisions of ss 69–74 are supplemented by the Company Names Adjudicator Rules 2008 (SI 2008/1738), made pursuant to s 71, which came into force on 1 October 2008. Section 82 is supplemented by the Companies (Trading Disclosures) Regulations 2008 (SI 2008/495), which came into force on 1 October 2008 and the Companies (Trading Disclosures) (Amendment) Regulations 2008 (laid in draft before Parliament) which come into force on 1 October 2009.

[131] 2006 Act Commencement Order No 7, arts 2(a)–(c); the Companies (Reduction of Share Capital) Order 2008 (SI 2008/1915).

[132] 2006 Act Commencement Order No 5, arts 5(2) and 8(b) and Schedule 3.

[133] 2006 Act Commencement Order No 8. 2006 Act, Part 13 (resolutions and meetings), ss 327(2)(c) and 330(6)(c) concerning polls are not being commenced for the time being.

### (3) Interpretation of the Companies Act 2006

**1.48** The Government's intention was that the Companies Act 2006 should be drafted 'in clear, concise and unambiguous language which can be readily understood by those involved in business enterprise'.[134] The 2006 Act not only includes the new reforming provisions, described in paragraphs 1.15–1.38 above, but also restates some of the provisions of the 1985 and 1989 Acts, rewriting them to make them simpler and easier to understand.[135] In February 2007 the Government published Explanatory Notes on the Act and tables of derivations and destinations. Three words are used in the table of derivations to identify provisions in the 2006 Act that do not re-enact the previous provisions without change:

'drafting'   This indicates a new provision of a mechanical or editorial nature (such as a definition used to avoid repetition).

'changed'   This means that the provision has been re-enacted with one or more primary, and not just consequential, changes.

'new'   This indicates a provision which has no predecessor in the repealed legislation or which is fundamentally different from its predecessor.

The table of destinations uses the word 'repealed' to identify provisions in the 1985 Act, the Business Names Act 1985, and the 1989 Act, in force on 8 November 2006, which are repealed by the 2006 Act and not re-enacted, even in amended form.

**1.49** Despite the Government's intentions and the assistance in understanding the 2006 Act it has provided, it is to be expected that unusual factual situations will expose difficulties of construction. In order to understand the background to, and objective of, particular provisions, reference may be made to the reports of the Law Commission, the reports of the CLR and the White Papers, which are described in Chapter 2, Section E, and also to the Explanatory Notes on the Act, published by the Government after it received the Royal Assent.[136]

**1.50** To give guidance on the new statutory statement of duties of company directors, in June 2007 the Government published extracts of statements made by Ministers in Parliament during the passage of the Bill. Whether or not any of these statements may be admissible in court proceedings under the rule established by *Pepper v Hart*[137] the statements are likely to be a useful guide to understanding the 2006 Act and so many of them are quoted in this work.

---

[134] *Modern Company Law for a Competitive Economy* (March 1998) at para 5.2(c).

[135] Explanatory memorandum to the 2006 Act Commencement Order No 1 at para 4.1.

[136] The court may refer to this material in order to interpret the Act: *Wilson v First County Trust Ltd (No 2)* [2004] 1 AC 816, HL, per Lord Nicholls at para 56; and for explanatory notes *R (Westminster County Court) v National Asylum Service* [2002] 1 WLR 2956, HL, per Lord Steyn at paras 4–6.

[137] [1993] AC 593, HL.

It is clear that the 2006 Act is intended to mark a new chapter in company law, **1.51** freed from many of the restrictions and complications of the previous law. Since the 2006 Act combines old and new provisions, difficulties of interpretation or of application of the provisions to particular circumstances may arise. If there are any ambiguities, the court will no doubt prefer the interpretation which furthers rather than hinders the Government's stated aim of providing a framework which 'facilitates enterprise and promotes transparency and fair dealing'.[138]

The 2006 Act may be compared with the Insolvency Act 1986, since the latter Act **1.52** includes not only reforms made by the Insolvency Act 1985 in the light of the report of the Cork Committee (1982, Cmnd 6659), but also provisions about insolvency which derived from the Companies Act 1985 and some provisions about personal bankruptcy which derived from the Bankruptcy Act 1914. The approach of the court to issues of interpretation of the Insolvency Act may be instructive in relation to the 2006 Act.

In *Smith v Braintree District Council*[139] Lord Jauncey of Tullichettle (with whom **1.53** the other Lords agreed) construed a section of the Insolvency Act 'as a piece of new legislation without regard to 19th century authorities or similar provisions of repealed Bankruptcy Acts', having regard to changes in policy shown by the new Act in relation to that provision.

In *Re a Debtor (No 784 of 1991)*[140] Hoffmann J, having referred to Lord Jauncey's **1.54** speech in *Smith* and other authorities, said: 'Those authorities show that, in approaching the language of the Act of 1986, one must pay particular attention to the purposes and policies of its own provisions and be wary of simply carrying over uncritically meanings which had been given to similar words in the earlier Act. It does not, however, mean that the language of the new Act comes to one entirely free of any of the intellectual freight which was carried by words and phrases in earlier bankruptcy or other legislation.' Where there is nothing in the policy of the new Act to indicate that words taken from the old Act should bear a different meaning, they should be interpreted in the same way as in the old Act.

In *Bishopsgate Investment Ltd v Maxwell*,[141] a case concerning an application for a **1.55** private examination under s 236, Dillon LJ said: '. . . there can be no doubt that the primary task of the court is to construe the Insolvency Act 1986 as it stands, without regard to the legislative histories of its various components . . . Even so,

---

[138] Foreword of the President of the Board of Trade (Margaret Beckett) to *Modern Company Law for a Competitive Economy* (March 1998); also paras 3.1, 3.8, 5.1, and 5.2.

[139] [1990] 2 AC 215, 238, HL.

[140] [1992] Ch 554, 558, 559; cited with approval by Ferris J in *Woodland-Ferrari v UCL Group Retirement Scheme* [2003] Ch 115 at para 41.

[141] [1993] Ch 1, 21, CA.

I have found it essential in the present case to consider the legislative antecedents of the Act of 1986, and the cases decided under them, partly to see how certain provisions of the Act of 1986 can, in the light of previous decisions under the earlier statutes, be expected to fit together, but even more to see what the mischief was in the old law which the Act of 1986 was intended to cure.'

# 2

# HISTORICAL INTRODUCTION TO THE LAW RELATING TO THE DUTIES AND LIABILITIES OF DIRECTORS

## A. Introduction

Directors of a company are identified by their functions, rather than their descrip-  **2.01**
tive title. The Joint Stock Companies Act 1844, the first of the Victorian statutes
on company law, defined directors as 'the persons having the direction, conduct,
management, or superintendence of the affairs of the company'.[1] The Companies
Act 1862 did not provide definitions, but since 1908 the Companies Acts have
provided that in those Acts a director 'includes any person occupying the position
of director, by whatever name called', thereby including de facto directors.[2]

---

[1] 1844 Act, s 3. Very recently Briggs J said that 'every director of a company has a responsibility,
shared with the other directors, for the management of the whole of the company's affairs. This
responsibility is imposed upon the directors not only by the general law, but by the standard form
articles of association': *Lexi Holdings plc v Luqman* [2008] 2 BCLC 725 at para 30.

[2] 1908 Act, s 285, 1929 Act, s 380, 1948 Act, s 455, 1985 Act, s 741(1), and 2006 Act, s 250.
See further Chapter 3 of this work.

Whereas the 1844 Act made it clear that the directors, not the shareholders, had the conduct of the ordinary management of the company, with power to make contracts, execute documents, and hire employees and agents,[3] subsequent Companies Acts have imposed duties on directors, but left it to the company's constitution to provide for the directors' functions and powers.

**2.02** Directors occupy a central position in the structure of company law, made up of statutory provisions supported by common law rules and equitable principles. The structure reflects three purposes.[4] The first purpose is that companies are formed and managed by the directors for the benefit of shareholders. This is achieved through the fiduciary obligations of directors and their duties of care and skill, remedies at law for their breach, and by the shareholders' powers of dismissal.[5] That purpose is subject to the second purpose, which is that there should be safeguards for the benefit of actual and potential creditors. This is achieved through directors' duties, insolvency law, and special provisions or rules about eg capital maintenance. Finally, as reflected in accounting and disclosure requirements, company law operates for the benefit of the community as a whole, including actual and potential shareholders and creditors.

**2.03** The following sections of this chapter trace the changing functions and obligations of directors as reflected in the default articles prescribed for companies, identify the common law rules and equitable principles which support the statutory framework, and finally outline the changes in statute law as they affect the functions, duties, and liabilities of directors. Two significant trends emerge. First, ever increasing statutory provision has largely replaced the common law rules and equitable principles. Those principles and rules will however remain influential in the interpretation and application of the Companies Act 2006, particularly in relation to the general duties of directors. The second trend concerns the role of directors. As expectations as to the amount of their participation in, and responsibility for, a company's affairs have increased, there has been a move away from comparing directors to trustees and instead emphasizing their commercial role. More powers have been delegated to directors and they have been expected to satisfy objective standards of skill, care, and diligence. At a mundane level the developing appreciation of the role of directors is reflected in the Companies Acts. The 1862 Act had little to say about directors, leaving those matters to the company's articles and the general law. The scheme of the 2006 Act gives directors a much more prominent position than they had enjoyed in any previous Companies Act.

---

[3] 1844 Act, s 27.

[4] CLR: *The Strategic Framework* at paras 5.1.4–5.1.7.

[5] This traditional relationship between directors and shareholders is described by Lord Oliver in *Caparo plc v Dickman* [1990] 2 AC 605, 630, HL.

## B. Articles of Association Relating to Directors

The Companies Acts of 1862, 1908, 1929, and 1948 prescribed articles of asso-  **2.04**
ciation in the form of Table A, which would stand as the default articles for
companies unless excluded or modified, as was frequently the case. Table A for the
1985 Act and the Model Articles for the 2006 Act have been prescribed by statutory instrument.[6] Under the 2006 Act there are separate Model Articles for private
companies limited by shares (pcls), private companies limited by guarantee (plg),
and public companies (plc). Many companies, particularly larger ones, adopt
bespoke articles which depart to a greater or lesser extent from the Table A model.
That will continue to be the case when the 2006 Model Articles become the
default articles.

The 1862 Act, Table A established the essential features of the office of director  **2.05**
which, with modifications, were repeated in the 1908, 1929, 1948, and 1985
Tables.[7] The significant developments have concerned directors with executive
functions and conflict of interest. The first directors were appointed by the subscribers and thereafter by the company in general meeting, subject to a power of
the board to fill casual vacancies. Directors received remuneration determined by
the company in general meeting. There were provisions for directors to retire by
rotation, but a director could only be removed by special resolution. The directors
managed the business of the company and could exercise all its powers except for
those reserved by the Act or the articles to the company in general meeting. They
would dispatch the business of the company at board meetings, but could delegate
their powers to a committee of one or more directors. They could recommend the
payment of dividends out of profits subject to the sanction of the company in
general meeting. They were responsible for keeping accounts and in each year
having them audited and laid before the company in general meeting.

Under the 1862 Act, Table A a director automatically vacated office if 'he holds  **2.06**
any other office or place of profit under the company', or 'if he is concerned in or
participates in the profits of any contract with the company'; subject to the proviso that he should not vacate office 'by reason of his being a member of any
company which has entered into contracts with or done any work for the company of which he is director; nevertheless he shall not vote in respect of such

---

[6] Companies (Tables A to F) Regulations 1985 (SI 1985/805); Companies (Tables A to F)
(Amendment) Regulations 2007 (SI 2007/2541); and Companies (Tables A to F) (Amendment)
(No 2)) Regulations 2007 (SI 2007/2826) which apply to companies incorporated after 1 October
2007; Companies (Model Articles) Regulations 2008 (SI 2008/3229) which apply to companies
incorporated after 1 October 2009.
[7] 1862 Act, Table A, regs 52–94; 1908 Act, Table A, regs 68–108; 1929 Act, Table A, regs
64–101; 1948 Act, Table A, regs 75–129 and 136; 1985 Act, Table A, regs 64–110, and 118.

contract or work; and if he does so vote his vote shall not be counted'.[8] It was not envisaged, therefore, that a director would be a full-time executive, remunerated under a contract of employment; hence references in the cases to the intermittent nature of the office. By the turn of the century this had begun to change and the role of executive directors who devoted the whole or a substantial amount of their time to the company's affairs was recognized in the 1908 Act, Table A. Under it the directors could appoint one or more of their body to the office of managing director or manager on terms and at remuneration fixed by the directors and a director so appointed was not subject to the rotation provisions and did not automatically vacate his office as director.[9]

**2.07** The 1948 Act, Table A acknowledged the obligations, expenses, and risks of the office of director by providing that in addition to remuneration directors might be paid all expenses properly incurred in attending meetings of directors, committees of directors, or general meetings of the company or in connection with the business of the company and that they were entitled to an indemnity in respect of all liabilities incurred in successfully defending civil or criminal proceedings or applying for relief under the 1948 Act, s 448.[10] Although a director's remuneration was to be determined by the company in general meeting, the directors could determine the terms, including remuneration, on which a director held other offices or places of profit under the company or provided professional services.[11] The 1985 Act, Table A for the first time expressly stated that the directors' powers of management were subject to any directions given by special resolution.[12]

**2.08** Under the 1948 Act, Table A conflict of interest was no longer a ground for vacating office. Instead a director who was in any way directly or indirectly interested in a contract or proposed contract with the company was to declare his interest to a meeting of the directors in accordance with the 1948 Act, s 199. With certain exceptions he was not to vote on the contract. The 1985 Act, Table A took this a stage further: a director could be directly or indirectly interested in transactions or arrangements with the company or in which the company was interested and was not accountable for benefits, provided that he disclosed the nature and extent of his interest to the directors.

---

[8] reg 57. He also vacated office if he became bankrupt or insolvent.

[9] regs 72 and 77, which also provided for a director to vacate office if he 'is found lunatic or becomes of unsound mind'.

[10] 1948 Act, Table A, regs 76 and 136.

[11] 1948 Act, Table A, regs 76, 84, and 88. Also 1985 Act, Table A, regs 85 and 94. 1985 Act, Table A, reg 87, gave the directors power to provide gratuities and pensions to former executive directors and their families.

[12] 1985 Act, Table A, reg 70.

The 2006 Act Model Articles follow the traditional structure, but directors are **2.09** given more powers in relation to appointment and remuneration and more flexibility in decision-making. The directors are responsible for the management of the company's business subject to directions given by special resolution, and they have full power to delegate to any person or committee.[13] Directors' decisions are to be taken collectively, either at a meeting or by written resolution.[14] Since the 2006 Act, ss 175, 177, and 182 deal expressly with conflicts of interest and interests in actual and proposed transactions; the Model Articles simply deal with the mechanics of decision-making in cases of conflict.[15] Directors may be appointed by ordinary resolution or by decision of the directors.[16] A director's remuneration for services as director and for any other service undertaken for the company is to be decided by the directors.[17]

## C. Common Law Rules and Equitable Principles Relating to the Management of Companies

### (1) The *ultra vires* doctrine

The memorandum of association of a company incorporated under the **2.10** Companies Acts 1862 to 1985 had to state the objects of the company with some degree of particularity.[18] Two consequences, of particular relevance to directors, followed from this. The first was that any transaction outside the scope of the company's objects, or what may fairly be regarded as incidental or consequential upon the stated objects, was void and incapable of ratification by shareholders.[19] A director who caused the company's property to be applied for purposes outside its objects would be personally liable for any loss caused.[20] The courts developed the *ultra vires* rule to protect investors in the company and creditors from

---

[13] Model Articles (pcls, plg, and plc) 3–6.

[14] Model Articles (pcls and plg) 7–13, 15, 16 and Model Articles (plc) 7–15, 17–19.

[15] Model Article (pcls and plg) 14 and Model Article (plc) 16.

[16] Model Article (pcls and plg) 17 and Model Article (plc) 20. Retirement by rotation only applies to directors of public companies (Model Article (plc) 21). Model Article (pcls and plg) 18 and Model Article (plc) 22 deal with automatic vacation of office for disqualification, bankrupty etc.

[17] Model Article (pcls and plg) 19 and Model Article (plc) 23. The company may also pay a director's reasonable expenses: Model Article (pcls and plg) 20 and Model Article (plc) 24.

[18] 1985 Act, s 2(1)(c). Also 1862 Act, s 10; 1908 Act, s 3; 1929 Act, s 2; 1948 Act, s 2(1)(c); *Re Crown Bank* (1890) 44 Ch D, 634, 644.

[19] *Eastern Counties Railway v Hawkes* (1855) 5 HLC 331, 346, 348; *The Ashbury Railway Carriage and Iron Co v Riche* (1875) LR 7 HL 653, 672, 673, 679, 689, 694; *A-G v Great Eastern Railway Co* (1880) 5 AC 473, 478, 481, 486.

[20] *Joint Stock Discount Co v Brown* (1869) LR 8 Eq 376; *Hardy v Metropolitan Land Co* (1872) 7 Ch App 427; *Great Eastern Railway Co v Turner* (1872) 8 Ch App 149; *Russell v Wakefield Waterworks Co* (1875) LR 20 Eq 474, 479; *Cullerne v London and Suburban Building Society* (1890) 25

loss resulting from the unauthorized use of company funds. A company could avoid the rigours of the rule by including in its memorandum a long list of objects, each of which was stated to be as an independent object, not limited or restricted by any other object.[21] The second consequence was that since the funds of a company were made by statute applicable only for the specific purposes set out in the memorandum, those funds were impressed with the qualities of a trust fund.[22] Directors were therefore considered to be in a position comparable to that of a trustee, although account had to be taken of the commercial nature of their engagement.[23]

**2.11** The *ultra vires* doctrine has now largely disappeared from view as a result of statutory reforms beginning in 1972, which have resulted in a company's capacity no longer being limited by the objects stated in its memorandum.[24] The 1985 Act, subs 35(1), which will be replaced without material change by the 2006 Act, subs 39(1),[25] provides that 'the validity of an act done by a company shall not be called into question on the ground of lack of capacity by reason of anything in the company's memorandum.' There are special rules for charitable companies.[26]

**2.12** Also, the objects clause has been liberalized. The 1985 Act, s 3A provides:[27]

> Where the company's memorandum states that the object of the company is to carry on business as a general commercial company—
> (a) the object of the company is to carry on any trade or business whatsoever, and
> (b) the company has power to do all such things as are incidental or conducive to the carrying on of any trade or business by it.

---

QBD 485; *Re George Newman & Co* [1895] 1 Ch 674, CA; *Re Claridge's Patent Asphalt Co Ltd* [1921] 1 Ch 543, CA.

[21] In *Cotman v Brougham* [1918] AC 514, 523 Lord Wrenbury deprecated the use of 'independent objects' clauses, but acknowledged that they were effective.

[22] *Selangor United Rubber Estates v Cradock (No 3)* [1968] 1 WLR 1555, 1575.

[23] Paragraph 2.19 below.

[24] The reforms began with the European Communities Act 1972, s 9 (giving effect to Article 9 of Council Directive 68/151/EEC), which became 1985 Act, s 35. A new s 35 was inserted into the 1985 Act by 1989 Act, s 108(1) as from 4 February 1991 to remove the limit of the protection in the original s 35, which only applied to third parties acting in good faith and to transactions decided on by the directors. The purpose of the 1972 Act and the Directive 'is to enable people to deal with a company in good faith without being adversely affected by any limits on the company's capacity or its rules for internal management'; per Sir Nicholas Browne-Wilkinson V-C in *TCB Ltd v Gray* [1986] Ch 621, 635.

[25] With effect from 1 October 2009. The only change is that the 2006 Act replaces 'memorandum' with 'constitution'. The other changes made by the 2006 Act are that 1985 Act, subs 35(2), concerning proceedings by members to restrain an act beyond the company's capacity, and subs (3), concerning the duty of directors to observe limitations on their powers flowing from the company's memorandum and ratification, are repealed and not replaced. Directors' duties and ratification are dealt with in 2006 Act, ss 170–181 and 239.

[26] 1985 Act, s 35(4); 2006 Act, ss 39(2) and 42.

[27] This was inserted by 1989 Act, s 110 with effect from 4 February 1991.

The 2006 Act, s 31(1) takes the process of liberalization a stage further by reversing the traditional rule that the memorandum must positively state the company's objects. It provides that 'unless a company's articles specifically restrict the objects of the company, its objects are unrestricted'.[28]

## (2) The indoor management rule

*Royal British Bank v Turquand*[29] established that, although it was to be assumed **2.13** that a person dealing with a company had read the company's public documents[30] and satisfied himself that the proposed transaction was not inconsistent with them, such a person was not required to inquire whether internal procedures had been duly carried out. The rule is supplemented by the rules of agency that a director or other officer may bind the company if he has ostensible or apparent authority to do so.[31]

The rule has been superseded by statutory provision now contained in the 1985 **2.14** Act, s 35A and s 35B,[32] which will be replaced without material change by the 2006 Act, s 40.[33] Subsection 35A(1) provides:

> In favour of a person dealing with a company in good faith, the power of the board of directors to bind the company, or authorise others to do so, shall be deemed to be free of any limitation under the company's constitution.

By subs 35A(2) a person is not regarded as acting in bad faith by reason only of his knowing that an act is beyond the powers of the directors and he is presumed to have acted in good faith unless the contrary is proved. Section 35B provides:

> A party to a transaction with a company is not bound to enquire as to whether it is permitted by the company's memorandum or as to any limitation on the powers of the board of directors to bind the company or authorise others to do so.

Subsection 35A(5) provides that the section does not deprive the company of claims against directors for exceeding their powers. These sections are discussed in Chapter 4, Section B of this work.

---

[28] This section will come into force on 1 October 2009.

[29] (1856) 6 El & Bl 327. In *Mahony v East Holyford Mining Co* (1875) LR 7 HL 869, 898 Lord Hatherley used the phrase 'the indoor management' in this context.

[30] eg its memorandum of association, articles of association, and special resolutions delivered to the Registrar.

[31] See further Chapter 4 of this work; *Freeman & Lockyer v Buckhurst Park Properties (Mangal) Ltd* [1964] 2 QB, 480, CA.

[32] In their original form these provisions were introduced by European Communities Act 1972, s 9 and became 1985 Act, s 35. The current ss 35A and 35B were inserted by 1989 Act, s 108 with effect from 4 February 1991.

[33] 2006 Act, s 40 will come into effect on 1 October 2009.

## (3) **Attribution**

2.15 For certain purposes it may be necessary for the court to determine whether the knowledge, mental state, or intentions of its directors, other officers, or employees are to be attributed to it. This issue may arise in civil contexts[34] and also in relation to the question whether the company has the necessary mental state (malice, dishonesty, or intention) to commit a criminal offence.[35] The dishonest intent will not, however, be attributed to the company where the fraud is committed upon the company.[36] In the leading case of *Lennard's Carrying Company v Asiatic Petroleum Ltd*[37] the House of Lords attributed the managing director's default to the company on the ground that he was the 'directing mind and will' or alter ego of the company. In a well-known passage Lord Haldane said:

> My Lords, a corporation is an abstraction. It has no mind of its own any more than it has a body of its own; its active and directing will must consequently be sought in the person of somebody who for some purposes may be called an agent, but who is really the directing mind and will of the corporation, the very ego and centre of the personality of the corporation. That person may be under the direction of the shareholders in general meeting; that person may be the board of directors itself, or it may be, and in some companies it is so, that that person has an authority co-ordinate with the board of directors given to him under the articles of association, and is appointed by the general meeting of the company, and can only be removed by the general meeting of the company.

2.16 In accordance with that principle the directors would normally be regarded as the directing mind and will of a company by virtue of their position under the company's constitution. But in *Meridian Global Funds Management Asia Ltd v Securities*

---

[34] *Lennard's Carrying Company v Asiatic Petroleum Ltd* [1915] AC 705, HL; *The Truculent* [1952] P 1; *The Lady Gwendolen* [1965] P 294, 355, CA (civil liability in collisions to which the Merchant Shipping Act 1894 applied); *DC Thompson & Co v Deakin* [1952] Ch 646, CA (inducing breach of contract); *Bolton (Engineering) Co Ltd v Graham & Sons* [1957] 1 QB 159 (intention to occupy premises for the purposes of the Landlord and Tenant Act 1954); *El Ajou v Dollar Land Holdings Ltd* [1994] 2 All ER 685, 695–8, 699, 700, 705, CA (knowledge for the purposes of a knowing receipt claim); *Odyssey Re (London) Ltd v OIC Run-Off Ltd*, 13 March 2000, CA (The Times, 17 March 2000 (perjury by company's key witness and member of case handling team); *Re Bank of Credit and Commerce SA (No 15)* [2005] 2 BCLC 328 at paras 114–124, 129, 130, CA (civil fraudulent trading under the Insolvency Act, s 213); *Moore Stephens v Stones & Rolls Ltd* [2008] 3 WLR 1146, CA (fraud on third party perpetrated by directors attributed to the company).

[35] *DPP v Kent & Sussex Contractors Ltd* [1944] KB 146, DC; *R v ICR Haulage* [1944] KB 551, 559, CA; *Moore v Bresler Ltd* [1944] 2 All ER 515, DC; *Melias Ltd v Preston* [1957] 2 QB 380, DC; *R v McDowell* [1966] 1 QB 233; *Tesco Supermarkets v Nattrass* [1972] AC 155, HL; *Knowles Transport v Russell* [1975] RTR 87, DC; *Re Supply of Ready Mixed Concrete (No 2)* [1995] 1 AC 456, HL; *Re Attorney General's Reference (No 2 of 1999)* [2000] 2 BCLC 257, 261, CA.

[36] *Re Hampshire Land Co* [1896] 2 Ch 743, 749, CA; *JC Houghton & Co v Nothard, Lowe and Wills Ltd* [1928] AC 1, 15, 19, HL; *Belmont Finance Corp v Williams Furniture Ltd* [1979] Ch 250, 261, 262, CA; *Moore Stephens v Stones & Rolls Ltd* [2008] 3 WLR 1146, CA.

[37] [1915] AC 705, HL.

*Commission*[38] Lord Hoffmann said that in an exceptional case where application of the 'directing mind and will' principle would defeat the intended application of a particular provision to companies, it may be necessary to attribute to the company the acts or knowledge of some other person, such as the person entrusted with conduct of a particular matter. Thus attribution becomes a question of construction of the substantive provision rather than the rigid application of an immutable principle.

### (4) The duties of directors

From the earliest times the duties of directors have been identified by comparing directors with trustees. In 1742 Lord Hardwicke LC had to determine the nature and extent of directors' duties in *The Charitable Corporation v Sutton*.[39] The corporation's affairs were a 'great scene of iniquity' in which its funds, rather than being applied for the relief of the industrious poor, had been misapplied in fraudulent and fictitious loans and other improper transactions, causing loss to the corporation of more than £350,000. The corporation brought proceedings to recover its losses from some 50 committeemen, directors, and other officers on the ground that they 'had been guilty of manifest breaches of trust, or at least of such supine and gross negligence of their duty'. Lord Hardwicke held that the office of director (or committeeman) was in the nature of a private trust, so that such officers were liable to the corporation for 'breaches of trust, either by commissions or omissions, for acts of misfeasance or nonfeasance' and that where 'there is a series of neglects, and breaches of trust are occasioned by their absence, then they are answerable for the misfeasance of others'. Even though the office of director is voluntary, it had to be discharged with 'fidelity, integrity, and diligence'. The five conspirators who had been directly responsible for the misapplication of the funds were primarily liable to make good the losses, but the other directors could be liable in the second degree if they connived in the affair by signing the false notes under which monies were misapplied, or if they failed to make use of 'the proper power invested in them by the charter, in order to prevent the ill consequences arising from such a confederacy'. Inquiries were ordered to determine the liability of the directors in the second degree. Thus *The Charitable Corporation v Sutton* established that directors owed the company fiduciary duties (fidelity and integrity) and a duty of diligence.

**2.17**

In relation to fiduciary duties the courts have always imposed exacting standards. Directors were liable to restore misapplied company property, whether they were

**2.18**

---

[38] [1995] 2 AC 500, 506–12, PC.
[39] (1742) 2 Atk 400; 9 Mod Rep 349. There are differences between the two reports and the quotations in this paragraph are taken from both reports.

recipients of the property or participants in the misapplication.[40] In *The York and North-Midland Railway Co v Hudson*[41] George Hudson, the 'Railway King', was liable to account to the company with interest at 5% for his secret profits and also for company monies for which he could not account, since they had been used in paying bribes to facilitate the passage through Parliament of a bill for the extension of the company's railway line. A director's fiduciary duty to promote the interests of the company precluded him from entering on behalf of the company into a contract with himself or a firm or company of which he was a member, regardless of the fairness or unfairness of the contract.[42] He could only be released from his position of conflict or duty to account by the assent of the members.[43] The fiduciary duties of a director were reflected in the 1862 Act, s 165, which gave the court a summary power, where a company was being wound up, to assess damages against a delinquent director or officer who had 'misapplied or retained or become liable or accountable for any moneys or property of the company, or been guilty of any misfeasance or breach of trust in relation to the company'.[44]

**2.19** The position of a director could not be equated entirely with that of a trustee. In 1878 Jessel MR said: 'Directors have sometimes been called trustees, or commercial trustees, and sometimes they have been called managing partners, it does not matter what you call them so long as you understand what their true position is, which is that they are really commercial men managing a trading concern for the benefit of themselves and all other shareholders in it' and that 'they are so bound to use fair and reasonable diligence in the management of the company's affairs, and to act honestly'.[45] In *City Equitable Fire Insurance Co*[46] Romer J said that he found the analogy with trustees wholly misleading. Directors stood in a fiduciary relationship to the company, but there was little resemblance between their duties and those of a trustee of a will or marriage settlement. The duties that a director owes to the company are determined by the functions he undertakes to perform, the nature of the company's business, and the way in which work is properly distributed among the directors and other officers.

---

[40]  *Benson v Heathorn* (1842) 1 Y&CC 326.

[41]  (1853) 16 Beav 485.

[42]  *Aberdeen Railway Co v Blaikie Bros* (1854) 1 Macq 461, HL.

[43]  *Regal (Hastings) Ltd v Gulliver* (1942) [1967] 2 AC 134n, 150, HL.

[44]  As restated by Companies (Winding Up) Act 1890, s 10. *Palmer's Handbook on Company Law* (4th edn, 1902) pp 170, 172 took the view that breach of trust was generally confined to misapplication of company funds (eg application for an *ultra vires* purpose), whereas misfeasance covered other breaches of duty (eg the allotment of shares to an infant, taking a bribe, or committing a fraudulent preference).

[45]  *Re Forest of Dean Coal Mining Co* (1878) 10 Ch D 450, 451, 452; *Re Lands Allotment Co* [1894] 1 Ch 616, 631, CA, per Lindley LJ.

[46]  [1925] Ch 407, 426–30.

In 1998 the Law Commission, chaired by Arden J, considered directors' fiduciary   **2.20** duties to the company under six heads:[47] (i) a duty of loyalty (to act in the best interests of the company),[48] (ii) a duty to act for proper purposes (to exercise powers for the purpose for which those powers were conferred),[49] (iii) a duty not to fetter their discretion,[50] (iv) the no conflict and no profit rules (under which a director could not keep profits from information, property, or opportunities that belong to the company),[51] (v) a duty to act in accordance with the company's constitution, and (vi) a duty to act fairly as between different shareholders.[52]

The amount of diligence expected of a nineteenth-century director was distinctly   **2.21** modest. A director who, by taking no part in the company's affairs and not attending board meetings, was unaware of wrongdoing or breaches of the company's constitution escaped liability to compensate the company for losses suffered.[53] Since a director could hold office while being largely ignorant of the company's affairs, he was free to take office as a director of a rival company.[54]

Consistently with the low standard of diligence tolerated by the court, a director   **2.22** could be found liable to compensate the company for breach of a duty of care and skill in relation to business decisions only if a high degree of negligence was shown.

---

[47] Law Commission *Company Directors: Regulating Conflicts of Interest and Formulating a Statement of Duties* (Consultation Paper No 153) at paras 11.4–11.20.

[48] *Re Smith and Fawcett Ltd* [1942] Ch 304, 306, CA, per Lord Greene MR. The best interests of the company may require account to be taken of the interests of creditors (*Winkworth v Edward Baron Development Co Ltd* [1986] 1 WLR 1512, 1516, HL, per Lord Templeman; *Facia Footwear Ltd v Hinchcliffe* [1998] 1 BCLC 218; *Yukong Line Ltd v Rendsburg Investments Corp (No 2)* [1998] 1 WLR 294) and employees (*Hutton v West Cork Railway Co* (1883) 23 Ch D 654, 672, 673, CA, per Bowen LJ, who said 'The law does not say that there are to be no cakes and ale, but there are to be no cakes and ale except such as are required for the benefit of the company', and 1985 Act, s 309).

[49] *Howard Smith Ltd v Ampol Petroleum Ltd* [1974] AC 821, 835, PC, per Lord Wilberforce; also *Spackman v Evans* (1868) LR 3 HL 171,186, per Lord Cranworth; *Alexander v Automatic Telephone Co* [1890] 2 Ch 233.

[50] *Fulham Football Club Ltd v Cabra Estates plc* [1994] 1 BCLC 363, 392, CA, per Neill LJ.

[51] *Regal (Hastings) Ltd v Gulliver* [1967] 2 AC 131n; *Industrial Development Consultants Ltd v Cooley* [1972] 1 WLR 443; *Movitex Ltd v Bullfield* [1988] BCLC 104, where Vinelott J said that the no profit rule imposed a disability not a duty.

[52] *Mutual Life Insurance v Rank Organisation Ltd* [1985] BCLC 11, 21, per Goulding J; *Re BSB Holdings Ltd (No 2)* [1996] 1 BCLC 155, 246–49, per Arden J.

[53] *Re Cardiff Savings Bank, the Marquis of Bute's Case* [1892] 2 Ch 100 is the best known illustration. In that case the Marquis had not attended any meetings of the bank's trustees and managers for the last seventeen years of the bank's trading life. During that period, through breach of the bank's regulations, its executive officer misapplied some £30,000 of the bank's funds. Stirling J held that the Marquis was not liable because, if he had read the notices of meetings sent to him, he would have seen that the bank's affairs appeared to be in order and he could rely on those who did attend the meetings to discharge their duties. *Re Denham* (1883) 25 Ch D 752 is to similar effect.

[54] *Re London and Mashonaland Exploration Co v New Mashonaland Exploration Co* [1891] WN 165, a case discussed in *In Plus Group Ltd v Pyke* [2002] 2 BCLC 201, CA. In fact the New Mashonaland Exploration Co soon collapsed into insolvent liquidation and the director whose appointment had been in dispute was fortunate to escape liability for misfeasance in making negligent loans of company money: *Re New Mashonaland Exploration Co* [1892] 3 Ch 577.

The negligence had to amount to *crassa negligentia*,[55] or 'it must be in a business sense culpable and gross'.[56] The standard of care was essentially subjective and dependent on the director's own capabilities: a director was required to show the degree of skill to be reasonably expected of a person with his knowledge and experience and to take such a care as an ordinary man might be expected to take on his own behalf, but he was not bound to give continuous attention to the affairs of the company and, in the absence of grounds for suspicion, was entitled to trust his fellow officers.[57] Therefore shareholders and creditors had to put up with the blunders of foolish and unwise directors[58] or of a board comprising 'a set of amiable lunatics'.[59]

**2.23** Subsequent changes to the Companies Acts, including provisions to enforce fair dealing, to strengthen the duties of directors, to maintain sufficient accounting records, and for the disqualification of unfit directors, have required directors to be more closely involved in a company's affairs. This has encouraged the court to apply an objective standard of care, skill, and diligence and to adopt the twofold test in the Insolvency Act, s 213(4) (wrongful trading).[60]

**2.24** Now the general duties of directors are codified by the 2006 Act, ss 170–177 (Chapters 9–16 of this work) and these duties are buttressed by provisions requiring directors to disclose interests in existing transactions and to obtain the approval of members for certain transactions in which they are interested (Chapters 17 and 18 of this work). The statutory statement of directors' fiduciary duties includes elements of reform in relation to the duty to promote the success of the company

---

[55] *Overend, Gurney & Co v Gibb* (1872) LR 5 HL 480, 487, HL, per Lord Hatherley, who explained that directors would be guilty of *crassa negligentia* if 'they were cognisant of circumstances of such a character, so plain, so manifest, and so simple of appreciation, that no men with any ordinary degree of prudence, acting on their own behalf, would have entered into such a transaction as they entered into'.

[56] *Lagunas Nitrate Co v Lagunas Syndicate* [1899] 2 Ch 392, 435, CA. *Re Brazilian Rubber Plantations and Estates Ltd* [1911] 1 Ch 425, discussed in Chapter 13, paragraph 13.14 of this work, is an extreme illustration of the difficulties of proving gross negligence. In that case the directors, who somewhat surprisingly were acquitted of negligence and were in any event entitled to rely on an exemption clause in the articles, consisted of a baronet who was 'absolutely ignorant of business', a banker from Bath who was 'seventy-five years of age and very deaf', a rubber broker who understood that his only function was to value the rubber if and when it arrived in England, and a businessman who joined because he considered that the banker and rubber broker were 'good men'.

[57] *Re City Equitable Fire Insurance Co* [1925] Ch 407, 428, 429, per Romer J; *Dorchester Finance Co Ltd v Stebbing* (1977) [1989] BCLC 498, 501, 502. As to relying on other officers: *Dovey v Corey* [1901] AC 477, 485, HL, per Lord Halsbury.

[58] *Turquand v Marshall* (1869) LR 4 Ch App 376, 386, per Lord Hatherley LC.

[59] In argument in *Pavlides v Jensen* [1956] Ch 565, 570.

[60] *Norman v Theodore Goddard* [1991] BCLC 1028, 1030, 1031, 1037, 1038, per Hoffmann J; *Bishopsgate Investment Management Ltd v Maxwell* [1994] 1 All ER 261, CA, per Hoffmann LJ; *Re D'Jan of London Ltd* [1994] 1 BCLC 561, 563, per Hoffmann LJ.

and in permitting the independent directors to authorize a matter in which a director has a conflict of interest.[61]

### (5) Shareholders' remedies

Where directors have misapplied company property or otherwise caused it loss, **2.25** the company can sue to recover its property or to obtain compensation even though it was party to the impugned transaction.[62] If the wrongdoers are in control of the company, they will be able to prevent it from suing. To prevent this injustice, in *Hichens v Congreve*,[63] decided in 1828, Lord Lyndhurst LC held that shareholders could sue on behalf of themselves and the other shareholders for the purpose of compelling the directors to refund monies improperly withdrawn by them. The limits of Lord Lyndhurst's decision were soon exposed by the well-known case of *Foss v Harbottle*,[64] decided in 1843, which established (i) the 'proper plaintiff' principle, by which prima facie the corporation is the proper claimant in proceedings in respect of a wrong alleged to have been done to it, and (ii) the 'majority rule' principle, by which an individual shareholder will not be allowed to pursue proceedings on behalf of himself and all other shareholders if the alleged wrong was within the powers of the company, since, in those circumstances, the majority of the shareholders might ratify the allegedly wrongful transaction; if they did not, they would be able to put the company in motion to bring the necessary proceedings.

The rule in *Foss v Harbottle* did not apply to claims to enforce a shareholder's per- **2.26** sonal rights, as distinct from rights belonging to the company. Nor did the rule prevent an individual shareholder from bringing proceedings (known as a 'derivative action') in respect of a wrong done by the directors to the company where (i) the transaction in question was beyond the powers of the company or illegal, (ii) there had been a fraud on the minority shareholders and the wrongdoers were in control, or (iii) the act required the sanction of a special majority which could not be obtained.[65] In relation to the 'fraud on the minority' exception the law was

---

[61] 2006 Act, s 175.
[62] *A-G v Wilson* (1840) Cr & Ph 1, 24, per Lord Cottenham.
[63] (1828) 4 Russ 562.
[64] (1843) 2 Hare 461. Followed by Lord Cottenham LC in *Mozley v Alston* (1847) 1 Ph 790.
[65] *Burland v Earle* [1902] AC 83, 93, HL, per Lord Davey; *Edwards v Halliwell* [1950] 2 All ER 1064, 1067, CA; *Daniels v Daniels* [1978] Ch 406, 408, 414, where Templeman J said that the minority could sue 'where directors use their powers, intentionally or unintentionally, fraudulently or negligently, in a manner which benefits themselves at the expense of the company'; *Prudential Assurance Co Ltd v Newman Industries Ltd* [1982] Ch 204, 210, CA; *Estmanco (Kilner House) Ltd v Greater London Council* [1982] 1 WLR 2, 12; *Smith v Croft (No 2)* [1988] Ch 114, 173. The minority have not been allowed to proceed on an allegation of mere negligence without fraud: *Pavlides v Jensen* [1956] Ch 565; *Heyting v Dupont* [1964] 1 WLR 843, CA.

'complex and obscure'.[66] Litigations could become protracted, expensive, and damaging to the company, which could be 'killed by kindness'.[67] Rules of court were introduced to control the procedure.[68]

**2.27**  In 1980 a new remedy, later embodied in the 1985 Act, s 459, was introduced to protect members from unfair prejudice (paragraph 2.58 below).[69] The new remedy meant that minority shareholders would seldom need to resort to a derivative action. The 2006 Act has reformed this area of the law in two further ways. First, s 239 prevents the director and those connected with him from voting on a resolution to ratify his own wrong. Secondly, Part 11, ss 260–264, has introduced a new statutory code for derivative actions, which replaces the rule in *Foss v Harbottle* and its exceptions. These new provisions are discussed in Chapters 19 and 21 of this work.

### (6)  Decision-making of members

**2.28**  A company's articles invariably provide that the directors have unfettered powers of management which cannot be interfered with by the members except by altering the articles, giving directions pursuant to a special resolution, or by removing and replacing directors.[70] The directors may need to obtain a resolution of the members, whether to alter the constitution, to consent to, approve, or authorize some transaction or arrangement, or to ratify acts of directors or for some other purpose. In this connection the courts have developed three rules. First, the notice of the meeting to consider the resolution (or statement accompanying the proposed written resolution) must give 'a fair and candid and reasonable explanation' of the proposed business and must not be misleading or tricky.[71] If it does not, any resolution purportedly passed will be invalid. The rule will remain relevant to the provisions of the 2006 Act about resolutions and meetings.[72] Decision-making by members is discussed in Chapter 22 of this work.

---

[66]  Law Commission Consultation Paper No 142 *Shareholder Remedies* at para 1.6.

[67]  *Prudential Assurance Co Ltd v Newman Industries Ltd* [1982] Ch 204, 221, CA.

[68]  RSC Order 15, rule 12A, replaced by CPR 19.9. In *Barrett v Duckett* [1995] 1 BCLC 243, 249, 250, CA, Peter Gibson LJ stated the general principles governing such actions.

[69]  1980 Act, s 75, which was replaced by 1985 Act, s 459. On 1 October 2007 the 2006 Act, Part 30, ss 994–999 came into force and replaced 1985 Act, s 459. 1980 Act, s 75 replaced 1948 Act, s 210, which provided the first statutory remedy for oppression, but in terms that were too onerous on the applicant.

[70]  Table A, reg 70; Model Article (pcls) 3 and Model Article (plc) 4.

[71]  *Kaye v Croydon Tramways Co* [1898] 1 Ch 358, 373, CA, per Rigby LJ; *Tiessen v Henderson* [1899] 1 Ch 861; *Baillie v Oriental Telephone and Electric Co Ltd* [1915] 1 Ch 503, CA; *Pacific Coast Coal Mines Ltd v Arbuthnot* [1917] AC 607, 618, PC; *Clarkson v Davies* [1923] AC 100, PC.

[72]  These provisions, ss 281–361, came into force on 1 October 2007, except for ss 308, 309, and 333, which came into force on 20 January 2007, and ss 327(2)(c) and 330(6)(3), which are not yet in force.

Secondly, closely linked to the fraud on the minority exception to the rule in *Foss v*   **2.29**
*Harbottle*, the court developed an equitable rule that, in order for a resolution to
be effective, the voting rights of the members in support of it must be exercised in
good faith in the interests of the company as a whole.[73] In *British America Nickel
Corp Ltd v MJ O'Brien Ltd*[74] Lord Haldane referred to 'a general principle, which
is applicable to all authorities conferred on majorities of classes enabling them to
bind minorities; namely, that the power given must be exercised for the purpose
of benefiting the class as a whole, and not merely individual members only'. When
applying the rule to a particular resolution, whether for the alteration of the company's articles, class rights, or to ratify a wrong to the company, the court would
only find that voting rights had been invalidly exercised if it was satisfied that no
reasonable person could have considered the resolution to be for the benefit of the
company.[75] Now the 2006 Act, s 239 regulates the position as described in paragraph 2.27 above, but the rule may continue to be relevant where directors procure the passing of the disputed resolution through the support of persons who are
not 'connected persons' and to matters not involving ratification of wrongdoing
by a director and so outside the scope of s 239.[76]

Thirdly, the courts have established a rule that the company is bound by the unan-   **2.30**
imous agreement of its members entitled to attend and vote on the matter without
the need for a formal resolution, whether in writing or at a meeting.[77] This rule,
which is expressly preserved by the 2006 Act, ss 239(6)(a) and 281(4), is subject
to exceptions, the scope of which is not clearly marked out, where a transaction is

---

[73] *Allen v Gold Reefs of West Africa Ltd* [1900] 1 Ch 656, 671, CA, per Lindley MR. Also: *Blisset
v Daniel* (1853) 10 Hare 493 (a partnership case); *Menier v Hooper's Telegraph Works* (1874) 9
Ch App 350; *Dominion Cotton Mills Co v Amyot* [1912] AC 546, 551–3, PC; *Cook v Deeks* [1916]
1 AC 554, 564, PC; *Greenhalgh v Arderne Cinemas Ltd* [1951] Ch 286, 291, CA, per Evershed MR;
*Re Holders Investment Trust Ltd* [1971] 1 WLR 583; *Estmanco (Kilner House) Ltd v Greater London
Council* [1982] 1 WLR 2, 16; *Smith v Croft (No 2)* [1988] Ch 114, 186. CLR described the rule as
'rather ill-defined' and limited it to alterations of articles and class right cases CLR: *Developing the
Framework* at para 4.142. In CLR: *Completing the Structure* at paras 5.94–5.101, 5.110 the CLR
proposed retaining the rule, but only in relation to changes to the constitution and class rights and
cases where the votes of the majority are tainted.
[74] [1927] AC 369, 371, PC; *Redwood Master Fund Ltd v TD Bank Europe Ltd* [2006] 1 BCLC
149 (both cases concerning the power to modify debentures or loan notes).
[75] *Shuttleworth v Cox Bros & Co (Maidenhead) Ltd* [1927] 2 KB 9, 18, 23, CA; *Greenhalgh v
Arderne Cinemas Ltd* [1951] Ch 286, 291, CA; *Citco Banking Corp NV v Pusser's Ltd* [2007] 2 BCLC
483, PC. In *Standard Chartered Bank v Walker* [1992] 1 WLR 561 Vinelott J invoked the court's
*Mareva* jurisdiction to restrain a shareholder from causing wilful damage to the value of his shares
by voting his shares to block a restructuring proposal.
[76] The CLR recommended the reform in s 239 to deal with this area CLR: *Final Report* at paras
7.52–7.62.
[77] *Re Duomatic Ltd* [1969] 2 Ch 365, 373; *Cane v Jones* [1981] 1 WLR 1451. The informal unanimous decision is attributed to the company: *Multinational Gas and Petrochemical Co v Multinational
Gas and Petrochemical Services Ltd* [1983] Ch 258, 269, 288–90, CA; *Meridian Global Funds
Management Asia Ltd v Securities Commission* [1995] 2 AC 500, PC.

beyond the powers of the company, such as a gift to directors out of capital,[78] or where the company is insolvent and creditors are prejudiced (see Chapters 11, Section E, and 19, Section D(4)).[79]

### (7) Accounts

**2.31** Like any other fiduciary a director is liable to account to the company. The 1844 Act stated the obligation of directors to keep books of account, prepare accounts to be laid before the members, and have them audited. The 1862 Act left those matters to Table A,[80] but the twentieth-century Companies Acts have regulated those obligations and provided for the public filing of accounts. The provisions concerning accounts, reports, and audit are now contained in the 2006 Act, Parts 15 and 16, ss 380–539.[81] Any failure of a director to comply with his statutory duties in relation to accounts is to be taken into account in determining his fitness to be a director for the purposes of disqualification proceedings.[82] The directors' functions and obligations relating to these matters are discussed in Chapter 23 of this work.

**2.32** In addition, if a company becomes subject to insolvency proceedings (administration, administrative receivership, or liquidation) or proposes a voluntary arrangement, directors become subject to additional duties to provide a statement of affairs and provide information to the officeholder or the official receiver. Furthermore directors may be called to account in a private or public examination.[83] If in the winding up it is found that directors have failed to keep proper books of account or have falsified or destroyed them, a criminal offence is committed which is punishable by imprisonment. These obligations are discussed in Chapter 29 of this work.

### (8) Maintenance of capital

**2.33** In their management of the company, directors are bound by the fundamental common law principle of maintenance of capital, breach of which exposes the directors responsible to liability for damages for breach of duty. Since, in most cases the liability of members is limited, the paid up share capital is the fund of last

---

[78] *Re George Newman & Co* [1895] 1 Ch 674, 686, CA; *Cook v Deeks* [1916] 1 AC 554, 564, PC.

[79] *Kinsela v Russell Kinsela Pty Ltd* (1986) 4 NSWLR 722, 730, per Street CJ, approved in *West Mercia Safetywear Ltd v Dodd* [1988] BCLC 250, 252, 253, CA, per Dillon LJ.

[80] 1862 Act, Table A, regs 78–94.

[81] These provisions came into force on 6 April 2008, except for s 463 which came into force on 20 January 2007 and ss 417 and 458–488 which came into force on 1 October 2007.

[82] CDDA, s 9 and Part I of Schedule 1.

[83] Private examinations are provided for by the Insolvency Act 1986, s 236 and can be traced back to the 1844 Winding Up Act, s 15. Public examination is provided for by the Insolvency Act, s 133 and can be traced back to the Companies (Winding Up) Act 1890, s 8.

resort available to meet the claims of creditors. The principle of maintenance of capital is therefore a principle for the protection of creditors.[84] Maintenance of capital is now entirely regulated by statute (see Chapter 24 of this work), but at common law it was manifest in four rules. First, shares could not be issued at a discount: the company must not be entitled to receive less than the nominal amount of the share, par value, in consideration for its allotment.[85] Secondly, a person who retained his shares, which he had been induced to take by fraud, could not claim damages, because that would infringe the principle of maintenance of capital. His only remedy was to rescind the contract on the ground of fraud and recover his money, provided he did so before the company went into liquidation.[86] The 1985 Act, s 111A reversed this principle by providing that holding shares was not a bar to obtaining damages or other compensation from a company.[87] Thirdly, a company could not return capital to its members except by a reduction of capital in accordance with the provisions of the Companies Acts. Nor could it acquire, or give financial assistance in the acquisition of, its own shares except in accordance with the provisions of those Acts.[88] Fourthly, although the way in which a company distributes its profits is a matter for its constitution, it could not pay dividends or make other distributions out of capital, since that would involve an unlawful distribution of capital.[89] The rules controlling the making of distributions are contained in the 2006 Act, ss 829–853.[90]

---

[84] *Trevor v Whitworth* (1887) 12 App Cas 409, 423, HL, per Lord Watson; *The Ooregum Gold Mining Company of India Ltd v Roper* [1892] AC 125, 133, HL, per Lord Halsbury LC.

[85] This principle is governed by statutory provision: 1985 Act, ss 99–111, 112–116 which will be replaced by 2006 Act, ss 580–609, 1150, and 1153 when those sections come into effect on 1 October 2009. The only changes are to the provisions of 1985 Act, subss 104(4), 108(1), and 113(2). Subsection 115(2) and s 116 are repealed.

[86] *Houldsworth v City of Glasgow Bank* (1880) 5 App Cas 317; *Re Addlestone Linoleum Co* (1887) 37 Ch D 191, CA. The principle also applied to claims under Misrepresentation Act 1967, s 2(2). It did not apply to purchases in the after-market: *Soden v British & Commonwealth Holdings plc* [1998] AC 298, HL. Note the departure from the principle taken by the High Court of Australia in *Sons of Gwalia Ltd v Margaretic* [2007] HCA 1.

[87] Introduced by 1989 Act, s 131 and re-enacted as 2006 Act, s 655 which comes into force on 1 October 2009.

[88] *Trevor v Whitworth* (1887) 12 App Cas 409. The provisions for reduction of capital, maintenance of capital, redeemable shares, and purchase by a company of its own shares are contained in 1985 Act, ss 135–181. These sections are replaced by 2006 Act, ss 641–723, which come into force on 1 October 2009. As from 1 October 2008 private companies no longer have to obtain court sanction for a reduction of capital. Except that the financial assistance provisions will no longer apply to private companies, the 2006 Act makes only a few minor changes.

[89] *MacDougall v Jersey Imperial Hotel Co* (1864) 2 Hem & M 528; *Dovey v Corey* [1901] AC 477; *Ammonia Soda Co v Chamberlain* [1918] 1 Ch 266, 292, CA.

[90] These provisions, which come into force on 6 April 2008, replace almost entirely without change provisions of the 1985 Act, ss 39–45, which were first introduced by the 1980 Act, ss 39–45.

# D. The Development of Statute Law Affecting Directors Before the Companies Act 2006

**2.34** The Companies Acts provide for the incorporation of companies and lay down the framework for their operation. To an ever increasing extent, in order to protect members and persons dealing with a company and improve standards of corporate governance, the Companies Acts have imposed restrictions on the management of companies, required public disclosure of information about the company, and imposed sanctions and provided remedies for default. To this end a number of techniques have been adopted: (i) certain conduct (eg fraudulent trading) or contraventions of the Companies Acts are made criminal offences; (ii) certain persons may be disqualified from being directors or concerned in the management of a company (bankrupts, fraudulent and unfit persons); and (iii) certain transactions are made unlawful (eg financial assistance in the purchase of a company's own shares and formerly tax-free payments to directors and loans to directors). To protect the interests of members, some transactions with directors have been made unlawful unless approved by the members (payments for loss of office and transactions with directors) and members in the minority have been given a statutory remedy for unfair prejudice (formerly oppression).

**2.35** Since 1844 winding up has been the process through which directors have been brought to account for their management of the company. Since 1890 the procedures have been strengthened to give creditors more control of the winding up where the company is insolvent, to improve the means of calling directors to account, and to make directors personally liable for fraudulent trading. The procedures have been extensively modernized by the Insolvency Act 1986, which has made directors personally liable for wrongful trading and contravention of the 'phoenix company' provisions.

**2.36** Since the 1856 Act the Board of Trade, or its successor Department, has had power, on the application of a specified proportion of members, to appoint inspectors to examine the affairs of the company. The 1967 Act extended these powers and enabled the Board of Trade to appoint inspectors whenever it had good reason to do so. Now the provisions are contained in the 1985 Act, Part XIV, ss 431–437, 439–453, as amended by the 2006 Act, Part 32.[91]

## (1) Legislation for companies 1844 to 1890

**2.37** The Joint Stock Companies Act 1844 provided the first general statutory scheme for companies to obtain corporate personality through registration with the

---

[91] The amendments came into effect on 1 October 2007.

Registrar of Companies. It suffered from two serious defects. First, the process of registration was cumbersome and the company could not enjoy the benefits of the Act until it was complete. Secondly, members were personally liable for the debts of the company.[92] In order to protect the members who were at risk, their approval was required for the purchase and sale of shares by directors, loans to directors, and contracts with directors outside the ordinary course of business and at least two directors had to sign larger contracts and bills.[93] Directors were responsible for maintaining the company's books of account and having the accounts confirmed by an auditor.

The 1844 Winding Up Act provided for the winding up of companies unable to meet their debts and was intended 'to make better provision for discovery of the abuses that may have attended the formation or management of the affairs' of companies and 'for ascertaining the causes of their failure'. Members would be the principal beneficiaries of these provisions since they were personally liable for the company's debts. Directors were to produce a balance sheet and provide information on which they would be examined and hand over company property.[94] The court would make a report on the causes of failure which could lead to criminal prosecution.[95]  **2.38**

The main defect of the 1844 Act, the failure to provide for limited liability, was remedied by the Limited Liability Act 1855, which allowed a company to be incorporated with limited liability if its name included the word 'limited'. The 1855 Act contained a number of provisions to protect persons dealing with the company, including one, which continued to be used in subsequent Companies Acts until repealed by the 2006 Act, making directors personally liable on all bills and other documents on which its correct name did not appear.[96]  **2.39**

The Joint Stock Companies Act 1856 consolidated and amended the law relating to companies, including winding up, in a way that identifies it as the precursor of the Companies Act 1862. The 1856 Act did not include many of the sanctions in the 1844 and 1855 Acts,[97] but included, for the first time, provisions for inspectors to examine the affairs of the company, either appointed by the Board of Trade on the application of members or by special resolution of members.[98]  **2.40**

---

[92] 1844 Act, s 25.
[93] 1844 Act, ss 27, 29, and 44–46.
[94] 1844 Winding Up Act, ss 12–15.
[95] 1844 Winding Up Act, ss 26 and 27.
[96] Limited Liability Act 1855, ss 4, 5, 9, 10, 13. The provision referred to last appeared as 1985 Act, s 349, which was repealed on 1 October 2008 by the 2006 Act Commencement Order No 5, Art 8(b) and Schedule 3.
[97] 1856 Act, ss 14 and 31.
[98] 1856 Act, ss 48–52.

**2.41**  The 1862 Act is generally regarded as the Act that 'laid down the foundation upon which subsequent legislation relating to companies has been built'.[99] The underlying philosophy was that a company should be free to determine the way in which it would be managed and administered, although default articles in the form of Table A were provided. A director could only be removed by special resolution.[100] Directors and managers were liable for a fine, along with the company, if they knowingly and wilfully authorized or permitted contravention of certain provisions for record-keeping and transparency.[101]

**2.42**  Among the provisions of the 1862 Act for winding up companies were provisions for the court to order officers and others to deliver up monies, books, papers, and other property to which the company is entitled,[102] for the private examination of, and production of books by, officers and others,[103] and for the court to assess damages against delinquent directors and officers.[104] If a director or other person was found to have falsified the company's books he was guilty of an offence, punishable by imprisonment.[105] There were also provisions for the prosecution of a director who had committed an offence in relation to the company, but on terms that the court could order that the costs and expenses of the prosecution could be paid out of the company's assets.[106]

**2.43**  The Companies Act 1867 amended the 1862 Act[107] and included a new provision for the memorandum of a company with limited liability to provide for directors,

---

[99]  Report of the Cork Committee at para 75.

[100]  1862 Act, s 51 and Table A, reg 65. That remained the position until 1948 Act, s 184 gave an overriding power to remove directors by ordinary resolution.

[101]  1862 Act, s 25 (register of members to be kept), s 27 (list of members and summary to be forwarded to the Registrar), s 32 (refusal of inspection of register of members), s 34 (notice of increase of capital and of number of members to be given to Registrar), s 43 (register of mortgages to be kept and inspection permitted), s 44 (statutory statement for banks and insurance companies), s 46 (register of directors to be kept), s 53 (special resolutions to be forwarded to Registrar), s 54 (special resolution to be forwarded to member on request), ss 58, 60 (books to be produced to inspector).

[102]  1862 Act, s 100. This section was the derivation of 1948 Act, s 258 and is the predecessor of Insolvency Act, s 234, which uses broader language.

[103]  1862 Act, ss 115–117. These sections were the derivation, subject to amendment by the 1928 Act, of 1948 Act, s 268 and are the predecessors of Insolvency Act, ss 236 and 237.

[104]  1862 Act, s 165. See paragraph 2.18 above. This section was replaced by the Companies (Winding Up) Act 1890, s 10, which was the derivation, subject to amendment by the 1893 and 1928 Acts, of 1948 Act, s 333 and is the predecessor of Insolvency Act, s 212, whose provisions are significantly broader.

[105]  1862 Act, s 166. This section was the derivation, subject to amendment by the 1947 Act, of 1948 Act, s 329, and is the predecessor of Insolvency Act, s 209.

[106]  1862 Act, ss 167 and 168. These sections were the derivation, subject to amendment by the 1928 and 1947 Acts (to remove the provision for the costs and expenses of prosecution to be borne by the company), of 1948 Act, s 334 and are the predecessors of Insolvency Act, ss 218 and 219.

[107]  The most significant amendments were provisions enabling a company to reduce its capital. 1867 Act, s 37 re-enacted 1856 Act, s 41, providing for the ways in which contracts on behalf of the company could be made, which had been inadvertently omitted from the 1862 Act.

managers, or managing directors to have unlimited liability and for the memorandum to be altered by special resolution to render unlimited the liability of those officers. Although the provision was seldom, if ever, used, it was retained in the successive Companies Acts, including the 1985 Act, ss 306 and 307, and is reflected in the Insolvency Act, s 75.[108]

In 1890 there were two major reforming statutes affecting directors. The first was **2.44** the Companies (Winding Up) Act 1890, which was 'clearly aimed at fraudulent and dishonest company promoters and directors'.[109] It improved the statutory powers for investigating the affairs of the company by requiring directors to make out and submit to the official receiver a statement of affairs and providing machinery for the public examination of promoters, directors, and officers of the company and gave the court somewhat wider powers to assess damages against delinquent directors and promoters than had been contained in the 1862 Act, s 165.[110] The second reforming statute was the Directors' Liability Act 1890, which was a prompt legislative response to the refusal by the House of Lords in *Derry v Peek*[111] to hold that a director could be personally liable for negligent misstatement in a prospectus. Section 3 made directors and others responsible for issuing a prospectus personally liable to subscribers for any false statement unless they could show that the untrue statement was made by an expert on whom they could reasonably rely or by an official person in a public document, or was one that they had reasonable grounds for believing was true.[112]

## (2) The Companies Acts 1900 to 1985

In the period between the end of the nineteenth century and the United Kingdom **2.45** joining the European Community in 1972 a pattern of company law reform emerged under which a committee would be appointed to report on amendments to company law, a Companies Act would give effect to the recommendations adopted by the Government, and a consolidating statute would follow. The committees' recommendations invariably responded to recently exposed scandals and mischief arising from the lack of regulation in the original 1862 Act. Thus in 1895 a committee under the chairmanship of Lord Davey reported on what amendments

---

[108] These provisions are not re-enacted in the 2006 Act and will be repealed on 1 October 2009.

[109] Cork Report at para 78.

[110] Companies (Winding Up) Act 1890, ss 7, 8, and 10.

[111] (1889) 14 App Cas 337. Directors were personally liable for their own deceits: *Barwick v English Joint Stock Bank* (1867) 2 Exch 259; *Standard Chartered Bank v Pakistan Shipping Corp* [2003] 1 AC 959, 968, HL, per Lord Hoffmann.

[112] This section was the derivation, subject to amendments made by the 1928 and 1947 Acts, of 1948 Act, ss 40, 43, and 46 and 1985 Act, ss 61, 62, 67–69, and 71. Those sections were repealed by Financial Services Act, s 212(3) and Schedule 17, Pt I and were replaced by s 150 of that Act. The current provisions are FSMA, s 90, discussed in Chapter 27 of this work.

to the Companies Acts were necessary 'with a view to the better prevention of fraud in relation to the formation and management of companies'.[113] Some of its recommendations, mainly concerning control of the abuse of the prospectus and registration of charges, were included in the 1900 Act.[114] The Loreburn Committee[115] reported in 1906. Its recommendations were enacted by the 1907 Act and consolidated with the surviving provisions of the Companies Acts 1862–1900 into the Companies (Consolidation) Act 1908. The Greene Committee, under the chairmanship of Wilfred Greene KC (later Lord Greene MR), published its report in 1926. Its recommendations were enacted by the Companies Act 1927 and brought into effect by the consolidating Companies Act 1929. Similarly the Cohen Committee, under the chairmanship of Cohen J (later Lord Cohen) reported in June 1945. Its recommendations were enacted by the Companies Act 1947 and its provisions consolidated into the Companies Act 1948. In June 1962 the Jenkins Committee, of which Lord Jenkins was chairman, published its report. The previous pattern of implementing recommendations was somewhat broken, because the Companies Act 1967 only implemented some of the Jenkins Committee recommendations (eg disclosure and accounts). Its recommendation for reform to give minority shareholders meaningful relief from unfair prejudice was not enacted until 1980, and a consolidating statute did not follow until 1985, by which time there had been several other reforming statutes.

**2.46**    The four twentieth-century Committees adopted broadly the same philosophy; namely that the great majority of companies were honestly and conscientiously managed and that, in the words of the Greene Committee, it was 'most undesirable, in order to defeat an occasional wrongdoer, to impose restrictions which would seriously hamper the activities of honest men and would inevitably re-act upon the commerce and prosperity of the country'.[116] The Cohen Committee took a more interventionist view, believing that the fullest practicable disclosure of information concerning a company's affairs should be made to shareholders, creditors, and the general public, that the requirements of the Companies Acts

---

[113] The committee was a distinguished one and included Chitty J, Vaughan Williams J, Mr HB Buckley QC, and Mr F Palmer.

[114] Companies Act 1900, ss 14–16 contained the provisions for registration of charges. The Davey Committee also recommended reforms to the law concerning qualification shares of directors and the particulars to be stated in a prospectus, which were enacted by the Companies Act 1900. In 1906 the Loreburn Committee found that these requirements were so stringent that they discouraged the use of a prospectus and deterred honest and prudent men from accepting directorships (para 16(3) of its Report). They were repealed and replaced by the less onerous requirements of the 1907 Act.

[115] The Loreburn Committee included Mr Gore-Browne and Messrs Palmer and Waterhouse who had been members of the Davey Committee.

[116] Report of the Loreburn Committee at para 8; Report of the Greene Committee at paras 7 and 9; Report of the Cohen Committee at para 5; Report of the Jenkins Committee at paras 11–14.

should be enforced more rigorously, and that improper or dishonest conduct should be investigated and prosecuted.[117]

None of the Committees made any recommendations in relation to a company's **2.47** capacity, the *ultra vires* rule, or the power of directors to bind the company.[118] Reform in that area had to await the implementation of the First EEC Directive on Harmonisation of Company Law (paragraph 2.11 above).

The process of reform that had been launched by the Greene Committee was **2.48** continued by the Insolvency Act 1976, s 9, and the Companies Acts 1976, 1980, and 1981 (the latter two Acts also giving effect to the Second and Fourth EEC Directives on Harmonisation of Company Law). The reforms made by those Acts were consolidated into the 1985 Act with provisions from the 1948 and 1967 Acts. The following paragraphs provide a brief summary of the course of the reform of the law relating to directors, following the order in which these matters are addressed in this work.

### Appointment and removal of directors

On the recommendation of the Cohen Committee every company had to have at **2.49** least one director and a secretary;[119] the appointment of a director was to be voted on individually, and the members were given an overriding power to remove a director by ordinary resolution, but without prejudice to the director's right to claim compensation and protest his removal.[120] Except that a private company need not have a secretary, these provisions have been adopted by the 2006 Act.[121]

### Directors' duties

In response to the unsatisfactory state of the law in relation to a director's duty of **2.50** care (paragraph 2.22 above), the Davey Committee recommended a statutory statement of a director's duty of care in objective terms: 'Every director shall be under an obligation to the company to use reasonable care and prudence in the exercise of his powers, and shall be liable to compensate the company for any

---

[117] Report of the Cohen Committee at paras 5 and 6.

[118] The Cohen Committee considered that 'the doctrine of ultra vires is an illusory protection for the shareholders and yet may be a pitfall for third parties dealing with the company' and favoured its abolition (para 12), but the Jenkins Committee disagreed (paras 35–41). On the recommendation of the Cohen Committee (para 12) a company could change its objects by special resolution without the need for court sanction; 1947 Act, s 76; 1948 Act, s 5.

[119] Report of the Cohen Committee at para 55 and 1948 Act, ss 177–179.

[120] Report of the Cohen Committee at para 130 and 1948 Act, ss 183 and 184. The Committee also recommended a compulsory retirement age of 70 for directors of public companies: Report at para 131 and 1948 Act, ss 185 and 186, which were re-enacted as 1985 Act, ss 293 and 294 (repealed by the 2006 Act on 1 October 2009). Instead the 2006 Act is concerned to prevent the appointment of under-age directors: ss 157–159.

[121] 2006 Act, ss 155, 160, 168, 270, 271.

damage incurred by reason of neglect to use such care and prudence.'[122] This recommendation was not adopted and the Loreburn Committee did not repeat it. Instead the Loreburn Committee recommended, and the Government accepted, that the court should have a statutory power to relieve directors who have acted honestly and reasonably, from liability for negligence or breach of trust.[123]

**2.51**  The Greene Committee said that 'to attempt by statute to define the duties of directors would be a hopeless task', but it observed that provisions in the articles or contract exempting directors from liability for negligence or breach of trust gave 'a quite unjustifiable protection to directors' and recommended that they should be void. It found the general law of negligence satisfactory, but recommended that, in exercising its power to relieve a director, the court should take into account all the circumstances of his appointment.[124] These recommendations were adopted in the 1929 Act, ss 152 and 372 and, in modified form continue in effect in the 2006 Act.[125]

**2.52**  The Cohen Committee did not address the issue of directors' duties, except to advocate strengthening their civil and criminal liability for false and misleading statements in a prospectus.[126]

**2.53**  The Jenkins Committee did not agree with the suggestion that the existing law on directors' duties should be codified, because of the danger that there might be gaps in the law as codified. Instead, it favoured a statement of the basic principles

---

[122]  Report of the Davey Committee at para 32 and draft clause 10(2). The Davey Committee recognized that the draft law went beyond any actual decision of the courts. The report contains an interesting appendix on German law from Dr Schuster in which he compared English law on the amount of diligence expected of a director unfavourably with German law: 'German law requires the diligence of a prudent trader, and presumes negligence in case of loss. English law recognises a shadowy liability for "crassa negligentia" and presumes diligence. German law makes a director liable for non-attendance to his duties; according to English law a director who never attends any board meetings cannot come under any liability, and a director who votes for a resolution sanctioning an "ultra vires" expenditure of the company's funds is not liable for such expenditure if he has not actually signed the cheque by which such expenditure is effected' (referring implicitly to *Re Cardiff Savings Bank* [1892] 2 Ch 100 and explicitly to *Cullerne v London and Suburban BS* (1890) 25 QBD 485, CA; pp 19 and 20 of the Appendix).

[123]  Report of the Loreburn Committee at para 24. The recommendation, modelled on Judicial Trustees Act 1896, s 3(1)(a), was enacted as Companies Act 1907, s 32, which is the derivation, with amendments made by the 1928 and 1947 Acts, of 1985 Act, s 727 and 2006 Act, s 1157, which came into force on 1 October 2007. Mr Edgar Speyer, a distinguished businessman and member of the Committee, added a note on para 24 of the Report in which he said that 'the immunity of directors from liability for negligence lies at the seat of the deplorable abuses in company matters in this country' and urged a statutory statement of a director's personal liability for negligence in the discharge of his duties.

[124]  Report of the Greene Committee at paras 46 and 47. Reference was made to *Re Brazilian Rubber Estates Ltd* [1911] 1 Ch 425.

[125]  1929 Act, s 152 is the derivation of 1985 Act, s 310 (as originally enacted). 2006 Act, ss 232–238 deal with provisions protecting directors from liability; see Chapter 19 of this work.

[126]  Report of the Cohen Committee at paras 41–46 and 1948 Act, ss 43 and 44.

underlying the fiduciary relationship of a director to his company; namely a duty to observe the utmost good faith and act honestly and a duty not to make, and to account for, secret profits.[127] Attempts were made to include a statutory statement of a director's fiduciary duties in Companies Bills of 1973 and 1978, but both were lost because of general elections. Instead, the 1980 Act, s 46 introduced a duty owed by a director to the company to have regard to the interests of the company's employees as well as the interests of its members.[128]

*Transactions with directors*

Following the recommendation of the Greene Committee, the 1929 Act, s 128 **2.54** required a company's accounts laid before the company in general meeting to contain particulars of loans to, and remuneration of, directors other than managing directors.[129] The 1929 Act included other new provisions to compel transparency in directors' dealings. A director had a duty to disclose his interests in a contract or proposed contract to the board and in default was liable to a fine.[130] It was not lawful for a director to receive a payment for loss of office in connection with a transfer of all or part of the company's undertaking or property without the approval of the company.[131]

On the recommendation of the Cohen Committee the tax-free payment of fees **2.55** and salaries to directors and loans to directors were made unlawful and absolutely prohibited,[132] and a payment to a director as compensation for loss of office was not lawful unless approved by the company.[133] The Cohen Committee also recommended that there should be more disclosure of share transactions by directors and that all directors' remuneration should be disclosed, including that earned as

---

[127] Report of the Jenkins Committee at paras 86, 87, and 99(a).

[128] This was re-enacted by 1985 Act, s 309. Employees' interests are now a factor to be considered in the duty to promote the success of the company (2006 Act, s 172(1)(b)).

[129] Report of the Greene Committee at paras 48–50. These provisions were the tentative precursors of provisions in 1985 Act, Part X, underpinning directors' duties and the provisions in the 2006 Act, Part 10, Chapter 4 (Chapter 18 of this work). A company could avoid the need to disclose directors' remuneration by appointing all its directors as managing directors: Cohen Report at para 89).

[130] 1929 Act, s 149, the precursor of 1985 Act, s 317 and 2006 Act, ss 177 and 182.

[131] 1929 Act, s 150, the precursor of 1985 Act, s 312; now 2006 Act, ss 215 and 217.

[132] Report of the Cohen Committee at paras 88 and 90 and 1948 Act, ss 189 and 190. The corresponding sections in 1985 Act (ss 311 and 330–342) have been repealed by 2006 Act and replaced in the case of loans by a requirement of members' approval (2006 Act, ss 197–214).

[133] Report of the Cohen Committee at para 92 and 1948 Act, s 191. This provision, with the related provisions brought into effect by the 1929 Act, were included in 1985 Act, Part 10. The corresponding provisions in the 2006 Act, but in different terms, are ss 215–222. Since the provisions concerning payment for loss of office did not apply to covenanted payments (*Taupo Totara Timber Co Ltd v Rowe* [1978] AC 537, PC), they were riddled with loopholes and easily evaded: Law Commission Joint Consultation Paper *Company Directors: Regulating Conflicts of Interest and Formulating a Statement of Duties* (No 153) at para 4.19.

managing director or executive, and pensions.[134] These disclosure requirements have been enhanced by subsequent Acts requiring details of remuneration to be disclosed in annual accounts and providing for directors' service contracts to be available for inspection.

**2.56** The Jenkins Committee recommended the prohibition of directors' dealing in options to buy or sell quoted shares or debentures of his company or its associated companies and made other recommendations for reform in relation to compensation for directors' loss of office, disclosure of directors' other interests, and loans to directors. The 1967 Act gave effect to these recommendations by making dealings by directors in options an offence, requiring directors' service contracts to be open to inspection by members, and imposing a duty on directors to notify the company of their interests in shares or debentures of the company or associated companies.[135]

**2.57** As 'a hasty legislative response' to a number of financial scandals in the 1970s,[136] the 1980 Act, ss 47–61 provided that certain transactions in which directors had a conflict of interest were invalid unless disclosed to and approved by the members; namely contracts of employment, substantial property transactions, and loans.[137] These provisions, which applied to shadow directors,[138] and the surviving provisions of the 1948 Act concerning transactions with directors were incorporated into the 1985 Act, Part 10. For discussion of the corresponding provisions of the 2006 Act, see Chapter 18 of this work.

*Shareholders' remedies*

**2.58** The Cohen Committee recognized the need to provide an alternative remedy to winding up for cases of minority oppression, particularly in private companies. The court should have power, if satisfied that a minority of shareholders was being oppressed and that a winding-up order would not do justice to the minority, to make such order as the court thought just, including an order that the minority be bought out at a fair price.[139] This recommendation was brought into effect by the 1948 Act, s 210, but, as interpreted by the court, the threshold test of oppression

---

[134] Report of the Cohen Committee at paras 89, 90, and 93 and 1948 Act, s 196.

[135] Report of the Jenkins Committee at paras 92–98 and 99(b)–(p), 1967 Act, ss 25–32 and 1976 Act, ss 24–27. The provisions about options and interests in shares, which were replaced by 1985 Act, ss 323–329 have been repealed by the 2006 Act.

[136] Law Commission Consultation Paper *Company Directors: Regulating Conflicts of Interest and Formulating a Statement of Duties* (No 153) at para 1.9.

[137] 1948 Act, s 190 was repealed.

[138] The concept of a 'shadow director' was not new to companies legislation. Its features had been used in the Companies (Particulars as to Directors) Act 1917, although the phrase 'shadow director' was not used. After 1980 more extensive use was made of the concept (see Chapter 3, Section C(3) of this work).

[139] Report of the Cohen Committee at paras 60, 152, and 153.

proved too onerous to give the section much practical value.[140] The Jenkins Committee doubted whether s 210 was intended to be interpreted so restrictively and recommended that the section be replaced by one that extended the court's powers and made it clear that it applied to isolated acts as well as to a course of conduct and to the conduct of the affairs of the company in a manner unfairly prejudicial to the interests of some part of the members and not merely in an oppressive manner.[141] The 1980 Act, s 75 replaced the 1948 Act, s 210 in the wide terms advocated by the Jenkins Committee and without reference to making a winding-up order.[142]

### Accounts

The Davey Committee recommended that there should be statutory obligations **2.59** to prepare annual accounts, which should be laid before the shareholders, and to appoint auditors, but it did not favour an obligation to file them with the Registrar.[143] The 1900 Act, in ss 22 and 23, only adopted the recommendation for the appointment of auditors. The Loreburn Committee recommended that private companies should be distinguished from public companies and exempt from the requirement to file with the Registrar an annual return and balance sheet, which was brought in by the 1907 Act, s 21.

After noting that there was no statutory obligation to keep proper accounts, the **2.60** Greene Committee recommended that the law be changed to make the keeping of such accounts compulsory, that a profit and loss account and balance sheet, with directors' report, should be laid before the general meeting every year, and that wilful default should be punishable by imprisonment. The recommendation was brought into effect by the 1929 Act, ss 122, 123.[144] The Cohen Committee recommended that the Companies Act should state the form and contents of a company's accounts and identify the matters to be stated in the auditors' report.[145] The provisions in the 1948 Act, which gave effect to the recommendations of the Cohen Committee, were substantially recast by the 1967 Act, on the recommendation of the Jenkins Committee, and further amended by the 1976 and

---

[140] *Scottish Co-operative Wholesale Society v Meyer* [1959] AC 324, 342, HL, per Viscount Simonds. In that case the claim for relief under s 210 succeeded. The only other reported successful application is *Re HR Harmer Ltd* [1959] 1 WLR 62.

[141] Report of the Jenkins Committee at paras 199–212.

[142] This was replaced by 1985 Act, s 459, which was amended by 1989 Act, s 145 and Schedule 19, para 11. The corresponding provisions now in force are 2006 Act, Part 30, ss 994–999. See Chapter 21 of this work.

[143] Report of the Davey Committee at paras 51–55.

[144] Report of the Greene Committee at paras 67 and 72. The current provisions are 2006 Act, ss 386–389 and 393–426.

[145] Report of the Cohen Committee at paras 96–114.

1981 Acts.[146] Failure to keep accounts and file returns is a factor to be taken into account in determining whether a director should be disqualified on the ground of unfitness.[147]

*Maintenance of capital*

**2.61** The only reform recommended by any of the four Committees concerning maintenance of capital was the prohibition on a company giving financial assistance in the purchase of its own shares. From the spectacular corporate collapses during and after the First World War,[148] the Greene Committee identified the 'highly improper' practice of a syndicate agreeing to buy from existing shareholders sufficient shares to acquire control of a company and arranging for the company to lend them the purchase money. Such a practice appeared to the Committee 'to offend against the spirit if not the letter of the law which prohibits a company from trafficking in its own shares and the practice is open to the gravest abuses'. The Committee recommended that a company should be prohibited from giving direct or indirect assistance in the purchase of their own shares.[149] This recommendation was adopted in the 1929 Act, s 45.[150] A director who caused or procured a company to misapply its money in contravention of the prohibition was in breach of his duties and liable to compensate the company for its loss and was also liable to criminal prosecution and imprisonment.[151]

**2.62** The Jenkins Committee referred to dissatisfaction with the provision, which had become the 1948 Act, s 54, and recommended that it be re-cast so that financial assistance could be given if sanctioned by a special resolution and if a declaration of solvency was filed with the Registrar, thereby protecting the interests of creditors.[152] The 1981 Act, Part III, ss 36–62 significantly reduced the restrictions on

---

[146]  Report of the Jenkins Committee at paras 330–435; 1967 Act, ss 3–14; 1976 Act, ss 1–20; 1981 Act, ss 1–21.

[147]  CDDA, s 9 and Schedule 1, para 4. See the observations of Sir Donald Nicholls V-C in *Re Swift 736 Ltd* [1993] BCLC 896, 900.

[148]  *Re Jubilee Cotton Mills Ltd* [1922] 1 Ch 100, [1923] 1 Ch 1, CA, [1924] AC 958, HL, is a well-known example.

[149]  Report of the Greene Committee at paras 30 and 31. Lord Greene described the offensive practice that the prohibition was designed to prevent in *Re VGM Holdings Ltd* [1942] Ch 235, 239, CA. In *Steen v Law* [1964] AC 287, 301, PC, Lord Radcliffe referred to the 'notorious objections' to the practice.

[150]  With amendments made by the 1947 Act, this section was re-enacted as 1948 Act, s 54. It was the precursor of 1985 Act, ss 151–158, which relaxed the rule for private companies. 2006 Act, ss 677–683, which restricts the rule to public companies, comes into force on 1 October 2009, but 1985 Act, ss 151–153, 155–158 ceased to apply to private companies on 1 October 2008 (2006 Act Commencement Order No 5, arts 5(2) and 8(b) and Schedule 3).

[151]  *Re VGM Holdings Ltd* [1942] Ch 235, CA; *Steen v Law* [1964] AC 287, PC; *Selangor United Rubber Estates Ltd v Cradock (No 3)* [1968] 1 WLR 1555, 1652–9; *Wallersteiner v Moir* [1974] 1 WLR 991, CA. As to criminal liability: *R v Lorang* (1931) 22 Cr App Rep 167.

[152]  Report of the Jenkins Committee at paras 170–186, 187(d).

companies giving financial assistance for the acquisition of shares and the purchase or redemption of its own shares, so that in certain cases such transactions were permitted provided creditors were protected by a declaration of solvency.

The 1980 Act, ss 39–45 for the first time imposed statutory restrictions on the **2.63** distribution of profits and assets, so that distributions to members could only be made out of profits available for the purpose.[153]

### Disqualification

The Greene Committee discovered that undischarged bankrupts used companies **2.64** through which to carry on business and incur credit, to the great risk of persons dealing with the company. It recommended that an undischarged bankrupt should be disqualified from being a director of a company or in any way concerned in its management without the leave of the bankruptcy court and that contravention of this prohibition should be an offence punishable with imprisonment. The recommendation was implemented in the 1929 Act, s 142 and continues in force as the CDDA, ss 11 and 13.[154]

Also, on the recommendation of the Greene Committee, the 1929 Act gave the **2.65** court power to disqualify a person from being a director or concerned in the management of a company for up to five years, but it limited the power to cases of fraudulent trading and other frauds in relation to the promotion or management of the company.[155] On the recommendation of the Cohen Committee the circumstances justifying disqualification were extended to cases of breach of trust and conviction of an offence in relation to companies.[156] The Jenkins Committee recommended further extensions to cover persons convicted on indictment of any offence involving fraud or dishonesty, persons who had been persistently in default in complying with the provisions of the Companies Act, and persons who had shown themselves to be unfit to be concerned in the management of companies through improper, reckless, or incompetent conduct.[157] Those recommendations were partially implemented by the Insolvency Act 1976, s 9 (disqualification for unfitness) and the Companies Act 1976, s 28 (disqualification for persistent default in relation to delivery of documents to Registrar) and are replaced by provisions in the CDDA.

---

[153] These provisions are now in 2006 Act, ss Part 23, ss 829–853, which came into force on 1 April 2008.

[154] Report of the Greene Committee at paras 56 and 57. 1929 Act, s 142 was re-enacted, with modifications, as 1948 Act, s 187 and 1985 Act, s 302 (repealed when the CDDA came into force).

[155] Report of the Greene Committee at paras 61 and 62 and 1929 Act, ss 217 and 275.

[156] Report of the Cohen Committee at paras 150 and 153 and 1948 Act, s 188.

[157] Report of the Jenkins Committee at paras 80–85.

*Winding up*

**2.66** The Davey Committee recommended radical reform to protect unsecured creditors through provisions making directors personally liable for debts incurred when there was no reasonable expectation that the company would be able to pay them, and also liable to the company for misfeasance for being party to a fraudulent preference and for pledging or disposing of property obtained on credit.[158] None of this was adopted at the time.

**2.67** The Greene Committee recommended the introduction of a provision to deal with fraudulent trading. There was evidence of persons in control of a company taking a floating charge over all its assets, obtaining goods on credit to 'fill up' the security, and then appointing a receiver who would pay them the sale proceeds. The recommendation was accepted. Directors responsible for carrying on the business of the company in fraud of creditors faced three sanctions: (i) personal liability for the debts and liabilities of the company, with the personal liability being charged on any debts owed to, or security held by, the director, (ii) imprisonment for a criminal offence, and (iii) disqualification for up to five years.[159]

**2.68** Also, on the recommendation of the Greene Committee, the 1929 Act provided that officers of a company in liquidation were liable for a range of offences, punishable with imprisonment, covering fraud and failure to keep proper accounts, and enforcing cooperation with the official receiver or liquidator.[160]

**2.69** The Jenkins Committee referred to widespread criticism that the Companies Act did not deal adequately with fraudulent or incompetent directors. It recommended more use of public examinations and extending the fraudulent trading section to reckless conduct, the misfeasance section to cover actionable negligence, and disqualification to cover acting as a receiver or liquidator.[161]

*Restructuring of the 1985 Act*

**2.70** The 1985 Act had only been in force for a little over one year when many of its sections were repealed and replaced by provisions in other Acts. Provisions about capital issues, including liability for false and misleading statements in listing particulars[162] were moved to the Financial Services Act 1986 and are now to be found in the Financial Services and Markets Act 2000. Provisions about

---

[158] Report of the Davey Committee at para 33 and draft clause 11. In *Re Washington Diamond Mining Co* [1893] 3 Ch 95 the Court of Appeal had held that a director was personally liable for misfeasance for causing the company to make a fraudulent preference.

[159] 1929 Act, s 275, which is the precursor of the civil liability in Insolvency Act, s 213 and the criminal offence in 2006 Act, s 993 (which replaced 1985 Act, s 458 on 1 October 2007).

[160] Report of the Greene Committee at paras 58, 60, 67, and 72 and 1929 Act, ss 271, 273, and 274. The corresponding provisions are in Insolvency Act, ss 206–211.

[161] Report of the Jenkins Committee at paras 496–503.

[162] 1985 Act, Part III, ss 56, 57, 61, 63–79.

disqualification[163] were repealed and are now to be found in the Company Directors Disqualification Act 1986. Provisions about receivers and winding up[164] were repealed and replaced by provisions in the Insolvency Act 1986.

### (3) The Insolvency Act and CDDA

As regards insolvency and disqualification, the catalyst for the restructuring of the **2.71** 1985 Act was the Report of the Cork Committee on Insolvency Law and Practice, published in June 1982. The Insolvency Act 1985 enacted the reforms made in light of the recommendations of the Cork Committee. The new provisions about insolvent companies were then brought into effect by the Insolvency Act 1986, which also included provisions from the 1985 Act about receivers and winding up. The new provisions about disqualification were included in the CDDA, which also includes disqualification provisions from the 1985 Act.[165]

The Cork Committee promoted the 'rescue culture',[166] but it also addressed the **2.72** public interest in the conduct of the management of companies, which included being satisfied (i) whether or not there is any fault or blame attaching to that conduct, (ii) if the conduct merits it, that those responsible for the management are suitably punished, (iii) that the opportunity to repeat that conduct is curtailed or restricted, and (iv) whether or not others are responsible for the insolvency. It found that the treatment of directors of insolvent companies was unduly lenient.[167] It recommended, among other measures, a new wrongful trading provision, automatic disqualification in certain cases, a general strengthening of the existing disqualification regime, and measures to deal with repeated abuse of limited liability through phoenix companies.[168]

The reforms in the Insolvency Act of particular relevance to directors are the pro- **2.73** visions requiring them to provide information and assistance to office holders (including ss 235 and 236), the new public examination provision (s 133), the new misfeasance section (s 212), personal liability for wrongful trading (s 214), the restriction on re-use of company names and personal liability for debts in the event of contravention (ss 216, 217), and the new transaction at undervalue, preference, and transactions defrauding creditors provisions (ss 238, 239, and 423).

---

[163] 1985 Act, Part IX, ss 295–302.
[164] 1985 Act, Parts XIX and XX, ss 488–650.
[165] These Acts have been amended by the Insolvency Act 1994, the Insolvency (No 2) Act 1994, the Insolvency Act 2000, and Enterprise Act 2002, Part 10.
[166] Report of the Cork Committee at paras [495] and [1980]; *Bristol Airport v Powdrill* [1990] Ch 744, 756, 758, CA, per Sir Nicholas Browne-Wilkinson V-C; and *Powdrill v Watson* [1995] 2 AC 394, 441, 442, HL, per Lord Browne-Wilkinson.
[167] Report of the Cork Committee at paras 1735, 1737, and 1739.
[168] Report of the Cork Committee at paras 1758–1766 and Chapter 45.

The CDDA, s 6 introduced a new and widely used power to disqualify unfit directors of an insolvent company for up to fifteen years.

### (4) Reforms to the 1985 Act regime

**2.74**  In the period after 1986 there were several strands in the reform and modernization of company law and governance under the 1985 Act regime. One strand concerned reform of parts of the 1985 Act. The 1989 Act, which implemented the Seventh and Eighth EC Company Law Harmonisation Directives, made a number of miscellaneous reforms of particular relevance to directors, which have been mentioned earlier in this chapter.[169] It also provided a measure of de-regulation for private companies by enabling them to pass written resolutions,[170] made reforms in relation to company contracts and the execution of documents,[171] and made it clear that the 1985 Act, s 310 did not prevent a company from purchasing and maintaining insurance for officers and auditors.[172] The Political Parties, Elections and Referendums Act 2000, s 139 and Schedule 19 inserted into the 1985 Act, ss 347A–347K, under which political donations were prohibited unless authorized by resolution of the company in general meeting and directors were personally liable for damages in respect of any unauthorized donations.[173] The Companies (Acquisition of own Shares) (Treasury Shares) Regulations 2003 inserted into the 1985 Act, ss 162A–162G which enabled a company to hold shares in its own capital that it had duly purchased as treasury shares.[174] The Companies (Audit, Investigations and Community Enterprise) Act 2004 was a response to weaknesses exposed by the accounting scandals associated with the US companies Enron and WorldCom. Of particular relevance to directors, it inserted

---

[169]  1989 Act, ss 108–110 inserted into 1985 Act, new ss 3A (statement of company's objects: general commercial company), 35 (a company's capacity not limited by its memorandum), 35A (power of directors to bind the company), 35B (no duty to inquire as to capacity of company or authority of directors), 36, 36A–C (company contracts, execution of documents, and 322A (preserving the invalidity of certain transactions with directors). See further paras 2.10–2.14 above. Section 131 inserted a new 1985 Act, s 111A (member's right to damages), which is mentioned in paragraph 2.33 above.

[170]  1989 Act, ss 113 and 114 inserting 1985 Act, ss 381A, 381B, 381C, and 382A and Schedule 15A. See further Chapter 22.

[171]  Section 130 inserted new 1985 Act, ss 36, 36A–36C (company contracts, execution of documents, pre-incorporation deeds and documents), which are discussed in Chapter 4 below.

[172]  1989 Act, s 137 replaced 1985 Act, subs 310(3) with a new provision and inserted a new para 5A in Schedule 7.

[173]  These provisions were inserted on the recommendation of the report of the Committee on Standards in Public Life, chaired by Lord Neill of Bladen, published in October 1998. They were replaced, with some minor changes, by 2006 Act, Part 14, ss 362–379, which came into force on 1 October 2007.

[174]  SI 2003/1116. These provisions are now in 2006 Act, ss 724–732, which come into effect on 1 October 2009.

new provisions restricting and controlling the indemnification of directors and auditors.[175]

A second strand concerned improvements in corporate governance. Following **2.75** reports on the role of non-executive directors[176] and directors' remuneration,[177] a Committee on Corporate Governance, chaired by Sir Ronald Hampel, published a *Final Report of the Committee on Corporate Governance* (1998) and drew up a Combined Code, stating a set of principles of corporate governance and a Code of Best Practice. The Combined Code was amended and updated in July 2003[178] and again in June 2006 and June 2008. In its current form, it is at Appendix 3 to this work. The Combined Code is appended to the Listing Rules, but does not form part of them. It is not legally binding,[179] but listed companies are expected to comply with it or explain departures. The Code requires listed companies to maintain a sound system of internal control to safeguard shareholders' investments and the company's assets. Aspects of the Combined Code are discussed in Chapters 3, 5, and 6 of this work.

The third and most important strand of reform has been the work of the Law **2.76** Commission on shareholder remedies and directors' duties and the work of the Company Law Review in setting out a framework for the fundamental modernization and restatement of company law now found in the 2006 Act.

## E.  Genesis of the Companies Act 2006

In 1992 the Department of Trade and Industry began a review of a number of areas **2.77** of company law. In February 1995 it asked the Law Commission to review shareholder remedies and make recommendations. The Law Commission, chaired by Arden J, published a Consultation Paper on *Shareholder Remedies* (1996, No 142) and a Report (1997, No 246). Among its recommendations was a new derivative action governed by court rules. This was not implemented at the time, because the

---

[175]  The C(AICE) Act replaced 1985 Act, s 310 with new 1985 Act, ss 309A–309C and 310 (provisions protecting directors from liability, qualifying third party indemnity provision, disclosure of qualifying third party indemnity provisions, and provisions protecting auditors from liability). The corresponding provisions of the 2006 Act are ss 232–238 in relation to directors (above and Chapters 19 and 20 of this work) and ss 532–538 in relation to auditors' liability.

[176]  *Report of the Committee on the Financial Aspects of Corporate Governance* chaired by Sir Adrian Cadbury (1992).

[177]  *Directors' Remuneration: Report of a Study Group* chaired by Sir Richard Greenbury (1995).

[178]  Following reports of a committee chaired by Derek Higgs on the effectiveness of non-executive directors and a committee chaired by Sir Robert Smith on audit committees.

[179]  Nor do departures constitute unfair prejudice for the purpose of a petition under 2006 Act, Part 30: *Re Astec (BSR) plc* [1998] 2 BCLC 556, 590.

issue of shareholder remedies was absorbed into the wider work of the Company Law Review described below.

**2.78**  In order to contribute to the work of the CLR, the Law Commission, chaired by Arden J, went on to review the 1985 Act, Part X (enforcement of fair dealing by directors) and consider the case for a statutory statement of directors' duties. In August 1998 the Law Commission published a Consultation Paper, *Company Directors: Regulating Conflicts of Interests and Formulating a Statement of Duties* (No 153). In September 1999 the Law Commission, now chaired by Carnwath J, published its Report (No 261), recommending a statutory statement, in broad and non-exhaustive terms, of a director's main fiduciary duties and duty of care and skill.[180] The terms of the statement in Appendix A reflected the duties identified in case law (paragraph 2.20 above). Thus a director could only make use of the company's property, information, or opportunities or have a position of conflict of interest if permitted by the company's constitution or if there has been disclosure to and approval by the company in general meeting. The Law Commission also recommended that a director's duty of skill, care, and diligence should be set out in the statute, that the test should be both objective (the knowledge and experience that may reasonably be expected of a person in the same position as the director) and subjective (the director's own knowledge and experience), and that regard should be had to the particular functions of the director and the circumstances of the company, but there was no need for a statutory business judgment rule or statement in relation to delegation or reliance on others.[181] The Law Commission also recommended the redrafting and simplifying of the 1985 Act, Part X and the repeal of prohibitions on tax-free payments to directors and option dealing by them, as well as the exemption from disclosure of directors' service contracts in respect of overseas employment.[182]

**2.79**  In March 1998 the Department of Trade and Industry launched a wide-ranging review of core company law by an independent steering group, the CLR, and issued a consultation paper *Modern Company Law for a Competitive Economy*. In her foreword to that paper, Margaret Beckett, President of the Board of Trade, described the then current framework of company law as 'a patchwork of regulation that is immensely complex and seriously out of date'. The goal was a framework that was up to date and competitive and which facilitated enterprise and promoted transparency and fair dealing.[183] This could be achieved through clarifying the language

---

[180] Report at para 4.48.

[181] Report at paras 5.6, 5.20, 5.29, and 5.37. This was accepted by the CLR (CLR: *Developing the Framework* at para 3.87) and carried into effect by repeals in the 2006 Act.

[182] Report at paras 7.99 and 11.3–11.7 deal with recommended repeals. The provisions about option dealing were repealed, because of duplication with the Criminal Justice Act 1993. For general recommendations about 1985 Act, Part X, see paras 16.07–16.58.

[183] The CLR's terms of reference are set out in the CLR: *Final Report*, Annex A, p 335.

and structure of the legislation, removing obsolescent and ineffective provisions, and making full use of electronic communication.

Under the general heading *Modern Company Law for a Competitive Economy* the **2.80** CLR produced three consultation papers: *The Strategic Framework* (February 1999, URN 99/654), *Developing the Framework* (March 2000, URN 00/656), *Completing the Structure* (November 2000, URN 00/1335) and a *Final Report,* with suggested draft clauses (July 2001, URN 01/942, 943).[184] The overall approach of the CLR was that modern company law should be in 'a coherent and accessible form, providing maximum freedom for participants to perform their proper functions, but recognising the case for high standards and for ensuring appropriate protection for all interested parties'.[185]

One of the core policies of the CLR was the 'think small first' approach to private **2.81** company regulation and legislative structure.[186] The CLR applied this approach when it proposed simplifying and modernizing the law for private companies, by (a) simplifying decision-making procedures (more use of written resolutions), (b) streamlining internal procedures (no need for AGMs or a secretary, and a simpler form of constitution), (c) reducing the burden of financial reporting and audit (extending the small companies regime and raising the audit exemption level), and (d) removing the ban on private companies giving financial assistance in the purchase of their own shares.[187]

Another core policy was to provide an inclusive, open, and flexible regime for **2.82** corporate governance. To this end the CLR proposed a statutory statement of directors' duties and a clarification and updating of the 1985 Act, Part 10, dealing with conflicts of interest. The duty of loyalty, by which directors are bound to promote the success of the company, should be informed by 'enlightened shareholder value', so that directors manage the business of the company in the long-term interests of shareholders, but in an enlightened and inclusive way, enabling the company to achieve productive relations with a range of interested parties, such as employees, suppliers, and customers. The CLR rejected the 'pluralist'

---

[184] In addition the CLR published consultation papers on *Company General Meetings and Shareholder Communication, Company Formation and Capital Maintenance, and Reforming the Law Concerning Overseas Companies* (October 1999, URN/1144–1146), *Capital Maintenance* (June 2000, URN 00/880), *Registration of Company Charges* (October 2000, URN 00/1213), and *Trading Disclosures* (October 2000).

[185] CLR: *Strategic Framework* at Executive Summary, para 2.

[186] CLR: *Strategic Framework* at Executive Summary para 2 and paras 2.25, 5.2.33; CLR: *Final Report* at paras 1.52–1.55.

[187] CLR: *Strategic Framework* at Executive Summary para 8; CLR: *Final Report* at paras 2.15–2.19, 2.21, 2.28–2.37, 4.3–4.7, 4.13–4.37, 10.06.

approach by which the interests of shareholders are merely balanced with the interests of others affected by the company.[188]

**2.83**   To protect the interests of shareholders the CLR recommended a statutory form of derivative action,[189] and that members with an interest in facilitating or condoning misconduct should be disenfranchised.[190] The CLR also made a number of recommendations to make sanctions more effective.[191]

**2.84**   The Government's response is contained in two White Papers *Modernising Company Law* (July 2002, Cm 5553) and *Company Law Reform* (March 2005, Cm 6456), each with draft clauses for a Companies Bill. The Government broadly adopted the approach of the CLR. There would be a statutory statement of directors' duties which would replace the existing common law and equitable rules and which would embed the concept of 'enlightened shareholder value' (but without codifying a duty to creditors). One change was that a director would be able to exploit a corporate opportunity with the consent of independent directors.[192] The Government did not agree to codify the *Duomatic* rule.[193]

**2.85**   On 1 November 2005 a Company Law Reform Bill was introduced into the House of Lords. The Under-Secretary of State, Department of Trade and Industry (Lord Sainsbury) said it had four key objectives: 'enhancing shareholder engagement and a long-term investment culture; ensuring better regulation and a "think small first" approach; making life easier to set up and run a company; and providing flexibility for the future'.[194] After extensive revision and a change of name to the Companies Bill, the Bill received the Royal Assent on 8 November 2006. The 2006 Act also repeals all the provisions of the Companies Act 1985, except for the provisions about investigations contained in Parts XIV and XV, which were amended.

---

[188] CLR: *Strategic Framework* at Executive Summary at paras 5 and 5.1.11–5.1.33; CLR: *Developing the Framework* at paras 2.7–2.26, 3.17–3.20, 3.37–3.58, 3.82; CLR: *Final Report* at paras 2.20, 3.5–3.11, 3.21–3.27, 4.8, 4.9, 6.2–6.16.

[189] CLR: *Final Report* at paras 2.23–2.26, 7.41–7.51.

[190] CLR: *Final Report* at paras 7.52–7.62.

[191] CLR: *Final Report* at paras 1.17, 15.1–15.77.

[192] 2005 White Paper at para 3.3.

[193] This was recommended by the CLR in the *Final Report* at paras 2.14, 7.17–7.26; 2005 White Paper at para 4.2. The CLR had recommended codifying a duty to creditors: *Developing the Framework* at paras 3.72, 3.73, 3.81; *Final Report* at paras 3.12–3.20.

[194] Hansard (HL Debate) Vol 677, 11 January 2006, col 182. In relation to flexibility for the future, Part 31 of the original Bill gave the Secretary of State wide law-making powers, but this Part was withdrawn. Instead the 2006 Act contains many provisions for the law to be stated in delegated legislation under the negative and affirmative resolution procedures or by the instrument being approved after being made; see ss 1288–1292.

# PART II

## THE OFFICE OF DIRECTOR

# 3

# DIRECTORS AND OTHER OFFICERS; REQUIREMENT AND DEFINITIONS

## A. The Requirement for a Company to Have Directors

Every private company must have at least one director and every public company **3.01** must have at least two directors.[1] The Model Articles[2] do not provide for minimum or maximum numbers of directors, leaving that matter to the Companies Act, but Table A, reg 64 provides: 'Unless otherwise determined by ordinary resolution, the number of directors (other than alternate directors) shall not be subject to any maximum but shall not be less than two.'[3]

There is a new rule[4] that every company must have at least one director who is a **3.02** natural person, although the requirement is met if the office of director is held by

---

[1] s 154, which restates 1985 Act, s 282(1) and (2), with changes.

[2] For companies registered before 1 October 2007, Table A of the Companies Act 1985 (SI 1985/805) continues to apply. For companies registered on or after 1 October 2007 (but before 1 October 2009), Table A with the amendments made by SI 2007/2541 and SI 2007/2826 apply. For companies registered on or after 1 October 2007, but before 1 October 2009, the 1985 Act Table A applies with amendments made by the Tables A to F Amendment Regulations 2007 and 2008.

[3] No change is made to reg 64 of Table A by the Tables A to F Regulations 2007 and 2008, which make changes applicable to companies registered between 1 October 2007 and 1 October 2009.

[4] s 155.

a natural person as a corporation sole (the Archbishop of Canterbury for example) or otherwise by virtue of an office. The White Paper *Modernising Company Law* (July 2002) originally proposed prohibiting corporate directors altogether, pointing out that (a) few countries other than the Netherlands and some offshore financial centres permit corporate directors on the same basis as individuals, (b) some jurisdictions (eg Australia, New Zealand, Canada, and Singapore) had recently introduced prohibitions, and (c) most US states, including Delaware and Maryland, require directors to be individuals.[5] The new rule ensures that there is at least one natural person responsible for the conduct of the company's affairs.

**3.03**  Section 156, which is new, gives the Secretary of State power to require a company to comply with s 154 (requirements as to number of directors) or s 155 (requirement to have at least one director who is a natural person). The Secretary of State's direction must specify (a) the statutory requirement the company appears to be in breach of, (b) what the company must do in order to comply with the direction, and (c) the period within which it must do so. That period must be not less than one month or more than three months after the date on which the direction is given.[6] The company must comply with the direction by making the necessary appointments and giving notice of them to the Registrar of Companies before the end of the period specified in the direction,[7] or if the company has already made the necessary appointment or appointments (or so far as it has done so), it must comply with the direction by giving notice of them under s 167 before the end of the period specified in the direction. If a company fails to comply with a direction, an offence is committed by (a) the company, and (b) every officer of the company who is in default (and for this purpose a shadow director is treated as an officer of the company).[8]

**3.04**  The civil consequences of the number of directors falling below the statutory minimum are discussed in Chapter 6 at paragraph 6.05.

## B. The Statutory Meaning

**3.05**  Section 250 provides: 'In the Companies Acts "director" includes any person occupying the position of director, by whatever name called'.[9] Thus the name or description of the role or position is not relevant in deciding whether someone is

---

[5]  p 9 and p 31, paras 3.32–3.35.
[6]  s 156(2).
[7]  ss 156(4) and 167.
[8]  s 156(6).
[9]  This restates 1985 Act, s 741. The definitions in the Model Article (plc) 1 and Model Article (pcls) 1 use similar wording stating 'director' means a director of the company, and includes any person occupying the position of director, by whatever name called. Insolvency Act, s 251 and

a director, and instead the court will examine the substance of the person's activities to decide whether he occupies the position of director. By s 1173 a director is an officer of a company.

The 1844 Act defined the word 'directors' as meaning 'the persons having the direction, conduct, management, or superintendence of the affairs of the company'. Subsequent Companies Acts have not included such a description of the 'position of director'. Instead the articles of the company have identified the directors' functions and powers. Thus Table A, reg 70 provides that, subject to the provisions of the 1985 Act, 'the business of the company shall be managed by the directors who may exercise all the powers of the company'. Model Article (plc) 3 and Model Article (pcls) 3 both provide: 'Subject to the articles, the directors are responsible for the management of the company's business, for which purpose they may exercise all the powers of the company'.[10] Chapter 4 describes a director's functions.

**3.06**

The phrase 'by whatever name called' (s 250) covers alternative descriptions in a company's constitution of the office of director, such as 'governor' or 'manager'.[11] Other descriptions of the persons managing the affairs of a company, occasionally found in company constitutions, are 'council', 'managing committee', or 'managers'. Such descriptions of persons occupying the position of directors are now unusual.

**3.07**

## C. Types of Director

### (1) Appointed directors

Anyone may be appointed to act as a director if willing to act, unless prohibited by law. As to those prohibited from acting as directors, see Chapter 6 below (minimum age requirements, disqualification, etc) and note also paragraphs 3.01 and 3.02 above. Chapter 6 also deals with appointment of directors.

**3.08**

---

CDDA s 22(4) both adopt the same inclusive meaning of 'director'. Chapter 28 deals with disqualification proceedings under the CDDA and Chapter 29 deals with the consequences of insolvency proceedings for directors.

[10] In the Government response to consultation on the model articles (URN 07/1227) the Government commented as regarded Model Article 3 'As set out in the February consultation document, previous wording used in the drafting of this article arguably gave rise to doubts as to whether the directors could dispose of the company's business without the consent of shareholders—we changed it to put this beyond doubt. One respondent to the February consultation considered that the article as drafted would not be applicable to dormant companies. We do not agree. The directors are still responsible for the activity of a company even if it is dormant—in deciding that it should be dormant and when it would cease to be dormant—therefore they are still managing the business. We do not therefore propose to change the drafting of this article.' (Paragraph 17, July 2007 response.)

[11] *Re Lo-Line Electric Motors Ltd* [1988] BCLC 698, 706.

**3.09** Model Article (pcls) 17 provides that for private companies, any person who is willing to act as a director, and is permitted by law to do so, may be appointed to be a director by ordinary resolution of the shareholders or by a decision of the directors. Model Article (plc) 20 is in identical terms for public companies.

### (2) De facto directors

**3.10** Persons who undertake the functions of directors, even though not formally appointed as such, are called de facto directors. In *Re Hydrodam (Corby) Ltd*[12] Millett J described a de facto director as

> a person who assumes to act as a director. He is held out as a director by the company, claims and purports to be a director, although never actually or validly appointed as such. To establish that a person was a de facto director of a company it is necessary to plead and prove that he undertook functions in relation to the company which could probably be discharged only by a director. It is not sufficient to show that he was concerned in the management of a company's affairs or undertook tasks in relation to its business which can probably be performed by a manager below board level.

**3.11** Whether a person 'assumes to act as a director' is determined by what he did, not what he calls himself.[13] For this purpose the court will take into account all the relevant factors, not merely statutory functions. Those factors include at least (a) directing others, (b) committing the company to major obligations, or (c) participating on an equal level in collective decisions made by the board, (d) whether or not there was a holding out by the company of the individual as a director, (e) whether the individual used the title 'director', (f) whether the individual had proper information (eg management accounts) on which to base decisions, and (g) whether the individual had to make major decisions.[14] In *Secretary of State for Trade and Industry v Hall* Evans-Lombe J declined to hold that an individual was a de facto director when he had

> taken none of the well recognized courses of action which would constitute him a de facto director of the subject company merely because, through a company he controls, he would be in a position to take those courses of action: this notwithstanding that, historically, the latter company has not, and was never intended to take such action.[15]

---

[12] [1994] 2 BCLC 180, 183.

[13] *Ultraframe (UK) Ltd v Fielding* [2005] EWHC 1638 (Ch) at paras 1255–1257.

[14] *Secretary of State for Trade and Industry v Tjolle* [1998] 1 BCLC 333, 343, where Jacob J cited with approval from the judgment of Judge Cooke in *Secretary of State for Trade and Industry v Elms* (unreported 16 January 1997). See also *Secretary of State for Trade and Industry v Hollier* [2007] BCC II at paras 61–81; *Re Mea Corporation Ltd* [2007] 1 BCLC 618 at paras 82–85; *Gemma Ltd v Davies* [2008] 2 BCLC at para 40; *Re Paycheck Services 2 Ltd* [2008] 2 BCLC 613 at paras 169–179.

[15] [2006] EWHC 1995 (Ch) at para 29.

In *Secretary of State for Trade and Industry v Tjolle* Jacob J said that it was necessary **3.12** for the court to bear in mind why it was asking itself whether a person was a de facto director. It would only be justifiable to disqualify a person for conduct making him unfit to be a director or to hold him liable for misfeasance for breach of a director's duties if that person was truly in a position to exercise the powers and discharge the functions of a director.[16]

A de facto director is not to be regarded as a director for all purposes of the **3.13** Companies Act.[17] Since a de facto director is within the definition of a director in s 251 he is subject to all the provisions in the 2006 Act, Part 10 about a company's directors, but the application of those provisions to a particular de facto director may depend on the circumstances.

### (3) Shadow directors

Section 251 defines 'shadow director':[18]  **3.14**

(1) In the Companies Acts 'shadow director', in relation to a company, means a person in accordance with whose directions or instructions the directors of a company are accustomed to act.
(2) A person is not to be regarded as a shadow director by reason only that the directors act on advice given by him in a professional capacity.
(3) A body corporate is not to be regarded as a shadow director of any of its subsidiary companies for the purposes of—
    Chapter 2 (general duties of directors),
    Chapter 4 (transactions requiring members' approval), or
    Chapter 6 (contract with sole member who is also a director),
    by reason only that the directors of the subsidiary are accustomed to act in accordance with its directions or instructions.

The concept of a 'shadow director' was introduced by the 1980 Act, s 63 to strengthen **3.15** the new provisions of Part IV of that Act, concerning duties of directors and conflicts of interest, which were later incorporated into Part X of the 1985 Act and have been replaced by provisions in the Companies Act, Part 10, Chapters 3–6.[19] 'Shadow

---

[16] [1998] 1 BCLC 333, 343. See the approving observations of Robert Walker LJ in *Re Kaytech International plc* [1999] 2 BCLC 351, 423e–424a, CA.

[17] *Re Lo-Line Electric Motors Ltd* [1988] BCLC 698, 706, 707.

[18] This restates the definition in 1985 Act, s 741(2).

[19] The philosophy behind 'shadow director' can be traced back to the First World War, when Companies (Particulars as to Directors) Act 1917 was enacted to provide for the disclosure of 'certain particulars respecting the Directors of Companies'. Section 3 provided that 'the expression "director" shall include any person who occupies the position of a director and any person in accordance with whose directions or instructions the directors of a company are accustomed to act'. The actual phrase 'shadow director' was not used in that 1917 Act. The same philosophy is to be found in the City Code, paragraph D.018 of which provides: 'Directors include persons in accordance with whose instructions the directors or a director are accustomed to act.'

director' therefore fulfils a statutory purpose. It applies to the following provisions of the Companies Act:[20]

(1) Part 5, ss 63, 68, 75, 76, and 84, concerning liability for offences in relation to a company's name;[21]

(2) Part 10, Chapter 1, concerning the appointment and removal of directors:

s 156 (criminal liability for default in complying with a direction from the Secretary of State under that section),

s 157 (saving of liability where a person under the minimum age for appointment as director purports to act as a director or acts as a shadow director),

ss 162, 165, and 167 (liability for offences in relation to the register of directors);[22]

(3) Part 10, Chapter 2, s 170(5) which provides that 'the general duties of directors apply to shadow directors where, and to the extent that, the corresponding common law rules or equitable rules so apply';

(4) Part 10, Chapter 3, s 187 which provides that a shadow director is under a duty to disclose an interest in an existing transaction;

(5) Part 10, Chapter 4, s 223 which provides that a shadow director is treated as a director for the purposes of the provisions of that Chapter concerning transactions requiring members approval;

(6) Part 10, Chapter 5, s 230 which provides that a shadow director is treated as a director for the purposes of the provisions of that Chapter concerning disclosure of directors' service contracts;

(7) Part 10, Chapter 6, s 231 which provides that a shadow director is treated as a director for the purposes of the provisions of that section concerning contracts with a sole member who is a director;

(8) Part 10, Chapter 7, s 239 which provides that a shadow director is treated as a director for the purposes of the provisions of that section concerning ratification by a company of acts of directors;

(9) Part 10, Chapter 9, s 247 which provides that a resolution of directors is not sufficient sanction for payments to or for the benefit of shadow directors under that section which gives directors power to make provision for employees on cessation or transfer of business in accordance with that section;[23]

---

[20] Unless otherwise indicated, these sections were brought into force on or before 1 October 2008.

[21] ss 63, 68, 75, and 76 do not come into force until 1 October 2009. Until then the corresponding provisions of 1985 Act, ss 28, 31, and 32, remain in force, but liability for default under them does not extend to shadow directors.

[22] ss 162, 165, and 167 do not come into force until 1 October 2009. Section 165 is a new section. 1985 Act, s 288, which corresponds with ss 162 and 167, remains in force and liability under it extends to shadow directors.

[23] s 247 does not come into force until 1 October 2009 and contains a new express provision to prevent the directors from authorizing payments for the benefit of directors, former directors, or

(10) Part 11, s 260 which provides that a shadow director is treated as a director for the purposes of derivative claims in England and Wales and Northern Ireland;

(11) Part 12, ss 272, 275, and 276 under which a shadow director may be liable for a criminal offence for default in appointing a secretary of a public company or keeping a register of secretaries;

(12) Part 14, s 379 by which 'director' includes a shadow director for the purposes of that Part concerning the control of political donations and expenditure;

(13) Part 24, s 859 which provides that a shadow director is treated as a director for the purposes of that Part concerning a company's annual return.[24]

**3.16** For the purposes of the Insolvency Act, Parts I to VII, s 251of that Act gives substantially the same definition of 'shadow director' as is contained in s 251(1) and (2) of the Companies Act. The definition applies to the following sections of the Insolvency Act:

(1) ss 206, 208, 210, and 211 which each provide that 'officer' includes a shadow director for the purposes of liability for criminal offences for fraud in anticipation of winding up, misconduct in the course of the winding up, material omissions from any statement relating to the company's affairs, and false representations to creditors;

(2) s 214, which provides that in that section, concerning directors' liability for wrongful trading, 'director' includes a shadow director;

(3) s 216 by which a shadow director who contravenes the provisions of that section concerning the re-use of a prohibited company name commits a criminal offence.

It should be noted that a person who is only a 'shadow director' does not appear to be amenable to a summary remedy for misfeasance under the Insolvency Act, s 212. For that purpose the shadow director would also have to be an officer of the company or to have taken part in its promotion, formation, or management. Nor is a person who is merely a shadow director necessarily liable for fraudulent trading under the Insolvency Act, s 213. For that purpose the shadow director must also have been knowingly party to the carrying on of the company's fraudulent business.

**3.17** The Insolvency Act, s 249 also provides that a person is connected with a company if he is a shadow director. This is relevant to the following provisions of the Insolvency Act:

(1) ss 165(6) and 167(2)(a) which require sanction for a disposition by a liquidator of property of the company to a person connected with the company;

---

shadow directors, which is not contained in 1985 Act, s 719, which remains in force until 1 October 2009.

[24] s 859 replaces 1985 Act, s 365(3) on 1 October 2009 without change.

(2) s 239(6) which presumes that a preference given to a person connected with the company was influenced by a desire to improve that person's position in the event of the company being wound up;

(3) s 240(a) which, in the case of a preference given to a person connected with the company, extends the preference period from six months to two years;

(4) s 240(2) which presumes that the company was unable to pay its debts at the time of or in consequence of a transaction at undervalue entered into with a person connected with the company;

(5) s 245(3)(a) and (4) which, in the case of a floating charge created in favour of a person connected with the company, extends the relevant time for avoidance from one to two years, without proof that the company was unable to pay its debts or became unable to pay its debts in consequence of the creation of the charge.

**3.18** The Company Directors Disqualification Act 1986, s 22(5) also adopts substantially the same definition of shadow director as is contained in the Companies Act, s 251(1) and (2). Shadow directors are liable to be disqualified for fraud in relation to a company being wound up, unfitness to be concerned in the management of a company, or following an investigation.[25]

**3.19** In *Re Hydrodam (Corby) Ltd* Millett J described the characteristics of a shadow director in contrast to a de facto director.

> A shadow director, by contrast, does not claim or purport to act as a director. On the contrary, he claims not to be a director. He lurks in the shadows, sheltering behind others who, he claims, are the only directors of the company to the exclusion of himself. He is not held out as a director by the company. To establish that a defendant is a shadow director of a company it is necessary to allege and prove: (1) who are the directors of the company, whether de facto or de jure; (2) that the defendant directed those directors how to act in relation to the company or that he was one of the persons who did so; (3) that those directors acted in accordance with such directions; and (4) that they were accustomed so to act. What is needed is first, a board of directors claiming and purporting to act as such; and secondly, a pattern of behaviour in which the board did not exercise any discretion or judgment of its own, but acted in accordance with the directions of others.[26]

**3.20** In *Re Kaytech International plc* Robert Walker LJ commented on Millett J's contrast between the characteristics of de facto and shadow directors and observed that they may have features in common in that 'an individual who was not a de jure director is alleged to have exercised real influence (otherwise than as a professional adviser) in the corporate governance of a company. Sometimes that

---

[25] CDDA, ss 4, 6, and 8.
[26] [1994] 2 BCLC 180, 183.

influence may be concealed and sometimes it may be open. Sometimes it may be something of a mixture, as the facts of the present case show.'[27]

The meaning of shadow director was considered by the Court of Appeal in **3.21** *Secretary of State for Trade and Industry v Deverell*.[28] Morritt LJ summarized the law in a number of propositions as follows:

(1) The definition of a shadow director is to be construed in the normal way to give effect to the parliamentary intention ascertainable from the mischief to be dealt with and the words used. In particular, as the purpose of the Act is the protection of the public and as the definition is used in other legislative contexts, it should not be strictly construed merely because it also has quasi-penal consequences in the context of the Company Directors Disqualification Act 1986 . . . .

(2) The purpose of the legislation is to identify those, other than professional advisers, with real influence in the corporate affairs of the company. But it is not necessary that such influence should be exercised over the whole field of its corporate activities . . . .

(3) Whether any particular communication from the alleged shadow director, whether by words or conduct, is to be classified as a direction or instruction must be objectively ascertained by the court in the light of all the evidence. In that connection it is not necessary to prove the understanding or expectation of either giver or receiver. In many, if not most, cases it will suffice to prove the communication and its consequence. Evidence of such understanding or expectation may be relevant but it cannot be conclusive. Certainly the label attached by either or both parties then or thereafter cannot be more than a factor in considering whether the communication came within the statutory description of direction or instruction.

(4) Non-professional advice may come within that statutory description. The proviso excepting advice given in a professional capacity appears to assume that advice generally is or may be included. Moreover the concepts of 'direction' and 'instruction' do not exclude the concept of 'advice' for all three share the common feature of 'guidance'.

(5) It will, no doubt, be sufficient to show that in the face of 'directions or instructions' from the alleged shadow director the properly appointed directors or some of them cast themselves in a subservient role or surrendered their respective discretions. But it is not necessary to do so in all cases. Such a requirement would be to put a gloss on the statutory requirement that the board are 'accustomed to act' 'in accordance with' such directions or instructions.[29]

In addition, Morritt LJ said that if (a) the directors usually took the advice of the **3.22** putative shadow director, it is irrelevant that on the occasions when he did not give advice the board did exercise its own discretion; and (b) if the board were accustomed to act on the directions or instructions of the putative shadow

---

27  [1999] 2 BCLC 351, 424c, CA.
28  [2001] Ch 340, CA at para 35.
29  Adopted by Lewison J in *Ultraframe (UK) Ltd v Fielding* [2005] EWHC 1638 (Ch) at paras 1260–1261. See also *Re Mea Corporation Ltd* [2007] 1 BCLC 618 at paras 86–91.

director it is not necessary to demonstrate that their action was mechanical rather than considered.[30]

**3.23**  In *Ultraframe (UK) Ltd v Fielding* Lewison J considered the phrase 'accustomed to act' in the definition of shadow director and concluded that (a) a person is capable of being a shadow director if a governing majority of the board is accustomed to act at his direction, (b) if a person becomes a shadow director as a result of the board being accustomed to act on his instructions or directions, transactions entered into before it can be said that the board is so accustomed cannot be retrospectively invalidated, and (c) the mere giving of instructions does not make someone a shadow director; it is only when they are translated into action by the board that the question can arise.[31]

**3.24**  Although it is possible for a bank, financier, or other creditor to be a shadow director, so far attempts to establish that such a person is a shadow director have been unsuccessful.[32] This is because the court readily accepts that a creditor is entitled to protect his own interests, by imposing conditions of continued support, without necessarily becoming a shadow director. Such a creditor is not dictating how the company is run, even if the directors have little choice but to accept his terms.[33]

**3.25**  Section 251(2) provides a measure of protection for professional advisers since '[a] person is not to be regarded as a shadow director by reason only that the directors act on advice given by him in a professional capacity'. Morritt LJ's fourth proposition in the *Deverell* case (paragraph 3.21 above)[34] shows that advice is capable of being a 'direction' or 'instruction' since they are all forms of 'guidance'. While lawyers who give legal advice to the board should be in no danger of being shadow directors, the same is not true of those who give financial advice, since in that context the dividing line between an adviser giving advice in a professional capacity and a shadow director may be difficult to draw.[35]

**3.26**  Since a parent company may well give directions and instructions to the directors of its subsidiaries, the parent is capable of being a shadow director within s 251(1).[36]

---

[30]  *Secretary of State for Trade and Industry v Deverell* [2001] Ch 340, CA at para 59.

[31]  [2005] EWHC 1638 (Ch) at paras 1270–1278.

[32]  *Re a Company No 005009 of 1987* (1988) 4 BCC 424 (where the claim of shadow directorship against a bank was abandoned at trial); *Re MC Bacon Ltd* [1990] BCLC 324, 325; and *In Re PTZFM Ltd* [1995] 2 BCLC 354.

[33]  *Ultraframe (UK) Ltd v Fielding* [2005] EWHC 1638 (Ch) at paras 1264–1269.

[34]  *Secretary of State for Trade and Industry v Deverell* [2001] Ch 340, CA at para 35.

[35]  *Re Tasbian Ltd (No 3)* [1991] BCLC 792, 802, (affirmed [1992] BCLC 297, CA).

[36]  But consider *Re Hydrodam (Corby) Ltd* [1994] 2 BCLC 180, 184a–b, where Millett J said that where a body corporate was a director of a company, it did not automatically follow that its own directors must *ipso facto* be shadow directors of that company. See also, by analogy, *MCA Records v Charly Records* [2003] 1 BCLC 93, CA at para 49, where Chadwick LJ said that a director will not be jointly liable with a company for torts if he does no more than carry out his constitutional role in the governance of the company.

Section 251(3) goes on to limit the statutory provisions for which a body corporate may be regarded as a shadow director of any of its subsidiaries. First, the parent is not to be regarded as a shadow director for the purposes of Part 10, Chapter 2 (general duties of directors). Without this provision, it could be argued that parent companies owe fiduciary duties and duties of care to their subsidiaries, thereby undermining the separate corporate personalities of group companies. Secondly, the parent is not to be regarded as a shadow director of any of its subsidiary companies for the purposes of Part 10, Chapter 4 (transactions requiring members' approval) and Chapter 6 (contract with sole member who is also a director).[37] These provisions are needed, because otherwise any group transaction between a subsidiary and a holding company might be classed as a transaction between the subsidiary company and a shadow director and so subject to the controls imposed by the relevant sections in those Chapters.

The issue whether a shadow director owes any, and if so what, duties to the company are considered in Chapter 9, Section C. **3.27**

## (4) Alternate directors

Save where a company's articles make special provision, a directorship is a personal **3.28** office and responsibility.[38] The 1985 Act Table A, regs 65–69 make provision for the appointment of alternate directors.[39] Alternate directors can be appointed in relation to any company, but are usually found in public companies. Thus Model Articles (plc) 25–27 contain provisions for public companies for the appointment, rights, and responsibilities of alternate directors and for termination of an alternate directorship, which are considered in Chapter 6 at paragraphs 6.57, 6.68, and 6.69. The Model Articles (pcls) do not include provision for private companies for alternate directors, because the Government considered it unlikely that directors of most private companies would want to appoint alternate directors.[40] Private companies that wish to adopt articles providing for the appointment of alternate directors may adopt the model articles for public companies or draft their own articles appropriately.

The appointment of an alternate director does not replace the appointing director **3.29** who remains in office. An alternate director is a person appointed by a director to (a) exercise that director's powers, and (b) carry out that director's responsibilities in relation to the taking of decisions by the directors in the absence of the alternate's

---

[37] This substantially re-enacts 1985 Act, s 741(3).
[38] A director therefore cannot delegate his powers under a power of attorney: *Mancini v Mancini* (1999) 17 ACLC 1, 570, SC (NSW).
[39] SI 1985/805 (with no change made by SI 2007/2541 or SI 2007/2826).
[40] *Implementation of the Companies Act 2006*, a DTI Consultative Document (February 2007) at para 3.107.

appointor.[41] The alternate director has the same rights in relation to any directors' meeting or directors' written resolution as the alternate's appointor.[42] Alternate directors are deemed for all purposes to be directors; they are personally liable for their own acts and omissions; they are subject to the same restrictions as their appointors; and they are not deemed to be agents of or for their appointors.[43]

**3.30**   An alternate director's appointment as an alternate terminates (a) when his appointor revokes his appointment by notice to the company in writing specifying when it is to terminate, (b) on the occurrence in relation to the alternate of any event which, if it occurred in relation to the alternate's appointor, would result in the termination of the appointor's appointment as director. The appointment of the alternate also terminates when his appointor dies or when the directorship of the appointor terminates (except that an alternate's appointment as an alternate does not terminate when the appointor retires by rotation at a general meeting and is then re-appointed as a director at the same general meeting).[44] An alternate director can only act where his appointor is not present and the alternate director has no powers, rights, or duties when the director for whom he is alternate is acting.[45]

### (5) Nominee directors

**3.31**   Whereas an alternate director is appointed by a director, a nominee director is appointed a director by a shareholder or, perhaps, by a major creditor. The shareholder may have the right to appoint a nominee director pursuant to a right attaching to shares or a contractual right in a joint venture or shareholders' agreement. A nominee director has the same duties to the company as any other director. It has to be recognized that the nomineeship may place him in particular difficulty in relation to the general duties to exercise independent judgment, to avoid conflicts of interest, not to accept benefits from third parties, and to declare his interest in proposed and existing transactions and arrangements (see Chapters 12, 14, 15, and 17 below).[46]

---

[41]   Model Article (plc) 25(1). An alternate director has no powers, rights, or duties when the director for whom he is alternate is acting: *Strathmore Group Ltd v Fraser* (1991) 5 NZCLC 67, 163, HC (NZ).

[42]   Model Article (plc) 26(1).

[43]   Model Article (plc) 26(2) and compare Table A, regs 66 and 69. The alternate director is not imputed with knowledge of a matter known to his appointor: *Re Associated Tool Industries Ltd* (1963) 5 FLR 55, 68 (SC (NSW)). The alternate director is not required to disclose an adverse interest in a transaction or disqualified from voting if the interest is not his own but that of his appointor: *Anaray Ltd v Sydney Futures Exchange Ltd* (1988) 6 ACLR 271 (SC (NSW)). It therefore follows that the alternate director will be disqualified from voting if he (the alternate director) has an adverse interest, even though his appointor has no adverse interest: *ASIC v Doyle* (2001) 38 ACSR 606, SC (WA).

[44]   Model Article (plc) 27.

[45]   *Strathmore Group Ltd v Fraser* (1991) 5 NZCLC 67, 163 HC (NZ).

[46]   ss 173, 175, 176, 177, 182.

In *Boulting and another v Association of Cinematograph Television and Allied*  **3.32**
*Technicians*[47] Lord Denning MR described the position of a nominee director:

> . . . take a nominee director, that is, a director of a company who is nominated by a
> large shareholder to represent his interests. There is nothing wrong in it. It is done
> every day. Nothing wrong, that is, so long as the director is left free to exercise his best
> judgment in the interests of the company which he serves. But if he is put upon terms
> that he is bound to act in the affairs of the company in accordance with the directions
> of his patron, it is beyond doubt unlawful (see *Kregor v. Hollins* (1913) 109 LT 225,
> 228 CA by Avory J.), or if he agrees to subordinate the interests of the company to
> the interests of his patron, it is conduct oppressive to the other shareholders for
> which the patron can be brought to book: see *Scottish Co-operative Wholesale Society
> Ltd. v. Meyer* [1959] AC 324, 341, 363, 366, 367. So, also, if a director of a company
> becomes a member of a trade union on the terms that he is to act in the company's
> affairs on the instructions of the trade union, or in accordance with the policy of the
> trade union (rather than according to what he thinks best in the interests of the com-
> pany), such an agreement of membership is unlawful. It is contrary to public policy
> that any director should be made to deny his trust and throw over the interests of
> those whom he is bound to protect. Take the converse. Suppose the employee of a
> company is an officer of a trade union. Would it be lawful for his employers to
> approach him and—by promises of promotion or threat of dismissal—get him to
> promise that he would act in the union's affairs on the instructions of his employers?
> It would in my judgment be unlawful. An officer of a trade union, too, is in a fidu-
> ciary position towards the members, and no employer would be justified in seeking,
> by promises or threats, to induce him to act disloyally towards them. In each one of
> these cases the reason is simple: it is wrong to induce another to act inconsistently
> with the duty of fidelity which he has undertaken by contract or trust to perform: cf.
> *Bents Brewery Co. Ltd. v. Hogan* [1945] 2 All ER 570 and *D. C. Thomson & Co. Ltd. v.
> Deakin* [1952] Ch 646, 694.

### (6) Executive and non-executive directors

The Companies Act does not distinguish between executive and non-executive  **3.33**
directors. Nor do the Insolvency Act and the CDDA. In small private companies
the practical distinction is between the directors who manage the daily business of
the company and receive remuneration for their executive services, so that they are
employees of the company, and those who do not. Similar arrangements may
apply in many public companies.

It is with listed companies that a formal distinction is drawn between executive  **3.34**
and non-executive directors under the provisions of the Combined Code discussed in paragraph 3.38 below. The former are executives, employed under service contracts, to work full time for the company. A non-executive director is a
director who is not employed under a contract of service. He may be a director of
several unconnected companies and his role is to provide the company with the

---

[47] [1963] 2 QB 606, 626–7, CA.

benefit of his advice and expertise on a part-time basis. The non-executive director of a listed company has an important role in providing independent supervision of the management of the executive directors, participating in audit and remuneration committees, and liaising with shareholders.

**3.35** Both executive and non-executive directors participate in decision-making by directors as members of the same board and they have the same access to the company's books and accounting records.

**3.36** Non-executive directors have the same general and particular duties under the Companies Act as executive directors, although the latter may owe additional duties by virtue of their contracts of service.[48] These duties are discussed in Chapters 9–15 below. While non-executive directors owe the same duty of care, skill, and diligence,[49] it is an essential feature of the non-executive director that in carrying out his functions he will necessarily have to rely on the executive directors and managers. In *Re Westmid Packing Services Ltd*[50] Lord Woolf MR said 'A proper degree of delegation and division of responsibility is of course permissible, and often necessary, but not total abdication of responsibility.'

**3.37** In *Equitable Life Assurance Society v Bowley*[51] Langley J accepted that the duty owed by a non-executive director will in expression be the same as the duty owed by an executive director, but in application the duty may and usually will differ. He went on to conclude that (a) a non-executive director could not place unquestioning reliance on others to do their job, (b) the extent to which a non-executive director may reasonably rely on the executive directors and other professionals to perform their duties is a developing area of the law and one which is 'fact sensitive', and (c) it arguable that a company may reasonably look to non-executive directors for independence of judgment and supervision of executive management. In reaching these conclusions Langley J found helpful the following statement of Jonathan Parker J, approved by Morritt LJ in *Re Barings plc (No 5), Secretary of State for Trade and Industry v Baker (No 5)*:[52]

> (i) Directors have, both collectively and individually, a continuing duty to acquire and maintain a sufficient knowledge and understanding of the company's business to enable them properly to discharge their duties as directors. (ii) Whilst directors are entitled (subject to the articles of association of the company) to delegate particular

---

[48] In *Dorchester Finance Co Ltd v Stebbing* [1989] BCLC 498, decided in 1977, Foster J rejected the proposition that non-executive directors had no duties to perform. In *Re Wimbledon Village Restaurant Ltd* [1994] BCC 753 a non-executive director was criticized, in the same way as executive directors, for failure to file accounts but no disqualification order was made.

[49] s 174.

[50] [1998] 2 All ER 124, CA.

[51] [2004] 1 BCLC 180 at paras 35–41.

[52] [2000] 1 BCLC 523, 535–6, CA at para 36 and at first instance [1999] 1 BCLC 433, 489. There is a useful discussion of the principles in *Lexi Holdings plc v Lugman* [2008] 2 BCLC 725 at paras 30–39, per Briggs J.

functions to those below them in the management chain, and to trust their competence and integrity to a reasonable extent, the exercise of the power of delegation does not absolve a director from the duty to supervise the discharge of the delegated functions. (iii) No rule of universal application can be formulated as to the duty referred to in (ii) above. The extent of the duty, and the question whether it has been discharged, must depend on the facts of each particular case, including the director's role in the management of the company.

Listed companies are expected to comply with the Combined Code containing **3.38** principles of good governance and a code of best practice (the current text of which is at Appendix 2 of this work).[53] This deals with the role of non-executive directors and indicates what level of commitment is to be expected of them and is likely to be relevant to any issues as to the role and duties of non-executive directors (see Schedule B to the Combined Code). Part A deals with directors.

(1) A.1 concerns the board. The main Principle is: 'Every company should be headed by an effective board, which is collectively responsible for the success of the company.' In relation to this the supporting principles state:

> As part of their role as members of a unitary board, non-executive directors should constructively challenge and help develop proposals on strategy. Non-executive directors should scrutinise the performance of management in meeting agreed goals and objectives and monitor the reporting of performance. They should satisfy themselves on the integrity of financial information and that financial controls and systems of risk management are robust and defensible. They are responsible for determining appropriate levels of remuneration of executive directors and have a prime role in appointing, and where necessary removing, executive directors, and in succession planning.

The Code provisions A.1.3 and A.1.4 state that non-executive directors should (a) hold meetings with the chairman without executives present, (b) meet with the senior independent director at least annually to appraise the chairman's performance, (c) ensure that any unresolved concerns are recorded in the board minutes, and (d) on resignation make a written statement to the chairman, for circulation to the board, if they have any concerns.

(2) A.3 concerns board balance and independence. The main principle is: 'The board should include a balance of executive and non-executive directors (and in particular independent non-executive directors) such that no individual or small group of individuals can dominate the board's decision taking.' The supporting principles include 'a strong presence on the board of both executive and non-executive directors'. Code provision A.3.1 states that (a) the annual report should identify each non-executive director considered to be independent in character

---

[53] The Combined Code, which is annexed to the Listing Rules, was first published in June 1998 and has been revised in July 2003, so as to apply to reporting years beginning on or after 1 November 2003; in June 2006, so as to apply to reporting years beginning on or after 1 November 2006; and in June 2008 for accounting periods beginning on or after 29 June 2008. For the origins of the Combined Code, see Chapter 2 at paragraph 2.74.

and judgment, (b) except for smaller companies[54] at least half the board, excluding the chairman, should comprise independent non-executive directors, and (c) one of the independent non-executive directors should be the senior independent director to whom shareholders should be able to express any concerns.

(3) A.4 concerns appointments to the board. Code provision A.4.4 states:

> The terms and conditions of appointment of non-executive directors should be made available for inspection.[55] The letter of appointment should set out the expected time commitment. Non-executive directors should undertake that they will have sufficient time to meet what is expected of them. Their other significant commitments should be disclosed to the board before appointment, with a broad indication of the time involved and the board should be informed of subsequent changes.

(4) A.5 concerns information and professional development. The main principle is: 'The board should be supplied in a timely manner with information in a form and of a quality appropriate to enable it to discharge its duties. All directors should receive induction on joining the board and should regularly update and refresh their skills and knowledge.' Code provision A.5.1 states 'The chairman should ensure that new directors receive a full, formal and tailored induction on joining the board. As part of this, the company should offer to major shareholders the opportunity to meet a new non-executive director.' Code provision A.5.2 states: 'The board should ensure that directors, especially non-executive directors, have access to independent professional advice at the company's expense where they judge it necessary to discharge their responsibilities as directors. Committees should be provided with sufficient resources to undertake their duties.'

(5) A.6 concerns performance evaluation of the board, committees, and individual directors. Code provision A.6.1 provides that 'the non-executive directors, led by the senior independent director, should be responsible for performance evaluation of the chairman, taking into account the views of executive directors'.

(6) A.7 concerns re-election, with directors being submitted for re-election at regular intervals, subject to satisfactory performance, and with a planned and progressive refreshing of the board. To this end code provision A.7.2. states that (a) non-executive directors should be appointed for specified terms (subject to re-election and removal), (b) in the event of a non-executive director being proposed for re-election, the board should give reasons why it considers that he should be re-elected and the chairman should confirm that evaluation of his performance shows him to be effective and committed, and (c) terms of

---

[54] Those below FTSE 350 throughout the year immediately prior to the reporting year.
[55] They should be made available for inspection by any person at the company's registered office during normal business hours and at the AGM (for 15 minutes prior to the meeting and during the meeting).

longer than six years should be subject to rigorous scrutiny (because of prejudice to independence).

(7) Part B concerns directors' remuneration and Part C concerns accountability
and audit. Code provision B.1.3 states that (a) 'levels of remuneration for non-
executive directors should reflect the time commitment and responsibilities of
the role', and (b) remuneration for non-executive directors should not include
share options, unless approved by shareholders in advance, since holding
options may impair independence. Code provisions B.2.1 and C.3.1 state that
the remuneration and audit committees should include 'at least three, or in the
case of smaller companies two, independent non-executive directors'.

(8) Part D deals with relations with shareholders. D.1 concerns dialogue with institutional shareholders. Code provision D.1.1 states that 'non-executive directors
should be offered the opportunity to attend meetings with major shareholders
and should expect to attend them if requested by major shareholders'. Code
provision D.1.2 indicates that non-executive directors are expected to 'develop
an understanding of the views of major shareholders about their company'.

## D.  Persons Connected with a Director

Sections 252 to 255 and Schedule 1 identify, for the purposes of Part 10, those **3.39**
persons, and only those persons, who are connected with a director of a company
or a director being connected with a person.[56] This identification is material to the
following sections (for all of which a shadow director is treated as a director):

(1) in Chapter 4: ss 190, 194, and 195 (substantial property transactions); ss 197,
200, 201, 203, 204, 210, 213 (loans, quasi-loans, and credit transactions);
s 215 (payments for loss of office);
(2) in Chapter 7: s 239 (ratification of acts of directors giving rise to liability).

Section 252(2) identifies five categories of persons who are regarded as connected **3.40**
with a director for the purposes of Part 10 if, but only if, they meet the requirements of the statutory definitions: (a) members of a director's family, (b) companies, (c) trustees, (d) partners, and (e) firms. Section 252(3) provides that for
those purposes a person connected with a director of a company does not include
a person who is himself a director of the company. Section 239(5)(d), however,
provides that s 252(3) does not apply for the purposes of s 239, which is concerned
with the power of the company to ratify acts of directors giving rise to liability.

---

[56] These provisions replace without material change, except to expand the categories of family
members, the provisions in 1985 Act, s 346 and Part 1 of Schedule 13. Note that Insolvency Act,
ss 249 and 435 explain for the purposes of Parts I–VII of that Act the meanings of 'connected' with
a company and 'associate'.

*Family members*

**3.41**   Section 253 defines what is meant by references to members of a director's family who are connected to him. Reflecting recommendations of the Law Commission the categories of family members has been extended.[57] The members of a director's family who are connected with him are:

(1)   the director's spouse or civil partner;

(2)   any other person (whether of a different sex or the same sex) with whom the director lives as partner in an enduring family relationship, but not where the person with whom the director lives is the director's grandparent or grandchild, sister, brother, aunt or uncle, or nephew or niece;[58]

(3)   the director's children or step-children;

(4)   any children or step-children of a person within (2) above (and who are not children or step-children of the director) who live with the director and have not attained the age of 18;

(5)   the director's parents.

*Connected companies*

**3.42**   Section 254, read with s 255 and Schedule 1, defines what is meant by references in Part 10 to a director being 'connected with a body corporate'. This is the case if, but only if, he and the persons connected with him together either (a) 'are interested in shares comprised in the equity share capital of that body corporate of a nominal value equal to at least 20% of that share capital', or (b) 'are entitled to exercise or control the exercise of more than 20% of the voting power at any general meeting of that body'. Those tests, based on interests in shares and voting power require considerable elaboration, as discussed in the following paragraphs.

**3.43**   For the purposes of ss 254 and 255 the provisions of Schedule 1 (references to interest in shares or debentures) have effect.[59] The general provisions of Schedule 1 are that a reference to an interest in shares includes any interest of any kind whatsoever in shares, and any restraints or restrictions to which the exercise of any right attached to the interest is or may be subject shall be disregarded; it is immaterial that the shares in which a person has an interest are not identifiable; and persons having a joint interest in shares are deemed each of them to have that interest.[60]

---

[57]   *Company Directors: Regulating Conflicts of Interests and Formulating a Statement of Duties* (Law Commission No 261) Part 14. Under 1985 Act, s 346 family members were limited to the director's spouse, child, or step-child. The Law Commission's recommendation to include a director's siblings was not adopted in the 2006 Act.

[58]   The exception is made by s 253(3).

[59]   s 254 (3). Schedule 1 applies to interests in debentures as well as shares.

[60]   Schedule 1, para 2.

Schedule 1, paragraphs 3–6 provide that a person is taken to have an interest in shares if:

(1)  he enters into a contract to acquire them;[61]

(2)  he has a right to call for delivery of the shares to himself or his order, or he has a right to acquire, or an obligation to take, an interest in shares (whether the right or obligation is absolute or conditional);[62]

(3)  not being the registered holder, he is entitled to exercise or control the exercise of rights conferred by the holding of the shares;

(4)  a body corporate is interested in them and (a) the body corporate or its directors are accustomed to act in accordance with his directions or instructions, or (b) he is entitled to exercise or control the exercise of more than one-half of the voting power at general meetings of the body corporate;[63]

(5)  he is a beneficiary of a trust, the property of which includes an interest in shares, subject to the provisions of paragraph 6.[64]

Section 255 explains what is meant by references to a director 'controlling' a body corporate.[65] A director of a company is taken to control a body corporate if, but only if (a) he or any person connected with him is interested in any part of the equity share capital of that body, or is entitled to exercise or control the exercise of any part of the voting power at any general meeting of that body, and (b) he, the persons connected with him, and the other directors of that company, together are interested in more than 50% of that share capital, or are entitled to exercise or control the exercise of more than 50% of that voting power.[66] The rules set out in Schedule 1 apply.[67] **3.44**

For both tests (interest in shares and control of the exercise of voting power), additional rules apply: **3.45**

(1)  References to voting power the exercise of which is controlled by a director include voting power whose exercise is controlled by a body corporate controlled by him.[68]

---

[61]  Schedule 1, para 3(1).

[62]  Schedule 1, para 3(2). Paras 3(3) and (4) contain further provisions for determining when a person is taken to have an interest in shares.

[63]  Schedule 1, para 5(2) contains further provisions for determining when voting power is taken to be exercisable.

[64]  Under para 6(a) an interest in the shares in reversion or remainder is disregarded so long as a person is entitled to receive, during the lifetime of himself or another, income from trust property comprising shares; (b) a person is treated as not interested in shares if and so long as he holds them as bare trustee or custodian trustee; (c) there shall be disregarded any interest of a person subsisting by virtue of certain unit trust, charitable church schemes.

[65]  s 255(1).

[66]  s 255(2).

[67]  s 255(3).

[68]  ss 254(4) and 255(4).

(2) Shares in a company held as treasury shares, and any voting rights attached to such shares, are disregarded.[69]

(3) To avoid circularity in the application of s 252 (a) a body corporate with which a director is connected is not treated for the purposes of s 254 as connected with him by virtue of s 252(2)(c) or (d) (connection as trustee or partner), and (b) a trustee of a trust the beneficiaries of which include (or may include) a body corporate with which a director is connected is not treated for the purposes of s 254 as connected with a director by reason only of that fact.[70]

*Trusts*

**3.46**　A person is connected with a director of a company if he is acting in his capacity as trustee of a trust (not being a trust for the purposes of an employees' share scheme or pension scheme) (a) the beneficiaries of which include the director or a person who by virtue of (1) or (2) above is connected with him, or (b) the terms of which confer a power on the trustees that may be exercised for the benefit of the director or any such person.[71]

*Partners*

**3.47**　A person is connected with a director of a company if he is acting in his capacity as partner (a) of the director, or (b) of a person who is connected with that director by virtue of subs 252(2)(a), (b), or (c) (family, company, or trust connection).[72]

*Firms*

**3.48**　A firm that is a legal person under the law by which it is governed is connected with a director of a company if it is one in which (a) the director is a partner, (b) a partner is a person who, by virtue of subs 252(2)(a), (b), or (c) (family, company, or trust connection) is connected with the director, or (c) a partner is a firm in which the director is a partner or in which there is a partner who, by virtue of subs 252(2)(a), (b), or (c) (family, company, or trust connection) is connected with the director.[73]

# E.　The Secretary

**3.49**　Part 12 of the Companies Act is concerned with company secretaries. The word 'secretary' is not defined in the Companies Act or the Model Articles. Table A, reg 1

---

[69] ss 254(5) and 255(5).
[70] ss 254(6) and 255(6).
[71] s 252(2)(c). Note *Re Kilnoore Ltd* [2006] Ch 489, where Lewison J held that a bare trustee of shares is not a person entitled to exercise the voting power attached to those shares, because the verb 'entitled' governed both the exercise of voting power and the control of voting power (Insolvency Act, s 435).
[72] s 252(2)(d).
[73] s 252(2(e).

states that in Table A 'secretary' means 'the secretary of the company or any other person appointed to perform the duties of the secretary of the company, including a joint, assistant or deputy secretary'.

Although the office of secretary is not defined (in the Model Articles where rele-  **3.50** vant (see below) or in the 2006 Act), his functions are usually ministerial and administrative, rather than managerial. He acts under the direction of the directors and it is for them to decide on his role and functions.[74] Outside Part 12 there are few references to the secretary:

(1) ss 12 and 16 contain provisions for the appointment of the first secretary or joint secretaries (see below);

(2) by s 44 he is an authorized signatory for the execution of documents by a company;[75]

(3) in the case of quoted companies, the secretary is required to provide an independent assessor, appointed to report on a poll, with information and explanations for the purposes of the report;[76]

(4) his signature on the record of a resolution of members passed otherwise than at a general meeting is evidence of the passing of the resolution;[77]

(5) he is an officer of the company for the purpose of being liable for offences committed by 'every officer of the company who is in default' in the event of contravention of an enactment in relation to a company,[78] and generally in the Companies Acts;[79]

(6) on the application of the Director of Public Prosecutions, the Secretary of State, or a chief officer of police, he may be ordered by a judge of the High Court to produce documents where there is reasonable cause to believe that any person has, while an officer of a company, committed an offence in connection with the management of the company's affairs;[80]

---

[74] The traditional view of a secretary was: 'A secretary is a mere servant; his position is that he is to do what he is told, and no person can assume that he has authority to represent anything at all . . .'; per Lord Esher MR in *Barnett, Hoares & Co v South London Tramways Co* (1887) 18 QBD 815, 817, CA, approved in *George Whitechurch Ltd v Cavanagh* [1902] AC 117, 124, HL, and supported by *Ruben v Great Fingall Consolidated* [1906] AC 439, HL. However, see also *Panorama Developments (Guildford) Ltd v Fidelis Furnishing Fabrics Ltd* [1971] 2 QB 711, CA, referred to in paragraph 3.51 below.

[75] ss 44(2)(a), (3) and (7), restating 1985 Act, s 36A(4) and (8).

[76] s 349(2).

[77] s 356(2), restating 1985 Act, s 382A(2).

[78] s 1121, which restates 1985 Act, ss 730(5) and 744, and s 1123, which is new.

[79] s 1173, restating 1985 Act, s 744. This makes the secretary an officer for the purposes of the Insolvency Act; see s 251 of that Act.

[80] s 1132, restating 1985 Act, s 721.

(7) he is a person on whom a document may be served by leaving it at, or sending it by post to, the secretary's registered address, whatever the purpose of the document in question.[81]

**3.51** The secretary will be regarded as having ostensible authority to make contracts concerning the administration of the company.[82] As an officer and, invariably an employee, of the company, the secretary will owe the company fiduciary duties and duties of skill, care, and diligence.[83]

*Private companies*

**3.52** The principal change from the 1985 Act is that private companies are not required to have a secretary.[84] The reasons for removing the requirement for private companies were explained in the White Paper, *Modernising Company Law*:

> The requirement represents a regulatory burden on small private companies, particularly those with only one director, which are forced to contract out the role to external advisers or appoint a family member, friend or associate to fill the position. While a company secretary can, for many companies, perform a highly valuable function, the specific role is not essential to good corporate governance; that is properly the responsibility of directors. It will, of course be open to private companies to appoint company secretaries if they choose, on the basis of the value that they add to the company; indeed, the Government believes that many companies will do so, and this will certainly be welcome.[85]

**3.53** A private company may keep a secretary if it wishes.[86] Anyone may be appointed a secretary of a private company. If a private company appoints a secretary the provisions of ss 274–280, described below, apply. Where a private company is to be formed and a person is to be the first secretary (or joint secretaries) of the company the required particulars must be given in the statement of the company's proposed officers and, on registration of the company, that person or persons will be deemed to have been appointed.[87] The Model Articles (pcls) do not contain any articles in relation to secretaries, but Table A, reg 99 provided 'the secretary

---

[81] s 1140, which is new.

[82] *Panorama Developments (Guildford) Ltd v Fidelis Furnishing Fabrics Ltd* [1971] 2 QB 711, CA. Indeed his authority may involve managerial matters; see *Re Maidstone Buildings Ltd* [1971] 1 WLR 1085, 1093. Whether a secretary has actual authority to enter into a transaction on behalf of the company is an issue of fact; see *UBAF Ltd v European American Banking Corp* [1984] QB 713 CA.

[83] For fiduciary duties, see *McKay's Case* (1876) 2 Ch D 1, CA, and *De Ruvigne's Case* (1877) 5 Ch D 306, CA. For a 'knowing assistance' claim against a company secretary, see *Brown v Bennett* [1999] 1 BCLC 649, CA.

[84] s 270.

[85] para 6.6. See also Lord Sainsbury (Hansard, 11 Jan 2006 (col 185)).

[86] As recommended by the Company Law Review Steering Group (CLR) in *Final Report*, paras 4.6 and 4.7. See also CLR: *Developing the Framework* at paras 7.34–7.36 and CLR: *Completing the Structure* at paras 2.18–2.22.

[87] ss 12(1)(b) and 16(6)(b). These sections derive, with changes, from 1985 Act, ss 10(2) and 13(5).

shall be appointed by the directors for such term, at such remuneration and upon such conditions as they may think fit; and any secretary so appointed may be removed by them'.

**3.54**  The removal by s 270(1) of the requirement for private companies to have a secretary necessitated modifications in relation to services and acts required or authorized to be done by or to the secretary. Where a private company is without a secretary (a) anything authorized or required to be given or sent to, or served on, the company by being sent to its secretary (i) may be given or sent to, or served on, the company itself, and (ii) if addressed to the secretary shall be treated as addressed to the company; and (b) anything else required or authorized to be done by or to the secretary of the company may be done by or to (i) a director, or (ii) a person authorized generally or specifically in that behalf by the directors.[88]

*Public companies*

**3.55**  Public companies are required to have a secretary.[89] Where a public company is to be formed and a person is, or persons are, to be the first secretary (or joint secretaries) of the company the required particulars must be given in the statement of the company's proposed officers and, on registration of the company, that person or persons will be deemed to have been appointed.[90] The Model Articles (plc) do not contain any provisions in relation to secretaries. Table A, reg 99 provides for the directors to appoint the secretary. The Companies Act imposes a duty on directors of a public company to appoint a secretary. It does so in two ways. First, if it appears that a public company is in breach of the requirement to have a secretary the Secretary of State can use enforcement powers in s 272 to require it to appoint a secretary. If the company fails to comply with the requirement, the company and every officer in default is guilty of an offence.[91] Secondly, the directors of a public company are under a duty to take all reasonable steps to secure that the secretary, or each joint secretary, (a) is a person who appears to them to have the requisite knowledge and experience to discharge the functions of secretary of the company, and (b) has one or more of the specified qualifications.[92]

---

[88] s 270(3).

[89] s 271.

[90] ss 12(1)(c) and 16(6)(b). These sections derive, with changes, from 1985 Act, ss 10(2) and 13(5).

[91] s 272(6) and (7). This is a new provision.

[92] s 273, restating 1985 Act s 286, with some changes in respect of s 273(1) and (2). The qualifications specified by s 273(2) and (3) are: (a) holding office as secretary of a public company for at least three of the immediately preceding five years; (b) membership of specified bodies (Institute of Chartered Accountants of England and Wales, Institute of Chartered Accountants of Scotland, Association of Chartered Certified Accountants, Institute of Chartered Accountants of Ireland, Institute of Chartered Secretaries and Administrators, Chartered Institute of Management Accountants, Chartered Institute of Public Finance and Accountancy), (c) UK barrister, advocate, or solicitor, (d) being a person who, by virtue of his holding or having held any other position or

**3.56** If there is a vacancy in office of the secretary, or there is for any other reason no secretary capable of acting, anything required or authorized to be done by or to the secretary may be done (a) by or to an assistant or deputy secretary (if any), or (b) if there is no assistant or deputy secretary or none capable of acting, by or to any person authorized generally or specifically in that behalf by the directors.[93]

**3.57** A company must keep a register of its secretaries, containing the required particulars and which is available for inspection at the place notified to the Registrar.[94]

# F. Officers

**3.58** Section 1173(1) defines an 'officer' in relation to a body corporate, as including a director, manager, or secretary.[95] Although not mentioned in this definition, an auditor, appointed under s 485,[96] is an officer of the company,[97] but not for the purposes of the independence requirements for acting as a statutory auditor.[98] A receiver and manager appointed by directors is not a manager within the definition of 'officer', since he does not manage on behalf of the company, but to enforce security over the company's property.[99] A liquidator, administrator, or administrative receiver would not be regarded as a manager within the definition of officer, since, although they have powers of management, they are separately identified in the Insolvency Act, s 212.

**3.59** In the Act the word 'officer' is used as a generic term for the directors and secretaries of a company.[100] Its most important function, however, is to identify persons who are guilty of an offence for contravention of the provisions of the Act. The Companies Act contains numerous offences, most of which provide a sanction for contravention of provisions requiring companies to maintain specified records, to

---

being a member of another body, appears to the directors to be capable of discharging the functions of secretary of the company.

[93] s 274, restating with changes 1985 Act, s 283(3).

[94] ss 275–279. Sections 275(4), 277(3) and (5), and 279 are new. The other provisions restate with changes 1985 Act, ss 288–290.

[95] This restates s 744(1).

[96] Formerly 1985 Act, s 384.

[97] *R v Shacter* [1960] 2 QB 252, CA. An auditor may therefore be subject to misfeasance proceedings under Insolvency Act, s 212; see *Re London and General Bank Ltd (No 2)* [1895] 2 Ch 166, *Re Kingston Cotton Mill Co* [1896] 1 Ch 6 and *(No 2)* [1896] 2 Ch 279, CA, *Re Thomas Gerrard Ltd* [1968] Ch 455.

[98] s 1214(5).

[99] *Re B Johnson & Co (Builders) Ltd* [1955] Ch 634, CA.

[100] s 9(4), which is new, and s 12, of which s 12(2) is new and the remainder restates s 10(2), with changes, and s 10(3), and s 16 (which is part new and part a restatement of 1985 Act, s 13(3)–(5)); also s 1078 (which is part new and part a restatement with changes of 1985 Act, s 711(1)) and s 1189, which is new.

make records available for inspection, and returns to be made to the Registrar. Criminal offences are discussed in Chapter 30. Directors, secretaries, and managers (and in some specified cases shadow directors) are all potentially liable as officers to criminal punishment for default by the company in complying with these requirements.

Section 1121 deals with the criminal liability of an officer in default.[101] It provides: **3.60**

(1) This section has effect for the purposes of any provision of the Companies Acts to the effect that, in the event of contravention of an enactment in relation to a company, an offence is committed by every officer of the company who is in default.

(2) For this purpose 'officer' includes—(a) any director, manager or secretary, and (b) any person who is to be treated as an officer of the company for the purposes of the provision in question.

(3) An officer is 'in default' for the purposes of the provision if he authorises or permits, participates in, or fails to take all reasonable steps to prevent, the contravention.

For particular provisions shadow directors and liquidators are treated as officers.[102] It should also be noted that s 1121(3) extends criminal liability to officers who (a) authorize, (b) permit, or (c) fail to take all reasonable steps to prevent the contravention, whereas the 1985 Act, s 730(5) only applied to officers who knowingly and wilfully authorized or permitted the contravention.

Section 1122 is a new provision dealing with the position where a company is an officer of another company. It provides: **3.61**

(1) Where a company is an officer of another company, it does not commit an offence as an officer in default unless one of its officers is in default.

(2) Where any such offence is committed by a company the officer in question also commits the offence and is liable to be proceeded against and punished accordingly.

(3) In this section 'officer' and 'in default' have the meanings given by section 1121.

The other uses of the word 'officer' in the Companies Act are to identify the persons (a) who may be ordered to provide information in connection with a shareholders' action to enforce directors' liabilities for unauthorized political donations or expenditure,[103] (b) who are entitled to inspect the company's accounting records,[104] (c) who may be required by an auditor of a company to provide information or explanations,[105] (d) who may certify on behalf of a company an instrument **3.62**

---

[101] s 1121 restates 1985 Act, 730(5) and 744(1), with a change as regards s 1121(3). By s 1123, s 1121 also applies to bodies other than companies.

[102] As regards shadow directors, see ss 63(2), 68(5), 75(5), 76(6), 84(2), 156(6), 162(6), 165(4), 167(4), 272(6), 275(6), 276(3). As regards liquidators, see ss 30(4) and 36(5).

[103] s 373, restating 1985 Act, s 347K.

[104] s 388, restating 1985 Act, s 221.

[105] ss 499 and 500, restating 1985 Act s 389A.

of transfer of shares,[106] (e) who may be required to give information in relation to an expert's report on a merger or division of a public company,[107] (f) who may be served with process where the company has no registered office,[108] and (g) in respect of whom the court may grant relief under s 1157 (discussed in Chapter 16, Section D).

---

[106] s 775, restating 1985 Act, s 184.
[107] ss 909 and 924, restating 1985 Act, Schedule 15B, para 5.
[108] s 1002 (concerning striking off), restating 1985 Act, s 652(7).

# 4

# DIRECTORS' POWERS AND RESPONSIBILITIES

## A. Directors' Authority to Manage Companies

### (1) Directors' general authority

Although the Companies Act contains much more provision about the nature of **4.01** directors' responsibilities than is found in previous Companies Acts, it does not state what the directors actually do. The only Act to have done so was the 1844 Act, which identified the directors as 'the persons having the direction, conduct, management, or superintendence of the affairs of the company'.[1] It has always been well understood that those are the functions of a director and that they have an internal and an external aspect. Internally, as between the directors and the shareholders, the directors' powers of management are left to the company's articles, as has always been the case since the 1856 Act. The exercise of the directors' powers is not solely a matter to be regulated by articles, since the conduct of a company's affairs affects wider interests. For this reason the Companies Acts have imposed

---

[1] 1844 Act, s 3.

particular responsibilities on directors. These internal aspects of the directors' powers and responsibilities are considered in Section A of this chapter. The external aspects of the management of a company are considered in Sections B and C.

### Companies incorporated under the 1985 Act

**4.02** Companies will continue to be incorporated under the 1985 Act until 1 October 2009, when the provisions in the 2006 Act about company formation and a company's constitution and its capacity come into effect.[2] A company limited by shares and incorporated under the 1985 Act, whether private or public, must have articles of association prescribing its regulations, which may be in the form registered with the Registrar, or in default of registration, the company will be deemed to have adopted Table A.[3] Companies that register their own bespoke articles invariably adopt at least some of the provisions of Table A for reasons of convenience and certainty. A company limited by guarantee and not having a share capital and an unlimited company having a share capital must register their articles with the Registrar and these must be as near to the forms of Tables C and E respectively as the circumstances admit.[4] Tables C and E adopt the provisions of Table A concerning the management of a company by directors and need not be considered further in this chapter.

**4.03** Table A, reg 70 states the powers of directors in these terms:

> Subject to the provisions of the Act, the memorandum and the articles and to any directions given by special resolution, the business of the company shall be managed by the directors who may exercise all the powers of the company. No alteration of the memorandum or articles and no such direction shall invalidate any prior act of the directors which would have been valid if that alteration had not been made or that direction had not been given. The powers given by this regulation shall not be limited by any special power given to the directors by the articles and a meeting of directors at which a quorum is present may exercise all powers exercisable by the directors.

**4.04** The first sentence of reg 70 gives the directors the responsibility for managing the business of the company, for which purpose they may exercise all the company's powers. Case law suggested some limits on the otherwise broad expression 'business of the company'. It was held not to cover fixing the directors' own remuneration,[5] but Table A goes on to provide expressly for the fixing of directors'

---

[2] 2006 Act Commencement Order No 8, arts 3(a)–(d).

[3] 1985 Act, ss 7 and 8. For companies registered before 1 October 2007, 1985 Act, Table A (SI 1985/805) continues to apply. For companies registered on or after 1 October 2007 (but before 1 October 2009), Table A (SI 1985/805) is amended by SI 2007/2541 and SI 2007/2826, to achieve consistency with provisions of the 2006 Act in force after that date.

[4] 1985 Act, ss 7 and 8.

[5] *Foster v Foster* [1916] 1 Ch 532.

remuneration. In general it is to be determined by ordinary resolution (reg 82), but by reg 84 the directors have power to determine the remuneration of the managing and executive directors. It was also held that the power to manage the business did not give the directors power to destroy it by presenting a winding-up petition,[6] but now directors have a statutory power to put a company into administration or present a winding-up petition.[7] Finally the directors' powers of management do not give them authority on behalf of members to give assurances to, or enter into understandings with, other members of the kind required for a petition under the 2006 Act, Part 30 (unfair prejudice).[8]

The powers of a company incorporated under the 1985 Act are controlled by the objects for which it was incorporated as stated in its memorandum.[9] The history of the expansion of companies' powers and the reducing role of the *ultra vires* doctrine has been described in Chapter 2. Most modern commercial companies have almost unlimited capacity either because they have adopted a very wide range of objects, empowering them to engage in every conceivable activity, or because the 1985 Act, s 3A applies to them. This provides: **4.05**

> Where the company's memorandum states that the object of the company is to carry on business as a general commercial company—
> (a) the object of the company is to carry on any trade or business whatsoever, and
> (b) the company has the power to do all such things as are incidental or conducive to the carrying on of any trade or business by it.[10]

Community interest and charitable companies will, of course, have restricted objects. Even if the fact that the directors have exceeded the company's powers has no external effect against third parties (see Section B below), it may have internal effect. The directors may be exposed to liability for breach of duty for failing to act

---

[6] *Smith v Duke of Manchester* (1883) 24 Ch D 611; *Re Emmadart Ltd* [1979] Ch 540. Although this is largely academic, it might be thought unduly restrictive to limit carrying on of business to active trading, not least because many companies are not trading companies. Also in bankruptcy it was well understood that a person carried on business until all his debts were paid: *Theophile v The Solicitor General* [1950] AC 186, HL; *Morphitis v Bernasconi* [2003] Ch 552, CA at para 41.

[7] For administration: Insolvency Act, Schedule B1, paras 12(1)(b) and 22(2). For winding up: Insolvency Act, s 124(1). See also *Re Instrumentation Electrical Services Ltd* [1988] BCLC 550; *Re Equiticorp International plc* [1989] 1 WLR 1010.

[8] *Re Benfield Greig Group plc* [2000] 2 BCLC 488 at para 43(7).

[9] The memorandum must (a) be subscribed by the persons forming the company (s 1), (b) state, among other things, the objects of the company, which can be altered in accordance with the 1985 Act (ss 2–6), and (c) be delivered to the Registrar for him to issue a certificate of incorporation (ss 10–13). From the moment the company is incorporated it is able to exercise all the functions of an incorporated company (s 13(3)).

[10] Some companies were reluctant to adopt the stand-alone objects clause provided by 1985 Act, s 3A due to uncertainties about a general objects clause (eg whether such a clause would allow a company to sell its entire undertaking or carry on charitable activities). Many preferred to continue with the established practice of adopting extensive express objects clauses.

in accordance with the company's constitution (the 2006 Act, s 171(a), discussed in Chapter 10, Section B).

**4.06** The directors' power to manage the business of the company is subject to three limitations: (a) the provisions of the 1985 and 2006 Acts, which provide that certain matters can only be undertaken by the company in general meeting; eg alterations of capital,[11] (b) restrictions contained in the company's memorandum or articles, which may impose limits on what the directors can do, either at all or without approval of the members, and (c) directions given by special resolution. The power of members to intervene in the management of the company is considered in paragraphs 4.14–4.20 below.

**4.07** The second sentence of reg 70 prevents an alteration of the company's memorandum or articles or any direction given by special resolution from retrospectively invalidating the prior exercise by the directors of their powers of management.[12] This provision protects directors as well as third parties, since, as noted above, directors owe a duty to obey the constitution of the company and could find themselves exposed to a breach of duty claim if the members could retrospectively interfere with the exercise of their powers. The third and final sentence of reg 70 makes clear the breadth of the directors' powers and goes on to deal with the manner of their exercise; a topic addressed in Chapter 5.

*Companies incorporated under the 2006 Act*

**4.08** As from 1 October 2009 companies will be incorporated under the 2006 Act. A company so incorporated must have articles of association prescribing its regulations. The articles must be registered, because otherwise, if the company is a limited company, the Model Article relevant to the company will apply by default.[13] Pursuant to the 2006 Act, s 19, the Companies (Model Articles) Regulations 2008[14] prescribe Model Articles for (a) private companies limited by shares (Model Article (pcls)), (b) private companies limited by guarantee (Model Article (pclg)), and public companies (Model Article (plc)). Companies not incorporated under the 2006 Act are able to adopt the Model Articles or provisions in them if they wish. It is likely that public companies will regard the Model Articles (plc) as containing a template of suitable provisions and will continue to have bespoke articles which adopt some but not all of the provisions of the Model Articles (plc).

---

[11] Chapter 22 of this work identifies matters required by the 2006 Act to be done by the members.
[12] This reflects the view of Buckley LJ in *Gramophone and Typewriter Ltd v Stanley* [1908] 2 KB 89, 105, 106, CA.
[13] 2006 Act, ss 18–20.
[14] SI 2008/3229.

The Model Articles (pcls), (pclg), and (plc) 3 each provide for the directors' general authority in the same terms:

> Subject to the articles, the directors are responsible for the management of the company's business, for which purpose they may exercise all the powers of the company.

**4.09**

The language of Model Article 3 is derived from Table A, reg 70. Thus the basic proposition is that the directors manage the company's business and may exercise all the powers of the company. As with Table A, reg 70 those powers are subject to the company's articles, which may include express restrictions on the exercise of the directors' powers, as well as the shareholders' reserve power to intervene by special resolution, contained in Model Article 4 (discussed in paragraph 4.16 below).[15] Model Article 3 does not include anything comparable to the second and third sentences of Table A, reg 70. This is because each Model Article 4(2) prevents a special resolution from having retrospective effect and each set of Model Articles contains express provision about decision-making by directors (Chapter 5 below).

**4.10**

Model Article 3 does not state that the directors' authority is subject to the company's memorandum of association, because under the 2006 Act that document is simply a record of the basis on which the company was incorporated. It is not part of the company's constitution and does not regulate the affairs of the company.[16]

**4.11**

Nor is it necessary for Model Article 3 to include the language in the third sentence of Table A, reg 70 as to the lack of limitation of the directors' powers. That lack of limitation is clear from the language of Model Article 3. Furthermore, companies incorporated under the 2006 Act have unlimited capacity. The 2006 Act, s 31(1) provides: 'Unless a company's articles specifically restrict the objects of the company, its objects are unrestricted.' Charitable companies and community interest companies may restrict their objects, but it is unlikely that any commercial company would do so. Where there are restrictions, persons dealing with a company may have the benefit of statutory protections (see Section B below).[17] Even so, directors who exceed the company's powers may be exposed to personal liability (paragraph 4.05 above).

**4.12**

Where the company has unrestricted capacity, Model Article 3 provides that the directors' authority to exercise its powers is similarly unrestricted. There should therefore be no question of the directors being unable to close down or dispose of all or part of the company's business (compare paragraph 4.04 above).[18]

**4.13**

---

[15] The same Article 4 applies to each of Model Article (pcls), (pclg), and (plc).

[16] 2006 Act, ss 8 and 17. See also Chapter 1 at paragraphs 1.39–1.46.

[17] 2006 Act, ss 39–42.

[18] This was certainly the Government's view of Model Article 3: *Implementation of Companies Act 2006* (Consultative Document, February 2007) at paras 3.46 and 3.47.

## (2) Shareholders' reserve power

**4.14**  Where, as with Table A, reg 70, and each Model Article 3, the articles confer on the directors power to manage the company's business, the shareholders cannot compel the directors, by ordinary resolution, to manage the business in a particular way.[19] On the other hand the shareholders can by ordinary resolution consent to, approve, or authorize the exercise of the directors' powers or they may ratify their acts so as to protect them from complaint by the company.[20] In these circumstances there is no conflict between the directors and the shareholders. For consent, approval, or authorization of acts of directors under the 2006 Act under s 180, see Chapters 9, Section D (generally) and 14, Section E (conflicts of interest). Ratification is discussed in Chapter 19, Section D.

**4.15**  Where the shareholders wish to intervene in the management of the company and the directors do not agree, four courses of action may be open to the shareholders. First, by ordinary resolution they may remove and replace the directors of whom they disapprove: 2006 Act, s 168 (Chapter 7 of this work).[21] The targeted director may be protected from removal from office by entrenched rights contained in the articles[22] or by weighted voting rights in favour of himself or shareholders who support him.[23]

**4.16**  Secondly, they may pass a special resolution directing the directors to take or refrain from taking specified action. This power is stated in the first sentence of Table A, reg 70, but the second sentence states that the special resolution cannot purport to operate retrospectively.[24] Each Model Article (pcls), (pclg), and (plc) 4 provides to the same effect:

(1) The shareholders may, by special resolution, direct the directors to take, or refrain from taking, specified action.
(2) No such special resolution invalidates anything which the directors have done before the passing of the resolution.

---

[19] *Automatic Self-Cleansing Filter Syndicate Co Ltd v Cunninghame* [1906] 2 Ch 34, CA; *Gramophone and Typewriter Ltd v Stanley* [1908] 2 KB 89, CA; *Salmon v Quin & Axtens* [1909] 1 Ch 311, 320, CA (affirmed in *Quin & Axtens Ltd v Salmon* [1909] AC 442, HL); *John Shaw and Sons (Salford) Ltd v Shaw* [1935] 2 KB 113, 134, CA; *Scott v Scott* [1943] 1 All ER 582; *Breckland Group Holdings Ltd v London and Suffolk Properties Ltd* [1989] BCLC 100.
[20] *Hogg v Crampthorn Ltd* [1967] Ch 254, 269; *Bamford v Bamford* [1970] Ch 212, CA.
[21] Replacing 1985 Act, s 303.
[22] 2006 Act, s 22.
[23] *Bushell v Faith* [1970] AC 1099 (HL); *Russell v Northern Bank Development Corporation Ltd* [1992] 1 WLR 588 (HL).
[24] Reflecting the judgment of Buckley LJ in *Gramophone and Typewriter Ltd v Stanley* [1908] 2 KB 89, 105, 106, CA.

The ability of shareholders to intervene by special resolution may be restricted by provisions for entrenchment in the articles or by weighted voting rights. [25]

Thirdly, the shareholders may pass a special resolution to alter the company's art- **4.17** icles to control or restrict the directors' powers of management, either generally or in relation to a particular matter. Again, the altered article could not have retrospective effect.[26]

Fourthly, if they are unanimous, the shareholders may informally take over the **4.18** management of the company for themselves.[27] The CLR expressed the principle in this way:

> The courts have established a rule that the members of a company may, by their unanimous agreement, bind or empower the company and its organs to do anything within its capacity, regardless of any limitations in the articles. This implies that the members may even decide unanimously to dispense with the division of powers between themselves and the directors and run the company themselves.[28]

If for some reason the directors are incapable of acting or the board has ceased to **4.19** exist, the company, through its shareholders, has a residual power to appoint new or additional directors to enable the company to function.[29] It will seldom be necessary to resort to this principle, since articles invariably give shareholders power to appoint directors by ordinary resolution.[30] See further, Chapter 6.

The foregoing paragraphs have described the steps that may be open to all or a **4.20** majority of the shareholders. If there is deadlock or if a minority shareholder complains of unfair prejudice in the management of a company, the aggrieved member may present a petition for relief under the 2006 Act, Part 30 (or less likely for winding up on the just and equitable ground) in which the court may grant appropriate interim relief, including injunctions and the appointment of a receiver.[31]

---

[25] 2006 Act, s 22. *Bushell v Faith* [1970] AC 1099, HL; *Russell v Northern Bank Development Corporation Ltd* [1992] 1 WLR 588, HL.

[26] For the position under the 1985 Act, see the second sentence of Table A, reg 70 and *Gramophone and Typewriter Ltd v Stanley* [1908] 2 KB 89, 105, 106, CA. For the position under the 2006 Act, see s 21.

[27] *Re Duomatic Ltd* [1969] 2 Ch 365. See further Chapter 22, Section B(4).

[28] CLR: *Developing the Framework* (March 2000) at [4.21].

[29] *Barron v Potter* [1914] 1 Ch 895; *Foster v Foster* [1916] 1 Ch 532; *Alexander Ward & Co v Samyang Navigation Co Ltd* [1975] 1 WLR 673.

[30] Table A, reg 78; Model Article (pcls) and (pclg) 17 (1)(a) and Model Article (plc) 20(a). If necessary the court can direct that a meeting of the company be held for this purpose: 2006 Act, s 306; see Chapter 22, paragraphs 22.47–22.51.

[31] As to interim relief, see *Re A Company (No 00596 of 1986)* [1987] BCLC 133; *Weir, Petitioners* [1990] BCC 761; *Re Milgate Developments Ltd* [1993] BCLC 291; *Wilton-Davies v Kirk* [1998] 1 BCLC 274; *Re Worldhams Park Golf Course Ltd* [1998] 1 BCLC 554.

### (3) Particular responsibilities of directors

**4.21**  In exercising their powers to manage the business of the company, directors must comply with their general duties under the Companies Act, Part 10 (discussed in Chapters 9–15 of this work). In addition, the Act imposes on directors numerous specific functions and duties to secure compliance with provisions of the Act. If the obligation is not complied with a director may be an officer in default and guilty of a criminal offence. The offences are for the most part intermediate or quasi-regulatory and triable summarily and punishable by a fine. For further discussion of offences under the 2006 Act, see Appendix 2 of this work, which lists the offences under the Act.

**4.22**  Many of these responsibilities concern record keeping, and, where required, delivering information to the Registrar or making the company's records open to inspection. These records include constitutional documents,[32] the register of the company's members, with an index if necessary,[33] the register of directors,[34] directors' service and indemnity contracts,[35] minutes of meetings of directors,[36] the register of secretaries,[37] records of company meetings and decisions of members,[38] information about interests in shares in a public company,[39] and the register of charges.[40] Model Article (plc) 82 gives a public company the right to destroy old documents relating to shares and dividends.

**4.23**  Directors are responsible for securing compliance by the company with directions from the Secretary of State in relation to the company's name,[41] the appointment of directors,[42] and the appointment of a secretary of a public company.[43]

**4.24**  In addition the directors are responsible for the proper conduct of company meetings as discussed in Chapter 22. They are responsible for maintaining proper accounting records and the preparation of accounts, audit, and annual return, as discussed in Chapter 23. They have a range of duties and responsibilities in relation to capital, as discussed in Chapter 24. They also have particular responsibilities in

---

[32]  2006 Act, ss 26, 30, 32, 34–36, and (following relief under Part 30) 998, 999. These provisions, apart from ss 998 and 999, do not come into force until 1 October 2009. Until then reference should be made to any corresponding provisions of the 1985 Act.

[33]  2006 Act, ss 113–115, 118, 120, 123, 130, 132, and 135.

[34]  2006 Act, ss 162, 165, 167, and 246

[35]  2006 Act, ss 228, 229, 231, 237, and 238.

[36]  2006 Act, s 248.

[37]  2006 Act, ss 275 and 276.

[38]  2006 Act, ss 355, 357, and 358.

[39]  2006 Act, ss 806–810, 813, 815, and 819.

[40]  2006 Act, s 877.

[41]  2006 Act, ss 63, 64, 68, 75, 76, and 84.

[42]  2006 Act, s 156.

[43]  2006 Act, s 272.

relation to reorganizations and takeovers, as discussed in Chapter 25. In each case default is a criminal offence.

Where a company, or any of its subsidiaries, is ceasing to carry on or is transferring **4.25** the whole or any part of its business, the directors have power to make provision for the employees or former employees of the company, provided that payments are made before the company goes into liquidation and are made out of distributable profits. The directors have power to make this provision with the sanction of an ordinary resolution of the company or if so authorized by the company's memorandum or articles.[44] When the 2006 Act, s 247 comes into force on 1 October 2009 the directors will not be able to use this power for the benefit of themselves, former directors, or shadow directors without the sanction of a resolution of the company.[45] The Model Articles include provisions authorizing the directors to make provision for employees and former employees, other than directors, former directors, and shadow directors.[46]

### (4) Directors' powers and responsibilities in relation to dissolution

Thus far this chapter has considered the powers and responsibilities of directors **4.26** while a company is in operation, whether or not it is actively carrying on business (but not when it is subject to insolvency proceedings as discussed in Chapter 29). Directors also have powers to have a company dissolved or to take steps to have it restored to life after it has been dissolved.

A company's existence is brought to an end when it is dissolved either because the **4.27** Registrar takes steps to strike off the register a company that appears to be defunct,[47] or because the company,[48] by its directors or a majority of them, takes the initiative and applies to be struck off the register and dissolved.[49] The procedure for dissolution on the application of the company has a number of safeguards to protect the interests of persons with dealings with the company: (a) three months must have elapsed since publication of notice of the proposed striking off was

---

[44] 1985 Act, s 719, which will be replaced by 2006 Act, s 247 on 1 October 2009: 2006 Act Commencement Order No 8, art 3(i). 2006 Act, s 247(3) makes special provision for charities.

[45] 2006 Act, s 247(5)(b), which was introduced on the recommendation of the CLR: *Final Report* at para 6.5.

[46] Model Article (pcls) 51; Model Article (pclg) 37; Model Article (plc) 84.

[47] 2006 Act, ss 1000, 1002 which replace 1985 Act, subss 652(1)–(3), (5)–(7) without change on 1 October 2009. The Registrar has a similar power where the company is in liquidation and he has reasonable cause to believe that no liquidator is acting or that the affairs of the company are fully wound up (1985 Act, subs 652(4)–(7), also replaced by 2006 Act, ss 1001 and 1002 on 1 October 2009).

[48] Until 1 October 2009 this procedure is only available to private companies. See next footnote.

[49] 2006 Act, ss 1003–1011 will replace 1985 Act, ss 652A–652F on 1 October 2009 without change, except to extend the voluntary striking-off procedure to public companies.

given in the Gazette, (b) the company must have been inactive for three months before the application for voluntary striking off, (c) the company must not be subject to ongoing insolvency proceedings or proceedings in relation to a scheme of compromise or arrangement, and (d) seven days' notice of the application for voluntary striking off must be given to members, employees, creditors, directors, pension fund trustees, and other persons specified by regulation.

**4.28** The consequence of the company being dissolved is that all its property and rights vest in the Crown as *bona vacantia*, but subject to a power of the Crown to disclaim and a power of the court to make a vesting order in favour of a person with an interest in the disclaimed property.[50] Sometimes it is necessary to have a company which has been struck off the register or dissolved restored to the register. The most common reasons for this are where it is discovered that the company had some valuable property, or where a third party needs to establish the company's liability for the purposes of making a claim against an insurer under the Third Parties (Rights against Insurers) Act 1930.[51]

**4.29** Under the 1985 Act a person who was simply a former director of the dissolved company could not apply for it to be restored to the register. Unless he is also a member or creditor he would not have a sufficient interest to apply for the dissolution to be declared void under the 1985 Act, s 651,[52] and only a member or creditor may apply to the court under s 653 for the company to be restored to the register.

**4.30** Under the provisions of the 2006 Act, which come into force on 1 October 2009, there are two ways of having a dissolved company restored to life; one is an administrative procedure and the other is by application to the court. Both may be invoked by a former director. Under the new administrative procedure an application for the restoration of the company to the register may be made to the Registrar by a former director or member of the company within six years of the date of dissolution provided that (a) the company was carrying on business or in operation at the time of striking off, (b) in respect of any property vested as *bona vacantia*, the Crown consents, and (c) records to be delivered to the Registrar are brought up to date and any penalties paid.[53] If that procedure is not available, the

---

[50] 2006 Act, ss 1012–1019, which replace 1985 Act, ss 654–658 and apply provisions in the Insolvency Act, ss 180–182 to Crown disclaimer.

[51] Asset overlooked: *Stanhope Pension Trust Ltd v Registrar of Companies* [1994] 1 BCLC 628; *Re Oakleague Ltd* [1995] 2 BCLC 624. Insured claims: *Re Harvest Lane Motor Bodies Ltd* [1969] 1 Ch 457; *Re Priceland Ltd* [1997] 1 BCLC 467; *Re Philip Powis Ltd* [1998] 1 BCLC 440, CA.

[52] *Re Waterbury Nominees Pty Ltd* (1986) 11 ACLR 348, SC (WA). Section 651 is repealed on 1 October 2009 and is not replaced: 2006 Act Commencement Order No 8. Under s 651 the application has to be made within two years of the date of dissolution.

[53] 2006 Act, ss 1024–1028, which are new provisions coming into force on 1 October 2009. These provisions were recommended by the CLR: *Final Report* at paras 11.17–11.20.

court has power to restore the company to the register under the 2006 Act, ss 1029–1032, which replace the 1985 Act, s 653. The new provision extends the classes of applicants to include, among others, former directors, but limits the time to six years from the date of dissolution (rather than 20 years under s 653), unless the application is for the purpose of bringing proceedings against the company for damages for personal injury, in which case it can be brought at any time (unless it appears that the claim is bound to fail).[54]

## B. Power of Directors to Bind the Company

A transaction will be binding on the company if (a) it has capacity to make it (ie it is within its power), (b) it is made by the company directly (ie under its seal) or on its behalf by persons capable of binding the company, and (c) it is formally valid. This had been an area of the law bedevilled by technicality, but reforms to the Companies Acts have greatly simplified it and there is less scope for companies avoiding their obligations on what might be seen as technical grounds. This Section B is concerned with capacity and the power of directors to bind the company. Section C considers formal validity.     **4.31**

### (1) A company's capacity

Under the *ultra vires* doctrine developed by the courts a company only had capacity to enter into transactions within the scope of its objects, set out in its memorandum of association. A transaction outside those objects was *ultra vires* and void and could not even be ratified by the unanimous assent of all the members.[55] The *ultra vires* doctrine was an impediment to the development of a company's business and so companies adopted a wide range of objects, usually stated to be separate objects, which enabled them to pursue an unlimited range of business activities with unrestricted powers (see also Chapter 2, paragraph 2.10). As noted in paragraph 4.05 above, the 1985 Act, s 3A enabled a company to state that its objects were those of a general commercial company, with the consequence that it was able to carry on any trade or business whatsoever with all necessary powers.[56]     **4.32**

---

[54] These provisions come into effect on 1 October 2009, as do the supplementary provisions in ss 1033 and 1034. The provisions of 1985 Act, s 651 which give the court power to declare a dissolution void on the application of the liquidator or a person interested made within two years from the date of dissolution are repealed and are not replaced (except for subss 651(5)–(7)), which made special provision for claims for damages for personal injuries which are restated in 2006 Act, s 1030.

[55] *Ashbury Railway Carriage and Iron Company Ltd v Riche* (1875) LR 7 HL 653; *A-G v Great Eastern Railway* (1880) 5 AC 473, HL.

[56] 1985 Act, s 3A was inserted by 1989 Act, s 110 with effect from 4 February 1991.

The 2006 Act, s 31(1)[57] provides that 'unless a company's articles specifically restrict the objects of the company, its objects are unrestricted'. In practice, the only companies that are likely to restrict their objects are charitable companies and community interest companies.

**4.33** In any event it became necessary to reform and largely do away with the *ultra vires* doctrine when the United Kingdom joined the EEC, because the First EEC Company Law Directive[58] states:

> 9.1 Acts done by the organs of the company shall be binding upon it even if those acts are not within the objects of the company, unless such acts exceed the powers that the law confers or allows to be conferred on those organs. However, Member States may provide that the company shall not be bound where such acts are outside the objects of the company, if it proves that the third party knew that the act was outside those objects or could not in view of the circumstances have been unaware of it; disclosure of the statutes shall not of itself be sufficient proof thereof.
>
> 9.2 The limits on the powers of the organs of the company, arising under the statutes or from a decision of the competent organs, may never be relied upon as against third parties, even if it had been disclosed.

Those provisions came to be reflected in the 1985 Act, ss 35, 35A, and 35B[59] and will be replaced by the 2006 Act, ss 39–42, with some changes as noted below. The manifest purpose of these provisions is 'to enable people to deal with a company in good faith without being adversely affected by any limits on the company's capacity or its rules of internal management.[60]

**4.34** The 1985 Act, s 35(1) deals with a company's capacity and provides:

> The validity of an act done by a company shall not be called into question on the ground of lack of capacity by reason of anything in the company's memorandum.

The 2006 Act, s 39(1) is in the same terms except that it substitutes 'the company's constitution' for 'the company's memorandum'. The 1985 Act, s 35(2) provides that a member may apply to restrain the doing of an act which would be beyond the company's capacity, unless the act is in fulfilment of a legal obligation arising from a previous act of the company. Subsection 35(3) recites that it is the duty of a director to observe any limitations flowing from the company's memorandum, but that actions by the directors beyond the company's capacity may be ratified by special resolution. Those subsections are not replicated in the 2006 Act, because by s 31(1) a company incorporated under it will have unlimited capacity,

---

[57] It comes into effect on 1 October 2009.

[58] 1968/151/EEC.

[59] The first attempt to meet the requirements of the Directive was the European Communities Act, s 9, later consolidated into 1985 Act, s 35. 1989 Act, ss 108 and 109, replaced the original s 35 with ss 35, 35A, and 35B with effect from 4 February 1991.

[60] *TCB Ltd v Gray* [1986] Ch 621, 635, per Sir Nicholas Browne-Wilkinson V-C (whose judgment was upheld on appeal: [1987] Ch 458).

unless it chooses to restrict its objects in which case the directors' powers are also restricted, and s 171(a) states the duty to act in accordance with the company's constitution.[61]

By s 35(4) the operation of s 35 is restricted in the cases of charitable companies and **4.35** transactions with directors. The 2006 Act, s 39(2) states that s 39 has effect subject to s 42 which contains special provisions for charities (paragraph 4.48 below).

### (2) The power of the directors to bind the company

Under the 'indoor management rule' third parties who dealt in good faith with a **4.36** company were entitled to assume that the company's internal procedures had been complied with.[62] As mentioned above, Article 9 of the First EEC Company Law Directive required reforms to be made in this respect. The current provision dealing with this matter is the 1985 Act, s 35A, whose provisions are restated by the 2006 Act, s 40 without material change, although there are some changes of language. The 1985 Act, s 35A(1) provides:

> In favour of a person dealing with a company in good faith, the power of the board of directors to bind the company, or authorise others to do so, shall be deemed to be free of any limitation under the company's constitution.

The 2006 Act, s 40 omits the words 'board of' and substitutes 'is' for 'shall be'.

It has been suggested that the change from 'the power of the board of directors to **4.37** bind the company' in s 35A(1) to 'the power of the directors to bind the company' in s 40(1) is a change of substance enabling a third party to rely on a transaction not decided on by the board, because, for example, it was inquorate.[63] It is respectfully suggested that there is no such change. First, none is indicated in the Explanatory Notes or Table of Derivations and none was suggested in the White Paper, *Modernising Company Law*[64] when commenting on its draft Bill: 'The basic rule . . . as under the present law, is that those doing business with the company are entitled to assume that the board of directors has authority to enter into commitments on the company's behalf and to authorise others to do so. They do not need therefore to worry about what is in the company's constitution.' Secondly, the deletion of the reference to the board is merely a return to the language used in the original

---

[61] Explanatory Notes to 2006 Act, s 39.

[62] *Royal British Bank v Turquand* (1856) 6 E & B 327. In *TCB Ltd v Gray* [1986] Ch 621, 635 Sir Nicholas Browne-Wilkinson V-C (whose judgment was upheld on appeal: [1987] Ch 458) said that the old doctrine of constructive notice of the company's memorandum and articles, mitigated by the *Turquand* case, caused commercial inconvenience and injustice and was largely swept away by the provisons giving effect to Article 9 of the First EEC Company Law Directive.

[63] *Palmer's Company Law Annotated Guide to the Companies Act 2006*, where it is suggested that such a change would reflect the view expressed by Robert Walker LJ in *Smith v Henniker-Major* [2003] Ch 182, CA at paras [23], [41]–[43].

[64] paras 28 and 29.

European Communities Act, s 9. Thirdly, the Model Articles, like Table A, are drafted on the basis that directors take decisions collectively, unless a matter has been delegated.[65] Finally the Insolvency Act, s 124(1) and Schedule B1 paras 12(1) (b) and 22(1), dealing with presentation of winding-up petitions and administration, refer to 'the directors' and it is well established that the taking of those steps must be decided on by the board.[66]

**4.38**    The 1985 Act, s 35A(2), read with s 35B, and the 2006 Act, s 40(2) both explain what is meant by a person dealing with the company in good faith. Section 35A(2) provides:

> For this purpose—
> (a) a person 'deals with' a company if he is a party to any transaction or other act to which the company is a party;
> (b) a person shall not be regarded as acting in bad faith by reason only of his knowing that an act is beyond the powers of the directors under the company's constitution; and
> (c) a person shall be presumed to have acted in good faith unless the contrary is proved.

Section 35B provides that 'A party to a transaction with a company is not bound to enquire as to whether it is permitted by the company's memorandum or as to any limitation on the powers of the board of directors to bind the company or authorise others to do so.' The 2006 Act, s 40(2)(a) is identical to the 1985 Act, s 35A(2)(a), but s 40(2)(b), dealing with the 'good faith' requirement uses slightly different and clearer language:

> (b) a person dealing with a company—
> > (i) is not bound to enquire as to any limitation on the powers of the directors to bind the company or authorise others to do so,
> > (ii) is presumed to have acted in good faith unless the contrary is proved, and
> > (iii) is not to be regarded as acting in bad faith by reason only of his knowing that an act is beyond the powers of the directors under the company's constitution.

**4.39**    The reference to a 'person dealing with a company in good faith' is wide enough to include insiders such as a director of the company,[67] although it does not

---

[65] Table A, regs 70–72, 84, 87–98, 102, 108, 110 (all of which refer to the directors, not the board); Model Articles (pcls) 5, 7–16; Model Articles (plc) 5, 7–19.

[66] *Re Equiticorp International plc* [1989] 1 WLR 1010.

[67] *Smith v Henniker-Major* [2003] Ch 182, CA at paras 45–52, 109, and 125. 1985 Act, s 35A(6) and 2006 Act, s 40(6) expressly restrict the application of the sections to directors and their associates. With respect to directors, see below (paragraphs 4.43–4.47). In *Cooperatieve Rabobank 'Vecht en Plassengebied' BA v Minderhoud* [1998] 1 WLR 1025 it was held that it was possible for directors to be treated differently by national law provisions and Article 8 of Council Directive 68/151/EEC should be so construed.

include a company's members as such.[68] To be 'dealing' with the company a person must be a party to any transaction 'or other act' to which the company is a party. The provisions therefore refer to wider arrangements than just contracts (because of the words 'or other act').[69] The requirement that the dealing must be 'in good faith' ensures that a defence based on absence of notice would not be available to someone who has not acted genuinely and honestly in his dealings with the company.[70] However, the statutory language means that it is possible for a person to act in good faith despite knowing that an act is beyond the powers of the directors under the company's constitution. Further, the person dealing is also protected by the statutory presumption that he acted in good faith unless the contrary is proved.[71]

The 1985 Act, s 35A(3) explains what is meant by limitations on the directors' powers under the company's constitution:  **4.40**

> The references above to limitations on the directors' powers under the company's constitution include limitations deriving—
> (a) from a resolution of the company or of any class of shareholders, or
> (b) from any agreement between the members of the company or of any class of shareholders.

The 2006 Act, s 40(3) is in the same terms. The limitations are therefore wider than limitations contained in the memorandum (in the case of a company incorporated before 1 October 2009) and the articles or imposed by special resolution.

The 1985 Act, s 35A(4) and (5) goes on to state the internal consequences of acts or intended acts beyond the directors' powers.  **4.41**

> (4) Subsection (1) does not affect any right of a member of the company to bring proceedings to restrain the doing of an action which is beyond the powers of the directors; but no such proceedings lie in respect of an act to be done in fulfilment of a legal obligation arising from a previous act of the company.

---

[68] *EIC Services Ltd v Phipps* [2004] 2 BCLC 589, CA, where the Court of Appeal decided that a bonus issue could not be validated by 1985 Act, s 35A(1) because shareholders receiving bonus shares were not persons 'dealing with the company'. At para 35 Peter Gibson LJ said that s 35A contemplated a bilateral transaction between the company and the person dealing with the company, and as a matter of ordinary language and having regard to the nature of a bonus issue and the fact that it was an internal arrangement in which there was no diminution or increase in the assets or liabilities of the company, a shareholder receiving bonus shares could not be regarded as a person dealing with the company.

[69] Thus for example a gratuitous act would presumably be included. See also *International Sales and Agencies Ltd v Marcus* [1982] 3 All ER 551; *EIC Services Ltd v Phipps* [2004] 2 BCLC 589, CA.

[70] See *Barclays Bank v TOSG Trust Fund* [1984] BCLC 1, 18; *Smith v Henniker-Major & Co* [2003] Ch 182, CA at para 108, where Carnwath LJ said that the general policy of the section 'seems to be that, if a document is put forward as a decision of the board by someone appearing to act on behalf of the company, in circumstances where there is no reason to doubt its authenticity, a person dealing with the company in good faith should be able to take it at face value'.

[71] Cf *El Ajou v Dollar Land Holdings plc* [1994] 1 BCLC 464, CA; *Guinness plc v Saunders* [1990] 2 AC 663, HL.

(5) Nor does that subsection affect any liability incurred by the directors, or any other person, by reason of the directors' exceeding their powers.

The 2006 Act, subss 40(4) and (5) are in the same terms, with stylistic changes of no material effect. Subsection (4) reflects the fact that a member has a right to see that the company's constitution is obeyed.[72] Subsection (5) preserves the directors' liability for breach of duty, including breach of the 2006 Act, s 171(a) and is without prejudice to the ability of the independent members to ratify the directors' conduct under s 239.

**4.42** Finally both the 1985 Act, s 35A(6) and the 2006 Act, s 40(6) restrict the application of the section to directors and their associates and to charitable companies (paragraph 4.48 below).

### (3) Transactions involving directors or their associates

**4.43** With regard to transactions between the company and its directors or their associates which depend for their validity on the 1985 Act, s 35A, or as the case may be, the 2006 Act, s 40 (because the transaction exceeded any limitation on the directors' powers under the company's constitution), there are special provisions contained in the 1985 Act, s 322A or the 2006 Act, s 41, to which the former sections are subject.[73] On 1 October 2009 the 2006 Act, s 41 replaces the 1985 Act, s 322A without material change, although there are differences to language and format. The effect of these special provisions is that the company may avoid transactions with directors and their associates and claim accounts and indemnity. Even where the sections apply, other remedies may be pursued; eg a derivative claim under the 2006 Act, Part 11, because the sections are not to be read as excluding the operation of any other enactment or rule of law by virtue of which the transaction may be called in question or any liability to the company may arise.[74]

**4.44** The 1985 Act, s 322A (or 2006 Act, s 40) applies where (a) the company enters into a transaction, including any act, which depends for its validity on s 35A (or the 2006 Act, s 39), in that the directors exceed any limitation on their powers under the company's constitution,[75] and (b) the parties to the transaction include (i) a director of the company or of its holding company,[76] or (ii) a person connected with any such director.[77] In these circumstances, the other party to the

---

[72] *Smith v Croft (No 2)* [1988] Ch 114, 169.
[73] 1985 Act, s 35A(6) and 2006 Act, s 40(6).
[74] 1985 Act, s 322A(4); 2006 Act, s 41(1).
[75] 1985 Act, s 322A(1) and (8); 2006 Act, s 41(1) and (7).
[76] Holding company is defined by 1985 Act, s 736; 2006 Act, s 1159.
[77] 1985 Act, s 322A(1)(b) also includes a person connected with a company with whom a director of the company or its holding company is associated. Under 2006 Act, s 41(7), the reference to a person connected with a director has the same meaning as in Part 10, ss 252–257, which are discussed in Chapter 3, Section D.

transaction is not protected even if he deals with the company in good faith (as explained by the 1985 Act, s 35A or the 2006 Act, s 39).

Where the 1985 Act, s 322A (or the 2006 Act, s 41) applies the consequence is **4.45** that the transaction is voidable at the instance of the company. This is subject to limitations. The first limitation is that the transaction ceases to be voidable if—

    (a) restitution of any money or other asset which was the subject-matter of the transaction is no longer possible, or

    (b) the company is indemnified for any loss or damage resulting from the transaction, or

    (c) rights acquired bona fide for value and without actual notice of the directors' exceeding their powers by a person who is not party to the transaction would be affected by the avoidance, or

    (d) the transaction is [ratified by the company in general meeting, by ordinary or special resolution or otherwise as the case may require/affirmed by the company].[78]

The list is not exhaustive and a company may be prevented from avoiding the transaction by laches. Paragraphs (a)–(c) may be compared with the 2006 Act, s 195 concerning the civil consequences of a contravention of the provisions of s 190 (substantial property transactions with directors). Paragraph (d) enables the members to affirm the transaction, with the support of votes of the directors who exceeded their powers,[79] but these votes could not be used to ratify the conduct of the directors in excess of their powers to save them from liability for breach of duty.[80] If the directors are unable to obtain ratification of their conduct they may obtain relief from the court under the 2006 Act, s 1157.[81]

The second limitation on the power of the company to avoid the transaction is **4.46** where a party to the transaction itself is not a director of the company or its holding company or connected with such a director.[82] In such a case the transaction would be valid under the 1985 Act, s 35A (or the 2006 Act, s 39) if the party had entered into the transaction on his own in good faith and his rights are not affected, but the court is given the power, on the application of the company or the independent party, to make an order affirming, severing, or setting aside the transaction on such terms as appear to the court to be just.[83]

Whether or not the transaction is avoided, any director of the company or its **4.47** holding company or person connected with such a director[84] who was party to the

---

[78] 1985 Act, s 322A(5), including the words in the first part in square brackets; 2006 Act, s 40(4), including the words in second part in square brackets.

[79] *North West Transportation Co v Beatty* (1887) 12 App Cas 589, PC.

[80] 2006 Act, s 239, which is in force.

[81] That section replaced 1985 Act, s 727 with effect from 1 October 2008.

[82] 1985 Act, s 322A(1) and (7); 2006 Act, s 41(2)(b) and (6).

[83] 1985 Act, s 322A(7); 2006 Act, s 41(6). In *Re Torvale Group Ltd* [1999] 2 BCLC 605, a case on s 322A(7) the court declined to avoid certain scheme debentures.

[84] 1985 Act, s 322A(1)(3); 2006 Act, s 41(2)(b) and (7)(b).

transaction and any director of the company who authorized it is liable '(a) to account to the company for any gain he has made directly or indirectly by the transaction, and (b) to indemnify the company for any loss or damage resulting from the transaction'.[85] But a person other than a director of the company is not liable to account or indemnify if he shows that at the time the transaction was entered into he did not know that the directors were exceeding their powers.[86]

### (4) Charities

**4.48** The Charities Act 1993, s 65(1) and the 1989 Act, s 112(3) made special provision for companies which are charities. The same restriction applies to the 2006 Act, because ss 39 and 40 have effect subject to s 42.[87] The effect of these provisions is that the 1985 Act, ss 35 and 35A (or the 2006 Act, ss 39 and 40) do not apply to the acts of a company that is a charity except in favour of a person who (a) does not know at the time the act is done that the company is a charity, or (b) gives full consideration in money or money's worth in relation to the act in question and does not know (as the case may be) (i) that the act is not permitted by the company's constitution, or (ii) that the act is beyond the powers of the directors.

### (5) Transactions of individual directors

*Actual authority, express or implied*

**4.49** The directors, (as the organ of the company vested with actual authority to manage its affairs), may delegate their authority to a committee of directors, a managing director, or any other director, so as to confer express actual authority and allow the company to be bound by such delegate.[88]

**4.50** The directors may also confer implied actual authority on a director when they appoint one of their number to be managing director. He will have implied actual authority to do all such things as fall within the usual scope of that office.[89] Persons dealing in good faith with a managing director are entitled to assume that he has all the powers that he purports to exercise, if they are powers which a managing

---

[85] 1985 Act, s 322A(3); 2006 Act, s 41(3). These provisions may be compared with 2006 Act, s 195(3).

[86] 1985 Act, s 322A(6); 2006 Act, s 41(5). These provisions may be compared with 2006 Act, s 195(7).

[87] 2006 Act, ss 39(2) and 40(6). Section 42 restates Charities Act 1993, s 65.

[88] eg Table A, reg 72; Model Article,(pcls) (pcg) (plc) 5. *Hely-Hutchison v Brayhead Ltd* [1968] 1 QB 549, 583, CA, per Lord Denning MR. Delegation is discussed further in Chapter 5.

[89] *Hely Hutchison v Brayhead Ltd* [1968] 1 QB 549, 583, CA, per Lord Denning MR.

director could have under the company's constitution.[90] In *Kreditbank Cassel GmbH v Schenkers Ltd* Atkin LJ said:[91]

> If you are dealing with a director in a matter in which normally a director would have power to act for the company you are not obliged to inquire whether or not the formalities required by the articles have been complied with before he exercises that power. Those are matters of internal management which an outsider is not obliged to investigate.

The same considerations apply to the appointment of a director with any other title such as finance director[92] or marketing director. Since directors should take decisions together,[93] an individual director, who has not been appointed to a particular office, will have little, if any, usual authority to act on behalf of the company beyond executing documents.[94] But if the board is to be taken to have impliedly authorized an individual director to deal with a particular matter he will have all the powers of the company that could have been delegated to him under the constitution and those powers are likely to be unlimited.[95] Thus an individual director may be able to bind the company to a bill signed by him.[96]  **4.51**

The directors may of course extend or restrict the authority of a director whom they have appointed to a particular office, but the extension will not assist, or the restriction prejudice, a third party unless he is aware of them.[97] If a director exceeds his authority, the board may ratify his conduct, but if the matter was beyond the powers of the board (which would be unusual) or involved a breach of duty, only the members could ratify under the 2006 Act, s 239 (Chapter 19 below).  **4.52**

A director's actual authority is limited to acting in the interests of the company, so that a director who acts not for the benefit of the company (fulfilling his duty to promote the success of the company under the 2006 Act, s 172), but for his own benefit is acting outside his authority.[98] The transaction is therefore void, as being outside the director's authority unless the third party can rely on apparent authority.[99]  **4.53**

---

[90] *Biggerstaff v Rowatt's Wharf Ltd* [1897] 2 Ch 93, CA. Under Table A, reg 72 and Model Article (pcls) and (plc) 5 all the powers of the directors may be delegated to a managing director, with the consequence that he can exercise all the powers of the company.

[91] [1927] 1 KB 826, 844, CA.

[92] *Kreditbank Kassel v Schenkers Ltd* [1927] 1 KB 826, CA; *British Bank of the Middle East v Sun Life Assurance Co of Canada Ltd* [1983] 2 Lloyd's Rep 9, HL.

[93] Table A, regs 70 and 88; Model Article (pcls) and (plc) 7.

[94] *Rama Corporation Ltd v Proved Tin & General Investments Ltd* [1952] 2 QB 147, following *Houghton & Co v Nothard, Lowe & Wills Ltd* [1927] 1 KB 246, CA (affirmed on other grounds [1927] AC 1, HL) and *Kreditbank Kassel v Schenkers Ltd* [1927] 1 KB 826, CA.

[95] Table A, reg 72 and Model Article (pcls) and (plc) 5.

[96] *Re Land Credit Company of Ireland* (1869) 4 Ch App 460, 473, per Sir GM Giffard LJ; *Dey v Pullinger Engineering Co* [1921] 1 KB 77.

[97] *Houghton & Co v Nothard, Lowe & Wills Ltd* [1927] 1 KB 246, CA.

[98] *Lysaght Bros & Co Ltd v Falk* (1905) 2 CLR 421, 430, per Griffiths CJ.

[99] *Hopkins v TL Dallas Group Ltd* [2005] 1 BCLC 543 at para 88.

**4.54**  A third party who deals with the company through the delegate so appointed is protected by the 1985 Act, ss 35 and 35A (and the 2006 Act, ss 39 and 40 when in force) as discussed in paragraphs 4.36–4.42 above. Furthermore, the third party has the protection of the 2006 Act, s 161, which provides:

(1) The acts of a person acting as a director are valid notwithstanding that it is after-
    wards discovered—
    (a) that there was a defect in his appointment;
    (b) that he was disqualified from holding office;
    (c) that he had ceased to hold office;
    (d) that he was not entitled to vote on the matter in question.
(2) This applies even if the resolution for his appointment is void under section 160
    (appointment of directors of public company to be voted on individually).

The only limit on the scope of s 161 is that a person who did not act in good faith may not rely on it.[100]

*Ostensible or apparent authority*

**4.55**  In *Freeman & Lockyer v Buckhurst Park Properties (Magnal) Ltd* Diplock LJ described the features of apparent or ostensible authority in these terms:[101]

> An 'apparent' or 'ostensible' authority . . . is a legal relationship between the principal
> and the contractor created by a representation, made by the principal to the contrac-
> tor, intended to be and in fact acted upon by the contractor, that the agent has
> authority to enter on behalf of the principal into a contract of a kind within the scope
> of the 'apparent' authority, so as to render the principal liable to perform any obliga-
> tions imposed upon him by such contract. To the relationship so created the agent is
> a stranger. He need not be (although he generally is) aware of the existence of the
> representation but he must not purport to make the agreement as principal himself.
> The representation, when acted upon by the contractor by entering into a contract
> with the agent, operates as an estoppel, preventing the principal from asserting that
> he is not bound by the contract. It is irrelevant whether the agent had actual author-
> ity to enter into the contract.

Diplock LJ went on to summarize four conditions which must be fulfilled to entitle a contractor to enforce against a company a contract entered into on behalf
of the company by an agent who had no actual authority to do so:[102]

(1) that a representation that the agent had authority to enter on behalf of the company
    into a contract of the kind sought to be enforced was made to the contractor;
(2) that such representation was made by a person or persons who had 'actual' author-
    ity to manage the business of the company either generally or in respect of those
    matters to which the contract relates;

---

[100] *Channel Collieries Trust Ltd v Dover, St Margaret's and Martin Mill Light Railway Co* [1914] 2
Ch 506, CA.
[101] [1964] 2 QB 480, 503, CA.
[102] [1964] 2 QB 480, 506, CA.

(3) that he (the contractor) was induced by such representation to enter into the contract, that is, that he in fact relied upon it; and

(4) that under its memorandum or articles of association the company was not deprived of the capacity either to enter into a contract of the kind sought to be enforced or to delegate authority to enter into a contract of that kind to the agent.

The first two conditions concern the representation on behalf of the company as to the agent's authority. The representation will usually involve, not words, but permitting the director or other officer to conduct the company's business with a third party.[103] That permitted conduct will entail a representation that the director or officer has all authority of an agent in that position. In the *Freeman & Lockyer* case the board allowed a director to deal with a project as if he was managing director, although never so appointed. A managing director would have authority to retain architects on behalf of the company and accordingly the company was liable to pay the architects' fees. While an agent cannot make an effective representation as to his own authority,[104] he may have been put in a position where he can make some other a representation on behalf of the company as to the authority of others.[105] Thus, although a branch manager of a bank may not have ostensible authority to agree a large loan facility, he may have such authority to communicate his superiors' approval of the loan to the prospective borrower.[106] **4.56**

As to the third condition, the third party would not be entitled to rely on the representation if he knew or ought reasonably to have appreciated that it was not made to him or for his benefit.[107] **4.57**

It will seldom be necessary to consider the fourth condition, since the 1985 Act, s 35A(1) and the 2006 Act, s 40(1) provide that in favour of a person dealing with a company in good faith, the power of the directors to bind the company, or authorize others to do so, is deemed to be free of any limitation under the company's constitution (see paragraphs 4.36–4.42 above) **4.58**

## C. Formalities of Doing Business

This section deals with company contracts and the execution of documents by or on behalf of a company. The 2006 Act, ss 43–47, 49, 50, and 52 contain provisions about the formalities of doing business by companies under the law of **4.59**

---

[103] *Freeman & Lockyer v Buckhurst Park Properties (Mangal) Ltd* [1964] 2 QB 480, 503, CA; *Hely-Hutchinson v Brayhead Ltd* [1968] 1 QB 549, 583, CA, per Lord Denning MR; *AMB Generali Holding AG v SEB TRYGG LIV* [2006] 1 Lloyd's Rep 318, CA at paras 31, 32, per Buxton LJ.

[104] *Armagas Ltd v Mundogas SA* [1986] AC 717, HL.

[105] *ING Re (UK) Ltd V R&V Verssicherung AG* [2007] 1 BCLC 108 at paras 100 and 101.

[106] *First Energy (UK) Ltd v Hungarian International Bank Ltd* [1993] 2 Lloyd's Rep 194, CA.

[107] *ING Re (UK) Ltd V R&V Verssicherung AG* [2007] 1 BCLC 108 at para 104.

England and Wales or Northern Ireland, which replace provisions in the 1985 Act, ss 36, 36A, 36AA, 37–40.[108] The new provisions come into effect on 1 October 2009, except that the 2006 Act, s 44 (execution of documents) replaced the 1985 Act, s 36A on 6 April 2008.[109]

**4.60** Among those groups of sections are the 1985 Act, s 40 and the 2006 Act, s 51,[110] which deal with pre-incorporation contracts, deeds, and obligations. A contract purportedly made on behalf of a company before it is formed takes effect, subject to any agreement to the contrary, as one made by the person purporting to act for the company or as agent for it, and he is personally liable on the contract accordingly. Since this topic gives rise to personal liability, it is discussed in Chapter 27, Section B(2) of this work. If the company wishes to be bound by the contract it must novate it or take an assignment of its benefit; it cannot simply ratify it.[111]

### (1) Company contracts

**4.61** The 1985 Act, s 36 (to be replaced by the 2006 Act, s 43) provides that there are two ways in which the directors may procure a company to make a contract. The first way is directly by the company itself: 'by a company, by writing under its common seal'. The second way is through the agency of its directors or other persons acting on its behalf: 'on behalf of a company, by a person acting under its authority, express or implied'. Such a contract may be made orally or in writing.

**4.62** The sections go on to provide that any formalities required by law in the case of a contract made by an individual also apply, unless a contrary intention appears, to a contract made by or on behalf of a company.[112] A guarantee given by a company must therefore be in writing and duly signed on its behalf.[113] Contracts for the sale or other disposition of an interest in land must be in writing in a document incorporating all the terms which the parties have expressly agreed, which is signed by

---

[108] 1985 Act, s 41 (authentication of documents) was repealed on 6 April 2007 and is not replaced (2006 Act Commencement Order No 1, art 4(2)(b)). 1985 Act, s 42 (events affecting a company's status) was replaced by 2006 Act, s 1079 on 1 January 2007 (2006 Act Commencement Order No 1, arts 2(1)(d) and 7(a)).

[109] 2006 Act Commencement Order No 5, art 3(1)(a).

[110] 2006 Act, s 51 comes into effect on 1 October 2009.

[111] *Kelner v Baxter* (1866) LR 2 CP 174; *Howard v Patent Ivory Manufacturing Co* (1888) 38 Ch D 156; *Natal Land and Colonization Co Ltd v Pauline Colliery and Development Syndicate Ltd* [1904] AC 120, PC.

[112] 1985 Act, s 36; 2006 Act, s 43(2).

[113] Statute of Frauds 1677, s 4. The court may not find an estoppel, so as to enforce the guarantor's liability, which is founded on an informal agreement which does not comply with s 4: *Actionstrength Ltd v International Glass Engineering IN.GL.EN SpA* [2003] 2 AC 541, HL.

or on behalf of each party or, where contracts are exchanged, in each exchanged document one of which must be signed by or on behalf of each party.[114]

## (2) The company seal

Where a contract is made by the company 'by writing under its common seal'[115] **4.63** the document embodying the contract is executed by the company by affixing its common seal.[116] A document so executed by the company satisfies one of the two requirements for valid execution by it as a deed for the purposes of the Law of Property (Miscellaneous Provisions) Act 1989, s 1(2)(b); the other requirement being delivery as a deed.[117] A document is presumed to be delivered as a deed upon its being executed, unless the contrary is proved.[118] Delivery in this context never meant 'handed over', but doing an act so as to evince an intention to be bound.[119]

It may not be possible for a company to make a contract directly under seal, **4.64** because there is no requirement for it to have a common seal.[120] Where a company does not have a common seal its documents are executed in the manner described in paragraphs 4.71 *et seq.* The advantages of a seal are that (a) it provides a greater degree of authenticity than execution by the officers alone, (b) since execution under seal involves more formality, it may help focus the attention of the company's officers on the transaction proposed, (c) provisions dealing with the safe-keeping of the seal and maintenance of a seal register may enhance internal controls, (d) foreign jurisdictions may require documents to be executed under seal, and (e) execution under seal may offer greater flexibility because the range of

---

[114] Law of Property (Miscellaneous Provisions) Act 1989, s 2. It is first necessary to identify the contract and then determine whether it falls within s 2: *Kilcarne Holdings Ltd v Target Follow (Birmingham) Ltd* [2004] EWHC 2547 (Ch) at paras 189, 190 and also 200–204. See also *Spiro v Glencrown Properties Ltd* [1991] Ch 537 (option agreement); *United Bank of Kuwait plc v Sahib* [1997] Ch 107 (equitable charge by deposit of title deeds must comply with s 2); *McCausland v Duncan Lawrie Ltd* [1997] 1 WLR 38, CA (variations must also comply with s 2); *Dolphin Quays Development Ltd v Mills* [2006] EWHC 931, CA (side letter).

[115] 1985 Act, s 36; 2006 Act, s 43 (1).

[116] 2006 Act, s 44(1). By s 44(8) the company may execute a document by affixing its seal where it executes it in the name and on behalf of another person whether or not that person is also a company.

[117] 1985 Act, s 36AA; 2006 Act, s 46.

[118] 2005 Act, s 36AA(2); 2006 Act, s 46(2). This effectively overrules the view expressed by Peter Gibson LJ in *Bolton Metropolitan BC v Torkington* [1994] Ch 66, CA at para 46 that to speak of a rebuttable presumption at common law may be going too far.

[119] *Vincent v Premo Enterprises Ltd* [1969] 2 QB 609, 619, CA, per Lord Denning MR.

[120] 1985 Act, s 36A(3); 2006 Act, s 45(1).

persons authorized to attest the sealing may be extended by the articles to persons other than directors and the secretary, such as solicitors.[121]

**4.65**  If the company does have a common seal, its name must be engraved on it in legible characters; otherwise an offence is committed, by the company, and every officer of the company who is in default.[122] However, a contract made by a company with a non-compliant seal may be enforced against it.[123]

**4.66**  The authority to use the common seal is a matter for the company's articles, which usually provide that it may only be used by the authority of the directors. Table A reg 101 provides:

> The seal shall only be used by the authority of the directors or of a committee of directors authorised by the directors. The directors may determine who shall sign any instrument to which the seal is affixed and unless otherwise so determined it shall be signed by a director and by the secretary or by a second director.

Where the instrument is so signed its validity cannot be contested by the company.[124]

**4.67**  In relation to the common seal the Model Articles give more flexibility as to the signing of the document to which the seal is affixed:[125]

(1) Any common seal may only be used by the authority of the directors.

(2) The directors may decide by what means and in what form any common seal is to be used.

(3) Unless otherwise decided by the directors, if the company has a common seal and it is affixed to a document, the document must also be signed by at least one authorized person in the presence of a witness who attests the signature.

(4) For the purposes of this article, an authorized person is—

    (a) any director of the company;

    (b) the company secretary (if any); or

    (c) any person authorized by the directors for the purpose of signing documents to which the common seal is applied.

---

[121] The Law Commission in *The Execution of Deeds and Documents by or on behalf of Bodies Corporate* (1996) Consultation Paper, No 143 and Report No 253 (1998), para 3.24.

[122] 1985 Act, s 350(1); 2006 Act, s 45(2); 1985 Act, s 350(1). Also an officer of the company, or a person acting on behalf of the company, commits an offence if he uses, or authorizes the use of, a seal purporting to be a seal of the company on which its name is not engraved as required by 1985 Act, s 350(1); see s 350(2); or 2006 Act, s 45(2); see s 45(4).

[123] *OTV Birwelco Ltd v Technical and General Guarantee Co Ltd* [2002] 4 All ER 668 at paras 45–59, where the company's trade name, not its registered name, was engraved on the seal.

[124] *County of Gloucester Bank v Rudry Merthyr Steam and House Coal Colliery Co* [1895] 1 Ch 629, CA; *Duck v Tower Galvanising Co* [1901] 2 KB 314, CA.

[125] Model Article 49 (pcls); Model Article (pclg) 35; Model Article (plc) 81(1)–(4) is in the same terms except that Article 81(2) also refers to the securities seal and Article 81(4)(b) omits the words '(if any)'.

Those requirements for authority to affix the common seal to a document are **4.68** consistent with the Law of Property Act 1925, s 74, which provides protection for purchasers where an instrument has been executed by a corporation (including a company) under seal:[126]

> (1) In favour of a purchaser an instrument shall be deemed to have been duly executed by a corporation aggregate if a seal purporting to be the corporation's seal purports to be affixed to the instrument in the presence of and attested by—
>    (a) two members of the board of directors, council or other governing body of the corporation, or
>    (b) one such member and the clerk, secretary or other permanent officer of the corporation or his deputy.
> (1A) Subsection (1) of this section applies in the case of an instrument purporting to have been executed by a corporation aggregate in the name or on behalf of another person whether or not that person is also a corporation aggregate.
> (1B) For the purposes of subsection (1) of this section, a seal purports to be affixed in the presence of and attested by an officer of the corporation, in the case of an officer which is not an individual, if it is affixed in the presence of and attested by an individual authorised by the officer to attest on its behalf.

A company may also have two other official seals, which when duly affixed to a **4.69** document have the same effect as the common seal. It may have a seal for use outside the United Kingdom. This seal must be a facsimile of the company's common seal, with the addition on its face of the place or places where it is to be used.[127] A company having an official seal for use outside the United Kingdom may, by writing under its common seal, authorize any person appointed for the purpose to affix the official seal to any deed or other document to which the company is a party. Model Article 81(5) (plc) provides that the company's official seal for use abroad may only be affixed to a document if its use on that document, or documents of a class to which it belongs, has been authorized by a decision of the directors. As between the company and a person dealing with such an agent, the agent's authority continues during the period mentioned in the instrument conferring the authority, or if no period is mentioned, until notice of the revocation or termination of the agent's authority has been given to the person dealing with him.[128] The agent affixing the official seal must certify in writing on the deed or other document to which the seal is affixed the date on which, and place at which, it is affixed.[129]

The other official seal that a company may have is a seal for use for sealing secur- **4.70** ities issued by the company or for sealing documents creating or evidencing securities so issued. This seal must be a facsimile of the company's common seal, but

---

[126] With effect from 15 September 2005 s 74 was amended by the Regulatory Reform (Execution of Deeds and Documents) Order 2005 (SI 2005/1906), art 3.
[127] 1985 Act, s 39(1) and (2); 2006 Act, s 49(1)–(3).
[128] 1985 Act, s 39(4); 2006 Act, s 49(5).
[129] 1985 Act, s 39(5); 2006 Act, s 49(6).

with the addition on its face of the word 'Securities'.[130] Model Article 81(6) (plc) provides that the company's securities seal may only be affixed to securities by the company secretary or a person authorized to apply it to securities by the company secretary.[131]

### (3) Execution of deeds and documents otherwise than under seal

*Execution of deeds and documents by directors and secretaries*

**4.71** Where the directors want to execute a document on behalf of the company (including where it executes the document on behalf of another person[132]) the alternative to affixing the company's common seal (as discussed in paragraphs 4.63–4.70 above) is by signature in accordance with s 44.[133] Subsections 44(2) and (3) set out how and by whom a document may be signed on behalf of a company:

(2) A document is validly executed by a company if it is signed on behalf of the company[134]—
   (a) by two authorised signatories, or
   (b) by a director of the company in the presence of a witness who attests the signature.

(3) The following are 'authorised signatories' for the purposes of subsection (2)—
   (a) every director of the company, and
   (b) in the case of a private company with a secretary or a public company, the secretary (or any joint secretary) of the company.[135]

---

[130] 1985 Act, s 40; 2006 Act, s 50.

[131] By Model Article 81(7) (plc) 'For the purposes of the articles, references to the securities seal being affixed to any document include the reproduction of the image of that seal on or in a document by any mechanical or electronic means which has been approved by the directors in relation to that document or documents of a class to which it belongs.'

[132] s 44(8) provides: 'This section applies to a document that is (or purports to be) executed by a company in the name of or on behalf of another person whether or not that person is also a company.' Thus, for example, a company, if acting as an agent for an individual (eg to effect a contract for that individual) must comply with the provisions of s 44.

[133] 2006 Act, 44(1) which is derived from 1985 Act, s 36A, but with two changes. The main change is the new s 44(2)(b) allowing one director to execute a document in the presence of a witness. Section 36A(4) provided: 'A document signed by a director and the secretary of a company, or by two directors of a company, and expressed (in whatever form of words) to be executed by the company has the same effect as if executed under the common seal of the company.' The other change is in s 44(5), which replaces 1985 Act, s 36A(6).

[134] subs 44(6) deals with the case where someone signs a document on behalf of more than one company: 'Where a document is to be signed by a person on behalf of more than one company, it is not duly signed by that person for the purposes of this section unless he signs it separately in each capacity.' Thus the same person can sign the document as agent for different companies, but separate entries will have to be made on the document for the names of each of the companies and to make clear that he is signing it separately in each capacity.

[135] subs 44(7) makes provision for where an office is held by a firm which is the signatory. It provides 'References in this section to a document being (or purporting to be) signed by a director or secretary are to be read, in a case where that office is held by a firm, as references to its being (or purporting to be) signed by an individual authorised by the firm to sign on its behalf.'

Subsection 44(4) provides that a document signed in accordance with subsection (2) and expressed, in whatever words, to be executed by the company has the same effect as if executed under the common seal of the company.

It is therefore logical to find that s 44(5) gives the same protection to purchasers as **4.72** the Law of Property Act 1925, s 74(1)–(1B) does for documents under seal: 'In favour of a purchaser a document is deemed to have been duly executed by a company if it purports to be signed in accordance with subsection (2).' The subsection goes on to provide: 'A "purchaser" means a purchaser in good faith for valuable consideration and includes a lessee, mortgagee or other person who for valuable consideration acquires an interest in property.'

Accordingly a document validly executed by signature in accordance with s 44 is **4.73** duly executed as a deed for the purposes of the Law of Property (Miscellaneous Provisions) Act 1989, s 1(2)(b) and will take effect as a deed if delivered as a deed.[136] See further paragraph 4.63 above.

Before turning to the execution of deeds and documents by an attorney, reference **4.74** should be made to the 1985 Act, s 37,[137] which provides that a bill of exchange or promissory note is deemed to have been made, accepted, or endorsed on behalf of the company if made, accepted, or endorsed in the name of, or by or on behalf or on account of, the company by a person acting under its authority. The company is bound by the bill or promissory note signed by a director, consistently with the company's articles, even though the director did not in fact have authority from the board to issue the bill.[138]

*Execution of deeds and documents by an attorney*

Rather than having a deed or document executed under seal or by signature of its **4.75** directors or secretaries, the directors may wish to have it executed by someone else. The 1985 Act, s 37(1) enables a company, by writing under its common seal, to empower any person, either generally or in respect of specified matters, as its attorney, to execute deeds on its behalf in any place elsewhere than in the United Kingdom. Subsection 37(2) provides that a deed executed by such an attorney on behalf of the company has the same effect as if it were executed by the company. Section 37 will be replaced by the 2006 Act, s 47, with significant changes. The new section provides:

(1) Under the law of England and Wales or Northern Ireland a company may, by instrument executed as a deed, empower a person, either generally or in respect of

---

[136] 2005 Act, s 36AA(1) (which was inserted by the Regulatory Reform (Execution of Deeds and Documents) Order 2005 (SI 2005/1906) art 6 as from 14 September 2005); 2006 Act, s 46.

[137] To be replaced by 2006 Act, s 37.

[138] *Dey v Pullinger Engineering Co* [1921] 1 KB 77.

specified matters, as its attorney to execute deeds or other documents on its behalf.

(2) A deed or other document so executed, whether in the United Kingdom or elsewhere, has effect as if executed by the company.

**4.76**   The new section makes several changes, which should be noted. First, the appointment may be made by instrument executed as a deed, rather than under seal. This may make no difference since the 2006 Act, s 44 is in force and provides that a document executed by signature has the same effect as if executed under the common seal of the company.[139] Secondly, the attorney may be given power to execute documents as well as deeds. Thirdly, and most significantly, the attorney may execute deeds and documents in the United Kingdom as well as outside it.

**4.77**   In addition, the Law of Property Act 1925, s 74(2) gives the directors power, by resolution or otherwise, to appoint an agent either generally or in a particular case, to execute on its behalf any agreement or other instrument which is not a deed in relation to any matter within the powers of the company.[140]

---

[139] 2006 Act, s 44(4).
[140] Law of Property Act 1925, s 74(3) and (4) deals with the conveyance of property by an attorney.

# 5

# DIRECTORS' DECISION-MAKING AND DELEGATION

## A. General Introduction

Chapter 4 explained how management powers are vested in directors. This **5.01** section A explains how directors, acting as a board or by delegation, take decisions to carry out those functions. The Companies Acts have always left the procedure for decision-making by directors to the constitution of the company, but have required records of decisions to be kept.[1]

The company's articles of association provide the rules regulating decision-mak- **5.02** ing by directors and committees to whom particular functions have been delegated. Sometimes the articles will contain special rules designed to meet the needs of the particular company: eg prescribing that certain matters cannot be done without the assent of particular directors. More often the company's articles adopt, with or without adaptation, the default articles prescribed by the Companies Acts, or at least those articles that deal with decision-making by directors. They do so for reasons of certainty and convenience. The discussion in this chapter therefore focuses on the procedures in those default articles.

For companies incorporated under the 1985 Act (which will continue to be **5.03** the case until 1 October 2009), Table A, regs 88–98 deal with proceedings

---

[1] 2006 Act, ss 248 and 249, which replace 1985 Act, s 382, with changes. These sections can be traced back to 1862 Act, s 67.

of directors.[2] For companies incorporated after 1 October 2009, the 2006 Act, s 19 provides that the Model Articles will be the default articles.[3] The Model Articles are significantly different to Table A. They are designed to promote efficiency of decision-making and to reflect more closely the commercial world in which private and public companies operate.

**5.04**   The Model Articles (pcls) for private companies limited by shares and the Model Articles (pclg) for private companies limited by guarantee are in the same terms in relation to delegation to committees (Articles 5 and 6) and decision-making by directors (Articles 7–16), so Model Articles (pclg) are not mentioned again in this chapter. The Model Articles (plc) for public companies, so far as they relate to those matters (Articles 5–19) are broadly the same as those for private companies. One important difference is that the directors of a private company may take unanimous decisions on an informal basis (Article 8), whereas for the directors of a public company the written resolution procedure is rather more formal (Articles 17 and 18). The Model Articles (plc) are likely to be used as a drafting source for public companies, which are more likely to adopt tailor-made articles.[4]

## B. Decisions to be Taken Collectively

**5.05**   Table A and the Model Articles reflect two general principles. The first is that decisions of directors are to be taken collectively, either by written decision, taken or agreed to by all directors, or made by a majority at a meeting. Once the decision has been taken, the directors, including dissenters, are bound by the decision and must carry it into effect (or resign).[5] This principle is expressly stated in Model Article (pcls) 7:

> (1) The general rule about decision-making by directors is that any decision of the directors must be either a majority decision at a meeting or a decision taken in accordance with article 8.

---

[2] For companies incorporated between 1 October 2007 and 1 October 2009 these have been amended by the Companies (Tables A to F) (Amendment) Regulations 2007 (SI 2007/2541), the Companies Act (Tables A to F) (Amendment) (No 2) Regulations 2007 (SI 2007/2826), and the Companies (Tables A to F) (Amendment) Regulations 2008 (SI 2008/739). These amendments enable Table A to conform to the provisions of the 2006 Act brought into force before 1 October 2009, but none of the amendments affect the regulations of Table A considered in this chapter. Different versions of Table A apply to companies incorporated under the 1948 Act or earlier Companies Acts.

[3] These are set out in the Companies (Model Articles) Regulations (SI 2008/3229).

[4] *Implementation of the Companies Act 2006, a Consultation Paper* (DTI, February 2007) at paras 3.31, 3.32.

[5] *Re Equiticorp International plc* [1989] 1 WLR 1010.

(2) If—
    (a) the company only has one director, and
    (b) no provision of the articles requires it to have more than one director,
    the general rule does not apply, and the director may take decisions without regard
    to any of the provisions of the articles relating to directors' decision-making.

Model Article (plc) 7 is in different terms:

(1) Decisions of the directors may be taken—
    (a) at a directors' meeting, or
    (b) in the form of a directors' written resolution.

The two Articles results are different because the unanimous decision procedure is not available for directors of public companies and a private company may have only one director, but a public company must have at least two.[6] Model Article (pcls) 7 does not require a private company which is entitled to have, and only has, one director to go through the fiction of requiring the sole director to have a meeting with himself.[7] The sole director must comply with his obligations under the 2006 Act, Part 10, Chapters 4–6, concerning transactions with directors requiring approval of members, directors' service contracts, and contracts with the sole member who is also a director (Chapter 18 of this work).

The second general principle is that, subject to the provisions of the company's **5.06** articles, which can only be altered by special resolution, 'the directors may regulate their proceedings as they see fit' (Table A, reg 88). This wording was 'generally taken to refer to fixing the timing of periodic meetings, the circulation of agendas and other administrative matters'.[8] Wording in terms of reg 88 does not enable a casual meeting of the only two directors of a company to be treated as a board meeting at the option of one, against the will of the other.[9]

Model Article (pcls) 16 and Model Article (plc) 19 both state the principle more **5.07** explicitly: 'Subject to the articles, the directors may make any rule which they think fit about how they take decisions, and about how such rules are to be recorded or communicated to directors.' The new wording is intended to make clear that the directors are able to 'fill in the gaps' which there may in particular circumstances turn out to be in the Model Articles' provisions on directors' decision-making.[10]

---

[6] 2006 Act, s 154, which replaced 1985 Act, s 282 on 1 October 2007.
[7] Contrast *Neptune (Vehicle Washing Equipment) Ltd v Fitzgerald* [1996] Ch 274.
[8] *Implementation of the Companies Act 2006, a Consultative Document* (DTI, February 2007) at para 3.84.
[9] *Barron v Potter* [1914] 1 Ch 895. See paragraph 5.08 below.
[10] *Implementation of the Companies Act 2006, a Consultative Document* (DTI, February 2007) at paras 3.85–3.86.

## C. Private Companies: Unanimous Decisions

**5.08**  Directors have always been able to take unanimous decisions on uncontentious matters in an informal way. In *Charterhouse Investment Trust Ltd v Tempest Diesels Ltd* Hoffmann J held that the informal acquiescence of all the directors sufficed for a binding resolution.[11] Table A, reg 93, however, required unanimous decisions not taken at a meeting to be in writing signed by all the directors (see paragraph 5.41 below). Unanimity is essential to the validity of informal decisions. If there is dissent or if the express assent of one or more directors cannot be obtained, the matter must be decided at a meeting. Such a meeting must be properly convened, because an informal meeting cannot take place against the will of one of the directors who happens to be present.[12] Nor is it sufficient to obtain the separate authority of a sufficient number of directors to constitute a quorum.[13] Where the matter has not been validly decided, the defect may be cured by ratification by a duly passed resolution at a meeting,[14] or indeed, by a later valid unanimous decision.

**5.09**  Model Article (pcls) 8 now gives directors of private companies more flexibility in decision making, because they are not required to do so simultaneously. They can do so over a period of time by an exchange of emails or text messages. It provides:

(1) A decision of the directors is taken in accordance with this article when all eligible directors indicate to each other by any means that they share a common view on a matter.

(2) Such a decision may take the form of a resolution in writing, copies of which have been signed by each eligible director or to which each eligible director has otherwise indicated agreement in writing.

(3) References in this article to eligible directors are to directors who would have been entitled to vote on the matter had it been proposed as a resolution at a director's metting.

(4) A decision may not be taken in accordance with this article if the eligible directors would not have formed a quorum at such a meeting.

**5.10**  Model Article (pcls) 8(1) indicates that a director may assent orally to the decision, perhaps by telephone. Furthermore, Model Article 8(2) is permissive: the

---

[11] *Charterhouse Investment Trust Ltd v Tempest Diesels Ltd* [1986] BCLC 1, 9. See also *Re Bonelli's Telegraph Co, Collie's Claim* (1871) LR 12 Eq 246, 258; *Runciman v Walter Runciman Plc* [1992] BCLC 1084, 1092; *Hunter v Senate Support Services Ltd* [2005] 1 BCLC 175, 208.

[12] *Barron v Potter* [1914] 1 Ch 895; *Glatzer and Warwick Shipping Ltd v Bradston Ltd* [1997] 1 Lloyd's Rep 449, 471, 472. However, there is a narrow dividing line. In *Smith v Paringa Mines Ltd* [1906] 2 Ch 193 one of the only two directors did not attend a meeting, though he had received proper notice. The other director met him in the corridor and proposed a resolution. He objected, whereby the other declared it passed by his casting vote (as chairman). The resolution was held to have been duly passed.

[13] *D'Arcy v Tanner, Kit Hill and Callington Railway Co* (1867) LR 2 Exch 158; *Re Haycraft Gold Reduction and Mining Co* [1900] 2 Ch 230, 235.

[14] *Re Portuguese Consolidated Copper Mines Ltd* (1890) 45 Ch D 16, CA; *Municipal Mutual Insurance Ltd v Harrop* [1998] 2 BCLC 540.

unanimous decision may take the form of a written resolution. While all the eligible directors must agree to the resolution, they can do so by signing it or in any other way (ie orally). By Model Article (pcls) 15 the directors must ensure that the company keeps a record of every unanimous decision for at least 10 years.

## D. Decisions Taken at Meetings

Where the decision cannot be taken unanimously, it must be taken at a meeting, properly called and constituted. **5.11**

### (1) Calling the meeting

Table A, reg 88 provides for the calling of a meeting of directors in these terms: **5.12**

> A director may, and the secretary at the request of a director shall, call a meeting of the directors. It shall not be necessary to give notice of the meeting to a director who is absent from the United Kingdom.[15]

Table A, reg 111 does not require notice of directors' meetings to be given in writing.[16]

The Model Articles follow Table A in providing that any director may call a meet- **5.13** ing by giving notice and that the secretary is to give notice on the request of a director. The language of the Model Articles (pcls) and (plc) is slightly different, reflecting the fact that a private company need not have a secretary. Model Article (pcls) 9(1) provides:

> Any director may call a directors' meeting by giving notice of the meeting to the directors or by authorising the company secretary (if any) to give such notice.

Model Article (plc) 8 explains who can or must call a directors' meeting in these terms:

> (1) Any director may call a directors' meeting.
> (2) The company secretary must call a directors' meeting if a director so requests.
> (3) A directors' meeting is called by giving notice of the meeting to the directors.

Model Article (pcls) 9(2)–(4) and Model Article (plc) 8(4)–(6) provide for the giv- **5.14** ing of notice of the directors' meeting in the same terms. Model Article 9 provides:

> (2) Notice of any directors' meeting must indicate—
> a) its proposed date and time;
> (b) where it is to take place; and

---

[15] Formerly 1948 Table A, art 98: 'a director may, and the secretary on the requisition of a director shall, at any time summon a meeting of the directors. It shall not be necessary to give notice of a meeting of directors to any director for the time being absent from the United Kingdom'.

[16] *Browne v La Trinidad* (1887) 37 Ch D 1, 9, CA.

  (c) if it is anticipated that directors participating in the meeting will not be in the same place, how it is proposed that they should communicate with each other during the meeting.

 (3) Notice of a directors' meeting must be given to each director, but need not be in writing.

 (4) Notice of a directors' meeting need not be given to directors who waive their entitlement to notice of that meeting, by giving notice to that effect to the company not more than 7 days after the date on which the meeting is held. Where such notice is given after the meeting has been held, that does not affect the validity of the meeting, or of any business conducted at it.

**5.15** Unlike Table A, reg 88, the Model Articles require the notice to give directors information about the arrangements for the meeting. Although there is no requirement for notice of the meeting to be given in writing,[17] that will be a sensible precaution in case there may be an issue about the validity of decisions taken at the meeting. There is no need for the notice to indicate the subject matter of the meeting.[18]

**5.16** Unlike Table A, reg 88, the Model Articles make no exception for directors absent from the United Kingdom.[19] This exception is no longer appropriate given modern communications technology.[20] The Model Articles recognize that in the days of mobile phones and email, the circumstances in which a director can be said to be out of reach have shrunk dramatically.[21] The Model Articles give effect to the general principle that each director is entitled to notice of the meeting.[22] Instead the Model Articles allow a director to waive his right to notice, by giving notice to the company not more than 7 days after the date on which the meeting is held.[23]

**5.17** As with Table A, reg 88, the Model Articles are silent as to length of notice. The case law has laid down various principles. Each board member should have reasonable

---

[17] *Browne v La Trinidad* (1887) 37 Ch D 1, 9, CA.

[18] *La Compagnie de Mayville v Whitley* [1896] 1 Ch 788, 797, CA.

[19] Even if a director is abroad and out of reach of notices, the meeting will be invalid if his absence means there is no quorum: *Davidson & Begg Antiques Ltd v Davidson* [1997] BCC 77, CS, Outer House.

[20] *Implementation of Companies Act 2006, a Consultative Document* (DTI, February 2007) at para 3.63.

[21] In *Halifax Sugar Refining Co Ltd v Francklyn* (1890) 59 LJ Ch 591, 593 a meeting was held to be valid where a director was genuinely 'out of reach'. In *Implementation of Companies Act 2006, a Consultative Document* (DTI, February 2007) at para 3.63, the DTI compared notification of a director on business in New York and a director 'holidaying on a remote island', but in the days of the Blackberry, that may no longer be a distinction of substance.

[22] *Smyth v Darley* (1849) 2 HL Cas 789; *Re Homer District Consolidated Gold Mines, ex p Smith* (1888) 39 Ch D 546.

[23] Compare *Re Portuguese Consolidated Copper Mines Limited* (1890) 42 Ch D 160, 168, CA, where Lord Esher MR said of a director that 'he could not waive his right to notice'; *Young v Ladies' Imperial Club* [1920] 2 KB 523, 528, 534, 536, CA. The approach in those cases is to be contrasted with that in *Browne v La Trinidad* (1887) 37 Ch D 1, 9, CA; *Bentley-Stevens v Jones* [1974] 1 WLR 638, 641.

notice of every meeting.[24] What is 'reasonable' may be determined by the board's previous course of conduct.[25] Reference should also be made to relevant circumstances such as urgency, subject matter, and location. In *Re Homer District Consolidated Gold Mines* three hours' notice was enough: in *Browne v La Trinidad* five minutes' notice was sufficient. If a director wishes to object to the shortness of notice, he should do so at once.[26]

Like Table A, reg 88, the Model Articles are silent about the effect of failure to give **5.18** notice. Though the practical consequences of this will most likely be limited, case law has established the following principles. A director cannot lawfully be excluded from a board meeting, and an excluded director can obtain an injunction restraining his continued exclusion (unless he is about to be removed, in which case an injunction would be pointless).[27] Where notice is not received by every director so entitled, business done at that meeting does not bind the company[28] and 'the failure to give requisite notice is an irregularity'.[29] This is so, even where directors without notice could not have changed the result.[30] Where a directors' meeting is rendered irregular, the irregularity will not prejudice persons acting in good faith.[31] An irregularity can be ratified at a subsequent board meeting.[32]

## (2) Conduct of the meeting

*Participation*

Whereas Table A, reg 88 assumes that the directors will meet in the same place, **5.19** Model Article (pcls) 10 and Model Article (plc) 9 recognize improvements in communication technology (such as conference calls and video conferencing) and

---

[24] *Re Homer District Consolidated Gold Mines* (1888) 39 Ch D 546.

[25] *Toole v Flexihire Pty Ltd* (1991) 6 ACSR 455, 461.

[26] *Browne v La Trinidad*, n 23 above at 9.

[27] *Pulbrook v Richmond Consolidated Mining Co* (1878) 9 Ch D 610, 612; *Hayes v Bristol Plant Hire Ltd* [1957] 1 WLR 499. In *Bentley-Stevens v Jones* [1974] 1 WLR 638 the court would not grant an injunction in respect of irregularities which could be cured by going through the right process (following *Browne v La Trinidad*). However, the board may exclude a director where the company has by resolution declared that it does not desire the director to act: *Bainbridge v Smith* (1889) 41 Ch D 462, 474, CA.

[28] *Re Homer District Consolidated Gold Mines* (1888) 39 Ch D 546.

[29] *Re Oriental Gas Co Ltd* [1999] BCC 237, 251, per Ferris J.

[30] *Young v Ladies' Imperial Club Limited* [1920] 2 KB 523. There is some debate as to whether notice must be given to a director with no vote under the articles: *John Shaw & Sons (Salford) v Shaw* [1935] 2 KB 113, CA (per Greer LJ at 133, per Slesser LJ at 138).

[31] 1985 Act, s 35A (to be replaced by 2006 Act, s 40 with changes). A director will not be able to rely on those sections, since the irregularity arose from his own failure to ensure that the transaction was properly authorized: *Smith v Henniker-Major & Co* [2003] Ch 182, CA. See Chapter 4, Section B.

[32] *Re Portuguese Consolidated Copper Mines Limited* (1890) 42 Ch D 160, 166, CA; *Re State of Wyoming Syndicate* [1901] 2 Ch 431, 437.

provide in the same terms for the directors to be in different locations from where they can communicate with each other. Model Article (pcls) 10 provides:

(1) Subject to the articles, directors participate in a directors' meeting or part of a directors' meeting when—
    (a) the meeting has been called and takes place in accordance with the articles, and
    (b) they can each communicate to the others any information or opinions they have on any particular item of the business of the meeting.
(2) In determining whether directors are participating in a directors' meeting, it is irrelevant where any director is or how they communicate with each other.
(3) If all the directors participating in a meeting are not in the same place, they may decide that a meeting is to be treated as taking place wherever any of them is.

*Quorum*

**5.20** Where a private company has only one director and is not required to have more, the provisions in the company's articles regulating meetings of directors have no application. The following discussion assumes that the company has, or must have, at least two directors. In such cases the articles usually provide for a quorum to be present, failing which business cannot be conducted. In the rare cases where the articles do not prescribe a quorum, the court has regarded the number of directors who usually conduct the company's business as being a de facto quorum.[33] In any event the business may be conducted by the majority of the directors.[34] Where business is conducted by one or more directors, being less than the quorum, the court may be entitled to infer that such business has been delegated to those directors as a committee.[35]

**5.21** Table A, reg 89 states that:

The quorum for the transaction of the business of the directors may be fixed by the directors and unless so fixed at any other number shall be two. A person who holds office only as an alternate director shall, if his appointor is not present, be counted in the quorum.

In such a case the alternate director will be entitled to vote. In fact, entitlement to vote is prerequisite to being counted in the quorum; a director who is not entitled to vote on a resolution (usually on the ground of conflict of interest) cannot be

---

[33] *Lyon's Case* (1866) 35 Beav 646; *Re Tavistock Iron Works Co, Lyster's Case* (1867) 4 Eq 233; *Re Regent's Canal Iron Co* [1867] WN 79.

[34] *York Tramways Co v Willows* (1882) 8 QBD 685, CA.

[35] Table A, reg 72; Model Articles (pcls) and (plc) 5 and 6; *Totterdell v Fareham Blue Brick and Tile Co* (1866) LR 1 CP 674; *Re Barned's Banking Co, ex p Contract Corp* (1867) 3 Ch App 105, 116; *Re Fireproof Doors Ltd* [1916] 2 Ch 142.

counted in the quorum for the purposes of the resolution.[36] Table A, reg 95 provides:

> A director shall not be counted in the quorum present at a meeting in relation to a resolution on which he is not entitled to vote.

Model Article (pcls) 11(1) and (2) and Model Article (plc) 10 set out the quorum **5.22** requirements for private and public companies in the same terms: Model Article (pcls) 11(1) and (2) provides:

> (1) At a directors' meeting, unless a quorum is participating, no proposal is to be voted on, except a proposal to call another meeting.
> (2) The quorum for directors' decision-making may be fixed from time to time by a decision of the directors, but it must never be less than two, and unless otherwise fixed it is two.

Model Article (pcls) 14(1) and Model Article (plc) 16(1) both provide that a director with a conflict of interest and who cannot vote is not included for quorum purposes (paragraph 5.38 below). Since Model Article (plc) 15 provides for an alternate director to be entitled to vote, he can be included for quorum purposes. It was not considered necessary for the Model Articles to include the second sentence of Table A, reg 89. The directors are free to alter the quorum provision, provided that it is never less than two. If the members want to fix the quorum provision in a way that the directors cannot alter their remedy is to make an appropriate alteration of the articles.

The general rule is that where there is no quorum, the board is unable to act.[37] **5.23** Further, the quorum must be satisfied both at the time the meeting opens, as well as when the resolution is voted upon.[38] As noted in paragraphs 5.21 and 5.22 above a director who cannot vote because of a conflict of interest is not to be counted for the quorum. This consequence cannot be evaded by splitting one resolution into two resolutions (in respect of each of which only one director is conflicted) or by reducing the quorum for a specific purpose.[39] It has been held (*obiter*)

---

[36] *Re Greymouth-Point Elizabeth Railway and Coal Co Ltd* [1904] 1 Ch 32, 34; *Victors Ltd (in liquidation) v Lingard* [1927] 1 Ch 323; *Re Cleadon Trust* [1939] Ch 286, CA; *Colin Gwyer & Associates Ltd v London Wharf (Limehouse) Ltd* [2003] 2 BCLC 153, 176.

[37] *Re Greymouth-Point Elizabeth Railway and Coal Co Ltd* [1904] 1 Ch 32, 34. In *Re Copal Varnish Co* [1917] 2 Ch 349 one of the company's two directors attempted to block the transfer of certain shares through non-attendance of board meetings (the quorum for the transaction of business being two). It was held that the transferees were entitled to an order directing the company to register the transfers.

[38] However, in *Re Hartley Baird Ltd* [1955] Ch 143, it was held that an article which provided that 'the quorum shall be two directors present when the meeting proceeds to business' did not require two directors to be present throughout the meeting.

[39] *Re North Eastern Insurance Co* [1919] 1 Ch 198, 205.

that where a director breaches his fiduciary duty in voting for a resolution, he is not included for quorum purposes.[40]

**5.24** A company's articles will usually provide that where the company has directors, but less than the number required to transact business, the remaining directors may act for limited purposes, such as appointing new directors or calling a general meeting.[41] Table A, reg 90 provides:

> The continuing directors or a sole continuing director may act notwithstanding any vacancies in their number, but, if the number of directors is less than the number fixed as the quorum, the continuing directors or director may act only for the purpose of filling vacancies or of calling a general meeting.

An article in these terms does not validate the acts of a board that was originally less than the prescribed minimum.[42] However, where an article, like reg 90, allows continuing directors to act notwithstanding vacancies, and the board was originally competent to transact business, the continuing directors (being less than the prescribed minimum) could act so as to bind the company.[43]

**5.25** Model Article (pcls) 11(3) makes similar provision:

> If the total number of directors for the time being is less than the quorum required, the directors must not take any majority decision other than a decision—
> (a) to appoint further directors, or
> (b) to call a general meeting so as to enable the shareholders to appoint further directors.

This article recognizes that the remaining directors may make a decision unanimously at the meeting, since they could do so informally under Model Article (pcls) 8.

**5.26** Model Article (plc) 11 makes slightly different provision for public companies where the total number of directors is less than the quorum, depending on whether there is one or more than one director in office at the time:

> (1) This article applies where the total number of directors for the time being is less than the quorum for directors' meetings.
> (2) If there is only one director, that director may appoint sufficient directors to make up a quorum or call a general meeting to do so.

---

[40] In *Colin Guyer & Associates Ltd v London Wharf (Limehouse) Ltd* [2003] 2 BCLC 153 the directors were found to have acted in their own, rather than the company's interests. The court held (*per curiam*) that where a director is shown to have acted in breach of his fiduciary duty, he should be treated as being incapable of voting on the business before the board, and not taken into account for quorum purposes. For new statutory provisions on directors' conflicts of interest, see Companies Act, s 175.

[41] *Channel Collieries Trust v Dover Light Railway Co* [1914] 2 Ch 506, CA. It is arguable that without such an article, the continuing directors may not be able to act: *York Tramways Co v Willows* (1883) 8 QBD 685, CA; *Re Bank of Syria* [1900] 2 Ch 272, 278; [1901] 1 Ch 115, 120, CA.

[42] *Re Sly, Spink & Co* [1911] 2 Ch 430.

[43] *Re Scottish Petroleum Co* (1883) 23 Ch D 413, 431, CA.

(3) If there is more than one director—
    (a) a directors' meeting may take place, if it is called in accordance with the articles and at least two directors participate in it, with a view to appointing sufficient directors to make up a quorum or call a meeting to do so, and
    (b) if a directors' meeting is called but only one director attends at the appointed date and time to participate in it, that director may appoint sufficient directors to make up a quorum or call a meeting to do so.

Where there are no directors at all, or they are unwilling to fill the vacancies, the **5.27** company in general meeting may make appointments until the board is properly reconstituted.[44] In *Alexander Ward v Samyang Navigation Co* the House of Lords held that the absence of validly appointed directors did not prevent a company taking proceedings to recover its debts (through an individual ratified by the members).[45]

### *Chairman*

The articles usually provide for the directors to have power to appoint a chairman to **5.28** conduct their meetings. A director does not have a common law right to hold the office of chairman during his period of office as a director.[46] The directors may terminate a chairman's appointment without any particular formality.[47] The chairman's role is limited to the conduct of meetings and it does not, as such, give him any particular power to transact business on behalf of the company.[48] The chairman must carry out his functions in good faith for the purpose for which he was appointed.

Table A, reg 91 deals with the appointment of the chairman: **5.29**

> The directors may appoint one of their number to be the chairman of the board of directors and may at any time remove him from that office. Unless he is unwilling to do so, the director so appointed shall preside at every meeting of directors at which he is present. But if there is no director holding that office, or if the director holding it is unwilling to preside or is not present within five minutes after the time appointed for the meeting, the directors present may appoint one of their number to be chairman of the meeting.

One of the chairman's important functions is to determine the eligibility of directors **5.30** to vote on particular matters, having regard to conflict of interest issues. Table A, reg 98 gives the chairman the power to rule conclusively on such matters:

> If a question arises at a meeting of directors or of a committee of directors as to the right of a director to vote, the question may, before the conclusion of the meeting,

---

[44] *Isle of Wight Railway Co v Tahourdin* (1883) 25 Ch D 320, 332, 335, CA; *Barron v Potter* [1914] 1 Ch 895, 902; *Foster v Foster* [1916] 1 Ch 532, 551.
[45] [1975] 1 WLR 673, HL.
[46] *Foster v Foster* [1916] 1 Ch 532, 551.
[47] *Cane v Jones* [1980] 1 WLR 1451.
[48] *Bell Houses Ltd v Wall Properties Ltd* [1966] 2 QB 656, 688, CA; *Hely-Hutchinson v Brayhead Ltd* [1968] 1 QB 549, CA.

be referred to the chairman of the meeting and his ruling in relation to any director other than himself shall be final and conclusive.

**5.31**   Subject to two minor variations Model Article (pcls) 12 and Model Article (plc) 12 deal with the appointment of chairman in the same terms. The directors do not have to appoint a chairman. Model Article (pcls) 12 provides:

(1)   The directors may appoint a director to chair their meetings.
(2)   The person so appointed for the time being is known as the chairman.
(3)   The directors may terminate the chairman's appointment at any time.
(4)   If the chairman is not participating in a directors' meeting within ten minutes of the time at which it was to start, the participating directors must appoint one of themselves to chair it.

Model Article (plc) 12(3) enables the directors of a public company 'to appoint other directors as deputy or assistant chairmen to chair directors' meetings in the chairman's absence'.[49] This leads to Model Articles (plc) 12(4) providing for the termination of the appoinment of the deputy or assistant chairman and 12(5) adapting the language of Model Article (pcls) 12(4) to refer to the absence of both the chairman and any director appointed under Model Article (plc) 12(3). One difference between Table A, reg 91 and both Model Article (pcls) 12(4) and Model Article (plc) 12(5) is that under the Model Articles the chairman must be more than ten minutes late (not five minutes) before the directors present may appoint another chairman.

*Voting*

**5.32**   Table A, reg 88 provides that 'questions arising at a meeting shall be decided by a majority of votes'. The Model Articles (pcls) do not prescribe any rules about voting, but assume that each director has one vote and that decisions are decided on a majority basis, subject to the chairman's casting vote and directors with conflicts of interest being disqualified from voting.[50] On the other hand Model Article (plc) 13 does prescribe general rules for voting at meetings of directors of public companies:

(1)   Subject to the articles, a decision is taken at a directors' meeting by a majority of the votes of the participating directors.
(2)   Subject to the articles, each director participating in a directors' meeting has one vote.
(3)   Subject to the articles, if a director has an interest in an actual or proposed transaction or arrangement with the company—
    (a)   that director and that director's alternate may not vote on any proposal relating to it, and
    (b)   this does not preclude the alternate from voting in relation to that transaction or arrangement on behalf of another appointor who does not have such an interest.

---

[49]   This was inserted in response to requests from consultees: *Implementation of the Companies Act 2006, a Consultation Document* (DTI, February 2007) at para 3.74.
[50]   Model Articles (pcls) 13 and 14.

The references in Model Article 13 to 'subject to the articles' would seem to be to Model Articles (plc) 14–16, dealing with the chairman's casting vote, votes of alternate directors, and conflicts of interest and any particular provisions restricting or enlarging directors' voting rights in the articles adopted by the company.

It is common for the chairman to have a casting vote to prevent the company being **5.33** paralysed by deadlock. At common law a chairman does not have a second casting vote.[51] Where the company is formed as a joint venture with shareholders having equal rights, a casting vote may not be appropriate. Table A, reg 88 provides: 'In the case of an equality of votes, the chairman shall have a second or casting vote.' Similarly both Model Article (pcls) 13 and Model Article (plc) 14 make provision, in the same terms, for the chairman's casting vote at directors' meetings:

(1) If the number of votes for and against a proposal are equal, the chairman or other director chairing the meeting has a casting vote.
(2) But this does not apply if, in accordance with the articles, the chairman or other director is not to be counted as participating in the decision-making process for quorum, or voting purposes.

Table A, reg 66 provides that an alternate director is entitled to vote at a directors' **5.34** meeting at which his appointor is not personally present. The Model Articles (pcls) do not deal with alternate directors on the ground that they are not frequently found in private companies.[52] Model Article (plc) 15 deals with the voting rights of a director who is also an alternate director for another director:

A director who is also an alternate director has an additional vote on behalf of each appointor who is—
(a) not participating in a directors' meeting, and
(b) would have been entitled to vote if they were participating in it.

Table A, reg 92 is a general provision validating acts done at a meeting of directors, **5.35** which operates as between the members themselves as well as being for the benefit of outsiders.[53] There is no comparable provision in the Model Articles, perhaps because the statutory protection given to outsiders dealing with the company, the 2006 Act, s 161 (validity of acts of directors) and the finality of the chairman's decision on directors' voting rights makes such a provision unnecessary.

*Conflicts of interest*

Articles have always contained detailed restrictions on participation by directors on **5.36** matters in which they are conflicted.[54] The purpose is to ensure that the other

---

[51] *Nell v Longbottom* [1894] 1 QB 767, 771; *Re Hackney Pavilion Ltd* [1924] 1 Ch 276, 280.
[52] *Implementation of the Companies Act 2006, a Consultation Document* (DTI, February 2007) at para 3.26. Alternate directors are discussed in Chapter 3 of this work.
[53] *Dawson v African Consolidated Land and Trading Co* [1898] 1 Ch 6. For further discussion of such provisions, see *British Asbestos Co v Boyd* [1903] 2 Ch 439; *Morris v Kanssen* [1946] AC 459, HL.
[54] There can be no conflict arising from the office of bare trustee, which involves no duties: *Cowan de Groot Properties Ltd v Eagle Trust Ltd* [1991] BCLC 1045, 1115.

directors are able to give their unbiased consideration to the matter and so discharge their duties to the company. The articles discussed below must be considered alongside the provisions of the 2006 Act regulating directors' duties: (a) s 175 (duty to avoid conflicts of interest, but subject to authorization by the directors), (b) s 177 (duty to declare interest in a proposed transaction or arrangement), and (c) s 182 (duty to declare interest in an existing transaction or arrangement).[55]

**5.37**   Table A, reg 94 provides that:

> Save as otherwise provided by the articles, a director shall not vote at a meeting of directors of a committee of directors on any resolution concerning a matter in which he has, directly or indirectly, an interest or duty which is material and which conflicts or may conflict with the interests of the company unless his interest or duty arises only because the case falls within one or more of the following paragraphs—
>
> (a)   the resolution relates to the giving to him of a guarantee, security, or indemnity in respect of money lent to, or an obligation incurred by him for the benefit of, the company or any or its subsidiaries;
>
> (b)   the resolution relates to the giving to a third party of a guarantee, security, or indemnity in respect of an obligation of the company or any of its subsidiaries for which the director has assumed responsibility in whole or part and whether alone or jointly with others under a guarantee or indemnity or by the giving of security;
>
> (c)   his interest arises by virtue of his subscribing or agreeing to subscribe for any shares, debentures or other securities of the company or any of its subsidiaries, or by virtue of his being, or intending to become, a participant in the underwriting or sub-underwriting of an offer of any such shares, for subscription, purchase or exchange;
>
> (d)   the resolution relates in any way to a retirement benefits scheme which has been approved, or is conditional upon approval, by the Board of the Inland Revenue for taxation purposes.

For the purpose of this regulation, an interest of a person who is, for any purpose of the Act (excluding any statutory modification thereof not in force when this regulation becomes binding on the company), connected with a director shall be treated as an interest of the director and, in relation to an alternate director, an interest of his appointer shall be treated as an interest of the alternate director without prejudice to any interest which the alternate director has otherwise.[56]

**5.38**   As already noted, if by reason of conflict a director cannot vote he is not counted in the quorum (Table A, reg 95) and the question whether the director may vote is to be determined by the chairman, whose decision is final and conclusive (Table A, reg 98). Table A, reg 96 gives the company the power to relax voting restrictions:

> A company may by ordinary resolution suspend or relax to any extent, either generally or in respect of any particular manner, any provision of the articles prohibiting a director from voting at a meeting of directors or of a committee of directors.[57]

---

[55] Chapters 14, 15, and 17 of this work.
[56] Formerly contained in 1948 Table A, art 84(2).
[57] Formerly contained in 1948 Table A, art 84(2).

Model Article (pcls) 14 makes provision for directors' conflicts of interest. Model **5.39**
Article (plc) 16 makes almost identical provision for public companies. Model
Article (pcls) 14 provides:

(1) If a proposed decision of the directors is concerned with an actual or proposed
transaction or arrangement with the company in which a director is interested, that
director is not to be counted as participating in the decision-making process for
quorum or voting purposes.

(2) But if paragraph (3) applies, a director who is interested in an actual or proposed
transaction or arrangement with the company is to be counted as participating in
the decision-making process for quorum and voting purposes.

(3) This paragraph applies when—
   (a) the company by ordinary resolution disapplies the provision of the articles
   which would otherwise prevent a director from being counted as participating
   in the decision-making process;
   (b) the director's interest cannot reasonably be regarded as likely to give rise to a
   conflict of interest; or
   (c) the director's conflict of interest arises from a permitted cause.

(4) For the purposes of this article, the following are permitted causes—
   (a) a guarantee given, or to be given, by or to a director in respect of an obligation
   incurred by or on behalf of the company or any of its subsidiaries;
   (b) subscription, or an agreement to subscribe, for shares or other securities of the
   company or any of its subsidiaries, or to underwrite, sub-underwrite, or guarantee subscription for any such shares or securities; and
   (c) arrangements pursuant to which benefits are made available to employees and
   directors or former employees and directors of the company or any of its subsidiaries which do not provide special benefits for directors or former
   directors.

(5) For the purposes of this article, references to proposed decisions and decision-
making processes include any directors' meeting or part of a directors' meeting.

(6) Subject to paragraph (7), if a question arises at a meeting of directors or of a committee of directors as to the right of a director to participate in the meeting (or part
of the meeting) for voting or quorum purposes, the question may, before the conclusion of the meeting, be referred to the chairman whose ruling in relation to any
director other than the chairman is to be final and conclusive.

(7) If any question as to the right to participate in the meeting (or part of the meeting)
should arise in respect of the chairman, the question is to be decided by a decision
of the directors at that meeting, for which purpose the chairman is not to be counted
as participating in the meeting (or that part of the meeting) for voting or quorum
purposes.

Issues may arise as to the materiality of the interest of the director which is said to **5.40**
give rise to a conflict. That will be for the chairman to determine and the finality
of his decision severely limits the scope for challenging his decision. In practice the
better course may be to refer the matter to the members if that is possible. Where

the director is permitted to vote in spite of his conflict he must do so in what he honestly considers to be the company's best interests.[58]

## E. Public Companies: Written Resolutions

**5.41**  The Model Articles (plc) 17 and 18 contain provisions for directors of public companies to make decisions by written resolution. These provisions may be compared with provisions in Table A, which are considered first. By Table A, reg 93, directors' decisions may also be taken through a written resolution signed by all the directors.

> A resolution in writing signed by all the directors entitled to receive notice of a meeting of directors or of a committee of directors shall be as valid and effectual as if it had been passed at a meeting of directors or (as the case may be) a committee of directors duly convened and held and may consist of several documents in the like form each signed by one or more directors; but a resolution signed by an alternate director need not also be signed by his appointor and, if it is signed by a director who has appointed an alternate director, it need not be signed by the alternate director in that capacity.[59]

A resolution passed pursuant to Table A, reg 93 would appear to be invalid where the number of directors 'entitled to receive notice' is less than the number required for a quorum.[60] Though the oral assent of a majority does not amount to a valid resolution, the defect may be ratified at a subsequent board meeting.[61]

**5.42**  The Model Articles (plc) contain a more detailed procedure for written resolutions of public companies, but in more permissive terms than Table A, reg 93. Model Article (plc) 17 deals with the means of giving notice of the proposed written resolution to the directors other than the director who proposes it:

(1) Any director may propose a directors' written resolution.

(2) The company secretary[62] must propose a directors' written resolution if a director so requests.

(3) A director's written resolution is proposed by giving notice of the proposed resolution to the directors.

(4) Notice of a proposed directors' written resolution must indicate—

    (a) the proposed resolution, and

    (b) the time by which it is proposed that the directors should adopt it.

---

[58] *Breckland Group Ltd v London and Suffolk Properties Ltd* [1989] BCLC 100.

[59] Formerly 1948 Table A, art 106. Unlike its predecessor, reg 93 allows for the resolution to be contained within several documents, and can be applied to meetings of a committee of directors as well as meetings of the full board.

[60] *Hood Sailmakers Ltd v Axford* [1997] 1 WLR 625.

[61] *Municipal Mutual Insurance Ltd v Harrop* [1998] 2 BCLC 540, 551 (applying *Re Portuguese Consolidated Copper Mines Ltd* (1890) 42 Ch D 160, CA).

[62] Unlike a private company, a public company must have a secretary: 2006 Act, ss 270, 271 (which came into force on 6 April 2008).

(5) Notice of a proposed directors' written resolution must be given in writing to each director.

(6) Any decision which a person giving notice of a proposed directors' written resolution takes regarding the process of adopting that resolution must be taken reasonably in good faith.

Model Article (plc) 18 provides for the adoption of the written resolutions pro-  **5.43**
posed by a director under Model Article (plc) 17:

(1) A proposed directors' written resolution is adopted when all the directors who would have been entitled to vote on the resolution at a directors' metting have signed one or more copies of it, provided that those directors would have formed a quorum at such a meeting.

(2) It is immaterial whether any director signs the resolution before or after the time by which the notice proposed that it should be adopted.

(3) Once a directors' written resolution has been adopted, it must be treated as if it had been a decision taken at a directors' meeting in accordance with the articles.

(4) The company secretary must ensure that the company keeps a record, in writing, of all directors' written resolutions for at least ten years from the date of their adoption.

The procedure under Model Articles (plc) 17 and 18 is similar to that under  **5.44**
Model Articles (pcls) 8, in that they both enable decisions to be taken by directors when some are travelling. The person giving notice of the proposed written resolution must give notice in writing to each director, but he may exercise a judgment as to how that notice may conveniently be given. Sending notice by email or fax to the place where the director is believed to be may be sufficient.

There are material differences between the directors' written resolution procedure  **5.45**
for public companies and unanimous decision-making by directors of private companies. Under Model Article (pcls) 8(1) the decision is taken when the directors indicate to each other their common view, whereas under Model Article (plc) 18(1) the decision is not adopted until all the directors have signed copies of the resolution. Also under Model Article (pcls) 8(2) the unanimous decision need not be in the form of a written resolution, but under Model Article (plc) 18 it must be.

## F.  Records of Decisions

The 2006 Act, s 248 requires minutes of directors' meetings to be kept for at least  **5.46**
10 years, failing which every officer of the company in default commits an offence.[63]
The substantive obligation is:

(1) Every company must cause minutes of all proceedings at meetings of its directors to be recorded.

(2) The records must be kept for at least ten years from the date of the meeting.

---

[63]  s 248(3) and (4).

By the 2006 Act, s 1135, 'company records'[64] may be kept in hard copy or electronic form, though where they are stored electronically they must be capable of being reproduced in hard copy form.

**5.47**  The 2006 Act, s 249 provides for the minutes to be evidence:

> (1) Minutes recorded in accordance with section 248, if purporting to be authenticated by the chairman of the meeting or by the chairman of the next directors' meeting, are evidence . . . of the proceedings at the meeting.
> (2) Where minutes have been made in accordance with that section of the proceedings of a meeting of directors, then, until the contrary is proved—
> (a) the meeting is deemed duly held and convened,
> (b) all proceedings at the meeting are deemed to have duly taken place, and
> (c) all appointments at the meeting are deemed valid.[65]

**5.48**  The Model Articles complement the 1985 Act, s 248 by imposing on directors a similar obligation, which is owed to the company and enforceable by members, to preserve records of informal unanimous decisions and written resolutions. Model Article (pcls) 15 provides that:

> The directors must ensure that the company keeps a record, in writing, for at least 10 years from the date of the decision recorded, of every unanimous or majority decision taken by the directors.

Model Article (plc) 18(4) contains a similar obligation for written resolutions of directors of public companies.

**5.49**  Finally, Table A, reg 100 provides that:

> Directors shall cause minutes to be made in books kept for the purpose—
> . . .
> (b) of all proceedings at meeting . . . of the directors, and of committees of directors, including the names of the directors present at each such meeting.[66]

A written resolution of directors under Table A, reg 93 is treated as if it had been passed at a meeting so as to fall within the obligation in reg 100.

**5.50**  Keeping records of decisions made by directors and of the factors taken into account has an additional significance in light of the duty under s 172 to promote the success of the company (Chapter 11 of this work). It is generally thought that this section will encourage detailed minutes, outlining the factors taken into account, as well as the decisions taken. It is possible to adduce evidence of decisions

---

[64]  s 1134 includes board minutes in its definition of 'company records'.
[65]  Restating 1985 Act, s 382(2) and (4) (with changes).
[66]  Formerly 1948 Table A, art 86, though omitting the requirement of that article that every director present at any meeting of directors or committee of directors should sign his name in a book kept for the purpose.

taken but not recorded in the minutes.[67] Draft minutes may also be admitted with evidence that they accurately reflect decisions made at the directors' meeting.[68]

## G.  Delegation to Committees

At common law the board may not delegate any of its powers to a committee, **5.51** unless the articles permit it to do so.[69] Subject to the construction of the articles, the delegation may be to a committee with a single member.[70] The directors may always revoke or alter the terms of the delegation to a committee and the board will be treated as having done so where it exercises the delegated power itself.[71] This is because a board cannot deprive itself of the power to control the company's business.[72]

Where the articles give a power to delegate, it is a fiduciary power. It may not **5.52** be used for an improper purpose, such as excluding one or more directors from the decision-making process.[73] A committee must take care not to act beyond the powers of delegation granted (as a matter of construction) by its articles. In the leading case of *Guinness plc v Saunders,*[74] the House of Lords found that a committee's powers did not extend to fixing the remuneration for one of its members.

Table A, reg 71 gives the directors power to delegate any of their powers to an **5.53** agent:

> The directors may, by power of attorney or otherwise, appoint any person to be the agent of the company for such purposes and on such conditions as they determine, including authority for the agent to delegate all or any of his powers.

Table A, reg 72 gives the directors power to delegate to a committee: **5.54**

> The directors may delegate any of their powers to any committee consisting of one or more directors. They may also delegate to any managing director or any director holding any other executive office such of their powers as they consider desirable to be exercised by him. Any such delegation may be made subject to any conditions the

---

[67] *Re Fireproof Doors Ltd* [1916] 2 Ch 142.
[68] *R (on the application of IRC) v Kingston Crown Court* [2001] 4 All ER 721.
[69] *Re County Palatine Loan and Discount Co, Cartmell's Case* (1874) 9 Ch App 691; *Re Leeds Banking, Howard's Case* (1886) 1 Ch App 561.
[70] *Re Taurine Co* (1884) 25 Ch D 118, CA; *Re Fireproof Doors Ltd* [1916] 2 Ch 142.
[71] *Huth v Clarke* (1890) 25 QBD 391, 394 (per Lord Coleridge CJ); *Gordon, Dadds & Co v Morris* [1945] 2 All ER 616, 622.
[72] *Horn v Henry Faulder & Co* (1908) 99 LT 524.
[73] *Pulbrook v Richmond Consolidated Mining Co* (1878) 9 Ch D 610; *Trounce and Wakefield v NCF Kaiapoi Ltd* (1985) 2 NZCLC 99.
[74] [1990] 2 AC 663, HL. In *UK Safety Group Ltd v Heane* [1998] 2 BCLC 208, 215, it was held (as a matter of construction) that the power to grant special terms of employment to a committee member cannot be delegated.

directors may impose, and either collaterally with or to the exclusion of their own powers and may be revoked or altered. Subject to any such conditions, the proceedings of a committee with two or more members shall be governed by the articles regulating the proceedings of directors so far as they are capable of applying.[75]

**5.55** Model Article (pcls) 5 and Model Article (plc) 5 give the directors power to delegate in identical terms:

(1) Subject to the articles, the directors may delegate any of the powers which are conferred on them under the articles—
  (a) to such person or committee;
  (b) by such means (including by power of attorney);
  (c) to such an extent;
  (d) in relation to such matters or territories; and
  (e) on such terms and conditions;
  as they think fit.
(2) If the directors so specify, any such delegation may authorise further delegation of the directors' powers by any person to whom they are delegated.
(3) The directors may revoke any delegation in whole or part, or alter its terms and conditions.

**5.56** Model Article (pcls) 6 and Model Article (plc) 6 prescribe the committees' powers and procedures in identical terms:

(1) Committees to which the directors delegate any of their powers must follow procedures which are based as far as they are applicable on those provisions of the articles which govern the taking of decisions by directors.
(2) The directors may make rules of procedure for all or any committees, which prevail over rules derived from the articles if they are not consistent with them.

## H. Listed Companies: Nomination, Audit, and Remuneration Committees

**5.57** The rest of this chapter reflects the Combined Code on Corporate Governance (June 2008),[76] which contains non-statutory requirements for listed companies to establish nomination, audit, and remuneration committees.[77] The Combined Code is at Appendix 3 to this work. The Code states that 'while it is expected that listed companies will comply with the Code's provisions most of the time, it is recognized that departure from the provisions of the Code may be justified in particular circumstances'.[78] These committees must be established in accordance with the company's constitution in the ordinary way.

---

[75] Formerly 1948 Table A, arts 103 and 109.
[76] For further discussion of developments in the Combined Code, see Chapter 2 at paragraph 2.75.
[77] The Association of British Insurers and the National Association of Pension Funds have also covered guidance on matters covered by the Code.
[78] Combined Code, Preamble, para 3.

*Nomination committee*

The Combined Code spells out the principle underlying board appointments: **5.58**
there should be a formal, rigorous, and transparent procedure for the appointment of new directors.[79]

There are two supporting principles.[80] First, 'appointments to the board should be **5.59**
made on merit and against objective criteria. Care should be taken to ensure that
appointees have enough time available to devote to the job. This is particularly
important in the case of chairmanships.' Secondly, 'the board should satisfy itself
that plans are in place for orderly succession for appointments to the board and to
senior management, so as to maintain an appropriate balance of skills and experience within the company and on the board'. These principles are discussed in
Chapter 6, Section C(2).

The Combined Code then sets out various provisions on board appointments.[81] **5.60**
There should be a nomination committee, which should lead the process for
board appointments and make recommendations to the board. A majority of
members of the nomination committee should be independent non-executive
directors. The chairman or an independent non-executive director should chair
the committee, but the chairman should not chair the nomination committee
when it is dealing with the appointment of a successor to the chairmanship. The
nomination committee should make available[82] its terms of reference, explaining
its role and the authority delegated to it by the board.

The Combined Code then sets out detailed provisions for the way in which it **5.61**
should set about its task of appointing directors. Its work should be described in a
separate section of the company's annual report.

*Audit committee*

The Combined Code lays down two bases for accountability and audit. As to finan- **5.62**
cial reporting, the board should present a balanced and understandable assessment
of the company's position and prospects. As to internal control, the board should
maintain a sound system of internal control to safeguard shareholders' investment
and the company's assets. It requires that 'the board should establish formal and
transparent arrangements for considering how they should apply the financial
reporting and internal control principles and for maintaining an appropriate

---

[79] Combined Code, A.4.
[80] At A.4.
[81] At A.4.1 *et seq.*
[82] The requirement to make the information available would be met by including the information on a website that is maintained by or on behalf of the company.

relationship with the company's auditors'.[83] The Combined Code then sets out how this should be achieved through the audit committee.[84]

**5.63** The board should establish an audit committee of at least three, or in the case of smaller companies,[85] two members, who should all be independent non-executive directors. The board should satisfy itself that at least one member of the audit committee has recent and relevant financial experience.

**5.64** The main role and responsibilities of the audit committee should be set out in written terms of reference, and should include:

(i) To monitor the integrity of the financial statements of the company, and any formal announcements relating to the company's financial performance, reviewing significant financial reporting judgments contained in them;

(ii) To review the company's internal financial controls and, unless expressly addressed by a separate board risk committee composed of independent directors, or by the board itself, to review the company's internal control and risk management systems;

(iii) To monitor and review the effectiveness of the company's internal audit function;

(iv) To make recommendations to the board, for it to put to the shareholders for their approval in general meeting, in relation to the appointment, re-appointment, and removal of the external auditor and to approve the remuneration and terms of engagement of the external auditor;

(v) To review and monitor the external auditor's independence and objectivity and the effectiveness of the audit process, taking into consideration relevant UK professional and regulatory requirements;

(vi) To develop and implement policy on the engagement of the external auditor to supply non-audit services, taking into account relevant ethical guidance regarding the provision of non-audit services by the external audit firm; and to report to the board, identifying any matters in respect of which it considers that action or improvement is needed and making recommendations as to the steps to be taken.

**5.65** The terms of reference of the audit committee, including its role and the authority delegated to it by the board, should be made available.[86] A separate section of the

---

[83] Combined Code, C.3.

[84] At C.3.1 *et seq.*

[85] A smaller company is one that is below the FTSE 350 throughout the year ending prior to the reporting year.

[86] The requirement to make information available would be met by including the information on a website that is maintained by or on behalf of the company.

annual report should describe the work of the committee in discharging those responsibilities.

Other functions of the audit committee are (a) reviewing arrangements by which   **5.66**
staff of the company may, in confidence, raise concerns about possible improprieties in matters of financial reporting or other matters, (b) monitoring and reviewing the effectiveness of the internal audit activities, and (c) having primary responsibility for the appointment, re-appointment, and removal of the external auditors.

*Remuneration committee*

The Combined Code sets out the following main principle with regard to   **5.67**
remuneration:

> levels of remuneration should be sufficient to attract, retain and motivate directors of the quality required to run the company successfully, but a company should avoid paying more than is necessary for the purpose. A significant proportion of executive directors' remuneration should be structured so as to link rewards to corporate and individual performance.[87]

This main principle is supplemented by a supporting principle, which requires   **5.68**
that:

> the remuneration committee should judge where to position their company relative to other companies. But they should use such comparisons with caution, in view of the risk of an upward ratchet of remuneration levels with no corresponding improvement in performance. They should also be sensitive to pay and employment conditions elsewhere in the group, especially when determining annual salary increases.[88]

Having set out detailed provisions on remuneration policy,[89] the Combined   **5.69**
Code proceeds to lay down the main principle of remuneration procedure: 'there should be a formal and transparent procedure for developing policy on executive remuneration and for fixing the remuneration packages of individual directors. No director should be involved in deciding his or her own remuneration.'[90]

There are two supporting principles: first,   **5.70**

> the remuneration committee should consult the chairman and/or chief executive about their proposals relating to the remuneration of other executive directors. The remuneration committee should also be responsible for appointing any consultants in respect of executive director remuneration. Where executive directors or senior management are involved in advising or supporting the remuneration committee, care should be taken to recognize and avoid conflicts of interest.

---

[87] At B.1.
[88] Ibid.
[89] At B.1.1 *et seq.*
[90] At B.1.

Secondly,

> the chairman of the board should ensure that the company maintains contact as required with its principal shareholders about remuneration in the same way as for other matters.[91]

**5.71**  The Combined Code then sets out further provisions on remuneration committees.[92] The board should establish a remuneration committee of at least three, or in the case of smaller companies two, independent non-executive directors. The company chairman may also be a member of, but not chair, the committee if he or she was considered independent on appointment as chairman. The remuneration committee should make available its terms of reference, explaining its role and the authority delegated to it by the board. Where remuneration consultants are appointed, a statement should be made available of whether they have any other connection with the company.

**5.72**  The remuneration committee should have delegated responsibility for setting remuneration for all executive directors and the chairman, including pension rights and any compensation payments. The committee should also recommend and monitor the level and structure of remuneration for senior management. The definition of 'senior management' for this purpose should be determined by the board but should normally include the first layer of management below board level.

**5.73**  The board itself or, where required by the articles of association, the shareholders should determine the remuneration of the non-executive directors within the limits set in the articles of association. Where permitted by the articles, the board may delegate this responsibility to a committee, which might include the chief executive.[93]

---

[91]  Ibid.

[92]  At B.2.1. *et seq.*

[93]  Further provisions on the design of performance-related remuneration are contained in Schedule A of the Combined Code.

# 6

# APPOINTMENT OF DIRECTORS

## A. Introduction

This chapter deals with directors who are formally appointed to the role (includ-  **6.01**
ing cases where the formal process is defective). It does not consider de facto or
shadow directors. It describes the rules relating to the required numbers of directors, their eligibility for appointment, the appointment process, and the publicity
rules relating to the appointment. Appointed directors may be either executive or
non-executive directors. The relevant statutory provisions are now found in Part 10
of the Companies Act. The provisions material to the appointment of directors,
ss 154–161, are all now in force.[1] The provisions material to publicity, concerning
the register of directors and directors' residential addresses, ss 162–167 and 240–246,
do not come into force until 1 October 2009.[2] Until then the corresponding

---

[1]  2006 Act Commencement Order No 3, art 2(1) brought ss 154, 160, and 161 into force on
1 October 2007. 2006 Act Commencement Order No 5, art 5(1) brought ss 155–159 into force on
1 October 2008.

[2]  2006 Act Commencement Order No 8, art 3(i).

provisions of the 1985 Act remain in force.[3] Reference should also be made to the company's own constitution.

## B. Numbers of Directors

**6.02**  There must be at least one director in every private company.[4] A sole director may serve also as company secretary.[5] There must be at least two directors in every public company.[6] Every company must now have at least one director who is a natural person.[7] A natural person who is a corporation sole, or who serves by virtue of holding some other office, will do for this purpose;[8] examples might be 'the Bishop of Winchester' (who is both a corporation sole and a natural person) or 'the Chairman of the Board of Governors of Anytown School' (who is a natural person but not a corporation sole).[9] These requirements were noted earlier (see Chapter 3, Section A). Chapter 3, Section C explains the difference between appointed directors (the subject of this chapter), de facto directors, shadow directors, alternate directors, nominee directors, and executive and non-executive directors. These categories are not mutually exclusive.

**6.03**  Although the Companies Act imposes a minimum number of directors, it does not impose any maximum. The Combined Code for listed companies says that 'the board should not be so large as to be unwieldy. The board should be of sufficient size that the balance of skills and experience is appropriate for the requirements of the business and that changes to the boards' composition can be managed without undue disruption.' Table A, reg 64 gives the members the power to determine any maximum number of directors by ordinary resolution, but provides that there is no maximum number until such a resolution is passed. The Model Articles (pcls) and (plc) do not contain any similar provision. It is not unusual for a limit to be specified in public company articles, although typically this may be increased by ordinary rather than special resolution. In a joint venture company, such a provision might be used in order to preserve a balance of voting power between the joint venture partners. However, balance is usually achieved in joint venture

---

[3]  1985 Act, ss 288, 289 (register of directors and secretaries and particulars of directors to be registered) and ss 723B–723E (confidentiality orders).

[4]  s 154(1).

[5]  This is because 1985 Act, s 283(2) has not been re-enacted.

[6]  s 154(2). This is so even in the case of public companies registered before 1 November 1929, because the exception formerly contained in 1985 Act, s 282(2) has not been re-enacted.

[7]  subs 155(2). 2006 Act Commencement Order No 5, Schedule 4, para 46 gives an extention of time for compliance with s 155 until 1 October 2010, if on 8 November 2006 none of the company's directors were a natural person and 1985 Act, s 282 was complied with in relation to the company.

[8]  subs 155(2).

[9]  For the corporation sole, see *Halsbury's Laws of England* (4th edn) (2006 Reissue) para 1111.

companies by having different classes of directors, with a requirement for a resolution to be supported by all classes.

The common law rule was that, if the number of directors fell below the fixed **6.04** minimum, the remaining directors could not, on the face of it, act at all.[10] But the articles may empower the continuing directors to act even when there is a vacancy or even if the number has fallen below the minimum.[11] Typically the articles provide that the quorum is two, unless set at some other number, and that where this quorum is not met, the remaining directors may only act for the purposes of appointing further directors or calling a general meeting.[12]

Even when the articles do not, strictly, empower the continuing directors to act in **6.05** the event of a lack of numbers,[13] their acts will still be valid in favour of a person dealing with the company in good faith, even if that person knows that the directors are acting beyond their powers under the company's constitution.[14] This will not, however, be the case when there are transactions with the directors themselves or with connected persons.[15] When the company is a charity, the terms of the good faith exemption are drawn more strictly.[16]

When the directors cannot act because the articles do not permit them to do so, **6.06** or because there are no directors (for example, the directors all resign), or because they are deadlocked, the default position is that their powers revert to the members.[17] Model Articles (pcls) 17(2) and (3) also give power to the personal representative of the last surviving shareholder in cases where there are no directors and no shareholders who might otherwise make the relevant appointment.

When the maximum number of directors prescribed by the articles has been **6.07** reached, any appointments over and above the prescribed limit will be void. However, the persons purportedly appointed might act as de facto or shadow directors if they purported to take up the void appointment. An appointment made by ordinary resolution may take effect as a valid appointment provided the articles allow the maximum to be increased by ordinary resolution; the resolution

---

[10] *Re Alma Spinning Co* (1880) 16 Ch D 681.
[11] *Re Scottish Petroleum Co* (1883) 23 Ch D 413; *Re Bank of Syria* [1900] 2 Ch 272, [1901] 1 Ch 115, CA.
[12] Table A, regs 89 and 90; Model Article (pcls) 11; and Model Articles (plc) 10 and 11.
[13] Ibid.
[14] 2006 Act, s 40, which comes into effect on 1 October 2009 and replaces 1985 Act, s 35A without change: 2006 Act Commencement Order No 8, art 3(d).
[15] 2006 Act, s 41, which comes into effect on 1 October 2009 and replaces 1985 Act, s 322A without change: 2006 Act, Commencement Order No 8, art 3(d).
[16] 2006 Act, s 42, which comes into effect on 1 October 2009 and replaces the Charities Act 1993, s 65 without change: 2006 Act Commencment Order No 8, art 3(d).
[17] *Barron v Potter* [1914] 1 Ch 895, per Warrington J. And see Model Article (pcls) 17(2) and (3), giving power to the personal representative of the last surviving shareholder in cases where there are no directors and no shareholders who might otherwise make the relevant appointment.

is taken to be an exercise of that power.[18] A resolution to reduce the maximum number of directors does not affect any existing directors (even in excess of the maximum) during the remainder of their current terms of office.[19] However, it prevents new directors being appointed until the number of directors has fallen below the new maximum.

**6.08**   If a company finds itself with no directors at all, it will be in breach of the 2006 Act, ss 154 and 155. It will be directed to appoint directors by the Secretary of State by virtue of s 156. The direction so given must include: (1) a statement of the section the company is in breach of; (2) the action the company must take in order to comply; and (3) the period within which the company must comply with the direction.[20]

## C.  Eligibility for Appointment as a Director

### (1)  Private and public companies

**6.09**   A significant aspect of the control of companies for the public interest is the prohibition of certain people (as a class, or specifically) from acting as company directors. Certain general disqualifications apply. These are considered below. In addition, the courts may declare specific individuals disqualified from directing or managing companies. This is done by making disqualification orders or accepting disqualification undertakings under the Company Directors Disqualification Act 1986 (CDDA) (see Chapter 28, Section D).

**6.10**   In all these cases, third parties are protected: s 161(1)[21] will render the acts of such persons, as directors, valid notwithstanding that there was a defect in their appointment, that they were disqualified from holding office, or that they had ceased to hold office. The purpose of s 161 is to protect third parties against a company relying on a person's lack of entitlement in order to avoid obligations. Its wording is more expansive than that contained in its predecessor section.[22]

### Age limits

**6.11**   Section 157 imposes a mandatory rule that persons under the age of 16 years may not be appointed as directors of a company unless the appointment is not to take

---

[18]   *Worcester Corsetry Ltd v Witting* [1936] Ch 640, CA.

[19]   *Foster v Greenwich Ferry Co Ltd* (1888) 5 TLR 16; *Worcester Corsetry Ltd v Witting* [1936] Ch 640, CA.

[20]   Under s 156(3) that period must be no less than one month or more than three months after the date on which the direction is given.

[21]   This provision replaces 1985 Act, s 285.

[22]   1985 Act, s 285 was applicable only where there was a procedural defect in the appointment of a director and not when there was not appointment at all (*Morris v Kanssen* [1946] AC 459, HL) or where a director had vacated office but continued to act.

effect until the qualification is met.[23] Appointments in breach of the rule are void. An under-age person may nevertheless be liable as a de facto or shadow director.[24]

The Secretary of State has power to make regulations providing for exceptions from the minimum age requirement.[25]    **6.12**

Anyone under the age of 16 who was a director when the age requirement came into force on 1 October 2008, and who was not exempted by regulations, automatically ceased to be a director.[26] The company's own register must be altered accordingly, but, interestingly, it is specified that there is no obligation to give notice to the Registrar of the change. The change will not appear on the register at Companies House until the Registrar is alerted in some other way.[27]    **6.13**

An under-age person is therefore prohibited by law from being a director for the purposes of the company's articles.[28] If under-age persons continue to act after their appointment is automatically terminated, then their acts remain valid,[29] and they may be liable as de facto or shadow directors. The section expressly preserves the liability of any de facto or shadow director who is under the age of 16.[30]    **6.14**

The Companies Act does not impose any maximum age for directors. The upper age limit of 70 years imposed by the 1985 Act, s 293 in relation to directors of public companies and their private company subsidiaries has been repealed as from 6 April 2007.[31]    **6.15**

### Disqualification

A person is prohibited by law from being a director of a company if he is subject to a disqualification order or undertaking under the CDDA, or is otherwise prohibited by law from acting as a director (see the detail below).[32] Under the CDDA, the courts may declare specific individuals disqualified from directing or managing companies. This is done by making disqualification orders or accepting    **6.16**

---

[23] The Secretary of State has power to make regulations specifying exceptions from this rule (s 158).

[24] subs 157(5).

[25] s 158. In Annex B to the Consultative Document *Implementation of the Companies Act 2006* (February 2007), the Government indicated that it did not intend to make regulations under s 158 and no such regulations have been made or published as a draft for consultation.

[26] s 159(2). Although the Government indicated that it would consider making transitional provisions to deal with special circumstances, relating to existing under-age directors (HC Comm D 6/7/06 col 501, HC Report Stage 17/10/06 Col 815), it has not actually done so.

[27] s 159(3), (4).

[28] Model Article (pcls) 17(1), Model Article (plc) 20 and Table A, reg 81(a).

[29] s 161 (validity of acts of directors).

[30] subs 157(5).

[31] 2006 Act, s 1295, Schedule 16; 2006 Act Commencement Order No 1, art 4(2)(c).

[32] 2006 Act, Part 40 contains provisions for disqualifying a person who is subject to a foreign disqualification order, which come into force on 1 October 2009 (see Chapters 28 and 31 of this work).

disqualification undertakings on the grounds of the following types of misconduct (see Chapter 28 for details):

(a) conviction of an indictable offence in connection with the promotion, formation, management, liquidation, or striking off of a company, or with the
receivership of a company's property or with being an administrative receiver
(CDDA, s 2);

(b) persistent breaches of the companies legislation (CDDA, s 3);

(c) fraud (CDDA, s 4);

(d) three convictions for failure to provide information to the Registrar
(CDDA, s 5);

(e) unfitness to be concerned in the management of a company as shown by conduct of a company that has gone into insolvent liquidation (CDDA, s 6);

(f) unfitness to be concerned in the management of a company as revealed by
investigation of a company (CDDA, s 8);

(g) participation in fraudulent or wrongful trading under the Insolvency Act,
ss 213 or 214 (CDDA, s 10);

(h) unfitness to be concerned in the management of a company as revealed by
breaches of competition law (CDDA, s 9A).

**6.17** Substantial additional restrictions (subject to some limited exceptions) have been
imposed by the Insolvency Act, s 216 to prevent the 'phoenix syndrome'.[33] The
goal is to prevent directors (including shadow directors) of companies that have
gone into insolvent liquidation[34] from being directors, or promoting or managing
or being involved in a company or an unincorporated business, that uses the same
or substantially the same registered or trading name as that used by the insolvent
company during the 12 months preceding insolvency. By the Insolvency Act,
s 216 breach of this restriction is an offence punishable by fine or imprisonment
or both.[35] Subsection 216(1) states that the section applies where a company
(known as the liquidating company) has gone into insolvent liquidation. It does
not apply to the company itself, but rather to any person who has been a director
or shadow director of that company at any time in the period of 12 months ending
with the day before it went into liquidation. Under s 216(3) the ex-director or
shadow director must not, during the period of five years beginning with the day
on which the company went into insolvent liquidation: (a) be a director of any
other company that is known by a prohibited name; (b) in any way, whether

---

[33] See Chapter 29, Section J for further discussion of these provisions.

[34] The restrictions apply to directors and shadow directors who held office at any time during
the 12 months before the insolvent company went into liquidation, and apply for five years from
that date, unless leave is obtained from the court (see Insolvency Rule 4.227) or certain prescribed
circumstances exist (Insolvency Rules 4.228–4.230).

[35] Insolvency Act, s 216(4).

directly or indirectly, be concerned or take part in the promotion, formation, or management of any such company; or (c) in any way, whether directly or indirectly, be concerned in the carrying on of a business under a prohibited name. A prohibited name is not only the name by which the company was actually known in the 12 months before its liquidation, but also a name which is so similar as to suggest an association with that company.[36] The test is not limited to an abstract comparison of the names themselves, but engages consideration of 'the context of all the circumstances in which they were actually used or likely to be used'.[37] In addition, by the Insolvency Act, s 217, the individual may be personally liable for the debts and liabilities incurred by the company during the period that he is involved in its management. Liability is strict and ignorance is no defence.[38] A person who is involved in the management of a company and acts on instructions given by someone he knows is in contravention of these restrictions may similarly incur personal liability.

The legislature has also imposed restrictions on bankrupts acting as directors. **6.18** Under the CDDA, ss 11 and 13, it is a criminal offence for an undischarged bankrupt to act as a director or to participate in or be concerned in the management of a company, whether directly or indirectly, except by leave of the court that made the bankruptcy order.[39] The offence of acting as a company director while bankrupt or subject to a bankruptcy restrictions order is an offence of strict liability (see Chapter 28, Section D).[40] The court may not give leave unless notice of the intention to apply is served on the official receiver in bankruptcy. It is his duty, if he is of the opinion that it is contrary to the public interest that the application should be granted, to attend the hearing of the application and oppose it.[41] 'Company', for the purposes of the section, includes an unregistered company and a company incorporated outside Great Britain which has an established place of business within Great Britain.[42] A defaulting director is liable to imprisonment or a fine, or both.[43]

---

[36] Insolvency Act, s 216(2).

[37] Per Mummery LJ in *Ricketts v Ad Valorem Factors Ltd* [2004] 1 All ER 894, CA at para 22; *Revenue & Customs Commissioners v Walsh* [2006] BCC 431, CA.

[38] *Thorne v Silverleaf* [1994] 2 BCLC 1637, CA; *Ricketts v Ad Valorem Factors Ltd* [2004] 1 All ER 894, CA; *Archer Structures v Griffiths Ltd* [2004] 1 BCLC 201; *Revenue & Customs Commissioners v Walsh* [2006] BCC 431, CA; *ESS Production Ltd v Sully* [2005] 2 BCLC 547, CA; *Revenue & Customs Commisioners v Benton-Diggins* [2006] 2 BCLC 255; *First Independent Factors Ltd v Churchill* [2007] 1 BCLC 293, CA.

[39] CDDA, s 11(1). Courts are unlikely to give leave: *Re McQuillan* (1988) 5 BCC 137; *Re Altim Pty Ltd* [1968] 2 NSWR 762; *Re Kingsgate Rare Metals Pty Ltd* [1940] QWN 42.

[40] *R v Doring* (2002) Crim LR 817.

[41] CDDA, s 11(3).

[42] CDDA, s 22.

[43] CDDA, ss 11(1), 13.

**6.19** In addition, under the Insolvency Act, s 281A and Schedule 4A restrictions may be imposed on individuals beyond the period of bankruptcy by bankruptcy restriction orders or undertakings operating for periods from two to 15 years. These are similar to director disqualification orders and undertakings under the CDDA. It is an offence for a person subject to such restrictions or undertakings to act as a director or, directly or indirectly, to take part in or be concerned in the promotion, formation, or management of a company, without the leave of the court which adjudged the bankrupt.[44]

**6.20** Finally, if an administration order (under which an individual's estate is administered by a court under the County Courts Act 1984, Part VI) is revoked because the individual has failed to make a payment required by the order, the court may order that CDDA, s 12 is to apply to that individual for a period not exceeding one year.[45] The individual is then prohibited from acting as a director of, or directly or indirectly taking part or being concerned in the management of, a company without leave of the court which ordered CDDA, s 12 to apply.

**6.21** In addition to these legislative provisions, a company's own articles usually provide that the office of director will be vacated automatically in certain events, such as the director becoming bankrupt or making arrangements with creditors. Model Article (pcls) 18 and Model Article (plc) 22, both provide that a person ceases to be a director of the company as soon as '. . . (b) a bankruptcy order is made against that person; (c) a composition is made with that person's creditors generally in satisfaction of that person's debts'. Similarly the 1985 Act, Table A, reg 81 provided for the office of director to be vacated if '. . . (b) he becomes bankrupt or makes any arrangement or composition with his creditors generally'. Articles in the above form do not prevent directors from holding office merely because they are in fact unable to pay their debts.[46] Articles may go further, and provide that bankrupts may not be appointed as directors, and that any purported appointments are void.

**6.22** Some commentators suggest that where a bankrupt is disqualified from *acting* as a director, but is not expressly disqualified from being appointed or holding office, then the bankrupt might continue to hold office, so preventing the appointment

---

[44] CDDA, ss 11 and 13; Insolvency Act, Schedule 4A, para 8.

[45] Insolvency Act, s 429(2)(b). This provision will be replaced from a day to be appointed by a new s 429(2) by the Tribunals, Courts and Enforcement Act 2007, s 106(2), Schedule 16, paras 3(1) and (2). The new s 429(A) specifies the grounds on which an administration order under the County Courts Act 1984, Part VI may be revoked, but the power to make a disqualification order is retained.

[46] Old cases are unlikely to have any continuing relevance: *London & Counties Assets Co v Brighton Grand Concert Hall* [1915] 2 KB 493, CA; *James v Rockwood Colliery Co* (1912) 106 LT 128; *Sissons & Co v Sissons* (1910) 54 SJ 802.

of new directors to fill the vacancy.[47] This is, however, inconsistent with the modern understanding of a director's continuing duties and obligations whilst in office. A director could not remain in office on the basis that he could and would do nothing at all, without being permanently in breach of all his duties as director. The assumption of duty which goes with the office must be associated with a power to act. Since a bankrupt lacks such power, he cannot properly serve in the office of director.

*Share qualification*

It used to be common for a company's articles to require its directors to hold a certain number of shares in the company. The 1985 Act, s 291[48] forced directors who failed to comply with this requirement to vacate their office and made them liable to a fine. But share qualifications are now much less common, and the 2006 Act repeals these provisions as obsolete with effect from 1 October 2009.[49] Share qualifications are not mentioned in the 1985 Act Table A or the Model Articles. The rationale behind the original requirement was to ensure that the director had a personal financial interest in the success of the company beyond his salary. However, although share qualifications are now rare as a formal obligation, in the context of public companies, shareholders may in practice expect directors (including non-executive directors) to hold shares as a demonstration of their commitment to the company and so as to align their financial interests with those of the shareholders. Shareholders will sometimes raise this issue at an AGM, or in correspondence with the company, with a view to embarrassing directors into making such investment. Many directors' compensation schemes include a Long Term Incentive Plan or Short Term Incentive Plan which will result in a holding of shares, and which may place restrictions upon disposal of those shares for a certain period. Alternatively, share options may be granted, or shadow options, both of which will depend for their value on share performance, although, in the case of share options, exercise is usually followed immediately by sale, in order to realize the difference between the share option strike price and the market value, with the result that the shares themselves are not retained for any significant period of time, and, in the case of shadow options, actual shares are not held at any time, although the rewards of the shadow option scheme will follow the performance of the shares.

**6.23**

---

[47] They refer to *Dawson v African Consolidated Land and Trading Co* [1898] 1 Ch 6, CA; *Re Northwestern Autoservices Ltd* [1980] 2 NZLR 302, CA (NZ).

[48] 1985 Act, s 291. CA 1985 requires a director who was subject to qualification shares provisions to obtain his qualification shares within two months after his appointment, or such shorter time as may be fixed by the company's articles. If the director failed to obtain the requisite number of shares within the prescribed time period he would cease to hold office automatically. If he continued to act whist being disqualified under s 291, he would be liable to a fine.

[49] s 1295 and Schedule 16; 2006 Act Commencement Order No 8.

**6.24** If such qualifications exist, they must be imposed by the articles. The articles must then provide time limits for compliance with the qualification, and state the consequences should the qualification never be complied with, or cease to be complied with. Where the articles do impose such a requirement, the following principles have been established.

(1) Articles which state that no person shall be 'eligible' as a director or 'qualified to become' a director, unless he hold[50] so many shares, impose a condition precedent to appointment. As a result, any appointment of a person not *already* holding such shares will be invalid.[51] Ratification is not possible (unless the articles are altered).[52]

(2) If, on the other hand (as is more usual), the provision is that '[a] director's qualification shall be' so many shares, this does not impose a condition precedent.[53] The articles should then make it clear when the condition should be complied with, with words such as 'A director may act before acquiring his qualification, but shall acquire the same within two months' or some other limited time.[54]

(3) The articles may authorize a director to act before acquiring his qualification, but, if they do not, it is his duty to qualify before he acts as a director,[55] and, in any event, within a reasonable time after his appointment.[56]

(4) Even if the articles authorize a director to act before acquiring his qualification, he automatically loses his office and his power to act in office if, upon expiry of the deadline, he has still failed to acquire the qualification.[57] However, s 161 validates the acts of de facto directors notwithstanding any defect which may subsequently be discovered.[58] The provision is wide enough to cover

---

[50] To 'hold' means to be registered as holder: *Spencer v Kennedy* [1926] 1 Ch 125. In *Pulbrook v Richmond Consolidated Mining Co* (1878) 9 Ch D 610 the articles required the person to hold the shares 'as registered member in his own right'. It was held that it was not necessary that he should also be the beneficial owner of the shares; cf *Venture Acceptance Corpn Ltd v Kirton* (1985) 9 ACLR 390, SC (NSW), affd on other grounds (1986) 10 ACLR 347, CA (NSW).

[51] *Barber's Case* (1877) 5 Ch D 963, CA; *Jenner's Case* (1877) 7 Ch D 132, CA.

[52] *Boschoek Proprietary Co v Fuke* [1906] 1 Ch 148.

[53] *Re Issue Co, Hutchinson's Case* [1895] 1 Ch 226, 234; *Brown's Case* (1873) 9 Ch App 102, 109 where Mellish LJ said 'according to the ordinary understanding of mankind it would be quite sufficient if a person acquired shares before he acted as a director'. But he must acquire them before acting: *Miller's Case* (1876) 3 Ch D 661, 665 (unless the articles otherwise provide).

[54] 1985 Act, s 291 makes two months the maximum time for compliance although it allowed the articles to prescribe a shorter period.

[55] *Miller's Case* (1876) 3 Ch D 661, 665, per Sir George Jessel MR.

[56] *Re Issue Co, Hutchinson's Case* [1895] 1 Ch 226, 234; *Molineaux v London, Birmingham and Manchester Insurance Co* [1902] 2 KB 589, CA, where signing a prospectus issued to the public was held to be acting as a director.

[57] *Craven-Ellis v Canons Ltd* [1936] 2 KB 403, CA.

[58] *Essendon Land & Finance Assn Ltd v Kilgour* (1897) 24 VLR 136, 146, 147, SC (Vic); *Oliver v Elliott* (1960) 23 DLR (2d) 486, SC (Alta); *Re Northwestern Autoservices Ltd* [1980] 2 NZLR 302, CA (NZ).

an appointment vacated by reason of failure to qualify. Typically, the articles themselves will also provide that the acts of an unqualified director are valid until the defect is discovered.[59]

(5) If, after a director has acquired his qualification, the amount required to qualify is increased, and he fails to acquire the additional amount, he retains his office but is deemed to have contracted to acquire the necessary qualification within a reasonable time.[60]

### Companies as directors

A company or other corporation may be appointed as director.[61] A company proposing to accept such an appointment should ensure that it is not *ultra vires* the company's constitution. At least one director, however, must be a natural person.[62]    **6.25**

### Conflicting offices or professional roles

Very few express restrictions operate to prevent those occupying certain offices, or    **6.26**
undertaking certain professional roles for the company, from being appointed as directors of that company. Of more concern for professionals is the possibility that, because of their professional activities, they may be deemed to be shadow directors of the company,[63] with all the potential liabilities that flow from that. However, a person will not be regarded as a shadow director by reason only that the directors act on advice given by him in a professional capacity.[64] This provision applies only to advice given in a professional capacity, so that the protection does not apply to commercial or other advice which may be given by a professional not acting in his professional capacity. This (limited) protection may, however, assist auditors, solicitors and, in particular circumstances, company doctors and venture capital providers from being deemed to be shadow directors. This issue is discussed in more detail in Chapter 3, paragraphs 3.14–3.27 above.

Directors may accept office with more than one company, but must in that event    **6.27**
recognize that they owe exactly the same general and fiduciary duties to each company (including those imposed by the 2006 Act, s 170(3)). Some disapplication or relaxation of duties is permitted by the 2006 Act, s 175 and s 180(4). However, subject to that, any dual appointment raises a question of possible conflicts of

---

[59] See 1985 Act, Table A, reg 92.

[60] *Molineaux v London, Birmingham, and Manchester Insurance Co* [1902] 2 KB 589.

[61] *Re Bulawayo Market and Offices Co Ltd* [1907] 2 Ch 58. The Government gave careful consideration to the question whether a company should be eligible to be appointed a director; see further Chapter 3, paragraph 3.02, of this work.

[62] 2006 Act, s 155.

[63] A shadow director is any person in accordance with whose directions or instructions the directors of the company are accustomed to act, s 251(1).

[64] s 251(2).

interest and duty which must be borne in mind in every such case. In some cases, the conflict of interest may be irreconcilable which would place the director in an impossible position. In addition, employment contracts may restrict or prohibit the acceptance of outside directorships. Breaches of duty may result in liability to one or even both companies.

**6.28**  Previously a sole director could not also be secretary of the company.[65] This restriction has been abolished in the 2006 Companies Act (see Chapter 3, paragraphs 3.49–3.57, above). Nevertheless, it remains the case that a provision requiring or authorizing a thing to be done by or to a director *and* the secretary is not satisfied by its being done by or to the *same person* acting both as director and as, or in place of, the secretary.[66]

**6.29**  An individual cannot act as both auditor and director. The 2006 Act, s 1214 restates the 1989 Act, s 27 and prescribes circumstances where a person must not act as a statutory auditor on grounds of lack of independence.[67] Indeed, an auditor cannot be an officer or employee (or a partner or employee of such an officer or employee) of the company or of any of its parent or subsidiary undertakings. For these purposes, and notwithstanding a company's articles, an auditor in his capacity as such is not regarded as an officer or employee of a company.[68]

**6.30**  Solicitors are not expressly prohibited from acting as directors, but a solicitor's first responsibility is to his client.[69] A solicitor who accepts an appointment as a company director must ensure that any possible conflict with other members of the board or with his employer or partners is clearly identified and understood by all concerned. If a conflict does arise, the solicitor must either refuse to advise the company professionally or resign his office as director.

**6.31**  It is increasingly common for people with appropriate skills or experience to be appointed on a short-term basis to rescue or turn around a company which is in difficulties.[70] Such directors are known as 'company doctors' or 'turnaround professionals'. Company doctors may be formally appointed as directors. However, they may also be appointed on a consultancy basis, without becoming directors, thereby avoiding the duties and liabilities of the directorship of what may be a failing

---

[65]  1985 Act, s 283.

[66]  s 280.

[67]  s 1214 came into force on 6 April 2008: 2006 Commencement Order No 5, art 2(1)(u).

[68]  2006 Act, s 1214(5). Section 1173(1) defines 'officer' in the Companies Acts as including 'any director, manager or secretary', but s 1121(1) extends the definition of 'officer in default' to include not only those persons, but also 'any person who is to be treated as an officer of the company for the purposes of a particular provision of the Act (which does, in particular cases, include for the purposes of liability a shadow director or a liquidator as an officer)'.

[69]  The Employed Solicitors Code, The Law Society's Guide to Professional Conduct of Solicitors.

[70]  V Finch, 'Doctoring in the Shadows of Insolvency' [2005] JBL 690–708.

company or allowing them to align themselves exclusively with the interests of a particular lender or shareholder,[71] provided they do not assume the position of a de facto or shadow director. A company doctor who does not wish to assume the obligations of a director must ensure that all decisions are made, ultimately, by the duly appointed directors, and should take care that his role is demonstrably advisory and not executive.[72]

Beneficed clergy of the Church of England have only recently become entitled to serve as company directors. This follows repeal of the prohibition in the Pluralities Act 1838, s 29, by the Statute Law (Repeals) Act 2004.   **6.32**

### (2) Additional requirements for listed companies

The Combined Code (set out in Appendix 3 of this work) contains a number of requirements relating to the appointment of directors of listed companies. A.3 requires the board to include a balance of executive and independent non-executive directors, with at least half of the board, excluding the Chairman, made up of independent non-executive directors, who should be identified as such in the Annual Report (A.3.1). However, the smaller company (below FTSE-350) need have no more than two independent non-executive directors in any event (A.3.2). A list of factors tending to suggest that a director might not be independent is set out in A.3.1; including the cases of a director who is or was recently employed by the company, a director with close family ties with any of the company's advisors, directors, or senior employees, a director with cross-directorships or other significant links with other directors, and a director who has or had material business relationships with the company. However, it allows the company to justify any determination that such a director is, nevertheless, independent in the annual report (A.3.1). In practice, investor representation bodies such as the Association of British Insurers, National Association of Pension Funds, and Pensions and Investment Research Consultants may apply more exacting standards of 'independence' in giving voting recommendations to their members. One of the non-executive directors should be appointed as the senior independent director, so as to provide a channel of communication for shareholders who have concerns not resolved through the normal channels of chairman, chief executive, or finance director (A.3.3.).   **6.33**

For listed companies, the Combined Code does not suggest (even on a 'comply or explain' basis) that directors of listed companies ought to have particular qualifications. It does, however, state in Supporting Principle A.3 that '[t]he board   **6.34**

---

[71] Steven Fennell and Susannah Dingly, 'Working with Companies in Financial Difficulties—Will You be Paid' (2006) 19(4) *Insolvency Intelligence* 49–53.
[72] *Re Tasbian Ltd (No 3)* [1992] BCLC 297, CA.

should be of sufficient size that the balance of skills and experience is appropriate for the requirements of the business and that changes to the board's composition can be managed without undue disruption'.

**6.35** The Combined Code also requires[73] the appointment of a Nomination Committee to make recommendations to the board on all new board appointments. The committee should be chaired by the Chairman of the board or by an independent non-executive director, and should have a majority of independent non-executive directors as members. The composition of the committee should be identified in the annual report, which should also record the numbers of meetings held and the attendance of members.[74]

**6.36** The Combined Code also states that every director should receive training on the first occasion that he or she is appointed to the board of a listed company, and subsequently as necessary. The extent of training, and by whom it should be given, is left open.

## D. The Appointment of Directors

### (1) Private companies

*Introduction*

**6.37** At the time the company is registered, the Companies Act requires delivery to the Registrar of a statement of the company's proposed officers, and their consents to act.[75] More generally, the Companies Act also requires particular details of all appointments to be registered and/or made available to the public.[76]

**6.38** The Companies Act does not prescribe who is responsible for appointing the directors of the company. That is left to the articles. Even when the Secretary of State acts under s 156 against a company which does not have the required number of directors, or which does not have the required minimum of one director who is a natural person, it is the company itself which is directed to make the appointment, and, in default of appointment, the remedy is enforcement against the company, and/or officers of the company (including shadow directors) by fines.

**6.39** Appointment of a person as a director of a company requires the proper agreement of the appointee before it takes effect.[77] Upon election, a director wishing to

---

[73] A.4.1.
[74] Combined Code, A.1.2.
[75] s 12, substantially repeating 1985 Act, s 10.
[76] See Section F, below.
[77] *Re British Empire Match Co Ltd* (1888) 59 LT 291.

withdraw can only resign and create a casual vacancy which must be filled by a new process; he cannot make way for the runner-up in the election once he has been elected.[78]

A person who has not been properly appointed but who nevertheless acts as a director may be sued by a member in order to restrain him from continuing to act.[79] Likewise, if a director who has been properly appointed is wrongly prevented from acting, he or any member may bring an action to enforce his right to act,[80] but not if the remedy would be pointless, because the director could and would be lawfully removed from office anyway.[81]

**6.40**

*Persons entitled to appoint a director*

Provision for the appointment of directors, other than upon the company's registration, is normally made in the company's articles. Model Article (pcls) 17 and Model Article (plc) 20 both provide simply that willing and qualified candidates may be appointed directors, either by ordinary resolution of the shareholders, or by decision of the directors. There are more detailed provisions in Table A, regs 73–80, but regs 73–75 and 80 do not apply to companies incorporated after 1 October 2007.[82] Table A, reg 76 requires advance notice to be given between 14 and 35 days before any general meeting of the company at which it is proposed to appoint a director who is not recommended by the existing directors, and reg 77 provides for this notice to be disseminated to those entitled to notice of the meeting. Table A, regs 73–75 and 80 provide for retirement by rotation (subject to any reappointment), and for retirement of all the original directors at the first AGM (also subject to any reappointment).

**6.41**

If the articles give exclusive power to appoint directors to a specific person or group (such as the board of directors, the vendor of a business,[83] or a major investor), then the general meeting has no power of appointment, although the general meeting does have the power to change the articles. If the articles make no provision, the inherent power to appoint directors lies with the general meeting by ordinary resolution.[84]

**6.42**

[78] *Hedges v NSW Harness Racing Club Ltd* (1991) 5 ACSR 291, SC (NSW).
[79] *Kraus v Lloyd* [1965] VR 232, SC (Vic).
[80] *Pulbrook v Richmond Consolidated Mining Co* (1878) 9 Ch D 610.
[81] *Bentley-Stevens v Jones* [1974] 1 WLR 638; *Conway v Petronius Clothin Co Ltd* [1978] 1 WLR 72.
[82] Companies (Tables A to F) (Amendment) Regulations 2007 (SI 2007/2541).
[83] eg *British Murac Syndicate Ltd v The Alperton Rubber Co* [1915] 2 Ch 186, and the court may enforce acceptance of the appointee by injunction unless the appointee is unsuitable on personal grounds.
[84] *Worcester Corsetry Ltd v Witting* [1936] Ch 640, CA.

*First directors*

**6.43** As noted above, the 1985 Act requires and the 2006 Act will require delivery to the Registrar at the time the company is registered of particulars of the company's first director or directors, and their consents to act.[85] The persons so named are deemed to have been appointed directors on the company's incorporation.[86] The articles may provide that none of the first directors can continue in office beyond the first annual general meeting[87] without being approved by the members.

*Subsequent directors*

**6.44** It will eventually be necessary to make further appointments after the first directors have been appointed, either to fill vacancies when a director vacates office for any reason, or to increase the size of the board. Depending upon the company's articles, these appointments may be made by either the directors or the members. Special rules may apply to the appointment of alternate directors and nominee directors (as discussed in Chapter 3). These issues are discussed below.

*Appointment by the directors*

**6.45** It is usual for the articles to empower the directors to appoint other directors, whether by board resolution or decision.[88]

**6.46** Even if there is only one director, he may exercise this power to increase the number of directors to the minimum required by statute or by the articles, or to constitute a quorum.[89] Sometimes directors are given power to fill vacancies which is exclusive, excluding, in particular, the usual power of appointment in the general meeting.[90] But the general meeting is always entitled to act to fill vacancies if the board cannot or will not act, even when an exclusive provision suggests otherwise.[91] Similarly, the general meeting has power to act if the directors are unable to appoint a managing director.[92]

---

[85] 1985 Act, s 10, which will be replaced in substantially the same terms by 2006 Act, s 12 on 1 October 2009.

[86] 2006 Act, s 16 which will replace 1985 Act, s 13(5).

[87] The Model Articles (pcls), do not do this, but see Table A, reg 73 and Model Article (plc) 21(1), which retain this provision for public companies.

[88] eg Table A, reg 79, Model Article (pcls) 17(1)(b) and Model Article (plc) 20(b).

[89] *Channel Collieries Trust Ltd v Dover St Margaret's and Martin Mill Light Railway Co* [1914] 2 Ch 506.

[90] *Blair Open Hearth Furnace Co v Reigart* (1913) 108 LT 665. Where power is given to the remaining directors to fill a casual vacancy, they may act by a majority: *Logan v Settlers Steamship Co* (1906) 26 NZLR 193, SC (NZ). Clear language is needed if the articles are to be construed so as to take away this inherent power: *Integrated Medical Technologies Ltd v Macel Nominees Pty Ltd* (1988) 13 ACLR 110, SC (NSW).

[91] *Barron v Potter* [1914] 1 Ch 895; *Isle of Wight Railway Co v Tahourdin* (1883) 25 Ch D 320.

[92] *Foster v Foster* [1916] 1 Ch 532.

The directors can only make appointments that are consistent with their powers. **6.47**
They must, therefore, respect any procedural requirements set out in the articles: for
example, requirements that they give notice.[93] In addition, any appointee must, at
the time of the appointment, meet the necessary qualifications for the role.[94]

In addition, the power to appoint must no doubt be exercised by the directors in **6.48**
a manner consistent with their general duties, including their fiduciary duties.
Abuse of the power which causes unfair prejudice to any member of the company
may justify a petition under s 994.[95]

*Appointment by the members*

The members have inherent power to appoint directors, unless the articles pro- **6.49**
vide otherwise.[96] In fact, the articles usually give them this power explicitly.[97]

In exercising this power, the members must act in accordance with the terms of **6.50**
the power granted to them. They must comply with any general or specific provisions in the Act or the company's articles relating to the general conduct of meetings or to the conduct of meetings specifically for the election or re-election of
directors. For example, if the members can only appoint persons recommended
by the board, this recommendation must be given by a properly constituted board
meeting. It will not be sufficient that a majority of the board are present at the
general meeting and assent to the appointment then.[98]

The power of the majority to appoint directors must 'be exercised for the benefit **6.51**
of the company as a whole and not to secure some ulterior advantage'.[99] The general meeting must, therefore, act for proper purposes. In *Theseus Exploration NL v
Mining and Associated Industries Ltd*,[100] the court issued an interim injunction to
prevent members of the company electing certain persons as directors, because
there was sufficient evidence that those persons intended to use the company's
assets solely for the benefit of the majority shareholder.[101]

---

[93] *Catesby v Burnet* [1916] 2 Ch 325. The relevant articles need to be interpreted carefully.
[94] *Jenner's Case* (1877) 7 Ch D 132, CA; *Spencer v Kennedy* [1926] 1 Ch 125 (both on share
qualifications).
[95] *Re Malaga Investments* (1987) 3 BCC 569.
[96] *Munster v Cammell Co* (1882) 21 Ch D 183; *Isle of Wight Railway Co v Tahourdin* (1883)
25 Ch D 320, 333, 335, CA; *Barron v Potter* [1914] 1 Ch 895; *Worcester Corsetry v Witting* [1936]
Ch 640, CA.
[97] eg Model Article (pcls) 17(1)(a), Model Article (plc) 20(a) and Table A, reg 78.
[98] *Barber's Case* (1877) 5 Ch D 963, CA.
[99] *Re HR Harmer Ltd* [1959] 1 WLR 62, 82.
[100] [1973] QdR 81.
[101] The case was considered more recently by *Remrose Pty Ltd v Allsilver Holdings Pty Ltd*, 2005
WASC 251 and *Minecom Australia Pty Ltd v Mine Radio Systems Inc*, 1999 TASC 116.

*Appointment by a nominated third party*

**6.52** In rare cases, a company's articles may give a third party (not even a shareholder) the right to appoint one or more directors[102] or may authorize the delegation of the power of appointment to a third party.[103] It seems, however, that the right may not be enforced by specific performance.[104] Moreover, the articles bind the company and the shareholders between themselves and do not constitute a covenant with the named third party.[105] They do not, therefore, confer rights on third parties which are directly enforceable against the company. This is confirmed by the Contract (Rights of Third Parties) Act 1999, s 6(2), which provides that 'Section 1 [which states the general principle of enforcement of third party rights] confers no rights on a third party in the case of any contract binding on a company and its members under section 14 of the Companies Act 1985'. If the relevant third party is to be sure that his right to appoint or remove a director is to be respected, he should seek a direct contractual undertaking from the shareholders in the company, confirming that they will act on his instructions. Finally it should be noted that, even if the agreement as to appointment is honoured, the shareholders have a statutory right to remove a director by ordinary resolution under the 2006 Act, s 168, notwithstanding any provision of the company's articles or any agreement between the company and the director.

**6.53** A shareholder who is not an executive director and who has a significant investment in a private company, usually ensures that he has the right to appoint one or more directors. This is typically done by dividing the company's shares into different classes, and amending the articles to provide that the different classes may appoint and remove a specific number of directors. This creates class rights, which must be operated in accordance with s 334, and which, under s 630, can be altered only with the written consent of at least 75% of the shareholders of that class by nominal value, or by a special resolution at a separate general meeting of the shareholders, unless, which is unusual, the articles otherwise provide.[106] The shareholder's power to appoint a director could be protected by a provision for entrenchment in the company's articles.[107]

---

[102] *Woodlands Ltd v Logan* [1948] NZLR 230, SC (NZ). Such a power, even if conferred on a named shareholder, is not constrained by any fiduciary or similar obligation and may be exercised in the shareholder's own interests: *Santos Ltd v Pettingell* (1979) 4 ACLR 110, SC (NSW).

[103] *British Murac Syndicate v Alperton Rubber Co* [1915] 2 Ch 186.

[104] *Plantations Trusts v Bila (Sumatra) Rubber Lands* (1916) 85 LJ Ch 801.

[105] 1985 Act, s 14, which will be replaced by 2006 Act, s 33 on 1 October 2009: 2006 Act Commencement Order No 8.

[106] 2006 Act, s 630 replaces 1985 Act, s 125 with changes on 1 October 2009: 2006 Act Commencement Order No 8, art 3(k).

[107] 2006 Act, s 22, which comes into force on 1 October 2009; 2006 Act Commencement Order No 8, art 3(c).

Formerly, when sole traders incorporated, the sole trader and vendor of the business to the company was typically appointed a director by the articles. He frequently had conferred upon him all the powers of a board of directors, with a right from time to time to appoint and remove other directors, and with a power to appoint a successor during his life, or by his will, or for his legal personal representatives to make such appointment after his death. Such powers appear to be effective as grants or delegations of the power to appoint new directors (rather than as powers to assign office[108]). Modern sole trader businesses which incorporate, however, are more likely simply to adopt Table A or the Model Articles and to exercise control through the shares. As control over the shares changes (for example, upon sale of the business), so would control over the board, and this would likely be required by any purchaser of the shares, who would not ordinarily expect an entrenched power over the board to exist independently. **6.54**

When the shareholders alone have the right to appoint, then the directors cannot by agreement with a stranger give the latter a power to appoint a director.[109] **6.55**

*Nominee directors: appointment*

The Companies Act does not provide specifically for nominee directors,[110] and nor do the various Model Articles. Nevertheless, it is common for large shareholders to have the right, under the articles, to appoint one or more directors to the board.[111] A nominee director may be either executive or non-executive. Although he reports to his appointor as to the activities of the company, he should not identify the interests of his appointor with those of the company.[112] Every director owes his fiduciary duties to the company and, in the absence of a specific disapplication or relaxation of those duties, they will override any duties the director may owe to the appointing shareholder. **6.56**

*Alternate directors: appointment*

There are no provisions in the Companies Act relating to alternate directors, nor in the draft model articles for private companies.[113] Nevertheless, a private company's articles may include provisions permitting a director to appoint an alternate; **6.57**

---

[108] In any event, the Companies Act repeals with effect from 1 October 2009, 1985 Act, s 308, which rendered the assignment of the office of director as such to another person of no effect unless and until approved by a special resolution of the company: 2006 Act Commencement Order No 8.

[109] *James v Eve* (1873) LR 6 HL 335.

[110] There is no statutory definition of the term 'nominee director.' Nor is there recognition of a nominee director as distinct from any other director for the purposes of the Companies Act, Part 10.

[111] Nominees are also discussed in Chapter 3, paragraph 3.31 above.

[112] *Scottish Co-Operative Wholesale Society Limited v Meyer* [1959] AC 324, HL.

[113] For public companies, and the provisions of Model Articles 25–27 in relation to alternate directors, see below.

ie a person who is typically authorized to attend meetings in place of the appointing director, and may also be generally authorized to act in place of the appointing director. Companies which have adopted Table A will have the benefit of such a provision (regs 65–69), but companies that adopt the Model Articles (pcls) will not.

### Retirement by rotation

**6.58** Articles of a private company may provide for a scheme of retirement by rotation, although the Model Articles (pcls) do not.[114] Table A regs 73–80 formerly made provision for automatic retirement by rotation (subject to reappointment) but, for companies incorporated after 1 October 2007, regs 73–75 and 80 are deleted, and references to rotation are excised from regs 76–79.[115]

### (2) Additional rules for public companies

### Introduction

**6.59** All of the powers and rules already described in relation to private companies also apply to public companies. Model Article (plc) 20 (methods of appointing directors) is drafted in the same terms as Model Article (pcls) 17(1).

**6.60** The two principal differences in the regime applied to the appointment of directors of public companies are in respect of rotation and the appointment of alternates. For those public companies which are also listed companies, the Combined Code imposes further requirements. The goal is to ensure, as far as possible, that the process is fair and transparent, and provides for appropriate renewal of talent and expertise, and that the boards of listed companies are sufficiently independent and well qualified for the task of managing the company.

### Appointment by directors

**6.61** As in the case of private companies, the articles usually give power to the directors of a public company to appoint additional directors,[116] typically exercisable by board decision or resolution. Any express limitations must be heeded. For example, the appointment may terminate automatically unless reappointed by the members at the next annual meeting,[117] or may be limited from the outset to appointments in specified circumstances.[118]

---

[114] But contrast Model Article (plc) 21 for public companies.
[115] Companies (Tables A to F) (Amendment) Regulations 2007 (SI 2007/2541).
[116] eg Model Article (plc) 20(b); and Table A, reg 79.
[117] Model Article 21(2).
[118] eg Table A, reg 79 limits appointments to those necessary to fill a vacancy or as an additional director. Model Article (plc) 20(b) contains no such limitation.

*Appointment by the members*

As with private companies, the members have inherent power to appoint direct- **6.62** ors, but are usually given such power explicitly in the articles.[119] In exercising this power, the members must comply with any general or specific provisions in the Act or the company's articles relating to the general conduct of meetings or to the conduct of meetings specifically for the election or re-election of directors.

Section 160 has already been considered above. It provides that a public company **6.63** in general meeting may not consider a single motion for the appointment of two or more directors unless it has first been agreed by the meeting, without any vote being cast against the proposal, that a single resolution is acceptable. In the absence of such unanimous agreement, a separate resolution must be proposed for the appointment of each candidate. Any resolution moved in contravention of the requirement is void, whether or not any objection was raised at the time. This statutory rule overrides any contrary provisions in the company's constitution.[120] Section 160 applies even if the resolution is for approving an appointment already made, or nominates a person for appointment, rather than making the appointment directly (s 160(3)). There is no corresponding ban on removing a number of directors by a single resolution.[121]

Although a resolution in contravention of s 160 is void, whether or not it was **6.64** objected to at the time, it may still have some result. First, s 161(2) provides that the acts of a director shall be valid notwithstanding any defect afterwards discovered in his appointment, specifically including defects arising by virtue of s 160 (void resolution to appoint). Secondly, s 160(2) specifically disapplies the application of any provision in the articles for the automatic reappointment of retiring directors in default of another appointment. Thus, if A and B retire under the articles, and a single resolution purports to pass for the election of C and D in their place, that resolution is void under the provisions of s 160, but the result will *not* be that A and B are automatically re-elected by virtue of an article providing that, in default of an election to the vacated offices, the retiring directors shall be deemed to have been re-elected.[122] Finally, s 160(4) specifically provides that nothing in the section is to apply to a resolution altering the articles, so it would not apply to a special resolution to introduce an article providing that both X and Y should be directors of the company, even when the proposal is made in a single resolution. In this case, s 160 does not make the resolution void at all because it does not apply.

---

[119] Model Article (plc) 20(a); and Table A, reg 78.
[120] The requirements of the predecessor of s 160 (1985 Act, s 292) were considered in *PNC Telecom plc v Thomas* [2004] 1 BCLC 88.
[121] *NRMA Ltd v Scandrett* (2002) 43 ACSR 401, SC (NSW).
[122] eg Table A, reg 73; Model Article (plc) 21 is more restrictive.

*Retirement by rotation*

**6.65**  In the case of public companies only, Model Article (plc) 21 provides for the retirement of directors by rotation. All directors must retire from office at the first annual general meeting unless specifically reappointed (Model Article (plc) 21(1)). All directors appointed by the directors since the last annual general meeting must retire from office unless specifically reappointed (Model Article (plc) 21(2)(a)). All directors not appointed at one of the preceding two annual general meetings must retire from office unless specifically reappointed (Model Article (plc) 21(2)(b)). This effectively provides for directors to offer themselves for reappointment at least every three years. However, it applies to each individually, rather than providing for a bloc of one-third of directors to retire at every annual general meeting as was the case with Table A, regs 73–75 (now deleted for companies incorporated after 1 October 2007 adopting Table A).

**6.66**  Regulation 73 of Table A, where applicable, provides that at every annual general meeting subsequent to the first one, one-third of directors subject to retirement by rotation (or if their number is not three or a multiple of three the number nearest one-third) shall retire from office and may put themselves up for re-election. In order to determine which of the directors are to retire at any particular annual general meeting from amongst those eligible, companies are directed by reg 74 to select for retirement those directors who have been in office longest since their last appointment or reappointment. If more than the required number of directors were last appointed or reappointed at the same time, those to retire are determined by lot, unless they agree amongst themselves who is to stand for re-election in that year.[123]

**6.67**  Where the articles provide for such a scheme of retirement by rotation, they typically also provide that a retiring director who is willing to act may be reappointed.[124] They may go further and provide that such a director will be deemed to have been reappointed if, at the general meeting at which the retirement takes effect, the company does not appoint someone else to fill the vacancy, unless the retiring director's reappointment was put to the meeting and rejected, or the meeting expressly resolves not to fill the vacancy.[125]

*Alternate directors*

**6.68**  Model Articles (plc) 25–27 provide for public companies to have alternate directors. Any director may appoint an alternate to act in his absence (Model Article (plc) 25)

---

[123]  Table A, reg 74.

[124]  Model Article (plc) 21; see also Table A, reg 80 (abolished for companies incorporated after 1 October 2007).

[125]  Model Articles (plc) do not, but see Table A, reg 75 (abolished for companies incorporated after 1 October 2007).

and the appointment may last (unless revoked) as long as, although no longer than, his own appointment (Model Article (plc) 27). The alternate director has the same rights, and owes the same responsibilities, as his appointor and is deemed to be a director for all purposes and not the agent of or for his appointor (Model Article (plc) 26). The appointment or removal of an alternate must be notified to the company in writing signed by the appointor, or in any other manner approved by the directors (Model Article (plc) 25). The notice must identify the alternate and contain his signed willingness to act (Model Article (plc) 25). Alternates are considered above at Chapter 3, paragraphs 3.28–3.30, of this work.

Table A, regs 65–69, also provide for the appointment of alternate directors[126] to **6.69** substantially the same effect. The first principal difference between the provisions of Table A and the corresponding provisions of Model Articles (plc) is that whereas Table A, reg 66 provides that the role of the alternate extends to all his appointor's functions, Model Article (plc) 25(1) stipulates that his appointment is 'in relation to the taking of decisions by the directors'. Model Article (plc) 26(1) also gives the alternate the appointor's rights 'in relation to any directors' meeting or directors' written resolution'. However, these provisions must be read with Model Article (plc) 26(2)(a), which provides that (except as the articles specify otherwise), alternate directors 'are deemed for all purposes to be directors'. The second principal difference is that whereas Table A, reg 66, provides that an alternate director is not entitled to any remuneration, Model Article (plc) 26(4) provides that the alternate's appointor may in writing direct the company to pay part of his own remuneration to the alternate.

### (3) Additional requirements for listed companies

Additional requirements for listed companies are contained in the Combined **6.70** Code. Main Principal A.4 of the Combined Code states that '[t]here should be a formal, rigorous and transparent procedure for the appointment of new directors to the board'. A listed company's board should establish a nomination committee to make recommendations to the board on all new appointments (para A.4.1). A majority of the members of the nomination committee should be independent non-executive directors, and the chair should be either the chair of the board (except when the nomination is of the chair's own successor) or an independent non-executive director.

The Combined Code (para A.7.1) requires all directors of listed companies to **6.71** submit themselves for re-election at least every three years, and sufficient biographical detail should be supplied on a person submitted for election so as to

---

[126] No change is made to these by any of the Companies (Tables A to F) (Amendment) Regulations 2007 (SI 2007/2541).

enable shareholders to take an informed decision on the election. The rules make specific reference to the need to refresh the board and maintain the independence of non-executive directors.

**6.72** These Combined Code provisions impose on listed companies a 'comply or explain', and the Listing Rules, LR 9.8.6R, require a listed company to include two governance-related statements in its annual report and accounts. The first must indicate how the company has applied the *principles* set out in Section 1 of the Combined Code, in a manner that would enable shareholders to evaluate how the principles have been applied. The second is a statement as to whether the company has complied with all relevant *provisions* set out in Section 1 of the Combined Code throughout the accounting period being reported upon, or a statement it has not so complied, together with details of, and reasons for, any non-compliance.

**6.73** The Combined Code distinguishes between 'Main' and 'Supporting' Principles. For example, it is a Main Principle (A.4) that '[t]here should be a formal, rigorous and transparent procedure for the appointment of new directors to the board'. To this, there are two Supporting Principles, namely, that '[a]ppointments to the board should be made on merit and against objective criteria. Care should be taken to ensure that appointees have enough time available to devote to the job. This is particularly important in the case of chairmanships,' and that '[t]he board should satisfy itself that plans are in place for orderly succession for appointments to the board and to senior management, so as to maintain an appropriate balance of skills and experience within the company and on the board'.

**6.74** A series of detailed Code Provisions then follow in relation to these principles.[127] These include the provision that there should be a nomination committee to lead the process and make recommendations to the Board (A.4.1). Independent non-executive directors should form a majority of the nomination committee (A.4.1). The nomination committee should make available[128] its terms of reference, explaining its role and the authority delegated to it by the board. The nomination committee should evaluate the balance of skills, knowledge, and experience on the board and, in the light of this evaluation, prepare a description of the role and capabilities required for a particular appointment (A.4.2).

**6.75** For the appointment of a chairman, the nomination committee should prepare a job specification, including an assessment of the time commitment expected, recognizing the need for availability in the event of crises. A chairman's other significant commitments should be disclosed to the board before appointment and

---

[127] The text of the Combined Code is reproduced in Appendix 3.
[128] The requirement to make the information available would be met by making it available on request and by including the information on the company's website.

included in the annual report. Changes to such commitments should be reported to the board as they arise, and included in the next annual report.

No individual should be appointed to a second chairmanship of an FTSE 100 **6.76** company (A.4.3).[129] Similarly, no full-time executive director should be allowed to take on more than one non-executive directorship in a FTSE 100 company or the chairmanship of such a company (A.4.5).

The terms and conditions of appointment of non-executive directors should be **6.77** made available for inspection. The letter of appointment should set out the expected time commitment. Non-executive directors should undertake that they will have sufficient time to meet what is expected of them. Their other significant commitments should be disclosed to the board before appointment, with a broad indication of the time involved and the board should be informed of subsequent changes (A.4.4).

A separate section of the annual report should describe the work of the nomin- **6.78** ation committee, including the process it has used in relation to board appoint- ments. If neither an external search consultancy nor open advertising has been used in the appointment of a chairman or a non-executive director, an explan- ation should be given (A.4.6).

Main Principle A.7 is that the board should ensure planned and progressive **6.79** refreshing of the board. The accompanying Code Provisions include provision for the names of directors submitted for election or re-election to be accompanied by biographical details and other relevant details for the information of the share- holders (A.7.1).

Any term beyond six years (eg two- three-year terms) for a non-executive director **6.80** should be subject to particularly rigorous review (A.7.2). Non-executive directors may serve longer than nine years (eg three three-year terms), subject to annual re-election. However, serving more than nine years could be relevant to the determin- ation of a non-executive director's independence (as set out in provision A.3.1).

## E. Validity of Acts and Defective Appointments

Section 161 provides for the validity of acts of directors. In particular, the acts of **6.81** a person acting as a director are valid notwithstanding that it is afterwards discov- ered (a) that there was a defect in his appointment; or (b) that he was disqualified from holding office; or (c) that he had ceased to hold office; or (d) that he was not

---

[129] Compliance or otherwise with this provision need only be reported for the year in which the appointment is made.

entitled to vote on the matter in question. Section 161(2) applies these provisions even if the resolution for his appointment is void under s 160 (appointment of directors of public company to be voted on individually).

6.82 Despite all the preceding comment on the appropriate process for the appointment of directors and the eligibility rules for such appointments, the acts undertaken by those acting as directors are generally valid. It follows that third parties dealing with the company are generally protected, and the company's remedy is to take action, if appropriate, against those responsible for the appointments and those acting improperly as directors.

6.83 Section 161 replaces the more limited provision in the 1985 Act, s 285, which was typically supplemented in the articles by wider terms such as those now appearing in s 161.[130] Third parties could only rely on the 1985 Act, s 285 if they had acted in good faith.[131] The material words in the new section are identical, so presumably the same limitation will apply.

6.84 Where a director has been properly appointed, he may obtain an injunction to restrain the company or other directors from preventing him acting as a director.[132] A director's shareholding and the possibility that he may be paid directors' fees may give him a sufficient interest for the court to have jurisdiction.[133] But whether the court exercises its discretion to grant the injunction is another matter. The wishes of the members of the company, expressed in general meeting, are highly material in this respect.[134] and it may also be relevant that he was appointed pursuant to some class right, but, in general, the court will not intervene when those able to remove the director wish to do so, since there is no point in merely making them go through the motions.[135]

6.85 Where it is not clear whether a director is entitled to act (ie whether he was properly appointed, or whether he remains a director), then, rather than litigating that preliminary issue, it seems preferable for the directors to convene an extraordinary general meeting to consider a resolution to dismiss the director under s 168, even if the resolution for dismissal is expressed to be conditional on the question of whether the person is indeed presently a director.[136]

---

[130] See, eg, Table A, reg 92, the provisions of which are codified by s 161.

[131] *Channel Collieries Trust Ltd v Dover, St Margaret's and Martin Mill Light Rly Co* [1914] 2 Ch 506, CA; *British Asbestos Co Ltd v Boyd* [1903] 2 Ch 439.

[132] *Pulbrook v Richmond Consolidated Mining Co* (1878) 9 Ch D 610; *Munster v Cammell Co* (1822) 21 Ch D 183.

[133] *Hayes v Bristol Plant Hire Ltd* [1957] 1 WLR 499.

[134] *Harben v Phillips* (1883) 23 Ch D 14; *Bainbridge v Smith* (1889) 41 Ch D 462.

[135] *Bentley-Stevens v Jones* [1974] 1 WLR 638.

[136] *Browne v Panga Pty Ltd* (1995) 120 FLR 34; but contrast *Currie v Cowdenbeath Football Club Ltd* 1992 SLT 407, where Lord Penrose allowed the alleged directors an interim interdict (interim

The purpose of s 161 is to protect third parties (both members[137] and outsiders) **6.86** against a company relying on a person's lack of entitlement to act as a director in order to avoid obligations. The predecessor section, the 1985 Act, s 285, referred only to 'any defect that may afterwards be discovered in his appointment or qualification', and specifically mentioning void resolutions to appoint (as in the new subs (2)). That wording had been interpreted narrowly so as to apply only when there is a procedural defect in the appointment, not when there has been no appointment at all,[138] or where a director had vacated office but continued to act.[139] The new section is explicitly more expansive, and, for example, covers directors who have vacated office and acts of under-age directors, notwithstanding that their appointment is void (by virtue of subs (1)(b)) or that they have been removed from office as a consequence of s 159 (by virtue of subs (1)(c)). Nevertheless, it would still seem that there must, at some stage, have been a purported appointment of the person to the role of director, and to that extent the words of Lord Simonds in *Morris v Kanssen*[140] remain apt:

> There is, as it appears to me, a vital distinction between (a) an appointment in which there is a defect or, in other words, a defective appointment, and (b) no appointment at all. In the first case it is implied that some act is done which purports to be an appointment but is by reason of some defect inadequate for the purpose; in the second case, there is not a defect, there is no act at all. The section does not say that the acts of a person acting as director shall be valid notwithstanding that it is afterwards discovered that he was not appointed a director.

## F. Publication of Appointment of Directors

### (1) Register of directors, etc

Under the 2006 Act, the register of directors and secretaries becomes two separate **6.87** registers, and only public companies are required to keep a register of secretaries.[141] The Secretary of State has power to amend by regulation the required registered particulars of directors.[142] The three significant changes from the 1985 Act,

---

injunction) against the holding of the meeting, saying this usurped the court's jurisdiction over the dispute and that it was not possible to pass a contingent resolution under the predecessor of s 168.

[137] *Dawson v African Consolidated Land and Trading Co* [1898] 1 Ch 6.
[138] *Morris v Kanssen* [1946] AC 459, HL.
[139] Ibid; *Tyne Mutual Steamship Insurance Association v Brown* (1896) 74 LT 283.
[140] [1946] AC 459, 471.
[141] 2006 Act, ss 162 and 275 replace 1985 Act, ss 288 with changes with effect from 1 October 2009: 2006 Act Commencement Order No 8, art 3(i) and (j), which applies to ss 162–167 and 275–279.
[142] s 166, which is a new provision, not due to come into force until October 2009; see n 141 above. The Secretary of State does not intend to make regulations on commencement of ss 162–167: *Implementation of the Companies Act 2006, a Consultative Document*, Annex B (February 2007).

s 289, which remains in force until 1 October 2009, are: (i) the director's address need not be a residential address but must be a service address (see below on the rules about residential addresses); (ii) particulars of any other directorships held are no longer required to be registered; and (iii) there is no longer an exception from the requirement for registering details of 'former names' for married women's maiden names.

**6.88** The reason for applying registration requirements to directors is that 'it is essential that the identities of those who control companies . . . should have their record in the public domain'[143] and 'to prevent the easy evasion of the legislation by persons who control companies but who either do not wish to be appointed to the board or, more typically, cannot be appointed because they are undischarged bankrupts or the subject of disqualification orders'.[144]

**6.89** To this end s 162,[145] like the 1985 Act, s 288, provides for the company to keep a register of directors, which is open to inspection by members without charge and by other persons on payment of the prescribed fee.[146] The location of the register is ordinarily the registered office (unless regulations specify otherwise) and must be notified to the Registrar. Failure to comply with the section is an offence, and the court may also enforce it by order compelling immediate inspection where there has been a refusal.

**6.90** In the case of individuals, under s 163, the register of directors must contain various particulars: name and any former name, a service address (which may be 'the company's registered office'),[147] country or state (including part of the United Kingdom where applicable) of usual residence, nationality, business occupation (if any), and date of birth.[148] When s 163 is in force it will no longer be necessary to give particulars of the director's other directorships and a former name need be given only if it was one by which the individual was known for business purposes.[149] Even that does not have to be provided if it relates to names used before the age of 16 years, or to activities conducted more than 20 years ago, or (in the case of the holder of a British title such as a peerage) to names pre-dating acquisition of the title.[150] The exception in relation to a woman's name before marriage has been removed.

---

[143] HC Comm D 6/7/07 cols 515–518.

[144] HL GC Day 2, Hansard HL 678 1/2/06 col 170.

[145] 2006 Act, s 163 replaces 1985 Act, s 289 on 1 October 2009; see n 141 above.

[146] Companies (Fees for Inspection of Company Records) Regulations 2008 (SI 2008/3007) (in draft).

[147] s 163(5), which is new.

[148] The main differences between s 163 and 1985 Act, s 289 have been noted in paragraph 6.86 above.

[149] s 163(3). Contrast 1985 Act, s 289(1)(a)(ii) and (vi).

[150] s163(4).

Section 164[151] provides for a similar list in the case of 'a body corporate, or a firm **6.91** that is a legal person under the law by which it is registered' including, in every case, the corporate or firm name, the registered or principal office, the register in which entered (if applicable), including details of the state and of the registration number, and, except in the case of registration in an EEA state, the legal form of the company or firm and the law by which it is governed.

Section 165 is a new provision, which provides for maintenance by the com- **6.92** pany of a separate register of individual directors' residential addresses which is not open for inspection, whether to shareholders or the public.[152] The information in the register is subject to the new provisions of ss 240–246, which protect directors' residential addresses from disclosure (see below). This separate register is necessary because directors' residential addresses no longer have to be included in the company's register of directors.[153] Section 165(4) makes it a criminal offence not to comply with this section, and liability extends to shadow directors.

## (2) Filing requirements with the Registrar of Companies

Within a period of 14 days from the date on which a person becomes or ceases to **6.93** be a director, or from the occurrence of any change in the particulars contained in its register of directors, or its register of directors' residential addresses, the company must give notice to the Registrar of Companies of the change and the date it occurred. Such notice must contain (in the case of the appointment of a new director) a statement of the particulars of the new director that are required to be included in the company's registers, as well as the consent of the new director to act in that capacity.[154]

The company and its defaulting officers (including shadow directors) are liable to **6.94** fines on conviction for any failure to comply with these provisions, and in the event of a refusal to allow inspection of the register, the court may order an immediate inspection.[155]

The extent of a person's responsibility for the company's failure to comply with **6.95** the duty to keep a register of directors and secretaries in accordance with these provisions is a matter to which the court must have regard in deciding whether

---

[151] This section replaces 1985 Act, s 289(1)(b), with changes, as from 1 October 2009; see n 141 above.

[152] Not due to come into force until October 2009; see n 141 above.

[153] s 163(1)(b), requires only a service address.

[154] s 167(2). Section 167 replaces s 288(2), with changes, so far as it relates to directors on 1 October 2009; see n 141 above.

[155] subss 162(6)–(8), which replace 1985 Act, subss 288(4) and (5) without change.

that person's conduct as a director or shadow director of the company makes him unfit to be concerned in the management of company.[156]

### (3) Directors' residential addresses: protection from disclosure

**6.96** The protection of directors' residential addresses from disclosure, despite the continuing requirement that they should be registered, is new in the 2006 Act. The reason for limiting disclosure of directors' residential addresses is simple. Directors have become increasingly concerned that public disclosure of their residential addresses endangers them and their families, in particular because of tactics used by campaigners and activists, for example, seeking to prevent the use of animals in biomedical research. In 2002, a limited system of confidentiality orders to protect directors who could demonstrate risk was introduced into the 1985 Act as ss 723B–723E, which remain in force until 1 October 2009.[157] Under the 1985 Act an individual had to apply to the Secretary of State for a confidentiality order protecting disclosure of his residential address on the ground that disclosure exposed him and persons living with him to a serious risk of violence or intimidation. By contrast, the 2006 Act, ss 240–246, contains a complete system of confidentiality for all directors' residential addresses.[158] The confidential register satisfies the need, considered to be important, to give creditors, the police, and regulatory authorities some ability to locate company directors. There is no requirement for the register of directors' residential addresses to be open for inspection. Although any change in a company's register of directors' residential addresses must be reported to Companies House (unless it concerns a shadow director), the information is subject to the confidentiality requirements of ss 240–246.

**6.97** The usual residential address of a director is 'protected information' within the meaning of s 240. It remains protected information after the director ceases to hold office.

**6.98** There are specific restrictions on use by companies and by the Registrar of Companies, and also specific exceptions to these restrictions.

**6.99** By s 241(1), a company must not use or disclose protected information about any of its directors except: (a) for communicating with the director concerned, (b) in order to comply with any requirement of the Companies Acts as to particulars to be sent to the Registrar, or (c) in accordance with s 244 (which provides for

---

[156] CDDA, s 9 and Schedule 1, para 4(c).

[157] 1985 Act, ss 723B–723E were introduced by the Criminal Justice and Police Act 2001. The provisions of 2006 Act, ss 240–246, will replace them on 1 October 2009; see n 141 above.

[158] The Bill originally included provisions to 'opt-in' to protection, but during the passage of the Bill through Parliament this was changed to the 'opt-out' scheme for reasons explained by Lord Sainsbury (Hansard, HL Report Stage, cols 873–874, 9 May 2006).

disclosure under court order). A company is not, however, prohibited from using or disclosing protected information if it has the consent of the director concerned.[159]

Companies House must withhold from public inspection all the information that **6.100** has been supplied to it as protected information. This includes directors' residential addresses provided to the Registrar of Companies after the relevant provisions of the Act come into force. Section 242(2)(b) provides that the Registrar is not obliged to omit anything from the public register that was registered before the Chapter came into force. Previously registered information will remain subject to any limited confidentiality orders applicable to that information under the former confidentiality regime.

The Registrar of Companies may disclose this information only (a) as permit- **6.101** ted by s 243 or (b) in accordance with a court order for disclosure under s 244. Section 243 allows the Registrar to use protected information for communicating with the director in question, and to disclose protected information to a public authority specified by regulations, or to a credit reference agency. Disclosure is subject to the conditions stated in the Companies (Disclosure of Address) Regulations 2008.[160]

Section 244 sets out the circumstances in which a court order may be granted for **6.102** disclosure of protected information. These are that (a) there is evidence that service of documents at a service address other than the director's usual residential address is not effective to bring them to the notice of the director, or (b) it is necessary or expedient for the information to be provided in connection with the enforcement of an order or decree of the court (and the court is otherwise satisfied that it is appropriate to make the order). An order for disclosure by the Registrar is to be made only if the company does not have the director's usual residential address, or has been dissolved. Application for the order may only be made by a person 'appearing to the court to have a sufficient interest' but application by a liquidator, creditor, or member of the company is permitted expressly. Any order has to specify the persons to whom, and purposes for which, disclosure is authorized.

Section 245 establishes a procedure by which the Registrar of Companies can put **6.103** a director's residential address on the public record, provided that the director and every company of which he is a director are notified and account is taken of representations made. The power to invoke this procedure is given to Companies House when (a) communications sent by the Registrar to the director and requiring a response within a specified period remain unanswered, or (b) there is evidence

---

[159] s 241(2).
[160] SI 2008. Laid in draft before Parliament and subject to affirmative resolution.

that service of documents at a service address provided in place of the director's usual residential address is not effective to bring them to the notice of the director. The Registrar's notice of the proposal to the director and to every company of which he is a director must state the grounds on which it is proposed to put the director's usual residential address on the public record, and specify a period within which representations may be made before that is done. It must be sent to the director at his usual residential address, unless it appears to the Registrar that service at that address may be ineffective to bring it to the individual's notice, in which case it may be sent to any service address provided in place of that address.

**6.104** Once the Registrar has decided to make this change, he must notify the director and the company, and the company must change its own registers. Failure to do so constitutes an offence committed by the company and every officer.[161] For directors whose residential addresses are put on the public record in this way, the publicity cannot be avoided by registering a service address other than the residential address for a period of five years from the Registrar's decision.[162]

**6.105** Section 242 sets out the extent of the Registrar's duty to guard against disclosure of protected information. The Registrar must omit protected information from the material on the register available for inspection where it is contained in a document delivered to him in which such information is required to be stated, and, in the case of a document having more than one part, it is contained in a part of the document in which such information is required to be stated. But he is not obliged to check other documents or (as the case may be) other parts of the document to ensure the absence of protected information. He is also not obliged to omit from the material that is available for public inspection anything registered before ss 240–246 come into force.

### (4) Additional publicity rules applying to listed companies

**6.106** A listed company must notify its Regulated Information Service[163] of any change in its board of directors. This is taken to include any important change in the role, functions, or responsibilities of the director (LR 9.6.11R(3)).

**6.107** Whenever a new director is appointed, a listed company must notify its Regulated Information Service of the director's name and whether the position is executive, non-executive, or chair, and the nature of any specific function or responsibility of the position (LR 9.6.11R(1)). This notification is required as soon as possible, and in any event by the end of the business day following the decision, or receipt of notice, about the change by the company.

---

[161] s 246(5)–(6).
[162] s 246(7).
[163] Such as the London Stock Exchange's Regulatory News Service.

Further information about a new director is required to be notified[164] as soon as **6.108** possible following the decision to appoint, and in any event within five business days of the decision, namely:

(1) details of all directorships he or she has held in any other publicly quoted company in the previous five years, including whether the position is still held;

(2) any unspent convictions in relation to indictable offences;

(3) details of any insolvencies etc which have been suffered by any company of which he or she was an executive director, or of any partnership in which he or she was a partner;

(4) details of any public criticism of the director by statutory or regulatory authorities and whether he or she has ever been disqualified from being a director, or from acting in the management or conduct of the affairs of any company.

Notification is also required of any change in these details (including any new **6.109** directorships in any other publicly quoted company) in relation to an existing director.[165]

---

[164] LR 9.6.13R.
[165] LR 9.6.14R.

# 7

# TERMINATION OF APPOINTMENT OF DIRECTORS

## A. Termination of Appointment of Directors of Private Companies

### (1) Introduction

It is an essential feature of the management of any company that directors' appoint- **7.01** ments are capable of termination, either voluntarily or upon the occurrence of some specified event, such as a resolution of the company. Termination provisions may be relied upon for a number of reasons: a director may be removed as part the process of accountability to company shareholders; a director may become incapacitated or otherwise unable to perform his duties; or from time to time a director may simply resign and move on or retire. This chapter considers the provisions of the Companies Act and company articles that govern termination, together with the rights and liabilities that arise in the event of termination.

### (2) Vacation of office under the Companies Act

In some circumstances it will be necessary for a company to remove a director **7.02** against his will, in particular because of unsatisfactory performance or behaviour.

Under the provisions of the Companies Act, s 168,[1] a director[2] can be removed by an ordinary resolution of the shareholders at any time. Section 168 provides:

(1) A company may by ordinary resolution at a meeting remove a director before the expiration of his period of office, notwithstanding anything in any agreement between it and him.

(2) Special notice is required of a resolution to remove a director under this section or to appoint somebody instead of a director so removed at the meeting at which he is removed.

(3) A vacancy created by the removal of a director under this section, if not filled at the meeting at which he is removed, may be filled as a casual vacancy.

(4) A person appointed director in place of a person removed under this section is treated, for the purpose of determining the time at which he or any other director is to retire, as if he had become director on the day on which the person in whose place he is appointed was last appointed a director.

(5) This section is not to be taken—

    (a) as depriving a person removed under it of compensation or damages payable to him in respect of the termination of his appointment as director or of any appointment terminating with that as director, or

    (b) as derogating from any power to remove a director that may exist apart from this section.

Section 168 is highly significant as part of the accountability of a company's directors to its owners. The power given to shareholders is unfettered[3] and may therefore be used for a number of aims. In particular, the power allows shareholders to remove directors who are performing poorly; but also to remove directors acting competently and within their powers, but in a way that may be contrary to the wishes of the shareholders. Further, the existence of the s 168 power has an influential effect upon the appointment of directors. There is little point in the directors attempting to override the hostility of shareholders, as any appointment may subsequently be terminated by a s 168 resolution. In short, s 168 constitutes an effective remedy for preserving the interests of shareholders as against directors.

**7.03** The power under the Companies Act to remove a director applies irrespective of any written agreement in the service contract.[4] As such, a resolution will override

---

[1] S 168 is derived from 1985 Act, s 303. The only change is that subs 168(1) includes the phrase 'at a meeting' to make it clear that the written resolution procedure cannot be used to remove a director.

[2] Or all of the company's directors simultaneously: *Taylor v McNamara* [1974] 1 NSWLR 164, SC (NSW); *Claremont Petroleum NL v Indosuez Nominees Pty Ltd* (1986) 10 ACLR 520, FC (Qld); *NRMA Ltd v Scandrett* (2002) 43 ACSR 401, SC (NSW). If the resolution takes effect from the election of the succeeding directors or if there is a small delay prior to the appointment of new directors, there will be no breach of the statutory requirement prescribing a minimum number of directors (see paragraphs 3.01 and 6.02 of this work).

[3] Although the shareholders are entitled to fetter their discretion by contract, and can agree not to use the s 168 power: *Holmes v Life Funds of Australia Ltd* [1971] 1 NSWLR 860.

[4] s 168(1). Removal of a director under s 168 will also override anything to the contrary in the articles.

any notice period or other contractual provision in the contract.[5] However, s 168(5)
(a) preserves any rights that a director may have in the event of termination to
compensation under the service agreement or to damages for breach of contract.[6]

The statutory power under s 168 expressly preserves any other right that a company      **7.04**
may have to dismiss a director, under common law or the articles.[7] Further, even
where a director, in his capacity as a member, may be entitled to petition for a just and
equitable winding up[8] on the principles stated by the House of Lords in *Re Westbourne
Galleries*,[9] he may still be dismissed from the board by a resolution within s 168.[10]

### Director's right to protest his removal

The Companies Act contains stringent procedural requirements, which are      **7.05**
intended to provide a director with a degree of protection. These are contained in
s 169,[11] which provides:

(1) On receipt of notice of an intended resolution to remove a director under section
    168, the company must forthwith send a copy of the notice to the director
    concerned.
(2) The director (whether or not a member of the company) is entitled to be heard on
    the resolution at the meeting. Where notice is given of an intended resolution to
    remove a director under that section, and the director concerned makes with respect
    to it representations in writing to the company (not exceeding a reasonable length)
    and requests their notification to members of the company, the company shall,
    unless the representations are received by it too late for it to do so—
    (a) in any notice of the resolution given to members of the company state the fact
        of the representations having been made; and
    (b) send a copy of the representations to every member of the company to whom
        notice of the meeting is sent (whether before or after receipt of the representa-
        tions by the company).
(4) If a copy of the representations is not sent as required by subsection (3) because
    received too late or because of the company's default, the director may (without
    prejudice to his right to be heard orally) require that the representations shall be
    read out at the meeting.
(5) Copies of the representations need not be sent out and the representations need not
    be read out at the meeting if, on the application either of the company or of any
    other person who claims to be aggrieved, the court is satisfied that the rights con-
    ferred by this section are being abused.

---

[5] See paragraph 7.34 *et seq.*
[6] In particular the right to payment for notice under s 86 of the Employment Rights Act 1996
will be preserved.
[7] s 168(5)(b).
[8] Pursuant to s 122(1)(g) of the Insolvency Act 1986.
[9] [1973] AC 360.
[10] *Bentley-Stevens v Jones* [1974] 1 WLR 638.
[11] Formerly 1985 Act, s 304 (with a minor change made in s 169(5)).

(6) The court may order the company's costs (in Scotland, expenses) on an application under subsection (5) to be paid in whole or in part by the director, notwithstanding that he is not a party to the application.

**7.06** The procedural requirements apply whenever a notice of a shareholders' resolution under s 168 is given. However, they do not apply where removal occurs pursuant to the articles,[12] which may provide for effective removal without any special protections for the director.[13]

**7.07** Special notice is required of a resolution to remove a director under s 168, or to appoint somebody instead of a director so removed at the meeting at which he is removed.[14] When the company receives notice of an intended resolution to remove a director under s 168, it must immediately send a copy of the notice to the director concerned.[15] The director has the right to protest his removal. He is entitled to be heard on the resolution at the meeting, even if he is not a member of the company.[16] In addition, provided the right is not abused,[17] a director is entitled to make representations in writing to the company (not exceeding a reasonable length) and request their notification to the members of the company. Unless the representations are received too late, the company must state that representations have been made; and send a copy of the representations to every member of the company to whom notice of the meeting is sent (whether before or after receipt of the representations by the company).[18] If a copy of the representations is not sent either because received too late or because of the company's default, the director may (without prejudice to his right to be heard orally) require that the representations shall be read out at the meeting.[19] Copies of the representations need not be sent out and need not be read out at the meeting if, on the application either of the company or of any other person who claims to be aggrieved, the court is satisfied that the rights conferred by this section are being abused.[20] In these circumstances, the court may order the company's costs of such an application under subsection (5) to be paid in whole or in part by the director, notwithstanding that he is not a party to the application.[21]

---

[12] See paragraph 7.14 *et seq.*

[13] *Browne v Panga Pty Ltd* (1995) 120 FLR 34. Removal pursuant to the articles is effective by reason of s 168(5)(b).

[14] s 168(2).

[15] s 169(1).

[16] s 169(2), and see below.

[17] s 169(5).

[18] s 169(3).

[19] s 169(4).

[20] s 169(5).

[21] s 169(6).

Unless these procedures are complied with, a removal pursuant to s 168 is likely **7.08**
to be ineffective. But if the company is able to cure the defects it would be pointless, for the court will not make orders reinstating the ousted director.[22] The special procedures permitting members of private companies to agree to written
resolutions, in Part 13 of the 2006 Act, are expressly excluded from applying to
resolutions under s 168.[23]

### Implied qualifications to s 168

As with the equivalent provisions in the earlier Companies Acts, the power under **7.09**
s 168 is subject to certain implied qualifications, alongside the express procedural
obligations set out above.

First, any removal of a director will not affect his rights under any agreement with **7.10**
the company. As such, the service agreement itself may contain certain rights or
liabilities, which arise when the s 168 power is used. The risk in such circumstances is that a director may have entrenched himself, such that any exercise of
the power of removal would result in significant financial liabilities. These are
considered in paragraph 7.35 *et seq* below.

Secondly, although s 168 overrides any contrary provision in a service agreement **7.11**
or the articles, there is no objection to shareholders agreeing by contract not to use
s 168,[24] either between themselves or in any agreement with a director. In appropriate circumstances, the court may intervene to uphold such an agreement by
way of injunctive relief.[25]

Thirdly, it is possible in private companies to put in place weighted voting rights **7.12**
that can make it difficult or impossible for the ordinary shareholders to use the
power in s 168. In *Bushell v Faith*,[26] the articles of a private company provided
that 'in the event of a resolution being proposed at any general meeting for the
removal from office of any director any shares held by that director shall on a poll
in respect of such resolution carry the right of three votes per share'. The House of
Lords, by a majority,[27] held that this was not an infringement of the rights of

---

[22] *Bentley-Stevens v Jones* [1974] 1 WLR 638.
[23] s 288(2)(1).
[24] *Holmes v Life Funds of Australia Ltd* [1971] 1 NSWLR 860.
[25] *Walker v Standard Chartered Bank plc* [1992] BCLC 535, CA.
[26] [1970] AC 1099. Cf *Swerdlow v Cohen* 1977 (3) SA 1050, PD (Tvaal) (article giving named
individual a veto). In *James North (Zimbabwe) (Pvt) Ltd v Mattinson* 1990 (2) SA 228, HC (Zim)
the articles conferred on the 'A' shareholders and the 'B' shareholders separate rights to appoint
and remove their own representative directors. It was held that only the 'B' shareholders could vote
on a resolution to remove a director representing that class, notwithstanding a statutory provision
equivalent to 1985 Act, s 303.
[27] Lord Morris of Borth-y-Gest dissenting.

members under the equivalent of what is now s 168, and did not contravene the principle that despite any contrary provision in the articles, any director may be removed by ordinary resolution. Lord Upjohn described the distinction between voting rights attached to shares and the policy of the Act as follows:[28]

> Parliament has never sought to fetter the right of the company to issue a share with such rights or restrictions as it may think fit. There is no fetter which compels the company to make the voting rights or restrictions of general application and it seems clear that such rights or restrictions can be attached to special circumstances and to particular types of resolution. This makes no mockery of [s 168]; all that Parliament was seeking to do thereby was to make an ordinary resolution sufficient to remove a director. Had Parliament desired to go further and enact that every share carrying an entitlement to vote should be deprived of its special right under the articles it should have said so in plain terms by making the vote on a poll one vote one share.

**7.13** The literal approach favoured by the majority of the House in theory constitutes a major limitation to the effect of s 168. In his forceful dissenting speech, Lord Morris of Borth-y-Gest[29] considered the decision to make a mockery of the law, in that its unconcealed effect, where the articles were so drafted, would be to make a director irremovable.[30] Lord Donovan,[31] justified the decision by reference to the need to protect shareholder-directors in small companies, which are 'conducted in practice as though they were little more than partnerships, particularly family companies running a family business', as, his Lordship held: 'it is, unfortunately, sometimes necessary to provide some safeguard against family quarrels having their repercussions in the boardroom'. In practice, the effect of the decision in *Bushell v Faith* is restricted to small private companies of this nature and has little widespread effect. Such articles are very rare in public companies (presumably because they render the shares unattractive to potential shareholders) and are prohibited in many sets of listing rules. As such, notwithstanding the strength of the criticism of *Bushell v Faith*, the 2006 Act does not reverse its effect.

## (3) Termination under the articles

**7.14** Articles may and usually do provide that the office of director is to be vacated upon the occurrence of certain specified events. Regulation 81 of Table A provides:

> The office of a director shall be vacated if—
> (a) he ceases to be a director by virtue of any provision of the Act or he becomes prohibited by law from being a director; or
> (b) he becomes bankrupt or makes any arrangement or composition with his creditors generally; or

---

[28] Ibid at 1109.
[29] At 1106.
[30] See also the criticism of Prentice (1969) 32 MLR 693.
[31] At 1110.

(c) he is, or may be, suffering from mental disorder and either—
    (i) he is admitted to hospital in pursuance of an application for admission for treatment under the Mental Health Act 1983 or, in Scotland, an application for admission under the Mental Health (Scotland) Act 1960, or
    (ii) an order is made by a court having jurisdiction (whether in the United Kingdom or elsewhere) in matters concerning mental disorder for his detention or for the appointment of a receiver, curator bonis or other person to exercise powers with respect to his property or affairs; or
(d) he resigns his office by notice to the company; or
(e) he shall for more than six consecutive months have been absent without permission of the directors from meetings of directors held during that period and the directors resolve that his office be vacated.

**7.15** Model Article (pcls) 18 provides that:

A person ceases to be a director as soon as:
(a) that person ceases to be a director by virtue of any provision of the Companies Act 2006 or is prohibited from being a director by law;
(b) a bankruptcy order is made against that person;[32]
(c) a composition is made with that person's creditors generally in satisfaction of that person's debts;
(d) a registered medical practitioner who is treating that person gives a written opinion to the company stating that that person has become physically or mentally incapable of acting as a director and may remain so for more than three months;
(e) by reason of that person's mental health, a court makes an order which wholly or partly prevents that person from personally exercising any powers or rights which that person would otherwise have;
(f) a notification is received by the company from the director that the director is resigning or retirement from office as director and such resignation or retirement has taken effect in accordance with its terms.

**7.16** Model Article (plc) 22 is in identical terms to that Article.

**7.17** Further, a company's articles may provide that the office of director will be vacated for any number of specified circumstances considered inappropriate or inconsistent with the role. In the past articles have provided that a director may be removed if he is concerned or interested in contracts made with the company,[33] accepts or holds an office of profit under the company,[34] or fails to acquire share qualification within a stated time or ceases to hold necessary share qualification.

---

[32] This does not bar from holding office an individual whose bankruptcy dates from the time of their appointment: *Dawson v African Consolidated Land and Trading Co* [1898] 1 Ch 6, CA; *Re Northwestern Autoservices Ltd* [1980] 2 NZLR 302, CA (NZ).

[33] This may apply where the director holds shares in a contracting company: *Turnbull v West Riding Club* (1894) 70 LT 92; *Todd v Robinson* (1884) 14 QBD 739; *Dimes v Grand Junction Canal Co* (1852) 3 HLC 759. However, modern articles commonly permit interests in contracts.

[34] *Astley v New Tivoli Ltd* [1899] 1 Ch 151; cf *Iron Ship Coating Co v Blunt* (1868) LR 3 CP 484 in which a director appointed as an unpaid company secretary was not disqualified. Modern articles now usually permit such activities, other than that of auditor.

Those provisions are unlikely to be considered suitable for modern companies, since few have share qualification requirements and the 2006 Act provides other means of dealing with conflicts of interest.[35] Articles may also provide for vacation of office if a director is convicted of an indictable offence,[36] or is absent from meetings of directors for a long period.

7.18 Interpretation of the particular provision for automatic vacation of office can be crucial. For example, in interpreting the words 'if he absents himself' (from board meetings), the courts have held that this means voluntary absence, and absence through sickness would not result in disqualification.[37] In interpreting articles providing for disqualification 'if he is concerned in any contract', it has been held that a director would be disqualified even though the contract he is concerned in is one that he could not profit from.[38]

7.19 If the articles provide for automatic vacation[39] when certain circumstances arise, the vacation is effective without a resolution and cannot be waived by the directors.[40] However, a person who is automatically removed from office by virtue of the company's articles may be reappointed when the disqualifying circumstances no longer apply.[41]

*Resignation of directors*

7.20 The company's articles and the director's contract of service generally specify the terms for retirement or resignation. Subject to those terms, however, the general rule is that a director is entitled to resign at any time by giving notice to the company. Resignation is effected by the giving of notice, and does not depend upon acceptance by the company. Even if the articles provide that notice of resignation is to be in writing, oral resignation is effective if accepted,[42] as is the submission of the appropriate form[43] to the Registrar by the resigning director, with resignation acknowledged in the annual return.[44] Once notice has been given, it cannot be withdrawn except by agreement with the company.[45] No minimum period of notice is required to resign the position of director.[46]

---

[35] See Chapter 14.
[36] Even if the indictable offence is tried summarily: *Hastings & Folkestone Glassworks v Kalson* [1949] 1 KB 214, CA.
[37] *Mack's Claim* [1900] WN 114; *McConnell's Case* [1901] 1 Ch 728.
[38] *Star Steam Laundry Co v Dukas* [1913] WN 39.
[39] For example where the articles provide that 'a director's office is vacated in the following circumstances . . .'.
[40] *Re Bodega Co Ltd* [1904] 1 Ch 276.
[41] Ibid.
[42] *Latchford Premier Cinema Ltd v Ennion* [1931] 2 Ch 409.
[43] Form 288b.
[44] *Aberdeen Water Technologists v Henderson* 2000 GWD 20-783 (Sheriff Court).
[45] *Glossop v Glossop* [1907] 2 Ch 370.
[46] *OBC Caspian Ltd v Thorp* 1998 SLT 653. Notice may however be required under the service contract. See paragraph 7.36 *et seq* below.

A director may resign his office at any time, even if the articles do not provide such **7.21** a power. The only exception is where the articles contain positive conditions for resignation. The resignation is complete when notice is given to the company (even though no acceptance has taken place) and it cannot subsequently be withdrawn except with the consent of the company.

Even though a person's resignation from the directorship of a company may seri- **7.22** ously damage the company, it is not in breach of the director's fiduciary duty to the company.[47] However, an executive director who breaches his service contract by leaving without giving the required period of notice may be liable to the company for damages suffered as a result.[48]

As noted, sometimes a company's articles will specify a procedure to be followed **7.23** for giving effect to a resignation from office of a director. Model Article (pcls) 18(f) and Model Article (plc) 22(f), for instance, provide that the office of a director shall be vacated upon the company receiving notice that he is resigning and such resignation has taken effect in accordance with its terms.[49] In such circumstances, resignation will be effective upon the completion of the notice period.

Retirement or resignation by rotation is considered at paragraph 7.26. **7.24**

## B. Additional Rules for Public Companies

*Dismissal by unanimous decision of directors*

Earlier drafts of the Model Articles (plc) included provision for the directors of **7.25** a public company to remove a director by unanimous decision, but this was not included in the final version. The rationale behind the inclusion of such a provision is that it allows directors, when acting unanimously, to deal with disruptive directors without the publicity and procedural difficulties of the Companies Act, s 168. Similar articles will often allow a company to detail procedures to remove a director by conferring a power of removal upon all, or a specified majority, of the directors. However in the absence of such a power, the board has no inherent right to remove a director from office, and a company will be obliged to use the power in s 168. Directors must act in the best interests of the company, and not for an

---

[47] *CMS Dolphin Ltd v Simonet* [2001] 2 BCLC 704. Although a director who no longer wishes to perform his duties or finds it impossible to do so may resign (*Re Galeforce Pleating Co Ltd* [1999] 2 BCLC 704, 716), he may be required to deal with pressing matters before he goes or, exceptionally, put relevant information into the hands of the hands of the proper organs of the company if he is not satisfied that the continuing directors will deal properly with the matter of concern (eg a fellow director's criminal convictions): *Lexi Holdings plc v Luqman* [2008] 2 BCLC 725 at para 39.

[48] Ibid.

[49] Table A, reg 81(d) provides for a director to vacate office if he resigns his office by notice to the company.

ulterior motive, when issuing such a notice, although the fact that they are acting for an ulterior motive does not itself invalidate a notice.[50]

*Retirement by rotation*

**7.26**  Private companies rarely choose to include articles providing for retirement of directors by rotation and there is no such provision in the Model Articles (pcls). Table A, regs 73–77 contain detailed provisions for the retirement of directors by rotation, which are seldom of relevance or benefit to private companies. However, public companies often do include an article providing for retirement by rotation. This is reflected in Model Article (plc) 21, which provides for retirement of directors by rotation:

(1)  At the first annual general meeting all the directors must retire from office.
(2)  At every subsequent annual general meeting any directors—
    (a)  who have been appointed by the directors since the last annual general meeting, or
    (b)  who were not appointed at one of the preceding two annual general meetings,
must retire from office and may offer themselves for reappointment by the members.

**7.27**  As such, the Model Articles envisage a period of office of no more than three years for any director, before he may offer himself for reappointment by the members. Further, any director appointed outside of the AGM must offer himself for reappointment at the next AGM, ensuring that shareholders have the opportunity to sanction any appointment at an early stage.

**7.28**  Articles which provide for retirement by rotation usually make special provision for the choice of the directors who will retire, and for the process of election of new directors. In every case, the articles are interpreted strictly. For example, where an article provides for the retirement of one-third of the directors (or the nearest number to one-third), and there are only two directors subject to such provision, neither is bound to retire.[51] Equally, a provision that a retiring director be deemed re-elected will operate notwithstanding that an express resolution to re-elect a retiring director has been defeated, even if a resolution, which proves to be invalid, is passed to appoint some other person in his place.[52] If a retiring director is re-elected, or deemed to be re-elected, his retirement does not constitute a vacation of office.[53]

**7.29**  A similar regime applies to listed companies. Paragraph A.7 of the Combined Code requires all directors to be submitted for re-election every three years (or one year in the case of an independent non-executive director in office for more than nine years), subject to continued satisfactory performance. Paragraph A.7.1

---

[50]  *Lee v Chou Wen Hsien* [1984] 1 WLR 1202, PC. Also see Ch 11.
[51]  *Re David Moseley & Sons* [1939] Ch 719.
[52]  *Holt v Catterall* (1931) 47 TLR 322; *Grundt v Great Boulder Proprietary Mines* [1948] Ch 145, CA, disapproving *Robert Batcheller & Son v Batcheller* [1945] Ch 169.
[53]  *Walker v Kenns* [1937] 1 All ER 566, CA.

provides that directors must submit themselves for election by shareholders at the first AGM after their appointment and thereafter at intervals of no more than three years. Sufficient biographical details of all directors subject to election must be provided to enable shareholders to make an informed decision as to their re-election.

## C. Effect of Termination of Appointment

Where directors continue to act as directors after their office is vacated, for whatever reason, their acts will continue to bind the company.[54]   **7.30**

Although a director may be validly removed as a matter of company law, he may still have the benefit of certain rights by reason of his status as an employee or worker of the company.[55] As such, many company articles provide that the appointment of managing director terminates if he ceases to be a director of the company.[56] In such circumstances, a company may incur liability to the director under his service contract. Further, a director employed under a service contract will have the benefit of statutory employment rights, which may apply in the event of his removal. As such, a valid removal of a director under the Companies Act or articles of association may still result in liabilities to the director under contract or statute.   **7.31**

Conversely, depending on the terms of his service contract, a director may still remain a company director despite being dismissed under the terms of his service agreement, until he resigns or is removed from office.   **7.32**

Where a director is removed from office, his right to inspect the company's books terminates.[57] This is because the right exists in order to allow a director to perform his duties, which lapse upon removal.   **7.33**

## D. Rights and Liabilities in the Event of Termination

In the event of removal, a company may have liabilities to a director arising under the terms of the service contract and by reason of employment legislation. Similarly, where a director resigns in breach of contract, he may also have liabilities to the company.   **7.34**

---

[54] s 161(1)(c); *Muir v Forman's Trustees* (1904) 5 F 546 (Court Sess Ca).
[55] See Chapter 8 regarding the employment status of a director.
[56] See *Southern Foundries Ltd v Shirlaw* [1940] AC 701, HL.
[57] *Conway v Petronius Clothing Co* [1978] 1 WLR 72.

### (1) Rights arising under the service contract

**7.35**  Service contracts for directors often make detailed provision regarding the consequences of termination. This section considers notice periods (statutory and contractual notice, PILON, and garden leave clauses), summary dismissal for gross
misconduct, and remedies for wrongful dismissal. The next section of this chapter
considers statutory rights in the event of termination.

*Notice periods*

**7.36**  Directors who are employed under service contracts are, normally,[58] entitled to
minimum periods of notice, either under statute or under the terms of the contract itself (either through express provision or by an implied term). However, no
notice is required to terminate a service contract by reason of gross misconduct, as
discussed below.[59]

**7.37**  A significant exception to this principle applies when the service contract is silent
as to notice and the articles of association at the time of appointment[60] provide
that the contract shall terminate automatically upon ceasing to be a director.
In such circumstances, if a company exercises its power under s 168, or any other
power under the articles, and removes a director, this will be effective to bring the
service contract to an end immediately.[61]

**7.38**  Under normal contractual principles, the giving of notice is operative to terminate the contract. As such, once notice is given by either side, there is no unilateral
right to rescind, notwithstanding that the director may remain in employment
whilst he serves his notice period.[62] Whether a director has in fact given notice will
not always be apparent. Where there is ambiguity, the issue of whether a director
has resigned must be determined objectively by reference to the understanding of
a reasonable recipient.[63]

---

[58] There may be no entitlement to notice where the parties agree to immediate termination
or the director is engaged to perform a specific task, which upon completion, discharges the
contract through performance: *Wiltshire County Council v NATFHE* [1980] ICR 455,
per Lord Denning MR. Further, there will be no entitlement to notice where the service contract is frustrated (which may occur for example when a director is imprisoned): *C Shepherd &
Co Ltd v Jerrom* [1987] QB 301, CA. See also *G F Sharp & Co Ltd v McMillan* [1998]
IRLR 632, EAT.

[59] At paragraph 7.48.

[60] If a company changes its articles to grant itself a power to dismiss which is contrary to the service agreement, it will be in breach of contract if it exercises the power: *Southern Foundries v Shirlaw*
[1940] AC 701, HL; *Shindler v Northern Raincoat Co Ltd* [1960] 1 WLR 1038.

[61] *Read v Astoria Garage (Streatham) Ltd* [1952] Ch 637, CA.

[62] *Riordan v War Office* [1959] 1 WLR 1046 (affirmed [1960] 1 WLR 210, CA).

[63] *Quarter Master UK Ltd v Pyke* [2004] EWHC 1815 (Ch), applying *Mannai Investment Co Ltd v
Eagle Star Life Assurance Co Ltd* [1997] AC 749, HL.

## Statutory minimum periods of notice

A director who has been employed for a month or longer is entitled to a minimum period of notice, based upon length of service. Directors who have been continuously employed for longer than one month are entitled to a notice period of one week, increasing by an additional week for each additional continuous year of service up to a maximum of 12 weeks.[64] As the statutory right to notice takes effect as an implied term of the service agreement, it can be enforced as an action for breach of contract.  **7.39**

A company also has a right to a minimum notice period of one week from a director who has been continuously employed for longer than one month.[65]  **7.40**

## Contractual notice periods

Depending on the terms of his service agreement, a director may (and usually will) be entitled to a longer period of notice than that provided by statute. Any termination by either party without the relevant period of notice is effective to terminate the contract, but will amount to a breach of contract (and therefore give rise to an action for damages).  **7.41**

Occasionally, a service contract will be silent as to the relevant period of notice. In such circumstances, the court will infer that the contract is capable of termination upon reasonable notice.[66] Factors that the court will take into account when determining what is reasonable in any given set of circumstances include seniority, nature of employment, and length of service.[67] Further, courts may take into account the frequency of salary payments[68] or any existing custom of the trade.[69] Any notice period implied by contract cannot, however, be less than the statutory minimum.[70]  **7.42**

## PILON clauses

Directors' service agreements will often include a clause allowing the company to make a PILON. The effect of a PILON clause is a matter of contractual construction in any given case. Typically, a PILON clause will confer upon the company  **7.43**

---

[64] Employment Rights Act 1996 (ERA), s 86.

[65] ERA, s 86(2).

[66] *Baxter v Nurse* (1844) 6 Man & G 935; *McClelland v Northern Ireland General Health Service Board* [1957] 1 WLR 594, per Lord Oaksey at 599; *Reda v Flag Ltd* [2002] IRLR 747, per Lord Millett at para 57.

[67] *CMS Dolphin Ltd v Simonet* [2001] 2 BCLC 704 (three months for an executive director of an advertising agency).

[68] *Marshall v English Electric Co Ltd* [1945] 1 All ER 653 (hourly); *Baxter v Nurse* (1844) 6 Man & G 935 (weekly); see also *Nokes v Doncaster Amalgamated Collieries Ltd* [1940] AC 1014, 1028 per Lord Atkin.

[69] See *Nokes v Doncaster Amalgamated Collieries Ltd* [1940] AC 1014, 1028.

[70] *Hill v C A Parsons & Co Ltd* [1972] Ch 305, CA.

a discretion to dismiss a director immediately, upon payment of the full amount of notice period salary as a lump sum.[71] Alternatively, a company may summarily dismiss the director, having previously agreed to offer a payment in lieu of notice (even where the service agreement does not confer an express right). In such circumstances, the parties have agreed to vary the contract and the payment is lawful.[72]

**7.44** If the contract does not contain a PILON clause, there is no common law right to tender payment in lieu of notice without the agreement of the director.[73] As such, payment of salary in lieu of notice without agreement would normally constitute wrongful dismissal on the part of the employer. There are potential implications for a company that takes this step. A director may still have suffered loss in such circumstances if, for example, he would have been entitled to a contractual bonus during the notice period.[74] Further, wrongful dismissal may have the effect of releasing a director from any restrictive covenants to which he would otherwise have been bound.[75]

*Garden leave*

**7.45** Many directors' service contracts include an express provision allowing the employer to suspend a director from his normal duties for the duration of his notice period. Alternatively, in the absence of a written provision in the service contract, the parties may agree that a director is not required to carry out any work. An express contractual suspension of this nature is commonly referred to as 'garden leave', as the director in question is expected not to carry out any work at all, and therefore might choose to spend his time in his garden. The benefit is that the director cannot enter into employment with a competitor for the period of garden leave, providing the company with an opportunity to recruit a successor (if no succession plan is in place). Further, any confidential information that the director might otherwise take to a rival is more likely to go stale if the director no longer has access to the company premises and records.

**7.46** In certain circumstances, a service contract may include an implied right to place a director on garden leave. However, whether it will be possible in any given instance depends upon the nature of the director's position together with the express terms of the service agreement. In *William Hill v Tucker*,[76] the Court of

---

[71] *Delaney v Staples* [1992] 1 AC 687, HL, per Lord Browne-Wilkinson.

[72] Ibid.

[73] See the decision of the Scottish Inner House of the Court of Session in *Morrish v NTL Group* [2007] CSIH 56 rejecting an argument that a PILON clause could be implied into a financial director/company secretary's service contract.

[74] *Morrish v NTL Group* [2007] CSIH 56.

[75] See paragraph 8.66 below.

[76] [1999] ICR 291, CA.

Appeal held that there was no implied right to place a senior employee on garden leave in circumstances where his seniority, unique position, and the presence of contractual terms encouraging development of personal skills, meant that the employee had a 'right to work'. However, as noted by the Court of Appeal in *Tucker*, where the service contract contains an express contractual provision allowing garden leave, there would be no need to consider whether the company had an implied right to place a director on garden leave. As such, to avoid this difficulty, garden leave clauses are now commonly found in directors' service contracts.

Where the service contract does not contain a garden leave clause, a company may **7.47** still have an implied right to place a director on garden leave where the director is himself in prior breach of contract. In *SG&R Valuation Service v Boudrais*,[77] Cranston J held that a company was entitled to place two directors on garden leave in the absence of an express power, where their earlier competitive activity had made it impossible for the company to offer continuing work.

*Summary dismissal for gross misconduct*

The main exception to the principle that notice must be given before termination **7.48** of a service agreement applies where the company dismisses a director for gross misconduct. Gross misconduct is the term used in employment law to describe any conduct on the part of the employee sufficiently serious to justify termination without notice[78] (including the statutory minimum period of notice).

The categories of gross misconduct have developed over time to reflect changing **7.49** values.[79] As held in *Neary v Dean of Westminster*[80] whether particular misconduct justifies summary dismissal is a question of fact. The character of the company, the role played by the director in the company, and the degree of trust required of the director vis-à-vis the company must all be considered in determining the extent of the duty of trust and the seriousness of any breach thereof.[81] Any director (and in particular a director occupying a central role in the management of the company, such as a managing director) will normally therefore be held to a higher standard than a mere employee.

A breach of fiduciary duty will inevitably constitute gross misconduct, whether or **7.50** not it was known to the employer at the time of dismissal.[82] However, a director will not be guilty of gross misconduct merely by indicating his intention to set up

---

[77] [2008] IRLR 770, QB.

[78] *Laws v London Chronicle (Indicator Newspapers) Ltd* [1959] 1 WLR 698, CA; *Wilson v Racher* [1974] ICR 428, CA.

[79] *Laws v London Chronicle (Indicator Newspapers) Ltd* [1959] 1 WLR 698, CA.

[80] [1999] IRLR 288, per Lord Jauncey sitting as Special Commissioner.

[81] Ibid.

[82] *Item Software v Fassihi* [2005] 2 BCLC 91, CA.

in competition in the future[83] providing any steps that he takes to do so do not go beyond preparatory steps.[84]

*Constructive dismissal*

**7.51**   Not all dismissals occur when a director is sacked by the company. A director is entitled to treat himself as having been dismissed, where he resigns in response to some sufficiently serious conduct on the part of the company (known as 'constructive dismissal').[85] However, mere unreasonable conduct is not enough; rather the conduct must be sufficient to constitute a breach of the service contract so as to justify the director treating the contract as at an end.[86] Further, the director must leave in response to the breach and must not delay unreasonably doing so.[87] If these conditions are not met, the director will be taken to have resigned.

**7.52**   The acts that may constitute constructive dismissal are wide and varied. Examples include subjecting an employee to insulting language;[88] imposing a disproportionate disciplinary sanction for a minor incident;[89] and arbitrarily imposing an inferior pay rise as compared to other employees.[90] Notably, any attempt to impose changes in conditions which are not permitted by the terms of the service contract may amount to a constructive dismissal, including changing a place of work without a mobility clause;[91] cutting pay;[92] or requiring an employee to relinquish his job in favour of another role.[93] The making of hostile comments in the boardroom cannot however constitute constructive dismissal, as the board is the controlling mind of the company and representations between individuals on the board is merely equivalent to the company thinking aloud to itself, which may include even negative and unworthy thoughts about a director.[94]

**7.53**   In *RDF Media Group plc v Clements*,[95] the court held that a director is not entitled to claim constructive dismissal, even where he meets all of the conditions discussed above, if he is himself in repudiatory breach of contract at the time of

---

[83]   *Adamson v B & L Cleaning Services Ltd* [1995] IRLR 193, EAT.
[84]   *Shepherds Investments v Walters* [2007] IRLR 110; *Helmet Integrated Systems Ltd v Tunnard* [2007] IRLR 126.
[85]   See also ERA, s 95(1)(c).
[86]   *Western Excavating (ECC) Ltd v Sharp* [1978] ICR 221.
[87]   *Walker v Josiah Wedgwood & Sons Ltd* [1978] IRLR 105. The breach need not be the sole cause, but may simply be an 'effective cause': *Jones v F Sirl & Son (Furnishers) Ltd* [1997] IRLR 493.
[88]   *Palmanor Ltd v Cedron* [1978] ICR 1008.
[89]   *Stanley Cole (Wainfleet) Ltd v Sheridan* [2003] IRLR 52.
[90]   *FC Gardner Ltd v Beresford* [1978] IRLR 43.
[91]   *Aparu v Iceland Frozen Foods plc* [1996] IRLR 119.
[92]   *Cantor Fitzgerald v Callaghan* [1999] IRLR 234.
[93]   *Hilton v Shiner Ltd Builders Merchants* [2001] IRLR 727.
[94]   *RDF Media Group plc v Clements* [2008] IRLR 207 at para 113.
[95]   [2008] IRLR 207.

his resignation.[96] This reasoning is highly doubtful; an unaccepted repudiation by a party does not normally bring a contract to an end, but rather gives the innocent party a right of election to treat the contract as terminated.[97] However, unless and until *Clements* is overturned, a company faced with a constructive dismissal claim may be able to take advantage of any anterior repudiatory breaches on the part of their former director. On a related point, in *Item Software (UK) Ltd v Fassihi*,[98] the court held that the director's breach of fiduciary duty could justify his dismissal irrespective of whether the breach was known to the company at the time of his dismissal and irrespective of whether his dismissal was otherwise justified.

*Remedies for wrongful dismissal*

Where a director is dismissed without due notice, he may bring a claim for damages[99] for wrongful dismissal. Normal principles of contract law apply to the measure of damages, meaning that a director will be entitled to damages equivalent to the amount of salary that he would otherwise have earned,[100] subject to the duty to mitigate his loss. **7.54**

Further, in assessing damages, it is to be assumed that a company would exercise any power available to it to bring the contract to an end in the way most beneficial to itself.[101] In *Laverack v Woods of Colchester*[102] a majority of the Court of Appeal held that the dismissed employee was not entitled to damages in respect of bonuses, which the directors of the company had made available from time to time, but which did not form part of his contractual entitlement. However, where a director's service contract provides for a discretionary annual pay rise or bonus, the director will be entitled to damages equivalent to the amount that he would have received if the company had exercised its discretion (which it cannot exercise capriciously or in bad faith).[103] A director's service agreement will often provide that there is no entitlement to a bonus if employment has terminated or notice has **7.55**

---

[96] Ibid.

[97] See *State Trading Corporation of India v Golodetz* [1989] 2 Lloyd's Rep 277 at 285, per Kerr LJ.

[98] [2005] 2 BCLC 91, CA.

[99] A claim may also be brought for debt if contract includes a PILON clause: *Abrahams v Performing Rights Society* [1995] IRLR 486, unless the payment in lieu is at the discretion of the company: *Cerberus Software Ltd v Rowley* [2001] IRLR 160, CA. An action for debt does not require the director to mitigate his loss and is therefore a valuable alternative remedy.

[100] Therefore taking account of matters such as any income tax, national insurance, or pension contributions that would have been payable on the outstanding salary and, if necessary, 'grossing up' to take account of any tax payable on the award of damages (payable where the award is in excess of £30,000 pursuant to ICTA 1988, s 148): *Shove v Downs Surgical plc* [1984] ICR 532.

[101] *Laverack v Woods of Colchester Ltd* [1967] 1 QB 278.

[102] [1967] 1 QB 278.

[103] *Clark v BET plc* [1997] IRLR 348; *Clark v Nomura International plc* [2000] IRLR 766; *Horkulak v Cantor Fitzgerald International* [2005] ICR 402.

been given by either side and in such circumstances, no damages will be recoverable.[104]

**7.56** Where a director is dismissed in breach of a contractual dismissal procedure, the court will calculate loss for the period during which the procedure would have been operated, together with damages for the notice period under the contract.[105]

**7.57** A director who is wrongfully dismissed is under a duty to take reasonable steps to mitigate his loss. However, the concept of reasonableness means that a director is not obliged to accept a position which would involve a significant loss of pay, seniority, or status.[106] Any salary, fees, or state benefits received after dismissal will go to reduce the amount payable by the company in damages.[107] Further, damages will be reduced to reflect the fact that damages are payable as a single lump sum and to reflect the potential for future salary to be curtailed by the 'vicissitudes of life'.[108]

**7.58** A claim for wrongful dismissal on the part of the director may be brought as an action for breach of contract in the High Court or county court, or in the employment tribunals. However, damages in the employment tribunals are limited to £25,000 and a director cannot bring a further claim in the High Court or county court for the balance of any outstanding sums.[109] There is no objection to a director pursuing a claim for unfair dismissal in the employment tribunals and a separate claim for wrongful dismissal in the High Court or county court. Any damages awarded will be subject to the principles of double recovery.[110] However, it is for the company to demonstrate that compensation awarded for unfair dismissal is attributable to the notice period for which damages for wrongful dismissal have been ordered. As the Court of Appeal made clear in *O'Laoire v Jackel International Ltd*,[111] this will only be the case when it is made clear from the judgment of the employment tribunal.

**7.59** The provisions of the Companies Act regulating payments for loss of office are considered in Chapter 18, Section E below.

---

[104] *Keen v Commerzbank AG* [2007] ICR 623.

[105] *Gunton v Richmond-upon-Thames LBC* [1980] ICR 755; *Dietman v Brent LBC* [1987] ICR 737; *Boyo v Lambeth LBC* [1995] IRLR 50.

[106] *Yetton v Eastwoods Froy Ltd* [1967] 1 WLR 104, where a managing director was entitled to reject an offer of the position of assistant managing director with the same salary, because of the loss of status that would entail.

[107] *Shove v Downs Surgical plc* [1984] ICR 532.

[108] ie if payment for the whole notice period may not actually have happened in certain circumstances. In *Bold v Brough Nicholson & Hall Ltd* [1964] 1 WLR 201 credit was given for the possibility of early lawful termination for illness.

[109] *Fraser v HLMAD Ltd* [2006] ICR 1395, CA.

[110] *O'Laoire v Jackel International Ltd* [1990] ICR 197. However, a basic award (as opposed to a compensatory award) for unfair dismissal does not fall to be deducted: *Shove v Downs Surgical plc* [1984] ICR 532.

[111] [1990] ICR 197.

## (2)  Statutory rights in the event of termination

A director who is removed from office may also have the benefit of certain other   **7.60**
protective rights, set out in the legislation. In particular, subject to certain qualifying requirements and the details of the relevant statutory provision, a director is
entitled to protection in the event of unfair dismissal, redundancy, and discrimination on certain specified grounds.

### Unfair dismissal

A company that dismisses a director may have liability for unfair dismissal.[112] The   **7.61**
concept of 'unfairness' in the legislation is not assessed by reference to the reasonable man on the street; rather protection under the legislation applies to breach of
the statutory tests of fairness as developed by the courts.[113] The statutory provisions impose a number of qualifying requirements for a claim, which can only be
brought in the employment tribunals. Unless the reason for dismissal is one of a
number of reasons specified in the legislation, the compensation that an employment tribunal can award is subject to a statutory cap.[114] Although rarely used in
practice, an employment tribunal can order a company to reinstate the director to
his previous position[115] or re-engage him elsewhere in the company.[116]

### Redundancy

If a director becomes surplus to the requirements of the business in which he is   **7.62**
employed, he may be dismissed on account of redundancy.[117] Although the term
'redundancy' is often used in practice when dismissing a director, he will only be
redundant for the purposes of the legislation if the statutory definition is met.[118]
The company is under specific duties prior to making a director redundant, notably the duty to consult at the earliest possible opportunity. A complaint of unfair
redundancy can be enforced as a claim for unfair dismissal in the employment
tribunals.[119]

---

[112]  For a comprehensive account of the law of unfair dismissal, see *Harvey on Industrial Relations and Employment Law*, section DI.

[113]  *W Devis & Sons Ltd v Atkins* [1976] 2 All ER 822, 828, per Phillips J, affirmed by [1977] AC 931.

[114]  Calculated by reference to a statutory basic award and compensatory award, capped at £66,200 from 1 February 2009: ERA, s 123.

[115]  ERA, s 114.

[116]  ERA, s 115.

[117]  For a comprehensive account of redundancy law, see *Harvey on Industrial Relations and Employment Law*, Division E.

[118]  ERA, s 139.

[119]  See paragraph 7.61 above.

**7.63**  Subject to his qualifying for the right, a director who is dismissed on account of redundancy will be entitled to a statutory redundancy payment.[120] If a service contract provides for enhanced terms in the event of redundancy (ie beyond the statutory minimum) the director will be entitled to enforce his entitlement by way of a claim for damages for breach of contract.

*Discriminatory termination*[121]

**7.64**  A company will also be liable to a director where a termination is discriminatory on the grounds of sex,[122] marital,[123] or civil[124] status, race (broadly defined),[125] disability,[126] age,[127] sexual orientation,[128] or religion and belief.[129] Liability may also arise where a director is removed on the grounds of trade union membership or non-membership.[130] A claim for discrimination can be brought in the employment tribunals, which have the power to award unlimited compensation, usually awarded in respect of lost earnings and injury to feelings.[131] Further, discrimination legislation may protect non-executive directors who fall within the restricted definition of an office-holder in the respective legislation from discriminatory removal from office.[132]

---

[120]  ERA, s 135.

[121]  For a comprehensive account of discrimination law, see *Harvey on Industrial Relations and Employment Law*, Division L.

[122]  Sex Discrimination Act 1975, s 6.

[123]  Sex Discrimination Act 1975, s 3.

[124]  In the sense of a civil partnership created by the Civil Partnership Act 2004: Sex Discrimination Act 1975, s 3.

[125]  Race Relations Act 1976, s 4.

[126]  Disability Discrimination Act 1995, ss 4–4A.

[127]  Employment Equality (Age) Regulations 2006, reg 7.

[128]  Employment Equality (Sexual Orientation) Regulations 2003, reg 6.

[129]  Employment Equality (Religion or Belief) Regulations 2003, reg 6.

[130]  Trade Unions and Labour Relations (Consolidation) Act 1992, s 152.

[131]  In line with the guidelines set out in *Vento v Chief Constable of West Yorkshire Police (No 2)* [2003] ICR 318, CA.

[132]  Sex Discrimination Act 1975, s 10A–10B; Race Relations Act 1976, s 76ZA; Disability Discrimination Act 1995, ss 4C–4F; Employment Equality (Age) Regulations 2006, reg 12; Employment Equality (Sexual Orientation) Regulations 2003, reg 10; Employment Equality (Religion or Belief) Regulations 2003, reg 10.

# 8

# DIRECTORS' TERMS OF SERVICE

## A. Introduction

The terms of service of a director will usually be a matter for negotiation between **8.01** the parties and incorporated within a written service agreement. The Companies Act imposes certain restrictions and controls upon directors' service agreements, which are discussed in Chapter 18. This chapter considers the rights and duties of directors which result from their contractual obligations, as opposed to the general duties (as now codified within the 2006 Act) which are discussed in Chapters 9 to 15. It examines the tests that the courts will apply to determine whether a director is employed under a service agreement, together with the sources of contractual rights. It also considers the typical contractual rights and restrictions that apply in service agreements, including the rights to remuneration and expenses, confidentiality, and post-termination restrictions.

## B. Employment Status of Directors

Depending on the nature of his role in the company, a director may, in addition **8.02** to holding the office of director, be employed by the company.[1] However, holding the office of director does not in itself confer employment status.[2] The company articles usually contemplate that directors may be appointed to executive office

---

[1] *Dunstan v Imperial Gas Light Co* (1832) 3 B & Ad 125; *Hutton v West Cork Railway* (1883) 23 Ch D 654, CA. See *Johnson v Ryan* [2000] ICR 236, explaining that office-holders may also be employees.
[2] *McMillan v Guest* [1942] AC 561, HL.

under the terms of a service agreement and receive remuneration.[3] In such circumstances, the director will also be an employee of the company. This will be the case with managing and other executive directors of most companies. However, in some instances, a director will not have the benefit of a written service agreement, but may still have the status of an employee, for the purposes of inter alia unfair dismissal and redundancy rights.[4] Further, if a director does not have the status of an employee, he may still be classified as a worker, a status that has the benefit of limited protection under employment legislation.

**8.03**   The significance of the following discussion is that both company and director will have different rights and obligations depending on the status of the director. For instance, the company's liability for tax and national insurance contributions will depend upon the director's position as an employee. Further, a company may make certain pension rights and share option schemes available to employees. Debts to employees may also constitute preferential debts in the event of a winding up of the company. Further, an employed director has certain protective rights, such as unfair dismissal, redundancy protection, maternity rights, and protection in the event of a transfer of undertaking, which a director who is not employed will not have. This section discusses the main tests that the courts apply to determine whether a director should also be considered an employee or worker.

**8.04**   The tests of employment have been the subject of continuing common law development. In many cases, the courts draw across a range of statutes and the common law itself in order to determine the status of an individual in question.[5] It should not however be concluded that a director who is not treated as an employee for tax purposes will not be treated as an employee under employment legislation or for the purposes of a company's pension scheme. It is possible for a director to be considered an employee in respect of, for example, a tax statute, but not an employee for the purposes of claiming unfair dismissal or redundancy payments.[6]

**8.05**   The courts will take as their starting point the question of whether there is a contract of employment between the company and director. Under the Employment Rights Act 1996 (ERA), s 230, a contract of employment is defined as a contract of service whether express or implied and (if it is express) whether oral or in writing. Applying the statutory definition, the existence of a written service agreement invariably confers employment status upon a director. Similarly, although unusual in the context of a director, where the court finds that a contract has been agreed orally between the parties, the director will be held to be an employee.

---

[3] Table A, article 84; Model Article (pcls), article 19, Model Article (plc), article 22.
[4] See Chapter 7, paragraphs 7.60–7.63.
[5] See eg the decision of Nolan LJ in the tax case of *Hall v Lorimer* [1994] 1 WLR 209, CA.
[6] See eg *Road Transport Industry Training Board v Readers Garage Ltd* (1969) 4 ITR 195, Div Ct.

The main difficulty arises in circumstances where the parties have not expressly agreed that a director is to be employed.

In order to determine whether a contract may be implied in such circumstances, **8.06** the courts apply a number of notoriously complicated common law tests.[7] Such tests include control of the director by the company;[8] integration into the workforce;[9] the economic reality of the relationship;[10] and an obligation on the director to provide work personally (and not through a substitute).[11]

Application of the control test presents certain difficulties in the case of directors. **8.07** For instance, a director will rarely be subject to control, in the sense of the company deciding the thing to be done, the means to be employed, and the time and place for doing it.[12] Rather, it will be the director himself, acting as the mind of the company who controls the activities and it is unreal to suggest that a director is subject to his own, or his fellow directors' control. Application of the other tests will present little difficulty in cases where a director does not act under a service contract, but carries out certain duties on behalf of the company on a full-time basis in return for a salary. Usually, the courts will presume that a contract of employment exists.[13] However, this will not always be the case and in *Albert J Parsons & Sons Ltd v Parsons*,[14] the Court of Appeal held that it was not possible to imply a service contract in respect of a full-time director, as he received remuneration by way of fees, was not treated as an employee for national insurance purposes, and no record of a service contract had been kept.[15]

There is no reason why a director, who is also the controlling or sole shareholder, **8.08** cannot also be an employee of a company.[16] Whether he will be an employee in

---

[7] For a comprehensive discussion of this area, see Deakin & Morris, *Labour Law*, (4th edn, Hart, 2005), chapter 3.

[8] *Yewens v Noakes* (1880) 6 QBD 530, CA; *Montgomery v Johnson Underwood Ltd* [2001] ICR 819.

[9] *Stevenson, Jordan & Harrison v MacDonald & Evans* [1952] 1 TLR 101, CA, per Denning LJ.

[10] *Market Investigations Ltd v Minister of Social Security* [1969] 2 QB 173.

[11] *Express and Echo Publications v Tanton* [1999] IRLR 367; a limited power to appoint substitutes is not inconsistent with an obligation of personal service: *Byrne Bros (Formwork) Ltd v Baird* [2002] IRLR 96.

[12] *Ready Mixed Concrete (South East) Ltd v Minister for Pensions and National Security* [1968] 2 QB 497, 515.

[13] *Trussed Steel Concrete Co Ltd v Green* [1946] Ch 115, per Cohen J; *Folami v Nigerline (UK) Ltd* [1978] ICR 277, EAT.

[14] [1979] ICR 271, CA.

[15] As then required under 1967 Act, s 26(1). See now 2006 Act, s 228.

[16] *Lee v Lee's Air Farming Ltd* [1961] AC 12, PC, referring to *Salomon v Salomon & Co* [1897] AC, 22, HL in holding that this was the case even in relation to one-man companies. See also *Secretary of State for Trade and Industry v Bottrill* [1999] ICR 592, doubting *Buchan v Secretary of State for Employment* [1997] IRLR 80; *Fleming v Secretary of State for Trade and Industry* [1997] IRLR 682; *Sellars Arenascene Ltd v Connolly* [2001] ICR 760; *Gladwell v Secretary of State for Trade and Industry* [2007] ICR 264, EAT; *Nesbitt v Secretary of State for Trade and Industry* [2007] IRLR 847,

any given case is a question of fact. The starting point for analysing this issue is the decision of the Court of Appeal in *Secretary of State for Trade and Industry v Bottrill* and the following guidance of Lord Woolf MR:[17]

> We are anxious not to lay down rigid guidelines for the factual inquiry which the tribunal of fact must undertake in the particular circumstances of each case, but we hope that the following comments may be of assistance.
>
> The first question which the tribunal is likely to wish to consider is whether there is or has been a genuine contract between the company and the shareholder. In this context how and for what reasons the contract came into existence (for example, whether the contract was made at a time when insolvency loomed) and what each party actually did pursuant to the contract are likely to be relevant consideration.
>
> If the tribunal concludes that the contract is not a sham, it is likely to wish to consider next whether the contract, which may well have been labelled a contract of employment, actually gave rise to an employer/employee relationship. In this context, of the various factors usually regarded as relevant . . . the degree of control exercised by the company over the shareholder employee is always important. This is not the same question as that relating to whether there is a controlling shareholding. The tribunal may think it appropriate to consider whether there are directors other than or in addition to the shareholder employee and whether the constitution of the company gives that shareholder rights such that he is in reality answerable only to himself and incapable of being dismissed. If he is a director, it may be relevant to consider whether he is able under the articles of association to vote on matters in which he is personally interested, such as the termination of his contract of employment. Again, the actual conduct of the parties pursuant to the terms of the contract is likely to be relevant. It is for the tribunal as an industrial jury to take all relevant factors into account in reaching its conclusion, giving such weight to them as it considers appropriate.

**8.09** The approach set out by Lord Woolf in *Bottrill* requires the court or tribunal to consider all of the relevant circumstances, including the existence of a controlling shareholding (which may or may not be determinative), whether the contract of employment was genuine or instead designed to confer employment status so as to take advantage of statutory rights, and whether the conduct of the parties is consistent with an employment relationship.

**8.10** In *Nesbitt v Secretary of State for Trade and Industry*,[18] Underhill J, considering the *Bottrill* guidance, suggested that the key issue would be whether or not the company is a 'mere simulacrum' defined as: 'something having merely the form or

---

EAT; *Clark v Clark Construction Initiatives Ltd* [2008] ICR 635; *Neufeld v A & N Communications In Print Ltd* [2008] All ER (D) 156 (Apr). At the time of writing, pursuant to a Practice Direction dated 9 September 2008 issued by the President of Employment Tribunals (England and Wales), HHJ Meeran, all claims in the employment tribunals raising the question of employment status in this context were stayed pending the outcome of the Court of Appeal's decision in *Secretary of State for BERR v Neufeld* CA Ref: 2008/1008.

[17] [1999] ICR 592, CA, at 604.
[18] [2007] IRLR 847, EAT at paragraphs 12, 27.

appearance of a certain thing, without possessing its substance or proper qualities', which applies 'where it appears that there is no real intention to vest the
business in the company in question or, therefore, to distinguish between the two
roles of director and employee'. This approach suggests that employment should
always be treated a valid where the arrangement is not a sham. In *Clark v Clark
Construction Initiatives Ltd*,[19] Elias P gave further guidance[20] as to the relevance of
sham company, as follows:

(1) Where there is a contract ostensibly in place, the onus is on the party seeking to
deny its effect to satisfy the court that it is not what it appears to be. This is particularly so where the individual has paid tax and national insurance as an employee; he
has on the face of it earned the right to take advantage of the benefits which employees may derive from such payments.

(2) The mere fact that the individual has a controlling shareholding does not of itself
prevent a contract of employment arising. Nor does the fact that he in practice is
able to exercise real or sole control over what the company does [*Lee v Lee's Air
Farming Ltd*].

(3) Similarly, the fact that he is an entrepreneur, or has built the company up, or will
profit from its success, will not be factors militating against a finding that there is a
contract in place. Indeed, any controlling shareholder will inevitably benefit from
the company's success, as will many employees with share option schemes [*Sellars
Arenascene Ltd v Connolly*].

(4) If the conduct of the parties is in accordance with the contract that would be a
strong pointer towards the contract being valid and binding. For example, this
would be so if the individual works the hours stipulated or does not take more than
the stipulated holidays

(5) Conversely, if the conduct of the parties is either inconsistent with the contract . . .
or in certain key areas where one might expect it to be governed by the contract is
in fact not so governed, that would be a factor, and potentially a very important
one, militating against a finding that the controlling shareholder is in reality an
employee

(6) In that context, the assertion that there is a genuine contract will be undermined if
the terms have not been identified or reduced into writing [*Fleming v Secretary of
State for Trade and Industry*]. This will be powerful evidence that the contract was
not really intended to regulate the relationship in any way.

(7) The fact that the individual takes loans from the company or guarantees its debts
could exceptionally have some relevance in analysing the true nature of the relationship, but in most cases such factors are unlikely to carry any weight. There is nothing intrinsically inconsistent in a person who is an employee doing these things.
Indeed, in many small companies it will be necessary for the controlling shareholder personally to have to give bank guarantees precisely because the company
assets are small and no funding will be forthcoming without them. It would wholly
undermine the [*Lee v Lee's Air Farming*] approach if this were to be sufficient to
deny the controlling shareholder the right to enter into a contract of employment.

---

[19] [2008] IRLR 364.
[20] At para 98.

(8) Although the courts have said that the fact of there being a controlling sharehold-ing is always relevant and may be decisive, that does not mean that the fact alone will ever justify a tribunal in finding that there was no contract in place. That would be to apply the [*Buchan v Secretary of State for Employment*] test which has been decisively rejected. The fact that there is a controlling shareholding is what may raise doubts as to whether that individual is truly an employee, but of itself that fact alone does not resolve those doubts one way or another.

**8.11** It is submitted that the guidance in *Clark v Clark Construction Initiatives* consti-tutes an accurate analysis of the tests to be applied in determining employment status in this context.

**8.12** A separate difficulty may arise where a director holds executive positions at a number of companies. Assuming the various appointments are all intended to operate over a period of time, the likely classification is that the director acts as an employee of each of the separate companies for which he acts.[21] Non-executive directors who do not provide labour or services to the company under a service agreement will rarely be employees, even if they receive written terms of appointment.

**8.13** If a director is not classified as an employee, he may still be classified as a worker under the ERA. A worker is defined under the ERA as any individual who works under a contract of employment (meaning that all employees are also workers) or any other contract 'whereby the individual undertakes to do or perform person-ally any work or services for another party to the contract whose status is not by virtue of the contract that of a client or customer of any profession or undertaking carried on by the individual'.[22] The concept of worker is used in relation to a number of statutes, including the unlawful deductions from wages provisions of ERA,[23] public interest disclosure (whistleblowing) protection,[24] the national minimum wage,[25] working time protection,[26] and the right to be accompanied to disciplinary hearings.[27] If therefore, an executive director is not an employee upon application of the tests discussed above, he will in all likelihood meet the defini-tion of a worker and have the benefit of these protective rights.

*Personal service companies*

**8.14** Where an individual is providing work through a personal service company the key consideration is whether he might additionally be an employee of the company

---

[21] This is consistent with the decision in *McMeechan v Secretary of State for Employment* [1997] ICR 549.

[22] s 230(3).

[23] ERA, Part II.

[24] ERA, Part IVA.

[25] National Minimum Wage Act 1998, s 54.

[26] Working Time Regulations 1998, reg 2.

[27] ERA, s 13.

to which the services are provided. The use of such a company has become less attractive with the introduction of the 'IR35' tax regime, removing the key tax benefits of the device. In appropriate cases, employment tribunals have been prepared to pierce the corporate veil and find that a contract of employment exists between the individual acting through the personal service company, and the company itself.[28]

## C. Sources of Contractual Terms

In most cases, the contract of a managing or other executive director will be set out in a detailed service agreement.[29] However, the written service agreement will rarely be the sole document that evidences terms and conditions and it will often be amended or supplemented by other sources, such as a company handbook, set of work rules, company policies, collective agreement, letters from the company, oral promises, or the conduct of the parties as time passes by, which the court will consider in order to determine the terms agreed by the parties.[30]    **8.15**

Whether the terms of any written document form part of the contract is a question of fact in any given set of circumstances. In particular, the terms of the service agreement may expressly state that a certain document, such as disciplinary or grievance policy, is not intended to have contractual effect, which will negate the possibility of it being incorporated into the contract. A service agreement may contain an 'entire agreement' clause, excluding reliance by either party on any other sources. Whether such a clause is conclusive will depend upon whether in all the circumstances the parties really intended the written instrument to reflect their whole bargain.[31]    **8.16**

As is particularly the case in relation to oral promises, the courts will consider whether any statement was intended to have legal effect (as distinct from words of comfort). As such, in *Judge v Crown Leisure*[32] the Court of Appeal upheld a finding that a casual conversation in the 'convivial spirit' of the Christmas party did not amount to a contractual promise.    **8.17**

---

[28] *Catamaran Cruisers v Williams* [1994] IRLR 386; cf *Hewlett Packard v O'Murphy* [2002] IRLR 4; *Lanksford v Business Post Ltd* [2004] All ER (D) 46 (Aug).

[29] Companies have a statutory obligation to provide all employed directors with a written statement of terms and conditions: ERA, Part I.

[30] See *Carmichael v National Power plc* [1999] 1 WLR 2042, HL, per Lord Hoffmann at 2048 *et seq.*

[31] *Bushaway v Royal National Lifeboat Institution* [2005] IRLR 674, EAT, in which the EAT held that the tribunal was entitled to look beyond the clause as there were inconsistencies between the contract and the parties' previous dealings; cf *White v Bristol Rugby Ltd* [2002] IRLR 204, in which the clause was held to be effective.

[32] [2005] IRLR 823.

**8.18** A contract of employment will contain terms implied under normal contractual principles. A term will be implied into a director's service agreement where it is obvious,[33] necessary for business efficacy,[34] or part of the custom of the industry or workplace in question.[35] Certain terms (particularly in relation to pay) are also implied by legislation.[36]

**8.19** Of particular importance is the implied term of mutual trust and confidence (otherwise described as the duty of fair dealing[37]), implied into all service agreements.[38] The term, recognized by the House of Lords in *Malik v Bank of Credit and Commerce International SA*,[39] is that a company must not without reasonable and proper cause, conduct itself in a manner calculated or likely to destroy or seriously damage the relationship of confidence and trust between itself and an employed director. In *Malik*, the House of Lords held that the term meant that the defendant bank was under an implied obligation not to conduct a dishonest or corrupt business. Any breach of the implied trust and confidence term by a company will be sufficient for a director to resign on account of constructive dismissal.[40]

**8.20** The overarching trust and confidence term regulates both a director's performance of his duties and a director's own contractual rights. Where an executive director carries out the managerial functions of the company itself, he must take care to do so in a manner that does not breach the trust and confidence term. Usually this will present little difficulty, as the director's fiduciary duty to act in the best interests of the company will in most cases require him to act consistently with the implied trust and confidence term, vis-à-vis the employees.[41]

**8.21** The trust and confidence term will often regulate discretionary clauses, commonly found in directors' service agreements. In particular, it will regulate express contractual provisions that purport to give the company a discretionary power, for instance in relation to pension provision,[42] a mobility clause,[43] and bonuses,[44] or

---

[33] *Shirlaw v Southern Foundries* (1926) Ltd [1939] 2 KB 206.
[34] *The Moorcock* (1889) 14 PD 64; *Reigate v Union Manufacturing Co (Ramsbottom) Ltd* [1918] 1 KB 592; *Marshall v Alexander Sloan & Co Ltd* [1981] IRLR 264.
[35] *Sagar v H Ridehalgh & Son Ltd* [1931] 1 Ch 310. For an example of custom being used as an aid to interpretation of an express term, see *Dunlop Tyres Ltd v Blows* [2001] IRLR 629.
[36] See paragraph 8.40 below.
[37] Usually described as such in the context of termination: see *Johnson v Unisys Ltd* [2003] 1 AC 518, HL, per Lord Steyn at para 24.
[38] *Malik v Bank of Credit and Commerce International SA* [1998] AC 20, HL.
[39] [1998] AC 20, HL.
[40] *Morrow v Safeway Stores plc* [2002] IRLR 9.
[41] See in particular the duty contained in s 172(1)(b), Companies Act 2006, discussed in Chapter 11.
[42] *Imperial Group Pension Trust Ltd v Imperial Tobacco Ltd* [1991] 1 WLR 589.
[43] *United Bank Ltd v Akhtar* [1989] IRLR 507.
[44] See *Horkulak v Cantor Fitzgerald* [2005] IRLR 502, CA.

to change duties.[45] Further, the duty may oblige a company to investigate complaints made by a director[46] or prevent its officers or employees from subjecting a director to foul and abusive language.[47]

As an implied term, there is no reason in principle why the term cannot be excluded **8.22** by a properly worded express term in a service contract. In practice, such exclusion may arise either directly or indirectly. An example of direct exclusion would be where the company purports to exclude the term itself; whereas indirect exclusion may arise where the terms of the contract provide that any discretionary power may be exercised on any basis whatsoever, whether irrationally or capriciously. Alternatively, the service contract might seek to deem otherwise repudiatory acts (such as a removal of duties or changing of status) as not constituting a repudiation of contract. It is unlikely that the courts would take a strong objection to any such terms (for example on public policy grounds) in the service agreements of directors, given their relatively strong bargaining power. Of greater significance may be the fact that any such term can indirectly cause the director to contract out of his protective rights, and may therefore be void.[48]

## D. Terms of Employment

At common law, company and director are free to enter into a service agreement **8.23** for any specified period of time or for an unlimited duration. Termination of service agreements is considered in Chapter 7. The provisions of the Companies Act regarding disclosure of details of long-term service agreements are discussed in Chapter 18 below.

### (1) Remuneration

The remuneration of directors comes from two separate sources. First, the direct- **8.24** ors (and in particular non-executive directors of public companies) may receive fees for acting as a director. Secondly, a director's service agreement, if there is one, will provide for payment of a salary and other benefits.

The regulation and disclosure requirements contained within the Companies Act **8.25** are considered in Chapter 18.

---

[45] See *Land Securities Trillium v Thornley* [2005] IRLR 765, in which the duty applied notwithstanding a broadly worded flexibility clause.

[46] *British Airways Corpn v Austin* [1978] IRLR 332.

[47] *Horkulak v Cantor Fitzgerald* [2005] ICR 502, CA, in which the court also held that high levels of remuneration cannot be used as justification for poor treatment.

[48] ERA, s 230.

*Remuneration permitted by the company articles*

**8.26**  Under most company articles, members must approve fees payable for holding office as directors, but directors may fix remuneration under the service agreement for executive functions.

**8.27**  Regulation 82 of Table A provides as follows:

> The directors shall be entitled to such remuneration as the company may by ordinary resolution determine and, unless the resolution provides otherwise, the remuneration shall be deemed to accrue from day to day.

**8.28**  Regulation 84 of Table A provides as follows:

> Subject to the provisions of the Act, the directors may appoint one or more of their number to the office of managing director or to any other executive office under the company and may enter into an agreement or arrangement with any director for his employment by the company or for the provision by him of any services outside the scope of the ordinary duties of a director. Any such appointment, agreement or arrangement may be made upon such terms as the directors determine and they may remunerate any such director for his services as they think fit. Any appointment of a director to an executive office shall terminate if he ceases to be a director but without prejudice to any claim to damages for breach of the contract of service between the director and the company. A managing director and a director holding any other executive office shall not be subject to retirement by rotation.

**8.29**  Model Article (pcls) 19 and Model Article (plc) 23 give authority to the directors to determine directors' remuneration and provide:

> (1) Directors may undertake any services for the company that the directors decide.
> (2) Directors are entitled to such remuneration as the directors determine—
>    (a) for their services to the company as directors, and
>    (b) for any other service which they undertake for the company.
> (3) Subject to the articles, a director's remuneration may—
>    (a) take any form, and
>    (b) include any arrangements in connection with the payment of a pension, allowance or gratuity, or any death, sickness or disability benefits, to or in respect of the director.
> (4) Unless the directors decide otherwise, directors' remuneration accrues from day to day.
> (5) Unless the directors decide otherwise, directors are not accountable to the company for any remuneration which they receive as directors of the company's subsidiaries or of any other body corporate in which the company is interested.

**8.30**  As such, the Model Articles provide for wide powers as to the form of any remuneration at the discretion of the directors, with such power delegated to the Board.

**8.31**  However, in the absence of a service contract, provision in the company articles or other approval by members,[49] a director does not have a right to be remunerated

---

[49] *Re George Newman and Co* [1895] 1 Ch 674, CA.

for services performed as a director for the company,[50] whether as a *quantum meruit* or otherwise.[51] As expressed by Bowen LJ in *Hutton v West Cork Railway*[52] a 'director is not a servant; he is a person doing business for the company, but not upon ordinary terms. It is not implied from the mere fact that he is a director that he is to be paid for it.' This general rule is an aspect of the fiduciary principle that a director is not allowed to make a profit unless expressly permitted.[53] However, where a director also provides services as a manager, he will be entitled to remuneration on a *quantum meruit* basis. Such issues rarely arise in practice, given the widespread use of service agreements authorized under the company articles.

Provided that remuneration is bona fide and not an improper return of capital to shareholders,[54] the court will not intervene with the company's exercise of discretion because 'it is not for the courts to manage the company'.[55] As such, there is no obligation to pay a 'going rate',[56] nor a restriction on high salaries. However, a failure by the directors to ensure that the board fixes salaries that are affordable by the company may show the directors' unfitness and be a ground for a disqualification order.[57] In addition, the payment of excessive remuneration bearing no reasonable relation to the services performed may be open to challenge as a 'fraud on the minority'.[58] Finally, excessive remuneration awarded when the company is in financial difficulties may be open to challenge by a liquidator under the misfeasance provision contained in the Insolvency Act.[59]

**8.32**

Remuneration is consideration for work done or to be done and as such it may take different forms. It will normally take the form of a salary, and may be supplemented by commissions, fees, or bonuses.[60] In every case, the entitlement that arises is a question of construction of the articles and any duly authorized agreement. Where a sum is dependent upon the performance of the company (for example by

**8.33**

---

[50] *Dunstan v Imperial Gas Light Co* (1832) 3 B & Ad 125; *Hutton v West Cork Railway* (1883) 23 Ch D 654, CA; *Guinness plc v Saunders* [1990] 2 AC 663, HL.

[51] See also *Re George Newman and Co* [1895] 1 Ch 674, CA; *Dunstan v Imperial Gas Light Co* (1832) 3 B & Ad 125; *Ex p Cannon* (1885) 30 Ch D 629; *In re Richmond Gate Property Co Ltd* [1965] 1 WLR 335.

[52] (1883) 23 Ch D 654, 671.

[53] '[E]very fiduciary is under a duty not to make a profit from his position (unless such profit is authorised)': *Henderson v Merrett Syndicates* [1995] 2 AC 145, HL, per Lord Browne-Wilkinson at 206. *Hutton v West Cork Railway* (1883) 23 Ch D 654.

[54] A disguised gift repaid out of capital is *ultra vires*: *Re Halt Garage (1964) Ltd* [1984] 3 All ER 1016.

[55] *Re Halt Garage (1964) Ltd* [1982] 3 All ER 1016, 1039, per Oliver J.

[56] *Secretary of State for Trade and Industry v Van Hengel* [1995] 1 BCLC 545.

[57] Ibid.

[58] *Nolan v Parsons* [1942] OR 358, CA (Ont); cf *Re Halt Garage (1964) Ltd* [1982] 3 All ER 1016.

[59] s 212.

[60] *Currencies Direct Ltd v Ellis* [2002] 2 BCLC 482, 487, per Mummery LJ.

reference to profits), then the director is not entitled to any sum where no profits are made.[61] However, where a sum is not dependent upon performance or any other measure, it will be payable irrespective of whether or not the company is making a profit.[62] In practical terms, a decrease in profits may result in the members resolving to cut or cancel directors' fees. However, absent express provision in the service agreement, any attempt to reduce contractual benefits will constitute a breach of contract, irrespective of the motive (and may amount to a repudiation of the agreement, entitling the director to resign on account of constructive dismissal). Sale of the bulk of the company's assets, so that the directors' duties are greatly reduced, does not disentitle them to their full remuneration.[63]

**8.34** If the articles are silent, the company in general meeting may vote remuneration; but in such case the remuneration is a gratuity, and not a matter of right.[64] In a going company, the general meeting may vote a gratuity at will,[65] but upon liquidation this cannot be done.[66]

**8.35** The 2006 Act has repealed an earlier provision[67] that made it unlawful for a company to agree to pay the director a certain sum net of tax, or to vary the director's income in line with changes in income tax rates.

*Position of directors with invalid appointments*

**8.36** If a director's appointment is not valid, he cannot recover remuneration as a director in accordance with the articles, even though he may have served for a long period.[68] However, depending on the terms of the service agreement, an invalid appointment will not necessarily affect the contractual position, which may be effective irrespective of the lack of a valid appointment. As noted below, however, compensation in all but name may often be recovered by an action for unjust

---

[61] Remuneration as a percentage of profits does not include a share of the profit made on the sale of the whole business of the company: *Frames v Bulfontein Mining Co* [1891] 1 Ch 140. It will include profits which exist in specie, even though these would not be converted into cash except on liquidation: *Re Spanish Prospecting Co* [1911] 1 Ch 92, CA.

[62] *Re Lundy Granite Co, Lewis's Case* (1872) 26 LT 673; *Nell v Atlanta Gold and Silver Consol Mines* (1895) 11 TLR 407, CA.

[63] *Re Consolidated Nickel Mines* [1914] 1 Ch 883.

[64] *Re Geo Newman and Co* [1895] 1 Ch 674, CA; *Dunstan v Imperial Gas Light Co* (1832) 3 B&Ad 125; *Ex p Cannon* (1885) 30 Ch D 629; *Putaruru Pine & Pulp Co (NZ) Ltd v MacCulloch* [1934] NZLR 639. Alternatively, in such a case, it may be paid with the unanimous consent of the shareholders: *D'Amore v McDonald* [1973] 1 OR 845 at 864, HC (Ont), affirmed (1974) 1 OR (2d) 370, CA (Ont).

[65] *Re Lundy Granite Co, Lewis's Case* (1872) 26 LT 673; *Re Geo Newman & Co* [1895] 1 Ch 674.

[66] *Hutton v West Cork Railway Co* (1883) 23 Ch D 654; *Stroud v Royal Aquarium, etc, Society* [1903] WN 143.

[67] 1985 Act, s 311.

[68] *Woolf v East Nigel Gold Mining Co* (1905) 21 TLR 660.

enrichment if the director acted in accordance with an implied invitation, one of the terms of which was for remuneration at the rate specified.[69]

In the unlikely event that it is discovered that fees have been paid after a director   **8.37** had vacated office, for whatever reason, and where the facts negative the probability of an intention to grant remuneration, the company can recover the amounts as money paid by mistake.[70]

*Agreement to forego fees*

It is open to directors by a resolution to renounce the right to future remuneration   **8.38** under such implied contracts.[71] An agreement by all the directors inter se and with the company to renounce the right to remuneration is binding on each director even at the suit of the company.[72] A resolution to forego fees may however be rescinded by a subsequent resolution, and if this is done, remuneration will be payable as from the date of the rescinding resolution.[73]

*The right to pay under the service agreement*

Under the terms of the service agreement, the entitlement to pay may comprise a   **8.39** number of different benefits, usually wider than those expressly referred to in the company articles. Almost always, the principal benefit will comprise salary, and will often be supplemented by further benefits such as bonuses, share options, a pension, medical care, company car, expenses incurred by reason of employment, sick pay, holiday pay, or any other specified entitlement.

Legislation (other than the Companies Act) imposes two restrictions upon the   **8.40** level of remuneration provided under a service contract. First, an equality clause will be implied into all service agreements, providing that a female director carrying out equal work is entitled to be paid the same as her male counterparts.[74] In *Villalba v Merrill Lynch & Co Inc*,[75] a former managing director brought a claim for equal pay alleging that her bonus payments constituted a breach of the implied equality clause.[76] For the purposes of the right to equal pay at least, the concept is

---

[69] *Swabey v Port Darwin Gold Mining Co* (1889) 1 Meg 385; *Isaacs' Case* [1892] 2 Ch 158; *Re Peruvian Guano Co* [1894] 3 Ch 690; *Re New British Iron Co, ex p Beckwith* [1898] 1 Ch 324; *Craven-Ellis v Canons* [1936] 2 KB 403, CA; *Re Richmond Gate Property Co* [1965] 1 WLR 335.

[70] *Re Bodega Co* [1904] 1 Ch 276. In this case the director was disqualified for having secretly participated in contracts with the company.

[71] *McConnell's Claim, re London and Northern Bank* [1901] 1 Ch 728.

[72] *West Yorkshire Darracq Agency v Coleridge* [1911] 2 KB 326.

[73] *Re Consolidated Nickel Mines* [1914] 1 Ch 883.

[74] Equal Pay Act 1970, s 1; the right to equal pay also applies by reason of Article 141 of the EC Treaty, which the European Court of Justice in Case 43/75 *Defrenne v SA Belge de Navigation Aérienne* [1976] ECR 455 held to be directly effective in English law.

[75] [2006] IRLR 437.

[76] See also *Barton v Investec Henderson Crosthwaite Securities* [2003] IRLR 332.

wide enough to encompass all of the benefits listed above which are payable as a condition of employment.[77] Secondly, where the director has the status of worker,[78] his contract will contain an implied term that he is entitled to the national minimum wage.

### Discretionary bonuses

**8.41** The entitlement to a bonus will often form the principal part of a director's remuneration. Such clauses are commonly described as discretionary and provide that an employer has an absolute discretion as to whether to award an employee a bonus, and, if it decides to make such an award, as to the amount and form of that bonus. In *Clark v Nomura*,[79] Burton J held that such a clause provided the employee with a right to have the discretion exercised, and that the discretion was subject to an implied obligation that it not be exercised irrationally or perversely. Further, the precise wording of the clause would constitute a 'contractual straitjacket' as to the factors that could be taken into consideration when exercising discretion.[80] Burton J went on to hold that in determining damages, the court should put itself in the position of the company as far as possible in order to reach a conclusion as to what position the employee would have been in had the employer performed its obligation. The Court of Appeal has since gone on to adopt the *Clark* test in a number of cases.[81] In the analogous context of a discretionary share option scheme, Peter Smith J in *McCarthy v McCarthy & Stone plc*[82] held that where a discretion had not been lawfully exercised (because of an absence of good faith) the court may conclude it to be a nullity and as a result may direct that the employer or the committee should reconsider the decision on a lawful basis.

**8.42** In *Commerzbank v Keen*,[83] the Court of Appeal recognized that a higher threshold would apply in cases where the company had exercised its discretion and determined the amount of the discretionary bonus (as opposed to deciding to make a nil award as in *Clark v Nomura*). There, Mr Keen sought to challenge bonus awards in the region of €3 million (making him amongst the highest paid employees of the company internationally) on the grounds of irrationality and perversity. Mummery LJ held that the burden upon an individual in such circumstances is a

---

[77] See *Barber v Guardian Royal Exchange Assurance Group* [1990] IRLR 240 in which the European Court of Justice held that the concept covered an occupational pension scheme.

[78] As defined in s 54 of the National Minimum Wage Act 1998.

[79] [2000] IRLR 766.

[80] As such, in *Clark v Nomura*, the discretionary bonus was based upon 'individual performance', which restricted the company from taking other factors into account.

[81] See eg *Mallone v BPB Industries Ltd* [2002] ICR 1045, CA and *Horkulak v Cantor Fitzgerald International* [2005] ICR 402, CA.

[82] [2006] 4 All ER 1127.

[83] [2007] ICR 623, CA.

'very high one' and would require an 'overwhelming case' to succeed.[84] As set out by Moses LJ, it is for the director to establish the irrationality of the decision, and he must, therefore, be able to demonstrate some feature of the award, or the circumstances in which it was made, which tends to show its perversity. However, in circumstances where the director has made out a prima facie case of irrationality, the company must meet that case by identifying the decision-maker and the reason for the decision.[85]

It is presently unclear (and will no doubt shortly be the subject of judicial consideration) whether a director may have a claim in circumstances where he is dismissed with the object of avoiding a bonus payment. The question arises as it is common for discretionary bonuses to provide that the director is in employment on the date that payment falls due. In *Commerzbank v Keen*, the Court of Appeal rejected an argument that such clauses were unenforceable by reason of the Unfair Contract Terms Act 1977, as that Act has no application to service agreements. In *Clark v Nomura*, Burton J held that dismissal with the aim of avoiding payment of a bonus might be ineffective, meaning that the director would either be able to keep the contract alive until the payment date or bring a claim for damages. Similarly, in *Reda v Flag*[86] the Privy Council was willing to assume that if employees had been capriciously or arbitrarily singled out for dismissal in order to deprive them of an entitlement to participate in a stock option plan, this might well constitute a breach of the implied term of trust and confidence and that an employee would not necessarily be without a remedy because the mechanism of victimization took the form of dismissal. That approach would have allowed the employees to pursue a free-standing contractual claim in respect of their non-participation in a stock option plan as damages for breach of the implied term of trust and confidence rather than a claim for damages for wrongful dismissal (ie for a free-standing anterior breach of contract). The Privy Council held that there had been no breach of the implied term of trust and confidence in that case because the employers were justified in treating the employees differently from and less favourably for commercially legitimate and objectively defensible reasons. **8.43**

*Apportionment of remuneration*

Under Table A, reg 82 and Model Article (pcls) 19(4) and Model Article (plc) 23(4) a director's remuneration accrues from day to day. As noted in *Item Software Ltd v Fassihi*,[87] the same outcome would apply under the Apportionment Act 1870, unless the parties otherwise stipulated in the service agreement. **8.44**

---

[84]  At 632.
[85]  At 639.
[86]  [2002] IRLR 747.
[87]  [2005] 2 BCLC 91.

*Remedies for breach of payments provisions*

**8.45**   A claim for non-payment of any contractual benefit can be enforced by way of an action for debt or damages for breach of contract.[88] If the claim is for unpaid wages, it can be enforced in the employment tribunals, and there is no limit on compensation.[89]

### (2)  Expenses

**8.46**   Regulation 82 of Table A provides:

> The directors shall be entitled to such remuneration as the company may by ordinary resolution determine and, unless the resolution provides otherwise, the remuneration shall be deemed to accrue from day to day.

**8.47**   Model Article (pcls) 20 and Model Article (plc) 24 each provide:

> The company must pay any reasonable expenses which the directors properly incur in connection with their attendance at—
> (a)  meetings of directors or committees of directors,
> (b)  general meetings, or
> (c)  separate meetings of the holders of any class of shares or of debentures of the company,
> or otherwise in connection with the exercise of their powers and the discharge of the their responsibilities in relation to the company.

**8.48**   Similar provisions are likely to be included within the service agreement, which may impose a procedure for reclaiming expenses. Where a director fails to claim expenses in accordance with an agreed contractual formula, they cannot be recovered.

**8.49**   Directors, as agents, are by law entitled to an indemnity in respect of all liabilities properly incurred by them in the management of the company's business.[90] No express provision is necessary, although the articles often give rights that are more extensive than those implied by law. This indemnity does not necessarily cover all expenses. Unless specially authorized by the articles or by resolution of a general meeting, expenses of travelling to or from board meetings must not be paid in addition.[91]

---

[88] Non-payment of salary will not necessarily constitute a repudiatory breach: *WPM Retail Ltd v Laing* [1978] ICR 787, EAT; *Gillies v Richard Daniels & Co Ltd* [1979] IRLR 457, EAT; *Cantor Fitzgerald International v Callaghan* [1999] ICR 639, CA. By contrast, denial of contractual obligations to pay normally will constitute a repudiation: *F Hill Ltd v Mooney* [1981] IRLR 258.

[89] However, a claim for a discretionary bonus cannot be enforced under the provisions of ERA, Part II where the discretion has not been exercised and the figure is not therefore quantifiable and due: *Coors Brewery v Adcock* [2007] ICR 983; *Mouradian v Tradition Securities and Futures SA* [2008] All ER (D) 224 (Jan).

[90] *Re German Mining Co* (1853) 4 De GM & G 19; *James v May* (1873) LR 6 HL 328.

[91] *Young v Naval and Military Co-operative Society* [1905] 1 KB 687; *Marmor v Alexander* 1908 SC 78.

## (3) Confidentiality[92]

A director will invariably be subject to a duty of confidentiality in respect of the **8.50**
company's trade secrets and confidential information. Inevitably, there will be a
significant degree of overlap between the duties imposed under the service agreement (whether expressly or impliedly) and a director's statutory duties under the
2006 Act.[93]

Typically, a service agreement will include an express confidentiality clause which **8.51**
will give contractual force to the director's statutory duties. In any event, all directors employed under service agreements are subject to an implied term not to disclose trade secrets or confidential information obtained by reason of employment[94]
and not to use any information obtained as a result of employment to the detriment of the company.[95] Such clauses can be enforced by an injunction, both before
and after termination of the service agreement.[96] However, contractual clauses
regarding confidentiality cannot restrict a director from making a public interest
disclosure within the meaning of the whistleblowing provisions of the ERA.[97]

Such clauses will often be used to protect trade secrets and confidential informa- **8.52**
tion. In *Herbert Morris v Saxelby*,[98] a distinction was drawn between information
that properly belongs to the company, and that forming part of the director's own
general knowledge. A company director will often be experienced and knowledgeable about the relevant industry in which his company operates, which he is
entitled to use for the benefit of a future company. The burden rests upon the
company to show that any specific body of information is outside that falling
within the director's own general knowledge.[99] Further, the company must be able
to show that the information is such as to the have the nature of confidentiality.
In *Thomas Marshall (Exports) Ltd v Guinle*,[100] Megarry V-C held that the issue of
confidentiality should be judged by reference to the potential injury to the company or advantage to a competitor, the reasonable belief of the company, and the
nature of the trade in question.

---

[92] See Goulding, *Employee Competition* (OUP, 2007), chapter 3.
[93] See Chapter 14 below.
[94] *Amber Size and Chemical Co v Menzel* [1913] 2 Ch 239; *Alperton Rubber Co v Manning*
(1917) 86 LJ Ch 377; *British Industrial Plastics v Ferguson* [1940] 1 All ER 479; *Initial Services Ltd
v Putterill* [1968] 1QB 396; *Thomas Marshall Ltd v Guinle* [1979] Ch 227.
[95] *Merryweather v Moore* [1892] 2 Ch.518; *Bent's Brewery Co v Hogan* [1945] 2 All ER 570;
*Cranleigh Precision Engineering Ltd v Bryant* [1965] 1 WLR 1293.
[96] An injunction may be granted where the breach of the duty of confidentiality or the duty of
good faith has occurred during the course of the employment even if the consequences of this only
occur after the employment has ended and, had it not been for the breach during the course of the
employment, the employee would have been free to use it afterwards: see *Roger Bullivant Ltd v Ellis*
[1987] ICR 464, CA.
[97] ERA, Part IVA.
[98] [1916] 1 AC 688, HL.
[99] *FSS Travel and Leisure Systems Ltd v Johnson* [1998] IRLR 382, CA.
[100] [1979] Ch 227.

**8.53** Often, a service contract will seek to impose more onerous restrictions upon a director, both in relation to the categories of information that should be treated as confidential, and in relation to restrictions after termination. Any attempt by a company to deem specific information as confidential, which would not otherwise be confidential (for example as forming part of the director's skill and general knowledge or not otherwise having the nature of confidentiality[101]) is ineffective.[102] However, such a clause may be useful as an aid in determining whether any information should properly be considered confidential.

**8.54** Many companies will also seek to impose restrictions on the use of confidential information after termination of a service agreement. Absent an express clause, the duty will continue in any event after employment.[103] This position is now enshrined in the 2006 Act, subs 170(2)(a), which provides that the director's duty to avoid conflicts of interest as regards the exploitation of property, information, or opportunity of which he became aware at a time when he was a director[104] continues when he ceases to be a director. Notwithstanding the existence of the duty, express contractual clauses are often useful as they will identify the restriction with precision and are more likely to be known to the director.

**8.55** There is no objection to the parties expressly identifying the category of information that is considered to be confidential.[105] However, where a deeming clause of this nature is so wide-ranging as to be in restraint of trade,[106] it will not be enforced, and it cannot be used as an alternative to an appropriate non-solicitation or non-competition clause.[107] As such, in circumstances where there is doubt as to whether the information in question would constitute a trade secret, a company would be well advised to include a well-drafted provision identifying the relevant information with precision and an appropriate duration for which it would remain confidential.

### (4) Restrictive covenants[108]

**8.56** The importance of a director to the success of the company means that it will often be common to include covenants restricting competition with the company after termination. Notably, a director will also be subject to subs 170(2)(b) which prevents him from receiving benefits from third parties as regards things done or

---

[101] See *Faccenda Chicken Ltd v Fowler* [1987] Ch 117.
[102] *Ixora Trading Inc v Jones* [1990] FSR 251.
[103] See *Printers and Finishers Ltd v Holloway (No2)* [1965] 1 WLR 1.
[104] 2006 Act, s 175.
[105] *Lansing Linde v Kerr* [1990] ICR 428.
[106] *Intelsec Systems v Grech-Chini* [2000] 1 WLR 1190.
[107] See *Balston v Headline Filters* [1987] FSR 330, 351–2.
[108] For a comprehensive discussion of this area, see Goulding, *Employee Competition* (OUP, 2007), chapter 5.

omitted before he ceased to be a director.[109] This may conceivably apply to remuneration received from a competitor company for whom a director subsequently goes to work.

As restrictive covenants restrict a director's ability to work, they will constitute an invalid restraint of trade unless reasonable and necessary to protect the company's legitimate business interests.[110] Restrictive covenants may be enforced by the company by way of a claim for damages in the event of breach or by way of an injunction, either before or after the termination of employment. **8.57**

The legitimate business interests of the company are determined by reference to the nature of its activities and the director's role in those activities.[111] The company can primarily use a restrictive covenant to protect trade secrets and confidential information, a director's connections, and workforce skills. However, the categories of legitimate interests are not closed and a reasonable covenant can be used in respect of any further legitimate interest that a company may have.[112] **8.58**

The business interests so far recognized as potentially requiring protection fall into three categories. First, as discussed above, the courts will act to protect confidential information and trade secrets that properly form part of the employer's property and not the general knowledge of the director. **8.59**

Secondly, typically, the director's contacts with customers and clients will constitute an asset of the company. This is particularly true in respect of companies offering professional services, where client relationships constitute a significant part of the company's income. It has long been the case that a company cannot restrict a director from soliciting clients with whom he has had no significant contact.[113] However, where a director has had significant contact, there will be little difficulty in most cases in establishing the legitimate interests capable of protection.[114] **8.60**

Thirdly, the courts have held that a company will have a legitimate interest in protecting the stability of its workplace. This interest is usually protected by way of a covenant restricting the solicitation or 'poaching' of existing directors or employees of the company. As such in *Alliance Paper Group plc v Prestwich*,[115] the court granted an injunction to prevent a managing director from attempting to recruit senior staff. In *Dawnay Day & Co Ltd v D'Alphen*,[116] the Court of **8.61**

---

[109] Companies Act, s 176.
[110] *Nordenfelt v Maxim Nordenfelt & Co* [1894] AC 535, HL.
[111] *Herbert Morris Ltd v Saxelby* [1916] 1 AC 688, HL.
[112] *Dawnay Day & Co Ltd v D'Alphen* [1998] ICR 1068, 1106, 1107, per Evans LJ.
[113] *Herbert Morris Ltd v Saxelby* [1916] 1 AC 688, HL.
[114] *Beckett Investment Management Group Ltd v Hall* [2007] ICR 1539.
[115] [1996] IRLR 25, Ch D.
[116] [1998] ICR 1068.

Appeal held that the restriction of such a clause to 'senior' staff was reasonable and therefore could be enforced. However, in *TSC Europe (UK) Ltd v Massey*[117] the court held that a similar non-solicitation clause constituted a legitimate interest, but on the facts of the case, the covenant was unenforceable as it extended to all employees of the company (including employees who had been recruited since the employee had departed) and was therefore too wide.

**8.62** The reasonableness of the covenant will depend very much upon the nature of the restriction. The courts are more likely to uphold restrictions in directors' service agreements for two reasons. First, as a high status employee, a director is more likely to have the knowledge and contacts that constitute a legitimate interest of the company. As such a restriction against competition entirely may be the only way of protecting the company's interest.[118] Secondly, a director, in contrast to a junior employee, is more likely to be able to protect his own interests when entering into an agreement and does not need the protection of the court.[119]

**8.63** However, notwithstanding the position of a director within the company, a court will still strike down a covenant, or any severable part of a covenant[120] where the restriction is more than is reasonably necessary to protect the interest of the company.[121] Covenants for longer durations and of wider scope will necessarily be more difficult to justify.[122] As such, care should be taken when deciding the interaction between area, duration, and specified restricted activities. In *Office Angels Ltd v Rainer-Thomas*,[123] the court struck down a one-kilometre area restriction in the contracts of a branch manager and consultant where the effect would be to restrict competition throughout most of the City of London. In *Beckett Investment Management v Hall*,[124] the Court of Appeal held that a 12-month non-competition clause was reasonable as it reflected the time required to recruit, organize, train, and project a suitable replacement director, and was consistent with industry practice. The enforceability of the covenants in any given case will turn upon its own facts.[125]

---

[117] [1999] IRLR 22, Ch D.

[118] *TFS Derivatives Ltd v Morgan* [2005] IRLR 246 at paras 15–17, 84, per Cox J; *Thomas v Farr plc* [2007] ICR 932, CA.

[119] 'A managing director can look after himself': *M and S Drapers v Reynolds* [1957] 1 WLR 9, CA, per Denning LJ. See also *Hanover Insurance Brokers Ltd v Schapiro* [1994] IRLR 82.

[120] On severance, see *Mason v Provident Clothing and Supply Co Ltd* [1913] AC 724, HL; *Rex Stewart Jeffries Parker Ginsberg Ltd v Parker* [1988] IRLR 483, CA; *Attwood v Lamont* [1920] 3 KB 571.

[121] *Nordenfelt v Maxim Nordenfelt & Co* [1894] AC 535, HL; *Mason v Provident Clothing Co* [1913] AC 724, HL; *Herbert Morris v Saxelby* [1916] 1 AC 688, HL.

[122] *Herbert Morris v Saxelby* [1916] 1 AC 688, 715, HL.

[123] [1991] IRLR 214, CA.

[124] [2007] ICR 1539.

[125] *Dairy Crest Ltd v Pigott* [1989] ICR 92, CA.

Any covenant must have been valid from the outset.[126] However, even where a **8.64** covenant was reasonable and necessary at the time of agreement, the court has a discretion as to whether to enforce it, which it is unlikely to exercise in respect of a covenant that has become obsolete. For this reason, continued review of the restrictive covenants in directors' service agreements will improve the likelihood that the restrictions remain reasonable and necessary. When drafting such clauses, it is useful to bear in mind Sedley LJ's comment in *Wincanton Ltd v Cranny*[127] that restrictive covenants are 'drafted with the comprehensive particularity of a conveyancer, and one of the morals of the many decided cases in this field of law is that those who live by this mode of drafting may find, when it comes to litigation, that they perish by it'.

### Group companies

Directors are often employed under a service agreement with one company, but in **8.65** fact perform their duties for a related company within the same group. In many cases, the director may be subject to a covenant that purports to restrict competition against an associated company, or any company within the Group. In *Henry Leetham & Sons Ltd v Johnstone-White*,[128] the Court of Appeal refused to uphold a covenant against competition against the Group on the grounds that it was wider than necessary for the company which actually employed the director. However, in *Stenhouse Australia Ltd v Phillips*,[129] the court upheld a similar covenant where subsidiary companies were agencies, handling the business of the parent. In *Beckett Investment Management v Hall*,[130] the Court of Appeal overturned a finding that a covenant was ineffective by reason that it applied to a holding company, notwithstanding the fact that the business in question was carried out by a subsidiary. Maurice Kay LJ referred back to the words of Lord Denning MR in *Littlewoods Organisation Ltd v Harris*[131] that the law should 'have regard to the realities of big business' and held that the parent did have an interest capable of protection, notwithstanding that the actual activities were performed by subsidiaries.

### Repudiation of restrictive covenants

Where the company repudiates the service agreement of a director, he will be **8.66** released from the restrictive covenants contained within the agreement.[132] In such

---

[126] *Gledhow Autoparts Ltd v Delaney* [1965] 1 WLR 1366.
[127] [2000] IRLR 716 at para 29.
[128] [1907] 1 Ch 322, CA.
[129] [1974] AC 391, PC.
[130] [2007] ICR 1539.
[131] [1978] 1 All ER 1026, CA.
[132] *General Billposting v Atkinson* [1909] AC 118, HL. See, however, the doubts expressed upon this decision in *Rock Refrigeration v Jones* [1997] ICR 938, per Phillips LJ at 959–60.

circumstances, a director may be entitled to any damages caused by the repudiation and, additionally, be released from otherwise enforceable restrictions. As such, the rule is of particular importance where the company may have committed a repudiatory breach, such as breach of the implied term of mutual trust and confidence, which would entitle the director to treat himself as constructively dismissed.

# PART III

# THE GENERAL DUTIES
# OF DIRECTORS

# 9

# GENERAL DUTIES OF DIRECTORS

## A. Scope and Nature of General Duties

### (1) Introduction

For the first time, general duties owed to a company by its directors are now **9.01** enshrined in statutory form, in Part 10, Chapter 2 of the Companies Act 2006. This followed the recommendation of the Law Commission and the Scottish Law Commission in their report in 1999,[1] which itself was but the latest in a distinguished line of reports spanning the previous hundred years, most of which had recommended the introduction of a statutory statement of directors' duties in one form or another,[2] and several previous attempts to do so, each of which had been unsuccessful.[3] As explained by Lord Goldsmith, the Attorney-General,

---

[1] *Company Directors: Regulating Conflicts of Interest and Formulating a Statement of Duties* (Law Com No 261).

[2] The Davey Committee (1895), the Greene Committee (1926) and the Jenkins Committee (1962). Of these, only the Greene Committee did not recommend the introduction of a statutory statement, concluding at para 46 of its report that '[t]o attempt by statute to define the duties of directors would be a hopeless task'.

[3] The Companies Bill 1973, which was lost due to the general election the following year, and the Companies Bill 1978, which was lost in similar circumstances in 1979.

the purpose of codification is 'to make what is expected of directors clearer and to make the law more accessible to them and to others'.[4]

**9.02** The general duties are identified as:

(1) the duty to act within powers (s 171);
(2) the duty to promote the success of the company (s 172);
(3) the duty to exercise independent judgment (s 173);
(4) the duty to exercise reasonable care, skill, and diligence (s 174);
(5) the duty to avoid conflicts of interest (s 175);
(6) the duty not to accept benefits from third parties (s 176);
(7) the duty to declare an interest in a proposed transaction or arrangement (s 177).[5]

These duties are considered separately in the chapters following.

**9.03** As they are formulated, the general duties specified in this part of the 2006 Act are based on, and take effect in place of, certain common law rules and equitable principles as they apply to directors.[6] The general duties are to be interpreted and applied in the same way as common law rules and equitable principles, and in interpreting and applying them, regard is to be had to the corresponding common law rules and equitable principles.[7] This presumably means that they may continue to develop over time, in the same way as they have been allowed to develop in the past, rather than remaining static and immutable according to the position reached by the time the Act came into force. It was certainly the Government's intention that the statement of general duties should be sufficiently flexible as to enable the law to respond to changing business circumstances and needs.[8]

**9.04** The statutory statement is, then, intended to be a codification of the existing position at common law, at least in so far as the general duties in their statutory form reflect the common law rules and equitable principles on which they are based. The codification does not, however, provide a complete code of the conduct to be expected of directors. This was confirmed by Lord Goldsmith, Attorney-General, who said:

> The statement of general duties . . . is not intended to be an exhaustive list of all the duties owed by a director to his company. The directors may owe a wide range of duties to their companies in addition to the general duties listed. Those are general,

---

[4] Lords Grand Committee, 6 February 2006, col 254.
[5] The duties set out in ss 171–173 came into force on 1 October 2007: 2006 Act Commencement Order No 3, art 2(d). The duties set out in ss 175–177 came into force on 1 October 2008: 2006 Act Commencement Order No 5, art 5(d).
[6] 2006 Act, s 170(3).
[7] 2006 Act, s 170(4).
[8] White Paper: Company Law Reform at p 21.

basic duties which it is seen as right and important to set out in this way. The statement that these are the general duties does not allow a director to escape any other obligation he has, including obligations under the Insolvency Act 1986.[9]

At least one significant duty remains uncodified, although its existence (or, at **9.05** least, the possibility of its existence) is recognized in s 172(3): namely, the duty owed to the company by directors to consider the interests of creditors when the company is insolvent or facing the threat of insolvency. This is considered further in Chapter 11, Section E below.

The general duties apply to directors appointed as such, as well as to de facto **9.06** directors.[10] In addition, they apply to shadow directors where, and to the extent that, the corresponding common law rules or equitable principles so apply:[11] see Section C below. Certain of the duties, namely the duties to avoid conflicts of interest and not to accept benefits from third parties, also apply to former directors in the manner described in Chapter 14, Section D.[12]

## (2) Distinction between fiduciary duties and other duties

Directors occupy a fiduciary position in relation to the company and owe duties **9.07** as such. A distinction has traditionally been drawn between fiduciary duties on the one hand, and other duties (including the duty to exercise reasonable care, skill, and diligence) on the other. The distinction is important because the duties are fundamentally different. In particular, not every breach of duty by a fiduciary is a breach of fiduciary duty,[13] and the consequences will be different.

It is necessary first to determine what a fiduciary is. According to Millett LJ in **9.08** *Bristol and West Building Society v Mothew*:[14]

A fiduciary is someone who has undertaken to act for or on behalf of another in a particular matter in circumstances which give rise to a relationship of trust and confidence. The distinguishing obligation of a fiduciary is the obligation of loyalty. The principal is entitled to the single-minded loyalty of his fiduciary. This core liability has several facets. A fiduciary must act in good faith; he must not make a profit out of his trust; he must not place himself in a position where his duty and his interest may conflict; he may not act for his own benefit or the benefit of a third person without the informed consent of his principal. This is not intended to be an exhaustive list, but it is sufficient to indicate the nature of fiduciary obligations.

---

9  Lords Grand Committee, 6 February 2006, col 249.
10  The statutory definition of 'director' in 2006 Act, s 250 includes a de facto director.
11  2006 Act, s 170(5).
12  2006 Act, s 170(2).
13  *Bristol and West Building Society v Mothew* [1998] Ch 1, 16D, CA, per Millett LJ.
14  [1998] Ch 1, 18A.

**9.09**   The badge of a fiduciary and, accordingly, of a fiduciary duty, therefore, is loyalty. As Millett LJ went on to say in *Mothew*:

> The various obligations of a fiduciary merely reflect different aspects of his core duties of loyalty and fidelity. Breach of fiduciary obligation, therefore, connotes disloyalty or infidelity. Mere incompetence is not enough. A servant who loyally does his incompetent best for his master is not unfaithful and is not guilty of a breach of fiduciary duty.[15]

**9.10**   Mr Jonathan Crow, sitting as a deputy judge of the Chancery Division, summarized the position in similar terms in *Extrasure Travel Insurance Ltd v Scattergood*, where he said:

> Fiduciary duties are concerned with concepts of honesty and loyalty, not with competence. In my view, the law draws a clear distinction between fiduciary duties and other duties that may be owed by a person in a fiduciary position. A fiduciary may also owe tortious and contractual duties to the cestui que trust: but that does not mean that those duties are fiduciary duties. Bearing all that in mind, I find nothing surprising in the proposition that crass incompetence might give rise to a claim for breach of a duty of care, or breach of contract, but not for a breach of fiduciary duty . . . The fact that his alleged belief was unreasonable may provide evidence that it was not in fact honestly held at the time: but if, having considered all the evidence, it appears that the director did honestly believe that he was acting in the best interests of the company, then he is not in breach of his fiduciary duty merely because that belief appears to the trial judge to be unreasonable, or because his actions happen, in the event, to cause injury to the company.[16]

**9.11**   The 2006 Act, s 178 perpetuates the distinction between fiduciary duties and other duties. It specifically excludes from the former the duty to exercise reasonable care, skill, and diligence (s 174), and confirms that the civil consequences of breach will fall to be determined according to different principles. This does not mean that there can be no interaction between fiduciary and other duties. As the 2006 Act, s 179 recognizes, more than one of the general duties may apply in any given case. This raises the possibility of the duty to exercise reasonable care, skill, and diligence arising in the performance of other duties, including the duty to promote the interests of the company (s 172), as discussed in paragraphs 9.23–9.26 below.

### (3) The relevance of common law rules and equitable principles

**9.12**   Questions of honesty and loyalty affect the conscience, which has traditionally been the preserve of equity. Such questions do not arise in relation to directors alone. They relate to all fiduciaries, including trustees and agents as well, with

---

[15] [1998] Ch 1, 18E–F.
[16] [2003] 1 BCLC 598, 617–18. See also *Ultraframe (UK) Ltd v Fielding* [2005] EWHC 1638 (Ch), per Lewison J at para 1300.

whose position that of directors has often been compared. The influence of equity has thus been keenly felt in the development of the nature and scope of fiduciary duties owed by directors and other fiduciaries. That it continues to do so in more modern times is clear from Millett LJ's judgment in *Bristol and West Building Society v Mothew* referred to at paragraphs 9.07–9.09 above, as well as *Ultraframe (UK) Ltd v Fielding*[17] considered below.

In contrast, the rules relating to duties of skill and care, even ones owed by fiduci- **9.13** aries, have been developed at common law. As will be seen in the context of the discussion of the general duty to exercise reasonable care, skill and diligence in Chapter 13, the nature and scope of such duties developed over the course of the last century as the functions of, and the role played by, directors changed, and as the Legislature recognized that more was to be expected of those who sought to take advantage of the benefits of trading with limited liability in the modern commercial world (apparent not only from the wrongful trading and other provisions of the Insolvency Act, but also from the enactment of the Company Directors Disqualification Act).

The general duties in their codified form are based on these common law rules **9.14** and equitable principles as they apply in relation to directors, and take effect in place of those rules and principles as regards the duties owed to a company by a director.[18] As already stated, those general duties are to be interpreted and applied in the same way as common law rules and equitable principles, and regard is to be had to the corresponding common law rules and equitable principles in interpreting and applying them.[19] Despite the apparent conflict between the concept of the general duties as codified having effect 'in place of' the relevant common law rules and equitable principles, while at the same time requiring those duties to be interpreted having regard to such rules and principles, the intended effect of subss 170(3) and (4) must be that the courts should interpret and give effect to the general duties by reference not only to the relevant rules and principles as they existed at the time of enactment, but as they continue to develop in the future. This recognizes the possibility, for example, that the rules and principles relating to agents, trustees and other fiduciaries may develop over time, and enables the courts to have regard to such developments. This was confirmed by Lord Goldsmith, the Attorney-General:

> Although the duties in relation to directors have developed in a distinctive way, they are often manifestations of more general principles. Subsection (4) is intended to enable the courts to continue to have regard to developments in the common law rules and equitable principles applying to these other types of fiduciary relationship.

---

[17] [2005] EWHC 1638 (Ch).
[18] 2006 Act, s 170(3).
[19] 2006 Act, s 170(4).

The advantage of that is that it will enable the statutory duties to develop in line with relevant developments in the law as it applies elsewhere.[20]

**9.15** Just how much regard shall be had to such rules and principles in any given case, however, is likely to depend upon the nature of the duty under consideration, and the extent to which the terms in which it is expressed in its codified form coincide with the corresponding rule or principle. In certain respects, the general duties in their codified form depart from existing common law duties or equitable principles. This is the case, for example, in relation to certain aspects of the general duty to promote the success of the company (s 172), the new conflict rules (s 175), and the new rules relating to disclosure of interests in proposed transactions or arrangements (s 177). Each of these general duties is discussed in the following chapters. Where these provisions change the law, the scope for having regard to the corresponding common law rules and equitable principles is obviously limited.

### (4) Directors as trustees

**9.16** The position of a director has historically been likened to that of a trustee. Since both are fiduciaries, their positions are analogous. Strictly speaking, however, a director is not a trustee, although he may become subject to the same liabilities as a trustee in certain circumstances. It is the actual control of assets belonging beneficially to a company which causes the law to treat directors as analogous to trustees of those assets.[21] As Lindley LJ put it in *Re Lands Allotment Company*:

> Although directors are not properly speaking trustees, yet they have always been considered and treated as trustees of money which comes to their hands or which is actually under their control; and ever since joint stock companies were invented directors have been held liable to make good moneys which they have misapplied upon the same footing as if they were trustees . . .[22]

**9.17** It is clear that this does not simply arise in relation to money which comes into the director's hands; rather it applies to all property (including rights[23]) coming under their control in their capacity as directors. As Kay LJ said in the same case:

> They are only trustees qua the particular property which is put into their hands or under their control.[24]

**9.18** Directors are not, however, to be treated, nor are they expected to behave, in the same way as trustees in every circumstance. Where the trustee may be expected to exercise caution in the conduct of trust affairs, the direction and control of

---

[20] Lords Grand Committee, 6 February 2006, cols 243–245.
[21] *Ultraframe (UK) Ltd v Fielding* [2005] EWHC 1638 (Ch), per Lewison at para 1253.
[22] [1894] 1 Ch 616, 631.
[23] *Ball v Eden Project Ltd* [2002] 1 BCLC 313.
[24] [1894] 1 Ch 616, 639. See also *Re Forest of Dean Mining Co* (1878) LR 10 Ch 450.

a trading company as a commercial profit-making enterprise will frequently call for a more robust exercise of commercial judgment at a strategic level as well as on a day-to-day basis. The courts have traditionally adopted a more relaxed attitude to the taking of commercial risk by directors in the exercise of their business judgment. This is perhaps most clearly demonstrated by the so-called business judgment rule.[25] For present purposes, it will suffice to illustrate the modern approach to the different functions of trustees on the one hand and directors on the other by reference to *Daniels v Anderson*, in which two members of the New South Wales Court of Appeal described the position in the following way:

> [W]hile the duty of a trustee is to exercise a degree of restraint and conservatism in investment judgments the duty of a director may be to display entrepreneurial flair and accept commercial risks to produce a sufficient return on the capital invested.[26]

### (5) The duties are owed to the company

The 2006 Act, s 170(1) provides as follows: **9.19**

> The general duties specified in sections 171 to 177 are owed by a director of the company to the company.

This reflects the position long recognized at common law that a director owes fiduciary duties and a duty to exercise reasonable care, skill, and diligence to the company and, in the absence of special circumstances,[27] to the company alone. Lord Goldsmith, the Attorney-General, explained that 'as in existing law, the general duties are owed by the director to the company. It follows that, as now, only the company can enforce them. Directors are liable to the company for loss to the company, and not more widely.'[28] A distinction is to be drawn here between the company and, in particular, its shareholders, which emanates from the company's separate legal personality. As Dillon LJ said in *Multinational Gas and Petrochemical Co Ltd v Multinational Gas and Petrochemical Services Ltd*:

> The directors indeed stand in a fiduciary relationship to the company, as they are appointed to manage the affairs of the company and they owe fiduciary duties to the company though not to the creditors, present or future, or to individual shareholders.[29]

Historically, the interests of the company have fallen to be determined by refer- **9.20** ence primarily to the interests of the shareholders (both present and future) as a general body, at least when the company is solvent. Even before the 2006 Act

---

[25] See Chapter 13.
[26] [1995] 13 ACLC 614, 657.
[27] See the discussion at paragraphs 9.21–9.23 below.
[28] Lords Grand Committee, 6 February 2006, col 242.
[29] [1983] Ch 258, 288. Also *Percival v Wright* [1902] 2 Ch 421; *Colin Gwyer v London Wharf* [2003] 2 BCLC 153 at para 72.

came into force, however, this was not exclusively so. The 1985 Act, s 309 obliged directors, in the performance of their functions, to have regard to the interests of the company's employees in general. In addition, in circumstances where the company was in financial difficulties so that its creditors were at risk, even if it was not technically insolvent, the interests of the company were extended so as to encompass the interests of the company's creditors as a whole, as well as those of its shareholders.[30] Whether and to what extent interests other than those of the members are to be taken into account must now be considered in the light of the 2006 Act, s 172 (as to which see Chapter 11 below).

**9.21** It is important to note, however, that the question whether and in what circumstances a director may owe a duty to someone other than the company, and what the nature and extent of any such duty may be, is neither addressed nor affected by the 2006 Act. To the extent, therefore, that any such duty existed before the 2006 Act was enacted, it will continue to apply.

**9.22** Although as a general rule, fiduciary duties owed by a director to the company do not necessarily extend to individual members, either individually or generally, the fact that a director owes fiduciary duties to the company does not necessarily preclude the coexistence of additional duties owed by the directors in special circumstances. Mummery LJ summarized the position in the following way in *Peskin v Anderson*:[31]

> The fiduciary duties owed to the company arise from the legal relationship between the directors and the company directed and controlled by them. The fiduciary duties owed to the shareholders do not arise from that legal relationship. They are dependent on establishing a special factual relationship between the directors and the shareholders in the particular case. Events may take place which bring the directors of the company into direct and close contact with the shareholders in a manner capable of generating fiduciary obligations, such as a duty of disclosure of material facts to the shareholders, or an obligation to use confidential information and valuable commercial and financial opportunities, which have been acquired by the directors in that office, for the benefit of the shareholders, and not to prefer and promote their own interests at the expense of the shareholders.

---

[30] *West Mercia Safetywear Ltd v Dodd* [1988] BCLC 250, 252; *Facia Footwear v Hinchcliffe* [1998] 1 BCLC 218, 228; *MDA Investment Management Ltd* [2004] 1 BCLC 217. See further the discussion in Chapter 11, Section E.

[31] [2001] 1 BCLC 372 at paras 33–34. See also *Allen v Hyatt* (1914) 30 TLR 444 (where the Privy Council held that the directors had held themselves out to the shareholders as acting as agents on their behalf and, accordingly, that they were liable to account to the shareholders for the profits they had made); *Howard Smith Ltd v Ampol Petroleum Ltd* [1974] AC 821 (directors' use of fiduciary power of allotment of shares for a different purpose than that for which it was granted, and so as to dilute the voting power of the majority shareholding of issued shares); *Coleman v Myers* [1977] 2 NZLR 225; *Heron International Ltd v Lord Grade* [1983] BCLC 244; *Re a Company (No 005136 of 1986)* [1987] BCLC 82; *Dawson International plc v Coats Patons plc* [1988] 4 BCC 305; *Re Chez Nico (Restaurants) Ltd* [1992] BCLC 192.

These duties may arise in special circumstances which replicate the salient features of well-established categories of fiduciary relationships. Fiduciary relationships, such as agency, involve duties of trust, confidence and loyalty. Those duties are, in general, attracted by and attached to a person who undertakes, or who, depending on all the circumstances, is treated as having assumed, responsibility to act on behalf of, or for the benefit of, another person. That other person may have entrusted or, depending on all the circumstances, may be treated as having entrusted, the care of his property, affairs, transactions or interests to him. There are, for example, instances of the directors of a company making direct approaches to, and dealing with, the shareholders in relation to a specific transaction and holding themselves out as agents for them in connection with the acquisition or disposal of shares; or making material representations to them; or failing to make material disclosure to them of insider information in the context of negotiations for a take-over of the company's business; or supplying to them specific information and advice on which they have relied. These events are capable of constituting special circumstances and of generating fiduciary obligations, especially in those cases in which the directors, for their own benefit, seek to use their position and special inside knowledge acquired by them to take improper and unfair advantage of the shareholders.

## (6) More than one of the general duties may apply

The 2006 Act, s 179 is in the following terms: **9.23**

> Except as otherwise provided, more than one of the general duties may apply in any given case.

This provision makes it clear that the general duties are generally to be regarded as **9.24** cumulative. Thus, when performing his duty to promote the success of the company (s 172), a director must presumably do so in compliance with his duty to exercise independent judgment (s 173) and with reasonable care, skill, and diligence, in accordance with his duty under s 174. Likewise, a director who accepts a bribe from a third party may simultaneously act in breach not only of the duty not to accept benefits from third parties (s 176), but also the duty to avoid conflicts of interest (s 175), and to promote the success of the company (s 172).

To take another example: a director who causes the company to sell property at an **9.25** undervalue to a company in which he holds shares may find himself in simultaneous breach of more than one of the general duties. He may be in breach of his duty to act within powers (s 171) to the extent that he does not exercise his powers for a legitimate purpose. He may be in breach of his duty to promote the success of the company (s 172). It may even be that he acts in breach of his duty to take account of the interests of the company's creditors (recognized by s 172(3)) if the company is insolvent or becomes insolvent as a result of the sale. He may act in breach of his duty to exercise reasonable care, skill, and diligence (s 174) to the extent that the undervalue results from negligence on his part. Similarly, he may be in breach of his duty to avoid conflicts of interest (s 175). If he receives a payment or other benefit from the recipient company, he may be in breach of his duty not to accept benefits from third parties (s 176), although it is unclear whether the fact that the value of his shareholding in the recipient company may increase would suffice for these purposes). Finally, he may also be in breach of his duty to declare an interest in a proposed transaction or arrangement (s 177).

**9.26** The general rule will not apply where provision is made to the contrary. Thus the duty to avoid conflicts of interest (s 175) does not apply to a conflict of interest arising in relation to a transaction or arrangement with the company, to which the duty to declare an interest (s 177) will apply instead.[32]

## B. The Application of the General Duties to Former Directors

**9.27** Section 170(2) provides that:

> A person who ceases to be a director continues to be subject—
> (a) to the duty in section 175 (duty to avoid conflicts of interest) as regards the exploitation of any property, information or opportunity of which he became aware at a time when he was a director, and
> (b) to the duty in section 176 (duty not to accept benefits from third parties) as regards things done or omitted by him before he ceased to be a director.
> To that extent those duties apply to a former director as to a director, subject to any necessary adaptations.

**9.28** The duties to avoid conflicts of interest and not to accept benefits from third parties are the only general duties capable of subsisting after a person has ceased to be a director and to be concerned in the management of a company. The application of these duties to former directors is discussed in Chapter 14, Section D.

## C. The Application of the General Duties to Shadow Directors

**9.29** The 2006 Act, s 170(5) provides as follows:

> The general duties apply to shadow directors where, and to the extent that, the corresponding common law rules or equitable principles so apply.

This begs an interesting question, namely whether and to what extent, according to those common law rules and equitable principles, duties of the kind now embodied in the 2006 Act are owed by shadow directors.

**9.30** Until recently it seems to have been assumed, in what little authority there was on the subject, that shadow directors owe the same fiduciary and other duties as

---

[32] 2006 Act, s 175(3).

*de jure* directors. In *Yukong Line v Rendsburg Investments*,[33] for example, Toulson J expressed himself in terms which do not appear to admit the possibility of debate:

> As to an unlawful means conspiracy, Mr [Y] undoubtedly owed a fiduciary duty to [the company]. Although he was not formally a director, he was a 'shadow director' and controlled the company's activities. To remove the funds in [the company's] bank account when it had a probable liability to [the Claimant] far in excess of its assets involved a clear breach of that fiduciary duty: *West Mercia Safetywear Ltd (in liq) v Dodd* [1988] BCLC 250.

Toulson J did not explain his reasoning and expressed his view in the context of the duty owed by a director to a company, which was insolvent, to take into account the interests of its creditors.[34] As appears from the discussion in Chapter 11 below, while such a duty exists at common law, the circumstances giving rise to it and its scope remain uncertain, and it is not one which has been codified in the 2006 Act, ss 171–177.

In *John v Price WaterhouseCoopers*,[35] Ferris J was minded to accept that a shadow **9.31** director owed a duty of care to the company, as appears from the following paragraph in his judgment:

> The case against Mr Haydon was that he was in breach of a duty of care owed by him to Bong as a shadow director and, to the extent that the salaries and expenses were debited to Bondi, in breach of a duty of care owed by him to Bondi. For reasons which I have already stated, I am satisfied that Mr Haydon did owe such a duty of care to Bondi. If it is correct that he was a shadow director of Bong I would accept that he owed a similar duty of care to Bong.

In the result, however, Ferris J concluded that Mr Haydon was not a shadow director of Bong. Accordingly, what he said in relation to a duty of care being owed by a shadow director was, strictly, *obiter*.

In neither case does it appear that the point was fully argued. The same cannot **9.32** be said of *Ultraframe (UK) Ltd v Fielding*.[36] In that case, it was alleged, and Lewison J held, that Mr Fielding was a shadow director of two companies. It was argued that this meant that he owed the same fiduciary obligations to those two companies as if he had been a *de jure* director of both of them. Lewison J disagreed. He concluded that the mere fact that a person falls within the statutory definition of 'shadow director' was not enough to impose upon him the same fiduciary duties to the relevant company as are owed by a *de jure* or de facto

---

[33] [1998] 2 BCLC 485, 502h.
[34] In *Ultraframe*, Lewison J referred to Toulson J's judgment in *Yukong*, but considered that he must be cautious before accepting that a shadow director 'undoubtedly' owes fiduciary duties to the company.
[35] Unreported, 11 April 2001 (Ferris J) at para 319.
[36] [2005] EWHC 1638 (Ch).

director,[37] but that on the facts of a particular case the activities of a shadow director may go beyond the mere exertion of indirect influence and subject him to particular fiduciary duties.[38]

**9.33** It is instructive to follow the line of reasoning which led Lewison J to this conclusion, not least because to do so amply demonstrates the influence equity has had on this area of the law and will continue to exercise by virtue of the 2006 Act, s 170(5). It may be summarized as follows:[39]

(1) The statutory definition of 'shadow director' was enacted for specific purposes of company legislation (including many prohibitions relating to transactions between companies and their directors, duties of disclosure, liability for wrongful trading, or to the making of disqualification orders). However, there was no specific statutory provision that said that a shadow director owes the same duties to a company as a *de jure* or de facto director.

(2) The term 'shadow director' was thus a limited statutory concept, not a concept of the general law.

(3) If the intention of Parliament had been to equate 'shadow directors' with 'directors' for all statutory purposes, this could have been simply achieved by extending the definition of 'director' to include a 'shadow director', but this had not been done.

(4) Instead, Parliament had specified those duties which apply to shadow directors, while remaining silent on others.

(5) The rationale for this distinction was that, unlike a *de jure* or de facto director, a shadow director does not undertake or agree to act in relation to the company in the same way.

(6) A shadow director directs or instructs those who themselves owe a fiduciary duty to the company. However, he does not thereby assume any obligation of loyalty to the company, and the company does not look to him to promote its interests. Instead, the company continues to look, at all times, to the de facto or *de jure* directors it has in place. It is against those persons that the company may have a complaint for breach of fiduciary duty.

(7) If the company has a complaint in equity against the 'shadow director' this can only be based upon an allegation of dishonest assistance by procuring a breach of fiduciary duty or for knowing receipt of trust property.

(8) The instructions that a shadow director gives (and which the *de jure* directors act upon) may be quite inimical to the company's interests, and it would be odd if, in those circumstances, a person who has no direct relationship with

---

37 [2005] EWHC 1638 (Ch) at paras 1284 and 1289.
38 Ibid at paras 1289–1290.
39 Ibid at paras 1279–1284.

the company and who consistently gives instructions inimical to its interests were nevertheless held to have undertaken a duty of loyalty to the company.

(9) The mere fact that a person falls within the statutory definition of 'shadow director', therefore, was not enough to impose upon him the same fiduciary duties to the relevant company as are owed by a *de jure* or de facto director.

The real question at issue[40] was this: in what circumstances will equity impose **9.34** fiduciary obligations on a person with regard to property belonging to another? After considering the authorities, Lewison J accepted the proposition that the key component of a fiduciary duty is the obligation of loyalty, and that he must look for facts which supported the inference that the company was in a direct relation of trust and confidence with the putative fiduciary.[41] Lewison J accepted that, on the facts of a particular case, the activities of a shadow director may go beyond the mere exertion of indirect influence. As sole signatory on the company's bank account, for example, it was indisputable that the shadow director was not entitled to draw on the account for his personal benefit. Taking it upon himself to assume control of an asset belonging to another carried with it a duty to use the asset for the benefit of the company, a duty which was properly called a fiduciary duty. Lewison J emphasized, however, that this fact alone did not mean that wider fiduciary duties were imposed upon him.[42]

Just as the 1985 Act did not extend the definition of 'director' so as to include **9.35** shadow director, neither does the 2006 Act.[43] Nor does the 2006 Act provide that shadow directors owe the same duties as are owed by *de jure* and de facto directors. Based on the wording of the relevant provisions, therefore, there is no reason why the position in relation to shadow directors, as Lewison J described it in *Ultraframe*, should not also obtain under the 2006 Act. Unless and until it is determined that Lewison J reached the wrong conclusion, therefore, the answer to the question prompted by the 2006 Act, s 170(5) will be: common law rules and equitable principles do not apply so as automatically to subject shadow directors to the same general duties as are imposed upon *de jure* and de facto directors, although on the facts of a particular case, the activities of a particular shadow director may go beyond the mere exertion of indirect influence and may accordingly give rise to one or more general duties on his part.

It is doubtful whether this position is that which was envisaged at the time the statu- **9.36** tory statement of general duties was being considered and formulated. For example, having referred to the statement in the edition of Pennington's *Company Law*

---

[40] [2005] EWHC 1638 (Ch) at para 1285.
[41] Ibid at paras 1286–1288.
[42] Ibid at paras 1289–1290.
[43] 2006 Act, s 250(1).

current at the time, to the effect that shadow directors are not subject to the common law or equitable duties of directors, the Law Commission and the Scottish
Law Commission said the following:

> However, the better view is that the shadow director is to be regarded as akin to a
> de facto director and that he can incur the liability of a de jure director under the
> general law where he effectively acts as a director through the people whom he can
> influence.[44]

They also considered that Toulson J had been correct to proceed on the basis that
a shadow director could be in breach of fiduciary duties as a director, in *Yukong
Line Ltd v Rendsburg Investments Corporation (No 2)*.[45] The Attorney-General,
Lord Goldsmith, was more equivocal, but evidently considered that some at least
of the general duties should apply to shadow directors:

> The law is still developing. It would not be right for the general duties not to apply
> at all to shadow directors, but the law may develop in such a way that some do and
> some don't. It is right to leave those areas, as now, to the courts . . .[46]

## D. Consent, Approval, or Authorization by Members

**9.37** The 2006 Act, s 180 contains provisions concerning the manner in which members of the company may give their consent, approval or authorization, or where
they may not be required to do so, in relation to the directors' general duties.

**9.38** Three general propositions are to be derived from the provisions of the 2006 Act,
s 180. First, the application of the general duties is not affected by the fact that the
case also falls within Chapter 4 (transactions requiring approval of members).[47] In
other words, the general duties and those set out in Chapter 4 are generally to be
regarded as being cumulative (save to the extent that the 2006 Act, s 180 otherwise provides, as discussed below), so that the general duties will apply even if
Chapter 4 also applies. It follows that compliance with the general duties does
not remove the need for approval under any applicable provision of Chapter 4.[48]

**9.39** Secondly, the general duties have effect subject to any rule of law enabling the
company to give authority, specifically or generally, for anything to be done
(or omitted) by the directors, or any of them, that would otherwise be a breach

---

[44] Law Commission, *Company Directors: Regulating Conflicts of Interests and Formulating a
Statement of Duties* at para 17.15 (Consultation Paper No 153, Scottish Law Commission Discussion
Paper No 105).
[45] [1998] 1 WLR 294; Joint Consultation Paper at para 17.15.
[46] Lords Grand Committee, 9 May 2006, col 828.
[47] 2006 Act, s 180(2). 2006 Act, Part 10, Chapter 4 is discussed in Chapter 18.
[48] 2006 Act, s 180(3).

of duty.[49] This means that members may still authorize what would otherwise constitute a breach of a general duty, for example by giving their unanimous consent informally.[50] However, it also means that such limitations as already exist on such powers to authorize acts or omissions by directors will remain. Thus consent, to be effective, must be properly informed.[51] Members could not authorize an act or omission that would be unlawful, or would constitute a breach of a statutory provision, the underlying purpose of which extends beyond the protection of members.[52] For similar reasons, members cannot authorize acts or omissions which are likely to affect the interests of the company's creditors, in circumstances where the company is insolvent or on the verge of insolvency.[53]

Careful consideration will have to be given, however, to the terms of the authority given by the members. The mere fact that directors may be authorized to act in a certain way, for example to enter into a certain transaction, will not obviate the need for them to continue to exercise reasonable care, skill, and diligence (2006 Act, s 174) when doing so, or to reconsider whether the transaction would promote the success of the company (2006 Act, s 172), if there were to be a material change of circumstances after authorization had been obtained.[54]    **9.40**

The 2006 Act, s 180(4)(a) must be read with the 2006 Act, s 239 (ratification of acts of directors), which is discussed in Chapter 19. The obvious difference is that ratification may only follow after the relevant act or omission that would otherwise constitute a breach of duty, whereas the 2006 Act, s 180(4)(a) contemplates prior authority being given. Subject to this, the essential distinction between the two is that, where ratification is sought, the vote of the director in breach of duty (if he is a member) and any member connected with him will be disregarded for the purposes of ascertaining whether the resolution has been passed by the requisite majority.[55] This is not so if the act or omission is authorized in advance. The reason for this is that an act or omission previously authorized cannot give rise to a breach of duty. On the other hand, the ratification of an act or omission which was not so authorized and which constitutes a breach of duty involves the company giving up a claim against the director concerned. It is to be noted that, whether the act or omission is previously authorized or subsequently ratified,    **9.41**

---

[49]  2006 Act, s 180(4)(a).

[50]  *Re Duomatic Ltd* [1969] 2 Ch 365; *Wright v Atlas Wright (Europe) Ltd* [1999] 2 BCLC 301, CA.

[51]  *Kaye v Croydon Tramways Co* [1989] 1 Ch 358, CA.

[52]  *Wright v Atlas Wright (Europe) Ltd* 1999 2 BCLC 301, CA.

[53]  *West Mercia Safetywear Ltd v Dodd* [1988] BCLC 250, 252h–253b, CA, per Dillon LJ; *Lexi Holdings plc v Luqman* [2007] EWHC 2652 (Ch), Briggs J at para 191.

[54]  eg *In re Brazilian Rubber Plantations and Estates Ltd* [1911] 1 Ch 425, 437 (a case where the company's articles conferred a discretion on the directors, which Neville J considered the directors were bound to exercise).

[55]  2006 Act, s 239(4).

a member will not be permitted to pursue a derivative claim against the director in respect of that act or omission.[56]

**9.42** The third general proposition set out in the 2006 Act, s 180 is that the general duties otherwise (ie subject to the other provisions of that section) have effect notwithstanding any enactment or rule of law, except as otherwise provided or where the context otherwise requires. [57]

**9.43** What the 2006 Act, s 180 also does, however, is make special provision in respect of cases which are concerned with the duty to avoid conflicts of interest (2006 Act, s 175), the duty not to accept benefits from third parties (2006 Act, s 176), and the duty to declare an interest in a proposed transaction or arrangement with the company (2006 Act, s 177). These are addressed separately below.

*The duty to avoid conflicts of interest*

**9.44** As more fully discussed in Chapter 14, the 2006 Act, s 175 contains a statutory statement of the duty to avoid conflicts of interest, which will include a conflict of interest and duty and a conflict of duties. It does not apply to a conflict of interest arising in relation to a transaction or arrangement with the company, to which the 2006 Act, s 177 and Chapters 3–6 apply instead. The duty is not infringed if the particular transaction or arrangement has been properly authorized by the directors.[58] Where this authorization has been obtained, the 2006 Act, s 180(1)(a) provides that the transaction or arrangement is not liable to be set aside by virtue of any common law rule or equitable principle requiring the consent or approval of the members of the company. However, if any other enactment requires the consent or approval of the members in respect of the particular transaction or arrangement, or if such consent or approval is required by the company's constitution, then it must be sought and obtained.[59]

**9.45** The 2006 Act, Part 10, Chapter 4 deals with transactions with directors which require the approval of members.[60] Where the transaction or arrangement under consideration falls within the provisions of Chapter 4, and either approval is given under that chapter or it is provided that approval is not needed, it is not necessary also to comply with s 175.[61] Otherwise, the application of the general duty to avoid conflicts of interest is not affected by the fact that the case also falls within Chapter 4.[62] This is an exception to the first general proposition discussed

---

[56] 2006 Act, s 263(2)(c).
[57] 2006 Act, s 180(5).
[58] 2006 Act subss 175(4)(b), (5), and (6).
[59] 2006 Act, s 180(1).
[60] The provisions of 2006 Act, Part 10, Chapter 4 are fully discussed in Chapter 18 below.
[61] 2006 Act, s 180(2).
[62] Ibid.

in paragraph 9.38 above. Conversely, however, the mere fact that the director complies with his general duty under s 175 does not remove the need for approval under any applicable provision of Chapter 4.[63]

Finally, in this context, it is to be noted that the general duties are not infringed by any act or omission on the part of the directors, when done (or omitted) in accordance with provisions contained in the company's articles for dealing with conflicts of interest.[64] It is suggested that this means that a director will not be in breach of a general duty merely by reason of a conflict of interest, if he acts (or omits to act) in accordance with the company's articles dealing with conflicts of interest. It is improbable, however, that the director will by virtue of this provision avoid liability for breach of one of the general duties altogether if, for example, he fails to exercise reasonable care, skill, and diligence, acts outside his powers, or fails to promote the success of the company.    **9.46**

### The duty to declare an interest in a proposed transaction or arrangement

With an important qualification, the 2006 Act, s 180 makes similar provision in relation to those cases which concern the duty to declare an interest in a proposed transaction or arrangement with the company. The duty is set out in the 2006 Act, s 177, which is fully discussed in Chapter 15. The section states that the declaration must be made before the company enters into the transaction or arrangement,[65] and explains how it may be made.[66] Where the requirements of s 177 are complied with, the transaction or arrangement is not liable to be set aside by virtue of any common law rule or equitable principle requiring the consent or approval of the members of the company.[67] Once again, however, if any other enactment requires the consent or approval of the members in respect of the particular transaction or arrangement, or if such consent or approval is required by the company's constitution, then it must be sought and obtained.[68]    **9.47**

Where the approach to this duty differs from the duty to avoid conflicts of interest, however, is in the application of the 2006 Act, s 180(2), which contains no exception in relation to a case to which the 2006 Act, s 177 applies. This means that, as with the remaining general duties (with the exception of the duty not to accept benefits from third parties discussed below), the application of the duty to declare an interest is not affected by the fact that the case also falls within Chapter 4. In other words, the requirements of the 2006 Act, s 177 will apply even    **9.48**

---

[63] 2006 Act, s 180(3).
[64] 2006 Act, s 180(4)(b).
[65] 2006 Act, s 177(3).
[66] 2006 Act, s 177(2). See generally the discussion in Chapter 15 below.
[67] 2006 Act, s 180(1)(a).
[68] 2006 Act, s 180(1).

if the provisions of Chapter 4 also apply and are complied with, just as compliance with s 177 will not remove the need for approval under Chapter 4.

### The duty not to accept benefits from third parties

**9.49**   The 2006 Act, s 176 sets out the general duty on the part of a director not to accept benefits from third parties.[69] The 2006 Act, s 180(2) provides that where the transaction or arrangement under consideration falls within the provisions of Chapter 4, and either approval is given under that chapter or it is provided that approval is not needed, it is not necessary also to comply with s 176.[70] This is the second exception to the general rule discussed in paragraph 9.39 above. Otherwise, however, the application of the general duty not to accept benefits from third parties is unaffected by the fact that the case also falls within Chapter 4.[71] Furthermore, the mere fact that the director complies with his general duty under s 176 does not remove the need for approval under any applicable provision of Chapter 4.[72]

## E.  Modifications for Charitable Companies

**9.50**   The 2006 Act, s 181(1) (which does not extend to Scotland) provides that, in their application to a company that is a charity, the provisions of s 175 (the duty to avoid conflicts of interest) and s 180(2)(b) are modified in certain respects. The Charities Act, s 26(5) is also amended so as to insert a new subsection 26(5A). In all other respects, the provisions of Chapter 10 of the 2006 Act apply to companies that are charities in the same way as they apply to companies that are not.

### The duty to avoid conflicts of interest

**9.51**   The effect of the 2006 Act, s 181(2) is that subss 175(3) and (5) (which impose the general duty to avoid conflicts of interest) are modified insofar as they relate to a company that is a charity. In the first place, the duty does not apply to a conflict of interest arising in relation to a transaction or arrangement with the company if or to the extent that the company's articles allow that duty to be so disapplied, which they may do only in relation to descriptions of transaction or arrangement specified in the company's articles.[73] Secondly, while the duty will not be infringed if the matter has been authorized by the directors,[74] such authorization may only be given by the directors where the company's constitution includes provision

---

[69]  2006 Act, s 176 is discussed in Chapter 14 below.
[70]  2006 Act, s 180(2).
[71]  Ibid.
[72]  2006 Act, s 180(3).
[73]  2006 Act, s 181(2)(a).
[74]  2006 Act, s 175(4)(b).

enabling them to authorize the matter, and the matter is proposed to, and authorized by, them in accordance with the company's constitution.

### Consent, approval, or authorization

Subsection 181(3) provides as follows:                                                    **9.52**

> Section 180(2)(b) (which disapplies certain duties under this Chapter in relation to cases excepted from requirement to obtain approval by members under Chapter 4) applies only if or to the extent that the company's articles allow those duties to be so disapplied, which they may do only in relation to descriptions of transaction or arrangement specified in the company's articles.

### The Charities Act 1993

The Charities Act 1993, s 26 confers powers on the Charities Commission to **9.53** sanction any action proposed or contemplated in the administration of a charity if it is expedient in the interests of the charity, whether or not it would otherwise be within the powers exercisable by the charity trustees in the administration of the charity. The 2006 Act, s 181(4) introduces by amendment a new subsection 26(5A) into the Charities Act 1993, the terms of which are self-explanatory:

> In the case of a charity that is a company, an order under this section may authorise an act notwithstanding that it involves the breach of a duty imposed on a director of the company under Chapter 2 of Part 10 of the Companies Act 2006 (general duties of directors).

# 10

## DUTY TO ACT WITHIN POWERS

## A. Introduction

Section 171 of the Companies Act provides that:                                     **10.01**

> A director of a company must—
> (a) act in accordance with the company's constitution, and
> (b) only exercise powers for the purposes for which they are conferred.

Paragraph (a) of the duty states a director's overriding duty of obedience to the       **10.02**
constitution.[1] Paragraph (b) requires a director to observe the spirit as well as the
letter of the constitution by which his powers of management are conferred.

The duty stated in s 171 applies to shadow directors to the extent that the com-        **10.03**
mon law rules or equitable principles corresponding to the duty to act within
powers applied to shadow directors (see Chapter 9, Section C).[2]

A director who, in relation to a particular transaction, wishes to be protected from    **10.04**
the risk of being in breach of the duty to act within powers may obtain the prior
consent, approval, or authorization of the members, as recognized by s 180(4)(a)
(see Chapter 9, Section D) or the subsequent ratification of his conduct under
s 239 (Chapter 19, Section D).

---

[1] CLR: *Final Report*, explanatory note 10 on p 350. Also see the Law Commission: *Company Directors: Regulating Conflicts of Interest and Formulating a Statement of Duties* (Consultation Paper, No 153; Scottish Law Commission Discussion Paper No 105) at paras 11.6–11.10 and 11.18.
[2] s 170(5).

## B. Duty to Act in Accordance with the Company's Constitution

**10.05**  The 2006 Act, s 171(a) codifies the director's duty to comply with the company's constitution. To the extent that the directors exceed their constitutional power in breach of s 171(a) they will be liable accordingly.

### (1) Meaning of the company's constitution

**10.06**  The constitution is defined for the purpose of the general duties by the 2006 Act, ss 17 and 257 and therefore includes:[3]

(1) the company's articles (s 17(a));

(2) any resolutions and agreements affecting a company's constitution (s 29), that is to say:

    (a) any special resolution;

    (b) any resolution or agreement agreed to by all the members of a company that, if not so agreed to, would not have been effective for its purpose unless passed as a special resolution;

    (c) any resolution or agreement agreed to by all the members of a class of shareholders that, if not so agreed to, would not have been effective for its purpose unless passed by some particular majority or otherwise in some particular manner;

    (d) any resolution or agreement that effectively binds all members of a class of shareholders though not agreed to by all those members;

    (e) and any other resolution or agreement to which Chapter 3 applies by virtue of any enactment.[4]

(3) In addition to (1) and (2): '(a) any resolution or other decision come to in accordance with the constitution, and (b) any decision by the members of the company, or a class of members, that is treated by virtue of any enactment or rule of law as equivalent to a decision by the company' (s 257).

**10.07**  It is important to note that the definitions of the term 'company's constitution' set out in ss 17 and 257 are non-exhaustive. In addition to the matters set out in those sections, the Companies Act clearly contemplates that the contents of certain other documents may be of constitutional relevance for certain purposes. What those other documents may encompass is presently unclear. Their ambit is, however, unlikely to be extensive. One example of an additional document that might be of constitutional relevance for certain purposes would be the company's

---

[3] 2006 Act Commencement Order No 3, para 2(3)(a) makes transitional provisions relating to the application of s 17 in connection with 2006 Act, ss 170 to 181.

[4] 2006 Act, s 29(2) provides that references to a member of a company, or a class of members of a company, do not include the company itself where it is such a member by virtue only of its holding shares as treasury shares.

certificate of incorporation, provision for which is made in the 2006 Act, s 15. This summarizes key information as to whether the company has been registered as a limited company or a public company and where the company is limited, whether it is limited by shares or by guarantee.

### The company's articles

The provisions of the 1985 Act Table A and the Model Articles (pcls) and (plc) are drafted such that the restrictions placed on the powers of directors to act are relatively limited. Of most relevance to this duty are those provisions concerning the procedure for declaring and paying dividends[5] and those concerning the participation of a director in the decision-making process for quorum, voting, or agreement purposes in circumstances where that director has a conflict of interest.[6]  **10.08**

Companies may, however, through their articles go further than the statutory duties by placing more onerous requirements on their directors (eg by requiring shareholder authorization of the remuneration of the directors). The articles may not, however, dilute the duties except to the extent that this is permitted by the following sections:[7]  **10.09**

(1) s 173 provides that a director will not be in breach of the duty to exercise independent judgment if he has acted in a way that is authorized by the constitution;

(2) s 175 permits authorization of some conflicts of interest by independent directors, subject to the constitution;

(3) subs 180(4)(a) preserves any rule of law enabling the company to give authority for anything that would otherwise be a breach of duty and compliments s 239;[8]

(4) subsection 180(4)(b) provides that a director will not be in breach of duty if he acts in accordance with any provisions in the company's articles for dealing with conflicts of interest;

(5) section 232 places restrictions on the provisions that may be included in the company's articles. But nothing in that section prevents companies from including in their articles any such provisions as are currently lawful for dealing with conflicts of interest.

---

[5] Table A, regs 102 to 108; Model Articles (pcls) 30–36; Model Articles (plc) 70–77.

[6] Table A, reg 85; Model Article (pcls) 14; Model Article (plc) 16. See also Chapter 14 below.

[7] 2006 Act, s 232.

[8] As to which see Chapter 19. Note also that subs 239(7) preserves the rule of uncertain ambit as to matters incapable of ratification because of prejudice to creditors where the company is insolvent or in the zone of insolvency. The relevant principles in this regard as discussed in full in Chapter 11, Section E.

**10.10**  In the context of the procedure for the declaration of dividends there are some older examples of the application of the duty which may remain instructive. In *Re Oxford Benefit Building and Investment Society*[9] the articles of association of a limited company provided that no dividends should be payable except out of realized profits and that no remuneration should be paid to the directors until a dividend of 7 per cent had been paid to the shareholders. The business of the company consisted chiefly in lending money to builders on mortgages payable by instalments, and the directors treated, as part of the profits available for dividends, the value (upon an estimate made by their surveyor who was also their secretary) of the instalments of principal and interest remaining unpaid by each mortgagor. Upon this footing the directors caused the company to pay out dividends and remuneration to themselves. The court held that the directors, having treated estimated profits as realized profits, had acted outside their constitutional powers and were jointly and severally liable to repay the dividends and remuneration. Such a situation would now, largely, be governed by the provisions of the 2006 Act, Part 23.[10] These statutory limitations on distributions make it much less likely than previously that provisions in the memorandum or articles will narrow down one or more of the possible sources of distributable profit. However, such provisions could be more narrowly drawn and if contravened could lead to personal liability on the part of the board under s 171(a).

*Resolutions and agreements*

**10.11**  Where a company passes a resolution or enters into an agreement affecting a company's constitution of the type listed in the 2006 Act, s 29, it must forward a copy of the resolution or agreement to the Registrar of Companies for registration within 15 days of the date on which the resolution was passed. If a company fails to do this, the company, and every officer of it who is in default, commits an offence. Where a resolution or agreement which affects a company's constitution is not in writing, the company is required to provide the Registrar with a written memorandum setting out the terms of the resolution or agreement in question.[11]

**10.12**  In this context, the directors should also have regard to those provisions (if any) of the company's articles which concern the shareholders' reserve power to control the actions of the directors by means of a special resolution. Model Article (pcls) 4 and Model Article (plc) 4 both provide that the shareholders may, by special resolution, direct the directors to take, or refrain from taking,

---

[9]  (1886) 35 Ch D 502.
[10]  2006 Act, Part 23 replaced 1985 Act, Part VIII, on 6 April 2008.
[11]  2006 Act, s 30, which came into force on 1 October 2007.

specified action.[12] Such a direction might be in general terms, eg relating to transactions of a particular class, or it might relate to a specific transaction, either requiring it to be carried out or prohibiting it.

### Informal unanimous consent

The 2006 Act, s 257 broadens the definition of the company's constitution for the **10.13** purposes of the general duties still further, by making it plain that informal unanimous decisions by the members are included.[13] The principle established in *Re Duomatic Ltd* provides that if all of the shareholders entitled to vote on a matter have informally assented to it then the formalities required by the Companies Act or by the company's articles can be dispensed with. The principle has been extended further in recent case law.[14]

In *Euro Brokers Holdings Ltd v Monecor (London) Ltd* [15] the Court of Appeal **10.14** considered whether the principle could be extended to a situation in which the procedural requirements existed outside the articles, specifically in a separate shareholders' agreement. The shareholders' agreement in question detailed how further financing of a joint venture should take place, setting out stated procedural requirements for the company to follow if it wished to make a capital call on the shareholders. The company did not follow these procedures, but sent out an email request instead. Both shareholders nevertheless agreed to this request, albeit that at a later stage one of the parties failed to pay the entire amount it had promised. That party argued that the capital call was invalid because it had not followed the procedure set out in the shareholders' agreement. It argued that the *Duomatic* principle was irrelevant because that principle only applied to internal corporate governance and to the issue of whether acts could be described as those of the company or not. The Court of Appeal disagreed allowing the application of the *Duomatic* principle to an act done with the consent of the shareholders and yet not in procedural compliance with a shareholders' agreement. The Court of Appeal rejected the appellant's attempts to confine *Duomatic* to 'internal governance' and to procedures placed in the articles of association. There was no difference between the contractual nature of the articles of association and a separate shareholders' agreement. It was the unanimous consent of the shareholders which was the key to the application of the principle and not the basis of the formal procedural requirement which it waived.[16]

---

[12] See also the provisions of Table A, reg 70.
[13] *Re Duomatic Ltd* [1969] 2 Ch 365.
[14] See Chapter 22, Section B(4).
[15] [2003] 1 BCLC 506.
[16] Cf *Russell v Northern Bank Development Corp Ltd* [1992] BCLC 1016.

(2) *Ultra vires*

**10.15** Where a director causes the company to act beyond its powers he will be in breach of the duty contained in s 171(a). This aspect of the duty set out in s 171(a) is not one that has featured greatly in recent case law. This is largely as a result of the enactment of the statutory predecessors to the 2006 Act, ss 39 and 40.[17] These sections (which are discussed in Chapter 4[18]) significantly reduced the effect of a breach of a director's duty to comply with the company's constitution in so far as it affects third parties. The 2006 Act, s 40 provides that, in favour of a person dealing with a company in good faith, the power of the directors to bind the company, or authorize others to do so, is deemed to be free of any limitation under the company's constitution.[19] In addition, s 39 provides that the validity of an act done by the company shall not be called into question on the ground of lack of capacity by reason of anything in the company's constitution.[20] Taken together the two provisions mean that a third party dealing with a company in good faith need not concern itself about whether the company is acting within its constitution and will be able to enforce an obligation incurred by the company even where a director causes the company to act in contravention of its constitution. The sections only operate to protect third parties dealing with the company or its directors. They do not alter any liability of a director to the company where he acts in excess of his constitutional powers in breach of s 171(a).

**10.16** The decision of the Court of Appeal in *Rolled Steel Products (Holdings) Ltd v British Steel Corpn*[21] has also impacted on the significance of the duty. In that case, the Court of Appeal emphasized that an important distinction needed to be drawn between acts which were genuinely *ultra vires* the company and acts which were within the company's capacity but were entered into by the directors for an improper purpose. Only the former acts will fall within the scope of s 171(a). The latter acts will now fall within the scope of s 171(b).

**10.17** Also of note is that the role of the memorandum of association is significantly reduced under the 2006 Act. Under the 2006 Act the purpose of the memorandum of association is to provide evidence of the intention of the subscribers to the memorandum to form a company and become members of that company on formation.[22] Information regarding the internal allocation of powers between

---

[17] 1985 Act, ss 35(1) and 35A. The provisions of 1985 Act, s 35A do not protect dealings with directors and their associates, to which 1985 Act, s 322A applies. These provisions of the 2006 Act replace the corresponding provisions of the 1985 Act on 1 October 2009.

[18] See also Chapter 2 at paragraphs 2.10–2.14.

[19] 2006 Act, s 40 is subject to the constitutional limitations concerning transactions involving directors or their associates to which s 41 applies (replacing 1985 Act, s 322A).

[20] This section has effect subject to 2006 Act, s 42 which relates to companies that are charities.

[21] [1986] Ch 246.

[22] 2006 Act, s 8.

the directors and members will now be found in the company's articles of association. Provisions in the memoranda of companies formed under the 1985 Act and its predecessors will be treated as provisions in the articles if they are of a type that will not now be in the memoranda of companies formed under the Companies Act.[23]

The 2006 Act, s 31 also provides for a new approach to the question of a company's objects. Under the 1985 Act all companies are required to have objects and these objects are required to be specified in the memorandum. The 1985 Act also makes specific provision for where a company states its objects to be to carry on business as a general commercial company.[24] Based on a recommendation of the Company Law Review Steering Group (CLR)[25] under the 2006 Act a different approach is taken. Instead of companies being required to specify their objects, companies will have unrestricted objects unless the objects are specifically restricted by the articles. This will mean that unless a company makes a deliberate choice to restrict its objects, the objects will have no bearing on what it can do. In most cases this is likely to further restrict the application of the duty contained in s 171(a).   **10.18**

In this regard, it is important to note that the expression '*ultra vires*' has been used to describe both acts which are invalid because they are not within the company's stated objects and acts which a company may not do because they are illegal, eg prohibited by the Companies Act (as in the case of the issue of shares not forming part of the authorized and unissued capital). The distinction is an important one because incapacity in the second sense remains unaffected by the 2006 Act, ss 39 and 40.[26] In most cases, however, it is likely that a transaction which is *ultra vires* in the second sense will also amount to a breach by the directors of their duties to the company. For example, in *MacPherson v European Strategic Bureau Ltd*[27] the Court of Appeal held that it was a breach of the duties owed by the directors to the company or alternatively an act which was *ultra vires* the company for them to enter into an arrangement which sought to achieve a distribution of assets to shareholders, as if on a winding up, without making proper provision for creditors, since to do so amounted to an attempt to circumvent the protection which the 1985 Act, s 263 aimed to provide. Such an arrangement failed the test of validity of a distribution of assets because it could not be described as being either for the benefit of the company or reasonably incidental to the carrying on   **10.19**

---

[23] 2006 Act, s 28.
[24] 1985 Act, s 3A.
[25] *Final Report*, para 9.10.
[26] The statement in *Aveling Barford Ltd v Perion Ltd* that 'a transaction which amounts to an unauthorised return of capital . . . is *ultra vires*' is probably best seen as example of the use of the term in the second sense.
[27] [2000] 2 BCLC 683.

of the company's business. Since the distribution of assets as if on a winding up but without making proper provision for creditors was not permitted by the 1985 Act, s 263 it was also an act outside the directors' powers.

## C.  Duty to Only Exercise Powers for the Purposes for Which They Are Conferred

**10.20**    The Companies Act, s 171(b) codifies the general duty of a director only to exercise his powers for the purposes for which they are conferred. The separation of this subsection from s 172 reflects the position previously established at common law that this duty exists independently of the duty to promote the success of the company.[28]

**10.21**    The section imposes a duty upon the directors to exercise each of the powers conferred on him only for their proper purpose. A proper purpose is one which, on a true construction of the constitution of the company, the power can be said to have been conferred.[29] It will not usually be possible to lay down in advance all of the exact limits beyond which directors must not exercise a particular power, since the variety of situations facing directors of different types of company in different situations cannot be anticipated. Instead, the court adopts a four-part test stage. The court must:[30]

(1)  identify the power whose exercise is in question;

(2)  identify the proper purpose for which that power was delegated to the directors;

(3)  identify the substantial purpose for which the power was in fact exercised. This involves a question of fact. It turns on the actual motives of the directors at the time; and

(4)  decide whether that purpose was proper.

**10.22**    Many of the cases concerning a breach by directors of their duty to use their powers for proper purposes concern situations where a section of the company's membership is given a special advantage or subjected to undue disadvantage, or where the directors act principally for their own benefit. Some examples are considered below.

---

[28] Although there were prior indications of the existence of the duty separate from the duty to act in good faith in the interests of the company, it is arguable that the duty was only established as a distinct duty in *Hogg v Cramphorn Ltd* [1967] Ch 254. The independent existence of the duty was confirmed in *Howard Smith Ltd v Ampol Petroleum Ltd* [1974] AC 821, 834–7.

[29]  *Smith v Fawcett* [1942] Ch 304, 306, per Lord Greene MR.

[30]  *Extrasure Travel Insurance Ltd v Scattergood* [2003] 1 BCLC 598 at paras 92–93; cf also the test set out in *Howard Smith Ltd v Ampol Petroleum Ltd* [1974] AC 821, 835.

### Misapplication of company funds

An example of a situation where directors act principally for their own benefit is **10.23** where they misappropriate or misapply company funds. Although directors are not strictly speaking trustees of a company's assets they are considered and treated as trustees of the company's property which comes into their hands or which is under their control.[31] In this regard, it is clear they owe a fiduciary duty to the company to apply its assets only for the proper purposes of the company. As Ungoed-Thomas J said in *Selangor United Rubber Estates Ltd v Cradock (No 3):*[32]

> ... property in [directors'] hands or under their control is theirs for the company, i.e., for the company's purposes in accordance with their duties, powers and functions. However much the company's purposes and the directors' duties, powers and functions may differ from the purposes of a strict settlement and the duties, powers and functions of its trustees, the directors and such trustees have this indisputably in common—that the property in their hands or under their control must be applied for the *specified purposes of the company or the settlement;* and to apply it otherwise is to mis-apply it in breach of the obligation to apply it to those purposes for the company or the settlement beneficiaries. So, even though the scope and operation of such obligation differs in the case of directors and strict settlement trustees, the nature of the obligation with regard to property in their hands or under their control is identical, namely, to apply it to specified purposes for others beneficially.

Accordingly, a director will breach this duty where he gives away company assets, **10.24** in the form of shares held by the company as trustee of a number of pension funds, for no consideration to a private family company of which he was a director.[33] Similarly it has been held that it is a misapplication for directors knowingly to pay or to recommend the unlawful payment of dividends.[34]

### Issue of shares

An issue or allotment of shares by the directors under exclusive powers conferred **10.25** in the articles, to themselves or their nominees, not for the purposes of raising further capital but to obtain or retain voting control at general meetings, may constitute a breach of duty.[35] Accordingly, in *Howard Smith Ltd v Ampol Petroleum*

---

[31] *Russell v Wakefield Waterworks Co* (1875) LR 20 Eq 474, 479; *Re Forest of Dean Coal Mining Co* (1879) 10 Ch D 450, 453; *Re Faure Electric Accumulator Co* (1888) 40 Ch D 141; *Flitcroft's Case* (1882) 21 Ch D 519, CA; *Re Sharpe, Re Bennett, Masonic and General Life Assurance Co v Sharpe* [1892] 1 Ch 154; *Belmont Finance Corpn Ltd v Williams Furniture Ltd (No 2)* [1980] 1 All ER 393, 404, CA, per Buckley LJ; *International Sales and Agencies Ltd v Marcus* [1982] 3 All ER 551; *Simtel Communications v Rebak* [2006] 2 BCLC 571 at para 15.

[32] [1968] 1 WLR 1555, 1575.

[33] *Bishopsgate Investment Management Ltd v Maxwell (No 2)* [1994] 1 All ER 261, CA.

[34] *Re Exchange Banking Co, Flitcroft's Case* (1882) 21 Ch D 536.

[35] *Punt v Symons & Co Ltd* [1903] 2 Ch 506; *Piercy v S Mills & Co* [1920] 1 Ch 77; *Hogg v Cramphorn Ltd* [1967] Ch 254; *Re Looe Fish Ltd* [1993] BCLC 1160.

*Ltd*[36] the Privy Council held that while in some circumstances it might be proper to issue shares for purposes other than to raise capital for the company 'it must be unconstitutional for directors to use their fiduciary powers over the shares in the company purely for the purpose of destroying an existing majority or creating a new majority which did not previously exist'.[37] At the other extreme, where directors unquestioningly follow the instructions of a majority of members without realistically exercising their discretion, which might have been exercised for the benefit of the company as a whole, they are in breach of this duty.[38]

**10.26**  The *Howard Smith* case was distinguished in *CAS (Nominees) Ltd v Nottingham Forest Football Club plc*.[39] In that case, the claimants presented a petition pursuant to the 1985 Act, s 459 claiming that an agreement between Nottingham Forest plc, which operated the football club, and a new investor, was unfairly prejudicial to their interests. This agreement involved an injection of cash by the new investor in return for control of the club and was arranged in a manner designed to avoid any opposition from the claimants, who held almost 25% of the issued share capital and could effectively block any special resolution. The restructuring of the company which followed had the inevitable effect of reducing their stake and removing this power. The power exercised by the board of the company in order to implement the transaction was the power of general management conferred by Article 110 of the company's articles. Hart J held that given the genuine desire on the part of the directors to raise capital for the club, it could not be said that the company's powers to reconstitute the board of the club and to increase and allot share capital in the club were being exercised for a purpose foreign to their proper ambit.[40]

*Other examples*

**10.27**  Other powers to which the duty has been held applicable include the forfeiture of shares,[41] making calls on shares,[42] approving transfers of shares,[43] and causing the company to enter into an agreement which deprived the directors of the

---

[36] [1974] AC 821, PC.

[37] At 837. Note also the provisions of 1985 Act, ss 80 and 89 and their replacements in 2006 Act, Part 17, Chapter 2, which come into force on 1 October 2009.

[38] *Scottish Co-operative Wholesale Society Ltd v Meyer* [1959] AC 324, 367.

[39] [2002] 1 BCLC 613.

[40] Ibid, 632–3.

[41] *Re Agriculturist Cattle Insurance Co, Stanhope's Case* (1866) 1 Ch App 161; *Re London and Provincial Starch Co, Gower's Case* (1868) LR 6 Eq 77; *The European Assurance Society Arbitration, Manisty's Case* (1873) 17 SJ 745.

[42] *Galloway v Hallé Concerts Society* [1915] 2 Ch 233.

[43] *Bennett's Case* (1867) 5 De GM&G 284.

managerial powers in circumstances where those directors knew the shareholders shortly intended to appoint new directors.[44]

*Extent to which court will substitute its own view for that of the director*

Traditionally, where the issue is one of management, the court will not seek to substitute its own view for that of the board.[45] However, more recent cases decided before the enactment of the 2006 Act have shown a greater tendency on the part of the court to intervene in corporate decision-making than was previously the case. In particular, the courts have done so by applying the *Wednesbury* principle familiar in public and administrative law. These principles derive from the decision of Lord Greene in *Associated Provincial Picture Houses Ltd v Wednesbury Corp*, a case of judicial review of the exercise of a public duty by a local licensing authority, in which Lord Greene MR summarized the principle as follows:[46]   **10.28**

> The court is entitled to investigate the action of the local authority with a view to seeing whether they have taken into account matters which they ought not to take into account, or, conversely, have refused to take into account or neglected to take into account matters which they ought to take into account. Once that question is answered in favour of the local authority, it may be still possible to say that, although the local authority have kept within the four corners of the matters which they ought to consider, they have nevertheless come to a conclusion so unreasonable that no reasonable authority could ever have come to it. In such a case, again, I think the court can interfere.

In *Byng v London Life Association Ltd*[47] the defendant company's AGM was convened at a location which proved of wholly inadequate capacity for the number of members who attended. The chairman adjourned the meeting until later that day at a different location with a greater capacity. The question then arose of whether the chairman exercised that discretion validly. As to that the Vice-Chancellor said:   **10.29**

> The chairman's decision will not be declared invalid unless on the facts which he knew or ought to have known he failed to take into account all relevant factors, took into account irrelevant factors, or reached a conclusion which no reasonable chairman, properly directing himself as to his duties, could have reached, ie the test is the same as that applicable on judicial review in accordance with the principles of *Associated Provincial Picture Houses Ltd v Wednesbury Corp*.[48]

---

[44] *Lee Panavision Ltd v Lee Lighting Ltd* [1992] BCLC 22, CA.
[45] *Howard Smith Ltd v Ampol Petroleum Ltd* [1974] AC 821, 832, PC.
[46] [1948] 1 KB 223, 233 to 234, CA.
[47] [1990] Ch 170.
[48] At 189. See also *Re a company, ex p Glossop* [1988] BCLC 570, 577; *Hunter v Senate Support Services Ltd* [2005] 1 BCLC 175 at paras 165 to 179; *Edge v Pensions Ombudsman* [2000] Ch 602, 627–8, per Chadwick LJ. Cf *Oxford Legal Group Ltd v Sibbasbridge Services plc* [2008] 2 BCLC 381, CA: Inspection of books by director under 1985 Act, s 222 (2006 Act, s 389) refused where purpose was improper.

**10.30**   Another example of the application of a concept familiar in public and administrative law to this aspect of a director's duty, is the extent to which the exercise by a director of his discretion will be void if he has failed to take into account a material consideration and that consideration might have materially affected his decision. This principle in so far as it applies to trustees is often referred to as the rule in *Re Hastings-Bass*.[49] Thus in *Hunter v Senate Support Services Ltd*[50] the deputy judge held that although the decisions of the directors to forfeit the claimant's shares for non-payment of a call and to transfer the forfeited shares to the group holding company were not made for any improper purpose they were nevertheless flawed because the directors had proceeded on the mistaken basis that the only course available to them was forfeiture of the shares. The directors regarded forfeiture as the inevitable result of non-payment of the second call notice and had acted without giving any consideration to possible alternative courses of action or exercising a genuine discretion whether to forfeit, as they were bound to do. In particular, they could have informed the claimant that his shares would not be forfeited but in the absence of payment he would be excluded from any future dividend. Their failure to consider the exercise of such a discretion amounted to a failure to take into account matters which they ought reasonably to have taken into account and the evidence showed that had they done so they would or might have reached a different decision. The directors' decision to forfeit the claimant's shares was therefore voidable at the instance of the claimant. It appears that the deputy judge viewed the application of the rule in *Hastings-Bass* to directors as a freestanding duty. However, this principle is probably now better seen as an aspect of the duty to only exercise powers for the purposes for which they are conferred.

**10.31**   This more interventionist approach is likely to continue after the enactment of the 2006 Act and is reflected in the positive formulation of the duty imposed by s 171(b) which provides that directors '*must* exercise their powers for the purposes for which they are conferred'.[51] This is to be contrasted with the negative formulation of the test used in some earlier cases.[52]

**10.32**   Section 171(b) does not seek to spell out all the characteristics of the duty and a number of questions have been left open for interpretation by the courts. In particular, questions will continue to arise where the board exercises a particular

---

[49] [1975] Ch 25.

[50] [2005] 1 BCLC 175.

[51] However, not all concepts familiar to public and administrative law will be directly applicable to this duty: see *Gaiman v National Association for Mental Health* [1971] Ch 317 where Megarry J held that the principles of natural justice were not applicable to the exclusion of a person from membership of company limited by guarantee.

[52] For instance *Re Smith & Fawcett Ltd* [1942] Ch 304, 306 where Lord Greene MR referred to the duty not to act for any collateral purpose.

power for several reasons, only one of which is improper. There are differing views as to whether the dominant motive must be improper or whether it is sufficient that any causative motive was improper. The traditional test has been that the court will seek to ascertain what was the primary or substantial purpose for which the power was exercised. This has been variously described as the 'dominant'[53] or 'substantial'[54] purpose. In *Howard Smith Ltd v Ampol Petroleum Ltd*[55] the Privy Council held that when a dispute arises as to whether the directors of a company made a particular decision for one purpose or for another, or whether there being more than one purpose, one or another purpose was the substantial or primary purpose, the court is entitled to look at the situation objectively in order to estimate how critical or pressing or substantial an alleged requirement may have been. If it finds that a particular requirement, though real, was not urgent or critical at the relevant time, it may have reason to doubt or discount the assertions of individuals. However, a stricter formulation of the principle has been suggested in Australia in *Whitehouse v Carlton Hotel Pty Ltd* where it has been suggested that it is not necessary to show that the dominant motive of the directors was improper, only that the improper purpose was a causative motive, in the sense that but for its presence the power would not have been exercised.[56]

Unlike the duty imposed by the 2006 Act, s 172(1), it will be no defence to an action that alleges that a director has acted in breach of s 171(1)(b) for the director to assert that he bona fide believed his conduct to be in the best interests of the company.[57]    **10.33**

*Effect of breach of the duty*

Where a director enters into a transaction in breach of his duty to act for proper purposes it will have both internal and external consequences. In so far as the transaction concerns the director himself or a third party not dealing in good faith with the company the transaction may be set aside. Accordingly, in the case of an improper allotment of shares or remuneration to a director the transaction may be set aside or declared invalid.[58] However, where the transaction involves a third party dealing with the company in good faith the question of whether or not the agreement will be binding on the company will depend upon the principles of the    **10.34**

---

[53] *Whitehouse v Carlton Hotel Pty Ltd* (1987) 162 CLR 285, 294.
[54] *Howard Smith Ltd v Ampol Petroleum Ltd* [1974] AC 821, 835.
[55] [1974] AC 821, 832D–G.
[56] *Whitehouse v Carlton Hotel Pty Ltd* (1987) 162 CLR 285 at 294.
[57] *Hardy v Metropolitan Land and Finance Co* (1872) 7 Ch App 427; *Great Eastern Rly Co v Turner* (1872) 8 Ch App 149; *Russell v Wakefield Waterworks Co* (1875) LR 20 Eq 474, 479; *Howard Smith Ltd v Ampol Petroleum Ltd* [1974] AC 821, 832; *Hogg v Cramphorn* [1967] Ch 254, 266–8; *Ultraframe (UK) Ltd v Fielding* [2005] EWHC 1638 (Ch) at paras 1292–1295.
[58] *Hogg v Cramphorn Ltd* [1967] Ch 254; *Howard Smith Ltd v Ampol Petroleum Ltd* [1974] AC 821.

law of agency with appropriate regard for the 2006 Act, ss 39 and 40.[59] In *Criterion Properties plc v Stratford UK Properties LLC*[60] the House of Lords held that the principles of 'knowing receipt' and 'dishonest assistance' do not apply to a contract entered into with a company in breach of the directors' duty to act for a proper purpose. 'Receipt' in 'knowing receipt' referred to the receipt by one person from another of assets. The creation by a contract of contractual rights did not constitute a receipt of assets in that sense. This position will remain the same under the 2006 Act.

---

[59] As to which see paragraph 10.15 above.
[60] [2004] 1 WLR 1846, HL.

# 11

# DUTY TO PROMOTE THE SUCCESS
# OF THE COMPANY

## A. Introduction

The Companies Act, s 172 provides that:                                    **11.01**

(1) A director of a company must act in the way he considers in good faith, would be
    most likely to promote the success of the company for the benefit of its members as
    a whole and in doing so have regard to (amongst other matters):
    (a) the likely consequences of any decision in the long term;
    (b) the interests of the employees;
    (c) the need to foster the company's business relationship with suppliers, custom-
        ers and others;
    (d) the impact of the company's operation on the community and the envir-
        onment;
    (e) the desirability of the company maintaining a reputation for high standards of
        business conduct; and
    (f) the need to act fairly as between members of the company.
(2) Where to the extent that the purposes of the company consist of or include purposes
    other than the benefit of its members, subsection (1) has effect as if the reference to

promoting the success of the company for the benefit of its members were to achieving those purposes.

(3) The duty imposed by this section has effect subject to any enactment or rule of law requiring directors, in certain circumstances, to consider or act in the interest of the creditors of the company.[1]

**11.02** The Companies Act, s 172 codifies the duty of a director to act in the way he considers, in good faith, would be most likely to promote the success of the company for the benefit of its members as a whole. The section is one of the more controversial in the Companies Act as can be gleaned from the considerable periods of time that debate surrounding the provisions of the section took up during the passage of the Bill through Parliament. In its review, the Company Law Review Steering Group (CLR) considered the issues surrounding the enactment of this section to be one of central importance.[2] It identified two possible approaches: 'the shareholder value approach' and 'the pluralist approach'. The shareholder value approach recognizes that companies are managed with the ultimate objective of generating maximum value for shareholders and advocates this as the best means of achieving overall prosperity and welfare. The pluralist approach argues that the ultimate objective of maximizing shareholder value will not necessarily achieve maximum prosperity and welfare. Advocates of the pluralist approach argue that company law should be modified to ensure that a company is required to serve a wider range of interests, not subordinate to, or as a means of achieving, shareholder value but as valid in their own right. The approach advocated by the CLR was referred to as an 'enlightened shareholder value approach'. This approach is based upon the shareholder value approach and involves directors having to act in the collective best interests of shareholders but does not focus on the exclusive consideration of short-term financial benefits but instead on the factors that will maximize shareholder value in the long term. The enlightened shareholder value approach was adopted by the Government in its White Papers, the Companies Bill, and ultimately in the Companies Act. One reason for this choice was that the pluralist approach risked leaving directors accountable to no one, since there would be no clear yardstick for judging their performance.[3]

**11.03** The adoption of the enlightened shareholder value approach is reflected in the language of s 172(1). The director must act in the way he considers, in good faith, would be most likely to promote the success of the company '*for the benefit of its members*'. This language clearly relates the success of the company to the interests of the members as a whole not to any individual shareholder or indeed the majority

---

[1] The section came into force on 1 October 2007: 2006 Act Commencement Order No 3, art 2(d).

[2] CLR: *The Strategic Framework*, para. 5.1.1.

[3] CLR: *Final Report*, para.1.17.

shareholder or shareholders. It follows that a director would be in breach of the duty if he were to promote the interests of only one section or class of shareholders.[4]

The duty stated in s 172 applies to shadow directors to the extent that the common law rules or equitable principles corresponding to the duty to promote the success of the company applied to shadow directors (see Chapter 9, Section C).[5]　**11.04**

A director who, in relation to a particular transaction, wishes to be protected from the risk of being in breach of the duty to promote the success of the company may obtain the consent, approval, or authorization of the members, as recognized by s 180(4)(a) (see Chapter 9, Section D) or ratification of his conduct under s 239 (Chapter 19, Section D).　**11.05**

## B. The Director's Judgment

The decision as to what will promote the success of the company is one for the director's good faith judgment. Section 172(1) grants an unfettered discretion to the directors provided they act in a way that they consider, in good faith, to be most likely to promote the success of the company. This reflects the position at common law, the classic statement of which is that of Lord Greene MR in *Re Smith and Fawcett Ltd*: 'The [directors] must exercise their discretion bona fide in what they consider—not what a court may consider—is in the interests of the company . . .'[6] More recently Jonathan Parker J referred to the relevant test in *Re Regentcrest plc v Cohen* as follows:　**11.06**

> The duty imposed on directors to act bona fide in the interests of the company is a subjective one. The question is not whether, viewed objectively by the court, the particular act or omission which is challenged was in fact in the interests of the company; still less is the question whether the court, had it been in the position of the director at the relevant time, might have acted differently. Rather, the question is whether the director honestly believed that his act or omission was in the interests of the company. The issue is as to the director's state of mind. No doubt, where it is clear that the act or omission under challenge resulted in substantial detriment to the company, the director will have a harder task persuading the court that he honestly believed it to be in the company's interest; but that does not detract from the subjective nature of the test.[7]

Accordingly, in *Extrasure Travel Insurance Ltd v Scattergood* Jonathan Crow, sitting as a deputy High Court judge, rejected an argument that a director acts in breach　**11.07**

---

[4] See the speech of Lord Goldsmith in the second passage quoted in paragraph 11.10 below: Hansard, HL, vol 678, col 256 (6 February 2006).

[5] s 170(5).

[6] [1942] Ch 304, 306, CA. See also *Charles Forte Investments Ltd v Amanda* [1964] Ch 240, CA.

[7] [2001] 2 BCLC 80, 105.

of his fiduciary duty if he honestly, but unreasonably and mistakenly, believed that he is pursuing the company's best interests.[8]

**11.08**    However, where it can be demonstrated that the director's belief was not well founded the situation will be different. Accordingly, in *Re W & M Roith Ltd*[9] the court accepted that the onus was on the liquidator to show that the service agreement in question was not entered into bona fide in the interests of the company, but that the presumption was displaced by the following matters (i) the director concerned had been in office for more than 30 years without a service contract, and the late change was only referable to his desire to benefit someone other than himself; (ii) while the director remained alive there was no benefit to the company resulting from the existence of the contract; and (iii) when the director took legal advice as to how to secure his widow's position, it was considered immaterial which of the companies with which he was associated was actually to provide the pension. Accordingly, notwithstanding no actual dishonesty or secret profit, the interests of the company were subordinated by the transaction and the test of bona fides was not satisfied. It is clear in this regard that a finding of bad faith does not require a finding of dishonesty.[10]

**11.09**    Similarly, in *Knight v Frost*[11] Hart J held that the directors had not acted bona fide in the interests of the company when they caused it to make loans to a third party corporation associated with one of the directors in circumstances where: (i) no steps had been taken to ensure that the company was entitled to a commercial rate of interest or to record or agree the currency in which repayment would be made; (ii) the third party had no assets of any significance apart from the one of the director's services which he could choose to provide on his own terms; and (iii) looked at from the company's viewpoint it stood to gain nothing from the transactions beyond a chance that it might be repaid if the third party flourished in the future.

**11.10**    Similar principles also apply as to what constitutes the 'success of the company'. The Companies Act does not seek to lay down any definition of this phrase. Instead, the decision as to what constitutes success is one for the members and directors using their good faith judgment.[12] Two extracts from a speech of Lord Goldsmith during the passage of the Companies Bill through Parliament are instructive in this regard:

> What is success? The starting point is that it is essentially for the members of the company to define the objective they wish to achieve. Success means what the members collectively want the company to achieve. For a commercial company, success will usually mean long-term increase in value. For certain companies, such as

---

8 [2003] 1 BCLC 598 at para 89. The relevant paragraph is quoted in Chapter 9 at paragraph 9.08.
9 [1967] 1 WLR 432.
10 *Wrexham Association Football Club Ltd v Crucialmove Ltd* [2008] BCLC 508, CA at para 37.
11 [1999] 1 BCLC 364.
12 Explanatory Notes to the Companies Act, para 327.

charities and community interest companies, it will mean the attainment of the objectives for which the company has been established. . . .

. . . it is for the directors, by reference to those things we are talking about—the objective of the company—to judge and form a good faith judgement about what is to be regarded as success for the members as a whole . . . they will need to look at the company's constitution, shareholder decisions and anything else that they consider relevant in helping them to reach that judgement . . . the duty is to promote the success for the benefit of the members as a whole—that is, for the members as a collective body—not only to benefit the majority shareholders, or any particular shareholder or section of shareholders, still less the interests of directors who might happen to be shareholders themselves. That is an important statement of the way in which directors need to look at this judgement they have to make.[13]

In this regard, it is permissible for directors to promote their own interests[14] or those of anybody else where to do so is in the company's interest (subject to any internal limitations on their powers). This permits the promoting of employees' interests under the 2006 Act, s 172(1)(b) or those of a group of companies of which the director's is one.[15]   **11.11**

As with the duty to only exercise powers for the purposes for which they were conferred the more recent cases decided before the enactment of the Companies Act have shown a growing tendency on the part of the court to intervene in corporate decision-making than was previously the case. Also, as with the duty to exercise powers for the purposes for which they were conferred, the courts have shown a growing tendency to apply the *Wednesbury* principle familiar in public and administrative law. For example, in *Re a company, ex p Glossop*[16] Harman J had before him an application to amend a petition for relief under the 1985 Act, s 459 (unfair prejudice) and in the alternative for a just and equitable winding up, to add allegations concerning the directors' alleged failure to recommend payment of a dividend. The application succeeded in part. Harman J said:   **11.12**

It is, in my judgment, vital to remember that actions of boards of directors cannot simply be justified by invoking the incantation 'a decision taken bona fide in the interests of the company' . . . If it were to be proved that directors resolved to exercise their powers to recommend dividends to a general meeting . . . without regard to the right of members to have profits distributed so far as was commercially possible, I am of opinion that the directors' decision would be open to challenge. This is an application, in a sense, of the principle affirmed in so many local government cases and usually called 'the *Wednesbury* principle'.[17]

---

[13] Hansard, HL, vol 678, cols 255–256 (6 February 2006).

[14] *Hirsche v Sims* [1894] AC 654, 660, per Lord Selborne.

[15] See paragraphs 11.22–11.24 and 12.17–12.18 below; *Charterbridge Corporation v Lloyds Bank* [1970] Ch 62.

[16] [1988] BCLC 570.

[17] [1988] BCLC 570, 577. See also *Byng v London Life Association Ltd* [1989] BCLC 400 considered in paragraph 10.29 above; and *Equitable Life Assurance Society v Hyman* [2002] 1 AC 408 at paras 17–21.

*Duty to report*

**11.13**  A director is not strictly speaking the agent of his co-directors. The mere fact that a particular director is liable to the company for a breach of duty is not enough of itself to render the remaining directors liable as well. Accordingly, it has been held that, in the absence of negligence, a director is not liable for a breach of duty by other directors of which he was ignorant, or which occurred before he became a director.[18] However, in certain circumstances the director's duty to promote the success of the company for the benefit of the members as a whole will require him to report breaches of duty either of his fellow directors or himself. Thus in *British Midland Tool Ltd v Midland International Tooling Ltd*[19] Hart J held that the director's duty to act so as to promote the best interests of his company includes a duty to inform the company of any activity, actual or threatened, which damages those interests. This in itself includes a duty to inform the company of any breaches of duty being carried out and perhaps even contemplated by other directors. Similarly, in *Item Software (UK) Ltd v Fassihi* the Court of Appeal held that a director was under a duty to disclose his own misconduct.[20] Where the decision is taken by the board to expel another director that decision too must be exercised in good faith and in the best interests of the company.[21]

## C.  Matters to Which the Directors Should Have Regard

**11.14**  Section 172(1) lays down a list of matters to which directors are to have regard when they exercise their duty to promote the success of the company. Whilst the wording of s 172(1) is mandatory (directors '*must* act . . . and in doing so *have* regard to') the list is not exhaustive, but is said to highlight areas of particular importance which reflect wider expectations of responsible business behaviour, such as the interests of the company's employees and the impact of the company's operations on the community and the environment.[22] The list is not ordered in any type of priority.

---

[18]  *Cullerne v London and Suburban General Permanent Building Society* (1890) 25 QBD 485. Cf *Green v Walkling* [2008] 2 BCLC 332: director not liable for breach of duty when he acted on legal advice and could not have done more to prevent misappropriation by others.

[19]  [2003] 2 BCLC 523 at para 89; *Lexi Holdings plc v Lugman* [2008] 2 BCLC 725 at para 32, concerning failure to report fellow director's criminal convictions.

[20]  [2005] 2 BCLC 91, CA. See also *Tesco Stores Ltd v Pook* [2003] EWHC 823; *Shepherds Investments Ltd v Walters* [2006] 2 BCLC 202 at paras 104–108, per Etherton J.

[21]  *Lee v Chou Wen Hsien* [1984] 1 WLR 1202, 1206, PC.

[22]  Explanatory Notes to the Companies Act, para 326. During the passage of the Bill though Parliament Lord Goldsmith said '. . . we have included the words "amongst other matters". We want to be clear that the list of factors is not exhaustive' (Hansard, HL Grand Committee (9 May 2006), col 846).

It is also important to note that that the factors set out in subs 172(1) are subsidi-   **11.15**
ary to the overall duty to promote the success of the company. Where the different
matters to which the director must have regard suggest a conflicting course of
action the director must take that action which he bona fide believes is consistent
with the overarching duty to promote the success of the company.

The duty is not owed to any of the persons specified in the subsection directly   **11.16**
(eg employees, suppliers, customers) but to the company.[23] Accordingly the duty to
have regard to the interests of employees, suppliers, and customers is not enforceable
by those individuals. The same is true of the duty to act fairly as between the members of the company. The duty is one owed to the company not to individual shareholders, although, as with other fiduciary duties owed to the company it may be
enforced indirectly by shareholders by a derivative claim, or, where the relevant
breach of duty is unfairly prejudicial to the interests of those shareholders within the
meaning of the 2006 Act, s 994, by petition under that section. When having regard
to the factors listed in subs 172(1), a director must also act in accordance with his
duty to exercise reasonable care, skill, and diligence (2006 Act, s 174).[24]

There is no statutory explanation of what the term 'have regard to' means in this   **11.17**
context. An indication of how the Government intended the expression to be
interpreted was given by Margaret Hodge, Minister of State for Industry and the
Regions:

> The words 'have regard to' mean 'think about'; they are absolutely not about just
> ticking boxes. If 'thinking about' leads to the conclusion, as we believe it will in many
> cases, that the proper course is to act positively to achieve the objectives in the clause,
> that will be what the director's duty is. In other words 'have regard to' means 'give
> proper consideration to' . . .[25]

Accordingly, where a director fails utterly to have regard to any of the specific matters set out in subsection (1) it appears likely he will act in breach of the duty.

However, where a director gives those matters due consideration and concludes in   **11.18**
good faith that the relevant action is likely to promote the success of the company
he will not act in breach of the duty. The weight to be given to the specific factors
will be a matter for the director's good faith judgment. This is confirmed by Lord
Goldsmith:

> We want the director to give such consideration to the factors identified as is neces-
> sary for the decision that he has to take, and no more than that. We do not intend

---

[23] 2006 Act, s 170(1).
[24] See Chapter 13 below.
[25] Hansard, HC, vol 450, col 789 (17 October 2006).

a director to be required to do more than good faith and the duty of skill and care require, nor do we want it to be possible for a director acting in good faith to be held liable for a process failure where it could not have affected the outcome.[26]

Similarly Margaret Hodge said:

> Consideration of the factors will be an integral part of the duty to promote the success of the company for the benefit of its members as a whole. The clause makes it clear that a director is to have regard to the factors in fulfilling that duty. The decisions taken by a director and the weight given to the factors will continue to be a matter for his good faith judgment.[27]

**11.19**  One perhaps unintended consequence of this approach is that the list of factors may be used by directors increasingly as a defence to an action by the company. For instance, where a director in good faith and in order to promote the success of the company for the benefit of its members as a whole, makes a decision in the wider interests of the community or the environment it may be arguable that he will be protected from reproach.

**11.20**  Few of the factors set out in subs 172(1) had ever specifically been recognized in case law prior to the enactment of the Companies Act.[28] However, they are clearly reconcilable with that case law. Indeed, one of the strengths of the common law duty was that it was expressed in very general terms and capable of application in cases where it has not previously been applied.

### (1) Likely consequences of any decision in the long term

**11.21**  Subsection 172(1)(a) reflects the importance placed by the Government on the long-term as opposed to the short-term approach that should be taken by directors. It provides that the directors are to have regard to the likely consequences of any decision in the long term. This is arguably what the general law required anyway, namely that directors should, in appropriate circumstances, seek to balance short-term considerations against long-term considerations. The subsection does not of course mean that directors are not allowed to have regard to the consequences in the short or medium term. Indeed in many circumstances short-term consequences may well outweigh long-term consequences. As Lord Goldsmith pointed out during the passage of the Bill through Grand Committee 'a particular decision may be an excellent long-term decision if only you could pay for it, but if

---

[26]  Hansard, HL Grand Committee (9 May 2006), col 846.

[27]  Hansard, HC (17 October 2006), col 789.

[28]  The Law Commission identified the relevant duties as (a) a duty of loyalty, to act in good faith in the best interests of the company, (b) a duty to have regard to the interests of the company's employees in general and its members, and (c) a duty to act fairly as between members: *Company Directors: Regulating Conflicts of Interest and Formulating a Statement of Duties*, Consultation Paper No 153 at paras 11.4–11.20; Report No 261 at Appendix A.

you try to pay for it today you may go completely bust'.[29] The important point is that directors are only to have *regard* to the likely consequences of a decision in the long term. If a director has regard to such long-term consequences but in good faith considers that other short-term factors outweigh those consequences the court will not interfere with his decision.

## (2) The interests of the company's employees

In requiring directors to have regard to the interests of employees, subs 171(1)(b) **11.22** replaces the 1985 Act, s 309.[30] This provided that the matters to which the direct-ors of a company were to have regard in the performance of their functions include the interests of the company's employees in general, as well as the inter-ests of its members. The employees' interests are various and may include non-discriminatory policies and safe systems of work, as well as job security and financial benfits. Although this section has been cited in a number of cases,[31] 'it has not been fully considered in any of these cases'.[32] In particular the courts have not expressed a view on the question of whether s 309 required directors in exer-cising their functions to have regard to the interests of employees in general even if their interests are not the same as those of the company.

In *Fulham Football Club Ltd v Cabra Estates plc*,[33] the Court of Appeal *obiter* were **11.23** minded to reject an argument that the company was bound by undertakings merely because all the shareholders had signed them on the basis that the duties owed by directors are to their company and the company is more than the sum of its members. The Court of Appeal held that creditors, both present and potential, were also interested, while the 1985 Act, s 309 imposed a specific duty on direct-ors to have regard to the interests of the company's employees in general. The Court of Appeal's decision could be read as suggesting that s 309 was not limited

---

[29] Hansard, HL Grand Committee (6 February 2006), col GC271.

[30] 1985 Act, s 309 re-enacted 1980 Act, s 46 which was the first statutory expression of the duty of directors to have regard to interests of employees. 1980 Act, s 74 for the first time gave a company power to provide for employees on cessation of business, so reversing *Parke v Daily News Ltd* [1962] Ch 927. Section 74 was re-enacted as 1985 Act, s 719 and will be replaced by 2006 Act, s 247 on 1 October 2009: 2006 Act Commencement Order No 8, art 3(i).

[31] *Fulham Football Club Ltd v Cabra Estates plc* [1994] 1 BCLC 363, CA; *Re Saul D Harrison & Sons plc* [1995] 1 BCLC 14, CA; *Dawson International plc v Coats Paton plc* [1989] BCLC 233, Ct of Sess; *Re London Life Association Ltd* (21 February 1989, unreported) (Hoffmann J); *Re A company, ex parte Burr* [1992] BCLC 724, 734.

[32] *Company Directors Regulating Conflicts of Interests and Formulating a Statement of Duties* (Law Com Paper No 153) at para 11.28. As to the circumstances in which the directors may cause the company to grant gratuities to the company's employees see: *Hampson v Price's Patent Candle Co* (1876) 45 LJ Ch 437; *Hutton v West Cork Rly Co* (1883) 23 Ch D 654, CA; *Kaye v Croydon Tramways Co* [1898] 1 Ch 358, 367, CA; *Parke v Daily News Ltd* [1962] Ch 927; *Re W and M Roith Ltd* [1967] 1 WLR 432; and *Re Halt Garage* [1982] 3 All ER 1016.

[33] [1994] 1 BCLC 363, CA.

to requiring directors to have regard to the interests of employees when to do so is conducive to the interests of the company.[34] In so far as this is an acceptable reading of the *Fulham Football Club* case it is submitted that it should not be adopted in relation to subs 172(1)(b). As noted above, the requirement that the director have regard to the interest of the company's employees is only a factor to which the company is to have regard. The overriding duty is to act in the way the director considers in good faith would be most likely to promote the success of the company for the benefit of its members as a whole. Often the interests of employees will be in conflict with the interests of the members as a whole; eg as to whether to close an unprofitable factory (but in such a case employees' interests will be respected by redundancy payments).[35]

**11.24**   The power to make provision for employees on cessation or transfer of the company's business (contained in the 1985 Act, s 719, which will be replaced by the 2006 Act, s 247) is exercisable notwithstanding the general duty imposed by s 172.

### (3)  The need to foster the company's business relationships with suppliers, customers, and others

**11.25**   Subsection 171(1)(c) provides that a director must have regard to the need to foster the company's business relationships with suppliers, customers, and others. In most cases the application of this duty will be relatively obvious. A reputation for bad commercial practices (eg late payment of bills and providing poor quality goods and services) can damage the company's business. Prior to enactment of s 171 the importance of maintaining a good relationship with customers and suppliers is something to which most directors would ordinarily have had regard. Such consideration will obviously be of crucial importance in maintaining the ongoing success of the company.

### (4)  The impact of the company's operations on the community and the environment

**11.26**   Subsection 172(1)(d) provides that the directors must have regard to the impact of the company's operations on the community and the environment. It is perhaps in this section that the 'pluralist approach' to directors' duties is most apparent. In many cases it may not be obviously apparent to a director how the impact of a company's operations on the wider community and the environment will be referable to the success of the company for the benefit of its members as a whole.

---

[34]  Ibid, para 11.28.

[35]  Margaret Hodge said: 'We do not, however, claim that the interests of the company and of its employees will always be identical; regrettably, it will sometimes be necessary, for example, to lay off staff. The drafting . . . must therefore clearly point directors towards their overarching objective' (Hansard, HC (17 October 2006), col 789).

However, the approach taken by the 2006 Act is that it is only if a director has regard to such factors that a company can ensure the success of the company particularly in the long term. There may also be short-term considerations in relation to this aspect of the duty. For example, where a director takes a decision which pays no regard to this consideration and this results in a fine or a claim for damages, for example, because of some breach of environmental legislation, it is possible that the director could be held to be liable to the company for the loss caused by the fine or claim for damages.

### (5) The desirability of the company maintaining a reputation for high standards of business conduct

Subsection 172(1)(e) provides that a director is to have regard to the desirability **11.27** of the company maintaining a reputation for high standards of business conduct. As with the need to foster the company's business relationships with suppliers, customers, and others the application of this aspect of the duty will be relatively obvious. Directors who cause their company not to maintain a high standard of business conduct are unlikely to be promoting the success of the company for the benefit of its members as a whole. As with subs 171(1)(d) consideration will need to be had as to the circumstances in which this subsection could lead to personal liability on the part of the director. In particular, where a director takes a decision which pays no regard to this consideration and this results in, for example, the production by the company of poorly manufactured goods, it is possible that he may be held liable for any fines or claims for damages arising in respect of those goods.

### (6) Need to act fairly as between members of the company

The duty on the part of a director to have regard to the need to act fairly as between **11.28** different shareholders set out in subs 171(1)(f) was identified in *Mutual Life v The Rank Organisation (No 2)*[36] and subsequently applied by Arden J in *Re BSB (Holdings) Ltd (No 2)*.[37] In *Mutual Life v The Rank Organisation* it was held that the directors were not in breach of their duty when after proper investigation they decided that it was in the interests of the company to proceed to make a rights issue to some only of the holders of ordinary shares. In *Re BSB (Holdings) Ltd* Arden J said 'the law did not require the interests of the company to be sacrificed in the particular interests of a group of shareholders.'[38] However, there would be a breach of the relevant duty where the directors fail completely to consider whether a proposal which is under consideration will be fair as between different

---

[36] [1985] BCLC 11, 21.
[37] [1996] 1 BCLC 155, 246–9.
[38] Ibid, 251.

groups of shareholders. Accordingly, it has been held that the directors must not use their powers of allotment, making calls, forfeiting shares, and so on to favour themselves above other shareholders,[39] or to favour particular classes of shareholders.[40] Likewise, where, before any dividend is declared, the directors cause the company to set aside a portion of profits to form a reserve, they should have regard to how the reserve may affect the respective rights of the preference and ordinary shareholders, particularly in cases where the preference dividend is not cumulative. In such cases, if the articles authorize the creation of a reserve, 'it will always be the duty of the directors to fix the amount of the fund to be retained with reference to the general interest of all classes of shareholders, and not to favour any one class at the expense of the other'.[41]

**11.29** The principle embodied with subs 171(1)(f) accords with the general principle that the fiduciary relationship of a director exists with the company not individual shareholders.[42] Directors will only be in a fiduciary relationship with individual shareholders in certain 'special circumstances'. The 'special circumstances' approach to the question of whether directors owe fiduciary duties to individual shareholders was indorsed by the Court of Appeal in *Peskin v Anderson*.[43] In that case the Court of Appeal refused to apply the principle so as to require directors to disclose to individual members plans which had not yet become firm, for the selling of a major business of the company, simply because the interests of the individual shareholders would have been furthered by such disclosure. This was particularly the case where there had been no dealing between the directors and the members in relation to those plans.

**11.30** However, where the directors seek to influence the exercise by the shareholders of their rights they may assume duties in relation to those shareholders. For example, where a company meeting has been summoned directors owe a specific duty in equity to give sufficient information to shareholders for them to make an informed decision about proposals to be put to them in the meeting.[44] Similarly, the courts

---

[39] *Hirsche v Sims* [1894] AC 654, PC (allotment); but cf *Re Jermyn Street Turkish Baths Ltd* [1971] 1 WLR 1042, CA; *Shaw v Holland* [1900] 2 Ch 305 (allotment to directors at an undervalue); *Harris v North Devon Rly Co* (1855) 20 Beav 384 (forfeiture); *Bennett's Case* (1854) 5 De GM & G 284, 297; *Re National Provincial Marine Insurance Co, Gilbert's Case* (1870) 5 Ch App 559 (calls); *Re European Central Railway Co, Sykes' Case* (1872) LR 13 Eq 255 (payments in advance of calls); *Parker v McKenna* (1875) 10 Ch App 96; *Alexander v Automatic Telephone Co* [1900] 2 Ch 56, 72–3, CA (payments on application and allotment).

[40] *Howard Smith Ltd v Ampol Petroleum Ltd* [1974] AC 821, PC.

[41] *Henry v Great Northern Railway* (1857) 1 De G&J 606, 638, per Lord Cranworth LC.

[42] See Chapter 9 at paragraphs 9.17–9.20 above; *Peskin v Anderson* [2001] 1 BCLC 372, CA; *Percival v Wright* [1902] 2 Ch 421.

[43] [2001] 1 BCLC 372, CA.

[44] *Residues Treatment & Trading Co Ltd v Southern Resources Ltd* (1988) 14 ACLR 375, 377–8, per White J; approved in *RAC Motoring Services Ltd* [2000] 1 BCLC 307, 326–7.

have held directors to be under a duty of good faith when giving advice whether to accept a take-over offer for their shares [45] or whether to sanction a scheme for the purchase of a large bloc of assets from another company. [46] Having given advice, if there is a change of circumstances it would normally be prudent of the directors to send out a circular in which its directors honestly state their views in the light of the change. [47] In *Prudential Assurance* this duty was classified as arising in tort and being 'no more than a particular application, to directors who assume responsibility for giving advice to shareholders, of the general duty to act honestly and with due care'. [48] However, in *Re A Company* [49] Hoffmann J was prepared to hold that, although directors were not obliged to give shareholders advice on whether to accept or reject a takeover offer, if such advice were given it should not only be accurate but 'given with a view to enabling the shareholders to sell, if they so wish at the best price and not in order to persuade the shareholders to accept or reject a bid which the directors, for their own reasons, wished to have accepted or rejected'. [50] This language echoes that used in the case law relating to the common law duty to promote the success of the company.

It has also been held that where directors have decided that it is in the interests of a company that it should be taken over, and where there are two or more bidders, it is the duty of the director to obtain the best price available. [51]　**11.31**

### (7) Practical effect on boardroom practice

There has been some debate as to the extent to which s 172 will alter practice in the boardroom, in particular, with regard to the documentation of board decisions. [52] Certainly in some cases it may be necessary for the board to review their decision-making processes to ensure that proper attention is given to each of the　**11.32**

---

[45] *Gething v Kilner* [1972] 1 WLR 337; *John Crowther Group plc v Carpets International plc* [1990] BCLC 460; cf *Goldex Mines Ltd v Revill* (1974) 54 DLR (3rd edn) 672.

[46] *Prudential Assurance Co Ltd v Newman Industries Ltd (No. 2)* [1981] Ch 257, Vinelott J.

[47] *Rackham v Peek Foods Ltd* [1990] BCLC 895.

[48] [1981] Ch 257, 302. Directors who fail to give factually accurate advice or who give advice otherwise then in the interests of the shareholders may also, in appropriate circumstances, expose themselves to a petition on grounds of unfairly prejudicial treatment: *Re A Company* [1986] BCLC 382.

[49] [1986] BCLC 382.

[50] See also rule 23 of the City Code on Take-overs and Mergers which states that: 'Shareholders must be given sufficient information and advice to enable them to reach a properly informed decision and must have sufficient time to do so. No relevant information should be withheld from them. The obligation of the offeror in these respects towards the shareholders of the offeree company is no less than an offeror's obligation towards its own shareholders.'

[51] See for example *Heron International Ltd v Lord Grade* [1983] BCLC 244, 265, CA.

[52] See in particular The Association for the General Counsel and Company Secretaries of FTSE100 Companies ('GC100')'s guidance on the Companies Act 2006 (Directors' Duties) dated 7 February 2007.

factors set out in subs 172(1) and that such considerations are properly documented. However, in most cases this will not be necessary.

**11.33**  The 2006 Act places no positive obligation on the board to evidence the thought processes that influence their thinking. Indeed, Margaret Hodge, the Minister for Trade and Industry, emphasized during the passage of the Bill through Parliament that 'the clause does not impose a requirement on directors to keep records . . . in any circumstances in which they would not have to do so now'.[53] Likewise, the Attorney-General, Lord Goldsmith, said in the Lords:

> There is nothing in this Bill that says there is a need for a paper trail . . . I do not agree that the effect of passing this Bill will be that directors will be subject to a breach if they cannot demonstrate that they have considered every element. It will be for the person who is asserting breach of duty to make that case good . . .[54]

**11.34**  A pragmatic and proportionate approach should be taken. In some cases, particularly in relation to a very significant decision being taken by the board, it may be appropriate for board minutes to state that each of the factors set out in subs 171(1) have been considered. In situations where litigation is possible or likely such an approach may even help to protect directors from criticism. However, in most other cases it will not be necessary to take such an approach. In particular, where one particular factor has been significant in causing the board to reach a decision it may be sufficient simply to note this. Each case will, however, depend upon its facts. GC100[55] has taken the lead in issuing best practice guidelines for companies expressing concern that the 2006 Act potentially increases bureaucracy, makes the decision-making process more cumbersome, and potentially increases the liability of directors. The approach suggested by GC100 is that:

(1)  Companies should ensure that all directors are aware of their duties under the 2006 Act.

(2)  Where the nature of the decision being taken by directors is such that it is supported by a formal process, that process need only specifically record consideration of those duties where the particular circumstances make it particularly necessary or relevant. The default position should be not to include these references. In this regard, GC100 emphasizes the importance of the preparation of briefing or background papers (the preparation of which can be properly delegated) in relation to important board decisions.

(3)  When decisions are taken by directors in circumstances other than at a formal board meeting, it should be for the company concerned to decide, in its particular circumstances, the best approach to be adopted. Where there is a clear

---

[53]  Hansard, HC Committee (11 July 2006), col 592.
[54]  Hansard, HL (9 May 2006), col 841.
[55]  See n 52 above.

scheme of delegation and a decision is to be taken by an individual director, it is unlikely to be appropriate for a paper to be prepared as described above. It has to be recognized that many decisions, even if taken in accordance with a formal scheme of delegation, have to be taken within a timeframe which does not allow for preparation of a formal paper; or for a formal minute of the decision. It is important that best practice recognizes this—lack of formal process should not lead to any inference that factors have not been properly considered.

## D. Special Purpose Companies

Subsection 172(2) provides that where or to the extent that the purposes of the **11.35** company consist of or include purposes other than the benefit of it members, the duty contained in subs (1) has effect as if the reference to promoting the success of the company for the benefit of its members were to achieving those purposes. This addresses the question of altruistic, or partly altruistic, companies. Where the purpose of the company is something other than the benefit of its members, the directors must act in the way they consider, in good faith, would be most likely to achieve that purpose. It is a matter for the good faith judgment of the director as to what those purposes are, and, where the company is operated partially for the benefit of its members and partly for other purposes, the extent to which those other purposes apply in place of the benefit of the members.

## E. The Duty to Take Account of the Interests of Creditors

The 2006 Act, s 172(3) provides that the duty to promote the success of the com- **11.36** pany 'has effect subject to any enactment or rule of law requiring directors, in certain circumstances, to consider or act in the interests of creditors of the company'.

It might be thought that, of all the situations in which directors and their advisors **11.37** would want to know as precisely as possible the nature and extent of their duties to the company, where the company is insolvent or at risk of insolvency would be amongst the most significant. At first blush, therefore, it may seem surprising that the 2006 Act does not contain a statutory statement of any such duty.

### Consideration by the CLR and Government

The principal reason for the omission appears from the CLR's Final Report. **11.38** Initially, the inclination of the CLR had been not to include in the statement of general duties reference to an obligation to have regard separately to the interests of creditors where the company was insolvent or threatened with insolvency, since the cases seemed capable of resolution on the basis of other principles and such a statement would cut across the Insolvency Act. Subsequently, they stated that it was generally agreed that the general duties must be subject to the overriding duties of directors towards creditors in an insolvency situation 'but also that it is undesirable to lay down any detailed new rule in this area: the law is developing and there is already a carefully balanced statutory provision, which operates *ex post* in a liquidation, in the Insolvency Act 1986 section 214 (wrongful trading)'.[56]

**11.39** In the Final Report the CLR considered that the wrongful trading rule should be included in the statement of general duties.[57] However, on the question whether reference should also be made to a special duty to take into account creditors' interests at an earlier stage when there was a substantial probability of an insolvent liquidation, at which point the directors should carry out a balancing exercise, they were unable to reach agreement.[58] On the one hand, it was said that such a rule would reflect what good directors should do, so that even where insolvency was less than inevitable but the risk substantial, directors should consider the interests of members and creditors together.[59] On the other hand, it was feared that such a 'balanced judgment' test would have a 'chilling effect', such that the directors might run down or abandon a going concern at the first hint of insolvency:

> The balanced judgement demanded is a difficult and indeterminate one. Fears of personal liability may lead to excessive caution. Small company directors in particular may feel driven to take expensive professional advice which may well be likely to err on the side of caution, with personal liabilities involved. Liquidation can, where there are means of saving the going concern, be as damaging to creditors as to shareholders. Break-up destroys value and employment. Arguably the first, 'no reasonable prospect', test will, in practice, influence directors to act more cautiously on the approach of insolvency.[60]

**11.40** In its White Paper: *Modernising Company Law*, the Government rejected the suggestion that any duties in relation to creditors should be included in the statutory statement of general duties. It considered that it would be inappropriate and unhelpful to make reference to a special duty arising where there is no reasonable prospect of avoiding insolvent liquidation, having regard to the provisions of the Insolvency Act.[61] As regards the suggestion that reference should be made to a special duty arising in circumstances where the company was likely to become insolvent and which would require the directors to carry out a balancing exercise, the Government stated that:

> Directors would need to take a finely balanced judgement, and fears of personal liability might lead to excessive caution. This would run counter to the 'rescue culture'

---

[56] CLR: *Completing the Structure* at para 3.12.
[57] CLR: *Final Report* at para 3.16.
[58] Ibid at para 3.20.
[59] Ibid at para 3.18.
[60] Ibid at para 3.19.
[61] White Paper: *Modernising Company Law* at paras 3.12–3.13.

which the Government is seeking to promote through the Insolvency Act 2000 and the Enterprise Bill now before Parliament.[62]

In fact, it has not yet been worked out at what point such a duty is triggered, nor **11.41** how the director can be expected to act in a situation where insolvent liquidation is short of inevitable, nor whether in such circumstances the interests of creditors are to be regarded as paramount, trumping all others. In the absence of clear answers to these issues, it is right that they be left to the courts to develop, at least for the moment, on a case-by-case basis.

### Enactments requiring consideration of interests of creditors

Turning to the 2006 Act, the reference in s 172(3) to 'any enactment . . . requiring **11.42** directors, in certain circumstances, to consider or act in the interests of creditors of the company' must be a reference to the Insolvency Act, the most directly relevant provision of which is that relating to wrongful trading (s 214).

Strictly speaking, s 214 only applies to fix a director with liability once a company **11.43** has gone into insolvent liquidation. Even where the company does go into insolvent liquidation, it may not be a straightforward matter for the liquidator to satisfy the requirements of s 214 so as to fix the director with liability. Nevertheless, the provisions of s 214 will inform the well-advised director how he should act before insolvent liquidation actually intervenes. This is because the possibility of liability is triggered as soon as the director knows or ought to conclude that there is no reasonable prospect that the company will avoid going into insolvent liquidation.[63] The facts which a director ought to know or ascertain and the conclusions he ought to reach are to be determined by reference to the matters set out in s 214(4) and (5), discussed at Chapter 29, Section I(3) below.

In the context of the duty to promote the success of the company imposed by the **11.44** 2006 Act, s 172, therefore, the effect of the proviso in s 172(3) is to render the duty to take every step to minimize the potential loss to the company's creditors paramount, in circumstances where the wrongful trading provisions apply, supplanting the matters listed in s 172(1). In other words, once the position is reached that the company has no reasonable prospect of avoiding insolvent liquidation, the mere fact that the director can show that he acted in a way which he considered, in good faith, would be most likely to promote the success of the company for the benefit of its members as a whole, having regard to the matters referred to in s 172(1), will not enable him to avoid liability for wrongful trading, if he failed to take every step that he ought to have taken to minimize the potential loss to the company's creditors.

---

[62] White Paper: *Modernising Company Law* at para 3.11.
[63] Insolvency Act, s 214(2)(b).

**11.45**  Section 214 is the only provision within the Insolvency Act which expressly requires directors to consider or act in the interests of creditors in certain circumstances. There are other provisions, however, which have as their clear purpose the protection of creditors' interests, most notably those which permit the court to set aside antecedent transactions in certain circumstances,[64] even though they do not in terms require separate consideration to be given to creditors' interests. The provisions relating to transactions at an undervalue and preferences are contained in the Insolvency Act, ss 238–241, which are discussed in Chapter 29, Section K below. The underlying purpose of the undervalue provisions is to prevent the assets of the company, which should properly be made available for distribution amongst the company's creditors in satisfaction of their debts, being improperly depleted. The evident purpose of the preference provisions is to ensure that, when the company is not in a position to pay all its creditors in full, the position of one or more of them is not improved to the detriment of the others.

**11.46**  It follows that, when considering whether the company should enter into a particular transaction or make a particular payment, the director must have proper regard for the interests of creditors so as to ensure that such interests are not prejudiced, even if the company is actually solvent immediately before the transaction or payment, if it would become insolvent in consequence. When deciding whether the company should enter into a transaction when it is insolvent, or will become insolvent as a result of doing so, therefore, the directors must ensure that the company will receive full value. Alternatively, if the company will not receive full value, or may not do so, the directors must satisfy themselves in good faith that the purpose of entering into the transaction is to enable the company to carry on its business and that there are reasonable grounds for believing that the transaction will benefit the company. In addition, the directors must ensure that the effect of the transaction or payment is not to prefer any of the company's creditors over the others. If the directors do not act in this way, they are at risk of being held in breach of their duty to take account of the interests of the company creditors, at least if the company then goes into administration or liquidation within the relevant period.[65]

**11.47**  In summary, therefore, it is clear from these provisions of the Insolvency Act that directors (i) must act so as minimize the potential loss to creditors once it has become clear, or ought to have become clear, that there is no reasonable prospect of the company avoiding insolvent liquidation; and (ii) must consider or act in the interests of creditors so as to cause the company to avoid entering into a transaction at an undervalue or giving a preference, when the company either is insolvent or will become insolvent in consequence of the transaction or preference. In such circumstances,

---

[64] Insolvency Act, ss 238–241.
[65] *Re Washington Diamond Mining Co* [1893] 3 Ch 95, CA; *West Mercia Safetywear Ltd v Dodd* [1988] BCLC 250, CA; *Re Cityspan Ltd* [2007] 2 BCLC 522.

the duty so to act will displace or, at the very least, take precedence over the duty to promote the interests of the company under the 2006 Act, s 172(1).

The question arises whether the directors of a company come under a duty to **11.48** consider or act in the interests of creditors at any earlier stage and, if so, in what circumstances that duty arises and how it is to be fulfilled. The Insolvency Act itself provides two instances where such a duty may arise even if, at the time, the company is solvent. The first is s 213, which enables the liquidator to pursue a claim for fraudulent trading against anyone (including any director) who was knowingly a party to the carrying on of the business of the company with (amongst other things) intent to defraud creditors of the company. The condition for relief under this section is not insolvency, but the presence of the intent to defraud creditors, which involves knowingly or recklessly exposing them to the risk that their debts will not be paid (see further Chapter 29 at paragraphs 29.154–29.157). The second is s 423, which applies in the event that the company enters into a transaction at an undervalue for the purpose of putting assets beyond the reach of a person (including a creditor) who is making, or may at some time make, a claim against the company, or otherwise prejudicing the interests of such a person in relation to such a claim. In such circumstances, s 423 permits the liquidator or administrator of the company or, in any other case, a victim of the transaction to seek relief. The condition for relief is not insolvency, but the presence of the purpose of defrauding creditors as defined by subs 423(3) (see further Chapter 29 at paragraphs 29.267–29.270).[66]

Apart from these two instances, however, the Insolvency Act is silent, and it is **11.49** necessary to look to the authorities for further guidance. As will appear from the discussion below, while the authorities recognize the existence of a duty to take into account the interests of the company's creditors in circumstances where the company itself is insolvent or at risk of insolvency, what triggers that duty, and its scope when it does arise, has not yet been fully worked out.

*Recognition by the courts of the duty to consider the interests of creditors*

Mason J adverted to such a duty in *Walker v Wimborne*,[67] noting that a failure on **11.50** the part of the directors to take account of such interests would have adverse consequences for the company as well as for them, but he did not elaborate on this. In *Lonrho Ltd v Shell Petroleum Ltd*,[68] Lord Diplock observed, in the context of

---

[66] A transfer of property could be set aside under the Fraudulent Conveyances Act 1571where the debtor was solvent at the time of the transfer but was about to embark on a hazardous venture and wanted to put the property out of the reach of his future creditors: *Crossley v Elworthy* (1871) 12 Eq 158; *Mackay v Douglas* (1872) 14 Eq 106; *Re Butterworth* (1882) 19 Ch D 588, CA.

[67] (1976) 137 CLR 1.

[68] [1980] 1 WLR 627, 634F, HL.

a request to allow inspection of the company's documents, that it was the duty of the board to consider whether to accede to the request would be in the best interests of the company, and that these were not exclusively those of the shareholders but might include those of its creditors as well. In *Winkworth v Baron Development Ltd*,[69] Lord Templeman described the position in the following terms:

> But a company owes a duty to its creditors, present and future. The company is not bound to pay off every debt as soon as it is incurred, and the company is not obliged to avoid all ventures which involve an element of risk but the company owes a duty to its creditors to keep its property inviolate and available for the repayment of its debts. The conscience of the company, as well as its management, is confided to its directors. A duty is owed by the directors to the company and to the creditors of the company to ensure that the affairs of the company are properly administered and that its property is not dissipated or exploited for the benefit of the directors themselves to the prejudice of the creditors.[70]

11.51 Lord Templeman considered that breach of any such duty would not have mattered if the solvency of the company had been maintained.[71] It is nevertheless implicit that he considered such a duty would exist even if the company were solvent. The fact that a duty to consider the interests of creditors exists even if the company is solvent, albeit that the interests of creditors in such circumstances should not count for very much, is supported by the following passage in the judgment of Nourse LJ in *Brady v Brady*:[72]

> The interests of a company, an artificial person, cannot be distinguished from the interests of the persons who are interested in it. Who are those persons? Where a company is both going and solvent, first and foremost come the shareholders, present and no doubt future as well. How material are the interests of creditors in such a case? Admittedly existing creditors are interested in the assets of the company as the only source for the satisfaction of their debts. But in a case where the assets are enormous and the debts minimal it is reasonable to suppose that the interests of the creditors ought not to count for very much. Conversely, where the company is insolvent, or even doubtfully solvent, the interests of the company are in reality the interests of existing creditors alone.

11.52 The reference to a company being 'doubtfully solvent' echoes language Templeman LJ had used in *Re Horsley & Weight Ltd*.[73] In that case, the directors caused the company to grant a pension to one of its directors, in the absence of any resolution of the board or of the company in general meeting. The Court of Appeal held that it was within the objects of the company to grant such a pension, that the grant could be ratified by the members and that it had been. The liquidator's misfeasance

---

69 [1986] 1 WLR 1512, HL.
70 [1986] 1 WLR 1512, 1516E–F.
71 Ibid, 1516G.
72 [1988] BCLC 20g–h, CA (reversed on different grounds, [1989] AC 755, HL).
73 [1982] Ch 442, CA.

claim against the recipient director was accordingly dismissed. While agreeing with the result, Templeman LJ considered what the position would have been if the company had been 'doubtfully solvent' at the time the pension was granted, which he described in the following words:

> If the company had been doubtfully solvent at the date of the grant to the knowledge of the directors, the grant would have been both a misfeasance and a fraud on the creditors for which the directors would remain liable.[74]

Even in the absence of fraud, Templeman LJ considered that there could have been gross negligence amounting to misfeasance (although, in the event, there was not):

> If the company could not afford to pay out £10,000 and was doubtfully solvent so that the expenditure threatened the continued existence of the company, the directors ought to have known the facts and ought at any rate to have postponed the grant of the pension until the financial position of the company was assured.[75]

Cooke J adopted similar language in *Nicholson v Permakraft (NZ) Ltd*,[76] where he said that:  **11.53**

> On the facts of particular cases this may require the directors to consider inter alia the interests of creditors. For instance creditors are entitled to consideration, in my opinion, if the company is insolvent, or near-insolvent, or of doubtful solvency, or if a contemplated payment or other course of action would jeopardise its solvency.[77]

*Re Horsley & Weight Ltd*[78] was an example of the application of the principle that  **11.54** the members of a company may assent to ratify any act done by the company so long as the act is one which is within the objects and powers of the company and is not done in fraud of the creditors. In *Kinsela v Russell Kinsela Pty Ltd*,[79] Street CJ adverted to the same principle, summarizing the position in two passages in his judgment, which have had a marked influence on the development of the duty in this country:

> In a solvent company the proprietary interests of the shareholders entitle them as a general body to be regarded as the company when questions of the duty of directors arise. If, as a general body, they authorise or ratify a particular action of the directors, there can be no challenge to the validity of what the directors have done. But where a company is insolvent the interests of the creditors intrude. They become prospectively entitled, through the mechanism of liquidation, to displace the power of the shareholders and the directors to deal with the company's assets. It is in a practical sense their assets and not the shareholders' assets that, through the medium of the

---

74 [1982] Ch 442, 455C–D.
75 [1982] 1 Ch 442, 455E.
76 [1985] 1 NZLR 242.
77 Ibid, 249.
78 [1982] Ch 442, 454D–E, per Buckley LJ.
79 (1986) 4 NSWLR 722, 730, 733.

company, are under the management of the directors pending either liquidation, return to solvency, or the imposition of some alternative administration . . .

Courts have traditionally and properly been cautious indeed in entering boardrooms and pronouncing upon the commercial justification of particular executive decisions. Wholly differing value considerations might enter into an adjudication upon the justification for a particular decision by a speculative mining company of doubtful stability on the one hand, and, on the other hand, by a company engaged in a more conservative business in a state of comparable financial instability. Moreover, the plainer it is that it is the creditors' money that is at risk, the lower may be the risk to which the directors, regardless of the unanimous support of all the shareholders, can justifiably expose the company.

**11.55** In *West Mercia Safetywear v Dodd* the Court of Appeal cited with approval the first of these passages from *Kinsela*.[80] In *West Mercia*, which was a pre-Insolvency Act case, the director had caused the company to make a payment to its parent, the effect of which (while reducing the debt owed by the company to the parent) was to reduce the parent's overdraft, which the director had guaranteed. The Court of Appeal concluded that the transfer constituted a fraudulent preference (under the pre-1986 legislation) and that the director was liable for misfeasance, on the basis of its earlier decision in *Re Washington Diamond Mining Co.*[81]

**11.56** Pausing in the review of the jurisprudence at this stage, it is to be noted that the duty to take account of the interests of creditors gives rise to three fundamental questions, namely (i) when the duty arises and whether it is triggered at a point short of inevitable insolvency; (ii) what behaviour on the part of the director will constitute a breach of the duty and what will not; and (iii) whether, when the duty arises, the interests of creditors are to be considered to the exclusion of other interests, or whether a balance is to be drawn. It is useful to bear these issues in mind when considering those cases which have followed *West Mercia*.[82]

### When does the duty arise?

**11.57** As to the first of these questions, the principles expressed in *Walker v Wimborne*, *Nicholson v Permakraft (NZ) Ltd*, *Kinsela v Russell Kinsela Pty Ltd*, and *West Mercia Safetywear v Dodd*, and set out above, were considered sufficient to justify the submission in *Facia Footwear v Hinchcliffe*[83] that the directors owed a duty to take

---

[80] [1988] BCLC 250, 252h–253b, CA, per Dillon LJ. See also *Bowthorpe Holdings v Hills* [2003] 1 BCLC 220 at paras 48–52.

[81] [1893] 3 Ch 95, CA.

[82] *Facia Footwear v Hinchcliffe* [1998] 1 BCLC 218; *Knight v Frost* [1999] 1 BCLC 364; *Official Receiver v Stern* [2002] 1 BCLC 119, CA at para [32]; *Bowthorpe Holdings* [2003] 1 BCLC 226 at paras 48–52; *Colin Gwyer & Associates Ltd v London Wharf (Limehouse) Ltd* [2003] 2 BCLC 153 at para 74; *Re Arena Corporation* [2004] BPIR 475 at para 118; *Ultraframe (UK) Ltd v Fielding* [2005] EWHC 1638 (Ch) at para 1304; *Re MDA Investment Management Ltd* [2004] 1 BCLC 217 at paras 69, 70, and 75; *Re Cityspan Ltd* [2007] 2 BCLC 522 at para 31.

[83] [1998] 1 BCLC 218, 228b.

into account the interests of creditors in circumstances where the company, and the group of which it was a member, were in a 'very dangerous' or 'parlous' financial position such that the future of the group probably depended on satisfactory refinancing arrangements becoming available.

While later cases have repeated the formulation adopted in *Facia Footwear v*   **11.58**
*Hinchcliffe*, however, it is fair to say that they provide only limited guidance on the all-important question when the duty to take account of the interests of creditors is triggered, short of the company's actual insolvency (in the sense of being unable to pay its debts on a cash-flow or balance sheet basis). While it was accepted in *Re MDA Investment Management Ltd*[84] that the duty arose when the company was in a 'dangerous' or 'precarious' financial position, the court also found that the company in that case was insolvent anyway (albeit in the context of the transaction at an undervalue claim, which failed for other reasons).[85] The company was also insolvent in *West Mercia Safetywear v Dodd*,[86] *Official Receiver v Stern*,[87] *Colin Gwyer & Associates Ltd v London Wharf (Limehouse) Ltd*,[88] and *Re Cityspan Ltd*.[89]

In any event, the words 'dangerous' and 'precarious' or even 'near-insolvent' or 'of   **11.59**
doubtful solvency', when applied to the financial position of a company, are imprecise terms. What will constitute a 'dangerous' or 'precarious' financial position sufficient to trigger the duty is likely to differ from case to case. The CLR sought to meet the problem by suggesting that the duty arose in circumstances where the directors 'know or ought to recognise that there is *a substantial probability* of an insolvent liquidation'.[90] The CLR's suggested clause, however, put the position more generally, such that the duty would arise '[a]t a time when the director of a company knows, or would know but for a failure of his duty to exercise due care and skill, that it is more likely than not that the company will at some point be unable to pay its debts as they fall due . . .'

As already explained,[91] the Government rejected the suggestion that any such   **11.60**
duty should be formulated and included in the statutory statement. It remains to be seen what approach the courts will adopt, given this rejection of the suggested formula. It will be necessary, therefore, to wait and see how the position is developed, albeit the cases where a claim is made against directors solely on the basis of their actions or inaction when the company was in such a position (rather than,

---

[84] [2004] 1 BCLC 217 at para 75.
[85] Ibid at paras 119–121, 122–124.
[86] [1988] BCLC 250.
[87] [2002] 1 BCLC 119.
[88] [2003] 2 BCLC 153 at para 80.
[89] [2007] 2 BCLC 522 at para 31.
[90] CLR: *Final Report*, para 3.17.
[91] Paragraph 11.40 above.

for example, wrongful trading or for breach of duty in circumstances giving rise to undervalue or preference claims) may be few and far between.

*How are the directors expected to behave when the duty does arise?*

**11.61** As the decision in *Facia Footwear v Hinchcliffe*[92] demonstrates, the manner in which the directors must act in the interests of creditors and whether the directors have acted in such a way as to be in breach of their duty by causing the company to continue trading, must inevitably depend upon the facts of the particular case. *Facia Footwear v Hinchcliffe* concerned a claim for breach of duty against directors for making payments to or for the benefit of group companies at a time when it was a claimed there was no realistic expectation that the group companies would be able to repay. One of the directors' defences was that at the time of the payments they considered that the group had a reasonable chance of weathering its financial difficulties.[93] In relation to that defence Sir Richard Scott V-C did not consider that the answer would always be clear-cut:

> It is clear enough that in continuing to trade ... [the directors] were taking a risk. But the boundary between an acceptable risk that an entrepreneur may properly take and an unacceptable risk the taking of which constitutes misfeasance is not always, perhaps not usually, clear cut ... I accept that, given the parlous financial state of the group, the directors had to have regard to the interests of creditors. But the creditors of the group, and of [the company] in particular, would clearly have been best served by a refinancing that could support a continuation of profitable trading. The cessation of trading followed by the disposal of the assets of the companies on a forced sale basis would, it was always realised, lead to heavy losses for the creditors. The creditors' only chance of being paid in full lay in a continuation of trading. A continuation of trading might mean a reduction in the dividend eventually payable to creditors but it represented the creditors' only chance of full payment. It is, therefore, not in the least obvious that in continuing to trade ... the directors were ignoring the interests of creditors.[94]

In *Facia Footwear v Hinchcliffe* itself, which was an application for summary judgment, the court concluded that a trial was necessary in order to determine this issue, so that the application must fail.

**11.62** Subsequent cases afford at least some guidance as to the type of conduct which has been found to constitute, or which might arguably constitute, a breach of duty on the part of the director. Examples include payments to the directors, whether in excess of that properly payable (*Official Receiver v Stern*[95]) or by way of preference (*Re Cityspan Ltd*[96]); the sale to a director of the company's shares in another

---

[92] [1998] 1 BCLC 218.
[93] Ibid, 225c–226a.
[94] Ibid, 228d–h.
[95] [2002] 1 BCLC 119 at paras 51–54.
[96] [2007] 2 BCLC 522.

company for substantially less than their market value (*Bowthorpe Holdings v Hills*[97]); causing the company to compromise on terms that meant the company would release valuable contractual rights against one of its members for no consideration (*Colin Gwyer & Associates v London Wharf (Limehouse) Ltd*[98]); and diverting consideration received from the sale of the company's business away from the company and causing the company to make payments to associated persons, which constituted preferences (*Re MDA Investment Management Ltd*[99]).

*Knight v Frost*[100] provides an example of conduct which was found not to constitute a breach of the duty. In that case, in reliance on *West Mercia Safetywear v Dodd*[101] and *Re Washington Diamond Milling Co*,[102] it was alleged that the de facto director had acted in breach of duty by causing payments to be made by the insolvent company to one of its creditors, which payments were said to involve an unlawful or improper preference of that creditor as against the plaintiff, another creditor. Although the court accepted that the company was insolvent at the time of the payment, however, it did not accept that the payments constituted preferences made in breach of duty because they had not been made within the relevant statutory period prior to the commencement of a winding up.[103]    **11.63**

Although the authorities referred to above give some guidance on the behaviour to be expected of directors, the question whether particular conduct will or will not attract liability will depend on the circumstances of each case. Where the conduct falls foul of well-known prohibitions on preferences and transactions at an undervalue the position is likely to be straightforward. Where the conduct complained of is more general, however, such as causing the company to continue to trade, the position is likely to be much less clear-cut.    **11.64**

*Are creditors' interests paramount or should a balance be drawn?*

The third issue concerns the degree to which directors must consider or act in the interests of creditors, in circumstances where the company is in a dangerous or precarious financial position short of actual insolvency. The question arises whether the interests of creditors are to be considered to the exclusion of all other matters, or whether a balancing exercise is to be undertaken such that creditors' interests form just one of a number of matters to which the directors ought to have regard. The authorities so far provide no real assistance in this respect, and the 2006 Act, s 172 itself is silent.    **11.65**

---

[97] [2003] 1 BCLC 220.
[98] [2003] 2 BCLC 153.
[99] [2004] 1 BCLC 217.
[100] [1999] 1 BCLC 364.
[101] [1988] BCLC 250.
[102] [1893] 3 Ch 95.
[103] [1999] 1 BCLC 364, 381f–382e.

**11.66**   It remains to be seen, therefore, whether the courts will expect the directors to perform a balancing exercise in such circumstances. Some members of the CLR advocated such an approach, such that 'the greater the risk of insolvency in terms of probability and extent, the more directors should take account of creditors' needs and the less those of members'.[104] Even if (as seems likely) such a balance is to be drawn, however, the weight to be attached to the competing interests will inevitably depend on the facts as they are perceived, or ought to be perceived, by the directors and will vary from case to case, rendering comprehensive guidance an unlikely prospect.

*Authorization and ratification*

**11.67**   Issues concerning the duty to consider the interests of the company's creditors are often coupled with issues as to whether the relevant transaction or conduct has been, or is capable of being, consented to, approved, authorized or ratified by the members of the company. Questions of consent, approval and authorization are considered in Chapter 9, paragraphs 9.37–9.49 and ratification is considered in Chapter 19, Section D.

---

[104]   CLR: *Final Report*, para 3.17.

# 12

# THE DUTY TO EXERCISE
# INDEPENDENT JUDGMENT

## A. Introduction

Section 173 of the Companies Act provides that:                                    **12.01**

  (1) A director of a company must exercise independent judgment.

  (2) This duty is not infringed by his acting:—

    (a) in accordance with an agreement duly entered into by the company that restricts the future exercise of discretion by its directors, or

    (b) in a way authorised by the company's constitution.

The 2006 Act, subs 173(1) codifies the established principle of law under which   **12.02**
directors must exercise their powers independently, without subordinating their
powers to the will of others, whether by delegation or otherwise (unless authorized by or under the constitution to do so).

The duty stated in subs 173(1) applies to shadow directors to the extent that the  **12.03**
common law rules or equitable principles corresponding to the duty to exercise
independent judgment applied to shadow directors (see Chapter 9, Section C).[1]

A director who, in relation to a particular transaction, wishes to be protected from  **12.04**
the risk of being in breach of the duty to exercise independent judgment may
obtain the consent, approval, or authorization of the members, as recognized by
s 180(4)(a) (see Chapter 9, Section D) or ratification of his conduct under s 239
(Chapter 19, Section D).

---

[1] s 170(5).

## B. The Duty

**12.05**  This duty under subs 173(1) is often closely linked with the duty under the 2006 Act, subs 175(1) to avoid conflicts of interest[2] and many cases that involve a breach of subs 173(1) will also involve a breach of subs 175(1). The reason for this is that breaches of a director's duty to use independent judgment often involve a director's relationship with third parties with whom that director is closely associated. For example, where a director makes a prior agreement to vote in a third party's interests on a particular transaction, thereby leaving himself no independent discretion as to how to act he will be in breach of subs 173(1).[3] Such a director is also likely to be in breach of subs 175(1) for placing himself in a position where he has, or can have, a direct or indirect interest that conflicts with, or possibly may conflict with, the interests of the company.

**12.06**  Another example is *Scottish Co-operative Wholesale Society Ltd v Meyer*.[4] In that case a holding company formed a subsidiary company to enable it to participate in the manufacture and sale of certain materials. The two respondents were appointed joint managing directors of the subsidiary company and became shareholders in it. The holding company then sought to purchase from the respondents their minority shares at less than their true value and, when this was rejected, they adopted a policy of transferring the company's business to a new department within the parent company, thereby forcing down the value of the shares. In addition to the respondents, there were nominee directors of the holding company on the subsidiary's board, and although they were aware of this new policy, they did not inform the respondents, but secretly promoted the holding company's plans. The House of Lords held that the interest of the respondents had been oppressed by the majority. In doing so it was said that the nominee directors were in breach of their duty to the subsidiary through their failure to take any positive steps to protect the subsidiary against the oppressive policy of the holding company.[5] This can be seen as an application of the duty to exercise independent judgment. There was also a conflict between the nominee directors' duty to the holding company and their duty to the subsidiary.[6]

**12.07**  Further examples of the particular situations in which this duty will arise, including in relation to nominee directors, are considered below.

---

[2] Chapter 14 of this work.
[3] *Re Englefield Colliery Co* (1878) 8 Ch D 388.
[4] [1959] AC 324, HL. See also *Gardner v Parker* [2004] 1 BCLC 417 at paras 18–19, per Blackburne J (affirmed [2004] 2 BCLC 554, CA).
[5] [1959] AC 324, 341, per Viscount Simonds; 347, per Lord Morton; 367, per Lord Denning.
[6] Ibid, 366, per Lord Denning.

*Delegation*

The duty does not confer a power on the directors to delegate, nor does it prevent  **12.08**
a director from exercising a power to delegate conferred by the company's
constitution provided that its exercise is in accordance with the company's constitution. Where the company's articles contain no power of delegation the court will
insist that it should be the directors and not some other person or body to whom
they have purported to delegate their powers, who should determine how those
powers are to be exercised.[7] Under the 1985 Act Table A and the Model Articles
the directors may delegate their functions in accordance with the articles.[8]

Where the company's constitution does allow a director to delegate his functions  **12.09**
to others the decision to delegate must be exercised in accordance with the general
duties. A director may only delegate his functions where it is appropriate to do so.
In particular, he must take reasonable care and skill in making his decision to
whom to delegate his functions. However, where it is appropriate for the director
to delegate he will not be expected to supervise every aspect of the delegate's
activities.[9]

In *Re Barings plc (No 5), Secretary of State for Trade and Industry v Baker (No 5)* the  **12.10**
Court of Appeal approved the following statement by Jonathan Parker J:[10]

(i) Directors have, both collectively and individually, a continuing duty to acquire
and maintain a sufficient knowledge and understanding of the company's business
to enable them properly to discharge their duties as directors.

(ii) Whilst directors are entitled (subject to the articles of association of the company)
to delegate particular functions to those below them in the management chain,
and to trust their competence and integrity to a reasonable extent, the exercise of
the power of delegation does not absolve a director from the duty to supervise the
discharge of the delegated functions.

(iii) No rule of universal application can be formulated as to the duty referred to in (ii)
above. The extent of the duty, and the question whether it has been discharged,
must depend on the facts of each particular case, including the director's role in the
management of the company.

Similarly, in *Re Westmid Packing Services Ltd* Lord Woolf MR said:[11]  **12.11**

A proper degree of delegation and division of responsibility is of course permissible,
and often necessary, but total abrogation of responsibility is not. A board of directors
must not permit one individual to dominate them and use them . . .

---

[7] *Re County Palatine Loan and Discount Co, Cartnell's Case* (1874) 9 Ch App 691.
[8] Table A, reg 72; Model Article (pcls) 5; Model Article (plc) 5.
[9] *Dovey v Cory* [1901] AC 477; *Re City Equitable Fire Insurance Co Ltd* [1925] Ch 407; *Norman
v Theodore Goddard* [1991] BCLC 1028; *Daniels v Anderson* (1995) 13 ACLC; *Ultraframe (UK) Ltd
v Fielding* [2005] EWHC 1638 (Ch) at paras 1296 to 1301.
[10] [2000] 1 BCLC 523, 536, CA.
[11] [1998] 2 BCLC 646, 653, CA.

*Advice*

**12.12**  Similar principles apply in respect of advice received by a director. The duty was expressed by Lord Goldsmith in the Lords Grand Committee stage of the Companies Bill as follows:

> . . . the clause does not mean that a director has to form his judgment totally independently from anyone or anything. It does not actually mean that the director has to be independent himself. He can have an interest in the matter . . . It is the exercise of the judgment of a director that must be independent in the sense of it being his own judgment . . . The duty does not prevent a director from relying on the advice or work of others, but the final judgment must be his responsibility. He clearly cannot be expected to do everything himself. Indeed, in certain circumstances directors may be in breach of their duty if they fail to take appropriate advice—for example, legal advice. As with all advice, slavish reliance is not acceptable, and the obtaining of outside advice does not absolve directors from exercising their judgment on the basis of such advice.[12]

*Nominee directors*

**12.13**  The duty is particularly important in the context of nominee directors. Particular examples of such directors include where a holding company has nominee directors on the board of its subsidiary or when a particular class of shareholder or a debenture holder has the right to appoint one or more directors on the board to represent their interests. There is nothing unlawful for a director to act in such a capacity. A director who, without concealment of his position and with the consent of the company[13] represents the interests of a third party on the board does not thereby breach his duty to the company. However, directors in such a position must take care to ensure that they continue to exercise their judgment independently and that no conflict of interest arises between their duty to the company and their obligations to their appointor. The law draws no distinction between the position of a nominee director and any other director. A nominee owes the same duties to the company and cannot blindly follow the judgment of those who appointed them. A nominee director may not plead any instruction from his appointor as a defence to an allegation of breach of duty.[14]

---

[12]  Hansard, HL vol 678, col 282 (6 February 2006); compare for instance *Davy-Chiesman v Davy-Chiesman* [1984] Fam 428 where, in the context of a solicitor's duty to the legal aid committee, the Court of Appeal held that although a solicitor was entitled to rely on the advice of properly instructed counsel that did not absolve him from his responsibility to exercise his own independent judgment. As to the extent to which taking legal advice may absolve a director for breaching his duty to the company see *Green v Walkling* [2008] 2 BCLC 332.

[13]  *Kregor v Hollins* (1913) 109 LT 225, 231, CA.

[14]  *Kuwait Asia Bank EC v National Mutual Life Nominees Ltd* [1991] 1 AC 187, 222, PC.

The position of nominee directors in general was considered in *Re Neath Rugby*  **12.14**
*Ltd* by HH Judge Havelock-Allan QC, who said as follows:[15]

> There is apparently no English authority which determines the extent to which a
> nominee director may or is obliged to follow the reasonable wishes of his appointor.
> However there are three Australian cases which have something to say on this topic.
> Bowen CJ commented on the position of nominee or representative directors in
> *Re News Corporation Ltd* (1987) 70 ALR 419 at 437 in these terms:
>
> > It is both realistic and not improper to expect that such directors will follow the
> > interests of the company which appointed them subject to the qualification that
> > they will not so act if of the view that their acts would not be in the interests of the
> > company as a whole.
>
> Similarly it was held in *Re Broadcasting Station 2GB Pty Ltd* [1964–5] NSWR 1648
> at 1663 that it is consistent with a director's duty for the director to follow the wishes
> of a particular interest which has brought about his appointment, without the need
> for a close personal analysis of the issues, unless the director is of the view that in
> doing so he or she is not acting in the best interests of the company as a whole.
> In *Canwest Global* (1997) 24 ACSR 405, the court observed uncritically that:
>
> > Directors usually act in accordance with the wishes and interests of a party that has
> > brought about their appointment and on whose goodwill their continuation in
> > office depends unless that places them in breach of their duties.
>
> The answer, in my judgment, is that the appointee's primary loyalty is to the com-
> pany of which he is a director. He is obliged to act in the best interests of that com-
> pany. He is quite entitled to have regard to the interests or requirements of his
> appointor to the extent those interests or requirements are not incompatible with his
> duty to act in the best interests of the company. Whether having regard to the appoin-
> tor's wishes is a matter of entitlement or obligation must depend on the terms, express
> or implied, of the agreement pursuant to which the director was appointed.

Accordingly, where a nominee director is placed in a position where the interests of  **12.15**
his appointer directly conflict with the interests of the company he may need to consider whether to vote against the interests of his appointer or to resign his position.

The provisions of s 173(2)(b) which provide that the duty is not infringed by a  **12.16**
director when he is acting in a way authorized by the company's constitution are
also highly relevant to nominee directors. The purpose of s 173(2)(b) appears to
have been to allow the position of nominee directors to be enshrined in a company's
constitution and provided the relevant provisions of the company's constitution
are properly worded for the nominee director to be released from the duty imposed
by subs 173(1). The nominee director will, however, remain obliged to comply
with his other duties to the company, including his duty to promote the success
of the company. The particular issues highlighted above in relation to nominee

---

[15] [2008] BCLC 527 at paras 26–27. The judge's decision was reversed in part by the Court of
Appeal at [2008] BCC 125 (reported under the name *Hawkes v Cuddy*). The Court of Appeal's decision did not, however, concern the judge's reasoning set out in these paragraphs.

directors will, therefore, continue to arise. The provisions of subs 173(2)(b) are considered in further detail in Section D below.

*Group companies*

12.17 Similar principles apply where the company is a member of a group. In *Charter-bridge Corporation Ltd v Lloyds Bank Ltd* Pennycuick J said that 'each company in the group is a separate legal entity and the directors of a particular company are not entitled to sacrifice the interest of that company'.[16] It follows that the directors of a holding company do not owe any duties to its subsidiary, at least if the subsidiary has different directors;[17] and that a director of a subsidiary owes his duties as such only to the subsidiary and cannot be compelled to exercise his powers in accordance with the holding company's wishes.[18] This is particularly the case where the subsidiary is not wholly owned by the parent. In such a case, where the directors of the subsidiary act in the interest of the parent and wholly without regard for the interests of the minority, issues of minority oppression may be relevant.[19] An example of such a case is *Scottish Co-operative Wholesale Society Ltd v Meyer* (the facts of which are set out in paragraph 12.06 above) where Viscount Simonds approved the statement of Lord President Cooper that: '[t]he truth is that, whenever a subsidiary is formed as in this case with an independent minority of shareholders, the parent company must, if it is engaged in the same class of business, accept as a result of having formed such a subsidiary an obligation so to conduct what are in a sense its own affairs as to deal fairly with its subsidiary'.[20]

12.18 In practice, however, it may be possible for the directors of a subsidiary to take into account the interests of the group more than the *Charterbridge* case suggests. Certainly, if the intended measure is likely to promote the success of the company for the benefit of its members as a whole, it is not a breach of duty for the director to take into account the benefit to the group as a whole. Moreover, in the case of a solvent company the interests of the subsidiary are likely to include the interests of its shareholders generally.[21] In the case of a wholly-owned subsidiary, the interests of the subsidiary will therefore include its holding company. In addition, where directors of a wholly-owned solvent subsidiary enter into a transaction which might prima facie amount to a breach of duty, the potential breach can in many

---

[16] [1970] Ch 62, 74. See also *Wallersteiner v Moir* [1974] 1 WLR 991, 1013, CA.
[17] *Lindgren v L & P Estates Limited* [1968] Ch 572, 595D–E, 604D–F.
[18] *Pergamon Press Limited v Maxwell* [1970] 1 WLR 1167, 1172.
[19] Chapter 21 of this work.
[20] [1959] AC 324, 343, HL.
[21] See 2006 Act, s 172 (considered in Chapter 11) which codifies the duty of a director to act in the way he considers, in good faith, would be most likely to promote the success of the company for the *benefit of its members as a whole*; see also *Greenhalgh v Arderne Cinemas* [1951] Ch 286, 291.

cases be cured by a resolution, or even an informal approval, of the holding company.[22] Difficulties may, however, arise in the case where the subsidiary is insolvent or in financial difficulties. In such circumstances, the holding company's ability to ratify a breach of duty by the directors is limited.[23]

## C. Contracts Restricting Future Exercise of Discretion

The duty imposed by s 173(1) will preclude a director from fettering his discretion by entering into a contract with a third party as to how he will exercise his discretion.[24] To do so would prevent the director from exercising an independent judgment at the appropriate time. However, the duty does not preclude the company from entering into, in good faith and in the interests of the company, a contract to take such further action as is necessary to carry out that contract. In *Fulham Football Club Ltd v Cabra Estates plc* the Court of Appeal stated:

**12.19**

> It is trite law that directors are under a duty to act bona fide in the interests of their company. However, it does not follow from that proposition that directors can never make a contract by which they bind themselves to the future exercise of their powers in a particular manner, even though the contract taken as a whole is manifestly for the benefit of the company. Such a rule could well prevent companies from entering into contracts which were commercially beneficial to them.

The Court of Appeal went on to hold:

> The true rule was stated by the High Court of Australia in *Thorby v Goldberg* (1964) 112 CLR 597. The relevant part of the headnote reads: 'If, when a contract is negotiated on behalf of a company, the directors bona fide think it in the interests of the company as a whole that the transaction should be entered into and carried into effect they may bind themselves by the contract to do whatever is necessary to effectuate it'.[25]

This position is confirmed by s 173(2)(a) which provides that the duty to exercise independent judgment is not infringed by the director if he is acting in accordance with an agreement duly entered into by the company that restricts the future exercise of discretion by the directors.

**12.20**

---

[22] As to the ratification of breaches of duty see Chapter 19, Section D.

[23] As to directors' duties in the case of an insolvent company or company in financial difficulties, see Chapter 11, Section E. For authorization and ratification where the duty to consider creditors' interests applies, see Chapter 9, Section D and Chapter 19, Section D.

[24] *Re Englefield Colliery Co* (1878) 8 Ch D 388; and see *Re London and South-Western Canal Ltd* [1911] 1 Ch 346, where directors were held liable for 'misfeasance' for holding their qualification shares on trust for promoters and giving them blank transfers, so that the promoters could dismiss them at any time.

[25] [1994] 1 BCLC 363, 392.

## D.  Authorization by the Constitution

**12.21**   The 2006 Act, s 173(2)(b) provides that the duty to exercise independent judgment is not infringed by the director acting in a way authorized by the company's constitution.[26] The Solicitor General explained the purpose of the subsection during consideration of the Bill in Standing Committee as follows:[27]

> . . . subsection (2)(b) will allow the status of the nominee director to be enshrined in the company's constitution so that the nominee is able to follow the instructions of the person who appointed him without breaching that duty. The extent to which that is possible under the existing law was unclear, but we have now made it clear. However, even when a nominee follows instructions, he must still comply with all his other duties—there may well be other duties—such as a duty to act broadly in the interests of the company.

**12.22**   Accordingly, when considering the appointment of nominee directors it will also be necessary to consider some amendment to the company's constitution in order to ensure that such directors are given the full protection afforded by subs 173(2)(b). However, as the passage from the speech of the Solicitor General set out above makes clear, even where a nominee or other director is released from the duty imposed by subs 173(1) by a provision in the company's constitution he will remain under a duty to comply with his other duties.

---

[26]  As to the meaning of the company's 'constitution' see CA 2006, ss 17, 257 and Chapter 10, paragraphs 10.06 to 10.07 above.

[27]  See the answer by the Solicitor General, HC Official Report, SC D (Company Law Reform Bill), 11 July 2006, col 601.

# 13

## THE DUTY TO EXERCISE
## REASONABLE CARE, SKILL,
## AND DILIGENCE

## A. Introduction

The 2006 Act, s 174 provides that: **13.01**

(1) A director of a company must exercise reasonable care, skill and diligence.
(2) This means the care, skill and diligence that would be exercised by a reasonably diligent person with—
   (a) the general knowledge, skill and experience that may reasonably be expected of a person carrying out the functions carried out by the director in relation to the company, and
   (b) the general knowledge, skill and experience that the director has.

The 2006 Act, s 174 thus codifies the director's duty to exercise reasonable care, **13.02** skill, and diligence. It reflects the current position at common law, which itself reflects the tests laid down in the context of wrongful trading, as set out in the Insolvency Act, s 214. Indeed, the wording of this section of the 2006 Act is substantially the same as that of the Insolvency Act, subs 214(4).

Whether a director has complied with the duty in any particular case will require **13.03** an assessment of his conduct which is both objective and subjective. It is objective in the sense that the director's conduct will be compared with that which may reasonably be expected of a person carrying out the same functions as those carried out by the director in relation to the company. If the director's conduct thus compared falls short of this standard, objectively ascertained, then he will have breached the duty. The fact that, having regard to the general knowledge, skill, and experience of the director concerned, nothing better could perhaps have been expected of him, will be nothing to the point. The objective standard may thus be regarded as imposing a minimum standard to be expected of all directors, which cannot be reduced further by reference to the general knowledge, skill, and experience of the particular director concerned.

**13.04**    The mere fact that the particular director meets the objective standard, however, will not mean that he has acted in accordance with his duty. In order to ascertain whether or not he has, it is also necessary to have regard to the general knowledge, skill, and experience of the director himself. It is in this respect that the assessment is subjective. If the director has greater knowledge, skill, and experience than might ordinarily be expected of someone carrying out the same functions as he carries out in relation to the company, a higher standard of conduct may be expected of him, and he must satisfy that higher standard. If he does not, he will have acted in breach of his duty. It will not suffice that he has reached the standard reasonably to be expected of someone carrying out the same functions but who does not have his greater knowledge, skill, and experience.

**13.05**    The dual assessment required by the duty as codified by the 2006 Act, s 174 thus confirms the rejection by the courts in the early 1990s[1] of the standard which had been prevalent earlier in the twentieth century, which did not require directors to exhibit a greater degree of skill than could reasonably be expected from a person with their knowledge and experience and which gave rise merely to a subjective assessment of the director's conduct in this respect.[2]

**13.06**    The duty to exercise care, skill, and diligence in its codified form replaces the common law rules and equitable principles upon which it is based.[3] Nevertheless, it is intended that it will be interpreted and applied in the same way as those corresponding common law rules and equitable principles which it replaces.[4]

**13.07**    It has been consistently emphasized by the courts on numerous occasions that the question whether a director has in fact acted in breach of his duty of care can only be determined upon consideration of the facts and circumstances of the particular case. Conduct which may be acceptable (in the sense that it does not give rise to actionable complaint) in one case may constitute an actionable breach of duty in another. In the event that concern arises as to the conduct of a director, therefore,

---

[1] *Re D'Jan of London Ltd, Copp v D'Jan* [1994] 1 BCLC 561 (Hoffmann LJ, sitting as an additional judge of the Chancery Division), 563d. In *Norman v Theodore Goddard* [1991] BCLC 1028, the same was assumed by Hoffmann J, but without argument: 1031b. See also *Lexi Holdings plc v Luqman* [2008] 2 BCLC 725 at paras 36 and 37.

[2] *Lagunas Nitrate Co v Lagunas Syndicate* [1899] 2 Ch 392; *Re Brazilian Rubber Plantations and Estates Ltd* [1911] 1 Ch 425; *Re City Equitable Fire Insurance Co* [1925] Ch 407; *Huckerby v Elliott* [1970] 1 All ER 189.

[3] 2006 Act, s 170(3).

[4] 2006 Act, s 170(4).

it will be necessary to form a clear understanding of the factual context so as to be able to identify the duty owed by the director and the manner in which it was breached, in order both to formulate the claim properly and determine whether it can be substantiated. It is likely to be necessary to have regard to the size of the company, and the nature of its business. It may also be necessary to have regard to the effect changes in the economy are likely to have on the company's business, and to the regulatory regime affecting the industry in which it operates. As far as the director himself is concerned, it will be necessary to ascertain the basis upon which his services have been retained by the company and, with an appropriate degree of precision, the functions he has been charged to undertake in relation to the company. It will be necessary to consider whether the director has any particular skill or skills, and the degree to which those skills relate, or were reasonably expected to relate, to the discharge of his functions. Likewise it will be necessary to have regard to the director's experience, both recent and over the course of his entire working life.

As conduct may constitute a breach of the director's duty of care in one case but not **13.08** in another, and since each case must therefore be considered on its own facts, it follows that the guidance to be derived from the authorities is necessarily limited.

## B. Nature of the Duty

The duty of care is not recognized at common law as a fiduciary duty and is not **13.09** enforceable as such. This is expressly recognized by the 2006 Act, s 178(2), which identifies the duty to exercise reasonable care, skill, and diligence as an exception to the rule that the duties codified in ss 171 to 177 are enforceable in the same way as any other fiduciary duty owed to a company by its directors.

The duty comprises three elements, namely care, skill, and diligence, which will **13.10** often overlap in practice. For the purposes of analysis, however, it may be helpful to distinguish between them. On the basis of the authorities discussed below, it is suggested that care is to be understood as carefulness, though not caution; skill denotes ability, while diligence may be understood as requiring the director to apply himself conscientiously to the affairs of the company and, in particular, the matter in hand.

## C. Scope of the Duty

Historically, it was considered that directors would only be liable for breach of **13.11** their duty of care if guilty of 'gross' negligence, or *crassa negligentia*. Some eminent judges regarded the use of the word 'gross' as unnecessary. In *Wilson v Brett*,[5]

---

[5] 11 M & W 11.

for example, Baron Rolfe (later Lord Cranworth) said that he 'could see no difference between negligence or gross negligence; that it was the same thing, with the addition of a vituperative epithet'. Others, however, considered that it was 'certainly not without its significance' and that it could usefully be retained.[6] In *Giblin v McMullen*, Lord Chelmsford considered that for the bank to have been negligent, it would need to have shown 'the want of that ordinary diligence which men of common prudence generally exercise about their own affairs'.

**13.12** The House of Lords adopted the same approach in relation to directors in *Overend & Gurney Co v Gibb*,[7] where Lord Hatherley LC identified the question in the following terms:

> [W]hether if [the directors] did not so exceed their powers they were cognisant of circumstances of such a character, so plain, so manifest, and so simple of appreciation, that no men with any ordinary degree of prudence, acting on their own behalf, would have entered into such a transaction as they entered into? Was there *crassa negligentia* on their part . . . ?[8]

**13.13** In *Lagunas Nitrate Company v Lagunas Syndicate*,[9] Lindley MR stated the position as follows:

> If directors act within their powers, if they act with such care as is reasonably to be expected from them, having regard to their knowledge and experience, and if they act honestly for the benefit of the company they represent, they discharge both their equitable as well as their legal duty to the company.[10]

He found that the amount of care to be taken was difficult to define. He continued:

> [B]ut it is plain that directors are not liable for all the mistakes they may make, although if they had taken more care they might have avoided them: see *Overend, Gurney & Co. v Gibb*. Their negligence must be not the omission to take all possible care; it must be much more blameable than that: it must be in a business sense culpable or gross. I do not know how better to describe it.[11]

**13.14** In *In re Brazilian Rubber Plantation and Estates Limited*,[12] Neville J explained the position in memorable terms by reference to the management of a rubber company:

> A director's duty has been laid down as requiring him to act with such care as is reasonably to be expected from him, having regard to his knowledge and experience.

---

[6] *Giblin v McMullen* (1868) 2 LR 2 PC 317, 336, 337, per Lord Chelmsford.
[7] (1872) LR 5 HL 480.
[8] Ibid, 487.
[9] [1899] 2 Ch 392, 422, CA.
[10] [1899] 2 Ch 392, 435.
[11] Ibid, CA.
[12] [1911] 1 Ch 425, 437.

He is, I think, not bound to bring any special qualifications to his office. He may undertake the management of a rubber company in complete ignorance of everything connected with rubber, without incurring responsibility for the mistakes which may result from such ignorance; while if he is acquainted with the rubber business he must give the company the advantage of his knowledge when transacting the company's business. He is not, I think, bound to take any definite part in the conduct of the company's business, but so far as he does undertake it he must use reasonable care in its despatch.

Such reasonable care must, I think, be measured by the care an ordinary man might be expected to take in the same circumstances on his own behalf. He is clearly, I think, not responsible for damages occasioned by errors of judgment.

This set the stage for Romer J's classical exposition in *Re City Equitable Fire* **13.15** *Insurance Co Ltd*.[13] He began by emphasizing the need to investigate all the relevant circumstances:

In order, therefore, to ascertain the duties that a person appointed to the board of an established company undertakes to perform, it is necessary to consider not only the nature of the company's business, but also the manner in which the work of the company is in fact distributed between the directors and the other officials of the company, provided always that this distribution is a reasonable one in the circumstances, and is not inconsistent with any express provisions of the articles of association. In discharging the duties of his position thus ascertained a director must, of course, act honestly: but he must also exercise some degree of both skill and diligence. To the question of what is the particular degree of skill and diligence required of him, the authorities do not, I think, give any very clear answer. It has been laid down that so long as a director acts honestly he cannot be made responsible in damages unless guilty of gross or culpable negligence in a business sense.[14]

Following the approach adopted in the *Lagunas* and *Brazilian Rubber* cases, Romer J **13.16** agreed that a director had to display reasonable care to be measured by the care an ordinary man might be expected to take in the circumstances on his own behalf, not all possible care. He continued:

There are, in addition, one or two other general propositions that seem to be warranted by the reported cases: (1) A director need not exhibit in the performance of his duties a greater degree of skill than may reasonably be expected from a person of his knowledge and experience. A director of a life insurance company, for instance, does not guarantee that he has the skill of an actuary or of a physician . . . It is perhaps only another way of stating the same proposition to say that directors are not liable for mere errors of judgment. (2) A director is not bound to give continuous attention to the affairs of his company. His duties are of an intermittent nature to be performed at periodical board meetings, and at meetings of any committee of the board upon which he happens to be placed. He is not, however, bound to attend all such meetings though he ought to attend, whenever, in the circumstances, he is reasonably able

---

[13] [1925] Ch 407.
[14] Ibid, 427.

to do so. (3) In respect of all duties that, having regard to the exigencies of business, and the articles of association, may properly be left to some other official, a director is, in the absence of grounds for suspicion, justified in trusting that official to perform such duties honestly . . .

**13.17** Three general observations may be made before considering separately care, skill, and diligence as they have developed since *City Equitable*. First, the courts were reluctant historically to formulate detailed rules for the guidance of directors in the conduct of business affairs. In the words of Lord Macnaghten in *Dovey v Cory*:[15]

> I do not think it desirable for any tribunal to do that which Parliament has abstained from doing—that is, to formulate precise rules for the guidance or embarrassment of business men in the conduct of business affairs. There never has been, and I think there never will be, much difficulty in dealing with any particular case on its own facts and circumstances: and, speaking for myself, I rather doubt the wisdom of attempting to do more.

**13.18** Secondly, although (as will appear from the discussion below) the standard of conduct to be expected of directors is no longer in all respects the same as that suggested by Romer J, it was the case then—and remains the case now—that the scope of the duty and, in particular, whether it has been discharged or breached, required a detailed consideration of all the relevant facts in any particular case. As the position was described more recently by the Supreme Court of New South Wales in *Daniels v Anderson*:[16]

> A person who accepts the office of director of a particular company undertakes the responsibility of ensuring that he or she understands the nature of the duty a director is called upon to perform. That duty will vary according to the size and business of the particular company and the experience or skills that the director held himself or herself out to have in support of appointment to the office. None of this is novel. It turns upon the natural expectations and reliance placed by shareholders on the experience and skill of a particular director . . . The duty includes that of acting collectively to manage the company.

**13.19** Finally, it is also fair to say that, if an issue arises as to the extent of a director's duties and responsibilities in any particular case, the level of reward he is entitled to receive may be a relevant factor in resolving that issue. As Jonathan Parker J put it in *Re Barings plc (No 5)*,[17] echoing what Sir Richard Scott V-C had previously said in *Re Barings plc, Secretary of State for Trade and Industry v Baker*:[18]

> The point is that the higher the level of reward, the greater the responsibilities which may reasonably be expected (prima facie, at least) to go with it.

---

[15] [1901] AC 477, 488, HL.
[16] (1995) 16 ACSR 607, 668 cited and adopted by Jonathan Parker J in *Re Barings plc (No 5)* [1999] 1 BCLC 433, 488, para B5.
[17] Ibid, para [B6].
[18] [1998] BCC 583, 586.

*Care*

The requirement that a director should exercise reasonable (though not all **13.20** possible) care necessarily introduced objective criteria in determining the standard of care he should exercise, the director's behaviour being compared with that to be expected of an ordinary man acting on his own behalf in similar circumstances. This is how Foster J interpreted the position in *Dorchester Finance Co Ltd v Stebbing*.[19] In that case, it was held that non-executive directors who were either qualified accountants or had considerable accountancy and business experience, and who had signed blank cheques, thereby allowing the managing director to misappropriate the company's money, had been negligent. Foster J distinguished between the duty of care, in relation to which a director was required to take such care in the performance of his duties as an ordinary man might be expected to take on his own behalf, and the duty of skill, which was to be determined subjectively.

It is unlikely to have been a coincidence that this distinction was one drawn in the **13.21** draft Companies Bill 1978,[20] published the year after *Dorchester Finance Co v Stebbing* was decided. As will be seen below, however, such a distinction did not survive *D'Jan of London Ltd, Copp v D'Jan*,[21] with the adoption of the test provided for by section 214(4) of the Insolvency Act 1986.

*Skill*

To the extent that Romer J identified the standard of skill required as a matter to **13.22** be determined subjectively, that is to say by reference only to the personal qualities of the director concerned, what he said was entirely consistent with the authorities at that time. As demonstrated by *Dorchester Finance Co Ltd v Stebbing*,[22] the test remained a subjective one into the late 1970s as Foster J accepted the proposition that a director is required to exhibit in the performance of his duties such a degree of skill as may reasonably be expected from a person with *his* knowledge and experience.

Within sixteen years of Foster J's decision, however, the skill to be expected of **13.23** a director fell to be determined not simply by reference to the knowledge and experience of the director himself (a subjective standard) but also by reference to an objective standard. In *D'Jan of London Ltd, Copp v D'Jan*,[23] Hoffmann LJ

---

[19] [1989] BCLC 498, 501d–e–502a (actually decided in July 1977).
[20] Clause 45(1) of the Companies Bill 1978 provided as follows: '(1) In the exercise of the powers and the discharge of the duties of his office in circumstances of any description, a director of a company owes a duty to the company to exercise such care and diligence as could reasonably be expected of a reasonably prudent person in circumstances of that description and to exercise such skill as may reasonably be expected of a person of his knowledge and experience.'
[21] [1994] 1 BCLC 561, 563d.
[22] [1989] BCLC 498, 501 (actually decided in July 1977).
[23] [1994] 1 BCLC 561, 563d.

(sitting as an additional judge of the Chancery Division) made the following statement as to the duty of care owed by a director at common law:

> In my view, the duty of care owed by a director at common law is accurately stated in section 214(4) of the Insolvency Act 1986. It is the conduct of—
>
> a reasonably diligent person having both—(a) the general knowledge, skill and experience that may reasonably be expected of a person carrying out the same functions as are carried out by that director in relation to the company, and (b) the general knowledge, skill and experience that that director has.

**13.24** It is not easy to discern the basis for this development of the standard of skill from the authorities of the time. It is true that Hoffmann J had himself previously stated the position in similar terms in *Norman v Theodore Goddard*.[24] In that case, however, he did not hear argument on the point as he was willing to assume that was the relevant test. In *D'Jan* itself, Romer J's judgment in *In Re City Equitable Fire Insurance Co* appears not to have been cited, perhaps because it was thought unnecessary by reason of its familiarity, and Hoffmann LJ did not elaborate on the reasoning which led him to take the view he did. It is also the case that in *Bishopsgate Investment Management Ltd v Maxwell (No 2)*,[25] Hoffmann LJ recognized that the law might be evolving in response to changes in public attitudes to corporate governance, but this statement was *obiter*.

**13.25** Nevertheless the development was plainly consistent with the changing role of directors and the Legislature's recognition that more was to be expected of those who sought to take advantage of the benefits of trading with limited liability in the modern commercial world, apparent not only from the specific terms of s 214 and other provisions of the Insolvency Act itself, but also from the enactment of the Company Directors Disqualification Act (CDDA) of the same year. These legislative developments had been intended to meet concerns which had been voiced increasingly vociferously over previous decades, including by the Jenkins Committee in its Report delivered in 1962 and the Report of the Cork Committee, delivered in 1982.[26] As Henry LJ said in *Re Grayan Building Services Ltd*:[27]

> The concept of limited liability and the sophistication of our corporate law offers great privileges and great opportunities for those who wish to trade under that regime.

---

[24] [1991] BCLC 1028, 1030h–1b.

[25] [1994] 1 All ER 261, 264b, CA.

[26] Report of the Jenkins Committee at paras 497–500, 503; report of the Cork Committee at chapter 45.

[27] [1995] Ch 241, 257–8, CA. In *Blackspur Group plc (No 2)* [1998] 1 BCLC 676, 680, CA, Lord Woolf MR described the purposes of the directors' disqualification legislation as 'the protection of the public, by means of prohibitory remedial action, by anticipated deterrent effect on further misconduct and by encouragement of higher standards of honesty and diligence in corporate management, from those who are unfit to be concerned in the management of a company'.

But the corporate environment carries with it the discipline that those who avail themselves of those privileges must accept the standards laid down and abide by the regulatory rules and disciplines in place to protect creditors and shareholders. And while some significant corporate failures will occur despite the directors exercising best managerial practice, in many too many [cases] there have been serious breaches of those rules and disciplines, in situations where the observance of them would or at least might have prevented or reduced the scale of the failure and consequent loss to creditors and investors. Reliable figures are hard to come by, but it seems that losses from corporate fraud and mismanagement have never been higher. At the same time the regulatory regime has never been more stringent—on paper even if not in practice. The Parliamentary intention to improve managerial safeguards and standards for the long term good of employees, creditors and investors is clear . . . The statutory corporate climate is stricter than it has ever been, and those enforcing it should reflect the fact that Parliament has seen the need for higher standards.

Such a development leads to a result which is both consistent and coherent, in the sense that the standard to be expected falls to be determined in the same way whether the company is carrying on business as usual or whether it is approaching, and has no reasonable prospect of avoiding, insolvent liquidation. This was recognized by the Law Commission.[28]  **13.26**

Regardless of the basis in authority for the position adopted in *D'Jan*, therefore, the decision to require the standard of skill to be ascertained by reference to objective (as well as subjective) criteria is obviously sensible,[29] both in principle and as a matter of policy. As the CLR subsequently recognized,[30] '[t]he community as a whole suffers if companies are run with less than objective standards of competence and it is appropriate to impose a mandatory standard'.  **13.27**

The dual test expounded in *D'Jan* has subsequently been widely recognized and applied by the courts,[31] including in the context of directors' disqualification cases.[32] It is no longer sufficient, therefore, for directors to bring to the performance of their functions the degree of skill they actually possess. Both collectively and individually, they have a continuing duty to acquire and maintain a sufficient knowledge and  **13.28**

---

[28] *Company Directors: Regulating Conflicts of Interests and Formulating a Statement of Duties* (Consultation Paper No 153, 1998), paras 15.27 and 15.29.

[29] According to the Law Commission, the movement in the case law to a dual subjective/objective test was a 'remarkable example of the modernisation of the law by the judges, facilitated of course by the changes in the insolvency legislation made by Parliament'. (*Company Directors: Regulating Conflicts of Interests and Formulating a Statement of Duties* (Consultation Paper No 153, 1998), para 13.19).

[30] CLR: *Developing the Framework* (March 2000) at para 3.68.

[31] *Cohen v Selby* [2001] 1 BCLC 176, CA at paras 10 and 21; *Re Westlowe Storage and Distribution Ltd* [2000] 2 BCLC 590, 611; *Bairstow v Queens Moat Houses plc* [2000] 1 BCLC 549, 559c–e; *Equitable Life Assurance Society v Bowley* [2004] 1 BCLC 180 at paras 36 and 37; *Lexi Holdings plc v Luqman* [2008] 2 BCLC 725 at paras 36 and 37.

[32] *Re Landhurst Leasing plc* [1999] 1 BCLC 286 at 344e–h.

understanding of the company's business to enable them properly to discharge their duties as directors.[33] As Jonathan Parker J noted in *Re Barings plc (No 5)*:

> It is a truism that if a manager does not properly understand the business which he is seeking to manage, he will be unable to take informed management decisions in relation to it.[34]

### Diligence

**13.29**  Romer J's summary of the position in relation to the degree of diligence to be expected of directors was not in practice a very exacting one. Apart from the authorities already referred to, perhaps the best-known illustration of the results to which such an unexacting requirement might lead was the *Marquis of Bute's Case*.[35] In that case, the bank went into liquidation following the discovery of a fraud perpetrated by its paid officer. The Marquis of Bute had been appointed president of the bank at the age of six months and attended only one board meeting in 39 years. He was found not liable for breach of duty. Stirling J distinguished between the failure to attend meetings and a neglect or omission of a duty which ought to be performed at those meetings. Even if he had read the reports sent to him, the Marquis would have been led to believe that the bank's affairs were being conducted in accordance with its rules.

**13.30**  Romer J's statement of the diligence to be expected of a director no longer accurately reflects modern standards or expectations save, possibly, in relation to non-executive directors. In practice, executive directors will generally be subject to contractual obligations which require that they give their constant and undivided attention to the affairs of the company in any event. The general expectation is that, so long as a director holds office and receives remuneration, it is incumbent upon that director to keep himself informed as to its financial affairs and to play an appropriate role in its management.[36]

**13.31**  In modern times, the company may reasonably look to non-executive directors for independence of judgment and supervision of the executive management.[37] Day-to-day involvement with the company will not generally be expected, and is

---

[33] *Re Barings plc (No 5)* [1999] 1 BCLC 433, 489, per Jonathan Parker J at para B7(i), and endorsed by the CA at [2000] 1 BCLC 523, 553–6 at para 36.

[34] *Re Barings plc (No 5)* [1999] 1 BCLC 489, 528g–h, per Jonathan Parker J.

[35] *Re Cardiff Savings Bank* [1892] 2 Ch 100. See also *Re Denham & Co* (1884) 25 Ch D 752, in which a director who was a 'country gentleman not a skilled accountant' was not liable for recommending payment of a dividend out of capital.

[36] *Re Galeforce Pleating Co Ltd* [1999] 2 BCLC 704, a disqualification case in which it was held that it was no answer to say, as the director had, that she 'had virtually a most negligible actual involvement in the running of the company' (716a). There is a useful discussion by Briggs J of the duty to take reasonable steps to prevent and detect fraud and other irregularities in *Lexi Holdings plc v Lugman* [2008] 2BCLC 725 at paras 30–39.

[37] *Equitable Life Assurance Society v Bowley* [2004] 1 BCLC 180 at para 41.

unlikely in any event to be possible or desirable. Just how much time and attention the non-executive director must devote to the company will inevitably depend on the facts and will vary from case to case. Nevertheless the diligence with which he will be expected to attend to the affairs of the company will be that which, in all the circumstances, is reasonably necessary to enable him properly to ensure that the judgment he exercises is not only independent but also properly informed, and to ensure that his supervision of the executive management is effective.

## D. Errors of Judgment

It has long been the case that directors are not to be held liable for 'mere errors of judgment'.[38] The courts historically have been reluctant to second-guess commercial decisions taken by the directors in good faith in what they honestly consider to be the best commercial interests of the company. It will certainly not be prepared to do so simply because, with the benefit of hindsight, the decision taken has turned out to be wrong. Any lingering doubt the court may have in such a case is likely to be resolved in favour of the director. As Lord Wilberforce said in *Howard Smith Ltd v Ampol Petroleum Ltd*[39] (in relation to the raising of finance):     **13.32**

> [Their Lordships] accept that it would be wrong for the court to substitute its opinion for that of the management, or indeed to question the correctness of the management's decision, on such a question, if bona fide arrived at. There is no appeal on merits from management decisions to courts of law; nor will courts assume to act as a kind of supervisory board over decisions within the powers of management honestly arrived at.

That is not to say that the court will always refuse to investigate the position. Indeed it will be necessary for it to determine whether what is complained of is a mere error of judgment or negligence amounting to breach of duty. It is implicit from what Lord Hatherley LC said in *Overend & Gurney Co v Gibb*[40] that his conclusion would have been different had he considered that the directors were 'cognisant of circumstances of such a character, so plain, so manifest, and so simple of appreciation, that no men with any ordinary degree of prudence, acting on their own behalf, would have entered into such a transaction as they entered into'. In modern times, and having regard to the 2006 Act, s 174, it is suggested that the     **13.33**

---

[38] *Overend & Gurney Co v Gibb* (1872) LR 5 HL 480, 494, per Lord Hatherley LC; *Lagunas Nitrate Company v Lagunas Syndicate* [1899] 2 Ch, 392, 435, CA, per Lindley MR; *In re Brazilian Rubber Plantations and Estates Limited* [1911] 1 Ch 425, 437; *In re City Equitable Fire Insurance Company Limited* [1925] 1 Ch 407, 429.

[39] [1974] AC 821, 832. See also *Re Smith & Fawcett Ltd* [1942] Ch 304; *Devlin v Slough Estates Ltd and others* [1983] BCLC 497, 504; *Runciman v Walter Runciman plc* [1992] BCLC 1084; *Re Tottenham Hotspur plc* [1994] BCLC 655, 660.

[40] (1872) LR 5 HL 480, 487.

courts' traditional reluctance to criticize errors of judgment will not extend to acts or omissions which no reasonable director or one possessing the particular director's expertise would have made.

**13.34** The hurdle is necessarily a high one. This is emphasized perhaps by the high burden of proof which falls to be discharged if the only complaint in support of an application for a director's disqualification is that he was incompetent.[41] Some caution is to be exercised in seeking to draw parallels in the context of disqualification, however. What may constitute a breach of duty in civil proceedings against the director, though it is a matter to which the court must have regard,[42] will not necessarily justify a finding of unfitness for the purposes of making a disqualification order against him, just as the director may be unfit even though no breach of duty is proved against him.[43] The position was perhaps best summed up by Jonathan Parker J in another passage in his judgment in *Re Barings plc (No 5)*:[44]

> Although in considering the question of unfitness the court had to have regard (among other things) to 'any misfeasance or breach of any fiduciary or other duty' by the respondent in relation to the company . . . it is not in my judgment a prerequisite of a finding of unfitness that the respondent should have been guilty of misfeasance or breach of duty in relation to the company. Unfitness may, in my judgment, be demonstrated by conduct which did not involve a breach of any statutory or common law duty: for example, trading at the risk of creditors may found a finding of unfitness even though it might not amount to wrongful trading under s 214 of the Insolvency Act 1986. Nor, in my judgment, would it necessarily be an answer to a charge of unfitness founded on allegations of incompetence that the errors which the respondent made can be characterised as errors of judgment rather than as negligent mistakes. It is, I think, possible to envisage a case where a respondent had shown himself so completely lacking in judgment as to justify a finding of unfitness, notwithstanding that he had not been guilty of misfeasance or breach of duty. Conversely, in my judgment, the fact that a respondent may have been guilty of misfeasance or breach of duty does not necessarily mean that he is unfit. As Sch 1 makes clear, there were a number of matters to which the court was required to have regard in considering the question of unfitness, in addition to misfeasance and breach of duty.

**13.35** The Law Commission considered whether, in the event that a statutory duty of care were to be introduced, there would also need to be a statutory statement of the principle of non-interference by the courts in commercial decisions made in

---

[41] *Re Sevenoaks Stationers (Retail) Ltd* [1991] Ch 164, 184, CA; *Re Barings plc (No 5)* [1999] 1 BCLC 433, 483–4 (para [A7]); *Re Cubelock* [2001] BCC 523, 535–6 (paras 50–53); *Re Bradcrown Ltd* [2001] 1 BCLC 547 at para 10; *Secretary of State for Trade and Industry v Walker* [2003] 1 BCLC 363 at paras 48–50. Though high, the degree of incompetence should not be exaggerated given the ability of the court to grant the director leave to act, notwithstanding the making of a disqualification order: *Re Barings plc (No 5)* [2000] 1 BCLC 523, CA at para 35.

[42] CDDA, s 9 and Schedule 1, Part I, para 1.

[43] *Re Barings plc (No 5)* [2000] 1 BCLC 523, CA at para 35.

[44] [1999] 1 BCLC 433, 486.

good faith,[45] but concluded that it would be unnecessary and also difficult to formulate so as to avoid narrowing the principle or making it too rigid.[46] The CLR agreed and likewise were opposed to a legislative business judgment rule. As they observed:

> Directors are employed to take risks, often under severe time pressures which prevent the fullest examination of all relevant factors. Some of these risks will not pay off. The directors' key skill is one of balancing the risk and time factors, recognising that their company's success and failure will depend on their not being unduly cautious as well as avoiding fool-hardiness. What risks are appropriate will depend on a multitude of factors, including the ethos of the company and the character of its business and markets.[47]

While they recognized a danger that the courts might apply hindsight, they noted that the courts had in fact shown 'a proper reluctance to enter into the merits of commercial decisions'.[48]

**13.36** In the event, the Act contains no statement of the principle, nor is any reference made to it.

## E. Delegation to and Reliance on Others

**13.37** The 2006 Act contains no statement to the effect that directors may delegate to, and rely on, third parties, nor any description of the circumstances in which they may do so. This follows the recommendation of the Law Commission that there should be no such statement, because the law was still developing, such a statement was likely to be too restrictive and, in any event, their research did not reveal any undue concern on the question. In the absence of a statutory statement, therefore, the position remains as it is at common law.

**13.38** The classical exposition of the position at common law, to be found in Romer J's third general proposition in *City Equitable*, is set out in paragraph 13.16 above. That statement has since been relied on, perhaps unfairly, in order to support the contention that the modern director is entitled to place unquestioning reliance upon others to do their job. That contention was decisively rejected, however, by Langley J in *Equitable Life Assurance Society v Bowley*.[49] The most authoritative summary of the modern position is to be found in the following extract from the

---

[45] Law Commission, *Company Directors: Regulating Conflicts of Interests and Formulating a Statement of Duties* (Consultation Paper No 153, 1998), paras 15.31 and 15.41.
[46] Law Commission, *Company Directors: Regulating Conflicts of Interests and Formulating a Statement of Duties* (Report No 261, 1999), paras 5.28–5.29.
[47] CLR: *Developing the Framework*, para 3.69.
[48] Ibid, para 3.70.
[49] [2004] 1 BCLC 180 at para 41.

judgment of Jonathan Parker J in *Re Barings plc (No 5)*,[50] in terms subsequently adopted verbatim by the Court of Appeal in that case:[51]

> ... (ii) While directors are entitled (subject to the articles of association of the company) to delegate particular functions to those below them in the management chain, and to trust their competence and integrity to a reasonable extent, the exercise of the power of delegation does not absolve a director from the duty to supervise the discharge of the delegated functions. (iii) No rule of universal application can be formulated as to the duty referred to in (ii) above. The extent of the duty, and the question whether it has been discharged, must depend on the facts of each particular case, including the director's role in the management of the company.

13.39  The duty to supervise is thus a continuing duty, which cannot be avoided. The extent of the supervision required will depend on all the circumstances. In some cases, the circumstances will be such that it will be incumbent on the director to take the initiative in satisfying himself that matters of concern have been properly dealt with and that delegated functions have been properly carried out, rather than expecting a colleague or senior subordinate charged with implementing improvements to raise any continuing concerns he may have.[52]

13.40  Directors can delegate functions. Their ability to do so, however, does not mean that they can delegate responsibility, nor that they are no longer under any duty in relation to the discharge of the particular function delegated, notwithstanding that the person to whom the function has been delegated may appear both trustworthy and capable of discharging it. As Sir Richard Scott V-C put it, in the context of disqualification proceedings following the collapse of Barings plc:[53]

> Overall responsibility is not delegable. All that is delegable is the discharge of particular functions. The degree of personal blameworthiness that may attach to the individual with the overall responsibility, on account of a failure by those to whom he has delegated a particular task, must depend on the facts of each particular case. Sometimes there may be a question whether the delegation has been made to the appropriate person; sometimes there may be a question of whether the individual with overall responsibility should have checked how his subordinates were discharging their delegated functions. Sometimes the system itself, in which the failures have taken place, is an inadequate system for which the person with overall responsibility must take some blame.

13.41  It follows from these statements of the law that the question whether, in any given case, delegation or reliance by the director is appropriate, will depend upon all the

---

[50] [1999] 1 BCLC 433, 489. As to the extent to which a director may fulfill his duty of care by taking and acting on legal advice, see *Lexi Holdings plc v Luqman* [2008] 2 BCLC 725.

[51] [2000] 1 BCLC 523, CA at para 36.

[52] *Re Barings plc (No 5)* [1999] 1 BCLC 433, 519c–h.

[53] Cited by Jonathan Parker J in *Re Barings plc (No 5)* [1999] 1 BCLC 433, 487 (para B3); *Re Queens Moat Houses plc (No 2)* [2005] 1 BCLC 136 at para 27.

circumstances of that case, and what may be appropriate in one case will not necessarily be appropriate in another.

## F. Non-executive Directors

The 2006 Act, s 174 does not distinguish between executive directors and non-executive directors: each owes the same duty to exercise reasonable care, skill, and diligence. The scope of the duty, however, will necessarily vary. What may reasonably be expected of an executive director, bound by the terms of his service contract to devote himself full-time to the business of the company, would be unrealistic to expect of a non-executive director. Moreover the purpose behind the appointment of non-executive directors to the board of the company, and the functions they will perform, are obviously different. As already noted, the company may reasonably look to non-executive directors for independence of judgment and supervision of the executive management: see paragraph 13.31 above.

**13.42**

Typically, the non-executive director will be appointed to the company's board by virtue of his particular knowledge, skill and experience. He must take care to apply such skills. Indeed the subjective element of the requirement laid down by the 2006 Act, s 174 requires him to do so. It is no part of the non-executive director's function, for example, to accept without question the reliability of management accounts and financial information presented to him. In order properly to supervise the executive management, it is to be expected that he would probe the financial information provided in order to test its reliability, deploying the care and skill reasonably to be expected of him, both subjectively and objectively ascertained in accordance with the requirements of the 2006 Act, s 174.

**13.43**

It has been said that such duties do not require non-executive directors to overrule the specialist directors, like the finance director, in their specialist fields.[54] Generally speaking, that may be so. What is to be expected of the non-executive director, however, will depend upon the facts and it is conceivable that the circumstances may be such as to require him so to act in an exceptional case. As Lord Woolf has recently put it, a non-executive director should act as a guard dog and be prepared to bark when necessary.[55]

**13.44**

---

[54] *Re Continental Assurance of London plc* [2007] 2 BCLC 287 at para 399.
[55] In reponse to a question from the audience following the COMBAR Annual Lecture 2008, 'Global companies can and should have the highest ethical standards', delivered by Lord Woolf on 21 October 2008.

# 14

## DUTIES TO AVOID CONFLICTS OF INTEREST AND NOT TO ACCEPT BENEFITS FROM THIRD PARTIES

## A. Introduction

The 2006 Act, ss 175 and 176 set out the duties to avoid conflicts of interest **14.01** and not to accept benefits from third parties. The sections are quoted in paragraphs 14.05 and 14.36 below. They are paradigm manifestations of a director's fiduciary duty of loyalty to the company and it is convenient to discuss them together. As Lord Upjohn said in *Phipps v Boardman* '[T]he fundamental rule of equity [is] that a person in a fiduciary capacity must not make a profit out of his trust which is part of the wider rule that a trustee must not place himself in a position where his duty and his interest may conflict.'[1]

A person who ceases to be a director continues to be subject to the duty to avoid **14.02** conflicts of interest as regards the exploitation of any property, information, or opportunity of which he became aware at a time when he was a director and also subject to a duty not to accept benefits from third parties as regards things done or

---

[1] [1967] 2 AC 46, 123, HL.

303

omitted by him before he ceased to be a director.[2] The application of these duties to former directors is discussed in Section D of this chapter.

**14.03**  The duties stated in ss 175 and 176 apply to shadow directors to the extent that the common law rules or equitable principles corresponding to those duties applied to shadow directors (see Chapter 9, Section C).[3]

**14.04**  A director who, in relation to a particular situation of conflict of interest, wishes to be protected from the risk of being in breach of the duty may now obtain the authorization of the directors, which, if given, has the consequence that the duty is not infringed.[4] This new power of the directors to authorize on behalf of the company a breach of the no conflict rule represents a significant change in the law. It enables directors to avoid the harsh consequences of that rule, as illustrated by the decision of the House of Lords in *Regal (Hastings) Ltd v Gulliver*.[5] Where the director does not obtain authorization from the directors he may obtain the protection of the consent, approval, or authorization of the members, as recognized by s 180(4)(a) (see Chapter 9, Section D) or ratification of his conduct under s 239 (Chapter 19, Section D). That protection is also potentially available in relation to benefits obtained from third parties.

## B.  Duty to Avoid Conflicts of Interest

**14.05**  The 2006 Act, s 175 provides that:

(1) A director of a company must avoid a situation in which he has, or can have, a direct or indirect interest that conflicts, or possibly may conflict, with the interests of the company.

(2) This applies in particular to the exploitation of any property, information or opportunity (and it is immaterial whether the company could take advantage of the property, information or opportunity).

(3) This duty does not apply to a conflict of interest arising in relation to a transaction or arrangement with the company.

(4) This duty is not infringed—

   (a) if the situation cannot reasonably be regarded as likely to give rise to a conflict of interest; or

   (b) if the matter has been authorised by the directors.

(5) Authorisation may be given by the directors—

   (a) where the company is a private company and nothing in the company's constitution invalidates such authorisation, by the matter being proposed to and authorised by the directors; or

---

[2]  s 170(2).
[3]  s 170(5).
[4]  subss 175(4)–(6), discussed in Section B(5) below.
[5]  [1967] 2 AC 134n, HL.

(b) where the company is a public company and its constitution includes provision enabling the directors to authorise the matter, by the matter being proposed to and authorised by them in accordance with the constitution.

(6) The authorisation is effective only if—

(a) any requirement as to the quorum at the meeting at which the matter is considered is met without counting the director in question or any other interested director, and

(b) the matter was agreed to without their voting or would have been agreed to if their votes had not been counted.

(7) Any reference in this section to a conflict of interest includes a conflict of interest and duty and a conflict of duties.

## (1) Avoidance of situations of conflict

A director of a company must avoid any situation in which he has, or can have, a direct or indirect interest that conflicts, or possibly may conflict, with the interests of the company.[6]    **14.06**

The rule is based upon the common law rule of equity that any person owing fiduciary duties must not put himself into a position in which he has or can have conflicting interests. The rule is a reformulation of the classic statement of the common law in *Aberdeen Railway Co v Blaikie Bros* by Lord Cranworth:[7]    **14.07**

> [It] is a rule of universal application, that no one, having [fiduciary] duties to discharge, shall be allowed to enter into engagements in which he has, or can have, a personal interest conflicting, or which may conflict, with the interests of those whom he is bound to protect. So strictly is this principle adhered to, that no question is allowed to be raised as to the fairness or unfairness of a contract so entered into.[8]

As is clear from the passage cited above the rule is strict.[9] As it relates to serving directors, it is 'an inflexible rule [which] must be applied inexorably by [the] court which is not entitled . . . to receive evidence, or suggestion, or argument as to whether the principal did or did not suffer any injury in fact by reason of the dealing of the agent . . .'[10]    **14.08**

---

[6] 2006 Act, s 175(1).

[7] (1854) 1 Macq 461, 471, HL. See also *Keech v Sandford* (1726) Sel Cas t King 61; *Bray v Ford* [1896] AC 44, 51, HL.

[8] This principle has been applied in numerous subsequent cases. See in particular: *Regal (Hastings) Ltd v Gulliver* [1967] 2 AC 134, 137–8, 147–50, 155–6, HL; *Boardman v Phipps* [1967] 2 AC 46, 94C–E, 112C–D, 123–5, HL; *Industrial Development Consultants Ltd v Cooley* [1972] 1 WLR 443, 447–53; *Canadian Aero Service v O'Malley* [1973] 40 DLR (3d) 371, 382ff and *Bhullar v Bhullar* [2003] 2 BCLC 241, CA at 27–42.

[9] *Boardman v Phipps* [1967] 1 AC 46, 111; and *New Zealand Netherlands Society 'Oranje' Inc v Keys* [1973] 1 WLR 1126, 1129–30, PC.

[10] *Parker v McKenna* (1874) LR 10 Ch App 96, 124–5, per James LJ, cited in *Regal (Hastings) Ltd v Gulliver* [1967] 2 AC 134n, 155, HL, per Lord Wright.

**14.09** It does not involve any enquiry into whether there has been an actual conflict between the interests of the director and that of the company. Instead, it is sufficient for there to have been a breach of the rule that the director has placed himself in a position where there is a possibility that he has or can have an interest that conflicts with that of the company. The phrase 'possibly may conflict' was considered by Lord Upjohn in *Boardman v Phipps* when he said: 'the reasonable man looking at the relevant facts and circumstances of the particular case would think that there was a real sensible possibility of conflict; not that you could imagine some situation arising which might, in some conceivable possibility in events not contemplated as real sensible possibilities by any reasonable person, result in conflict.'[11]

**14.10** That test has been applied more recently by the Court of Appeal in *Bhullar v Bhullar* where Jonathan Parker LJ stated that the test was whether: 'reasonable men looking at the facts would think that there was a real sensible possibility of conflict'.[12] This test has been reformulated in the 2006 Act, s 175(4)(a), which provides that the duty of a director to avoid a conflict of interest is not infringed if the situation cannot reasonably be regarded as likely to give rise to a conflict of interest.[13]

**14.11** A director can be in breach of the rule even though his or her conduct has caused no loss to the company.[14] Similarly the fairness or otherwise of the transaction is not a relevant consideration.[15] The honesty or otherwise of the director is also irrelevant.[16]

**14.12** The statutory duty to avoid conflicts of interest replaces the equitable 'no conflict rule' and 'no profit' rule by a single rule. This approach (where the no profit rule is regarded as part of the no conflict rule) is evident in a number of cases.[17] But other cases have regarded the rules as distinct.[18]

---

[11] [1967] 2 AC 46, 124, HL.

[12] [2003] 2 BCLC 241 at paras 30 and 27–39; for other similar restatements see *Guinness v Saunders* [1990] 2 AC 663, HL, 689–92, per Lord Templeman; 700, per Lord Goff; *Neptune (Vehicle Washing Equipment) v Fitzgerald (No. 2)* [1995] BCC 1000, 1015–16.

[13] See paragraphs 14.26–14.29 below.

[14] *Aberdeen Railway Co v Blaikie Bros* (1854) 1 Macq 461, 472, HL; *Regal (Hastings) Ltd v Gulliver* [1967] 2 AC 134n, 153, HL.

[15] *Aberdeen Railway Co v Blaikie Bros* (1854) 1 Macq 461, 471–2, HL.

[16] *Regal (Hastings) Ltd v Gulliver* [1967] 2 AC 134n, 153, HL.

[17] *Bray v Ford* [1896] AC 44, 51–2, HL; and *Boardman v Phipps* [1967] 2 AC 46, 123, HL.

[18] *Regal (Hastings) Ltd v Gulliver* [1967] 2 AC 134n, 153, 159, HL. For a consideration of the difference between the 'no conflict rule' and the 'no profit rule' see *Re Allied Business and Financial Consultants Ltd* [2008] EWHC 1973 (Ch) at 175 to 204; *Ultraframe (UK) Ltd v Fielding* [2005] EWHC 1638 at 1305 to 1306. The objective of the 'no conflict rule' is to preclude the fiduciary from being swayed by considerations of personal interest. The objective of the 'no profit rule' is to preclude the fiduciary from actually his position for his personal advantage.

*Competing directorships*

Subsection 175(7) provides that any reference in s 175 to a conflict of interest **14.13** includes a conflict of interest and duty and a conflict of duties. This provision raises a number of questions in relation to the position where a director acts in relation to two or more companies which are in competition with each other. In such a situation the director does not prefer or potentially prefer his own interest to that company but may prefer his duty to one company to his duty to the other. Similar questions may arise where a director holds shares in or enters into a transaction with a company which competes with the company of which he is a director.

The position in relation to fiduciaries generally was discussed by Millett LJ in **14.14** *Bristol and West BS v Mothew*, where he said: 'A fiduciary who acts for two principals with potentially conflicting interests without the informed consent of both is in breach of the obligation of undivided loyalty; he puts himself in a position where his duty to one principal may conflict with his duty to the other . . . This is sometimes described as "the double employment rule." Breach of the rule automatically constitutes a breach of fiduciary duty.'[19]

In so far as the position in relation to directors is concerned it was held by a major- **14.15** ity of the Court of Appeal in *Plus Group Ltd v Pyke*[20] that there is no completely rigid rule that a director may not be involved in the business of a company which is in competition with another company of which he was a director.[21] This proposition was based upon the decision in *London and Mashonaland Exploration Co Ltd v New Mashonaland Exploration Co Ltd*.[22] That principle was approved *obiter* by Lord Blanesburgh in *Bell v Lever Bros Ltd*.[23] However, the *Mashonaland* decision has been subjected to criticism including by Sedley JL in *Re Plus Group*. It is submitted that *Mashonaland* has to be understood as being a case of its time. The better view now is that a director must not, like other fiduciaries, act for two companies with potentially competing interests unless he does so with the informed consent of both companies or the authorization of the directors within the meaning of subss 174(4)–(6).[24]

This was the view of Lord Goldsmith who said that: **14.16**

> there is currently no absolute rule prohibiting directors from holding multiple directorships or even from engaging in business that competes with the company of which

---

[19] [1998] Ch 1, 18, CA. Cf the position in relation to solicitors: *Clark Boyce v Mouat* [1994] 1 AC 428, PC; *Hilton v Barker Booth & Eastwood* [2005] 1 WLR 567, HL.
[20] [2002] 2 BCLC 201.
[21] Ibid, at para 72.
[22] [1891] WN 165.
[23] [1932] AC 161, 195.
[24] As to authorization by the company, see s 180 and Chapter 9, Section D above. As to ratification, see 2006 Act, s 239 and Chapter 19, Section D below.

they are a director, but obviously a tension results from that degree of tolerance and the fiduciary duties which the director owes. The solution to it is . . . there is no prohibition of a conflict or potential conflict as long as it has been authorised by the directors in accordance with the requirements set out in the [Act].[25]

## (2) Exploitation of property, information, or opportunity

**14.17**  Subsection 175(2) provides that the duty to avoid conflicts or possible conflicts of interest applies in particular to the exploitation of any property, information, or opportunity.

**14.18**  It is clear that misappropriation, diversion, or exploitation of the company's property by a director will amount to a breach of the duty imposed by s 175(1). Although directors are not strictly speaking trustees of a company's assets they owe a duty not to misapply those assets.[26]

**14.19**  Arguably the juxtaposition of the term 'information' next to the term 'property' in subs (2) suggests that there is an intention to treat information in a similar manner to property. However, this is far from clear. In *Boardman v Phipps* Lord Upjohn was clear that 'in general information is not property at all' as 'it is normally open to all who have eyes to read and ears to hear'.[27] Instead, the reference to the exploitation of information in subs (2) is best viewed in similar terms to the exploitation of an opportunity of the company.

**14.20**  Deciding whether information has been exploited in breach of a director's duty to avoid conflict of interest will largely be a question of fact. No single factor is likely to be determinative. The court will need to weigh all the relevant factors and decide whether the information is sufficiently closely connected to the company such that the exploitation of that information constitutes a conflict of interest. In this regard the information exploited need not be confidential to fall within the scope of the duty. The legal rationale for the doctrine is separate from the doctrine of breach of confidence: 'The fact that breach of confidence . . . may itself afford a ground of relief does not make [it] a necessary ingredient of a successful claim for breach of a fiduciary duty.'[28] By contrast where the information forms part of the

---

[25] Hansard, HL Grand Committee (6 February 2006), col 288.

[26] *Cook v Deeks* [1916] AC 554, PC; *Selangor United Rubber Estates Ltd v Craddock* [1968] 1 WLR 1555, 1575–6; *CMS Dolphin Ltd v Simonet* [2002] 2 BCLC 704, 733. See also paragraphs 10.23 and 10.24 above.

[27] [1967] 2 AC 46, 127.

[28] *Canadian Aero Service Ltd v O'Malley* (1973) 40 DLR (3d) 371, 390; this analysis was confirmed by Collins J in *CMS Dolphin v Simonet* [2001] 2 BCLC 704 at [94]. See also *Crown Dilmun v Sutton* [2004] 1 BCLC 468 at para 187: 'Whether or not the information is confidential, if the opportunity that arises by reason of the acquisition of the information puts the fiduciary in a position of conflict, he cannot take that opportunity.' As to action for breach of confidence see for example *Saltman Engineering Co Ltd v Campbell Engineering Co Ltd* [1963] 3 All ER 413n, CA; *Printers and Finishers Ltd v Holloway* [1964] 3 All ER 731. It has been held that the principle that where a

general knowledge and expertise of the director acquired during the course of his work there is unlikely to be any conflict of interest.[29]

The concept of the exploitation of information is probably best illustrated by the **14.21** facts of *Industrial Development Consultants Ltd v Cooley*.[30] In that case, the defendant was an architect who was also the managing director of the plaintiff company, which was in a group supplying construction services. One of his duties was to procure new business, particularly in connection with the gas industry and the gas boards. The company had unsuccessful negotiations with the Eastern Gas Board for a contract to design and build depots. Subsequently the deputy chairman of the Eastern Gas Board made a tentative approach to the defendant in his private capacity about the design and construction of new depots. In the course of the meeting, the defendant acquired knowledge that the company did not have, and would have wanted to have. The defendant realized that if he could obtain his release from his position with the company he could acquire a valuable contract from the board. He falsely told the company that he was ill and obtained a release. He was subsequently awarded a contract by the board. That contract was substantially the same business as the company had been attempting to obtain. Roskill J found that there was no doubt that Mr Cooley got the contract for himself as a result of work that he did while still the company's managing director. He said:[31]

> Therefore, I feel impelled to the conclusion that when the defendant embarked on this course of conduct of getting information . . . using that information and preparing those documents . . . and sending them off . . ., he was guilty of putting himself into the position in which his duty to his employers, the plaintiffs, and his own private interests conflicted and conflicted grievously. There being the fiduciary relationship I have described, it seems to me plain that it was his duty once he got this information to pass it to his employers and not to guard it for his own personal purposes and profit. He put himself into the position when his duty and his interests conflicted.

A director will also be guilty of a breach of fiduciary duty if he diverts to himself **14.22** or for anyone else's benefit a business opportunity of the company.[32] There is no single accepted statement of the doctrine. It has been said that the doctrine

---

person has obtained confidential information from another he must not use that information to the prejudice of the person who gave it applies with particular force as between a director and his company by reason of the fiduciary character of the duty owed by the director: *Baker v Gibbons* [1972] 1 WLR 693, 700. See also *Cranleigh Precision Engineering Ltd v Bryant* [1965] 1 WLR 1293; *Thomas Marshall (Exports) Ltd v Guinle* [1979] Ch 227; *Dranez Anstalt v Hayek* [2002] 1 BCLC 693.

[29] *Islands Export Finance Ltd v Umunna* [1986] BCLC 460, 482.
[30] [1972] 1 WLR 443.
[31] Ibid, 452H–453B.
[32] *Regal (Hastings) Ltd v Gulliver*, n 5 above at 137G and 149F; *IDC v Cooley*, n 30 above at 382 and 391; *Canadian Aero Service v O'Malley*, n 8 above at 382 and 391; *CMS Dolphin Ltd v Simonet* [2001] 2 BCLC 704; *Ball v Eden Project Ltd* [2002] 1 BCLC 313; *Kingsley IT Consulting v McIntosh* [2006] BCC 875; *Simtel Communications v Rebak* [2006] 2 BCLC 571.

precludes a director or senior officer from 'obtaining for himself, either secretly or without the informed approval of the company . . . any property or business advantage either belonging to the company or for which it has been negotiating'.[33] This is especially the case where the director or officer is a participant in those negotiations.[34] Like the position in relation to the exploitation of information deciding whether a business opportunity 'belongs to a company' is largely a question of fact. The application of the 'no conflict rule' does not depend on establishing that the company has a proprietary interest in the business opportunity that has been diverted.[35] The court has to weigh all the relevant factors and decide whether the opportunity is sufficiently closely connected to the company to be considered an opportunity of the company.[36]

**14.23**   Subsection 175(2) makes it clear that it is immaterial whether the company could take advantage of the property, information, or opportunity. This reflects the position at common law.[37] A director 'must not be allowed to use his position as such to make a profit even if it was not open to the company, as for example, by reason of a legal disability, to participate in the transaction'.[38] The reasoning behind the rule is to act as a deterrent to discourage fiduciaries from placing themselves in a conflict of interest.[39] To allow a director to advance the argument that it would have been impossible for the company to enter into the transaction in question would create the risk that directors might be tempted to characterize an opportunity as one the company could not obtain in order that they may obtain it for themselves.

**14.24**   The liability of the director also does not depend upon proof of mala fides.[40] Neither does it matter that the original proposals put forward by the company for the acquisition of the opportunity are different from the proposals subsequently

---

[33]   *CMS Dolphin v Simonet* [2001] 2 BCLC 704 at [91].
[34]   *Canadian Aero Service Ltd v O'Malley* (1973) 40 DLR (3d) 371, 382, 391.
[35]   *Ultraframe (UK) Ltd v Fielding* [2005] EWHC 1638 (Ch) at [1355].
[36]   *Canadian Aero v O'Malley*, above at 390–1; *Regal (Hastings) Ltd v Gulliver*, n 5 above at 153E–F; *Pacifica Shipping Co Ltd v Andersen* [1986] 2 NZLR 328; *SEA Food Internal Pty Ltd v Lam* (1998) 130 FCA (27 February 1998) at §137–§144. Compare also 'the line of business test' in the United States as formulated in *Guth v Loft, Inc* 5 A2d 503 (Del 1939) where it was held that an opportunity was a corporate opportunity if it was closely related to the corporation's existing or prospective activities.
[37]   *IDC v Cooley*, n 30 above at 453; *Regal (Hastings) Ltd v Gulliver*, above at 139; *Canadian Aero v O'Malley*, above at 383–4; *Natural Extracts Pty Ltd v Stotter* (1997) 24 ASCR 10, 141; *Crown Dilmun v Sutton* [2004] 1 BCLC 704 at paras 49 and 182.
[38]   *Canadian Aero Service Ltd v O'Malley* (1973) 40 DLR (3d) 371, 383–4; see also Struan Scott, 'Corporate Opportunity Doctrine and Impossibility Arguments' (2003) 66 MLR 852; Pearlie Koh, 'Principle 6 of the Proposed Statement of Directors Duties' (2003) 66 MLR 894; D D Prentice 'The Corporate. Opportunity Doctrine' (1974) 37 MLR 464.
[39]   *Murad v Al-Saraj* [2005] EWCA Civ 959 at para 74, per Arden LJ.
[40]   *Regal (Hastings) Ltd v Gulliver* [1967] 2 AC 134, 137G.

put forward by the director.[41] So also, it is not a pre-condition of liability that the director had 'special knowledge' of the opportunity or had acquired knowledge of that opportunity only by reason of his position as an officer of the company.[42] It is further irrelevant that the party offering the opportunity has first approached the defendant in his personal capacity and expressed a desire to work with him, and not the company.[43]

### (3) Transactions and arrangements with the company

Subsection 175(3) provides that the duty does not apply to a conflict of interest arising in relation to a transaction or arrangement[44] with the company. This would include such matters as the remuneration received by a director and director's loans. Instead, such transactions or arrangements with the company must be declared under s 177 in the case of proposed transactions or under s 182 in the case of existing transactions unless an exception applies under those sections. These provisions are considered in further detail in Chapters 15 and 17.

**14.25**

### (4) Situations where there is no reasonable likelihood of a conflict

Subsection 175(4) provides that the duty is not infringed if the situation cannot reasonably be regarded as likely to give rise to a conflict of interest. This reflects the position at common law.[45]

**14.26**

In this regard, it has been held that there is no duty on a director to disclose competitive activity unless he had used his position to further that activity. To investigate the possibility of setting up a business in competition with the company does not, of itself, constitute a breach of fiduciary duty provided the director does not engage in any actual competitive activity.[46]

**14.27**

In this regard, the precise point at which preparations by a departing director for the establishment of a competing business become unlawful will turn on the facts of the case. As set out above, merely making a decision to set up a competing business will not be sufficient, but soliciting customers would be in breach of the

**14.28**

---

[41] *Canadian Aero Service Ltd v O'Malley* (1973) 40 DLR (3d) 371, 390–1.

[42] Ibid; this analysis was also confirmed by Collins J in *CMS Dolphin v Simonet* [2001] 2 BCLC 704 at §94.

[43] *IDC v Cooley,* n 30 above at 451.

[44] As to the meaning of arrangement see Chapter 15.

[45] *Queensland Mines Ltd v Hudson* (1978) 52 ALJR 399, 400, PC ('a real sensible possibility of conflict'); and see *Peso Silver Mines Ltd v Cooper* (1966) 58 DLR (2d) 1. The later decision has, however, not been without criticism: S M Beck, 'The Saga of Peso Silver Mines: Corporate Opportunity Reconsidered' (1971) 49 *Can Bar Review* 80; see also D D Prentice, 'Regal Hastings Ltd v Gulliver—The Canadian Experience' (1967) 30 MLR 450; and J A VanDuzer, *The Law of Partnerships and Corporations* (2nd edn, Canada) p 282.

[46] *Balston Ltd v Headline Filters Ltd* [1990] FSR 385; *Coleman Taymar Ltd v Oakes* [2001] 2 BCLC 749; *Framlington Group plc v Anderson* [1995] BCC 611, 629.

director's duties. In between, there is a wide spectrum of possible activity which must be considered on a case-by-case basis.[47]

**14.29**    The question of whether a situation can reasonably be regarded as likely to give rise to a conflict of interest can sometimes be a difficult one and it is suggested that in cases of doubt the director in question should disclose the matter to the board and seek authorization where appropriate.

### (5) Authorization by the directors of infringement of duty to avoid conflict

**14.30**    Subsection 175(4)(b) modifies the position at common law. It provides that the duty to avoid conflicts of interests will not be infringed if the matter has been authorized by the directors. The circumstances in which authorization may be granted are set out in subss 175(5) and (6). Traditionally conflicts of interest could be resolved only by disclosure to and with the consent of the members of the company, although in practice standard articles often replaced this by a requirement of disclosure to the board of directors. The CLR were concerned that this strict requirement might stifle entrepreneurial activity; and therefore recommended that, in the case of a private company, it should be possible for conflicts to be authorized by independent directors unless the company's constitution prevents this.[48] This recommendation was adopted by the Government. The change gives proper effect to the delegation of all powers of the company to the directors found in the articles of most companies.[49]

**14.31**    As a result of the provisions of subss 175(5) and (6) decisions such as that in *Regal (Hastings) Ltd v Gulliver*[50] would now be likely to be decided differently provided the provisions of those subsections are complied with. In that case, the plaintiff company had formed a subsidiary company that was to take up a lease of two cinemas. The owner of the cinemas insisted that the subsidiary should have a paid-up capital that, in the honest opinion of the plaintiff's board, was greater than the plaintiff company could afford to subscribe. The ordinary directors accordingly subscribed at par for part of the balance themselves, the remainder being taken up by 'outsiders' in the name of the chairman of directors and by the plaintiff's solicitor. The whole transaction had been carried out with a view to a sale of the two cinemas, together with another cinema that the plaintiff itself owned, as a going concern. Ultimately, however, the shares of the plaintiff and of the subsidiary were purchased at a price substantially above par. The plaintiff company sued the ordinary directors, the chairman, and the solicitor for an account of their profits on the resale. It was found that they had all acted honestly

---

[47]    *Shepherds Investments Ltd v Walters* [2006] 2 BCLC 202.
[48]    CLR: *Final Report* at paras 3.21–3.27; *Completing the Structure* at paras 3.26 and 3.27.
[49]    Table A, reg 70; Model Article (pcls) 3; Model Article (plc) 3.
[50]    [1967] 2 AC 134n.

throughout, but none the less the ordinary directors were in a fiduciary capacity in relation to the company and, as such, were accountable to the company for the profit that they made on the sale of the shares. The decision in *Regal (Hastings)* has been the subject of criticism; in particular, as the directors in question had acted honestly throughout. Following the introduction of subss 175(5) and (6) such a transaction would now have been likely to have been authorized by the board.

Subsection 175(5) provides that authorization may be given by the directors **14.32** (a) where the company is a private company and nothing in the company's constitution invalidates such authorization, by the matter being proposed to and authorized by the directors; or (b) where the company is a public company and its constitution includes provisions enabling the directors to authorize the matter, by the matter being proposed to and authorized by them in accordance with the constitution. The 2006 Act, s 180(1) makes clear that if s 175 is complied with any transaction or arrangement is not liable to be set aside by virtue of any common law rule or equitable principle requiring the consent or approval of the company in general meeting. However, if any other enactment requires the consent or approval of the members in respect of the particular transaction or arrangement, or if such consent or approval is required by the company's constitution, then it must be sought and obtained.[51]

Under subs 175(6), board authorization is effective only if the conflicted directors **14.33** or 'any other interested director' have not participated in the taking of the decision or if the decision would have been valid even without the participation of the conflicted directors: the votes of the conflicted directors in favour of the decision are ignored and the conflicted directors are not counted in the quorum. In this regard, what amounts to an interested director may well not always be clear. Equally, and particularly in the context of smaller and family companies, it may be difficult to find any directors who are independent in the requisite sense. In such cases authorization or ratification by a majority of the shareholders of the company at a general meeting in accordance with the 2006 Act, ss 180 or 239 may well be useful.[52]

The use of the word 'only' in subs 175(6) makes it clear that these are the mini- **14.34** mum procedural requirements for authorization. Any further rules imposed by the company's constitution or the common law must be complied with. As Lord Goldsmith said during the passage of the Bill through Parliament:

[A]ny requirements under the common law for what is necessary for a valid authorisation remain in force. I draw the Committee's attention to Clause 159(6), which says: 'The authorisation is effective only if'. It then sets out certain specific requirements.

---

[51] s 180(1).
[52] See *North-West Transportation Co Ltd v Beatty* (1887) 12 App Cas 589, 593–4, PC; *Boulting v Association of Cinematograph, Television and Allied Technicians* [1963] 2 QB 606; and Chapters 9 and 19, Section D of this work.

It deliberately does not say that if those requirements are met the authorisation is effective. There might be other conditions in relation to the authorisation that would be required—for example, the company's constitution may have some specific provision with which it would be necessary to comply. Those formalities and those conditions need to be complied with as well.[53]

*The articles*

**14.35**  In so far as the articles of association of the company are concerned the 2006 Act, s 232(4) provides that nothing in that section prevents a company's articles from making such provision as has previously been lawful for dealing with conflicts of interest. This is a deviation from the normal rule contained in s 232 which prohibits a company from exempting a director from, or indemnifying him against, any liability in connection with any negligence, default, breach of duty, or breach of trust by him in relation to the company. This leaves open the possibility that the company's articles of association may relieve or modify a director's duty under s 175.[54] It has long been the practice, in this regard, for articles to provide that in certain circumstances, and subject to certain conditions, a director may put himself in a position of conflict or make a profit from the use of the company's property, information, or opportunities.

## C. Duty Not to Accept Benefits from Third Parties

**14.36**  The Companies Act, s 176 provides that:

(1) A director of a company must not accept a benefit from a third party conferred by reason of—
  (a) his being a director, or
  (b) his doing (or not doing) anything as director.

(2) A 'third party' means a person other than the company, an associated body corporate or a person acting on behalf of the company or an associated body corporate.

(3) Benefits received by a director from a person by whom his services (as a director or otherwise) are provided to the company are not regarded as conferred by a third party.

(4) This duty is not infringed if the acceptance of the benefit cannot reasonably be regarded as likely to give rise to a conflict of interest.

(5) Any reference in this section to a conflict of interest includes a conflict of interest and duty and a conflict of duties.

**14.37**  This section codifies the rule prohibiting the exploitation of the position of director for personal benefit.[55] The duty prohibits the acceptance of benefits (including

---

[53]  Hansard, HL, vol 678, col 326 (9 February 2006).

[54]  See for instance *Movitex Ltd v Bulfield* [1988] BCLC 460.

[55]  As to the position in relation to fiduciaries generally see *A-G for Hong Kong v Reid* [1994] 1 AC 324, PC; and *Daradayan Holdings Ltd v Solland International Ltd* [2005] Ch 119.

bribes). This provision is not a codification of the so-called 'no profit rule' which is broader and is instead subsumed within s 175.[56] Lord Goldsmith said that the section codifies the 'long-standing rule, prohibiting the exploitation of the position of director for personal benefit. It does not apply to benefits that the director receives from the company, or from any associated company, or from any person acting on behalf of those companies' and he added that 'benefits are prohibited by the duty only if their acceptance is likely to give rise to a conflict of interest'.[57]

'Benefit' is generally a word of wide import.[58] The benefit may be financial or non-financial and may include gifts and hospitality. During the passage of the Bill through Parliament the Solicitor General suggested that 'in using the word "benefit" we intend the ordinary dictionary meaning of the word. The Oxford English Dictionary defines it as a favourable or helpful factor, circumstance, advantage or profit.'[59] Earlier Lord Goldsmith made the same point when he said 'the word "benefit"... includes benefits of any description, including non-financial benefits'.[60]   **14.38**

A third party is defined by subs 176(2) as a person other than the company, an associated body corporate, or a person acting on behalf of the company or an associated body corporate.[61] Accordingly, benefits conferred by the company (and its holding company or subsidiaries) do not fall within this duty. In addition, benefits received by a director from a person by whom his services (as a director or otherwise) are provided to the company are not regarded as conferred by a third party.[62]   **14.39**

The use of the expression 'by reason of his being a director, or his doing (or not doing) anything as director' is an important limitation on the duty contained in s 176(1). As Lord Goldsmith said 'the purpose of the clause ... is to impose on a director a duty not to accept benefits from third parties. It applies only to benefits conferred because the director is a director of the company or because of something that the director does or doesn't do as director.'[63]   **14.40**

The duty is not infringed if the acceptance of the benefit cannot reasonably be regarded as likely to give rise to a conflict of interest.[64] For example, where a director is offered a gift or hospitality in the normal course of business which can be considered trivial there will be no difficulty in him accepting. However, where such an offer is made with the specific intent to influence decision-making or to   **14.41**

---

[56] See paragraph 14.12 above.
[57] Hansard, HL Grand Committee (9 February 2006) col 330.
[58] See, eg, *Cronin v Grierson* [1968] AC 895, 909, per Lord Upjohn.
[59] Hansard, HC (11 July 2006) cols 621–622.
[60] Hansard, HL Grand Committee (9 February 2006) col 330.
[61] As to the meaning of an associated body corporate, see 2006 Act, s 256.
[62] 2006 Act, s 176(3).
[63] Hansard, HL Grand Committee (9 February), col 330.
[64] 2006 Act, s 176(4).

obtain information there may be a breach of the duty where the director decides to accept the offer.

**14.42**   In this regard the reference to conflict of interest includes a conflict of interest and duty and a conflict of duties.[65] Accordingly, the acceptance of a benefit giving rise to an actual or potential conflict of interest will fall within the duty to avoid conflicts of interests (s 175) as well as this duty. However, unlike s 175 this duty is not subject to any provision for board authorization.

## D.  The Application of the General Duties to Former Directors

**14.43**   Section 170(2) provides that:

> A person who ceases to be a director continues to be subject—
> (a)  to the duty in section 175 (duty to avoid conflicts of interest) as regards the exploitation of any property, information or opportunity of which he became aware at a time when he was a director, and
> (b)  to the duty in section 176 (duty not to accept benefits from third parties) as regards things done or omitted by him before he ceased to be a director.
> To that extent those duties apply to a former director as to a director, subject to any necessary adaptations.

**14.44**   Whether or not, as discussed in Section B above, the no conflict rule remains as stringent in relation to serving directors, it appears from pre-2006 Act authorities that, so far as former directors were concerned, the courts were inclined to adopt a more sensitive approach by reference to the particular facts of each case.[66] Nevertheless, it remained clear that the incidence of liability on the part of the former director would not depend upon the company being shown to have suffered loss; it would suffice if the former director had, directly or indirectly, made a profit, for which he would be made liable to account.[67]

**14.45**   A helpful starting point is the summary of the principles of Bernard Livesey QC, sitting as a deputy judge of the High Court) in *Hunter Kane Ltd v Watkins*,[68] itself

---

[65]   2006 Act, s 176(5). Subsection 176(5) appears to explain subs 176(4), which is the only subsection to refer to conflict of interest.

[66]   *Industrial Development Consultants v Cooley* [1972] 1 WLR 443; *Canadian Aero Service Ltd v O'Malley* (1973) 40 DLR (3d) 371; *Island Export Finance Ltd v Ummuna* [1986] BCLC 460; *Balston Ltd v Headline Filters Ltd* [1990] FSR 385; *Framlington Group plc v Anderson* [1995] 1 BCLC 475; *CMS Dolphin Ltd v Simonet* [2001] 2 BCLC 704; *Hunter Kane Ltd v Watkins* [2002] EWHC 186 (Ch); *In Plus Group Ltd v Pyke* [2002] 2 BCLC 201, CA; *British Midland Tool Ltd v Midland International Tooling Ltd* [2003] 2 BCLC 523; *Shepherds Investments Ltd v Walters* [2006] EWHC 836, [2007] IRLR 110; *Foster Bryant Surveying Ltd v Bryant* [2007] 2 BCLC 239, CA.

[67]   *Foster Bryant Surveying Ltd v Bryant* [2007] 2 BCLC 239, per Rix LJ at para [88]; per Buxton LJ at para [101].

[68]   [2002] EWHC 186 (Ch); for point 3 see now *Lexi Holdings plc v Lugman* [2008] 2 BCLC 725, at para 39.

based on the earlier analysis of Lawrence Collins J in *CMS Dolphin Ltd v Simonet*,[69] and described as 'perceptive and useful' by the Court of Appeal in *Foster Bryant Surveying Ltd v Bryant* (subject to the qualification that each case will depend on its facts):[70]

1. A director, while acting as such, has a fiduciary relationship with his company. That is he has an obligation to deal towards it with loyalty, good faith and avoidance of the conflict of duty and self-interest.

2. A requirement to avoid a conflict of duty and self-interest means that a director is precluded from obtaining for himself, either secretly or without the informed approval of the company, any property or business advantage either belonging to the company or for which it has been negotiating, especially where the director or officer is a participant in the negotiations.

3. A director's power to resign from office is not a fiduciary power. He is entitled to resign even if his resignation might have a disastrous effect on the business or reputation of the company.

4. A fiduciary relationship does not continue after the determination of the relationship which gives rise to it. After the relationship is determined the director is in general not under the continuing obligations which are a feature of the fiduciary relationship.

5. Acts done by the directors while the contract of employment subsists but which are preparatory to competition after it terminates are *not necessarily* in themselves a breach of the implied term as to loyalty and fidelity.

6. Directors, no less than employees, acquire a general fund of skill, knowledge and expertise in the course of their work, which [it] is plainly in the public interest that they should be free to exploit [. . .] in a new position. After ceasing the relationship by resignation or otherwise a director is in general (and subject of course to any terms of the contract of employment) not prohibited from using his general fund of skill and knowledge, the 'stock in trade' of the knowledge he has acquired while a director, even including such things as business contacts and personal connections made as a result of his directorship.

7. A director is however precluded from acting in breach of the requirement at 2 above, even after his resignation where the resignation may fairly be said to have been prompted or influenced by a wish to acquire for himself any maturing business opportunities sought by the company and where it was his position with a company rather than a fresh initiative that led him to the opportunity which he later acquired.

8. In considering whether an act of a director breaches the preceding principle the factors to take into account will include the factor of position or office held, the nature of the corporate opportunity, its ripeness, its specificness and the director's relation to it, the amount of knowledge possessed, the circumstances in which it was obtained and whether it was special or indeed private, the factor of time in the continuation of the fiduciary duty where the alleged breach occurs after termination of the

---

[69] [2001] 2 BCLC 704.

[70] *Foster Bryant Surveying Ltd v Bryant* [2007] 2 BCLC 239, per Rix LJ at para 76. Mr Livesey QC's summary of the principles is quoted at para 8.

relationship with the company and the circumstances under which the [relationship] was terminated, that is whether by retirement or resignation or discharge.

9. The underlying basis of the liability of a director who exploits after his resignation a maturing business opportunity of the company is that the opportunity is to be treated as if it were the property of the company in relation to which the director had fiduciary duties. By seeking [to] exploit the opportunity after resignation he is appropriating to himself that property. He is just as accountable as a trustee who retires without properly accounting for trust property.

10. It follows that a director will not be in breach of the principle set out as point 7 above where either the company's hope of obtaining the contract was not a 'maturing business opportunity' and it was not pursuing further business orders nor where the director's resignation was not itself prompted or influenced by a wish to acquire the business for himself.

11. As regards breach of confidence, although while the contract of employment subsists a director or other employee may not use confidential information to the detriment of his employer, after it ceases the director/employee may compete and may use know-how acquired in the course of his employment (as distinct from trade secrets—although the distinction is sometimes difficult to apply in practice).

**14.46**  The authorities have been concerned with a wide variety of differing circumstances and conduct, and were the subject of extensive review by the Court of Appeal in *Foster Bryant Surveying Ltd v Bryant* itself.[71] Rix LJ, who delivered the leading judgment in that case, was in no doubt that the underlying principles, namely that a director must act towards his company with honesty, good faith, and loyalty and must avoid any conflicts of interest 'are firmly in place, and are exacting requirements, exactingly enforced'.[72] Nevertheless, emphasizing that each case depended on its own facts and that it was difficult accurately to encapsulate the circumstances in which a retiring director may be found to have breached his fiduciary duty, Rix LJ considered that the courts had developed merits-based solutions, having regard to the fact that the circumstances in which directors retire are so various.[73]

**14.47**  Thus, at one extreme, was *In Plus Group Ltd v Pyke*,[74] which Rix LJ described as being a case where the defendant was a director in name only. The director concerned set up his own company and began competing with the existing company, even to the extent of working for its major client. On the facts, however, the Court of Appeal agreed that the director had not acted in breach of duty. The company had unsuccessfully sought over many months to force the director to resign, following a period of serious illness. It deprived him of remuneration and information, and refused to repay loans he had made to it. The relationship between him and his fellow director had completely broken down. The director had, the Court

---

[71] [2007] 2 BCLC 239 at paras 48–77.
[72] Ibid, per Rix LJ at para 76.
[73] [2007] 2 BCLC 239, per Rix LJ at para 77.
[74] [2002] 2 BCLC 201.

of Appeal considered, effectively been expelled from the company, was not using any of the company's property, and was not making use of any confidential information which had come to him as a director of the company. In the words of Buxton LJ, the exclusion of the director from the company 'eliminates the duality of interest or duty which the law seeks to guard against . . . Quite exceptionally, the defendant's duty to the [company] had been reduced to vanishing point by the acts (explicable and even justifiable though they may have been) of his sole fellow director and fellow shareholder . . .'[75]

At the other extreme, Rix LJ put cases where the director had 'planned his resignation having in mind the destruction of the company or at least the exploitation of its property in the form of business opportunities' in which the director was currently involved. Into this category, Rix LJ placed *Industrial Development Consultants v Cooley*,[76] *Canadian Aero Service Ltd v O'Malley*,[77] *CMS Dolphin Ltd v Simonet*,[78] and *British Midland Tool Ltd v Midland International Tooling Ltd*.[79]   **14.48**

In *Industrial Development Consultants v Cooley*,[80] the director had resigned in order to obtain for himself a business opportunity for which he, as managing director of the company and the person responsible for procuring new business, had been negotiating on the company's behalf, and he subsequently did obtain that opportunity for himself. He resigned as a director on the basis of dishonest and untrue misrepresentations. He was found liable for breach of duty and ordered to account for his profits, even though there was only a 10% chance that the company would itself have obtained the contract.   **14.49**

In *Canadian Aero Service Ltd v O'Malley*,[81] the directors or senior officers had resigned in order to take the benefit of a project for which they had been negotiating on behalf of their company. They were held to be in breach of duty. Laskin J summarized the position in the following terms:   **14.50**

> An examination of the case law in this Court and in the Courts of other like jurisdictions on the fiduciary duties of directors and senior officers shows the pervasiveness of a strict ethic in this area of the law. In my opinion, this ethic disqualifies a director or senior officer from usurping for himself or diverting to another person or company with whom or with which he is associated a maturing business opportunity which his company is actively pursuing; he is also precluded from so acting even after his resignation where the resignation may fairly be said to have been prompted or influenced by a wish to acquire for himself the opportunity sought by the company,

---

[75] [2002] 2 BCLC 201, per Buxton LJ at para 90.
[76] [1972] 1 WLR 443.
[77] (1983) 40 DLR (3d) 371.
[78] [2001] 2 BCLC 704.
[79] [2003] 2 BCLC 523.
[80] [1972] 1 WLR 443.
[81] (1983) 40 DLR (3d) 371.

*or where it was his position with the company rather than a fresh initiative that led him to the opportunity which he later acquired.*[82] (emphasis added)

(It is to be noted in relation to the italicized part of this extract from Laskin J's judgment that the courts in this country have interpreted the 'or' as 'and'.[83])

**14.51**  In *CMS Dolphin Ltd v Simonet*,[84] the director had resigned (without notice) in order to profit from the company's business. Having made plans beforehand, he immediately set up in competition after his resignation and set about poaching the company's staff and clients. The director was found to have acted in breach of duty: by resigning, he had exploited the company's maturing business opportunities. Lawrence Collins J found that the director had been prompted or influenced to resign by a wish to acquire for himself, directly or indirectly, the business opportunities which he had previously obtained or was actively pursuing with the company's clients, and which he had then actually diverted for his own profit. The judge emphasized that '[t]here must be some relevant connection or link between the resignation and the obtaining of the business'.[85]

**14.52**  In *British Midland Tool Ltd v Midland International Tooling Ltd*,[86] one director resigned in order to compete, while his three former colleagues remained in office and conspired with him to poach the company's employees. Hart J concluded that the director who had resigned had not acted in breach of fiduciary duty, but that the others had.

**14.53**  All the cases so far mentioned being at either extreme, Rix LJ said that in the middle there were 'more nuanced' cases which went both ways. Thus *Shepherds Investments Ltd v Walters*[87] (where, he said, the combination of disloyalty, active promotion of the planned business, and exploitation of a business opportunity, all while the directors remained in office, brought liability) was to be compared with cases such as *Island Export Finance Ltd v Umunna*,[88] *Balston Ltd v Headline Filters Ltd*,[89] and *Framlington Group plc v Anderson*,[90] where the resignations were unaccompanied by disloyalty and there was no liability.

**14.54**  In *Shepherds Investments Ltd v Walters*,[91] Etherton J concluded that the former directors had acted in breach of duty by reason of what they did while still directors

---

[82] [1986] BCLC 460 at 480a–b, 481c–e.
[83] *Island Export Finance Ltd v Umunna* [1986] BCLC 460; *CMS Dolphin Ltd v Simonet* [2001] BCLC 704, per Lawrence Collins J at para 91.
[84] [2001] 2 BCLC 704.
[85] [2001] 2 BCLC 704, per Lawrence Collins J at para 91.
[86] [2003] 2 BCLC 523.
[87] [2007] IRLR 110.
[88] [1986] BCLC 460.
[89] [1990] FSR 385.
[90] [1995] 1 BCLC 475.
[91] [2007] IRLR 110.

in anticipation of the competition they planned after their resignations. In that case, the directors had, prior to their respective resignations, formed the irrevocable intention to establish a business which they knew would fairly be regarded by the companies to which they owed fiduciary duties as a competitor to the business carried on by another company, for which those companies acted as manager (responsible for sales and marketing) and investment advisor. Nevertheless, the directors continued to take steps to bring into existence that rival business, contrary to what they knew to be the best interests of the companies, and without the consent of those companies after full disclosure of all material facts. After reviewing the authorities, Etherton J said the following:

> What the cases show, and the parties before me agree, is that the precise point at which preparations for the establishment of a competing business by a director become unlawful will turn on the actual facts of any particular case. In each case, the touchstone for what, on the one hand, is permissible, and what, on the other hand, is impermissible unless consent is obtained from the company or employer after full disclosure, is what, in the case of a director, will be in breach of the fiduciary duties to which I have referred or, in the case of an employee, will be in breach of the obligation of fidelity. It is obvious, for example, that merely making a decision to set up a competing business at some point in the future and discussing such an idea with friends and family would not of themselves be in conflict with the best interests of the company and the employer. The consulting of lawyers and other professionals may, depending on all the circumstances, equally be consistent with a director's fiduciary duties and the employee's obligation of loyalty. At the other end of the spectrum, it is plain that soliciting customers of the company and the employer or the actual carrying on of trade by a competing business would be in breach of the duties of the director and the obligations of the employee. It is the wide range of activity and decision making between the two ends of the spectrum which will be fact sensitive in every case. In that context, Hart J may have been too prescriptive in saying, at paragraph [89] of his judgment, that the director must resign once he has irrevocably formed the intention to engage in the future in a competing business and, without disclosing his intentions to the company, takes any preparatory steps. On the facts of *British Midland Tool*, Hart J was plainly justified in concluding, in paragraph [90] of his judgment, that the preparatory steps had gone beyond what was consistent with the directors' fiduciary duty in circumstances where the directors were aware that a determined attempt was being made by a potential competitor to poach the company's workforce and they did nothing to discourage, and at worst actively promoted, the success of that process, whereas their duty to the company required them to take active steps to thwart the process.[92]

In *Island Export Finance Ltd v Umunna*,[93] the director, who had resigned because **14.55** of his dissatisfaction with the company, and not in order to appropriate its business for himself, subsequently obtained an order from a client of the company.

---

[92] [2007] IRLR 110, per Etherton J at para 108.
[93] [1986] BCLC 460.

Hutchison J found that the director was not in breach of duty: the mere fact that a defendant's position as director led to a post-resignation opportunity was not sufficient to found a breach of duty (retreating from the apparent width of the italicized section of Laskin J's judgment in the *Canadian Aero* case set out above).

**14.56** In *Balston Ltd v Headline Filters Ltd,*[94] the defendant, being both a director and an employee of the company, gave notice as employee and then resigned with immediate effect as director. Despite the fact that he took preparatory steps to set up a company of his own in anticipation of engaging in competing activities, it was found that the defendant did not act in breach of duty as a director, as there had been no maturing business opportunity for the acquisition of which he had resigned. (As an employee, however, the defendant had acted in breach of his duty of good faith to the company by engaging in active competition (in the form of successful tendering for the business of a client of the company) before the notice terminating his employment had expired.)

**14.57** In *Framlington Group plc v Anderson,*[95] the directors of the company resigned and took up employment with a competing company, to which the company had sold a fund management business. Under remuneration packages negotiated before their resignation from the company, the directors were to receive benefits from the competing company, which related to the value of the managed funds transferred. The company complained that it was unaware that the directors would receive such benefits from the competing company. It was held, however, that the directors were not in breach of duty: they had played no role in the negotiations for the sale of the business (indeed, they had been instructed not to), there was no duty to inform the company of their own arrangements, and they were free to negotiate whatever price they could from the competing company for their future services; there was no question of a secret bribe or commission, and nor had they diverted any kind of maturing business opportunity.

**14.58** In *Foster Bryant Surveying Ltd v Bryant* itself, the Court of Appeal concluded that the defendant did not act in breach of fiduciary duty: his resignation had been forced upon him and had no ulterior purpose. The acceptance of an offer of future employment was innocent, and there had been no diversion of any property or any maturing business opportunity from the company to the defendant.

**14.59** It remains to be seen whether, having regard to the provisions of the 2006 Act, ss 170(2), 175, and 176, the approach adopted by the courts to the no conflict rule in so far as it applies to former directors, as exemplified by the authorities

---

[94] [1990] FSR 385.
[95] [1995] 1 BCLC 475.

considered above, will now change. As a matter of principle, there would seem to be no reason why it should. Doubtless, however, careful consideration will have to be given to the question whether the potential conflict is one which may be, or has been, authorized in the manner for which s 175 provides.

## E. Need for Consent, Approval, or Authorization of Members

One situation where it will be necessary to obtain the consent, approval, or **14.60** authorization of members to avoid infringement of the duty to avoid conflicts of interest within subs 175(1) is where it is not possible to obtain authorization from the directors under subss 175(4)–(6). This may be because a majority of the other directors are not willing to agree to authorization being given or because provisions of the company's constitution prevent them from doing so. In such circumstances the director can only avoid infringing s 175 if he obtains the consent, approval, or authorization of the members in advance of his becoming subject to a conflict of interest. The disclosure made by the director to the shareholders must be full and frank such that the shareholders have full knowledge of the conflict.[96] If he is subject to a conflict of interest, he must seek ratification under s 239, but then the votes of himself and persons connected with him are not counted (see Chapter 19, Section D).

Any current ability of the members of a company to authorize the acceptance of **14.61** benefits which would otherwise be a breach of the duty under s 176 is preserved by s 180(4). The provisions of the Companies Act, s 239 regarding ratification also apply to the duty.[97] In addition, it appears that the company's articles may contain specific provisions concerning benefits from third parties.[98]

The 2006 Act, Part 10, Chapter 4 deals with transactions with directors which **14.62** require the approval of members.[99] Where the transaction or arrangement under consideration falls within the provisions of Chapter 4, and either approval is given under that Chapter or it is provided that approval is not needed, it is not necessary also to comply with ss 175 and 176.[100] Otherwise, the application of the general duties to avoid conflicts of interest and not to accept benefits from third parties are unaffected by the fact that the case also falls within Chapter 4.[101] Conversely, the mere fact that the director complies with his general duties under ss 175

---

[96] *Kaye v Croydon Tramways Company* [1898] 1 Ch 358; *Herrman v Simon* (1990) 8 ACLC 1094 at 1096–7.
[97] Chapter 19.
[98] 2006 Act, s 232(4).
[99] The provisions of Chapter 4 are fully discussed in Chapter 18 below.
[100] 2006 Act, s 180(2).
[101] 2006 Act, s 180(2).

and 176 does not remove the need for approval under any applicable provision of Chapter 4.[102]

## F. Charitable Companies

**14.63** The 2006 Act, s 181 reverses the relaxations made to the no-conflict rule as it applies to the directors of charitable companies. Subsection 181(2)(a) replaces subs 175(3) which excludes conflicts of interest arising out of transactions or arrangements with the company. The replacement excludes such conflicts of interest from the duty only if or to the extent that the charitable company's articles so allow. The articles must describe the transactions or arrangements which are to be so excluded from the duty. Subsection 181(2)(b) replaces s 175(5) which allows authorization for conflicts of interest to be given by the directors. The replacement only allows authorization to be given by the directors where the charitable company's constitution expressly allows them to do so.

**14.64** Subsection 181(4) amends the Charities Act 1993 to give the Charity Commission the power to authorize acts that would otherwise be in breach of the general duties. This was necessary to preserve the current power of the Charity Commissioners to do so, in the light of the statutory statement of the general duties.

---

[102] s 180(3).

# 15

# DUTY TO DECLARE INTEREST IN PROPOSED TRANSACTION OR ARRANGEMENT

## A. Introduction

The 2006 Act, s 177 provides that:                                                      **15.01**

(1) If a director of a company is in any way, directly or indirectly, interested in a proposed transaction or arrangement with the company, he must declare the nature and extent of that interest to the other directors.

(2) The declaration may (but need not) be made:
   (a) at a meeting of the directors, or
   (b) by notice to the directors in accordance with:
      (i) section 184 (notice in writing), or
      (ii) section 185 (general notice).

(3) If a declaration of interest under this section proves to be, or becomes, inaccurate or incomplete, a further declaration must be made.

(4) Any declaration required by this section must be made before the company enters into the transaction or arrangement.

(5) This section does not require a declaration of an interest of which the director is not aware or where the director is not aware of the transaction or arrangement in question.
   For this purpose a director is treated as being aware of matters of which he ought reasonably to be aware.

(6) A director need not declare an interest:
   (a) if it cannot reasonably be regarded as likely to give rise to a conflict of interest;
   (b) if, or to the extent that, the other directors are already aware of it (and for this purpose the other directors are treated as aware of anything of which they ought reasonably to be aware); or

      (c) if, or to the extent that, it concerns terms of his service contract that have been or are to be considered:
         (i) by a meeting of the directors, or
         (ii) by a committee of the directors appointed for the purpose under the company's constitution.

**15.02** One of the consequences of the common law principle that a director must avoid conflicts of interest was that a director could not have interests in transactions with the company unless the interest was authorized by the company in a general meeting.[1] Company articles often modified the common law rule, requiring disclosure of the conflict instead.[2] In addition, the 1985 Act, s 317 required disclosure at a meeting of the directors of the company. The 2006 Act, s 177 replaces the common law principles and, in so far as it relates to proposed transactions, the 1985 Act, s 317.

**15.03** It is important to note the relationship between the duty contained in section 177 with the other obligations imposed by the 2006 Act, Part 10, Chapters 2 and 3. In particular:

(1) Section 177 relates to interests in *proposed* transactions or arrangements with the company and is to be contrasted with the obligations contained in the 2006 Act, ss 182–187 which related to *existing* transactions or arrangements with the company.[3] A director who fails to declare an interest in a transaction or arrangement already entered into with the company as required by s 182 is guilty of an offence; a director who fails to declare an interest in a proposed transaction or arrangement is not.[4] On the other hand, whereas a breach of s 177 attracts civil consequences, a breach of s 182 does not. The reason for the distinction appears to be that a failure to make the relevant disclosure under s 177 has the potential to prejudice the company's decision to enter into a proposed transaction whereas a failure to make the relevant disclosure under s 183 has no such potential.[5]

(2) Section 177 relates to proposed transactions or arrangements *with* the company and is to be contrasted with the 2006 Act, s 175 which does not apply to

---

[1] *Aberdeen Ry Co v Blaikie* (1854) 1 Macq 461, HL (SC); *North-West Transportation Co Ltd v Beatty* (1887) 12 App Cas 589, PC. Authorization by the board is not sufficient: *Benson v Heathorn* (1842) 1 Y&CCC 326, 341, 342; *Re Cardiff Preserved Coke and Coal Co* (1862) 32 LJ Ch 754; *Imperial Mercantile Credit Association v Coleman* (1871) 6 Ch App 556 at 567 (revd on other grounds (1873) LR 6 HL 189); *Gray v New Augarita Porcupine Mines Ltd* [1952] 3 DLR 1, 13, PC.

[2] Table A, reg 85; Model Article (plc) 16.

[3] The provisions of 2006 Act, ss 182 to 187 replace the provisions of s 317 in so far as they relate to existing transactions with the company. See Chapter 17 below.

[4] 2006 Act, s 183.

[5] For example, Lord Goldsmith said that s 177 'is deliberately intended to apply only to proposed transactions . . . if a company is told that a director has an interest in a proposed transaction, it can decide whether to enter into the transaction, on what terms and with what safeguards' (Hansard, HL Grand Committee (9 February 2006), col 334.

a conflict of interest arising in relation to a transaction or arrangement with the company: see Chapter 14, Section B(3) above.

The duty stated in s 177 applies to shadow directors to the extent that the common law rules or equitable principles corresponding to the duty to declare an interest in a proposed transaction or arrangement applied to shadow directors (see Chapter 9, Section C).[6]  **15.04**

## B.  The Duty

Section 177 provides that if a director of a company is in any way, directly or indirectly, interested in a proposed transaction or arrangement with the company, he must declare the nature and extent of that interest to the other directors. This replaces the equitable rule that directors may not have interests in transactions with the company unless the interest has been authorized by the members. As proposed by the CLR, shareholder approval for the transaction is not a requirement of the statutory duty.[7] The members of the company may, however, still impose requirements for shareholder approval in the articles. However, the statutory duty imposed by s 177 cannot be ousted by the company's articles.[8]  **15.05**

Section 177 requires a director to disclose any interest, direct or indirect, that he has in relation to a proposed transaction or arrangement[9] with the company. Any declaration required by the section must be made before the company enters into the transaction or arrangement.[10] This is to allow the company to decide whether to enter into the transaction, on what terms, and with what safeguards.  **15.06**

Where a director fails to comply with the provisions of s 177 two consequences follow. First, as with the 1985 Act, s 317, the failure to comply will not render the contract void or unenforceable, but only voidable at the instance of the company against any party thereto who has notice of the breach of duty,[11] so that, if it is no  **15.07**

---

[6]  s 170(5).

[7]  CLR: *Final Report* at paras 3.21–3.27; *Completing the Structure* at paras 3.26, 3.27.

[8]  2006 Act, s 232.

[9]  The word 'arrangement' is wider than the word 'transaction': *Re British Basic Slag Ltd's Agreements* [1963] 1 WLR 727; *Re Duckwari plc* [1999] Ch 253, CA; *Murray v Leisureplay plc* [2004] EWHC 1927 (QB), per Stanley Burnton J.

[10]  2006 Act, s 177(4).

[11]  *Transvaal Lands Co v New Belgium (Transvaal) Land and Development Co* [1914] 2 Ch 488, CA; *Boulting v ACTAT* [1963] 2 QB 606, 648, CA; *Hely-Hutchinson v Brayhead Ltd* [1968] 1 QB 549, 585 CA, per Lord Denning MR; *Guinness plc v Saunders* [1990] 2 AC 663, 697, HL, per Lord Goff of Chieveley; *Cowan de Groot Properties Ltd v Eagle Trust plc* [1991] BCLC 1045, 1116, 1117; *Craven Textile Engineers Ltd v Batley Football Club Ltd* [2001] BCC 679, 688; *Re Marini Ltd* [2004] BCC 172 at paras 62–66.

longer possible to restore the parties to their former position, rescission is impossible.[12] Secondly, any profit which the director derives from the contract is recoverable from him by the company.[13] This is so even if he can show that the transaction was fair and reasonable and/or that he would have made the same amount of profit after disclosure.[14]

**15.08**  Provided a declaration has been made the conflicted director may, subject to the company's articles of association and compliance with his other duties, participate in decision-taking relating to such transactions with the company.

## C.  Direct and Indirect Interests in a Proposed Transaction or Arrangement

**15.09**  Case law relating to the 1985 Act, s 317 and the common law principles have considered what constitutes a direct or indirect interest. That case law is likely to continue to be instructive in considering what constitutes a direct or indirect interest in a transaction or arrangement under s 177. However, care will obviously need to be taken where the case law considers those parts of the 1985 Act, s 317 which do not form part of s 177.

**15.10**  The director does not need to be a party to the transaction for the duty to apply. An interest of another person in a contract with the company may require the director to make a disclosure under this duty, if that other person's interest amounts to a direct or indirect interest on the part of the director. For example, a director is 'interested' in a contract with a firm of which he was a member;[15] and a director is 'interested' in a contract between the company of which he is director and another company in which he owns shares, even though he holds such shares *qua* trustee.[16]

**15.11**  A director is not automatically interested in a contract, or proposed contract, for the purposes of s 177 by reason of some interest in that contract or proposed contract

---

[12]  *Erlanger v New Sombrero Phosphate Co* (1878) 3 App Cas 1218, HL; *Victors Ltd v Lingard* [1927] 1 Ch 323.

[13]  Formerly, under 1985 Act, s 217 a failure to comply with the statute did not give a separate right of action to the company for damages against a director. Such liability depended upon a breach of the director's fiduciary obligations: *Coleman Taymar Ltd v Oakes* [2001] 2 BCLC 749. However, since 2006 Act, s 177 replaces both 1985 Act, s 317 and the common law rules such a distinction is no longer likely to be relevant.

[14]  *Costa Rica Ry Co v Forwood* [1901] 1 Ch 746, 761, CA. In fashioning the account the court may have regard to just allowances for the time, skill, labour, or assumption of business risk undertaken by the director in relation to the transaction: *O'Sullivan v Management Agency and Music Ltd* [1985] QB 428, CA; *Ultraframe (UK) Ltd v Fielding* [2005] EWHC 1638 (Ch) at para 1588.

[15]  *Imperial Mercantile Credit Association v Coleman* (1873) LR 6 HL 189; *Aberdeen Rly Co v Blaikie Bros* (1854) 1 Macq 461.

[16]  *Transvaal Lands Co v New Belgium Co* [1914] 2 Ch 488.

held by a person 'connected' to him within the meaning of the 2006 Act, s 252: persons so connected with a director are not specifically mentioned in s 177. Clearly, however, sometimes such interests will fall within the terms of s 177 and consequently disclosure of such interests is advisable as a matter of caution.[17]

An expectation of benefit by reason of, rather than under, a contract or proposed **15.12** contract can constitute an 'interest' in that contract though the strength of the expectation will be material in deciding whether it does in fact constitute such an interest.[18] Also, a director's expectation of some benefit as a result of the company rejecting a proposed contract could also result in the director having an interest in the contract.[19]

Under the 1985 Act, s 317 it was held to be irrelevant that the proposed contract **15.13** would not otherwise come before the board for approval.[20] It is thought that the same position will be true under s 177.

Subsection 177(5) makes it clear that a declaration is not required of an interest of **15.14** which the director is not aware or where the director is not aware of the transaction or arrangement in question.[21] For this purpose a director is treated as being aware of matters of which he ought reasonably to be aware.

## D.  The Declaration

Section 177 does not impose any rules on how the declaration of an interest must **15.15** be made, but subs (2) allows the declaration to be made (a) at a meeting of the directors, or (b) by notice to the directors in accordance with s 184 (notice in writing), or s 185 (general notice).[22] It seems, however, that disclosure only to a committee of board is not sufficient.[23]

Disclosure to the members is not sufficient (although if disclosure is made to **15.16** all members, it is hard to imagine why it would not be duly declared to directors).

---

[17]  *Re Dominion International Group plc (No 2)* [1996] 1 BCLC 572, 597–8.
[18]  Ibid, 597.
[19]  *Item Software (UK) Ltd v Fassihi* [2004] EWCA Civ 1244 at [36], per Arden LJ.
[20]  *Guinness plc v Saunders* [1988] BCLC 607, 612, per Fox LJ, CA; affirmed on other grounds [1990] 2 AC 663, HL suggests that disclosure 'at a meeting of the directors of the company' means disclosure to a duly convened meeting of the main board, rather than disclosure to a committee of the board. See also *Gwembe Valley v Koshy* [2004] 1 BCLC 131, CA at para 59 and *Re MDA Investment Management Ltd* [2004] 1 BCLC 217 at para 97. However, disclosure 'at a meeting of the directors of the company' does not necessarily entail disclosure to a meeting of the board at which all members of it are present.
[21]  Cf *J Harrison (Properties) Ltd v Harrison* [2001] 1 BCLC 158 (affirmed [2002] 1 BCLC 162).
[22]  2006 Act, s 177(2).
[23]  *Guinness plc v Saunders* [1988] BCLC 607; *Gwembe Valley Development Co Ltd v Koshy* [2004] 1 BCLC 131 at paras 51 and 59.

It is also not enough for the director merely to state that he has an interest. The director must declare the nature and extent of his interest to the other directors. The requirement is for full and frank disclosure.[24] Disclosure must be for the purposes of allowing the board to consider and approve the contract, that is, it must be more than a mere presentation to the board of a fait accompli.[25] Similarly, informal disclosure made piecemeal, or proof of the knowledge of individual board members, does not comply with the formal requirements of disclosure to the board, which would involve an opportunity for consideration of the matter by the board as a body.[26] As the duty requires disclosure to be made to the other directors, no disclosure is required where the company has only one director.[27]

**15.17** If a declaration of interest under s 177 proves to be, or becomes, inaccurate or incomplete, a further declaration must be made.[28] However, this is only necessary if the company has not yet entered into the transaction or arrangement at the time the director becomes aware of the inaccuracy or incompleteness of the earlier declaration (or ought reasonably to have become so aware). Where the company has entered into the transaction or arrangement the provisions of the 2006 Act, ss 182–187 apply.

## E. Where a Declaration is not Required

**15.18** There are various exemptions from the duty to make a declaration pursuant to s 177. Section 177 does not require a declaration of an interest of which the director

---

[24] *Ultraframe (UK) Ltd v Fielding* [2005] EWHC 1638 at [1432], citing *Neptune (Vehicle Washing Equipment) Ltd v Fitzgerald* [1996] Ch 274, 282; *Fine Industrial Commodities Ltd v Powling* (1954) 71 RPC 253, 259, 261–2.

[25] *Re A Company (No 00789 of 1987); Nuneaton Borough Association Football Club Ltd (No 2)* [1991] BCLC 267 44, 60D.

[26] *Gwembe Valley Development Co Ltd v Koshy (No 3)*, [2004] 1 BCLC 131, CA at 59, per Mummery LJ; *Guinness plc v Saunders* [1988] 1 WLR 863, 868–9, CA, per Fox LJ (on appeal but not affected on this point [1990] 2 AC 663); *Neptune (Vehicle Washing Equipment) Ltd v Fitzgerald* [1996] Ch 274, 282–4; *Re MDA Investment Management Ltd* [2004] 1 BCLC 217. But cf *Lee Panavision Ltd v Lee Lighting Ltd* [1992] BCLC 22, CA (where the court hesitated to find that the failure formally to declare at a board meeting an interest common to all members and *ex hypothesi* already known to all of the members of the board, was a breach of 1985 Act, s 317). See also *Runciman v Walter Runciman plc* [1992] BCLC 1084, 1093; *MacPherson v European Strategic Bureau Ltd* [1999] 2 BCLC 203, 219 (revsd but not on this point [2000] 2 BCLC 683, CA); *Re Marini Ltd* [2004] BCC 172 at paras 59–64.

[27] See the Explanatory Notes to the Companies Act, para 352 (compare the position under 1985 Act, s 317): *Neptune (Vehicle Washing Equipment) Ltd v Fitzgerald* [1996] Ch 274 (followed in *Neptune (Vehicle Washing Equipment) Ltd v Fitzgerald (No 2)* [1995] BCC 1000). However, note the provisions of 2006 Act, s 231 which impose obligations where a director who is its only member contracts with the company.

[28] 2006 Act, s 177(3).

is not aware or where the director is not aware of the transaction or arrangement in question. For this purpose a director is treated as being aware of matters of which he ought reasonably to be aware.[29] The test is an objective one.[30] Accordingly, a director will breach the duty if he fails to declare something he ought reasonably to have known, but the duty does not otherwise require a director to declare anything he does not know.

A director need not declare an interest if it cannot reasonably be regarded as likely **15.19** to give rise to a conflict of interest. A director also need not declare an interest if, or to the extent that, the other directors are already aware of it (and for this purpose the other directors are treated as aware of anything of which they ought reasonably to be aware).

Subsection 177(6)(c) makes special provision for service contracts[31] that are con- **15.20** sidered by a meeting of the directors or a committee appointed for the purpose (such as a remuneration committee). It provides that a director need not declare an interest if, or to the extent that, it concerns terms of his service contract that have been or are to be considered (i) by a meeting of the directors, or (ii) by a committee of the directors appointed for the purpose under the company's constitution.[32]

## F. Consent, Approval, or Ratification of Members

If s 177 is complied with, the transaction or arrangement is not liable to be set **15.21** aside for failure to obtain the consent or approval of the members. Section 180(1) of the Companies Act makes clear that if s 177 is complied with any transaction or arrangement is not liable to be set aside by virtue of any common law rule or equitable principle requiring the consent or approval of the company in general meeting. However, if any other enactment requires the consent or approval of the members in respect of the particular transaction or arrangement, or if such consent or approval is required by the company's constitution, then it must be sought and obtained.[33]

The application of the general duty to declare an interest in the proposed transac- **15.22** tion or arrangement is not affected by the fact that the case also falls within the

---

[29] 2006 Act, s 177(5).
[30] This was the view of Lord Goldsmith (Hansard, HL Grand Committee (9 February 2006), col 334).
[31] As to the meaning of the terms 'service contract' see 2006 Act, s 227.
[32] 2006 Act, s 177(6).
[33] s 180(1).

2006 Act, Chapter 4 (transactions with directors requiring approval of members).[34] Conversely, in such a case, compliance with the general duty under s 177 does not remove the need for approval under any applicable provisions of Chapter 4.[35]

**15.23** Where s 177 has not been complied with, the director may obtain the protection of ratification by the members under s 239 (discussed in Chapter 19, Section D).

---

# 16

# THE COMPANY'S REMEDIES FOR BREACH OF DIRECTORS' GENERAL DUTIES

## A. Introduction

The Companies Act 2006 has effected no change to the remedies which lie against **16.01** a director for breach of duty. Subsection 178(1) provides that 'the consequences of breach (or threatened breach) of ss 171 to 177 are the same as would apply if the corresponding common law rule or equitable principle applied', and subs 178(2) provides that the duties set out in ss 171 to 173 and 175 to 177 'are, accordingly, enforceable in the same way as any other fiduciary duty owed to a company by its directors'.[1] No separate express provision is made in respect of the duty to exercise reasonable care, skill, and diligence (set out in s 174), but it is clear that the remedies for breaches of that duty are those provided by the common law.

---

[1] ss 170–174 and 178 came into force on 1 October 2007: 2006 Act Commencement Order No 3, para 2(d). Sections 175–177 come into force on 1 October 2008: 2006 Act Commencement Order No 5, para 5(1)(d).

**16.02**    This chapter is concerned with the remedies available to the company. They are also applicable to a derivative claim under Part 11. The company's remedies may be pursued in conjunction with contractual claims for breach of the director's service contract, which may contain additional obligations supplementing the general duties, and also with claims arising from a failure to obtain members' approval to a transaction in accordance with Part 10, Chapter 4, ss 188–226 (Chapter 18 below).

**16.03**    In addition, where the director has been guilty of a breach of duty he may be removed from office under s 168 and the company's articles (Chapter 7 above). A breach of fiduciary duty will constitute grounds for summary dismissal under his service contract without compensation, except for unpaid salary payable for the period up to the date of termination.[2]

## B.  Remedies for Breach of Fiduciary Duty

### (1)  Introduction

**16.04**    Breach by a director of a fiduciary duty owed to the company may give rise to a number of remedies. First, the company may avoid a transaction entered into as a result of the breach of fiduciary duty or it may obtain an injunction to prevent it from occurring or being carried into effect. Secondly, the company may pursue a proprietary claim to recover its property from a director or third party. Thirdly, the company may pursue personal claims against a director or third party for compensation or an account of profits.[3] The nature of these claims may require the court to consider three key concepts: (a) the nature of the fiduciary or trustee-like obligations of a director or a third party in relation to the company's property (which also affects defences such as limitation and perhaps set-off), (b) the extent of the company's property, and (c) tracing and following to identify what has become of the company's property.

---

    [2] In *Boston Deep Sea Fishing and Ice Co Ltd v Ansell* (1889) 39 Ch D 339 a director was found to have accepted a secret commission in relation to a contract entered into by the company. The Court of Appeal held that this entitled the company summarily to dismiss him, since his conduct revealed that he was incompetent faithfully to discharge his duties to the company. Moreover, the Court of Appeal held that the director was not entitled to payment of any outstanding salary. In *Item Software (UK) Ltd v Fassihi* [2005] 2 BCLC 91 the Court of Appeal distinguished the *Boston* case and held that where the director was summarily dismissed for breach of fiduciary duty during a pay period he was entitled to be paid a proportionate part of his salary for the period up to his summary dismissal under the Apportionment Act 1870.

    [3] Worthington, 'Corporate Governance: Remedying and Ratifying Directors' Breaches' (2000) 116 LQR 638, 659–74, contains a discussion of the personal and proprietary remedies for breach of directors' fiduciary duties, and a discussion of the extent to which directors can be made liable to disgorge profits acquired in breach of duty.

*Fiduciary or trustee-like obligations*

Directors are not trustees of the company's property, but a breach by a director of **16.05** a fiduciary duty owed to the company is treated as a breach of trust. In *J J Harrison (Properties) Limited v Harrison*,[4] Chadwick LJ identified the following four propositions which he regarded as beyond argument:

> (a) that a company incorporated under the Companies Acts is not a trustee of its own property; it is both legal and beneficial owner of that property; (ii) that the property of a company so incorporated cannot lawfully be disposed of other than in accord-ance with the provisions of its memorandum and articles of association; (iii) that the powers to dispose of the company's property, conferred upon the direc-tors by the articles of association, must be exercised by the directors for the purposes, and in the interests, of the company; (iv) that, in that sense, the directors owe fidu-ciary duties to the company in relation to those powers and a breach of those duties is treated as a breach of trust.

This has the effect of bringing into play certain proprietary remedies applicable to breaches of trust so that, for example, 'a person who receives that property with knowledge of the breach of duty is treated as holding it upon trust'.[5]

Millett LJ, in *Paragon Finance v Thakerar*,[6] identified two separate classes of con- **16.06** structive trustee. The first covers the case where a person (though not expressly appointed a trustee) has assumed the duties of a trustee by a lawful transaction which was independent of and preceded the breach of trust and is not impeached by the beneficiary. A director will fall within this class, in relation to the company's property, since he assumes the duties of a trustee in relation to the company's property upon appointment to the office of director so that, if he subsequently takes possession of the company's property, his possession is 'coloured from the first by the trust and confidence by means of which he obtained it'.[7]

The second class of constructive trustee covers the case where the trust obligation **16.07** arises as a direct consequence of the unlawful transaction which is impeached by the claimant, such as deceit. In this case the defendant is not a trustee at all, having never assumed the duties of a trustee, but because of his implication in a fraud he is held liable to account: he is liable to account as if he were a constructive trustee in respect of property which he has received adversely to the claimant by an unlaw-ful transaction impugned by the claimant.[8] A third party recipient of property

---

[4] [2002] 1 BCLC 162, CA at para 25. See also *In re Forest of Dean Coal Mining Co* (1878) 10 Ch D 450, 453, per Sir George Jessel.

[5] *J J Harrison (Properties) Limited v Harrison* [2002] 1 BCLC 162, CA at para 26, per Chadwick LJ.

[6] [1999] 1 All ER 400, CA. See *JJ Harrison* (above) at para 27, per Chadwick LJ.

[7] See *JJ Harrison* (above) at para 29.

[8] *Gwembe Valley Development v Koshy* [2004] 1 BCLC 131, CA at paras 88 and 91 of the judg-ment of Mummery LJ.

acquired from a company as a consequence of a director's breach of fiduciary duty will fall within this class.

*Company property*

**16.08**  The property of the company includes, for this purpose, property treated as such even though it is not strictly the company's property. For example, a secret commission or bribe acquired as a consequence of a breach of duty is regarded as the company's property and held on constructive trust for the company: see *Daraydan Holdings v Solland International*,[9] following *A-G of Hong Kong v Reid*.[10]

**16.09**  It also includes an asset which the company had the opportunity of acquiring, but which is acquired by a director for himself in breach of his fiduciary obligations: see, for example, *Cook v Deeks*,[11] where the directors wrongfully obtained the benefit of a contract in their own names. On the other hand, it appears that where the opportunity exploited in breach of fiduciary duty consists of a business, it is not regarded as property belonging to the company (as opposed to where specific business assets, whether tangible, eg, shares, or intangible, eg, good will, are appropriated by the director). Whilst there is Australian authority going the other way,[12] the better view appears to be that, so far as English law is concerned, a proprietary claim is not available in the case of an exploitation of a business opportunity and does not apply to profits made from such a business. This was certainly the view taken in *Ultraframe (UK) Ltd v Fielding*,[13] where Lewison J pointed out that the process of fashioning an account of profits, including making just allowances or limiting the period within which profits from a business were to be accounted for, was inconsistent with a non-discretionary proprietary remedy. Lewison J also concluded that it was not possible to trace into the profits of a business, given that the identification of profits involved a balance of income and expenditure over an extended period, including notional items such as depreciation, whereas tracing depended upon the 'identification of specific inputs and outputs of substitution'.[14]

---

[9]  [2005] Ch 119.

[10]  [1994] 1 AC 324, in which the Privy Council held that *Lister v Stubbs* (1890) 45 Ch D 1 was wrongly decided. In *Allied Business and Financial Consultants Ltd* [2008] EWHC 1973 (Ch) it was held that under the 'no profit' rule it is necessary to consider whether the profit derived from information or properly acquired for purposes within the scope of the company's business.

[11]  [1916] 1 AC 554, PC; referred to by Morritt LJ in *Brown v Bennett* [1999] 1 BCLC 649, 656, CA.

[12]  *Timber Engineering Co Pty Ltd v Anderson* [1980] 2 NSWLR 488.

[13]  [2005] EWHC 1638 at [1547]: 'a proprietary remedy is not available in the case of an alleged misappropriation of a business (as opposed to a proprietary claim to shares in a company or to a specific business asset, including an intangible but proprietary asset)'. See also *Warman v Dyer* [1994] 128 ALR 201.

[14]  *Ultraframe v Fielding* [2005] EWHC 1638 at paras 1472–1475. The liability of a dishonest assistant for any loss suffered by the company as a result of breach of fiduciary duty is joint and several with the liability of the defaulting fiduciary. A dishonest assistant is not, however, liable

### Tracing and following

The trust-like nature of directors' obligations leads to the possibility that property **16.10** of the company (including under the extended definition referred to above) transferred away as a result of a breach of directors' duties can be followed or traced into the hands of third parties. The basic principle is that the company, in the same way as the beneficiary of a trust, is entitled to a continuing beneficial interest not merely in the trust property, but in its traceable proceeds. That interest binds everyone who acquires the property, or its traceable proceeds, except a bona fide purchaser for value without notice: see, for example, *Foskett v McKeown*.[15]

## (2) Avoiding the transaction

### Internal matters

Where the consequence of a director's breach of fiduciary duty is a transaction **16.11** between the company and a third party, it will normally follow that the director acted in excess of the powers conferred on him by the company's constitution in causing the company to enter into the transaction.[16] This will typically be the consequence of a breach of s 171, but may also arise in case of breach of s 172.

Following the House of Lords' decision in *Criterion Properties*,[17] it is clear that the **16.12** relevant question is whether or not the director who caused the company to enter into the transaction had actual or apparent authority to do so.[18] According to Lord Scott (with whom the remainder of their Lordships agreed) if the director had either actual or apparent authority then the transaction was enforceable by the third party, but otherwise it was not.[19]

Lord Nicholls (with whom Lord Walker agreed) explained the position as follows: **16.13**

> If a company (A) enters into an agreement with B under which B acquires benefits from A, A's ability to recover these benefits from B depends essentially on whether the agreement is binding on A. If the directors of A were acting for an improper purpose when they entered into the agreement, A's ability to have the agreement set aside depends upon the application of familiar principles of agency and common law.

---

(whether jointly or jointly and severally) for any *profits* which the fiduciary alone has made: ibid at paras 1600–1601.

[15] [2001] 1 AC 102, 127, HL, per Lord Millett.

[16] *Rolled Steel Products (Holdings) Ltd v British Steel Corporation* [1986] Ch 246, CA.

[17] [2004] 1 WLR 1846.

[18] The House of Lords in this regard disagreed with the Court of Appeal in the same case, where the liability of the third party to disgorge benefits received under the transaction was assumed to depend upon the principles derived from the cases dealing with knowing receipt of property disposed of in breach of fiduciary duty.

[19] [2004] 1 WLR 1846 at para 30. At 31 he explained that a person who dealt with the director knowing or having reason to believe that the contract is contrary to the commercial interests of the company is unlikely to be able to assert with any credibility that he believed the director had actual authority, and lack of such a belief would be fatal to a claim that the agent had apparent authority.

If, applying these principles, the agreement is found to be valid and is therefore not set aside, questions of 'knowing receipt' by B do not arise. So far as B is concerned there can be no question of A's assets having been misapplied. B acquired the assets from A, the legal and beneficial owner of the assets, under a valid agreement made between him and A. If, however, the agreement is set aside, B will be accountable for any benefits he may have received from A under the agreement. A will have a proprietary claim, if B still has the assets. Additionally, and irrespective of whether B still has the assets in question, A will have a personal claim against B for unjust enrichment, subject always to a defence of change of position. B's personal accountability will not be dependent upon proof of fault or 'unconscionable' conduct on his part. B's accountability, in this regard, will be 'strict'.[20]

**16.14**  If the court concludes that the director did not have authority, then it simply declares the transaction invalid. Other personal or proprietary remedies may follow and, if necessary, an injunction may be granted to prevent the transaction from being acted on.

**16.15**  This is a remedy which is frequently employed in the context of the improper issue or forfeiture of shares: see, for example *Re Agriculturist Cattle Insurance*[21] (where an arrangement between the company and a shareholder that his shares should be forfeited on his retirement for non-payment of a call was declared invalid, as being beyond the powers of the directors); *Re European Central Rly Co*[22] (where the action of the directors in appropriating an amount uncalled upon their shares to pay their unpaid fees was declared to be a breach of duty to act in the proper interests of the company and not allowed to stand); *Re County Palatine Loan*[23] (where a purported delegation from the directors to a manager of authority to buy back shares was held to be beyond the powers of the directors, and a transfer of shares following a purchase by the manager acting under his supposed delegated authority was declared invalid); *Punt v Symons*[24] (where an injunction was granted to restrain the holding of a meeting at which new shares were to be issued in breach of duty to act for the proper purposes of the company); *Galloway v Halle*[25] (in which an injunction was granted to restrain a call being made on certain shareholders where the exercise of the power to make calls was found to be invalid as carried out in breach of duty); *Piercy v Mills*[26] (where the purported exercise of a power to issue shares was declared void, it having been exercised by the directors for the improper purpose of seeking to maintain control); *Hogg v Cramphorn*[27]

---

[20]  See also *Ultraframe v Fielding* [2005] EWHC 1638 at paras 1492–1494; *Allied Carpets Group PLC v Nethercott* [2001] BCC 81.
[21]  (1866) 1 Ch App 161.
[22]  (1872) 13 Eq 255.
[23]  (1874) 9 Ch App 691.
[24]  [1903] 2 Ch 506.
[25]  [1915] 2 Ch 233.
[26]  [1920] 1 Ch 77.
[27]  [1967] Ch 254.

(where a purported issue of shares and a connected loan were declared invalid, unless ratified by general meeting, as having been made for an improper purpose); *Bamford v Bamford*[28] (where an allotment of shares for the improper purpose of blocking a takeover bid was saved from invalidity only by subsequent ratification); *Hunter v Senate*[29] (where the decision by the directors to forfeit shares for non-payment of a call was found to be the product of a failure to take into account matters they ought to have taken into account, and thus voidable).

It is also relevant in cases involving unlawful dividends or unlawful distributions **16.16** of assets: see, for example, *Macpherson v European Strategic Bureau*,[30] in which the court of appeal invalidated a transaction pursuant to which members of the company were paid an amount by way of remuneration which had the effect, at a time when the company was insolvent, of distributing the company's assets to them as members without making proper provision for creditors.

Similarly, the remedy has been employed to invalidate resolutions approving **16.17** remuneration or pension payments for directors: see, for example, *Hutton v West Cork Rly Co*[31] (in which a resolution authorizing payments to directors for their services after the time at which the company had ceased as a going concern and only existed for the purpose of its winding up was held to be invalid); *Re Lee Behrens & Co*[32] (where a pension granted in favour of the widow of a director was declared invalid, in the subsequent winding up of the company, on the grounds that the transaction was not one for the benefit of the company or reasonably incidental to the carrying on of its business); *Parke v Daily News*[33] (where the court declared that the proposed payment of ex gratia payments to employees was a breach of duty by the directors, as it was not reasonably incidental to the company's business and thus invalid); *Re W&M Roith*[34] (where the court invalidated a service agreement with a director, where it concluded that its sole purpose had been to benefit the director's widow, by providing a pension after the director's death, and not the company).

### Transactions with third parties

Where the result of a director's breach of duty is a transaction with a third party, **16.18** then the ability of the third party to uphold the transaction is likely to depend on whether he can bring himself within the protection of s 40 (previously the 1985 Act, s 35A) or s 44 (previously the 1985 Act, s 36A), and whether he can avoid a

---

[28] [1970] Ch 212, CA.
[29] [2005] 1 BCLC 175.
[30] [2000] 2 BCLC 683.
[31] (1883) 23 Ch D 654, CA.
[32] [1932] 2 Ch 46.
[33] [1962] Ch 927.
[34] [1967] 1 WLR 432.

finding of lack of good faith, or failure to make enquiries having been put on enquiry, as in *Wrexham Association Football Cub Ltd v Crucialmove Ltd*,[35] applying *Rolled Steel Products (Holdings) Ltd v British Steel Corporation*,[36] in which a guarantee entered into in breach of the directors' authority was held to be unenforceable, on the basis that a person dealing with a company on notice that the directors are exercising a power of the company for purposes other than the purpose of the company cannot rely on the ostensible authority of the directors and cannot hold the company to the transaction.

### (3) Proprietary claims to recover the company's property

*Recovery from a director*

**16.19**  As noted above, the fact that a director is treated as if he were a trustee of the company's assets has the consequence that if the director acquires any assets of the company (or assets which are treated as belonging to the company, as in the case of a bribe, secret commission, or asset which it was the company's opportunity to acquire) as a result of a breach of fiduciary duty he will hold those assets on trust for the company. Such a trust arises by virtue of his pre-existing position as 'trustee', and not as a consequence of the transaction pursuant to which he acquired the assets.[37] See, for example, *Cook v Deeks*,[38] where a contract obtained by the directors in breach of their duty to acquire it for the company was declared to be held by them on trust for the company.

**16.20**  This proprietary remedy against the director depends upon his receipt of the company's property, and his retention of either the property or its traceable proceeds. If and to the extent that the company's property can be traced into assets retained by the director, then the company has an absolute (as opposed to a discretionary) right to that property.[39] Where, therefore, a director has wrongfully misappropriated property and used it to purchase other property then the company can, at its option, either assert its beneficial ownership in the asset or bring a personal claim against the director and enforce an equitable lien or charge on the proceeds of the property.[40] Where the director has mixed the misappropriated property with other

---

[35]  [2007] BCC 139, CA.

[36]  [1986] Ch 246, CA.

[37]  *JJ Harrison (Properties) Ltd v Harrison* [2002] 1 BCLC 162, CA at paras 25–29, per Chadwick LJ; *Paragon Finance plc v D B Thakerar & Co* [1999] 1 All ER 400, 408, 409, CA.

[38]  [1916] 1 AC 554, PC.

[39]  *Foskett v McKeown* [2001] 1 AC 102.

[40]  Ibid, per Lord Millett at 130. The property itself may be 'followed' into the hands of third party recipients. This is considered in more detail below when dealing more generally with claims against third parties.

property then the company has the option of taking a proportionate part of the new property or a lien upon it.[41]

An orthodox view of proprietary remedies depends upon first identifying prop-  **16.21** erty of the company, or its proceeds, in the hands of the director. A note of unorthodoxy was introduced, however, by the Court of Appeal in *United Pan-European Communications NV v Deutsche Bank AG*,[42] where it appeared to accept that the circumstances in which a proprietary remedy could be granted against a director for breach of a fiduciary duty of loyalty was not limited to cases where it was possible to trace into property over which the remedy was sought. Instead, the answer to the question whether the remedy was proprietary or personal depended upon all the circumstances.[43]

### Recovery from third parties

A proprietary claim may lie against a third party to whom property of the com-  **16.22** pany has been transferred and who still retains that property or its traceable proceeds.[44] It is unnecessary for the company to establish that the receipt or retention of the property would be 'unconscionable'. Such a claim will lie against any person who retains the property, or its traceable proceeds, save for the bona fide purchaser for value without notice of the breach of fiduciary duty.[45]

A recent example of a proprietary remedy is *Clark v Cutland*,[46] where one of the  **16.23** directors of the company misappropriated funds and transferred them to the trustees of a pension fund, the beneficiaries of which were the director and his family. The Court of Appeal held that the company was entitled to trace the payments into the pension fund assets and granted a charge over those assets, notwithstanding that the pension trustees were unaware of the breach of duty at the time of receipt of the funds.

Where the relevant property is transferred to a bona fide purchaser for value with-  **16.24** out notice, and that purchaser further transfers the property on to another person, the fact that the ultimate purchaser has notice of the breach of fiduciary duty is

---

[41] Ibid, per Lord Millett at 130.

[42] [2000] 2 BCLC 461.

[43] This analysis borders on adopting a 'remedial' constructive trust approach which has generally been rejected in English law: see, for example, *Re Polly Peck International (No 4)* [1998] 2 BCLC 185 (CA). See also *Sinclair Investment Holdings v Versailles Trading Finance* [2007] EWHC 915 at para 128; and *Westdeutsche Landesbank v Islington BC* [1996] AC 669, 716.

[44] In contrast, the mere fact that a third party has dishonestly assisted in a breach of fiduciary duty does not lead to the imposition of a proprietary claim: *Sinclair Investment Holdings v Versailles Trading Finance* [2007] EWHC 915.

[45] *Re Loftus (deceased); Green v Gaul* [2005] 2 All ER 700 at paras 172–174. The onus is on the defendant to plead and prove the defence: *Barclays Bank plc v Boulter* [1998] 1 WLR 1, 8.

[46] [2004] BCC 27, CA.

irrelevant (unless that person was himself previously bound by the equity). If this were not so, it would unduly restrict the ability of the bona fide purchaser for value to deal with the property as his own.[47]

**16.25**  Whether a proprietary claim is brought against the director or against third parties, the claimant company has within its armoury the possibility of obtaining a proprietary injunction to restrain dealings with the claimed property pending its right being established by action.[48]

### (4) Personal remedies against a director

**16.26**  There are three categories of personal claim against a director who is guilty of actual, or threatened, breach of fiduciary duty: (i) equitable compensation, (ii) an account of profits, and (iii) injunctive relief.

*Equitable compensation*

**16.27**  Claims for equitable compensation are more likely to arise in cases of breach of the duties referred to in s 171, s 172, or s 273, as opposed to the conflict-based duties in ss 175–177.

**16.28**  Equitable compensation differs in material respects from a common law claim for damages, as explained by the House of Lords in *Target Holdings Ltd v Redferns*.[49] Whilst the House of Lords noted that the common law principles of causation and quantification do not apply to claims for equitable compensation, nevertheless the two principles fundamental to an award of damages at common law are applicable as much in equity as at common law. Those principles are (1) the defendant's wrongful act must cause the damage complained of, and (2) the claimant is to be put 'in the same position as he would have been in if he had not sustained the wrong for which he is now getting compensation or reparation'.[50]

**16.29**  Lord Browne-Wilkinson described the approach of equity to ordering compensation for breach of fiduciary duty as follows.[51] The rules have developed in relation to traditional trusts 'where the only way in which all the beneficiaries' rights can be protected is to restore to the trust fund what ought to be there'. Accordingly, the basic rule is that a trustee in breach of trust must restore or pay to the trust estate either the assets which have been lost to the estate or compensation for such loss. 'If specific restitution of the trust property is not possible, then the liability of

---

[47]  *Barrow's Case* (1880) 14 Ch D 432.

[48]  See below at paragraph 16.57.

[49]  [1996] 1 AC 421, a case involving mortgage fraud, and not concerned specifically with breaches of duty by company directors. Nevertheless, the principles set out in the case relating to equitable compensation are of general application.

[50]  At 432, per Lord Browne-Wilkinson.

[51]  At 434.

the trustee is to pay sufficient compensation to the trust estate to put it back to what it would have been had the breach not been committed.' Whilst the common law rules of remoteness of damage and causation do not apply, there must be some causal connection between the breach of trust and the loss to the trust estate for which compensation is recoverable, ie 'the fact that the loss would not have occurred but for the breach'.

Lord Browne-Wilkinson approved the following statement of the law by McLachlin J in *Canson Enterprises Ltd v Boughton & Co*:[52]  **16.30**

> In summary compensation is an equitable monetary remedy which is available when the equitable remedies of restitution and account are not appropriate. By analogy with restitution, it attempts to restore to the plaintiff what has been lost as a result of the breach, i.e. the plaintiff's loss of opportunity. The plaintiff's actual loss as a consequence of the breach is to be assessed with the full benefit of hindsight. Foreseeability is not a concern in assessing compensation, but it is essential that the losses made good are only those which, *on a common sense view of causation*, were caused by the breach.

The emphasis was added by Lord Browne-Wilkinson, who went on:[53] 'In my view this is good law. Equitable compensation for breach of trust is designed to achieve exactly what the word compensation suggests: to make good loss in fact suffered by the beneficiaries and which, using hindsight and common sense, can be seen to have been caused by the breach.'

Writing extra-judicially, Lord Millett has criticized the reasoning of the House of Lords in *Target Holdings*.[54] According to Lord Millett, it is wrong and misleading to speak of a breach of trust as if it were the equitable counterpart of breach of contract at common law, and equally wrong to regard equitable compensation as 'common law damages masquerading under a fancy name'.[55] Unlike a contracting party, whose primary obligation is to perform the contract and whose secondary obligation is to pay damages if he does not, a trustee's primary obligation is to account for his stewardship of the trust, so that the primary remedy of the beneficiary is to have an account taken, '. . . to surcharge and falsify the account, and to require the trustee to restore to the trust estate any deficiency which may appear when the account is taken'. The liability of the trustee is strict, and the account must be taken 'down to the date that it is rendered'.  **16.31**

Lord Millett's approach has the advantage of clarity and lends itself to a more consistent application, in contrast to the less principled approach of the House of  **16.32**

---

[52] (1991) 85 DLR (4ᵗʰ) 129, 163.
[53] At 438, 439.
[54] 'Equity's Place in the Law of Commerce' (1998) 114 LQR 214.
[55] This approach nevertheless continues to be adopted: *Shepherds Investment Ltd v Walters* [2007] 2 BCLC 202, where Etherton J spoke in terms of 'damages' for breach of fiduciary duty. He does not appear to have been referred to *Target Holdings*.

Lords in *Target Holdings*. The 'common sense view' test for causation is necessarily more susceptible to inconsistent application.[56]

**16.33** Where the breach of fiduciary duty consists of the removal of property from the beneficiary pursuant to an unauthorized transaction between the fiduciary and the beneficiary, then the above difficulties are largely avoided. In *Gidman v Barron & Moore*[57] Patten J held that in such a case the fiduciary is simply not entitled to enforce the transaction, the transaction can be set side, and the fiduciary is required to restore the property removed from the beneficiary. It is, in particular, not relevant to enquire whether the beneficiary nonetheless would have entered into the transaction if the fiduciary had not breached his duty (for example, in the case of a transaction between a director and the company, if the director had obtained the informed consent of the company before entering into the transaction). Even if it could be shown that the fiduciary's principal would have consented, if asked, the fiduciary is required to make restitution.

**16.34** In *Gwembe Valley v Koshy*,[58] however, Mummery LJ drew a contrast in this regard between the remedies of account of profits or rescission on the one hand and the remedy of equitable compensation on the other. Where the relevant breach of fiduciary duty by the director consists of failing to disclose an interest in a transaction, then the strictness of the rule in equity that a fiduciary should not profit from a breach of trust means that the transaction should be set aside, or the director should be made to account for the profit made by him, irrespective of whether the company would have entered into the transaction if there had been proper disclosure. Where, on the other hand, equitable compensation was claimed, it was right, in asking whether compensation should be paid for the loss claimed to have been suffered as a result of the actionable non-disclosure, to consider what would have happened if disclosure had been made. On the facts, the Court of Appeal upheld the judge's decision to refuse to order equitable compensation where the evidence showed that the disclosure by the director would probably have made no difference.[59]

**16.35** A director guilty of breach of fiduciary duty can be made liable to pay compensation for the loss caused by his own breach, but not for the loss attributable only to

---

[56] In *Fyffes Group v Templeman* [2000] 2 Lloyd's Rep 643, Toulson J noted that it was accepted in that case that the same principles applied in assessing damages in tort for fraud as in assessing equitable compensation for knowingly assisting in a breach of fiduciary duty. See also *Queen's Moat House v Bairstow* [2001] 2 BCLC 531, where the Court of Appeal held that a case where directors had been guilty of dishonest payment of dividends was wholly different from the circumstances in *Target Holdings*. As such, no question of 'stopping the clock' arose (as in *Target*), and the directors were liable to pay compensation for their breach of fiduciary duty notwithstanding that the company could have paid the dividends lawfully had its relevant accounts been properly prepared.

[57] [2003] EWHC 153.

[58] [2004] 1 BCLC 131, CA at paras 142–147.

[59] See also *Murad v Al Saraj* [2005] EWCA Civ 959.

breaches of fiduciary duty committed by other directors. Where, however, two or more directors are in breach of fiduciary duty which has caused the same loss to the company, then each of them is jointly and severally liable to pay equitable compensation[60] and any one of them who is required to repay the whole of the loss is entitled to proceed against the others for a contribution.

Although in *Gluckstein v Barnes*, the House of Lords recognized that it may be **16.36** appropriate to proceed against all the defaulting directors instead of proceeding against one, leaving it to that director to seek to recover against the others, on the facts, however, they refused to show any indulgence to the sole director against whom proceedings had been brought.[61] In *Gidman v Barron & Moore*,[62] Patten J refused to allow a contribution in favour of defaulting directors against another director whose alleged default was to permit the others to carry out their acts of default, saying:

> I have no difficulty in accepting that a director cannot sit in silence and allow his fellow directors to act in breach of duty, without making reasonable attempts to curtail their activities. But for the otherwise innocent director to become liable for the consequences of the breaches of duty by the other directors, there must be culpable inactivity on his part.

In many cases the company may have a claim either for an account of profits or for **16.37** equitable compensation. In those circumstances the company may elect which remedy to pursue.[63] An example of such a case is *Crown Dilmun v Sutton*[64] where Peter Smith J refused to force the claimant to elect whether to adopt a transaction entered into in breach of fiduciary duty and claim an account of profits, or claim equitable compensation, on the basis that the claimant did not yet have sufficient information to make an informed choice.

Examples of cases where directors have been ordered to pay equitable compensa- **16.38** tion to the company for breach of fiduciary duty include those where directors have caused the company to make *ultra vires* payments (such as unauthorized payments out of capital),[65] to pay unlawful dividends,[66] or to enter into transactions

---

[60] *Re Englefield Colliery Co* (1878) 8 ChD 388; *Re Duckwari plc* [1999] Ch 253, 262. In both *Cullerne v London & Suburban Building Society* (1890) 25 QBD 485 and *Young v Naval, Military, and Civil Service Co-operative Society of South Africa* [1905] 1 KB 687 the court refused to impose liability on directors who, though they had been party to resolutions authorizing the company to make payments of a type which were held to be *ultra vires*, were not themselves privy to the actual payments made.

[61] [1900] AC 240, 255, per Lord MacNaghton.

[62] [2003] EWHC 153 at para 131. See also *Lexi Holdings v Lugman* [2008] EWHC 1639 (Ch).

[63] *Sinclair Investment Holdings SA v Versailles Trade Finance Ltd* [2007] EWHC 915 at para128, per Rimer J.

[64] [2004] 1 BCLC 468.

[65] *Re Sharpe* [1892] 1 Ch 154.

[66] *Queen's Moat House v Bairstow* [2001] 2 BCLC 531.

which were unlawful, as being in breach of the financial assistance provisions of the Companies Acts.[67] Further examples include: *Re Oxford Benefit Building and Investment Society*[68] (where directors were ordered to pay compensation to the company equal to the amount of dividends they had wrongly caused the company to pay out of capital, plus 4 per cent interest); *Hirsche v Sims*[69] (where directors were ordered to pay compensation in the sum equal to the discount at which they had wrongly caused shares to be issued; in the absence of fraud or evidence of further damage to the company from the transaction, compensation was limited to the amount of the discount and did not extend, for example, to the profit made by the directors from the sale of the shares); *Knight v Frost*[70] (where compensation was ordered in the sum which the director wrongly caused the company to loan to a company connected with the director, and which was subsequently irrecoverable); *Extrasure Travel Insurance Ltd v Scattergood*[71] (where directors had, in breach of fiduciary duty, caused the company to transfer £200,000 to a company associated with the directors, without any honest belief that it benefited the transferring company; the court ordered (at least on a provisional basis) compensation to be assessed by reference to the amount that the transferring company's assets had been diminished as a consequence of the wrongful transfer; moreover, the court held that there was no duty to mitigate).

*Account of profits*

**16.39**    Claims to an account of profits will usually involve a breach of ss 175–177.

**16.40**    A defaulting fiduciary is liable to account for any unauthorized profit made by him. This is an aspect of the obligation of a trustee to account for his stewardship of the trust assets.[72] The fiduciary is treated as having made the unauthorized profit for the benefit of his principal (the trust in the case of a trustee, and the company in the case of a director).[73] Where a director acquires, as a consequence of the breach of duty, an asset which fluctuates in value, then he can be made liable

---

[67]  *Selangor United Rubber Estates v Craddock (No 3)* [1968] 1 WLR 1555.

[68]  (1886) 35 Ch D 502.

[69]  [1894] AC 654, HL.

[70]  [1999] 1 BCLC 364.

[71]  [2003] 1 BCLC 598.

[72]  Lord Millett, 'Equity's Place in the Law of Commerce' (1998) 114 LQR 214, 225: 'The primary obligation of a trustee is to account for his stewardship.' In *Ultraframe (UK) Ltd v Fielding* [2005] EWHC 1638 at para 1550 Lewison J said: 'Where a fiduciary makes an unauthorised profit he is liable to account for that profit. He is treated as having made the profit for the benefit of the trust; and hence the account may be surcharged with that profit.' See also *Allied Business and Financial Consultants Ltd* [2008] EWHC 1973 (Ch).

[73]  *Cook v Deeks* [1916] 1 AC 554, 565, PC; *Regal (Hastings) Ltd v Gulliver* [1967] 2 AC 134, 143, HL, per Lord Russell of Killowen: '[the directors] may be liable to account for the profits which they have made, if, while standing in a fiduciary relationship to Regal, they have by reason and in course of that fiduciary relationship made a profit'; *Boardman v Phipps* [1967] 2 AC 46, HL.

to account to the company for the value of the asset at its highest value in the intervening period.[74]

The liability to account for profits is a personal liability of the defaulting fiduciary. **16.41**
A director is liable to account for (ie to pay over to the company) the profits made by him as a consequence of his breach of duty whether or not he retains the profits (or their traceable proceeds). The extent to which a proprietary claim lies in favour of the company against either the director who retains unauthorized profits, or against a third party who has received, and retains, profits arising as a consequence of a director's breach of fiduciary duty is considered above.

Each fiduciary is liable for the unauthorized profit made by him. The question **16.42**
whether a fiduciary is obliged to account for profit made by others was considered in *Regal (Hastings) v Gulliver*. In that case, one of the director fiduciaries, Gulliver, who had himself made no profit, had nevertheless participated in the acquisition of shares by others, upon which those others made a profit. The House of Lords held that Gulliver, not having made any profit himself, was not liable to account for the profit made by those others[75] (distinguishing, in the process, cases where partners have been held liable to account for profits made by the partnership as a result of the breach by one of the partners of a fiduciary obligation owed to a third party[76]).

More recently, in *Ultraframe (UK) Ltd v Fielding* Lewison J re-affirmed that a fidu- **16.43**
ciary is only liable to account for profits that he himself has made and is not liable to account for profits made by a third party, save for the case where a company which is a mere cloak or alter ego of the fiduciary makes the relevant profit, in which case it may be appropriate to pierce the corporate veil and treat the company's receipt as the fiduciary's receipt.[77] Lewison J declined to follow, in this respect, a decision of Lawrence Collins J in *CMS Dolphin v Simonet*[78] to the effect that a fiduciary was liable to account for an unauthorized profit made by a company in which the fiduciary had a substantial interest.[79] Lawrence Collins J's reasoning,

---

[74] *Nant-y-glo and Blaina Ironworks Co v Grave* (1878) 12 Ch D 738; *Target Holdings Ltd v Redferns* [1996] AC 421.

[75] [1967] 2 AC 134, 151–2, per Lord Russell of Killowen.

[76] *Liquidators of Imperial Mercantile Credit Association v Coleman* (1873) LR 6 HL 189.

[77] [2005] EWHC 1638 at paras 1550–1576. Cases in which the court has been willing to pierce the corporate veil and treat the profits of a company under the control of the defaulting fiduciary as having been made by the fiduciary include: *Trustor AB v Smallbone (No 2)* [2001] 1 WLR 1177; *Gencor ACP Ltd v Dalby* [2000] 2 BCLC 734.

[78] [2001] 2 BCLC 704; also *Quarter Master UK Ltd v Pyke* [2005] 1 BCLC 245.

[79] *Cook v Deeks* [1916] 1 AC 554 was said by Lawrence Collins J to support the proposition that directors could be jointly liable to account for profits made by a company under their control, even though it was not their alter ego. In contrast, Lewison J, in *Ultraframe* at para 1574 regarded *Cook v Deeks* as establishing no more than that the defaulting fiduciary was liable to account for his own profits.

that directors are jointly liable with the corporate vehicle formed by them because they have 'jointly participated' in the breach of trust, was expressly disapproved by Lewison J, who considered that the concept of 'joint participation' in a breach of trust has no place in English law.[80]

**16.44**  Where the court orders an account of profits, the form of the account will vary depending upon the precise circumstances of the case.[81] 'In each case the form of inquiry to be directed is that which will reflect as accurately as possible the true measure of the profit or benefit obtained by the fiduciary in breach of duty.'[82] There is some debate in the authorities as to whether the court can order an account of less than the entire profit made by the defaulting fiduciary,[83] or whether the fiduciary is liable for the whole of the profit but the court is able to fashion the account by defining the profit by reference to the precise circumstances of the breach of duty.[84] In *Ultraframe (UK) Ltd v Fielding*[85] Lewison J derived the following principles from the authorities:

(1) The fundamental rule is that a fiduciary must not make an unauthorized profit out of his fiduciary position.

(2) The fashioning of an account should not be allowed to operate as the unjust enrichment of the claimant.

(3) The profits for which an account is ordered must bear a reasonable relationship to the breach of duty proved.

(4) It is important to establish exactly what has been acquired.

(5) Subject to that, the fashioning of the account depends on the facts. In some cases it will be appropriate to order an account limited in time;[86] or limited to profits derived from particular assets or particular customers; or to order an account of all the profits of a business subject to just allowances for the fiduciary's skill, labour, and assumption of business risk.[87] In some cases it may be appropriate to order the making of a payment representing the capital value of the advantage in question, either in place of or in addition to an account of profits.[88]

---

[80] *Ultraframe (UK) Ltd v Fielding* [2005] EWHC 1638 at paras 1573, 1574. The concepts of 'dishonest assistance' in a breach of trust and 'knowing receipt' of trust property are, in contrast, well known to English law.

[81] *Re Jarvis* [1958] 1 WLR 815, 820, per Upjohn J.

[82] *Hospital Products Ltd v United States Surgical Corp* (1984) 156 CLR 41, 110, per Mason J.

[83] In *Satnam Investments Ltd v Dunlop Heywood* [1999] 3 All ER 652 the Court of Appeal held that, in determining whether to order an account, the court should apply a principle of proportionality. In that case, because an account would have been a disproportionate response to the nature of the breach of duty committed, the Court of Appeal declined to order any account at all.

[84] *CMS Dolphin v Simonet* [2001] 2 BCLC 704, 732, per Lawrence Collins J.

[85] [2005] EWHC 1638 at para 1588.

[86] *Warman v Dwyer* (1995) 182 CLR 544.

[87] But see *Guinness v Saunders* below, on whether it would ever be appropriate to permit a defaulting director an allowance by way of remuneration for the work carried out by him.

[88] *Lindsley v Woodfull* [2004] 2 BCLC 131, CA.

For example, in *Gwembe Valley Development v Koshy*[89] the Court of Appeal ordered **16.45**
a director guilty of a dishonest breach of fiduciary duty to account for all of the
profits made by him, overturning the judge who, it was held 'failed to follow
through the consequences of his finding of dishonesty on the part of Mr Koshy
when he declined to order an account against him of *all* the profits obtained by
him from the pipeline loan transactions'. The order included profits that were
made by the director indirectly through the increase in value of shares in a company which itself received profits, as well as profits that were made by him directly.
'The point,' said Mummery LJ, 'is that Mr Koshy was not, as a fiduciary vis a vis
GVDC, entitled to retain for his personal benefit any of the unauthorised profits
dishonestly made from transactions between him and the company.'[90]

In *Gencor ACP Ltd v Dalby*[91] Rimer J held that a director guilty of diverting a busi- **16.46**
ness opportunity in breach of fiduciary duty was liable to account for the benefit
he received from that business, irrespective of whether the company would have
been able to take up the opportunity. Rimer J also lifted the corporate veil in
respect of an offshore company so that the benefits received by it were treated as
benefits received by the director for which he had to account.[92]

In the case of trustee fiduciaries, it is open to the court to permit a fiduciary who is **16.47**
liable to account for unauthorized profits to claim an allowance for reasonable
remuneration for work carried out in effecting the transaction giving rise to the
secret profit. In *Boardman v Phipps*,[93] where it was found that the defaulting trustees acted in good faith throughout, the House of Lords agreed with the view of the
trial judge that the trustees should be permitted an allowance 'on a liberal scale'.

In theory, the possibility exists of a similar allowance being permitted in the case **16.48**
of directors who act in breach of fiduciary duty. In *Guinness Plc v Saunders*,[94]
however, the House of Lords drew an unfavourable contrast between directors

---

[89] [2004] 1 BCLC 131, CA.
[90] At para 137. See also *Murad v Al Saraj* [2005] EWCA Civ 959 where the Court of Appeal ordered
the defaulting fiduciary to account for the whole of the profit made as a consequence of the breach
of duty; it was irrelevant that the consent of the beneficiary might have been forthcoming: 'it is only
actual consent which obviates the liability to account', per Arden LJ at para 71; moreover, liability to
account did not depend on whether the beneficiary had suffered any loss, per Arden LJ at para 80.
In *Condliffe and Hilton v Sheingold* [2007] EWCA Civ 1043, a director sold, after liquidation of the
company, a business which she had formerly run via the company. This was held to be a misappropriation of the goodwill of the business which belonged to the company. The court held that once
the director had been found liable to account, it was up to her to raise any matter that could be raised
as a proper deduction from profits she actually received. Having agreed, in the sale of the business,
a price for the goodwill, the court decided that the price so agreed on was the value of the goodwill,
for the purpose of fixing the quantum of the obligation to account.
[91] [2000] 2 BCLC 734.
[92] See also *Industrial Development Consultants v Cooley* [1972] 1 WLR 443.
[93] [1967] 2 AC 46, 104, per Lord Cohen.
[94] [1990] 2 AC 663.

and trustees. Lord Goff considered that to permit a fiduciary an allowance, even in the case of a trustee, was on its face irreconcilable with the 'fundamental principle that a trustee is not entitled to remuneration for services rendered by him to the trust except as expressly provided in the trust deed'. He considered, therefore, that 'it can only be reconciled with it to the extent that the exercise of the equitable jurisdiction to permit an allowance does not conflict with the policy underlying the rule. And, as I see it, such a conflict will only be avoided if the exercise of the jurisdiction is restricted to those cases where it cannot have the effect of encouraging trustees in any way to put themselves in a position where their interests conflict with their duties as trustees.' He expressly left open the question whether this was ever possible in the case of a director fiduciary, but could not see any possibility of an allowance being permitted to the director in the *Guinness* case itself. Lord Templeman, in the same case, could not envisage any circumstances in which a court of equity would exercise a power to award remuneration to a director when the relevant articles of association confided that power to the board of directors.[95]

16.49　It is to be noted, however, that in *Kingsley IT Consulting v McIntosh*,[96] an account of profits was ordered against a former director who had diverted a corporate opportunity to himself, but an allowance of £3,000 per month was given to the former director for the work he had undertaken in exploiting the opportunity. In *Quarter Master UK v Pyke*,[97] on the other hand, Paul Morgan QC applied the approach of Lord Goff in the *Guinness* case (to the effect that the exercise of the jurisdiction to award an allowance was restricted to those cases where it could not have the effect of encouraging trustees or directors in any way to put themselves in a position where their interests conflict with their duties) and, on the facts, refused to make any allowance.

*Interest*

16.50　The power of the court to award interest was recently summarized by the Court of Appeal in *Black v Davies*[98] as follows:

(1) the court has no power at common law to award interest;

(2) the statutory power to award interest, pursuant to the Supreme Court Act 1981, s 35A is limited to simple interest;

(3) the court had an equitable jurisdiction to award compound interest in certain cases, those cases being limited to (a) those involving the obtaining and retention

---

[95] Above at 694.
[96] [2005] BCC 875.
[97] [2005] 1 BCLC 245, 271–2.
[98] [2005] EWCA Civ 531.

of money by fraud and (b) the withholding or misapplication of money by a trustee or fiduciary who was liable to account for the profit made by him.[99]

The inability of the common law to award compound interest was addressed to a large extent by the House of Lords in *Sempra Metals v IRC*.[100] It was there decided that the common law jurisdiction to grant restitutionary relief permitted the court in an appropriate case to award compound interest as part of its restitutionary relief. The House of Lords also held that the court had jurisdiction at common law to award compound interest as damages for breach of any contractual or tortious duty.

In cases involving breach by misapplication of the company's money by a director in breach of fiduciary duty, accordingly, the court may (and often will) award compound interest.[101] On the other hand, in *Knight v Frost*[102] the court refused to award compound interest on the basis that such an award is usually intended to ensure that as far as possible the defendant retains no profit for which he ought to account, and on the facts it was plain that the defendant had not retained any of the money transferred to it in breach of duty, but had immediately defrayed it on expenses. **16.51**

In the case of liability for breach of an express trust, the Court of Appeal, in *Bartlett v Barclays Trust Co (No 2)*,[103] held that the appropriate rate of interest was that received from time to time on the courts' short-term investment account. In the case of breach of duty by directors, however, it would appear that the more commercial approach advocated in *Sempra Metals* (above) is appropriate; on this basis the rate of interest would be calculated by reference to the benefit actually received (if interest is awarded in a restitution context, eg where it is awarded in conjunction with an account of profits made) or by reference to the loss actually suffered by the company being kept out of its money (if interest is awarded in the context of an award for compensation). **16.52**

### Injunctions

The court has wide-ranging powers to grant injunctive relief against directors guilty of actual or threatened breaches of duty, both on a final and interlocutory basis. **16.53**

A final injunction may take one of two forms, or a combination of both. Where it is established that particular proposed conduct on the part of a director would **16.54**

---

[99] *Westdeutsche Landesbank v Islington LBC* [1996] AC 669, HL; *Wallensteiner v Moir* [1975] QB 373, CA; *President of India v LaPintanda Compania Navigacion SA* [1985] AC 104, HL.
[100] [2007] 3 WLR 354, HL.
[101] *BCCI v Saadi* [2005] EWHC 2256 (Forbes J).
[102] [1999] 1 BCLC 364.
[103] [1980] Ch 515, CA.

constitute a breach of fiduciary duty the court may grant a permanent injunction to restrain the director from committing the breach. This is an inherently less likely possibility, given the practical difficulties in identifying possible breaches of fiduciary duty before they are committed. Alternatively, where it is established that a director has committed a breach of fiduciary duty then injunctive relief may be available to prevent the director from continuing the breach. An injunction may be granted, for example, to restrain a director from continuing a business which it is proved constituted a corporate opportunity wrongly acquired by him in breach of duty, or to restrain a director from exploiting information acquired in breach of confidence.[104]

16.55　The most common form of interim injunction is the freezing order. This, as the name suggests, 'freezes' assets of the defendant (either particular assets, or assets up to the value of the claim), thereby preventing him from dealing with those assets in a way which would prevent them from being available to satisfy any judgment obtained by the claimant. This is not confined to cases in which a proprietary claim is made, but is potentially available wherever a judgment for the payment of money is sought against a defendant. A freezing order could therefore be relevant in any case where damages, equitable compensation, or an account of profits are sought against a director, whether the claim is for a breach of fiduciary duty or breach of a duty to exercise reasonable skill and care.

16.56　In essence, a freezing order may be granted where the court is satisfied that the claimant has a good arguable case and there is a real risk that in the absence of an injunction any judgment ultimately obtained may go unsatisfied. A freezing order may also be obtained following judgment, to ensure that assets of the defendant against which the judgment could be executed are not dissipated pending enforcement of the judgment.[105]

16.57　In any case where a proprietary claim is made against a director or third party arising out of a breach of fiduciary duty by the director, the court's equitable jurisdiction extends to granting an injunction to preserve the property over which the company claims a beneficial interest and correspondingly to restrain dealing with the particular asset. Such an injunction may be available in circumstances which

---

[104] See the analogous line of cases dealing with misuse of confidential information or trade secrets by former employees: *Faccenda Chickens v Fowler* [1987] Ch 117; *Lancashire Fires Ltd v SA Lyons & Co Ltd* [1997] IRLR 117; *Take v BSM Marketing* [2006] EWHC 1085; *Dranez Anstalt v Hayek* [2002] 1 BCLC 693, in which Evans-Lombe J held that an ex-director who set up a competing business was in no worse position than an ex-employee so far as concerned his exploitation of the skills and experience acquired while he was a director (although the judge's decision on the facts was reversed by the Court of Appeal [2003] 1 BCLC 278).

[105] See Gee, *Commercial Injunctions* (5th edn, 2004) for a full description of the circumstances in which freezing orders may be granted.

would not satisfy a claim for a freezing order, for example because there is insufficient evidence of a risk of dissipation of the defendant's assets.[106]

As an adjunct to injunctive relief in the context of a proprietary claim, the court **16.58** has, in a number of cases, ordered the defendant to disclose the whereabouts of property or money claimed to belong in equity to the claimant.[107]

Where a simple freezing order is sought, it is common to permit the defendant to **16.59** use his funds (otherwise frozen) for payment of reasonable legal costs. Where an injunction is sought in support of a proprietary claim over specific funds of the defendant, then the position is more problematic. The court is naturally reluctant to permit a defendant to use funds which, if the claimant's claim turns out to be correct, belong beneficially to the claimant. On the other hand, the court is also reluctant to deprive a defendant of the ability to use funds which are only arguably subject to a proprietary claim in favour of the claimant, in order to defend that very claim. These competing considerations were discussed in *PCW (Underwriting Agencies) v Dixon*.[108] The proprietary claim in that case extended to the entirety of the defendant's assets. Lloyd J considered, in those circumstances, that it would be unjust to deprive the defendant of the use of his assets, notwithstanding the pending proprietary claim, and therefore held that the balance came down in favour of permitting the use of the funds in order to pay legal expenses. In the unreported case of *Sundt Wrigley & Co v Wrigley*,[109] Sir Thomas Bingham MR said that:

> a careful and anxious judgment has to be made in a case where a proprietary claim is advanced by the plaintiff as to whether the injustice of permitting the use of the funds by the defendant is out-weighed by the possible injustice to the defendant if he is denied the opportunity of advancing what may of course turn out to be a successful defence.

In that case, the Court of Appeal did not interfere with the first instance judge's decision to allow the defendant to use a very substantial portion of the claimed funds in order to pay his legal expenses.[110]

It was made clear by the Court of Appeal, however, in *Fitzgerald v Williams*,[111] that **16.60** a defendant who wished to obtain permission to use funds covered by a 'proprietary' interim injunction would first have to satisfy the court, on proper evidence,

---

[106] *Polly Peck International plc v Nadir* [1992] 4 All ER 769, 784, CA.

[107] *Bankers Trust Co v Shapira* [1980] 1 WLR 1274; *A v C (No 1)* [1981] QB 956; *PCW (Underwriting Agencies) Ltd v Dixon* [1983] 2 Lloyd's Rep 197.

[108] [1983] 2 Lloyd's Rep 197.

[109] Court of Appeal, 23 June 1993.

[110] In *Phillips v Symes*, 1 May 2001, Neuberger J said: 'it seems to me that the court should be very slow indeed before it makes an order the effect of which will be to deprive a party of the ability to obtain legal representation, especially in complex litigation involving large sums of money and a great deal of evidence such as the present case'.

[111] [1996] QB 657, CA.

that there were no funds or assets available to him to be utilized for the payment of his legal fees other than the assets to which the claimants maintained an arguable proprietary claim.

**16.61** Moreover, in *United Mizrahi Bank v Doherty*,[112] it was held that even where the court (in the exercise of its discretionary jurisdiction relating to the grant of injunctions) does permit a defendant to use funds that are the subject of a proprietary claim to pay legal expenses incurred in defending proceedings, that merely precludes an action for contempt being brought against the defendant (since it would cause the use of the funds not to be a breach of the injunction). In particular, such order of the court would not necessarily mean that third parties (eg the lawyers instructed to defend the proceedings) who received funds from the defendant could not be found to hold those funds on constructive trust for the claimant.

### (5) Personal claims against third parties

**16.62** Personal claims against third parties arising out of a breach of fiduciary duty by a director fall into two categories: (i) dishonest assistance in breach of fiduciary duty and (ii) unconscionable receipt of trust property.

*Dishonest assistance*

**16.63** A third party who dishonestly assists in a breach of fiduciary duty may be personally liable to pay compensation to the company.[113] The claim is a personal, fault-based one and has nothing to do with the receipt of trust property.[114]

**16.64** In order to impose liability on a defendant for dishonest assistance in a breach of fiduciary duty, three matters must be established. First, the fiduciary must have committed a breach of fiduciary duty, although it is not necessary to show that the breach was committed dishonestly.[115]

---

[112] [1998] 1 WLR 435.

[113] *Royal Brunei Airlines Sdn Bhd v Tan* [1995] AC 378, PC; *Twinsectra v Yardley* [2002] 2 AC 164, HL. Rattee J, in *Brown v Bennett* [1998] 2 BCLC 97 had held that liability for dishonest assistance was applicable only in cases of breach of trust, and not breaches of fiduciary duty. The Court of Appeal in the same case [1999] 1 BCLC 649 doubted that this was correct, but did not decide the point. The Privy Council in the *Tan* case stated the principle as covering dishonest assistance both in a breach of trust and in a breach of fiduciary duty (see [1995] AC 378, per Lord Nicholls at 392). Subsequent decisions have assumed that dishonest assistance in the breach of a fiduciary duty attracts liability under this principle: see, eg, *Caring Together Ltd v Bauso* [2006] EWHC 2345 (Ch); *Attorney-General of Zambia v Meer Care & Desai* [2007] EWHC 952 (Ch).

[114] *Twinsectra v Yardley* [2002] 2 AC 164, 194, per Lord Millett; *Royal Brunei Airlines Sdn Bhd v Tan* [1995] AC 378, 387, per Lord Nicholls.

[115] *Royal Brunei Airlines v Tan* [1995] AC 378, 384, 385, PC.

Secondly, the defendant must have assisted in that breach. The mere receipt of trust property does not count as assistance: *Brown v Bennett*.[116] In *Brink's Ltd v Abu-Saleh*,[117] the fact that the wife of the defaulting fiduciary accompanied him on money laundering trips was not considered sufficient assistance to impose liability on her.

**16.65**

Thirdly, the defendant must have acted 'dishonestly'. In *Royal Brunei Airlines v Tan*[118] Lord Nicholls defined dishonesty as '. . . simply not acting as an honest person would in the circumstances' and explained that this involved both subjective and objective elements. This appears to have been interpreted, in *Twinsectra v Yardley*[119] as a two-fold test: (a) that what was done was dishonest by the standards of ordinary people, and (b) that the assistant knew that what he was doing was, by those standards, dishonest.[120] This precluded the assistant from relying on his own (non-standard) concept of what was acceptable. In *Barlow Clowes International Ltd v Eurotrust International Ltd*,[121] however, the Privy Council disagreed with this two-fold analysis of *Twinsectra*. According to Lord Hoffmann in *Barlow Clowes*, the House of Lords in *Twinsectra* had not intended to depart in this respect from the decision of the Privy Council in *Tan* and, in particular, the House of Lords in *Twinsectra* had not intended to suggest that an assistant must have had 'reflections' or 'thoughts' about what the normally acceptable standards of honest conduct were. Accordingly, in order to find a person liable for dishonest assistance it must be shown that he had knowledge of the elements of the transaction which rendered his participation contrary to ordinary standards of honest behaviour, but it did not require him to have reflections on what those normally acceptable standards were.[122] A person who deliberately shuts his eyes so as to avoid confirming a suspicion that the relevant facts exist is dishonest (provided that the suspicion is 'firmly grounded and targeted on specific facts'): *Manifest Shipping Co Ltd v Uni-Polaris Insurance Co Ltd*.[123]

**16.66**

---

[116] [1999] 1 BCLC 649, 659, CA, per Morritt LJ.

[117] [1999] CLC 133.

[118] [1995] AC 378, 389, PC.

[119] [2002] 2 AC 164, HL.

[120] This was followed in *Ultraframe v Fielding* [2005] EWHC 1638 at para 1498.

[121] [2006] 1 WLR 1476, PC.

[122] *Barlow Clowes International Ltd v Eurotrust International Ltd* [2006] 1 WLR 1476, PC. In *Adnan Shaaban Abou-Rahmah v Abacha* [2006] EWCA Civ 1492, the majority of the Court of Appeal appear to have accepted that the *Barlow Clowes* decision must be taken as representing English law. Lewison J, in *Mullarkey v Broad*, Chancery Division, 3 July 2007, took the same view. See also: *Barnes v Tomlinson* [2006] EWHC 3115; *Attorney-General of Zambia v Meer Care & Desai* [2007] EWHC 952; Sir Anthony Clarke MR, 'Claims against Professionals: Negligence, Dishonesty and Fraud' [2006] 22 *Professional Negligence* 70/85; T Yeo, 'Dishonest Assistance: A Restatement from the Privy Council' [2006] 122 LQR 171–4.

[123] [2003] 1 AC 469, HL at para 116, per Lord Scott.

*Knowing receipt*

**16.67** A third party who receives property as a consequence of a director's breach of fiduciary duty may be liable to pay compensation to the company. This is a personal liability which is dependent upon *receipt* of the relevant property but not upon the *retention* of that property.[124] In order to impose liability, it must be established that:[125]

(1) there was a disposal of assets of the company in breach of fiduciary duty;

(2) there was beneficial receipt by the defendant of assets which are traceable as representing the assets of the company;[126] and

(3) the defendant acted with knowledge that the assets are traceable to a breach of fiduciary duty.

**16.68** After considerable debate in the authorities,[127] the Court of Appeal in *BCCI (Overseas) Ltd v Akindele*[128] held that there was a single test of 'knowledge' for the purposes of knowing receipt cases, namely that the defendant's state of knowledge should be such as to make it 'unconscionable' for him to retain the benefit of the receipt.

**16.69** The use of 'unconscionability' as the touchstone of liability is surprising in the light of the following passage from Lord Nicholls' opinion in *Royal Brunei Airlines v Tan*:[129]

It must be recognised, however, that unconscionable is not a word in everyday use by non-lawyers. If it is to be used in this context, and if it is to be the touchstone for liability as an accessory, it is essential to be clear on what, in this context, unconscionable means. If unconscionable means no more than dishonesty, then dishonesty is the preferable label. If unconscionable means something different, it must be said that it is not clear what that something different is. Either way, therefore, the term is better avoided in this context.

**16.70** In *Criterion Properties v Stratford UK Properties LLC*[130] the House of Lords held that the test of unconscionability had no application to a case where challenge was

---

[124] *Ultraframe v Fielding* [2005] EWHC 1638 at para 1486.

[125] *El Ajou v Dollar Land Holdings* [1994] 2 All ER 685, 700, CA, per Hoffmann LJ.

[126] The receipt must be the direct consequence of the breach of fiduciary duty: *Brown v Bennett* [1999] 1 BCLC 649, 655, CA.

[127] eg as to whether 'constructive knowledge' was sufficient: see *Re Montagu's Settlement Trusts* [1987] Ch 264; *Eagle Trust plc v SBC Securities Ltd* [1993] 1 WLR 484; *Cowan de Groot Properties Ltd v Eagle Trust plc* [1992] 4 All ER 700; *Baden v Société Générale pour Favoriser le Développement du Commerce et de l'Industrie en France SA* [1993] 1 WLR 509.

[128] [2001] Ch 437. Followed by the Court of Appeal in *City Index Ltd v Gawler* [2007] EWCA Civ 1382.

[129] [1995] 2 AC 378, 392, PC.

[130] [2004] 1 WLR 1846.

made to a transaction which a director had procured the company to enter into in breach of fiduciary duty. The question in such a case (see above at paragraph 16.12) was not one of knowing receipt at all, but related to the enforceability of a transaction entered into in excess of the directors' powers (see further below). The House of Lords did not, however, disapprove of the single test of 'unconscionability' for true cases of knowing receipt, and that test has been followed and applied in subsequent cases: see, for example, *Pakistan v Zardani*,[131] *Ultraframe v Fielding*,[132] *Wexham Drinks v Corkery*.[133]

## C.  Remedies for Breach of Duty of Care

A director who breaches his duty to exercise reasonable skill and care is liable to pay damages for that breach, in accordance with the common law principles applicable to negligence claims, including the common law principles of causation, foreseeability, and quantification of damages.[134]    **16.71**

Examples of cases where directors have been ordered to pay damages for breach of a duty of care include: *Dorchester Finance Co v Stebbing*[135] (where an enquiry as to damages was ordered); *Re D'Jan of London*[136] (where, taking into account the defence available to the director under the 1985 Act, s 727, Hoffmann LJ ordered the director to pay compensation limited to an amount equal to any further dividends which he would otherwise have received from the company's liquidation); and *Re Simmons Box (Diamonds) Ltd, Cohen v Selby*[137] (a case under the Insolvency Act s 212, where the Court of Appeal emphasized that the amount which a director should be ordered to contribute under that section must be specifically related to the amount of damage which his breach of duty caused the company).    **16.72**

---

[131]  [2006] EWHC 2411.

[132]  [2005] EWHC 1638.

[133]  [2005] EWHC 1731.

[134]  It is necessary, for example, to show that the loss claimed fell within the scope of the director's duty of care: see *South Australia Asset Management Corporation v York Montague Ltd* [1997] AC 191, 124, per Lord Hoffmann. Note that s 1 of the Compensation Act 2006 modifies the common law by requiring a court—when considering whether a person ought to have taken particular steps to meet a standard of care—to have regard to the fact that a requirement that those steps be taken might prevent a desirable activity from being undertaken at all, or discourage persons from undertaking a desirable activity. This is unlikely, however, to have any material impact on the scope of duty owed by directors to the company itself.

[135]  [1989] BCLC 498.

[136]  [1994] 1 BCLC 561.

[137]  [2001] 1 BCLC 176.

# D. Relief from Liability

**16.73**    The Companies Act, s 1157 re-enacts the 1985 Act, s 727 without change.[138] Subsection 1157(1) provides as follows:

> If in proceedings for negligence, default, breach of duty or breach of trust against—
> (a) an officer[139] of a company, or
> (b) a person employed by a company as auditor (whether or not he is an officer of the company),
>
> it appears to the court hearing the case that the officer or person is or may be liable but that he acted honestly and reasonably, and that having regard to all the circumstances of the case (including those connected with his appointment) he ought fairly to be excused, the court may relieve him, either wholly or in part, from his liability on such terms as it thinks fit.

**16.74**    As the wording of the section makes plain, relief may be granted in relation to breaches of fiduciary duty as much as in relation to breaches of a duty of care. It would include, therefore, relief against liability to account for profits made as a result of a breach of fiduciary duty.[140] It does not include, however, liability imposed on a director imposed by legislation other than that regulating his duties to the company.[141] It has also been held that the section cannot be used to relieve from a liability to repay, for example, remuneration wrongly received by a director, where the apparent contract under which the remuneration was paid was void: see *Guinness Plc v Saunders*,[142] where Lord Templeman held that s 727, if it were to have applied, would have entitled the director to remuneration in circumstances where such entitlement depended on the authority of the board and there had in fact been no such authority. The section also does not apply to claims for wrongful trading under the Insolvency Act, s 214.[143]

---

[138] s 1157 replaced 1985 Act, s 727 on 1 October 2008; 2006 Act Commencement Order No 5, para 5(1)(f).

[139] It was held in *Ultraframe v Fielding* [2005] EWHC 1638 at para 1452 that 'officer' did not include a shadow director, who was thus outside the scope of the section.

[140] *Coleman Taymar v Oakes* [2001] 2 BCLC 749.

[141] *Customs & Excise Commissioners v Hedon Alpha Ltd* [1981] 1 QB 818, CA, which related to liability under the Betting and Gaming Duties Act 1972. Cf the position in Australia: *Edwards v Attorney-General* (2004) 60 NSWLR 667.

[142] [1990] 2 AC 663.

[143] *Re Produce Marketing Consortium (No 1)* [1990] 1 WLR 745; *Re Brian D Pierson (Contractors) Ltd* [2001] 1 BCLC 275. In *IRC v McEntaggart* [2006] 1 BCLC 476, Patten J held that the section did not apply to relieve a person from liability under the CDDA, s 15 (which imposes liability on an undischarged bankrupt, who acts as a director of a company, for the debts of that company), because 'the provisions of s 727 applied only where the essential nature of the proceedings, whether they be brought in equity or under the provisions of the companies legislation, was to enforce, at the suit of or for the benefit of the company, the duties which the director owed to the company'. Whether or not the section can be used to grant relief from liability under the Insolvency Act, s 217

In order to be relieved from liability a director must establish three things: (i) that    **16.75**
he acted honestly, (ii) that he acted reasonably, and (iii) that having regard to all
the circumstances he ought fairly to be excused. The first of these is a subjective
requirement, the second an objective requirement.[144] It might be thought odd
that a director could establish that he had acted reasonably in circumstances so as
to relieve him of a liability in negligence where, by definition, the court will have
found him to have breached a duty to act with reasonable skill and care. There is
no doubt, however, that the court can grant relief under the section from liability
in negligence.[145] In *Barings plc v Coopers & Lybrand*,[146] for example, Evans-Lombe J
held that auditors whom he had found guilty of relatively technical breaches of a
duty to take reasonable care were entitled to be partially relieved of liability in
proceedings brought by the company's liquidators. Their conduct could be
described as reasonable given that their breaches of duty were not 'pervasive and
compelling'.[147]

The burden of establishing honesty and reasonableness lies on the director.[148] In a    **16.76**
case decided before the introduction of the new Civil Procedure Rules in England
and Wales, it was held that the defence may be raised at trial, and that there was
no requirement specifically to plead the defence, so that no particulars of the
defence would be ordered.[149] It remains to be seen whether a court would require
details of the facts and matters which a defendant sought to rely on in support of
the defence pursuant to the court's powers to order further information or clarification of a party's case under CPR Part 18.

It is only if both of the first two requirements are established that the court needs to    **16.77**
consider the third requirement, that in all the circumstances the director ought

---

(which imposes liability on a director for use of a prohibited name) was expressly left open by the
Court of Appeal in *ESS Production Ltd v Sully* [2005] 2 BCLC 547.

[144]  *Coleman Taymar Ltd v Oakes* [2001] 2 BCLC 749, 770; *Re MDA Investment Management Ltd*
[2004] 1 BCLC 217.

[145]  The words of the section make this plain; and see *Re D'Jan of London* [1994] 1 BCLC 561;
*Re MDA Investment Management Ltd* [2004] 1 BCLC 217.

[146]  [2003] EWHC 1319, [2003] PNLR 34.

[147]  See also *Maelor Jones Inv v Heywood-Smith* (1989) 54 SASR 285, where express consideration
was given by Olsson J, in the South Australian Supreme Court, to whether there is any limitation
(both in terms of scope and time frame) to the South Australian equivalent to s 727. He concluded
(at 295) that: 'Whilst it may be that, in a particular situation, the very circumstances which give rise
to a finding of negligence may be so pervasive and compelling as also to demand a conclusion that a
person had acted unreasonably for the purposes of the exculpatory section, nevertheless that section
is to be taken to directing its attention to a much wider area of concern—both in point of scope and
time frame.'

[148]  *Bairstow v Queens Moat Houses plc* [2001] 2 BCLC 531, CA, at para 58; *Re Loquitur Ltd*
[2003] 2 BCLC 442 at para 228. *Re In A Flap Envelope Company Ltd* [2004] 1 BCLC 64 is an example of a case where the director's refusal to give oral evidence meant that he was unable to discharge
the burden of establishing that he acted honestly.

[149]  *Re Kirby's Coaches Ltd* [1991] BCLC 414.

fairly to be excused. 'All the circumstances' has been widely interpreted by the courts. In the Australian case of *AWA Ltd v Daniels*[150] Rogers CJ rejected a submission on behalf of the company that the phrase 'all the circumstances of the case' in the Australian equivalent of the section should be construed narrowly so as to limit it to a consideration of the way in which the default or breach occurred. He found that the phrase was broad enough to encompass the circumstances of a release given by a company to its former directors, in the context of a negligence claim by the company against its auditors. In *Re D'Jan of London Ltd*,[151] Hoffmann LJ, in exercising his discretion under the 1985 Act, s 727, took into account the fact that in light of the company's solvent position at the time of the breach of duty of care by the director and the fact that he and his wife owned all the shares in the company, he had been foreseeably putting only his and his wife's interests at risk. In *Re Barry and Staines Linoleum Limited*[152] Maugham J considered that the current views of the shareholders and other directors of the company (which was solvent) would be relevant to the question whether the particular director found to be in breach of duty should be granted relief. Finally, in *Re Duomatic Ltd*,[153] Buckley J relieved a director from liability in respect of unauthorized drawings having regard to the fact that he was in control of the company, could have passed a resolution in general meeting permitting the drawings, and it was a mere oversight that he had not passed the requisite resolution.

**16.78** Examples of the application of the 1985 Act, s 727 in practice include the following. In a case involving the payment of an unlawful dividend, the court found that the directors had acted honestly and reasonably where they had taken advice before paying the dividend. Nevertheless the court refused to grant relief against liability imposed under the 1985 Act, s 263 where the consequences of granting relief would have been to leave the directors in enjoyment of benefits, at the expense of creditors, which they would never have received but for the default.[154] On the other hand, where directors, guilty of causing the company to enter into an *ultra vires* transaction, had acted in good faith having taken advice that the transaction was *intra vires* the court relieved them of liability.[155] In a case where the court found that the companies' failure was the result of mismanagement and disastrous

---

[150] (1992) 7 ACSR 463.

[151] [1994] 1 BCLC 561.

[152] [1934] 1 Ch 227.

[153] [1969] 2 Ch 365.

[154] *Re Marini Ltd* [2004] BCC 172. 1985 Act, s 263 was replaced by 2006 Act, ss 829, 830, 849, and 850 on 6 April 2008: Companies Act 2006 Commencement Order No 5, para 3(1)(k). In *Inn Spirit Ltd v Burns* [2002] 2 BCLC 780 Rimer J could not see that the court could or should grant relief from liability at the expense of creditors, but that it was arguable that the directors should be relieved from having to repay to the company any more than was necessary to enable creditors' claims to be paid in full.

[155] *Re Claridge's Patent Asphalte Co Ltd* [1921] 1 Ch 543.

financial handling, most of which was the responsibility of the defendant director, the court would have refused to exercise its discretion to grant relief, even if it had found that the director's conduct was reasonable.[156] Similarly, in *Re Westlowe Storage and Distribution Ltd*[157] the court refused to grant relief where, although the director had acted in good faith and in what he believed to be the interests of the company in intermingling its affairs with a separate joint venture, his failure to put in place proper accounting procedures was not reasonable. Where the directors of a company consisted of a husband and wife, but where the wife in fact undertook no executive management functions, the court relieved her from liability in respect of misfeasance claims involving the transfer of goodwill and other assets of the company shortly before its liquidation.[158] In contrast, where directors acted blindly at the behest of the majority shareholders, who had appointed them to the board, in disposing of large sums without any regard for the minority shareholders, the court held that the directors had not acted reasonably even if they had been acting in good faith.[159]

Section 1157(2) enables directors or officers of a company to apply to the court for relief in advance of any finding of breach of duty against them. It provides as follows:  **16.79**

> If any such officer or person has reason to apprehend that a claim will or might be made against him in respect of negligence, default, breach of duty or breach of trust—
> (a) he may apply to the court for relief, and
> (b) the court has the same power to relieve him as it would have had if it had been a court before which proceedings against him for negligence, default, breach of duty or breach of trust had been brought.

It is only permissible to make an application for prospective relief, however, in circumstances where proceedings have not already been commenced against the director or officer for breach of the relevant duty.[160] By the Companies Act, ss 232 and 234((3)(iii) a company may not indemnify a director in respect of an application under s 1157 if the court refuses to grant him relief.

## E.  Defences

There are a number of potential defences open to directors against whom proceedings are brought for breach of duty. The following are considered in this section: (i) limitation, (ii) set-off, and (iii) contributory negligence.  **16.80**

---

[156]  *Re MDA Investment Management Ltd* [2004] 1 BCLC 217.
[157]  [2000] 2 BCLC 590.
[158]  *Re Brian D Pierson (Contractors) Ltd* [2001] 1 BCLC 275.
[159]  *Selangor United Rubber Estates Ltd v Craddock (No 3)* [1968] 1 WLR 1555.
[160]  *Barry and Staines Linoleum Ltd* [1934] Ch 227.

**(1) Limitation**

16.81 A director may be entitled to plead limitation as a defence to a claim brought against him by the company or a derivative claim brought under Part 11 or pursuant to an order of the court in proceedings under s 994 (proceedings for protection of members against unfair prejudice). Whether (and the extent to which) he will be able to do so depends on the nature of the claim brought against him.

16.82 Misfeasance claims brought by a liquidator pursuant to the Insolvency Act, s 212 in respect of any breach of duty by a director of the company are no different, substantively, from claims by the company in respect of the same breach of duty. Section 212 merely provides an alternative procedure for asserting such claims, once the company is in liquidation. As such, even though a claim pursuant to s 212 cannot be brought until after the company has gone into liquidation, there is no new limitation period for such claims: the relevant limitation period is that which would have applied as if the claim had been brought by the company.[161]

*Negligence*

16.83 If the claim against a director is based on his failure to act with reasonable skill and care, then the claim will be barred six years after the date on which it accrued. This is either because the claim is analogous to a claim in tort[162] or because the claim might be for breach of a term (express or implied) of the contract between the director and the company.[163]

*Breach of fiduciary duty*

16.84 A director's 'trustee-like' position has the consequence that the provisions of the Limitation Act 1980, s 21 (dealing with actions against trustees) apply, either directly or by analogy to certain claims arising out of a breach of fiduciary duty by the director.[164]

---

[161] This was recently re-affirmed by Blackburne J in *Re Eurocruit Europe Ltd* [2007] 2 BCLC 598, following *Re Lands Allotment Company* [1894] 1 Ch 616, CA. See also *Canadian Land Reclaiming and Colonizing Company* (1880) 14 Ch D 660; *Cohen v Selby* [2001] 1 BCLC 176.

[162] Any claim in tort is statute barred six years after the cause of action accrued: Limitation Act 1980, s 2. Where a claim to equitable relief mirrors a common law claim, then the common law limitation period applies by analogy: the Limitation Act 1980, s 36 and *Cia Imperio v Heath Ltd* [2001] 1 WLR 112.

[163] Any claim in simple contract is also statute barred six years after the cause of action accrued: Limitation Act 1980, s 5.

[164] *Gwembe Valley Development v Koshy* [2004] 1 BCLC 131, CA at paras 111, 112, per Mummery LJ.

Section 21 provides (materially) as follows:                                                        **16.85**

(1) No period of limitation prescribed by this Act shall apply to an action by a
    beneficiary under a trust, being an action—
    (a) in respect of any fraud or fraudulent breach of trust to which the trustee was a
        party or privy; or
    (b) to recover from the trustee trust property or the proceeds of trust property in
        the possession of the trustee, or previously received by the trustee and con-
        verted to his use

    . . . .

(3) Subject to the preceding provisions of this section, an action by a beneficiary to
    recover trust property or in respect of any breach of trust, not being an action for
    which a period of limitation is prescribed by any other provision of this Act, shall
    not be brought after the expiration of six years from the date on which the right of
    action accrued.

The application of this section to proceedings against a director was considered by   **16.86**
the Court of Appeal in *JJ Harrison (Properties) Limited v Harrison*,[165] in which the
director had, as a result of a breach of fiduciary duty owed to the company, received
land and then sold it on. There was no claim to trace the proceeds of sale of the
land in the director's hands. The Court of Appeal held as follows.

(1) A director who in breach of the fiduciary duty owed by him to the company
    had taken a transfer of the company's property to himself was a 'trustee' of
    property of which the company was the 'beneficiary' for the purposes of the
    Limitation Act 1980, s 21.[166]

(2) The action was not one to recover trust property or its proceeds in the posses-
    sion of the director (since neither was retained by him).

(3) It was, however, an action to recover '. . . the proceeds of trust property previ-
    ously received by the trustee and converted to his use'. In reaching this con-
    clusion, Chadwick LJ applied the decision of Kekewich J in *In re Timmis,
    Nixon v Smith*[167] who considered that the intention of the provisions now
    found in the Limitation Act 1980, s 21 was:

    > to give a trustee the benefit of the lapse of time when, although he had done
    > something legally or technically wrong, he had done nothing morally wrong or
    > dishonest, but it was not intended to protect him where, if he pleaded the stat-
    > ute, he would come off with something he ought not to have, i.e. money of the
    > trust received by him and converted to his use.

The Court of Appeal's decision in *JJ Harrison* was premised on the finding that the   **16.87**
director was a 'trustee' within the first of the two classes of constructive trustee

---

[165] [2002] 1 BCLC 162.
[166] Ibid at para 39, per Chadwick LJ.
[167] [1902] 1 Ch 176, 186.

identified by Millett LJ in *Paragon Finance v Thakerar*.[168] A constructive trustee within the first class is treated as a 'trustee' for the purposes of (and thus caught by the provisions of) the Limitation Act 1980, s 21, whereas a constructive trustee within the second class is not.[169] Accordingly, a proprietary claim to recover property held on constructive trust by a director of the company will fall within the Limitation Act 1980, subs 21(1)(b) and will not therefore be subject to any statutory limitation period.

**16.88**   In the second class of case the defendant (not being a trustee at all) is liable to account as if he were a constructive trustee in respect of property which he has received adversely to the claimant by an unlawful transaction impugned by the claimant.[170] Claims against a 'constructive trustee' in the second category are therefore subject to limitation defences by analogy with common law claims. On the other hand, as shown by *Gwembe Valley* itself, a claim for an account of profits made by a fiduciary does not fall within the first class of constructive trust cases, and is therefore subject to the six-year limitation period under the Limitation Act 1980, subs 21(3) unless there is some other reason for disapplying that period.[171]

**16.89**   In *Gwembe Valley* the claim against the director was for an account of profits made by him from his fiduciary position. This claim was not dependent on showing that he had received any money or other property belonging to the company. He was, however, under a personal liability to account for the unauthorized profits made by him. The Court of Appeal analysed this as a constructive trust within the second of Millett LJ's two classes: the director's liability to account for profits did not depend on any pre-existing responsibility for any property of the company. The claim did not, therefore, fall within the Limitation Act 1980, subs 21(1)(b) which would have disapplied the six-year limitation period otherwise applicable because of subs 21(3).[172]

---

[168]   [1999] 1 All ER 400. See *JJ Harrison* (n 165 above) at para 27, per Chadwick LJ. The two classes described by Millett LJ are considered further at paragraphs 16.06 and 16.07 above.

[169]   *Gwembe Valley Development v Koshy* [2004] 1 BCLC 131, CA at para 157, per Mummery LJ.

[170]   Ibid, at paras 88 and 91 of the judgment of Mummery LJ.

[171]   See per Mummery LJ at para 91 of his judgment in *Gwembe Valley*. Where a claim is based on the fraud of the defendant, or where facts material to the claim have been concealed, then the time period does not begin to run until the fraud or concealment could with reasonable diligence have been discovered: Limitation Act 1980, s 32.

[172]   In fact, the Court of Appeal went on to hold that the director had acted dishonestly, such that the claim fell within subs 21(1)(a) and the six-year limitation period was disapplied for that reason instead. A further example of a case which the court decided fell within the second category of constructive trust is *Halton International Inc v Guernroy Ltd* [2006] 1 BCLC 78, in which Patten J held at para 165 that a liability to account for shares received was based on the recipient's breach of fiduciary duty in circumstances 'which gave rise to what amounts to a remedial constructive trust' and was therefore outside the ambit of s 21. The Court of Appeal upheld his judgment; [2006] EWCA

### Statutory claims

Claims against a director pursuant to particular sections of the Companies Act[173] (or pursuant to any other statutory provision) are also governed by a six-year limitation period by virtue of the Limitation Act 1980, s 9. **16.90**

### Laches

It has long been a defence to a claim in equity that the claimant has through his conduct and neglect, whilst not constituting a waiver of the claim, put the defendant in a situation where it would not be reasonable to assert the claim against him.[174] **16.91**

It is sometimes said that the defence of laches is not available in a case where there is a statutory limitation period which applies either directly or, possibly, by analogy.[175] The issue was considered recently by the Court of Appeal in *P&O Nedlloyd BV v Arab Metals Co*.[176] It was there held that the defence of laches might be available where an applicable limitation period was still extant, although it was likely that something more than mere delay was required in support of the laches defence. **16.92**

### (2) Set-off

There are three kinds of set-off: (i) legal set-off, where both the claim and the cross-claim are liquidated; (ii) equitable, or transaction set-off, which may operate in respect of unliquidated or even contingent claims, and which requires the cross-claim to flow out of and be inseparably connected with the dealings and transactions which give rise to the claim;[177] and (iii) insolvency set-off under either Insolvency Rule 4.90, in the case of the liquidation of the company,[178] which **16.93**

---

Civ 801. See also *Frawley v Neill* [2000] CP Reports 20, cited with approval in *Green v Gaul* [2007] 1 WLR 591.

[173] For example, pursuant to the following provisions of the Companies Act: s 41(3) (liability of directors to indemnify the company for loss suffered as a result of a transaction entered into in excess of the directors' powers); s 213 (liability to account for gains made by transactions in breach of ss 197, 198, 200, 201, or 203, relating to members' approval for loans etc); s 222 (liability to indemnify company in respect of payments made for loss of office in contravention of s 217); s 369 (liability to make good to the company the amount of an unauthorized political donation or expenditure, and to compensate the company for any loss suffered as a result thereof); s 767 (joint and several liability of the directors to indemnify the counterparty to a transaction entered into in contravention of s 761, which prohibits a public limited company from transacting business without a trading certificate); and s 847 (liability to repay an unauthorized distribution made in contravention of Part 23).

[174] *The Lindsay Petroleum Co v Hurd* (1874) LR 5 PC 221, 240, per Lord Selborne LC.

[175] See, for example, *Snell's Equity*, 31st edn at [5]–[16]. But see Halsbury's Laws, Vol 28 at [806], citing the Limitation Act 1980, s 36(2) ('Nothing in this Act shall affect any equitable jurisdiction to refuse relief on the ground of acquiescence or otherwise').

[176] [2007] 1 WLR 2288.

[177] *Bank of Boston Connecticut v European Grain and Shipping Ltd* [1989] 1 AC 1056.

[178] Rule 4.90 applies only if the company is in liquidation (the Insolvency Act, s 323 is the comparable provision for bankruptcy). If the company is in administration then, unless and until

operates in respect of mutual credits, mutual debts, or other mutual dealings between the company and the director, or Insolvency Act, s 323 in the case of the bankruptcy of the director.[179]

**16.94**   Prior to either the company going into liquidation (or administration and the administrator giving notice of an intention to make a distribution to creditors) or the director becoming bankrupt, there is unlikely to be much scope for set-off as between a claim for breach of duty against a director and any claim which the director may have against the company. This is because it is unlikely either that the claim against the director will be liquidated (which is necessary for legal set-off to operate) or that the claim and cross-claim would be sufficiently closely connected for equitable set-off to operate.

**16.95**   There is a further difficulty in relation to set-off as between a claim for breach of duty against a director, and any cross-claim that the director may have against the company, once the company has gone into liquidation. This is due to long-standing authority to the effect that a director may not rely on a claim against the company by way of set-off against a claim in misfeasance brought against him: *ex parte Pelly*.[180] It is, however, difficult to identify a satisfactory justification for this rule.

**16.96**   In *Pelly* itself, Brett LJ sought to justify the rule on the basis that set-off was only permissible where there was an action at law, and a misfeasance claim (under what is now the Insolvency Act s 212) is a summary remedy without an action. This is not satisfactory, however, since an action at law is not a pre-requisite of set-off under Insolvency Rule 4.90 (which is the only applicable basis of set-off once a company is in liquidation). An alternative justification, also referred to in *Pelly*, is that misfeasance was a creature of statute and as a matter of statutory construction there was no reason to imply into the statutory remedy of misfeasance a right of set-off under the separate statutory provision permitting insolvency set-off.[181] If this is correct, then the rule could not have any application to a situation where the claim was brought by way of action by the company prior to the liquidation of the company.[182]

---

the administrator gives notice of an intention to make a distribution to creditors (pursuant to Insolvency Rule 2.95) then set-off between the company and a third party is governed by the principles relating to legal or equitable set-off. Where, however, the administrator has given notice of an intention to make a distribution to creditors, then Insolvency Rule 2.85 provides for set-off of mutual credits, mutual debts, or other mutual dealings in much the same way as Insolvency Rule 4.90 operates in respect of a company in liquidation.

[179]   For a fuller treatment of the principles of legal and equitable set-off, generally, see Dereham, *Set-off* (3rd edn), and Philip Wood, *English and International Set-off*.

[180]   (1882) 21 Ch D 492.

[181]   Ibid, per Brett LJ at 507 and per Jessel MR at 502.

[182]   In *Re Bassett* (1895) 2 Mans 177 it was indeed held that if an action is brought against a director for breach of duty by way of proceedings, as opposed to by way of summons for misfeasance, then set-off is available as a defence.

More recently, in *Manson v Smith*,[183] Millett LJ has offered two further justifica-  **16.97**
tions for the rule. First, that misappropriation of a company's assets is not a
'dealing' between the director and the company. Dereham[184] has argued that this
is unconvincing, in light of the fact that insolvency set-off may be based on a prior
debt which is not the result of a dealing between the parties. Secondly, Millett LJ
suggested that the rule can be justified on the basis that the misfeasance claim only
arises after the company goes into liquidation. This, however, is inconsistent with
the fact that the Insolvency Act, s 212 does not create a new right, but is merely a
procedure for enforcing an existing claim (paragraph 16.82 above).

A further explanation for the rule is found in the judgment of Maugham J in  **16.98**
*Re Etic*.[185] He considered that the 1908 Act, s 215 (the equivalent then of the
Insolvency Act, s 212) only applied to claims against officers in the nature of
breach of trust. In so doing, he relied on the fact that set-off was not available in
defence to a misfeasance claim: he reasoned that the section ought to be confined
to cases in which set-off was not available. This reasoning is undermined by the
fact that the wording of the Insolvency Act, s 212 is wider than the wording of the
1908 Act, s 215.[186] Moreover, the assumption that set-off is not available as a
defence to claims in the nature of a breach of trust is incompatible with the notion
that the defence would be available where a claim was pursued by a company by
action, prior to liquidation.[187]

As a matter of principle, there is something to be said for limiting the non-avail-  **16.99**
ability of set-off to claims in misfeasance brought after the company has gone into
liquidation. The justification is that a delinquent director ought to contribute to
the insolvent estate formerly under his stewardship and be left to prove along with
all other creditors for his debt.[188] A good example of a case where the result accords
with such a principle is provided by *Reliance Wholesale (Toys, Fancy Goods and
Sports) Ltd*[189] in which the director had loaned £7,500 to the company on terms
that it should be repaid as soon as the company could afford it. The director
caused the company to pay him the balance owing by filling in and countersign-
ing a cheque which had been signed in blank by his co-director. The director was
found to be guilty of misfeasance and ordered to repay the money without set-off
of his loan.

---

[183] [1997] 2 BCLC 161.
[184] *Set-off* (3rd edn) at para 8.66.
[185] [1928] Ch 861.
[186] The former section referred only to misfeasance or breach of trust, whereas s 212 extends to
a breach of any other duty and therefore includes negligence under the Companies Act, s 174.
[187] See above.
[188] Dereham advances a similar justification on policy grounds (*Set-off* (3rd edn) at para 8.69),
although limits it to misfeasance claims in the nature of a breach of trust (*Re Etic Ltd* above).
[189] (1979) 76 Law Soc Gazette 731.

### (3) Contributory negligence

**16.100**   A director guilty of dishonest breach of fiduciary duty would not be able to plead a defence of contributory negligence.[190] Whilst in theory a director might be entitled to raise a defence of contributory negligence as a defence to a claim that he failed to exercise reasonable skill and care, in reality it is difficult to envisage circumstances in which such a defence could operate, given the difficulty in practice of identifying any negligence on the part of the company that was not attributable to the actions of the defendant director.

---

[190]   *Standard Chartered Bank v Pakistani National Shipping Corp* [2003] 1 AC 959. See also *Corpn nel Cobre de Chile v Sogernu* [1997] 1 WLR 1396.

# 17

# DECLARATION OF INTEREST IN EXISTING TRANSACTION OR ARRANGEMENT

## A. The Substantive Provisions

The Companies Act, Part 10, Chapter 3 contains provisions requiring a director **17.01** to declare his interest in existing transactions or arrangements of the company unless any of the exceptions apply.[1] Subsections 182(1)–(4) provide:

(1) Where a director of a company is in any way, directly or indirectly, interested in a transaction or arrangement that has been entered into by the company, he must declare the nature and extent of the interest to the other directors in accordance with this section. This section does not apply if or to the extent that the interest has been declared under section 177 (duty to declare interest in proposed transaction or arrangement).[2]

(2) The declaration must be made—(a) at a meeting of the directors, or (b) by notice in writing (see section 184), or (c) by general notice (see section 185).

(3) If a declaration of interest under this section proves to be, or becomes, inaccurate or incomplete, a further declaration must be made.[3]

(4) Any declaration required by this section must be made as soon as is reasonably practicable. Failure to comply with this requirement does not affect the underlying duty to make the declaration.

---

[1] ss 182–187 came into force on 1 October 2008: 2006 Act Commencement Order No 5, art 5(1)(e) with the transitional provisions in Schedule 4, Part 4, para 50.

[2] See Chapter 15 for discussion of s 177.

[3] See Chapter 15 above as to the transitional provisions relating to s 177(3).

The nature and form of the required declaration are discussed in Part C of this chapter. Subsubsections 182(5) and (6) identify the circumstances in which a declaration is not required or need not be made (see Part D of this chapter).

**17.02**   Section 183 provides that a director who fails to comply with these requirements commits an offence, for which he is liable to a fine.[4] In contrast, a director who fails to comply with s 177 (duty to declare interest in proposed transaction or arrangement) commits no offence. The reasoning behind the distinction appears to have been that if the duty under s 177 is not complied with, the company will or may have civil remedies under s 178, whereas it will not for breach of s 182. This was confirmed by the Attorney-General who said:[5]

> As regards why the remedies are different . . . there is only one consequence of breach of [s 182]—because one is here concerned with an existing transaction or arrangement, the failure to declare cannot affect the validity of the transaction or give rise to any other civil consequences. That is to be contrasted with the position where there is the failure to disclose an interest in relation to a proposed transaction where the law can say that as a result of the failure to disclose that interest—and the company then enters into the transaction in ignorance of that—consequences can follow. The transaction may be voidable, to be set aside. The company may wish to claim financial redress in one form or another as a result of what has taken place. But, as I say, that is different from a failure to declare an interest in an existing transaction where those considerations probably cannot arise. That is why a criminal offence is created.

**17.03**   Section 186 adapts the requirement for a declaration to cases where the company has a sole director, but is required to have more than one director (see paragraphs 17.27–17.29 below). Section 187 applies the provisions of Chapter 3 to shadow directors, but with modifications as to the means of giving the notice (see paragraphs 17.15 and 17.18 below).

## B. Comparison with the 1985 Act, s 317 and with the 2006 Act, s 177

**17.04**   The provisions summarized above represent, substantially, a re-enactment of the 1985 Act, s 317.[6] That section applied not only to declarations of an interest in existing transactions or arrangements, but also to an interest in proposed transactions or arrangements. The duty to declare an interest in a proposed transaction

---

[4] By subs (2) on conviction on indictment the fine is unlimited, but on summary conviction the fine may not exceed the statutory maximum.

[5] Hansard, HL GC Day 4, vol 678 col 338 (9 February 2006).

[6] 1985 Act, s 317 derived from (i) 1948 Act, s 199, which in turn derived from 1947 Act, s 41(5) and 1929 Act, s 149 (introducing the provisions of 1928 Act, s 81), and (ii) 1980 Act, ss 60, 63(3), and Schedule 3, para 25.

or arrangement is now one of the general duties of directors set out in Part 10 Chapter 2 of the Act. Section 177 is in similar terms to the duty in respect of actual transactions and arrangements set out above.[7] However, although a director who fails to declare an interest in a transaction or arrangement already entered into with the company as required by s 182 is guilty of an offence, a director who fails to declare an interest in a proposed transaction or arrangement is not. On the other hand, whereas a breach of s 177 attracts civil consequences, a mere breach of s 182 does not.

**17.05** The 1985 Act, s 317 had to be understood against the background of the then applicable general law relating to directors and conflicts of interest and duty. Under that general law, a director of a company was precluded from dealing on behalf of that company in respect of transactions or arrangements in which he had an interest, or in respect of which he owed a duty to another party to the transaction, save where he had made full disclosure of all material facts to the members of the company.[8] If the other party to the transaction had notice of the irregularity, the company might rescind the contract.[9] The director might also be liable for breach of duty and under a duty to account for profits obtained by reason of such dealings.[10]

**17.06** The prohibition on such dealings[11] could be, and in practice almost invariably was, relaxed by the company's articles. The effect of such articles was permissive, permitting a director to carry out dealings which would otherwise have been precluded under the general law. Generally, that permission under the articles was subject to compliance by the interested director with certain conditions,

---

[7] A comparison of 1985 Act, s 317 with Companies Act, ss 177 and 182 suggests that the latter two sections are essentially a splitting up of the composite s 317 into separate sections dealing with proposed and actual transactions. Despite the similarity in wording, Companies Act, s 177, dealing with proposed transactions, has substantive effects which go well beyond those of 1985 Act, s 317. The table of origins of the 2006 Act gives 1985 Act, s 317 as the origin of s 182 but not of s 177

[8] *Aberdeen Railway Co v Blaikie Bros* (1854) 1 Macq 461, 471, 472, HL; *Transvaal Lands Company v New Belgium (Transvaal) Land and Development Company* [1914] 2 Ch 488; *Gwembe Valley Development Co Ltd v Koshy (No 3)* [2004] 1 BCLC 131, CA at para 65; as to shareholder approval, see *North-West Transportation Co Ltd v Beatty* (1887) 12 App Cas 589, 593, 594, PC.

[9] The *Transvaal Lands Company* case, above.

[10] Ibid; *Hely-Hutchinson v Brayhead Ltd* [1968] 1 QB 549, 589, 590, CA per Lord Wilberforce; *Regal (Hastings) Ltd v Gulliver* [1967] 2 AC 134n.

[11] There was some support in the case law for the proposition that a principle of equity *disabled* a director from entering into such dealings (without full disclosure), as opposed to his being under a fiduciary duty not to make a secret profit: *Movitex Ltd v Bulfield* [1988] BCLC 104, 119–21, referring to *Tito v Waddell (No 2)* [1977] Ch 106. CLR: *Developing the Framework* para 3.62, n 43, explained that the 'disability' analysis had been preferred due to the need to reconcile Table A, reg 85 with 1985 Act, s 309A (see now 2006 Act, s 232), which rendered void any provision purporting to exempt a director from liability for breach of duty. In *Gwembe Valley Development Co Ltd v Koshy* [2004] 1 BCLC 131 at paras 104–109 the Court of Appeal described the distinction between disability and duty in *Tito v Waddell* as 'a needless complication'.

including, in particular, conditions as to disclosure of the relevant interest to the board.[12] If the conditions were complied with, the director was not accountable to the company for any benefit which he derived from the transaction or arrangement, and the transaction or arrangement was not voidable on the basis of the director's interest.

**17.07**  A director who failed to comply with the 1985 Act, s 317 was liable to a fine, but s 317 did not specify any other consequences of a failure to comply. Subsection 317(9) provided that nothing in the section prejudiced the operation of any rule of law restricting directors of a company from having an interest in contracts with the company. Although not wholly free from doubt, the legal position under the Companies Act 1985, s 317 was, therefore, probably as follows:

(1) In and of itself, any failure by a director to comply with its provisions had no civil consequences. The effect of a failure by a director to comply with s 317 was merely that he thereby committed an offence.[13]

(2) The civil consequences of a director having an interest in a transaction, and his failure to disclose the same, were therefore determined exclusively by the general law and the company's articles of association. The general law prohibited a director, absent full disclosure of his interest to the members, from dealing on behalf of the company in respect of any transaction in which he had an interest, imposed a duty to account on the director if he did so, and rendered the contract entered into absent such disclosure potentially voidable.[14] A company's articles could, however, permit such dealings provided that certain preconditions relating to disclosure by the interested director were

---

[12]  eg Table A, regs 85 and 86.

[13]  *Hely-Hutchinson v Brayhead Ltd* [1968] 1 QB 549, 588–91, 594, CA, per Lord Wilberforce and Lord Pearson (Lord Denning at 585, 586 is equivocal); *Guinness Plc v Saunders* [1990] 2 AC 663, 697, 698, HL, per Lord Goff, who approved the reasoning of Lord Pearson. At 694 Lord Templeman stated that the Court of Appeal in *Hely-Hutchinson* had held that s 317 rendered a contract voidable by the company if the director did not declare his interest. In *Lee Panavision Ltd v Lee Lighting Ltd* [1991] BCLC 575, 583, Harman J described Lord Templeman's observation as 'surprising', adding that 'quite plainly *Hely-Hutchinson* never said anything of the sort at all'. The Court of Appeal upheld the decision in *Lee Panavision* on other grounds ([1992] BCLC 22), but, at 33, refused to enter into the 'scholastic exercise' of discerning whether 'true doctrine' was to be discerned in the judgments of Lords Pearson and Wilberforce, as opposed to Lord Denning MR, in the *Hely-Hutchinson* case, or in the speech of Lord Templeman rather than Lord Goff in the *Guinness* case. In *Cowan de Groot Properties Ltd v Eagle Trust Plc* [1991] BCLC 1045, 1113 Knox J stated that it was clear that the statutory duty of disclosure under the 1985 Act, s 317 and its predecessors did not of itself affect the validity of a contract. In *Re Marini Ltd* [2004] BCC 172, 195, 196 it was said to be common ground that a breach of the 1985 Act, s 317 rendered the contract voidable, though it is unclear from the limited references to the company's articles, at 176, whether this would have resulted from the company's articles in any event. Under s 317 a director was not liable for damages for breach of statutory duty if he failed to comply with its requirements: *Coleman Taymar Ltd v Oakes* [2001] 2 BCLC 749, 769; *Castlereagh Motels v Davies-Roe* (1967) 67 SR (NSW) 279.

[14]  Paragraph 17.05 above.

complied with. Those preconditions might (and, in the case of the 1985 Table A, reg 85, implicitly did) include compliance with s 317.

The legal landscape under the Companies Act is very different. The general law **17.08** prohibiting a director from dealing on behalf of a company in respect of a transaction in which he has an interest, and rendering the transaction voidable if the informed consent of the members has not been obtained, has been superseded by a combination of the Companies Act, ss 177, 178, and 180, discussed in Chapters 15 and 16 above. Section 177 imposes a general duty on a director to declare the nature and extent of his interest in a proposed transaction or arrangement to the other directors. If the director complies with that general duty, the transaction or arrangement is not liable to be set aside by reason of his not obtaining the consent or approval of the members of the company (as was the case previously under the general law).[15] Disclosure to the board, under the general duty embodied in s 177, is now key to the validity of the transaction, rather than disclosure to the members (or compliance with the company's articles[16]). If a director fails to comply with his general duty of disclosure under s 177, the consequence is that the transaction may be voidable, and the director accountable for breach of fiduciary duty.[17]

One consequence of the change to the legal landscape is that the Articles will gen- **17.09** erally no longer play the crucial role they once did, ie of permitting that which would otherwise be prohibited. The Model Articles thus make reference to conflicts of interest only in the context of voting at board meetings.[18] The articles may, however, contain a provision requiring the consent or approval of the members to any proposed transaction in which a director has an interest.[19]

Returning to the 2006 Act, s 182, dealing with declarations of an interest in an **17.10** existing (as opposed to proposed) transaction or arrangement, there is little doubt that the sole consequence of a failure by a director to comply with this duty of disclosure is to render the director liable to a fine under section 183.[20] It is difficult to see what remedies a company could expect to have in respect of non-disclosure

---

[15] s 180.

[16] Save where the company's constitution requires the consent or approval of members: s 180(1).

[17] s 178. The imposition of a positive fiduciary duty to declare the relevant interest, in default of which the relevant transaction may be avoided and the director accountable for any profit, is in some ways a statutory formulation of the general law as, perhaps, it was expressed by Lord Denning MR in the *Hely-Hutchinson* case, [1968] 1 QB 549, 585.

[18] See Model Article (plc) 16, Model Article (pcls) 14 and Model Article (pclg) 14.

[19] subs 180(1).

[20] Failure to comply with s 182 may also be taken into account in proceedings taken against a director under CDDA; see s 9 and Schedule 1, Part 1, para 1. In *Re Dominion International Group Plc (No 2)* [1996] 1 BCLC 572, 597–600 a breach of the disclosure requirements under 1985 Act, s 317 was relied on in disqualification proceedings, but was discounted as purely technical.

of an interest in an existing transaction in any event.[21] Section 182 will primarily apply in two contexts:

(1) Where a new director, interested in a transaction or arrangement already entered into by the company, joins the board. Mere non-disclosure of the director's interest could not, of itself, give the company a civil remedy in respect of the contract itself or against the director. A criminal sanction is imposed by s 183 to compel disclosure of the director's interest in the transaction or arrangement in order to enable the other directors to preserve the integrity of their decision-making and to protect the company's position, eg by protecting its confidential information. If, while concealing his interest in the transaction or arrangement, the director's conduct causes the company harm, it may have civil remedies for breach of the director's general duties under ss 171–174 or s 176[22] or possibly arising from any related breach of its articles.

(2) Where a director has failed to declare his interest in a proposed transaction or arrangement under s 177 and the company has since entered into that transaction or arrangement. The company will or may have remedies by reason of the breach of s 177 itself. Continuing non-disclosure of the director's interest after the company has entered into the transaction or arrangement will expose the director to criminal sanction under s 183.

## C. Nature and Form of the Declaration

**17.11** The wording of s 182(1) (and s 177) has been expanded, compared to the 1985 Act, s 317. Whereas s 317 required a director to declare merely the 'nature' of his interest to a meeting of the directors, the requirement is now to declare the nature 'and extent' of that interest to the other directors.[23] The reference to 'a transaction or arrangement' has been retained: although the 1985 Act, s 317(1) referred to a 'contract or proposed contract', the inclusive definition in s 317(5), defined

---

[21] See the statement of the Attorney-General, quoted in paragraph 17.02 above.

[22] Compare cases under the previous law: *Neptune (Vehicle Washing Equipment) Ltd v Fitzgerald (No 2)* [1995] BCC 1000; *Ultraframe (UK) Ltd v Fielding* [2005] EWHC 1638 (Ch) at para 1436. By subs 175(3), the general duty to avoid conflicts of interest does not apply to conflicts of interest arising in relation to a transaction or arrangement with the company.

[23] It had been held that s 317 required a full and frank declaration by the director not of 'an' interest but of the precise nature of the interest: *Neptune (Vehicle Washing Equipment) Ltd v Fitzgerald* [1995] 1 BCLC 352, 358; *Ultraframe (UK) Ltd v Fielding* [2005] EWHC 1638 (Ch) at para 1432. The permission under Table A, reg 85 applied only if the nature and extent of the interest was disclosed. Full disclosure was also required as matter of general law: see *Imperial Mercantile Credit Association v Coleman* (1873) LR 6 HL 189, 201; *Gray v New Augarita Porcupine Mines Ltd* [1952] 3 DLR 1, PC; *Gwembe Valley Development Co Ltd v Koshy (No 3)* [2004] 1 BCLC 131, CA at para 65.

'contract' as including any transaction or arrangement.[24] Under the 1985 Act it has been held that, for the purposes of s 317, an interest in a transaction or arrangement included real and substantial expectations.[25]

If a declaration of interest proves to be or becomes inaccurate or incomplete, **17.12** a further declaration must be made.[26] Since the duty is to disclose both the nature and the extent of the interest, a director who is, for example, interested in a contract between the company and a third party by reason of his holding of shares in that third party will be obliged to make a new declaration if and when his shareholding in that third party increases or, it appears, decreases. Any declaration must be made as soon as is reasonably practicable, but failure to make the declaration as soon as reasonably practicable does not affect the underlying duty to make the declaration.[27]

As with subs 177(2) of the Act, the declaration of interest must be made in one of **17.13** three ways: at a meeting of the directors,[28] by a notice in writing, or by general notice.[29]

### Declaration at a meeting of directors

It had been held under the 1985 Act, s 317 that the requirement for disclosure at **17.14** a meeting of the directors meant a duly convened meeting of directors.[30] The point is now largely irrelevant, since if there is disclosure to the directors making up the board outside a formally convened board meeting, there will be no duty to disclose at a formal board meeting by reason of s 182(6)(b). Under the 1985 Act,

---

[24] The words 'transaction or arrangement' are not defined. Compare the broad inclusive definition of 'transaction' in Insolvency Act, s 436; and Chapter 18 at paragraph 18.42 on 'arrangement' under the Companies Act, s 190 (Substantial property transactions). Whilst 'transaction or arrangement' are words of broad meaning, the words themselves, and the requirement that the transaction or arrangement must have been 'entered into by' the company, perhaps connote an element of mutual dealing and suggest that a gift, or any unilateral dealing, would not fall within s 182: compare *Re Taylor Sinclair (Capital) Ltd* [2001] 2 BCLC 176, 184.

[25] *Re Dominion International Group Plc* [1996] 1 BCLC 572, 597. Given that the expectation in that case was 'comparable to that of a healthy young person entitled as the sole next of kin on the prospective intestacy of an incurable lunatic in the last stages of a fatal disease', Knox J held that there was an interest which ought to have been disclosed under 1985 Act, s 317. It appears that even a nominal interest had to be disclosed: *Todd v Robinson* (1884) 14 QBD 739, CA, though this is now subject to s 182(6).

[26] subs 182(3).

[27] subs 182(4).

[28] A shadow director may not give notice in this way: paragraphs 17.15 and 17.18 below.

[29] subs 182(2).

[30] *Guinness Plc v Saunders* [1988] 1 WLR 863, 868, CA (appeal to the House of Lords dismissed on other grounds: [1990] 2 AC 663); *Gwembe Valley Development Co Ltd v Koshy (No 3)* [2004] 1 BCLC 131, CA at [59]; Re *MDA Investment Management Ltd* [2004] 1 BCLC 217, 255, 6. In *Re Marini Ltd* [2004] BCC 172, 194, it was held that 1985 Act, s 317 did not require disclosure at a formal board meeting, but the decision of the Court of Appeal in the *Guinness* case was not, it appears, cited.

s 317, disclosure to a committee of the board was insufficient.[31] It is thought that the position is the same under s 182.

**17.15**   A shadow director may not declare his interest at a meeting of directors.[32] Instead there must be a written record of the declaration of the shadow director's interest.

### Notice in writing

**17.16**   Where the declaration is made by notice in writing, the director must send the notice to the other directors.[33] The notice may be sent in hard copy form or, if the recipient has agreed to receive it by electronic means, in an agreed electronic form: s 184(3).[34] The notice may be sent by hand or by post or, if the recipient has agreed to receive it by electronic means, by agreed electronic means: s 184(4).[35] Where a director declares an interest by notice in writing in accordance with s 184, the making of the declaration is deemed to form part of the proceedings at the next meeting of the directors after the notice is given, and the provisions of s 248 (minutes of meetings of directors) apply as if the declaration had been made at that meeting.[36] These provisions are new, having no equivalent under the 1985 Act or other previous Companies Acts.

### General notice

**17.17**   General notice is notice given to the directors of the company to the effect that the director has an interest (as member, officer, employee, or otherwise) in a specified body corporate or firm and is to be regarded as interested in any transactions or arrangement that may, after the date of the notice, be made with that body corporate or firm, or is connected with a specified body (other than a body corporate or firm) and is to be regarded as interested in any transaction or arrangement that may, after the date of the notice, be made with that person.[37] The notice must state the nature and extent of the director's interest in the body corporate or firm or, as the case may be, the nature of his connection with the person.[38] General notice is not effective unless it is given at a meeting of the directors, or the director takes reasonable steps to secure that it is brought up and read at the next meeting of the directors after it is given.[39] Where general notice is given in accordance with these

---

[31]   *Guinness Plc v Saunders* [1988] 1 WLR 863 (CA), 868. Again, the point was not addressed when the case went to the House of Lords: [1990] 2 AC 663.
[32]   subs 187(2).
[33]   subs 184(2).
[34]   subs 184(3).
[35]   subs 184(4).
[36]   subs 184(5).
[37]   subs 185(2).
[38]   subs 185(3).
[39]   subs 185(4).

provisions, it is a sufficient declaration of interest in relation to the matters to which it relates.[40]

A shadow director may not give a general notice of his interest at a meeting of directors and a general notice is not effective unless given in writing.[41]    **17.18**

## D. Circumstances in which a Declaration Need not be Made

As already noted the 2006 Act, s 182 does not apply if and to the extent that the interest has already been declared under s 177. Further, the requirement to disclose an interest in an existing transaction or arrangement is subject to the same qualifications as apply to the duty to disclose an interest in a proposed transaction or arrangement under s 177(5) and (6). These qualifications are entirely new, having no equivalent under the 1985 Act. For the most part, the qualifications have the sensible effect that no duty of disclosure is imposed where it would be pointless to impose such a duty. The possibility of a director being guilty of an offence by reason of a technical breach of the disclosure provisions is therefore significantly lessened, compared to the position under s 317.    **17.19**

No declaration is required where the director is not aware of his interest or of the transaction or arrangement.[42] Subsection 182(5) thus provides:    **17.20**

> This section does not require a declaration of an interest of which the director is not aware or where the director is not aware of the transaction or arrangement in question. For this purpose a director is treated as being aware of matters of which he ought reasonably to be aware.

Subsection 182(5) provides for an objective test.[43] The Solicitor General said:[44]    **17.21**

> The Government take the view that directors have some substantial obligations and that they ought to declare those things about which they should reasonably have been aware. That is an objective test applied to directors concerned. So it will take into account any relevant circumstances relating to that director; it will focus on the individual director. This is the question that will be asked: what is it reasonable to expect a director in those circumstances to have been aware of? For example, a non-executive director might be expected generally to be less aware of the individual transactions or arrangements entered into by a company. I repeat that directors are

---

[40] subs 185(1). These provisions re-enact, with some modifications, 1985 Act, s 317(3) and (4).

[41] subss 187(3) and (4).

[42] Following the Law Commission recommendation: Law Commission, *Company Directors: Regulating Conflicts of Interest and Formulating a Statement of Duties*, No 261, para 8.57. Under Table A, reg 85, an interest of which the director had no knowledge, and of which it was unreasonable to expect him to have knowledge, was not treated as an interest of his which needed to be disclosed if he was to take advantage of the permission in reg 85: see reg 86(b).

[43] Hansard, HL GC Day 4, Vol 678, col 334 (9 February 2006).

[44] Hansard HC Standing Committee D col 628 (11 July 2006).

not expected to disclose things that they do not know. One of the purposes of the clause is to ensure that the board is aware of anything that might influence a director's decision. The director can disclose only what he is aware of, and if he is aware of it, he ought to declare it. The clause will therefore be clear enough, but anyone who wants clarification can read the notes on the clause or, on the basis of Pepper v Hart, read my comments in Hansard.

**17.22**   Subsection 182(6) identifies three circumstances where a declaration need not be made.[45] Subsection 182(6) provides:

> A director need not declare an interest under this section—
> (a) if it cannot reasonably be regarded as likely to give rise to a conflict of interest;
> (b) if, or to the extent that, the other directors are already aware of it (and for this purpose the other directors are treated as aware of anything of which they ought reasonably to be aware); or
> (c) if, or to the extent that, it concerns terms of his service contract[46] that have been or are to be considered—(i) by a meeting of the directors, or (ii) by a committee of the directors appointed for this purpose under the company's constitution.

This express provision should make it unnecessary for the court to have to consider whether mere technical breaches of disclosure requirements have substantive consequences.[47] Three particular features of s 182(6) deserve comment.

**17.23**   First, s 182(6)(a) imposes no duty if the interest cannot reasonably be regarded as likely to give rise to a conflict of interest.[48] The test is not whether the interest is in fact likely to give rise to a conflict of interest, but whether it cannot reasonably be regarded as likely to give rise to such an interest, a narrower limitation on the duty. The test has no subjective component. The word 'likely' has several different shades of meaning, varying from 'more likely than not' to 'may well'.[49] Given the importance which the law has traditionally ascribed to the need to avoid conflict

---

[45] Again a recommendation of the Law Commission: Law Commission, *Company Directors: Regulating Conflicts of Interest and Formulating a Statement of Duties*, No 261, paras 8.33, 8.44, and 8.45.

[46] See s 227 for the expansive definition of 'service contract'.

[47] This issue was considered in a number of cases all concerned with prospective transactions: *Runciman v Walter Runciman plc* [1992] BCLC 1084, 1093, 1095–6; *Lee Panavision Ltd v Lee Lighting Ltd* [1992] BCLC 22, 33, CA; *Re Dominion International Group Plc (No 2)* [1996] 1 BCLC 572, 598–600 (a directors' disqualification case); *MacPherson v European Strategic Bureau Ltd* [1999] 2 BCLC 203, 219; *Re Marini Ltd* [2004] BCC 172, 194–6. In each case, no substantive effect was given where the breach was merely technical by refusing to grant any equitable remedy even where recognized defences such as acquiescence, delay, and impossibility of *restitutio in integrum* were not available. A strict approach to construction was adopted in *Neptune (Vehicle Washing Equipment) Ltd v Fitzgerald* [1995] 1 BCLC 352, and followed through to trial ([1995] BCC 1000). No declaration would be necessary if the facts of *Neptune* were to recur in the context of the Act ss 182 or 177: see below at paragraph 17.27.

[48] This is to some degree a reflection of Table A, reg 85, which required disclosure only of any 'material' interest of the director.

[49] *Cream Holdings Ltd v Banerjee* [2005] 1 AC 253, 259, HL, per Lord Nicholls.

of duty and interest,[50] it is thought that s 182(6)(a) should be interpreted narrowly, and a director under a duty to disclose the interest even where the possibility of a conflict is somewhat remote.

Secondly, s 182(6)(b) appears to have the effect that a director is under no duty to declare an interest if, or to the extent that, the other directors ought reasonably to be aware of the interest and its extent. It appears, therefore, that a director who knows or suspects that his fellow directors are in fact unaware of his interest (even though they ought to know of it) is, on a strict reading of s 182(6)(b), under no duty to disclose it.

**17.24**

Thirdly, s 182(6)(c) confirms that s 182 applies in respect of directors' service contracts.[51] It was thought to be the law under the predecessors of s 182 and s 177 that the section did not apply solely to contracts which were to go before the board for approval.[52] This is, to some extent, implicitly confirmed by s 182(6)(c)(ii), since it limits the duty to disclose in circumstances in which the relevant contract has been or is to be approved by a committee of the board, and not the board itself.[53]

**17.25**

It is likely that, ordinarily, a director who fails to disclose his interest in respect of his service contract or a variation of it will not be required to disclose that interest in any event, because the other directors will normally be aware of his interest with the consequence that s 182(6)(b) will apply. However, where the service contract or variation to it is not agreed by the board, but, for example, the chief executive alone, or a remuneration committee of the directors, or the composition of the board changes, directors other than the chief executive or members of the committee may not be aware of the relevant transaction or arrangement or of the director's interest in it. In those circumstances, s 182(6)(b) would not, it seems, apply. Thus, a further limitation on the duty to disclose is created by s 182(6)(c), so that there is no duty of disclosure where the relevant interest concerns terms of his service contract that have been or are to be considered by a meeting of directors or a remuneration committee.

**17.26**

---

[50] In *Guinness Plc v Saunders* [1990] 2 AC 663, 694 Lord Templeman said 'section 317 [of the 1985 Act] shows the importance which the legislature attaches to the principle that a company should be protected against a director who has a conflict of interest and duty'.

[51] As was held in respect of 1948 Act, s 199, the predecessor of 1985 Act, s 317, in the *Runciman* case. Simon Brown J was much struck by the absurdity of a director having to disclose his interest in a service contract at a meeting of directors, when all other directors were plainly aware of the director's interest in his own service contract—an absurdity now removed by s 182(6)(b).

[52] *Neptune (Vehicle Washing Equipment) Ltd v Fitzgerald* [1995] 1 BCLC 352, 359.

[53] In line with the Law Commission's recommendation: Law Commission, *Company Directors: Regulating Conflicts of Interest and Formulating a Statement of Duties*, No 261, para 8.38.

# E. Companies with a Sole Director

**17.27**  Where a director of a company is its sole director, and the company is not required to have more than one director, the sole director is under no obligation to declare any interest in an existing transaction or arrangement under s 182 of the Act. The obligation under s 182 is to declare the interest to 'the other directors', and thus where there are no other directors, the section cannot apply.[54] This was confirmed by the Attorney-General who said:[55]

> The Company Law Review recommended that the requirement should be disapplied in respect of a sole director. The Bill implements that recommendation, but only where the company legitimately has just one director . . . this is a common-sense approach. Plainly, a requirement of a sole director to make disclosure to himself is a nonsense. But the position is different where, at that point in time, the company has only one director where it should have more than one—for example, if it were a public company. In that circumstance, [s 186] provides that the sole director must record in writing the nature and extent of his interest in any transaction or arrangement that has been entered into, and that the declaration has to form part of the proceedings at the next meeting of the directors after the notice has been given. The consequence is that there will be a record so that when another director comes along, as should be the case, the position is clear and has been seen. However, I repeat that if a sole director is entitled to be a sole director, the provision does not apply.

**17.28**  Section 186 deals with the position where at the time the company only has one director, but is required to have more than one director.[56] In such a case the sole director's duty to declare his interest is effectively the same as if the other directors had been appointed (except that s 182(6)(b) cannot apply). Section 186(1) provides that the declaration must be recorded in writing, the declaration is deemed to form part of the proceedings at the next meeting of the directors after the notice is given, and the provisions of s 248 of the Act (minutes of meetings of directors) apply as if the declaration had been made at that meeting: s 186(1). In this way the declaration will be made available to the new directors following their appointment.

**17.29**  Nothing in s 186 affects the operation of s 231 of the Act (contract with sole member who is also a director: terms to be set out in writing or recorded in minutes).[57]

---

[54]  The obligation under 1985 Act, s 317 was to declare the interest 'at a meeting of the directors of the company'. It had been held by Lightman J in *Neptune (Vehicle Washing Equipment) Ltd v Fitzgerald* [1995] 1 BCLC 352 that a sole director of a company was under a duty to make the relevant declaration to himself at a duly convened meeting with himself, pause for thought 'though it may be that the declaration does not have to be out loud', and record the declaration in the minutes.

[55]  Hansard, HL GC (9 February 2006) day 4, cols GC 343–344.

[56]  A public company is required to have at least two directors: s 154 of the Act.

[57]  See Chapter 18, paragraphs 18.174–18.182.

# 18

# TRANSACTIONS WITH DIRECTORS REQUIRING APPROVAL OF MEMBERS

# A. Introduction

**18.01**   This chapter covers the provisions in the Companies Act, Part 10, Chapter 4, ss 182–230, which underpin the duties of directors by requiring certain transactions with directors to be approved by the members.[1] It also deals with the special rules, set out in s 231, that apply to contracts with a sole member who is a director.[2]

# B. Directors' Service Contracts

## (1) Requirement of approval of members

*The substantive provisions*

**18.02**   Section 188 of the Act requires the prior approval of members before a company enters into certain long-term service contracts. Section 189 sets out the civil consequences in the event that such approval is not obtained.[3]

**18.03**   Section 188(1)–(4) provides:

(1)  This section applies to provision under which the guaranteed term of a director's employment—
   (a)  with the company of which he is a director, or
   (b)  where he is the director of a holding company, within the group consisting of that company and its subsidiaries,is, or may be, longer than two years.

(2)  A company may not agree to such provision unless it has been approved—
   (a)  by resolution of the members of the company, and
   (b)  in the case of a director of a holding company, by resolution of the members of that company.

(3)  The guaranteed term of a director's employment is—
   (a)  the period (if any) during which the director's employment—
      (i)  is to continue, or may be continued otherwise than at the instance of the company (whether under the original agreement or under a new agreement entered into in pursuance of it), and
      (ii)  cannot be terminated by the company by notice, or can be so terminated only in specified circumstances, or

---

[1]  These sections came into force on 1 October 2007: 2006 Act Commencement Order No 3, art 2(1)(d).

[2]  This section also came into force on 1 October 2007: 2006 Act Commencement Order No 3, art 2(1)(d).

[3]  ss 188 and 189 apply to agreements made on or after 1 October 2007: 2006 Act Commencement Order No 3, Schedule 3, para 6(1). A resolution passed before that date approving the provision made by such an agreement is effective for the purposes of those sections if it complies with the requirements of those sections: ibid para 6(2). 1985 Act, s 319 continues to apply to agreements made before 1 October 2007: ibid, para 6(4).

(b) in the case of employment terminable by the company by notice, the period of
notice required to be given,

or, in the case of employment having a period within paragraph (a) and a period
within paragraph (b), the aggregate of those periods.

(4) If more than six months before the end of the guaranteed term of a director's
employment the company enters into a further service contract (otherwise than in
pursuance of a right conferred, by or under the original contract, on the other party
to it[4]), this section applies as if there were added to the guaranteed term of the new
contract the unexpired period of the guaranteed term of the original contract.

Subsection 188(5) deals with approval by members (paragraph 18.18 below).
Subsection 188(6) provides that no approval is required under s 188 on the part
of the members of a body corporate that is not a UK-registered company, or is a
wholly-owned subsidiary of another body corporate.[5]

Under s 188(7), 'employment' for the purposes of s 188 means any employment **18.04**
under a 'director's service contract', which for the purposes of the 2006 Act,
Part 10, is defined by s 227:

(1) For the purposes of this Part a director's 'service contract', in relation to a company,
means a contract under which—
(a) a director of the company undertakes personally to perform services (as director
or otherwise) for the company, or for a subsidiary of the company, or
(b) services (as director or otherwise) that a director of the company undertakes
personally to perform are made available by a third party to the company, or to
a subsidiary of the company.
(2) The provisions of this Part relating to directors' service contracts apply to the terms
of a person's appointment as a director of a company.

They are not restricted to contracts for the performance of services outside the
scope of the ordinary duties of a director

Lord Sainsbury explained the operation of s 227:[6] **18.05**

In line with the recommendations of the Law Commissioners and the Company
Law Review, the definition of 'service contracts' is expressly extended so that, in
addition to covering contracts of service and contracts for services, it includes letters
of appointment to the office of director. As a result, it covers the terms under which
a director is appointed to that office alone. It operates as follows; subs(1)(a) covers
contracts of service such as any employment contract that the director may hold with
a company or a subsidiary of the company of which he is a director, for example, as
an executive director, or any contract for services that he personally undertakes to

---

[4] In such a case, there is no need for any provision such as s 188(4) to apply, as the contract will
fall within s 188(3)(a)(i).
[5] Where the company is a charity, the prior written consent of the Charity Commission is
necessary notwithstanding this exemption: s 226.
[6] (Hansard, HL GC Day 4, Vol 678, cols 361, 362 (9 February 2006)). Contrary to the apparent
sense of the first clause of the quoted passage, no such recommendation appears to have been made
by either the Law Commissioners or the CLR.

perform as such. Subsection (1)(b) covers the case where those services are made available to the company through a third party such as a personal services company. In either case, the contract must require the director personally to perform the service or services in question. Subsection (2) brings within the definition of a service contract letters of appointment to the office of director. Many directors will have no contract of service or for services with the company. Historically . . . an office has been regarded as a kind of property, with the fees attaching to that office being regarded as an incident of that office. The second sentence of subs (2) ensures that the definition of 'service contracts' includes arrangements under which the director performs duties within the scope of the ordinary duties of the director, as well as contracts to perform duties outside the scope of the ordinary duties of a director. Without that, the term 'service contract' might be interpreted as applying only to the latter type of contract.

**18.06**   Under s 189, if a company agrees to provision in contravention of s 188, the provision is void, to the extent of the contravention (s 189(a)), and the contract is deemed to contain a term entitling the company to terminate it at any time by the giving of reasonable notice (s 189(b)).

**18.07**   For the purposes of ss 188 and 189, a shadow director is treated as a director.[7]

*Comparison with the 1985 Act, s 319*

**18.08**   The Companies Act, ss 188 and 189 derive ultimately from the 1980 Act, ss 47 and 63(1), a White Paper having recommended that directors' service contracts for longer than five years should be approved by the company in general meeting.[8] The purpose of the immediate predecessor of ss 188 and 189 (1985 Act, s 319) was to ensure that a company should not be bound by an obligation to employ a director for more than (at that time) five years unless its members had considered and approved the relevant term, but the purpose was limited to protecting the shareholders.[9] A company is empowered by ordinary resolution at a meeting to remove a director before the expiration of his period of office, notwithstanding anything in any agreement between it and him;[10] but this power does not deprive a person removed of compensation or damages payable to him in respect of the termination of his appointment as director or of any appointment terminating with that as director.[11] Sections 188 and 189 seek to ensure that, save where the members have approved the director's long-term service contract, a company's hands are not tied in deciding whether to remove a director by the prospect of very considerable sums payable by the company by way of compensation or damages.

---

[7]   subs 223(1) and also s 230.
[8]   The Conduct of Company Directors (1977) Cmnd 7037.
[9]   *Wright v Atlas Wright (Europe) Ltd* [1999] 2 BCLC 301, 310, 315, per Potter LJ.
[10]   2006 Act, s 168(1).
[11]   subs 168(5).

Sections 188 and 189 are, in large part, a re-enactment of the 1985 Act, s 319. **18.09**
Section 188 has been re-worded with the aim of clarifying the law: in particular,
the reference to 'guaranteed term' makes the essential purpose clearer. Four
substantive changes should be noted.

First, the duration of the 'guaranteed term' has been significantly reduced from **18.10**
five to two years.[12]

Secondly, although broadly speaking the provisions of the 1985 Act, s 319 for **18.11**
determining when (under that legislation) the five-year limit was exceeded are
repeated in s 188, there are new provisions dealing with the situation where the
company is entitled to terminate the employment by notice. In such a case, the
period of notice required to be given by the company is taken into account in
determining the 'guaranteed term', hence whether the two-year limit is or may be
exceeded. Under subs 188(3)(b), where the director's employment is terminable
by notice, the period of notice required to be given is the 'guaranteed term'. If
the period of notice is, or may be, longer than two years, prior members' approval
is necessary. A service contract for five years, terminable by the company on
12 months' notice, does not require prior members' approval. Under the final two
clauses of subs 188(3), in the case of employment having periods which fall
within both paragraphs 188(3)(a) and 188(3)(b), the two periods are aggregated
for the purposes of determining the 'guaranteed term'. Hence, if the relevant
service contract were for three years, with a provision whereby the company could
give the director notice of termination at the earliest 18 months from commencement, such notice period being 12 months, without the final two clauses of subs
188(3) the guaranteed term of the employment would not exceed two years: the
guaranteed term under subs 188(3)(a) would be only 18 months (ie the period of
the contract during which the company could not give notice), and the guaranteed term under subs 188(3)(b) would be only 12 months (ie the requisite notice
period). By virtue of the aggregation under the final two clauses of s 188(3), the
'guaranteed term' would be two years six months.

---

[12] Despite recommendations of various shorter periods. The Law Commission (in *Company
Directors: Regulating Conflicts of Interest and Formulating a Statement of Duties*, No 261, paras 9.30
and 9.35) recommended three years. CLR: *Final Report*, paras 6.10–6.14 generally recommended
one year, which was consistent with the objective of one year stated in the Combined Code. The
Companies Bill started life by retaining the five-year period, but it was reduced to two years after
an Opposition amendment proposed in House of Lords Grand Committee stage: Hansard, HL
GC Day 4, Vol 678, cols 344–345 (9 February 2006). Lord Hodgson of Astley Abbotts supporting
the amendment and stating: 'Out there in UK Plc or among the general public, if they were to see
us considering long-term contracts of five years, they would consider it an amazing length of time.
It would be laughable against the background of modern corporate governance and practice.'

**18.12**  Thirdly, by means of the new definitions of 'employment' and 'director's service contract',[13] ss 188 and 189 apply to contracts under which a director undertakes to perform services as director or otherwise, apply to the terms of a person's appointment as a director of the company, and are not restricted to contracts for the performance of services outside the scope of the ordinary duties of a director. Under the 1985 Act, subs 319(7), 'employment' was defined as including employment under a contract for services, and hence, explicitly at least, applied only to contracts of service and for services. The new Act will therefore cover, for example, letters of appointment to the office of director.[14]

**18.13**  Fourthly, the Companies Act largely re-enacts the provisions of the 1985 Act relating to approval given (in respect of private companies) by written resolution, and the requirement for a written memorandum incorporating the relevant provision to be sent or submitted to eligible members at or before the time that the proposed resolution is sent or submitted.[15] In a change to the law, the Companies Act, s 224 now provides that, subject to any provision of the company's articles, any accidental failure to send or submit the memorandum to one or more members shall be disregarded for the purpose of determining whether the requirement has been met.

**18.14**  The legal landscape underpinning ss 188 and 189 remains similar to that which obtained under the 1985 Act. At common law, a director is not entitled to remuneration for his services, as he is treated as a trustee and hence, prima facie, not entitled to profit from the trust.[16] That common law rule is abrogated where the articles of association so provide just as, in the case of a trustee *strictu sensu*, the trust instrument so provides.[17] Articles of Association almost invariably make such provision; eg Table A, reg 82, Model Article (pcls) 19 and Model Article (plc) 23. Section 188, however, prohibits the inclusion of provisions under which the guaranteed term of a director's employment exceeds two years unless the prior approval of the members is obtained, whilst s 189 renders the provision void to the extent of the contravention, and deems the contract to contain a term entitling the company to terminate it at any time by the giving of reasonable notice.

**18.15**  A number of features of ss 188 and 189 may be noted. First, the director need not be a party to the relevant contract. A combination of ss 188(7) and 227(1)(b) make clear that the sections apply equally to a contract to which the director is

---

[13]  subs 188(7) and s 227, set out in paragraph 18.04 above.
[14]  Explanatory Notes, para 399.
[15]  subs 188(5)(a), substantially re-enacting 1985 Act, Schedule 15A, para 7.
[16]  *Guinness Plc v Saunders* [1990] 2 AC 663, 689, 700, HL, per Lord Templeman and Lord Goff.
[17]  *Guinness Plc v Saunders*, above.

not a party—for example where the director's services are provided by a service company which he controls.[18]

Secondly, the sections do not, it appears, apply to certain 'rolling contracts'.[19] The **18.16** Law Commission had pointed out that the predecessor of ss 188 and 189 could be, and was in fact being, circumvented by the use of rolling contracts, and thus recommended that, as a matter of necessity, those contracts should be subject to the relevant statutory limit.[20] This recommendation appears not to have been adopted by Parliament.

Where the terms of a service contract are approved by the directors (or any of **18.17** them), and irrespective of ss 188 and 189 of the Act, such directors owe general duties to the company as set out in the 2006 Act, Part 10, Chapter 2, breach of which may render them, as well as the relevant director whose terms of employment are under consideration, liable to the company if such duties are breached. For example, any director has a duty to promote the success of the company (s 172), a duty which applies equally to the agreement of a director's service contract.[21]

### Approval of members

The resolution of the members of the company or holding company may be a **18.18** written resolution or a resolution at a meeting,[22] but subs 188(5) lays down certain requirements for a valid resolution under subs 188(2):

> (5) A resolution approving provision to which this section applies must not be passed unless a memorandum setting out the proposed contract incorporating the provision is made available to members—
>
> (a) in the case of a written resolution, by being sent or submitted to every eligible[23] member at or before the time at which the proposed resolution is sent or submitted to him;
>
> (b) In the case of a resolution at a meeting, by being made available for inspection by members of the company both—
>
> (i) at the company's registered office for not less than 15 days ending with the date of the meeting, and
>
> (ii) at the meeting itself.

---

[18] See the quotation from Lord Sainsbury in paragraph 18.05 above.

[19] Law Commission Consultation Paper *Company Directors: Regulating Conflicts of Interest and Formulating a Statement of Duties*, No 153, paras 4.161–4.162.

[20] *Company Directors: Regulating Conflicts of Interest and Formulating a Statement of Duties*, No 261, paras 9.33 and 9.35.

[21] See, under the old law where the equitable duty upon the directors was to act bona fide in the interests of the company: *Runciman v Walter Runciman Plc* [1992] BCLC 1084, 1097–8.

[22] For resolutions of members, see Chapter 22 of this work.

[23] For the definition of 'eligible member' see s 289: essentially, it means those members entitled to vote on the resolution on the circulation date of the resolution (as itself defined in s 290). As was the case under the 1985 Act, where the written resolution procedure is used, it is only those members entitled to vote who are entitled to the memorandum: whereas, if an actual meeting is held, all members can inspect the memorandum.

Eligible members are those members entitled to vote on the resolution on the circulation date of the resolution (as itself defined in s 290).[24] As was the case under the 1985 Act, where the written resolution procedure is used, it is only those members entitled to vote who are entitled to the memorandum: whereas, if an actual meeting is held, all members can inspect the memorandum. Subject to any provision of the company's articles, any accidental failure to send or submit the memorandum to one or more members shall be disregarded for the purpose of determining whether the requirement has been met.[25]

**18.19**　In relation to the 1985 Act, the Court of Appeal held that the properly informed unanimous consent of all shareholders entitled to attend and vote at the general meeting of the company, given informally, overrode the statutory formalities for member approval under s 319, given that the sole purpose of s 319 was to protect the shareholders.[26] There is no reason to believe that the position has altered under the Act.

### (2) Service contracts to be available for inspection

**18.20**　Section 228 provides for a copy of a director's service contract or memorandum of terms to be available for inspection. Subsection 228(1) provides:

> A company must keep available for inspection a copy of every director's service contract with the company or with a subsidiary of the company, or if the contract is not in writing, a written memorandum setting out the terms of the contract.[27]

Lord Sainsbury explained that 'a memorandum is nothing more than a proper written record of the terms of the contract or agreement', which is required to prevent avoidance of the requirements of ss 228 and 229 by use of an oral contract.[28] The provisions apply to a variation of a director's service contract as they apply to the original contract.[29]

---

[24]　s 289 defines 'eligible member' and s 290 identifies the circulation date.

[25]　s 224.

[26]　*Wright v Atlas-Wright (Europe) Ltd* [1999] 2 BCLC 301, CA.

[27]　A director includes a shadow director: s 230. 'Service contract' is defined by s 227. 2006 Act, ss 228 to 230 apply to contracts within s 227(1) of that Act entered into on or after 1 October 2007, appointments within s 227(2) made on or after that date, and contracts to which 1985 Act, s 318(1) applied immediately before that date: 2006 Act Commencement Order No 3, para 13(1). The provisions of 1985 Act, s 318 continue to apply in relation to any default made before 1 October 2007 in complying with s 318(1) or (5); any request for inspection under s 318(7) made before that date; and any duty to give notice under s 318(4) arising before that date: ibid, para 13(4).

[28]　Hansard, HL GC Day 4, cols 362–363 (9 February 2006). There followed some debate in which certain members of the Committee expressed some doubts as to whether the requirement for a memorandum meant that all the terms of the contract had to be accurately set out: ibid, Lords Wedderburn and Freeman.

[29]　subs 228(7).

All such copies and memoranda must be available for inspection at the company's **18.21** registered office, or a place specified in regulations.[30] The copies and memoranda must be retained by the company for at least one year from the date of termination or expiry of the contract and must be kept available for inspection during that time.[31] The company must give notice to the Registrar of Companies of the place at which the copies and memoranda are kept available for inspection, and of any change in that place, unless they have at all times been kept at the company's registered office.[32]

If default is made in complying with the provisions of subss 228(1)–(3) (or in the **18.22** case of the obligation to give notice to the registrar of companies under s 228(4), if default is made for 14 days in complying with that obligation), an offence is committed by every officer of the company who is in default.[33]

Section 229 states the right of every member to inspect and take a copy of a **18.23** director's service contract or memorandum of terms.

(1) Every copy or memorandum required to be kept under section 228 must be open to inspection by any member of the company without charge.
(2) Any member of the company is entitled, on request and on payment of such fee as may be prescribed, to be provided with a copy of any such copy or memorandum.

The copy must be provided within seven days after the request is received by the company.

If an inspection required under s 229(1) is refused, or default is made in comply- **18.24** ing with s 229(2), an offence is committed by every officer of the company who is in default.[34] In the case of any such refusal or default the court may by order compel an immediate inspection or, as the case may be, direct that the copy required be sent to the person requiring it.[35]

---

[30] subs 228(2). The regulations are made by the Secretary of State under s 1136. Until regulations are made under that section specifying a place for the purposes of s 228(2)(b), the copies and memoranda referred to in s 228 may be kept by a company at any place where its register of members is kept, or at its principal place of business, provided that place is situated in the part of the United Kingdom in which the company is registered: 2006 Act Commencement Order No 3, Schedule 3, para 13(2).

[31] subs 228(3).

[32] subs 228(4). See 2006 Act, s 1068 for delivery by electronic means. Until s 1068(1) comes into force the notice referred to in s 228(4) must be given on the form prescribed for the purposes of 1985 Act, s 318(4): 2006 Act Commencement Order, Schedule 3, para 13(3).

[33] subs 228(5). Unlike 1985 Act, s 318(8) the company is not guilty of an offence. A person guilty of an offence is liable on summary conviction to a fine under subs 228(6).

[34] subs 229(3). Unlike 1985 Act, s 318(8) the company is not guilty of an offence. A person guilty of an offence is liable on summary conviction to a fine under subs 229(4).

[35] subs 229(5). In *Pelling v Families Need Fathers Ltd* [2002] 1 BCLC 645, CA, the Court of Appeal considered the similarly worded provision relating to the enforcement of a member's right to inspect the register of members under 1985 Act, s 356(6) (replaced and substantially altered by 2006 Act, ss 116 and 117). The Court of Appeal there decided that the court's power to order

*Discussion and comparison with the 1985 Act, s 318*

**18.25**  Sections 228 and 229 are substantially re-enactments of the 1985 Act, s 318, having their ultimate origin in the 1967 Act, s 26.[36] The following are the main changes.

**18.26**  The obligation to retain copies and memoranda and allow inspection persists for longer than under the 1985 Act, and the scope of the copies and memoranda to be kept is broader in one respect. Under s 228(3), the copies and memoranda must be retained, and inspection allowed, whilst the contract is in force and for a year beyond its termination or expiry; whereas under the 1985 Act, s 318(11) no copy had to be kept or inspection allowed of any copy contract or memorandum which had less than a year to run, or in relation to a contract which could be terminated by the company on 12 months' notice or less without payment of compensation.[37]

**18.27**  Under the 2006 Act, members have a new right of requesting a copy of the copy contract or memorandum on payment of the prescribed fee.[38] The right under the 1985 Act, s 318 was to inspect, though by statutory instrument the person inspecting was permitted to copy any information made available for inspection by means of the taking of notes or the transcription of the information.[39]

**18.28**  The new definition of director's 'service contract' incorporated in ss 228 and 229 by reason of s 227 expressly covers contracts of service, contracts for service and letters of appointment. A contract whereby the director's services are provided through a service company is now expressly covered.

**18.29**  The 1985 Act did not apply if the contract required the director to work wholly or mainly outside the United Kingdom, merely requiring the company to keep and allow inspection of a memorandum specifying the director's name, the provisions of the contract relating to its duration, and (if the contract was with a

---

inspection was discretionary. Although the court would normally make a mandatory order to give effect to a legal right (by analogy, the legal right of inspection or to a copy under s 229(1) and (2)), and although the criminal sanctions attaching to the failure to allow inspection (by analogy, the criminal sanctions contained in subs 229(3)) underscored the importance of the right and obligation of the company, the grant of a mandatory order was not a matter of unqualified right, and in special circumstances could be refused. The order could be made subject to terms and conditions.

[36]  Which applied only to contracts with the company itself. The provisions were extended to contracts with a subsidiary by 1980 Act, s 61.

[37]  Enacting a recommendation of the Law Commission: Law Commission Report, *Company Directors: Regulating Conflicts of Interest and Formulating a Statement of Duties*, No 261, para 9.17.

[38]  subs 229(2); the Companies (Fees for Inspection and Copying of Company Records) Regulations (SI 2007/2612).

[39]  Companies (Inspection and Copying of Registers, Indices and Documents) Regulations 1991 (SI 1991/1998), reg 3(2)(b). That regulation was not to be construed as obliging a company to provide any facilities additional to those provided for the purposes of facilitating inspection: ibid, reg 3(3).

subsidiary) the name and place of incorporation of that subsidiary, but no such limitations on the obligation to keep and allow inspection appear in the 2006 Act.[40]

**18.30** The copies and memoranda must be kept at the company's registered office or a place specified under regulations by the Secretary of State. Previously, the company and its officers had the option of keeping the contracts or memoranda at the registered office, or the place where its register of members was kept (if different) or its principal place of business (provided that was situated in that part of Great Britain in which the company was registered and that all copies and memoranda are kept at the same place). Although the wording of s 228 is less explicit in this regard, subss 228(2) and (4) implicitly mandate that all copies and memoranda must be similarly kept in the same place.

**18.31** Finally some limitations on the obligations on the company to keep and allow inspection of copy contracts or memoranda, and on the right of inspection may be noted. There is no obligation on the company to keep and allow inspection of documentation collateral to the contract. The obligation extends, it appears, in the case of a written contract only to documents which contain the terms of the contract (and in the case of a memorandum, thus where the contract is unwritten, the memorandum must contain the terms, hence apparently all terms, of the contract).[41]

## C. Substantial Property Transactions

### (1) The substantive provisions

**18.32** The Companies Act, Part 10, Chapter 4, ss 190–196 contains provisions prohibiting a company from entering into an arrangement under which a director of the company or its holding company, or a person connected with such a director, directly or indirectly acquires or is to acquire a 'substantial non-cash asset' from the company, or the company acquires or is to acquire such an asset from such a person, unless the arrangement is approved by resolution of the members.[42]

---

[40] 1985 Act, subs 318(5). The change enacts a recommendation of the Law Commission: Law Commission Report, *Company Directors: Regulating Conflicts of Interest and Formulating a Statement of Duties*, No 261, para 9.14.

[41] Law Commission Consultation Paper, *Company Directors: Regulating Conflicts of Interest and Formulating a Statement of Duties*, No 153, para 9.18–9.20. CLR: *Completing the Structure*, recommended the extension to such documents, apparently under the impression that the Law Commission had itself made that recommendation. Parliament did not act on the recommendation.

[42] ss 190 to 196 apply to arrangements or transactions entered into on or after 1 October 2007: 2006 Act Commencement Order No 3, Schedule 3, para 7(1). A resolution passed before that date approving an arrangement or transaction is effective if it complies with the requirements of those

**18.33**    Subsection 190(1) provides:

> (1) A company may not enter into an arrangement under which—
>
>     (a) a director of the company or of its holding company, or a person connected with such a director, acquires or is to acquire from the company (directly or indirectly) a substantial non-cash asset, or
>
>     (b) the company acquires or is to acquire a substantial non-cash asset (directly or indirectly) from such a director or a person so connected,
>
> unless the arrangement has been approved by a resolution of the members of the company or is conditional on such approval being obtained.[43]

For the purposes of this section a director includes shadow director.[44] The prohibition is subject to a number of exceptions: see paragraphs 18.54–18.59 below.

**18.34**    'Non-cash asset' means 'any property or interest in property, other than cash', and 'cash' includes foreign currency.[45] A reference to the transfer or acquisition of a non-cash asset includes '(a) the creation or extinction of an estate or interest in, or a right over, any property, and (b) the discharge of the liability of any person, other than a liability for a liquidated sum'. [46]

**18.35**    'Substantial non-cash asset' is explained in s 191, whereby a non-cash asset is a substantial asset in relation to a company if its value exceeds 10% of the company's asset value and is more than £5,000, or exceeds £100,000.[47] For this purpose, a company's 'asset value' at any time is the value of the company's net assets determined by reference to its most recent statutory accounts, or if no statutory accounts have been prepared, the amount of the company's called up share capital.[48] Whether an asset is a substantial asset is to be determined as at the time the arrangement is entered into.

**18.36**    If the director or connected person is a director of the company's holding company or a person connected with such a director, the arrangement must also

---

sections: ibid, para 7(2). 1985 Act, ss 330–342 continue to apply in relation to arrangements or transactions entered into before that date: ibid, para 7(3).

    [43] Where a company is a charity, any approval given by members of the company under this section is ineffective without the prior written consent of the Charity Commission: s 226.

    [44] subs 223(1)(b). 'Holding company' is defined in Companies Act, s 1159: see also s 1160 and Schedule 6. Section 252 explains when a person is connected with a director (see further Chapter 3, Section D of this work).

    [45] subs 1163(1).

    [46] subs 1163(2). It has been held under the predecessor of subs 1163(2) that 'any person' does not include the company itself, so that the predecessor of s 190 applied only where the company discharges the liability of another person, not its own liability: *Gooding v Cater* (unreported) 13 March 1989, Edward Nugee QC.

    [47] The Secretary of State has power to vary the sum under 2006 Act, s 258.

    [48] A company's 'statutory accounts' means its annual accounts prepared in accordance with 2006 Act, Part 15, and by s 191(4) its 'most recent' statutory accounts are those in relation to which the time for sending them out to members under s 424 is most recent.

have been approved by a resolution of the members of the holding company or conditional on such approval being obtained.[49]

**18.37**  The civil consequences of contravention of s 190 are set out in s 195: see paragraphs 18.66–18.78 below.

### (2) Comparison with the Companies Act, s 320

**18.38**  Subsections 190(1) and (2) very substantially re-enact the 1985 Act, s 320(1). Three main changes have been made. First, the prohibition applies where the director or the person connected with the director acquires or is to acquire *directly or indirectly* the substantial non-cash asset from the company, and likewise where the company acquires or is to acquire the substantial non-cash asset *directly or indirectly* from a director or person connected.

**18.39**  Secondly, whereas the 1985 Act, s 320 required prior approval of the company in general meeting, a company may now enter into such an arrangement conditional on approval by members' resolution.[50] A company is not subject to any liability by reason of a failure to obtain approval required by s 190.[51]

**18.40**  Thirdly, by reason of s 190(5), an arrangement involving more than one non-cash asset, or an arrangement that is one of a series involving non-cash assets, is treated as if they involved a non-cash asset of a value equal to the aggregate value of all the non-cash assets involved in the arrangement or, as the case may be, the series. The purpose is to avoid the artificial structuring of arrangements and transactions so as to bring each individual arrangement or transaction under the financial minima set out in s 191, and hence outside the scope of the Act.

### (3) The prohibition: essential elements

**18.41**  The similarity between the 1985 Act, ss 320–322 and the 2006 Act ss 190–196 suggests that case law decided under the 1985 Act will generally continue to be authoritative. Sections 190–196 constitute the latest enactment of parts of a fasciculus of provisions first enacted in the 1980 and 1981 Acts intended to sharpen up the protections of companies against being improperly exploited to the companies' detriment.[52] The thinking behind the requirement for members'

---

[49] subs 190(2).

[50] subs 190(1). The Law Commission found that the requirement of prior members' approval under the 1985 Act placed the company at a commercial disadvantage if the other party to the arrangement was not willing to wait whilst approval was obtained: Law Commission Consultation Paper, *Company Directors: Regulating Conflicts of Interest and Formulating a Statement of Duties*, No 153, para 4.192.

[51] subs 190(3).

[52] *NBH Ltd v Hoare* [2006] 2 BCLC 649, 662, per Park J. A fasciculus means 'a group of sections or paragraphs [of an Act] marked by a cross-heading' (Bennion, *Statutory Interpretation* (5th edn),

approval of substantial property transactions is that if a company by its directors enters into a substantial commercial transaction with one of their number, there is a danger that their judgment may be distorted by conflicts of interest. The requirement of members' approval is designed to protect a company against such distortions.[53]

### An 'arrangement'

**18.42**  For s 190 to apply, first, there must be an 'arrangement' within the meaning of subs 190(1). 'Arrangement' is not defined by the Act. It was decided under the 1985 Act that it was a word widely used by Parliament to include arrangements or understandings having no contractual effect.[54]

### 'Acquire'

**18.43**  Secondly, the arrangement entered into by the director, connected person, or company must be one under which such person acquires or is to acquire a substantial non-cash asset. The reference in s 190 to the acquisition of a non-cash asset is given a broad inclusive definition of 'acquire' given by s 1163(2) of the Act. The breadth of the definition is such that non-cash assets can, in certain circumstances, be deemed to have been acquired for the purposes of s 190 in circumstances where, as a matter of normal usage, no acquisition of the asset would be considered to have taken place at all.[55]

**18.44**  In *Duckwari plc v Offerventure Ltd*,[56] a company (O) had agreed to purchase real property from a third party, and paid a 10% deposit. Prior to completion of the sale, O agreed that another company (D) should take over the purchase contract. D was connected with one of the directors of O. The approval of the members of D was not obtained. After D had acquired the property, the property market fell and D sued O for breach of the 1985 Act, s 320, the predecessor of s 190. The precise legal nature of the 'taking over' was in dispute. O contended that, on its true analysis, the contract of purchase between the third party and O must have been novated in favour of D. The Court of Appeal decided that, as a matter of fact,

---

p 749) and which, through its ultimate Latin root, has given us both fascism and faggot (in most of its current meanings, including the slang).

[53]  *British Racing Drivers' Club v Hextall Erskine* [1997] 1 BCLC 182, 198, per Carnwath J, remarking that the requirement for members' approval did not necessarily mean that the members would exercise a better commercial judgment: but it did make it likely that the proposed arrangement would be more widely ventilated and a more objective decision reached.

[54]  *Re Duckwari Plc* [1998] Ch 253, 260, CA, per Nourse LJ; *Murray v Leisureplay plc* [2004] EWHC 1927 (QB), per Stanley Burnton J at para 106 referring to the Restrictive Practices Act 1976 (not affected by the decision of the Court of Appeal [2005] EWCA Civ 963).

[55]  *Ultraframe (UK) Ltd v Fielding* [2005] EWHC 1638 (Ch) at paras 1369–1387, referring to the acquisition of the licence in respect of intellectual property rights.

[56]  [1997] 2 BCLC 713, Ch and CA.

the nature of the arrangement was a bilateral agreement whereby O agreed to allow D to acquire the rights under the contract by directing the third party to convey to D. Millett LJ, however, considered it arguable that even if the true nature of the arrangement had been a novation, this did not mean that there was no acquisition of an asset by D. By reason of the 1985 Act, s 739(2) (the predecessor of s 1163(2)), by which acquisition includes the 'extinction . . . of an estate or interest in, or right over, any property . . .', a novation, which would necessarily involve the consent of the initial contracting party, might constitute the acquisition of an asset from that contracting party. The addition of the words 'directly or indirectly' in s 190(1)(a) suggests that, were an arrangement similar to that undertaken in the *Duckwari* case to occur now, but effected by a novation, such an arrangement would indeed fall within s 190(1).

Section 190 applies not only to arrangements whereby the company, director, or **18.45** connected person actually acquires a substantial non-cash asset, but also to arrangements whereby such person is to acquire such an asset. The company may have remedies for non-compliance with s 190 even where the relevant asset is never in fact acquired by the company. Thus, if the company enters into an arrangement for the acquisition of an asset, the requisite members' approval under s 190 is not obtained, and the acquisition is never completed, the company may still be able to recover for any loss or damage suffered by it resulting from the arrangement, for example money spent on due diligence.[57]

### 'Non-cash asset'

Thirdly, the director, connected person, or company must acquire a 'non-cash **18.46** asset'. The definition is given in s 1163(1) of the Act: see paragraph 18.34 above. In straightforward cases, the identification of the asset acquired will be obvious: if the arrangement is a contract of sale, for example. The characterization of the relevant assets in other arrangements may be more difficult. On the facts of *Duckwari*, the Court of Appeal held that the asset acquired was a single asset which could be described in one of two ways with equal accuracy, namely the benefit of the purchase contract, or company O's beneficial interest in the property subject of the purchase contract.[58]

---

[57] *Murray v Leisureplay Plc* [2005] IRLR 946, CA.
[58] [1997] 2 BCLC 713, 724, 725, per Millett LJ. A similar conclusion was reached by Lewison J in *Ultraframe (UK) Ltd v Fielding* [2005] EWHC 1638 (Ch) at paras 1395–1410, when considering whether 1985 Act, s 320 applied to the sale by a receiver of a company's charged assets. The judge held that in such circumstances, the relevant 'non-cash asset' for the purposes of s 320 was not the assets themselves, but the equity of redemption in the charged assets, since this alone was owned by the company: see paragraph 18.50 below.

**18.47**   In *Lander v Premier Pict Petroleum Ltd*,[59] a director's service contract was amended so as to provide that if control of the company's share capital was taken by a third party, the director had the option of terminating the service contract whereupon he would become entitled to payment of three times his annual salary from the company and various pension contributions. Following the exercise of the option by the director, he sued for payment of these various sums, and proceedings were defended on the basis, inter alia, that the amendment was voidable under the 1985 Act, s 320 since the option granted by the amendment was a non-cash asset. The Court of Session (Outer House) rejected that defence on several bases. The court held that since the option was incapable of assignment, it did not constitute 'property or [an] interest in property, other than cash' within the meaning of what is now s 1163(1); further, the rights granted under the option were rights to cash payments, so that the rights were not rights to property 'other than cash'.[60]

**18.48**   In *Ultraframe (UK) Ltd v Fielding*,[61] issues arose as to whether a number of different arrangements involved the acquisition of a 'non-cash asset' within the meaning of the 1985 Act, s 320. The grant by the directors of a company of a lease to that company was held to fall within s 320, and the relevant non-cash asset was the lease itself, not the right to possession granted to the company under the lease.[62] A licence to exploit certain intellectual property rights was held not to constitute 'any property or interest in property' within the meaning of what is now s 1163(1), on the basis that the licence was a mere authority and created no proprietary interest in the intellectual property rights. Nonetheless, Lewison J held that the grant of the licence did constitute the acquisition of a non-cash asset within the meaning of what is now s 1163(2), as the grant constituted 'the creation . . . of . . . a right over, any property' under what is now s 1163(2). Hence what is now s 190 applied.[63] By reason of the broad inclusive definition in s 1163(2), the meaning of the word 'acquire' is thus extended well beyond its typical application. In effect, Lewison J reasoned that whilst the licence itself was not property or an interest in property, and hence not itself a 'non-cash asset' under what is now s 1163(1), the trade marks in respect of which the licence was granted were

---

[59]   [1998] BCC 248.

[60]   [1998] BCC 248, 254. This conclusion is questionable. The definition in what is now s 1163 indicates that cash means cash (including foreign currency): the Court of Session's reasoning would suggest that a debt, for example, would not be a non-cash asset. Contrast *Sylfaen Constructions Ltd v Davies* (HHJ Nicholas Chambers QC, 18 August 2000, unreported) at para 16: 'The fact that an asset may be turned into cash does not make it a cash asset.'

[61]   [2005] EWHC 1638 (Ch).

[62]   *Ultraframe (UK) Ltd v Fielding* [2005] EWHC 1638 (Ch) at paras 1369–1372. This led to the conclusion that the value of that asset was the capital value of the lease itself, not the value of the right to occupy: see paragraph 18.50 below. In *Joint Receivers and Managers of Niltan Carson Ltd v Hawthorne* [1988] BCLC 298, decided under 1980 Act, s 48 (the predecessor of 1985 Act, s 320) the parties and Hodgson J assumed that the section applied to a lease.

[63]   Ibid at paras 1373–1387.

undoubtedly property and thus non-cash assets. The grant of the licence in respect of that property (ie the trade marks) created a right over that property in favour of the licensee within the meaning of what is now s 1163(2)(a). Hence, for the purposes of what is now s 190, the trade marks themselves were acquired (within the meaning ascribed to that word by what is now s 1163(2)(b)) by the licensee by virtue of the grant of the licence.

*'Substantial' non-cash asset*

The meaning of 'substantial' is explained in s 191 of the Act: see paragraph 18.35 **18.49** above.[64] Whether an asset is a substantial asset is determined as at the time that the arrangement is entered into. The focus of s 190 is on the members approving the arrangement at inception, and therefore if s 190 is to apply at all, the requisite value of the non-cash asset must be established at that time. Thus, if a company enters into a trading arrangement with one of its directors, under which the director is obliged to supply an indeterminate amount of, say, raw materials to the company, if the minimum value of those supplies determined as at the date of the arrangement cannot be shown to exceed the requisite values under s 191, the section will not apply and member approval is unnecessary.[65] For s 190 to apply, it is not necessary to establish what the value of the non-cash asset is: but it is necessary to establish that, at a minimum, its value exceeds those set out in s 191.[66] The burden of establishing that the value of the non-cash asset exceeds those minima lies on the party seeking relief.[67]

The value of the non-cash asset will, of course, depend on what non-cash asset is **18.50** acquired, which may depend on the characterization of the arrangement or transaction by the court. Thus, for example, in the *Duckwari* case the non-cash asset was the benefit of the purchase contract or (another way of describing the same thing) the transferring company's beneficial interest in the property. Hence the value was the value of the property less the unpaid element of the purchase price, or (the same thing) the value of the property less the unpaid vendor's lien. In *Ultraframe*, as concerns the sale by a receiver of the assets of the company, the non-cash asset was the company's equity of redemption in those assets, and hence it was the value of that equity which had to be proven for the purposes of what is now s 191, not the value of the assets themselves. Also in *Ultraframe*, concerning the creation of a lease by directors in favour of the company, the non-cash asset was the lease itself, not the right to possession acquired under the lease, and hence the

---

[64] Derived with changes from 1985 Act, s 320(2).
[65] Cf the *Ultraframe* case at paras 1390–1393.
[66] Ibid at para 1392; *Sylfaen Constructions Ltd v Davies* (HHJ Nicholas Chambers QC, 18 August 2000, unreported) at para 19.
[67] *Joint Receivers and Managers of Niltan Carson Ltd v Hawthorne* [1988] BCLC 298, 321.

relevant value was the capital value of the lease, not the value of the right to possession as evidenced by the rental covenant.[68]

**18.51**  Section 191 gives no guidance as to how the value of the non-cash asset is to be determined. There may be cases where the value of the non-cash asset to the company, and indeed its market value, is significantly less than the value of the non-cash asset to the acquiring director or connected person. For example, a strip of land transferred by the company to one of its directors may have little value in itself, but may have considerable value to the owner of adjoining land if the strip is necessary for the development of that other land. Similar circumstances came before the Court of Session (Outer House) in *Micro Leisure Ltd v County Properties & Developments Ltd*.[69] The issue arose on an application to amend pleadings so as to allege that the value of land transferred by a company to entities connected with its directors was higher than the value of the land in isolation, by reason of its 'marriage value' with adjacent land also owned by the connected entities. Allowing the amendment, Lord Hamilton reasoned that since the purpose behind what is now s 190 was to afford protection to members in respect of transactions which might benefit directors to the benefit of the company, Parliament intended that the value of a non-cash asset had to be determined in the context of the particular circumstances of the arrangement, which circumstances would include the fact that the land had a particular increased value to the owners of adjacent land—at least where the board of the company was aware of that fact.[70] That reasoning is, it is submitted, correct. It is further submitted that the knowledge of the directors is irrelevant.

**18.52**  In the *Ultraframe* case, the grant of a debenture by a company was held not to fall within the 1985 Act, s 320 on the basis that 'the company parts with nothing of value when it grants a debenture; and the consideration it receives is incapable of being valued in money or money's worth, and cannot therefore be a "non-cash asset" of the requisite value'.[71] In so deciding, Lewison J relied on the decision in *Re MC Bacon Ltd*,[72] where it was held on similar grounds that the grant of a

---

[68] In *Joint Receivers and Managers of Niltan Carson Ltd v Hawthorne* Hodgson J reached the same conclusion at 321.

[69] [2000] BCC 872.

[70] [2000] BCC 872, 874, 875.

[71] Ibid at paras 1388–1389. The passage quoted deals with two different analyses whereby the grant of a debenture might fall within what is now s 190. First, the charge itself in favour of the chargee might constitute the acquisition of a substantial non-cash asset by the chargee (the first clause of the passage quoted); secondly, whatever consideration is given by the chargee might constitute the acquisition of a substantial non-cash asset by the company (the second clause). As to the latter, given that (as in *MC Bacon*) the consideration in question was constituted by such nebulous expectations as the forbearance of the creditor, it appears to have been inherently incapable of valuation on the facts: and in any event, it is difficult to see that any 'non-cash asset' was acquired by the company.

[72] [1990] BCLC 324.

debenture could not constitute a transaction at an undervalue within the meaning of Insolvency Act, s 238. It appears that Lewison J did not reason that the grant of a debenture in favour of a director or connected person was not the acquisition of a 'non-cash asset' within the meaning of what is now s 1163: rather, his reasoning was that no *value* could be ascribed to that non-cash asset (or to the consideration moving from the chargee), and hence there was no acquisition of a *substantial* non-cash asset. Indeed, in the context of s 1163(1), it is difficult to see why the interest of a chargee is not 'property or an interest in property',[73] or in any event (and following the reasoning of Lewison J on the licence issue, above) why the grant of a debenture by a company is not 'the creation of . . . a right over . . . any property' (the relevant property being the property which is charged to the chargee) within the meaning of s 1163(2). If so, the grant of debentures to a person could constitute the acquisition of a non-cash asset by that person within the meaning of s 190(1)(a).

Whether the grant of the debenture in *Ultraframe* could constitute the acquisition of a *substantial* non-cash asset by the chargee thus depended on whether the requisite value could be ascribed to the debenture for the purposes of what is now s 191. Relying on *MC Bacon*, Lewison J stated that 'the company parts with nothing of value when it grants a debenture'. This contention, which appears to have been conceded by counsel, is doubtful. Security is of undoubted value to any creditor of a company, and hence the ability to grant security must have value. In *Hill v Spread Trustee Ltd*[74] Arden LJ stated that there was no reason why the value of a right to have recourse to security and to take priority over other creditors should be left out of account when considering the value of the consideration moving between the parties to a putative transaction defrauding creditors under Insolvency Act 1986 s 423.[75] If, therefore, a charge has value, the next issue is whether it can be ascribed a value in excess of one of the statutory minima found in s 191. There might in many cases be difficulties in proving that the value of a charge exceeded the statutory minima: though since, for example, a grant of security might be reflected in an interest rate differential between secured and unsecured lending, in principle a certain value in excess of the statutory minima might be ascribed. **18.53**

---

[73] This is obviously so in the case of a mortgage or specific charge: and in the case of a floating charge, it creates a present proprietary interest albeit in a fund of circulating capital rather than over any specific asset: see eg *National Westminster Bank Plc v Spectrum Plus Ltd* [2005] 2 AC 680, 729, 730, HL, per Lord Walker.

[74] [2007] 1 WLR 2404, CA.

[75] Ibid at para 138. To some degree, the reasoning in *MC Bacon* was doubted. It is not clear to what extent Arden LJ relied on the fact that the relevant charges in the *Hill* case were by way of mortgage, though her reasoning on value would apply equally to a floating charge.

### (4) Exceptions to the requirements for member approval

**18.54** No approval is required under s 190 on the part of the members of a body corporate that is not a UK-registered company or is a wholly-owned subsidiary of another body corporate.[76]

**18.55** Section 190 does not apply to a transaction so far as it relates to anything to which a director of a company is entitled under his services contract, or to payment for loss of office as defined in s 215 (payments requiring members' approval).[77] This provision is new, but probably merely clarifies rather than changes the law.[78]

**18.56** By s 192 approval is not required under s 190:

(a) for a transaction between a company and a person in his character as a member of that company, or

(b) for a transaction between—
   (i) a holding company and its wholly-owned subsidiary, or
   (ii) two wholly-owned subsidiaries of the same holding company.[79]

Exception (a) was explained by Lord Sainsbury as being:

> . . . intended to cover transactions such as the payment of the [sic] dividend in specie as well as the distribution of assets to a member of a company during the winding-up of the company and in satisfaction of his rights qua member in the liquidation. Likewise a duly sanctioned return of capital in the form of non-cash assets would fall within this exception. It is also intended to put beyond doubt that the issue of shares or other rights to a member does not require approval under the rules for substantial property transactions.[80]

**18.57** By s 193, where a company is being wound up (unless the winding up is a members' voluntary winding up), or the company is in administration,[81] members' approval is not required under s 190 on the part of the members of a company or for an arrangement entered into by a company. The exception relating to a company which is being wound up is substantially a re-enactment of the 1985 Act, s 321(2)(b), albeit that its precise method of operation differs. The exception relating to a company in administration is new. If the purpose underlying s 190 is to protect a company against the danger that the directors'

---

[76] subs 190(5); substantially a re-enactment of 1985 Act, s 321(1). For the meaning of 'subsidiary', see 2006 Act, s 1159, also s 1160 and Schedule 6. Where the company is a charity, the prior written consent of the Charity Commission is necessary notwithstanding this exemption: s 226.

[77] subs 190(6).

[78] *Gooding v Cater* (unreported) 13 March 1989; also *Lander v Premier Pict Petroleum Ltd* [1998] BCC 248.

[79] Substantially a re-enactment of 1985 Act, s 321(2)(a) and (3), although the scope of s 321(3) has been extended. For the definitions of 'holding company' and 'wholly-owned subsidiary' see 2006 Act, s 1159, also s 1160 and Schedule 6.

[80] Hansard HL GC Day 4 (9 February 2006) col 347.

[81] Within the meaning of Insolvency Act, Schedule B1.

judgment may be distorted by conflicts of interest when the transaction is with one of their number, that danger does not exist where the company is in insolvent winding up or administration, nor is it likely that the shareholders have any interest in the transaction in any event. This was confirmed by Lord Sainsbury:[82]

> The point of the exception [ie under s 193] is that when a company is being wound up or is in administration, the conduct of the company's affairs is no longer in the hands of the members. If a liquidator or administrator is content with the substantial property transaction, it is not appropriate to require approval under [s 190], either by the members of the company being wound up or in administration, or by the members of its holding company.

There is no exception where the company is in administrative (or other) receiver-  **18.58**
ship.[83] The failure of Parliament to create such an exception[84] is unlikely to create practical difficulties, certainly as time passes. First, since the relevant provisions of the Enterprise Act 2002 came into force on 15 September 2003, the holder of a qualifying floating charge may now appoint an administrator, who will of course benefit from the statutory exemption. Secondly, Lewison J has decided in the *Ultraframe* case that the relevant 'non-cash asset' which is sold by an administrative receiver when he sells the business of a company in administrative receivership is the equity of redemption in those assets, not the assets unencumbered (paragraph 18.50 above).[85] If this decision is correct (as, it is submitted, it is in the result), members' approval under s 190 will only be required where the

---

[82] Hansard, HL Report Stage, Vol.681, col 870 (9 May 2006).

[83] In *Demite Ltd v Protec Health Ltd* [1998] BCC 638, Park J had held that 1985 Act, s 320 applied to a sale of the business of a company in administrative receivership. The Law Commission considered whether there should be such an exception, first in the consultation paper on directors' duties, then in the Report itself. The Law Commission recommended that there should be no exemption for administrative receivers, apparently on the basis that a company in administrative receivership was not necessarily insolvent on a balance sheet basis (thus the shareholders might have a residual interest in the assets), and because of the possibility of abuse where the receiver was appointed by a director or connected person. Against this, the Law Commission recognized that often shareholders would have no residual interest, and the most appropriate buyer would sometimes be a connected person or director. The Law Commission sought to balance these factors by recommending the enactment of a power to apply to court for approval of a transaction where there is reason to believe that the company's assets are insufficient to make a payment to shareholders or for some other good reason, a proposal accepted in CLR: *Developing the Framework*, para 26. Parliament did not adopt this recommendation. It may be that such a power existed already by reason of Insolvency Act, s 35(2): see the *Demite* case [1998] BCC 638, 647.

[84] An amendment was proposed by the Opposition so that the exception would apply to a company 'in receivership' but was withdrawn after Margaret Hodge, Minister for Industry and the Regions, explained the Government's position that there would be a risk of abuse, as a receiver could be appointed by a director or connected person and would not necessarily be a licensed insolvency practitioner: HC SD D (11 July 2006) cols 631–632.

[85] This point was not argued in the *Demite* case.

value of the equity of redemption exceeds one of the statutory minima in s 191.[86] This latter point applies equally, of course, to non-administrative receivers.

**18.59** By subs 194(1), approval is not required under s 190 for a transaction on a recognized investment exchange effected by a director, or a person connected with him, through the agency of a person who in relation to the transaction acts as an independent broker.[87]

### (5) Approval by the members

**18.60** In order to comply with s 190, the arrangement must have been approved by a resolution of the members of the company or be conditional on such approval being obtained.[88]

**18.61** Under the 1985 Act, s 320 it was eventually held that the *Duomatic* principle[89] applied to the requirement for member approval so that the informal consent of members of the company satisfied the requirement for prior approval of the arrangement.[90] Whether informal approval can be given in circumstances where the company is insolvent was undecided under the 1985 Act.[91]

---

[86] Lewison J considered that this result was appropriate as a matter of policy, given that shareholders should only have a veto on sale where there is the prospect of a surplus, and thus '... if ... there is the prospect of a surplus [sc. after payment of the secured debt] which exceeds the requisite value, then there is every point in requiring the shareholders to approve the sale'. The dovetailing of s 320 with such policy arguments may not be exact. Where there is the prospect of a surplus after repayment of the secured debt, but no prospect of a surplus for shareholders by reason of the existence of unsecured liabilities, as may well be the case in a receivership, shareholders will have a right of veto by reason of s 190 even where they have no interest in the assets sold.

[87] This exception is, very substantially, a re-enactment of 1985 Act, s 321(4). By subs 194(2) 'independent broker' means 'a person who, independently of the director or any person connected with him, selects the person with whom the transaction is to be effected' and 'recognised investment exchange' has the same meaning as in FSMA, Part 18.

[88] subs 190(1).

[89] *Re Duomatic Ltd* [1969] 2 Ch 365, 373, per Buckley J: '... where it can be shown that all shareholders who have a right to attend and vote at a general meeting of the company assent to some matter which a general meeting of the company could carry into effect, that assent is as binding as a resolution in general meeting would be'.

[90] *Re Conegrade Ltd* [2003] BPIR 358; *NBH Ltd v Hoare* [2006] 2 BCLC 649, 665, 666, following *Wright v Atlas Wright (Europe) Ltd* [1999] 2 BCLC 301, CA, where the principle was applied in the context of 1985 Act, s 319 (now s 188—Directors' long-term service contracts: requirement of members' approval). *Conegrade* was not apparently cited in the *NBH* case, but the court came to the same conclusion.

[91] This issue is discussed in Chapter 22, Section B(4) of this work. In *Walker v WA Personnel Ltd* [2002] BPIR 621, 639, 642, it was held to be seriously arguable that the *Duomatic* principle did not operate where the company was insolvent: see paragraph 18.64 below. In *Re Conegrade Ltd* [2003] BPIR 358, the *Duomatic* principle was applied to an arrangement under 1985 Act, s 320 notwithstanding that the company was insolvent at the time of the transaction (and thus the transaction was set aside as a preference), but the possible non-application of the principle where the company was insolvent does not appear to have been argued.

## (6) Subsequent affirmation

By s 196 where a transaction or arrangement is entered into by a company in **18.62** contravention of s 190 but, within a reasonable period, it is affirmed by resolution of the members of the company (in the case of a contravention of subs 190(1)) or of the holding company (in the case of a contravention of subs 190(2)) the transaction or arrangement may no longer be avoided under s 195.[92]

Section 196 is, substantially, a re-enactment of the 1985 Act, s 322(2)(c). One **18.63** change should be noted. Under the 1985 Act, s 320, as under s 190(1) and (2), where the arrangement was with a director of the company's holding company (or a person connected with such a director), there was a dual requirement of resolutions of both the members of the company and of its holding company. Under s 322(2)(c), in order for the arrangement to be affirmed in such circumstances, there was a dual requirement that both the company and its holding company affirm the arrangement. A consequence of these dual requirements (presumably unintended) was that where the members of the company itself approved the arrangement before it was entered into, but the members of the holding company affirmed the arrangement within a reasonable period after it had been entered into, or vice versa, s 320 was not complied with.[93] Under s 190, this is no longer the case. Whilst there remains a requirement for dual approval, where s 190 is contravened solely by reason of the members of the company failing to approve the arrangement before it is entered into, the members of the company alone can affirm the arrangement under s 196(a), and likewise, where the contravention of s 190 arises by reason of the members of the holding company failing to approve the arrangement before it is entered into, the members of the holding company alone can affirm the arrangement under s 196(b).

Under the 1985 Act, s 322(2)(c) it had implicitly been held that it was seriously **18.64** arguable that the ability of a company in general meeting to ratify the arrangement abated when the company was insolvent or close to insolvency.[94] It is submitted that the members of the company or holding company should be able to ratify the transaction in accordance with s 196 whether the company is solvent or not. The statutory wording contains no limit on the power to ratify, explicit or implicit. There can be no question but that the requisite approval at the time of the arrangement in question can be given whether or not the company is insolvent or near insolvent. Further, to introduce limitations into statutory wording based

---

[92] Where a company is a charity, any affirmation by members of the company under this section is ineffective without the prior written consent of the Charity Commission: s 226.

[93] *Sylfaen Constructions Ltd v Davies* (HHJ Nicholas Chambers QC, 18 August 2000, unreported) at paras 27–40.

[94] *Walker v WA Personnel Ltd* [2002] BPIR 621. The issue arose on an application for a continuation of an injunction, thus the court reached no concluded view as to the issue.

on indeterminate concepts such as near insolvency, or even insolvency itself, is to introduce uncertainty.

**18.65**   It appears that, in certain circumstances, the arrangement may be affirmed by a method outside of s 196. In the *Ultraframe* case, Lewison J held that an arrangement which was voidable through failure to comply with the 1985 Act, s 320 could be affirmed by the liquidator when the company subsequently entered insolvent liquidation.[95] The judge reasoned that failure to comply with the 1985 Act, s 320 rendered the arrangement voidable at the instance of the company, that this right to avoid was a chose in action within the control of the liquidator and thus the liquidator could decide to affirm the arrangement. In the context of affirmation by a liquidator in an insolvent liquidation, the result is unexceptionable. The reasoning could lead to the conclusion that the right to affirm could be exercised by the board of the company, an absurd result: though apart from being implicit in s 196 that such affirmation is not possible, such affirmation itself might possibly be subject to s 195.

### (7) Civil consequences of contravention

**18.66**   Section 195 states:[96]

(1) This section applies where a company enters into an arrangement in contravention of section 190 . . .

(2) The arrangement, and any transaction entered into in pursuance of the arrangement (whether by the company or any other person), is voidable at the instance of the company, unless—

   (a) restitution of any money or other asset that was the subject matter of the arrangement or transaction is no longer possible,

   (b) the company has been indemnified in pursuance of this section by any other persons for the loss or damage suffered by it, or

   (c) rights acquired in good faith, for value and without actual notice of the contravention by a person who is not a party to the arrangement or transaction would be affected by the avoidance.

(3) Whether or not the arrangement or any such transaction has been avoided, each of the persons specified in subsection (4) is liable—

   (a) to account to the company for any gain that he has made directly or indirectly by the arrangement or transaction, and

   (b) (jointly and severally with any other person so liable under this section) to indemnify the company for any loss or damage resulting from the arrangement or transaction.

(4) The persons so liable are—

   (a) any director of the company or of its holding company with whom the company entered into the arrangement in contravention of section 190,

---

[95] *Ultraframe (UK) Ltd v Fielding* [2005] EWHC 1638 (Ch) at paras 1440, 1441.
[96] s 195 is very substantially a re-enactment of 1985 Act, s 322. The wording has been changed in places but not so as to change the substance.

(b) any person with whom the company entered into the arrangement in contravention of that section who is connected with a director of the company or of its holding company,

(c) the director of the company or of its holding company with whom any such person is connected, and

(d) any other director of the company who authorised the arrangement or any transaction entered into in pursuance of such an arrangement.

(5) Subsections (3) and (4) are subject to the following two subsections.

(6) In the case of an arrangement entered into by a company in contravention of section 190 with a person connected with a director of the company or of its holding company, that director is not liable by virtue of subsection (4)(c) if he shows that he took all reasonable steps to secure the company's compliance with that section.

(7) In any case—

(a) a person so connected is not liable by virtue of subsection (4)(b), and

(b) a director is not liable by virtue of subsection (4)(d),

if he shows that, at the time the arrangement was entered into, he did not know the relevant circumstances constituting the contravention.

(8) Nothing in this section shall be read as excluding the operation of any other enactment or rule of law by virtue of which the arrangement or transaction may be called in question or any liability to the company may arise.

Broadly speaking, the remedies available under s 195 reflect those which would be available under the general law if s 190 stood alone, thus the remedies available in respect of a misapplication of the company's assets by its directors.[97] Section 195 is in very similar terms to s 213, which sets out the civil consequences of contravening the 2006 Act ss 197, 198, 200, 201, and 203 (loans to directors, etc). Reference may therefore be made to the commentary on s 213 at paragraphs 18.122–18.126 below in addition to the following commentary. **18.67**

*Avoidance*

The first remedy which is, in principle, available to the company is to avoid the arrangement, and any transaction entered into in pursuance of the arrangement, under s 190(2). The company may avoid the arrangement or any transaction unless, first, restitution of any money or other asset that was the subject matter of the arrangement or transaction is no longer possible. The statutory remedy is similar to, but not the same as, the right to rescind in equity. For example, whereas in equity delay in exercising the right to rescind may provide a defence to the purported exercise of that right, there is no limitation on the right to avoid under s 195(2) arising by reason of lapse of time alone.[98] **18.68**

---

[97] *Re Duckwari Plc* [1998] Ch 253, 260–2, CA, per Nourse LJ, dealing specifically with the liability to account and indemnify under what is now s 195(3).

[98] *Demite Ltd v Protec Health Ltd* [1998] BCC 638, 650.

**18.69**   Further, it has been held under the 1985 Act, s 322(1) and (2) that the company could avoid the arrangement or transaction notwithstanding that complete restitution of the assets transferred under the arrangement in question was no longer possible.[99] A purposive approach to construction was adopted since otherwise the right to avoid granted by Parliament was likely to be incapable of exercise in a large number of cases: and in the case of a business sale agreement, where assets are necessarily changing from time to time as the business is carried on, the 1985 Act s 322(1) and (2) would have had no scope.[100] The word 'unless' which now appears in s 195(2) was thus read in the sense of 'except to the extent that', so that the arrangement or transaction could be avoided (and the transferred property ordered to be returned) except to the extent that the property no longer existed.[101] It was further held that an incident of the company's right to avoid is that the company must repay to the other party to the arrangement or transaction the consideration which passed to the company: though if complete restitution were not possible, the repayment would be reduced pro tanto.[102]

**18.70**   The right to avoid is otherwise lost when the company has been indemnified under s 195(3) and (4) (s 195(2)(b)), and when the avoidance would affect rights acquired by a person who is not a party to the arrangement or transaction in good faith, for value and without actual notice of the contravention (s 195(2)(c)). If 'unless' is read in the sense of 'except to the extent that' for the purposes of s 195(2)(b) and (c) also, it may be that partial avoidance is possible.

*Liability to account for any gain*

**18.71**   Whether or not the arrangement or any transaction entered into in pursuance of the arrangement has been avoided, each of the persons specified in s 195(4) (the Specified Persons) is liable to account to the company for any gain that he has made directly or indirectly by the arrangement or transaction.

**18.72**   It was held under the similarly worded 1985 Act, s 322(3)(a) that this provision corresponded to s 320(1)(a) of that Act (now s 190(1)(a)).[103] Thus, where it is the director (or connected person) that acquires the substantial non-cash asset, the relevant entitlement of the company under s 195(3) is a right to an account of the gains made directly or indirectly by the Specified Persons by the arrangement or transaction under s 195(3)(a). Where it is the company that acquires the

---

[99] *Demite Ltd v Protec Health Ltd* [1998] BCC 638; *Demite Ltd v Protec Health Ltd (No 2)* (7 July 1998, unreported, Park J) ('*Demite (No 2)*').

[100] *Demite (No 2)*.

[101] Ibid.

[102] Ibid.

[103] *Re Duckwari Plc* [1998] Ch 253, 261, CA, per Nourse LJ; *NBH Ltd v Hoare* [2006] 2 BCLC 649, 667, 668.

substantial non-cash asset under s 190(1)(b), the relevant entitlement of the company is to be indemnified for any loss or damage resulting from the arrangement or transaction under s 195(3)(b).

The use of the words 'directly or indirectly' in s 195(3)(a) means that Parliament intended to cast its net wide:[104] the liability to account is potentially extremely broad. The gain must however have been made by the arrangement or transaction, so the arrangement or transaction must, in some sense, have caused the gain.[105] **18.73**

### Liability to indemnify for loss or damage

Again, whether or not the arrangement or any transaction entered into in pursu-ance of the arrangement has been avoided, each of the Specified Persons is liable to indemnify the company for any loss or damage resulting from the arrangement or transaction. As stated above, the liability to indemnify arises where it is the company that has acquired the substantial non-cash asset under s 190(1)(b). The scope of the liability to indemnify under s 190(1)(b) was held, under the 1985 Act, to mirror in large part the scope of the liability of directors of a company to make good a company's losses arising from a misapplication by them of the company's assets.[106] Such liability treats the directors as if they were trustees of those assets.[107] Hence, prima facie, they (and other Specified Persons) are liable to make good any losses which the company would not have suffered *but for* the transaction which constitutes the misapplication.[108] **18.74**

Therefore, if a company acquires a substantial non-cash asset of the requisite value from a director or person connected without complying with the formalities of s 190, and pays the market value for that asset, the Specified Persons will in principle be liable to indemnify the company under s 195(3)(b) in the event that the asset depreciates. But for the acquisition, the company would not have suffered the loss or damage which it in fact suffered by reason of the acquisition. In the *Duckwari* case,[109] the right to acquire a property was acquired by the company, and the company then completed the acquisition. The price paid was not, as at the date of acquisition, excessive. Property prices generally fell, and the value of the property fell far below the acquisition price. The court of first instance had concluded that in those circumstances, the Specified Persons were not liable **18.75**

---

[104] *Murray v Leisureplay plc* [2004] EWHC 1927 (QB), per Stanley Burnton J (at first instance) para 110.
[105] *NBH Ltd v Hoare* [2006] 2 BCLC 649, 666.
[106] *Re Duckwari Plc* [1998] Ch 253, 260–2, CA, per Nourse LJ.
[107] Ibid, 262.
[108] *Murray v Leisureplay Plc* [2005] IRLR 946, CA, 960, per Arden LJ, referring to *Target Holdings Ltd v Redferns* [1996] AC 421, HL.
[109] [1999] Ch 253, CA.

to indemnify the company in respect of the loss in value which followed acquisition, stating that '. . . the mischief, and only mischief, addressed by these provisions [ie the 1985 Act, ss 320 ff.] is acquisition[s] by the company at an inflated value or disposals by the company at an undervalue'.[110] The Court of Appeal overruled that decision, holding the Specified Persons liable for the loss to the company caused by the fall in property values.

**18.76** In order for the Specified Persons to be liable to indemnify under s 195(3)(b), the relevant loss or damage suffered by the company must be loss or damage 'resulting from' from the arrangement or transaction. This wording contrasts with that used in s 195(3)(a), where the liability of the Specified Persons to account for any gain is for any gain that he has made 'directly or indirectly' by the arrangement or transaction. In *Re Duckwari (No 2)*,[111] one of the issues was whether the borrowing costs incurred by the company for the purpose of acquiring the property, but before it had actually acquired the property, were recoverable under s 195(3)(b). The analysis of the Court of Appeal in *Re Duckwari*[112] itself, whereby the predecessor of s 195 was interpreted as reflecting the remedies which would have been available to a company against its directors in respect of a misapplication of the company's assets, suggested that the borrowing costs ought to be recoverable. But for the acquisition, the borrowing costs would not have been incurred. Notwithstanding, the Court of Appeal held that the borrowing costs were irrecoverable. The loss or damage recoverable under the predecessor of s 195(3)(b) was only that 'resulting from' the arrangement or transaction, and on the basis that the relevant arrangement or transaction was the actual acquisition of the property by the company, the borrowing costs were not recoverable. If the decision is correct, and the same interpretation placed on s 195(3)(b), the parallel between remedies under trust law and under s 195(3) is less than exact. Further, there is a marked contrast between the scope of the gain for which account must be made under s 195(3)(a) (which covers gains made directly or indirectly by the arrangement or transaction) and the scope of the indemnity under s 195(3)(b) (which would not include loss or damage resulting indirectly from the arrangement or transaction).[113]

**18.77** Some doubt has been cast on the decision in *Duckwari (No 2)* by a differently constituted Court of Appeal in *Murray v Leisureplay Plc*.[114] Arden LJ stated that it was open to question whether the interpretation of the predecessor of s 195(3)(b) was consistent with the decision in the earlier *Duckwari* case as to the parallel

---

[110] *Re Duckwari Plc* [1997] Ch 201, 206.
[111] [1999] Ch 268.
[112] [1999] Ch 253, CA. The Court of Appeal was identically constituted.
[113] See the comments of Arden LJ in *Murray v Leisureplay Plc* [2005] IRLR 946, 960.
[114] [2005] IRLR 946.

between remedies under the statute and remedies for misapplication by directors. She nonetheless considered herself bound by *Duckwari (No 2)*. Buxton LJ also remarked that *Duckwari (No 2)* caused difficulties in interpreting the predecessor of s 195.[115] It remains to be seen whether s 195(3)(b) will ultimately be interpreted in line with *Duckwari (No 2)*. Although there is no change of substance to the wording in the new Act, it is possible that the courts will not consider themselves bound by *Duckwari (No 2)*.[116]

If the decision in *Duckwari (No 2)* is correct, greater importance is placed on defining the relevant arrangement or transaction at issue.[117] On the interpretation in that case, in order for loss and damage to result from an arrangement or transaction, the arrangement or transaction must predate the loss or damage. In *Duckwari (No 2)*, the Court of Appeal defined the relevant arrangement or transaction as the acquisition of the property itself, and hence the borrowing costs incurred to enable that acquisition were irrecoverable. Had the relevant arrangement been defined differently, it seems that the borrowing costs might have been recoverable.[118]    **18.78**

## D. Loans and Quasi-loans, Credit Transactions, and Related Arrangements

The 2006 Act, ss 197–214 prohibit a company (in the case of loans to directors under s 197, and 'related arrangements' under s 203), or a public company or company associated with a public company (in the case of quasi-loans to directors under s 198, loans or quasi-loans to persons connected with directors under s 200, and credit transactions under s 201), from entering into loans to directors, quasi-loans to directors, quasi-loans to persons connected with directors, or credit transactions with directors or persons connected with such directors unless the prior approval of members has been obtained.[119] The prohibitions are subject to a number of exceptions.    **18.79**

---

[115] Ibid, 963–4.

[116] Cf *Power v Sharp Investments Ltd* [1994] 1 BCLC 111, 122, CA.

[117] See paragraph 18.50 above.

[118] See in particular the judgment of Buxton LJ in *Murray v Leisureplay Plc* [2005] IRLR 946, 963, 964.

[119] ss 197 to 214 apply to transactions or arrangements entered into on or after 1 October 2007: 2006 Act Commencement Order No 3, Schedule 3, para 8(1). A resolution passed before that date approving a transaction or arrangement is effective for the purposes of those sections if it complies with the requirements of those sections: ibid, para 8(2). 1985 Act, ss 330 to 342 continue to apply in relation to a contravention occurring before that date: ibid, para 8(3). Approval is not required under ss 197, 198, 200, or 201 for anything done by the company in pursuance of an agreement entered into before 1 October 2007 that, by virtue of 1985 Act, s 337A (funding of director's expenditure on defending proceedings), would not have required approval if done before

**18.80** The Law Commission described the statutory predecessors of these sections as 'complex and inaccessible'.[120] The CLR also identified the need to simplify the provisions.[121] Sections 197–214 of the Act have succeeded, to some limited extent, in this regard. In broad terms, ss 197–214 re-enact the 1985 Act, ss 330–344, subject to one significant change: whereas under the 1985 Act, loans, etc made in breach of the Act were illegal, and attracted criminal penalties, the Act merely imposes a requirement of prior member approval (and under s 214 permits subsequent affirmation by the members).

### (1) Loans to directors: requirement of members' approval

**18.81** The substantive provisions are contained in subss 197(1) and (2), which provide:

> (1) A company may not—
> (a) make a loan to a director of the company or of its holding company, or
> (b) give a guarantee[122] or provide security in connection with a loan made by any person to such a director,
> unless the transaction has been approved by a resolution of the members of the company.
>
> (2) If the director is a director of the company's holding company,[123] the transaction must also have been approved by a resolution of the members of the holding company.

For the purposes of s 197 the person for whom the transaction is entered into is the person to whom the loan is made or, in the case of a guarantee or security, the person for whom the transaction is made in connection with which the guarantee or security is entered into,[124] and a director includes a shadow director.[125]

**18.82** Subsections 197(3) and (4) state the requirements for obtaining members' approval.

---

that date: ibid, para 9. There are further specific transitional provisions relating to the application of 2006 Act, ss 204 and 205, noted under the relevant sections below.

[120] *Company Directors: Regulating Conflicts of Interest and Formulating a Statement of Duties* A Joint Consultation Paper (No 153) para 6.6.

[121] CLR: *Developing the Framework* Annex C, para 28.

[122] This is undefined. Section 331(2) of the 1985 Act provided: "'Guarantee'" includes indemnity, and cognate expressions are to be construed accordingly.' Presumably the Act will be construed so as to apply to indemnities, if not through a wide reading of the word 'guarantee', then by interpreting 'security' as including personal security.

[123] Defined in s 1159; and see s 1160 and Schedule 6.

[124] s 212(a) and (c).

[125] subs 223(1)(c).

(3) A resolution approving a transaction to which this section applies must not be passed unless a memorandum setting out the matters mentioned in subsection (4) is made available to members—

    (a) in the case of a written resolution, by being sent or submitted to every eligible member at or before the time at which the proposed resolution is sent or submitted to him;

    (b) in the case of a resolution at a meeting, by being made available for inspection by members of the company both—

        (i) at the company's registered office for not less than 15 days ending with the date of the meeting, and

        (ii) at the meeting itself: s 197(3)(a).

(4) The matters to be disclosed are—

    (c) the nature of the transaction,

    (d) the amount of the loan and the purpose for which it is required, and

    (e) the extent of the company's liability under the transaction connected with the loan.

Eligible members are those members entitled to vote on the resolution on the circulation date of the resolution (as itself defined in s 290).[126] As was the case under the 1985 Act, where the written resolution procedure is used, it is only those members entitled to vote who are entitled to the memorandum: whereas, if an actual meeting is held, all members can inspect the memorandum. The 2006 Act, s 224 applies where there is an accidental failure to send the memorandum.

By subs 197(5) no approval is required under s 197 on the part of the members of **18.83** a body corporate that is not a UK-registered company, or is a wholly-owned subsidiary[127] of another body corporate.[128] There are also exceptions (discussed in paragraphs 104–117 below) for (a) expenditure on company business, (b) expenditure on defending proceedings, (c) expenditure in connection with regulatory action or investigation, (d) for minor and business transactions, (e) for intra-group transactions, and (f) for money-lending companies.

'Loan' in s 197 is not defined; nor was it under s 330 of the 1985 Act. In *Champagne* **18.84** *Perrier-Jouet SA v HH Finch Ltd*,[129] Walton J construed the word 'loan' for the purposes of a company's articles and the 1948 Act, s 190 (a predecessor of s 197). He held that the correct meaning of loan was to be found in the then current edition of the Shorter Oxford English Dictionary: 'A sum of money lent for a time, to be returned in money or money's worth . . .' The judge held, therefore, that if a person paid money to B at the request of A, although A would be indebted to B, there was no loan. The indebtedness would now be a 'quasi-loan' within the meaning of the 2006 Act, ss 198 and 199 (paragraphs 18.87–18.92 below). A contract of

---

[126] s 289 defines 'eligible member' and s 290 identifies the circulation date.
[127] Defined in s 1159; and see s 1160 and Schedule 6.
[128] Where the company is a charity, the prior written consent of the Charity Commission is necessary notwithstanding this exemption: s 226.
[129] [1982] 1 WLR 1359.

loan is a consensual transaction, and hence for there to be a loan the lender must, objectively, have consented to the lending.[130]

**18.85** In practice, difficulties can arise in deciding whether a transaction entered into by a company with a director is indeed a loan (in which case the company will be able to recover the loan in the normal way, in addition to having the remedies now found in the 2006 Act, s 213 if the loan falls within s 218 and no relevant exception applies), or whether the relevant payment is by way of remuneration (in which case, prima facie, the company has no remedy), or a misapplication of company funds (in which case, the company has no remedies under any contract of loan nor under s 213, but has the usual remedies available to it in respect of a misapplication of company funds).[131]

**18.86** Whether the members can approve the relevant transaction informally, under the *Duomatic* principle, is unclear.[132] Under the 1985 Act, given that the relevant transaction was illegal, there was no question of member approval, formal or informal. The answer may depend on whether the provisions of the Act are interpreted as being for the protection of members or for creditors also.[133]

### (2) Quasi-loans to directors: requirement of members' approval

**18.87** Section 198 contains provisions in respect of 'quasi-loans', which are very similar to the provisions about loans in s 197, but s 198 applies only to a public company

---

[130] *Re Ciro Citterio Menswear Plc* [2002] 1 BCLC 672.

[131] See, under 1985 Act, *Currencies Direct Ltd v Ellis* [2002] 1 BCLC 193, Gage J, and [2002] 2 BCLC 482, CA (where the issue was whether certain payments were made by way of loan to the director, or by way of remuneration); *Re Westminster Property Management Ltd (No 3)* [2004] BCC 599 (where an issue arose as to whether certain payments were loans, and hence unlawful, or the misapplication of company funds). Those cases illustrate that such issues can only be decided by a close analysis of the facts. It appears that the mere fact that a director has signed a company's accounts recording the relevant transaction as a loan will not necessarily bind him, since he will ordinarily have signed such accounts in his capacity as director, not borrower: *John Shaw and Sons (Salford) Ltd v Shaw* [1935] 2 KB 113; and see *Currencies Direct Ltd v Ellis* [2002] 1 BCLC 193 (where a certificate under s 232(3) of the 1985 Act bound the director). It appears that, as a mere admission out of court, a director could in any event explain and contradict such admission, unless the accounts constituted an account stated: *Camillo Tank Steamship Company Ltd v Alexandria Engineering Works* (1921) 38 TLR 134. In *Re DPR Futures Ltd* [1989] BCLC 634, 638, Millett J relied on the fact that that the directors had acknowledged their indebtedness in a statement of affairs in concluding that it was difficult to see any possible defence to a claim for repayment of the loans.

[132] *Re Duomatic Ltd* [1969] 2 Ch 365, and see paragraphs 18.62–18.64 above.

[133] See *Wright v Atlas-Wright (Europe) Ltd* [1999] 2 BCLC 301 (CA) decided under 1985 Act, s 319. The Law Commission interpreted the provisions of the 1985 Act as being for the protection of creditors as well as members: but that interpretation was based, in part at least, on the fact that the relevant transactions were illegal, and attracted criminal penalties: Joint Consultation Paper, *Company Directors: Regulating Conflicts of Interest and Formulating a Statement of Duties*, No 153, paras 6.33–6.43. Under the Act, the transactions are not illegal, no criminal sanctions attach, and whether the transactions can be entered into depends on member approval.

or a company associated with a public company.[134] Subsections 198(2) and (3) contain the substantive provisions:

> (2) A company to which this section applies may not—
>  (a) make a quasi-loan to a director of the company or of its holding company, or
>  (b) give a guarantee or provide security in connection with a quasi-loan made by any person to such a director,
>
> unless the transaction has been approved by a resolution of the members of the company.
>
> (3) If the director is a director of the company's holding company, the transaction must also have been approved by a resolution of the members of the holding company.

For the purposes of s 198 the person for whom the transaction is entered into is the person to whom the quasi-loan is made, or, in the case of a guarantee or security, the person for whom the transaction is made in connection with which the guarantee or security is entered into,[135] and a director includes a shadow director.[136]

Sections 198(4) and (5), relating to the necessary resolution of members and disclosure to those members regarding the quasi-loan, mirror, *mutatis mutandis*, s 197(4) and (5) in the context of loans to directors, and s 224 (accidental failure to send memorandum) applies (paragraphs 18.82–18.83 above). **18.88**

By subs 198(6) no approval is required under s 198 on the part of the members of a body corporate that is not a UK-registered company, or is a wholly-owned subsidiary[137] of another body corporate.[138] There are also exceptions (discussed in paragraphs 18.104–18.121 below) for (a) expenditure on company business, (b) expenditure on defending proceedings, (c) expenditure in connection with regulatory action or investigation, (d) for minor and business transactions, (e) for intra-group transactions, and (f) for money-lending companies. **18.89**

Section 198 is in large part a re-enactment of the 1985 Act, s 330 so far as it applied to the making of quasi-loans to directors, but with the significant change that quasi-loans are not illegal, and attract no criminal penalties. Instead, members' approval is required, in default of which the civil consequences of contravention set out in s 213 apply (paragraphs 18.122–18.126 below). **18.90**

The restriction of the prohibition on making quasi-loans to public companies and companies associated with public companies, as per s 198(1) of the Act, broadly **18.91**

---

[134] subs 198(1). For the meaning of 'associated', see s 256.
[135] s 212(a) and (c).
[136] subs 223(1)(c).
[137] Defined in s 1159; and see s 1160 and Schedule 6.
[138] Where the company is a charity, the prior written consent of the Charity Commission is necessary notwithstanding this exemption: s 226.

re-enacts the restriction in the 1985 Act, s 330 to 'relevant' companies.[139] Until a late stage in the passage of the Companies Bill through Parliament, it had been intended that the prohibition contained in s 198 (as well as similar prohibitions in s 200 (loans or quasi-loans to persons connected with directors), and s 201 (credit transactions), which also apply only to public companies or companies associated with a public company) should apply to all companies, following a recommendation of the Law Commission as endorsed by the CLR.[140] The Government changed its mind following informal consultation with unspecified 'stakeholders',[141] and hence the requirement for members' approval in respect of quasi-loans, loans, and quasi-loans to persons connected with directors and credit transactions apply only to public companies or companies in the same group as a public company.

**18.92**  'Quasi-loan' and related expressions are defined under s 199:[142]

(1) A 'quasi-loan' is a transaction under which one party 'the creditor' agrees to pay, or pays otherwise than in pursuance of an agreement, a sum for another 'the borrower' or agrees to reimburse, or reimburses otherwise than in pursuance of an agreement, expenditure incurred by another party for another ('the borrower')—

(a) on terms that the borrower (or a person on his behalf) will reimburse the creditor; or

(b) in circumstances giving rise to a liability on the borrower to reimburse the creditor.

(2) Any reference to the person to whom a quasi-loan is made is a reference to the borrower.

(3) The liabilities of the borrower under a quasi-loan include the liabilities of any person who has agreed to reimburse the creditor on behalf of the borrower

### (3) Loans or quasi-loans to persons connected with directors: requirement of members' approval

**18.93**  Under s 200 of the Act, similar provisions to those in ss 197 and 198 apply to a public company or a company associated with a public company in respect of loans and quasi-loans made to persons connected with a director of the company

---

[139] As defined by 1985 Act, s 331(6).

[140] Law Commission Report, *Company Directors: Regulating Conflicts of Interest and Formulating a Statement of Duties*, No 261, para 12.17; CLR: *Developing the Framework* Annex C, para 28.

[141] Hansard HC Debates cols 797–798 (17 October 2006), Margaret Hodge: 'Although that recommendation [ie of the Law Commission, that all rules on loans, quasi-loans and credit transactions should extend to all companies] was endorsed by the company law review, we have carried out further informal consultation in light of the discussion in Committee. Stakeholders clearly supported the proposal that the requirements that currently apply only to relevant companies should not be extended to all private companies.' The reference to the discussion in Committee may be to Hansard HC Standing Committee D cols 632–633 where the Opposition spokesman raised a query, specifically in respect of credit transactions, as to why, if the Bill was intended to be deregulatory, it extended rules which previously applied solely to 'relevant companies' to all companies.

[142] A re-enactment, without substantive change, of 1985 Act, ss 331(3) and (4).

or its holding company, and the giving of guarantees or provision of security in connection with such loans or quasi-loans.[143] Subsections 200(2) and (3) contain the substantive provisions:

> (2) A company to which this section applies may not—
>   (a) make a loan or quasi-loan to a person connected with[144] a director of the company or of its holding company, or
>   (b) give a guarantee or provide security in connection with a loan or quasi-loan made by any person to a person connected with such a director,
>
> unless the transaction has been approved by a resolution of the members of the company.[145]
>
> (3) If the connected person is a person connected with a director of the company's holding company, the transaction must also have been approved by a resolution of the members of the holding company.

For the purposes of s 200, the person for whom a transaction is entered into is the person to whom the loan or quasi-loan is made, or, in the case of a guarantee or security, the person for whom the transaction is made in connection with which the guarantee or security is entered into,[146] and a director includes a shadow director.[147]

**18.94** Subsections 200(4) and (5), relating to the necessary resolution of members and disclosure to those members regarding the loan or quasi-loan, mirror, *mutatis mutandis*, ss 197(4) and (5), and 198(4) and (5), in the context of loans and quasi-loans to directors.

**18.95** By subs 200(6) no approval is required under s 200 on the part of the members of a body corporate that is not a UK-registered company, or is a wholly-owned subsidiary[148] of another body corporate.[149] There are also exceptions (discussed in paragraphs 18.104–18.121 below) for (a) expenditure on company business, (b) expenditure on defending proceedings, (c) expenditure in connection with regulatory action or investigation, (d) for minor and business transactions, (e) for intra-group transactions, and (f) for money-lending companies.

---

[143] s 200 derives from s 330(3)(b) of the 1985 Act. The criminal sanctions applicable under the 1985 Act have been removed, and the prohibition under the 1985 Act replaced by a requirement for members' approval. Subsection 200(1) restricts the application of s 200 to public companies and companies associated with a public company. For the meaning of 'associated', see s 256. As with ss 198 and 201, the provisions were originally intended to apply to all companies.

[144] For the definition of 'connected person' see s 252 (Persons connected with a director).

[145] Where a company is a charity, any approval given by members of the company under this section is ineffective without the prior written consent of the Charity Commission: s 226.

[146] s 212(a) and (c).

[147] subs 223(1)(c).

[148] Defined in s 1159; and see s 1160 and Schedule 6.

[149] Where the company is a charity, the prior written consent of the Charity Commission is necessary notwithstanding this exemption: s 226.

### (4) Credit transactions: requirement of members' approval

**18.96** Under s 201, similar provisions to those relating to loans and quasi-loans to directors or connected persons apply in respect of a public company or a company associated with a public company entering into a 'credit transaction' with a director or person connected with a director.[150] Subsections 201(2) and (3) contain the substantive provisions:

> (2) A company to which this section applies may not—
>
> > (a) enter into a credit transaction as creditor for the benefit of a director of the company or of its holding company, or a person connected with such a director, or
> >
> > (b) give a guarantee or provide security in connection with a credit transaction entered into by a person for the benefit of such a director, or a person connected with such a director,
>
> unless the transaction (that is, the credit transaction, the giving of the guarantee or the provision of security, as the case may be) has been approved by a resolution of the members of the company.
>
> (3) If the director or connected person is a director of its holding company or a person connected with such a director, the transaction must also have been approved by a resolution of the members of the holding company.

For the purposes of s 201 the person for whom a transaction is entered into is the person to whom goods, land, or services are supplied, sold, hired, leased, or otherwise disposed of under the transaction, or, in the case of a guarantee or security, the person for whom the transaction is made in connection with which the guarantee or security is entered into,[151] and a director includes a shadow director.[152]

**18.97** Subsections 201(4) and (5) state the requirements for obtaining members' approval of the credit transaction:

> (4) A resolution approving a transaction to which this section applies must not be passed unless a memorandum setting out the matters mentioned in subsection (5) is made available to members[153]—
>
> > (a) in the case of a written resolution, by being sent or submitted to every eligible member at or before the time at which the proposed resolution is sent or submitted to him;
> >
> > (b) in the case of a resolution at a meeting, by being made available for inspection by members of the company both—

---

[150] s 201 derives from 1985 Act, s 330(4). The prohibition under the 1985 Act has been replaced by the requirement of prior member approval and the criminal sanctions applicable under the 1985 Act have been removed. Subsection 201(1) restricts the application of s 201 to public companies and companies associated with a public company. For the meaning of 'associated', see s 256. As with ss 198 and 200, the provisions were originally intended to apply to all companies.

[151] s 212(b) and (c).

[152] subs 223(1)(c).

[153] Where there is an accidental failure to send the memorandum, s 224 applies.

       (i)  at the company's registered office for not less than 15 days ending with the date of the meeting, and

      (ii)  at the meeting itself:

  (4)  The matters to be disclosed are—

     (a)  the nature of the transaction,

     (b)  the value of the credit transaction and the purpose for which the land, goods or services sold or otherwise disposed of, leased, hired or supplied under the credit transaction are required, and

     (c)  the extent of the company's liability under any transaction connected with the credit transaction.

**18.98**   By subs 201(6) no approval is required under s 201 on the part of the members of a body corporate that is not a UK-registered company, or is a wholly-owned subsidiary[154] of another body corporate.[155] There are also exceptions (discussed in paragraphs 18.104–18.115 below) for (a) expenditure on company business, (b) expenditure on defending proceedings, and (c) expenditure in connection with regulatory action or investigation.

**18.99**   Section 202 gives the meaning of 'credit transaction'.[156]

  (1)  A 'credit transaction' is a transaction under which one party ('the creditor')—

     (a)  supplies any goods or sells any land under a hire-purchase agreement or a conditional sale agreement,[157]

     (b)  leases or hires any land or goods in return for periodical payments, or

     (c)  otherwise disposes of land or supplies goods or services[158] on the understanding that payment (whether in a lump sum or instalments or by way of periodical payments or otherwise) is to be deferred.

  (2)  Any reference to the person for whose benefit a credit transaction is entered into is to the person to whom goods, land or services are supplied, sold, leased, hired or otherwise disposed of under the transaction

### (5) Related arrangements: requirements of members' approval

**18.100**   Section 203 is an anti-avoidance provision,[159] which prevents a company from evading the requirements for members' approval by entering into an arrangement whereby another person gives the director a loan, quasi-loan, or credit transaction, and in return that person obtains a benefit from a company or subsidiary of the company.[160] For example, a 'back-to-back' arrangement, whereby a company

---

[154] Defined in s 1159; and see s 1160 and Schedule 6.

[155] Where the company is a charity, the prior written consent of the Charity Commission is necessary notwithstanding this exemption: s 226.

[156] The definition is a re-enactment, without substantive change, of 1985 Act, ss 331(7), (8), (9)(b), and (10).

[157] 'Conditional sale agreement' has the same meaning as in the Consumer Credit Act 1974: s 202(3).

[158] 'Services' means anything other than goods or land.

[159] It is derived from 1985 Act, s 330(6) and (7).

[160] Hansard HL GC Day 4 vol 678 cols 349–350 (9 February 2006), Lord Sainsbury.

agrees to make loans to the directors of another company in return for that other company making loans to its own directors, will be caught.

**18.101**   The substantive provisions of s 203 are:

> (1) A company may not—
>> (a) take part in an arrangement[161] under which—
>>> (i) another person enters into a transaction that, if it had been entered into by the company, would have required approval under sections 197, 198, 200 or 201, and
>>> (ii) that person, in pursuance of the arrangement, obtains a benefit from the company or a body corporate associated with it, or
>> (b) arrange for the assignment to it, or assumption by it, of any rights, obligations or liabilities under a transaction that, if it had been entered into by the company, would have required such approval,
>
> unless the arrangement in question has been approved by a resolution of the members of the company.[162]
>
> (2) If the director or connected person for whom the transaction is entered into is a director of its holding company or a person connected with such a director, the arrangement must also have been approved by a resolution of the members of the holding company.
>
> . . .
>
> (6) In determining for the purposes of this section whether a transaction is one that would have required approval under section 197, 198, 200 or 201 if it had been entered into by the company, the transaction shall be treated as having been entered into on the date of the arrangement.

For the purposes of s 203 the person for whom the arrangement is entered into is the person for whom the transaction is made to which the arrangement relates,[163] and a director includes a shadow director.[164]

**18.102**   Under s 203(4) and (5), a resolution approving an arrangement to which s 203 applies must not be passed unless a memorandum setting out the matters that would have to be disclosed if the company were seeking approval of the transaction to which the arrangement relates, the nature of the arrangement, and the extent of the company's liability under the arrangement or any transaction connected with it, is made available to members in the same way, *mutatis mutandis*, as under ss 197(3), 198(4), 200(4), and 201(4).[165]

---

[161] 'Arrangement' is not defined. It is a word of wide import and, given the purpose of the section, it is thought that it will be widely construed: compare paragraph 18.42 above, as to the meaning of 'arrangement' in the context of s 190 (substantial property transactions).

[162] Where a company is a charity, any approval given by members of the company under this section is ineffective without the prior written consent of the Charity Commission: s 226.

[163] s 212(d).

[164] subs 223(1)(c).

[165] Where there is an accidental failure to send the memorandum s 224 applies.

As under ss 197(3), 198(4), 200(4), and 201(4), no approval is required on the **18.103** part of the members of a body corporate that is not a UK-registered company, or is a wholly-owned subsidiary of another body corporate.[166]

## (6) Exceptions

Sections 204–209 create six exceptions from the requirement for member approval **18.104** of loan and quasi-loan transactions, namely (a) for expenditure on company business (s 204), (b) for expenditure on defending proceedings etc (s 205), (c) for expenditure in connection with regulatory action or investigation (s 206), (d) for minor and business transactions (s 207), (e) for intra-group transactions (s 208), and (f) for money-lending companies (s 209). None of the exceptions applies to related arrangements. The exceptions apply to shadow directors.[167]

### (a) Expenditure on company business

Section 204 provides as follows:[168]                                                              **18.105**

> (1) Approval is not required under section 197, 198, 200 or 201 (requirement of members' approval for loans etc) for anything done by a company—
>   (a) to provide a director of the company or of its holding company, or a person connected with any such director, with funds to meet expenditure incurred or to be incurred by him—
>     (i) for the purposes of the company, or
>     (ii) for the purpose of enabling him properly to perform his duties as an officer of the company, or
>   (b) to enable any such person to avoid incurring such expenditure.
> (2) This section does not authorise a company to enter into a transaction if the aggregate of—
>   (a) the value of the transaction in question, and
>   (b) the value of any other relevant transactions or arrangements,[169] exceeds £50,000.[170]

---

[166] subs 203(5). For the meaning of subsidiary, see ss 1159 and 1160 and Schedule 6. Where the company is a charity, the prior written consent of the Charity Commission is necessary notwithstanding this exemption: s 226.

[167] s 223(1)(c).

[168] Where before 1 October 2007 a company has done anything pursuant to 1985 Act, s 337(1) or (2) (funding of director's expenditure on duty to the company), and on the condition mentioned in 1985 Act, s 337(3)(b) (condition requiring repayment of loan etc if approval of company in general meeting not given within six months), if that condition has not been satisfied before that date, it continues to apply notwithstanding the repeal of that section, but subject as follows. In the case of a private company that by reason of the repeal of 1985 Act, s 366 with effect from that date ceases to be required to hold an annual general meeting, the condition shall be read as if it provided that the approval of the company is required on or before the last date on which the company would have been required to hold an annual general meeting but for the repeal, and that the loan is to be repaid within six months from that date if such approval is not forthcoming: 2006 Act Commencement Order No 3, Schedule 3, para 10(1)–(3).

[169] See s 210.

[170] The Secretary of State has power to increase this limit under 2006 Act, s 256.

**18.106**  Section 204 re-enacts the 1985 Act, s 337, with significant changes. Under the 1985 Act, s 337(3), the exception applied only if the members in general meeting had given prior approval to the loan, etc, or the loan, etc was made on condition that if such approval was not given at or before the next AGM, the loan was to be repaid, or any other liability arising under such transaction was discharged, within six months from the conclusion of that AGM. The 1985 Act, s 337(3) and (4) provided for the disclosure of certain matters at the relevant AGM. These limitations on the exception have now gone, with the result that a loan, etc for expenditure on company business need not be repayable or disclosed, provided it is less than £50,000 in aggregate.

**18.107**  The provisions of ss 210 and 211 are material for determining whether the loan, quasi-loan, or credit transaction is within the £50,000 limit.[171] For this purpose it is necessary to add up the transaction in question and any other relevant existing transactions or arrangements.[172] Section 211 provides the rules for determining the value of a transaction or arrangement, of which subss (2)–(5) and (7) are relevant to the value of the transaction in question (subs 204(2)(a)):

> (2)  The value of a loan is the amount of its principal.
> (3)  The value of a quasi-loan is the amount, or maximum amount, that the person to whom the quasi-loan is made is liable to reimburse the creditor.
> (4)  The value of a credit transaction is the price that it is reasonable to expect could be obtained for the goods, services or land to which the transaction relates if they had been supplied (at the time the transaction is entered into) in the ordinary course of business and on the same terms (apart from price) as they have been supplied, or are to be supplied, under the transaction in question.
> (5)  The value of a guarantee or security is the amount guaranteed or secured.
> (6)  The value of an arrangement to which section 203 (related arrangements) applies is the value of the transaction to which the arrangement relates.
> (7)  If the value of a transaction or arrangement is not capable of being expressed as a specific sum of money—
> > (a)  whether because the amount of any liability arising under the transaction or arrangement is unascertainable, or for any other reason, and
> > (b)  whether or not any liability under the transaction or arrangement has been reduced,
>
> its value is deemed to exceed £50,000.

**18.108**  Subsection 204(2)(b) requires the value of any other relevant transactions or arrangements to be added to the value of the transaction in question. Other relevant transactions or arrangements are identified in accordance with s 210.

---

[171]  These sections derived from 1985 Act, ss 339 and 340 without material change.
[172]  Lord Sainsbury, Hansard, HL GC Day 4, vol 678 (9 February 2006).

(2) Other relevant transactions or arrangements are those previously entered into, or entered into at the same time as the transaction or arrangement in question in relation to which the following conditions are met.

(3) Where the transaction or arrangement in question is entered into—

(a) for a director of the company entering into it, or

(b) for a person connected with such a director,

the conditions are that the transaction or arrangement was (or is) entered into for that director, or a person connected with him, by virtue of the relevant exception by that company or by any of its subsidiaries.

(4) Where the transaction or arrangement in question is entered into—

(a) for a director of the holding company of the company entering into it, or

(b) for a person connected with such a director,

the conditions are that the transaction or arrangement was (or is) entered into for that director, or a person connected with him, by virtue of the relevant exception[173] by the holding company or by any of its subsidiaries.

(5) A transaction or arrangement entered into by a company that at the time it was entered into—

(a) was a subsidiary of the company entering into the transaction or arrangement in question, or

(b) was a subsidiary of the company's holding company,

is not a relevant transaction or arrangement if, at the time the question arises whether the transaction or arrangement in question falls within a relevant exception, it is no longer such a subsidiary.

Having determined whether a transaction or arrangement is relevant for the **18.109** purposes of 204(2)(b) it is necessary to value it in accordance with s 211. By subs 211(1)(b) its value is taken to be the value determined in accordance with subss (2)–(7), reduced by any amount by which the liabilities of the person for whom the transaction or arrangement was made have been reduced.

---

[173] By subs 210(1) 'the relevant exception' means the exception under ss 204–209 for the purposes of which it falls to be determined what are 'other relevant transactions or arrangements'.

*(b) Defending proceedings etc*

**18.110** Section 205 provides as follows:[174]

(1) Approval is not required under section 197, 198, 200 or 201 (requirement of members' approval for loans etc) for anything done by a company—

    (a) to provide a director of the company or of its holding company with funds to meet expenditure incurred or to be incurred by him—

        (i) in defending any criminal or civil proceedings in connection with any alleged negligence, default, breach of duty or breach of trust by him in relation to the company or an associated company,[175] or

        (ii) in connection with an application for relief (see subsection (5)), or

    (b) to enable any such director to avoid incurring such expenditure,

    if it is done on the following terms.

(2) The terms are—

    (a) that the loan is to be repaid, or (as the case may be) any liability of the company incurred under any transaction connected with the thing done is to be discharged, in the event of—

        (i) the director being convicted in the proceedings,

        (ii) judgment being given against him in the proceedings, or

        (iii) the court refusing to grant him relief on the application; and

    (b) that it is to be so repaid or discharged not later than—

        (i) the date when the conviction becomes final,

        (ii) the date when the judgment becomes final, or

        (iii) the date when the refusal of relief becomes final.

(3) For this purpose a conviction, judgment or refusal of relief becomes final—

    (a) if not appealed against, at the end of the period for bringing an appeal;

    (b) if appealed against, when the appeal (or any further appeal) is disposed of.

(4) An appeal is disposed of—

    (a) if it is determined and the period for bringing any further appeal has ended, or

    (b) if it is abandoned or otherwise ceases to have effect.

(5) The reference in subsection (1)(a)(ii) to an application for relief is to an application for relief under—

    section 661(3) or (4) (power of court to grant relief in case of acquisition of shares by innocent nominee), or

    section 1157 (general power of court to grant relief in case of honest and reasonable conduct).[176]

---

[174] Approval is not required under ss 197, 198, 200, or 201 for anything done by the company in pursuance of an agreement entered into before 1 October 2007 that, by virtue of 1985 Act, s 337A (funding of director's expenditure on defending proceedings), would not have required approval if done before that date: 2006 Act Commencement Order No 3, Schedule 3, para 9. Where before 1 October 2007 a company has done anything pursuant to 1985 Act, s 337A(1) or (3) and on the terms mentioned in s 337A(4) (terms requiring repayment of loan etc if the defendant convicted, has judgment given against him or refused relief), if immediately before 1 October 2007 it is not yet known whether repayment will be required, or repayment is required but had not been made, those terms continue to apply notwithstanding the repeal of that section: 2006 Act Commencement Order No 3, Schedule 3, para 11(1) and (2).

[175] See s 256.

[176] 2006 Commencement Order No 3, art 6, Schedule 1, para 11 provides that in subs (5), for the words 'section 661(3)' to the end is to be substituted 'section 144(3) or (4) of the Companies Act 1985 . . ., or section 727 of the Companies Act 1985 . . .'.

Section 205 largely re-enacts the exception in the 1985 Act, s 337A. Section 205 **18.111** is complemented by s 206, an express exception for expenditure in connection with regulatory action or investigation. The Government considered that the latter expenditure fell within s 205 in any event, but the Government followed Opposition calls for clarification, resulting in s 206.[177] The exception applies not only in respect of expenditure incurred or to be incurred in actually defending criminal or civil proceedings but also, as appears from s 205(1)(b), expenditure incurred or to be incurred in respect of, for example, the instruction of legal advisers prior to the issue of any proceedings.

The reference to associated companies in s 205(1)(a)(i) makes clear that the **18.112** exception applies, in principle, to loans made by one company to the director of another company in the same group.[178] Where the prohibition applies, the board of the associated company should not fall into the trap of thinking that, merely because the exception in s 205 extends to associated companies, a loan for the purposes set out in s 205 can be made by the associated company without further consideration. Hence, before authorizing the loan, the board of the associated company must consider their general duties and thus, for example, whether the making of the loan promotes the success of the lending company (see s 172 and Chapter 11 above).

There is no financial limit on the exception for expenditure on defending **18.113** proceedings. The loan must be repaid if the defence is unsuccessful in that (a) he is convicted in criminal proceedings, (b) judgment is given against him in civil proceedings, or (c) he is refused relief under s 1157. This is consistent with the provisions permitting third party indemnity provision and qualifying pension scheme indemnity provision under ss 234 and 235 (Chapter 19 of this work). If civil proceedings against a director are settled, without judgment being entered against him, it will not be necessary for the purposes of s 205 for the loan to be repaid. The directors may need to consider whether a loan on those terms is in the interests of the company or whether it should be repayable where the director has effectively 'lost'.

---

[177] Hansard, HL GC Day 4, Vol 678, cols 351–352 (9 February 2006)

[178] The Government recognized the convenience of the extension, but was keen to emphasize that the exception '. . . should only be used for matters that are properly connected to the company. It would be inappropriate for the exceptions to be available for company funds to be used without member approval to defend a director against proceedings unconnected with company business': Hansard, HC Report Stage 17, col 799 (17 October 2006), Margaret Hodge. Hence, the exceptions are narrower than the circumstances in which a director can be granted a qualifying third party indemnity provision under s 234.

*(c) Regulatory action or investigation*

**18.114** Section 206 provides:

Approval is not required under section 197, 198, 200 or 201 (requirement of members' approval for loans etc) for anything done by a company—

(a) to provide a director of the company or of its holding company with funds to meet expenditure incurred or to be incurred by him in defending himself—

(i) in an investigation by a regulatory authority, or

(ii) against action proposed to be taken by a regulatory authority,

in connection with any alleged negligence, default, breach of duty or breach of trust by him in relation to the company or an associated company, or

(b) to enable any such director to avoid incurring such expenditure.

**18.115** Section 206 is new and complements s 205. It was introduced in the circumstances described in paragraph 18.111 above. There is no financial limit on expenditure in relation to regulatory actions or investigations, nor need any loan be repaid even if the director is found to have been negligent or in default, breach of duty, or breach of trust in relation to the company or an associated company.

*(d) Minor and business transactions*

**18.116** Section 207 provides:

(1) Approval is not required under section 197, 198 or 200 for a company to make a loan or quasi-loan, or to give a guarantee or provide security in connection with a loan or quasi-loan, if the aggregate of—

(a) the value of the transaction, andf

(b) the value of any other relevant transactions or arrangements, does not exceed £10,000.[179]

(2) Approval is not required under section 201 for a company to enter into a credit transaction, or to give a guarantee or provide security in connection with a credit transaction, if the aggregate of—

(a) the value of the transaction (that is, of the credit transaction, guarantee or security), and

(b) the value of any other relevant transactions or arrangements,

(3) Approval is not required under section 201 for a company to enter into a credit transaction, or to give a guarantee or provide security in connection with a credit transaction, if—

(a) the transaction is entered into by the company in the ordinary course of the company's business, and

---

[179] The Secretary of State has power to increase this limit under 2006 Act, s 256.

(b) the value of the transaction is not greater, and the terms on which it is entered into are not more favourable, than it is reasonable to expect the company would have offered to, or in respect of, a person of the same financial standing but unconnected with the company.

Section 207 largely re-enacts the 1985 Act, ss 332, 334, and 335, with the **18.117** exception extended to quasi-loans and includes connected persons. The monetary limits have also been increased. In order to determine whether the loan, quasi-loan, guarantee, or security or credit transaction is within the relevant monetary limit, it is necessary to assess values under ss 210 and 211 as described in paragraph 18.109 above. A credit transaction may come within the exception even though it exceeds the £15,000 limit, provided that it is on normal business terms within subs 207(3).

*(e) Intra-group transaction*

Section 208 provides: **18.118**

(1) Approval is not required under section 197, 198 or 200 for—
   (a) the making of a loan or quasi-loan to an associated body corporate,[180] or
   (b) the giving of a guarantee or provision of security in connection with a loan or quasi-loan made to an associated body corporate.
(2) Approval is not required under section 201—
   (a) to enter into a credit transaction as creditor for the benefit of an associated body corporate, or
   (b) to give a guarantee or provide security in connection with a credit transaction entered into by any person for the benefit of an associated body corporate.

Section 208 re-enacts the 1985 Act, ss 333 and 336, though the exception is **18.119** somewhat broader. Section 256 defines an 'associated body corporate'.

*(f) Money-lending companies*

Section 209 provides: **18.120**

(1) Approval is not required under section 197, 198 or 200 for the making of a loan or quasi-loan, or the giving of a guarantee or provision of security in connection with a loan or quasi-loan, by a money-lending company if—
   (a) the transaction (that is, the loan, quasi-loan, guarantee or security) is entered into by the company in the ordinary course of the company's business, and
   (b) the value of the transaction is not greater, and its terms are not more favourable, than it is reasonable to expect the company would have offered to a person of the same financial standing but unconnected with the company.
(2) A 'money-lending company' means a company whose ordinary business includes the making of loans or quasi-loans, or the giving of guarantees or provision of security in connection with loans or quasi-loans.

---

[180] See s 256.

(3) The condition specified in subsection (1)(b) does not of itself prevent a company from making a home loan—

    (a) to a director of the company or of its holding company, or

    (b) to an employee of the company,

if loans of that description are ordinarily made by the company to its employees and the terms of the loan in question are no more favourable than those on which such loans are ordinarily made.

(4) For the purposes of subsection (3) a 'home loan' means a loan—

    (a) for the purpose of facilitating the purchase, for use as the only or main residence of the person to whom the loan is made, of the whole or part of any dwelling-house together with any land to be occupied and enjoyed with it,

    (b) for the purpose of improving a dwelling-house or part of a dwelling-house so used or any land occupied and enjoyed with it, or

    (c) in substitution for any loan made by any person and falling within paragraph (a) or (b).

**18.121** Section 209 re-enacts the 1985 Act, s 338 with changes. Whereas s 338 imposed a financial limit of £100,000 on the value of the aggregate of the loans, etc, no such limit appears in s 209. The exception in respect of home loans in s 209(3) has been broadened by s 209(3)(b). The purpose of that exception is to allow directors to take advantage of any employee home loan schemes operated by a money-lending company on the same terms as are offered to employees. Whereas under the 1985 Act, s 338 the exception did not apply in respect of a home loan to an employee connected with a director, s 209 applies in such circumstances—the Government considered it unfair for certain employees to be excluded from the benefit of schemes run by their employers for their benefit merely because of a connection with a director.[181]

### (7) Civil consequences of contravention

**18.122** Section 213 states:

(1) This section applies where a company enters into a transaction or arrangement in contravention of section 197, 198, 200, 201 or 203 (requirement of members' approval for loans etc).

(2) The transaction or arrangement is voidable at the instance of the company, unless—

    (a) restitution of any money or other asset that was the subject matter of the transaction or arrangement is no longer possible,

    (b) the company has been indemnified for any loss or damage resulting from the transaction or arrangement, or

    (c) rights acquired in good faith, for value and without actual notice of the contravention by a person who is not a party to the arrangement or transaction would be affected by the avoidance.

---

[181] Hansard, HL GC Day 4, vol 678 col 353 (9 February 2006), Lord Sainsbury.

(3) Whether or not the transaction or arrangement has been avoided, each of the persons specified in subsection (4) is liable—

(a) to account to the company for any gain that he has made directly or indirectly by the transaction or arrangement, and

(b) (jointly and severally with any person so liable under this section) to indemnify the company for any loss or damage resulting from the transaction or arrangement.

(4) The persons so liable are—

(a) any director of the company or of its holding company with whom the company entered into the transaction or arrangement in contravention of section 197, 198, 201 or 203,

(b) any person with whom the company entered into the transaction or arrangement in contravention of any of those sections who is connected with a director of the company or of its holding company,

(c) the director of the company or of its holding company with whom any such person is connected, and

(d) any other director of the company who authorised the transaction or arrangement.

(5) Subsections (3) and (4) are subject to the following two subsections.

(6) In the case of a transaction or arrangement entered into by a company in contravention of section 200, 201 or 203 with a person connected with a director of the company or of its holding company, that director is not liable by virtue of subsection (4)(c) if he shows that he took all reasonable steps to secure the company's compliance with the section concerned.

(7) In any case—

(a) a person so connected is not liable by virtue of subsection (4)(b), and

(b) a director is not liable by virtue of subsection (4)(d),

if he shows that, at the time the arrangement was entered into, he did not know the relevant circumstances constituting the contravention.

(8) Nothing in this section shall be read as excluding the operation of any other enactment or rule of law by virtue of which the transaction or arrangement may be called in question or any liability to the company may arise.

Section 213 is in terms almost identical to s 195 (property transactions: civil consequences of contravention) and reference may be made to paragraphs 18.66–18.78 above on that section.[182]   **18.123**

The two main remedies created by s 213 are the right to avoid the transaction or arrangement (under s 213(2)) and the right, as against directors and others, to an account and indemnity (under ss 213(3) and (4)). The right to avoid under s 213(2) is subject to there having been no subsequent affirmation under s 214: see paragraphs 18.127–18.128 below. It may not be necessary for the company to rely on the statutory remedies at all: for example, if a loan is made by a company to one of its directors without prior member approval, and thus in breach   **18.124**

---

[182] S 213 derives from 1985 Act, s 341. There are no longer any criminal penalties for breach of ss 197, 198, 200, 201, or 203, as were previously contained, in relation to those sections' predecessors, in 1985 Act, s 342.

of s 197, the company may choose simply to sue on the loan rather than seeking to avoid it: see eg *Re Westminster Property Management Ltd (No 3)*.[183] In certain circumstances, however, even where the remedy sought is simply repayment of monies advanced by way of loan, there may be an advantage in avoiding first, for example where the debtor maintains that the loan is not yet repayable.[184] Under the 1985 Act, s 341, under which Act the making of a prohibited loan was illegal, it had been argued that any loan made in breach of s 330 of that Act was irrecoverable on grounds of illegality, a contention which was, naturally, rejected.[185]

**18.125**  Section 213(8) preserves remedies which might exist in respect of the transaction or arrangement outside of s 213. In *Re Ciro Citterio Meanswear Plc*,[186] it was contended that a loan made to a director under s 330 of the 1985 Act was held by that director as constructive trustee for the company by reason solely of the fact that the loan was made in contravention of s 330. In the absence of facts rendering the making of the loan a breach of fiduciary duty by the directors of the company,[187] the argument was rejected.[188]

**18.126**  In *Neville v Krikorian*,[189] the Court of Appeal held that a director who authorized the practice of the company making loans to a fellow director (in breach of the 1985 Act, s 330), and who took no steps to cause the company to recover the indebtedness, was in breach of his duty as a director. In addition, despite the fact that it had not been proven that the director had known of each loan which the company advanced, since he had authorized the practice of making such loans, he was liable to indemnify the company for any loss or damage resulting

---

[183]  [2004] BCC 599.

[184]  See *Tait Conisbee (Oxford) Ltd v Tait* [1997] 2 BCLC 349, where the director alleged that the loan was repayable only out of dividends to be declared by the company. The Court of Appeal held that, were that the case, the letter of demand for repayment served by the company avoided the loan and hence the amount of the loan was in any event due to the company.

[185]  *Currencies Direct Ltd v Ellis* [2002] 1 BCLC 193 (Gage J). The argument was not pursued on appeal: *Currencies Direct Ltd v Ellis* [2002] 2 BCLC 482, 484, CA. Under the Act, there are no criminal sanctions and the making of a loan is no longer illegal.

[186]  [2002] 1 BCLC 672

[187]  As may have been the case in *Budge v AF Budge (Contractors) Limited* [1997] BPIR 366, CA, discussed in *Ciro Citterio* at [2002] 1 BCLC 672, 688–9.

[188]  This rejection did, however, involve a questionable treatment of dicta in *Wallersteiner v Moir* [1974] 1 WLR 991, 1015, CA, where Lord Denning MR stated that a director who authorized the lending of money to a company which was his 'puppet', in breach of 1948 Act, s 190 (a predecessor of 2006 Act, s 197), was guilty of misfeasance. The Master of the Rolls appears to have relied on the unlawfulness of the loan, however: under the Act, loans, etc, in breach of ss 197, 198, 200, and 201 are no longer unlawful. In *Re a Company (No 1641 of 2003)* [2004] 1 BCLC 210 it was held that a debtor in respect of a loan made in breach of 1985 Act, s 330 could not set off monies alleged to have been owing from the company to the debtor under rule 4.90 of the Insolvency Rules. However, this was on the basis that the taking of an unlawful loan was a misappropriation, and thus there was no 'dealing' within rule 4.90. Since a loan made without prior member approval is no longer unlawful, if the only circumstances relied upon were such failure to obtain approval, rule 4.90 would probably apply.

[189]  [2007] 1 BCLC 1, CA.

from the loans under the 1985 Act, s 341(2)(b) (the predecessor of the 2006 Act, s 213(3)(b)). Under s 341(2)(b), the director was liable to make good the difference between the amount outstanding to the company as at the date that he authorized the practice, and the amount ultimately outstanding when the company entered administration. The director who received the loans was unable to make any repayment. In respect of his breach of duty as director, the director was liable to pay to the company the difference between the sum which could have been recovered by the company if it had sought repayment of the loans when the director first got to know of them, and the amount recoverable at the date of judgment (the latter sum being nil).

### (8) Effect of subsequent affirmation

Section 214 provides:                                                                    **18.127**

> Where a transaction or arrangement is entered into by a company in contravention of section 197, 198, 200, 201 or 203 (requirement of members' approval for loans etc) but, within a reasonable period, it is affirmed—
>
> (a) in the case of a contravention of the requirement for a resolution of the members of the company, by a resolution of the members of the company,[190] and
> (b) in the case of a contravention of the requirement for a resolution of the members of the holding company,
>
> the transaction or arrangement may no longer be avoided under section 213.

This is a new provision, very similar to section 196 (property transactions: effect   **18.128**
of subsequent affirmation): see paragraphs 18.62–18.64 above. Since the making of loans, etc, in contravention of s 330 of the 1985 Act was illegal, they were incapable of ratification by the shareholders.[191] In *Ultraframe (UK) Ltd v Fielding*,[192] Lewison J held that an arrangement which was voidable through failure to comply with the 1985 Act, s 320 (the predecessor of s 190) could be affirmed by the liquidator when the company subsequently entered insolvent liquidation: see paragraph 18.65 above. Similar reasoning may apply to transactions and arrangements entered into in breach of ss 197, 198, 200, and 201.

---

[190] Where a company is a charity, any affirmation by members of the company under this section is ineffective without the prior written consent of the Charity Commission: s 226.

[191] *Re DPR Futures Ltd* [1989] BCLC 634, 638.

[192] [2005] EWHC 1638 (Ch) at paras 1440–1441.

# E.  Payments for Loss of Office

## (1)  The meaning of 'payment for loss of office'

**18.129**  Sections 215–222 deal with payments for loss of office.[193] These are payments made to a director (or former director) to compensate him for ceasing to be a director, or for losing any other office or employment with the company or a subsidiary of the company. They also include payments made in connection with retirement. Members' approval is required for these payments.

**18.130**  Section 215(1) states that, for the purposes of these provisions, 'payment for loss of office' means a payment made to a director or past director of a company:[194]

   (a)  by way of compensation for loss of office as director of the company,

   (b)  by way of compensation for loss, while director of the company or in connection with his ceasing to be a director of it, of—

      (i)  any other office or employment in connection with the management of the affairs of the company, or

      (ii)  any office (as director or otherwise) or employment in connection with the management of the affairs of any subsidiary undertaking of the company,

   (c)  as consideration for or in connection with his retirement from his office as director of the company, or

   (d)  as consideration for or in connection with his retirement, while director of the company or in connection with his ceasing to be a director of it, from—

      (i)  any other office or employment in connection with the management of the affairs of the company, or

      (ii)  any office (as director or otherwise) or employment in connection with the management of the affairs of any subsidiary undertaking of the company.

**18.131**  By subs 215(2) references to 'compensation' and 'consideration' include benefits otherwise than in cash and references to 'payment' have a corresponding meaning. By subs 215(3) payment to a person connected with a director, or payment to any person at the direction of, or for the benefit of, a director or a person connected with him, is treated as payment to the director. By subs 215(4) references to

---

[193]  ss 215 to 222 apply in relation to any loss of office or employment as is mentioned in s 215(1)(a) or (b), or any retirement as is mentioned in s 215(1)(c) or (d), occurring on or after 1 October 2007: 2006 Act Commencement Order No 3, Schedule 3, para 12(1). A resolution passed before that date approving a payment is effective for the purposes of those sections if it complies with the requirements of those sections: ibid, para 12(2). 1985 Act, ss 312–316 continue to apply in relation to loss of office or retirement within the meaning of those provisions occurring before that date: ibid, para 12(3). For these purposes, loss of office or retirement is regarded as occurring in the case of a directorship, when the person ceases to be a director; in the case of any other office, when the person ceases to hold that office; and in the case of employment, when the employment comes to an end: ibid, para 12(4).

[194]  s 215 is a new provision.

payment by a person include payment by another person at the direction of, or on behalf of, the person referred to.

For the purposes of these provisions, references to a director include a shadow **18.132** director, but any reference in those provisions to loss of office as a director does not apply in relation to loss of a person's status as a shadow director.[195] They also apply to former directors, so that it is not possible to evade the provisions by resigning prior to payment. The court would be expected to treat resignation and payment as part of a single operation.[196]

There are three categories of payments, which categories may overlap. **18.133**

(1) Under s 217, members' approval is required if a company wishes to make a payment for loss of office to one of its directors or a director of its holding company.

(2) Under s 218, members' approval is required if any person (including the company or anyone else) wishes to make a payment for loss of office to a director of the company in connection with the transfer of the whole or any part of the undertaking of the property of the company or of a subsidiary of the company.

(3) Under s 219, in the case of a payment for loss of office to a director of the company in connection with the transfer of shares in the company or in a subsidiary of the company resulting from a takeover bid, approval is required of the holders of the shares to which the bid relates and of any other holder of shares of the same class.

In what follows, payments by a company for loss of office under s 217 are dealt with first, followed by payments in connection with transfer of undertaking etc (s 218) and payment in connection with share transfer (s 219).

### (2) Payments by company

Section 217 states the prohibition: **18.134**

(1) A company may not make a payment for loss of office to a director of the company unless the payment has been approved by a resolution of the members of the company.[197]

(2) A company may not make a payment for loss of office to a director of its holding company unless the payment has been approved by a resolution of each of those companies.

Subsection 217(3) deals with the requirements for obtaining members' approval **18.135** in much the same way as applied to ss 197, 198, 200, and 201:[198]

---

[195] subss 223(1)(d) and (2).

[196] Hansard, HL GC Day 4 Vol 678, cols 355–356 (9 February 2006).

[197] Where a company is a charity, any approval given by members of the company under this section is ineffective without the prior written consent of the Charity Commission: s 226.

[198] For the meaning of 'eligible member' see Part 13, Chapter 2, s 289 and paragraph 18.18 above. Where there has been an accidental failure to send the requisite memorandum s 224 applies.

(3) A resolution approving a payment to which this section applies must not be passed unless a memorandum setting out particulars of the proposed payment (including its amount) is made available to the members of the company whose approval is sought

(a) in the case of a written resolution, by being sent or submitted to every eligible member at or before the time at which the proposed resolution is sent or submitted to him;

(b) in the case of a resolution at a meeting, by being made available for inspection by the members both—

(i) at the company's registered office for not less than 15 days ending with the date of the meeting, and

(ii) at the meeting itself.

**18.136** No approval is required under s 217 on the part of the members of a body corporate that is not a UK-registered company, or is a wholly-owned subsidiary of another body corporate.[199]

**18.137** The provisions requiring prior[200] approval of members before a company makes a payment for loss of office now embodied in s 217 are derived from the 1985 Act, ss 312 and 316(3).[201] The Act makes very significant amendments, bolstering considerably the protection given by the 1985 Act. Some understanding of the law as it appeared to be under the 1985 Act assists in understanding the new provisions.

**18.138** The 1985 Act, s 312 stated that:

It is not lawful for a company to make to a director of the company any payment by way of compensation for loss of office, or as consideration for or in connection with his retirement from office, without particulars of the proposed payment (including its amount) being disclosed to members of the company and the proposal being approved by the company.

Very broadly (and somewhat inaccurately) speaking, s 312 thus covered, in abbreviated form, what is now included in s 217(1). By reason of the 1985 Act, s 316(3), such payments did not include '. . . any bona fide payment by way of damages for breach of contract or by way of pension in respect of past services'.

---

[199] subs 217(4). Where the company is a charity, the prior written consent of the Charity Commission is necessary notwithstanding this exemption: s 226.

[200] The fact that approval must be given before payment is made is clear from the reference to 'proposed payment' in s 217(3). No provision is made in ss 215–222 for ratification or affirmation of a payment made without prior approval: compare and contrast s 196 of the Act regarding affirmation of substantial property transactions, and s 214 regarding affirmation of loans, etc, made without prior member approval. It might nonetheless be possible for the company (presumably acting in general meeting, and not by its board), or a liquidator or administrator, to waive any remedies that it holds arising from failure to comply with s 217: compare *Ultraframe (UK) Ltd v Fielding* [2005] EWHC 1638 (Ch) at paras 1440–1441, decided under the predecessor of ss 190–196 of the Act (substantial property transactions) and discussed at paragraph 18.65 above.

[201] They have their origin in Companies Act 1947, s 36(1).

Section 220 of the Act covers similar ground, though is much expanded from the 1985 Act, s 316(3).

The 1985 Act, ss 312 and 316(3) had never been interpreted by the House of Lords or Court of Appeal, and, it appears, had only twice been interpreted by the English courts at all.[202] A similar provision in New Zealand legislation had, however, come before the Privy Council in *Taupo Totara Timber Co Ltd v Rowe*.[203] The Privy Council interpreted that provision restrictively, apparently concluding, first, that the only payments which were covered by the equivalent of s 312 were payments made to the director for the loss of his office *as director*, and thus the section did not cover payments made, for example, in respect of the termination of a contract of service held by that director; and secondly, the provisions only applied to uncovenanted (ie voluntary) payments. Thus, if the company was legally liable to make certain payments under the contract or terms of office of the director, s 312 did not apply at all. This interpretation was adopted and applied by the English and Scottish Courts in deciding the scope of the 1985 Act, ss 312 and 316(3).[204]

18.139

The second finding in the *Taupo* case, that the provisions do not apply to uncovenanted payments, has been adopted, clarified, and expanded somewhat in the new legislation.[205] By reason of s 220(1)(a), approval is not required under s 217 for a payment made in good faith in discharge of an existing legal obligation.

18.140

As to the other conclusion in the *Taupo* case (ie the legislation covered only payments made to the director for the loss of his office *as director*), this has been reversed by the new provisions. The limited operation of the previous legislation as reflected in the *Taupo* case is now covered by s 215(1)(a) (and s 215(1)(c) in respect of retirement). The broad wording of s 215(1)(b) (and in connection with retirement from office, 215(1)(d)) make clear that payments for loss of office include not only loss of office as director, but also loss of any other office or employment[206] in connection with the management of the affairs of the company.

18.141

---

[202] *Re Duomatic Ltd* [1969] 2 Ch 365 (considering 1948 Act, s 191, the predecessor of 1985 Act, s 312) and *Gooding v Cater* (unreported) 13 March 1989, Edward Nugee QC.

[203] [1978] AC 537.

[204] In England in *Gooding v Cater* (unreported) 13 March 1989, Edward Nugee QC followed the second holding in the *Taupo* case. He also held that the payment of damages for wrongful dismissal or of an agreed sum in settlement of a right to compensation for premature termination of a contract of employment were payments which a company was legally obliged to make, and thus fell outside s 312. *Sed quaere*: such payments would have fallen within 1985 Act, s 316(3), now s 220. In Scotland: *Lander v Pict Petroleum Ltd* [1998] BCC 248, 253, 254, OH; *Mercer v Heart of Midlothian Plc* [2002] SLT 945, 951–3, OH.

[205] By reason of the reference to 'good faith' in s 220(1), and the wording of s 220(1)(a), it appears that no members' approval will be required where the company in good faith but mistakenly miscalculates the extent of the existing legal obligation (s 220(1)(a)).

[206] 'Employment' is not defined: compare s 188(7) in the context of directors' long-term service contracts. The context suggests that 'employment' will be interpreted broadly.

Subsection 215(1)(b)(ii) also covers payments made by way of compensation for loss of any office (as director or otherwise) or employment in connection with the management of the affairs of any subsidiary undertaking of the company. There will in all cases remain the preliminary question as to whether any payment is indeed made by way of compensation for loss of office, etc, or as consideration for or in connection with a director's retirement from office, as opposed, for example, to some new role which the director might be taking up with the company.[207]

**18.142**  The ambit of the provisions has been extended from those under the 1985 Act in several other ways:

(1)  By reason of s 217(2), payment for loss of office is prohibited where the payment is made to a director of the holding company, and in such case the members of both the company and the holding company must approve the payment. This covers the situation where a director of a holding company is employed by the subsidiary, as not infrequently occurs where one subsidiary in a group employs all employees in the group.

(2)  Section 217 applies both to directors and to *past* directors of a company.[208] The wording is designed to close a possible loophole under the 1985 Act whereby, if the director resigned his office prior to payment, arguably members' approval was not required.

(3)  Section 217 treats payments to a person connected with a director, or payment to any person at the direction of, or for the benefit of, a director or a person connected with him, as payment to the director.[209]

(4)  References to 'compensation' and 'consideration' include benefits[210] otherwise than in cash, and references to 'payment' in Part 10, Chapter 4 have a corresponding meaning.[211] Under the 1985 Act, it had been held that the

---

[207]  See *Mercer v Heart of Midlothian plc* [2002] SLT 945, 952, where the benefits to the retiring director were held referable not to his retirement, but to his new appointment as life president. Lord MacFayden held, following *Lincoln Mills (Aust) Ltd v Gough* [1964] VR 193, that the court must have regard to 'the nature and circumstances' of the payment in order to determine 'its true character'.

[208]  subs 215(1).

[209]  subs 215(3).

[210]  During debates on what is now s 176 of the Act, the Solicitor General stated: 'In using the word "benefit", we intend the ordinary dictionary definition of the word. The "Oxford English Dictionary" defines it as a favourable or helpful factor, circumstance, advantage or profit' (HC Comm D, 11 July 2006, col 622). Reference was also made to the wide interpretation of 'benefit' in another context in *Cronin v Grierson* [1968] AC 895, HL.

[211]  subs 215(2). In *Mercer v Heart of Midlothian plc* [2002] SLT 945, 953, Lord MacFayden provisionally concluded that 'payment' under s 312 of the 1985 Act did not include solely transfers of money.

focus of s 312 was on the depletion of assets of the company as opposed to the benefit received by the director.[212]

*Exceptions*

There are two main exceptions, namely (a) exception for payments in discharge of legal obligations, etc and (b) exception for small payments. **18.143**

Section 220(1) provides that members' approval is not required under s 217[213] for a payment[214] made in good faith **18.144**

(a) in discharge of an existing legal obligation...,
(b) by way of damages for breach of such an obligation,
(c) by way of settlement or compromise in connection with the termination of a person's office or employment, or
(d) by way of pension in respect of past services.[215]

By subs 220(2), in relation to a payment within s 217, 'an existing legal obligation' means 'an obligation of the company, or any body corporate associated with it, that was not entered into in connection with, or in consequence of, the event giving rise to the payment for loss of office'.[216] This definition applies where the payment is also within ss 218 or 219.[217] A payment part of which falls within s 220(1) and part of which does not is treated as if the parts were separate payments.[218]

The wording of subs 220(1)(c) will cover settlement or compromise of any statutory claims for unfair dismissal and redundancy which were, it seems, outside the wording of the 1985 Act, s 316(3), which referred only to 'bona fide payment by way of damages for breach of contract . . .'; **18.145**

---

[212] The *Mercer* case, above. The benefits to the former director included two seats in the directors' box at Tynecastle on match days to watch Hearts, and Lord MacFayden concluded, perhaps unsurprisingly, that no cost to the company in allowing the director to enjoy such privileges was properly alleged.

[213] s 220 applies also to payments under s 218 (payment in connection with transfer or undertaking, etc) and 219 (payment in connection with share transfer): see further below.

[214] By reason of s 215(3), 'payment' in s 220 has the extended meaning given by s 215(2), and hence extends to the provision of benefits otherwise than in cash.

[215] The wording 'by way of pension in respect of past services' repeats the wording found in 1985 Act, s 316(3). 'Pension' was there defined as including 'any superannuation allowance, superannuation gratuity or similar payment'. The Act includes no definition of 'Pension', though it will doubtless be interpreted as covering all payments specifically mentioned in the former definition. The exception in s 220(1)(d) presumably applies where the director had no entitlement to any pension.

[216] The point of s 220(2) is to close a potential loophole whereby s 217 could be circumvented by the company entering into a binding agreement with the director shortly before his loss of office, and then making the payment in discharge of the company's legal obligations under that agreement. The possible existence of this loophole under the 1985 Act was discussed in *Mercer v Heart of Midlothian Plc* [2002] SLT 945, 952, OH.

[217] subs 220(4).

[218] subs 220(5).

**18.146**  By subs 221(1), which is a wholly new provision, approval is also not required under s 217 if:

(a) the payment in question is made by the company or one of its subsidiaries, and

(b) the amount or value of the payment, together with the amount or value of any 'other relevant payments', does not exceed £200.[219]

In s 221, 'payment' has the extended meaning given in subss 215(3) and (4) (paragraph 18.131 above). By subs 221(2) 'other relevant payments' are payments for loss of office in relation to which, in relation to s 217, the conditions of subs 221(3) are met, namely that the other payment was or is paid:

(a) By the company making the payment in question or any of its subsidiaries;[220]

(b) To the director to whom that payment is made,[221] and

(c) In connection with the same event.

*Civil consequence of payments made without approval*

**18.147**  By s 222, if a payment is made in contravention of s 217:

(a) it is held by the recipient on trust for the company making the payment, and

(b) any director who authorised the payment is jointly and severally liable to indemnify the company that made the payment for any loss resulting from it.

If the payment is in contravention of s 217 and also of ss 218 or 219, the civil consequences in respect of the latter provisions apply (paragraphs 18.162–18.164 below), unless, in the case of s 219, the court otherwise orders.[222]

**18.148**  The civil consequences of a payment made in contravention of s 217 have been spelt out for the first time.[223] The provision whereby any payment is held on trust by the recipient for the company which made the payment (s 221(1)(a)) applies not only to any director recipient, but to any person who falls within s 215(3) of the Act.

**(3) Payment in connection with transfer of undertaking etc**

**18.149**  Section 218[224] requires members' approval of any payment for loss of office in connection with the transfer of the whole or any part of the undertaking or

---

[219]  s 221 applies also to payments under section 218 (payment in connection with transfer or undertaking, etc) and 219 (payment in connection with share transfer): see further below. The Secretary of State has the power to raise the £200 limit: s 258.

[220]  See preceding note.

[221]  For these purposes, payment to a person connected with a director, or payment to any person at the direction of, or for the benefit of, a director or person connected with him, is treated as payment to the director: s 215(3).

[222]  subss 222(4) and (5).

[223]  Under the former law (where payment without prior approval was not lawful), the remedies available were those which applied to a misapplication of the company's funds: *Re Duomatic Ltd* [1969] 2 Ch 365, 374–5.

[224]  s 218 derives from 1985 Act, ss 313 and 316 and ultimately the Companies Act 1928.

property of the company. 'Payment for loss of office' has the meaning stated in s 215 (paragraphs 18.129–18.132 above).

Under subs 216(1)[225] the provisions of subs (2) apply to identify amounts to be taken to be payments for loss of office where in connection with any transfer as is mentioned in s 218 a director of the company: **18.150**

    (a) is to cease to hold office, or
    (b) is to cease to be the holder of—
        (i) any other office or employment in connection with the management of the affairs of the company, or
        (ii) any office (as director or otherwise) or employment in connection with the management of the affairs of any subsidiary undertaking of the company.

Subsection (2) provides:

If in connection with any such transfer—

    (a) the price to be paid to the director for any shares in the company held by him is in excess of the price which could at the time have been obtained by other holders of like shares, or
    (b) any valuable consideration is given to the director by a person other than the company,
the excess or, as the case may be, the money value of the consideration is taken for the purposes of [s 218][226] to have been a payment for loss of office.

Section 216 effectively ensures that certain 'disguised' payments for loss of office do not slip through the net, and require prior members' approval. Thus, where, in connection with a transfer of undertaking or property of a company,[227] a director is paid an inflated price in respect of shares held by him in the company (s 216(2)(a)), the excess value of the consideration is taken to have been a payment for loss of office; and if a person other than the company gives any valuable consideration to the director in connection with such a transfer, the value of the consideration is taken to have been a payment for loss of office (s 216(2)(b)). **18.151**

The conditions for the requirement of members' approval are stated in subss 218(1), (2), and (5): **18.152**

    (1) No payment for loss of office may be made by any person to a director of a company in connection with the transfer of the whole or any part of the undertaking or

---

[225] The section, which is substantially derived from 1985 Act, s 316(2), also applies to payments within s 219 (payment in connection with share transfer): see paragraph 18.165 below.

[226] s 216(2) also applies to s 219 (payment in connection with share transfer): see paragraph 18.165 *et seq* below.

[227] s 216(2) in part achieves its expansive effect by applying wherever the excessive price for the shares, or the valuable consideration given by a person other than the company, is 'in connection with' the transfer identified in s 218—the payment need not, it appears, be by way of compensation, etc, as specified in the opening words of each of s 215(1)(a)–(b). It is not clear what the addition of the words 'by a person other than the company' are intended to add to s 216(2)(b): such words did not appear in s 316(2)(b) of the 1985 Act, and ss 218 and 219 apply to payments 'by any person'.

property of the company unless the payment has been approved by a resolution of the members of the company.[228]

(2) No payment for loss of office may be made by any person to a director of a company in connection with the transfer of the whole or any part of the undertaking or property of a subsidiary of the company unless the payment has been approved by a resolution of the members of each of the companies.

...

(5) A payment made in pursuance of an arrangement—[229]

(a) entered into as part of the agreement for the transfer in question, or within one year before or two years after that agreement, and

(b) to which the company whose undertaking or property is transferred, or any person to whom the transfer is made, is privy,

is presumed, except in so far as the contrary is shown, to be a payment to which this section applies.

**18.153** The requirements for members' approval in respect of payments for loss of office in connection with transfers of undertaking, set out in s 218(3), are the same as those applicable to payments for loss of office under s 217 (paragraph 18.135 above). Section 224, dealing with an accidental failure to send the requisite memorandum, also applies.

**18.154** Section 218(4) of the Act creates the same exception as s 217(4) in respect of members of a body corporate that is not a UK-registered company or is a wholly-owned subsidiary of another body corporate.[230]

**18.155** By s 218(2) of the Act, the requirement for prior members' approval is extended so as now to cover payments to a director of a company in connection with the transfer of the whole or any part of the undertaking or property of the subsidiary of the company. In contrast to s 219, where a director or his associate are precluded from voting on the resolution, a transferee who also holds shares in the company, and his associates, are permitted to vote.[231]

**18.156** No reported decision had considered the 1985 Act, ss 313 and 316 in so far as they applied to company approval for payments for loss of or retirement from office. The case law cited at paragraphs 18.139–18.141 above, which considered statutory predecessors of the current s 216, was of persuasive authority on s 313.

---

[228] Where a company is a charity, any approval given by members of the company under this section is ineffective without the prior written consent of the Charity Commission: s 226.

[229] On the meaning of 'arrangement' in the context of s 190 of the Act (substantial property transactions) see paragraph 18.135 above.

[230] Where the company is a charity, the prior written consent of the Charity Commission is necessary notwithstanding this exemption: s 226.

[231] See Law Commission Report, *Company Directors: Regulating Conflicts of Interest and Formulating a Statement of Duties*, No 261, paras 7.64 for the distinction between the two sections: the Law Commission considered that if the effect of a resolution under s 218 was to confer a benefit on the majority who caused it to be passed at the expense of the minority, the resolution was likely to be ineffective on the ground that it is a fraud on the minority.

In particular, the decision of the Privy Council in *Taupo Totara Timber Co Ltd v Rowe*,[232] and those cases which followed its reasoning, suggested that s 313 did not apply to covenanted payments, reasoning which was endorsed by the Law Commission and CLR. Parliament followed this reasoning, and as with s 217, s 218 does not apply to covenanted payments: see s 220(1)(a).

As to the other aspect of the decision in the *Taupo* case, limiting the scope of the 1985 Act, s 312 to payments made to the director for the loss of his office *as director*, it is doubtful that that reasoning ever applied to the predecessor of s 218 by reason of the wide wording of s 316(2)(b) of the 1985 Act. In any event, by reason of s 215 of the Act, the scope of s 218 extends to the offices and employment covered by the broad wording of s 215(1). It is further made express that s 218 applies to past directors (s 215(1)), that references to 'compensation' and 'consideration' include benefits otherwise than in cash, references to 'payment' having a corresponding meaning (s 215(2)), that s 218 includes payment to persons connected with the director, and to any person at the direction of, or for the benefit of, a director or a person connected with him (s 215(3)) and to any person at the direction of, or for the benefit of, a director or a person connected with him (s 215(3)) and that references to payment by a person include payment by another person at the direction of, or on behalf of, the person referred to (s 215(4)). **18.157**

A rebuttable statutory presumption is created by s 218(5) whereby certain payments are presumed to be covered by s 218.[233] Despite the fact that s 218 applies to payments for loss of office to a director of a company in connection with the transfer of a subsidiary's undertaking or property, the presumption will apply only where, inter alia, the company whose undertaking or property is transferred (and not the company in respect of which the director holds office for the purposes of s 218(2)) is privy to the arrangement.[234] **18.158**

*Exceptions*

As with payments falling within ss 217 and 219, there are two exceptions, namely exception for payments in discharge of legal obligations, etc and exception for small payments, but with some modifications. **18.159**

By subs 220(1), members' approval is not required under s 218 for a payment made in good faith in discharge of 'an existing legal obligation', by way of damages for breach of such an obligation, by way of settlement or compromise in **18.160**

---

[232] [1978] AC 537.
[233] s 218(5) is substantially a re-enactment of 1985 Act, s 316(1), in so far as that subsection applied to payments in respect of a transfer of undertaking or property. 1985 Act, s 316(1) was limited in its operation to proceedings for recovery of a payment received by any person in trust by virtue of s 313(2): s 218(5) is not so limited.
[234] subs 218(5)(b).

connection with the termination of a person's office or employment, or by way of pension in respect of past services (paragraph 18.144 above). However, in relation to payments within ss 218 and 219, the words 'an existing legal obligation' have a different meaning from that which applies in respect of payments within s 217. In relation to payments under ss 218 and 219, subs 220(3) provides that 'an existing legal obligation' means 'an obligation of the person making the payment that was not entered into for the purposes of, in connection with or in consequence of, the transfer in question'. In the case of a payment within both ss 217 and 218, the definition in subs 220(2) (paragraph 18.144 above) applies and subs 220(3) does not apply.[235]

**18.161** Subsection 221(1) provides that approval is not required under s 218 if the payment in question is made by the company or one of its subsidiaries, and the amount or value of the payment, together with the amount or value of any 'other relevant payments', does not exceed £200 (paragraph 18.146 above). However, where the payment is one to which s 218 applies, the conditions which must be met for a payment for loss of office to be 'other relevant payments' differ from the conditions applicable to payments falling within s 217 and are stated in subs 221(4):[236]

> (4) Where the payment in question is one to which section 218 or 219 applies (payment in connection with transfer of undertaking, property or shares), the conditions are that the other payment was (or is) paid in connection with the same transfer—
> (a) to the director to whom the payment in question was made, and
> (b) by the company making the payment or any of its subsidiaries.

*Civil consequences of payments made without approval*

**18.162** Subsection 222(2) provides:

> If a payment is made in contravention of section 218..., it is held by the recipient on trust for the company whose undertaking or property is or is proposed to be transferred.[237]

**18.163** Section 222(2) is substantially a re-enactment of the 1985 Act, s 313(2). The wording has been altered and expanded in line with the new provisions found in s 218(2) (ie members' approval is now required for payment to a director where it is a subsidiary's undertaking or property which is transferred) and s 215(3) (whereby payments to persons connected with the director, and payments to third

---

[235] subs 220(4).
[236] subss 221(2) and (4).
[237] Compare and contrast s 222(1) at paragraph 18.147 above, setting out the civil consequences of a payment made in contravention of s 217, where the payment is held on trust for the company making the payment, and any director who authorized the payment is jointly and severally liable to indemnify that company for any loss resulting from it.

parties at the direction of, or for the benefit of, a director or person connected with him, are now treated as payments to the director). In contrast to the civil consequences applicable where a payment is made in breach of s 217, directors who authorized the payment are not liable under any provision of the statute to indemnify the company in respect of any loss resulting from it.

**18.164** If a payment is made in contravention of both ss 217 and 218, s 222(2) applies rather than s 222(1).[238] It is not wholly clear how this provision is intended to apply. Presumably the remedies set out in s 222 operate to the exclusion of remedies under the common law:[239] though since ss 217, 218 (and 219) prohibit payments without the requisite approval, it is not beyond argument that, where the payments are made by the company, the usual remedies apply where directors misapply a company's property, and s 222 does not specifically exclude this conclusion. Assuming that s 222 implicitly excludes such common law remedies, the surprising effect of s 222(4) appears to be that where a payment falls within both ss 217 and 218, the liability of directors under s 222(1)(b) which would arise if the payment fell within s 217 alone is excluded.

### (4) Payment in connection with share transfer: requirement of members' approval

**18.165** Section 219 deals with payment to a director for loss of office in connection with share transfers resulting from a takeover bid.[240] Payment for loss of office has the meaning in s 215 and s 216 also applies to determine the amounts to be taken to be payments for loss of office (paragraphs 18.130–18.150 above). Subsections 219(1), (2), and (7) provide:

(1) No payment for loss of office may be made by any person to a director of a company in connection with a transfer of shares in the company, or in a subsidiary of the company, resulting from a takeover bid unless the payment has been approved by a resolution of the relevant shareholders.

(2) The relevant shareholders are the holders of the shares to which the bid relates and any holders of shares of the same class as any of those shares.

. . .

(7) A payment made in pursuance of an arrangement[241]—

    (a) entered into as part of the agreement for the transfer in question, or within one year before or two years after that agreement, and

---

[238] subs 222(4).

[239] Unlike, for example, s 195 (property transactions: civil consequences of contravention) and 213(8) (loans etc: civil consequences of contravention), s 222 does not specifically preserve remedies which might arise under the general law.

[240] s 219 dervies from 1985 Act, ss 314–316 and ultimately the Companies Act 1928.

[241] On the meaning of 'arrangement' in the context of s 190 of the Act (substantial property transactions) see paragraph 18.42 above.

    (b) to which the company whose shares are the subject of the bid, or any person to whom the transfer is made, is privy,

is presumed, except in so far as the contrary is shown, to be a payment to which s 219 applies.

**18.166** The requirements for members' approval in respect of payments for loss of office in connection with share transfers, set out in s 219(3), are the same as those applicable to payments for loss of office under ss 217 and 218 (paragraphs 18.134–18.164 above).[242] However, subss 219(4) and (5) contain special provisions to protect shareholders by preventing the person making the offer and his associates from voting on the resolution to approve the payment to the director:[243]

    (4) Neither the person making the offer, nor any associate of his (as defined in section 988), is entitled to vote on the resolution, but—

        (a) where the resolution is proposed as a written resolution, they are entitled (if they would otherwise be so entitled) to be sent a copy of it, and

        (b) at any meeting to consider the resolution they are entitled (if they would otherwise be so entitled) to be given notice of the meeting, to attend and speak and if present (in person or by proxy) to count towards the quorum.

    (5) If at a meeting to consider the resolution a quorum is not present, and after the meeting has been adjourned to a later date a quorum is again not present, the payment is deemed to have been approved.

**18.167** No approval is required under s 217 on the part of the members of a body corporate that is not a UK-registered company, or is a wholly-owned subsidiary of another body corporate.[244]

**18.168** Under the 1985 Act, ss 314–316, where a takeover offer or similar conditional offer for shares was made in respect of shares in a company, a director to whom a payment was to be made by way of compensation for loss of office in connection with such offer was obliged to take all reasonable steps to secure that particulars of the proposed payment were included in any notice to the shareholders of the offer made for the shares.[245] If the director failed to comply with this duty, or the making of the payment was not approved by a meeting by the shareholders to whom the offer related (and those in the same class) the payment was held in trust for the shareholders who sold their shares as a result of the offer, and the costs of distributing the payment to such persons was again to be borne by the director. Section 219 removes the duty on the director to disclose particulars of a proposed payment for loss of office in connection with a share transfer to the target shareholders.

---

[242] Where the company is a charity, the prior written consent of the Charity Commission is necessary notwithstanding this exemption: s 226. Where there is an accidental failure to send the requisite memorandum, s 224 applies.

[243] This was on the recommendation of the Law Commission (Hansard HL GC Day 4, Vol 678, cols 358, 359 (9 February 2006)).

[244] subs 219(6).

[245] 1985 Act, subss 314(1) and (2).

The requirement that the relevant shareholders (ie the shareholders to whom the bid relates, or who are in the same class) should approve the proposed payment by resolution is retained, consonant with the similar requirements for prior approval in ss 217 and 218.[246] The rationale is to avoid the risk that directors may obtain advantageous payments from the persons launching the takeover bid which should in fact go towards the members in return for their shares.[247]

**18.169** The observations in paragraphs 18.157–18.158 concerning the scope of s 218 apply equally to s 219.

**18.170** A rebuttable statutory presumption is created by s 219(7) whereby certain payments are presumed to be covered by s 219. Subsection 219(7) is substantially a re-enactment of the 1985 Act, s 316(1), in so far as that subsection applied to payments held on trust in consequence of a director's failure to disclose a payment for loss of office to be made in connection with a takeover.[248]

*Exceptions*

**18.171** As with payments falling within ss 217 and 218, there are two exceptions, namely an exception for payments in discharge of legal obligations, etc (s 220) and an exception for small payments (s 221). In respect of both exceptions, the position under s 219 is the same as under s 218 (paragraphs 18.152–18.158 above).

*Civil consequence of payments made without approval*

**18.172** Subsection 222(3) provides:

> (3) If a payment is made in contravention of section 219 . . . —
> (a) it is held by the recipient on trust for persons who have sold their shares as a result of the offer made, and
> (b) the expenses incurred by the recipient in distributing that sum amongst those persons are to be borne by him and not retained out of that sum.[249]

---

[246] Under 1985 Act, s 314(3), if the director failed to take the steps set out in s 314 (ie inclusion of particulars of the proposed payment in the offer document), or any person properly required by the director to include such particulars failed to do so, they were liable to a fine. No such provision is included in the Act. Lord Sainsbury described such a provision, and the duty cast upon a director under 314(2), as 'over-regulatory', and stated that the civil consequences of failure to obtain approval should be sufficient, in line with the removal of criminal sanction for all breaches in this Chapter of the Act: Hansard, HL GC Day 4, Vol 678, cols 358–359 (9 February 2006).

[247] Per Lord Sainsbury, Hansard, HL GC Day 4, Vol 678, col 358 (9 February 2006).

[248] 1985 Act, s 316(1) was limited in its operation to proceedings for recovery of a payment received by any person in trust by virtue of s 315(1): s 219(7) is not so limited.

[249] Compare and contrast s 222(1) at paragraphs 18.147–18.148 above, setting out the civil consequences of a payment made in contravention of s 217, where the payment is held on trust for the company making the payment, and any director who authorized the payment is jointly and severally liable to indemnify that company for any loss resulting from it; and s 222(2) at paragraphs 18.162–18.164 above, setting out the civil consequences of a payment made in contravention of

**18.173**   Section 222(3) is substantially a re-enactment of the 1985 Act, s 315(1). The wording has been altered and expanded in line with the new provisions found in s 215(3) (whereby payments to persons connected with the director, and payments to third parties at the direction of, or for the benefit of, a director or person connected with him, are now treated as payments to the director). In contrast to the civil consequences applicable where a payment is made in breach of s 217, directors who authorized the payment are not liable under any provision of the statute to indemnify the company in respect of any loss resulting from it. The 1985 Act imposed no such liability either.[250] If a payment is made in contravention of s 217 and s 219, s 222(3) applies rather than s 222(1), unless the court directs otherwise.[251] This provides clarification of the law: it is plainly right that where ss 217 and 219 both apply, it is the shareholders who have lost out who should be compensated, not the company as such (since of course benefit to the company will not benefit the shareholders who have sold their shares). For reasons similar to those above at paragraph 18.164, in certain respects it is not clear how s 222(5) will operate in practice.

## F.  Contracts with Sole Members who are Directors

**18.174**   The Companies Act, s 231[252] regulates contracts between a company and its sole member where:

(a)  a limited company having only one member enters into a contract with the sole member,

(b)  the sole member is also a director of the company, and

(c)  the contract is not entered into in the ordinary course of the company's business.[253]

**18.175**   Where s 231 applies, subs 231(2) provides:

> The company must, unless the contract is in writing, ensure that the terms of the contract are either:
>
> (a)  set out in a written memorandum, or
>
> (b)  recorded in the minutes of the first meeting of the directors of the company following the making of the contract.

---

s 218, where the payment is held on trust for the company whose undertaking is or is proposed to be transferred.

[250]  1985 Act, s 315(1). The Law Commission recommended that s 315(1) be expanded so as to impose liability on authorizing directors: Law Commission Report, *Company Directors: Regulating Conflicts of Interest and Formulating a Statement of Duties*, No 261, paras 7.81–7.86.

[251]  subs 222(5).

[252]  s 231 applies to contracts entered into on or after 1 October 2007: 2006 Act Commencement Order No 3, Schedule 3, para 14(1). 1985 Act, s 322B continues to apply to contracts entered into before that date: ibid, para 14(2).

[253]  subs 231(1). Section 3 defines limited and unlimited companies. For the purposes of s 231 a shadow director is treated as a director.

If a company fails to comply with the requirements set out above, every officer **18.176** of the company who is in default commits an offence, which is punishable on summary conviction by a fine.[254]

Failure to comply with s 231 in relation to a contract does not affect the validity **18.177** of the contract.[255] Nothing in s 231 is to be read as excluding the operation of any other enactment or rule of law applying to contracts between a company and a director of the company.[256]

Section 231 substantially re-enacts the 1985 Act, s 322B and gives effect to Article **18.178** 5 of the 12th EEC Company Law Directive.[257] That Directive ultimately sought to harmonize divergences that had occurred between Member States permitting single-member private limited-liability companies, the aim being to encourage enterprise amongst small firms. The preamble to the Directive specifically provided for contracts between the company and sole member to be recorded in writing.

The main change introduced by s 231 is that the section now applies to any **18.179** limited company having only one member, and thus applies to a public limited company with only one member.[258] A further change is that under s 231(3), the company itself commits no offence if s 231 is not complied with, and hence is not itself liable to a fine.[259]

The purpose of s 231 is to ensure that records are kept in those cases where **18.180** there is a high risk of the lines becoming blurred between where a person acts in his personal capacity and when he acts on behalf of the company.[260] This may be of particular interest to a liquidator should the company become insolvent.[261]

The purpose and scope of s 231 is thus rather different to the purpose and scope **18.181** of the provisions in the Companies Act, Part 10, Chapter 4 discussed in the

---

[254] subss 231(3) and (4).

[255] subs 231(6).

[256] subs 231(7).

[257] Which was inserted into the 1985 Act by the Companies (Single Member Private Limited Companies) Regulations 1992 (SI 1992/1699), reg 2, Schedule, para 3, as from 15 July 1992, so as to give effect to Article 5 of the 12th EEC Company Law Directive (89/667/EEC) [1989] OJ L395/40.

[258] See the Explanatory Notes, para 422. Under 1985 Act, ss 1(1) and 24 a public limited company had to have two members as a minimum. Such requirement in respect of private limited companies was removed by the 12th EEC Company Law Directive as made clear by, inter alia, 1985 Act, s 1(3A).

[259] Explanatory Notes, para 424.

[260] Explanatory Notes, para 421.

[261] Ibid; a point repeated by the Attorney-General: Hansard, HL GC Day 4, Vol 678, col 344. (9 February 2006).

previous sections of this chapter. Section 231 only applies to contracts whereas the provisions in Part 10, Chapter 4 apply to transactions and arrangements. Section 231 applies to any contract outside the ordinary course of business and is not limited to service contracts, substantial property transactions, loans, quasi-loans and credit transactions, or payments for loss of office. Since its purpose is limited to ensuring that there is a record of the contract, it does not apply to written contracts. Whereas Part 10, Chapter 4 set out the civil consequences of non-compliance, there are no civil consequences of non-compliance with s 231. This is not surprising since the sole member can consent to, authorize, approve, or ratify any contract into which the company may lawfully enter, so as to make it binding on the company and protect directors from personal liability. Compliance with s 231 is irrelevant to the merits of a claim under the provisions in the Insolvency Act for relief in respect of antecedent transactions.

**18.182**   Section 231 is complemented by the Companies Act, s 357,[262] which again applies to a company limited by shares or by guarantee that has only one member.[263] Where the member takes any decision that may be taken by the company in general meeting, and has effect as if agreed by the company in general meeting, he must (unless that decision is taken by way of a written resolution) provide the company with details of that decision.[264] A person who fails to comply with the section commits an offence, and is liable on summary conviction to a fine, but failure to comply with s 357 does not affect the validity of any decision taken where s 357 is not complied with.[265]

---

[262]  s 357 re-enacts s 382B of the Act, which again resulted ultimately from the 12th EEC Law Company Law Directive (n 257 above).

[263]  subs 357(1).

[264]  subs 357(2).

[265]  subss 357(3)–(5).

# 19

# DIRECTORS' LIABILITIES: EXEMPTION, INDEMNIFICATION, AND RATIFICATION

## A. Introduction

The 2006 Act, Part 10, Chapter 7, ss 232–239, contains provisions relating to exemption and protection of directors from liabilities incurred in discharge of their functions.[1] Sections 232–234 and 236–238 largely restate or preserve the former law,[2] providing for general prohibitions on the exemption and indemnification of a director from liability or against liability that would otherwise attach to him in connection with any negligence, default, breach of trust, or breach of duty in relation to the company, subject, in the case of indemnification, to specified exceptions relating to insurance and certain third party indemnity provision.

**19.01**

---

[1] These sections came into force on 1 October 2007: 2006 Act Commencement Order No 3, art 2(1)(d).

[2] As contained in 1985 Act, ss 309A–309C. These sections were inserted in the 1985 Act by the Companies (Audit, Investigations and Community Enterprise) Act 2004 (C(AICE) Act), s 19(1), with effect from 6 April 2005. Until then 1985 Act, s 310 provided for a general prohibition on provisions exempting officers and auditors from liability attaching in respect of any negligence, default, breach of duty, or breach of trust in relation to the company. Section 310 derived from the 1948 Act, s 205, and was first brought into effect by 1929 Act, s 152. With effect from 6 April 2005 s 310 ceased to apply to officers of a company. In the 2006 Act, the provisions in s 310 relating to auditors have been replaced by the largely new provisions contained in Part 16, Chapter 6, ss 532–538.

Section 235 is a new provision dealing with the indemnification of a director of a company that is a trustee of an occupational pension scheme.

**19.02**  Section 239 is another new provision which reforms the law as to the circumstances in which a company may ratify the conduct of a director amounting to negligence, default, breach of duty, or breach of trust. In effect the conduct can only be ratified if shareholders who are independent of the wrongdoer assent. Section 239 does, however, preserve the current law on the validity of decisions taken by unanimous consent of members, the power of the directors not to sue or to settle or release claims, and existing rules which impose additional requirements for ratification or render certain acts incapable of ratification.

**19.03**  This chapter deals with the general prohibition on exemptions and indemnities, qualifying third party and pension scheme indemnity provision, and ratification. The provision of insurance for directors, which is made lawful by s 233, is dealt with in Chapter 20.

## B. General Prohibition on Exemptions and Indemnities

**19.04**  Section 232 sets out the general prohibition on the exemption and indemnification of directors in relation to their negligence, default, breach of duty, or breach of trust in relation to the company, identifies the exceptions to the general prohibition on indemnification (discussed in Sections C and D below), and preserves the effectiveness of provisions in a company's articles dealing with conflicts of interest. It provides:

(1) Any provision that purports to exempt a director of a company (to any extent) from any liability that would otherwise attach to him in connection with any negligence, default, breach of duty or breach of trust in relation to the company is void.

(2) Any provision by which a company directly or indirectly provides an indemnity (to any extent) for a director of a company, or of an associated company, against any liability attaching to him in connection with any negligence, default, breach of duty or breach of trust in relation to the company of which he is a director is void, except as permitted by—
  (a) section 233 (provision of insurance),
  (b) section 234 (qualifying third party indemnity provision) or
  (c) section 235 (qualifying pension scheme indemnity provision).

(3) This section applies to any provision, whether contained in a company's articles or in any contract with the company or other otherwise.

(4) Nothing in this section prevents a company's articles from making such provision as has previously been lawful for dealing with conflicts of interest.

**19.05**  Until the 1929 Act, s 152 brought into effect provisions recommended by the Greene Committee,[3] it was common for the articles of a company to exempt

---

[3] Report of the Greene Committee, paras 46 and 47.

directors from loss except when it was due to their 'wilful neglect or default' or, in some cases, due to actual dishonesty, and the court gave effect to these exemptions from liability.[4] Since 1929 provisions for exemption or indemnification falling within the scope of the successive statutory provisions have been void.

The Attorney-General, Lord Goldsmith, explained the principle underlying the prohibition on exempting and indemnifying directors for negligence, default, breach of duty, and breach of trust:[5]    **19.06**

> . . . the starting point for our reform package was a principle . . . that companies should be prohibited from exempting directors from, or indemnifying them against, liability for negligence, default, breach of duty or breach of trust in relation to the company. However the reform package also recognised that companies should be permitted to indemnify directors in respect of third party claims in most circumstances . . . There are four main possible exceptions to indemnification: criminal penalties; penalties imposed by regulatory bodies; costs incurred by the director in defending criminal proceedings in which he is convicted; and costs incurred by the director in defending civil proceedings brought by the company in which final judgment is given against him.

Thus there is nothing to prevent a company from indemnifying a director for liability incurred through, for example, giving a guarantee.[6]

The conduct of a director to which subss 232(1) and (2) apply is any negligence, default, breach of duty, or breach of trust in relation to the company. This formulation has been used since the 1929 Act, s 152, and is used also in Part 11, s 260(3), in relation to the new procedure for bringing derivative claims[7] and in s 1157 (power of court to grant relief in certain cases).[8] The misconduct described in subss 232(1) and (2) may be compared with the misconduct in the Insolvency Act, s 212 (summary remedy against delinquent directors, liquidators, etc), which applies where a director 'has misapplied or retained, or become accountable for, any money or other property of the company, or has been guilty of any misfeasance or breach of any fiduciary or other duty in relation to the company'.[9] The words 'breach of any fiduciary or other duty' in s 212 replaced the words 'breach    **19.07**

---

[4] *Re Brazilian Rubber Plantations and Estates Ltd* [1911] 1 Ch 425; *Re City of London Insurance Co Ltd* (1925) 41 TLR 521; *Re City Equitable Fire Insurance Co Ltd* [1925] Ch 407; *Re Home and Colonial Insurance Co Ltd* [1930] 1 Ch 102.

[5] Hansard, Lords Grand Committee, 9 February 2006, col 364.

[6] The company's articles usually contain a power of indemnity: Table A, reg 118; Model Article (pcls) 52; Model Article (plc) 85. Since directors are fiduciaries in respect of their powers, as a matter of general law, by analogy with the position of trustees, they may be entitled to an indemnity from the company for expenses incurred in good faith and for the benefit of the company: *Re German Mining Co* (1853) 4 De G M & G 19, 52, per Turner LJ (where the directors guaranteed *ultra vires* borrowing).

[7] Chapter 21 below.

[8] Chapter 16, Section D.

[9] For discussion on Insolvency Act, s 212 see Chapter 29, Section I.

of trust' found in its predecessor, the 1948 Act, s 333, and are wide enough to include claims based on negligence.[10] Thus the difference in scope between the Companies Act, s 232, and the Insolvency Act, s 212, is that the former extends to defaults, whereas the latter does not. This is not surprising, since in the context of s 232 'default' would seem to apply to acts or omissions of a director, which expose him to liability to criminal penalty or penalty imposed by a regulatory authority. Those are matters for which a director might wish to be indemnified, but which are prohibited as a matter of policy.

**19.08**   The 1985 Act, s 309A, introduced by the C(AICE) Act 2004, made three changes from the language of the 1985 Act, s 310: (i) it deleted the phrase 'by virtue of any rule of law', so that there can be no question that statutory as well as common law liability is covered; (ii) it added the words in brackets 'to any extent' to make it clear that that partial exemption or indemnification was prohibited; and (iii) it extended the prohibition to indemnities to a director of an associated company. These changes are restated in s 232(1) and (2). Section 256 defines 'associated bodies corporate' for the purposes of Part 10:

> For the purposes of this Part—
> (a) bodies corporate are associated if one is a subsidiary of the other or both are subsidiaries of the same body corporate, and
> (b) companies are associated if one is a subsidiary of the other or both are subsidiaries of the same body corporate

The Attorney-General, Lord Goldsmith, explained the significance of the extension of the prohibition of indemnification to associated companies:[11]

> The 2004 Act . . . closed an important loophole concerning the indemnification of directors by third parties. It used to be the practice in some groups that one group company would indemnify the director of another group company. It was possible thereby in effect to circumvent the rule that the company could not indemnify its own directors. We take the view that that should continue to apply and that what we consider is an important prohibition—to continue to make directors properly accountable for what they do in relation to the company—should stand.

---

[10] *Re D'Jan of London Ltd* [1994] BCLC 561. In *Re B Johnson & Co (Builders) Ltd* [1955] Ch 634, CA, the Court of Appeal had held that the language used in 1948 Act, s 333 did not cover negligence claims.

[11] Hansard, Lords Grand Committee, 9 February 2006, col 366. Lord Sainsbury of Turville explained why the Government was not persuaded to provide a carve-out so that a parent company could indemnify a director of a subsidiary (Lords Report, 23 May 2006, col 724): 'It is also important to remember that at the same time as the loophole was closed, important reforms were introduced that permit all companies to indemnify directors against third-party claims, subject to . . . [certain] requirements. Although we agree that indemnification by a parent company of the directors is less likely to result in attempts at circumvention of the prohibition than indemnification by a wholly owned subsidiary company of the director of a holding company, we still believe there is scope for mischief. We cannot . . . accept [any] amendment.'

Section 232(3) makes it clear that the prohibitions in s 232 apply to exemptions **19.09** and indemnities contained in the company's articles as well as to contracts.[12] Provisions in the company's articles are not automatically incorporated into a contract between the company and a director, but, if not expressly incorporated, relatively little may be required for an indemnity in the articles to be impliedly incorporated.[13] The words 'or otherwise' are limited to exemptions and indemnities given by the company and do not extend to indemnities given by third parties.[14]

Section 232(4) is a new provision, which preserves the existing law by which a **19.10** company's articles may continue to make provision for dealing with conflicts of interest without them being void under subss 232(1) and (2). Sections 175–177 deal with the duties of directors to avoid conflicts of interest, not to accept benefits from third parties, and to declare interests in a proposed transaction or arrangement. Section 180(4)(b) provides that, where the company's articles contain provisions for dealing with conflicts of interest, a director's general duties are not infringed by anything done or omitted by him in accordance with those provisions.[15] It would seem that provisions in a company's articles that deal with conflicts of interest are not rendered void as exempting a director from liability for breach of duty or breach of trust, and that the director will not be liable to the company provided that he complies with the articles and the Companies Act, as the case may be. Section 232(4) does not apply to the directors' other duties under ss 171–174, namely to act within his powers, to promote the success of the company, to exercise independent judgment, and to exercise reasonable care, skill, and diligence.

Notwithstanding that s 232 renders void provisions in a contract, the articles or **19.11** otherwise that purport to exempt or indemnify the director from or against liability before the relevant conduct has occurred, there are a number of ways in which

---

[12] Articles often include indemnity provisions: Table A, reg 118; Model Article (pcls) 52; Model Article (plc) 85.

[13] *John v Price Waterhouse* [2002] 1 WLR 953 at [26]; *Gobalink Telecommunications Ltd v Wilmbury* [2003] 1 BCLC 145 at [29]–[31].

[14] *Burgoine v London Borough of Waltham Forest* [1997] 2 BCLC 612, 626.

[15] Table A, reg 85, Model Article (pcls) 14, and Model Article (plc) 16 all make express provision for dealing with conflicts of interest. In *Movitex Ltd v Bulfield* [1988] BCLC 104 Vinelott J resolved the apparent conflict between 1948 Act, Table A, regs 78 and 84 (now 1985 Act, Table A, reg 85) and 1948 Act, s 205 (a predecessor of s 232) by distinguishing (i) the self-dealing rule, which disabled a director from entering into contracts with the company, which could be modified by the articles, and (ii) liability for breach of trust, which could not be exempted by virtue of the 1948 Act, s 205. In *Gwembe Valley Development Co Ltd v Koshy (No 3)* [2004] 1 BCLC 131, CA at [107] the Court of Appeal described this distinction as 'an unnecessary complication' and inconsistent with the exposition of the nature of fiduciary duties given by Millett LJ in *Bristol and West BS v Mothew* [1998] Ch 1, CA, and *Paragon Finance plc v DB Thackerar & Co* [1999] 1 All ER 400, CA. In the context of the 2006 Act it should not be necessary to refer to this distinction.

a director may achieve practical exemption from liability to the company for negligence, default, breach of trust, or breach of duty:

(1) The directors may cause the company not to make a claim against him and in due course the claim will become barred by limitation. If the directors act in this way, they expose themselves to a claim for negligence, breach of duty, or breach of trust if the company suffers any loss from the non-pursuit of the claim.

(2) The directors may agree not to sue, or to settle or to release a claim made by them on behalf of the company.[16] In exercising their powers in this respect the directors must of course comply with their fiduciary duties and duty of care, skill, and diligence. If they do not and the wrongdoing director has the requisite knowledge of the other directors' breach of duty, the agreement may be set aside. Also, if creditors' interests are prejudiced, the agreement may be vulnerable under the Insolvency Act, ss 238 and 423.

(3) The company may ratify the director's conduct under s 239 or by informal unanimous consent and so release him from liability (but again subject to the impact on creditors' interests).[17]

(4) Finally by s 1157 the court has a discretion to relieve the director, either wholly or in part, from any liability for negligence, default, breach of duty, or breach of trust where it appears to the court that he has acted honestly and reasonably and ought fairly to be excused.[18]

## C. Qualifying Indemnity Provision

### (1) Qualifying third party indemnity provision

**19.12** As foreshadowed by s 232(2)(b), s 234[19] provides an exemption from the general rule, contained in s 232(2), making void any provision by which a company directly or indirectly provides an indemnity (to any extent) for a director of the company, or of an associated company, against any liability attaching to him in connection with any negligence, default, breach of duty, or breach of trust in relation to the company of which he is a director. Section 234(1) states that s 232(2) does not apply to a qualifying third party indemnity provision and subss 234(2) and (3) explain what the requirements for that provision are:

(2) Third party indemnity provision means provision for indemnity against liability incurred by the director to a person other than the company or an associated company.

---

[16] s 239(6)(b).
[17] Section D below and Chapter 22, Section B.
[18] s 1157 replaces 1985 Act, s 727. This is discussed in Chapter 16, Section D.
[19] It restates 1985 Act, s 309B without substantial change.

Such provision is qualifying third party indemnity provision if the following requirements are met.

(3) The provision must not provide indemnity against—
  (a) any liability of the director to pay—
      (i) a fine imposed in criminal proceedings, or
      (ii) a sum payable to a regulatory authority by way of a penalty in respect of non-compliance with any requirement of a regulatory nature (howsoever arising); or
  (b) any liability incurred by the director—
      (i) in defending criminal proceedings in which he is convicted, or
      (ii) in defending civil proceedings brought by the company, or an associated company in which judgment is given against him,[20] or
      (iii) in connection with an application for relief (see subsection (6)) in which the court refuses to grant him relief.[21]

Therefore the first requirement for qualifying third party indemnity provision is **19.13** that it does not indemnify the director against liability incurred by him to the company or an associate company[22] in connection with any negligence, default, breach of duty, or breach of trust in relation to the company of which he is director. The company may indemnify the director against liability incurred by him to any third party in connection with those wrongs, provided that the second requirement is met: the liability is not a criminal or civil liability within subs (3), as discussed in the following paragraphs. The liabilities against which the company may indemnify the director include liability to a third party under a guarantee or for misrepresentation in relation to the company and liabilities arising as a result of an accident relating to the company's affairs.

Subsections 234(3)(a)(i) and (b)(i) deal with criminal proceedings. A company **19.14** may not indemnify a director against liability to pay a fine imposed in criminal proceedings or a liability incurred by him in defending criminal proceedings in which he is convicted (after exhausting all appeals). A company can, however, indemnify the director against costs liabilities incurred by him in successfully defending criminal proceedings.

---

[20] subs (4) explains that the references in subs (3)(b) to a conviction, judgment, or refusal of relief are to the final decision in the proceedings. Subsection (5) provides:
  For this purpose—
  (a) a conviction, judgment, or refusal of relief becomes final—(i) if not appealed against, at the end of the period for bringing an appeal, or (ii) if appealed against, at the time when the appeal (or any further appeal) is disposed of; and
  (b) an appeal is disposed of—(i) if it is determined and the period for bringing any further appeal has ended, or (ii) if it is abandoned or otherwise ceases to have effect.
[21] subs (6) explains that the reference in subs (3)(b)(iii) to an application for relief is to an application for relief under subss 661(3) or (4) (power of court to grant relief in case of acquisition of shares by innocent nominee), or s 1157 (general power of court to grant relief in case of honest and reasonable conduct).
[22] 'Associate company' is defined by s 256; see paragraph 19.08 above.

**19.15** Subsection 234(3)(a)(ii) prevents a company from indemnifying the director against liability to pay a penalty imposed by a regulatory authority in respect of non-compliance with any requirement of a regulatory nature, but curiously subs 234(3)(b) does not expressly prevent the company from indemnifying the director in respect of the costs of unsuccessfully defending the regulatory proceedings.

**19.16** Subsection 234(3)(b)(ii) and (iii) deal with liabilities incurred by the director in relation to certain civil proceedings concerning the company. They prevent a company from indemnifying the director against any liability, including a liability to pay any costs, incurred by him in defending civil proceedings brought by the company or an associate company in which final judgment is given against him or in unsuccessfully applying for relief under ss 661(3) or (4) or 1157. On the other hand the company may indemnify the director in respect of his costs, whether pursuant to an order or by agreement, if he succeeds in his defence of the proceedings brought against him by the company or an associate company or if he succeeds in obtaining relief from the court under ss 661(3) or (4) or s 1157.[23] It may be difficult to apply subs 234(3)(b) to a case where the director settles or compromises proceedings. By so doing he may avoid a final judgment, but can it be said that he has succeeded in his defence? Furthermore the director may be protected by indemnity under a directors' and officers' insurance policy as discussed in Chapter 20 below.

**19.17** Although a company's ability to indemnify the director in respect of liabilities incurred in civil and criminal proceedings is controlled and restricted by s 234, it should be noted that a company may lend the director money to defend civil or criminal proceedings, provided that the requirements of s 205 are complied with.[24]

### (2) Qualifying pension scheme indemnity provision

**19.18** As foreshadowed by subs 232(2)(c), s 235 enables a company that is a trustee of an occupational pension scheme to indemnify a director against liability for negligence, default, breach of duty, or breach of trust incurred in connection with the company's activities as trustee of the scheme in slightly broader terms than apply to third party indemnities. Subsection 235(6) provides that in s 235 'occupational pension scheme' means an occupational pension scheme as defined in the Finance Act 2004, s 150(5) that is established under a trust, namely:

> a pension scheme established by an employer or employers and having or capable of having effect so as to provide benefits to or in respect of any or all of the employees of—
> (a) that employer or those employers, or
> (b) any other employer,

---

[23] Applications for relief under s 1157 are discussed in Chapter 16, Section D above.
[24] Chapter 18, Section D above.

(whether or not it also has or is capable of having effect so as to provide benefits to or in respect of other persons).

The liabilities facing directors of companies that are trustees of such schemes are discussed in Chapter 26 of this work.

The section was introduced by the Government at the committee stage in the House of Commons, in response to concerns expressed in the House of Lords as to the importance of the role performed by such directors, the limited protection currently offered by D&O Insurance policies, and the difficulties of recruiting high-quality directors for companies acting as trustees of occupational pension schemes.[25]     **19.19**

Section 235(1) states that s 232(2) does not apply to a qualifying pension scheme indemnity provision and subss 235(2) and (3) explain what the requirements for that provision are:     **19.20**

(1) Pension scheme indemnity provision means provision indemnifying a director of a company that is a trustee of an occupational pension scheme against liability incurred in connection with the company's activities as trustee of the scheme.

Such provision is qualifying pension scheme indemnity provision if the following requirements are met.

(2) The provision must not provide indemnity against—
    (a) any liability of the director to pay—
        (i) a fine imposed in criminal proceedings, or
        (ii) a sum payable to a regulatory authority by way of a penalty in respect of non-compliance with any requirement of a regulatory nature (howsoever arising); or
    (b) any liability incurred by the director in defending criminal proceedings in which he is convicted.

Subsections (4) and (5) explain that the reference to a conviction is to a final conviction after any appeal process has been exhausted.[26]

---

[25] The Solicitor General explained why the Government amended the Company Law Reform Bill by adding a clause in terms of s 235 (Hansard, HC Comm D, cols 636–637 (11 July 2006)):

The amendments concern indemnification of a director of a company acting as a trustee of an occupational pension scheme. They deal with worries that were raised in another place. It was said that such directors perform a vital role, often for little direct financial reward, and that directors' and officers' liability insurance policies currently available afford limited protection. We made it clear in another place that the Government attach importance to the work of such directors and that we were aware that it can sometimes be difficult to recruit high-quality directors for companies acting as trustees of occupational pension schemes. In view of that, and following consultation with key stakeholders, we agreed in principle to table amendments that would permit companies to indemnify the directors of associated companies acting as trustees of occupational pension schemes.

[26] The language used in subss 235(4) and (5) is the same as that used in subss 234(4) and (5) (see n 20 above), except that s 235 is only concerned with criminal convictions.

**19.21**  Unlike a qualifying third party indemnity provision, a qualifying pension scheme indemnity provision may indemnify the director against liability incurred by him in connection with the company's activities as trustee of the scheme (1) to the company or an associate company in connection with any negligence, default, breach of duty, or breach of trust, (2) in defending civil proceedings brought by the company or associate company even if judgment is given against him, and (3) in connection with an unsuccessful application for relief under s 1157 (general power of court to grant relief in case of honest and reasonable conduct). In connection with its activities as trustee of an occupational pension scheme, a company may grant its directors effective immunity from suit. A company may also indemnify the director against liability incurred by him to any third party in connection with the company's activities as trustee of an occupational pension scheme, provided that the liability is not a criminal or regulatory liability within subs (3). The position in respect of criminal fines, regulatory penalties, and the costs of unsuccessfully defending criminal proceedings is the same as for a qualifying third party indemnity provision (paragraphs 19.14 and 19.15 above).

### (3) Disclosure and inspection of qualifying indemnity provision

**19.22**  Sections 236–238[27] impose requirements for disclosure of any qualifying third party or pension scheme indemnity provision in the directors' report, for copies of such provision to be available for general inspection, and for members' entitlement to inspect and be provided with copies. Breach of the requirements to have copies available for inspection and for members' entitlements is an offence.

**19.23**  If a qualifying indemnity provision[28] is in force for the benefit of one or more directors of the company (or an associated company) at the time of the directors' report, or was in force at any time during the financial year to which the report relates for the benefit of one or more persons who were then directors of the company (or an associated company), the directors' report must state that such provision is or was in force.[29]

**19.24**  A copy of the qualifying indemnity provision (or, if it is not in writing, a written memorandum setting out its terms) must be kept available for inspection at the company's registered office or a place specified in regulations under s 1136.[30]

---

[27] Except for ss 237(4) and (9) and 238(4), which are new, these sections derive, with minor changes, from 1985 Act, ss 309C and 318.

[28] Meaning qualifying third party indemnity provision and qualifying pension scheme indemnity provision (s 236(1)).

[29] subss 236(2) and (3) in relation to the company and subss 236(3) and (4) in relation to an associated company.

[30] subss 237(2) and (3). By s 237(1), the section applies to the company (whether provision is made by the company or an associated company), and where the provision is made by as associated company, to that company.

The copy or memorandum must be retained and kept available for inspection for a year after expiry or termination.[31] Unless the copy or memorandum has at all times been kept at the company's registered office, the company must give notice to the Registrar of the place where it is kept and of any changes to that place.[32] Every copy or memorandum required to be kept under s 237 must be open to inspection by any member without charge and any member is entitled, on request and on payment of the prescribed fee, to be provided with a copy of the copy or memorandum, to be supplied within seven days.[33] Default in complying with these provisions is an offence.[34] Further, the court may, in case of refusal or default in providing a requested copy, make an order for immediate inspection or direct despatch of a copy to the person requesting it.[35]

## D. Ratification of Acts of Directors

### (1) The reform made by section 239

Section 239 is a new provision regulating the means by which a company may decide to ratify any conduct (ie acts or omissions) of a director, former director, or shadow director, which amount to negligence, default, breach of duty, or breach of trust in relation to the company. The section does not alter the law as to the acts or omissions of directors that are incapable of being ratified by the company.[36] Provided that the conduct is capable of being ratified by the company, the section gives the members, either unanimously or by a resolution in which the votes of the director and persons connected with him are not counted, the power to decide whether the company should relieve the director of liability in respect of his misconduct. If they do so decide, the company is bound by their decision and there is an absolute bar to the continuation of a derivative action under the Companies Act, Part 11.[37] If the untainted members do not agree to ratify the director's conduct, he will remain exposed to a claim by the company or a derivative action until the expiry of the relevant limitation period,[38] unless and to the extent that the

**19.25**

---

[31] s 237(4).
[32] s 237(5).
[33] subss 238(1) and (2).
[34] subss 237(6) and (7) and subss 238(3) and (4).
[35] s 238(5).
[36] subs 239(7).
[37] s 263(2)(c)(ii).
[38] By the Limitation Act 1980, ss 2, 5, 23 the limitation period for cases of negligence, breach of duty, or breach of trust is six years (eg *Re Lands Allotments Ltd* [1894] 1 Ch 616, CA), unless the claim is one in respect of fraud or trust property within s 21, for which there is no limitation period, or the limitation period is extended by s 32 on the ground of fraud, concealment, or mistake. For the proper scope of trust claims within s 21, see *Paragon Finance plc v Thackerar & Co* [1999] 1 All ER 400, CA; *JJ Harrison (Properties) Ltd v Harrison* [2002] 1 BCLC 162, CA; *Gwembe Valley*

court grants relief under s 1157 on the ground that he acted honestly and reasonably and ought fairly to be excused.[39]

**19.26** Section 239 provides for the ratification of acts of directors as follows:

(1) This section applies to the ratification by a company of conduct by a director amounting to negligence, default, breach of duty or breach of trust in relation to the company.

(2) The decision of the company to ratify such conduct must be made by resolution of the members of the company.

(3) Where the resolution is proposed as a written resolution neither the director (if a member of the company) nor any member connected with him is an eligible member.

(4) Where the resolution is proposed at a meeting, it is passed if the necessary majority is obtained disregarding votes in favour of the resolution by the director (if a member of the company) and any member connected with him. This does not prevent the director or any such member from attending, being counted towards the quorum and taking part in proceedings at any meeting at which the decision is considered.

(5) For the purposes of this section—

(a) 'conduct' includes acts or omissions;

(b) 'director' includes a former director;

(c) a shadow director is treated as a director; and

(d) in section 252 (meaning of 'connected person'), subsection (3) does not apply (exclusion of person who is himself a director).

(6) Nothing in this section affects—

(a) the validity of a decision taken by unanimous consent of the members of the company, or

(b) any power of the directors to agree not to sue, or to settle or release a claim made by them on behalf of the company.

(7) This section does not affect any other enactment or rule of law imposing additional requirements for valid ratification or any rule of law as to acts that are incapable of being ratified by the company.

**19.27** Under the old law a director and persons connected with him were entitled to vote at a general meeting of the company to ratify his conduct or to approve a transaction procured through the director's breach of duty. If the meeting decided by the requisite majority, including the votes of the director and persons connected with him, to approve the transaction and ratify the director's conduct, the transaction would be binding on the company and the director relieved of liability.[40] This was

---

*Development Co Ltd v Koshy* [2004] 1 BCLC 131, CA; *Halton International Inc v Guernroy Ltd* [2006] EWCA Civ 801, CA.

[39] Chapter 16, Section D of this work.

[40] *North West Transportation Co Ltd v Beatty* (1887) 12 AC 589, PC; *Burland v Earle* [1902] AC 83, 94, PC; *Cook v Deaks* [1916] 1 AC 554, 561, PC; *Bamford v Bamford* [1970] Ch 212, 239, CA. Third parties would in any event be able to rely on 1985 Act, ss 35 and 35A to uphold the validity of the transaction (to be replaced by ss 39 and 40 on 1 October 2009).

an element of the rule in *Foss v Harbottle*[41] and was subject to exceptions, two of which are discussed in this chapter: (1) where the transaction was beyond the powers of the company, and (2) where the transaction was a fraud on the minority and the wrongdoers were in control.[42] The first exception is discussed in paragraphs 19.49 and 19.50 below and the second in the next two paragraphs.

The precise scope of the second exception was more difficult to identify. In *Burland* **19.28** *v Earle* Lord Davy gave as an example of a fraudulent transaction within the second exception, a case 'where the majority are endeavouring directly or indirectly to appropriate to themselves money, property, or advantages which belong to the company, or in which other shareholders are entitled to participate'.[43] Some cases took a broader view of the second exception, holding that it applied where the justice of the case required it,[44] or where there was a breach of duty from which the wrongdoing director and majority shareholder benefited.[45] These decisions have focused on the transaction or conduct of the director, rather than on the question whether the company in general meeting could properly exercise its authority to ratify.

Professor Sarah Worthington has argued that it is more profitable to concentrate **19.29** on the decision by the company organ to authorize or ratify, rather than on the nature of the transaction or conduct in question. Her thesis is that a decision will not be effective to bind the company unless it is taken bona fide and for proper purposes.[46] This equitable restriction on the exercise of voting rights is recognized in the context of the alteration of a company's articles,[47] improper share issues,[48]

---

[41] (1843) 2 Hare 461.

[42] For further discussion of the rule and its exceptions, see Chapter 2, paragraphs 2.25, 2.26 and Chapter 21 of this work.

[43] [1902] AC 83, 93, PC. Other cases on the 'fraud on the minority' exception are noted in the next two footnotes and also: *Atwool v Merryweather* (1867) LR 5 Eq 464n; *Gray v Lewis* (1873) LR 8 Ch App 1035; *Menier v Hooper's Telegraph Works* (1874) LR 9 Ch App 350; *MacDougall v Gardiner* (1875) 1 Ch D 13, 25; *Mason v Harris* (1879) 11 Ch D 97; *Cook v Deeks* [1916] 1 AC 554, 563–5, PC; *Edwards v Halliwell* [1950] 2 All ER 1064, 1067, CA; *Prudential Assurance Co Ltd v Newman Industries Ltd* [1982] Ch 204, 210, CA; *Estmanco (Kilner House) Ltd v Greater London Council* [1982] 1 WLR 2, 12; *Smith v Croft (No 2)* [1988] Ch 114. Mere negligence was not enough to bring the case within the exception; *Turquand v Marshall* (1869) LR 4 Ch App 376, 386; *Pavlides v Jensen* [1956] Ch 565; *Heyting v Dupont* [1964] I WLR 843, CA.

[44] *Russell v Wakefield Waterworks Co* (1875) LR 20 Eq 474, 480, 482; but see *Prudential Assurance Co Ltd v Newman Industries Ltd (No 2)* [1982] Ch 204, 221 CA.

[45] *Alexander v Automatic Telephone Co* [1900] 2 Ch 56, CA; *Daniels v Daniels* [1978] Ch 406, 408, 414.

[46] 'Corporate Governance: Remedying and Ratifying Directors' Breaches' (2000) 116 LQR 638, 646. See *British America Nickel Corp Ltd v MJ O'Brien* [1927] AC, 369, 371, PC; *Redwood Master Fund Ltd v TD Bank Europe Ltd* [2006] 1 BCLC 149 (both cases on modification of loan notes).

[47] *Allen v Gold Reefs of West Africa Ltd* [1900] 1 Ch 656, 671, CA; *Shuttleworth v Cox Bros & Co (Maidenhead) Ltd* [1927] 2 KB 9, 18, 23, 24, CA; *Greenhalgh v Arderne Cinemas Ltd* [1951] Ch 286, 291, CA; *Citco Banking Corp NV v Pusser's Ltd* [2007] 2 BCLC 483, PC.

[48] *Hogg v Cramphorn Ltd* [1967] Ch 254; *Bamford v Bamford* [1970] Ch 212, CA (although this is not to say that any shareholder is disenfranchised); *Mason v Harris* (1879) 11 Ch D 97).

and sometimes more generally in the 'fraud on the minority' cases.[49] It does not mean that shareholders are subject to fiduciary obligations. They can vote in their own interests except where they would be using their voting power to achieve a purpose outside the scope of the power granted them to vote at general meetings. The court would only interfere if satisfied that no reasonable person could have considered the resolution would benefit the company.[50] The burden is on those who allege that a shareholder has or will cast his vote in bad faith or for an improper purpose.[51]

**19.30**  The new s 239 takes this approach a stage further by disenfranchising the wrong-doer and persons connected with him in relation to the decision to ratify.[52] The Attorney-General, Lord Goldsmith, said of the new provision:[53]

> It seeks to exclude the votes of the wrongdoer and those persons most likely to be biased in favour of the director or under his influence—namely, the persons connected with him—and make it easier to identify those persons when the votes are counted.

So, in relation to the decision whether or not to ratify a director's conduct, it is no longer necessary for minority shareholders to impugn the exercise of voting rights by the majority. By the section certain votes are excluded. It will seldom, if ever, be necessary to return to the difficult issues discussed in the preceding paragraphs. The second important change made by s 239 is that, provided that the transaction is within the powers of the company and creditors' interests are not affected, it is no longer necessary to consider the nature of the director's conduct to determine whether or not it is capable of being ratified by the shareholders. If the independent shareholders are content to ratify the director's conduct, he will be safe from a derivative action.[54]

### (2)  The scope of ratification

**19.31**  Section 239 is concerned with the decision of the company, by its members, to ratify the conduct of a director, former director, or shadow director. It is not explicitly concerned with ratifying or adopting a transaction entered into or apparently entered into as a result of the acts or omissions of the director. Indeed it

---

[49] *Atwool v Merryweather* (1867) LR 5 Eq 464n; *Cook v Deeks* [1916] 1 AC 554, PC; *Smith v Croft (No 2)* [1988] Ch 114.
[50] *Shuttleworth v Cox Bros & Co (Maidenhead) Ltd* [1927] 2 KB 9, 18, 23, 24, CA; *Greenhalgh v Arderne Cinemas Ltd* [1951] Ch 286, 291, CA; *Citco Banking Corp NV v Pusser's Ltd* [2007] 2 BCLC 483, PC.
[51] *Peter's American Delicacy Co Ltd v Heath* (1939) 61 CLR 457, 482, 511; *Citco Banking Corp NV v Pusser's Ltd* [2007] 2 BCLC 483, PC at [18].
[52] This reform was recommended in the CLR *Final Report* at paras 7.52–7.62.
[53] Hansard, HL Report Stage, cols 872–3 (9 May 2006).
[54] s 263((2)(c).

is possible for the company to affirm or adopt a transaction as against the other party to it, while preserving its breach of duty claims against the director who caused the company to enter into it.

The Companies Act does not define 'ratification', but an effective ratification is **19.32** generally understood to mean that the director's wrong is cured so that there is no cause of action in respect of which the company can bring proceedings and, equally, no derivative action may be pursued by a minority shareholder.[55] In *Bamford v Bamford* Harman LJ said that where directors find that they have misconducted themselves 'such directors can, by making a full and frank disclosure and calling together the general body of shareholders, obtain absolution and forgiveness of their sins'.[56]

So long as the decision to ratify subsists, the director is certainly safe from pro- **19.33** ceedings by the company or a derivative action. But it is not entirely clear whether the decision of the company to ratify is, on its own, sufficient to protect the director at all times. Following a change of control or insolvency, the company may change its mind and wish to sue the director. A director would be well advised to obtain a deed of release or enter into a compromise agreement, including a release of claims.

A director may wish to obtain ratification of his conduct where he is exposed to **19.34** the civil consequences of a breach of his general duties (s 178) or where he has been guilty of specific defaults under the Companies Act, which have caused the company loss and damage; eg by having to pay fines for failure to deliver returns to the Registrar. A director will not be exposed to civil liability to the company for breach of the duty and will therefore not need to obtain ratification if:

(1) in relation to the director's conflict or possible conflict of interest, the matter is authorized by the directors in accordance with s 175;[57]

(2) the director duly declares the nature and extent of his interest in a proposed transaction or arrangement with the company to the other directors in accordance with s 177;[58]

(3) the director complies with any provisions in the company's articles dealing with conflicts of interest;[59]

(4) the director obtains from the company, acting by its directors, an agreement not to sue or a settlement or release of a claim; provided of course that the

---

[55] Law Commission, *Shareholder Remedies*, No 246, at para 6.80.
[56] [1970] Ch 212, 238, CA.
[57] Companies Act, s 180(1).
[58] Ibid.
[59] Companies Act, s 180(4)(b).

directors act in accordance with their general duties in agreeing not to sue, to settle, or to release the claim.[60]

**19.35** Finally a director will not need to resort to ratification if he acts in accordance with a specific or general authority of the company; as where the company, by its members, consents to, approves, or authorizes a transaction before it is entered into in accordance with s 180(4)(a).[61] But s 180(4)(a) appears to preserve any rule of law to the effect that a resolution of the members will not be valid if the vote was carried by votes that were not cast in good faith and for the proper purposes of the company. If it were otherwise, a director and the majority shareholders could use prior authorization as a means of avoiding the provisions of s 239.

### (3) The decision of the company to ratify

**19.36** There are three ways in which the company may decide to ratify a director's conduct: by written resolution, by resolution passed at a meeting, and unanimously.

*Ratification by resolution*

**19.37** Chapter 22, Section C, describes the written resolution procedure. Where the proposed resolution is for ratification of a director's conduct, subs 239(3) varies the procedure in that the director (if a member of the company) and any member connected with him is not an eligible member within s 289.

**19.38** Chapter 22, Section D, describes the procedure where a decision is taken by resolution at a meeting of the members of the company. Where the proposed resolution is for ratification of a director's conduct, subs 239(4) varies the procedure in that the votes in favour of the resolution by the director (if a member of the company) and any member connected with him are disregarded.

**19.39** Where ratification is sought by way of a written resolution or a resolution at a meeting, the relevant circumstances must be fully and frankly disclosed to the shareholders.[62]

**19.40** Section 252 identifies the persons connected with the director whose conduct is the subject of the proposed ratification, but, for the purposes of s 239 a person

---

[60] Companies Act, s 239(6)(b). There would have to be a deed of release unless there was consideration for the company's agreement to release or not pursue the claim.

[61] *Queensland Mines Ltd v Hudson* (1978) 18 ALR 1, PC; *Re Horsley & Weight Ltd* [1982] Ch 442, CA; *Multinational Gas and Petrochemical Co v Multinational Gas and Petrochemical Services Ltd* [1983] Ch 258, CA.

[62] *Kaye v Croydon Tramway Co* [1898] 1 Ch 358, CA; *Tiessen v Henderson* [1899] 1 Ch 861; *Baillie v Oriental Telephone and Electric Co Ltd* [1915] 1 Ch 503, 514, CA; *New Zealand Netherlands Society 'Oranje' Inc v Kuys* [1973] 1 WLR 1126, PC; *Knight v Frost* [1999] 1 BCLC 364; *Re RAC Motoring Services Ltd* [2000] 1 BCLC 307.

who is himself a director is included among those connected with the director.[63] Persons connected with the director are members of the director's family and certain companies, trustees, partners, and partnerships.[64]

Section 253 identifies the members of a director's family as being:  **19.41**

(a)  the director's spouse or civil partner;

(b)  any other person (whether of a different sex or the same sex) with whom the director lives as partner in an enduring family relationship, unless that person is the director's grandparent or grandchild, sister, brother, aunt or uncle, or nephew or niece;

(c)  the director's children or step-children;

(d)  any children or step-children of a person within (b), not being the children or step-children of the director, who live with the director and have not attained the age of 18;

(e)  the director's parents.

It follows that members of the director's broader family, such as his brothers and sisters, may be able to force a ratification of the director's conduct against the wishes of the wholly independent minority members, unless that minority could challenge the votes as not being cast in good faith and for proper purposes.[65]

A body corporate is connected with the director in the circumstances described in  **19.42**
s 254 and Schedule 1. In essence a director is connected with a body corporate if the director and persons connected with him together (a) are interested in at least 20% of the equity share capital or (b) control the exercise of more than 20% of the voting power at any general meeting.

A member is also connected with the director if:  **19.43**

(1)  he is a person acting in his capacity as trustee of a trust and (a) the beneficiaries of the trust include the director, a member of the director's family, or a connected body corporate connected, or (b) the terms of the trust confer a power on the trustees that may be exercised for the benefit of any such person;[66]

(2)  he is acting in his capacity as a partner of (a) the director or (b) a member of the director's family, a connected body corporate, or a connected trustee;[67]

---

[63]  subss 239(5)(d) and 252(3). Sections 252–255 replace 1985 Act, s 346 without substantive change.

[64]  See also Chapter 3, Section D.

[65]  Paragraph 19.29 above.

[66]  subs 252(2)(c).

[67]  subs 252(2)(d).

(3) it is a firm that is a legal person under the law by which it is governed and in which (a) the director is a partner, (b) a partner is a member of the director's family, a connected body corporate, or a connected trustee, or (c) a partner is a firm in which the director is a partner or in which there is a partner who is a member of the director's family, a connected body corporate, or a connected trustee.[68]

*Unanimous consent*

**19.44**  The power of all the members of the company unanimously to consent to the director's conduct, so as to ratify it, is preserved by subs 239(6)(a). The members may also unanimously consent to, approve, or authorize in advance a particular transaction or conduct, so that no question of breach of duty arises: the director simply carries out the company's will. In both cases this is subject to the transaction or conduct being capable of ratification, as discussed below.

**19.45**  The unanimous consent procedure is discussed in Chapter 22, Section B.[69] In *Re D'Jan of London Ltd*[70] Hoffmann LJ said that the principle that the members could bind the company by unanimous consent to ratify a breach of duty or mandate particular conduct 'requires that the shareholders should have, whether formally or informally, mandated or ratified the act in question. It is not enough that they probably would have ratified if they had known or thought about it before the liquidation removed their power to do so.' It is therefore difficult to see what scope there could be for any attempt to establish ratification by acquiescence.[71]

### (4) Limits on ratification

**19.46**  Subsection 239(7) preserves the existing law as to additional requirements for a valid ratification and as to acts that are incapable of being ratified by the company. The Attorney-General, Lord Goldsmith, explained that 'the requirements of this section are additional and not alternative to any other requirements as to ratification imposed by statute or under the common law'.[72]

**19.47**  The reference in subs (7) to additional requirements probably refers to acts which to be valid require a special resolution or the taking of some other procedural step. By way of exception to the rule in *Foss v Harbottle*, an individual shareholder was entitled to maintain an action where the resolution could only be passed by

---

[68]  subs 252(2)(e).
[69]  *Re Duomatic Ltd* [1969] 2 Ch 365 is the case that gives its name to this form of authorization or ratification.
[70]  [1994] 1 BCLC 561, 564 (where Hoffmann LJ was sitting as an additional judge of the Chancery Division).
[71]  Consider *Re Bailey Hay & Co Ltd* [1971] 1 WLR 1357.
[72]  Hansard, HL Report Stage, col 873 (9 May 2006).

a special resolution (assuming the majority could not obtain it) or where the wrong done to the company infringed the individual's own rights.[73] Section 239 is not a means of avoiding the requirements of other provisions of the Companies Act.

The acts which are incapable of being ratified by the company so as to prevent the **19.48** minority from suing have been described as being 'of a fraudulent character or beyond the powers of the company'.[74] Equally such acts could not be ratified so as to prevent a liquidator, administrator, or administrative receiver from suing or causing the company to sue. More recently the courts have identified a duty owed by directors to have regard to the interests of creditors and have developed from that the view that, where the company is insolvent,[75] the members are not able to ratify a director's breach of duty which adversely affects the interests of creditors. The precise scope of this duty and of the limitation on the power to ratify remain uncertain.

*Acts beyond the power of the company*

It is plain that an act which is beyond the corporate capacity of the company can-  **19.49** not be ratified,[76] but given the unrestricted objects of a modern company, this issue will seldom arise.[77] The principle also applies to acts which infringe statutory or common law rules as to the preservation of capital and which are therefore unlawful. Thus the members cannot ratify a distribution paid out of capital in breach of ss 830 and 831 or an act constituting financial assistance given by a public company in breach of the 1985 Act, s 151.[78] At common law it was established that the shareholders could not authorize or ratify the payment of gifts to directors out of capital or money borrowed by the company, for, as Lindley LJ explained:[79] 'Such money cannot be lawfully divided amongst shareholders themselves, nor can it be given away by them for nothing to their directors so as to bind the company in its corporate capacity.'

The court may recharacterize a transaction as being a disguised distribution to  **19.50** or at the direction of the shareholders which is unlawful and incapable of being

---

[73] *Edwards v Halliwell* [1950] 2 All ER 1064, 1066, 1067, CA, per Jenkins LJ; *Baillie v Oriental Telephone and Electric Co Ltd* [1915] 1 Ch 503, CA; *Cotter v National Union of Seamen* [1929] 2 Ch 58, 69, 70.

[74] Lord Davey in *Burland v Earle* [1902] AC 83, 93, PC.

[75] For the purposes of the Insolvency Act, 'insolvency' refers to the process (s 247(1)). That Act, s 123, refers instead to a company being unable to pay its debts on either balance sheet basis (liabilities exceed assets) or a cash-flow basis (inability to pay debts as they fall due).

[76] *Rolled Steel Ltd v British Steel Corpn* [1986] Ch 246, 296, CA.

[77] 1985 Act, s 3A; 2006 Act, s 31(1).

[78] *Precision Dippings Ltd v Precision Dippings Marketing Ltd* [1986] Ch 447, CA (an unlawful distribution of profits). 1985 Act, s 151 is replaced by 2006 Act, s 678 on 1 October 2009, but the private company exemptions came into force on 1 October 2008.

[79] *Re George Newman & Co* [1895] 1 Ch 674, 686, CA; *Official Receiver v Stern* [2002] 1 BCLC 119, CA at para 32.

ratified if not made out of distributable profits.[80] This is exemplified by the decision of Hoffmann J in *Aveling Barford Ltd v Perion Ltd*,[81] which concerned 'a sale at a gross undervalue for the purpose of enabling a profit to be realised by an entity controlled and put forward by [the company's] sole beneficial shareholder'. The company did not have sufficient distributable profits and so the sale could not be validated by the unanimous approval of the shareholder. Hoffmann J went on to say that: '[i]t was the fact that it was known and intended to be a sale at an undervalue which made it an unlawful distribution'.[82]

### Fraudulent transactions

19.51 A fraudulent transaction necessarily involves a victim.[83] In the present context that may be the company itself or its constituents: ie its shareholders and creditors. A company which has been defrauded by its directors and shareholders may pursue a claim against them for compensation.[84] Similarly a company may be the victim of a theft committed by all its shareholders and it is no defence for the shareholders to say that they all agreed to take the company's property.[85] In these cases the shareholders' participation in the conspiracy or theft could not be regarded as a corporate act equivalent to a resolution authorizing or ratifying the directors' conduct.

19.52 If a director defrauds some of the shareholders by misapplying company property available for distribution to shareholders, the question whether his conduct is capable of being ratified needs to be reconsidered in the light of s 239. If the director seeks ratification, he will have to disclose his misconduct to the shareholders

---

[80] *Ridge Securities v Inland Revenue Commissioners* [1964] 1 WLR 479, 495 (interest payments recharacterized as distributions); *Re W & M Roith Ltd* [1964] 1 WLR 432 (widow's pension in a service contract a disguised distribution at the direction of the shareholder); *Re Halt Garage Ltd* [1982] 3 All ER 1016 (excessive remuneration paid to a director who performed no services treated as a disguised distribution); *Sasea Finance Ltd v KPMG* [2002] BCC 574 at paras 25–31 (circular transaction involving loan for purchase of shares).

[81] [1989] BCLC 626, 632, 633.

[82] Note the reform made by 2006 Act, s 845.

[83] In *Welham v Director of Public Prosecutions* [1961] AC 103, 123, HL Lord Radcliffe said:
Now, I think that there are one or two things that can be said with confidence about the meaning of the word 'defraud'. It requires a person as its object: that is, defrauding involves doing something to someone. Although in the nature of things it is almost invariably associated with the obtaining of an advantage for the person who commits the fraud, it is the effect upon the person who is the object of the fraud that ultimately determines its meaning.
That passage was quoted by Lord Lane CJ in the fraudulent trading case *R v Grantham* [1984] QB 675, 683, CA.

[84] *Belmont Finance Corporation Ltd v Williams Furniture Ltd* [1979] Ch 250, CA.

[85] *Attorney-General's Reference (No 2 of 1982)* [1984] QB 624, CA. Fraud prevents valid authorization or ratification by unanimous consent; see *Attorney-General for Canada v Standard Trust Company of New York* [1911] AC 498, 504, 505, PC, per Viscount Haldane; *Re Express Engineering Works Ltd* [1920] 1 Ch 466, 471, CA, per Younger LJ; *Multinational Gas and Petrochemical Co v Multinational Gas and Petrochemical Services Ltd* [1983] Ch 258, 280, CA, per May LJ.

and it will be for the shareholders who are not connected with the director to decide whether or not to grant ratification. If the majority of the independent shareholders agree to ratify, then, unless their votes were cast in bad faith or for an improper purpose,[86] there seems no reason why there should not be ratification.

More often the creditors are the direct or indirect victims of the fraud. Where the transaction or conduct of the directors involves a fraud on creditors the members have no power to cause the company to authorize or ratify it.[87] The courts have given a flexible meaning to the concept of fraud on creditors, so that conduct amounting to 'sharp practice' may be considered fraudulent.[88]  **19.53**

*Insolvency and the interests of creditors*

There are two distinct, albeit connected, matters to consider. The first is whether, and in what circumstances, a director owes the company a duty to consider or act in the interests of creditors of the company.[89] The second is whether insolvency or harm to creditors prevents the members from authorizing or ratifying a breach of duty by a director, whether the breach is in respect of the duty to have regard to the interests of creditors or any other breach of the general duties of a director.[90]  **19.54**

Section 172 states the duty of a director to promote the success of the company for the benefit of its members as a whole, but subs (3) provides that the duty imposed by that section 'has effect subject to any enactment or rule of law requiring directors, in certain circumstances, to consider or act in the interests of creditors of the company'. The Insolvency Act, s 214 (wrongful trading) is an enactment requiring directors to take every step with a view to minimizing the potential loss to the company's creditors, but that section only applies when the company has reached the point when there is no reasonable prospect that the company will avoid going into insolvent liquidation. A number of cases have recognized a rule of law to the effect that a director has a duty to the company to consider and act  **19.55**

---

[86] See paragraph 19.29 above. The majority of shareholders not connected with the director in accordance with s 252 might nevertheless have close associations with the director; eg as brothers or sisters or as business associates. As a result they might have had some collateral reason for voting to ratify.

[87] *Re Halt Garage (1964) Ltd* [1982] 3 All ER 1016, 1037; *Rolled Steel Ltd v British Steel Corp* [1986] Ch 246, 296, CA.

[88] *Lloyds Bank Ltd v Marcan* [1973] 1 WLR 1387, CA; *Agricultural Mortgage Corp Ltd v Woodward* [1995] 1 BCLC 1, CA. See also Chapter 29, Section K.

[89] This aspect is discussed in more detail in Chapter 11, Section E.

[90] These issues have been considered by the CLR in *Developing the Framework* at paras [3.72], [3.73], [3.79]–[3.81] and in the *Final Report* at paras paras 3.12–3.20. Also see the White Paper *Modernising Company Law* (July 2002) at paras 3.8–3.14 and articles by Andrew Keay, 'The director's duty to take into account the interests of company creditors: when is it triggered?' [2001] MULR 11 and 'Directors' duties to creditors: contrarian concerns relating to efficiency and over-protection of creditors' (2003) 66 MLR 665.

in the interests of its creditors when it is insolvent or on the verge of insolvency.[91] The duty is owed to the company, not directly to creditors.[92]

**19.56**  In *Re Horsley & Weight Ltd*[93] Cumming-Bruce and Templeman LLJ said, *obiter*, that it would be surprising and unsatisfactory if the members of an insolvent company could ratify conduct of its directors which amounted to serious but not fraudulent misconduct so as to provide the directors with a defence to a breach of duty claim. But *obiter dicta* of Slade LJ in *Rolled Steel Ltd v British Steel Corp*[94] tend to support the view that the limitation on the power of members to ratify acts which are within the power of a company is restricted to frauds on creditors. He said:

> However the clear general principle is that any act that falls within the corporate capacity of a company will bind it if it is done with the unanimous consents of all the shareholders or is subsequently ratified by such consents . . . . This last-mentioned principle certainly is not an unqualified one. In particular, it will not enable the shareholders of a company to bind the company itself to a transaction which constitutes a fraud on its creditors.

**19.57**  In the Australian case *Kinsela v Russell Kinsela Pty Ltd*[95] the court had to determine whether the members of a company could effectively authorize or ratify a transaction which occurred at a time when the company was insolvent or on the verge of insolvency and prejudiced creditors. In that case, at a time when the company was in severe financial difficulties and shortly before the court made a winding-up order, the directors caused the company to grant them a lease of its property at a rent that was substantially below the market rate. The liquidator did not allege that the lease was a fraud on creditors. Although all the members assented to the lease, the New South Wales Court of Appeal held that it was void, since the members of a company did not have power to authorize or ratify conduct which is or, but for the members' assent, would be a breach of a director's duty and which has the effect of prejudicing the company's creditors. In two influential paragraphs

---

[91]  This duty has been referred to in *Walker v Wimborne* (1976) 137 CLR 1 at [13]; *Lonrho Ltd v Shell Petroleum Co Ltd* [1980] 1 WLR 627, 634, HL, per Lord Diplock; *Nicholson v Permakraft (NZ) Ltd* (1985) 3 ACLC 453; *Kinsela v Russell Kinsela Pty Ltd* (1986) 4 NSWLR 722; *Winkworth v Edward Baron Development Ltd* [1986] 1 WLR 1512, 1516, HL; *Brady v Brady* (1987) 3 BCC 535, 552, CA; *West Mercia Safetywear Ltd v Dodd* [1988] BCLC 250, CA; *Facia Footwear Ltd v Hinchcliffe* [1998] 1 BCLC 218, 228; *Knight v Frost* [1999] 1 BCLC 364, 381, 382; *Re Pantone 485 Ltd* [2002] 1 BCLC 266 at [70]; *Colin Gwyer Associates Ltd v London Wharf (Limehouse) Ltd* [2003] 2 BCLC 153 at [74]; *Re MDA Investment Management Ltd* [2004] 1 BCLC 217 at [70]. For further discussion of these cases, see Chapter 11, Section E of this work.

[92]  *Re Horsley & Weight Ltd* [1982] Ch 442, 454, per Buckley LJ; *Kuwait Asia Bank EC v National Mutual Life Nominees Ltd* [1991] 1 AC 187, 219, PC; *Yukong Line Ltd v Rendsburg Investments Corp (No 2)* [1998] 1 WLR 294, 311, 312.

[93]  [1982] Ch 442, 455, 456, CA.

[94]  [1986] Ch 246, 296, CA.

[95]  (1986) 4 NSWLR 722, New South Wales Court of Appeal.

Street CJ distinguished between the power of the members to authorize or ratify conduct of the directors when the company is solvent and the position when it is not:[96]

> In a solvent company the proprietary interests of the shareholders entitle them as a general body to be regarded as the company when questions of the duty of directors arise. If, as a general body, they authorise or ratify a particular action of the directors, there can be no challenge to the validity of what the directors have done. But where a company is insolvent the interests of the creditors intrude. They become prospectively entitled, through the mechanism of liquidation, to displace the power of the shareholders and directors to deal with the company's assets. It is in a practical sense their assets and not the shareholders' assets that, through the medium of the company, are under the management of the directors pending either liquidation, return to solvency or the imposition of some alternative administration.

> It is, to my mind, legally and logically acceptable to recognise that, where directors are involved in a breach of duty to the company affecting the interests of shareholders, then shareholders can either authorise that breach in prospect or ratify it in retrospect. Where, however, the interests at risk are those of creditors I see no reason in law or logic to recognise that the shareholders can authorise the breach. Once it is accepted, as in my view it must be, that the directors' duty to a company as a whole extends in an insolvency context to not prejudicing the interests of creditors . . . the shareholders do not have the power or authority to absolve the directors from that breach.

**19.58**  In *West Mercia Safetywear Ltd v Dodd*[97] the English Court of Appeal approved the first of those paragraphs in the judgment of Street CJ in support of its decision that a director was liable for breach of duty for causing a company to make a payment in fraudulent preference of a related company, when he knew both companies were insolvent and had been advised by the prospective liquidator not to operate the bank accounts.

**19.59**  The second of those paragraphs in the judgment of Street CJ has also been quoted with approval by Sir Andrew Morritt V-C in *Bowthorpe Holdings Ltd v Hills*,[98]

---

[96] At 730 and 732. Hope and McHugh JJA agreed with Street CJ who drew support from the *obiter dicta* of Cumming-Bruce and Templeman LLJ in *Re Horsley & Weight Ltd* [1982] Ch 442, 455, 456, CA and the judgment of Cooke J in *Nicholson v Permakraft (NZ) Ltd* (1985) 3 ACLC 453, 457–60, New Zealand Court of Appeal.

[97] [1988] BCLC 250, CA, a decision on the pre-Insolvency Act law. The director does not appear to have defended the claim on the ground that the payment was authorized or ratified by all the shareholders. Instead his defence was that he was not in breach of duty in causing the company to pay a due debt. The defence failed because it was a breach of duty and fraud on the creditors for a director to cause a company to make a fraudulent preference; *Re Washington Diamond Mining Co* [1893] 3 Ch 95, 115, CA. In *Official Receiver v Stern* [2002] 1 BCLC 119, CA at paras 32, 51, and para 52 Sir Andrew Morritt V-C also quoted with approval the first of the paragraphs from Street CJ's judgment in *Kinsela*. The *Stern* case concerned disqualification proceedings, where the director withdrew sums for his own benefit when he knew the company was insolvent and was found unfit to be concerned in the management of a company.

[98] [2003] 1 BCLC 226 at paras 51–55.

when holding that the company had an arguable claim to rescind a sale of shares on terms that gave rise to a deficiency against its creditors.

**19.60** The precise extent of the limitation on the power of the members to authorize or ratify conduct of a director when the company is insolvent has therefore not been developed by the English courts. If it does arise for determination, the following three matters may need to be considered. First, the duty to consider creditors' interests and the question whether or not shareholders can authorize or ratify conduct that may breach the duty overlaps with the scope of the Insolvency Act, s 214 (wrongful trading). That section was introduced to fill a gap in English law [99] and it would be anomalous if the rule of law developed by the court was more extensive than the statutory rule.

**19.61** Secondly, many of the transactions or conduct which cause harm to creditors, because they occur when the company is insolvent or cause it to become insolvent, are within the reach of the provisions of the Insolvency Act for adjusting prior transactions on the grounds of transaction at undervalue, preference, or defrauding creditors.[100] If the court sets aside the transaction, it would follow that any authorization or ratification of the transaction or a director's conduct was ineffective, with the result that the director is exposed to a breach of duty claim.[101] Again, it would be anomalous if the rule of law developed by the court was more far reaching than the express provisions of the Insolvency Act. In *Knight v Frost*[102] Hart J declined to apply *West Mercia* in order to hold that a director was liable for a breach of duty claim in respect of an alleged preference which occurred outside the relevant statutory period.

**19.62** Thirdly, in cases not covered by the provisions of the Insolvency Act it may be necessary to look more closely at (a) the transaction and conduct in question, (b) the extent of the insolvency of the company, and (c) the way in which the transaction or conduct was authorized or ratified.

**19.63** In relation to the transaction itself, the Companies Acts recognize a distinction between a transaction with directors or their associates and a transaction with other persons.[103] Even in the former case the transaction ceases to be voidable if affirmed by the company. If the conduct may be characterized as a fraud on

---

[99] Cork Report, Chapter 44.

[100] Insolvency Act, ss 238–241, 423–425. In fact *West Mercia* could have been decided in this way had a defence of shareholder assent been relied on. Similarly, had the circumstances of *Kinsela* been brought before an English court after 1986, the lease could have been set aside under the Insolvency Act, s 238 and/or s 423. As to the latter section, consider *Agricultural Mortgage Corp Plc v Woodward* [1995] 1 BCLC 1, CA and *Lloyd's Bank Ltd v Marcan* [1973] 1 WLR 1387, CA.

[101] *Re Washington Diamond Mining Co* [1893] 3 Ch 95, CA.

[102] [1999] 1 BCLC 364, 381, 382. *West Mercia* was also distinguished in *Re Brian D Pierson Ltd* [2001] 1 BCLC 275, 299.

[103] 1985 Act, ss 35A and 322A (to be replaced by 2006 Act, ss 40 and 41 on 1 October 2009).

creditors, then it will not be ratifiable (paragraphs 19.51–19.53 above). Where the conduct falls short of being fraudulent, it will be helpful in most cases to determine which of the general duties (ss 171–177) has been broken and whether the court would grant relief under s 1157. A breach of duty involving a disposition of company property at an undervalue to a director or his associates may be viewed differently to a breach of the duty of care, skill, and diligence (s 174) or a conflict of interest case (ss 175, 177). Since in the latter case, the directors may relieve the director from liability (s 180(1)), there seems no reason why the members should not do so as well, regardless of the financial position of the company. If the court would grant relief, it would seem that the conduct should be ratifiable regardless of the interests of creditors. Where the court would not grant relief and ratification would deprive creditors of an asset (the claim against the director), the effectiveness of the purported ratification may turn on an assessment of the respective interests of the creditors and the members.

Turning to the financial position of the company, it should be borne in mind that **19.64** the issue only arises where a wrongful trading claim is not available against the director and the transaction cannot be impugned under the Insolvency Act (paragraph 19.61 above). Thus, the case under consideration will be one where there is a real prospect that the company may avoid entering an insolvency procedure and the members have a real interest in the fortunes of the company and the goodwill of the directors.[104]

Thus the reasons why the members ratify or purport to ratify the director's con- **19.65** duct may be important. There may be a distinction between a case where the members purport to exercise the power to vote for ratification in the genuine belief that to do so is in the best interests of the company and one where they purport to exercise their voting power in bad faith and not for the purposes for which they were given the power.[105] The latter case, where there is no reason to believe that ratification could benefit the company, will invariably involve a fraud on creditors, since the members would be ratifying conduct amounting to a breach of duty so as to protect the director from a claim brought by an administrator or liquidator of the company (paragraphs 19.51–19.53 above). It therefore seems that the scope for the development of a broad common law principle, as enunciated in the second paragraph of Street CJ's judgment in *Kinsela* (paragraph 19.57 above) is limited.

---

[104] The consideration given to this issue by the CLR should be borne in mind: *Developing the Framework* at paras 3.72, 3.73, 3.79–3.81; *Final Report* at paras 3.12–3.20.

[105] Paragraph 19.29 above and the discussion of the CLR referred to in the preceding footnote.

# 20

# DIRECTORS' LIABILITIES:
# PROVISION OF INSURANCE

## A. Introduction

The Companies Act, s 233 deals with the provision of insurance as a valid means **20.01** of indemnifying a director against liability attaching to him in connection with any negligence, default, breach of duty, or breach of trust.[1] It provides:

> Section 232(2) (voidness of provisions for indemnifying directors) does not prevent a company from purchasing and maintaining for a director of the company, or of an

---

[1] s 233 came into force on 1 October 2007: 2006 Act commencement Order No 3, art 2(1)(d). It restates without change the provisions in 1985 Act, s 309A(5), which were inserted with effect from 6 April 2005 by C(AICE) Act, s 19(1). Until then the relevant provision was contained in 1985 Act, s 310 which applied to directors as well as officers. With effect from 1 April 1990 the 1985 Act, was amended by 1989 Act, s 137 to make it clear that s 310 did not prevent a company from purchasing and maintaining for any officer or auditor insurance against liability which by virtue of any rule of law would attach to him in respect of any negligence, default, breach of duty, or breach of trust. The original form of s 310 contained provisions first brought into effect by 1929 Act, s 152 and there had been some doubt as to whether a company was permitted to provide liability insurance for its officers without breaching the general prohibition on exempting from liability or indemnifying against liability any officer of the company.

associated company, insurance against any such liability as mentioned in that subsection.

**20.02** Section 233 permits, but does not oblige, a company to purchase and maintain insurance for a director of the company or an associated company, against any liability attaching to the director in connection with any negligence, default, breach of duty, or breach of trust in relation to the company of which he is a director. The rationale for permitting liability insurance for the directors of companies can be seen from the White Paper: Company Law Reform 2005, where it was explained that:

> the law on directors' liability needs to strike a careful balance: on the one hand, the law must be firm and robust to deal fairly with cases where something has gone wrong, as a result of either negligence or of dishonesty: on the other, Britain needs a diverse pool of high-quality individuals willing to assume the role of company director, and a willingness by directors to take informed and rational risks.[2]

Furthermore, the Government agreed with the CLR that 'ultimately it [was] a matter for the board [of a company] to determine the conditions of employment of senior employees'.[3]

**20.03** The Model Articles for public and private companies contain a short permissive article dealing with the provision of insurance to directors and former directors as well as employees and former employees of a company.[4] It is open to the company to adopt more detailed articles regulating the circumstances in which the directors of a company are permitted to purchase Directors and Officers Liability Insurance (D&O Insurance) in accordance with the provisions of the Companies Act.[5]

---

[2] Chapter 3, (Enhancing Shareholder Engagement and a Long Term Investment Culture), p 23.

[3] Hansard—Standing Committee A, 14 September 2004, Col 9.

[4] Model Article (pcls) 53 and Model Article (plc) 86 each provide:

  (1) The directors may decide to purchase and maintain insurance, at the expense of the company, for the benefit of any relevant officer in respect of any relevant loss.

  (2) In this article—

    (a) a 'relevant officer' means any director or former director of the company or an associated company, any other officer or employee or former officer or employee of the company or an associated company (but not its auditor) or any trustee of an occupational pension scheme (as defined in section 235(6) of the 2006 Act) for the purposes of an employees' share scheme of the company or an associated company,

    (b) a 'relevant loss' means any loss or liability which has been or may be incurred by a relevant officer in connection with that relevant officer's duties or powers in relation to the company, any associated company (within the meaning of [relevant article]) or any pension fund or employees' share scheme of the company or an associated company, and

    (c) Companies are associated if one is a subsidiary of the other or both are subsidiaries of the same body corporate.

[5] 1985 Act, Table A does not contain any provision about purchasing or maintaining insurance for directors or other officers. The Companies Act does not contain any restriction on providing such insurance to officers, as opposed to directors. A company can therefore purchase D&O Insurance for its officers without reference to ss 232 and 233.

# B. The Policy

## (1) Available cover

D&O Insurance is a product. It is subject to fluctuations in price and to variations **20.04** in the terms and conditions that insurers are prepared and permitted to offer. Insurance against certain risks may be permissible in one jurisdiction but prohibited in another.[6] Competition for business between insurers, and factors such as loss history (both an insured's own and the insurance industry's as a whole), may lead to terms differing materially from year to year and from insured to insured. The terms of any D&O Insurance will depend upon the commercial circumstances in which it is negotiated. The discussion that follows is intended to highlight the key concepts and issues around which the commercial discussion will revolve.

## (2) The risks covered

The purpose of D&O Insurance is, in broad terms, to provide indemnity for **20.05** liabilities incurred by directors and officers (and, in most cases, specified categories of employee) as a result of their acting in the course of the business of a company. Such liabilities can arise from breach of duty to the company and from breach of duty to third parties. A third category of potential liability is that arising from regulatory investigation. In most cases cover will extend not only to the amount of any judgment or settlement, but also to the legal and certain other costs incurred by the insured individual in defending claims and otherwise seeking to avoid liability.

The range of duties which may be owed to a company by a director or officer are **20.06** covered elsewhere in this book. It is usual for the clause specifying the scope of cover to be cast in wide terms, with insurers then specifically excluding matters which they are not prepared to cover. Exclusions may relate to issues specific to the insured, such as exclusions of cover for the financial consequences of problems of which the insured was aware prior to the commencement of cover. Exclusions may also relate to general issues of concern to the insurance markets, such as claims arising out of incidents involving pollution of the environment. Insurers will usually look to exclude liabilities to the company arising from wilful misconduct on the part of the individual and also losses arising out of breaches of duty which result in an individual making a personal profit.[7]

---

[6] The prohibition may be a matter of law driven by public policy or a matter of regulation.

[7] Where the remedy sought against the insured is that he surrenders a profit he should not have made then an express exclusion of losses of that nature is likely to feature in the policy. Insurers are reluctant to treat as financial 'loss' the giving up of a profit.

**20.07** The provision of cover against regulatory intervention is an increasingly important component of the protections available to individuals working for companies operating in regulated industries. Depending on its powers, a regulator may be involved in the investigation of an individual in respect of alleged breaches of duty to the company, breaches of duty to third parties, and breaches of the regulators' own rules. Regulators may impose restrictions on the extent to which it is permissible to insure against the consequences of their interventions; by the General Provisions (Prohibition of Insurance Against Fines) Instrument 2003 the FSA amended its General Provisions to provide that no FSA-regulated firm could 'enter into, arrange, claim on or make a payment under a contract of insurance that is intended to have, or has or would have, the effect of indemnifying' an FSA-regulated individual against all or part of a financial penalty imposed by the FSA. The prohibition does not extend to insurance in respect of defence costs incurred in defending FSA enforcement action nor to insuring against having to pay the FSA's costs of such action.

### (3) The period of cover

**20.08** Most D&O Insurance is written with a policy period of one year. D&O Insurance is also usually written on the so-called 'claims made' basis. In broad terms the effect of this is that the coverage provided by the policy applies to those claims of which the insured becomes aware during the policy period.[8]

**20.09** The first key feature to note about the 'claims made' concept is that it does not matter when the conduct complained of took place, or when the claimant suffered the loss out of which his claim arises.[9] It is the making of the claim against the insured within the policy period that potentially triggers the operation of the cover.

**20.10** The second key feature of the 'claims made' concept is that the insured being aware of the claim will not usually, in and of itself, be sufficient to trigger policy coverage. An insured must also notify his insurer of the claim within a prescribed time of the insured becoming aware of it. Because of this, it might be more accurate to refer to such insurances as 'claims made and notified' policies. Both the

---

[8] The standard, but now rarely used, alternative to 'claims made' policies are so-called 'losses occurring during' policies which are triggered when the conduct potentially giving rise to liability occurs during the policy period, even if no claim is advanced until much later.

[9] Any insured will be expected to advance limitation defences that are available to him in respect of the claim. However, the fact that a claim is or may be time barred is not usually a justification for the insured failing to notify his insurer of the claim. Notification of claims to insurers is a key component to activating cover under a 'claims made' policy and the insured may sacrifice the ability to recover the costs of striking out a time-barred claim if he fails to notify.

'claims made' and the 'notified' elements of this concept merit further consideration.[10]

What is a 'claim' and when is it 'made'? A well-drafted policy will make this clear. **20.11** Both insurer and insured risk considerable uncertainty in the operation of the policy if they are unable to identify what constitutes a claim being made. Service of suit upon the insured is the clearest indication that a claim has been made. However, policies do not usually set the threshold so high as to require actual service of proceedings before a claim is treated as 'made'. A more informal indication of an actual or potential dispute may suffice. That said, the policy will normally require some form of communication of intent by the potential claimant to the insured. The nature of that communication, and the nature of the intention evidenced thereby are matters which the insurer and insured may wish to specify in order to introduce maximum certainty into their obligations. For instance, some policies will treat the receipt of a pre-action demand as the making of a claim and, indeed, in certain cases the receipt of a complaint seeking redress will be deemed a claim even though litigation is not expressly threatened.

Once a claim has been made against him, the insured will be obliged to notify his **20.12** insurer of that claim. The time permitted between the insured becoming aware of the claim and his having to notify his insurer, and the sanctions which will apply if he fails to notify within the relevant period, are vital elements of D&O Insurance. The policy will set a maximum period which it will permit to elapse between the insured being aware of the claim and the receipt of notification of that claim by insurers. The consequences which flow from failure to notify within that period will depend on the policy language. Frequently the obligation to notify the insurer of a claim is expressed as a condition precedent to the insurer's liability. Condition precedent language necessitates strict compliance with the term in question. In such circumstances any failure to meet the deadline, no matter how narrow the margin of failure, will entitle the insurer to refuse to meet the claim, even though the insurer has in no way been prejudiced by the delay.[11]

When a time period for notification is specified this will normally require steps to **20.13** be taken within a matter of days rather than within a number of months. Alternatively, the policy may adopt a test such as 'as soon as reasonably practicable'

---

[10] An exhaustive discussion of this difficult subject is beyond the scope of this chapter. What follows is by way of introduction only.

[11] See eg *Pioneer Concrete (UK) Ltd v National Employers' Mutual General Insurance Association* [1985] 2 All ER 395. In this case the policy required the insured to give timeous notice of 'any accident or claim or proceedings' Bingham J rejected a disjunctive construction of this clause and said at 400: 'The obvious commercial purpose of this clause is to enable the insurer to perform his role as *dominus litus* and to investigate accidents and claims at the earliest possible opportunity, and that purpose would clearly be frustrated by the construction contended for.'

which allows potentially greater flexibility, while still permitting an objective assessment of whether the requirement has been met. Much will depend on commercial considerations but also on what the insured believes is achievable. This is a particular concern in the context of D&O Insurance where it cannot be assumed that any individual insured will be sufficiently conversant with the subtleties of what the policy regards as a claim, or necessarily familiar with his notification obligations. Ensuring that the individual insureds are sufficiently aware of the steps necessary to satisfy their policy obligations is one of the risk management challenges associated with D&O Insurance.

20.14 The position may be complicated further if a policy imposes a requirement that, notwithstanding any specified period for notification, the notification must in any event be made before the end of the policy period. A claim may emerge at a time when the remainder of the policy period is shorter than the amount of time usually permitted to elapse between the insured becoming aware of the claim and being obliged to notify it. In view of this, well drafted policies will allow a period of time after the expiry of the policy in which claims can be notified. However, insurers will seek to ensure that the claim must still have been made during the policy period. Otherwise they risk extending the period for which the policy provides cover.

20.15 What of matters of which the insured becomes aware during the policy period, and which suggest that he may face a claim in the future, but which do not currently meet the policy threshold for a claim being made? It is common for policies to give the insured the option to notify such matters, but without subjecting him to an obligation so to do. If the insured exercises the option then the policy will cover any claim which subsequently emerges out of the notified matter, even if that claim does not emerge until after the end of the policy period.

20.16 The difficulty of defining what, short of a claim, may nevertheless merit notification is reflected in the arcane law which has developed around it. For instance, defining such matters as circumstances 'likely to give rise to a claim' has been held to create a different threshold for notification than a policy which requires notification of circumstances 'which may give rise to a claim'.[12]

20.17 It is important for the insurers to exercise some control over just what, other than claims, the insured is entitled to notify. A primary commercial consideration behind insurers writing policies on the 'claims made' basis is that, at the end of

---

[12] The former has been held to mean that a claim was more likely than not, so that the mere possibility that a claim will be made is not sufficient to give rise to a claim; see *Layher v Lowe* [2000] Lloyd's Rep IR 510 (CA). The latter is a weaker test, and has been held to be satisfied where 'it was at least possible' that a claim would arise; see *J Rothschild v Collyear* [1999] Lloyd's Rep IR 6.

the policy period, insurers will have a complete list of their sources of potential exposure and so can quantify and manage those potential exposures. Allowing an insured to notify everything of which they became aware during the year that might conceivably become a problem, no matter how currently unclear the concern or its basis might be, would leave insurers in a significant, and commercially unappealing, state of uncertainty. The insurer will wish the insured to be able to show some identifiable and objectively verifiable basis for concern in order that the subject matter of the notification can be circumscribed. The insurer will want some clarity as to the subject matter of the notification: at the very least he will want details of the facts which are causing the insured concern. In addition he will want to impose some relatively close connection between the facts notified and any subsequent claim in order for that claim to be covered: the insurer will, for example, want the claim to 'arise out of' or 'relate to' the notified circumstance. In the absence of clear definition of the notified circumstance, insurers face the potential for attempts by the insured to exploit any lack of clarity as a means of widening the range of subsequent claims that might be brought under the policy by reference to the notified circumstance.

Insurers' objectives as outlined above potentially pose problems for the insured **20.18** and, in this regard, the insured has to exercise particular care. When entering into a policy for any one year he will be in no position to know what exclusions he may face as and when he comes to buy his cover for the following year. He will not wish to encounter a position where an emerging matter which does not qualify for notification under the current policy might also fall within an exclusion to be imposed in a successor policy. If that happens then he will be without cover. Therefore, his objective will be to secure the maximum scope for notifying circumstances which have not yet matured into claims.

### (4) The structure of D&O Insurance

D&O Insurance may be purchased to provide protection to individuals, or to **20.19** companies, or to both.

The coverage offered to individuals is widely known by the shorthand 'Side A **20.20** Cover'. The cover available to companies is, broadly, of two distinct types. One type, often referred to as 'Side B Cover', provides an indemnity to a company to the extent that it has indemnified certain individuals against specified liabilities. Side B Cover does not operate in respect of a company's own liability to third parties: it is triggered by the company's performance of an obligation to indemnify the insured individuals against such liabilities. Whether a particular indemnity is recoverable from insurers via Side B Cover will hinge upon the nature of the underlying conduct indemnified against, not the scope of the company's agreement to indemnify. If an insurer would not be prepared to insure an individual directly for a particular liability, it is unlikely to be prepared to insure a company against having to indemnify that individual for that liability.

**20.21** The second type of cover available to companies is generally known as 'Entity Cover' and is offered in respect of a company's own liability to third parties. As insurers offer a range of specific products tailored to cover the third party liabilities of companies, any Entity Cover element of D&O Insurance may be restricted: most usually it is confined to liabilities arising from so-called 'Securities Claims'. In essence, these are claims by investors in the shares of a company. Such claims generally arise when investors allege that, due to the concealment of information by the company, the price they paid for their shares was in excess of their true value. Such claims are usually triggered by a decline in the share price of the company. As Securities Claims are frequently pursued against both a company and its directors, the inclusion of Entity Cover against such claims in a D&O Insurance policy has a certain logic.

**20.22** It is not necessary to purchase Side A Cover, Side B Cover, and Entity Cover in the same policy. Side A and Side B Covers are often bought on a stand-alone basis. The decision as to what to purchase and in what combinations will be a commercial one driven by the risk profile and coverage requirements of a company and its directors. However, the combinations in which these covers are purchased can have very significant implications for the scope and efficacy of cover. Those implications are dealt with later in this chapter.

### (5) The level of cover

**20.23** D&O Insurance will provide cover subject to a policy 'limit of liability'. That limit will almost certainly be expressed to represent the maximum amount for which insurers will be liable under the policy for all claims by all insureds. It is sometimes assumed, incorrectly, that the limit of liability represents an amount which is available in full to each insured in respect of his own liabilities. In certain circumstances that may be the case. It is not, however, the norm. Normally, the limit of liability is a single 'pot' of money, and once it is exhausted by payments there will be no further funds available to any insured. Subject to certain modifications which may appear in the wording of the policy,[13] claims are met in the order in which the insureds' liabilities are established by judgment or settlement, not in the order in which the claims were made or notified. Furthermore, it is the norm for payments by insurers in respect of defence costs to reduce the 'pot' such that, in exceptional circumstances or because a low limit of liability has been purchased,

---

[13] Often in coverages involving both Side A and Side B there is a provision whereby the policyholder may elect for all Side A claims to be paid prior to settlement of any Side B claims.

the entire amount of insurance available may have been used up by defence costs before any liability to pay compensation is established or agreed.

The size of a policy's limit of liability is a decision influenced by a number of **20.24** factors. One factor will be the insurer's willingness to provide cover and the price it wishes to charge for it. From the purchaser's perspective, the amount of cover it feels it needs will be determined by such factors as its appetite for retaining risk and the scale of its operations, particularly in jurisdictions where exposure to claims is seen as high. There are also corporate governance questions: is there a point at which the availability of D&O Insurance may cease to be reassuring but, rather, come to be seen as a licence to take risks in the management of the company? Will a company wish to purchase a level of D&O cover which may induce complacency or unnecessary risk taking on the part of directors?

The decision as to who and what to cover may also be influenced by simple eco- **20.25** nomics. The more individuals who have the benefit of the cover, the more potential claimants upon the limit of liability, and so the more thinly spread the contents of the 'pot' may become. This can also influence which covers to buy. In a Side A only policy, the individual insureds know that only they have the potential to make a claim under the policy. Once Side B Cover is added, indemnifying companies have potential claims on the policy funds. This may not matter to the directors who have been indemnified, but the reduction in the amount of insurance otherwise available after a Side B payment might give them pause for thought. Some may form the view that it is preferable to have the benefit of a corporate indemnity to the extent it can be given, plus a Side A only policy for all other eventualities. This issue is thrown into even sharper relief if Entity Cover is added into the mix. If Entity Cover is purchased the directors may be surprised to discover that a policy which, on the face of it, has been purchased for their benefit is, as it turns out, completely exhausted by a claim against the company.

### (6) The insured under the policy

*The companies in respect of which cover is provided*

Which individuals within an organization will have the benefit of D&O Insurance? **20.26** To answer that question, one needs to begin by identifying the 'organization'. The principal purpose of D&O Insurance is, in broad terms, to provide indemnity for liabilities incurred by individuals as a result of their acting in the course of the business of a company. Consequently, the policy needs to identify accurately the company or companies whose directors, officers, and employees are to be insured.

If a single company is purchasing D&O Insurance then this question is easily **20.27** answered. In the context of D&O Insurance purchased for a group of companies the position is more complex. The usual way of resolving the issue is to identify one company as the 'policyholder'. The policyholder is normally identified as having responsibility for a number of administrative functions under the policy, not least paying premium. The policyholder is also usually the entity which forms the basis of the policy's definition of the companies whose directors, officers, and employees are intended to be insured.

20.28    A standard policy may identify the 'company' in respect of which the insurance is provided as the 'policyholder and its subsidiaries'. Two basic issues flow from this. The first is the need to check that the definition of 'subsidiaries' is sufficiently comprehensive to encompass all of the entities to which the cover is intended to apply.[14] The second is that any cover which operates by reference to 'the policyholder and its subsidiaries' contains an inherent assumption that the 'policyholder' is at the apex of the corporate structure pyramid. If the policyholder is not the ultimate holding company, and there are companies of which it is a subsidiary and to which it is intended that the D&O Insurance should apply, then either the identity of the policyholder will need to be changed or the means of defining the 'group' modified.

### *'Outside entities'*

20.29    D&O Insurance frequently distinguishes between the cover provided to individuals acting on behalf of 'group' companies (ie the policyholder and its subsidiaries) and the cover provided for directors, officers, and employees of group companies when acting in roles for companies which fall outside the group as defined. Such companies are frequently referred to as 'outside entities'. A company may appoint one of its directors, officers, or employees to sit on the board of a company in which it has invested, but that investment may be insufficient to bring that company within the policy definition of the 'group'. In those circumstances, because the individual is taking up that appointment in furtherance of the interests of the appointing company, it would seem appropriate that he should be covered for any liabilities that he thereby incurs under the D&O Insurance purchased by the appointing company.[15]

20.30    Where such cover is provided, most D&O Insurances draw some important distinctions between activities undertaken on behalf of companies regarded as part of the covered 'group' and those undertaken for 'outside entities'. One of the more obvious distinctions is as to which individuals are covered. All of the members of a board of a 'group' company will be covered by the D&O Insurance, unless specifically excluded by the policy. However, the D&O Insurance of the group will

---

[14]    Policies issued in the London insurance market have tended to adopt as the policy definition of 'subsidiary' that used in the Companies Acts and which now appears in Companies Act, s 1159.

[15]    The interaction between any D&O insurance of the outside entity of which the individual has the benefit and the 'group' insurance is considered below at paragraph 20.43.

only cover board members of an outside entity if they have been appointed to that outside entity by or with the consent of the insurance buying group.[16]

In addition, the policy may limit the type of companies which it is prepared to regard as qualifying automatically as 'outside entities'. The insurer may not be prepared to offer automatic cover to someone who undertakes their 'outside entity' role with a company that has a share listing in the United States of America or which is engaged in an area of commercial activity regarded by insurers as high risk. Often a company will not qualify as an 'outside entity' unless and until identified in a schedule or endorsement to the policy. This may cause considerable difficulties if, for instance, a claim is made against an individual who has been appointed to an 'outside entity' but that entity has accidentally been omitted from the relevant policy schedule. **20.31**

In order to obtain cover as an 'outside entity' director an individual will often not only have to show that the company to which he is appointed meets the definition of 'outside entity', but also that he meets any policy requirement as to the reason for and the form of his appointment to that role. For example, the policy may only cover appointments to outside entities if those appointments are made either for certain limited purposes or by certain formal means. The policy may not provide cover where the role has nothing to do with the business of the group that purchased the policy. A director of a group company who has directorships with non-group companies should not therefore assume that those roles will be covered automatically by the 'outside entity' provisions of the D&O Insurance which the group arranges. Furthermore, there may be procedural requirements, such that the appointment be in writing, which do not reflect the reality of how individuals come to join those outside boards. It is important to ensure that the outside entity cover is not defeated because of some procedural requirement in relation to an appointment that is not met in practice. **20.32**

*The insured individuals*

Once the relevant companies have been identified, which individuals within those companies have the benefit of cover? As one would expect, 'directors' and 'officers' **20.33**

---

[16] This is an important consideration when companies are determining how wide they wish to cast the definition of what constitutes the 'group' for the purposes of a D&O policy. Because of the limitations upon cover for roles with outside entities there may be a temptation to bring all such entities within the scope of the 'group' for the purpose of the policy definitions. However, the company purchasing the policy may thereby bring within the scope of its cover numerous individuals who, as board members of the outside entity with no other link to the group, would not otherwise be covered as directors of 'outside entities'. The increase in the number of potential claimants on the policy limit may thereby prejudice the coverage available for the 'group' directors. Furthermore, those individuals would thereby become 'insureds' with obligations to give pre-contractual disclosure in respect of the D&O Insurance which the 'group' may not be able to monitor effectively, thereby potentially prejudicing the cover for the other directors.

are usually covered. However, elaboration on what constitutes a 'director' or 'officer' is often not provided. Consideration needs to be given as to whether the policy language should make clear that both de facto and *de jure* appointments will be covered.[17] Another refinement, of particular relevance in the 'claims made' policy context, is ensuring that cover is provided for directors who have already retired when the policy commences, but against whom a claim may be made during the policy period in respect of conduct undertaken when in office.

20.34   It is a question for the company purchasing the insurance to decide to what extent it requires cover for employees who are not directors or officers. Some individuals may, as a result of seniority, face potential exposures equivalent to those of directors and officers. Indeed, in a heavily regulated industry, all employees or a significant number thereof may be subject to the jurisdiction of the regulator and it may be necessary to extend the cover to them to provide some protection in the case of regulatory investigation, primarily in relation to the payment of any legal fees. Further, those appointed to 'outside entity' boards are often not directors or officers of their 'home' organization. A crucial consideration for the company is how wide it wishes to cast the net of potential claimants upon the policy, thereby potentially reducing the policy funds available to senior executives.

## C.  Pre-contractual Disclosure

20.35   Insurance contracts are subject to their own special rules by reason of being contracts of utmost good faith. One example of those rules is the obligation imposed upon potential insureds to give disclosure of certain facts to the insurer in advance of the policy becoming binding. The duty of disclosure and its consequences is a vast topic. For present purposes, the following basic propositions should suffice:

(1) everyone who is to be an insured under a policy of insurance has an obligation to make disclosure to the insurer in advance of that contract coming into effect;

(2) the obligation to give disclosure is an obligation to provide the insurer with all facts known to the insured which are material to the risk that the insurer will assume under the policy;

(3) a fact is material if it is something of which the notional 'prudent insurer' might wish to take account in determining whether or not to provide the insurance or, if he wishes to provide it, the terms on which it will be provided;

---

[17]  That is, those occupying the position of director, whether or not formally appointed.

(4) if the insured fails to disclose a material fact, and the insurer would have made a different decision about whether to write the risk, or would have written it on different terms, had he known the true position, then the insurer is entitled to avoid the policy: ie to treat it as if it never existed.

**20.36** The reason why the question of 'who is insured' is important in this context is that the obligations of disclosure fall upon insureds. Given the consequences of breach of the duty of utmost good faith disclosure, it is important to ensure that adequate disclosure is given. This creates challenges in the D&O Insurance context given the potential number of individual insureds. There can be no substitute for a full and frank discussion between those arranging the insurance and the proposed insurer as to the steps that are being taken to identify material information. The insurer may be prepared to agree to some 'short cuts' to allow focus on the information which he regards as essential (the burden of reviewing extensive disclosure is not one which insurers necessarily assume with relish). However, the taking of short cuts in the absence of agreement risks insurers being able to avoid the policy.

**20.37** What happens if one of the insureds is guilty of non-disclosure: are insurers entitled to avoid the policy in respect of all insureds, or just in respect of the one responsible for the non-disclosure? This will depend on whether the policy is construed to be a 'joint' insurance or a 'composite' insurance. A joint insurance treats all individual insureds as if they were one, with the result that a non-disclosure by one insured renders the policy voidable against all insureds. A composite insurance proceeds on the basis that each insured is insured individually for his own interest, with the result that a non-disclosure by one insured can only result in the avoidance of his cover and not that of the other insureds.

**20.38** Whether a policy is to be construed as a joint or a composite insurance can often turn upon detailed and difficult analysis of the intention behind its provisions.[18] In order to circumvent this analysis policies will often include a provision intended to make the insurance composite. Whether the provision achieves that will turn upon the detail of its wording which will need to be construed with care.

**20.39** Care will also be needed to ensure that such provisions are not limited to pre-contractual disclosure. Although the duty to make utmost good faith disclosure ceases at the moment the policy becomes binding, it can revive to a degree during the course of the life of a policy in certain instances: for example, if new insureds are to be added to the policy. A company may make acquisitions during a policy year, potentially bringing individuals working for the acquired companies into

---

[18] As to the complications that may arise see, for example, *New Hampshire Insurance Co v Mirror Group Newspapers* [1997] LRLR 24, CA.

the scope of the acquiring company's D&O Insurance. The policy may automatically extend cover to new subsidiaries but, in some cases, a risk presentation to insurers will be required before the insurer is prepared to extend cover. The duty of utmost good faith disclosure will revive at that point in relation to the new company. It is therefore important to ensure that any provisions seeking to provide mitigation against the harsh rules relating to disclosure are drafted to apply to any revival of the disclosure duties post-inception. Indeed, all provisions seeking to modify the duty of disclosure or to mitigate the consequence of breach, or to achieve both, need to be approached with care to ensure that all relevant duties are catered for and that the mitigation is adequate and permissible.[19]

## D. The Interaction between D&O Insurance and Indemnities from the Company

20.40 A director who has the benefit of indemnities from the companies of which he is a director, and who also has D&O Insurance in respect of those directorships, may feel that he is in a fortunate position. However, he needs to be conscious of how those protections will interrelate.

20.41 One of the advantages of Side A Cover is that it is usually provided to directors on the basis that they will have to meet no part of any loss from their own pockets. The absence of any self-insured retention or excess is of considerable value to directors. However, because insurers will pay Side A claims without the benefit of any self-insured retention, they are keen to limit the scope of claims which will fall within Side A. The most effective way of achieving this is for the insurer to look at the indemnities which are, or which could be, available to a director to meet a loss which is otherwise within the scope of the insurance. Insurers can seek to limit their Side A exposures by the inclusion in the policy of what is often referred to as a 'presumption of indemnity'. In essence, this is a stipulation that whenever a particular loss could have been recovered by an individual insured under another indemnity then, for policy purposes, he shall be deemed to have effected such recovery. The Side A Cover will only respond to the extent that the deeming provision does not apply. The most obvious source of indemnity is an indemnity from the company; but a presumption of indemnity will not necessarily be limited to such indemnities and may call into account all and any other potential sources of indemnification.

---

[19] As to the difficulties that can arise in the drafting of clauses mitigating the harshness of the law relating to disclosure see *HIH Casualty & General Ins Ltd v Chase Manhattan Bank* [2003] 1 All ER (Comm) 349, HL; *Arab Bank Ltd v Zurich Insurance Co* [1999] 1 Lloyd's Rep 262.

While a presumption of indemnity can apply in a stand alone Side A Cover, **20.42** it affects fundamentally the operation of a policy combining Side A Cover with Side B Cover. By way of contrast with the Side A Cover, the Side B Cover is likely to have a significant retention: companies who have the benefit of the Side B Cover will have to bear for themselves a portion of the financial consequences of their decision to indemnify their directors. In such circumstances, the insurer is exposed 'from the ground up' on Side A but not exposed on Side B until the insured loss exceeds the retention.

A presumption of indemnity may not be limited to stipulating that an insured **20.43** cannot recover under the insurance any part of his loss which has actually been paid by an alternative source of indemnity. The presumption may treat that alternative source of indemnity as having responded to the claim whether or not it actually has done. In such circumstances, a director may find a gap opening up in his protections between the amount of indemnity he actually receives from the company, if any, and the amount of indemnity which, for policy recovery purposes, he is deemed to have received. If the latter exceeds the former then the director will find himself personally responsible for the amount of the gap between the two. This is a genuine practical concern. For example, the company which is supposed to be providing the relevant indemnity may be insolvent. An important feature of the commercial negotiation between the parties to a D&O Insurance will be whether, and to what extent, insurers will be prepared to modify the presumption of indemnity to reflect directors' difficulties should other sources of indemnity prove unwilling or unable to pay.[20] The position can be particularly complex in relation to outside directorship roles: a policy may presume

---

[20] It is far from clear whether the insured individuals could make use of the Third Parties (Rights against Insurers) Act 1930 if the policy does not permit the directors to claim for a loss indemnifiable by the company in circumstances where the potential indemnifier is insolvent. The 1930 Act, s 1 provides that where, under a contract of insurance, the insured is insured against liabilities to third parties which he may incur then, in the event of the insured becoming insolvent, the insured's rights against the insurer under the contract of insurance are transferred to the third party to whom the liability is incurred. If the individuals are insured under the same policy as the insolvent company (ie the cover is both Side A and Side B) it is not immediately obvious that the individuals are 'third parties' within the contemplation of the 1930 Act. This potentially produces the somewhat peculiar result that the ability of the individuals to invoke the provisions of the 1930 Act may depend upon whether the policy is a Side B cover only. It is also open to question whether the contractual liability to indemnify is the kind of insured liability which the 1930 Act contemplates. Even if these issues can be surmounted, the Side B cover will often be conditional upon the company having actually indemnified the individual for his loss. As the 1930 Act vests in the third party no greater rights than the insured itself possessed, the third party will also be subject to this condition of cover. Consequently, the vesting of rights in the individual may be of no assistance in the absence of an indemnity being provided (unless, perhaps, the courts were prepared to approach that issue on lines similar to those adopted in *Charter Reinsurance Co Ltd v Fagan* [1997] AC 313 (HL)). Furthermore, the individual who succeeded in enforcing the company's rights would have to bear the company's retention: with the consequence that the irrecoverable loss of the individual may be too great to make invoking the 1930 Act worthwhile.

indemnification of an individual not only by the company appointing but also by the outside entity in which he serves.

20.44 Many policies contain deeming provisions which operate not by reference to the indemnity which the company has actually agreed to give to the individual, but by reference to the indemnity which the company could have given had it provided the maximum indemnity permitted by law. If the company has agreed to indemnify, but stopped short of agreeing to indemnify to the maximum extent which the law permits, then a gap in the protections available will also emerge.[21] This is a particular concern for officers. It is unusual for a D&O Insurance to make any distinction of substance between its treatment of directors and its treatment of officers. However, English law permits companies to indemnify their officers to a much greater extent than they are permitted to indemnify their directors.[22] In determining the extent to which it is appropriate to indemnify directors and officers, companies may take the decision that officers should not be placed in a more advantageous position than directors, notwithstanding that the company is legally entitled to put them in such a position. In such circumstances, and where a policy has a presumption of indemnity expressed by reference to 'the maximum extent permitted by law', the danger of a gap opening up in the protections available is even more acute for officers of an English company than it is for directors.

## E. The Policy in Operation

### (1) Claims by the company

20.45 The circumstances in which a company can indemnify one of its own directors against a claim by the company are now very restricted.[23] Consequently, Side A D&O Insurance is all the more important to directors. It may be their principal, or sole, protection against the financial consequences of such claims. That said, the policy may not provide unqualified cover against them.

20.46 Insurers argue that claims by a company against its own directors are of particular concern to them. The essence of the concern is that a company may wish to institute a weak or hopeless claim against its own directors with a view to extracting a settlement from insurers. Insurers do not wish their policy to be exploited in this way and so become a potential source of income in a difficult year for the company. Insurers consider that they are at risk of such conduct because the board

---

[21] It should not be assumed that a company will agree to provide directors with the maximum indemnity that the law will allow.

[22] Companies Act, s 232 applies to directors, not to officers.

[23] Companies Act, ss 232–236; see Chapter 14.

represents both the potential object of litigation by the company and the principal day-to-day decision-making body of the company. In short, the board has the opportunity to launch claims against itself.

Regardless of whether the scenario envisaged by insurers is a realistic one, it is **20.47** clearly not the case that directors will only face claims by the company brought at the instigation of a board on which they sit. Claims by a company can be brought by a successor board after the retirement of an insured director; or by way of derivative action; or at the behest of an administrator or liquidator. In none of these instances will the director have been in a position to influence the decision to bring proceedings against himself and the limited basis of the insurer's concern ought not to be allowed to influence the policy's approach to all and any claims by the company.

Many D&O policies proceed on the basis that any claim by a company against its **20.48** own directors is excluded.[24] Whether the director has cover at all will then depend on whether he can bring himself within any exceptions to that exclusion. The exceptions will usually preserve cover in the event of actions brought at the behest of administrators or liquidators or by way of derivative action. Any exclusion will need to be read with care in order to understand its scope and in order ensure that the exceptions to the exclusion identify ways of proceeding that are practicable. For instance, it may be that a policy will exclude all claims against the directors brought by the company except in so far as the directors can show that they have not been party to a decision to bring the claim or have not in some way incited or solicited the claim. However, in order to take advantage of an exception drafted in such terms, the directors necessarily assume the considerable burden of proving a negative. Such a burden should not be assumed lightly.

## (2) The funding of a director's defence

How and when the policy will fund the legal costs of individuals incurred in deal- **20.49** ing with actual or potential claims against them is one of the most important aspects of D&O Insurance. Directors of major companies are exceptionally unlikely to be able to find sufficient affordable insurance to cover the full financial consequences of that company becoming insolvent by reason of their actions or experiencing some other calamity of equivalent severity. Not all risks are capable of being laid off in their entirety to the insurance market. However, no director will wish to be forced to liquidate his own assets to meet legal costs incurred in defending a claim for which the ultimate liability may be well within the policy limits, especially if he has a good defence to that claim. Directors will want to

---

[24] At present, it is more likely than not that the exclusion will be limited to claims brought in the United States of America.

ensure that the policy provides an adequate mechanism for paying regular and potentially significant lawyers' fees.

**20.50** It is not unusual for a policy to provide that insurers will advance defence costs prior to the resolution of the claim. While that will be of some comfort to individual insureds, it falls short of a commitment that lawyers' invoices will be paid as and when submitted. In order to ensure proper protection for the individual insureds the policy should provide a clear mechanism for the submission, agreement, and payment of legal fees as and when they are incurred.[25]

**20.51** Usually legal costs will be covered insofar as they are incurred with the insurer's prior written consent. This is, on the whole, an adequate arrangement when insured individuals are faced with a claim which is proceeding through the courts in the usual way. Notwithstanding the advances which have been made in the light of the CPR, court proceedings generally progress at a pace which allows for advance communication with insurers as to steps which are required and, perhaps most importantly in this respect, court proceedings have a relatively predictable course.

**20.52** Where a D&O Insurance provides cover for the costs incurred in connection with regulatory action it will be necessary for it to recognize the practicalities for companies and individuals operating in a regulated environment. It is not unusual for regulators to have significant powers of intervention and coercion. An invitation to attend an interview with a regulator at short notice may not be an invitation that an individual will be able or will wish to ignore. The individual may have time to consult with his lawyers in advance of the meeting, but possibly not with his insurers.[26] However, on the traditional approach to policy drafting, he will be at

---

[25] Some policies do provide that, in respect of certain types of claim, defence costs will be advanced pending a finding of liability against the insured notwithstanding that some or all of that liability, if established, will be excluded by the policy terms and conditions. Particular care will need to be exercised in the drafting of such provisions. The legal issues underpinning and resulting from such drafting have been explored by the High Court of Australia in *Rich v CGU Insurance Limited* and *Silberman v CGU Insurance Limited* [2005] HCA 16 and in *Wilkie v Gordian Runoff Ltd* [2005] HCA 17. These cases do not address the question of whether defence costs will be advanced in circumstances where the insurer is denying liability for reasons other than the application of a particular exclusion or is challenging policy validity generally. In the absence of specific provision an insurer is unlikely to agree to advance defence costs in such circumstances: by performing the contract the insurer will risk waiving its rights to refuse to pay or to avoid the policy. Further, it will assume the credit risk of not recovering the amount of the advanced costs if it is ultimately found not to be liable. This latter consideration is fundamental to why, except in limited circumstances, insurers are unlikely to be prepared to agree policy wordings which allow insureds to receive policy funds while insurer's liability to indemnify is unresolved.

[26] Whether this is an issue will depend upon the scope of the cover for costs incurred in connection with regulatory action. Some policies will only provide cover once formal regulatory enforcement action commences. Depending on the industry in which the insured operates this may mean that some regulatory action in relation to which it is necessary to take legal advice will not be covered and so the associated legal costs will not be paid by insurers. It will be for the organization to satisfy

risk of having his claim for any legal costs incurred in preparing for that meeting denied for want of prior written consent from the insurer. Any insureds who are looking to buy cover to deal with potential regulatory action need to take account of the realities of operating in a regulated industry, in order to ensure that the policy will respond as they wish to the situations which they may face. One solution is to have a pre-determined level of costs which can be spent in the absence of consent in emergency situations.

### (3) Continuing obligations of the company

The policy is likely to include ongoing obligations and other terms of which the **20.53** insured must take note in the event that significant developments in the company's business take place during the period in which the policy is in force. Examples of such terms include the following:

(1) Cover for outside entity appointments may be conditional upon the names of the relevant outside entities being notified to the insurer. If that obligation exists, then means will need to be put in place to monitor appointments to ensure that the necessary details are conveyed to the insurers to ensure that cover is effective from the date of appointment.

(2) While the policy may grant an automatic extension of cover to directors and officers of newly acquired subsidiaries this is likely to be subject to thresholds. In particular, policies are unlikely to confirm cover automatically in respect of subsidiaries whose capital exceeds certain limits or whose operations involve certain jurisdictions, particularly the USA. Acquisitions will need to be monitored to determine whether an extension of cover for the new subsidiary needs to be specifically negotiated.

(3) Some mergers and acquisitions may terminate cover. The policy may specify that if the company engages in transactions of a particular kind or scale then, as of the effective date of that transaction, the policy will cease to cover claims made except insofar as they arise out of conduct which took place prior to the effective date of the transaction.

(4) During the course of any policy year any number of directors, officers, and employees will resign and retire. The retirement or resignation will not bring to an end their potential liability for conduct which took place before they left the company. They will be exposed to the risk of claims up until such time as any relevant periods of limitation take effect. A director may resign or retire at a time when the D&O Insurance of his company provides cover for claims made against former directors. However, if the policy is an annual contract

---

itself where its directors' exposures may arise and engage in debate with insurers as to whether appropriate cover can be provided.

then its terms and conditions may change from year to year. The company may decide in future not to purchase cover for former directors. The director will need to consider, prior to his departure, whether he needs to extract a contractual commitment from the company to ensure that future D&O policies include cover designed to respond to claims he may face after he leaves.

### (4) Conduct of claims

20.54 While all of the above issues are important, it is in the conduct of claims that the policy will provide ongoing obligations which individual insureds may regard as of greatest significance to them.

20.55 A familiar feature of liability policies is the requirement that an insured who is defending a claim shall consult with his insurers as to his conduct of the defence. It is self-evident that insurers have an interest in the conduct of that defence: they are probably paying for it and they may well find themselves having to meet the ultimate liability if the defence is unsuccessful. The mechanics of that relationship and the respective degrees of control which the insurer and insured will have over the litigation are matters for which the policy ought to make specific provision.

20.56 It may be helpful if the policy specifies when, and in what respects, the insured is obliged to consult his insurers as to the conduct of the litigation. Certain decisions, in particular the admission of liability or the negotiation of a settlement, will almost certainly be specified as matters requiring the input of insurers. It is not unusual to see a 'QC clause' whereby any dispute between the insured and insurers as to whether an offer to settle should be put or accepted is referred to the binding decision of a QC.[27]

20.57 In the context of D&O Insurance two potential consequences of a claim merit particular comment. The first is that policies will often contain an allocation provision to regulate what happens when a claim is made for which some of the defendants are insured under the policy and some are not and, or alternatively, where some of the causes of action are covered and some are not. Insurers will wish to be able to determine the extent to which they are obliged to contribute to a damages award or settlement encompassing insured and uninsured causes of action, and to the costs of defending a claim where the lawyers' fees may not identify with precision on whose behalf and on what issues those fees were incurred. Allocation provisions can confer a very broad discretion on insurers to determine what their contribution should be: in extreme cases, that discretion may come perilously close to a unilateral right on the part of the insurer to determine whether

---

[27] Where the policy provides cover for companies with international operations it may not always be appropriate to have reference to an English QC. For multinational operations it is often prudent to 'internationalize' the QC clause to allow referral to a senior lawyer in any relevant jurisdiction.

or not he makes any payment at all. However, seeking to provide for every eventuality in advance may lead to tortuous drafting or to the policy not catering for unexpected developments. The extent to which the policy prescribes the allocation process will, largely, depend on personal taste. The key consideration from the perspective of insureds is to try to achieve a means of ensuring an objective and logical determination of the extent of insurers' obligation to contribute.

The second consequence arises from the fact that in most cases the D&O Insurance **20.58** will have been purchased for the directors by the company. The day-to-day administration of the policy will be performed by the company. Indeed, and as recognized above, the policy normally confers upon a corporate 'policyholder' the right and obligation to act on behalf of all insureds when dealing with insurers. From an administrative perspective such arrangements are difficult to argue with. However, a key risk against which the policy may provide cover is claims against directors by the policyholder. In the event that such a claim arises there will be a clear conflict of interest between the party authorized to deal with insurers on the directors' behalf and the director. As with allocation, this is an area in respect of which it may be problematic to be too prescriptive as to what will happen in the event that a conflict emerges. However, those negotiating the policy will need to consider to what extent they wish to recognize the potential for conflicts and make provision for it: at the very least in recognizing that the policyholder's authority on behalf of an individual insured will terminate in the event that a claim is brought against that insured by the policyholder.

# F. Conclusions

The operation of directors' and officers' liability insurance has not been subject to **20.59** extensive exploration by the English courts. That said, the policies involve terms, conditions, and features of other forms of liability policy in respect of which the courts have given considerable guidance over time. It remains to be seen whether a detailed examination of a D&O Insurance policy by the courts will produce conclusions which take the insurance industry and its customers by surprise. For present purposes, the drafting and operation of those policies remains guided by general principles of insurance law and common sense. At the heart of these lie perhaps two fundamental questions:

(1) What are the exposures which the policy will cover? and,
(2) Will the policy provide the insured with the funds the insured needs at the time he needs them?

The first of the above questions is a risk management issue for the insured and a **20.60** product development issue for insurers. Both parties need to explore what risks need to be covered. However, the insured should not rely upon his insurer to tell him what cover he needs. The second question is one of policy mechanics and necessitates consideration of what will happen when a claim arises. The insured may have negotiated a policy which covers every conceivable risk that he might face. However, that cover will be of no use to him if, as a matter of practical mechanics, the policy leaves the insurer with the option of whether and when he might pay. Both insureds and insurers have entirely legitimate interests to protect. In reaching their bargain it is essential that each of them understands what is expected of them, and that each of them has an adequate contractual means of enforcing his expectations of the other.

# 21

# PROCEEDINGS BY MEMBERS ARISING FROM CONDUCT OF DIRECTORS

## A. Introduction

This chapter is concerned with proceedings brought by members who have suf- **21.01**
fered or may suffer damage or prejudice to their shareholding arising out of the
conduct of directors. Section B deals briefly with personal claims by shareholders
against directors and the principle of reflective loss, which affects most such claims.
Section C deals with the new statutory procedure, introduced by the 2006 Act,
Part 11, Chapter 1, ss 260–264,[1] for bringing a derivative claim or action arising
out of an act or omission (or threatened act or omission) involving negligence,
default, breach of duty, or breach of trust by a director. For the first time derivative

---

[1] Part 11 came into effect on 1 October 2007. The old law will apply to cases where the claimant
has applied for permission to continue the claim before that date. Where the claim arises out of acts
or omissions occurring before that date, the court must not allow a claim to continue which would
not have been allowed under the previous law. See 2006 Act Commencement Order No 3,
para 20.

claims brought by members of a company against wrongdoing directors have been placed on a statutory footing. This change follows the recommendations of the Law Commission and the Company Law Review Steering Group (CLR),[2] the terms of which have been adopted to a significant extent.

21.02   Section D sets out the circumstances, prescribed by the 2006 Act, Part 14, ss 362–379, in which shareholders may enforce directors' liabilities for unauthorized political donations or expenditure. These provisions largely restate provisions in the 1985 Act.[3]

21.03   Section E deals with the statutory remedy in respect of acts or omissions that constitute unfair prejudice of a member, which is contained in the 2006 Act, Part 30, ss 994–999. These provisions substantially restate or preserve the law relating to petitions for relief against acts or omissions that constitute unfair prejudice in relation to members.[4]

21.04   Finally, Section F considers the statutory remedy under the Insolvency Act, which is available to members to wind up the company on the ground that it is just and equitable.[5]

## B. Personal Claims; Reflective Loss

21.05   The 2006 Act does not affect the law relating to when a member can bring a personal action to enforce his individual rights against the company. Section 260(1) defines a derivative claim in terms which preclude a cause of action vesting in a person other than the company.[6] As such, the new statutory procedure under Part 11 does not extend to a member seeking to enforce personal rights which derive from the articles of association of the company.

21.06   Nor do the new provisions in Part 11 affect the rare cases where a member has a direct claim against a director or cases where a member has a claim against a third party in relation to his shares in the company. Such claims invariably raise difficult

---

[2] *Shareholder Remedies* (1997, Law Com No 246), which was preceded by a Consultation Paper No 142 (1996); CLR: *Developing the Framework* at paras 4.65–4.144; CLR: *Final Report* at paras 7.46–7.51.

[3] 1985 Act, ss 347A–K. Those sections were inserted into the 1985 Act by the Political Parties, Elections and Referendums Act 2000, Schedule 19, to control political donations and political expenditure by companies. The provisions of the 2006 Act came into force on 1 October 2007, except for the provisions in relation to independent election candidates, which came into force on 1 October 2008.

[4] As provided in 1985 Act, ss 459–461. 2006 Act, Part 30 came into force on 1 October 2007.

[5] ss 122(1)(g) and 124(1).

[6] By contrast, s 265(6)(a) expressly recognizes the non-application of those provisions to the personal rights of a member to raise proceedings and obtain a remedy on his own behalf, in relation to Scotland.

issues and are almost always defeated by the 'reflective loss principle'. That principle dictates that where a company suffers loss caused by a breach of duty owed to it, only the company may sue in respect of that loss. No action lies at the suit of a member suing in that capacity to make good a diminution in the value of his shareholding, where it is merely a reflection of the loss suffered by the company.[7]

The interplay between personal claims and derivative claims was considered at **21.07** length by the House of Lords in *Johnson v Gore Wood & Co*.[8] In that case, claims were brought against a firm of solicitors by a majority (and virtually the only) shareholder and the company. The plaintiff was in principle entitled to recover damages in respect of all heads of non-consequential loss, arising in relation to duties owed to him personally as shareholder. Lord Millett held that where the company suffers a loss caused by the breach of a duty owed both to the company and the shareholder, then the shareholder's loss merely reflects that suffered by the company—and in respect of which the company has its own cause of action. Further, Lord Millett said:

> If the shareholder is allowed to recover in respect of such loss, then either there will be double recovery at the expense of the defendant or the shareholder will recover at the expense of the company and its creditors and other shareholders. Neither course can be permitted. This is a matter of principle; there is no discretion involved. Justice to the defendant requires the exclusion of one claim or the other; protection of the interests of the company's creditors requires that it is the company which is allowed to recover to the exclusion of the shareholder.

On that broad proposition, the reflective loss is not limited to the diminution in value of the shareholding. Rather, Lord Millett said that it includes a loss of dividends and all other payments which a member might have obtained from the company if it had not been deprived of its funds.[9]

Accordingly, a personal claim may only be brought by a member where he can **21.08** demonstrate (a) a breach of a duty owed to him personally, and crucially (b) personal loss separate and distinct from that suffered by the company.[10] That notwithstanding, it is difficult to conceive of circumstances in which a member would have a personal claim against the directors which was not defeated by reflective loss. This is one of the reasons why a petition for relief from unfair prejudice is likely to be the more suitable procedure for an aggrieved member. A notable exception would arise where a claim against the directors and/or company in

---

[7] *Prudential Assurance Co Ltd v Newman Industries Ltd (No. 2)* [1982] Ch 204, 222–3, CA, as cited by Lord Bingham in *Johnson v Gore Wood & Co* [2002] 2 AC 1, 35, HL.

[8] [2002] 2 AC 1, 35, 62, HL. Subsequent cases: *Ellis v Property Leeds (UK) Ltd* [2002] 2 BCLC 175, CA; *Barings plc v Cooper & Lybrand (a firm) (No 1)* [2002] 2 BCLC 364; *Giles v Rhind* [2003] Ch 618, CA; *Shaker v Al-Bedrawi* [2003] Ch 350, CA; *Gardner v Parker* [2004] 2 BCLC 554, CA.

[9] [2002] 2 AC 1, 35, 66H, HL.

[10] *Johnson v Gore Wood & Co* [2002] 2 AC 1, 35H, HL.

deceit or negligence arises out of the issue of a false prospectus.[11] That is dealt with in Chapter 27.

# C. Derivative Claims

## (1) Introduction

*New provisions: the statutory derivative claim*

**21.09**  A derivative claim is a claim by a member of a company in respect of a cause of action vested in the company and seeking relief on behalf of the company, which arises out of an act or omission (actual or proposed) involving negligence, default, breach of duty, or breach of trust by a director.[12] Such a claim is now subject to a successful application to the court for permission, since s 260(2) states that a derivative claim may only be brought under Part 11 or pursuant to a court order in proceedings under s 994.[13] To that extent, the rule in *Foss v Harbottle*,[14] described in paragraph 21.13 below, is displaced.

**21.10**  However, the substantive change to the existing rules should not be overstated. Part 11, Chapter 1 does not introduce a substantive rule to replace the rule in *Foss v Harbottle*. Rather, it introduces a new statutory procedure for bringing a derivative claim by way of exception to that rule.[15] It will be seen that the common law principles have been codified so as to render them at once both accessible and flexible and that they are supplemented by a new CPR 19.9.

**21.11**  The rationale of derivative claims is not difficult to explain. Where the company has suffered a wrong by reason of the conduct of a director, leaving the decision of whether to bring an action or not to the board would create room for a conflict of interest. The derivative claim is best viewed as an action commenced by a minority shareholder seeking relief *on behalf of* the company in respect of a wrong done to the company: his rights are 'derived' from the company. By s 260(3), a derivative claim may be brought only in respect of a cause of action arising from an

---

[11]  Cf *Prudential Assurance Co Ltd v Newman Industries Ltd (No 2)* [1982] Ch 204, CA. In that case, the claim against the directors involved inter alia a claim for conspiracy arising out of the distribution of a false circular to shareholders. The Court of Appeal considered that the directors owed the shareholders a duty to give advice in good faith and not fraudulently. It went on to accept that if directors convened a meeting on the basis of a fraudulent circular, a shareholder would have a right of action to recover any loss which he had been personally caused as a result, for example, of the expense of attending the meeting.

[12]  2006 Act, s 260(1), (3).

[13]  ie as a remedy in a successful unfair prejudice action.

[14]  (1843) 2 Hare 461.

[15]  It is to be noted that Chapter 1 uses the term 'derivative claim' and assumes that there is already a right to bring such claims in England and Wales and Northern Ireland. It therefore regulates the conduct of a derivative claim rather than conferring the right to bring a claim.

actual or proposed act or omission involving negligence, default, breach of duty, or breach of trust by a director of the company. The definition of 'director' for these purposes extends to a former[16] or shadow[17] director (ss 260(5)(a) and (b)).

Notwithstanding that such acts or omissions are attributed to the director, the derivative claim may also be brought against a third party (in addition to or in lieu of the director). Section 260(3) states that the cause of action may be against the director *or* another person (or both). That will be appropriate where a third party has knowingly received corporate property as a result of a breach of duty by a director. In this context, the common law rules relating to dishonest assistance or knowing receipt of corporate property remain applicable.[18]     **21.12**

### The old law: 'fraud on a minority'

The previous common law principles relating to derivative actions will be of continuing relevance. The derivation of the shareholder's remedy was the rule established in the case of *Foss v Harbottle*.[19] That rule established two general propositions: (i) the 'proper plaintiff' principle, by which prima facie the corporation is the only proper claimant in proceedings in respect of a wrong alleged to have been done to it or to recover money or damages alleged to be due to it; and (ii) the 'majority rule' principle, by which an individual shareholder will not be allowed to pursue proceedings on behalf of himself and all other shareholders if     **21.13**

---

[16] s 170(2) provides that a person who ceases to be a director continues to be subject to the duty to avoid conflicts of interests in s 175 as regards the exploitation of any property, information, or opportunity of which he became aware at the time he was a director. He also continues to be subject to the duty in s 176 (duty not to accept benefits from third parties) as regards things done or omitted by him before he ceased to be a director.

[17] How significant this will be in practice is not clear, since it cannot be said with any certainty that shadow directors owe fiduciary duties to the company. See Chapter 9, Section C. The extension of s 260 to shadow directors was recommended by the Law Commission in *Shareholder Remedies* (1997, Law Com No 246) at para 6.36. This was on the basis that it should be possible to base a claim against a shadow director on the grounds of breach of a statutory obligation (for example, for non-compliance with Part 10, where many of the provisions do apply to shadow directors). Naturally the derivative claimant will still need to satisfy the court that the putative defendant is in fact a shadow director.

[18] No attempt has been made in the Act to prescribe the circumstances in which the company has such a claim against third parties.

[19] (1843) 2 Hare 461. In that case, an action was brought by two minority shareholders against the directors for misapplication, alienation, and waste of company property. Sir James Wigram VC considered (at 491) the only question to be whether the facts of the case justified a departure from the rule which prima facie would require the company to sue in its own name (or that of its representative). He observed (at 494) that a simple majority of shareholders in general meeting had the power to bind the entire body of shareholders, and thus waive the complaints against the directors. His reasoning was that the shareholders were the ultimate proprietors of the company and in most cases would act by majority rule. Accordingly, were the court to allow the minority shareholder action to proceed, the company could defeat the judgment by way of majority vote. Its power to do so demonstrated that the action was not sustainable. Only where it could be demonstrated that 'there is no such power' on the part of the majority, could the action be pursued.

the alleged wrong was within the powers of the corporation, since, in those circumstances, the majority of the shareholders might lawfully ratify the allegedly wrongful transaction; if they did not, they would be able to put the corporation in motion to bring the necessary proceedings.

**21.14** Put differently, minority shareholders could not complain of irregularities in the conduct of the company's internal affairs if the irregularity was one which could be cured by a vote of the company in general meeting.[20] As such, the rule prevented the court from interfering with the internal management of a company at the instance of a minority shareholder, dissatisfied with the conduct of the company's affairs by the majority or the board of directors.

**21.15** Both those propositions can be found in cases decided after *Foss v Harbottle*.[21] In *Edwards v Halliwell*[22] Jenkins LJ explained the relationship between those two propositions. The assertion that the company is prima facie the proper plaintiff in an action the subject of which is the company's affairs, is equivalent to holding that the majority have the sole right to determine whether or not the action shall be brought.[23]

**21.16** It was eventually recognized that the principle of majority rule could not be equitably applied in the case of wrongdoing directors who were, or formed part of, the majority shareholders. The effect would be to allow the majority to 'cure' by way of ratification a breach of duty committed by the majority. In relation to the proper plaintiff principle, it was also recognized that reliance on the shareholders in general meeting to bring a claim in the name of the company would be unrealistic in such circumstances. In this way, an otherwise meritorious claim could be stultified by reason of wrongdoer control. As such, it was thought that an individual member ought in certain (limited) circumstances to be allowed to bring a derivative action. Several exceptions to the rule in *Foss v Harbottle* consequently grew up, of which the most significant turned on whether the action taken was a 'fraud on the minority'. The exceptions dictated the circumstances in which a derivative action could be brought.

---

[20] *Prudential Assurance Co Ltd v Newman Industries Ltd (No 2)* [1982] Ch 204, 210–11, CA.

[21] *Mozley v Alston* (1847) 1 Ph 790; *Burland v Earle* [1902] AC 83, PC; *Pavlides v Jensen* [1956] Ch 565.

[22] [1950] 2 All ER 1064, 1066H, CA.

[23] For judicial justification of the rule by reference to practical considerations, see *Gray v Lewis* (1873) 8 Ch App 1035, 1051, CA; *MacDougall v Gardiner* (1875) 1 Ch D 13, 25, CA. In the latter case, Mellish LJ considered that 'if something has been done irregularly which the majority are entitled to do regularly, or if something has been done illegally which the majority of the company are entitled to do legally, there can be no use having litigation about it the ultimate end of which is that a meeting is called and then ultimately the majority gets its wishes'. As such, ignoring the majority's power to ratify was futile.

In *Burland v Earle*[24] Lord Davey considered the development of the exceptions to **21.17** the rule and said:

> [it] is mere matter of procedure in order to give a remedy for a wrong which would otherwise escape redress, and it is obvious that in such an action the plaintiffs cannot have a larger right to relief than the company itself would have if it were plaintiff, and cannot complain of acts which are valid if done with the approval of the majority of the shareholders, or are capable of being confirmed by the majority. The cases in which the minority can maintain such an action are, therefore, confined to those in which the acts complained of are of a fraudulent character or beyond the powers of the company.

The rule thus evolved to recognize certain limited situations in which a member **21.18** could bring a derivative action. Specifically, the claimant was required to prove that the case came within at least one of three exceptions to the rule: (i) the nature of the wrong committed by the directors was beyond the powers of the company or illegal (hence it could not be ratified),[25] (ii) the wrong constituted a fraud on the minority shareholders and the alleged wrongdoers had control of the general meeting which was or would be exercised to preclude the bringing of an action against the wrongdoers,[26] or (iii) the act required the sanction of a special majority which could not be obtained.[27] More recently, it became important to demonstrate that the majority of the independent shareholders favoured the litigation.[28] Thus, even when a prima facie case existed under exceptions (i), (ii), or (iii), the court would not permit a derivative claim to proceed where the majority of shareholders who were independent of the wrongdoers, did not wish the proceedings to continue.[29] As a result, remedy by way of derivative claim was available only in the most restricted circumstances.[30]

---

[24] *Burland v Earle* [1902] AC 83, 93, PC.

[25] *Edwards v Halliwell* [1950] 2 All ER 1064, 1067, CA; *Smith v Croft (No 2)* [1988] Ch 114; *Australian Agricultural Co v Oatmont Pty Ltd* (1992) 8 ACSR 255 (CA).

[26] *Prudential Assurance Co Ltd v Newman Industries Ltd (No 2)* [1982] Ch 204, CA.

[27] Ibid, 210–11, CA: '. . . because a simple majority cannot confirm a transaction which requires the concurrence of a greater majority'.

[28] *Smith v Croft (No 2)* [1988] Ch 114. In that case, the minority shareholders brought an action against the directors of a company on the ground that they had caused the company to make certain illegal and *ultra vires* payments. The question before the judge was whether the plaintiffs could proceed with their action and as such, whether the company was entitled to the relief claimed and whether the action fell within the exception to the rule in *Foss v Harbottle*. Knox J held that it was proper to have regard to the views of independent shareholders, and applying that proposition to the facts at issue, the statement of claim was struck out.

[29] Cf *Smith v Croft (No 2)* [1988] Ch 114.

[30] For examples of court intervention in this context, see: *Duckett v Gover* (1877) 6 Ch D 82; *Daniels v Daniels* [1978] Ch 406; *Estmanco (Kilner House) Ltd v Greater London Council* [1982] 1 WLR 2; *Bamford v Bamford* [1970] Ch 212, CA.

**21.19** The second exception to the rule that alleged wrongdoers who control the majority of shares may prevent the company from bringing an action by refusing to authorize proceedings in the company's name merits particular attention. If the court denied the minority the right to bring proceedings 'their grievance could never reach the court because the wrongdoers themselves, being in control, would not allow the company to sue'.[31] The principal question therefore became: 'Is the plaintiff being improperly prevented from bringing these proceedings on behalf of the company?'[32] Under the old law, the question of control was to be decided as a preliminary issue before the claim was allowed to proceed. In taking that decision, it was not considered enough for the court to say that there was no plain and obvious case for striking out. Rather, it was for the shareholder to establish to the satisfaction of the court that he should be allowed to sue on behalf of the company.[33] It was not left for determination at trial, although the court could also grant a sufficient adjournment to enable a meeting of shareholders to be convened by the board, to decide whether proceedings should continue in the company's name.[34] The votes of the persons complained of could not however be excluded.[35]

**21.20** In this way the general principle that the court has no jurisdiction to interfere with the internal management of companies acting within their powers remained intact.[36] Nor would claimants have a more extensive right to relief than the company in its capacity as claimant. For example, they could not complain of acts which were valid if done with the approval of the majority of shareholders or were capable of being confirmed by the majority. In other words, mere irregularity or informality which was capable of cure was insufficient to found a derivative action.[37] Further, where those seeking to bring a derivative claim in fact controlled the company, such that they were in a position to cause the company to bring the claim itself, any such claim was judged wholly misconceived.[38]

---

[31] *Prudential Assurance Co Ltd v Newman Industries Ltd (No 2)* [1982] Ch 204, 210–11, CA.
[32] *Smith v Croft (No 2)* [1988] Ch 114, 185B.
[33] *Barrett v Duckett* [1995] 1 BCLC 243, 249–50, CA.
[34] *Prudential Assurance Co Ltd v Newman Industries Ltd (No 2)* [1982] Ch 204, 222, CA; *Danish Mercantile Co Ltd v Beaumont* [1951] Ch 680, 687.
[35] *Mason v Harris* (1879) 11 Ch D 97, CA; *North West Transportation Co Ltd v Beatty* (1887) 12 App Cas 589, PC.
[36] Cf *Alexander v Automatic Telephone Co* [1900] 2 Ch 56, 69. See also *MacDougall v Gardiner* (1875) 1 Ch D 13, CA; *Burland v Earle* [1902] AC 83, 93, PC.
[37] Ibid; *MacDougall v Gardiner* (1875) 1 Ch D 13, CA, per Mellish LJ. In the latter case, although the decision itself was reversed, Malins VC said that there had to be something at least bordering upon fraud to found a minority shareholders' action.
[38] *Watts v Midland Bank plc* [1986] BCLC 15, where there was no obstacle to the company bringing the action.

## (2) Scope of derivative claims

Section 260(1) defines a derivative claim as:                                    **21.21**

> proceedings in England and Wales or Northern Ireland by a member[39] of a company[40]—
> (a) in respect of a cause of action vested in the company, and
> (b) seeking relief on behalf of the company.

Since this definition reflects existing case law on derivative claims, it seems that past authorities will continue to be relevant. In practice, the member will be a minority shareholder unable to persuade the company to bring proceedings. This may include a 50 per cent shareholder, where he can be treated as being under the same disability as a minority shareholder.[41] Further, the section addresses the situation where the directors have refused to enter the name of a transferee of shares in the register of members: s 260(5)(c) operates to include within the definition under s 260(1) a person who is not a member but to whom shares in the company have been transferred or transmitted by operation of law.

Section 260(2) delineates the scope for bringing a derivative claim. As already **21.22** noted, it makes the statutory remedy under s 260 the exclusive procedure for bringing the claim, save for orders granted in proceedings under s 994 of the Companies Act. In practice, however, a successful petitioner under s 994 is most unlikely to seek such an order under s 996(2)(c), since a buy-out order will usually be more appropriate (see below).[42]

---

[39] By 1985 Act, s 22 the members of a company are the subscribers of its memorandum and every other person who agrees to become a member of a company and whose name is entered in its register of members. On 1 October 2009, 2006 Act, s 112 replaces s 22 with minor changes.

[40] 1985 Act, s 735 defines 'company' as a company formed and registered under that Act or previous Companies Acts, thus excluding overseas companies. 2006 Act, s 1, which replaces 1985 Act, s 735 on 1 October 2009, is to the same effect. These definitions also exclude a derivative claim being brought by a shareholder in a parent company on behalf of a subsidiary company to whom the duty is owed (known as multiple derivative claims). The Law Commission considered that it would be neither helpful nor practicable to include such claims (Law Com No 246 at para 6.110). However, the Commission at the same time considered that the question was best left to the courts to resolve, if necessary using its remedial power upon a successful unfair prejudice petition to allow the commencement of derivative proceedings. This is most likely to be invoked in the case of wholly-owned subsidiaries formed for a specific purpose or activity. Where, however, it is manifest that control of the subsidiary lies with persons independent of its parent, the court may be less likely to allow such a claim.

[41] *Barrett v Duckett* [1995] 1 BCLC 243, 250, CA.

[42] Attempts were made during the Bill's passage through Parliament to remove the provision under s 260(2)(b) (679 HL Official Report (5th series) col GC6 (27 February 2006)). The Government rejected them and accepted the view of the Law Commission that, despite the fact that a shareholder is unlikely to use s 996(2)(c) to bring a derivative claim, the better approach is to maintain both routes (Law Com No 246 at para 6.55). Furthermore, where relief is given under s 996 to bring a derivative claim, the threshold for permission to continue the claim laid down in s 261 will not apply.

**21.23**　By s 260(4) it is immaterial whether the cause of action arose before or after the person seeking to bring or continue the derivative claim became a member of the company. This provision retains the common law rule.[43] It reflects the fact that the rights being enforced are those of the company rather than the member. It is also commercially realistic. If the company receives a windfall from previous events just after a shareholder disposes of shares, it is the new shareholder who takes the benefit. Similarly, it is the new shareholder who will suffer detriment where the company suffers an unexpected loss arising out of past events.

**21.24**　Nor is any minimum shareholding stipulated.[44] In theory, therefore, the putative claimant could purchase one share for the purpose of bringing a derivative claim. Concern was voiced during the parliamentary debates that vulture funds, environmentalists, animal rights activists, and US litigators would seek to take advantage of the absence of any such provision, and that this would be damaging to commercial activity.[45] Those fears were somewhat allayed by the potential disadvantages to any such litigant. Specifically, any recovery will inure to the benefit of the company and the claimant will risk being penalized in costs in the absence of an indemnity order. Such differences in incentive were viewed as preventing American-style class actions.

**21.25**　Of greater significance is s 260(3). That section sets out the various categories of 'wrongs' out of which the cause of action will arise:

> A derivative claim under this Chapter may be brought only in respect of a cause of action arising from an actual or proposed act or omission involving negligence, default, breach of duty or breach of trust by a director of the company.[46]

In both form and substance it marks a striking change of approach. The restrictive requirements of fraud on the minority and control by the alleged wrongdoers do not appear.[47] As a result, the ambit of the derivative claim is now much wider than under the previous regime and extends to any cause of action falling within those four categories of conduct. Three points should be noted.

**21.26**　First, a derivative claim may now be brought in respect of negligence. It was previously the case that no such action would lie where mere negligence on the part of

---

[43] Cf *Seaton v Grant* (1867) 2 Ch App 459. See further Law Com No 246 at para 6.98 and 679 HL Official Report (5th Series) col GC15 (27 February 2006).

[44] Cf *Seaton v Grant* (1867) 2 Ch App 459.

[45] 679 HL Official Report (5th Series) cols GC11–13 (27 February 2006).

[46] The same language is used in 2006 Act, s 239. See the discussion in Chapter 19 at paragraph 19.07.

[47] It was considered that the requirement of wrongdoer control may make it impossible for a derivative claim to be brought successfully by a member of a widely held company: 681 HL Official Report (5th series) col 883 (9 May 2006) (Lord Goldsmith).

the directors was alleged.[48] The CLR noted however that a general concern had been voiced in relation to breaches of the duty of care and skill.[49] The CLR considered that 'the developments in the law in relation to directors' duties of skill and care should have their counterpart in policing procedures'.[50] Against that it was argued that the court should adopt a restrictive approach, since the board is responsible for management, and problems may arise where there is a clear breach of duty by a director but the board takes a commercial decision not to pursue it. The CLR did not consider this latter suggestion to pose any difficulties. If an untainted majority of the board takes the decision, in compliance with their duties, then it should stand. If not, then whether an action should proceed would be determined in accordance with the principles on directors' duties.[51] In practice, therefore, it will be a matter for the courts to distinguish between commercial misjudgement and negligent conduct.

The second important change is that a claim may now be brought in respect of a **21.27** breach of duty, including negligence, without having to prove some personal benefit accruing to the alleged wrongdoers. The position at common law was that as a mere breach of a fiduciary duty owed to the company is ratifiable, a derivative action could not be brought in respect of any such breach.[52] Only (in the absence of fraud) where the directors and majority shareholders were guilty of a breach of duty which not only harms the company but *benefits* those shareholders, could a derivative claim be brought.[53] The absence of personal benefit is however likely

---

[48] *Pavlides v Jensen* [1956] Ch 565 (approved in *Multinational Gas and Petrochemical Co v Multinational Gas and Petrochemical Services Ltd* [1983] Ch 258, CA); *Heyting v Dupont* [1964] 1 WLR 843, CA. In *Pavlides v Jensen*, it was alleged that the directors had been guilty of gross negligence in effecting a sale of a valuable asset of the company at a price greatly below its true market value. It was also alleged that the directors knew or ought to have known that it was below market value. It was found that the sale was not *ultra vires* the powers of the company and no allegation of fraud was made. Danckwerts J held (at 576) that it was open to the company, on the resolution of the majority of shareholders, to sell the asset at a price decided by the company in that manner. Further, that it was open to the company by a vote of the majority to decide that, if the directors by their negligence had sold the asset at an undervalue, proceedings should not be taken by the company against the directors. See, however, Robin Hollington QC, *Shareholders' Rights* (5th edn) at para 6-16 for an argument that *Pavlides v Jensen* may have been wrongly decided.

[49] CLR: *Final Report* at para 7.47. See also Law Com No 246 at paras 6.38–6.41 in relation to the risks of extending the scope of derivative claims to include negligence of directors.

[50] CLR: *Developing the Framework* at para 4.127.

[51] In a similar vein, the Law Commission took the view that, whilst investors take the risk that those who manage companies may make mistakes, they do not have to accept that directors will fail to comply with their duties (Law Com No 246 at para 6.41).

[52] *Burland v Earle* [1902] AC 83, PC; *Pavlides v Jensen* [1956] Ch 565; *Heyting v Dupont* [1964] 1 WLR 843, CA.

[53] *Daniels v Daniels* [1978] Ch 406. In that case, it was contended by the minority shareholders that any breach of fiduciary duty by directors could found a derivative action. The defendants contended that no cause of action was shown because the statement of claim did not allege fraud. Further, that in the absence of fraud, the minority shareholders were unable to maintain a derivative claim. Templeman J rejected this proposition as not consistent with the authorities. He relied on

to be taken into account by the court in the exercise of its discretion as to whether to grant permission to continue.

**21.28** Finally, it might be thought that the inclusion of 'breach of duty' is no more than a reference to breaches of the general duties set out in Part 10, Chapter 2.[54] However: (i) the section does not so provide in terms; (ii) the general thrust of the text is to widen the ambit of the derivative claim;[55] and (iii) the inclusion of 'default' as a ground for a derivative claim is a direct reference to a breach of other statutory obligations, which cause loss to the Company (eg through being fined).

### (3) Procedure for derivative claims

*The need for procedural reform*

**21.29** Not only was the availability of the derivative claim under the common law narrowly circumscribed: the exceptions to the rule in *Foss v Harbottle* were also unclear and difficult to apply to particular cases. Complex disputes ensued. The decision in *Prudential v Newman (No 2)*[56] had emphasized the importance of determining whether the member had *locus standi* to bring a derivative claim in advance of and separately from the hearing on the substantive merits of the claim. The derivative claimant was required to establish that: (i) the wrong could not be ratified by the majority; and (ii) the wrongdoing majority's control of the company prevented the company itself bringing an action in its own name.[57]

**21.30** Therefore it is hardly surprising that putative claimants were deterred by the prospect of having to establish both *locus standi* (on the above grounds) and the absence of personal relief. In consequence, derivative claims were rarely brought and few were successful. The need to satisfy the court at an early stage that the action

---

previous cases for the proposition (at 414) that 'a minority shareholder who has no other remedy may sue where directors use their powers intentionally or unintentionally, fraudulently or negligently, in a manner which benefits themselves at the expense of the company'. He also emphasized that neither allegations that directors have appropriated property belonging in equity to the company nor that they have acted in bad faith in exercising a director's power to sell the company's property, amount to an allegation of fraud. See also *Estmanco v Greater London Council* [1982] 1 WLR 2, 12F and 15H–16A, per Megarry V-C: 'Apart from the benefit to themselves at the company's expense, the essence of the matter seems to be an abuse or misuse of power. "Fraud" in the phrase "fraud on a minority" seems to be being used as comprising not only fraud at common law but also fraud in the wider equitable sense of that term, as in the equitable concept of a fraud on a power'.

[54] Despite the inclusion of former and shadow directors in s 260(5)(a) and (b), there are certain limitations on the circumstances in which the general duties apply to former (s 170(2)) or shadow directors (s 170(5)).

[55] 679 HL Official Report (5th Series) col GC2 (27 February 2006).

[56] [1982] Ch 204, CA.

[57] *Prudential Assurance Co Ltd v Newman Industries Ltd (No 2)* [1982] Ch 204, CA; *Smith v Croft (No 2)* [1988] Ch 114.

should be permitted to proceed represented a substantial barrier and many claims failed at this first hurdle.[58] The changes made by Part 11 need to be set in the context of past practice, with the result that obtaining permission will remain a substantial challenge.[59]

It is in that context that in 1997 reform was recommended by the Law Commission **21.31** and the CLR.[60] It was considered that the rule in *Foss v Harbottle*, which could only be found in case law, was 'complicated and unwieldy'. The scope of the exception to the rule was uncertain. Further, the way in which a member was required to prove *locus standi* as a preliminary issue by evidence which shows a prima facie case on the merits, could amount to a mini-trial which increased the length and cost of litigation.[61] Rather than determining availability of the derivative claim by reference to a set of rules which defined whether the claim could be brought at all, it was proposed to transfer that discretion to the court.

The statutory derivative procedure proposed by the Law Commission envisaged **21.32** the imposition of criteria for determining whether a shareholder may pursue a claim: criteria which were 'more modern, flexible and accessible'.[62] In this way, the Law Commission considered that the proposals would put the derivative action on a much clearer and more rational basis. Further, that they would give courts the flexibility to allow cases to proceed in appropriate circumstances, while giving advisers and shareholders the necessary guidance on matters which the court will take into account in deciding whether to grant leave.[63] It was further considered that a statutory procedure would give greater transparency to the requirements for a claim, in that it would alert shareholders, directors, and other interested parties to the existence of the provision and would ensure (along with the unfair prejudice remedy) that the Companies Act constituted a complete code with regard to shareholders' remedies.[64]

---

[58] Grounds for refusal included the availability of alternative remedies, the fact that no independent board would sanction the action and concerns about whether the applicant was acting in good faith. See: *Portfolios of Distinction Ltd v Laird* [2004] 2 BCLC 741; *Jafari-Fini v Skillglass Ltd* [2005] BCC 842; *Mumbray v Lapper* [2005] BCC 990; *Harley Street Capital Ltd v Tchigirinsky* [2006] BCC 209. Most recently, Lewison J in *Reeves v Sprecher* [2007] 2 BCLC 614 refused leave to continue a derivative claim on the basis that the English court was not the appropriate forum.

[59] It is too early to state whether claims will have a better prospect of obtaining permission to continue under the 2006 Act. At the time of writing there have been two reported decisions under the new regime: *Mission Capital Plc v Sinclair* [2008] BCC 866 and *Franbar Holdings Ltd v Patel* [2008] BCC 885. In both cases permission to continue was refused.

[60] Law Com No 246, which was preceded by a Consultation Paper No 142 (1996).

[61] Law Com No 246 at para 6.4.

[62] Ibid at para 6.15.

[63] Ibid at para 6.14.

[64] Ibid at paras 6.16–6.18. The Law Commission also considered that it was important to remain consistent with the legislation of other jurisdictions such as Canada, New Zealand, and Australia,

**21.33**  The Law Commission recommended that the court should have a discretion at the leave stage, which should not be confined to the application of the rule in *Foss v Harbottle* and its exceptions, and that the rules governing the exercise of judicial discretion should be set out in the CPR, in terms identified in Appendix B to the Report. These took account of relevant factors identified in existing case law.

**21.34**  Part 11 contains provisions which adopt the Law Commission's proposals to a significant extent.[65] For example, the absence of a requirement to demonstrate control of the general meeting by wrongdoing directors. That notwithstanding, a certain amount of unease was expressed over the prescription by statute of the substantive criteria according to which a claim may be brought. In this respect Part 11 extends further than envisaged by the Commission. During the Bill's passage through Parliament, amendments were effected so as to prescribe yet further the circumstances in which the court's discretion could be exercised.[66] Debate has for a long time reigned over whether the rule in *Foss v Harbottle* ought to be regarded as purely procedural.[67] The consequence of comprehensive provision in Part 11 has been that much less falls to be dealt with in the CPR or delegated legislation.

**21.35**  Further apprehension surrounded the operation of Part 11 in tandem with Part 10, which contains a statutory statement of directors' duties, certain of which may be thought to widen the obligations to which directors were subject at common law.[68]

### The permission application

**21.36**  Section 261 places the procedure for an application for permission to continue a derivative claim on a statutory footing. It sets out the procedure to be observed once a claimant has initiated a derivative action. Subsection 1 requires a member of a company who brings a derivative claim to apply to the court for permission to

---

cf Canadian Business Corporation Act 1975, s 239; New Zealand Companies Act 1993, ss 165–168; and Australian Corporations Act 2001, Part 2F.1A, ss 236–242.

[65] *Final Report* at para 7.46.

[66] 681 HL Official Report (5th series) col 883 (9 May 2006).

[67] *Konamaneni v Rolls Royce Industrial Power (India) Ltd* [2002] 1 WLR 1269, 1284E. See also the comments of Knox J in *Smith v Croft (No 2)* [1988] Ch 114, 170F: '. . . the whole doctrine whereby a minority shareholder is permitted to assert claims on behalf of the company is rooted in a procedural expedient and adopted to prevent a wrong going without redress'.

[68] The Explanatory Notes, para 483, in addressing Part 11, open with a reference to s 170. In *Litigating domestic disputes within companies: continuity or change?* (Sweet and Maxwell Company Law Newsletter, Issue 220 (22/2007) 1, 2) David Milman contends that the wider range of directors' duties under ss 170 *et seq* may open up greater opportunities for shareholder litigation. He goes on, however, to reach the conclusion that there is unlikely to be a flood of shareholder litigation, but merely an enhanced opportunity to launch derivative claims.

continue it.[69] Part 11 thus assumes that the claimant may commence the claim without any court intervention, but must then seek permission to continue.

The new CPR 19.9[70] supplements the substantive provisions of Part 11 and requires the derivative claimant to apply for permission to continue.[71] By CPR 19.9(2) the claim is commenced by the issue of a claim form. Rule 19.9(3) provides that the company for the benefit of which a remedy is sought must be made a defendant to the claim. After the issue of the claim form, the claimant must not take any further step in the proceedings without the permission of the court, other than: (a) a step permitted or required by rule 19.9A or 19.9C; or (b) making an urgent application for interim relief.[72]    **21.37**

Rule 19.9A deals with the application for permission. When the claim form is issued, the claimant must file an application notice under Part 23 for permission to continue the claim and the written evidence on which he relies in support of the permission application.[73] The claimant must not make the company a respondent to the permission application.[74] As such, the claim form may be issued without any prior notice or request to the company. However, the claimant must notify the company of the claim and permission application by sending to the company as soon as reasonably practicable after the claim form is issued: (a) a notice in the form set out in the practice direction supplement to r 19.9;[75] (b) copies of the claim form and the particulars of claim; (c) the application notice; and (d) a copy of the evidence filed by the claimant in support of the permission application.[76] The claimant must file a witness statement confirming that he has notified the company in accordance with the rule.[77] The requirement for notice to be given to    **21.38**

---

[69] The court is defined by s 1156 as the High Court and also a county court in England and Wales, subject to the power of the Lord Chancellor to re-define the jurisdictions of the county courts for the purposes of the Companies Acts.

[70] Brought into effect by SI 2007/2204 on 1 October 2007.

[71] With effect from 1 October 2007.

[72] CPR 19.9(4).

[73] CPR 19.9A(2).

[74] CPR 19.9A(3).

[75] Practice Direction 19C sets down further details on certain procedural requirements.

[76] CPR 19.9A(4).

[77] CPR 19.9A(6). Interestingly the Law Commission also recommended that a shareholder wishing to bring a derivative claim be required to serve a notice on the company at least 28 days before the commencement of the proceedings, specifying the grounds of the proposed claim (Law Com No 246 at paras 6.58–6.59). That recommendation was not followed, despite such a requirement being imposed under 2006 Act, s 371 (unauthorized political donations). During the Bill's passage through Parliament it was also proposed that a derivative claim be allowed to be brought only where the directors have been requested by a member of the company to bring a claim and have refused to do so (679 HL Official Report (5th Series) cols GC6–7 (27 February 2006)). That proposed amendment was designed to decrease the number of unmeritorious claims being brought for tactical reasons. It was, however, similarly rejected. The Government stressed that it did not wish to reintroduce an element of the 'wrongdoer control' test—one of the very reasons the Law Commission proposed a new statutory remedy (679 HL Official Report (5th Series) cols GC7–8

the company is subject to the court's discretion to permit notification to be delayed where it would be likely to frustrate some part of the remedy sought.[78]

**21.39** Section 261 in essence provides that a prima facie case is required to continue a derivative claim or the application will be struck out. The section appears to contemplate that the permission application is dealt with in two stages: the first under subss 261(2) and (3) and the second under subs 261(4).

**21.40** By s 261(2):

> If it appears to the court that the application and the evidence filed by the applicant in support of it do not disclose a prima facie case for giving permission . . ., the court—
> (a) must dismiss the application, and
> (b) may make any consequential order it considers appropriate.

That is the first stage of the hearing of the application. The provision was introduced after debate in the House of Lords, with a view to reducing the burden on directors in defending unmeritorious cases.[79] It reflects to a substantial extent the test laid down by the Court of Appeal in *Prudential v Newman (No 2)*.[80] The court's power to dismiss the application at this stage is reinforced by s 261(2)(b) which enables the court to penalize an applicant with costs orders or deter a nuisance applicant with a civil restraint order. At this first stage the court considers, on a prima facie basis only, whether the applicant has standing and has shown that (i) the directors have committed the wrong alleged against the company, and (ii) permission to continue the case should be given, having regard to the criteria set out in s 263. CPR 19.9A(9) contemplates that the first stage is dealt with by the court as a paperwork exercise without a hearing, although representations by, and evidence from, the company and other potential respondents are not excluded

---

(27 February 2006)). Lord Goldsmith felt that this may create scope for directors to spin out the claim in order to buy time. Further, that that is an issue better dealt with by the court when exercising its discretion under s 263(3).

[78] CPR 19.9A(7). Such an application may be made without notice (r 19.9A(8)).

[79] 681 HL Official Report (5th Series) cols 883 (9 May 2006). As to earlier concerns that the reform would burden companies with frivolous or unmeritorious claims, see 679 HL Official Report (5th series) col GC14 (27 February 2006); 681 HL Official Report (5th Series) cols 883–884 (9 May 2006). This power to dismiss the claim subsists alongside the ability of a defendant to apply to have the claim struck out under CPR 3.4. The principal difference is that an application to strike out requires a positive response from the company, whereas s 261(2) requires the court to dismiss the application without hearing from the company.

[80] [1982] Ch 204, CA. In that case, the Court of Appeal found (at 221) that the judge at first instance erred in failing to determine as a preliminary issue whether the plaintiffs were entitled to proceed by way of derivative action. Further (at 221–2), that the plaintiff ought to be required before proceeding with his action to to establish a 'prima facie case (i) that the company is entitled to the relief claimed, and (ii) that the action falls within the proper boundaries of the exception to the rule in *Foss v Harbottle*'. See also *Estmanco v Greater London Council* [1982] 1 WLR 2, 14H.

from consideration. If the application is dismissed, then the claimant has the right to apply for an oral hearing (CPR 19.9A(10)).[81]

Where a prima facie case is made out and the application is not dismissed under subs 261(2), the court gives directions for the hearing of the permission application. It will: (a) order that the company and any other appropriate party must be made respondents to the permission application; and (b) give directions for the service on the company and other appropriate party of the application notice and the claim form.[82] By subs 261(3) the court '(a) may give directions as to the evidence to be provided by the company, and (b) may adjourn the proceedings to enable the evidence to be obtained'. **21.41**

Subsection 261(4) deals with the second stage of the permission application at a hearing, which will determine whether the substantive action can be pursued. It provides: **21.42**

> On hearing the application, the court may—
> (a)  give permission to continue the claim on such terms as it thinks fit,[83]
> (b)  refuse permission . . . and dismiss the claim, or
> (c)  adjourn the proceedings on the application and give such directions as it thinks fit.

At this stage the court will have before it the evidence of the claimant member, the company, and that of the defendant directors. It thus affords the court a very wide discretion to manage the case in the manner it deems appropriate to the particular facts. As to the third of those routes, an adjournment would: (i) allow the company to seek authorization or ratification of the wrongdoing[84] (see below); or (ii) enable the parties to reach a settlement.[85]

*Permission to take over company's claim by members*

If the company has brought a claim against a director, there should be no reason for a member to have to resort to a derivative claim. However, sometimes it may be necessary; eg where the directors have caused the company to institute the **21.43**

---

[81]  The company and the claimant will be notified of the court's decision, but the court may make an order not to notify the company of a decision to dismiss on paper (rr 19.9A(9) and (10)). CPR 19.9A(8)–(11) addresses the situation where the court dismisses the permission application either without a hearing or at an oral hearing.

[82]  CPR 19.9A(12).

[83]  This will presumably include the power to make an order for costs under CPR 19.9E (see paragraph 21.49 below).

[84]  Cf the guidance given by the Court of Appeal in *Prudential Assurance Co Ltd v Newman Industries Ltd (No 2)* [1982] Ch 204, 222, CA, that in his assessment of whether the plaintiff is entitled to bring a derivative action, it may be right for the judge trying the preliminary issue to grant a sufficient adjournment to enable a meeting of shareholders to be convened by the board, so that he can reach a conclusion in the light of the conduct of, and proceedings at, that meeting.

[85]  See paragraph 21.52 below.

claim in order to frustrate the member and prevent a successful claim being brought,[86] or where a change of control in the company results in the board wanting to discontinue the claim. Section 262 deals with the circumstances in which a member may take over a claim initiated by the company. By s 262(1), it applies where: '(a) a company has brought a claim, and (b) the cause of action on which the claim is based could be pursued as a derivative claim under [Part 11]'.[87]

21.44    By s 262(2) a member may apply to court for permission to continue the claim as a derivative claim on the ground that:

    (a)  the manner in which the company commenced or continued the claim amounts to an abuse of the process of the court,

    (b)  the company has failed to prosecute the claim diligently, and

    (c)  it is appropriate for the member to continue the claim as a derivative claim.

21.45    Subsections 262(3) to (5) repeat the provisions of subss 261(2)–(4). Accordingly, the application to the court is treated in the same way as if the member was applying from the outset to bring a derivative claim under s 261. The same two-stage process applies. CPR 19.9B applies to permission applications under s 262(1) the provisions of CPR19.9A, except for paras (1), (2) and (4)(b), and para (12)(b) so far as it applies to the claim form and references in rule 19.9A are to be read as references to the person who seeks to take over the claim.

21.46    The effect is that even if the requirements of s 262(2) are met, the member may still be precluded from taking over the claim if it cannot satisfy the court that permission would have been granted if the claim had originally been brought as a derivative action. That interpretation is also borne out by the wording of s 262(1)(b): 'the cause of action on which the claim is based could be pursued as a derivative claim under this Chapter'.

*Permission to take over derivative claim brought by another member*

21.47    In a similar vein, s 264 deals with the circumstances in which a member may take over a claim already commenced by another member. By s 264(1) this will extend to the situation where 'a member of a company ("the claimant"): (a) has brought a derivative claim; (b) has continued as a derivative claim a claim brought by the company; or (c) has continued a derivative claim under this section'. The grounds upon which the member may seek to take over the claim and the attendant procedure are set out in ss 264(2) and (3), and are the same as those set out for the taking

---

[86]  See Law Com No 246 at para 6.63. The Law Commission considered that any such action on the part of the directors would amount to an abuse of the process of the court for the purposes of the new rule.

[87]  There is no equivalent provision for a company seeking to take over a claim commenced by a member, since the company always has this right: 679 HL Official Report (5th Series) col GC34 (27 February 2006).

over of an action commenced by the company under s 262. CPR 19.9B applies to permission applications under s 264(1) the provisions of CPR19.9A in the same way as it does to permission applications under s 262(1) (paragraph 21.45). The court's powers under subs 264(5) are the same as under subs 261(4).

There is one significant difference between ss 262 and 264. The court is not, when **21.48** proceeding under s 264, formally required to take the additional step of exercising its discretion under s 263. Section 263 does not refer to s 264, presumably because s 264 assumes that the original claimant has already obtained permission to continue under s 263. However, subs 264(1) applies where a member has *brought* a derivative claim and this may simply mean that the member has instituted the claim. It is therefore possible to invoke the s 264 procedure before the original claimant has obtained permission. This might be appropriate if a limitation issue was relevant.

*Costs*

CPR 19.9E anticipates the making of *Wallersteiner v Moir (No 2)*[88] indemnity **21.49** orders. It provides that the court may order the company for the benefit of which a derivative claim is brought to indemnify the claimant against liability for costs incurred in the permission application or in the derivative claim or both.

The indemnity for costs afforded by the decision in *Wallersteiner v Moir (No 2)*[89] **21.50** has in practice rarely been granted by the courts. The case is authority for the proposition that where a shareholder has in good faith sued as plaintiff in a minority shareholder's action, the benefit of which will inure to the company and only indirectly to the plaintiff in his capacity as member, and which action it would be reasonable for an independent board of directors to bring in the company name, then the court may order the company to pay the plaintiff's costs. The Court of Appeal in *Wallersteiner v Moir* held that the application should in the first instance be made *ex parte*, although other parties could still be joined. The decision has been the subject of both restrictive and wide interpretation.[90] It was later held that the derivative claimant had to demonstrate that an order for costs was genuinely needed.[91] Further, under the old law, where the judge considered that a claimant would have a right to an indemnity out of the assets recovered, it was more commonly refused.[92] In *Smith v Croft (No 1)*[93] it was held that an order should not

---

[88] [1975] QB 373, CA.
[89] Ibid.
[90] *Smith v Croft (No 1)* [1986] 1 WLR 580 adopted a narrow interpretation, whereas *Jaybird v Greenwood Ltd* [1986] BCLC 319 was more generous.
[91] *Smith v Croft (No 1)* [1986] 1 WLR 580, 597.
[92] *Mumbray v Lapper* [2005] BCC 990.
[93] *Smith v Croft (No 1)* [1986] 1 WLR 580, 588.

normally be made *ex parte*, and that as a rule the company should have revealed to it the relevant evidence, save to the extent that it consists of matters covered by legal professional privilege or there exists some other reason for its non-disclosure. In determining whether to make an order, the court must decide whether an independent board of directors—exercising the standard of care which prudent businessmen would exercise in their own affairs—would in the circumstances consider that it ought to bring the action.[94]

**21.51** As to the position of a defendant director, under the 2006 Act, s 205, companies may fund expenditure incurred by him in defending derivative proceedings. If, however, he is unsuccessful then those funds must be returned to the company.

### *Discontinuance and settlement*

**21.52** CPR 19.9F provides that where the court has given permission to continue a derivative claim, it may order that the claim may not be discontinued or settled without the permission of the court. Such a direction is appropriate where the company has other members, not party to the proceedings, whose interests may need to be considered before the derivative claim is discontinued or settled.

### *Remedies*

**21.53** Part 11 does not deal with remedies if the derivative claim is permitted to continue. Section 178 deals with remedies available to the company for breach of duty. These issues are discussed in Chapter 16. However, a member considering bringing a derivative claim may find the more direct remedies available under Part 30 more attractive, since they include an order that he be bought out at a fair price.

### (4) Permission

**21.54** Section 263 sets out the criteria to which the court should have regard in determining leave on a s 261 or s 262 application. Two types of criteria are stipulated: (i) those laid out in subs 263(2) which *require* the court to refuse leave to commence or continue the claim; and (ii) those set out in subs 263(3) which contain a list of factors the court must take into account if it does not refuse permission under subs 263(2). This prescription of the substantive criteria according to which a claim may be brought is an important innovation. By subss 263(5)–(7) the Secretary of State is given power to alter or add to the circumstances in subs 263(2) and the matters in subs 263(3).

---

[94] *Smith v Croft (No 1)* [1986] 1 WLR 580, 590F.

*Absolute bars to permission*

The factors in s 263(2) thus constitute an absolute bar to the court giving permis-    **21.55**
sion to continue the derivative claim. By subs 2, permission must be refused if the
court is satisfied:

(a) that a person acting in accordance with section 172 (duty to promote the success of
    the company) would not seek to continue the claim, or
(b) where the cause of action arises from an act or omission that is yet to occur, that the
    act or omission has been authorised by the company,[95] or
(c) where the cause of action arises from an act or omission that has already occurred,
    that the act or omission—
    (i)  was authorised by the company before it occurred, or
    (ii) has been ratified by the company since it occurred.

As such, there are effectively two grounds on which permission will be refused.    **21.56**
The first ground requires the court to apply the standard of the objective, reasonable director under s 172(1), which defines the director's core duty of loyalty.[96]
This standard emphasizes the fact that a derivative action will only be allowed to
continue if it is for the benefit of the company. In this way, the court itself is
required to decide whether the litigation is required to promote the success of the
company, by reference to the test of what a hypothetical director would decide in
the same circumstances. Further, the restatement in Part 11 of the duty in s 172(1)
emphasizes that the overriding obligation of directors is to promote the success of
the company for the benefit of its members as a whole.

How this test will operate in practice when subject to judicial interpretation, is far    **21.57**
from certain. Numerous scenarios can be anticipated in which the arguments are
evenly weighted. Some may not be suitable for summary determination, as envisaged by ss 261 and 262. The court will have to consider the prospects of success,
whether the cost of litigation or time involved would be disproportionate to the
relief recoverable, the impact on relationships within the company or even on the
company's share price, the risk of reputational damage if the claim is or is not
pursued and whether shareholders are exploiting the procedure as a platform to
pursue their own agenda. It is also likely to consider the views of other independent shareholders or directors.[97]

Since the second ground is simpler to apply, the court would only have to apply    **21.58**
the objective director test if the second ground was not established. The second
ground requires the court to see if the act or omission has been authorized

---

[95] ie whoever has the right to decide matters for the company, be they directors or members; see
679 HL Official Report (5th Series) col GC29 (27 February 2006).
[96] See Chapter 11 of this work. Proposals to draft this requirement in terms merely of a director
acting in good faith in what he considers to be in the interests of the company were rejected (679
HL Official Report (5th Series) col GC23–24 (27 February 2006)).
[97] Cf *Smith v Croft (No 2)* [1988] Ch 114.

or ratified. The provisions of ss 263(2)(b) and (c) reflect established principles, which the Law Commission recommended should not be changed.[98] The rule in *Foss v Harbottle* was premised on the ratifiability of the wrongful act or omission: ratifiability by simple majority remains fundamental. If the act has been duly authorized or ratified, it no longer constitutes a wrong on the part of the director. Either the director never was liable to the company or his liability is extinguished.[99] If the act or omission has not yet been authorized or ratified, but might be, the court will consider that as a discretionary factor under subs 263(3)(c) and (d) and may adjourn the permission application under subs 261(4)(c) or 262(5)(c).

21.59   Two points should be noted in relation to ratification and authorization. The first is that the act or omission must be one capable of being authorized or ratified by the members. Section 239(7) recognizes that some acts or omissions are incapable of being ratified, but, as discussed in Chapter 19, Section D, there are few acts or omissions affecting members' interests that are incapable of being ratified. Acts which are beyond the power of the company cannot be ratified. Since most companies have unrestricted objects, the acts which are incapable of ratification are likely to be limited to acts which breach the Companies Act (eg unlawful distributions or financial assistance). The other acts which are incapable of ratification concern transactions which prejudice creditors. But if the company is insolvent or on the verge of insolvency a member would have difficulty in showing a tangible interest in pursuing the derivative claim and it might be struck out on that ground.[100]

21.60   The second point to note is a difference between authorization and ratification. Section 180(4)(a) preserves the rule of law under which the company may give authority, specifically or generally, for anything to be done or omitted by the directors or any of them, that would otherwise be a breach of duty. If there is such authorization there could be no breach of duty and a derivative claim alleging breach of duty could not succeed. In relation to authorization, there is no restriction on the voting rights of any member. Where the act or omission has occurred without prior authorization, so that the directors require the protection of ratification, ss 239(3) and (4) prevent the director and members connected with him from voting.[101] If a member is prevented from bringing a derivative claim by

---

[98]   See Law Com No 246 at 6.85–6.86.

[99]   See s 175 on authorization of conflicts of interest (Chapter 14), s 180(4) on authorization generally (Chapter 9, Section D), and s 239 on ratification of acts of directors (Chapter 19, Section D).

[100]   Cf *Re Rica Goldwashing Co* (1879) 11 Ch D 36, 42, 43 CA; *Cavendish-Bentinck v Fenn* (1887) 12 App Cas 652, HL; *Deloitte & Touche v Johnson* [1999] 1 WLR 1605, PC.

[101]   This changes the law as stated in cases such as *MacDougall v Gardiner* (1875) 1 Ch D 13, 25, CA; *North West Transport Co Ltd v Beatty* (1887) 12 AC 589, PC; *Burland v Earle* [1902] AC 83, 93–4, PC.

reason of prior authorization, he may be able to obtain relief by application under Part 30.[102]

*Discretionary factors*

**21.61** Even where the claim is not prohibited by s 263(2), a discretion still resides in the court to refuse permission under s 263(3). A non-exhaustive list of factors is set out in that subsection. By s 263(3), in considering *whether to* give permission the court must take into account, *'in particular'*—

  (a)  whether the member is acting in good faith in seeking to continue the claim;

  (b)  the importance that a person acting in accordance with section 172 (duty to promote the success of the company) would attach to continuing it;

  (c)  where the cause of action results from an act or omission that is yet to occur, whether the act or omission could be, and in the circumstances would be likely to be—

    (i)  authorised by the company before it occurs, or

    (ii)  ratified by the company after it occurs;

  (d)  where the cause of action arises from an act or omission that has already occurred, whether the act or omission could, and in the circumstances would be likely to be, ratified by the company;

  (e)  whether the company has decided not to pursue the claim;

  (f)  whether the act or omission in respect of which the claim is brought gives rise to a cause of action that the member could pursue in his own right rather than on behalf of the company.

**21.62** The factors identified in subs 263(3) can be considered under three heads: (i) the personal position of the member wishing to pursue the claim, (ii) the views of a hypothetical director acting in accordance with his duty under s 172, and (iii) the views of members.

**21.63** Subsection 263(4) emphasizes the relevance of the views of independent members when deciding whether to grant leave. It provides:

> In considering whether to give permission . . . the court shall have particular regard to any evidence before it as to the views of members of the company who have no personal interest, direct or indirect, in the matter.[103]

As such, it builds upon the decision of Knox J in *Smith v Croft (No 2)*,[104] who said that if the bringing of proceedings is prevented by an expression of the corporate

---

[102] The aggrieved member could also consider applying to restrain an act which is beyond the powers of the directors: 1985 Act, 35A(4) (to be replaced by 2006 Act, s 40(4)).

[103] As with certain other requirements in Part 11, this provision was added to the Bill during its passage through the House of Lords with a view to deterring vexatious claims. See 681 HL Official Report (5th series) cols 883–884 (9 May 2006).

[104] [1988] Ch 114, 183. Knox J also said (at 166) that: '[t]he usual reason in practice for wanting to abandon such an action is that there is far more to lose financially by prosecuting the right to redress than by abandoning or not pursuing it, and that view will be reinforced in the minds of those who wish to abandon the claim if their opinion is that it is a bad claim anyway'. Knox J also held (at 186) that votes should be disregarded only if the court is satisfied either that the vote or

will of the company by an appropriate independent organ, then the plaintiff is not improperly but properly prevented. He did not consider that a just result will be achieved by a single minority shareholder having the right to involve a company in a derivative action if all the other minority shareholders are, for disinterested reasons, satisfied that the proceedings will be productive of more harm than good. The court thus looked to an independent 'majority within the minority' to reach its conclusion on grounds generally thought to advance the company's interests. It will remain the case that the views of independent members will carry great weight with the court. There are some problems. First, if the claimant is genuinely pursuing a claim for the benefit of members as a whole, should his views be included among those of independent members? Secondly, it may not be practical to obtain the views of members of a large quoted company on directors' commercial decisions.[105] Thirdly, there may be issues as to whether particular shareholders are 'persons who have no personal interest, direct or indirect, in the matter'. Finally, the court considers views, including the reasons for the views, and does not merely count heads.[106]

**21.64**  (i)  **The personal position of the member.**    The personal position of the member who wishes to pursue the claim is identified as a factor in subss 263(3)(a) and (f). The good faith requirement is designed to prevent frivolous, vexatious, or abusive claims from being brought. In most cases the court will be satisfied as to the claimant's good faith where the claim appears to have merit. The problem arises where it is alleged that the claim is being advanced to pursue personal interests of the member as distinct from the company. It is suggested that provided that a successful outcome would bring benefits to the company, the claim should not be excluded on good faith grounds. The Law Commission did not intend that an interest in the commercial benefits of litigation should rule out a claim if the court otherwise considers that it is in the company's interests.[107]

**21.65**  Under the old law the member had to satisfy the court that he was acting in good faith, pursuing the interests of the company and not some personal agenda,[108] and the defendant could raise against the claimant any defence which could have been

---

its equivalent is actually cast with a view to supporting the defendants rather than securing benefit to the company, or that the situation of the person whose vote is considered is such that there is a substantial risk of that happening. Further, that the court should not substitute its own opinion but should assess whether the decision-making process is vitiated by being or being likely to be directed to an improper purpose.

[105]  681 HL Official Report (5th series) col 884 (9 May 2006).
[106]  Compare cases on the Insolvency Act, s 190 and its predecessors, such as *Re JD Swain Ltd* [1965] 1 WLR 909, CA.
[107]  See Law Com No 246 at para 6.76.
[108]  *Barrett v Duckett* [1995] 1 BCLC 243, 250, CA.

raised had the action been one brought by the shareholder personally.[109] Accordingly, under the new law, the court may refuse to allow a claim to proceed where the behaviour of the minority shareholder would render it inequitable for the claim to succeed (ie he has not come to court with 'clean hands').

**21.66**   Subs 263(3)(f) enables the court to stop a derivative claim where the member has a personal claim that could be pursued without involving the company.[110] In particular this factor brings into question the interplay between s 994 of the Act and Part 11.[111]

**21.67**   **(ii) The views of a director complying with his duty under s 172.** Subsection 263(3)(b) requires the court to take into account the importance that a person (a director) acting in accordance with s 172 (duty to promote the success of the company) would attach to continuing the claim. This factor is to be considered on the footing that the court has not been satisfied under subs 263(2)(a), negatively, that such a person would not seek to continue the claim.[112] Subsection 263(3)(b)

---

[109] *Nurcombe v Nurcombe* [1984] BCLC 557, CA.

[110] The existence of an alternative remedy did not prevent the commencement of a derivative claim under the previous law: *Konamaneni v Rolls-Royce* [2002] 1 WLR 1269, 1279B, per Lawrence Collins J, although he declined to express a final view on the matter. In *Jafari-Fini v Skillglass* [2005] BCC 842, however, the court refused permission to proceed with the derivative claim where a personal claim could be brought by the claimant to determine the same issue. Similarly in *Mumbray v Lapper* [2005] BCC 990, the court refused permission to proceed with the derivative claim under CPR 19.9, as more appropriate remedies were available (specifically, winding up on the just and equitable basis). The Law Commission recommended that the court should take into account the availability of alternative remedies, but that their availability should not necessarily be conclusive on the issue of leave: see Law Com No 246 at 6.91. The Government resisted an amendment which would have required the court to address the question whether an alternative remedy exists. This was on the basis that: (i) an offer to buy the claimant's shares is not an appropriate remedy in the circumstances of a derivative claim; and (ii) such a provision could encourage vulture funds to tell companies that they must either buy them out or face a possible derivative claim. See further 682 HL Official Report (5th series) cols 726–728 (23 May 2006).

[111] *Airey v Cordell* [2006] EWHC 2728 (Ch). The unfair prejudice remedy formerly available under 1985 Act, s 459 and now under Part 30 has proved attractive and, as a result, it has seldom been desirable or necessary to use the derivative claim procedure.

[112] For example in *Mission Capital Plc v Sinclair* [2008] BCC 866, a case decided under the 2006 Act, Floyd J (at [43] in considering the discretionary factors under subs 263(3)) said that although he could not be satisfied that the notional s 172 director would not continue the claim, he did not (on the particular facts) believe that he would attach that much importance to it. This was largely attributed to the facts that the company would be more likely to replace the directors rather than take action against those responsible for the damage it has suffered, and that the damage the company was to suffer was speculative. A similar approach was adopted in *Franbar Holdings Ltd v Patel* BCC 885. In that case, Mr William Trower QC, sitting as a Deputy Judge of the High Court, in reaching a determination under subs 263(2)(a), summarized (at 30) the different stances which could be adopted by the hypothetical director. He observed that: '[d]irectors are often in the position of having to make what is no more than a partially informed decision on whether or not the institution of legal proceedings is appropriate, without having a very clear idea of how the proceedings will turn out. Some directors might wish to spend more time investigating and strengthening the company's case before issuing process, while others would wish to press on with proceedings straight away; in a case such as this one, both approaches would be entirely appropriate'. Mr. William Trower QC went

therefore enables the court to give some weight, when exercising its discretion under the section, to the broader commercial considerations for and against continuing the claim.[113]

**21.68**   The views of directors are also to be considered under subs 263(3)(e), because they may have decided that the company should not pursue the claim.[114] In considering that decision the court would have regard to the independence, or otherwise, of the directors who took the decision and the reasons why they took it.[115] If the decision had been taken some time previously and had not been challenged, that might be a factor against permitting the claim to continue.

**21.69**   **(iii) Views of other members.**   Where there has not been authorization or ratification so as to constitute an absolute bar to continuance of the claim under subs 263(2)(b) or (c), the court takes account of the views of other members in three ways. First, it does so by considering the evidence before it as to the views of independent members under subs 263(4) as to whether the claim should continue, as discussed in paragraph 21.63 above.

**21.70**   Secondly, it considers under subs 263(3)(c) and (d) how, on the evidence before it, the members would be likely to vote, if asked to authorize or ratify the act

---

on (at 36), in his approach to subs 263(3)(b), to refer to certain of the considerations the hypothetical director would take into account when assessing the importance of continuing the claim: 'These would include such matters as the prospects of success of the claim, the ability of the company to make a recovery on any award of damages, the disruption which would be caused to the development of the company's business by having to concentrate on the proceedings, the costs of the proceedings and any damage to the company's reputation and business if the proceedings were to fail. A director will often be in the position of having to make what is no more than a partially informed decision on continuation without any very clear idea of how the proceedings might turn out.' In that case, it was further considered (at 37) that the hypothetical director would be less likely to attribute importance to continuation of the derivative claim where: (i) the complaints were not yet in a form in which the hypothetical director might be expected to conclude that there were obvious breaches of duty which ought to be pursued; (ii) several of the complaints could more naturally be formulated as breaches of a shareholders' agreement that was in existence between the parties and acts of unfair prejudice which were already the subject matter of proceedings commenced by the minority shareholder; and (iii) all parties sought and had offered a buy-out of the minority by the majority and the principal issue was one of valuation. Also see *Fanmailuk.com Ltd v Cooper* [2008] BCC 877.

[113] Interestingly in *Developing the Framework*, the CLR suggested that the best test of whether the action should proceed was whether the minority's views were the best available evidence of what was in the best interests of the company. Reactions to that proposal were mixed. Thus the CLR went on to suggest conferring on the court a discretion to consider all the circumstances in determining whether a derivative action should proceed, and in so doing pay particular regard to the issue of whether it was in the best interests of the company in accordance with the criterion set out in the principles on directors' duties (CLR: *Final Report* at para 7.48). In practice, the considerations under ss 263(3)(b) and 263(4) may well be the same, cf the statement of Lord Goldsmith: 'What is success? The starting point is that it is essentially for the members of the company to define the objective they wish to achieve. Success means what the members collectively want the company to achieve' (678 HL Official Report (5th series) col GC255 (6 February 2006)).

[114] 679 HL Official Report (5th series) col GC29 (27 February 2006).

[115] Law Com No 246 at para 6.87.

or omission. As to that, the court may prefer to adjourn the permission application to enable the matter to be put to the vote of the members. Even if satisfied that the members would authorize or ratify the act or omission, the court retains a discretion to permit the claim to continue. It might take the view that pursuit of the claim plainly furthered the interests of the company and that the majority of members would be acting irrationally in voting against it. Also the court might take the view that a majority against continuing the claim would be made up of persons favouring the defendant director and hostile to the claimant, even though not sufficiently connected to the director to have their votes excluded under s 239(3) and (4) (eg the director's brothers and sisters).

Thirdly, under subs 263(3)(e) it will take account of a decision by the members of **21.71** the company that the company should not pursue the claim. More weight would be given to such a decision than to a decision by the directors, at least where the decision was supported by independent members. It should be noted that such a decision is different from a decision to authorize or ratify the act or omission. The decision not to pursue the claim does not affect the liability of the director to the company until the claim becomes barred by limitation.

**(iv) Other matters.** One factor not mentioned in s 263 is that the company is **21.72** in or is about to enter liquidation or administration. A member may wish to pursue a derivative claim in these circumstances in the hope that the relief obtained may restore the company to solvency or enable the company to be rescued as a going concern. Under the previous regime a claim did not lie once the company was in liquidation.[116] It was the impossibility of relief being obtained for the company in any other manner which had originally persuaded the courts to allow derivative claims to be brought. It follows that once the right to bring a claim in the name of the company has passed to an administrator or liquidator, then the premise on which such a claim was allowed disappears.[117] There is no reason to think that the court would allow a claim to continue if the company was in administration or liquidation (solvent or insolvent) or about to enter into one of those proceedings.[118] If the company is insolvent but not in liquidation or administration, the court might permit a shareholder to bring a derivative claim in order to

---

[116] *Ferguson v Wallbridge* [1935] 3 DLR 66, PC; *Fargo Ltd v Godfroy* [1986] 3 All ER 279; *Barrett v Duckett* [1995] 1 BCLC 243, 250–2, CA.

[117] Insolvency Act, Schedule B1, para 60 and Schedule 1, para 5 gives the administrator power to bring proceedings in the name of the company. A liquidator has the same power under the Insolvency Act, s 165 and Schedule 4, para 4, subject to directions of the court under ss 112 or 167(3) giving conduct to a creditor or member.

[118] See 'Can derivative proceedings be commenced when a company is in liquidation?' ((2008) 21 *Insolvency Intelligence* 49), in which Andrew Keay concludes that the arguments for allowing permission to be given to members in these circumstances are evenly balanced.

obtain the benefit of recovering a debt, provided the debt was closely connected to the shareholding.[119]

# D. Shareholder's Action to Enforce Directors' Liabilities for Unauthorized Political Donations or Expenditure

## (1) The requirement for authorization by resolution of the members

**21.73**  The 2006 Act, Part 14, preserves the current law on the liability of directors to compensate the company for unauthorized political donations. As originally enacted the rationale of these provisions was to regulate conflicts of interest. The Government did not consider it acceptable for directors to support political parties that promote policies with which they personally agree, rather than policies that will benefit the company.[120] In October 1998 the Neill Committee (Committee on Standards in Public Life) recommended that a company intending to make a donation (whether in cash or in kind, and including any sponsorship, or loans or transactions at a favourable rate) to a political party or organization should be required to have the prior authority of its shareholders.[121] The Government accepted that recommendation. It was implemented principally through the Political Parties, Elections and Referendums Act 2000 (the 'PPER Act'), by inserting a new regime for the control of political donations and expenditure as Part XA of the 1985 Act.

**21.74**  Part 14 largely restates the provisions of the 1985 Act, Part XA, in a manner consistent with other sections of the Companies Act. Of greatest import for directors are the provisions of s 369, which make directors personally liable for unauthorized political donations and expenditure, and ss 370–373, which enable a shareholder to bring proceedings to enforce that liability. Part 14 makes two changes to provide greater flexibility from the perspective of the company.[122] A holding company may seek authorization in respect of both itself and one or more subsidiaries through a single approval resolution. Also, the provision preventing subsequent ratification from nullifying a contravention of the 1985 Act, Part XA has been repealed.[123]

---

119  *Gamlestaden Fastigheter AB v Baltic Partners Ltd* [2007] 4 All ER 164, PC.
120  See 678 HL Official Report col GC139–140 (1 March 2006).
121  Ibid. See also the Explanatory Notes at para 611.
122  See 678 HL Official Report col GC139–140 (1 March 2006).
123  1985 Act, s 347C(5).

Part 14 governs: (a) political donations made by companies to political parties,[124] **21.75**
to other political organizations,[125] and to independent election candidates;[126] and
(b) political expenditure incurred by companies (s 362). In relation to a political
party or other political organization, a 'political donation' is defined by reference
to the PPER Act, ss 50–52 as anything that in accordance with those sections
constitutes a donation for the purposes of Chapter 1 of Part 4 of the PPER Act
(control of donations to registered parties) or would constitute such a donation
reading references in those sections to a registered party as references to any political party or other political organization.[127] A similar definition applies to a political donation to an independent election candidate.[128]

In relation to a company, 'political expenditure' means expenditure, not being **21.76**
a political donation incurred by the company on:[129]

   (a)  the preparation, publication or dissemination of advertising or other promotional
      or publicity material—
      (i)  of whatever nature, and
      (ii)  however published or otherwise disseminated,
      that, at the time of publication or dissemination, is capable of being reasonably
      regarded as intended to affect public support for a political party or other political
      organisation, or an independent election candidate; or
   (b)  activities on the part of the company that are capable of being reasonably regarded
      as intended—
      (i)  to affect public support for a political party or other political organisation, or
      an independent election candidate, or
      (ii)  to influence voters in relation to any national or regional referendum held
      under the law of a member State.

A loan at a commercial rate will not fall within the ambit of Part 14.[130] Also, it **21.77**
seems that payment to a political party for the promotion or advertisement of that

---

[124] By s 363(1) a party is a 'political party' if: (a) it is registered under the PPER Act, Part 2; or
(b) it carries on, or proposes to carry on, activities for the purposes of or in connection with the
participation of the party in any election or elections to public office held in a member state other
than the United Kingdom.

[125] By s 363(2) an organization is a 'political organisation' if it carries on, or proposes to carry on,
activities that are capable of being reasonably regarded as intended: (a) to affect public support for
a political party to which, or an independent election candidate to whom, Part 14 applies; or (b) to
influence voters in relation to any national or regional referendum held under the law of the United
Kingdom or another member state.

[126] By s 363(3) Part 14 applies to an 'independent election candidate' at any election to public
office held in the United Kingdom or another member state.

[127] s 364(2)(a). By s 364(2)(b) the PPER Act, s 53 applies, in the same way, for the purpose of
determining the value of a donation.

[128] s 364(3). This is a new provision.

[129] s 365.

[130] This is because s 364(4) provides that the PPER Act, ss 50 and 53 (definition of 'donation'
and value of donations) shall be treated as if the amendments to those sections made by the Electoral
Administration Act 2006 had not been made. Lord McKenzie explained that the amendment

company's product or services, would not be construed as a political donation if it is genuinely commensurate with the value of the service provided by the political party.[131]

**21.78**   By reason of s 366(1) a company must not: (a) make a political donation to a political party or other political organization, or to an independent election candidate; or (b) incur any political expenditure, unless the donation or expenditure is authorized in accordance with ss 366(2) to (5). Subsection 366(2)(a) institutes the general rule that the donation or expenditure must be authorized, in the case of a company that is not a subsidiary of another company, by a resolution of the members of the company. It must be passed before the donation is made or the expenditure incurred (s 366(5)(b)).[132] Where the donation or expenditure is to be made or incurred by a subsidiary company it must be authorized by (i) a resolution of the members of the company and (ii) a resolution of the members of any relevant holding company.[133] However, no resolution is required on the part of a company that is a wholly-owned subsidiary of a UK-registered company.[134] In spite of these provisions it seems that a breach of the rules may be ratified in accordance with the 2006 Act, s 239 and a director may apply for relief under s 1157 (power of court to grant relief in certain cases).[135]

**21.79**   Section 367 deals with the form of authorizing resolutions. There are four matters to be addressed in the resolution.

---

ensures that the scope of s 364 is not altered by the changes to the PPER Act made by the Electoral Administration Act: 'In other words, [Pt 14] of this Bill will continue to apply only to political donations, which are defined as including loans at a non-commercial rate' (HL Report Stages col 912 (10 May 2006)).

[131]   Lord McKenzie said that the PPER Act, Part IV already recognizes that companies may interact with political parties on commercial terms, and that s 50(2) of that Act states that 'donation' means 'any gift to the party of money or other property' (678 HL Official Report cols GC145–146 (1 March 2006)).

[132]   s 366(5)(b). During the Company Law Reform Bill's passage through Parliament, there was a debate as to why a director cannot make a political donation or incur political expenditure without a resolution if he considers it would promote the success of the company, or why board authorization is not sufficient. The Government responded by emphasizing the nuisance that Part 14 is trying to avoid, namely the need to regulate donations that might be seen to reflect the director's personal viewpoint rather than the interests of the company (678 HL Official Report col 149 (1 March 2006)).

[133]   s 366(2)(b). A 'relevant holding company' is a company that, at the time the donation was made or the expenditure was incurred: (a) was a holding company of the company by which the donation was made or the expenditure was incurred; (b) was a UK-registered company; and (c) was not a subsidiary of another UK-registered company (s 366(4)).

[134]   s 366(3).

[135]   Lord McKenzie stated: 'It is our intention—and we believe the effect of these clauses—that members will be able to ratify an unauthorised donation or political expenditure and that, in such cases, the director will not continue to have any liability for the failure to obtain authorisation. Similarly [Part 14] will not prevent a director applying for relief under section 1157 (678 HL Official Report col 149 (1 March 2006)).

(1) It should identify the company or companies to which it relates.[136] A holding company may seek authorization of political donations and expenditure in respect both of itself and one or more of its subsidiaries, including non-wholly-owned subsidiaries, in a single approval resolution. Subsection 367(2) provides that a resolution may be expressed to relate to all companies that are subsidiaries of the company passing the resolution without identifying them individually.[137]

(2) The resolution may authorize the following heads of donations or expenditure: '(a) donations to political parties or independent election candidates; (b) donations to political organisations other than political parties; (c) political expenditure'.[138] The resolution is to be expressed in general terms and must not purport to authorize particular donations or expenditure.[139]

(3) The donations or expenditure must be authorized up to a specified amount.[140] A holding company is permitted to state one aggregate amount to cover the total amounts paid or incurred by all the companies for, on the one hand, political donations and, on the other, political expenditure.[141]

(4) The period of authorization must be specified. That is a period of four years beginning with the date on which it is passed unless the directors determine, or the articles require, that it is to have effect for a shorter period beginning with that date.[142]

Sections 374–378 set out various exemptions to the requirement for shareholder authorization of political donations and expenditure. In broad terms, those exceptions relate to trade unions, membership of trade associations, all-party parliamentary groups, political expenditure exempted by order of the Secretary of State, and donations amounting to not more than £5,000 in any twelve-month period.  **21.80**

### (2) Enforcement of directors' liability

Section 369 provides that where a company has made a political donation or incurred political expenditure without the authorization required by Part 14[143]  **21.81**

---

[136] 2006 Act, subs 367(1), (2), (4), and (5).
[137] Further, the resolution may relate to companies that are subsidiaries of the company passing the resolution (a) at the time the resolution is passed, or (b) at any time during the period for which the resolution has effect.
[138] subss 367(3), (4).
[139] subs 367(5).
[140] subs 367(6)(7).
[141] subs 367(6)(7). Subsection 3 details the three different heads under which donations or expenditure may be authorized.
[142] subss 367(6) and s 368.
[143] subs 369(6) provides that where only part of a donation or expenditure was unauthorized, s 369 applies only to so much of it as was unauthorized.

the directors[144] in default are jointly and severally liable: '(a) to make good to the company the amount of the unauthorised donation or expenditure, with interest,[145] and (b) to compensate the company for any loss or damage sustained by it as a result of the unauthorised donation or expenditure having been made'.

**21.82** The directors in default are:

(a) those who, at the time the unauthorised donation was made or the unauthorised expenditure was incurred, were directors of the company by which the donation was made or the expenditure was incurred, and

(b) where—

(i) that company was a subsidiary of a relevant holding company, and

(ii) the directors of the relevant holding company failed to take all reasonable steps to prevent the donation being made or the expenditure incurred, the directors of the relevant holding company.[146]

**21.83** Section 370 gives the right to enforce a director's liability for contravention of Part 14 to an authorized group of members[147] of the company or holding company subject to the controls in s 371. This right is necessary, because the directors responsible for the unauthorized donation or expenditure control the relevant board. It is however additional to the company's own right to enforce the liability[148] and to any member's right to bring or continue a derivative claim under Part 11.[149] Subsection 370(1) provides:

Any liability of a director under section 369 is enforceable—

(a) in the case of a liability of a director of a company to that company, by proceedings brought under [s 370] in the name of the company by an authorised group of its members;

(b) in the case a liability of a director of a holding company to a subsidiary, by proceedings brought under [s 370] in the name of the subsidiary by—

(i) an authorised group of members of the subsidiary, or

(ii) an authorised group of members of the holding company.

---

[144] By s 379(1), this includes a shadow director.

[145] That means interest on the amount of the unauthorized donation or expenditure so far as not made good to the company (a) in respect of the period beginning with the date when the donation was made or the expenditure was incurred, and (b) at such rate as the Secretary of State may prescribe by regulations (s 369(5)).

[146] subs 369(4) defines 'relevant holding company' in terms that are consistent with earlier sections: 'a company that, at the time the donation was made or the expenditure was incurred— (a) was a holding company of the company by which the donation was made or the expenditure was incurred, (b) was a UK-registered company, and (c) was not a subsidiary of another UK-registered company'.

[147] By subs 370(3) an 'authorised group' of members of a company means—'(a) the holders of not less than 5% in nominal value of the company's issued share capital, (b) if the company is not limited by shares, not less than 5% of its members, or (c) no less than 50 of the company's members'.

[148] subs 370(2).

[149] subs 370(5).

By s 371 the court[150] is afforded a supervisory role. Section 371(1) lays down cer-  **21.84**
tain procedural formalities to be observed in relation to the giving of notice to the
company. Subsection 371(2) allows any director to apply to the court within
28 days of the giving of the notice for an order directing that the proposed proceedings shall not be brought on one or more of the following grounds:

(a) that the unauthorised amount has been made good to the company;
(b) that proceedings to enforce the liability have been brought, and are being pursued
with due diligence, by the company;
(c) that the members proposing to bring proceedings do not constitute an authorised
group.

In relation to subs 371(2)(b), subs 371(3) permits the court as an alternative to
direct: (a) that such proceedings may be brought on such terms and conditions as
the court thinks fit; and (b) that the proceedings brought by the company (i) shall
be discontinued or (ii) may be continued on such terms and conditions as the
court thinks fit.

For the purpose of enforcing the director's liability the authorized group may  **21.85**
apply to the court for an order directing the company to indemnify them in respect
of their costs.[151] The group is not entitled to be paid any such costs out of the assets
of the company except by virtue of such a court order.[152] If no such order is made,
the group is entitled to be paid any costs of the proceedings awarded or agreed to
be paid to the company and the group is liable to pay any costs awarded or agreed
to be paid to a defendant.[153]

The authorized group of members is bound to need information from the com-  **21.86**
pany in order to pursue the claim. Section 373 obliges the company to provide the
group 'with all information relating to the subject matter of the proceedings that
is in the company's possession or under its control or which is reasonably obtain-
able by it'.[154]

# E.  Unfair Prejudice Petition

## (1)  Introduction

The 2006 Act, Part 30, ss 994–999 contains the provisions protecting members  **21.87**
from unfair prejudice arising from the conduct of the affairs of the company.

---

[150] The court is defined by s 1156 as the High Court and also a county court in England and
Wales, subject to the power of the Lord Chancellor to redefine the jurisdictions of the county courts
for the purposes of the Companies Acts.
[151] subss 372(1) and (2).
[152] subs 372(3).
[153] subs 372(4).
[154] subs 373.

These provisions came into force on 1 October 2007 and replaced provisions in the 1985 Act, ss 459–461 without change, except for the introduction of the 2006 Act, s 999, which contains new supplementary provisions where the company's constitution is altered.

**21.88**   Part 30 derives from the 1948 Act, s 210, which was brought into force on the recommendation of the Cohen Committee[155] to provide minority shareholders who were being oppressed with an alternative remedy to winding up. Where the conditions of the section were satisfied the court had power to make such order as it thought just, including an order that the minority be bought out at a fair price. Under s 210 the applicant had to show that 'the affairs of the company are being conducted in a manner oppressive to some part of the members (including himself)' and that a winding-up order would not do justice to the minority. The court interpreted the reference to oppression as requiring the applicant to satisfy it that the majority were exercising their powers in a manner that was 'burdensome, harsh and wrongful'.[156] As a result there were only two reported successful applications under s 210.[157] The Jenkins Committee doubted whether this restrictive interpretation had been intended, preferring the meaning of oppression given by Lord Cooper in *Elder v Elder & Watson Ltd*:[158]

> the essence of the matter seems to be that the conduct complained of should at the lowest involve a visible departure from the standards of fair dealing, and a violation of the conditions of fair play on which every shareholder who entrusts his money to a company is entitled to rely.

The Jenkins Committee recommended that s 210 be replaced by a section based on unfair prejudice and which did not require the applicant to show that winding up would not be a just remedy.[159]

**21.89**   After some delay the 1980 Act, s 75 was enacted to replace s 210 in the terms recommended by the Jenkins Committee. The provisions of s 75 were re-enacted as the 1985 Act, ss 459–461. These sections have been widely used. The availability of a statutory remedy for unfair prejudice is significant for directors, because their conduct of the affairs of the company or acts or omissions may justify a member's application for relief. Where the petition is well founded the court has wide powers to give relief in ways which may affect the directors. As described below, the court may, and frequently does, order the respondents (who are usually

---

[155] Report of the Cohen Committee at paras 60, 152, and 153.
[156] *Scottish Co-operative Wholesale Society Ltd v Meyer* [1959] AC 324, 342, HL (Sc), per Lord Simonds.
[157] The *Scottish Co-operative* case and *Re HR Harmer Ltd* [1959] 1 WLR 62, CA. Also see *Re Belador Silk Ltd* [1965] 1 WLR 1051.
[158] [1952] SC 49, referred to by Hoffmann LJ in *Re Saul D Harrison & Sons Plc* [1995] 1 BCLC 14, 18, CA.
[159] Report of the Jenkins Committee at paras 199–212.

directors and shareholders) to buy the petitioner's shares at a fair price. The court can also sanction a derivative action and may even short-circuit the process by ordering compensation to be paid or property restored to the company.

## (2)  The statutory provisions

### *Petition by company member*

Section 994(1) provides:

**21.90**

> A member of a company may apply to the court[160] by petition for an order under this Part on the ground—
>
> (a)  that the company's affairs are being or have been conducted in a manner that is unfairly prejudicial to the interests of members generally or some part of its members (including at least himself),[161] or
>
> (b)  that an actual or proposed act or omission of the company (including an act or omission on its behalf) is or would be so prejudicial.

The normal meaning of 'member of a company' applies,[162] but subs 994(2) **21.91** extends the provisions of Part 30 to 'a person who is not a member of a company but to whom shares have been transferred or transmitted by operation of law' in the same way as they apply to a member of a company. This enables a trustee in bankruptcy or executor to petition.[163] In the past the court has struck out petitions presented by a person who had agreed to take a transfer of shares, but had not obtained registration.[164] In *Alipour v Ali*[165] the Court of Appeal took a more flexible approach to disputes as to standing in a member's winding-up petition, saying that such issues could be determined in the petition if in all the circumstances it was convenient to do and not harmful to the company. The same approach may be applied to Part 30 petitions. In the recent case of *Re Starlight*

---

[160]   The court is defined by s 1156 as the High Court and also a county court in England and Wales, subject to the power of the Lord Chancellor to redefine the jurisdictions of the county courts for the purposes of the Companies Acts.

[161]   With effect from 4 February 1991 the 1989 Act, s 145 and Schedule 19, para 11 substituted the phrase 'unfairly prejudicial to the interests of members generally or some part of its members' for the phrase in 1985 Act, s 459 'unfairly prejudicial to the interests of some part of the members' in order to make it clear that the section was engaged where all members were harmed, so avoiding the outcome of *Re a Company (No 00370 of 1987), ex p Glossop* [1988] 1 WLR 1068. In fact *ex p Glossop* was not followed on this point by Peter Gibson J in *Re Sam Weller & Sons Ltd* [1990] Ch 682.

[162]   By 1985 Act, s 22 the members of a company are the subscribers of its memorandum and every other person who agrees to become a member of the company and whose name is entered in its register of members. On 1 October 2009, 2006 Act, s 112 replaces s 22 with minor changes. See *Re Nuneaton Borough Association Football Club Ltd* [1989] BCLC 454, CA; *Jaber v Science and Information Technology Ltd* [1992] BCLC 764.

[163]   *Murray's Judicial Factor* [1992] BCC 596.

[164]   *Re Garage Door Associates Ltd* [1984] 1 WLR 35 (a winding-up case); *Re a Company (No 007828 of 1985)* (1986) 2 BCC 98,951; *Re a Company (No 003160 of 1986)* [1986] BCLC 391; *Re Quickdome Ltd* [1988] BCLC 370.

[165]   [1997] 1 BCLC 557, 568, CA.

*Developers Ltd*[166] Briggs J exercised case management powers to stay, rather than strike out, an unfair prejudice petition brought by a transferee of shares who was not registered, because he was satisfied that the petitioner had a reasonable case for obtaining rectification of the register. On the other hand a registered member who has agreed to transfer his shares still has standing to petition,[167] but his interest may be limited to receiving the agreed purchase price.[168]

**21.92** It has been held that a member is not debarred from presenting an unfair prejudice petition because he has agreed that disputes with the respondent members should be referred to arbitration.[169]

**21.93** Subsection 994(3) explains that in s 994 and other provisions of Part 30 applicable to that section 'company' means a company within the meaning of the 2006 Act and a statutory water company. As with the statutory provisions for derivative claims, s 994 therefore does not apply to foreign companies.[170]

**21.94** The grounds to support an unfair prejudice petition are discussed in Sections (3)–(5) below.

### Petition by Secretary of State

**21.95** The 2006 Act, s 995(2) gives the Secretary of State power to present a petition for an order under Part 30 on the same grounds of unfair prejudice to members as are set out in s 994(1), where (a) the Secretary of State has received an inspector's report under the 1985 Act, s 437, (b) the Secretary of State has exercised his powers to require documents or information or to enter and search premises under the 1985 Act, ss 447 or 448, (c) the Secretary of State or the FSA has exercised his or its powers under FSMA, Part 11 (information gathering and investigations), or (d) the Secretary of State has received a report from an investigator appointed by him or the FSA under FSMA, Part 11.[171] The Secretary of State may present such a petition in addition to, or instead of, presenting a petition for the winding up of the company.[172] In s 995 'company' means any body corporate that is liable to be wound up under the Insolvency Act.[173] Unlike s 994, the scope of s 995 therefore

---

[166] [2007] BCC 929.

[167] *Atlasview Ltd v Brightview Ltd* [2004] 2 BCLC 191 (where it was considered arguable that the interests of the nominee shareholder included the interests of the beneficial owner); *Re McCarthy Surfacing Ltd* [2006] EWHC 832 (Ch).

[168] *Baker v Potter* [2005] BCC 855 (where specific performance of the sale and purchase agreement was ordered).

[169] *Exeter Football Club Ltd v Football Conference Ltd* [2004] 1 WLR 2910, not following *Re Vocam Europe Ltd* [1998] BCC 396. In the same way a company's articles cannot restrict a member's right to petition for winding up: *Re Peveril Gold Mines Ltd* [1898] 1 Ch 122, CA.

[170] See paragraph 21.21 above.

[171] 2006 Act, s 995(1).

[172] 2006 Act, s 995(3).

[173] 2006 Act, s 995(4).

extends to foreign companies. It is not thought that the Secretary of State has ever used the power now contained in s 995.

*Powers of the court under Part 30*

Section 996 provides for the orders that may be made on a well-founded petition under Part 30: **21.96**

> (1) If the court is satisfied that a petition presented under this Part is well founded it may make such order as it thinks fit for giving relief in respect of the matters complained of.
> (2) Without prejudice to the generality of subsection (1), the court's order may—
>   (a) regulate the company's affairs in the future;
>   (b) require the company—
>     (i) to refrain from doing or continuing an act complained of, or
>     (ii) to do an act that the petitioner has complained it has omitted to do;
>   (c) authorise civil proceedings to be brought in the name and on behalf of the company by such person or persons and on such terms as the court may direct;
>   (d) require the company not to make any, or any specified, alterations in its articles without the leave of the court;
>   (e) provide for the purchase of the shares of any members of the company by other members or by the company itself and, in the case of a purchase by the company itself, the reduction of the company's capital accordingly.

Relief for unfair prejudice is discussed in Section (6) below. The remedies are not dependent on a case being made for winding up the company. Rather, s 996 gives the court a full range of powers to apply 'an appropriate remedy during the continuing life of the company'.[174]

Subsections 998(1) and (2) provide for a copy of an order affecting the company's constitution[175] to be delivered to the Registrar within 14 days from making the order or such longer period as the court may allow. Section 999, which is a new section, adds that (a) the copy of the order altering the company's constitution delivered to the Registrar must be accompanied by a copy of the company's articles or the resolution or agreement in question, and (b) every copy of a company's articles issued by it after the order is made must be accompanied by a copy of the order unless the effect of the order has been incorporated into the articles by amendment.[176] If the company makes default in complying with these sections, it and every officer in default commits an offence and is liable for a fine.[177] **21.97**

---

[174] *Re a Company (No 00314 of 1989), ex p Estate Acquisition and Development Ltd* [1991] BCLC 154, 161, per Mummery J; approved by Lord Hoffmann in *O'Neill v Phillips* [1999] 1 WLR 1092, 1100, HL.

[175] By s 17 a company's constitution includes its articles and the resolutions and agreements identified in s 29.

[176] Subsections 999(1)–(3).

[177] Subsections 998(3) and (4) and 999(4) and (5).

*Procedure*

**21.98**  Section 997 provides for rules to be made under the Insolvency Act, s 411. The rules so made to govern the procedure for Part 30 petitions are still the Companies (Unfair Prejudice Applications) Rules 1986,[178] and, subject to them, the Civil Procedure Rules. Particular points on procedure are discussed in Section (7) below.

### (3) The concept of unfair prejudice

**21.99**  The grounds to support an unfair prejudice petition have been the subject of authoritative explanation by Hoffmann LJ in *Re Saul D Harrison Ltd*[179] and later as Lord Hoffmann in the leading case of *O'Neill v Phillips*.[180] It is convenient to identify the statements of principle made in these cases before turning to the detail of the grounds in Sections E(4) and (5) of this chapter.

**21.100**  In those cases Lord Hoffmann considered what was required to show unfairly prejudicial conduct:

(1)  The concept of unfair prejudice was chosen 'to free the court from technical considerations of legal right and to confer a wide power to do what appeared just and equitable'.[181]

(2)  The court applies an objective standard of fairness.[182] 'The concept of fairness must be applied judicially and the content which it is given by the courts must be based on rational principles.'[183]

(3)  Fairness is considered in a commercial context in which the company's articles govern the relationships of the shareholders with the company and each other. Sometimes there are collateral agreements between shareholders. The starting point is therefore to ask whether the conduct complained of was in accordance with the articles or the collateral agreement.[184]

(4)  Therefore 'a member of a company will not ordinarily be entitled to complain of unfairness unless there has been some breach of the terms on which he agreed that the affairs of the company should be conducted'.[185]

---

[178]  SI 1986/2000. 2006 Act, s 997 applies the rule-making power in the Insolvency Act, s 411 to petitions under Part 30. The 1986 Rules continue to have effect in relation to petitions under Part 30 by virtue of the continuity of law provision in 2006 Act, s 1297.

[179]  [1995] 1 BCLC 14, CA.

[180]  [1999] 1 WLR 1092, HL.

[181]  [1999] 1 WLR 1092, 1098D.

[182]  [1995] 1 BCLC 14, 17f–g.

[183]  [1999] 1 WLR 1092, 1098E.

[184]  [1995] 1 BCLC 14, 17i–18a; [1999] 1 WLR 1092, 1098G–H.

[185]  [1999] 1 WLR 1092, 1098H–1099A.

(5) Whether there has been some such breach may turn on the exercise by the directors of the fiduciary powers entrusted to them under the articles. A breach of their fiduciary duties may entitle a shareholder to a remedy under the unfair prejudice section even though, as a matter of general law the directors would be protected by the principle of majority rule. This is because 'enabling the court in an appropriate case to outflank the rule in *Foss v Harbottle* was one of the purposes of the section'.[186]

(6) Not every breach of the articles or breach of duty will amount to unfairly prejudicial conduct. Trivial or technical infringements should not give rise to an unfair prejudice petition.[187]

(7) On the other hand 'there will be cases in which equitable considerations make it unfair for those conducting the affairs of the company to rely upon their strict legal rights'.[188] In this part of the analysis Lord Hoffmann asserted the role of equity 'to restrain the exercise of strict legal rights in certain relationships in which it considered it to be contrary to good faith'[189] and drew support from the speech of Lord Wilberforce in *Ebrahimi v Westbourne Galleries Ltd*[190] (quoted in paragraph 21.132 below).

(8) In the interests of legal certainty the control of the exercise of legal rights should be governed by established principles of equity, rather than some 'indefinite notion of fairness'.[191] As to the concept of 'legitimate expectations' used in *Re Saul D Harrison & Sons Plc*,[192] Lord Hoffmann said that 'it was probably a mistake to use this term' and that 'the concept of legitimate expectation should not be allowed to lead a life of its own, capable of giving rise to equitable restraints in circumstances to which the traditional equitable principles have no application'.[193]

(9) The application of equitable principles may mean that

> there may be some event which puts an end to the basis upon which the parties entered into association with each other, making it unfair that one shareholder should insist upon the continuance of the association. The analogy of contractual frustration suggests itself. The unfairness may arise not from what the parties have positively agreed but from a majority using its legal powers to maintain the association in circumstances to which the minority can reasonably say it did not agree.[194]

---

[186] [1995] 1 BCLC 14, 18a–g.
[187] Ibid, 18g–i.
[188] [1995] 1 BCLC 14, 19a–20b; [1999] 1 WLR 1092, 1099A.
[189] [1999] 1 WLR 1092, 1098H.
[190] [1973] AC 360, 379.
[191] [1999] 1 WLR 1092, 1099F–H.
[192] [1995] 1 BCLC 14, 19. It was used in many other cases.
[193] [1999] 1 WLR 1092. 1102E–F.
[194] Ibid, 1101H–1102A.

(10)  It follows that it is not fair for a member who has been excluded from participation in management to keep his assets locked up in the company. There
should therefore be an offer to buy the excluded member's shares at a fair
price or some other fair arrangement.[195]

(11)  A fair price will ordinarily be at a value representing an equivalent proportion of the total issued share capital without any discount on account of it
being a minority holding. If the price is not agreed it should be fixed by
an expert acting as such, with the parties having equal access to information.
The majority shareholder should have a reasonable time to make an offer
before being at risk as to costs.[196]

(12)  Lord Hoffmann emphatically rejected the idea of 'no-fault divorce' as running counter to the contractual basis underlying the shareholders' relationship. Accordingly 'a member who has not been dismissed or excluded
[cannot] demand that his shares be purchased simply because he feels that
he has lost trust and confidence in the others'.[197]

(13)  He also affirmed that 'the requirement that prejudice must be suffered as
a member should not be too narrowly or technically construed'.[198]

**21.101**  In *Grace v Biagioli*[199] the Court of Appeal deduced the following principles from
Lord Hoffmann's speech in *O'Neill v Phillips*:

(1)  The concept of unfairness, although objective in its focus, is not to be considered
in a vacuum. An assessment that conduct is unfair has to be made against the legal
background of the corporate structure under consideration. This will usually take
the form of the articles of association and any collateral agreements between shareholders which identify their rights and obligations as members of the company.
Both are subject to established equitable principles which may moderate the exercise of strict legal rights when insistence on the enforcement of such rights would
be unconscionable;

(2)  It follows that it will not ordinarily be unfair for the affairs of a company to be
conducted in accordance with the provisions of its articles or any other relevant and
legally enforceable agreement, unless it would be inequitable for those agreements
to be enforced in the particular circumstances under consideration. Unfairness
may, to use Lord Hoffmann's words, 'consist in a breach of the rules or in using the
rules in a manner which equity would regard as contrary to good faith' (see [1999]
2 BCLC 1 at 8, [1999] 1 WLR 1092 at 1099); the conduct need not therefore be
unlawful, but it must be inequitable;

---

[195]  [1999] 1 WLR 1092, 1104G, 1107B.
[196]  Ibid, 1107C–1108B.
[197]  Ibid, 1104G–1105B.
[198]  Ibid, 1105G.
[199]  [2006] 2 BCLC 70, CA at para 61. There is a useful analysis of Lord Hoffmann's speech by
Jonathan Parker J in *Re Guidezone Ltd* [2000] 2 BCLC 321, 354–6 and another summary by Auld
LJ in *Re Phoenix Office Supplies Ltd* [2003] 1 BCLC 76, CA at para 19.

(3) Although it is impossible to provide an exhaustive definition of the circumstances in which the application of equitable principles would render it unjust for a party to insist on his strict legal rights, those principles are to be applied according to settled and established equitable rules and not by reference to some indefinite notion of fairness;

(4) To be unfair, the conduct complained of need not be such as would have justified the making of a winding-up order on just and equitable grounds as formerly required under s 210 of the Companies Act 1948;

(5) A useful test is always to ask whether the exercise of the power or rights in question would involve a breach of an agreement or understanding between the parties which it would be unfair to allow a member to ignore. Such agreements do not have to be contractually binding in order to found the equity;

(6) It is not enough merely to show that the relationship between the parties has irretrievably broken down. There is no right of unilateral withdrawal for a shareholder when trust and confidence between shareholders no longer exist. It is, however, different if that breakdown in relations then causes the majority to exclude the petitioner from the management of the company or otherwise to cause him prejudice in his capacity as a shareholder.

**21.102**  The CLR considered, but rejected, submissions that the 1985 Act, s 459 should be amended to give the court more flexibility to grant relief to minority shareholders than Lord Hoffmann's analysis permitted.[200] The CLR agreed with the House of Lords in *O'Neill v Phillips* that 'the basis for a claim should be a departure from an agreement, broadly defined, between those concerned, to be identified by their words or conduct. This is necessary in the interests of certainty and the containment of the scope of section 459 actions.' The Government agreed and hence Part 30 re-enacts without change the comparable provisions of the 1985 Act.

**21.103**  Section 994 emphasizes the need for a connection between the conduct complained of and the relief sought, so distinguishing unfair prejudice petitions from derivative claims.[201] Nevertheless it is helpful to consider (a) the conduct of the affairs of a company, including acts or omissions, actual or proposed, of which complaint may be made before turning to (b) the unfair prejudice to the interests of members, and (c) remedies.

### (4) Conduct of the affairs of the company

**21.104**  Complaints about the conduct of a company's affairs usually concern a course of conduct.[202] Subsection 994(1)(b) makes it clear, however, that individual acts or omissions, actual or proposed, are capable of being the subject of legitimate

---

[200] *Final Report* at para 7.41.
[201] *Re Charnley Davies Ltd (No 2)* [1990] BCLC 760, 783, 784 (a case on the Insolvency Act, s 27).
[202] *Re Macro (Ipswich) Ltd* [1994] 2 BCLC 354, 406.

complaint.[203] Threats of acts or omissions may not be enough to persuade the court to act.[204]

### The position of the petitioner

**21.105**  The petitioner is entitled to complain about conduct before he became a member,[205] even though he was aware of it when he acquired his shares,[206] and about matters arising after the petition was presented.[207]

**21.106**  Although the language of s 994 does not preclude the possibility of a majority shareholder petitioning for relief, such a procedure is most unlikely to be necessary or appropriate, because the majority shareholder can readily put an end to the unfair prejudice alleged.[208]

**21.107**  The petitioner does not have to come to court with clean hands, but his own conduct may prevent him from establishing the grounds of the petition in that it may render the conduct of the other parties, even if prejudicial, not unfair, and it may affect the relief, if any, that the court is prepared to grant.[209] Delay may be a bar to relief,[210] as may fraudulent conduct or abuse of the process of the court.[211]

### The affairs of the company

**21.108**  Complaint may not be made of conduct which is outside the company and does not involve corporate acts or omissions. Matters outside the scope of Part 30 include the payment by a respondent shareholder from his own money of a debt

---

[203] *Re Legal Costs Negotiators Ltd* [1999] 2 BCLC 171, 200, CA. Proposed acts were taken into account in *Re Kenyon Swansea Ltd* [1987] BCLC 514 and *Re a Company (No 00314 of 1989), ex p Estates Acquisition and Development Ltd* [1991] BCLC 154, 160 (threats to alter articles to remove director/shareholder).

[204] Cases where threats were not enough are: *Re Astec (BSR) plc* [1998] 2 BCLC 556, 571; *Re John Reid & Sons Ltd* [2003] 2 BCLC 319.

[205] *Lloyd v Casey* [2002] 1 BCLC 454.

[206] *Bermuda Cablevision Ltd v Colica Trust Co Ltd* [1998] AC 198, PC.

[207] *Cobden Investments Ltd v RWM Langport Ltd* [2007] EWHC 3048 (Ch), Warren J.

[208] *Re Legal Costs Negotiators Ltd* [1999] 2 BCLC 171, 200, 201, CA, where Peter Gibson LJ discusses the cases of *Re Baltic Real Estate Ltd (No 1)* [1993] BCLC 498 and *Re Baltic Real Estate Ltd (No 2)* [1993] BCLC 503, where this issue had been raised. In each of those cases the petitioner, who was the majority shareholder, unsuccessfully attempted to use 1985 Act, s 459 as a means of forcing the minority shareholder to sell his shares.

[209] *Re London School of Electronics Ltd* [1986] Ch 211, 222; *Re Baumler (UK) Ltd* [2005] 1 BCLC 92 at para 181; *Richardson v Blackmore* [2006] BCC 277, CA at para 53. Also see *Vujnovich v Vujnovich* [1990] BCLC 227, PC (a winding-up case).

[210] *Re Grandactual Ltd* [2006] BCC 73 (where the delay was nine years). In *Re a Company (No 5134 of 1986), ex p Harries* [1989] BCLC 383 the delay did not prevent the petitioner from obtaining relief. The same result was achieved in *Rahman v Malik* [2008] 2 BCLC 403, 425 where the learned judge accepted there had been considerable chronological delay, but was not persuaded in the circumstances that this justified excluding the petitioner from any remedy to which he might otherwise be entitled. An important factor was the absence of prejudice to the respondents by the passage of time.

[211] *Arrow Nominees Inc v Blackledge* [2000] 2 BCLC 167, CA. Also see *Rock (Nominees) Ltd v RCO (Holdings) Plc* [2004] 1 BCLC 439, CA, where at para 81 Jonathan Parker LJ considered that the petition was being used as a 'weapon in a tactical battle' and might have been struck out as an abuse.

owed by the company to its bank,[212] and theft, or unauthorized taking, by a director of company money or property (but the failure by the directors to take steps to recover the money or property would be within the scope of Part 30).[213] Also acts of a shareholder in dealing with his shares (such as refusing to sell his shares to another member) are outside the affairs of a company; although the company may become involved in share dealings, through sanctioning a share transfer or registering it.[214] Similarly an offer by one member to buy another's shares is outside the conduct of the company's affairs.[215] The line is often a fine one, because the company will necessarily be involved in giving effect to the transfer of shares (see paragraph 21.118 below).

**21.109** An unsuccessful attempt by the majority shareholder in a listed company, through its nominee directors to persuade the board to stop dividend payments and support its offer to buy the remaining shares, was not conduct of the affairs of the company, since the company's affairs were reflected in the decision of the board; nor was an announcement by the majority shareholder of its desired dividend policy conduct of the affairs of the company.[216]

**21.110** While the general position is that the complaint must concern the conduct of the affairs of the company which is the subject of the petition and not the conduct of directors of a connected company or trustees of a pension scheme,[217] or the conduct of the affairs of some other company, which holds shares in it or supplies it with goods,[218] a more flexible approach is necessary where the subject company is the parent of a company whose management is the subject of complaint. In *Rackind v Gross*[219] the Court of Appeal held that the affairs of a company can include the affairs of a subsidiary, in a case where the two companies had common directors. Sir Martin Nourse held that 'the expression "the affairs of the company" is one of the widest import which can include the affairs of a subsidiary'.[220] In *Re Grandactual Ltd*[221] the judge limited that statement to cases where a company controls, or is controlled by, another company, so that a petitioner for relief in respect of one company could not complain about the affairs of another company which the respondent shareholders controlled.

---

[212] *Re a Company (No 001761 of 1986)* [1987] BCLC 141, 144, 145.

[213] Ibid, 148.

[214] *Re Unisoft Group Ltd (No 3)* [1994] 1 BCLC 609, 623; *Re Leeds United Holdings plc* [1996] 2 BCLC 545; 559, 560; *Re Legal Costs Negotiators Ltd* [1999] 2 BCLC 171, 196, 197, CA.

[215] *Re Estate Acquisition & Development Ltd* [1995] BCC 338, 349.

[216] *Re Astec (BSR) plc* [1998] 2 BCLC 556.

[217] *Re Blackwood Hodge plc* [1997] 2 BCLC 650, 673.

[218] *Arrow Nominees Inc v Blackledge* [2000] 2 BCLC 167, CA at para 21.

[219] [2005] 1 WLR 3505, CA.

[220] [2005] 1 WLR 3505, 3512. Keene and Jacob LJJ agreed.

[221] [2006] BCC 73 at para 29. These authorities were considered by Lewison J in *Hawkes v Cuddy (No 2)* [2008] BCC 390 at paras 208–213.

**21.111**  The flexibility of the expression 'affairs of the company' has enabled the court to hold that when a company which held 75% of the shares in the company, the subject of the petition, withheld payments due to the company it was conducting the affairs of the company.[222]

*Breach of the company's constitution or shareholders' agreement*

**21.112**  The company's articles of association and memorandum, and any shareholders' agreements, govern the relationships of the shareholders with the company and each other. As such, unfairness may consist in a breach of the articles or the terms of any such agreement. A failure by the directors to recognize the appointment of a director by a shareholder pursuant to its entitlement under a shareholders' agreement would be unfairly prejudicial conduct.[223] A repeated failure to hold AGMs and lay accounts before the company depriving the members of their right to consider and question those accounts and to consider the affairs of the company, may amount to conduct unfairly prejudicial to the interests of all the members.[224] The holding of extraordinary general meetings, which have been invalidated by short notice, may also be unfairly prejudicial to shareholders who subscribed for shares which did not exist because of the procedural irregularity.[225]

**21.113**  There are certain other infringements of shareholders' rights which have founded successful unfair prejudice petitions. A proposed act which affects the rights of different groups of shareholders *inter se* might amount to unfairly prejudicial conduct where the directors have not exercised their powers fairly as between the different groups.[226] An allotment of shares in breach of statutory pre-emption

---

[222] *Nicholas v Soundcraft Electronics Ltd* [1993] BCLC 360, 364, 368, CA. In that case the group was in financial difficulties and payment was withheld to support the group, from which the company would benefit. Accordingly there was no unfair prejudice.

[223] *Re A&BC Chewing Gum Ltd* [1975] 1 WLR 579 (a winding-up case, where these facts entitled the petitioner to a winding-up order).

[224] *Re a Company (No 00789 of 1987), ex p Shooter* [1990] BCLC 384. In that case, the repeated failure to hold AGMs deprived the company of any proper board of directors. Harman J observed that one instance of such failure might not be enough; here, the resultant absence of any proper authority to look after the company's affairs was prejudicial to the interests of members. In *Fisher v Cadman* [2006] 1 BCLC 499 the respondents had failed to hold regular AGMs without valid reason. As a result, they deliberately frustrated the petitioner's reasonable efforts to obtain information about the conduct of the company's business and allowed the inclusion of (what were held to be) unreasonable directors' remuneration in the company accounts which had not been approved by the company in general meeting.

[225] *Re a Company (No 00789 of 1987), ex p Shooter* [1990] BCLC 384, in which Harman J's finding that the majority shareholder was unfit to control the company led him to order the majority shareholder to sell his shares to the petitioner.

[226] *Re BSB Holdings Ltd (No 2)* [1996] 1 BCLC 155; *Re McCarthy Surfacing Ltd* [2008] EWHC 2279 (Ch) at paras 77–81; cf *Mutual Life Insurance Co of New York v Rank Organisation Ltd* [1985] BCLC 11. The duty to promote the success of the company in 2006 Act, s 172 requires directors to have regard to the need to act fairly as between members of the company. In *Re BSB Holdings Ltd (No 2)*, there was no finding of unfair prejudice. Notwithstanding the fact that the directors had

rights and an unequal allotment in breach of fiduciary duty which discriminates between shareholders *inter se* have both been found to be conduct amounting to unfair prejudice.[227] Where, however, capital has been raised legitimately and there is no unfairness in the subsequent allotment of share capital, there will be no finding of unfair prejudice.[228]

The interests of members may also be unfairly prejudiced where the majority ignore an agreement made or an understanding reached between shareholders and on which the minority has acted in reliance.[229] In *Re Guidezone Ltd* Jonathan Parker J, in analysing Lord Hoffmann's speech in *O'Neill v Phillips*, held that:[230]

21.114

> Applying traditional equitable principles, equity will not hold the majority to an agreement, promise or understanding which is not enforceable at law unless and until the minority has acted in reliance on it. In the case of an agreement, promise or understanding made or reached when the company was formed, that requirement will almost always be fulfilled, in that the minority will have acted on the agreement, promise or understanding in entering into association with the majority and taking the minority stake. But the same cannot be said of agreements, promises or understandings made or reached subsequently, which are not themselves enforceable at law. In such a case, the majority will not as a general rule be regarded in equity as having acted contrary to good faith unless and until it has allowed the minority to act in reliance on such an agreement, promise or understanding. Absent some special circumstances, it will only be at that point, and not before, that equity will intervene by providing a remedy to the minority which is not available at law.

---

failed to address as they should have done whether the proposed acts had different effects on different groups of shareholders, on the facts this did not produce a result which was unfairly prejudicial to the interests of the petitioner.

[227] *Re a Company (No 005134 of 1986), ex p Harries* [1989] BCLC 383; *Dalby v Bodilly* [2005] BCC 627 (breach of duty in the allotment of shares to himself by a controlling director).

[228] *CAS (Nominees) Ltd v Nottingham Forest FC plc* [2002] 1 BCLC 613 (shares allotted without infringing the company's articles of association and where the directors could not be said to have exercised their powers for an improper purpose).

[229] *Re Regional Airports Ltd* [1999] 2 BCLC 30 (decided before *O'Neill v Phillips*, where the petitioner was held to have acted on common understandings, as to the way that the company should be run, which were based on the relationship of mutual trust and confidence between the parties, and which entitled him to complain of unfair prejudice when the understandings were departed from); *Re Guidezone Ltd* [2000] 2 BCLC 321 (alleged failure to sell property in breach of understanding); *Re Phoneer Ltd* [2002] 2 BCLC 241 (breach of shareholders' agreement that the petitioner should continue to manage and develop the company's business and act as its managing director, when the petitioner withdrew from management and wanted to renegotiate the basis of an agreed salary). See, more recently, *Re Southern Countries Fresh Foods Ltd* [2008] EWHC 2810 (Ch); *Rahman v Malik* [2008] 2 BCLC 403 (breach of agreement in failing to appoint petitioner as director and thereafter excluding him from real and effective participation in the affairs of the company).

[230] [2002] 2 BCLC 321 at para 175. See *Yeomans Row Management Ltd v Cobbe* [2008] UKHL 55 for a recent discussion by the House of Lords of the application of equitable principles to incomplete agreements and understandings.

### Breach of fiduciary duties

**21.115** The breach by a director of his fiduciary duties, whether or not the breaches were ratifiable under the rule in *Foss v Harbottle*, may amount to unfairly prejudicial conduct for the purposes of s 994 as a breach of the bargain between shareholders and the company.[231] 'Enabling the court in an appropriate case to outflank the rule in *Foss v Harbottle* was one of the purposes of [Part 30].'[232] The codification of directors' general duties in the 2006 Act, Part 10, Chapter 2[233] will affect directors in that any alleged unfairly prejudicial conduct arising out of a breach of duty will be identified with greater ease. Invariably the conduct complained of amounts to a breach of more than one of the general duties of directors.

**21.116** It is not enough to prove a breach of fiduciary duty to establish a claim for relief under Part 30; it must also cause unfair prejudice to the interest of the petitioner as member.[234] It is necessary in each case to show that the breach of fiduciary duty constitutes unfairly prejudicial management of the affairs of the company, since the petition will seek 'relief from mismanagement, not a remedy for misconduct'.[235] Usually the unfairness to the petitioner or shareholders will be inherent in the nature of the breach of duty complained of and the harm caused to the company and thereby to shareholders.[236] As the following discussion shows the breaches of duty which constitute unfairly prejudicial conduct invariably involve dishonesty, concealment, conflict of interest, partisan, or discriminatory behaviour. Where those breaches occur the petitioner will have good grounds for saying he has lost trust and confidence in the management of the company. On the other hand a breach which is trivial or technical may not be enough to support an unfair prejudice petition.[237] Nor is it likely to be enough to point to bad business decisions or acts of incompetence, because every shareholder takes the risk that they will occur (paragraph 21.131 below).

### The fiduciary duty to act within powers

**21.117** Directors of a company must only exercise powers for the purposes for which they are conferred.[238] The corollary of that rule is that they must not exercise those

---

[231] *O'Neill v Phillips* [1999] 1 WLR 1098H–1099A, HL.

[232] *Re Saul D Harrison Ltd* [1995] 1 BCLC 14, 18g–i, CA.

[233] See Chapters 9–15 and 17–18.

[234] *Re Saul D Harrison & Sons plc* [1995] 1 BCLC 14, 31, CA, per Neill LJ; *Re Blackwood Hodge plc* [1997] 2 BCLC 650, 673.

[235] *Re Charnley Davies Ltd (No 2)* [1990] BCLC 760, 783, 784, per Millett J (a case on the Insolvency Act, s 27).

[236] *Anderson v Hogg* [2002] BCC 923.

[237] *Re Saul D Harrison Ltd* [1995] 1 BCLC 14, 18g–i, CA. See also *Re a Company (No 008699 of 1985)* [1986] BCLC 382, 387 where Hoffmann J said that the concept of unfairness 'cuts across the distinction between acts which do or do not infringe rights attached to the shares by the constitution of the company'.

[238] 2006 Act, s 171.

powers for an improper or collateral purpose.[239] There have been a number of instances in which the management by directors of the company's assets or reserves were found to be motivated by collateral purposes and as such, unfairly prejudicial.[240] Directors of a company have a duty to consider what proportion of a company's trading profits they can properly distribute to members, as the owners of the company, and a failure to pay reasonable dividends may, in the particular circumstances of the company, support an allegation of unfair prejudice,[241] albeit one that may be difficult to make good. Such an allegation is invariably accompanied by an allegation that the directors have paid excessive remuneration to themselves or paid other benefits to the majority shareholders.[242]

Where the directors use their powers as such to enable the majority shareholders **21.118** to sell their shares, they may breach their fiduciary duties and their obligations of good faith to the minority shareholder and director from whom they deliberately concealed the sale.[243]

---

[239] *McGuiness, Petitioner* (1988) 4 BCC 161 (directors exercising power to postpone EGM at which resolutions to change the constitution of the board were to be considered; held capable of being unfairly prejudicial conduct).

[240] *Re a Company (No 007623 of 1984)* [1986] BCLC 382 (directors proposed a rights issue at par to raise capital that the company needed, but this was arguably unfairly prejudicial conduct, because the shares were worth more than par and the directors knew the minority shareholder could not afford to subscribe for his shares); *Re a Company (No 002612 of 1984)* (1986) 2 BCC 99,453, 99,478–99,480; on appeal as *Re Cumana Ltd* [1986] BCLC 430, 434, CA (rights issue to depress petitioner's stake); *Jesner v Jarrad Properties Ltd* [1993] BCLC 1032 (threatened use of company's assets to pay the liabilities of an associated company, in which the petitioner had a smaller shareholding); *Grace v Baglioli* [2006] 2 BCLC 70, CA (failure to pay dividends and distribution of profits by majority shareholders to themselves under the guise of management expenses in breach of profit sharing agreement).

[241] *Re a Company (No 00370 of 1987), ex p Glossop* [1988] 1 WLR 1068, 1076–7 (allegation by a minority shareholder that the directors of the company had failed to pay reasonable dividends out of the very large profits accruing to the company could justify a winding-up order, but held in *Re Saul D Harrison Ltd* [1995] 1 BCLC 14, CA, per Hoffmann LJ to apply to an unfair prejudice petition as well). In *Re McCarthy Surfacing Ltd* [2008] EWHC 2279 (Ch) at paras 77–84 the court found unfairly prejudicial conduct where the directors had paid themselves substantial bonuses while failing to consider whether or not they should declare dividends.

[242] In *Re Sam Weller & Sons Ltd* [1990] Ch 682 it was held that the payment of the same derisory dividend over many years and the failure of the majority shareholders of a family company to pay reasonable dividends, whilst continuing to draw an income from the company and to accumulate profits and cash in hand, combined with a proposed significant capital expenditure, could amount to conduct unfairly prejudicial to the interests of the minority shareholders. Also: *Re a Company* [1997] 1 BCLC 479; *Irvine v Irvine (No 1)* [2007] 1 BCLC 349; *Re McCarthy Surfacing Ltd* [2008] EWHC 2279 (Ch).

[243] *Richardson v Blackmore* [2006] BCC 277, CA at paras 23, 24, and 65. In that case, the sale altered the petitioner's position in the company from that of being an equal shareholder with two people who had been partners (or quasi partners in the context of the company), to that of being a true minority shareholder with an individual who was a competitor of the company's business. In respect of a number of the individual steps involved in completing the sale, the directors were held to have breached their duties of good faith to the company and their conduct was held to be unfairly prejudicial.

*The fiduciary duty to promote the success of the company*

**21.119**  Directors have an overriding duty to act in good faith in what they consider to be the interests of the company [244] and are not bound to pursue the interests of minority shareholders contrary to those interests. A director of a company must act in the way he considers, in good faith, would be most likely to promote the success of the company for the benefit of its members as a whole.[245] The breaches of this duty capable of sustaining an unfair prejudice petition are likely to involve conflict of interest or discriminatory treatment of shareholders.[246] Where a proposed act will have an effect not only on the company itself, but also on the interest of some of the shareholders, the duty to act in the best interests of the company requires them also within limits to act fairly as between different groups of shareholders.[247] Where the act has different effects on different groups of shareholders, however, the directors must consider whether this is justified in the particular circumstances by the overriding need to act in the interests of the company: they are not bound to pursue the interests of minority shareholders contrary to the interests of the company itself.[248]

**21.120**  The need to act in the interests of the company pervades all transactions into which the directors propose to enter.[249] The duty is subject to the company's constitution. If a particular transaction required the approval of a particular majority of shareholders, which could not be obtained, the failure by the company to enter into the transaction could not put the directors in breach of the duty to promote the success of the company or amount to unfair prejudice.[250]

**21.121**  Where the directors take the view that it is in the interests of the company for all the shares to be transferred to an outside bidder, their fiduciary duty extends to not misleading shareholders, when advising shareholders on rival takeover bids,

---

[244] *Re Saul D Harrison Ltd* [1995] 1 BCLC 14, 18; *Mutual Life Insurance Co of New York v Rank Organisation Ltd* [1985] BCLC 11. This duty has been codified in 2006 Act, s 172.

[245]  2006 Act, s 172.

[246]  The conduct in *Scottish Co-operative Wholesale Society Ltd v Meyer* [1959] AC 324, HL (Sc), a case under the 1948 Act, s 210, is an example of a breach of the duty to promote the success of the company which would amount to unfairly prejudicial conduct. There the director deliberately ran down the company so that another company in which he was interested could prosper.

[247]  2006 Act, s 172(1)(f); *Re BSB Holdings Ltd (No 2)* [1996] 1 BCLC 155.

[248]  *Re BSB Holdings Ltd (No 2)* [1996] 1 BCLC 155. Arden J held that had the directors considered and detected the effects on different groups of shareholders, they would doubtless have taken the view that it was imperative to approve the proposed act in the interests of the company having regard to the urgency of the situation and the almost certain absence of other sources of funding.

[249]  *Re Metropolis Motor Cycles Ltd* [2007] 1 BCLC 520 (alleged non-disclosure of information material to transaction at the time of its implementation and allegedly unfair cessation of drawings in breach of arrangement between former partners where there were insufficient profits to support those drawings); *Bermuda Cablevision Ltd v Colica Trust Co Ltd* [1998] AC 198, PC (application to strike out petition dismissed where petitioner alleged that the carrying on of the business of the company unlawfully constituted unfairly prejudicial conduct).

[250]  *Wilkinson v West Coast Capital* [2007] BCC 717 at paras 295–304.

and providing them with sufficient information to reach a properly informed decision, and a breach of this duty is prima facie capable of founding an unfair prejudice petition.[251]

In *Re Blackwood Hodge plc*[252] the petitioners, who held preference shares, estab-  **21.122**
lished that the former directors had breached their duties to the company by failing to give adequate consideration to the terms of a merger of the company's pension scheme with the pension scheme of the company that bought all its ordinary share capital, but failed to establish unfair prejudice, because they could not show that the company had suffered any loss.

Where the petition alleges that the directors are continuing to trade when the  **21.123**
company is trading at a loss and when it should have been apparent that there was no real prospect that the company would return to profitability, the court would conclude that its affairs were being conducted in a manner unfairly prejudicial to its members if it is able to infer that the directors' decision was improperly influenced by their desire to continue in office and to draw remuneration and other benefits for themselves and that no reasonable board would consider it to be in the interests of the company and its members for it to continue to trade.[253]

### The fiduciary duty to avoid conflicts of interest

The strict and inflexible rule of equity that a director must not place himself in  **21.124**
a position of conflict of interest and duty may found an allegation of unfairly prejudicial conduct.[254] Unfair prejudice in this context may consist in diversion of the company's business by the majority shareholders to another business owned by them,[255] charging the company's assets to support another company connected with the directors,[256] misapplication of the company's assets for the personal

---

[251] *Re a Company (No 008699 of 1985)* [1986] BCLC 382 (motion to strike out petition dismissed where chairman's circular to shareholders was arguably misleading and arguably impaired the chances of shareholders being able to sell their shares to the highest bidder).

[252] [1997] 2 BCLC 650.

[253] *Re a Company, ex p Burr* [1992] BCLC 724; on appeal, reported as *Re Saul D Harrison Ltd* [1995] 1 BCLC 14. The Court of Appeal found that the evidence did not support the allegation that the directors had carried on the business with no or no substantial expectation that they would succeed in making a profit which would reflect the value of the assets employed. Nor could the court accept the allegation that the directors had carried on the business simply to further their own interests.

[254] Now codified under 2006 Act, ss 175–177 in the form of three distinct duties. See *Bhullar v Bhullar* [2003] 2 BCLC 241, per Jonathan Parker LJ for a detailed exposition of this rule.

[255] *Re London School of Electronics Ltd* [1986] Ch 211; *Re a Company (No 002612 of 1984)* (1986) 2 BCC 99,453, 99,477, 99,478; on appeal as *Re Cumana Ltd* [1986] BCLC 430, 434, CA; *Lowe v Fahey* [1996] 1 BCLC 262.

[256] *Re Brenfield Squash Racquets Club Ltd* [1996] 2 BCLC 184.

benefit of its director and his family and friends,[257] misappropriation by a director of the company's business and assets for the benefit of a new business in which he is interested,[258] payment of 'management charges' which had no commercial justification to a company wholly owned by the majority shareholder and his wife,[259] and a transfer of company property to majority shareholders at an undervalue.[260] Subjecting a company to a loan on onerous and uncommercial terms from a company connected with directors and without obtaining shareholder approval as had been agreed could amount to unfairly prejudicial conduct.[261] It has also been held that a director will be placed in a position of conflict with his duties as a director where he attempts to negotiate the purchase of a potential competitor, without any disclosure or discussion with his fellow directors and shareholders, and attempts to conceal the negotiations.[262]

**21.125** A prima facie conflict of interest on the part of the directors will not constitute unfair prejudice to the interests of the minority, where in the particular circumstances no prejudice can be found to have been suffered.[263] In the absence of a breach of fiduciary duties, petitioners will be forced to demonstrate unfair prejudice on the basis of their rights under the company's constitution or collateral

---

[257] *Re Elgindata Ltd* [1991] BCLC 959 (notwithstanding that there was no serious diminution in value of the minority's shares): see *Bhullar v Bhullar* [2003] 2 BCLC 241 as to the relevant question being simply whether the circumstances attract application of the rule against conflicts of interest.

[258] *Allmark v Burnham* [2006] 2 BCLC 43 at para 96.

[259] *Wilson v Jaymarke Estates Ltd* [2007] BCC 883, HL (Sc).

[260] *Re Little Olympian Each-Ways Ltd (No 3)* [1995] 1 BCLC 636 (transfer of company's business at an undervalue to a company under the same de facto control as part of a hiving up operation, depriving the petitioner of any further interest in those assets); *Guinness Peat Group plc v British Land Co plc* [1999] 2 BCLC 243, CA (petition based on an alleged transfer by the company of its sole asset at an undervalue was not struck out, as the questions of valuation of the minority shareholding merited a full hearing in order to determine whether prejudice had in fact been suffered by the petitioner).

[261] *Atlasview Ltd v Brightview Ltd* [2004] 2 BCLC 191.

[262] *Grace v Biagioli* [2006] 2 BCLC 70, CA, paras 64–70, in which such misconduct was held to justify the removal of the petitioner as a director of the company.

[263] *Nicholas v Soundcraft Electronics Ltd* [1993] BCLC 360, CA; see paragraph 21.111. In that case, the Court of Appeal held that the minority shareholder had not been 'unfairly' prejudiced because the decision to withhold payments represented a reasonable commercial judgment necessary to support the group. In a similar vein, see *Re Grandactual Ltd* [2006] BCC 73, para 31 where it was held that the alleged diversion of the company's assets to the benefit of the majority was in fact a valid payment of licence fees to a related company and such payment was necessary to keep the company subject to the petition in business. As a result, unfair prejudice could not be established. See also: *Re Blackwood Hodge plc* [1997] 2 BCLC 650 (no prejudice caused by directors' treatment of employees' pension schemes following a takeover in breach of fiduciary duties) and *Rock Nominees Ltd v RCO (Holdings) plc* [2004] 1 BCLC 439, CA at paras 73 *et seq* (sale by the directors of the company of its subsidiary was not found to be at an undervalue and in consequence the petitioner had not suffered prejudice; the Court of Appeal considered it inappropriate to make a finding of a breach of fiduciary duty in the abstract, notwithstanding that the directors were in a position of conflict).

shareholders' agreements. In such circumstances, it has been held that non-voting minority shareholders who complain about a sale of their company's assets (indirectly) to its directors, which gives rise to a prima facie conflict of interest, will be precluded from establishing unfair prejudice where the company has complied with both the provisions of the articles of association and the Companies Act dealing with conflicts of interest,[264] and no other agreement or understanding of the shareholders *inter se* is demonstrated.[265]

A shareholders' agreement may in certain circumstances preclude a finding of unfair prejudice even though there has been a prima facie breach of a directors' fiduciary duties. In *North Holdings Ltd v Southern Tropics Ltd*[266] the shareholders' agreement provided that the majority shareholders were free to engage in any other business for their own benefit or set up any competing business using a specified trading name. The Court of Appeal held that, notwithstanding the fact that the majority's development and promotion of a competing business was not a breach of their fiduciary duties as directors of the company, it was arguable that they had acted in breach of their fiduciary duties by using the company's assets for their own benefit as shareholders in the competing business. **21.126**

That notwithstanding, the putative petitioner must still satisfy the court that he has suffered some prejudice in consequence of the breach of fiduciary duty, which is unfair. In *Wilkinson v West Coast Capital*[267] the shareholders had made an agreement to the effect that no other company or business would be acquired without the consent of 65 per cent of the holders of issued shares. Warren J interpreted the shareholders' agreement as evincing an intention that the company was to be a single purpose vehicle. As such, he held that a director's pursuit of a corporate opportunity in his personal capacity did not amount to a breach of the no conflict rule since the company was prevented by its constitution from taking up the same opportunity. Accordingly, no prejudice for the purposes of s 994 could be said to exist. **21.127**

*Transactions with directors*

A director who is in any way, directly or indirectly, interested in a proposed or existing transaction or arrangement with the company must declare the nature and extent of that interest to the other directors.[268] Service contracts, substantial **21.128**

---

[264] Now 2006 Act, ss 175(4)(b), 177, 180, 182, and Part 10, Chapter 4.

[265] *Re Posgate and Denby (Agencies) Ltd* [1987] BCLC 8 (shareholder approval as required by 1985 Act, s 320 having been obtained).

[266] [1999] 2 BCLC 625, CA.

[267] [2007] BCC 717 at paras 305–313.

[268] 2006 Act, ss 177, 182–187.

property transactions, loans, quasi-loans and credit transactions, and payments for loss of office all require the approval of members.[269]

**21.129**  Conduct consisting in the drawing of excessive levels of remuneration and other benefits,[270] payment of unauthorized remuneration,[271] the procurement by a director of consultancy fees and remuneration in breach of the articles of association,[272] the payment by directors of company money for their own personal expenditure,[273] and gifts described as bonuses and payment to assist a shareholder to pay calls[274] may all amount to unfair prejudice on the part of the directors. In *Re Regional Airports Ltd*,[275] the conduct complained of concerned inter alia an excessive claim to remuneration and the proposal of a share rights issue by the majority shareholder and director. It was found that his proposal of the rights issue was motivated by a desire to achieve a situation where: (a) he stood a good chance of being able to increase his proportionate equity stake at effectively no cost to himself; (b) certain desirable aspects of his remuneration package would be settled retrospectively subject only to upwards renegotiation in the future; and (c) the remaining shareholders and directors would be forced either to increase their financial investment in the company or allow their existing stakes to be significantly diluted.

---

[269] 2006 Act, ss 188–226.

[270] *Re a Company (No 004415 of 1996)* [1997] 1 BCLC 479; *Irvine v Irvine (No 1)* [2007] 1 BCLC 349 (payment of excessive levels of remuneration by a director to himself without seeking the approval of the company in general meeting and without reference to the board of directors, thus depriving the petitioner of his dividend entitlement); *Re McCarthy Surfacing Ltd* [2008] EWHC 2279 (Ch) (unjustified bonuses). In such circumstances the court may hear expert evidence as to 'objective commercial criteria' to determine whether the remuneration was in fact excessive and thus founds an allegation of unfair prejudice. Note the observations on remuneration levels in *Smith v Croft* [1986] 1 WLR 580. See also: *Re Phoneer Ltd* [2002] 2 BCLC 241 in relation to an attempt by the majority shareholder and director to renegotiate an agreed salary structure and his simultaneous withdrawal from management of the company; *Allmark v Burnham* [2006] 2 BCLC 43 at para 96.

[271] *Clark v Cutland* [2003] 2 BCLC 393, CA; *Anderson v Hogg* [2002] BCC 923 (where the payments were described as redundancy payments).

[272] *Re Ravenhart Service (Holdings) Ltd* [2004] 2 BCLC 376 at para 86, cf *Guinness plc v Saunders* [1990] 2 AC 663.

[273] *Re Jayflex Construction Ltd* [2004] 2 BCLC 145 at para 71. In that case, Sir Donald Rattee (sitting as a judge of the High Court) held that such payments by both directors of the company were improper and a breach of the duty of each to the company as a director. Such payments, albeit to a minor degree, prejudiced the company and, therefore, the shareholders. However, on the facts he found that since both directors had adopted a practice of making such payments (and there were no other shareholders), neither could complain as against the other that the making of such payments was unfairly prejudicial conduct. Even though the aggregate quantum of payments to each director were not equal, the judge found that there was an understanding as between the directors that an equalization process would be carried out in the future.

[274] *Re Hailey Group Ltd* [1993] BCLC 459, 471.

[275] [1999] 2 BCLC 30.

### Breach of duty of care, skill, and diligence

A director of a company must exercise the care, skill, and diligence that may rea-    **21.130**
sonably be expected of a person carrying out the functions carried out by the
director in relation to the company and the general knowledge, skill, and experience that the director has.[276]

It is unlikely that a simple breach of this duty will be sufficient to make out a com-    **21.131**
plaint of unfair prejudice. In *Re Elgindata Ltd*[277] Warner J identified two reasons
for this. The first is the general reluctance of the court to resolve disputes over
particular managerial decisions. Not only is the court ill-qualified to do so, but
'there can be no unfairness to the petitioners in those in control of the company's
affairs taking a different view from theirs on such matters'. Secondly, shareholders
acquire their shares knowing that their value will depend on the competence of
management. They take a risk that management will make mistakes. The position
might be different if, for example, a director known to be incompetent was kept
in office for family reasons. In *Re Macro (Ipswich) Ltd*[278] Arden J applied Warner
J's analysis and held there was a distinction between a difference of opinion on
commercial decisions and serious mismanagement. The latter could justify intervention under Part 30, particularly where steps were not taken to prevent or
rectify it.

### Equitable restraints on lawful conduct

As Lord Hoffmann explained in *Re Saul D Harrison Ltd*[279] and *O'Neill v Phillips*[280]    **21.132**
equitable principles may make it unfair for those in control of the company to
exercise their legal rights in a particular way. The company may remove a director
by ordinary resolution,[281] but if the director is a minority shareholder, it may be
unfair to remove him without making a fair offer for his shares. To identify the
considerations that make equitable principles applicable in the context of unfair
prejudice petitions, Lord Hoffmann applied the reasoning of Lord Wilberforce in
*Ebrahimi v Westbourne Galleries Ltd*[282] (a contributory's winding-up petition on
the just and equitable ground) in the two passages:

> The words ['just and equitable'] are a recognition of the fact that a limited company
> is more than a mere legal entity, with a personality in law of its own: that there is
> room in company law for recognition of the fact that behind it, or amongst it, there

---

[276] 2006 Act, s 174.
[277] [1991] BCLC 959, 993, 994.
[278] [1994] 2 BCLC 354, 405, 406. See also *Re Saul D Harrison & Sons plc* [1995] 1 BCLC 14,
31, per Neill LJ.
[279] [1995] 1 BCLC 14, 19a–20b, CA.
[280] [1999] 1 WLR 1092, 1098H–1099A, 1104G, 1107B, HL.
[281] 2006 Act, s 168.
[282] [1973] AC 360, 379, HL.

are individuals with rights, expectations and obligations inter se which are not necessarily submerged in the company structure. That structure is defined by the Companies Act and by the articles of association by which shareholders agree to be bound. In most companies and in most contexts, this definition is sufficient and exhaustive, equally so whether the company is large or small. The 'just and equitable' provision does not, as the respondents suggest, entitle one party to disregard the obligation he assumes by entering a company, nor the court to dispense him from it. It does, as equity always does, enable the court to subject the exercise of legal rights to equitable considerations; considerations, that is, of a personal character arising between one individual and another, which may make it unjust, or inequitable, to insist on legal rights, or to exercise them in a particular way.

It will be impossible, and wholly undesirable, to define the circumstances in which these considerations may arise. Certainly the fact that the company is a small one, or a private company, is not enough. There are very many of these where the association is a purely commercial one, of which it can safely be said that the basis of association is adequately and exhaustively laid down in the articles. The superimposition of equitable considerations requires something more . . .

**21.133** Where the company is a public company with many shareholders it is improbable that equitable considerations will apply.[283] In relation to listed companies the public dealing in the market for the company's shares must be entitled to proceed 'on the footing that the constitution of the company is as it appears in the company's public documents, unaffected by any extraneous equitable considerations and constraints'.[284]

**21.134** Equally with private companies there may be no scope for equitable considerations to be applied. *Re Saul D Harrison Ltd*[285] was a case where there was 'nothing more' to prevent the company and the board from exercising powers of management. In *Posgate and Denby Agencies Ltd*[286] Hoffmann J rejected the petitioner's case that certain property would not be sold without shareholder approval as being inconsistent with (a) the directors' powers of management conferred by the articles, (b) a particular article dealing with conflicts of interest, and (c) the fact shareholders must be taken to accept that the best commercial decisions may not

---

[283] *Re Blue Arrow plc* [1987] BCLC 585, 590 (petition of president of quoted company to prevent it from altering its articles to remove her was struck out); *Re Tottenham Hotspur plc* [1994] 1 BCLC 655, 659 (no expectation that nominee of minority shareholder in quoted company would retain office as chief executive); *Re Leeds United Holdings plc* [1996] 2 BCLC 556, 559; *Re Benfield Greig Group plc* [2000] 2 BCLC 488, 507, 508; *Re CAS (Nominees) Ltd v Nottingham Forest FC plc* [2002] 1 BCLC 613 at para 37.

[284] *Re Astec (BSR) plc* [1998] 2 BCLC 556, 589, 590 (where the judge rejected the petitioner's submission that it had a legitimate expectation that the listed company would comply with the Listing Rules, the City Code, and the Cadbury Code).

[285] [1995] 1 BCLC 14, 20, CA. In that case the complaint, which was dismissed, was that the directors were continuing a loss-making business in order to earn remuneration, whereas a reasonable board would stop trade and sell the company's property.

[286] [1987] BCLC 8, 14.

be taken. Similarly the existence of detailed agreements may preclude any expectation inhibiting the exercise of legal rights.[287]

As Lord Hoffmann explained in *O'Neill v Phillips* [288] it is usually unfair for a member who has been removed from participation in management to keep his investment locked up in the company, but 'that does not mean that a member who has not been dismissed or excluded can demand that his shares be purchased simply because he feels that he has lost trust and confidence in the others'.[289] In *Hawkes v Cuddy (No 2)*,[290] Lewison J accepted that the petition was well founded because, in addition to loss of confidence in management, it relied on the consequent deadlock and inability of the company to conduct its business as initially contemplated.

**21.135**

The 'something more' referred to by Lord Wilberforce (paragraph 21.132 above) may be satisfied by showing '(i) a business association formed or continued on the basis of a personal relationship of mutual trust and confidence, (ii) an understanding or agreement that all or some of the shareholders should participate in the management of the business and (iii) restrictions on the transfer of shares so that a member cannot realise his stake if he is excluded from the business'.[291] As a convenient shorthand an association in a company which has these features is usually called a 'quasi-partnership'. Relationships in relation to a company may change so that it becomes a quasi-partnership,[292] or ceases to be one.[293] The fact that the minority shareholder is employed by the company under a service agreement does not preclude a quasi-partnership relationship, although the dividing line between

**21.136**

---

[287] *Re a Company (No 005685), ex p Schwarcz* [1989] BCLC 427, 440, 441 (no expectation that a director would not be removed from office in a case where there were detailed agreements covering the relationship between the parties). Also see *Re Elgindata Ltd* [1991] BCLC 959, 985; *Re Estate Acquisition & Development Ltd* [1995] BCC 338, 345–9, 355.

[288] [1999] 1 WLR 1092, 1104F–H, HL (where the petitioner unsuccessfully relied on loss of confidence in management in support of a petition to be bought out).

[289] In *Re a Company (No 004475 of 1982)* [1983] Ch 178, 191 Lord Granchester said that he did not consider that the unfair prejudice section was enacted 'so as to enable a "locked-in" minority shareholder to require the company to buy him out at a price which he considered adequately to reflect the value of the underlying assets referable to his shareholding, providing the company held sufficient resources so to do'. Also see *Re Jayflex Construction Ltd* [2004] 2 BCLC 145 at para 55.

[290] [2008] BCC 390 at para 231 (a case containing a full review of the authorities at paras 198–242).

[291] *CVC/Opportunity Equity Partners Ltd v Demarco Almeida* [2002] 2 BCLC 108, PC (a just and equitable winding-up case) at para 32, per Lord Millett, who summarized the factors identified by Lord Wilberforce at [1973] AC 360, 379.

[292] As was the case in *O'Neill v Phillips* [1999] 1 WLR 1092, HL.

[293] *Re a Company (No 005134 of 1986)* [1989] BCLC 383; *Re McCarthy Surfacing Ltd* [2008] EWHC 2279 (Ch) at paras 95–99.

a master and servant relationship and the more equal one of quasi-partnership may be a fine one.[294]

**21.137**  There have been many cases of exclusion from management where, in the absence of a fair offer to buy the petitioner's shares, the court has taken into account equitable considerations and given the petitioner relief from unfair prejudice by ordering the purchase of his shares at a fair price.[295] In *Re Kenyon Swansea Ltd*[296] the petitioner was a minority shareholder and managing director of the company and had an option to buy the majority shareholder's shares. The court refused to strike out a petition which complained that the majority shareholder was taking steps to alter the company's articles to prevent the option from being exercisable and to have the petitioner removed from office.

**21.138**  The petitioner's misconduct or threatened breach or departure from the company's constitution or associated agreements may prevent him from complaining that his exclusion from management was unfair.[297] Even in a case of a quasi-partnership, if a director voluntarily resigns for personal reasons, or indicates his wish to do so, it is not unfair for him to be excluded from management and such a departing director cannot force a purchase of his shares at their full undiscounted value when he had no contractual right to do so.[298]

**21.139**  As Lord Hoffmann also explained in *O'Neill v Phillips*,[299] 'there may be some event which puts an end to the basis upon which the parties entered into association with each other, making it unfair that one shareholder should insist upon the continuance of the association'. Thus where the parties joined together to operate a nightclub, which was sold, it may be unfair to the minority shareholder, who

---

[294] There was a quasi-partnership relationship in *Quinlan v Essex Hinge Co Ltd* [1996] 2 BCLC 417; *Richards v Lundy* [2000] 1 BCLC 376; *Brownlow v GH Marshall Ltd* [2000] 2 BCLC 655, but not in the Scottish case *Third v North East Ice & Cold Storage Co Ltd* [1998] BCC 242.

[295] *Re a Company (No 00477 of 1986)* [1986] BCLC 376; *Tay Bok Choon v Tahansan Sdn Bdh* [1987] 1 WLR 413, PC (a just and equitable winding-up case); *Re Ghill Beck Driving Range Ltd* [1993] BCLC 1126; *R&H Electric Ltd v Haden Bill Electrical Ltd* [1995] 2 BCLC 280, 295 (participation through a representative); *Quinlan v Essex Hinge Co Ltd* [1996] 2 BCLC 417; *Re a Company (No 002015 of 1996)* [1997] 2 BCLC 1 (even though there were formal agreements between the parties); *Richards v Lundy* [2000] 1 BCLC 376; *Brownlow v GH Marshall Ltd* [2000] 2 BCLC 655 (even though the director had a service agreement); *Parkinson v Eurofinance Group Ltd* [2001] 1 BCLC 720; *Richardson v Blackmore* [2006] BCC 276, CA at paras 64–68; *Strahan v Wilcock* [2006] 2 BCLC 555, CA at paras 27–30.

[296] [1987] BCLC 514.

[297] *Re London School of Electronics Ltd* [1986] Ch 211, 222; *Parkinson v Eurofinance Group Ltd* [2001] 1 BCLC 720 at para 87; *Mears v R Mears & Co (Holdings) Ltd* [2002] 2 BCLC 1 at paras 34–36; *Grace v Biagioli* [2006] 2 BCLC 70, CA at para 64 (petitioner's removal justified by putting himself in a position of conflict and attempted concealment of actions).

[298] *Re Guidezone Ltd* [2000] 2 BCLC 321 at paras 185–192; *Mears v R Mears & Co (Holdings) Ltd* [2002] 2 BCLC 1; *Re Phoenix Office Supplies Ltd* [2003] 1 BCLC 76, CA; *Re Jayflex Construction Ltd* [2004] 2 BCLC 145.

[299] [1999] 1 WLR 1092, 1101H–1102A, HL.

wished to recover his investment, for the directors and majority shareholders to use their powers to invest the proceeds in another club or business.[300] Similarly, where a company paid management charges to one of its shareholder's companies while both shareholders were engaged in management, it may be unfair to continue to do so after the relationship in the business has ended.[301]

Where it was understood or agreed that a shareholder would participate in man-  **21.140**
agement and the venture for which the association between the parties was formed has come to an end, it will ordinarily be unfair for the shareholder's investment to be locked into the company. In *O'Neill v Phillips*[302] Lord Hoffmann explained that fairness required the purchase of the shareholder's shares at a price fixed pro rata to the value of the company without any discount and that, if the parties cannot agree on price, an independent expert should be appointed to fix it (paragraph 21.100(10) and (11) above). If the other shareholders offer to buy out the (potential) petitioner in accordance with the principles stated by Lord Hoffmann there will be no unfairness and no need for any relief to be granted by the court. Any petition presented by the shareholder will be struck out.[303]

Sometimes the company's articles provide a mechanism for the purchase of shares,  **21.141**
but in a case where equitable considerations apply and the shareholder is not a willing seller, the court will not expect him to invoke the procedures in the articles if their terms are, or may be in their implementation, less favourable to him than the principles stated by Lord Hoffmann.[304] Where however the articles provide a mechanism which conforms to Lord Hoffmann's principles, it would normally be an abuse of the process of the court for the excluded shareholder to proceed with a Part 30 petition rather than invoking the articles.[305] Indeed, where, by the articles or otherwise, the excluded shareholder has contractually bound himself to sell his shares on agreed terms in the applicable circumstances, the other shareholders' case for the petition being an abuse is stronger.[306] The two exceptions

---

[300] See the facts of *Virdi v Abbey Leisure Ltd* [1990] BCLC 342, CA, which were considered by Lord Hoffmann at [1999] 1 WLR 1092, 1101H–1102A, HL.

[301] *Wilson v Jaymarke Estates Ltd* [2007] BCC 883, HL (Sc).

[302] [1999] 1 WLR 1092, 1104G, 1107C–H. Also *Re Bird Precision Bellows Ltd* [1984] Ch 419, CA.

[303] *Re a Company (No 003843 of 1986)* [1987] BCLC 562; *Re a Company (No 005685 of 1988), ex p Schwarcz* [1989] BCLC 427, 437; *West v Blanchet* [2000] 1 BCLC 795; *Re Belfield Furnishings Ltd* [2006] 2 BCLC 707.

[304] *Re Boswell & Co (Steels) Ltd* (1989) 5 BCC 145; *Virdi v Abbey Leisure Ltd* [1990] BCLC 342, 349, CA; *Re a Company (No 00330 of 1991) ex p Holden* [1991] BCLC 597; *Re Benfield Greig Group plc* [2000] 2 BCLC 488, CA.

[305] *Re Belfield Furnishings Ltd* [2006] 2 BCLC 705 at para 38(1).

[306] Ibid at para 38(2). See also *Re a Company (No 007623 of 1984)* [1986] BCLC 362; *Re a Company No 004377 of 1986)* [1987] 1 WLR 102; *Re a Company (No 003096 of 1987)* (1988) 4 BCC 80; *Re a Company (No 006834 of 1988), ex p Kremer* [1989] BCLC 365; *Re Castleburn Ltd* [1991] BCLC 89. Indeed in *Holt v Faulks* [2000] 2 BCLC 816 the minority shareholder was bound

to this, which would justify pursuing a Part 30 petition are where (a) there has been misapplication of company assets which might affect the value of the shares, unless it is agreed that the value of the misapplied assets is restored for the purposes of valuation, or (b) there is an issue as to the independence of the valuer.[307]

### (5) Unfair prejudice to interests of members

**21.142**  The conduct complained of must be both prejudicial to the interests of the member and unfairly so.[308] The unfairness of the conduct has been considered in Section (4) above. Lawful conduct in relation to the management of the company, which is subjected to equitable considerations and may found an unfair prejudice petition, is unlikely to have caused loss to the company. Similarly, where the petition relies on breach of the articles, breach of a shareholders' agreement, or breach of duty, it is not necessary to show loss to the company (although many of the breaches of duty discussed in paragraphs 21.117–21.131 will have caused loss to the company which thereby causes prejudice to shareholders' interests). This is because the wrongful conduct may cause the petitioner to have a justifiable loss of confidence in management.[309]

**21.143**  The court does not take a narrow or technical approach to the interests of which account is taken.[310] With large companies it may be easy to distinguish a person's interest as a shareholder from his interest as an executive director under a service contract. With smaller companies it may not be appropriate to separate a member's expectation of participation in management from his shareholding.[311] In *R & H Electric Ltd v Haden Bill Electrical Ltd*[312] Robert Walker J took into account a member's legitimate expectation of participation in management in a company so long as loans made to that company by another company with which he was

to sell his shares in accordance with the articles, since their terms applied expressly to a shareholder who had been wrongfully dismissed. In relation to his ability to petition under Part 30, such a shareholder would seem to be in the position described in the last sentence of paragraph 21.91.

[307] *Re Benfield Greig Group plc* [2000] 2 BCLC 488, CA; *Re Belfield Furnishings Ltd* [2006] 2 BCLC 705 at para 38(3).

[308] *Re Saul D Harrison & Sons Plc* [1995] 1 BCLC 14, 31, CA, per Neill LJ.

[309] *Re Baumler (UK) Ltd* [2005] 1 BCLC 92 at paras 180 and 181, per Mr George Bompas QC. See also *Loch v John Blackwood Ltd* [1924] AC 783, 788, PC, a winding-up case, where Lord Shaw said that 'whenever the lack of confidence is rested on lack of probity in the conduct of the company's affairs, then the former is justified by the latter and it is, under the statute, just and equitable that the company be wound up'.

[310] *O'Neill v Phillips* [1999] 1 WLR 1092, 1105G, HL, per Lord Hoffmann.

[311] *Re a Company (No 00477 of 1986)* [1986] BCLC 376, 379; *Re a Company (No 00314 of 1989), ex p Estate and Acquisition and Development Ltd* [1991] BCLC 154, 160; *Re Phoenix Office Supplies Ltd* [2003] 1 BCLC 76, CA at para 23, per Auld LJ.

[312] [1995] 2 BCLC 280, 292–4, where Robert Walker J said that he would order the purchase of the petitioner's shares at a fair price without discount and that the loans should be repaid as soon as reasonably possible. Robert Walker J's broad approach to a member's interests was endorsed by Lord Hoffmann in *O'Neill v Phillips* [1999] 1 WLR 1092, 1105G, HL.

connected remained unpaid. In *Gamlestaden Fastigher AB v Baltic Partners Ltd*[313]
Lord Scott, giving the judgment of the Privy Council in a case concerning the
Jersey equivalent of Part 30, followed the approach in *R & H Electric Ltd* and held
that a shareholder who was also a loan creditor could obtain relief which, because
of the company's insolvency, could only benefit it as loan creditor and not as shareholder. Such relief would amount to 'a real financial benefit' for the petitioner.[314]

Sometimes it is material to distinguish other interests, because Part 30 is not to be   **21.144**
used as a means of enforcing rights which are distinct from the member's shares,
such as enforcing a member's consultancy agreement against the company,[315] or
obtaining possession of property let by the member to the company.[316]

## (6) Remedies

A petitioner will usually succeed in obtaining relief if he shows that 'the value of   **21.145**
his shareholding in the company has been seriously diminished or at least seriously jeopardised by reason of a course of conduct on the part of those persons
who have had de facto control of the company, which has been unfair to him'.[317]
But those are not the only reasons why the court may consider it just to grant
relief. Relief may be granted provided the applicant is a member and the court is
satisfied that the affairs of the company have been conducted in a manner unfairly
prejudicial to his interests.[318] Even if the petition is well founded, the petitioner's
conduct may affect the relief given to him (paragraph 21.107 above).

### The general power

Most unfair prejudice petitions concern closely held private companies. If suc-   **21.146**
cessful the court invariably makes an order for the purchase of the petitioner's
shares, exercising its power under s 996(2)(e), but the power of the court to grant
relief is not limited. Subsection 996(1) provides:

> If the court is satisfied that a petition under this Part is well founded, it may make
> such order as it thinks fit for giving relief in respect of the matters complained of.

In *Re a Company (No 005287 of 1985)*[319] Hoffmann J said of similar words in
the predecessor of subs 996(1): 'Those words appear to give the widest possible

---

[313] [2007] 4 All ER 164, PC.
[314] *Gamlestaden Fastigher AB v Baltic Partners Ltd* [2007] 4 All ER 164, PC at para 36.
[315] *Re a Company (No 003843 of 1986)* [1987] BCLC 562, 572, 573; *Re a Company (No 005685 of 1988), ex p Schwarcz* [1989] BCLC 424, 442.
[316] *Re JE Cade & Son Ltd* [1992] BCLC 213, 228, 229.
[317] *Re Bovey Hotels Ltd* (31 July 1981, unreported), per Slade J; adopted and applied by Nourse J in *Re RA Noble & Sons (Clothing) Ltd* [1983] BCLC 273; by Warner J in *Re Elgindata Ltd* [1991] BCLC 959, 984; and by Hart J in *Re Regional Airports Ltd* [1999] 2 BCLC 30, 79.
[318] *Gamlestaden Fastigher AB v Baltic Partners Ltd* [2007] 4 All ER 164, PC at para 24.
[319] [1986] 1 WLR 281, 283; *Re Little Olympian Each-Ways Ltd* [1994] 2 BCLC 420, 423, 424.

discretion.' Similarly in *Re Bird Precision Bellows Ltd*[320] Oliver LJ said of the same section that it confers on the court 'a very wide discretion to do what is considered fair and equitable in all the circumstances of the case, in order to put right and cure for the future the unfair prejudice which the petitioner has suffered at the hands of the other shareholders of the company'. The court's powers of granting relief are not limited to the particular heads of relief identified in subs 996(2). Nor need the relief be directed solely towards remedying the particular things that have happened.[321]

**21.147** Thus where the conduct complained of is misappropriation of company property or other conduct causing it loss, the court has recognized that on an unfair prejudice petition it may order a party before it to make a payment to the company.[322] This short-circuits a derivative claim, as mentioned in subs 996(2)(c). However, in *Re Chime Corporation Ltd*[323] Lord Scott of Foscote NPJ said that such a claim should not be included in an unfair prejudice petition, as distinct from a derivative claim, unless it is clear at the pleading stage that the claim can be dealt with conveniently in the petition, so that, if the claim is upheld, the company receives the amount, if any, to which it is entitled and the person liable receives a good discharge as against the company.

**21.148** In *Atlasview Ltd v Brightview Ltd*[324] the deputy judge considered that the provision now in s 996(1) would enable the court to order the person liable to the company to make a payment direct to the petitioner. In *Re Chime Corporation Ltd*[325] Lord Scott of Foscote NPJ pointed out that this could only be done in a winding up or by a distribution duly made, in each case having regard to creditors' interests.

*Regulation of the affairs of the company*

**21.149** Subsections 996(2)(a)(b) and (d) (quoted in paragraph 21.96 above) give the court wide powers to regulate the affairs of the company and put right the matters

---

[320] [1986] Ch 658, 669, CA.

[321] *Re Hailey Group Ltd* [1993] BCLC 459, 472.

[322] *Lowe v Fahey* [1996] 1 BCLC 262; *Anderson v Fahey* [2002] BCC 923; *Clark v Cutland* [2003] 2 BCLC 393; *Atlas Ltd v Brightview Ltd* [2004] 2 BCLC 191 at paras 56 and 63; *Re Chime Corporation Ltd* [2004] HKFCA 73 at para 49, per Lord Scott of Foscote NPJ; *Gamlestaden Fastigher AB v Baltic Partners Ltd* [2007] 4 All ER 164, PC at para 28; *Rahman v Malik* [2008] 2 BCLC 403, 426–427 (reconciliation of funds diverted to respondent's company, as well as payment to petitioner of his proper share of profits and of dividends and buy-out order).

[323] [2004] HKFCA 73 at para 62.

[324] [2004] 2 BCLC 191 at para 63.

[325] [2004] HKFCA 73 at para 46. In *Richardson v Blackmore* [2006] BCC 276 the Court of Appeal set aside an order under which £60,000 of company money was to be applied towards payment for the petitioner's shares as being unlawful financial assistance.

complained of. In a case under the 1948 Act, s 210, *Re HR Harmer Ltd*,[326] the court ordered the principal respondent not to interfere in the affairs of the company otherwise than in accordance with valid decisions of the board. The power has been used to prevent the issue and allotment of shares and the company disposing of property pending a meeting.[327]

These powers have been little used, however, because a buy-out order is usually **21.150** the most satisfactory means of disposing of a successful unfair prejudice petition. In *Grace v Biagioli*[328] the directors had breached their duties by withholding a dividend from the petitioner and paying themselves management fees. The Court of Appeal took the view that relations between the parties had broken down to such an extent that making good the default by paying the petitioner the dividends he should have been paid was not sufficient and that the respondents should be ordered to buy the petitioner's shares.

In *Hawkes v Cuddy (No 2)*,[329] which was a deadlock case concerning a company **21.151** which operated a rugby club, Lewison J considered that an order that one member should sell his shares to the other was disproportionate to the unfair prejudice that had been established; instead the court would make an order regulating the affairs of the company in a way that gave the other member a more effective role in the company's affairs.

*Derivative claim*

The power under subs 996(2)(c) to 'authorise civil proceedings to be brought in **21.152** the name and on behalf of the company by such person or persons and on such terms as the court may direct' has also been little used.[330] Where the petitioner's purpose is to obtain relief for the benefit of the company and the intended defendant to the derivative claim is a respondent to the Part 30 petition, the court, if satisfied that the petition is well founded, may make an immediate order in favour of the company, so avoiding the cost and delay of a derivative claim (see paragraph 21.147 above).

*Buy-out orders*

The usual order made on a successful unfair prejudice petition is an order that the **21.153** respondent(s) buy the petitioner's shares at a fair price. The respondent ordered to buy the shares need not have been involved in the conduct complained of.[331] Exceptionally the court may order the respondent to sell his shares to the

---

[326] [1959] 1 WLR 62, CA.
[327] *Malaga Investments Ltd, Petitioners* (1987) 3 BCC 569.
[328] [2006] 2 BCLC 70, CA.
[329] [2008] BCC 390.
[330] See paragraph 21.22 above.
[331] *Re Little Olympian Each-Ways Ltd (No 3)* [1995] 1 BCLC 636, 666.

petitioner.[332] A buy-out order must be proportionate to the matters complained of and it will be refused where such an order would be disproportionate.[333] The court may also refuse to make an order for the purchase of the petitioner's shares (taking a value at an early date) after the company has become insolvent for reasons unconnected with the conduct complained of, since to do so would amount to imposing a fine on the respondent and would be unjust.[334]

**21.154** Usually the fair price will represent a pro rata share of the total value of the company, without any discount on account of minority holding.[335] In quasi-partnership cases, a valuation on a non-discounted basis is well established.[336] In *CVC/ Opportunity Equity Partners Ltd v Almeida*[337] Lord Millett explained that the reason for this rule derived from the law of partnership under which the value of the outgoing partner's interest was 'based on a notional sale of the business as a whole to an outside purchaser' and that in the case of a quasi-partnership company:

> the majority can exclude the minority only if they offer to pay them a fair price for their shares. In order to be free to manage the company's business without regard to the relationship of trust and confidence which formerly existed between them, they must buy the whole, part from themselves and part from the minority, thereby achieving the same freedom to manage the business as an outside purchaser would enjoy.

**21.155** These considerations do not apply where the company is not a quasi-partnership. Then a fair price may include a discount on account of a minority interest. Indeed Arden LJ has said: 'It is difficult to conceive of circumstances in which a non-discounted basis of valuation would be appropriate where there was unfair prejudice for the purposes of the 1985 Act but such a relationship [of quasi-partnership] did not exist.'[338] In *Irvine v Irvine (No 2)*[339] Blackburne J summarized the position:

> A minority shareholding, even one where the extent of the minority is as slight as in this case, is to be valued for what it is, a minority shareholding, unless there is some

---

[332] *Re a Company (No 00789 of 1987), ex p Shooter* [1990] BCLC 384, 394, 395; *Re a Company (No 00789 of 1987), ex p Shooter (No 2)* [1991] BCLC 267; *Re Brenfield Squash Racquets Club Ltd* [1996] 2 BCLC 184, 190.

[333] *Re Full Cup International Trading Ltd* [1995] BCC 683; on appeal *Antoniades v Wong* [1997] 2 BCLC 419, CA (no order made in a case where a winding-up order would have been the appropriate remedy, but was not sought); *Re Metropolis Motorcycles Ltd* [2007] 1 BCLC 520 (no order made); *Hawkes v Cuddy (No 2)* [2008] BCC 390 (see paragraph 21.151 above).

[334] *Re Hailey Group Ltd* [1993] BCLC 459.

[335] *O'Neill v Phillips* [1999] 1 WLR 1092, 1107C–1108B, HL. If necessary the price may be fixed by an expert.

[336] *Re Bird Precision Bellows Ltd* [1984] Ch 419, 431 (affirmed [1986] Ch 658, CA); *Strahan v Wilcock* [2006] 2 BCLC 555, CA at para 55; *Rahman v Malik* [2008] 2 BCLC 403, 426.

[337] [2002] 2 BCLC 108, PC at paras 41, 42.

[338] *Strahan v Wilcock* [2006] 2 BCLC 555, CA at para 17.

[339] [2007] 1 BCLC 445 at para 11. See also *Re McCarthy Surfacing Ltd* [2008] EWHC 2279 (Ch).

good reason to attribute to it a pro rata share of the overall value of the company. Short of a quasi-partnership or some other exceptional circumstance, there is no good reason to accord to it a quality it lacks.

The overriding requirement is that the valuation should be fair on the facts of the **21.156** case. The date of valuation may be an important factor and two considerations affect its selection.[340] One consideration is that the shares should be valued at a date as close as possible to the date of sale; ie the date on which the shares are ordered to be purchased.[341] The other consideration favours the date of the petition as being the date when the petitioner elected to treat the unfair conduct as destroying the basis on which he agreed to continue as a shareholder.[342] If an early date is chosen the court has power under s 996 to include a sum equivalent to interest.[343] In *Profinance Trust SA v Gladstone*[344] Robert Walker LJ concluded that the starting point was that the valuation date should be the date of the order to purchase, but that in the interests of fairness to one side or the other a different date might be selected. He illustrated the circumstances where that might be appropriate.

(i) Where a company has been deprived of its business, an early valuation date (and compensating adjustments) may be required in fairness to the claimant.[345]

(ii) Where a company has been reconstructed or its business has changed significantly, so that there is a new economic identity, an early valuation date may be required in fairness to one or both parties.[346] But an improper alteration in the issued share capital, unaccompanied by any change in the business, will not necessarily have that outcome.[347]

(iii) Where a minority shareholder has a petition on foot and there is a general fall in the market, the court may in fairness to the claimant have the shares valued at an early date, especially if it strongly disapproves of the majority shareholder's prejudicial conduct.[348]

---

[340] *Profinance Trust SA v Gladstone* [2002] 1 WLR 1024, CA at paras 33–45, per Robert Walker LJ.

[341] *Re London School of Electronics Ltd* [1986] Ch 211, 224; *Re a Company (No 005134 of 1986)* [1989] BCLC 383, 399; *Re Elgindata Ltd* [1991] BCLC 959; *Re Regional Airports Ltd* [1999] 2 BCLC 30, 83.

[342] *Re a Company (No 002612 of 1984)* (1986) 2 BCC 99, 453, 99,492–99,493; on appeal as *Re Cumana Ltd* [1986] BCLC 430, 436, 445, CA; *Re OC (Transport) Services* [1984] BCLC 251, 258.

[343] *Profinance Trust SA v Gladstone* [2002] 1 WLR 1024, CA at paras 31 and 32, where Robert Walker LJ said that the power to include interest was to be exercised sparingly and that a petitioner had to plead the claim and support it with evidence to persuade the court that including interest produced a fair result.

[344] [2002] 1 WLR 1024, CA at paras 60 and 61.

[345] *Scottish Co-operative Wholesale Society Ltd v Meyer* [1959] AC 324, HL (Sc).

[346] *Re OC (Transport) Services* [1984] BCLC 251; *Re London School of Electronics Ltd* [1986] Ch 211.

[347] *Re a Company (No 005134 of 1986)* [1989] BCLC 383.

[348] *Re Cumana Ltd* [1986] BCLC 430, CA.

(iv) But a claimant is not entitled to what the deputy judge called a one way bet, and the court will not direct an early valuation date simply to give the claimant the most advantageous exit from the company, especially where severe prejudice has not been made out.[349]

(v) All these points may be heavily influenced by the parties' conduct in making and accepting or rejecting offers either before or during the course of the proceedings.[350]

**21.157** Valuing the shares in a private company as a going concern on the open market is not a straightforward task, since there is no known applicable price/earnings ratio to be applied to the company's maintainable profits.[351] The valuation may add back losses caused by the unfairly prejudicial conduct[352] where the facts are clear.[353] Where the unfairly prejudicial conduct included failure to consider paying dividends, the value may compensate the petitioner for having lost the chance to receive pro rata dividends.[354] Where the issue is not clear, the issue should be determined by the court, not the valuer.[355] It is possible that difficulties in the way of valuing the shares mean that a fair price is not ascertainable; in such a case no order for purchase will be made and a winding-up order may be the only appropriate relief.[356]

*Interim orders*

**21.158** The court does not have power to make an interim order in exercise of its jurisdiction under Part 30, s 996 until it is satisfied that the petition is well founded.[357] Once an order for the purchase of shares has been made, the court can order an interim payment on account.[358]

---

[349] *Re Elgindata Ltd* [1991] BCLC 959.

[350] *O'Neill v Phillips* [1999] 1 WLR 1092, HL.

[351] *Re Planet Organic Ltd* [2000] 1 BCLC 366; *Parkinson v Eurofinance Group Ltd* [2001] 1 BLC 720.

[352] *Lloyd v Casey* [2002] 1 BCLC 454; *Wilson v Jaymarke Estates Ltd* [2007] BCC 883, HL (Sc) (where improper management charges were added back).

[353] *Macro v Thompson (No 3)* [1997] 2 BCLC 36, 72.

[354] *Re McCarthy Surfacing Ltd* [2008] EWHC 2279 (Ch) at paras 100, 101.

[355] *North Holdings Ltd v Southern Tropics Ltd* [1999] 2 BCLC 625, 637, CA.

[356] *Re Full Cup International Trading Ltd* [1995] BCC 683; on appeal *Antoniades v Wong* [1997] 2 BCLC 419, 427, CA.

[357] *Re a Company (No 004175 of 1986)* [1987] 1 WLR 585 (where Scott J noted that what is now the Insolvency Act, s 125(1) gives the court power to make an interim order on hearing a winding-up petition). Harman J followed this decision in *Re a Company (No 004502 of 1988), ex p Johnson* [1992] BCLC 701, 706, 707, when refusing to make an interim order that the respondent shareholders restore to the company its money, which had been wrongly used by them in responding to the unfair prejudice petition. *Malaga Investments Ltd, Petitioners* (1987) 3 BCC 569 appears to be a case where the injunction was granted on the footing that the petition was well founded.

[358] *Re Clearsprings (Management) Ltd* [2003] EWHC (Ch) 2516 at paras 43–45 (recording that the court's power to make such an order was common ground).

In a petition under Part 30, the court may grant an interim injunction in exercise of its general jurisdiction under the Supreme Court Act 1981, s 37.[359] The court's normal consideration of the balance of convenience[360] has to be modified to a consideration of the appropriateness of the interim relief sought in the context of relief sought under s 996.[361] Since in general the petitioner will be compensated in the price he receives for his shares, it is seldom necessary for the court to grant injunctions imposing controls on the management of the company.[362]

**21.159**

Under the same jurisdiction (the Supreme Court Act, s 37) the court may appoint a receiver in a quasi-partnership case where it is not clear which party will be ordered to buy out the other and there is evidence of mismanagement by the respondents.[363] In most cases it is clear who will be bought out if the petition succeeds and there is no need for an order interfering with management by the party who will retain control of the company.

**21.160**

There are difficulties in the way of making freezing orders in Part 30 petitions before the court has been satisfied that the petition is well founded and made an order to which a freezing order would be appropriate ancillary relief. The general principle is that a freezing order can only be made in support of an existing cause of action.[364] In *Re Premier Electronics (GB) Ltd*[365] Pumfrey J applied this principle when refusing to make a freezing order against the respondents in support of relief in an unfair prejudice petition, which alleged that the respondents as directors of the company had conducted its affairs in an unfairly prejudicial manner by misappropriating £250,000 of the company's money. In the meantime the company

**21.161**

---

[359] In *Re Milgate Developments Ltd* [1993] BCLC 291 (decided in 1990) the court granted an interim injunction restraining the respondent shareholders from causing or procuring the companies to be represented on petitions for relief from unfair prejudice or a winding-up order, except for any applications under the Insolvency Act, s 127. In *Re a Company (No 004502 of 1988), ex p Johnson* [1992] BCLC 701, 704, Harman J affirmed that decision. In *Rutherford, Petitioner* [1994] BCC 876 an interim injunction restraining the company from proceeding with a buy-back of its shares was discharged on the balance of convenience. In *Re Ravenhart Service (Holdings) Ltd* [2004] 2 BCLC 376 an interim injunction was granted restraining the company from making payments to directors of fees and remuneration. In *Jones v Jones* [2003] BCC 226 the Court of Appeal granted an interim injunction in an unfair prejudice petition, restraining the company from pursuing a separate action against the petitioner until after the disposal of the unfair prejudice petition.

[360] *American Cyanamid Co v Ethicon Ltd* [1975] AC 396, HL.

[361] *Re Posgate & Denby (Agencies) Ltd* [1987] BCLC 8.

[362] Ibid; *Trident European Fund v Coats Holdings Ltd* [2003] EWHC 2471 (Ch); *Pringle v Callard* [2008] 2 BCLC 505.

[363] *Re a Company (No 00596 of 1986)* [1987] BCLC 133; *Wilton-Davies v Kirk* [1998] 1 BCLC 274.

[364] *Veracruz Transportation Inc v VC Shipping Inc* [1992] 1 Lloyd's Rep 353, CA; *Zucker v Tyndall Holdings plc* [1992] 1 WLR 1127, CA. But note the dissenting speech of Lord Nicholls in *Mercedes Benz AG v Leiduck* [1996] AC 284, 310–12, PC under the heading 'Causes of action and prospective rights'. The principle has been eroded by the Civil Jurisdiction and Judgments Act 1982, s 25 and the Civil Jurisdiction and Judgments Act 1982 (Interim Relief) Order 1997.

[365] [2002] 2 BCLC 634, 638.

had gone into administration. It is not clear from the report what relief was sought in the petition. If it was an order that the respondents buy the petitioner's shares, the judge was right to disregard it as a basis for a freezing order, since the respondents would have no liability to the petitioner until the order was made (and then only if there was a real risk that the respondents would deal with their assets so as to avoid paying the petitioner). It seems, however, that the petitioner sought to justify the freezing order by reference to the respondents' liabilities to the company, but, as the judge observed, they had not brought, or obtained leave to bring, a derivative claim in the name of the company under what is now s 996(2)(c).[366] If the relief sought in the petition had been payment by the respondents to the company (see paragraph 21.147 above) a freezing order might have been supportable as a matter of jurisdiction.

### (7) Procedure

**21.162**    As mentioned in paragraph 21.98 above, the Unfair Prejudice Application Rules govern the procedure for Part 30 Petitions.[367] Paragraph 3 of these rules provides for the petition to 'specify the grounds on which it is presented and the nature of the relief which is sought by the petitioner' and for the petition to be filed at court, which fixes a return day. The petitioner should not include a petition for winding up as an alternative to relief under s 996 unless the petitioner prefers winding up or considers it to be the only relief to which he is entitled.[368] By paragraph 4 the petition is to be served on the company and every respondent named in the petition. On the return day, by paragraph 5, the court gives directions for the conduct of the petition, including any directions required for pleadings and evidence.[369] A common response to service of an unfair prejudice petition is an application to strike it out, either on the ground that it is unsustainable (and many of the issues

---

[366] This is consistent with the view expressed by Harman J in *Re a Company (No 004502 of 1988), ex p Johnson* [1992] BCLC 701, 707. In any event it is improbable that they would be able to bring such claims after the company had gone into administration; see paragraph 21.72 above.

[367] A claim under Part 30 brought otherwise than by petition (eg by claim form) will be struck out: *Re Osea Road Camp Sites Ltd* [2005] 1 WLR 760.

[368] *Practice Direction—Order under Section 127 Insolvency Act 1986* (supplementing CPR Part 49), para 1 (*Civil Procedure* (Vol 2, 2008) at para 2G-47; [1999] BCC 741).

[369] As to pleadings, see *Re Unisoft Group Ltd* [1994] 1 BCLC 609. As to disclosure, see *Arrow Trading & Investments Est 1920 v Edwardian Group Ltd* [2005] 1 BCLC 696, referring at para 24 to the general rule that a shareholder is entitled to disclosure of all documents obtained by the company in the course of its administration, including advice by solicitors to the company about its affairs. But not where the advice relates to hostile proceedings between the company and its shareholders: *Re Hydrosan Ltd* [1991] BCLC 418; *CAS (Nominees) Ltd v Nottingham Forest plc* [2002] 1 BCLC 613. As to disclosure of connected company documents, see *Re Technion Investments Ltd* [1985] BCLC 434, CA.

discussed in sections (4) and (5) have arisen on strike out applications) or on the ground that a fair offer has been made (paragraph 21.140 above). Paragraph 6 deals with the drawing up of any order made on the petition.

One matter affecting the directors is what role, if any, the company should play in the proceedings. In the normal case where the petitioner is seeking relief against the respondent shareholders, so that as a matter of substance the dispute is between shareholders, it is well established that the company should not be involved or incur costs in relation to the proceedings and that the directors would be in breach of their duties if they applied company money for such a purpose.[370] There are exceptions to this rule where the petition involves the company in giving disclosure of documents or where the relief sought involves the company (eg in being ordered to buy the petitioner's shares).[371] Also, where the relief sought in the petition is for the direct benefit of the company (paragraph 21.147 above) or is for an order under s 996(2)(c) the legitimate participation of the company and the burden in costs on it may be greater.[372]    **21.163**

While the petitioner must be a member of the company (paragraph 21.91 above), there is flexibility as to the joinder of respondents. That is inherent in the broad language of Part 30.[373] In deciding who are proper respondents, the court considers both the allegations of unfairly prejudicial conduct and who may be affected by the relief sought.[374] A former member may be joined as a respondent,[375] but only if relief may properly be claimed against him.[376] On the other hand the petitioner is not obliged to join as respondents all the other shareholders or all persons whose conduct is criticized.[377]    **21.164**

---

[370] *Re Kenyon Swansea Ltd* [1987] BCLC 514, 521; *Re Crossmore Electrical and Civil Engineering Ltd* [1989] BCLC 137; *Re a Company (No 005685 of 1988), ex p Schwarcz* [1989] BCLC 424 (a case on the Insolvency Act, s 127, where the petitioner sought relief for unfair prejudice and a winding-up order in the alternative); *Re Hydrosan Ltd* [1991] BCLC 418, 420; *Re a Company (No 004502 of 1988), ex p Johnson* [1992] BCLC 701; *Re Milgate Developments Ltd* [1993] BCLC 291.

[371] *Re a Company (No 004502 of 1988), ex p Johnson* [1992] BCLC 701, 703; *Re a Company (No 1126 of 1992)* [1994] 2 BCLC 146. As to disclosure of documents in an unfair prejudice petition, see *Re Technion Investments Ltd* [1985] BCLC 434, CA.

[372] *Re Chime Corporation Ltd* [2004] HKFCA 73 at paras 53–55, per Lord Scott of Foscote NPJ.

[373] *Re Little Olympian Each-Ways Ltd* [1994] 2 BCLC 420, 429.

[374] *Re BSB Holdings Ltd* [1993] BCLC 246 (where a party was properly joined since it had been involved in the transactions complained of and would be affected by the relief sought).

[375] *Re a Company (No 005287 of 1985)* [1986] 1 WLR 281.

[376] *Re Baltic Real Estate Ltd (No 1)* [1993] BCLC 498 (petition of majority shareholder sought purchase of the minority's shares; former shareholders wrongly joined). As to service out of the jurisdiction; see *Re Baltic Real Estate Ltd (No 2)* [1993] BCLC 503.

[377] *Re Ravenhart Service (Holdings) Ltd* [2004] 2 BCLC 376 at para 103.

# F. Just and Equitable Winding Up

**21.165**  By the Insolvency Act, s 122(1)(g) a company[378] may be wound up by the court[379] if 'the court is of the opinion that it is just and equitable that the company should be wound up'.[380] A member or members (referred to as a contributory[381]) may petition the court for the company to be wound up[382] on this ground provided that he satisfies a statutory condition and a common law condition. The company's articles cannot restrict the ability of a member to petition.[383]

*Standing to petition*

**21.166**  The statutory condition, contained in subs 124(2), prevents a member from presenting a winding-up petition unless either (a) the number of members is reduced below two,[384] or (b) the shares in respect of which he is a contributory, or some of them, either were originally allotted to him, or have been held by him, and registered in his name, for at least six months during the 18 months before the commencement of the winding up,[385] or have devolved on him through the death of a former holder. For the requirement that the member is a registered shareholder, reference should be made to paragraph 21.91 above.

**21.167**  The common law condition is that the member must have a legitimate interest in obtaining a winding-up order.[386] For this purpose he must satisfy the court that there is a real prospect of a surplus being available for distribution to members.[387] The court will however allow a member to proceed where he complains that accounts or information to which he is entitled have not been provided, so that he

---

[378]  For the jurisdiction of the English court to wind up a solvent foreign company on the application of a member, reference should be made to the discussion in *Dicey & Morris, The Conflict of Laws* (14th edn) at rule 163.

[379]  By the Insolvency Act, s 117 the High Court has jurisdiction to wind up any company registered in England and Wales and the county court has concurrent jurisdiction where the company's paid up share capital does not exceed £120,000 (subject to increase under subs 117(3)) and its registered office is situated in the district of the county court.

[380]  The other grounds for petitioning for a winding-up order specified in s 124(1) that might be of relevance to a member are in fact almost never invoked and are not discussed in this chapter.

[381]  Defined by the Insolvency Act, s 79(1) as 'every person liable to contribute to the assets of a company in the event of it being wound up', but does include the holder of fully paid shares: *Re National Savings Bank Association* (1866) 1 Ch App 547.

[382]  Insolvency Act, s 124(1).

[383]  *Re Peveril Gold Mines Ltd* [1898] 1 Ch 122.

[384]  This does not apply where the company has always had only one member: *Re Pimlico Capital Ltd* [2002] 2 BCLC 544. This condition reflects s 122(1)(e).

[385]  In *Re Gattopardo Ltd* [1969] 1 WLR 619 a premature petition was struck out.

[386]  *Deloitte & Touche AG v Johnson* [1999] 1 WLR 1605, PC.

[387]  *Re Rica Gold Washing Co* (1879) 11 Ch D 36, CA; *Re WR Willcocks* [1974] Ch 163; *Re Chesterfield Catering Co Ltd* [1977] Ch 373; *Re Martin Coulter Enterprises Ltd* [1988] BCLC 12, 18.

does not know whether or not the company is solvent.[388] Outside quasi-partnership cases, this relaxation of the rule is limited by the fact that members do not have a general right to information from a company or to access to its documents.

### The just and equitable ground

As noted in paragraph 21.162 above a member should not petition for winding **21.168** up unless he prefers winding up to the relief that may be granted under the Companies Act, Part 30 or he considers it to be the only relief to which he is entitled. The reasons why members' winding-up petitions are discouraged are that (a) they put the company to the cost of applying for relief under the Insolvency Act, s 127, and (b) the court is limited to imposing a 'death sentence' on the company, whereas under Part 30 'the appropriate remedy [can be] applied during the course of the continuing life of the company'.[389]

The jurisdiction to wind up a company on the just and equitable ground is no **21.169** wider than the jurisdiction under Part 30. If the matters relied on as constituting unfairly prejudicial conduct are insufficient to obtain relief under Part 30, they will not be sufficient to justify a winding-up order.[390] This reflects the fact that the principles stated by Lord Wilberforce in *Ebrahimi v Westbourne Galleries Ltd*[391] (quoted in paragraph 21.132 above) in relation to a member's petition for winding up on the just and equitable ground apply equally to Part 30 petitions in cases of quasi-partnership. It also reflects the fact that where the petition is grounded on breaches of duty by the directors, the breaches must be sufficient to cause the member who petitions to have lost confidence in management. In *Loch v John Blackwood Ltd*[392] Lord Shaw said that 'whenever the lack of confidence is rested on lack of probity in the conduct of the company's affairs, then the former is justified by the latter and it is, under the statute, just and equitable that the company be wound up'. Since the remedies available under Part 30, including an order that one member purchases the shares of another, are more flexible and responsive to the needs of the parties, a petition under Part 30 alone is the invariable practice. The court has no hesitation in striking out an unnecessary claim for a winding-up order.[393]

---

[388] *Re Newman and Howard Ltd* [1962] Ch 257; *Re Chesterfield Catering Co Ltd* [1977] Ch 373; *Re Commercial and Industrial Insulation Ltd* [1986] BCLC 191; *Re Wessex Computer Stationers Ltd* [1992] BCLC 366; *Re a Company (No 007936 of 1994)* [1995] BCC 705, 713.

[389] *Re a Company (No 00314 of 1989), ex p Estates Acquisition and Development Ltd* [1991] BCLC 154, 161.

[390] *Re Guidezone Ltd* [2000] 2 BCLC 321 at para 179.

[391] [1973] AC 360, 379, HL.

[392] [1924] AC 783, 788, PC.

[393] *Re a Company (No 004415 of 1996)* [1997] 1 BCLC 479.

**21.170** The court is therefore only likely to make a winding-up order in preference to an order under Part 30 where the circumstances of the company are such that none of the parties wants to carry on the business of the company and buy out another party and it is not fair for the court to make an order that one party buys out another.[394]

*Alternative remedy*

**21.171** The Insolvency Act, s 125(2) restricts the power of the court to make a winding-up order on a member's petition on the just and equitable ground. It provides:

> If the petition is presented by members of the company as contributories on the ground that it is just and equitable that the company should be wound up, the court, if it is of the opinion—
> (a) that the petitioners are entitled to relief either by winding up the company or by some other means, and
> (b) that in the absence of any other remedy it would be just and equitable that the company should be wound up,
> shall make a winding-up order; but this does not apply if the court is also of the opinion both that some other remedy is available to the petitioners and that they are acting unreasonably in seeking to have the company wound up instead of pursuing that other remedy.

**21.172** The approach of the court under this provision is much the same as its approach to fair offers in the context of Part 30 petitions (as to which see the principles stated by Lord Hoffmann in *O'Neill v Phillips* summarized in paragraph 21.100(10) and (11) and their application as discussed in paragraphs 21.140 and 21.141 above).[395]

*Procedure*

**21.173** The procedure for presentation of a winding-up petition by a contributory is dealt with under rules 4.22–4.24 of the Insolvency Rules 1986. They are broadly the same as those applicable to Part 30 petitions discussed in paragraph 21.162 above.

**21.174** Unlike the position in relation to Part 30 petitions, the court has jurisdiction under the Insolvency Act, s 125(1) to make an interim order.

---

[394] Recent cases where the court has made a winding-up order rather than making an order giving relief from unfair prejudice are: *Re Perfectaire Holdings Ltd* [1990] BCLC 423; *Re Worldhams Park Golf Course Ltd* [1998] 1 BCLC 554. Also see *Re Full Cup International Trading Ltd* [1995] BCC 683; on appeal *Antoniades v Wong* [1997] 2 BCLC 419, CA, where the court regarded winding up as the appropriate remedy and refused to give relief for unfair prejudice.

[395] Cases on the exercise of this power not mentioned in the footnotes to paragraphs 21.140 and 21.141 are: *Re a Company (No 002567 of 1982)* [1983] 1 WLR 927; *Re Copeland & Craddock Ltd* [1997] BCC 294, CA; *Re a Company (No 004415 of 1996)* [1997] 1 BCLC 479; *Fuller v Cyracuse Ltd* [2001] 1 BCLC 187; *CVC/Opportunity Equity Partners Ltd v Demarco Almeida* [2002] 2 BCLC 108, PC; *Apcar v Aftab* [2003] BCC 510.

# PART IV

## DIRECTORS' PARTICULAR FUNCTIONS AND DUTIES

# 22

# DECISION-MAKING BY MEMBERS

## A. Introduction

This chapter describes the ways in which members make decisions for a company **22.01** and the procedures for obtaining their decisions. The members of the company are the subscribers and any other person who agrees to become a member, by allotment or transfer, and whose name is entered on the register of members.[1]

---

[1] 1985 Act, s 22; 2006 Act, s 112. A person agrees to become a member if he assents; a binding contract is not required: *Re Nuneaton Borough Association Football Club Ltd* [1989] BCLC 454, CA. 1985 Act, s 23 contains provisions prohibiting a subsidiary from being a member of its holding company, which are replaced by provisions in 2006 Act, ss 136–144. These provisions of the 2006 Act come into force on 1 October 2009. 1985 Act, ss 80–116 contain provisions about allotment of shares, pre-emption rights, and payment for shares, which are replaced by 2006 Act, ss 549–609 with a few minor changes on 1 October 2009. 2006 Act, ss 544, 768–790 came into force on 6 April 2008 and contain provisions about share certificates, transfers, including paperless transfers, and warrants.

The company is required to keep a register of members, which the court has power to rectify.[2]

**22.02**   Directors are concerned with decision-making by members, because (a) the Companies Act provides that certain transactions must be authorized or approved by the company, acting by the decision of its members, (b) a company's articles may require other transactions to be authorized or approved by decision of the members, (c) in other cases the directors may wish to have a transaction authorized, approved, or ratified by the company, in order to protect themselves from criticism or liability, (d) members may use the procedures to change or influence the management of the company,[3] (e) the directors have duties and powers in relation to the obtaining and recording of members' decisions, and (f) directors may face criminal liability for certain defaults.

**22.03**   The necessary procedures and requirements by which the directors may obtain the authorization, approval, or ratification of the company are to be found primarily in the Companies Act, Part 13, ss 281–361[4] and the company's articles of association.[5] The Companies Act reflects a structural change in that some provisions that formerly appeared in Table A are now included in the Companies Act.[6] The rule of law by which the company is bound by certain decisions taken by informal unanimous consent of the members of the company is preserved by s 281(4).

**22.04**   The reforms to decision-making by members made by the Companies Act, Part 13, have two broad purposes, both recommended by the CLR: (i) the deregulation

---

[2]   1985 Act, ss 352–362, which are replaced by provisions in 2006 Act, ss 113–135 on 1 October 2009, except that ss 116–119 came into force on 1 October 2007 and ss 121 and 128 on 6 April 2008.

[3]   By 2006 Act, s 518 a resigning auditor also has the right to requisition a general meeting to explain the circumstances of his resignation (Chapter 23, paragraphs 23.143–23.145 below).

[4]   Part 13 came into force on 1 October 2007 (2006 Act Commencement Order No 3, para 2(1)(f)), except for ss 308, 309, and 333, which came into force on 20 January 2007 (2006 Act Commencement Order No 1, para 3(1)(a) and (b)), and subss 327(2)(c) and 330(6)(c), which have not yet come into force. The provisions of Part 13 that came into force on 1 October 2007 did so subject to the transitional adaptations specified Schedule 1 of the 2006 Act Commencement Order No 3, reflecting the fact that certain provisions of the 1985 Act had not yet been replaced by provisions in the 2006 Act. Part 13 replaces 1985 Act, Chapter 4, ss 366–383, which were repealed on 1 October 2007 by 2006 Act Commencement Order No 3, Schedule 2.

[5]   Decision-making by members is dealt with by Model Articles (pcls) 37–47, Model Articles (pclg) 23–33, which are in the same terms, and Model Articles (plc) 28–42. By the Companies Act, s 17, these will be the default articles for companies incorporated after 1 October 2009. Table A, regs 36–63 contain provisions dealing with general meetings. With effect from 1 October 2007 Table A has been amended for companies incorporated on or after that date by the 2007 Tables A to F Amendment Regulations.

[6]   s 284 derives in part from Table A, reg 54; s 302 derives from Table A, reg 37; ss 310 and 311 derive in part from Table A, reg 38; s 313 derives from Table A, reg 39; and s 320 derives in part from Table A, regs 47 and 48.

and simplification of procedures for private companies, and (ii) the improvement of communications with members.[7] The main changes made by the 2006 Act to the law relating to decision-making by members may be summarized as follows.

(1) Private companies no longer have to hold AGMs.[8]

(2) The written resolution procedure is now only available to private companies, but may be used to pass a resolution by a simple resolution rather than unanimously.[9]

(3) The concept of extraordinary resolutions has been abolished and only ordinary and special resolutions remain.[10]

(4) All company meetings may be convened on 14 days' notice, including a meeting to consider a special resolution, but a company's articles may require a longer period of notice and public company AGMs require 21 days' notice.[11] For private companies 90%, rather than 95%, of the members can agree to short notice.[12]

(5) The use of electronic communication and record keeping in relation to meetings has been extended.[13]

(6) There are reforms in relation to corporate representation at meetings and proxies.[14]

(7) In order to improve confidence in the integrity and effectiveness of voting processes and to promote greater transparency, quoted companies are

---

[7] CLR: *Company General Meetings and Shareholder Communications* at paras 24–27, 51, 52; CLR: *Developing the Framework* at paras 4.19–4.64, 7.6–7.15; the CLR: *Final Report* at paras 2.15, 4.3, 6.39, 7.5–7.26; White Paper: *Modernising Company Law* at paras 2.6–2.35; White Paper: *Company Law Reform* at paras 3.1, 4.2.

[8] The provisions about AGMs apply only to public companies; ss 336–340. White Paper: *Company Law Reform* at para 4.2 rejected the CLR's recommendation that public companies should be able to opt out of having to hold AGMs.

[9] Sections 281(1) and (2) and ss 288–300. Under 1985 Act, ss 381A–381C the written resolution procedure could be used by private and public companies but only if all the members agreed to the resolution. The elective resolution procedure has been removed as no longer needed (formerly 1985 Act, ss 80A, 252, 366A, 369(4), 378(3), 379A, and 386). Table A, reg 53 has been deleted in respect of companies registered on or after 1 October 2007 (2007 Tables A to F Amendment Regulations, reg 6).

[10] By 1985 Act, s 378(1) and (2) extraordinary and special resolutions both required a majority of not less than three-fourths of members voting in person or by proxy, but a special resolution also required not less than 21 days' notice, specifying the intention to propose the resolution as a special resolution (rather than the normal 14 days (1985 Act, s 369)). The extraordinary resolution procedure was used in relation to voluntary winding up (Insolvency Act, s 84(1)(c) and Table A, reg 117), and the variation of class rights (1985 Act, s 125). Now the relevant procedures can be effected by a special resolution.

[11] s 307. Note that special notice requires 28 days.

[12] s 307.

[13] ss 296, 308, 309, 314, 333, 338, 1143–1148, and Schedules 4 and 5.

[14] ss 323–331.

required to publish the results of a poll on a website and there are provisions for an independent audit of a poll taken in general meeting.[15]

**22.05** Two other reforms made by the 2006 Act which concern decision-making by members should be mentioned here. First, the 2006 Act, s 22 will enable a company's articles to contain entrenched provisions if they are made in the company's articles on formation or if an amendment to the articles to include them is made with the agreement of all the members of the company.[16] Once a provision has been entrenched it can only be amended by agreement of all the members of the company or by order of a court or other authority having power to alter the company's articles.[17] Secondly, the Companies Act, Part 9, ss 145–153, sets out important new rights for indirect investors, whose shares are held through nominees, to enable them to play a greater role in company proceedings.[18] These apply where the company's articles make provision enabling a member to nominate another person or persons as entitled to enjoy or exercise specified rights of the member in relation to the company, including, in the case of companies whose shares are admitted to trading on a regulated market, specified information rights.

## B. General Provisions about Resolutions

### (1) Means of passing resolutions

**22.06** Section 281[19] identifies or recognizes three means by which a resolution of the members of a company may be passed: (i) as a written resolution, (ii) at a meeting of the members, or (iii) by informal unanimous assent. Subsection 281(1) gives private companies the option of passing a resolution as a written resolution or at a meeting, unless the decision concerns the removal of a director or auditor.[20] The attractions of the written resolution procedure (described in Section C of this chapter) should mean that private companies will seldom need to convene

---

[15] ss 341–351. See the comments of Lord Sainsbury in Hansard HL GC day 6 (60301-28).

[16] This section will come into effect on 1 October 2009. CLR: *Final Report* recommended provisions for entrenchment at [16.68]–[16.70].

[17] subs 22(3).

[18] Part 9, which is new, is discussed in paragraph 17.92 below. It came into force on 1 October 2007; 2006 Act Commencement Order No 3, para 2(1)(c). For discussion of the need for these provisions, see the DTI paper: *Modern Company Law for a Competitive Economy* (March 1998) at [3.7]; CLR: *Developing the Framework* at paras 4.7–4.18; CLR: *Final Report* at paras 7.1–7.4 and 7.13; White Paper: *Company Law Reform* (2005) at para 3.2, and the DTI and Treasury Consultative document: *Private Shareholders: Corporate Governance Rights* (November 2006).

[19] s 281 is a new provision, although subs 281(4) derives from 1985 Act, s 381C(2), which applied only to private companies.

[20] s 288(2).

meetings of members. In contrast subs 281(2) insists that public companies must pass resolutions of members at meetings.[21] These subsections provide:

(1) A resolution of the members (or of a class of members) of a private company must be passed—
   (a) as a written resolution in accordance with Chapter 2, or
   (b) at a meeting of the members (to which the provisions of Chapter 3 apply).
(2) A resolution of the members (or of a class of members) of a public company must be passed at a meeting of the members (to which the provisions of Chapter 3 and, where relevant, Chapter 4 of this Part apply).

Although both subss 281(1) and (2) are expressed in mandatory terms, they are **22.07** subject to the provisions of subs (4) which preserves two established rules of law, by which decisions of members may be effective and binding on the company: (i) the informal unanimous consent or *Duomatic*[22] principle, and (ii) the principle that in certain circumstances a person may be precluded from alleging that a resolution has not been duly passed.[23] Subsection 281(4) provides:

Nothing in this Part affects any enactment or rule of law as to—
   (a) things done otherwise than by passing a resolution,
   (b) circumstances in which a resolution is or is not treated as having been passed, or
   (c) cases in which a person is precluded from alleging that a resolution has not been duly passed.

## (2) Ordinary resolutions

The ordinary resolution is the normal means for making decisions of members of **22.08** a company. A company's articles may provide for certain matters to be decided on by ordinary resolution.[24] The Companies Acts expressly provide for certain matters to be decided on by ordinary resolution[25] and in other cases merely require a

---

[21] This represents a change in the law; see paragraph 22.04(2) above.

[22] *Re Duomatic Ltd* [1969] 2 Ch 365.

[23] See *Re Bailey, Hay & Co Ltd* [1971] 1 WLR 1357, in which the shareholders who abstained from voting did not object to the passing of the resolution.

[24] (i) The issue of different classes of shares (Table A, reg 2, Model Article (pcls) 22 and Model Article (plc) 43); (ii) appointment of directors (Table A, reg 78, Model Article (pcls) 17 and Model Article (plc) 20); (iii) payment of dividends recommended by directors (Table A, reg 102, Model Article (pcls) 31 and Model Article (plc) 72); (iv) authorization of inspection by member of accounting records and other records or documents (Table A, reg 109, Model Article (pcls) 50 and Model Article (plc) 83); (v) capitalization of profits (Table A, reg 110, Model Article (pcls) 36 and Model Article (plc) 78); (vi) amendment of special resolution in cases of obvious error (Model Article (pcls) 47(2) and Model Article (plc) 40(2)).

[25] (i) The removal of a director (2006 Act, s 168(1)); (ii) quoted company: approval of directors' remuneration report (2006 Act, s 439(1)); (iii) appointment and removal of auditors and fixing their remuneration (2006 Act, ss 485(4), 489(4), 492(1), and 510(2)); (iv) public company: approval of the transfer of a non-cash asset as consideration for shares (1985 Act, s 104(4)(c), which will be replaced by 2006 Act, s 601(1)); (v) reconversion by limited company of stock into shares (1985 Act, s 121(4), which will be replaced by 2006 Act, s 620(2)); (vi) terms and manner of redemption of shares in limited company (1985 Act, s 160(3) which will be replaced by 2006 Act,

resolution of a company, without specifying what kind of resolution is required.[26] In those cases, s 281(3) provides that what is required is an ordinary resolution, unless the company's articles require a higher majority or unanimity. The following matters of particular relevance to directors require an ordinary resolution.

(1) A company's articles invariably provide that a director may be appointed by ordinary resolution.[27]

(2) During a director's period of office, certain transactions between him and the company require the approval of an ordinary resolution (as discussed in Chapter 18),[28] and an ordinary resolution is one of the ways in which a company may ratify conduct of a director amounting to negligence, default, breach of duty, or breach of trust, as discussed in Chapter 19, Section D.[29]

(3) By s 168(1) an ordinary resolution is the means for removing a director before the expiration of his period of office, notwithstanding anything in any agreement between the company and him.[30] Special notice of the resolution to remove the director must be given and the written resolution procedure may not be used, since the director has a right to protest against his removal.[31] Although a director cannot rely on any provision in the company's constitution or agreement with the company to override the right of the members to remove him by ordinary resolution, in *Bushell v Faith* the House of Lords held

---

s 685(2)); (vii) the adoption of arrangements under which title to securities is required to be evidenced or transferred (or both) without a written instrument (2006 Act, s 786(1)); (viii) approval of the articles of the new transferee company in case of merger or division (2006 Act, ss 912 and 928). The replacements in (iv)–(vi) will occur on 1 October 2009.

[26] (i) Transactions with directors requiring approval (2006 Act, Part 10, Chapter 4); (ii) ratification of acts of directors (2006 Act, s 239); (iii) power to make provision for employees on cessation or transfer of business (2006 Act, s 247); (iv) authorization of political donations and expenditure (2006 Act, ss 366–368, 377, and 378); (v) omission of name of auditor in published copies of auditor's report (2006 Act, s 506); (vi) authorization of limited liability agreement with auditor (2006 Act, s 536); (vii) sub-division or consolidation of shares (1985 Act, s 121 which will be replaced by 2006 Act, s 618 on 1 October 2009); (viii) authorization for market purchase of a company's own shares (1985 Act, s 166 which will be replaced by 2006 Act, s 701 on 1 October 2009).

[27] 1985 Act, Table A, reg 78; Model Article (pcls) 17(1)(a); Model Article (plc) 20(1)(a).

[28] These transactions are long-term service contracts, substantial property transactions, loans, and quasi-loans to directors or persons connected with them, credit transactions for the benefit of directors or persons connected with them, related arrangements, and payments for loss of office as director (ss 188, 190, 196–198, 200, 201, 203, 214, 217–219, 224, and 225).

[29] s 239. The other ways are unanimous consent of members and an agreement made by the directors of the company not to sue, or to settle or release a claim made by them on behalf of the company (subs 239(6)).

[30] Chapter 7 above.

[31] subs 168(2), s 169, and subs 288(2)(a). It is doubtful whether an informal decision of all the members to remove a director from office would comply with ss 168, 169, and 288(2)(a), but the director would gain nothing by challenging the formality of the procedure for his removal, since the company could cure any defects by ratification and the court would not grant an injunction; *Bentley-Stevens v Jones* [1974] 1 WLR 638.

that a provision in the company's articles giving weighted voting rights could be relied on to entrench the director in office and defeat his removal by ordinary resolution.[32]

Section 282 describes what is meant by an ordinary resolution.[33]                    **22.09**

(1) An ordinary resolution of the members (or of a class of members) of a company means a resolution that is passed by a simple majority.

(2) A written resolution is passed by a simple majority if it is passed by members representing a simple majority of the total voting rights of eligible members (see Chapter 2).

(3) A resolution passed at a meeting on a show of hands is passed by a simple majority if it is passed by a simple majority of—

   (a) the members who, being entitled to do so, vote in person on the resolution, and

   (b) the persons who vote on the resolution as duly appointed proxies of members entitled to vote on it.

(4) A resolution passed on a poll taken at a meeting is passed by a simple majority if it is passed by members representing a simple majority of the total voting rights of members who (being entitled to do so) vote in person or by proxy on the resolution.

(5) Anything that may be done by ordinary resolution may also be done by special resolution.

Subsection (2) changes the law to enable private companies to use the written resolution procedure to pass a resolution by a simple majority, rather than unanimously as had been the case under the 1985 Act, ss 381A–381C.

A proposal may be made to amend an ordinary resolution if the amendment does   **22.10** not materially alter the scope of the resolution, but the company's articles may restrict amendments to those of which notice has been given before the meeting.[34]

---

[32] [1970] AC 1099, HL. Applying *Bushell v Faith*, a Hong Kong court has held that an unqualified agreement not to remove a particular person as a director constitutes an unlawful fetter on the statutory power of removal (*Muir v Lampl* [2004] 4 HKC 626 in respect of s 157B of the Companies Ordinance).

[33] s 282 is a new provision. Previous Companies Acts defined extraordinary and special resolutions, but not ordinary resolutions. At common law an ordinary resolution was passed by a simple majority of the persons present and entitled to vote. In *Att-Gen v Davy* (1741) 2 Atk 212 Lord Hardwicke CJ said: 'It cannot be disputed, that wherever a certain number are incorporated, a major part of them may do any corporate act; so if all are summoned, and part appear, a major part of those that appear may do a corporate act, though nothing be mentioned in the charter of the major part.' Also see *Grant v United Kingdom Switchback Railways Co* (1880) 40 Ch D 135; *Merchants of the Staple v Bank of England* (1887) 21 QB 160, 165.

[34] Model Article (pcls) 47(2) and Model Article (plc) 40(1) provide that an ordinary resolution may be amended if (i) notice of the proposed amendment is given to the company in writing by a person entitled to vote at the general meeting at which it is to be proposed 48 hours before the meeting is to take place, or at such time as the chairman of the meeting may direct and (ii) the proposed amendment does not, in the reasonable opinion of the chairman, materially alter the scope of the resolution. For the general law relating to amendments of ordinary resolutions: *Clinch v Financial Corporation* (1868) LR 5 Eq 450, 481; *Wright's Case* (1871) LR 12 Eq 335n, 341n; *Henderson v Bank of Australasia* (1890) 45 Ch D 330, CA; *Wall v London and Northern Assets Corp (No 1)* [1898]

If there is an irregularity in the passing of an ordinary resolution, it can be cured by subsequent ratification.

**22.11** Special notice of the intention to move an ordinary resolution is required to be given to the company if the resolution is (i) to remove a director under s 168 or to appoint somebody instead of a director so removed at the meeting at which he is removed,[35] (ii) to remove an auditor from office under s 510,[36] and (iii) in certain cases, to appoint a person as auditor in place of an auditor whose term of office has ended or is to end.[37] Since special notice is for the protection of the director or auditor who is to be removed, members cannot waive compliance with the requirements for special notice set out in s 312 (paragraph 22.61 below).[38]

### (3) Special resolutions

**22.12** The Companies Acts requires the sanction of a special resolution for changes to the constitution,[39] name,[40] status,[41] and share capital of a company[42] and also for a change of the registered office of a Welsh company[43] and for takeovers.[44] A special resolution is required to put a company into voluntary liquidation or, in the

---

2 Ch 469, 483, CA; *Re Teede & Bishop Ltd* (1901) 70 LJ Ch 409; *Stroud v Royal Aquarium Soc* (1903) 89 LT 243; *Betts & Co v Macnaghten* [1910] 1 Ch 430; *Baillie v Oriental Telephone and Electric Co Ltd* [1915] 1 Ch 503, CA.

[35] s 168(2) which restates 1985 Act, s 303(2).

[36] s 511, which restates 1985 Act, s 391A (which was inserted by 1989 Act, s 122).

[37] s 515, which is derived from 1985 Act, s 391A. Where the written resolution procedure is adopted, s 514 applies.

[38] The director has a right to protest his removal under s 169 and the auditor has rights under ss 502 and 513. See n 31 above.

[39] (i) Altering objects as stated in the memorandum (1985 Act, s 4); (ii) amendment of articles etc (1985 Act, s 9 which will be replaced by 2006 Act, s 21); (iii) altering conditions contained in the memorandum which could have been contained in the articles (1985 Act, s 17); (iv) substitution of memorandum and articles for deed of settlement company (1985 Act, s 690). In each case the sections of the 1985 Act will be repealed on 1 October 2009, when 2006 Act, s 21 comes into effect.

[40] 1985 Act, s 28, which will be replaced by 2006 Act, ss 77 and 78 on 1 October 2009.

[41] 1985 Act, ss 43(1), 51, 53, which will be replaced by 2006 Act, ss 90(1), 97(1), 105 on 1 October 2009. These sections concern change of status by which a private company becomes public, a public company becomes private, and an unlimited private company becomes limited.

[42] (i) Disapplication of pre-emption rights (1985 Act, s 95 and 2006 Act, ss 569–573); (ii) reduction of capital in connection with redenomination (2006 Act, s 626); (iii) uncalled capital only to be called up on winding up (1985 Act, s 120 which will be repealed); (iv) variation of class rights (1985 Act, s 125 and 2006 Act, s 630); (v) reduction of capital (1985 Act, 135 and 2006 Act, s 641); (vi) authority for off-market purchase of a company's own shares (1985 Act, ss 164, 165, and 167 and 2006 Act, ss 694–697 and 700); (vii) payment out of capital by a private company for the redemption or purchase of its own shares (1985 Act, ss 173–175 and 2006 Act, ss 713, 716–719). In each case the sections of the 1985 Act will be repealed and, where appropriate, replaced by sections of the 2006 Act on 1 October 2009.

[43] 1985 Act, s 2(2) which will be replaced by 2006 Act, s 88.

[44] 2006 Act, ss 966, 967, 970–972.

case of a company proposed to be, or being, wound up voluntarily, to sanction the transfer of the whole or part of the company's business or property to another company in consideration for shares, policies, and like interests in the transferee company for distribution among the members of the transferor company.[45] The court may wind up a company if it has by special resolution resolved that it be wound up by the court.[46] The company's articles may provide that where the members wish to direct the directors to take or refrain from taking specified action they can do so by special resolution.[47]

Section 283 explains what is meant by a special resolution:[48]                     **22.13**

(1) A special resolution of the members (or of a class of members) of a company means a resolution passed by a majority of not less than 75%.

(2) A written resolution is passed by a majority of not less than 75% if it is passed by members representing not less than 75% of the total voting rights of eligible members (see Chapter 2).

(3) Where a resolution of a private company is passed as a written resolution—
   (a) the resolution is not a special resolution unless it stated that it was proposed as a special resolution, and
   (b) if the resolution so stated, it may only be passed as a special resolution.

(4) A resolution passed at a meeting on a show of hands is passed by a majority of not less than 75% if it is passed by not less than 75% of—
   (a) the members who, being entitled to do so, vote in person on the resolution, and
   (b) the persons who vote on the resolution as duly appointed proxies of members entitled to vote on it.

(5) A resolution passed on a poll taken at a meeting is passed by a majority of not less than 75% if it is passed by members representing not less than 75% of the total voting rights of the members who (being entitled to do so) vote in person or by proxy on the resolution.

(6) Where a resolution is passed at a meeting—
   (a) the resolution is not a special resolution unless the notice of the meeting included the text of the resolution and specified the intention to propose the resolution as a special resolution, and
   (b) if the notice of the meeting so specified, the resolution may only be passed as a special resolution.

---

[45] Insolvency Act, ss 84(1)(b) and 110.

[46] Insolvency Act, s 122(1)(a).

[47] Table A, reg 70, Model Article (pcls) 4, and Model Article (plc) 4. An ordinary resolution is sufficient if the members wish to authorize or ratify a transaction or conduct of the directors: *Bamford v Bamford* [1970] Ch 212, CA, but not if the members are adverse to the directors: *Automatic Self-Cleansing Filter Syndicate Co Ltd v Cunninghame* [1906] 2 Ch 34, CA; *Gramophone and Typewriter Co Ltd v Stanley* [1908] 2 KB 89, CA; *Salmon v Quin & Axtens Ltd* [1909] 1 Ch 311; *John Shaw & Sons (Salford) Ltd v Shaw* [1935] 2 KB 113, CA..

[48] This section is derived from 1985 Act, s 378(1)–(3), (5). Subss (2) and (3) are new and the other subss incorporate changes. 21 days' notice is no longer required; instead all meetings are subject to a standard 14-day notice period.

**22.14**   Since a private company may pass a special resolution by the written resolution procedure and the period of notice for both ordinary and special resolutions is 14 days, the differences between the two types of resolution are that (i) a special resolution requires a majority of 75% rather than a simple majority, and (ii) the formalities for obtaining a special resolution are stricter than for an ordinary resolution. Where the written resolution procedure is adopted, the resolution must state that it is proposed as a special resolution.[49] Where the resolution is passed at a meeting the notice of the meeting must have included the text of the resolution and specified the intention to propose the resolution as a special resolution.[50] Once the resolution has been specified as a special resolution, it can only be passed as a special resolution.

**22.15**   In *Re Moorgate Mercantile Ltd* [51] Slade J held that a resolution is not validly passed as a special resolution if there has been any departure between the text as proposed and the text of the resolution as purportedly passed, unless (i) the departure is not one of substance, such as correcting grammatical or clerical errors or making the language more formal, or (ii) all the members of the company, or relevant class of members, agree to waive compliance with the statutory requirements for a special resolution now contained in s 283. A company's articles may deal with errors in the proposal of a special resolution by providing that a special resolution proposed at a meeting may be amended by ordinary resolution if the chairman proposes the amendment at the meeting at which the resolution is proposed and the amendment does not go beyond what is necessary to correct an obvious error in the resolution.[52] A company cannot by ordinary resolution ratify and make good an invalid special resolution.[53]

### (4) Informal unanimous consent

**22.16**   Subsection 281(4), quoted in paragraph 22.06 above, preserves the rule of law that the informal unanimous consent of all the members of the company who have a right to attend and vote at a general meeting of the company can override formal, including statutory, requirements and is as effective to bind the company as a duly passed resolution.[54] The rule is founded on the dictum of Lord Davey in *Salomon v*

---

[49]   subs 283(3).

[50]   subs 283(6).

[51]   [1980] 1 WLR 227.

[52]   Model Article (pcls) 47(2) and Model Article (plc) 40(2).

[53]   *Baillie v Oriental Telephone Co* [1915] 1 Ch 503, CA.

[54]   This rule of law is also recognized in 2006 Act, ss 29, 239, and 257. The Government decided against codifying this rule, considering that the benefits of codification (clarity and certainty) were outweighed by the disadvantages that would result from loss of flexibility; White Paper: *Modernising Company Law* at paras 2.31–2.35; White Paper: *Company Law Reform* at para 4.2. For discussion and recommendations of the CLR, see CLR: *Developing the Framework* at paras 4.21–4.23; CLR: *Final Report* at para 2.14.

*Salomon* that 'the company is bound in a matter intra vires by the unanimous agreement of its members'.[55] The rule has come to be known as the *Duomatic* principle, in reference to the case decided by Buckley J who stated the principle:

> I proceed upon the basis that where it can be shown that all shareholders who have a right to attend and vote at a general meeting of the company assent to some matter which a general meeting of the company could carry into effect, that assent is as binding as a resolution in general meeting would be.[56]

The principle is most likely to be relevant to private companies where there is an identity or close connection between the directors and shareholders, but in theory it applies equally to public companies; provided in all cases that all members with a right to vote agree.[57] It has also been held to be applicable to matters affecting the class rights of particular shareholders and to shareholders' agreements.[58]

More recently Neuberger J described the *Duomatic* principle in rather wider terms: **22.17**

> The essence of the *Duomatic* principle, as I see it, is that, where the articles of a company require a course to be approved by a group of shareholders at a general meeting, that requirement can be avoided if all members of the group, being aware of the relevant facts, either give their approval to that course, or so conduct themselves as to make it inequitable for them to deny that they have given their approval. Whether the approval is given in advance or after the event, whether it is characterised as agreement, ratification, waiver, estoppel, and whether members of the group give their consent in different ways at different times does not matter.[59]

The *Duomatic* principle is not a general panacea. If the shareholders are not competent to effect the act formally, the *Duomatic* principle does not enable them to do it informally without a meeting.[60] A distinction may be drawn between (i) statutory or other controls which exist for the protection of shareholders, or the relevant class, and which may be waived by the informal unanimous consent of all **22.18**

---

[55] [1897] 1 AC 22, 59, HL.

[56] See *Re Duomatic Ltd* [1969] 2 Ch 365, 373 (where the shareholders with a right to vote signed the accounts). See also *Parker Cooper Ltd v Reading* [1926] 1 Ch 975; *Re Express Engineering Works* [1920] 1 Ch 466; *Re Oxted Motor Co* [1921] 3 KB 32; *Re Bailey, Hay & Co Ltd* [1971] 1 WLR 1357 (where the assent was acquiescence); *Re Gee & Co Ltd* [1975] Ch 52; *Cane v Jones* [1980] 1 WLR 1451; *Multinational Gas and Petrochemical Co v Multinational Gas and Petrochemical Services Ltd* [1983] Ch 258, CA; *Wright v Atlas Wright (Europe) Ltd* [1999] 2 BCLC 301, CA.

[57] *Demite Ltd v Protec Health Ltd* [1998] BCC 638; *Knopp v Thane Investments Ltd* [2003] 1 BCLC 380; *Extrasure Travel Insurance Ltd v Scattergood* [2003] 1 BCLC 634 at para 153.

[58] *Re Torvale Group Ltd* [1999] 2 BCLC 605 (class meeting); *Euro Brokers Holdings Ltd v Monecor (London) Ltd* [2003] 1 BCLC 506, CA (shareholders' agreement, where the assent was through a corporate representative).

[59] *EIC Services Ltd v Phipps* [2004] 2 BCLC 589 at para 122. In the same report the Court of Appeal reversed the judgment of Neuberger J on different grounds.

[60] *Re New Cedos Engineering Co Ltd* (1975) [1994] 1 BCLC 797, 814, per Oliver J; approved by the Court of Appeal in *Wright v Atlas Wright (Europe) Ltd* [1999] 2 BCLC 301, 314, 315.

the shareholders or members of the relevant class and, (ii) statutory or other controls which exist to protect the interests of other persons, such as creditors, which may not be waived.[61] In each case it is necessary to consider the purpose and underlying rationale of the particular formality, statutory or otherwise, that has been overlooked.[62] The *Duomatic* principle has been invoked to validate the payment of remuneration to a director or of pension contribution for his benefit.[63] The court has also accepted that the members may informally but unanimously alter the articles of the company,[64] approve the reduction of the company's share capital,[65] sanction a transaction with a director,[66] or disapply pre-emption rights.[67] In contrast, the informal unanimous assent of shareholders does not enable the company to avoid compliance with a provision for the protection of creditors.[68] Other limitations on the ability of members to authorize or ratify transactions or conduct of the directors are discussed in Chapter 19, Section D.

**22.19**  For the *Duomatic* principle to apply the court must be satisfied that all the shareholders whose consent is required have in fact assented.[69] The court would not accept that assent has been given where the shareholder was unaware that his assent was necessary or being sought,[70] or where inadequate disclosure is given.[71] Since the written resolution procedure makes it simple for private companies to obtain a recorded decision of its members and companies are obliged to keep records of written resolutions and minutes of general meetings, the courts may become more sceptical about attempts to set up informal unanimous agreements that are not properly recorded, particularly when the alleged agreement is claimed to have the same effect as a special resolution.[72]

---

[61]  *Precision Dippings Ltd v Precision Dippings Marketing Ltd* [1986] Ch 447, CA; *BDG Roof Bond Ltd v Douglas* [2000] 1 BCLC 401; *Bairstow v Queens Moat Houses plc* [2001] 2 BCLC 531 at para 36, CA; *Kinlan v Crimmin* [2007] 2 BCLC 67. The reasoning in *Re Peak (RW) (Kings Lynn) Ltd* [1998] 1 BCLC 193 is influenced by the failure to comply with the provisions of 1985 Act, s 381A which are no longer in force.

[62]  *Wright v Atlas Wright (Europe) Ltd* [1999] 2 BCLC 301 at 315, per Potter LJ.

[63]  *Re Duomatic Ltd* [1969] 2 Ch 365; *Re Horsley & Weight Ltd* [1982] Ch 442, CA.

[64]  *Cane v Jones* [1980] 1 WLR 1451.

[65]  *Re Barry Artist plc* [1985] BCLC 283, where Nourse J reluctantly sanctioned a reduction of capital for which a special resolution was required (1985 Act, s 135 to be replaced by 2006 Act, s 641).

[66]  Under what is now 2006 Act, Part 9, Chapter 4 (transactions with directors): *Wright v Atlas Wright (Europe) Ltd* [1999] 2 BCLC 301, CA; *NBH Ltd v Hoare* [2006] 2 BCLC 649 at para 43.

[67]  *Pena v Dale* [2004] 2 BCLC 509.

[68]  *Precision Drippings Ltd v Precision Drippings Marketing Ltd* [1986] Ch 447, CA. In *Kinlan v Crimmin* [2007] 2 BCLC 67 the informal unanimous consent of the shareholders was effective to dispense with compliance with one statutory provision for the protection of shareholders, but not another provision which had a wider purpose, including the protection of creditors.

[69]  *Re D'Jan of London Ltd* [1994] 1 BCLC 561, 564.

[70]  *EIC Services Ltd v Phipps* [2004] 2 BCLC 589 at paras 138 and 146.

[71]  *Clark v Cutland* [2004] 1 WLR 783 at [21], CA.

[72]  Section 355(1)(a) requires a company to keep records of all resolutions of members passed otherwise than at general meetings. Section 356(2) provides that the record of a resolution passed

There is some uncertainty whether the assent must be that of the registered share-  **22.20**
holder or whether the assent of the beneficial owner is sufficient. The orthodox
position is that the consent of the registered shareholder is required.[73] However,
in *Deakin v Faulding* Hart J held that the *Duomatic* principle could apply where
the beneficial owner, not the registered shareholder, assented, and the beneficial
owner was also regarded as acting as agent for his nominee.[74] In *Sharar v Tsitsekkos*
Mann J held, for the purposes of a summary judgment application, that the proposition that the *Duomatic* principle could never apply to the consent of a beneficial, but not registered owner, was not clearly right.[75]

## C. Written Resolutions

### (1) General provisions about written resolutions

A written resolution is a resolution of a private company proposed and passed in  **22.21**
accordance with Part 13, Chapter 2. A public company cannot pass a written resolution, although it could under the 1985 Act. The new written resolution provisions set out in Chapter 2 are intended to simplify procedures for private companies
and should be the normal means by which members of such companies make
decisions, whether by ordinary or special resolution.[76] Private companies may use
the written resolution procedure to ratify acts of directors under s 239, but not to
pass a written resolution to remove a director or auditor before the expiration of
his term of office.[77] A written resolution may be proposed by the directors of a
private company in accordance with s 291 or by the members of a private company in accordance with ss 292–295. A written resolution has effect as if passed by
the company in general meeting or, as the case may be, by a meeting of a class of
members of the company.[78]

---

otherwise than at a general meeting, if purporting to be signed by director of the company or by
the company secretary, is evidence of the passing of the resolution. 1985 Act, s 380, which is to be
replaced by 2006 Act, ss 29 and 30 on 1 October 2009, requires any resolution or agreement agreed
to by all the members of a company that, if not so agreed to, would not have been effective for its
purpose unless passed as a special resolution (or which varies class rights) to be forwarded to the
Registrar within 15 days after it is passed or made.

[73] *Domoney v Godhino* [2004] 2 BCLC 15.
[74] 31 July 2001, [2001] All ER (D) 463.
[75] [2004] EWHC 2659 (Ch) at paras 62–67.
[76] ss 281(1), 292(2), 283(2) and (3), 284, and ss 288–300. These provisions replace 1985
Act, ss 381A–381C, which applied to all companies but required the unanimous consent of all
members.
[77] s 288(2). 2006 Act Commencement Order No 3, Schedule 1, para 13(2)(b) adds an additional subs 288(2)(c): 'a resolution under section 80A of the Companies Act 1985 . . . revoking,
varying or renewing the authority of the directors to allot securities'. 1985 Act, s 80A is due to be
repealed on 1 October 2009.
[78] s 288(5). 2006 Act Commencement Order No 3, Schedule 1, para 13(3) adds an additional subs
288(6): 'A written resolution under any of the provisions of the Companies Act 1985 . . . mentioned in

**22.22**  A resolution proposed as a written resolution of a private company is to be circulated among the eligible members, who are the members who would have been entitled to vote on the resolution on the circulation date.[79] The circulation date of a written resolution is the date on which copies of it are sent or submitted to members (or if copies are sent or submitted to members on different days, the first of those days).[80] There is no express provision for sending or submitting the proposed written resolution to the company's auditor, but s 502 provides that the company's auditor is entitled to receive all such communications relating to the written resolution proposed to be agreed to by a private company as are required to be supplied to a member of the company.[81]

**22.23**  Section 300 has the effect that a private company cannot in its articles provide for an alternative written resolution procedure or prevent the company from using the written resolution procedure in Chapter 2 by insisting on meetings. It states:

> A provision of the articles of a private company is void in so far as it would have the effect that a resolution that is required by or otherwise provided for in an enactment could not be proposed and passed as a written resolution.[82]

Table A, reg 53 is inconsistent with s 281(1) for private companies and s 281(2) for public companies and ceased to have effect for companies incorporated on or after 1 October 2007.[83] The Model Articles do not contain any provisions for

---

sections 300A to 300D is not effective unless the procedural requirements specified in those sections are complied with.' Sections 300A–300D concern respectively (a) disapplication of pre-emption rights under 1985 Act, s 95(2), (b) financial assistance for the purchase of a company's own shares or those of its holding company under 1985 Act, s 155, (c) authority for off-market purchase or contingent purchase contract of company's own shares under 1985 Act, s 164, and (d) the approval of payment out of capital under 1985 Act, ss 173 and 174. Those sections of the 1985 Act are due to be repealed on 1 October 2009 when, except for s 155, they will be replaced by provisions in the 2006 Act.

[79]  s 289(1). If the persons entitled to vote on a written resolution change during the course of the day that is the circulation date of the resolution, the eligible members are the persons entitled to vote on the resolution at the time that the first copy of the resolution is sent or submitted to a member for his agreement (subs 289(2)).

[80]  s 290.

[81]  1985 Act, s 381B is not restated in the 2006 Act and s 502 re-enacts 1985 Act, s 390. It is therefore not entirely clear what should be sent to the auditor in relation to a proposed written resolution, although BERR guidance indicates that the proposed written resolution does not have to be sent to the auditor.

[82]  Attempts were made to amend s 300 prior to enactment, so as to allow private and public companies to make alternative provisions in their articles. The Government rejected these attempts on the basis that: (i) the statute provides detailed procedures which are not onerous and therefore should be followed; (ii) for public companies certain decisions need to be taken in a meeting rather than by written resolution, pursuant to the Second Company Law Directive; (iii) there is nothing in the Act which stops non-statutory resolutions from being passed in whatever way the articles envisage. If the articles require members' agreement, there is no need to comply with the statutory procedures: see Hansard HoC Debate, 18 October 2006, 2nd day, col 978.

[83]  Table A, reg 53 states: 'A resolution in writing executed by or on behalf of each member who would have been entitled to vote upon it if it had been proposed at a general meeting at which he was present shall be as effectual as if it had been passed at a general meeting duly convened and held

written resolutions, since Chapter 2 is a self-contained code. Since subs 281(4) preserves the *Duomatic* principle it is possible for all the members of a private company to dispense with compliance with Chapter 2 and instead make an informal unanimous agreement in relation to the matter that might have been proposed as a written resolution (and such a course is also available to a public company).

### (2) Circulation of written resolutions

Where the directors propose a resolution as a written resolution the company **22.24** must send or submit a copy of the resolution to every eligible member either (a) by sending copies at the same time (so far as reasonably practicable) to all eligible members in hard copy form, in electronic form, or by means of a website, or (b) if it is possible to do so without undue delay, by submitting the same copy to each eligible member in turn (or different copies to each of a number of eligible members in turn), or (c) by sending copies to some members in accordance with (a) and submitting a copy or copies to other members in accordance with (b).[84] The copy of the resolution must be accompanied by a statement informing the member how to signify agreement to the resolution, as provided in s 296, and as to the date by which the resolution must be passed if it is not to lapse in accordance with s 297.[85]

The members of a private company may require the company to circulate a resolu- **22.25** tion that may properly be moved and is proposed to be moved as a written resolution and, if they do, they may also require the company to circulate with the resolution a statement of not more than 1,000 words on the subject matter of the resolution.[86] The rights of the members to require the company to circulate the resolution and statement are subject to three restrictions.

First, the resolution and accompanying statement must command the requisite **22.26** support from members. This is the threshold requirement and the company is not required to circulate the resolution and accompanying statement until it receives

---

and may consist of several instruments in the like form each executed by or on behalf of one or more members.'

[84] subss 291(1)–(3). Options (b) and (c) allow the company to pass round a document or email instead of sending out several copies. Section 299 provides that where a company sends a written resolution or a statement relating to a written resolution to a person by means of a website, the resolution or statement is not validly sent for the purposes of Chapter 2 unless the resolution is available on the website throughout the period beginning with the circulation date and ending on the date on which the resolution lapses under s 297. Also see 2006 Act, s 1144(2) and Schedule 5, Part 3 for communications in electronic form and para 4 for communications by means of a website.

[85] subs 291(4).

[86] subss 292(1) and (3). These provisions are intended to enhance shareholder engagement (Hansard HL GC day 5 (60227-51)).

requests that it do so from members representing not less than the requisite percentage of the total voting rights of all members entitled to vote on the resolution.[87] The requisite percentage is 5% or such lower percentage as is specified for this purpose in the company's articles.[88]

**22.27**   Secondly, members must not abuse their power to require the company to circulate the written resolution and accompanying statement. The resolution is not capable of being properly moved as a written resolution if (a) it would, if passed, be ineffective (whether by reason of inconsistency with any enactment or the company's constitution or otherwise), (b) it is defamatory of any person, or (c) it is frivolous and vexatious.[89] The company is not required to circulate the accompanying statement if it or any other person who claims to be aggrieved applies to the court under s 295 and the court is satisfied that the rights conferred by ss 292 and 293 are being abused.[90]

**22.28**   Thirdly, the members who request the company to circulate the resolution and statement under s 293 must pay the company's expenses, unless the company has resolved otherwise, and must deposit with, or tender to, the company a sum sufficient to meet the company's expenses.[91]

---

[87]   subs 292(4). By subs 292(6) the request (a) may be in hard copy form or electronic form, (b) must identify the resolution and accompanying statement, and (c) must be authenticated by the person or persons making it. As to hard copy form and electronic form, see s 1144 and Schedule 4. As to authentication, see s 1146.

[88]   subs 292(5).

[89]   subs 292(2). If the directors take the view that the proposed resolution is ineffective, defamatory, or frivolous or vexatious and the resolution is accompanied by a statement, the issue of abuse will be determined on an application under s 294. Where there is no accompanying statement, the directors could apply to the court for a declaration that they are not liable to circulate it under s 293, or they could inform the members of their decision and leave it to the members to apply to court for an order that they do so, or require a meeting under ss 303–305, or conceivably apply to the court under s 306. Since subs 292(1) requires the members to identify the resolution, rather than merely the general nature of the business to be considered (as under subs 303(4)), it may be easier for directors to conclude that the proposed resolution would, if passed, be ineffective; *Isle of White Railway Co v Tahourdin* (1883) 25 Ch D 320, 329, 330, per Cotton LJ, and 334, per Lindley LJ; *Rose v McGivern* [1998] 2 BCLC 593, 605–12.

[90]   subss 293(1) and 295(1). Subsection 295(1) is in similar terms to subs 317(1) and may be compared with subs 520(4). If the court considered that the company's application under s 295 was tactical, it might order the company to pay the members' costs on the indemnity basis; *Jarvis plc v PricewaterhouseCoopers* [2000] 2 BCLC 368, a case on 1985 Act, s 394, the predecessor of s 520 (concerning circulation of auditor's statement on ceasing to hold office). On the other hand, subs 295(2) provides that the court may order members who requested the circulation of the statement to pay the whole or part of the company's costs of the application, even if they are not parties to the application. Members who support the circulation of a resolution and statement should therefore satisfy themselves that the statement is not abusive.

[91]   subs 293(1) and s 294. A demand for an unreasonable deposit would not be regarded as compliance with s 293 (HC Comm D, col 316). Sections 316 and 340 are the equivalent provisions for general meetings and AGMs.

Not more than 21 days after it becomes subject to the requirement under s 292 to **22.29** circulate the resolution, the company must send or submit to every eligible member a copy of the resolution and a copy of any accompanying statement in the same manner and with the same guidance as applies to the circulation of written resolutions proposed by the directors.[92] The duties imposed on the company (and the directors) by s 293 in respect of the circulation of the resolution proposed by members largely mirror the requirements set out in s 291 for the circulation of written resolutions proposed by directors. An additional requirement under s 293 is that the resolution must be circulated within 21 days of the request being made by the member to the company pursuant to section 292.[93]

Where the company's articles include a provision enabling a member to nominate **22.30** another person or persons as entitled to enjoy or exercise all or any specified rights of the member in relation to the company, any nominated person has the right to be sent the proposed written resolution under ss 291 and 293 and to require circulation of a written resolution under s 292.[94] If the company is a traded company, in that its shares are admitted to trading on a regulated market, a member of the company who holds shares on behalf of another person may nominate that person to enjoy information rights, which include the right to receive communications that the company sends to its members concerning written resolutions.[95]

The validity of the resolution, if passed, is not affected by a failure to comply with **22.31** ss 291 or 293.[96] If the vote is carried, it will be valid even if a member who would have been in the minority was not circulated with the proposed resolution. Such a member may have a remedy by unfair prejudice petition under the 2006 Act, Part 30. Instead, to secure compliance with ss 291 and 293, in the event of default in complying with them, an offence is committed by every officer of the company in default who is liable to a fine on conviction.[97]

---

[92] subss 293(1)–(4). The company's obligations under subs 293(1) are subject to ss 294(2) (deposit or tender of sum in respect of circulation) and 295 (application not to circulate members' statement).

[93] See subs 293(3).

[94] Part 9, s 145, which is a new provision concerning the exercise of members' rights.

[95] Part 9, ss 146–148, which are new provisions. See paragraph 22.92 below. Section 147 prescribes the form in which copies are to be provided to the nominated person.

[96] subss 291(7) and 293(7). The reason for subs 291(7) is that a company must have certainty to be able to pursue its business effectively and efficiently irrelevant of whether or not errors are made: see Hansard HoC, Standing Committee, day 5, col 306. For the same reason, the validity of a written resolution is not affected by an accidental failure to send a memorandum required under Part 10, Chapter 4 (transactions with directors requiring approval of members); s 224.

[97] subss 291(5) and (6) and 293(5) and (6). For officer in default, see s 1121.

### (3) Agreeing to written resolutions

**22.32**  A member signifies his agreement to a proposed written resolution when the company receives from him, or someone acting on his behalf, an authenticated document, which may be in hard copy form or in electronic form, identifying the resolution to which it relates and indicating his agreement to the resolution.[98] Once agreement to the resolution has been signified to the company it cannot be withdrawn.[99]

**22.33**  A written resolution is passed when the required majority of eligible members have signified agreement to it.[100] A simple majority is required for an ordinary resolution and a majority of not less than 75% is required for a special resolution.[101] On a vote on a written resolution and subject to any provision of the company's articles (a) in the case of a company having a share capital, every member has one vote in respect of each share or £10 of stock held by him, and (b) in any other case every member has one vote.[102] Subject to any provision of the company's articles, where there are joint holders of shares, only the vote of the senior holder who votes may be counted.[103]

**22.34**  A proposed written resolution lapses if it is not passed before the end of the period specified for this purpose in the company's articles, or, if none is specified, the period of 28 days beginning with the circulation date. The agreement of a member to a written resolution is ineffective if signified after the expiry of that period.[104] This means that there is a definite date after which the company can say that a resolution with insufficient support has not been passed.

---

[98]  subss 296(1) and (2). For the authentication of the document signifying consent, see s 1146. A signature is not required. For communication of the consent in hard copy form or electronic form, see s 298, which provides that where the company has given an electronic address the document signifying agreement may be sent electronically to that address, and ss 1143, 1144(1), and 1168 and Schedule 4. Subject to voting agreements, a member may vote as he pleases (paragraph 22.79 below), but on a resolution to ratify the acts of a director under s 239 the director (if a member) and members connected with him are not eligible to vote; subss 239(3) and (5) and s 252.

[99]  subs 296(3).

[100]  subs 296(4). Eligible members are those members who are entitled to vote on the resolution; s 289.

[101]  subss 282(1) and (2) and 283(1) and (2).

[102]  subss 284(1) and (4), which derive from 1985 Act, subss 370(1) and (6). Account must be taken of any weighted voting rights, as in *Bushell v Faith* [1970] AC 1099. Section 287 provides that nothing in Chapter 2 affects (a) any provision of a company's articles requiring an objection to a person's entitlement to vote on a resolution to be made in accordance with the articles, and for the determination of any such objection to be final and conclusive, or (b) the grounds on which such a determination may be questioned in legal proceedings. Table A, reg 58 is a provision for determining the admissibility of votes for the purposes of a meeting. Model Article (pcls) 43 and Model Articles (plc) 35 provide for the determination of errors and disputes in relation to votes at meetings.

[103]  s 286, which is derived from Table A, reg 55. The senior holder of a share is determined by the order in which the names appear in the register of members.

[104]  s 297. The circulation date is identified in accordance with s 290.

If the written resolution is passed the company must keep a record of it and if **22.35** the resolution is a special resolution a copy of it must be forwarded to the Registrar within 15 days after it is passed.[105] A copy of the written resolution signed by a director of the company or by the company secretary is evidence of the passing of the resolution.[106] Where there is a record of a written resolution of a private company, the requirements of the Companies Act with respect to the passing of the resolution are deemed to be complied with unless the contrary is proved.[107]

## D. Resolutions at Meetings

The default provisions for obtaining the authorization of the company at a meet- **22.36** ing are set out in the Companies Act, Chapter 3, ss 301–335.[108] These provisions apply equally to private and public companies. Additional provisions which apply only to public companies and quoted companies are then set out in Chapters 4 and 5 (which are discussed in Sections E and F below).

A resolution of the members of a company is validly passed at a general meeting if **22.37** notice of the meeting and of the resolution is given and the meeting is held and conducted in accordance with the provisions of Chapter 3 (and where relevant, Chapter 4) and the company's articles.[109]

### (1) Calling meetings

*Meetings called by the directors*

The directors of a company may call a general meeting of the company or a meet- **22.38** ing of a class of members.[110] The directors may informally and unanimously agree

---

[105] subs 355(1)(a) and 1985 Act, s 380, which will be replaced by 2006 Act, ss 29 and 30 on 1 October 2009. The provisions of subss 355(1)(a) and 356(2) and (3) also apply to class meetings.

[106] subs 356(2).

[107] subs 356(3).

[108] These sections are derived from and replace 1985 Act, ss 368–377, 379, and 381. They also derive from Table A, regs 37–39, 47, 48, and 63. The new provisions on resolutions in general meeting reflect the fact that private companies will no longer be required to hold AGMs. 1985 Act, s 367, which gave the Secretary of State a power to call a meeting where there had been no AGM, has been repealed.

[109] s 301.

[110] ss 302, 334, and 335 and also Table A, reg 37. Section 335, dealing with class meetings of companies without a share capital, is a new section. Table A, reg 37 also provides that if there are not within the United Kingdom sufficient directors to call a general meeting, any director may call a meeting. The secretary of a company has no power to call a general meeting under the Companies Act or under the general law: *In re State of Wyoming Syndicate* [1901] 2 Ch 431.

to call a meeting, but if they are not unanimous they should make a majority decision in accordance with the company's articles.[111]

22.39 The directors will use the power to call a general meeting where they wish to obtain the assent, authorization, or ratification of the members to a particular transaction or conduct and the written resolution procedure is not available and they cannot obtain the informal unanimous consent of all the members. The directors' power to call a general meeting is a fiduciary power to be exercised for the purpose for which it is conferred.[112] Pursuant to their duties to the company the directors will invariably prepare a circular explaining their opinion that the resolutions proposed by them should be supported by the members.

*Meetings requisitioned by members*

22.40 The members of a company may require the directors to call a general meeting of the company, but not a meeting of a class of members.[113] The company's articles may give members additional powers to call meetings.[114] Under s 303 the directors are required to call a general meeting once the company has received requests[115] to do so from members which satisfy two conditions.

22.41 First, the resolution must command the requisite support from members. The members making the request must represent at least the required percentage of such of the paid-up capital of the company as carries the right of voting at general meetings of the company (excluding any paid-up capital held as treasury shares).[116] The required percentage is 10%, but for private companies the percentage may be reduced to 5% if more than 12 months have elapsed since the end of the last general meeting called under s 303 or in relation to which members could have

---

[111] Table A, regs 88–98, Model Articles (pcls) 7–14 and Model Articles (plc) 7–16; *Harben v Phillips* (1883) 23 Ch D 14, *Re Haycraft Gold Reduction Co* [1900] 2 Ch 230; *Bolton Engineering Ltd v TJ Graham & Sons Ltd* [1957] 1 QB 159, CA. Irregularities in convening a general meeting may be cured by ratification by the board or provisions in the company's articles: *Hooper v Kerr Stuart & Co* (1900) 83 LT 729; *Transport v Schomberg* (1905) 21 TLR 305; *Boschoek Proprietary Co v Fuke* [1906] 1 Ch 148.

[112] s 171 and *Pergamon Press Ltd v Maxwell* [1970] 1 WLR 1167. The power would be abused if the directors called a meeting for a time and place when they knew that a member or members could not attend.

[113] ss 303 and 334(2)(a) and 335(2)(a).

[114] Table A, reg 37 provides that if there are not within the United Kingdom sufficient directors to call a meeting, any member of the company may call a meeting. Model Article (plc) 28 provides that if a company has fewer than two directors, and the director (if any) is unable or unwilling to call a meeting to appoint further directors, then two or more members may call a general meeting (or instruct the company secretary to do so).

[115] A request may be in hard copy form or in electronic form and must be authenticated by the person or persons making it (subs 303(6)).

[116] s 303(2). If the company does not have a share capital, the requests must have been received from members who represent at least the required percentage of the total voting rights of all members having a right to vote at general meetings.

exercised rights under that section.[117] Where the company's articles include a provision enabling a member to nominate another person or persons as entitled to enjoy or exercise all or any specified rights of the member in relation to the company, any nominated person has the right to require directors to call a general meeting under s 303.[118]

Secondly, the request must identify the general nature of the business to be dealt **22.42** with at the meeting, and may include the text of the resolution that may properly be moved and is intended to be moved at the meeting.[119] A resolution may not be properly moved if (a) it would, if passed, be ineffective, (b) it is defamatory of any person, or (c) it is frivolous or vexatious.[120]

Directors required under s 303 to call a general meeting of the company must call **22.43** a meeting within 21 days from the date on which they become subject to the requirement, and the meeting must be held on a date not more than 28 days after the notice convening the meeting.[121] Subsections 304(2)–(4) contain further provisions designed to ensure that the members' requests are properly considered at the meeting: (a) the notice of the meeting must include notice of any resolution identified in the request, (b) the business that may be dealt with at the meeting includes a resolution of which notice is given under s 304, and (c) if the resolution proposed is a special resolution, the directors are treated as not having duly called the meeting if they do not give the required notice of the resolution in accordance with s 283.

If the directors are required under s 303 to call a meeting, and do not do so in **22.44** accordance with s 304, the members who requested the meeting, or any of them representing more than one half of the total voting rights of all of them, may themselves call a general meeting which must be called for a date not more than three months after the date on which the directors become subject to the requirement to call a meeting.[122] The meeting must be called in the same manner,

---

[117] subs 303(3). The reduced threshold for private companies in certain circumstances is new and is intended to assist engagement by members in the affairs of a private company (Hansard HoC, Standing Committee, day 5, col 320).

[118] Part 9, s 145, which is a new provision concerning the exercise of members' rights.

[119] subs 303(4). The phrase 'general nature of the business' is broader than the phrase 'objects of the meeting' in 1985 Act, s 368(3), but that flexibility is balanced by the option to include the text of the proposed resolution, which is new. If the requests merely state the general nature of the business, rather than the text of the proposed resolution, it may be more difficult for the directors to conclude that any resolution, if passed, would be ineffective; paragraph 22.26 above and n 87.

[120] subs 303(5), which is in the same terms as subs 292(2) concerning written resolutions (paragraph 17.26 above). If the resolution may not properly be moved, the directors will not act on the request, leaving it to the members to call, or purport to call the meeting under s 305 or apply to court under s 306.

[121] subs 304(1), which continues the time limits in 1985 Act, s 368.

[122] subss 305(1) and (3). Section 305 re-enacts part of 1985 Act, s 368.

as nearly as possible, as that in which meetings are required to be called by directors of the company and the notice of the meeting must include notice of any resolution included in the members' requests.[123] The business that may be dealt with at the meeting includes a resolution of which notice is given in accordance with s 305,[124] but the members are not entitled to raise other business at the meeting that was not identified in the requests.[125]

22.45 The sanction on the directors for failing to comply with the members' requests is that the company is obliged to reimburse the reasonable expenses incurred by the members requesting the meeting by reason of the directors' failure duly to call a meeting and any sum so reimbursed must be retained by the company out of any sums due or to become due from the company by way of fees or other remuneration in respect of the services of such of the directors as were in default.[126]

22.46 The directors should not be passive in relation to the meeting requisitioned by the members. If the directors consider that the resolution is contrary to the best interests of the company, their fiduciary duties require them to take proper steps to oppose it, by circulating a statement of their views and soliciting votes and proxies, for which purposes they may use the company's funds.[127]

### Meetings ordered by the court

22.47 Section 306 gives the court power to order a meeting of the company to be called, held, and conducted in any manner the court thinks fit whenever it is impracticable to call or conduct a meeting, but not a meeting of holders of a class of share.[128] It provides:

> (1) This section applies if for any reason it is impracticable—
> (a) to call a meeting of a company in any manner in which meetings of that company may be called, or
> (b) to conduct the meeting in the manner prescribed by the company's articles or this Act.
> (2) The court may, either of its own motion or on the application—
> (a) of a director of the company, or
> (b) of a member of the company who would be entitled to vote at the meeting,
> order a meeting to be called, held and conducted in any manner the court thinks fit.
> (3) Where such an order is made, the court may give such ancillary or consequential directions as it thinks expedient.

---

[123] subss 305(2) and (4).
[124] subs 305(5).
[125] *Ball v Metal Industries* [1957] SC 315.
[126] subss 305(6) and (7).
[127] *Peel v London and North-Western Railway* [1907] 1 Ch 5, CA; *Wilson v London Midland and Scottish Railway Co* [1940] Ch 393, CA.
[128] s 306 re-enacts 1985 Act, s 371 without change, and subss 334(2)(b) and 335(2)(b).

(4) Such directions may include a direction that one member of the company present at the meeting be deemed to constitute a quorum.

(5) A meeting called, held and conducted in accordance with an order under this section is deemed for all purposes to be a meeting of the company duly called, held and conducted.

The court may order a meeting to be held of its own motion, or on the application of a director or a member who would be entitled to vote at a meeting. The jurisdiction to make an order is founded on it being for any reason impracticable to call or conduct a meeting. The circumstances in which the calling or conducting of a meeting are impracticable are unlimited and may arise from an absence of directors or members or where there are practical difficulties in giving notice to members overseas.[129] It is not, however impracticable to conduct a meeting, simply because the chairman is a director and shareholder, giving rise to a conflict between his duty to the company and his interests as a shareholder.[130]  **22.48**

There have been several cases where the impracticability has resulted from a director and minority shareholder abusing the quorum provisions by absenting himself and preventing an effective meeting from taking place in which he would be removed from office or another director would be appointed. In those circumstances the court has directed that a meeting be called, if necessary with a direction that one member present shall constitute a quorum.[131] Those cases are to be distinguished from ones where the court has declined to exercise its powers under s 306, because to do so would override an entrenched or class right or affect substantive voting rights by breaking the deadlock between two equal shareholders.[132]  **22.49**

---

[129] *Re Consolidated Nickel Mines Ltd* [1914] 1 Ch 883; *Re Noel Tedman Holdings Pty Ltd* [1967] Qd R 561; *Harman v BML Group Ltd* [1994] 1 WLR 893, 896, CA, per Dillon LJ.

[130] *Might SA v Redbus Interhouse plc* [2004] 2 BCLC 449. In *Monnington v Easier plc* [2006] 2 BCLC 283 the court refused an order, because it was not impracticable to call or conduct a meeting, even though the board might frustrate its intended purpose by appointing new directors, and the applicant could not use the statutory power to achieve an alteration of the company's articles.

[131] *Re El Sombrero Ltd* [1958] Ch 900; *Re HR Paul & Sons Ltd* (1974) 118 Sol Jo 166; *Re Opera Photographic Ltd* [1989] 1 WLR 634; *Re Woven Rugs Ltd* [2002] 1 WLR 324; *Union Music Ltd v Watson* [2003] 1 BCLC 453, CA; *Vectone Entertainment Holding Ltd v South Entertainment Ltd* [2004] 2 BCLC 224.

[132] *Harman v BML Group Ltd* [1994] 1 WLR 893, CA; *Ross v Telford* [1998] 1 BCLC 82, CA. The dividing line between these cases and those in the preceding footnote is a narrow one. In *Alvona Developments Ltd v Manhattan Loft Corporation (AC) Ltd* [2006] BCC 119, on a summary judgment application, the judge held that an alleged right of a minority shareholder to be a director was a class right, which if established would prevent an order from being made. That decision is difficult to reconcile with s 168 and its predecessor, 1985 Act, s 303.

**22.50** The following propositions may be derived from the judgment of Peter Gibson LJ in the leading authority, *Union Music Ltd v Watson*.[133]

(1) Section 306 is a procedural section intended to enable company business which needs to be conducted at a general meeting of the company to be so conducted. The management of its affairs should not be frustrated by the impracticability of calling or conducting a general meeting in the manner prescribed by the articles and the Companies Act.

(2) The section confers on the court a discretion, which must be exercised properly having regard to the relevant circumstances.[134]

(3) The fact that there are quorum provisions in the company's articles requiring two members' attendance will not in itself be sufficient to prevent the court making an order under s 306, where the applicant is seeking a proper order such as the appointment of a director, something which a majority shareholder would have the right to procure in ordinary circumstances. The order would not affect the substantive voting rights of the minority shareholder who may choose whether or not to attend the meeting.

(4) The machinery of s 306 is not to be used to override entrenched or class rights, or rights in the nature of class rights, by imposing a new shareholder agreement on the parties.[135] A quorum provision is not a class right.

(5) Section 306 is a procedural section not designed to affect substantive voting rights or to shift the balance of power between shareholders where they have agreed that power should be shared equally and where potential deadlock must be taken to have been agreed for the protection of each shareholder.[136]

**22.51** The existence of an unfair prejudice petition under Part 30 or the likelihood of litigation if an order is made are not factors that will prevent the court from making an order under s 306 if other circumstances justify it, but the court may impose conditions.[137]

### (2) Notice of meetings

*Length of notice*

**22.52** A general meeting of a private company must be called by notice of at least 14 days (excluding the day of the meeting and the day on which notice is given), but the

---

[133] [2003] 1 BCLC 453 at paras 32–43. Buxton LJ and Morland J agreed with the judgment of Peter Gibson LJ.

[134] An applicant for an order is not entitled to an order as of right, nor is the respondent entitled to resist the order as of right: *Re El Sombrero Ltd* [1958] Ch 900.

[135] Explaining *Harman v BML Group Ltd* [1994] 1 WLR 893, CA.

[136] Referring to *Ross v Telford* [1998] 1 BCLC 82, CA.

[137] *Re Sticky Fingers Restaurant Ltd* [1992] BCLC 84; *Re Whitchurch Insurance Consultants Ltd* [1993] BCLC 1359; *Harman v BML Group Ltd* [1994] 1 WLR 349, CA; *Re Woven Rugs Ltd* [2002] 1 BCLC 324; *Vectone Entertainment Holding Ltd v South Entertainment Ltd* [2004] 2 BCLC 224.

company's articles may require a longer period.[138] A majority of the members may however agree to shorter notice if they are a majority in number of the members having a right to attend and vote at the meeting, being a majority who together hold not less than 90% (or such higher percentage not exceeding 95% as may be specified in the company's articles) in nominal value of the shares giving a right to attend and vote at the meeting (excluding any shares of the company held as treasury shares).[139]

A general meeting of a public company must also be called by notice of at least 14 days (excluding the day of the meeting and the day on which notice is given), but the company's articles may require a longer period.[140] A majority of the members may also agree to shorter notice if they are a majority in number of the members having a right to attend and vote at the meeting, being a majority who together hold not less than 95% in nominal value of the shares giving a right to attend and vote at the meeting (excluding any shares of the company held as treasury shares).[141]   **22.53**

The AGM of a public company must be called by notice of at least 21 days (excluding the day of the meeting and the day on which notice is given), but the company's articles may require a longer period of notice.[142] The members may only agree to shorter notice if they all agree.[143]   **22.54**

### Form and content of the notice

Section 308 provides that notice of a general meeting of a company must be given in hard copy form, in electronic form, or by means of a website in accordance with s 309.[144] Section 309 states the requirements for valid notification to a member of the presence of the notice of the meeting on the website: (i) the notification must state that it concerns a notice of a company meeting, specify the place, date and   **22.55**

---

[138] subss 307(1)–(3) and s 360. Section 307 re-enacts with changes 1985 Act, s 369. Note the draft directive COM (2005) 865 final, Article 5. Section 360 is a new provision, which enacts the former common law rule in *Re Hector Whaling Ltd* [1936] Ch 208, and was introduced by amendment after the 2nd Reading of the Bill in the House of Commons: Hansard HoC, Standing Committee, day 5, cols 322–323). Table A, reg 115 provides: 'A notice shall be deemed to be given at the expiration of 48 hours after the envelope containing it was posted or, in the case of electronic communication, at the expiration of 48 hours after the time it was sent.'

[139] subss 307(4)–(6). The reduction in the requisite percentage to 90%, subject to the company's articles, is a change from the 1985 Act. See Table A, reg 38. In the case of a company not having a share capital the majority must represent not less than the requisite percentage of the total voting rights at that meeting of all the members (subs 307(5)(b).

[140] subss 307(2)(b), (3), and s 360.

[141] subss 307(4)–(6). Subsection 307(5)(b) applies to a company not having a share capital.

[142] subss 307(2)(a), (3), and s 360.

[143] subss 307(4), (7), and 337(2).

[144] ss 308 and 309 are derived from 1985 Act, subss 369(4A)–(4C), with changes. See also s 1144(2) and Schedule 5 for communications by a company in hard copy form, electronic form, and by means of a website. Sections 308 and 309 came into force on 20 January 2007 (2006 Act Commencement Order No 1).

time of the meeting, and, in the case of a public company, state whether the meeting will be an AGM, and (ii) the notice must be available on the website throughout the period beginning with the date of notification and ending with the conclusion of the meeting. The mandatory terms of s 308 would seem to preclude provision in the company's articles for giving notice of a general meeting by advertisement in an appropriate newspaper (a form of communication mentioned in subs 312(3)(a)). In the unlikely event that it is impracticable to give notice to all members by at least one of the three methods specified in s 308, it will be necessary to apply to the court under s 306 for directions as to the manner in which the meeting should be called.

22.56    The notice must state the place, date, and time of the meeting and the general nature of the business to be dealt with at the meeting.[145] The notice must contain a 'fair, candid, and reasonable explanation' of the business to be dealt with at the meeting.[146] If it does not and, for example benefits to directors are concealed, any resolution purportedly passed will be invalid and the company will be restrained from acting on it.[147]

22.57    In every notice calling a meeting of a company there must appear, with reasonable prominence, a statement informing the member of his right under s 324 to appoint a proxy and any more extensive rights conferred by the company's articles to appoint more than one proxy.[148] To achieve certainty in the outcome of the meeting, failure to comply with s 325 does not affect the validity of the meeting or of anything done at the meeting.[149] The sanction for non-compliance is that every officer of the company who is in default commits an offence and if convicted is liable to a fine.[150]

22.58    Where a traded company sends a copy of a notice of a meeting to a person nominated under s 146 the copy of the notice must be accompanied by a statement that he may have a right under an agreement between him and the member by whom he was nominated to be appointed, or to have someone else appointed, as a proxy for the meeting, and, if he has no such right or does not wish to exercise it, he may have a right under such agreement to give instructions to the member as to the

---

[145]   s 311, which states provisions in 1985 Act, Table A, reg 38.
[146]   *Kaye v Croydon Tramways Co* [1898] 1 Ch 358, CA.
[147]   *Re Hampshire Land Co* [1896] 2 Ch 743; *Kaye v Croydon Tramways Co* [1898] 1 Ch 358, CA; *Normandy v Ind Coope & Co* [1908] 1 Ch 84; *Pacific Coast Coal Mines v Arbuthnot* [1917] AC 607, PC.
[148]   subs 325(1). Section 325 is derived from 1985 Act, s 372(3) and (4) with changes. Table A, reg 59 allows a member to appoint more than one proxy and regs 61 and 62 provide for the form of proxy. Model Articles (pcls) 45 and 46 and Model Articles (plc) 38 and 39 deal with the content and delivery of proxy notices.
[149]   subs 325(2).
[150]   subss 325(3) and (4).

exercise of voting rights. Section 325 does not apply to the copy of the notice sent to the nominated person, and the company must either omit the notice required by s 325, or include it but state that it does not apply to the nominated person.[151]

### To whom notice must be sent

Notice of a general meeting must be sent to every member of the company, every director, and also to any person who is entitled to a share as a consequence of the death or bankruptcy of a member, subject to any enactment and any provision of the company's articles.[152] A company's auditor is also entitled to receive all notices and communications of general meetings.[153] Notice is given to a personal representative and trustee in bankruptcy for information since the company's articles may exclude them from the meeting and they will not be counted in any vote.[154]     **22.59**

Where the company's articles include a provision enabling a member to nominate another person or persons as entitled to enjoy or exercise all or any specified rights of the member in relation to the company, any nominated person has the right to be sent the notice of the general meeting under s 310.[155] If the company is a traded company, a member of the company who holds shares on behalf of another person may nominate that person to enjoy information rights, which include the right to receive communications that the company sends to its members concerning notice of meetings.[156]     **22.60**

### Resolutions requiring special notice

An ordinary resolution for the removal of a director or auditor or, in certain circumstances, to appoint a person as auditor in place of a person whose term of     **22.61**

---

[151] Part 9, s 149. See paragraph 22.92 below.

[152] s 310 re-enacts 1985 Act, s 370 and restates part of Table A, reg 38. The relevant part of reg 38 provides: 'Subject to the provisions of the articles and to any restrictions imposed on any shares, the notice shall be given to all members, to all persons entitled to a share in consequence of the death or bankruptcy of a member and to the directors and auditors.' Table A, reg 112, deals with service of notices on members and provides that a member whose registered address is not within the United Kingdom is not entitled to receive any notice of the company if he does not give the company an address within the United Kingdom at which notices may be given to him, or an address to which notices may be sent using electronic communications. Section 310 and the part of Table A, reg 38 quoted above reverse the position at common law under which the personal representatives of a deceased shareholder were not entitled to receive notice: *Allen v Gold Reefs of West Africa Ltd* [1900] 1 Ch 656, CA. Table A, reg 116 deals with service of notices on personal representatives and trustees in bankruptcy.

[153] ss 498 to 502 state the duties and rights of auditors. Section 502 re-enacts 1985 Act, s 390.

[154] 1985 Act, Table A, reg 31 and ss 282 and 283.

[155] Part 9, s 145, which is a new provision concerning the exercise of members' rights.

[156] Part 9, ss 146–148, which are new provisions. Section 147 prescribes the form in which copies are to be provided to the nominated person. See paragraphs 22.92 and 22.93 below.

office has ended requires special notice to be given to the company.[157] By subs 312(1) such a resolution is not effective unless notice of the intention to move it has been given to the company at least 28 days before the meeting at which it is moved.[158] The company must give its members notice of the resolution in the same manner and at the same time as it gives notice of the meeting, but if that is not practicable, the company must give its members notice at least 14 days before the meeting by advertisement in a newspaper having an appropriate circulation, or in any other manner allowed by the company's articles.[159] If after the notice of the intention to move the resolution has been given to the company, a meeting is called for a date 28 days or less after notice has been given, the notice is deemed to have been properly given, though not given within the time required.[160]

### Accidental failure to give notice of resolution or meeting

**22.62**   Subsection 313(1) states the general rule that where a company gives notice of a general meeting or a resolution intended to be moved at a general meeting any accidental failure to give notice to one or more persons shall be disregarded for the purpose of determining whether notice of the meeting or resolution is duly given.[161] The general rule is subject to any provision in the company's articles, except that, to ensure certainty, it cannot be modified in respect of s 304 (notice of meetings required by members), s 305 (notice of meetings called by members), or s 339 (notice of resolutions at AGMs proposed by members).[162] Where information rights have been conferred on a nominated person in respect of a traded company, a failure to give effect to the rights conferred by the nomination does not affect the validity of anything done by or on behalf of the company.[163]

**22.63**   A person who claims that the meeting is valid has the burden of proving that the failure to give notice was accidental.[164] The court has been satisfied that the

---

[157]   Paragraph 22.10 above.

[158]   s 312 is derived from 1985 Act, s 379, with changes to take account of the fact that 14 days is the normal period for notice of a general meeting.

[159]   subss 312(2) and (3). These subsections are machinery designed to ensure that members, as well as the director or auditor concerned, have notice of the proposed resolution, but nothing in s 312 gives an individual member the right to compel inclusion in the agenda of a company meeting of a resolution of the type that requires special notice: *Pedley v Inland Waterways Association Ltd* [1977] 1 All ER 209. If the company is a traded company, a member of the company who holds shares on behalf of another person may nominate that person to enjoy information rights, which include the right to receive communications that the company sends to its members concerning notice of meetings, such as notice of a resolution requiring special notice (s 146).

[160]   subs 312(4).

[161]   subs 313(1) is derived from the Table A, reg 39, which is in these terms: 'The accidental omission to give notice of a meeting to, or non-receipt of notice of a meeting by, any person entitled to receive notice shall not invalidate the proceedings at that meeting.'

[162]   subs 313(2).

[163]   subs 150(6).

[164]   *POW Services Ltd v Clare* [1995] 2 BCLC 435, 450.

failure to give notice to certain members was accidental when inadvertently records of their addresses had become separated from the rest, but a deliberate decision not to give notice to a member, based on a mistaken belief that the member is not entitled to notice is not an accidental failure.[165] Independently of s 313, a failure to give notice to a member for any reason can be cured by the assent of all the members of the company entitled to vote[166] or by the presence at the meeting of the member who had not been given notice and his acquiescence in the business conducted at it.[167]

### (3) Members' statements

The members of a company may require the company to circulate, to members of **22.64** the company entitled to receive notice of a general meeting, a statement of not more than 1,000 words with respect to a matter referred to in a proposed resolution to be dealt with at that meeting, or other business to be dealt with at that meeting.[168] The rights of the members to require the company to circulate the resolution and statement are subject to three restrictions.

First, the statement must command the requisite support from members. This is **22.65** the threshold requirement and the company is not required to circulate the statement until it receives requests[169] that it do so from (a) members representing at least 5% of the total voting rights of all the members who have a relevant right to vote (excluding any voting rights attached to any shares in the company held as treasury shares), or (b) at least 100 members who have a relevant right to vote and hold shares in the company on which there has been paid up an average sum, per member, of at least £100.[170] Where the company's articles enable a member to nominate another person or persons as entitled to enjoy or exercise all or any specified rights of the member in relation to the company, a nominated person

---

[165] *Re West Canadian Collieries Ltd* [1962] Ch 370; *Royal Mutual Benefit Society v Sharman* [1963] 1 WLR 581; *Musselwhite v CH Musselwhite & Sons Ltd* [1962] Ch 964.

[166] This is an application of the *Duomatic* principle (paragraphs 22.16–22.21 above): *Re Express Engineering Works Ltd* [1920] 1 Ch 466; *Re Oxted Motor Co* [1921] 3 KB 32; *Parker and Cooper v Reading* [1926] Ch 975.

[167] *Re Bailey, Hay & Co Ltd* [1971] 1 WLR 1357.

[168] subss 314(1), which is derived from 1985 Act, subss 376(1) and (2) and 377(1)(a) with changes. Members have a similar right in respect of written resolutions proposed by them; s 292(2) and paragraph 22.24 above.

[169] By subs 314(4) each request (a) may be in hard copy form or in electronic form, (b) must identify the statement to be circulated, (c) must be authenticated by the person or persons making it, and (d) must be received by the company at least one week before the meeting to which it relates. For hard copy form and electronic form, see ss 333 and 1144(1) and Schedule 4. For authentication, see s 1146.

[170] subs 314(2). By subs 314(3) a 'relevant right to vote' means '(a) in relation to a statement with respect to a matter referred to in a proposed resolution, a right to vote on that resolution at the meeting to which the requests relate, and (b) in relation to any other statement, a right to vote at the meeting to which the requests relate'.

may request the company to circulate the statement.[171] If the company is a traded company, a member may nominate another person to enjoy information rights, in which case the nominated person may be included among the 100 members for the purpose of requesting the company to circulate the statement if the conditions in subs 153(2) are satisfied with respect to the nominated person.[172]

**22.66** Secondly, members must not abuse their power to require the company to circulate a statement. The company is not required to circulate the statement if, on an application by the company or another person who claims to be aggrieved, the court is satisfied that the rights conferred by ss 292 and 293 are being abused.[173]

**22.67** Thirdly, unless the meeting to which the requests to circulate the statement relate is an AGM of a public company and requests sufficient to require the company to circulate the statement are received before the end of the financial year preceding the meeting, the members who request the company to circulate the statement must pay the companies' expenses of complying with s 315, unless the company has resolved otherwise, and must deposit with, or tender to, the company a sum sufficient to meet the company's expenses in doing so.[174]

**22.68** A company that is required under s 314 to circulate a statement must send a copy of it to each member of the company entitled to receive notice of the meeting in the same manner as the notice of the meeting, and at the same time as, or as soon as reasonably practicable after, it gives notice of the meeting.[175] There is no reason to think that failure duly to circulate the members' statement of itself affects the validity of any resolution passed at the meeting.[176] Instead, in the event of default in complying with s 315, an offence is committed by every officer of the company in default who is liable to a fine on conviction.[177]

---

[171] s 145.

[172] ss 146 and 153. Reference should be made to the Companies Act for the conditions in subs 153(2). See paragraph 22.92 below.

[173] subs 315(2) and s 317, which is derived from 1985 Act, s 377(3) with changes. Subsection 317(2) provides that the court may order members who requested the circulation of the statement to pay the whole or part of the company's costs of the application, even if they are not parties to the application. Members who support the circulation of a members' statement should therefore satisfy themselves that the statement is not abusive. Section 295 is the equivalent provision for written resolutions, discussed in paragraph 22.26 above.

[174] subs 315(2) and s 316, which may be compared with s 294 in relation to written resolutions and statements, discussed in paragraph 17.27 above, and s 340 in relation to public company AGMs. Section 316 is derived from 1985 Act, ss 376 and 377 with changes.

[175] subs 315(1). The company's obligations under subs 315(1) are subject to subs 315(2) (deposit or tender of sum in respect of circulation) and s 317 (application not to circulate members' statement). If the company is a traded company, a member of the company who holds shares on behalf of another person may nominate that person to enjoy information rights, which include the right to receive communications that the company sends to its members concerning notice of meetings; ss 146–148.

[176] There is no equivalent to s 293(7).

[177] subss 291(5) and (6) and 293(5) and (6). For officer in default, see s 1121.

## (4) Procedure at meetings

### Attendance and business at the meeting

A company's articles invariably provide that the directors are entitled to attend **22.69** and speak at general meetings even if they are not shareholders.[178] The business at the meeting will however be decided on by three classes of person: (i) the individual members, who are entitled to vote, (ii) representatives of companies appointed in accordance with s 323, and (iii) proxies appointed in accordance with ss 324–331.[179]

The meeting is held at the place identified in the notice, but all the members of a **22.70** company may informally agree to change the location of the meeting. With modern technology it is possible for persons located elsewhere to be connected by audio-visual links to the place of the meeting, so that they are regarded as being present.[180]

All the members of a company may decide what business to conduct at a general **22.71** meeting, but in the absence of unanimity, the business will be limited to the resolutions proposed, or business of the general nature described, in the notice of the meeting.[181]

### Quorum

For the purposes of the quorum provisions in s 318 a qualifying person is (i) an **22.72** individual who is a member of the company, (ii) a person who is authorized to represent a corporation which is a member of the company, who has been appointed under s 323, or (iii) a person appointed as proxy for a member in relation to the meeting.[182] The quorum provisions in s 318 do not apply to a variation of class rights meeting.[183]

In the case of a company limited by shares or guarantee which has only one mem- **22.73** ber, one qualifying person present at the meeting is a quorum.[184] If the sole member does not take a decision by way of written resolution, s 357 provides that he must provide the company with details of any decision made by him that may be

---

[178] Table A, reg 44; Model Article (pcls) 40 and Model Article (plc) 32.
[179] Table A, regs 59–63, Model Articles (pcls) 45 and 46, and Model Articles (plc) 38 and 39 deal with proxies or proxy notices and votes by proxies. In the case of traded companies, regard should be had to the interests in the appointment of proxies of nominated persons with information rights under Part 9; ss 146 and 149.
[180] *Byng v London Life Association Ltd* [1990] Ch 170, 183, 192, CA.
[181] ss 304 and 311 and Table A, reg 38.
[182] subs 318(3). Section 318 is derived from 1985 Act, s 370(1) and (4) and 370(A) with changes.
[183] subss 334(3) and 335(3); instead the quorum is as stated in subss 334(4) or 335(4), as the case may be.
[184] subs 318(1).

taken by the company in general meeting or which has effect as if agreed by the company in general meeting, so that the company has a written record of the decision.[185] Section 231 provides for a written record to be made of any contract between the company and a sole member who is also sole director which is not entered into in the ordinary course of business. There are criminal sanctions for failure to comply with ss 231 and 357, although non-compliance does not affect the validity of the transaction or decision.[186]

**22.74** If a company limited by shares or guarantee has more than one member, or in any other case, subject to the provisions of the company's articles, two qualifying persons present at the meeting are a quorum. But a quorum cannot be achieved by a member appointing two or more corporate representatives or proxies.[187] A single person present in two capacities (as an individual member and as a corporate representative) counts as two persons.[188] Unlike the 1985 Act, subs 370(4), subss 318(1) and (2) do not include the phrase 'personally present', which suggests that it is not necessary for the two qualifying persons to be physically present in the same meeting room.[189] The quorum provision in Table A is slightly different to subss 318(1) and (2): 'Save in the case of a company with a single member two persons entitled to vote upon the business to be transacted, each being a member or a proxy for a member or a duly authorised representative of a corporation, shall be a quorum.'

**22.75** No business other than the appointment of the chairman of the meeting can be transacted at a general meeting if the persons attending do not constitute a quorum and, in such a case, the meeting has to be adjourned.[190] Subject to the

---

[185] s 357 re-enacts 1985 Act, s 382B, and 2006 Act, subs 355(1)(c).

[186] subss 231(3), (4), and (6) and 357(3)–(5). These provisions go a long way to avoiding the unsatisfactory position of a sole director and member 'purporting to continue the business and effectively bind everyone else who is interested in it by anything to which, in his private thoughts, he cares to assent', which Oliver J rejected and, with a homage to Wordsworth, described as 'the self-sufficing power of solitude'; *Re New Cedos Engineering Co Ltd* (1976) [1994] 1 BCLC 797, 813.

[187] subs 318(2).

[188] *Neil McLeod & Sons Ltd, Petitioners* [1967] SC 16.

[189] This accords with modern commercial practice (*Byng v London Life Association Ltd* [1990] Ch 170, CA) and is reflected in Model Article (pcls) 37(4) and Model Article (plc) 29(4), which both provide: 'In determining attendance at a general meeting, it is immaterial whether any two or more shareholders attending it are in the same place as each other.' Further Model Article (pcls) 37(3) and Model Article (plc) 29(3) enable the directors to make whatever arrangements they consider appropriate to enable those attending a general meeting to exercise their rights to speak or vote at it. This issue was addressed in the CLR: *Company General Meetings and Shareholder Communications* at [29]–[30] and the CLR: *Developing the Framework* at [4.30]–[4.35], and the White Paper: *Company Law Reform* at [4.2].

[190] Table A, regs 40–42; Model Articles (pcls) 39(2) and 41(1) and Model Articles (plc) 31(2) and 33(1).

company's articles, the quorum has to be present for the duration of the meeting.[191] A resolution purportedly passed at an inquorate meeting will be invalid.[192] Abuse of the quorum provisions can be overcome by applying to the court under s 306 to order a meeting at which a quorum may be one person present (paragraphs 22.47–22.51 above).

*Chairman*

Section 319 provides a default rule for the appointment of the chairman of a general meeting, by which, subject to any provision in the company's articles, a member may be elected to be chairman by ordinary resolution of the company passed at the meeting.[193] In fact the company's articles invariably make provision for the chairman of the board to be chairman of the meeting, or for a director to be chairman, or, in default of a director being appointed chairman, for the members to choose one of their number to be chairman.[194]   **22.76**

The chairman's responsibilities are to supervise the conduct of the meeting, to determine whether the meeting should be adjourned, and to take any votes that are required. It is the chairman's responsibility to secure the proper, fair, and orderly conduct of the meeting so that the meeting can make its decision on any matter before it.[195] The chairman will introduce any directors' report or members' statement that is to be put before the meeting. The chairman will direct the order of speeches by directors and members, corporate representatives, and proxies.[196] He may also have a discretion to allow non-members to attend and speak at   **22.77**

---

[191] *Sharp v Dawes* (1876) 2 QBD 26 (CA); *Re Sanitary Carbon Co* [1877] WN 223; *Re London Flats Ltd* [1969] 1 WLR 711. Table A, reg 41 provides that the meeting has to be adjourned if the meeting ceases to be quorate. Under the 1948 Table A, reg 53, if a quorum was present at the commencement of the meeting, the departure of members reducing the numbers present to below the quorum figure did not invalidate resolutions passed at the meeting: *Re Hartley Baird Ltd* [1955] Ch 143.

[192] *Re Cambrian Peat, Fuel and Charcoal Ltd* (1875) 31 LT 773.

[193] s 319 re-enacts 1985 Act, subss 370(1) and (5) without change.

[194] Table A, regs 42 and 43; Model Article (pcls) 39 and Model Article (plc) 31. On the power under the general law of the members present to appoint a chairman, when the chairman does not attend: *Re Salcombe Hotel Development Co Ltd* [1991] BCLC 44. A proxy may be elected chairman; s 328. In *Re Bradford Investments Ltd* [1991] BCLC 224 it was held that the members could choose a solicitor who held a proxy but was not a member to act as temporary chairman to supervise the election of a proper chairman.

[195] *National Dwellings Society v Sykes* [1894] 2 Ch 159; *Carruth v Imperial Chemical Industries* [1937] Ch 707, 761, 767, PC.

[196] The articles usually provide for directors to be entitled to speak, whether or not they are members; Table A, reg 44; Model Article (pcls) 40(1) and Model Article (plc) 32(1). A member has a prima facie right to speak (*Const v Harris* (1824) Turn & R 496, 525) and this right to speak is reflected in Model Article (pcls) 37(2), (3), and (5) and Model Article (plc) 29(2), (3) and (5). A corporate representative and a proxy have rights to speak on behalf of the member: ss 323 and 324.

the meeting.[197] Once a resolution has been properly debated, the chairman may end the debate and take the vote or close the meeting.[198]

**22.78** The company's articles usually provide that the chairman must adjourn the meeting if a quorum is not present within half an hour from the time appointed for the meeting,[199] but that, where a quorum is present, the chairman may with the consent of the meeting adjourn it to a later date.[200] The chairman also has a residual power to adjourn the meeting where the circumstances are such that the consent of the meeting cannot be ascertained, but his decision to do so may be challenged on the same grounds as apply to judicial review cases.[201] If the articles provide for the chairman to have power to adjourn with the consent of the meeting, the members cannot compel an adjournment against the wishes of the chairman.[202] The new Model Articles, however, give the members an independent right to direct the chairman to adjourn the meeting.[203] If the chairman purports to adjourn the meeting without the consent of the members and leaves the meeting, declaring it closed, the members may appoint another chairman and continue the meeting.[204]

**22.79** An adjourned meeting is a continuation of the original meeting and it will conduct the same business as could have been conducted at the original meeting. The articles invariably provide that if the adjournment is for more than fourteen days, notice should be given, but subject to that, and unless the articles otherwise provide, no further notice is necessary, the quorum is the same, and the proxies for the original meeting can be used.[205] Where a resolution is passed at an adjourned meeting of a company, the resolution is for all purposes to be treated as having been passed on the date on which it was in fact passed, and is not to be deemed passed on any earlier date.[206]

---

[197] Model Article (pcls) 41(2) and Model Article (plc) 32(2).

[198] *Wall v London and Northern Assets Corp* [1898] 2 Ch 649, CA; *Carruth v Imperial Chemical Industries* [1937] AC 707, 767, PC.

[199] Table A, reg 41 provides that the meeting shall 'stand adjourned to the same day in the next week at the same time and place or to such time and place as the directors may determine'. Model Article (pcls) 42 and Model Article (plc) 33 both provide for the meeting to be adjourned in such circumstances (subpara (1)), but the adjournment date is to be fixed in accordance with subpara (3) in the same way as for any other adjournment.

[200] Table A, reg 45; Model Article (pcls) 42(2)(a) and Model Article (plc) 33(2)(a). In *Re Abbey National plc* [2005] 2 BCLC 15 the articles required a poll on a resolution to adjourn.

[201] *Byng v London Life Association Ltd* [1990] Ch 170, CA; Model Article (pcls) 42(2)(b) and Model Article (plc) 33(2)(b).

[202] *Salisbury Gold Mining Co v Hathorn* [1897] AC 268, PC.

[203] Model Article (pcls) 42(3) and Model Article (plc) 33(3).

[204] *National Dwellings Society v Sykes* [1894] 3 Ch 159; *John v Rees* [1970] Ch 345.

[205] *Wills v Murray* (1850) 4 Ex 843; *Scadding v Lorant* (1851) 3 HLC 418; *McLaren v Thomson* [1917] 2 Ch 261. Table A, reg 45; Model Article (pcls) 42(5) and (6) and Model Article (plc) 33(5) and (6).

[206] s 332, which re-enacts 1985 Act, s 381 without change.

*Votes*

The chairman is responsible for taking the vote on resolutions at the meeting. The **22.80** articles usually provide that, unless a poll is duly demanded, votes shall be decided on a show of hands.[207] When the vote is on a show of hands, subject to any provision of the company's articles, every member present in person has one vote, and every proxy present who has been duly appointed by a member entitled to vote on the resolution has one vote.[208] Where the resolution is to ratify acts of a director, the votes of the director (if a member) and persons connected with him are disregarded.[209] Articles invariably provide that in the event of equality of votes, the chairman has a casting vote, but such a provision is considered to be inconsistent with ss 281 and 282.[210] On a vote on a resolution at a meeting on a show of hands (unless a poll is demanded and the demand is not subsequently withdrawn), a declaration by the chairman that the resolution has or has not been passed, or passed with a particular majority, is conclusive evidence of that fact without proof of the number or proportion of the votes recorded in favour of or against the resolution.[211] The articles usually provide that the chairman's decision on entitlement

---

[207] Table A, reg 46; Model Article (pcls) 42 and Model Article (plc) 34.

[208] s 284, which is derived from 1985 Act, subss 370(1) and (6) and Table A, reg 54, with changes. The articles may provide that a share may not be voted if there are monies owed in respect of it; Table A, reg 57 and Model Article (plc) 41. A proxy has one vote for each member represented; see also subss 285(1) and (2), which are new. There are possible difficulties of interpretation of s 284 when a corporate member appoints several representatives. Where there are joint holders of shares, only the vote of the senior holder who votes, in person or by proxy, is to be counted and seniority is determined by the order of names in the register of members; s 286, which restates Table A, reg 55. Provisions about proxies are to be found in ss 324–331; Table A, regs 59–63; Model Articles (pcls) 45, 46 and Model Article (plc) 38, 39. The right to appoint a proxy to act at a meeting is one of the rights that a nominated person may enjoy where s 145 applies. In the case of a traded company a nominated person may also be entitled to appoint a proxy, depending on his agreement with the nominee member; ss 146 and 149.

[209] subss 239(4) and (5) and s 252. Subject to s 239, as far as the company is concerned, if a member is entitled to vote on a resolution, he may vote as he pleases even if he is interested in the transaction being voted on: *North-West Transportation Co v Beatty* (1887) 12 AC 589, PC; *Burland v Earle* [1902] AC 83, PC; *Northern Counties Securities Ltd v Jackson & Steeple Ltd* [1974] 1 WLR 1133. A member may, however, enter into a valid agreement as to the exercise of voting rights, which may be enforced by injunction: *Russell v Northern Bank Development Corporation Ltd* [1992] 1 WLR 588, HL. For limitations on the effectiveness of a vote, see Chapter 19 at paras 19.25–19.30 above.

[210] The Tables A to F Amendment Regulations 2007 therefore delete Table A, reg 50 for companies incorporated on or after 1 October 2007. But 2006 Act Commencement Order No 5, Schedule 5, para 2(b) amends 2006 Act Commencement Order No 3, Schedule 3, by inserting a new para 23A, which provides that where, immediately before 1 October 2007 a company's articles provided for a chairman's casting vote, unless it had subsequently been removed, such provision continued to have effect notwithstanding 2006 Act, ss 281(3) and 282.

[211] subss 320(1) and (3), which re-enacts 1985 Act, 378(4), without change, and restates Table A, regs 47 and 48 with changes. Evidence tendered to the effect that the chairman's declaration was wrong is inadmissible, but the chairman's declaration can be challenged if (a) there is a manifest error on the face of the declaration (if it identifies insufficient votes for the resolution to be passed), (b) there was an error in the procedure (if a member was wrongly excluded from voting), or (c) fraud

to vote is final and conclusive.[212] Further, an entry in respect of the chairman's declaration in minutes of the meeting recorded in accordance with s 355 is also conclusive evidence of that fact without proof.[213]

**22.81** Where the outcome or likely outcome of a vote is contentious, a poll may be demanded. Section 321 makes void any provision in a company's articles in so far as it would have the effect of:

(1) excluding the right to demand a poll at a general meeting on any question other than the election of the chairman of the meeting or the adjournment of the meeting; and

(2) making ineffective a demand for a poll on any such question which is made—

(a) by not less than 5 members having the right to vote on the resolution; or (b) by a member or members representing not less than 10% of the total voting rights of all the members having the right to vote on the resolution (excluding any voting rights attached to any shares in the company held as treasury shares); or (c) by a member or members holding shares in the company conferring a right to vote on the resolution, being shares on which an aggregate sum has been paid up equal to not less than 10% of the total sum paid up on all the shares conferring that right (excluding shares in the company conferring a right to vote on the resolution which are held as treasury shares).[214]

A demand by a proxy is taken into account for the purpose of determining the qualification to demand a poll under paragraphs (a)–(c) above.[215] The articles usually give the chairman and members (if certain conditions are met, which conditions cannot be less extensive than required by s 321) the right to demand a poll.[216] If the chairman has the right to demand a poll, he should exercise that right when he is unable to determine the outcome of a vote on a show of hands.[217]

---

is shown: *Re Hadleigh Castle Gold Mines* [1900] 2 Ch 419; *Arnot v United African Lands* [1901] 1 Ch 518, CA; *Re Caratal (New) Mines Ltd* [1902] 2 Ch 498; *Clark & Co* [1911] SC 243.

[212] Table A, reg 58; Model Article (pcls) 43(2) and Model Article (plc) 35(2). These provisions are effective; s 287, which is new.

[213] subs 320(2), which restates Table A, reg 47.

[214] s 321, which re-enacts 1985 Act, subs 373(1) with changes. Section 321 does not apply to variation of class rights meetings; ss 334(3)(b) and 335(30(b).

[215] s 329, which re-enacts 1985 Act, s 373(2) with changes.

[216] Table A, reg 46; Model Article (pcls) 44(1) and (2) and Model Article (plc) 36(1) and (2). The Model Articles provide that a poll may be demanded (a) before the meeting, (b) before the show of hands, or (c) immediately after the result of the show of hands is declared. They also give a director the right to demand a poll (which may be significant on a vote for his removal).

[217] *Second Consolidated Trust v Ceylon Amalgamated Tea & Rubber Estates Ltd* [1943] 2 All ER 567.

The demand for a poll may be withdrawn with the chairman's consent before it is taken.[218]

**22.82** Subject to provisions of the company's articles, the chairman will determine when and how to take the poll. He may wish to have the assistance of scrutineers. The articles usually provide for the poll to be taken immediately or, if it does not concern the election of the chairman of the meeting or adjournment, at a future date within 30 days of the meeting of which at least seven days' notice is given, and that the result of the poll shall be the decision of the meeting in respect of the resolution on which the poll was demanded.[219]

**22.83** On a vote on a resolution on a poll taken at a meeting, subject to any provisions of the company's articles, in the case of a company having a share capital, every member has one vote in respect of each share or £10 of stock held by him, and in any other case, every member has one vote.[220] When a poll is taken it is the votes conferred by each share that are counted, so that it is irrelevant whether the member is voting in person or by proxy.[221] A member who is entitled to more than one vote on a poll need not, if he votes, use all his votes or cast all the votes he uses in the same way.[222] For special provisions about polls of quoted companies, see paragraphs 22.94–22.102 below.

*Minutes of general meetings*

**22.84** A company must keep minutes of all proceedings of general meetings and if a resolution is a special resolution a copy of it must be forwarded to the Registrar within 15 days after it is passed.[223] The minutes of proceedings of a general meeting, if purporting to be signed by the chairman of that meeting or by the chairman of the next general meeting, are evidence of the proceedings of the meeting.[224]

---

[218] Table A, reg 48; Model Article (pcls) 44(3) and Model Article (plc) 36(3).

[219] Table A, regs 51 and 52; Model Article (plc) 37. Model Article (pcls) 44(4) provides that for private companies polls must be taken immediately and in such manner as the chairman of the meeting directs. Subject to the articles, a chairman has an inherent power to adjourn for a poll; *Jackson v Hamlyn* [1953] Ch 577.

[220] subss 284(3) and (4) re-enact 1985 Act, subss 370(1) and (6) and restate Table A, reg 54 with changes. Note also subs 285(3). Companies' articles frequently provide for weighted voting rights and effect will be given to them on a poll; *Bushell v Faith* [1970] AC 1099, HL. For provisions about joint holders of shares and proxies, see n 208 above.

[221] Hansard HoC, Standing Committee, day 5, col 297.

[222] s 322, which re-enacts 1985 Act, s 374 without change. It allows members who hold shares on behalf of different clients to act on their clients' instructions, by voting in different ways or not voting. Section 152 is to similar effect.

[223] subs 355(1)(b) and 1985 Act, s 380, which will be replaced by 2006 Act, ss 29 and 30 on 1 October 2009. The provisions of subss 355(1)(b) and 356(4) and (5) also apply to class meetings.

[224] subs 356(4). Table A, reg 100 provides that the directors shall cause minutes to be made in books kept for the purpose of all proceedings at meetings of the company and class meetings, including the names of the directors present at each such meeting.

Where there is a record of proceedings of a general meeting of a company, then, until the contrary is proved the meeting is deemed duly held and convened, all proceedings at the meeting are deemed to have duly taken place, and all appointments at the meeting are deemed valid.[225]

## E. Public Companies: Additional Requirements for AGMs

**22.85**  A private company does not have to hold AGMs unless required to do so by its memorandum or articles.[226] Every public company must, by subs 336(1), hold an AGM within six months of its financial year end.[227] If the company fails to comply with subs 336(1) an offence is committed by every officer of the company in default and a person guilty of an offence is liable to a fine.[228]

**22.86**  A notice calling an AGM must state that the meeting is an AGM.[229] The AGM must be called by notice of at least 21 days, and that period can only be reduced if all the members entitled to attend and vote at the meeting agree to shorter notice.[230]

**22.87**  The members of a public company may require the company to give, to members of the company entitled to receive notice of the next AGM, notice of a resolution which may properly be moved and is intended to be moved at the meeting.[231] The proposed resolution may be supported by a members' statement under ss 314–317, subject to the restrictions there mentioned (paragraphs 22.64–22.68 above). The members' right to require circulation of a resolution for an AGM is subject to three restrictions.

**22.88**  First, the resolution must command the requisite support from members. This is the threshold requirement and the company is not required to circulate the

---

[225]  subs 356(5).

[226]  2006 Act Commencement Order No 3, Schedule 3, para 32. By 2006 Act, Commencement Order No 3, Schedule 3, para 32, as amended by 2006 Act Commencement Order No 5, Schedule 5, para 2(b) an elective resolution under 1985 Act, s 366A is not regarded as a provision requiring a private company to hold an AGM.

[227]  s 336(1), which is subject to the qualification in subs 336(2) and to 2006 Act Commencement Order No 3, Schedule 1, para 15, which extends the period to seven months, and Schedule 3, paras 33–38. Section 336 is derived from 1985 Act, s 366 with changes and new provisions. The period within which the AGM must be held has been reduced from ten to six months. For discussion of the reforms in relation to AGMs, see CLR: *Company General Meetings and Shareholder Communication* at paras 31, 32, 41, 46; CLR: *Developing the Framework* at paras 4.25–4.28, 4.39; CLR: *Completing the Structure* at paras 4.2–4.5; CLR: *Final Report* at paras 6.39, 7.6, and 7.8; White Paper: *Company Law Reform* at para 4.2.

[228]  subss 336(3) and (4).

[229]  subs 337(1) which re-enacts 1985 Act, subs 366(1) without change.

[230]  subss 307(2)(a) and 337(2), which re-enact subs 369(3)(a) without change.

[231]  subs 338(1), which re-enacts 1985 Act, s 376(1)(b).

resolution until it receives requests[232] that it do so from (a) members representing at least 5% of the total voting rights of all the members who have a relevant right to vote on the resolution at the AGM to which the requests relate (excluding any voting rights attached to any shares in the company held as treasury shares), or (b) at least 100 members who have a right to vote on the resolution at the AGM to which the request relates and hold shares in the company on which there has been paid up an average sum, per member, of at least £100.[233] The level of support required for the resolution is the same as the level of support required for the circulation of a members' statement for a general meeting and nominated persons have the same rights to be included in the support for the resolution as are described in paragraph 22.65 above.[234]

Secondly, members must not abuse their power to require the company to circulate the resolution. The resolution is not capable of being properly moved at an AGM if (a) it would, if passed, be ineffective (whether by reason of inconsistency with any enactment or the company's constitution or otherwise), (b) it is defamatory of any person, or (c) it is frivolous and vexatious.[235] **22.89**

Thirdly, unless requests sufficient to require the company to circulate the resolution are received before the end of the financial year preceding the meeting, the members who request the company to circulate the resolution must pay the company's expenses of complying with s 339, unless the company has resolved otherwise, and must deposit with, or tender to, the company, not later than six weeks before the AGM to which the request relates, or, if later, the time at which notice is given of that meeting, a sum sufficient to meet the company's expenses in complying with s 339.[236] **22.90**

A company that is required under s 338 to give notice of a resolution must send a copy of it to each member of the company entitled to receive notice of the AGM in the same manner as the notice of the meeting, and at the same time as, or as **22.91**

---

[232] By subs 338(4), each request (a) may be in hard copy form or in electronic form, (b) must identify the statement to be circulated, (c) must be authenticated by the person or persons making it, and (d) must be received by the company at least one week before the meeting to which it relates. Subsection 338(4) may be compared with subss 292(6), 303(6), and 314(4). For hard copy form and electronic form, see ss 333 and 1144(1) and Schedule 4. For authentication, see s 1146.

[233] subs 338(3), which derives from 1985 Act, subs 376(2) with changes.

[234] ss 146 and 153. Reference should be made to the Companies Act for the conditions in subs 153(2).

[235] subs 338(2), which is new. This is the same restriction as applies to members' requests for circulation of a written resolution under subs 292(2); see paragraph 22.28 above.

[236] s 340, which is part new and part derived from 1985 Act, subss 376(1) and 377(1)(b) with changes and which may be compared with ss 294 and 316 in relation to written resolutions and statements. See paragraph 22.27 above.

soon as reasonably practicable after, it gives notice of the meeting.[237] The business which may be dealt with at an AGM includes a resolution of which notice is given in accordance with s 339.[238] To secure compliance with s 339, in the event of default in complying with it, an offence is committed by every officer of the company in default who is liable to a fine on conviction.[239]

## F. Additional Requirements for Quoted Companies

**22.92** In relation to decision-making by members, the Companies Act contains particular provisions relevant to quoted companies, being companies whose equity share capital is officially listed in the UK under FSMA, Part 6, or in an EEA state, or on either the New York Stock Exchange or Nasdaq.[240] Directors of quoted companies must be aware of the special rights of members of quoted companies, and of the rights of indirect investors in their shares, which in several respects are enforced through criminal penalties.

### (1) Traded companies: information rights

**22.93** The first set of provisions is in Part 9, ss 146–153, concerning the exercise of members' rights, which are new provisions. A quoted company, which is a traded company, in that its shares are admitted to trading on a regulated market, may be subject to information rights in favour of a nominated person.[241] A member of the quoted company who holds shares on behalf of another person may nominate that person to enjoy information rights, which include the right to receive communications that the company sends to its members generally or to any class of its members that includes the person making the nomination.[242] The member may enforce the information rights against the company for the benefit of the nominated person.[243] When the company sends notice of a meeting to a nominated person it must provide information as to possible rights in relation to voting at the meeting.[244] Subject to the requirements of subs 153(2) a nominated person may be included among the 100 persons for the purposes of determining whether

---

[237] subss 339(1). Section 339 re-enacts 1985 Act, subss 376(1), (6), and (7) and Schedule 24 without change. The company's obligations under subs 339(1) are subject to subs 340(2) (deposit or tender of sum in respect of expenses of circulation).

[238] subs 339(3).

[239] subss 339(4) and (5). The liability of an officer 'in default' is dealt with in s 1121.

[240] ss 361 and 385.

[241] Its articles should provide for it to recognize nominations and keep records of them; s 145.

[242] s 146.

[243] s 150.

[244] s 149.

the company is required to (a) circulate a members' statement under s 314, (b) circulate a resolution for a public company AGM under s 338, or (c) have an independent report on a poll under s 342. These provisions are referred to elsewhere in this chapter.[245]

## (2) Disclosure of, and independent report on, polls

The second set of provisions is in Part 13, Chapter 5, ss 341–354, concerning the validation of polls at general meetings of quoted companies through publication of poll results on a website and, in certain circumstances, requiring the company to obtain an independent report on a poll.[246] These are new provisions. The latter provisions are detailed and the following paragraphs focus on the provisions directly concerning directors.

**22.94**

### *Website publication of poll results*

Section 341 provides for the results of a poll taken at a meeting or class meeting of a quoted company to be made available on a website in accordance with the requirements of s 353.[247] The information about the results of the poll required to be made available on the website are (a) the date of the meeting, (b) the text of the resolution or description of the subject matter of the poll, (c) the number of votes cast in favour, and (d) the number of votes cast against. In the event of default in complying with ss 341 and 353 an offence is committed by every officer of the company in default and a person guilty of an offence is liable to a fine.[248] Failure to comply with ss 341 and 353 does not affect the validity of the poll or the resolution or other business (if passed or agreed) to which the poll relates.[249]

**22.95**

### *Independent report on poll*

The members of a quoted company may require the directors to obtain an independent report on any poll taken, or to be taken, at a general meeting or class

**22.96**

---

[245] Paragraphs 22.29, 22.57, 22.59, 22.64, and 22.95.

[246] These two measures were recommended by the CLR: *Final Report* at [6.39]. By s 354 the Secretary of State may limit or extend the types of company to which the provisions of Chapter 5 apply; eg to extend it to other companies with a large shareholder base, which are not private companies, or to narrow the application of the Chapter if the definition of quoted company were to be extended; Hansard HL GC Day 6 (60301-29).

[247] s 341 enacts the proposed EU Directive COM (2005) 685 final, Article 15. Section 352 applies s 341 to the results of a poll in respect of a class meeting. The requirements of s 353 are that (i) the website is maintained by or on behalf of the company, and identifies the company, (ii) there is no charge for access to the website or obtaining hard copies of information on it, and (iii) the information is made available as soon as reasonably practicable and remains on the website for two years.

[248] subss 341(3) and (4). The liability of an officer 'in default' is dealt with in s 1121.

[249] subs 341(5).

meeting of the company.[250] The directors are only required to obtain an independent report if, in respect of each poll, they receive requests[251] that they do so from (a) members representing at least 5% of the total voting rights of all the members who have a right to vote on the matter to which the poll (excluding any voting rights attached to any shares in the company held as treasury shares), or (b) at least 100 members who have a right to vote on the matter to which the poll relates and hold shares in the company on which there has been paid up an average sum, per member, of at least £100. The level of support required to obtain the report is the same as the level of support required for the circulation of a members' statement for a general meeting and a members' resolution at an AGM and nominated persons have the same rights to be included in the support for the request for a report as are described in paragraphs 22.64 and 22.87 above.[252]

**22.97** Unless no poll on which a report is required is in fact taken, the directors who are required by s 342 to obtain an independent report on a poll or polls, must appoint an independent assessor to prepare a report for the company on it or them within one week after the company being required to obtain the report.[253] The directors must not appoint as the independent assessor a person who does not meet the independence requirements in s 344, or who has another role in relation to any poll on which he is to report (including, in particular, a role in connection with collecting or counting votes or with the appointment of proxies).[254] In the event of default in complying with s 343 an offence is committed by every officer of the company in default and a person guilty of an offence is liable to a fine.[255]

**22.98** The independent assessor's report must state the independent assessor's name and his opinion whether (a) the procedures adopted in connection with the poll or polls were adequate; (b) the votes cast (including proxy votes) were fairly and

---

[250] ss 342 and 352. Sections 342–353 were introduced to address what was said to be a lack of confidence in the integrity and effectiveness of counting proxies; CLR: *Final Report* at [6.39(iv)]; White Paper: *Modernising Company Law* at [2.19]; White Paper: *Company Law Reform* at [3.1]; Paul Myner's *Review of impediments to voting United Kingdom shares*; and the debate at Hansard HL GC Day 6, Vol 679, col 134; HL Report, Vol 682, col 731; HC Comm D, col 336.

[251] By subs 342(4), each request (a) may be in hard copy form or in electronic form, (b) must identify the statement to be circulated, (c) must be authenticated by the person or persons making it, and (d) must be received by the company at least one week before the meeting to which it relates. For hard copy form and electronic form, see ss 333 and 1144(1) and Schedule 4. For authentication, see s 1146.

[252] ss 146 and 153. Reference should be made to the Companies Act for the conditions in subs 153(2).

[253] s 343.

[254] s 344 identifies persons who may not be appointed as an independent assessor, having regard to specified connections of themselves or their associates (as explained by s 345) with the company. An auditor of the company is not excluded from being an independent assessor. Section 346 deals with the appointment of a partnership as an independent assessor.

[255] subss 341(3) and (4). The liability of an officer 'in default' is dealt with in s 1121.

accurately recorded and counted; (c) the validity of members' appointments of proxies was fairly assessed; (d) the notice of the meeting complied with s 325 (notice of meeting to contain statement of rights to appoint proxies); and (e) s 326 was complied with in relation to the meeting (company-sponsored invitations to appoint proxies).[256] The report must give the independent assessor's reasons for the opinions stated, or record that he is unable to form an opinion on any of those matters and state his reasons for that.

**22.99**    For the purpose of preparing his report, s 348 entitles the independent assessor to attend the meeting at which the poll is to be taken and any subsequent proceedings in connection with the poll and to be provided with a copy of the notice of the meeting and other communications provided by the company in connection with it. For the same purpose, s 349 provides that the independent assessor (a) is entitled to access to the company's records relating to any poll on which he is to report and the meeting at which the poll or polls may be, or were, taken; and (b) may require anyone who at any material time was, among others,[257] a director or secretary of the company, to provide him with information or explanations. There are two protections for persons required to give information and explanations. First, a statement made by a person in response to a requirement under s 349 may not be used in evidence against him in criminal proceedings except proceedings under s 350. Secondly, the person is not required to disclose information in respect of which a claim to legal professional privilege could be maintained in legal proceedings.

**22.100**    The independent assessor may enforce his rights under ss 348 and 349 by applying for an injunction.[258] Section 350 enforces compliance with s 349 by imposing criminal sanctions.

(1) A person who fails to comply with a requirement under s 349 without delay commits an offence, unless it was not reasonably practicable for him to provide the required information or explanation, and if convicted is liable to a fine.[259]

(2) A person commits an offence if he knowingly or recklessly makes to an independent assessor a statement, oral or written, that conveys or purports to convey any information or explanations which the independent assessor requires, or is entitled to require under s 349, and is misleading, false, or

---

[256] s 347.
[257] The other person who may be required to provide information are: an employee of the company, a person holding or accountable for any of the company's records, a member of the company, and an agent of the company including the company's bankers, solicitors, and auditor.
[258] This is acknowledged by subs 350(5).
[259] subs 350(3).

deceptive in a material particular. On conviction a person is liable to a fine or imprisonment.[260]

**22.101** Section 351 provides for information about the appointment of an independent assessor to be made available on a website in accordance with the requirements of s 353 (paragraph 22.95 above). The information about the independent assessor required to be made available on the website are (a) the fact of his appointment, (b) his identity, (c) the text of the resolution or, as the case may be, a description of the subject matter of the poll to which his appointment relates, and (d) a copy of a report by him which complies with s 347. In the event of default in complying with ss 351 and 353 an offence is committed by every officer of the company in default and a person guilty of an offence is liable to a fine.[261] Failure to comply with ss 351 and 353 does not affect the validity of the poll or the resolution or other business (if passed or agreed) to which the poll relates.[262]

**22.102** Sections 342–353 do not identify the civil consequences of a report by an independent assessor of inadequacies, unfairness, or procedural defects in the meeting or the taking of the poll. In a clear case, a member may be able to obtain a declaration that a resolution was not passed or other business not agreed. The admissibility of the report as evidence in civil proceedings is uncertain.[263] Civil proceedings following a critical report may not be needed, however, because an adverse report may have consequences for the company's listing unless changes are made to the governance of the company.

## G. Records of Resolutions and Meetings

**22.103** By s 355, every company must keep records comprising (a) copies of all resolutions of members passed otherwise than at general meetings (written resolutions and resolutions passed by informal unanimous consent), (b) minutes of all proceedings of general meetings, and (c) details provided to the company in accordance with s 357 of decisions of a sole member (paragraph 22.73 above); and these records must be kept for at least ten years from the date of the resolution, meeting, or decision.[264] By s 1135, records of the resolutions, minutes, and details required

---

[260] subs 350(4).
[261] subss 351(3) and (4). The liability of an officer 'in default' is dealt with in s 1121.
[262] subs 351(5).
[263] Contrast 1985 Act, 441(1), in relation to an inspector's report.
[264] subs 355(1) and (2). The provisions of Chapter 6, ss 355–359 replace 1985 Act, ss 318(2), 382A, 382B, and 383 with changes and new provisions. The main changes are that subs 355(2) requires records to be kept for at least 10 years and that s 359 also applies Chapter 6 to meetings of a class of members. Table A, reg 100 requires the directors to cause minutes to be made in books kept for the purpose of, among other things, all proceedings at meetings of the company and of the

to be kept under s 355 may be kept in hard copy or electronic form, and may be arranged in such manner as the directors of the company think fit, provided that (a) the information in question is adequately recorded for future reference, and (b) records kept in electronic form are capable of being reproduced in hard copy form.[265] Section 1138 provides that where those records are kept otherwise than in bound books, adequate precautions must be taken to guard against falsification, and to facilitate the discovery of falsification. Compliance with these provisions is enforced by criminal sanction. If the company fails to comply with ss 355, 1135, or 1138 an offence is committed by every officer of the company in default and a person guilty of an offence is liable to a fine.[266]

A company's articles will usually provide that a member has no right of inspection **22.104** of company records except as conferred by statute or authorized by the directors or by ordinary resolution of the company.[267] But s 358 provides for the records of resolutions and meetings referred to in s 355 to be open to inspection. Those records relating to the previous ten years must be kept available for inspection at the company's registered office, or at a place specified in regulations under s 1136. By subs 358(2) the company must give notice to the Registrar of the place at which the records are kept available for inspection, and of any change in that place, unless they have at all times been kept at the company's registered office. By subs 358(3) the records must be open to the inspection of any member of the company without charge, and by subs 358(4) any member may require a copy of any records on payment of such fee as may be prescribed.[268] If default is made for 14 days in complying with subs 358(2) or an inspection under subs 358(3) is refused, or a copy requested under subs 358(4) is not sent, an offence is committed by every officer of the company in default and a person guilty of an offence is liable to a fine.[269]

Where a special resolution is passed or any resolution or agreement is agreed to by **22.105** all the members of a company that, if not agreed to, would not have been effective

---

holders of any class of shares in the company, including the names of the directors present at each such meeting.

[265] subss 1135(1) and (2). Subsection 1135(1) is derived from 1985 Act, subss 722(1) and 723(1) with changes and subs 1135(2) is new.

[266] Subsections 355(3) and (4), 1135(3) and (4), which are new, and 1138(2) and (3), which re-enact 1985 Act, subs 722(2) and Schedule 24. The liability of an officer 'in default' is dealt with in s 1121.

[267] Table A, reg 109; Model Article (pcls) 50 and Model Article (plc) 83.

[268] A member may be accompanied by an adviser; *McCusker v McRrae* [1966] SC 253. The prescribed charge is 10p per 500 words or part thereof copied and the reasonable costs incurred by the company in delivering the copy; the Companies (Fees for Inspection and Copying of Company Records) Regulations 2007 (SI 2007/2612), reg 4.

[269] subss 355(3) and (4), 1135(3) and (4), which are new, and 1138(2) and (3), which re-enact 1985 Act, subs 722(2) and Schedule 24. The liability of an officer 'in default' is dealt with in s 1121.

for its purpose unless passed as a special resolution, a copy of the resolution or agreement, or (in the case of a resolution or agreement that is not in writing) a written memorandum setting out its terms, must be forwarded to the Registrar within 15 days after it is passed or made.[270] If the company fails to comply with these requirements an offence is committed by every officer of the company in default and a person guilty of an offence is liable to a fine.[271]

---

[270] 1985 Act, subss 380(1)(4) and (4A), which also apply to class meetings, and which will be replaced by 2006 Act, ss 29 and 30 on 1 October 2009.

[271] subss 355(3) and (4), 1135(3) and (4), which are new, and 1138(2) and (3), which re-enact 1985 Act, subs 722(2) and Schedule 24. The liability of an officer 'in default' is dealt with in s 1121.

# 23

## ACCOUNTING RECORDS, REPORTS, AND AUDIT

# A. Introduction

**23.01**  This chapter deals with the functions, responsibilities, and liabilities of company directors in relation to accounting records, reports, and audit. This broad subject area breaks down into several parts. First, it is necessary to consider the functions, responsibilities, and liabilities of directors in connection with the 'raw materials'—ie the accounting records themselves—which must be kept by the company in accordance with the statutory provisions. Secondly, it is necessary to consider the functions, responsibilities, and liabilities of directors in connection with the forming of those raw materials into a finished product—ie the preparation of accounts and reports. Thirdly, this chapter deals with the functions, responsibilities, and liabilities of directors in connection with the checking of the finished product. This is the work of auditors, who must be supplied with information by the company's directors. Fourthly, and finally, this chapter concentrates on the functions, responsibilities, and liabilities of directors in connection with the annual return, which must be filed in accordance with the provisions of the Act.

*Key concepts*

**23.02**  The relevant statutory provisions make use of a number of concepts which are defined in the Act. The main distinctions for this purpose are: (1) the distinction between companies subject to the 'small companies regime' and those which are not subject to that regime; and (2) the distinction between 'quoted companies' and companies that are not quoted.[1]

*The small companies regime*

**23.03**  The small companies regime for accounts and reports applies to a company for a financial year in relation to which the company: (1) qualifies as small; and (2) is not excluded from the regime. Qualification as 'small' is dealt with by the 2006 Act, s 382 (as amended by the Companies Act 2006 (Amendment) (Accounts and Reports) Regulations 2008 (SI 2008/393)). In summary, the company must satisfy two or more of the following requirements: (1) turnover of not more than £6.5 million; (2) balance sheet total[2] of not more than £3.26 million; and (3) not more than 50 employees.[3]

---

[1]  2006 Act, s 380(3).

[2]  The 'balance sheet total' is the aggregate of the amounts shown as assets in the company's balance sheet: see 2006 Act, s 382(5).

[3]  The employee number must be the average number of persons employed by the company in the year, determined in accordance with 2006 Act, s 382(6).

A parent company will not qualify as a small company unless the group which it **23.04** heads qualifies as a small group. A 'small group' is a group which meets two or more of the following requirements: (1) aggregate[4] turnover of not more than £6.5 million net[5] (or £7.8 million gross[6]); (2) aggregate balance sheet total of not more than £3.26 million net (or £3.9 million gross); and (3) aggregate number of employees of not more than 50.

A public company is not capable of qualifying as a small company.[7] The term **23.05** 'public company' is defined in the 2006 Act, s 4.[8] Furthermore, a company will be excluded[9] from the small companies regime if it is an authorized insurance company,[10] a banking company,[11] an e-money issuer,[12] an ISD investment firm,[13] a UCITS management company,[14] or a company that carries on insurance market activity.[15]

The most significant exclusion from the small companies regime relates to mem- **23.06** bers of ineligible groups. In short, the small companies regime will not apply to any company which is a member of an ineligible group.[16] A group will be 'ineligible' for these purposes if any of its members is (inter alia[17]) a public company.[18] This means that any company, however small, which forms part of a group headed by a public company, will be ineligible for the small companies regime.

---

[4] Aggregate figures must be ascertained by aggregating the relevant figures determined in accordance with 2006 Act, s 382 for each member of the group.

[5] The term 'net' means after any set-offs and other adjustments made to eliminate group transactions.

[6] The term 'gross' means without the set-offs and adjustments mentioned in the preceding footnote.

[7] 2006 Act, s 384(1)(a).

[8] See generally Chapter 24 below.

[9] 2006 Act, s 384(1)(b).

[10] See 2006 Act, s 1165(2) for a definition of the term 'authorised insurance company'.

[11] The term 'banking company' is defined in 2006 Act, s 1164.

[12] See 2006 Act, ss 474(1) and 539.

[13] Ibid.

[14] Again, see 2006 Act, ss 474(1) and 539.

[15] 2006 Act, s 1165(7).

[16] 2006 Act, s 384(1)(c).

[17] A group will also be ineligible if any of its members is a body corporate (other than a company) whose shares are admitted to trading on a regulated market in an EEA state, a person (other than a small company) who has permission under Part 4 of the FSMA 2000 to carry on a regulated activity, a small company that is an authorized insurance company, a banking company, an e-money issuer, an ISD investment firm or a UCITS management company, or a person who carried on insurance market activity; see 2006 Act, s 384(2)(b), (c), (d), (e).

[18] 2006 Act, s 384(2)(a).

*Quoted companies*

**23.07** A quoted company is a company whose equity share capital:[19] (1) has been included in the official list[20] in accordance with the provisions of Part 6 of the FSMA 2000; or (2) is officially listed in an EEA state; or (3) is admitted to dealing on either the New York Stock Exchange or Nasdaq. Companies quoted on the AIM fall outside this definition. Perhaps unsurprisingly, an 'unquoted company' is 'a company that is not a quoted company'.[21]

*Medium sized companies*

**23.08** A company is 'medium sized' if: (1) two or more of the qualifying conditions are met; and (2) it is not excluded. The qualifying conditions are: (1) turnover of not more than £25.9 million; (2) balance sheet total[22] of not more than £12.9 million; (3) not more than 250 employees.[23] A parent company will qualify as a medium sized company only if the group which it heads is a 'medium sized group'.[24] A group qualifies as 'medium sized' if two or more of the following conditions are met: (1) aggregate[25] turnover of not more than £25.9 million net[26] (or £31.1 million gross[27]); (2) aggregate balance sheet total of not more than £12.9 million net (or £15.5 million gross); (3) aggregate number of employees of not more than 250.[28]

**23.09** Public companies are expressly precluded from being 'medium sized' companies.[29] Further exclusions relate to companies which have permission under Part 4 of the FSMA 2000 to carry on a regulated activity or which carry on insurance market activity.[30]

---

[19] The term 'equity share capital' is defined by 2006 Act, s 548 to mean a company's entire issued share capital excluding any part which has limits on the right to participate in a distribution by way of dividend or capital; see generally Chapter 24 below.

[20] The term 'official list' has the meaning given by s 103(1) of the FSMA 2000.

[21] 2006 Act, s 385(3).

[22] Again, the 'balance sheet total' is the aggregate of the amounts shown as assets in the company's balance sheet; see 2006 Act, s 465(5).

[23] 2006 Act, s 465 (as amended by the Companies Act 2006 (Amendment) (Accounts and Reports) Regulations 2008 (SI 2008/393)).

[24] 2006 Act, s 466(1).

[25] The aggregate figures are to be ascertained by aggregating the relevant figures for each member of the group; see 2006 Act, s 466(5).

[26] The term 'net' means after any set-offs and other adjustments made to eliminate group transactions; see 2006 Act, s 466(6).

[27] The term 'gross' means without such set-offs or adjustments.

[28] 2006 Act, s 466(4).

[29] 2006 Act, s 467(1)(a).

[30] 2006 Act, s 467(1)(b).

Equally significant is the fact that a company cannot be a 'medium sized' company **23.10** if it is a member of an ineligible group.[31] A group will be ineligible if any of its members is (inter alia[32]) a public company.[33] As with the small companies regime, this means that any company which is a member of a group headed by a public company may not take the benefit of any provision relating to medium sized companies.

## B. Directors' Functions, Responsibilities, and Liabilities in Relation to Accounting Records

It is essential for the officers of a company to ensure that the company maintains **23.11** proper accounting records so that business decisions are made on the basis of reliable information and so that, if the business fails, the liquidator's administration of the winding up is facilitated.[34] Provisions designed to ensure that proper records are kept may now be found in the 2006 Act, Part 15, Chapter 2, which replaced the corresponding provisions in the 1985 Act (Part VII, Chapter 1 and specifically ss 221 and 222) on 6 April 2008. The importance of these provisions was emphasized by Chadwick J in *Secretary of State for Trade and Industry v Arif*:[35]

> Section 221 of the 1985 Act has, at the least, two purposes. First, to ensure that those who are concerned in the direction and management of companies which trade with the privilege of limited liability do maintain sufficient accounting records to enable them to know what the position of the company is from time to time. Without that information, they cannot act responsibly in making decisions whether to continue trading. But equally important is a second purpose. If the company fails, a licensed insolvency practitioner will become office holder; as liquidator or as administrator or as administrative receiver. The office holder requires information as to the company's trading and transactions which is sufficient to enable him to identify and recover or exploit the company's assets. His task is made extremely difficult, if not impossible, if the company has failed to comply with its obligations under s 221 of the 1985 Act.

---

[31] 2006 Act, s 467(1)(c).

[32] A group will also be ineligible if any of its members is a body corporate (other than a company) whose shares are admitted to trading on a regulated market in an EEA state, a person (other than a small company) who has permission under Part 4 of the FSMA 2000 to carry on a regulated activity, a small company that is an authorized insurance company, a banking company, an e-money issuer, an ISD investment firm or a UCITS management company, or a person who carries on insurance market activity; see 2006 Act, s 467(2)(b), (c), (d), (e).

[33] 2006 Act, s 467(1)(a).

[34] *Secretary of State for Trade and Industry v Arif* [1997] 1 BCLC 34; see also *Re Firedart Ltd, Official Receiver v Fairall* [1994] 2 BCLC 340.

[35] [1997] 1 BCLC 34.

**23.12**   The importance of the requirement to keep proper accounting records is emphasized by the criminal penalties imposed for non-compliance with these provisions, and also by the 2006 Act, s 498(1), which requires a company's auditors to form an opinion as to whether adequate accounting records have been kept by the company.[36] If the auditor is of the opinion that adequate accounting records have not been kept, he is required to state that fact in his report.[37]

### (1)  Duty to keep accounting records

**23.13**   Every company is required to keep adequate accounting records.[38] The accounting records must be sufficient to show and explain the company's transactions,[39] to disclose with reasonable accuracy, at any time, the financial position of the company at that time,[40] and to enable the company's directors to ensure that any accounts required to be prepared[41] comply with the requirements of the 2006 Act.[42,43]

**23.14**   The term 'accounting records' is broadly expressed and will encompass, for example, purchase invoices, sales invoices, paying-in books, and bank statements; and documents do not cease to be accounting records simply because their contents have been summarized or included in another document such as the final accounts.[44] The obligation is to ensure that the accounting records disclose the financial position at any time; in other words, they must be up to date to the current time.

*Contents of accounting records*

**23.15**   A company's accounting records must, in particular, contain: (1) entries from day to day of all sums of money received and expended by the company and the matters in respect of which the receipt and expenditure takes place; and (2) a record of the assets and liabilities of the company.[45] If the company's business involves dealing in goods, the accounting records must also contain: (1) statements of stock held by the company at the end of each financial year; (2) all statements of stock-taking from which any statement of stock has been or is to be prepared; and

---

[36]  2006 Act, s 498(1)(a).

[37]  2006 Act, s 498(2).

[38]  2006 Act, s 386(1).

[39]  2006 Act, s 386(2)(a).

[40]  2006 Act, s 386(2)(b).

[41]  See paragraphs 23.34–23.48 below.

[42]  2006 Act, s 386(2)(c).

[43]  In the case of 'publicly traded' companies, the accounting records must also be sufficient to ensure that consolidated accounts are prepared in accordance with Article 4 of the IAS Regulation: see Regulation (EC) No 1606/2002 of the European Parliament and of the Council of 19 July 2002 on the application of international accounting standards.

[44]  *DTC (CNC) Ltd v Gary Sargeant & Co* [1996] 1 BCLC 529.

[45]  2006 Act, s 386(3).

(3) except in the case of goods sold by way of ordinary retail trade, statements of all goods sold and purchased, showing the goods and the buyers and sellers in sufficient detail to enable them to be identified.[46]

### Where records must be kept

A company's accounting records must be kept at its registered office or such other **23.16** place as the directors think fit and must at all times be open to inspection by the company's officers.[47] If a company's accounting records are kept outside the United Kingdom, it will be necessary for all accounts and returns to be sent to, and kept at, a place in the United Kingdom, and the accounts and returns must at all times be open to inspection by the company's officers.[48] The accounts and returns sent to the United Kingdom must be such as to: (1) disclose with reasonable accuracy the financial position of the business at intervals of not more than six months; and (2) enable the directors to ensure that the accounts required to be prepared[49] comply with the requirements of the 2006 Act and, where applicable, Article 4 of the IAS Regulation.[50,51]

### For how long records must be kept

In the case of a private company, accounting records must be kept for three years **23.17** from the date on which they are made.[52] In the case of a public company, accounting records must be kept for six years from the date on which they are made.[53]

### Computerized records

The 2006 Act, s 1135(1), provides that a company's accounting records may be **23.18** kept in hard copy or electronic form, provided the information in question is adequately recorded for future reference. However, where accounting records are kept in electronic form, they must be capable of being reproduced in hard copy form.[54]

---

[46] 2006 Act, s 386(5).
[47] 2006 Act, s 388(1). A director has a common law right to apply to the court for an order requiring the company to make its accounting records available to him: *McCusker v Rae* (1966) SC 253; *Conway v Petronius Clothing Co Ltd* [1978] 1 WLR 72.
[48] 2006 Act, s 388(2).
[49] See paragraphs 23.34–23.48 below.
[50] Regulation (EC) No 1606/2002 of the European Parliament and of the Council of 19 July 2002 on the application of international accounting standards. See paragraph 23.40 below as to the companies required to prepare their accounts in accordance with Article 4 (ie in accordance with international accounting standards). Other companies may choose to prepare their accounts in accordance with Article 4—see paragraphs 23.40 and 23.44.
[51] 2006 Act, s 388(3).
[52] 2006 Act, s 388(4)(a).
[53] 2006 Act, s 388(4)(b).
[54] 2006 Act, s 1135(2).

*Delivery of records to liquidator or administrator*

**23.19**   It should be noted that additional requirements are imposed in the event of the company going into administration, administrative receivership, liquidation or, provisional liquidation.[55] In such circumstances, any officer or former officer of the company who has in his possession or control any books, papers, or records to which the company appears to be entitled,[56] or which relate to the promotion, formation, business, dealings, affairs, or property of the company, may be ordered by the court to deliver the relevant books, papers, or records to the administrator, administrative receiver, liquidator, or provisional liquidator (as the case may be).[57]

### (2)  Liabilities of directors in relation to accounting records

*Criminal sanctions*

**23.20**   If a company fails to keep accounting records in the form and place required by the 2006 Act, an offence is committed[58] by every officer of the company who is in default.[59] However, it is a defence for a person charged with such an offence to show that he acted honestly and that in the circumstances in which the company's business was carried on such default was excusable.[60] If a company fails to keep accounting records for the duration required by the 2006 Act, an officer of the company commits an offence if he fails to take all reasonable steps for ensuring compliance with the statutory requirements, or intentionally causes non-compliance with the statutory requirements.[61] The penalty for any of these offences is, on conviction on indictment, imprisonment for a term not exceeding two years or a fine or both, and, on summary conviction, imprisonment for a term not exceeding 12 months or a fine not exceeding the statutory maximum.[62]

**23.21**   In addition, where a company keeps accounting records in electronic form which are not capable of being reproduced in hard copy form, an offence is committed[63]

---

[55]   Insolvency Act, s 234(1). See Chapter 29 at paragraphs 29.97–29.100.

[56]   In *Walker Morris v Khalastchi* [2001] 1 BCLC 1, the applicants, who had been requested by the liquidator to hand over files of documents relating to the company, wished to impose conditions that the liquidator should not release any of the documents or disclose their contents to the Inland Revenue without an order of the court, but it was ruled that, since the files were the property of the company, the liquidator was entitled to possession of them and that it was for the liquidator to decide whether or not to make voluntary disclosure of the documents to any person.

[57]   Insolvency Act, ss 234(2) and 235(2) and (3).

[58]   2006 Act, s 387(1), s 389(1).

[59]   ie who authorizes or permits or participates in or fails to take all reasonable steps to prevent the commission or continuation of the offence: see 2006 Act, s 1121.

[60]   2006 Act, s 387(2), s 389(2).

[61]   2006 Act, s 388(3).

[62]   2006 Act, s 387(3), s 389(4).

[63]   2006 Act, s 1135(3).

by every officer in default.[64] This offence is triable summarily and the penalty is a fine not exceeding level 3 on the standard scale and, for continued contravention, a daily default fine not exceeding one-tenth of level 3 on the standard scale.[65]

*Additional criminal sanctions in the event of winding up*

It should also be noted that various offences may arise on the company's wind- **23.22** ing up. The Insolvency Act, s 206, provides that an offence is 'deemed to have [been] committed' by an officer [66] who:

(1) within the period of 12 months prior to the commencement of the winding up,[67] either:

---

[64] ie who authorizes or permits or participates in or fails to take all reasonable steps to prevent the commission or continuation of the offence: see 2006 Act, s 1121. The definition of 'officer in default' in 2006 Act, s 1121, is far wider than the definition of the same phrase in the Companies Act 1985, s 730, which provided that an 'officer in default' was a person who 'knowingly and wilfully' authorized or permitted the contravention in question. The words 'knowingly and wilfully' do not appear in 2006 Act, s 1121. When the Company Law Reform Bill was going through the House of Lords, Lord Sharman proposed that the definition of the term 'officer in default' should be amended to include the words 'knowingly and wilfully'. His concern was to ensure that officers who were ignorant of the contravention did not commit an offence. Lord Sainsbury, the Parliamentary Under-Secretary of State for the Department of Trade and Industry, answered this concern by saying that the draftsman was concerned to ensure that the definition did not exclude reckless officers, officers who deliberately closed their eyes to their responsibilities, or officers who claimed that they did not know that their act or omission constituted an offence. He said: 'I understand the concern underlying the amendment; namely, that an innocent officer could in theory permit a contravention by being ignorant of its commission. But I would emphasise that an officer would be liable under this provision only if his ignorance constituted a tacit authorisation, permission or failure to take reasonable steps. I would say that any officer who is so deliberately or recklessly ignorant of his responsibilities as to be liable in this way cannot be described as "innocent" and it is right that he should be liable under this clause.' Lord Sharman said that he understood Lord Sainsbury's arguments, and, although remaining unconvinced by those arguments, begged leave to withdraw his amendment: see Hansard, House of Lords, 30 March 2006. The implications of the omission of the words 'knowingly and wilfully' will no doubt be considered by the courts in due course. The word 'manager' in s 1121(2) could well be a source of difficulty. It has been held that the word 'manager' should not be too narrowly construed, that it is not to be equated with a managing or other director or general manager, and that the term describes any person who in the affairs of the company exercises a supervisory control which reflects the general policy of the company for the time being or which is related to the general administration of the company: *Re A Company (No 00996 of 1979)* [1980] Ch 138, 144 per Shaw J.
[65] 2006 Act, s 1135(4).
[66] The term 'officer' is discussed in Chapter 3, Section F above. For the purposes of s 206 of the Insolvency Act, 'officer' includes a shadow director: see Insolvency Act, s 206(3); see also the definition of the term 'shadow director' in the Insolvency Act, s 251, which is in materially the same terms as 2006 Act, s 251. For further analysis of this concept, see *Secretary of State for Trade and Industry v Deverell* [2001] Ch 340 and Chapter 3, Section C(3). Offences under the Insolvency Act are discussed in Chapter 30, Section I.
[67] The term 'commencement of the winding up' is defined by the Insolvency Act, ss 86 and 129. In a voluntary liquidation, the winding up is 'deemed to commence at the time of the passing of the resolution for voluntary winding up'; Insolvency Act, s 86. In a compulsory liquidation, the winding up is prima facie deemed to commence at the time of the presentation of the petition for winding up; Insolvency Act, s 129(3); see also s 129(1) and (2).

   (a)  has:

       (i)  'concealed, destroyed, mutilated or falsified any book or paper affecting or relating to the company's property or affairs';[68] or

      (ii)  'made any false entry in any book or paper affecting or relating to the company's property or affairs';[69] or

    (iii)  'fraudulently parted with, altered or made any omission in any document affecting or relating to the company's property or affairs';[70] or

   (b)  has been 'privy to the doing by others of any of [these] things';[71] or

(2)  after the commencement of the winding up, either:

   (a)  does any of these things;[72] or

   (b)  is 'privy to the doing by others of any of [these] things'.[73]

**23.23**  Furthermore, where a company is being wound up, whether by the court or voluntarily, any person, being a past or present officer of the company,[74] commits an offence if he 'does not deliver up to the liquidator (or as he directs) all books and papers in his custody or under his control belonging to the company and which he is required by law to deliver up'[75] or 'prevents the production of any book or paper affecting or relating to the company's property or affairs'.[76]

**23.24**  The seriousness of these offences is underlined by two factors. First, a penal sentence may be imposed: the statute provides that a person guilty of any of these offences is liable to imprisonment or a fine or both.[77] Secondly, the burden of proof in respect of *mens rea* is placed on the defendant, rather than on the prosecution: Parliament has provided that a person charged with these offences will be liable unless he is able to prove[78] that he had no intent to conceal the state of affairs of the company or defeat the law.[79]

---

[68] Insolvency Act, s 206(1)(c).

[69] Insolvency Act, s 206(1)(d).

[70] Insolvency Act, s 206(1)(e).

[71] Insolvency Act, s 206(2).

[72] Ibid. The 'commencement of the winding up' falls to be determined in accordance with Insolvency Act, ss 86 and 129.

[73] Insolvency Act, s 206(2).

[74] Here the term 'officer' again includes shadow directors: Insolvency Act 1986, s 208(3). For discussion of the term 'officer' see Chapter 3, Section F above.

[75] Insolvency Act, s 208(1)(c). The legal requirement to deliver up books and papers to a liquidator may be found in Insolvency Act, ss 234 and 236.

[76] Insolvency Act, s 208(1)(e).

[77] Insolvency Act, ss 206(6) and 208(5).

[78] Insolvency Act, ss 206(4) and 208(4). As to whether such a 'reverse burden' is compatible with Article 6 of the Convention for the Protection of Human Rights and Fundamental Freedoms, as scheduled to the Human Rights Act 1998, see *Attorney-General's Reference (No 1 of 2004)* [2004] BPIR 1073 and *Sheldrake v Director of Public Prosecutions, Attorney-General's Reference (No 4 of 2002)* [2005] 1 AC 264.

[79] The reference to 'intent . . . to defeat the law' is somewhat obscure and it may be doubted whether it is a true alternative: if a defendant has done one of the things set out in s 206(1)(c), (d) or (e)

An additional offence, which will in practice overlap significantly with the offences **23.25** already considered, is created by the Insolvency Act, s 209, which applies to officers and contributories, but not expressly to shadow directors, where such a person 'destroys, mutilates, alters or falsifies any books, papers or securities, or makes or is privy to the making of any false or fraudulent entry in any register, book of account or document belonging to the company with intent to defraud or deceive any person'.[80] This offence is punishable by imprisonment or fine or both.[81]

The Insolvency Act does not itself define the word 'document' at all; rather, it **23.26** adopts (for the purpose of Parts I to VII, which relate to corporate insolvency) the definition in s 1114 of the 2006 Act, which provides that the word 'document' means 'any information recorded in any form'. This appears to be sufficiently wide to cover computer records.

Such an approach would be consistent with the authorities on the meaning of the **23.27** word 'document' in other contexts. In *Derby & Co Ltd v Weldon (No 9)*,[82] which related to the meaning of the word 'document' in RSC Ord 24, Vinelott J held that computer records held in electronic form were 'documents' provided that they contained information capable of being retrieved and converted into readable form.[83] In *Alliance & Leicester Building Society v Ghahremani*,[84] Hoffmann J rejected a submission that Vinelott J's view as to the scope of the word 'document' was restricted to questions of discovery under the rules of court. He applied the extended meaning to the question whether the deliberate deletion of information stored on the disc of an office computer was a contemptuous breach of an order restraining a solicitor from destroying or altering any documents relating to a conveyancing transaction.

In *Rollo v HM Advocate*,[85] the High Court of Justiciary took the same view in rela- **23.28** tion to the meaning of the word in the context of the seizure of an electronic notebook under the powers conferred by s 23(3)(b) of the Misuse of Drugs Act 1971. Lord Milligan said: 'It seems to us that the essential essence of a document is that it is something containing recorded information of some sort. It does not matter if, to be meaningful, the information requires to be processed in some way

---

or s 208(1)(c) or (e) but has proved that he did not intend to conceal the state of the company's affairs, it is hard to see how he could be convicted on the ground that he has failed to prove that he did not intend to defeat the law.

[80] Insolvency Act, s 209(1).
[81] Insolvency Act, s 209(2).
[82] [1991] 1 WLR 652.
[83] See also *Grant v Southwestern and County Properties Ltd* [1975] Ch 185, *Alliance and Leicester Building Society v Ghahremani* (1992) 32 RVR 198, *Rollo v HM Advocate* [1997] JC 23.
[84] (1992) 32 RVR 198.
[85] [1997] JC 23, 26.

such as translation, decoding or electronic retrieval.' Similarly, in *Victor Chandler International Ltd v Customs and Excise Commissioners*,[86] the Court of Appeal held that to construe s 9(1)(b) of the Betting and Gaming Duties Act 1981 as only applying to advertisements in documentary form took insufficient account of the technological advances since the statutory language first appeared. Chadwick LJ held: 'A compact disc or floppy diskette . . . on which information is stored in electronic form must, in the age in which we now live, be treated by the law as a document.'[87]

**23.29**   These authorities suggest that the word 'document' in s 209(2) includes information held in electronic form. A contrary view is suggested by the definition of the word 'records' in s 436 of the Insolvency Act 1986, which provides that the word 'records' includes 'computer records and other non-documentary records'. Although this definition does not directly affect the meaning of s 209, which does not use the word 'records', the reference 'non-documentary records' could be taken to suggest that a computer record is not a 'document' within the meaning of the Insolvency Act. It is important to note, however, that s 1114(1) of the 2006 Act, which applies to Parts I to VII of the Insolvency Act by virtue of s 251 of the Insolvency Act, defines the expression 'document' to mean 'information recorded in any form'.

**23.30**   Under the Insolvency Act, s 209, an intent to deceive is sufficient but not essential: an intent to defraud will do.[88] If the defendant destroys records in order to suppress evidence of dishonest transactions, it might be difficult to argue that he intends to deceive others, who have never suspected that such transactions might have taken place, into believing that they have not; but fraud does not require

---

[86] [2000] 1 WLR 1296.

[87] Ibid at 1307.

[88] In respect of the term 'intent to defraud', see *Welham v DPP* [1961] AC 103, which concerned the meaning of the words 'intent to defraud' under s 4 of the Forgery Act 1913. Lord Radcliffe held as follows at 123–4: 'Now, I think that there are one or two things that can be said with confidence about the meaning of this word "defraud". It requires a person as its object: that is, defrauding involves doing something to someone. Although in the nature of things it is almost invariably associated with the obtaining of an advantage for the person who commits the fraud, it is the effect upon the person who is the object of the fraud that ultimately determines its meaning . . . Secondly, popular speech does not give, and I do not think ever has given, any sure guide as to the limits of what is meant by 'to defraud.' It may mean to cheat someone. It may mean to practise a fraud upon someone. It may mean to deprive someone by deceit of something which is regarded as belonging to him or, though not belonging to him, as due to him or his right . . . There is nothing in any of this that suggests that to defraud is in ordinary speech confined to the idea of depriving a man by deceit of some economic advantage or inflicting upon him some economic loss.' The House of Lords subsequently made clear that the speeches in *Welham* were directed to the meaning of 'intent to defraud' in general and were not limited to its meaning in the Forgery Act 1913: *R v Terry* [1984] AC 374, 380–1, per Lord Fraser of Tullybelton.

deception, and a dishonest intention to avoid the consequences of his misconduct would probably suffice.

*Civil liability for wrongful trading*

If a company fails to keep adequate accounting records, the directors of that com-    **23.31**
pany may have no reliable means of assessing the company's financial position and may continue trading when in fact there is no reasonable prospect of the company avoiding insolvent liquidation. In those circumstances, in the event of the company being wound up, the directors will face the prospect of civil liability to contribute to the company's assets under s 214 of the Insolvency Act. The knowledge to be imputed in testing whether or not directors knew or ought to have concluded that there was no reasonable prospect of the company avoiding insolvent liquidation is not limited to the documentary material actually available at the given time, but will include any information which, given reasonable diligence and an appropriate level of general knowledge, skill, and experience, would have been ascertainable by the company's directors.[89] Wrongful trading is discussed in Chapter 29, Section I(3).

*Disqualification*

It should also be noted that one of the matters to which the court must have regard    **23.32**
on an application by the Secretary of State for the disqualification of a director under s 6 of the CDDA is the extent of the director's responsibility for any failure to keep proper accounting records in the place and for the duration required by the 2006 Act.[90] In practice, non-compliance with the requirement to keep accounting records is a very common basis for a finding of unfitness warranting disqualification.[91]

# C. Directors' Functions, Responsibilities, and Liabilities in Relation to Annual Accounts and Reports

## (1) Introduction

This section deals with the functions, responsibilities, and liabilities of company    **23.33**
directors in relation to annual accounts and reports, including: (1) the preparation of annual accounts; (2) the directors' report; (3) in the case of quoted

---

[89] *Re Produce Marketing Consortium Ltd (No 2)* [1989] BCLC 520.
[90] CDDA, Schedule 1, para 4.
[91] See, for example, *Re New Generation Engineers Ltd* [1993] BCLC 435; *Secretary of State for Trade & Industry v Ettinger, Re Swift 736 Ltd* [1993] BCLC 896; *Re Firedart Ltd, Official Receiver v Fairall* [1994] 2 BCLC 340; *Secretary of State for Trade & Industry v Arif* [1997] 1 BCLC 34; *Re Galeforce Pleating Co Ltd* [1999] BCLC 704.

companies, the directors' remuneration report; (4) the duty to publish accounts and reports; (5) in the case of public companies, the laying of accounts before general meeting; (6) in the case of quoted companies, approval of directors' remuneration report; (7) the filing of accounts and reports; and (8) the revision of defective accounts and reports.

## (2) Preparation of annual accounts

**23.34** The 2006 Act, ss 390–414, which came into force on 6 April 2008 require companies to prepare individual accounts and, in the case of parent companies which are not subject to the small companies regime or able to take the benefit of any exemption, group accounts. These sections establish three core principles with regard to a company's or group's financial statements. First, they must comply with specific statutory requirements as to disclosure, format, and accounting principles. Secondly, the balance sheets and profit and loss accounts must give a 'true and fair view' of the company's or group's financial position and its profit or loss for a given period. Thirdly, within a group of companies, accounting standards should prima facie be consistently applied.

### *Duty to prepare individual accounts*

**23.35** The directors of every company must prepare accounts for the company for each of its financial years.[92] The accounts may either be prepared in accordance with the 2006 Act or IAS.[93] The former are referred to as 'Companies Act individual accounts' and the latter as 'IAS individual accounts'. Once a company has switched to IAS, all subsequent accounts must be prepared in accordance with IAS unless there is a 'relevant change of circumstance'.[94] There are also rules on consistency within groups. See paragraph 23.45 below. A company's financial year must be determined in accordance with s 390 of the 2006 Act. In summary, it will be the same as the company's accounting period,[95] subject to the directors' discretion to alter the last day of the period by plus or minus seven days. The duty to prepare accounts is an obligation of the directors and the duty is owed to the company and not to individual shareholders.[96]

---

[92] 2006 Act, s 394.

[93] 2006 Act, s 474(1) refers to the definition in the IAS Regulation (EC) 1606/2002. This includes International Accounting Standards, International Financial Reporting Standards, and related interpretations (SICs or IFRICs) issued or adopted by the International Accounting Standards Board and adopted by the European Commission in accordance with the IAS Regulation.

[94] 2006 Act, s 395(4) provides that there is a 'relevant change of circumstance' if, broadly, the company becomes the subsidiary of another undertaking that does not prepare IAS consolidated accounts or the company (or its parent undertaking) ceases to have securities admitted to trading on a regulated market in the EEA.

[95] 2006 Act, s 391.

[96] *Devlin v Slough Estates Ltd* [1983] BCLC 497.

### Requirement for individual accounts to show a true and fair view

The directors of a company must not approve a company's individual accounts **23.36** (whether Companies Act or IAS individual accounts) unless they are satisfied that they give a true and fair view of the company's assets, liabilities, financial position, and profit or loss.[97] Ultimately this will be a matter of judgment; there may be more than one method of presenting the financial position of a company in a way which is true and fair.[98] The European Court of Justice has held that '[t]he principle of the true and fair view requires that the accounts reflect the activities and transactions which they are supposed to describe and that the accounting information be given in the form judged to be the soundest and most appropriate for satisfying third parties' needs for information, without harming the interests of the company'.[99] In general, the obligation to give a true and fair view means that a company should follow any applicable accounting standard unless there is a good reason not to do so.[100]

### Contents of individual accounts

A company's individual accounts must contain a balance sheet as at the last day of **23.37** the financial year and a profit and loss account.[101] In relation to Companies Act individual accounts, the balance sheet must give a true and fair view of the state of affairs of the company as at the end of the financial year[102] and the profit and loss account must give a true and fair view of the profit or loss of the company for the financial year.[103] IAS individual accounts must achieve a fair presentation.

Save for companies subject to the small companies regime, a company's annual **23.38** accounts must also contain details of the monthly average number of employees, both in total and broken down into appropriate categories.[104] The accounts must also contain the aggregate amounts of sums paid out by way of wages and salaries and social security costs, and any costs incurred by the company in respect of any company pension scheme.[105]

In the case of a company which does not prepare group accounts, details of **23.39** advances and credits granted by the company to its directors, and guarantees of

---

[97] 2006 Act, s 393(1). This provision helps to reinforce the true and fair concept for companies who prepare their accounts using IAS. IAS 1.13 requires accounts to achieve a fair presentation but does not use the 'true and fair' formulation.

[98] *Devlin v Slough Estates Ltd* [1983] BCLC 497 at 503.

[99] *DE&ES Bauunternehmung v Finanzamt Bergheim (Case C-275/97)* [2000] BCC 757.

[100] *Lloyd Cheyham & Co Ltd v Littlejohn & Co* [1987] BCLC 303.

[101] 2006 Act, s 396(1).

[102] 2006 Act, s 396(2)(a). See The Small Companies and Groups (Accounts and Directors' Reports) Regulations (SI 2008/409) and The Large and Medium-Sized Companies and Groups (Accounts and Reports) Regulations (SI 2008/410), both made under s 396(3) and other sections.

[103] 2006 Act, s 396(2)(b).

[104] 2006 Act, s 411(1), (2).

[105] 2006 Act, s 411(5).

any kind entered into by the company on behalf of its directors, must be shown in the notes to the individual accounts.[106] In addition, the 2006 Act, s 412 provides that the Secretary of State may make regulations requiring information to be given in the notes to a company's annual accounts about directors' remuneration.[107]

*Preparation of group accounts*

**23.40** If a parent company is subject to the small companies regime, the preparation of group accounts is optional.[108] If a parent company is not subject to the small companies regime, the preparation of group accounts is mandatory, and, in addition to the preparation of the parent company's individual accounts, the directors are expressly required to prepare group accounts at the end of every financial year, unless the company is exempt.[109] The exemptions are located in s 400 (company included in the EEA accounts of larger group), s 401 (company included in non-EEA accounts of larger group), and s 402 (company none of whose subsidiary undertakings need be included in consolidation).

Group accounts of UK publicly traded companies[110] are required by Article 4 of the IAS Regulation to be prepared in accordance with IAS (IAS group accounts). The group accounts of other companies may be prepared in accordance with the 2006 Act (Companies Act group accounts) or IAS.[111] Once a parent company has switched to IAS in its group accounts, all subsequent accounts must be prepared in accordance with IAS unless there is a 'relevant change of circumstance'.[112] There are also rules on consistency within groups. See paragraph 23.45 below.

*Subsidiary undertakings to be included in group accounts*

**23.41** Where a parent company prepares group accounts, all the subsidiary undertakings of the company must be included in the consolidation,[113] unless: (1) the inclusion of the subsidiary undertaking is not material for the purposes of giving a true and fair view:[114] or (2) severe long-term restrictions substantially hinder the

---

[106] 2006 Act, s 413(1).

[107] 2006 Act, s 412(1). As per addition 102 until 'both made' when the section no should be 412(1)–(3).

[108] 2006 Act, s 398.

[109] 2006 Act, s 399(1), (2).

[110] UK-incorporated companies whose securities are admitted to trading on an EU-regulated market such as the FSA's Official List.

[111] The AIM Rules require parent companies incorporated in the UK to prepare their consolidated accounts in accordance with IAS for financial years commencing on or after 1 January 2007.

[112] 2006 Act, s 403(5). There is a relevant change of circumstance if, broadly, the company becomes a subsidiary undertaking of another undertaking that does not prepare IAS group accounts, or if the company (or its parent undertaking) ceases to be an undertaking with securities admitted to trading on a regulated market in the EEA.

[113] 2006 Act, s 405(1).

[114] 2006 Act, s 405(2). Note that two or more undertakings may be excluded only if they are not material taken together.

exercise of the rights of the parent company over the assets or management of that undertaking;[115] or (3) the information necessary for the preparation of group accounts cannot be obtained without disproportionate expense or undue delay;[116] or (4) the interest of the parent company is held exclusively with a view to subsequent resale.[117]

### *Requirement for group accounts to show a true and fair view*

The directors must not approve group accounts unless they are satisfied that they give a true and fair view of the assets, liabilities, financial position, and profit or loss of the undertakings included in the consolidation as a whole, so far as concerns members of the company.[118]     **23.42**

### *Contents of group accounts*

Companies Act group accounts must comprise: (1) a consolidated balance sheet dealing with the state of affairs of the parent company and its subsidiary undertakings; and (2) a consolidated profit and loss account dealing with the profit or loss of the parent company and its subsidiary undertakings.[119] The accounts must give a true and fair view of the state of affairs as at the end of the financial year, and the profit or loss for the financial year, of the undertakings included in the consolidation as a whole, so far as concerns members of the company.[120] IAS accounts must achieve a fair presentation.     **23.43**

In the case of a parent company that prepares group accounts, details of any advances and credits granted to the directors of the parent company by that company or by any of its subsidiary undertakings and any guarantees of any kind entered into on behalf of the directors of the parent company by that company or by any of its subsidiary undertakings must be shown in the notes to the group accounts.[121]     **23.44**

### *Consistency of financial reporting within group*

The directors of a parent company must secure that the individual accounts of the parent company and each of its subsidiary undertakings are all prepared using the same financial reporting framework, ie UK GAAP, or IAS, except to the extent that in the opinion of the directors there are good reasons for not doing so.[122]     **23.45**

---

[115] 2006 Act, s 405(3)(a).
[116] 2006 Act, s 405(3)(b).
[117] 2006 Act, s 405(3)(c).
[118] 2006 Act, s 393(1)(b); where group accounts are prepared in accordance with IAS, this is helpful to reinforce the true and fair standard—see paragraph 23.36 above.
[119] 2006 Act, s 404(1).
[120] 2006 Act, s 404(2).
[121] 2006 Act, s 413(2).
[122] 2006 Act, s 407.

However, a parent company that prepares both individual and group accounts using IAS is not required to ensure that all its subsidiary undertakings use IAS, provided that they all use the same framework.[123]

### Approval and signing of accounts

**23.46** A company's annual accounts must be approved by the board of directors and signed on behalf of the board by a director of the company.[124] The signature must appear on the company's balance sheet.[125] If the accounts are prepared in accordance with the provisions applicable to companies subject to the small companies regime, the balance sheet must contain a statement to that effect in a prominent position above the signature.[126]

### Criminal liability of directors

**23.47** If annual accounts are approved that do not comply with the requirements of the 2006 Act (and, where applicable, the requirements of the IAS Regulation), every director of the company who knew that they did not comply, or was reckless as to whether they complied, and failed to take reasonable steps to secure compliance with those requirements or, as the case may be, to prevent the accounts from being approved, commits an offence.[127] A person guilty of any such offence is liable on conviction on indictment, to a fine, or, on summary conviction, to a fine not exceeding the statutory maximum.[128]

### Disqualification

**23.48** One of the matters to which the court must have regard on an application by the Secretary of State for the disqualification of a director under s 6 of the CDDA is the extent of the director's responsibility for any failure to prepare annual accounts[129] or for any failure for the accounts so prepared to be approved and signed.[130] Disqualification is discussed in Chapter 28, Section D.

### (3) The directors' report

**23.49** Since 2005, as part of the implementation of the Modernisation Directive into English law, all companies (other than small companies) have been required to prepare a business review as part of their directors' report. A requirement for quoted companies to produce more strategic and forward-looking disclosure in the form of an 'operating and financial review' or 'OFR' was also introduced at the

---

[123] 2006 Act, s 407(5).
[124] 2006 Act, s 414(1).
[125] 2006 Act, s 414(2).
[126] 2006 Act, s 414(3).
[127] 2006 Act, s 414(4).
[128] 2006 Act, s 414(5).
[129] CDDA, Schedule 1, para 5(a).
[130] CDDA, Schedule 1, para 5(b).

same time, then unexpectedly repealed in January 2006, on the grounds it went beyond the requirements of the Modernisation Directive. Nonetheless, more meaningful narrative reporting remained the policy of the Government and investor bodies and other stakeholders have continued to call for better and more forward-looking disclosure. Many of old OFR disclosure requirements have now been reinstated for quoted companies by the 2006 Act, s 417(5); see paragraph 23.54 below. The 2006 Act also includes a new liability regime (see Section C(11) below) which clarifies the liability of directors and issuers by setting out the limited circumstances where liability arises for the reports and accounts which they publish and excluding liability in other circumstances.

*Duty to prepare a directors' report*

The directors of a company are expressly required to prepare a directors' report for **23.50** each financial year of the company.[131] Where a parent company prepares group accounts, the directors' report must be a consolidated report (a 'group directors' report') relating to the undertakings included in the consolidation.[132] A group directors' report may, where appropriate, give greater emphasis to the matters that are significant to the undertakings included in the consolidation, taken as a whole.[133]

*Contents of directors' report*

The directors' report must state the names of the persons who, at any time during **23.51** the financial year, were directors of the company.[134] It must also state the principal activities of the company (or, in the case of a group directors' report, the group) in the course of the year.[135] Except in the case of companies subject to the small companies regime, the directors' report must also state the amount (if any) which is recommended by the directors to be paid by way of dividend.[136]

In addition, the directors' report of all companies (other than small companies) **23.52** must contain a business review. This must, in turn, contain a fair review of the company's business and a description of the principal risks and uncertainties facing the company.[137] It must also provide a balanced and comprehensive analysis of the development and performance of the company's business during the

---

[131] 2006 Act, s 415(1). The 2006 Act, Part 15, Chapter 5, ss 415–419, concerning the directors' report came into force on 6 April 2008, except for s 417, which was brought into force on 1 October 2007: 2006 Act Commencement Orders No 3, art 2(1)(g), and No 5, art 3(1)(d).

[132] 2006 Act, s 415(2).

[133] 2006 Act, s 415(3).

[134] 2006 Act, s 416(1)(a). See The Small Companies and Groups (Accounts and Directors' Reports) Regulations (SI 2008/409) and The Large and Medium-Sized Companies and Groups (Accounts and Reports) Regulations (SI 2008/410), both made under s 416(4) and other sections.

[135] 2006 Act, s 416(1)(b), (2).

[136] 2006 Act, s 416(3).

[137] 2006 Act, s 417(3).

financial year, and the position of the company's business at the end of the year.[138] The level of detail should be commensurate with the size and complexity of the company's business. Analysis using financial and, where appropriate, other key performance indicators, including information relating to environmental and employee matters, must also be included to the extent necessary for an understanding of the development, performance, or position of the company's business.

**23.53**   A number of changes to the business review disclosure requirements are made by the 2006 Act. These include additional disclosure obligations for quoted companies (often referred to as the enhanced business review)[139] and a new statement of the purpose of the business review.[140] These changes take effect for financial years commencing on or after 1 October 2007.

**23.54**   The additional disclosures required by a quoted company are, to the extent necessary for an understanding of the development, performance, or position of the company's business, (1) the main trends and factors likely to affect the future development, performance, and position of the company's business, (2) information about: environmental matters (including the impact of the company's business on the environment), the company's employees, and social and community issues, including information about any policies of the company in relation to those matters and the effectiveness of those policies, and (3) information about persons with whom the company has contractual and other arrangements which are essential to the business of the company.

**23.55**   If the business review does not contain information about environmental matters, employees, social and community issues, and essential contractual or other arrangements, it must state which of those kinds of information it does not contain.

**23.56**   As a result of these disclosures, quoted companies will have to include more forward-looking information in the business review and their disclosures in the area of corporate social responsibility will need to become more robust because of the requirement to give information about corporate social responsibility policies and their effectiveness. They will also need to consider whether there are any contractual or other arrangements essential to the business of the company which need to be disclosed for an understanding of the development, performance, or position of the business. Disclosure is not required if the disclosure would be seriously prejudicial to the person and contrary to the public interest.[141] This is likely to be rarely used. It protects the subject of the disclosure, rather than the company,

---

[138]   2006 Act, s 417(4).
[139]   2006 Act, s 417(5).
[140]   2006 Act, s 417(2).
[141]   2006 Act, s 417(11).

and would involve the directors in making a difficult judgment about the public interest. However, only essential contractual arrangements need to be disclosed, so many companies may decide that no disclosure is required.

Quoted and unquoted companies can omit information about impending developments or matters in the course of negotiation if the disclosure would be seriously prejudicial to the company's interests. This may be of little benefit to quoted companies because of the requirement under the Disclosure and Transparency Rules for issuers to give a responsibility statement in their report and accounts (see paragraph 23.74). This imports a true and fair override so that such companies will not be able to omit information if it would result in the responsibility statement failing the true and fair test. **23.57**

The 2006 Act, s 417(2), states that the purpose of the business review (for both quoted and unquoted companies) is to inform members of the company and help them assess how the directors have performed their duty to promote the success of the company, having regard to factors such as employees, the community, and the environment. This new provision will provide the directors with an annual opportunity to demonstrate that they are performing their duties. But equally, the review may be scrutinized closely by non-governmental organizations, activist shareholders, and others with an interest in looking for failings in directors' strategy or policies and, potentially, evidence to make a derivative claim. **23.58**

Unless a company is exempt from audit and the directors have taken advantage of that exemption, the directors' report must also contain a statement to the effect that, in the case of each of the persons who are directors at the time the report is approved, (1) so far as each director is aware, there is no information required by the auditor in connection with preparing his report of which the company's auditor is unaware, and (2) each director has taken all the steps that he ought to have taken as a director in order to make himself aware of any such information and to establish that the company's auditor is aware of that information.[142] **23.59**

*Approval and signing of directors' report*

The directors' report must be approved by the board of directors.[143] In addition, it must be signed on behalf of the board by a director[144] or, alternatively, by the company secretary.[145] If the report is prepared in accordance with the small **23.60**

---

[142] 2006 Act, s 418(1), (2). This restates the 1985 Act, s 234ZA, introduced for financial years commencing on or after 1 April 2005, as one of the measures aimed at improving the audit and accounting process following the fall of Enron.

[143] 2006 Act, s 419(1).

[144] Ibid.

[145] 2006 Act, s 419(1).

companies regime, it must contain a statement to that effect in a prominent position above the signature.[146]

### Criminal liability of directors

**23.61**  In the case of failure to comply with the requirement to prepare a directors' report, an offence is committed by every person who was a director of the company immediately before the end of the period for filing accounts and reports for the financial year in question and who failed to take all reasonable steps for securing compliance with that requirement.[147] The penalty for such an offence is a fine on conviction on indictment or a fine not exceeding the statutory maximum on summary conviction.[148]

**23.62**  Where a directors' report contains a statement that the auditor is aware of all relevant audit information and that the director has taken all the steps that he ought to have taken as a director in order to make himself aware of all relevant audit information and to establish that the company's auditor is aware of it, but the statement is false, every director of the company who knew that the statement was false (or was reckless as to whether it was false) and failed to take reasonable steps to prevent the report from being approved, commits an offence[149] punishable on conviction on indictment to imprisonment for a term not exceeding two years or a fine or both or on summary conviction to imprisonment for a term not exceeding 12 months or to a fine not exceeding the statutory maximum or both.[150]

**23.63**  If a directors' report is approved which does not comply with the statutory requirements imposed by the 2006 Act, ss 415–419, every director of the company who knew that it did not comply (or was reckless as to whether it complied) and failed to take reasonable steps to ensure compliance with those requirements or, as the case may be, to prevent the report from being approved, commits an offence[151] punishable on conviction on indictment by a fine or on summary conviction by a fine not exceeding the statutory maximum.[152]

### Civil liability of directors

**23.64**  Pursuant to the 2006 Act, s 463,[153] if a company suffers loss as a result of an untrue or misleading statement in a directors' report, or by reason of the omission from

---

146  2006 Act, s 419(2).
147  2006 Act, s 415(4).
148  2006 Act, s 415(5).
149  2006 Act, s 418(5).
150  2006 Act, s 418(6).
151  2006 Act, s 419(3).
152  2006 Act, s 419(4).
153  This section was brought into force on 20 January 2007 by the 2006 Act Commencement Order No 1, art 3(1)(c).

the report of anything which ought properly to have been included, any director who knew the statement to be untrue or misleading (or was reckless as to whether the statement was untrue or misleading), or knew the omission to be dishonest concealment of a material fact, will be liable to compensate the company.[154] However, no person shall be subject to any liability to any person other than the company as a result of reliance by any person on the untrue or misleading or omitted information.[155]

### (4) Quoted companies: directors' remuneration report

The requirement for the directors of a quoted company to produce a remuner-  **23.65**
ation report was introduced by the Directors' Remuneration Report Regulations 2002 (SI 2002/1986). The requirement for such a report has been preserved and now appears in the 2006 Act, ss 420–422, which came into force on 6 April 2008: 2006 Act Commencement Order No 5, art 3(1)(d). However, whereas previously the particulars required to be contained in such report were contained in Schedule 7A to the Companies Act 1985, it is now the case that such particulars will be specified in regulations made by the Secretary of State,[156] which largely replicate Schedule 7A (although there is a new requirement for the remuneration report to contain a statement of how pay and employment conditions of employees of the company and other undertakings within the same group as the company were taken into account when determining directors' remuneration for the relevant financial year).

*Directors' duty to keep company informed*

To support the requirement of directors of quoted companies to prepare a remu-  **23.66**
neration report, every director of the company, and every person who was a director in the preceding five years, is under a specific statutory duty to ensure that the company is informed of such matters relating to himself as must be contained in the directors' remuneration report.[157]

*Approval and signing of directors' remuneration report*

The directors' remuneration report must be approved by the board of directors  **23.67**
and signed on behalf of the board, either by a director or by the company secretary.[158]

---

[154] 2006 Act, s 463(1), (2), (3).
[155] 2006 Act, s 463(4).
[156] The Large and Medium-sized Companies and Groups (Accounts and Reports) Regulations 2008 (SI 2008/410).
[157] 2006 Act, s 421(3).
[158] 2006 Act, s 422(1).

*Criminal liability of directors*

**23.68** If a company's directors fail to comply with the requirement to prepare a directors' remuneration report, every person who was a director of the company immediately before the end of the period for filing accounts and reports for the financial year in question and who failed to take all reasonable steps for securing compliance with that requirement commits an offence[159] punishable on conviction on indictment by a fine and on summary conviction by a fine not exceeding the statutory maximum.[160]

**23.69** Additionally, any director or any person who has in the preceding five years been a director of the company will commit an offence (punishable by fine) if he fails to provide the company with such matters relating to himself as ought to appear in the directors' remuneration report.[161]

**23.70** If a directors' remuneration report is approved which does not comply with the requirements of the 2006 Act, ss 420 to 422, every director of the company who knew that it did not comply (or was reckless as to whether it complied) and who failed to take reasonable steps to secure compliance or, as the case may be, to prevent the report from being approved, commits an offence[162] punishable on conviction on indictment to a fine or on summary conviction to a fine not exceeding the statutory maximum.[163]

*Civil liability of directors*

**23.71** If a directors' remuneration report is untrue or misleading or contains any material omission which results in the company suffering a loss, any director who knew of the untrue or misleading nature information (or was reckless as to whether it was untrue or misleading) or who knew the omission to be a dishonest concealment of a material fact is liable to compensate the company.[164] See also Section C(11) below.

### (5) Listed companies: additional periodic reporting obligations

**23.72** The Transparency Directive,[165] implemented in the UK through the Disclosure and Transparency Rules made by the FSA, imposes additional periodic reporting

---

[159] 2006 Act, s 420(2).
[160] 2006 Act, s 421(3).
[161] 2006 Act, s 421(4).
[162] 2006 Act, s 422(2).
[163] 2006 Act, s 422(3).
[164] 2006 Act, s 463(1), (2), (3). Although this provision is capable of rendering a director liable in damages for untrue or misleading information or material omissions in a directors' remuneration report, it is suggested that it will be rare for a company to suffer a loss by reason of such untrue or misleading information or material omission.
[165] Directive 2004/109/EC of the European Parliament and of the Council of 15 December 2004.

obligations on listed companies[166] for financial years commencing on or after 20 January 2007. Such companies must produce (1) an annual financial report consisting of consolidated audited accounts, a management report and responsibility statement, (2) a half-yearly report consisting of condensed financial statements, an interim management report, and a responsibility statement, and (3) approximately midway through each half-year period an interim management statement. Many of the requirements overlap with existing statutory disclosure requirements but the requirement for a responsibility statement in each of the annual financial report and half-yearly report, a more forward looking interim management report in the half-yearly report and the requirement for interim management statements are new. Also, the periods for publishing annual and half-yearly reports have been shortened.

Responsibility statements must be given by 'persons responsible' within the issuer. **23.73** With respect to liability attaching to responsibility statements, s 90A of FSMA imposes liability on an issuer (rather than on the directors) to pay compensation to any person who relies on, and suffers loss as a result of, an untrue or misleading statement in (or omission from) a report. Such liability will only arise where a director knew (or was reckless as to whether) the report was untrue or misleading, or knew the omission to be a dishonest concealment of a material fact. Therefore, despite the requirement for responsibility statements to be given under the Disclosure and Transparency Rules, the position with respect to directors' liability will not change significantly. See Section C(11) for more information.

## (6) Duty to publish accounts and reports

The 2006 Act, Part 15, Chapter 7, ss 423–436, contain provisions for the publica- **23.74** tion of accounts and reports. Every company[167] is required by statute to send a copy of its financial accounts and reports for each financial year to every member of the company, every debenture holder, and every person who is entitled to receive notice of general meetings.[168] The accounts and reports sent out in compliance with this requirement must identify the signatory by name on the balance sheet, directors' report, and, in the case of a quoted company, directors' remuneration report.[169]

---

[166] The Disclosure and Transparency Rules apply to issuers with securities admitted to trading on a regulated market in the UK (or outside the UK where the UK is the home state for the purposes of the Transparency Directive). This will include issuers with securities admitted to the FSA's Official List, whether incorporated in the UK or elsewhere, but not AIM issuers.

[167] In *Re Allen Craig & Co (London) Ltd* [1934] Ch 483, Bennett J confirmed that the obligation is that of the company and not that of the auditors.

[168] The 2006 Act, ss 423–426 came into force on 6 April 2008: 2006 Act Commencement Order No 5, art 3(1)(d). 2006 Act, s 423(1). Copies need not be sent to a person for whom the company does not have a 'current address': s 423(2). The term 'current address' is defined in 2006 Act, s 423(3).

[169] 2006 Act, s 433(1), (2), (3).

Statutory accounts must be accompanied by the auditor's report on those accounts (unless the company is exempt from audit and the directors have taken advantage of that exemption).[170] If group accounts are prepared, a company must not publish individual accounts unless they are accompanied by the group accounts.[171]

**23.75** If a company publishes any financial information (non-statutory accounts) in addition to the statutory accounts required to be filed with the Registrar of Companies, it must take care to ensure that readers of the non-statutory accounts do not confuse them with the statutory accounts. To this end, the company must state clearly that the non-statutory accounts are not the statutory accounts[172] and must ensure that the auditor's report on the statutory accounts is not published alongside the non-statutory material.[173]

**23.76** In the case of a private company, the requirement to send out copies of accounts and reports must be complied with by the end of the period for filing accounts and reports or, if earlier, the date on which the company actually delivers its accounts and reports to the Registrar.[174] A public company must circulate accounts and reports at least 21 days[175] before the date of the relevant accounts meeting.[176] If a public company's accounts and reports are despatched less than 21 days before the accounts meeting, the members may agree to waive the default at the accounts meeting, and upon such agreement the accounts and reports will be deemed to have been duly sent.[177] However, it is not possible for the members to agree prospectively to waive late service of accounts and reports which have not yet been sent out.

*Option to provide summary financial statement*

**23.77** The 2006 Act, s 426, enables the Secretary of State to make regulations allowing companies to provide a summary financial statement, instead of the accounts and reports which otherwise would be required to be sent out. Where a summary financial statement is provided, members and debenture holders will continue to have a statutory right to demand a copy of the full accounts and reports,[178] and accounts and reports must be sent out to any member or debenture holder or person who is entitled to receive notice of general meetings who requests them.[179]

---

[170] 2006 Act, s 434(1).

[171] 2006 Act, s 434(2).

[172] 2006 Act, s 435(1)(a).

[173] 2006 Act, s 435(2).

[174] 2006 Act, s 424(2).

[175] At least 21 clear days means 21 clear days' notice, excluding the day of service and the day on which the meeting is to be held: *Re Railway Sleepers Supply Co* (1885) 29 Ch D 204.

[176] 2006 Act, s 424(3). In the 2006 Act, the term 'accounts meeting' means, in relation to a public company, a general meeting of the company at which the company' annual accounts and reports are to be laid in accordance with s 437: see, specifically, s 437(3).

[177] 2006 Act, s 424(4).

[178] 2006 Act, s 431, s 432.

[179] 2006 Act, s 426(2). See The Companies (Summary Financial Statements) Regulations (SI 2008/374) made pursuant to ss 426(1), 427(2)–(5), and 428(2)–(5).

In the case of an unquoted company, the summary financial statement must com-   **23.78**
ply with the requirements of s 427. In the case of a quoted company, it must
comply with the requirements of s 428. These sections provide, inter alia, that the
summary financial statement must be derived from the company's annual accounts
and must state on its face that it is a summary only.

*Quoted companies: website publication*

The 2006 Act, s 430, introduces a new requirement for quoted companies (as   **23.79**
defined in s 385) to put the full accounts and reports on a website. This requirement came into force on 6 April 2008 and is in addition to sending out the full
accounts and reports to members under s 423. The annual accounts must be made
available as soon as reasonably practicable on a website that is maintained by or on
behalf of the company and that identifies the company in question. Access to the
website must be available to all members of the public and not just to members,
and there must be continuous access to the website without charge. The annual
accounts and reports for a financial year must remain available until the accounts
and reports for the next financial year are published on the website.

*Criminal liability of directors*

If a company fails to circulate its accounts and reports to members, debenture   **23.80**
holders, and such others as may be entitled to receive notice of general meetings
by the statutory deadline, an offence[180] (punishable by way of fine) is committed
by every officer in default.[181] It should be noted that an odd situation arises in the
case of a public company which sends out its accounts and reports less than
21 days before the accounts meeting: the officers in default will be guilty of an
offence unless the members agree at the accounts meeting to waive the default, in
which case the accounts and reports will be deemed to have been duly sent, and
the offence will no longer exist. Generally it is not possible to cure an illegality by
ratification; however, as a result of the 'deeming' language of s 424(4), a public
company's tardiness despatching accounts and reports presents an exception to
this general rule.

Offences may also be committed in connection with the failure of a quoted com-   **23.81**
pany to make its accounts and reports available on a website in accordance with
the statutory requirements;[182] a failure by any company to identify the signatory
by name on the balance sheet, directors' report, and, in the case of a quoted company, the directors' remuneration report;[183] failure to enclose the auditor's report

---

[180] 2006 Act, s 425(1), (2).
[181] ie who authorizes or permits or participates in or fails to take all reasonable steps to prevent
the commission or continuation of the offence: see 2006 Act, s 1121.
[182] 2006 Act, s 430(5), (6).
[183] 2006 Act, s 433(4).

or, where group accounts are prepared, copies of the group accounts;[184] or failure to comply with the statutory requirements aimed at preventing confusion between statutory and non-statutory accounts.[185] These offences are triable summarily and punishable by fine.[186]

**23.82** It is also a summary offence punishable by fine, committed by any officer in default, for a company's summary financial statement prepared under s 426 to fail to comply with the requirements of s 427 or s 428 (as the case may be) or any regulations made thereunder.[187] Similarly, it is a summary offence punishable by a fine not exceeding level 3 on the standard scale, committed by every officer in default, for a company to fail to comply within seven days with a demand by a member or debenture holder for a copy of accounts and reports.[188]

### (7) Public companies: laying accounts before general meeting

**23.83** The directors of a public company must lay before the company in general meeting copies of its annual accounts and reports.[189] This requirement must be complied with not later than the end of the period for filing the accounts and reports in question.[190] If this requirement is not complied with by the deadline, a summary offence punishable by fine is committed by every director of the company.[191] However, it is a defence for a person charged with such offence to prove that he took all reasonable steps for securing that those requirements would be complied with before the end of the applicable period.[192] It is not a defence to prove that the documents in question were not in fact prepared.[193]

### (8) Quoted companies: approval of directors' remuneration report

**23.84** In the case of a quoted company, the directors' remuneration report[194] for the financial year must be approved at the company's accounts meeting[195] in respect of that financial year. To that end, s 439(1) provides that a quoted company must, prior to the accounts meeting, give to the members of the company entitled to be sent notice of the meeting notice of the intention to move at the meeting, as an ordinary

---

[184] 2006 Act, s 434(4).
[185] 2006 Act, s 435(5).
[186] 2006 Act, s 430(7), s 430(5), s 434(5), s 435(6).
[187] 2006 Act, s 429(1), (2).
[188] 2006 Act, s 431(3), (4), s 432(3), (4). Sections 437 and 438 came into force on 6 April 2008. 2006 Act Commencement Order No 5, art 3(1)(d).
[189] 2006 Act, s 437(1).
[190] 2006 Act, s 437(2).
[191] 2006 Act, s 438(1), (4).
[192] 2006 Act, s 438(2).
[193] 2006 Act, s 438(3); cf *Stockdale v Coulson* [1974] 1 WLR 1192.
[194] See paragraphs 23.65 to 23.71 above.
[195] The term 'accounts meeting' is defined in s 437(3); see n 176 above.

resolution, a resolution approving the directors' remuneration report for the financial year. The business of that meeting must then include the resolution;[196] this is the case even where the company has defaulted in sending out the resolution as required by s 439(1). Pursuant to s 439(4), the directors of a quoted company are expressly required to ensure that the resolution is put to the vote at the meeting.

If the resolution is not sent out as required by s 439(1), an offence is committed **23.85**
by every officer in default.[197] If the resolution is not put to the vote at the meeting, an offence is committed by every director of the company,[198] save that it is a defence for a person charged with such an offence to prove that he took all reasonable steps for securing that the resolution was put to the vote at the meeting.[199] These offences are both summary and punishable by fine.[200]

### (9) Filing of accounts and reports

The directors of a company must deliver to the Registrar, for each financial **23.86**
year, the accounts and reports required by the 2006 Act, Part 15, Chapter 10, ss 441–453.[201] The precise content of the filing obligation will depend on whether the company in question is small[202] or medium sized,[203] or quoted;[204] different requirements are in place for different types of company. Directors of companies subject to the small companies regime should ensure that the requirements of s 444 are satisfied. For directors of medium-sized companies, the relevant requirements which must be observed are contained in s 445. Unquoted companies are dealt with in s 446, and quoted companies in s 447. In summary: (1) small companies must deliver a copy of the balance sheet, but it is not mandatory to deliver a copy of the profit and loss account or the directors' report; (2) medium-sized companies must file the annual accounts (which may be in an abbreviated form) and the directors' report and the auditors' report (unless exempt from audit); (3) other unquoted companies must file the annual accounts, the directors' report, and the auditors' report; and (4) quoted companies must file the annual accounts, the directors' report, the directors' remuneration report, and the auditors' report. Unlimited companies are exempt from the obligation to file accounts.[205]

---

[196] 2006 Act, s 439(3). Sections 439 and 440 came into force on 6 April 2008: 2006 Act Commencement Order No 5, art 3(1)(d).

[197] 2006 Act, s 440(1).

[198] 2006 Act, s 440(2).

[199] 2006 Act, s 440(3).

[200] 2006 Act, s 440(4).

[201] 2006 Act, s 441(1). Chapter 10 came into force. Sections 439 and 440 came into force on 6 April 2008: 2006 Act Commencement Order No 5, art 3(1)(d).

[202] 2006 Act, s 382.

[203] 2006 Act, s 465.

[204] 2006 Act, s 385.

[205] 2006 Act, s 448.

**23.87**   The accounts and reports required to be filed must be delivered to the Registrar by the applicable deadline.[206] For private companies, this will be nine months after the end of the relevant accounting reference period.[207] For public companies, it will be six months after the end of that period.[208] However, if the relevant accounting reference period is the company's first and is a period of more than 12 months, the deadline for the filing of accounts will be nine months (in the case of a private company) or six months (in the case of a public company) from the first anniversary of incorporation, or three months after the end of the accounting reference period, whichever is the later.[209]

### Criminal liabilities of directors

**23.88**   If the directors' duty to file accounts and reports is not complied with by the applicable deadline, an offence is committed by every director of the company,[210] save that it is a defence for any person charged with such an offence to show that he took all reasonable steps for securing that the duty would be complied with before the end of the relevant period.[211] However, it is not a defence to show that the relevant documents were not actually prepared.[212]

### 14-day notices, civil proceedings, and contempt of court

**23.89**   If the directors fail to comply with the duty to file accounts and reports by the deadline, the Registrar may serve a notice requiring those duties to be complied with within 14 days.[213] If after 14 days the duty has still not been complied with, the Registrar (or any member or creditor of the company) may apply to the court for an order directing the directors to make good the default within such time as may be specified by the court.[214] Any director who fails to comply with such an order will be liable to be committed to prison for contempt of court. In addition, a director may be ordered to pay the costs of the proceedings.[215]

### Civil liability of company; company's claim against directors

**23.90**   In addition, where the directors of a company fail or neglect to comply with the duty to file accounts and reports by the applicable deadline, the company is liable,

---

[206] 2006 Act, s 442(1). Months are to be reckoned in accordance with s 443 which reverses the 'corresponding date rule' laid down by the House of Lords in *Dodds v Walker* [1981] 1 WLR 1027.
[207] 2006 Act, s 442(2)(a).
[208] 2006 Act, s 442(2)(b).
[209] 2006 Act, s 442(3).
[210] 2006 Act, s 451(1).
[211] 2006 Act, s 451(2).
[212] 2006 Act, s 451(3); cf *Stockdale v Coulson* [1974] 1 WLR 1192.
[213] 2006 Act, s 452(1)(b).
[214] 2006 Act, s 452(1).
[215] 2006 Act, s 452(2).

automatically by operation of law,[216] to pay a civil penalty to the Registrar, who must pay it into the Consolidated Fund.[217] The quantum of the liability will fall to be determined in accordance with regulations which will be made by the Secretary of State. The civil liability of a company under these provisions will give rise to the possibility of a claim for indemnification by the company against its directors; such a claim could be framed in terms of negligence or breach of fiduciary duty.

### (10) Revision of defective accounts and reports

Where accounts or reports do not comply with the requirements of the 2006 Act (or, where applicable, with the requirements of the IAS Regulation[218]), the directors may prepared revised accounts in accordance with Part 15, Chapter 11, ss 454–462.[219] If the accounts and reports in question have been circulated to members or filed with the Registrar, the revisions must be confined to the correction of the respects in which the previous documents failed to comply with the applicable requirements, and any necessary consequential alterations.[220]    **23.91**

Where the directors of a company do not take the initiative to revise defective accounts and reports, they may find that they become subject to the unwelcome attention of the Secretary of State or the Financial Reporting Review Panel.    **23.92**

*Involvement of Secretary of State*

The 2006 Act, s 455, provides that the Secretary of State may serve a notice on the directors of a company requiring them (1) to provide an explanation, within    **23.93**

---

[216] In *R (on the application of POW Trust) v Chief Executive and Registrar of Companies* [2002] EWHC 2783 (Admin), a company sought judicial review of the Registrar's decision to recover the penalty. The company contended that the liability arose by reason of the Registrar's decision, which was susceptible to judicial review. Lightman J said: 'The liability is strict: there is no defence to a claim to payment if there has been non-compliance with the filing obligation. The role of the Registrar is confined to recovery of the penalty: he has no role in respect of the liability to pay or the quantum of the penalty. I accordingly hold that the statutory penalty is immediately payable without more on non-compliance.' See also *Registrar of Companies v Radio-Tech Engineering Ltd* [2004] BCC 277.

[217] 2006 Act, s 453(1), (2). Also see The Companies (Late Filing Penalities) and Limited Liability Partnerships (Filing Periods and Late Filing Penalities) Regulations (SI 2008/497). It is not a defence in recovery proceedings by the Registrar to show that the documents in question were never prepared: 2006 Act, s 453(4).

[218] Regulation (EC) No 1606/2002 of the European Parliament and of the Council of 19 July 2002 on the application of international accounting standards.

[219] 2006 Act, s 454(1). Chapter 11 came into force on 6 April 2008. Also see The Companies (Revision of Defective Accounts and Reports) Regulations (SI 2008/373), made under s 454(3). The ability to prepare revised accounts is limited to cases of non-compliance with mandatory requirements; accounts may not be revised on other grounds (eg inadvertent disclosure of legally privileged information): *Re A Company (No 1389920)* [2004] EWHC 35 (Ch).

[220] 2006 Act, s 454(2).

a period of one month, of the aspects of the accounts or reports which the Secretary of State considers to be non-compliant, or alternatively (2) to prepare revised accounts or a revised report.[221] If the directors fail to comply with such a notice, the Secretary of State has the ability to apply to court under s 456 for a declaration that the accounts or reports in question are defective in the manner alleged and for an order requiring the directors to prepare compliant accounts and reports.[222] On the hearing of such an application, the court may give directions as to (1) the auditing of the accounts and/or reports, (2) the revision of the accounts and/or reports, (3) the taking of steps by the directors to bring the making of the order to the notice of anyone who might rely on the defective accounts and/or reports, and (4) such other matters as the court thinks fit.[223] The court may also order the directors to pay the costs of the proceedings.[224]

### The Financial Reporting Review Panel

**23.94**  The 2006 Act, s 457, enables the Secretary of State to delegate his powers to 'a fit and proper person'. For this purpose the FRRP is appointed to exercise the powers.[225]

**23.95**  The person appointed by the Secretary of State (the 'authorized person') is given extensive powers to obtain documents,[226] information, and explanations from the officers of the company.[227] The 2006 Act, s 459 provides that the 'authorized person' may require any officer, employee, or auditor of the company to produce any document, or to provide him with any information or explanations, that he may reasonably require for the purpose of discovering whether there are grounds for an application to the court under s 456 or deciding whether or not to make such an application.[228] If a person fails to comply with a request by the authorized person for documents, information, or explanations, the authorized person may apply to the court for an order requiring that the request be complied with.[229] Failure to comply with such an order will amount to contempt of court rendering the contemnor liable to be committed to prison.

---

[221]  2006 Act, s 455(1), (2), (3).

[222]  2006 Act, s 455(4), s 456(1).

[223]  2006 Act, s 456(3), (4).

[224]  2006 Act, s 456(5).

[225]  See the Companies (Defective Accounts and Directors' Reports) (Authorised Person) and Supervision of Accounts and Reports (Prescribed Body) Order 2008 (SI 2008/623).

[226]  For these purposes, 'document' includes information recorded in any form: s 459(8).

[227]  These powers were originally introduced by the C (AICE) Act 2004 further to a recommendation of the Coordinating Group on Audit and Accounting Issues, which was established by the Government following the collapse of Enron.

[228]  2006 Act, s 459(1), (2), (3).

[229]  2006 Act, s 459(4), (5).

### (11) Liability of directors and issuers for accounts and reports

A new liability regime for financial reporting disclosures was inserted in the **23.96**
Companies Act 2006 and FSMA, with effect for financial years commencing
20 January 2007. This was introduced to deal with concerns that (1) fear of liability for forward-looking statements in the enhanced business review would deter
meaningful disclosures and lead to defensive reporting by quoted company directors and (2) the Transparency Directive overturned existing principles of English
law and makes directors liable to investors.

Before the implementation of the Transparency Directive on 20 January 2007, it **23.97**
was generally understood, using the principles laid down by the House of Lords
in *Caparo Industries plc v Dickman*[230] (which concerned the liability of auditors),
that directors had a duty of care to shareholders as a whole to enable them to exercise their governance rights but not, in the absence of circumstances creating
proximity or a special relationship, to individual shareholders in relation to their
investment or to potential investors or other third parties.

The Transparency Directive requires issuers to publish periodic financial informa- **23.98**
tion, consisting of annual financial reports, half-yearly reports, and interim management statements (see paragraph 23.72), with the objective of allowing investors
to make an 'informed assessment' of an issuer's position and to increase investor
protection within the EU. Periodic financial information must be made generally
available throughout the EU. For annual financial reports and half-yearly reports,
a statement of responsibility must be given by 'persons responsible'.

In the absence of legislative intervention, there was the risk that the implementa- **23.99**
tion of the Transparency Directive would extend the scope of liability under
English law for annual accounts and other financial reporting to investors and the
public in general across the EU. However, while Member States were required to
impose liability for information published under the Directive on at least the
issuer or its directors, the Directive allows Member States to determine the extent
of that liability.

The Government therefore took the opportunity to include two provisions in the **23.100**
Companies Act to clarify the liability of directors for narrative reports and the
liability of companies for periodic financial information (including narrative
reports). Both provisions operate so as to define the limited circumstances in
which liability will arise, and to exclude liability in all other circumstances.

The first provision (2006 Act, s 463) relates to the directors' report (including the **23.101**
business review), directors' remuneration report, and information in summary

---

[230] [1990] 2 AC 605.

financial statements derived from either of these reports. It provides that a director will be liable to compensate the company for any loss it suffers as a result of any untrue or misleading statement in, or omission from, such a report, but only if he knew (or was reckless as to whether) the statement was untrue or misleading, or knew the omission to be dishonest concealment of a material fact. Furthermore, no director, auditor, or other person will have any liability to anyone other than the company resulting from reliance on these reports.

**23.102** The second provision (2006 Act, s 1270) inserts s 90A into FSMA and deals with liability in relation to annual financial reports, half-yearly reports, and interim management statements published by issuers under the Disclosure and Transparency Rules.[231] It also extends to preliminary announcements of results, where issuers choose to publish them, but only to the extent that the information contained in the preliminary announcement is of a kind appearing in the subsequent annual report.

**23.103** The provision imposes on an issuer of securities liability to pay compensation to an investor who acquires securities of the issuer and suffers loss as a result of an untrue or misleading statement in, or omission from, a report but only if a 'person discharging managerial responsibilities'[232] within the issuer knew (or was reckless as to whether) the report was untrue or misleading, or knew the omission to be a dishonest concealment of a material fact.

**23.104** The provision exempts the issuer and any other person from any other liability, subject to limited exceptions described below.

**23.105** The existing power under FSMA for a court or the FSA to require restitution to be paid to investors or others who have suffered loss resulting from a breach of FSA rules is not affected by the new provision. Although never yet used in the context of a breach by an issuer or director of the Listing, Disclosure and Transparency, or Prospectus Rules, this power does leave open at least a possibility of personal liability to investors on the part of directors. Similarly, the provision does not exclude civil or criminal liabilities such as under the market abuse regime, penalties for Listing Rule breaches, or criminal acts under s 397 of FSMA.

**23.106** The liability regime was devised somewhat hurriedly to ensure that there was something on the statute books by 20 January 2007, the deadline for implementing

---

[231] The Disclosure and Transparency Rules apply to issuers with securities admitted to trading on a regulated market in the UK (or outside the UK where the UK is the home state for the purposes of the Transparency Directive). This will include issuers with securities admitted to the FSA's Official List, whether incorporated in the UK or elsewhere, but not AIM issuers.

[232] 'Persons discharging managerial responsibilities' will generally mean directors. It will only catch senior executives of non-corporate issuers.

the Transparency Directive. Since the division between disclosures within the liability regime and those which are not is quite arbitrary, the Government appointed Professor Paul Davies to conduct a review of the liability regime. Professor Davies published his final report in June 2007. He recommended that the regime should be extended to cover all announcements of 'inside' and other information made to the market by issuers through their Regulatory Information Service and to issuers on AIM and PLUS and that liability should be introduced for dishonest delay in making Regulatory Information Service announcements. However, he rejected suggestions that the bar for liability to third parties should be brought down from the fraud threshold to negligence.

Professor Davies also suggested that there should be a single legal regime applied to investor claims. This is because the liability regime in the UK does not protect issuers or directors from being sued in other jurisdictions. However, the point was beyond the terms of reference for Professor Davies's review, so he did not deal with it in any detail and merely raised a flag for the Government that this point should be addressed in the context of a pan-European securities market. **23.107**

The Treasury will consult on Professor Davies's recommendations before exercising its powers under s 90B of FSMA to amend the scope of the regime by statutory instrument. **23.108**

## D. Directors' Functions and Responsibilities in Relation to Audit

### (1) Introduction

This section deals with the functions, responsibilities, and liabilities of company directors in relation to audit. Specifically, it deals with: (1) the requirement for audited accounts; (2) directors' functions in relation to appointment of auditors; (3) directors' functions in relation to auditors' remuneration; (4) directors' functions and responsibilities in relation to the functions of the auditors; (5) directors' functions and responsibilities in relation to the removal or resignation of auditors; (6) in respect of quoted companies, the directors' functions in relation to the right of members to raise concerns at the accounts meeting; and, finally, (7) directors' functions and responsibilities in relation to provisions protecting auditors from liability. **23.109**

Part 16 of the Companies Act governing audit matters took effect on 6 April 2008 except for provisions relating to the appointment of auditors by private companies ss 485–488 which took effect on 1 October 2007. **23.110**

## (2) Requirement for audited accounts

**23.111**  A company's annual accounts for a financial year must be audited, unless the company is exempt from audit.[233] The statutory purpose of this provision is to secure for shareholders independent and reliable information on the true financial position of the company at the time of the audit.[234] The importance of audited accounts is now reinforced by the Fourth Company Law Directive,[235] which states that companies must have their annual accounts audited by one or more persons authorized by national law to audit accounts.[236]

**23.112**  The exemptions relate to small companies,[237] dormant companies,[238] and non-profit-making companies subject to public sector audits.[239] The provisions relating to qualification for exemption are considered below.

**23.113**  However, in the case of small companies and dormant companies which are entitled to claim exemption from audit, the members of the company representing not less in total than 10 per cent in nominal value of the company's issued share capital (or any class of it) are entitled by the 2006 Act, s 476, to serve a notice requiring that the company's accounts be audited. The notice may not be given before the financial year to which it relates and must not be given later than one month before the end of that year.[240] If such a notice is served, the directors must not claim exemption from audit, but must ensure instead that the company's accounts are audited in accordance with the requirements of the 2006 Act, Part 16.

**23.114**  In the case of a small or dormant company where no such notice is given by members requiring audit, and in the case of non-profit-making companies subject to public sector audits, the right to claim exemption from audit must be exercised by election; in other words, it is an 'opt in' system, rather than an 'opt out' system. To elect to take advantage of the exemption, the directors of the company must ensure that the company's balance sheet contains a statement (which must appear above the signature[241]) that the company is exempt from audit; failure to include such a statement on the balance sheet will cause the company to lose its right to claim exemption, and the company will be liable to audit.[242] In addition, in the

---

233  2006 Act, s 475(1).
234  *Re London & General Bank (No 2)* [1895] 2 Ch 673, 682, per Lindley LJ.
235  78/660/EEC.
236  Art 51(1)(a).
237  2006 Act, s 477.
238  2006 Act, s 480.
239  2006 Act, s 482.
240  2006 Act, s 476(3).
241  2006 Act, s 475(4).
242  2006 Act, s 475(2).

case of a small or dormant company, the balance sheet must record (again by way of statement appearing above the signature) that the company's members have not required the company to obtain an audit, and that the directors acknowledge their responsibilities for complying with the requirements of the Companies Act with respect to accounting records[243] and the preparation of accounts;[244] failure to ensure that the balance sheet contains this statement will result in the company losing its exemption, and an audit will be required.[245]

*Exemption from audit: small companies*

In order to be exempt from audit as a small company, the company must (1) qualify as a small company,[246] (2) have turnover of no more than £6.5 million, and (3) have a 'balance sheet total' (ie aggregate asset value; see s 382(5)) of not more than £3.26 million.[247] If the company is part of a group, it may not claim exemption from audit unless (1) the group is a 'small group' (as determined in accordance with s 383), (2) the group is not an ineligible group (as defined by s 384(2) and (3)), (3) the group's aggregate turnover is not more than £6.5 million net (or £7.8 million gross), and (4) the group's aggregate balance sheet total for the year is not more than £3.26 million net (or £3.9 million gross).[248] Public companies and insurers may not take advantage of this exemption, if they would otherwise qualify for it.[249]

**23.115**

*Exemption from audit: dormant companies*

To be exempt from audit as a dormant company, the company must have been either (1) dormant since its formation, or (2) dormant since the end of the previous financial year, provided (a) it is entitled to prepare individual accounts in accordance with the small companies regime (or would be so entitled but for having been a public company or a member of an ineligible group) and (b) it is not required to prepare group accounts for that year.[250]

**23.116**

*Exemption from audit: companies subject to public sector audit*

A non-profit-making company is not subject to the audit requirements imposed by Part 16 of the Companies Act if (but only if) its accounts are subject to audit by the Auditor General under the Government Resources and Accounts Act 2000

**23.117**

---

[243] See paragraphs 23.13–23.19 above.
[244] See paragraphs 23.34–23.48 above.
[245] 2006 Act, s 475(3).
[246] See paragraph 23.03 above.
[247] 2006 Act, s 477(2). The amounts referred to in paragraph 23.115 reflect amendments made to the 2006 Act, ss 477 and 479 by the Companies Act 2006 (Amendment) (Accounts and Reports) Regulations 2008 (SI 2008/393), reg 5, which were made pursuant to ss 468(1) and (2) and 473(2).
[248] 2006 Act, s 479(1), (2), (3), (4).
[249] 2006 Act, s 478.
[250] 2006 Act, s 480(1), (2).

(or, in Wales, by the Auditor General for Wales under the Government of Wales Act 1998).[251]

### (3) Directors' functions in relation to appointment of auditors

**23.118**  The 2006 Act, Part 16, Chapter 2, relates to the appointment of auditors. The requirement to appoint an auditor applies to both private and public companies, unless exempt from audit. In either case, failure to appoint an auditor is not an offence, but an offence is committed by any officer in default if the company fails to notify the Secretary of State that no auditor has been appointed. It should be noted that a person may be appointed to carry out a particular audit exercise without being appointed to the office of auditor.[252]

*Private companies*

**23.119**  In the case of a private company, an auditor (or auditors) must be appointed for each financial year of the company,[253] unless the directors reasonably resolve otherwise on the ground that audited accounts are unlikely to be required.[254] The appointment must be made before the end of the period of 28 days[255] (the 'period for appointing auditors'; s 485(2)) beginning with the end of the time allowed for sending out copies of the company's annual accounts and reports for the previous financial year,[256] or, if earlier, the day on which copies of the company's annual accounts and reports for the previous financial year are circulated to members.[257]

**23.120**  At any time before the company's first period for appointing auditors, or following a period in which (by reason of being exempt from audit) the company did not have any auditor, or to fill a casual vacancy, the company's directors may appoint an auditor.[258] Otherwise, the auditor must be appointed by the members by ordinary resolution.[259] However, if auditors are not appointed by the directors or the members, the Secretary of State has power to appoint an auditor.[260] In order to ensure that the Secretary of State is aware that the power to appoint an auditor has arisen, the company is required by statute to give notice to the Secretary of State that no auditor has been appointed and that the Secretary of State's power to appoint has accordingly become exercisable.[261] Such a notice must be given within

---

251  2006 Act, s 482.
252  *Mutual Reinsurance Co Ltd v Peat Marwick Mitchell & Co* [1997] 1 BCLC 1.
253  2006 Act, s 485(1).
254  ie by reason of an exemption; see paragraphs 23.111–23.117 above.
255  2006 Act, s 485(2).
256  2006 Act, s 424; see paragraph 23.76 above.
257  2006 Act, s 423; see paragraph 23.74 above.
258  2006 Act, s 485(3).
259  2006 Act, s 485(4).
260  2006 Act, s 486(1).
261  2006 Act, s 486(2).

one week of the end of the period for appointing auditors. Failure to give the notice to the Secretary of State when required is an offence committed by every officer of the company who is in default.[262] The offence is summary and punishable by fine.[263]

An auditor of a private company will not take office until any previous auditor ceases to hold office, and will cease to hold office at the end of the next period for appointing auditors, unless re-appointed.[264] However, where no successor has been appointed, the auditor in office will be deemed to be re-appointed, unless (1) he was appointed by the directors, (2) the company's articles require actual re-appointment, (3) the deemed re-appointment is prevented by the members (ie under s 488, which enables members representing 5 per cent of the total voting rights of all members to give notice that the auditor should not be automatically re-appointed), (4) the members have resolved that he should not be re-appointed, or (5) the directors have resolved that no auditor should be appointed for the financial year in question.[265]

*Public companies*

In the case of a public company, auditors must be appointed for each financial year of the company, unless the directors reasonably resolve otherwise on the ground that audited accounts are unlikely to be required.[266] The auditors must generally be appointed by the members at a meeting at which accounts are to be laid. There is no provision for deemed re-appointment. The auditors of a public company will not take office until any previous auditor ceases to hold office, and will cease to hold office at the end of the accounts meeting next following their appointment, unless re-appointed.[267] The requirement to notify the Secretary of State if no auditor is appointed and the power of the Secretary of State to appoint the auditor is the same for public companies as for private companies except the Secretary of State must be notified within a week of the accounts meeting.[268]

**(4) Directors' functions in relation to auditors' remuneration**

If the auditor is appointed by the members, the auditor's remuneration must be fixed by the members.[269] However, if the auditor is appointed by the directors, the

23.121

23.122

23.123

---

[262] 2006 Act, s 486(3).
[263] 2006 Act, s 486(4).
[264] 2006 Act, s 487(1).
[265] 2006 Act, s 487(2).
[266] 2006 Act, s 489(1).
[267] 2006 Act, s 491(1).
[268] 2006 Act, s 490.
[269] 2006 Act, s 492(1).

directors have a specific statutory duty to fix the auditor's remuneration.[270] For these purposes, 'remuneration' includes sums paid in respect of expenses.[271]

**23.124**  In determining the level of remuneration payable to an auditor, the directors should be mindful of their duty to promote the success of the company[272] (which will involve ensuring that the company's assets are not expended unnecessarily in paying excessive sums to auditors by way of remuneration) and their duty to act with reasonable care, skill, and diligence[273] (which will involve ensuring that the company's auditors are not remunerated in excess of the going rate).

### (5) Directors' functions and responsibilities in relation to the functions of the auditors

*The auditor's functions: in general*

**23.125**  A company's auditor must make a report to the company's members on all annual accounts of the company which are, in the case of a private company, sent out to members, or, in the case of a public company, laid before the company in general meeting.[274]

*The auditor's functions: preparation of auditors' report*

**23.126**  In order to prepare the report, the auditor must carry out such investigations as will enable him to form an opinion as to (1) whether adequate accounting records have been kept by the company and returns adequate for the audit have been received from branches not visited by him, (2) whether the company's individual accounts are in agreement with the accounting records and returns, and (3) in the case of a quoted company, whether the directors' remuneration report is consistent with the accounting records and returns.[275]

*The auditors' functions: contents of the report*

**23.127**  The report must include an introduction, which must identify the annual accounts which are the subject of the audit and the financial reporting framework which has been applied in their preparation, and a description of the scope of the audit, which must identify the auditing standards in accordance with which the audit was conducted.[276] The body of the report must state clearly whether, in the auditor's opinion, the annual accounts (1) give a true and fair view,[277] (2) have been

---

[270]  2006 Act, s 492(3).
[271]  2006 Act, s 492(4).
[272]  2006 Act, s 172.
[273]  2006 Act, s 174.
[274]  2006 Act, s 495(1).
[275]  2006 Act, s 498(1).
[276]  2006 Act, s 495(2).
[277]  See paragraph 23.36 above.

properly prepared in accordance with the relevant financial reporting framework, and (3) have been prepared in accordance with the requirements of the Companies Act (and, where applicable, the requirements of the IAS Regulation).[278] The auditor's report must be either 'qualified' or 'unqualified' and must include a reference to any matters to which the auditor wishes to draw attention by way of emphasis without qualifying the report.[279]

**23.128** The auditor must also state whether or not the directors' report is consistent with the company's annual accounts.[280] In the case of a quoted company, the auditor must also report to the members in respect of the auditable part of the directors' remuneration report; specifically, he must state whether the directors' remuneration report has been properly prepared in accordance with the requirements of the Companies Act.[281]

**23.129** If the accounting records and returns have not been kept adequately, or if adequate returns have not been received from unvisited branches, or if the individual accounts are not consistent with the accounting records and returns, or if the auditable part of the directors' remuneration report is not consistent with the accounting records and returns, the auditor must state that fact in his report.[282] Furthermore, if the auditor fails to obtain all the information and explanations which, to the best of his knowledge and belief, are necessary for the purposes of his audit, he must state this fact in his report.[283]

*Specific duties of directors in respect of the auditor's function*

**23.130** A company's directors are likely to be one of the auditor's main sources of information. Accordingly the directors' duties in relation to the preparation and contents of the auditors' report relate chiefly to the provision of information to the auditor. To that end, an auditor is expressly entitled to require any officer of the company to provide such information or explanations as he thinks necessary for the performance of his duties as auditor.[284] He may also ask any officer of a subsidiary undertaking to provide him with books, accounts, or vouchers relating to the subsidiary undertaking.[285] He is also entitled to all communications relating to written resolutions[286] and general meetings.[287]

---

[278] 2006 Act, s 495(3).
[279] 2006 Act, s 495(4).
[280] 2006 Act, s 496.
[281] 2006 Act, s 497.
[282] 2006 Act, s 498(2).
[283] 2006 Act, s 498(3).
[284] 2006 Act, s 499(1), (2).
[285] 2006 Act, s 499(2)(d).
[286] 2006 Act, s 502(1).
[287] 2006 Act, s 502(2).

**23.131** An offence is committed by any officer (or, for that matter, any other person) who knowingly or recklessly makes any statement to an auditor, whether oral or written, which conveys or purports to convey any information required by the auditor, but which is misleading, false, or deceptive in a material particular.[288] Such an offence is triable on indictment and punishable by imprisonment for up to two years or a fine or both, or summarily and punishable by imprisonment for up to 12 months or a fine not exceeding the statutory maximum or both.[289]

**23.132** In addition, a summary offence punishable by fine is committed by any person who fails without delay to comply with an auditor's requirement for information, unless it was not reasonably practicable for him to provide the required information.[290]

**23.133** Furthermore, where a parent company fails to comply with an auditor's request for information, a summary offence punishable by fine is committed by every officer of the company who is in default.[291]

**23.134** The obligations in the Companies Act to provide auditors with information are supported by the statement that must be included in the directors' report that, so far as each director is aware, there is no relevant audit information of which the company's auditor is unaware and that each director has taken all steps to make himself aware of any relevant audit information and to establish that the auditor is aware of such information.[292]

### (6) Directors' functions and responsibilities in relation to the removal or resignation of auditors

*Introduction*

**23.135** The 2006 Act, Part 16, Chapter 4, contains provisions relating to the removal or resignation of auditors and imposes certain duties on companies to notify the Registrar of such events. Failure to notify the Registrar results in offences on the part of officers in default.

*Removal of auditor from office*

**23.136** Under the 2006 Act, s 510, the members of a company may remove an auditor from office by ordinary resolution at a meeting, provided that the special notice required by s 511 has been (1) given to the company and (2) forwarded by the company to the auditor proposed to be removed.

---

[288] 2006 Act, s 501(1).
[289] 2006 Act, s 501(2).
[290] 2006 Act, s 501(3), (5).
[291] 2006 Act, s 501(4).
[292] 2006 Act, s 418. See also paragraph 23.59 above.

*Duties and liabilities of directors in connection with removal of auditor from office*

Where the members resolve to remove an auditor in accordance with these provisions, the company is required to give notice of that fact to the Registrar within 14 days.[293] If a company fails to comply with this requirement, an offence is committed by every officer in default.[294] This offence is triable summarily and punishable by a fine not exceeding level 3 on the standard scale; in addition, a daily default fine not exceeding one-tenth of level 3 on the standard scale is applicable for continued contravention.[295]

**23.137**

*Resignation of auditor*

A company's auditor has an express statutory right to resign at any time. However, the resignation will not be effective unless the auditor complies with the provisions of the 2006 Act, ss 516 and 519, by depositing at the company's registered office: (1) a notice of resignation; and (2) a statement of the circumstances connected with his resignation (unless, in the case of an unquoted company, the auditor considers that there are no circumstances in connection with his resignation which ought properly to be brought to the attention of the company's members and creditors[296]).

**23.138**

*Duties and liabilities of directors in connection with resignation of auditor*

Where an auditor resigns in accordance with these provisions, the company must send a notice to the Registrar of Companies. If the company fails to comply with this requirement, an offence is committed by every officer in default.[297] The offence is punishable on conviction on indictment by a fine or summarily by a fine not exceeding the statutory maximum (and, for continued contravention, a daily default fine not exceeding one-tenth of the statutory maximum).[298]

**23.139**

*Duties and liabilities of directors in connection with auditor's statement*

Where the resigning auditor serves on the company a notice under s 519, the company must within 14 days of the deposit of the statement either (1) send a copy of the statement to every person who is entitled to be sent copies of the

**23.140**

---

[293] 2006 Act, s 512(1).
[294] 2006 Act, s 512(2)(b); for the meaning of the term 'officer in default' see s 1121. A director is in default if he 'authorises or permits, participates in, or fails to take all reasonable steps to prevent the contravention'.
[295] 2006 Act, s 512(3).
[296] If the auditor considers that there are no circumstances in connection with his ceasing to hold office which ought properly to be brought to the attention of the company's members and creditors, he is required to deposit at the company's registered office a statement to that effect: 2006 Act, s 519(2).
[297] 2006 Act, s 517(2).
[298] 2006 Act, s 517(3).

accounts[299] or (2) apply to the court (on notice to the auditor[300]) for a ruling that the auditor is seeking to obtain 'needless publicity for defamatory matter'.[301]

23.141  The obligation to send out the statement is suspended for as long as the application is pending. If the court grants such a ruling, the company is relieved of the obligation to send out copies of the statement; however, the company must within 14 days of the court's decision send (to every person who is entitled to be sent copies of the accounts[302]) 'a statement setting out the effect of the order'.[303] If the court declines to rule in the company's favour, the obligation to send out the statement is reinstated, and the company must comply within 14 days of the court's decision.[304] If the company decides to discontinue the proceedings, the obligation to send out the statement is reinstated and the company must comply within 14 days of discontinuance.[305]

23.142  If the company defaults in complying with its obligations under this section,[306] an offence (punishable by fine[307]) is committed by every officer of the company who is in default.[308] However, it is a defence for a person charged with such an offence to show that he took all reasonable steps and exercised all due diligence to avoid the commission of the offence.[309]

*Duties and liabilities of directors in connection with auditor's requisition*

23.143  In addition, where the resigning auditor serves on the company a notice under s 519 setting out the circumstances connected with his resignation, the auditor has a statutory right to serve with the notice a 'signed requisition' calling on the directors of the company forthwith to convene a general meeting of the company for the purpose of receiving and considering the auditor's explanation.[310] In addition, the auditor may request the company to circulate to its members a statement in writing 'not exceeding a reasonable length' dealing with the circumstances

---

[299]  See paragraphs 23.74–23.82 above.
[300]  2006 Act, s 520(3).
[301]  2006 Act, s 520(2), (3). See also *Jarvis v PricewaterhouseCoopers* [2000] 2 BCLC 368.
[302]  See paragraphs 23.74–23.82 above.
[303]  2006 Act, s 520(4).
[304]  2006 Act, s 520(5).
[305]  Ibid.
[306]  ie by failing to send out the statement within 14 days of its deposit, or within 14 days of a ruling against the company, or within 14 days of discontinuance, or, in the event of a ruling in the company's favour, by failing to send out a statement explaining the effect of the court's decision within 14 days.
[307]  2006 Act, s 520(8).
[308]  2006 Act, s 520(6).
[309]  2006 Act, s 520(7).
[310]  2006 Act, s 518(1), (2).

connected with his resignation;[311] the company is prima facie[312] required to draw the existence of the statement to the attention of the members[313] and provide the members with a copy of the statement.[314]

Within 21 days from the date of the deposit of a requisition, the directors must **23.144** 'proceed duly to convene a meeting'[315] for a day not more than 28 days after the date on which the notice convening the meeting is given.[316] If the directors fail to comply with this requirement, an offence is committed by 'every director who fails to take all reasonable steps to ensure that a meeting was convened'.[317] The offence is indictable or triable summarily and punishable by way of fine.[318]

However, the company (or 'any other person who claims to be aggrieved') may **23.145** apply to the court under s 518(9) for a ruling that the auditor is using the provisions of s 518 'to secure needless publicity for defamatory matter'; such a ruling has the effect of disapplying the requirement for the statement to be sent out or read out at the meeting.[319]

### Duty to notify audit authority

Finally, it should be noted that where an auditor ceases to hold office before the **23.146** end of his term of office, the company must notify the appropriate audit authority[320] that the auditor has ceased to hold office.[321] The notice must be accompanied by: (1) a statement by the company of the reasons for the auditor ceasing to hold office; or (2) if the company of the statement deposited by the auditor at the company's registered office under s 519 contains a statement of circumstances in connection with the auditor's ceasing to hold office that need to be brought to the

---

[311] 2006 Act, s 518(3).

[312] An exception exists where the statement is 'received too late for [the company] to comply': s 518(4). However, if a copy of the statement is not sent out because received too late, the auditor may require the statement to be read out at the meeting: s 518(8).

[313] s 518(4)(a).

[314] 2006 Act, s 518(4)(b).

[315] It is suggested that the words 'proceed duly to' are superfluous.

[316] 2006 Act, s 518(5).

[317] 2006 Act, s 518(6).

[318] 2006 Act, s 518(7).

[319] 2006 Act, s 518(9).

[320] The term 'appropriate audit authority' is defined by s 525. In the case of a major audit, ie a statutory audit in respect of (a) any company whose securities have been admitted to the official list within the meaning of Part 6 of the FSMA or (b) any other company 'in whose financial condition there is a major public interest', the 'appropriate audit authority' is the Secretary of State (or any person to whom the Secretary of State's functions may have been delegated under s 1252, ie the Professional Oversight Board of the Financial Reporting Council; see The Statutory Auditors (Delegation of Functions etc) Order 2008 (SI 2008/496)). Otherwise, the 'appropriate audit authority' is the 'relevant supervisory body' as defined by Part 42.

[321] 2006 Act, s 523(2)(a).

attention of the members or creditors of the company, a copy of that statement.[322] The notice must be given not later than 14 days after the date on which the auditor's statement is deposited at the company's registered office under s 519.

**23.147**  If a company fails to comply with these requirements, an offence (punishable by fine[323]) is committed by every officer in default.[324] A defence will be available if the accused is able to show that he took all reasonable steps and exercised all due diligence to avoid the commission of the offence.[325]

### (7) Quoted companies: directors' functions in relation to the right of members to raise concerns at accounts meeting

*Duties in relation to website publication*

**23.148**  Pursuant to the 2006 Act, s 527 the members of a company representing at least 5 per cent of the total voting rights of all members[326] (or, alternatively, at least 100 members who hold shares on which there has been paid up an average sum, per member, of £100[327]) may require[328] the company to publish on a website[329] a statement setting out any matter relating to the audit of the company's accounts or the ceasing of the auditor to hold office that the members propose to raise at the next accounts meeting[330] of the company.[331] These provisions are new and came into force on 6 April 2008.

**23.149**  The statement must be made available on the website within three working days of the company being required to publish it on a website[332] and must be kept available until after the meeting to which it relates,[333] although a failure to make information available on a website throughout the relevant period will be disregarded if (1) the information was made available on the website for part of the period and (2) the failure is wholly attributable to circumstances that it would not be reasonable to have expected the company to prevent or avoid.[334]

---

[322]  2006 Act, s 523(2)(b).
[323]  2006 Act, s 523(6).
[324]  For the meaning of 'officer in default', see n 294 above.
[325]  2006 Act, s 523(5).
[326]  2006 Act, s 527(2)(a).
[327]  2006 Act, s 527(2)(b).
[328]  The request may be sent to the company in hard copy of electronic form and must be received by the company at least one week before the meeting to which it relates: s 527(4)(a), (d).
[329]  The technical requirements as regards the website are contained in s 528. In short, the website must (a) be maintained on behalf of the company, (b) identify the company in question, and (c) be accessible free of charge.
[330]  See n 176 above.
[331]  2006 Act, s 527(1).
[332]  2006 Act, s 528(4)(a).
[333]  2006 Act, s 528(4)(b).
[334]  2006 Act, s 528(5).

It should be noted that a quoted company is not required to place on a website    **23.150**
a statement under this section if, on an application by the company or another
person who claims to be aggrieved, the court is satisfied that the rights conferred
by this section are being abused.[335]

*Liabilities of directors in respect of website publication*

Where a company fails to comply with s 528 and/or s 529, an offence (punishable    **23.151**
by fine[336]) is committed by every officer in default.[337]

### (8) Directors' functions and responsibilities in relation to provision protecting auditors from liability

Any provision protecting an auditor from liability is prima facie void and un-    **23.152**
enforceable.[338] However, exceptions are provided by s 533, which relates to indemnification for costs of successfully defending proceedings where the auditor
obtains judgment in his favour or is acquitted and by ss 534–536, which permit
auditors to limit their liability to the audited company by means of a liability limitation agreement or 'LLA' and which came into force on 6 April 2008. An LLA is
only effective in relation to acts or omissions occurring in the course of the audit
for one financial year. It must be authorized by members of the company (though
a private company can waive the need for approval) and the company that has
entered into an LLA must disclose its principal terms in the annual report, in
accordance with regulations to be made by the Secretary of State. The limitation
cannot reduce the auditors' liability to less than such an amount as is fair and
reasonable in all circumstances, having regard to the auditors' responsibilities,
their contractual obligations to the company, and the professional standards
expected of them. The Secretary of State also has the power to make regulations about the kind of provisions that LLAs should, or should not, contain but
this is a reserve power to be used only if LLAs develop in such a way that would
damage competition in the audit market.[339] See The Companies (Disclosure of
Auditor Remuneration and Liability Limitation Agreements) Regulations 2008
(SI 2008/489).

In causing a company to enter into a defence costs indemnification agreement or    **23.153**
LLA, a company's directors must ensure that they comply with their general duties
under the 2006 Act, Part 10, Chapter 2.[340]

---

[335] 2006 Act, s 528(5).
[336] 2006 Act, s 530(2).
[337] 2006 Act, s 520(1). For the meaning of the phrase 'officer in default', see n 294 above.
[338] 2006 Act, s 532.
[339] 2006 Act, ss 535(2) and (3).
[340] As to which see Chapters 9–15 of this work.

## E. Directors' Functions and Responsibilities in Relation to the Annual Return

### (1) Introduction

**23.154**   The 2006 Act, Part 24, ss 854–859, contains provisions dealing with the filing of a company's annual return. These provisions, come into force on 1 October 2009, when they replace the corresponding provisions in the 1985 Act, ss 363–365, with changes.

**23.155**   The text has been simplified, and the Secretary of State has been given a specific power to make exceptions from the statutory requirements,[341] but otherwise the provisions remain unchanged.

**23.156**   Part 24 applies to all companies, whether public or private, limited (whether by shares or by guarantee), or unlimited. It also applies to dormant companies.[342] However, it does not apply to overseas companies.

### (2) Duty to submit an annual return

**23.157**   Every company is required to make a return (called the annual return) to the Registrar made up to a date which is not later than the date which is from time to time the company's 'return date'.[343]

*The 'return date'*

**23.158**   The concept of a 'return date' was introduced by the 1989 Act. It will be either (1) the anniversary of the company's incorporation or (2) if the company's last return was made up to a different date, the anniversary of that date.[344] Since the annual return must be made up to a date which is 'not later than' the existing return date,[345] it is possible to adjust a company's return date so as to harmonize return dates within a group of companies.

*Time limit for delivering the annual return*

**23.159**   The return must be delivered to the Registrar within 28 days after the date to which it is made up.[346] It should be accompanied by the appropriate filing fee. Prior to the 1976 Act, the annual accounts of a company were required to be

---

[341] 2006 Act, s 857(2)(b). Sections 854–859 are brought into force on 1 October 2009 by the 2006 Act Commencement Order No 8, art 3(m).
[342] As defined by s 1169.
[343] 2006 Act, s 854(1).
[344] 2006 Act, s 854(2).
[345] 2006 Act, s 854(1).
[346] 2006 Act, s 854(3)(b).

annexed to the annual return; this is no longer the case. Annual accounts and associated reports have to be delivered to the Registrar separately. Failure to deliver the return within 28 days of the date to which it is made up renders the company guilty of an offence and liable to a fine;[347] the directors, secretary, and shadow directors will also prima facie be guilty of an offence.[348]

*Contents of the annual return*

A company's annual return must contain the information required by or under the 2006 Act, ss 855 to 857. **23.160**

In summary, every annual return must contain: (1) the date to which it is made up;[349] (2) the address of the company's registered office;[350] (3) the type of company it is and its principal business activities;[351] (4) the prescribed[352] particulars of directors and secretary of the company;[353] (5) if the register of members is not kept available for inspection at the company's registered office, the address of the place where it is kept available for inspection;[354] and (6) if any register of debenture holders (or a duplicate of any such register or any part of it) is not kept available for inspection a the company's registered office, the address of the place where it is kept available for inspection.[355] **23.161**

In the case of a company which has a share capital, the annual return must also contain: (1) a statement of capital[356] which must state with respect to the company's share capital at the date to which the return is made up (a) the total number of shares of the company,[357] (b) the aggregate nominal value of those shares,[358] (c) for each class of share, prescribed particulars of the rights attached to the shares, the total number of shares of that class, and the aggregate nominal value of shares of that class,[359] and (d) the amount paid up and the amount (if any) unpaid on each class (whether on account of the nominal value of the share or by way of **23.162**

---

[347] 2006 Act, s 858(1)(a).
[348] See paragraph 23.166 below.
[349] 2006 Act, s 855(1).
[350] 2006 Act, s 855(1)(a).
[351] 2006 Act, s 855(1)(b). Particulars of 'the type of company it is' must be given by reference to 'the classification scheme prescribed for the purposes of this section': s 855(2). The information as to the company's principal business activities 'may be given by reference to one or more categories of any prescribed system of classifying business activities': s 855(3).
[352] The Secretary of State may by regulations make further provision as to the information to be given in a company's annual return: s 857(1).
[353] 2006 Act, s 855(1)(c).
[354] 2006 Act, s 855(1)(d).
[355] 2006 Act, s 855(1)(e).
[356] 2006 Act, s 856(1)(a).
[357] 2006 Act, s 856(2)(a).
[358] 2006 Act, s 856(2)(b).
[359] 2006 Act, s 856(2)(c).

premium);[360] and (2) in respect of the company's members,[361] (a) the prescribed particulars of every person who is a member of the company on the date to which the return is made up[362] or has ceased to be a member of the company since the date to which the last return was made up (or, in the case of the first return, since the incorporation of the company),[363] (b) the number of shares of each class held by each member of the company at the date to which the return is made up,[364] (c) the number of shares of each class transferred since the date to which the last return was made up (or, in the case of the first return, since the incorporation of the company) by each member or person who has ceased to be a member,[365] and (d) the dates of registration of any such transfers.[366] If these requirements have been satisfied in respect of either of the two immediately preceding returns, the return need contain only such particulars as relate to persons ceasing to be or becoming members since the date of the last return and to shares transferred since that date.[367]

*No requirement for signature*

**23.163**   It was formerly a requirement that a company's annual return be signed by a director or or the secretary of the company.[368] However, the requirement for signature by a director or secretary has not been retained in the 2006 Act.[369]

**(3) Liabilities of directors and shadow directors in relation to the annual return**

**23.164**   The directors of a company are responsible for ensuring that the company delivers a return containing the necessary information to the Registrar by the applicable deadline. Failure to comply with these requirements will amount to a criminal offence on the part of the company and its directors.[370] It will also put the directors at risk of an application by the Registrar under s 1113 and, ultimately, an application for the directors to be committed to prison for contempt of court.[371] Failure to submit an annual return may also result in the company being struck off

---

360   2006 Act, s 856(2)(d).
361   2006 Act, s 856(1)(b).
362   2006 Act, s 856(3)(a).
363   2006 Act, s 856(3)(b).
364   2006 Act, s 856(4)(a).
365   2006 Act, s 856(4)(b).
366   2006 Act, s 856(4)(c).
367   2006 Act, s 856(5).
368   1985 Act, s 363(2)(c).
369   2006 Act, s 854(3) provides merely that the return must contain the necessary information and be delivered to the Registrar within 28 days after the date to which it is made up.
370   See paragraph 23.166 below.
371   See paragraph 23.168 below.

the register[372] and/or disqualification proceedings against the defaulting directors under the CDDA.[373]

### Application to shadow directors

The requirements to file an annual return and the sanctions for failure to comply **23.165** with these requirements apply not only to *de jure* and de facto directors of the company but also to any shadow directors. Section 859 provides: 'For the purposes of this Part a shadow director is treated as a director.' The term 'shadow director' is defined by s 251 to mean 'a person in accordance with whose directions or instructions the directors of the company are accustomed to act'.[374]

### Criminal sanction for failure to submit annual return

The return must be delivered to the Registrar within 28 days of the date to which **23.166** it is made up.[375] Failure to do so renders the company guilty of an offence.[376] Every director of the company and the company secretary will also be prima facie guilty of an offence. A director or secretary charged with such an offence will have a defence if he is able to prove that he took all reasonable steps to avoid the commission or continuation of the offence.[377] However, it is no defence for an individual to say that he himself was not the person required to make the return if in fact he should have summoned the persons who were required and he failed to do so.[378] A person guilty of the offence of failing to file the annual return is liable on summary conviction to a fine not exceeding level 5 on the standard scale and, for continued contravention, a daily default fine not exceeding one-tenth of level 5 on the standard scale.[379]

The contravention continues until such time as an annual return made up to the **23.167** applicable return date is delivered by the company to the Registrar.[380] In the case of continued contravention, an offence is also committed by every officer of the

---

[372] See paragraph 23.169 below.
[373] See paragraph 23.170 below.
[374] However, 'A person is not to be regarded as a shadow director by reason only that the directors act on advice given by him in a professional capacity': s 251(2).
[375] 2006 Act, s 854(3).
[376] 2006 Act, s 858(1)(a), (2); *R v Tyler & International Commercial Co* [1891] 2 QB 588.
[377] 2006 Act, s 858(4). Under the Companies Act 1985 as originally enacted, liability was restricted to officers in default, which required the prosecution to prove that the director in question knowingly and wilfully authorized or permitted the contravention. Under the 1985 Act, however, the burden is on the directors and the secretary to prove that they took all reasonable steps to avoid the commission or continuation of the offence.

As a result of s 858(1)(c) and s 1121, a manager of the company will also be guilty of an offence if he authorizes or permits or participates in or fails to take all reasonable steps to prevent the commission or continuation of the offence.
[378] *Gibson v Barton* (1875) LR 10 QB 329.
[379] 2006 Act, s 858(2).
[380] 2006 Act, s 858(3).

company who did not commit an offence in respect of the initial contravention (ie who is able to prove that he took all reasonable steps to avoid the contravention) but who is 'in default' in relation to the continued contravention (ie who is shown to have authorized or permitted or participated in or failed to take all reasonable steps to prevent the continuation).[381] A person guilty of the offence of this form of continued contravention is liable on summary conviction to a fine not exceeding one-tenth of level 5 on the standard scale for each day on which the contravention continues and he is in default.[382]

*14-day notices, civil proceedings, and contempt of court*

23.168    If a company fails to file an annual return, the Registrar may serve a notice on the company requiring it to do so within 14 days.[383] If the company fails to file an annual return within 14 days after the service of the notice, the Registrar or any member or creditor of the company may apply to the court for an order directing the company and its directors to file an annual return within a specified time.[384] The court's order may also provide that all costs of and incidental to the application are to be borne by the company or by any officers of the company responsible for the default.[385] If the directors or secretary fail to comply with an order of the court requiring them to file the company's annual return, they may be committed to prison for contempt of court.[386]

*Striking off by Registrar for failure to make returns*

23.169    In addition, the Registrar may treat a company's omission to file an annual return as reasonable cause for belief that the company is not carrying on business or in operation, and, after certain formalities, strike its name off the register of companies.[387] As soon as the Registrar publishes a notice in the Gazette stating that the company's name has been struck off the register,[388] the company will be dissolved automatically by operation of law.[389] Every year large numbers of companies are struck off the register for this reason.

*Disqualification*

23.170    Failure to file annual returns will constitute misconduct on the part of a director for the purposes of proceedings by the Secretary of State under s 6 of the CDDA

---

381  2006 Act, s 858(5), s 1121.

382  2006 Act, s 858(5).

383  2006 Act, s 1113(1), (2). Section 1113 comes into force on 1 October 2009: 2006 Act Commencement Order No 8, art 3(o).

384  2006 Act, s 1113(3) (coming into force on 1 October 2009).

385  2006 Act, s 1113(4) (coming into force on 1 October 2009).

386  *Re George Downman Ltd*, The Times, 26 July 1960.

387  2006 Act, s 1000 (coming into force on 1 October 2009).

388  2006 Act, s 1000(5).

389  2006 Act, s 1000(6).

for the disqualification of a director on the ground that he is unfit to be concerned in the management of a company.[390] Although '[d]efaults of this kind are not to be brushed off as trivial',[391] it has been said that '[o]n their own, although misconduct, they would not warrant a finding of unfitness. They add some weight to the other findings of misconduct when overall consideration is given to the issues of fitness and the appropriate period of disqualification.'[392] However, under s 3 of the CDDA, 'persistent' failure to file a return may lead to disqualification on that ground alone.[393] Persistent failure may be proved conclusively (without prejudice to proof in any other manner) 'by showing that in the 5 years ending with the date of the application [the director] has been adjudged guilty (whether or not on the same occasion) of three or more defaults'.[394]

---

[390] *Re Churchill Hotel (Plymouth) Ltd* [1988] BCLC 341; *Secretary of State for Trade and Industry v Goldberg* [2004] 1 BCLC 597.

[391] *Reynard v Secretary of State for Trade and Industry* (unreported, 22 June 2001, Blackburne J).

[392] Ibid.

[393] CDDA, s 3(1): 'The court may make a disqualification order against a person where it appears to it that he has been persistently in default in relation to provisions of the companies legislation requiring any return, account or other document to be filed with, delivered or sent, or notice of any matter to be given, to the registrar of companies.'

[394] CDDA, s 3(2).

for the disqualification of a director on the ground that he is unfit to be concerned in the management of a company.[...] Although '[in]fractions of this kind are not to be brushed off as trivial,'[...] it has been said that '[o]n their own, although minor in nature, they would not warrant a finding of unfitness. They add some weight to the other findings of misconduct when overall consideration is given to the issues of fitness and the appropriate period of disqualification.'[...] However, under s.3 of the CDDA, 'persistent' failure to file a return may lead to disqualification on that ground alone.[...] Persistent failure may be proved conclusively (without prejudice to proof in any other manner) 'by showing that in the 5 years ending with the date of the application [the director] has been adjudged guilty (whether or not on the same occasion) of three or more defaults.'[...]

[...] Re Barings Plc (No 5), Secretary of State for Trade and Industry v Baker (No 5) [1988] BCC 583, Secretary of State per Jonathan Parker J, upheld at [2000] 1 BCLC 523.

[...] Re Secretary of State for Trade and Industry v Tjolle (unreported, 22 June 2001: Weald Lucid).

[...] ibid.

[...] CDDA, s 3(1). 'The court may make a disqualification order against a person on the ground that he has been persistently in default in relation to provisions of the companies legislation requiring any return, account or other document to be filed with, delivered or sent, or notice of any matter to be given, to the registrar of companies.'

[...] CDDA, s 3(2).

# 24

# CAPITAL AND DISTRIBUTIONS

## A. Introduction

This chapter is primarily concerned with the functions, responsibilities, and **24.01** liabilities of directors in respect of shares. The provisions of the 2006 Act, Parts 17 and 18, concerning a company's share capital and the purchase by a limited company of its own shares (including financial assistance), are due to come into force on 1 October 2009,[1] except for (a) s 544 (transferability of shares), which came into force on 6 April 2008,[2] and (b) the provisions enabling a private company to reduce its capital without having to obtain a court order, which came into force on 1 October 2008.[3] Also on 1 October 2008 the restrictions under the 1985 Act, ss 151–153 and 155–158, on the giving by a private company of financial assistance for the acquisition of its own shares, including the 'whitewash' procedure

---

[1] Pursuant to 2006 Act Commencement Order No 8 (in draft, at the time of writing).

[2] 2006 Act Commencement Order No 5, art 3(1)(f).

[3] 2006 Act, ss 641(1)(a), (2)–(6), 642–644, 652(1) and (3), and 654; pursuant to 2006 Act Commencement Order No 7, art 2(a)–(c).

were repealed.[4] Apart from those provisions, the provisions in Parts 17 and 18 re-enact provisions in the 1985 Act almost entirely without change. Although the provisions of the 1985 Act remain in force until 1 October 2009 this chapter describes the law by reference to the 2006 Act, but indicating the provisions of the 2006 Act which are replaced. The provisions of the 2006 Act, Parts 20–23, concerning private and public companies, certification and transfer of securities, information about interests in a company's shares, and distributions are all in force.[5]

**24.02** This chapter also deals with directors' functions, responsibilities, and liabilities in respect of loan capital. The provisions in Part 19 concerning debentures came into force on 6 April 2008.[6] The provisions in Part 25, containing the provisions about company charges, are due to come into force on 1 October 2009.[7]

## B. Allotment and Issue of Shares

### (1) The nature of a share

**24.03** A share is personal property (not real estate)[8] in the nature of a chose in action[9] comprising 'the interest of a shareholder in the company measured by a sum of money, for the purpose of liability in the first place, and of interest in the second, but also consisting of a series of mutual covenants entered into by all the shareholders inter se'.[10] In the 2006 Act, the term 'share' in relation to a company means share in the company's share capital.[11] A certificate under the common seal of a company specifying any shares held by a member is prima facie evidence of his title to those shares.[12]

**24.04** Shares in a limited company having a share capital must each have a fixed nominal value.[13] An allotment of a share that does not have a fixed nominal value is void.[14]

---

[4] 2006 Act Commencement Order No 5, arts 5(2) and 8(b) and Schedule 3.

[5] Parts 20–23 were brought into force on 6 April 2008 by 2006 Act Commencement Order No 5, arts 3(1)(h)–(k), except for ss 791–810, 811(1)–(3), 813, and 815–828 (information about interests in shares) which came into force on 20 January 2007 (2006 Act Commencement Order No 1, art 3(1)(d)).

[6] 2006 Act Commencement Order No 5, art 3(1)(g).

[7] Pursuant to the 2006 Act Commencement Order No 8, art 3(n).

[8] 2006 Act, s 541, restating 1985 Act, s 182(1)(a). Sections 540 and 541 come into force on 1 October 2009.

[9] *R v Williams* [1942] AC 541, 549; *Colonial Bank v Whinney* (1886) 11 App Cas 426.

[10] *Borland's Trustee v Steel Bros & Co Ltd* [1901] 1 Ch 279, 288, per Farwell J.

[11] 2006 Act, s 540(1), restating the definition of 'share' in 1985 Act, s 744. Subsection 540(2) is a new provision which states that a company's shares may no longer be converted into stock.

[12] 2006 Act, s 768(1), restating 1985 Act, s 186 and in force from 6 April 2008. For articles concerning share certificates, see Table A regs b and 7; Model Articles (pcls) 24 and 25; Model Article (plc) 46 and 47. Model Article (plc) 50 contemplates that a public company may wish to issue uncertificated shares (2006 Act, ss 783–790).

[13] 2006 Act, s 542(1). Section 542 is a new section, which comes into force on 1 October 2009.

[14] 2006 Act, s 542(2).

Further, such an allotment is an offence (punishable by fine) committed by every officer in default.[15] Shares in a limited company having a share capital may be denominated in any currency, and different classes of shares may be denominated in different currencies.[16]

Each share must be designated with a specific number, unless all the issued shares **24.05** in the company or in any particular class are fully paid up and rank *pari passu* for all purposes, in which case numbering is not required.[17]

For the purposes of the 2006 Act, shares in a company are taken to be allotted **24.06** when a person acquires the unconditional right to be included in the company's register of members in respect of the shares.[18] A share is not issued until the processes of application, allotment, and registration have been completed.[19]

## (2) General rules

### *Authorization of allotment*

Where a private company has a single class of shares, no specific authorization to **24.07** allot shares is necessary, and the directors may exercise any power of the company to allot shares or grant rights to subscribe for or to convert any security into such shares, except to the extent that they are prohibited from doing so by the company's articles.[20]

In the case of a private company with more than one class of shares, and in the case **24.08** of a public company, the position is different, and specific authorization to allot shares, or to grant subscription/conversion rights, is required, either by way of authorization in the articles, or by way of authorization by resolution.[21] Such authorization may be specific or general and conditional or unconditional.[22] The

---

[15] 2006 Act, s 542(4) and (5).

[16] 2006 Act, s 542(3), codifying existing practice: *Re Scandinavian Bank Group Plc* [1988] Ch 87. But see s 765 (initial authorized minimum share capital requirement for public company to be met by reference to share capital denominated in sterling or euros). A company's articles usually give it power to issue shares with such rights or restrictions as the company may by ordinary resolution determine: Table A reg 2; Model Article (pcls)22; Model Article (plc) 43.

[17] 2006 Act, s 543, restating 1985 Act, s 182(2) without change (in force 1 October 2009).

[18] 2006 Act, s 558, restating 1985 Act, s 738(1) (in force 1 October 2009).

[19] *National Westminster Bank Plc v Inland Revenue Commissioners* [1995] 1 AC 119, HL.

[20] 2006 Act, s 550, which is a new provision recommended by the CLR: *Final Report* at para 4.5. The term 'subscribe for' is considered to possess its ordinary meaning of taking shares for cash: *Government Stocks & Other Securities Investment Co Ltd v Christopher* [1956] 1 WLR 237. Until this section takes effect on 1 October 2009 directors must comply with 1985 Act, s 80. Table A and the Model Articles do not restrict the power of the directors to allot shares, but members of private companies may require articles containing such restrictions in order to preserve their proportionate interests in the company

[21] s 551(1). Section 551 replaces 1985 Act, s 80, which restated the 1980 Act, s 14, which first introduced a statutory restriction on the authority of the directors to allot shares. Until 1 October 2009 1985 Act, s 80 remains in force.

[22] s 551(2).

authorization must: (1) state the maximum number of shares to which it relates; and (2) specify a date within the next five years on which the authority is to expire.[23] The shares must be allotted, or the subscription/conversion rights granted, within the period of the authorization's validity, although there is nothing to prevent the allotment of shares after the expiration of the authorization pursuant to an agreement entered into prior to that time, if the authorization itself expressly permits this.[24] In the case of subscription/conversion rights, no authority is required for the allotment of shares pursuant to exercise of the rights.[25]

**24.09** In either case, the power to allot shares must be exercised bona fide in the best interests of the company at a whole and not for a collateral purpose[26] and fairly as between different shareholders.[27]

**24.10** If the statutory rules relating to authorization of allotment are not observed, any director of the company who knowingly contravened the statutory requirements or permitted or authorized the contravention is guilty of an offence punishable by fine.[28] In addition, attempts by directors to use the power of allotment to increase or consolidate their own control of a company, or to prevent a rival from gaining control of a company, are likely to be held to be invalid.[29]

*Commissions etc*

**24.11** The general rule[30] is that a company must not apply any of its shares or capital money,[31] either directly or indirectly, in payment of any commission, discount, or allowance to any person in consideration of his agreeing to subscribe for shares in the company or procuring or agreeing to procure subscriptions.[32] To 'subscribe

---

[23] 2006 Act, s 551(3). It should be noted that an authority which is about to expire may be extended for a further five years: s 551(4). A resolution renewing such authority must comply with the same requirements, ie it must state the maximum number of shares to which it relates and specify an expiry date which must be a date within the next five years: s 551(5).

[24] 2006 Act, s 550(7).

[25] 2006 Act, s 549(3).

[26] *Howard Smith Ltd v Ampol Petroleum Ltd* [1974] AC 821, PC.

[27] *Mutual Life Insurance Co of New York v Rank Organisation Ltd* [1985] BCLC 11.

[28] 2006 Act, s 549(4) and (5), which will replace 1985 Act, s 80(9) and Schedule 24 without change on 1 October 2009.

[29] *Fraser v Whalley* (1864) 2 Hem & M 10; *Punt v Symons & Co Ltd* [1903] 2 Ch 506; *Piercy v S Mills & Co Ltd* [1920] 1 Ch 77; *Hogg v Cramphorn Ltd* [1967] Ch 254; *Bamford v Bamford* [1970] Ch 212, CA; *Howard Smith Ltd v Ampol Petroleum Ltd* [1974] AC 821, PC. See also 2006 Act, s 171.

[30] Which was a rule at common law prior to its statutory formulation: see *Ooregum Gold Mining Co of India v Roper* [1892] AC 125, in which the House of Lords held that the payment of such commissions was *ultra vires*. See also *Australian Investment Trust Ltd v Strand & Pitt Street Properties Ltd* [1932] AC 735.

[31] The phrase 'shares or capital money' means unissued shares or money derived from the issue of shares: *Hilder v Dexter* [1902] AC 474. Premium paid over par value falls within the scope of the term 'capital money': *Shorto v Colwill* [1909] WN 218.

[32] 2006 Act, s 552(1), which will replace 1985 Act, s 98(1) without change on 1 October 2009.

for' shares generally means to take up shares for cash and does not include a purchase of issued shares.[33] In deciding whether the general rule has been contravened, the court will look at the substance of the transaction, not the form.[34] Where shares are issued partly in consideration of subscribing or procuring subscriptions and partly for other consideration, the whole issue falls within the prohibition.[35]

The exception to this rule is that commissions may be paid if, but only if, the payment of commission is authorized by the company's articles and the commission does not exceed 10 per cent of the price at which the shares are issued or the amount or rate authorized by the articles, whichever is the less.[36]   **24.12**

It has been held that commission paid in contravention of the statutory provisions is not recoverable unless the recipient had notice of the illegality.[37] In such circumstances, it may be the case that the directors are liable in damages to compensate the company for its loss, depending on the facts.   **24.13**

*Registration of allotment*

An allotment of shares must be registered as soon as practicable and in any event within two months after the date of the allotment.[38] Further, the company[39] must, within one month of making the allotment, deliver a return to the Registrar[40] and the return must contain such information as may be prescribed by the Secretary of State and must be accompanied by a statement of capital.[41]   **24.14**

---

[33] *Government Stock & Other Securities Investment Co v Christopher* [1956] 1 WLR 237.

[34] *Booth v New Afrikander Gold Mining Co Ltd* [1903] 1 Ch 295; *Keatings v Paringa Consolidated Mines Ltd* [1902] WN 15.

[35] *Banking Service Corporation Ltd v Toronto Finance Corpn Ltd* [1928] AC 333.

[36] 2006 Act, s 553(2), which will replace 1985 Act, s 97(2)(a) without change on 1 October 2009. The exception was first introduced by the Companies Act 1900. Authorization in the memorandum is not sufficient: *Re Republic of Bolivia Exploration Syndicate* [1914] 1 Ch 139. Table A reg 4 and Model Article (plc) 44 provide for a company to which those articles apply to pay commission on subscription for its shares.

[37] *Andreae v Zinc Mines of Great Britain Ltd* [1918] 2 KB 454.

[38] 2006 Act, s 554(1). Section 554 is a new section which comes into force on 1 October 2009. 1985 Act, s 185 imposed a duty on the company to issue certificates within two months after the allotment of its shares, but did not impose a time limit for the first step of registration.

[39] Similar provisions apply as regards unlimited companies: 2006 Act, s 556, which replaces 1985 Act, s 128 with changes on 1 October 2009.

[40] 2006 Act, s 555(2), which replaces 1985 Act, s 88(2) with changes. Section 555 comes into force on 1 October 2009.

[41] 2006 Act, s 555(3), which, with s 555(4), is a new provision, recommended by the CLR: *Final Report* at para 7.30. It implements the requirement in the Second Company Law Directive (77/91/EEC) that 'the statutes or instruments of incorporation of the company shall always give at least the following information . . .(c) when the company has no authorised capital, the amount of the subscribed capital . . .' The statement of capital must contain the usual particulars, as specified in s 555(4) (ie total number of shares, aggregate nominal value, rights attached, total number in each class, aggregate nominal value of each class, and amounts paid up).

**24.15**  If the company fails to register an allotment within two months, an offence (punishable by fine) is committed by every officer in default.[42] If the company fails to deliver a return containing the appropriate particulars and the statement of capital to the Registrar within one month, an offence (punishable by fine) is committed by every officer in default[43] although there is special provision enabling such person to apply to the court for relief on the grounds that the omission to deliver the document was accidental or due to inadvertence.[44] The court may grant such relief as it considers to be just and equitable; such relief will ordinarily take the form of an extension of time in which to deliver the document.[45] Relief may be granted on the basis of ignorance or misunderstanding of the statutory provisions.[46]

*Payment for shares*

**24.16**  The general rule is that shares must not be allotted gratuitously[47] or at a discount[48] (ie for less than the nominal value of the shares in question). The allottee must pay at least the nominal value of the shares: 'the liability of a member continues so long as anything remains unpaid upon his shares. Nothing but payment, and payment in full, can put an end to the liability.'[49]

**24.17**  Any shares allotted in contravention of the Act give rise to a liability[50] on the part of the allottee to pay the company an amount equal to the discount,[51] with interest.[52] Any subsequent holder of the shares will be similarly liable, save for a bona fide purchaser for value without notice of the contravention.[53] An allotment of

---

[42]  2006 Act, s 554(3) and (4). Section 554 is a new section; see n 38 above.

[43]  2006 Act, s 557(1) and (2).

[44]  2006 Act, s 557(3). Accordingly the legislation envisages that a person may be 'in default' within s 1121(3) by accidentally or inadvertently authorizing, permitting, participating in, or failing to take all reasonable steps to prevent the contravention.

[45]  2006 Act, s 557(3).

[46]  See *Re Jackson & Co Ltd* [1899] 1 Ch 348, *Re Tom Tit Cycle Co Ltd* (1899) 43 Sol Jo 334, *Re Whitefriars Financial Co Ltd* [1899] 1 Ch 184.

[47]  *Re Wragg Ltd* [1897] 1 Ch 796; *Ooregum Gold Mining Co of India Ltd v Roper* [1892] AC 125; *Re Eddystone Marine Insurance Co* [1893] Ch 9. Note that Model Articles (pcls) 21 contemplates that shares in a private company will be issued fully paid up, whereas Model Articles (plc) 52–62 contemplate that a public company may issue partly paid shares (as may a company to which Table A applies (regs 8–22)).

[48]  2006 Act, s 590(1), which replaces 1985 Act, s 114 without change on 1 October 2009.

[49]  *Ooregum Gold Mining Co of India v Roper* [1892] AC 125, 145 (Lord Macnaghten). See also *Re Eddystone Marine Insurance Co* [1893] 3 Ch 9 and *Welton v Saffery* [1897] AC 299.

[50]  *Re Bradford Investments plc* [1991] BCLC 224.

[51]  2006 Act, s 580(2), which replaces 1985 Act, s 100(2) without change on 1 October 2009.

[52]  2006 Act, s 609(1), which replaces 1985 Act, s 107 without change on 1 October 2009. The rate of interest is 5% per annum or such other rate as may be specified by order made by the Secretary of State.

[53]  2006 Act, s 588(1), (2), which replace 1985 Act, s 112(1), (3), and (5)(a) without change on 1 October 2009.

shares at par subsequent to allotment at a premium does not constitute an allotment at a discount.[54]

A company may, if so authorized by its articles, make arrangements on the issue of shares for a difference between the allottee shareholders in the amounts and time of payment of calls on their shares and may accept payment of the amount remaining at any time.[55] Further, the company may, if so authorized by its articles, pay a dividend in proportion to the amount paid up on each share where a larger amount is paid up on some shares than on others.[56] **24.18**

The general rule as to payment (subject to special rules for public companies discussed below) is that shares allotted by a company and any premium on them may be paid up in money or money's worth (including goodwill and know-how).[57] A debt due from the company and payable so that the demands could be set off will suffice,[58] as will property handed over pursuant to a binding contract.[59] **24.19**

However, as Lord Watson said in *Ooregum Gold Mining Co of India v Roper*:[60] **24.20**

> The court 'would doubtless refuse effect to a colourable transaction, entered into for the purpose or with the obvious result of enabling the company to issue its shares at a discount; but it has been ruled that, so long as the company honestly regards the consideration given as fairly representing the nominal value of the shares in cash, its estimate ought not to be critically examined'.[61]

It is only where the consideration is 'colourable' or illusory or where it is manifest on the face of the instrument that the shares are issued at a discount that the court will be prepared to consider the adequacy of the consideration.[62] Whether the consideration is colourable is a question of fact in each case.[63]

Directors who allot shares at a discount are guilty of a breach of duty to the company and are liable to pay the amount of the discount and interest to the company if that amount cannot be recovered from the allottee or holder of the shares, as **24.21**

---

[54] *Hilder v Dexter* [1902] AC 474.

[55] 2006 Act, s 581, which replaces 1985 Act, s 119 without change on 1 October 2009.

[56] 2006 Act, s 581.

[57] 2006 Act, s 582(1), which replaces 1985 Act, s 99(1) without change on 1 October 2009. See *Drummond's Case* (1869) 4 Ch App 772, *Pell's Case* (1869) 5 Ch App 11, *Re Baglan Hall Colliery Co* (1870) 5 Ch App 346, *Schroder's Case* (1870) LR 11 Eq 131, *Jones' Case* (1870) 6 Ch App 48, *Key's Case* (1868) 16 WR 1103, *Re Wragg Ltd* [1897] 1 Ch 796.

[58] *Forbes and Judd's Case* (1870) 5 Ch App 270.

[59] *Re Baglan Hall Colliery Co* (1870) 5 Ch App 346; see also *Dent's Case* (1873) LR 15 Eq 407, *Fothergill's Case* (1873) 8 Ch App 270.

[60] [1892] AC 125, 137.

[61] *Ooregum Gold Mining Co of India v Roper* [1892] AC 125, 137 (Lord Watson).

[62] *Re White Star Line Ltd* [1938] Ch 458; *Mosely v Koffyfontein Mines Ltd* [1904] 2 Ch 108; *Re Wragg Ltd* [1897] 1 Ch 769.

[63] *Re Innes & Co Ltd* [1903] 2 Ch 254.

where the shares have passed into the hands of a bona fide purchase for value from the original allottee.[64]

### Share premiums

**24.22**  If a company issues shares at a premium, whether for cash or otherwise, a sum equal to the aggregate amount or value of the premium on those shares must be transferred to an account called the 'share premium account'.[65] Sums transferred to the share premium account may be used to write off the expenses of issuing those shares and any commission lawfully paid on the issue of those shares.[66] The company may also use the share premium account to pay up new shares to be allotted to members as fully paid bonus shares.[67] Otherwise, and subject to specific provisions applicable in respect of group reconstruction relief[68] and merger relief,[69] the balance standing to the credit of the share premium account is subject to the ordinary rules relating to reduction of capital, and the share premium account is treated for these purposes as though it were merely part of the company's paid up share capital.[70] It follows that directors may incur civil or criminal liability in respect of the share premium account in precisely the same circumstances as may result in liability upon any unlawful reduction of the company's capital generally.

### (3) Pre-emption rights

**24.23**  Pre-emption rights in respect of newly issued shares may exist in the company's articles or under statute. Alternatively, pre-emption rights may be excluded by the company's articles, or excluded from operating in certain circumstances, or disapplied for various reasons. These various possibilities will be considered before considering the procedure to be followed where such rights exist and apply and the liability of directors for contravention of pre-emption rights. The relevant statutory provisions, which provide the over-arching code for pre-emption rights, including such rights in the articles, apply to 'equity securities' (defined to mean ordinary shares or rights to subscribe for or convert securities into ordinary shares; 'ordinary shares' being defined in turn to mean shares which are uncapped as to dividend and capital). These provisions have no application

---

[64] *Hirsche v Sims* [1894] AC 654.

[65] 2006 Act, s 610(1). Section 610 replaces 1985 Act, s 130, with changes made by subss (2) and (3), on 1 October 2009.

[66] 2006 Act, s 610(2).

[67] 2006 Act, s 610(3).

[68] 2006 Act, s 611, which replaces 1985 Act, s 132 without change on 1 October 2009.

[69] 2006 Act, s 612, which replaces 1985 Act, s 131 and s 132(8) without change on 1 October 2009.

[70] 2006 Act, s 610(4).

to the taking of shares by subscribers to the memorandum on the formation of the company.[71]

### Pre-emption rights in the articles

In many cases, a company's articles will contain a pre-emption provision, prohibiting the company from allotting ordinary shares of a particular class unless it has offered those shares to existing shareholders.[72]    **24.24**

### Pre-emption rights under statute

The 2006 Act, s 561(1),[73] states the general rule, giving existing shareholders a right of pre-emption:    **24.25**

> A company must not allot equity securities to a person on any terms unless—
> (a) it has made an offer[74] to each person who holds ordinary shares in the company to allot to him on the same or more favourable terms a proportion of those securities that is as nearly as practicable equal to the proportion in nominal value held by him of the ordinary share capital of the company, and
> (b) the period during which any such offer may be accepted has expired or the company has received notice of the acceptance or refusal of every offer so made.

Treasury shares are disregarded for these purposes, so that the company is not treated as a person who holds ordinary shares, and any treasury shares are not treated as forming part of the ordinary share capital of the company.[75] The offer period must be at least 21 days and must not be withdrawn prior to its expiry.[76]

The pre-emption rights contained in the 2006 Act, s 561 are subject to:[77]    **24.26**

(1) exceptions to pre-emption rights in relation to the allotment of bonus shares, the allotment of equity securities for non-cash consideration (in whole or in part), or in the case of employees' share schemes:[78]

(2) exclusion of pre-emption rights for private companies, as described in paragraph 24.27 below;

---

[71] 2006 Act, s 577, which replaces 1985 Act, s 94(2) without change on 1 October 2009.

[72] Such provisions fall within 2006 Act, s 568, which replaces 1985 Act, ss 89(2) and (3), 90(1) and 92(1) and (2) without change on 1 October 2009. 1985 Act Table A and the draft Model Articles do not include pre-emption provisions, leaving that matter to statutory control and to any additional provisions desired by the parties. Table A to earlier Companies Acts did include pre-emption provisions: see, eg the 1862 Table A, reg 27; the 1908 Table A, reg 42; the 1929 Table A, reg 35.

[73] 2006 Act, s 561(1) replaces 1985 Act, s 89(1) without change on 1 October 2009.

[74] The offer may be in hard copy of electronic form: s 562(2). This is a new provision.

[75] 2006 Act, s 561(4), which replaces 1985 Act, s 89(6) without change on 1 October 2009.

[76] 1985 Act, s 562(4) and (5), which replace 1985 Act, s 90(6) with changes on 1 October 2009.

[77] 2006 Act, s 561(5), which is a drafting provision, not changing the law.

[78] 1985 Act, ss 564–566, which replace provisions contained in 1985 Act, ss 89(4) and (5) and 94(2) without change on 1 October 2009.

(3) the disapplication of pre-emption rights in the circumstances described in paragraph 24.28 below;

(4) savings in relation to certain pre-emption requirements under the 1985 Act.[79]

**24.27** The statutory pre-emption rights are excluded in two cases:

(1) A private company's articles may exclude the provisions contained in the 2006 Act, ss 561 by provisions[80] either (a) generally in relation to the allotment by the company of equity securities, or (b) in relation to allotments of a particular description.[81] Furthermore, any requirement or authorization contained in the articles of a private company that is inconsistent with the statutory provisions is treated as excluding them.[82]

(2) Also, the pre-emption rights in s 561 do not apply where the company's articles contain a corresponding right in accordance with which the company makes an offer to allot to the holder of ordinary shares of the particular class and the holder or anyone in whose favour he has renounced his right accepts the offer.[83]

**24.28** The directors of a private company that has only one class of shares may be given power by the articles, or by special resolution of the company, to allot shares/equity securities of that class as if the statutory right or pre-emption did not apply, or applied subject to modification.[84] Similarly, where the directors of a public or private company (with one or more classes of shares) are generally authorized to allot shares, they may be given power by the articles, or by a special resolution to allot equity securities pursuant to the authorization in a manner which would otherwise contravene the statutory pre-emption provisions.[85] Alternatively, where the directors of a public or private company are authorized (whether generally or specifically) to allot shares, the company may by special resolution disapply the statutory pre-emption rights, or apply them subject to modification, in respect of a 'specified allotment' of equity securities.[86] A special resolution in respect of a specific allotment must not be proposed unless it is recommended by the directors[87] and before it is proposed the directors must make a written statement setting out their reasons for making the recommendation, the amount to be paid to the

---

[79] 2006 Act, s 576, which preserves requirements in 1985 Act, s 96.
[80] 2006 Act, s 567(1). Section 567 replaces 1985 Act, s 91 without change on 1 October 2009.
[81] 2006 Act, s 567(2).
[82] 2006 Act, s 567(3).
[83] 2006 Act, s 568, which replaces 1985 Act, ss 89(3), 90(1), and 92 with change on 1 October 2009.
[84] 2006 Act, s 569. This is a new provision which comes into effect on 1 October 2009. Until then the directors must obtain an authorization to disapply pre-emption rights in the ordinary way.
[85] 2006 Act, s 570. Sections 570–573 replace 1985 Act, s 95 without material change on 1 October 2009.
[86] 2006 Act, s 571.
[87] 2006 Act, s 571(5).

company in respect of the equity securities to be allotted, and the directors' justification of that amount.[88] It is an offence for a person knowingly or recklessly to authorize or permit the inclusion of any matter that is misleading, false, or deceptive in a material particular in such a statement.[89]

Where pre-emption rights apply, whether pursuant to statute or by reason of a **24.29** pre-emption provision in the company's articles, the statutory requirements as to communication of the pre-emption offer must be observed,[90] save to the extent that the company's articles provide otherwise.[91] Accordingly, the offer may be made in hard copy or electronic form (or, where the holder's address is not known, by way of advertisement in the Gazette[92]) and must be open for acceptance for at least 21 days[93] (and may not be withdrawn prior to its expiry date). The power is given to the Secretary of State to reduce the period for acceptance to not less than 14 days, and it is expected that advantage will be taken of this power.[94]

Where applicable pre-emption requirements are contravened, the company and **24.30** every officer who knowingly authorized or permitted the contravention are jointly and severally liable to compensate any person to whom an offer should have been made in accordance with those provisions for any loss, damage, costs, or expense which the person has sustained or incurred by reason of the contravention.[95] Proceedings against the company and/or the directors must be commenced within two years.[96] In addition, there is authority to support the proposition that a failure to comply with pre-emption provisions may provide grounds for an unfair prejudice petition.[97]

### (4) Private companies: prohibition of public offers

A private company limited by shares or limited by guarantee and having a share **24.31** capital must not offer to the public[98] any securities[99] of the company or allot or agree to allot any securities of the company with a view to their being offered to

---

[88] 2006 Act, s 571(6). The statement must be sent with the resolution if it is a written resolution or circulated with the notice calling the meeting: s 571(7).

[89] 2006 Act, s 572(2).

[90] 2006 Act, s 562.

[91] 2006 Act, s 567.

[92] 2006 Act, s 562(3).

[93] 2006 Act, s 562.

[94] 2006 Act, s 562(6).

[95] 2006 Act ss 563(2), 568(4).

[96] 2006 Act, ss 563(3), 568(5).

[97] *Re A Company (No 005134 of 1986) ex p Harris* [1989] BCLC 383.

[98] Or any section of the public: 2006 Act, s 756(2) which replaced provisions in 1985 Act, s 742A(1) without change on 6 April 2008. See, generally, *Sherwell v Combined Incandescent Mantels Syndicate Ltd* [1907] WN 110 and *Re South of England Natural Gas & Petroleum Co* [1911] Ch 573.

[99] The word 'securities' means shares or debentures: 2006 Act, s 755(5), which came into effect on 6 April 2008.

the public.[100] An offer is not regarded as an offer to the public if it can properly be regarded, in all the circumstances, as not being calculated to result, directly or indirectly, in securities of the company becoming available to persons other than those receiving the offer or otherwise being a private concern[101] of the person receiving it and the person making it.[102] A private company will not breach the prohibition if it makes an offer to the public in good faith in pursuance of arrangements under which it is to re-register as a public company before the shares are allotted, or if it undertakes to, and does, re-register as a public company within six months of the offer being made.[103]

**24.32**  If it appears to the court that a private company is proposing to make an offer to the public in contravention of the prohibition, the court may restrain the company from so doing.[104] Where the contravention has already occurred, the court may make an order requiring the company to re-register as a public company[105] or make a winding-up order in respect of the company[106] or make a 'remedial order'. A 'remedial order' is an order for the purpose of putting a person affected by a contravention of the prohibition in the position he would have been in if the contravention had not occurred and may require any person knowingly concerned in the contravention to offer to purchase any of the securities at such price and on such other terms as the court thinks fit.[107] Officers of the company are obvious targets for remedial orders, but the court's powers are wide, and a remedial order may be made against any person knowingly involved in the contravention, whether or not an officer of the company.[108] Where a remedial order is made against the company itself, the court may provide for the reduction of the company's capital accordingly.[109]

---

[100]  2006 Act, s 755(1), which replaced 1985 Act, s 81(1) with changes on 6 April 2008. There is a rebuttable statutory presumption that an allotment or agreement to allot securities was made with a view to their being offered to the public if an offer of the securities (or any of them) to the public is made within six months after the allotment or agreement to allot or before the receipt by the company of the whole of the consideration to be received in respect of the securities: 2006 Act, s 755(2), which replaced 1985 Act, s 58(3) without change on 6 April 2008.

[101]  The term 'private concern' is rebuttably presumed where an offer is made to a person already connected with the company (eg an existing member or employee or family member or widow of such a person or existing debenture holder of the company: s 756(5)) or where the offer is made in the context of an employees' share scheme: s 756(4). 2006 Act, s 756; 1985 Act, s 742A with changes on 6 April 2008.

[102]  2006 Act, s 756(4).

[103]  2006 Act, s 755(3).

[104]  2006 Act, s 757(2). Sections 757–759 are new provisions, which came into effect on 6 April 2008.

[105]  2006 Act, s 758(2).

[106]  2006 Act, s 758(3).

[107]  2006 Act, s 759(3).

[108]  2006 Act, s 759(4).

[109]  2006 Act, s 759(5).

## (5) Public companies: particular rules

### *Minimum capital requirements*

A public company must not do business or exercise any borrowing powers unless **24.33** the Registrar has issued it with a trading certificate which will be issued on an application by the company if the Registrar is satisfied that the nominal value of the company's allotted share capital is not less than the authorized minimum.[110] The 'authorized minimum' is currently £50,000 or the prescribed euro equivalent.[111]

An application for a certificate must (a) state that the nominal value of the com- **24.34** pany's allotted share capital is not less than the authorized minimum, (b) specify the amount, or estimated amount, of the company's preliminary expenses, (c) specify any amount or benefit paid or given, or intended to be paid or given, to any promoter[112] of the company, and the consideration for the payment or benefit, and (d) be accompanied by a statement of compliance.[113] It should be noted that a false representation as to the capital position for the purpose of securing a certificate is grounds for disqualification of directors under the CDDA.[114]

Once obtained, a trading certificate is conclusive evidence that the company is **24.35** entitled to do business and exercise any borrowing powers.[115] However, if a company does business or exercises any borrowing powers without a trading certificate, an offence (punishable by fine) is committed by every officer in default as well as by the company itself. [116] Furthermore, in addition to this criminal liability, the directors may incur civil liability for trading or borrowing without a trading certificate: the 2006 Act, s 767(3) provides that the directors of a public company will be jointly and severally liable to provide indemnification to any person who suffers loss by reason of the fact that the company has traded with or borrowed from such person without a trading certificate and then failed to perform the contractual obligations owed to such person and arising from such trade

---

[110] 2006 Act, s 761(1) and (2). Sections 761–767 replaced provisions in 1985 Act, ss 117–118 with changes and new provisions on 6 April 2008.

[111] 2006 Act, s 763(1), (2).

[112] The term 'promoter' is a 'short and convenient way of designating those who set in motion the machinery by which the [Companies] Act enables them to create an incorporated company': *Erlanger v New Sombrero Phosphate Co* (1878) 3 App Cas 1218, 1268, per Lord Blackburn. It is someone who 'undertakes to form a company with reference to a given project and to set it going, and who takes the necessary steps to accomplish that purpose': *Twycross v Grant* (1877) 2 CPD 469, 541, per Cockburn CJ.

[113] 2006 Act, s 762.

[114] *Re Kaytech International plc* [1999] 2 BCLC 351.

[115] 2006 Act, s 761(4).

[116] 2006 Act, s 767(1) and (2). Section 767(1)–(3) replaced provisions in 1985 Act, s 117 (7) and (8) and Schedule 24 without change on 6 April 2008.

or borrowing within 21 days of being called on to do so.[117] The directors liable in this manner will be those who were directors at the time the company entered into the transaction in question.[118]

*Liability to return allotment money when issue not fully subscribed*

**24.36** Where shares in a public company are offered[119] for subscription, no allotment may be made unless the issue is subscribed in full or the offer is made on terms that the shares subscribed for may be allotted in any event or upon satisfaction of specified conditions which are in fact satisfied.[120]

**24.37** If money has been received from applications for shares which are not allotted by reason of this prohibition, that money must be repaid to the applicants forthwith (without interest).[121] If any money is not repaid within 48 days after the first making of the offer, the directors and the company are jointly and severally liable to repay it together with interest at the judgment rate.[122] However, liability will not attach to any director who proves that the default in repayment was not due to any misconduct or negligence on his part.[123]

**24.38** If the shares are wrongly allotted in contravention of this prohibition, the allotment is voidable (by notice[124]) at the instance of the application within one month of the date of the allotment, and not later.[125] A director of a public company who knowingly contravenes or permits or authorizes the contravention of the prohibition regarding allotment is liable to compensate the company and the allottee

---

[117] 2006 Act, s 767(3), which came into force on 6 April 2008.

[118] 2006 Act, s 767(4). This is a new provision, which came into effect on 6 April 2008.

[119] Whether for cash or non-cash consideration: see 2006 Act, s 578(4). Where the shares have been offered for non-cash consideration, the provisions of s 578(5) modify the statutory language so as to make it applicable to non-cash assets. If it is not reasonably practicable to return the non-cash consideration, the company must return its value in money at the time it was received. Section 578 replaces provisions in 1985 Act, s 84 with changes on 1 October 2009.

[120] 2006 Act, s 578(1), which restates 1985 Act, s 84(1) and comes into force on 1 October 2009.

[121] 2006 Act, s 578(2) (restating 1985 Act, s 84(2); in force from 1 October 2009). In fact, where the money was paid into a separate account pursuant to an express term to that effect in the offer, the money may already be impressed with a trust for the applicants and should be returned to them as beneficiaries in any event, irrespective of the statutory provision to that effect: *Re Nanwa Gold Mines Ltd* [1955] 1 WLR 1080; *Moseley v Cressey's Co* (1865) LR 1 Eq 405; see also *Quistclose Investment Ltd v Rolls Razor Ltd* [1970] AC 567.

[122] 2006 Act, s 578(3) (replacing 1985 Act, s 84(3), with changes; in force from 1 October 2009); Judgments Act 1838, s 17.

[123] 2006 Act, s 578(5) (which comes into force on 1 October 2009), restating 1985 Act, s 84(4) and (5) without change.

[124] *Re National Motor Mail Coach Co Ltd* [1908] 2 Ch 228. The allotment may be avoided even where the company is in winding up.

[125] 2006 Act, s 579(1), which replaces 1985 Act, s 85 without change on 1 October 2009.

respectively for any loss, damages, costs, or expenses that the company or allottee may have sustained or incurred by the contravention.[126] The term 'knowingly' means with knowledge of the facts on which the contravention depends, but it does not extend to knowledge of the legal effect of the facts.[127] Proceedings to recover such loss, damages, costs, or expenses must be brought within two years or not at all.[128]

### Payment for shares in cash

Additional rules apply in the case of shares in a public company. First, shares taken by a subscriber to the memorandum of a public company and any premium on the shares must be paid up in cash.[129] For the purpose of the Act, a 'cash consideration' includes a cheque received by the company in good faith that the directors have no reason for suspecting will not be paid and an undertaking to pay cash at a future date.[130] The cash need not be pounds sterling but may be in a foreign currency.[131]   **24.39**

Furthermore, a public company must not accept at any time, in payment up of its shares or any premium thereon, an undertaking given by any person that he or another should do work or perform services for the company or any other person.[132] If any such undertaking is accepted, s 585(2) imposes a liability[133] on the holder of the shares to pay the nominal value, any premium and interest (subject to any relief from liability which may be granted by the court; s 589). However, s 591 provides that such an undertaking will remain enforceable by the company notwithstanding the fact that it ought properly not to have been accepted by the company.[134]   **24.40**

---

[126] 2006 Act, s 579(3) (which comes into force on 1 October 2009, replacing and restating 1985 Act, s 85(2) without change). Where the allotment has occurred, the matter is governed by s 579, and s 578 is no longer applicable: *Burton v Bevan* [1908] 2 Ch 240.

[127] *Burton v Bevan* [1908] 2 Ch 240; see also *Twycross v Grant* (1877) 2 CPD 469; *Shepherd v Broome* [1904] C 342; *MacLeay v Tait* [1906] AC 24.

[128] 2006 Act, s 579(4) (which comes into force on 1 October 2009), restating 1985 Act, s 85(3) without change.

[129] 2006 Act, s 584, which replaces 1985 Act, s 106 without change on 1 October 2009.

[130] 2006 Act, s 583(3). Section 583 replaces provisions in 1985 Act, s 738 with new provisions in subss (3(e), (4), and (7) on 1 October 2009. An 'undertaking to pay cash . . . at a future date' does not include the assignment of an earlier debt: *System Control plc v Munro Corporate plc* [1990] BCLC 659.

[131] 2006 Act, s 583(6).

[132] 2006 Act, s 585(1), which replaces 1985 Act, s 99(2) without change on 1 October 2009.

[133] The effect is to create an immediate liability as if the allottee had agreed to take up the shares for cash: *Re Bradford Investments plc* [1991] BCC 224.

[134] 2006 Act, s 591(1). Section 591 replaces 1985 Act, s 115(1) without change on 1 October 2009.

**24.41**  Additionally, a public company must not allot a share except as paid up at least to one-quarter of its nominal value and the whole of any premium on it.[135] If a company allots shares in contravention of this provision, the share is to be treated as if one-quarter of its nominal value, together with the whole of any premium on it, had been received, and the allottee is liable to pay such an amount as would be required to render the shares one-quarter paid up[136] with interest.[137] Relief under s 589 is not available in such a case.

**24.42**  Finally, a public company must not allot shares as fully paid up (as to their nominal value or any premium on them) otherwise than in cash if the consideration for the allotment is or includes an undertaking which is to be or may be performed more than five years after the date of the allotment.[138] If shares are allotted in contravention of this rule, the allottee is liable to pay the company an amount equal to the aggregate of their nominal value and the whole of any premium (or, if the case so requires, so much of that aggregate as is treated as paid up by the undertaking) with interest[139] (subject to any relief from liability which may be granted by the court: s 589).

**24.43**  If the statutory rules relating to payment for shares and additional requirements in the case of public companies are contravened, an offence (punishable by fine) is committed by every officer in default.[140]

*Independent valuation of non-cash consideration*

**24.44**  A public company must not allot shares as fully or partly paid up (as to their nominal value or any premium on them) otherwise than in cash unless (a) the consideration for the allotment has been independently valued in accordance with the Act,[141] (b) the valuer's report has been made to the company during the six months immediately preceding the allotment of the shares, and (c) a copy of the report has been sent to the proposed allottee.[142]

---

[135]  2006 Act, s 586(1). This provision does not apply to shares allotted in pursuance of an employees' share scheme: s 586(2). Section 586 replaces 1985 Act, s 101 without change on 1 October 2009. Model Articles (plc) 52–62 contemplate that a public company may issue partly paid shares (as does Table A regs 8–22).

[136]  2006 Act, s 586(3).

[137]  2006 Act, s 609(1). Section 609 replaces 1985 Act, s 107 without change on 1 October 2009.

[138]  2006 Act, s 587(1). Section 587 replaces provisions in 1985 Act, s 102 without change on 1 October 2009.

[139]  1985 Act, s 587(2); for interest see s 609(1).

[140]  2006 Act, s 590(1) and (2), which replace 1985 Act, s 114 and Schedule 24 without change on 1 October 2009.

[141]  The valuer's report must comply with the requirements of s 596(3). 2006 Act, ss 593–609, concerning independent valuation of non-cash consideration replace provisions in 1985 Act, ss 88(6), 103–114, and Schedule 24 with some changes on 1 October 2009.

[142]  2006 Act, s 593(1). There are exceptions for takeovers, schemes of arrangement, and mergers: ss 594, 595.

If the allottee has not received the valuer's report required or there is some other **24.45** contravention of the statutory requirements, and the allottee knew or ought to have known of the contravention,[143] then the allottee is liable to pay the company an amount equal to the aggregate of the nominal value of the shares and the whole of any premium with interest.[144] The court has power to grant relief subject to quite stringent conditions.[145]

A copy of the valuer's report must be delivered to the Registrar.[146] This must occur **24.46** at the same time as the filing of the return of the allotment.[147] The company's directors must ensure that this occurs. If these requirements are not satisfied, an offence (punishable by fine) is committed by every officer in default.[148] Where a director fails to file the report, it is possible to apply to the court for relief.[149] If the court is satisfied that the omission to deliver the documents was accidental or due to inadvertence,[150] or that it is just and equitable to grant relief,[151] it may make an order extending the time for delivery of the document for such period as the court thinks proper.[152]

It is important for directors of public companies to ensure that the statutory **24.47** requirements as to non-cash consideration are complied with, since contravention of the statutory requirements amounts to an offence committed by every officer in default and such offence is punishable by fine.[153]

### Transfer of non-cash asset in initial period

A public company formed as such must not enter into an agreement with a person **24.48** who is a subscriber to the company's memorandum for the transfer by him to the

---

[143] Liability is imposed if the allottee knew or ought to have known of the facts which constitute the contravention: *Systems Control plc v Munro Corporate plc* [1990] BCLC 659. It is not a requirement that the allottee knew the requirements of the law as to valuation.

[144] 2006 Act, s 593(3) (which comes into force on 1 October 2009, replacing s 103(6) of 1985 Act without change).

[145] 2006 Act, s 606 (which comes into force on 1 October 2009, replacing s 113 of 1985 Act with changes). See also *Systems Control plc v Munro Corporate plc* [1990] BCLC 659.

[146] 2006 Act, s 597(1) (which comes into force on 1 October 2009, restating part of s 111(1) of 1985 Act without changes).

[147] 2006 Act, s 597(2) (which comes into force on 1 October 2009, restating the remaining part of s 111(1) of the 1985 Act without changes).

[148] 2006 Act, s 597(3) and (4) (coming into force on 1 October 2009, restating s 111(3) of the 1985 Act without changes).

[149] 2006 Act, s 597(5) (which comes into force on 1 October 2009, restating ss 88(6) and 111(3) of the 1985 Act without changes).

[150] *Re Jackson & Co Ltd* [1899] 1 Ch 348.

[151] *Re Tom-Tit Cycle Co Ltd* (1899) 43 Sol Jo 334; *Re Whitefriar's Financial Co Ltd* [1899] 1 Ch 184.

[152] 2006 Act, s 597(6) (which comes into force on 1 October 2009, restating ss 88(6) and 111(3) of the 1985 Act without changes).

[153] 2006 Act, s 607(2) and (3) (which comes into force on 1 October 2009, replacing 1985 Act, s 114, Schedule 24, without changes).

company, or another, before the end of the company's initial period of one or more non-cash assets and under which the consideration for the transfer to be given by the company is at the time of the agreement equal in value to one-tenth or more of the company's issued share capital, unless (a) the requirements as to independent valuation are complied with, and (b) the requirements of member approval are complied with.[154]

**24.49** The requirements for independent valuation are laid down by the 2006 Act, ss 599–600. In short, the consideration must have been independently valued, and the valuer's report must have been made to the company during the six months preceding the date of the agreement, and a copy of the report must have been sent to the proposed transferor. The specific requirements as to the contents of the valuer's report are contained in s 600.

**24.50** The requirements for member approval are laid down by the 2006 Act, s 601. In summary (a) the terms of the agreement must have been approved by an ordinary resolution of the company, (b) the valuer's report must have been circulated to members, and (c) a copy of the proposed resolution must have been sent to the proposed transferor.

**24.51** If the transferor does not receive the valuer's report, or if there has been some other contravention of the statutory requirements and the transferor knew or ought to have known that there was a contravention, the company is entitled to recover any consideration given by it for the transfer, and the agreement is void.[155]

**24.52** A company that has passed a resolution under s 601 with respect to the transfer of an asset must, within 15 days of doing so, deliver to the Registrar a copy of the resolution together with the valuer's report.[156] If the company fails to comply with this requirement, an offence (punishable by fine) is committed by every officer in default.[157] Further, any contravention of the statutory requirements amounts to an offence committed by every officer in default and such offence is punishable by fine.[158]

---

[154] 2006 Act, s 598(1) (which comes into force on 1 October 2009, replacing 1985 Act, s 104(1) without changes).

[155] 2006 Act, s 604(2) (which comes into force on 1 October 2009, replacing 1985 Act, s 105(2) without changes).

[156] 2006 Act, s 602(1) (which comes into force on 1 October 2009, replacing 1985 Act, s 111(2) without changes).

[157] 2006 Act, s 602(2) and (3) (coming into force on 1 October 2009, replacing 1985 Act, s 111(4) and Schedule 24 without changes).

[158] 2006 Act, s 607(2) and (3) (which comes into force on 1 October 2009, replacing 1985 Act, s 114, Schedule 24, without changes).

## (6)  Quoted companies: particular rules

*Directors' functions and responsibility in relation to official listing*

The FSA, acting as the competent authority for listing, is referred to as the UKLA **24.53** and maintains the Official List. To gain admission of securities to the Official List an issuer must make an application for Listing to the UKLA's Listing Applications team.[159] Detailed application and eligibility requirements and ongoing obligations of listed companies are contained in the UKLA's Listing Rules, which have been made under the FSMA, s 73A.[160] Listing particulars are only required in limited circumstances.[161]

The contents of a company's listing particulars are primarily the responsibility of **24.54** the company's directors. FSMA, s 79(3), provides that the 'persons responsible for listing particulars' are to be determined in accordance with regulations made by the Treasury. The Treasury's regulations under this provision are the Financial Services and Markets Act 2000 (Official Listing of Securities) Regulations 2001.[162] Regulation 6 provides that the 'persons responsible for listing particulars' will include 'where the issuer is a body corporate, each person who is a director of that body at the time when the particulars are submitted to the [UKLA]'.[163]

A company's directors must take steps to ensure that the company complies with **24.55** the general duty of disclosure in respect of its listing particulars. FSMA, s 80, provides that listing particulars:

> must contain all such information as investors and their professional advisers would reasonably require, and reasonably expect to find there, for the purpose of making an informed assessment of (a) the assets and liabilities, financial position, profits and losses, and prospects of the issuer of the securities, and (b) the rights attaching to the securities.[164]

---

[159]  See in particular FSMA, s 75.

[160]  The term 'listing particulars' is defined to mean 'a document in such form and containing such information as may be specified in the Listing Rules': see FSMA, s 79(2).

[161]  See Maurice Button (ed), *A Practitioner's Guide to the Financial Services Authority Listing Regime 2008/2009* (City & Financial Publishing, June 2008), para 2.3.

[162]  SI 2001/2956.

[163]  However, a director is not to be treated as responsible for any particulars if they are published without his knowledge or consent and on becoming aware of their publication he forthwith gives reasonable public notice that they were published without his knowledge or consent: see reg 6(2).

[164]  Disclosure may be exempted under FSMA, s 82, if disclosure would be contrary to the public interest or seriously detrimental to the issuer or, in the case of securities of a kind specified in listing rules, if disclosure would be unnecessary for persons of the kind who may be expected normally to buy or deal in securities of that kind. However no exemption may be granted in respect of 'essential information'—ie information which a person considering acquiring securities of the kind in question would be likely to need in order not to be misled about any facts which it is essential for him to know in order to make an informed assessment.

**24.56**   In determining what information should be included in listing particulars, regard must be had (in particular) to (a) the nature of the securities and their issuer, (b) the nature of the persons likely to consider acquiring them, (c) the fact that certain matters may reasonably be expected to be within the knowledge of professional advisers of a kind which persons likely to acquire the securities may reasonably be expected to consult, and (d) any information available to investors or their professional advisers as a result of requirements imposed on the issuer of the securities by a recognized investment exchange, by listing rules, or by or under any other enactment.[165] If the company's directors are not aware of the relevant information, they must make reasonable enquiries.[166] Supplementary listing particulars must be prepared if there is a significant change in circumstances prior to listing.[167]

*Liabilities of directors in respect of listing particulars*

**24.57**   FSMA, s 90(1), provides that any person responsible for listing particulars or supplementary listing particulars (which will generally include a company's directors; see paragraph 24.53 above) will be liable to pay compensation to a person who has (a) acquired securities to which the particulars or supplementary particulars apply, and (b) suffered loss in respect of them as a result of any untrue or misleading statement in the particulars supplementary particulars or the omission from the particulars supplementary particulars of any matter required to be included therein.

**24.58**   FSMA, s 90(4), provides that failure to prepare supplementary listing particulars where necessary will also give rise to liability to pay compensation to any person who has (a) acquired securities of the kind in question, and (b) suffered loss in respect of them as a result of the failure.

**24.59**   If the UKLA considers that a company director (or other person discharging managerial responsibilities within an issuer or a person connected with any person discharging managerial responsibilities) has contravened any provision of disclosure rules, it may impose on him a penalty of such amount as it considers appropriate.[168] Alternatively the UKLA may issue a public statement censuring the person who would otherwise be liable to a financial penalty.[169] The UKLA may not take action against a person after the end of the period of two years beginning with the first day on which it knew of the contravention unless proceedings against

---

[165]   FSMA, s 80(4).
[166]   FSMA, s 80(3).
[167]   FSMA, s 81.
[168]   FSMA, s 91(1A).
[169]   FSMA, s 91(3).

that person, in respect of the contravention, were begun before the end of that period.[170]

Any person who, in purported compliance with any requirement imposed by or under FSMA, knowingly or recklessly gives the FSA information which is false or misleading in a material particular is guilty of an offence[171] punishable on summary conviction, to a fine not exceeding the statutory maximum or on conviction on indictment, to a fine.

**24.60**

*Directors' functions and responsibilities in relation to the company's prospectus*

A request for admission to trading on a regulated market (such as the London Stock Exchange's Main Markets for official listed securities) and/or an offer of securities to the public will, unless exempt, require a prospectus, which must be approved by the UKLA. Detailed requirements in respect of the form and contents of a company's prospectus are contained in the FSA's Prospectus Rules made under FSMA, s 73A, to which the reader is referred. Further, if before the closure of the offer or the commencement of trading there arises or is noted a significant new factor, material mistake, or inaccuracy relating to the information included in a prospectus approved by the UKLA, the person on whose application the prospectus was approved must, in accordance with prospectus rules, submit a supplementary prospectus containing details of the new factor, mistake, or inaccuracy to the UKLA for its approval.[172]

**24.61**

The procedure for approval is laid down by FSMA.[173] A prospectus will not be approved unless (a) the United Kingdom is the home state in relation to the issuer of the transferable securities to which it relates, (b) the prospectus contains the information necessary to enable investors to make an informed assessment of the assets and liabilities, financial position, profits and losses, and prospects of the issuer of the transferable securities and of any guarantor and the rights attaching to the transferable securities,[174] and (c) there has been compliance with all other applicable requirements. A prospectus must include a summary (unless the transferable securities in question are ones in relation to which prospectus rules provide that a summary is not required). The summary must, briefly and in non-technical

**24.62**

---

[170] FSMA, s 91(6).
[171] FSMA, s 398.
[172] FSMA, s 87G.
[173] See in particular ss 87C and 87D. Sections 84–87R replaced previous provisions in ss 84–87 with effect from 1 July 2005 (Prospectus Regulations 2005 (SI 2005/1433)).
[174] Disclosure of information may be exempted if the inclusion of the information would be contrary to the public interest or seriously detrimental to the issuer, provided that the omission would be unlikely to mislead the public with regard to any facts or circumstances which are essential for an informed assessment, or if the information is only of minor importance for a specific offer to the public or admission to trading on a regulated market and unlikely to influence an informed assessment: see FSMA, s 87B.

language, convey the essential characteristics of, and risks associated with, the issuer, any guarantor, and the transferable securities to which the prospectus relates.[175]

**24.63** As a condition of approving a prospectus, the UKLA may by notice in writing (a) require the inclusion in the prospectus of such supplementary information necessary for investor protection as the UKLA may specify, (b) require a person controlling, or controlled by, the applicant to provide specified information or documents, (c) require an auditor or manager of the applicant to provide specified information or documents, and (d) require a financial intermediary commissioned to assist either in carrying out the offer to the public of the transferable securities to which the prospectus relates or in requesting their admission to trading on a regulated market, to provide specified information or documents.[176]

*Consequences of failure to comply with rules*

**24.64** A company's directors must be astute to ensure that the detailed requirements regarding the production of a prospectus are observed, because failure to comply with these requirements will have serious consequences. First, it will be an offence. Secondly, it may give rise to a civil action. Thirdly, the UKLA may impose a suspension of the offer or request for admission. Fourthly, the UKLA may issue a public censure of the issuer. These possibilities are considered in detail below.

**24.65** There are two relevant offences. First, it is unlawful for transferable securities to be offered to the public in the United Kingdom unless an approved prospectus has been made available to the public before the offer is made.[177] Secondly, it is unlawful to request the admission of transferable securities to trading on a regulated market situated or operating in the United Kingdom unless an approved prospectus has been made available to the public before the request is made.[178] A person who contravenes either of these provisions is guilty of an offence and liable on summary conviction, to imprisonment for a term not exceeding three months or a fine not exceeding the statutory maximum or both or on conviction on indictment to imprisonment for a term not exceeding two years or a fine or both.[179]

**24.66** It is specifically provided in FSMA that a contravention of these provisions is actionable, at the suit of a person who suffers loss as a result of the contravention, subject to the defences and other incidents applying to actions for breach

---

175 FSMA, s 87A.
176 FSMA, s 87J.
177 FSMA, s 85(1).
178 FSMA, s 85(2).
179 FSMA, s 85(3).

of statutory duty.[180] The possibility of civil liability is considered further in paragraphs 24.70–24.72 below.

If the UKLA has reasonable grounds for suspecting that an applicable provision[181] **24.67** has been infringed, it may (a) require the offeror to suspend the offer for a period not exceeding 10 working days, and (b) require a person not to advertise the offer, or to take such steps as the authority may specify to suspend any existing advertisement of the offer, for a period not exceeding 10 working days.[182] The UKLA may require the offeror to withdraw the offer if it has reasonable grounds for suspecting that it is likely that an applicable provision will be infringed, or if it finds that an applicable provision has been infringed.[183] Similar provisions apply in respect of requests for the admission of transferable securities to trading on a regulated market situated or operating in the United Kingdom.[184] In such a case, as well as being able to suspend the request for 10 days, the UKLA may require a person not to advertise the securities to which it relates, or to take such steps as the authority may specify to suspend any existing advertisement in connection with those securities, for a period not exceeding 10 working days.

Further, if the UKLA has reasonable grounds for suspecting that an applicable **24.68** provision has been infringed and the securities have been admitted to trading on the regulated market in question, it may (a) require the market operator to suspend trading in the securities for a period not exceeding 10 working days, and (b) require a person not to advertise the securities, or to take such steps as the authority may specify to suspend any existing advertisement in connection with those securities, for a period not exceeding 10 working days. If the UKLA finds that an applicable provision has been infringed, it may require the market operator to prohibit trading in the securities on the regulated market in question.

If the UKLA finds that an issuer of transferable securities, a person offering trans- **24.69** ferable securities to the public or a person requesting the admission of transferable securities to trading on a regulated market is failing or has failed to comply with his obligations under an applicable provision, it may publish a statement to that effect. If the UKLA proposes to publish a statement, it must give the person a warning notice setting out the terms of the proposed statement. If, after considering any representations made in response to the warning notice, the UKLA decides to make the proposed statement, it must give the person a decision notice setting out the terms of the statement.

---

[180]  FSMA, s 85(4).
[181]  An 'applicable provision' is every applicable provision of FSMA or the prospectus rules or any other applicable provision made in accordance with the Prospectus Directive.
[182]  FSMA, s 87K(2).
[183]  FSMA, s 87K(3) and (4).
[184]  FSMA, s 87L.

*Exemptions*

**24.70**    Offers will be exempt from these provisions if (a) the offer is made to or directed at qualified investors[185] only, (b) the offer is made to or directed at fewer than 100 persons, other than qualified investors, per EEA state, (c) the minimum consideration which may be paid by any person for transferable securities acquired by him pursuant to the offer is at least 50,000 Euros (or an equivalent amount), (d) the transferable securities being offered are denominated in amounts of at least 50,000 Euros (or equivalent amounts), or (e) the total consideration for the transferable securities being offered cannot exceed 100,000 Euros (or an equivalent amount).[186]

*Liabilities of directors in respect of contents of prospectus*

**24.71**    A company's directors are, in the case of a prospectus for equity securities, responsible for the contents of the prospectus. The persons responsible for prospectuses are laid down in the Prospectus Rules (PR 5.5) made by the FSA pursuant to s 84(1)(d) of FSMA and include the company itself. Pursuant to FSMA, s 90(11), any person responsible for a company's prospectus or supplementary prospectus will be liable to pay compensation to a person who has (a) acquired securities to which the prospectus or supplementary prospectus applies, and (b) suffered loss in respect of them as a result of any untrue or misleading statement in the prospectus or supplementary prospectus or the omission from the prospectus or supplementary prospectus of any matter required to be included therein. However, a person is not to be subject to civil liability solely on the basis of a summary in a prospectus unless the summary is misleading, inaccurate, or inconsistent when read with the rest of the prospectus; and, in this subsection, a summary includes any translation of it.

**24.72**    Similarly, failure to prepare a supplementary prospectus where necessary will also give rise to liability to pay compensation to any person who has (a) acquired securities of the kind in question, and (b) suffered loss in respect of them as a result of the failure.[187]

**24.73**    If the UKLA considers that (inter alia) a person offering transferable securities to the public or requesting their admission to trading on a regulated market (or

---

[185]   The term 'qualified investor' means: (a) an entity falling within Article 2.1(e)(i), (ii), or (iii) of the Prospectus Directive; (b) an investor registered on the register maintained by the UKLA under section 87R; (c) an investor authorized by an EEA state other than the United Kingdom to be considered as a qualified investor for the purposes of the Prospectus Directive.

[186]   FSMA, s 86(1). For these purposes, the making of an offer of transferable securities to trustees of a trust, members of a partnership in their capacity as such, or two or more persons jointly is to be treated as the making of an offer to a single person: FSMA, s 86(3).

[187]   FSMA, s 90(11).

a director of such a person[188]) or an applicant for the approval of a prospectus in relation to transferable securities (or a director of such a person[189]) has contravened a provision of this Part or of prospectus rules, or a provision otherwise made in accordance with the Prospectus Directive or a requirement imposed on him under such a provision, it may impose on him a penalty of such amount as it considers appropriate.[190] Alternatively the UKLA may issue a public statement censuring the person who would otherwise be liable to a financial penalty.[191] The UKLA may not take action against a person after the end of the period of two years beginning with the first day on which it knew of the contravention unless proceedings against that person, in respect of the contravention, were begun before the end of that period.[192]

**24.74** Any person who, in purported compliance with any requirement imposed by or under FSMA, knowingly or recklessly gives the FSA information which is false or misleading in a material particular is guilty of an offence[193] punishable on summary conviction, to a fine not exceeding the statutory maximum or on conviction on indictment, to a fine.

### Functions and responsibilities of directors in respect of transparency

**24.75** The UKLA's Transparency Rules, which have been made under FMSA, s 89A[194] for the purposes of the Transparency Obligations Directive, lay down a detailed code for the provision of certain information including (for example): (a) 'vote-holder information' (ie information relating to the proportion of voting rights held by a person in respect of the shares); (b) information relating to the rights attached to transferable securities, including information about the terms and conditions of those securities which could indirectly affect those rights; and (c) information about new loan issues and about any guarantee or security in connection with any such issue.[195]

---

[188] FSMA, s 91(2).
[189] FSMA, s 91(2).
[190] FSMA, s 91(1A).
[191] FSMA, s 91(3).
[192] FSMA, s 91(6).
[193] FSMA, s 398.
[194] 2006 Act, s 1266 introduced new Transparency Rules in FSMA, ss 89A–89G, which came into force on enactment of the 2006 Act on 8 November 2006 pursuant to s 1300.
[195] Detailed analysis of the Transparency Rules is outside the scope of this work; the reader is referred to the Transparency Rules for further details.

**24.76**   FSMA, s 89H, enables the UKLA to call for information.[196] The section applies to directors and similar officers, but it also applies to auditors and vote holders.[197] It provides that the UKLA may by notice in writing given to a person to whom the section applies require him (a) to provide specified information or information of a specified description, or (b) to produce specified documents or documents of a specified description. The UKLA may also require (a) such information to be provided in such form as it may reasonably require, (b) any information provided, whether in a document or otherwise, to be verified in such manner as it may reasonably require, and (c) any document produced to be authenticated in such manner as it may reasonably require. The UKLA may also require an issuer to make public any information provided under these provisions or may itself make that information public, if the issuer fails to do so.

**24.77**   If the UKLA finds that an issuer of securities admitted to trading on a regulated market is failing or has failed to comply with an applicable transparency obligation,[198] it may publish a statement to that effect.[199] If the UKLA proposes to publish a statement, it must give the issuer a warning notice setting out the terms of the proposed statement. If, after considering any representations made in response to the warning notice, the UKLA decides to make the proposed statement, it must give the issuer a decision notice setting out the terms of the statement.

**24.78**   If the UKLA has reasonable grounds for suspecting that an applicable transparency obligation has been infringed by an issuer, it may (a) suspend trading in the securities for a period not exceeding 10 days, (b) prohibit trading in the securities, or (c) make a request to the operator of the market on which the issuer's securities are traded to suspend trading in the securities for a period not exceeding 10 days or to prohibit trading in the securities.[200]

**24.79**   Further, if the UKLA has reasonable grounds for suspecting that a provision required by the Transparency Obligations Directive has been infringed by a vote holder of an issuer, it may (a) prohibit trading in the securities, or (b) make a request to the operator of the market on which the issuer's securities are traded to prohibit trading in the securities. If the UKLA finds that an applicable transparency obligation has been infringed, it may require the market operator to prohibit trading in the securities.

---

[196] 2006 Act, s 1267 introduced new provisions in FSMA, ss 89H–89J, giving the FSA power to call for information. Again these provisions came into effect on 8 November 2006 pursuant to s 1300.

[197] The term 'voteholder' means a person who holds voting rights in respect of any voting shares or is treated as holding such rights.

[198] The term 'transparency obligation' means an obligation under a provision of Transparency Rules or any other provision made in accordance with the Transparency Obligations Directive.

[199] FSMA, s 87K. 2006 Act, s 1268 introduced new provisions in FSMA, ss 89K–89N, exercisable in the case of infringement of transparency obligations, which came into force on enactment on 6 November 2006 pursuant to s 1300.

[200] FSMA, s 87L.

*Civil liability in respect of transparency*

In relation to any annual, half-yearly, or interim reports or preliminary statements **24.80** published under the FSA's Transparency Rules, the issuer of securities will be liable to pay compensation to a person who has (a) acquired such securities issued by it; (b) suffered loss in respect of them as a result of any untrue or misleading statement in such a publication or the omission from any such publication of any matter required to be included in it.[201] The issuer is so liable only if a person discharging managerial responsibilities within the issuer[202] in relation to the publication (a) knew the statement to be untrue or misleading or was reckless as to whether it was untrue or misleading; (b) knew the omission to be dishonest concealment of a material fact. A loss is not regarded as suffered as a result of the statement or omission in the publication unless the person suffering it acquired the relevant securities (a) in reliance on the information in the publication; (b) at a time when, and in circumstances in which, it was reasonable for him to rely on that information. See also the 2006 Act, s 463, which provides that where a company suffers loss as a result of errors or omissions in a directors' report (which will be part of the annual report published under the Transparency Rules), the knowing or reckless director may be liable to the company.[203]

*Financial penalties in respect of transparency*

If the UKLA considers that a person (or a director of a person[204]) has contravened **24.81** a provision of Transparency Rules or a provision otherwise made in accordance with the Transparency Obligations Directive, it may impose on the person a penalty of such amount as it considers appropriate.[205] Alternatively the UKLA may issue a public statement censuring the person who would otherwise be liable to a financial penalty.[206] The UKLA may not take action against a person after the end of the period of two years beginning with the first day on which it knew of the contravention unless proceedings against that person, in respect of the contravention, were begun before the end of that period.[207]

---

[201] FSMA, s 90(1).
[202] Persons 'discharging managerial responsibilities' in relation to a publication will be: (1) any director of the issuer (or person occupying the position of director, by whatever name called); (2) in the case of an issuer whose affairs are managed by its members, any member of the issuer; (3) if there are no persons falling within these two categories, any senior executive of the issuer having responsibilities in relation to the publication.
[203] s 463 came into force on 20 January 2007 pursuant to 2006 Act Commencement Order No 1, art 3(1)(c).
[204] FSMA, s 91(2).
[205] FSMA, s 91(1B).
[206] FSMA, s 91(3).
[207] FSMA, s 91(6).

*Market abuse*

**24.82** Market abuse is behaviour (whether by one person alone or by two or more persons jointly or in concert) which (a) occurs in relation to qualifying investments admitted to trading on a prescribed market, qualifying investments in respect of which a request for admission to trading on such a market has been made, or, in categories 1 and 2 below, investments which are related investments in relation to such qualifying investments; and (b) falls within any one or more of the types of behaviour set out in FSMA, s 118.

**24.83** FSMA, s 118, specifies seven different types of behaviour.

(1) The first type of behaviour is where an insider[208] deals, or attempts to deal, in a qualifying investment or related investment on the basis of inside information[209] relating to the investment in question.[210]

(2) The second is where an insider discloses inside information to another person otherwise than in the proper course of the exercise of his employment, profession, or duties.[211]

(3) The third is where the behaviour (not falling within the first two categories) is based on information which is not generally available to those using the market but which, if available to a regular user of the market, would be, or would be likely to be, regarded by him as relevant when deciding the terms on which transactions in qualifying investments should be effected, and is likely to be regarded by a regular user of the market as a failure on the part of the person concerned to observe the standard of behaviour reasonably expected of a person in his position in relation to the market.[212]

(4) The fourth is where the behaviour consists of effecting transactions or orders to trade (otherwise than for legitimate reasons and in conformity with

---

[208] An 'insider' is any person who has inside information: (1) as a result of his membership of an administrative, management, or supervisory body of an issuer of qualifying investments; (2) as a result of his holding in the capital of an issuer of qualifying investments; (3) as a result of having access to the information through the exercise of his employment, profession, or duties; (4) as a result of his criminal activities; or (5) which he has obtained by other means and which he knows, or could reasonably be expected to know, is inside information: see FSMA, s 118B.

[209] The concept of 'inside information' is not entirely straightforward but may in general terms be said to involve information 'of a precise nature' which is not 'generally available: see FSMA, s 118C. Information is precise if it indicates circumstances that exist or may reasonably be expected to come into existence or an event that has occurred or may reasonably be expected to occur and is specific enough to enable a conclusion to be drawn as to the possible effect of those circumstances or that event on the price of qualifying investments or related investments. Information which can be obtained by research or analysis conducted by, or on behalf of, users of a market is to be regarded, for the purposes of this Part, as being generally available to them.

[210] FSMA, s 118(2).
[211] FSMA, s 118(3).
[212] FSMA, s 118(4).

accepted market practices on the relevant market) which give, or are likely to give, a false or misleading impression as to the supply of, or demand for, or as to the price of, one or more qualifying investments, or secure the price of one or more such investments at an abnormal or artificial level.[213]

(5) The fifth is where the behaviour consists of effecting transactions or orders to trade which employ fictitious devices or any other form of deception or contrivance.[214]

(6) The sixth is where the behaviour consists of the dissemination of information by any means which gives, or is likely to give, a false or misleading impression as to a qualifying investment by a person who knew or could reasonably be expected to have known that the information was false or misleading.[215]

(7) The seventh is where the behaviour (not falling within subsection categories 4, 5, or 6) is likely to give a regular user of the market a false or misleading impression as to the supply of, demand for or price or value of, qualifying investments or would be, or would be likely to be, regarded by a regular user of the market as behaviour that would distort, or would be likely to distort, the market in such an investment, and the behaviour is likely to be regarded by a regular user of the market as a failure on the part of the person concerned to observe the standard of behaviour reasonably expected of a person in his position in relation to the market.[216]

In each case the behaviour in question will be relevant only if it occurs in the United Kingdom or in relation to qualifying investments which are admitted to trading on a prescribed market situated in, or operating in, the United Kingdom, qualifying investments for which a request for admission to trading on such a prescribed market has been made, or, in categories 1 and 2 above, investments which are related investments in relation to such qualifying investments.[217] **24.84**

*Penalties for market abuse*

If the FSA is satisfied that a person (A) is or has engaged in market abuse or, by taking or refraining from taking any action, has required or encouraged another **24.85**

---

[213] FSMA, s 118(5).

[214] FSMA, s 118(6).

[215] FSMA, s 118(7).

[216] FSMA, s 118(8).

[217] FSMA, s 118(1A). Further, behaviour does not amount to market abuse for the purposes of FSMA if: (1) it conforms with a rule which includes a provision to the effect that behaviour conforming with the rule does not amount to market abuse; (2) it conforms with the relevant provisions of Commission Regulation (EC) No 2273/2003 of 22 December 2003 implementing Directive 2003/6/EC of the European Parliament and of the Council as regards exemptions for buy-back programmes and stabilization of financial instruments; or (3) it is done by a person acting on behalf of a public authority in pursuit of monetary policies or policies with respect to exchange rates or the management of public debt or foreign exchange reserves: FSMA, s 118(5).

person or persons to engage in behaviour which, if engaged in by A, would amount to market abuse, it may impose on him a penalty of such amount as it considers appropriate.[218] However, the FSA may not impose a penalty on a person if, having considered any representations made to it in response to a warning notice, there are reasonable grounds for it to be satisfied that he believed, on reasonable grounds, that his behaviour did not amount to market abuse or he took all reasonable precautions and exercised all due diligence to avoid behaving in a way which amounted to market abuse.[219] If the FSA is entitled to impose a penalty on a person, it may, instead of imposing a penalty on him, publish a statement to the effect that he has engaged in market abuse.[220]

**24.86** Further, the FSA may on an application to the court under FSMA, ss 381 or 383 request the court to consider whether the circumstances are such that a penalty should be imposed on the person to whom the application relates. The court may, if it considers it appropriate, make an order requiring the person concerned to pay to the FSA a penalty of such amount as it considers appropriate.[221]

*Injunctions and restitution*

**24.87** In cases of contravention of the provisions of FSMA, the FSA (and the Secretary of State) are able to apply for injunctions and restitution orders. In practice the targets of such action are likely to include company directors and for that reason these provisions are summarized below.

**24.88** FSMA, s 380, enables the FSA or the Secretary of State to obtain injunctions against the contravention of any 'relevant requirement'. The FSA or the Secretary of State is required to satisfy the court that there is a 'reasonable likelihood' of any such contravention occurring or continuing or being repeated.[222] Additionally the FSA or the Secretary of State may obtain an order requiring any person who has contravened the requirement, and any other person who appears to have been knowingly concerned in the contravention, to take such steps as the court may direct to remedy the contravention.[223]

**24.89** The FSA and the Secretary of State may also take steps to prevent the dissipation of assets. FSMA, s 380(3), enables the FSA or the Secretary of State to apply for an order restraining any person who may have contravened a relevant requirement or been knowingly concerned in the contravention of such a requirement from

---

218 FSMA, s 123(1).
219 FSMA, s 123(2).
220 FSMA, s 123(3).
221 FSMA, s 129.
222 FSMA, s 380(1).
223 FSMA, s 380(2).

disposing of, or otherwise dealing with, any assets of his which it is satisfied he is reasonably likely to dispose of or otherwise deal with.

In the case of an application by the FSA, the term 'relevant requirement' means **24.90** any requirement imposed by FSMA or any directly applicable Community regulation made under the Markets in Financial Instruments Directive or which is imposed by or under any other Act and whose contravention constitutes an offence which the FSA has power to prosecute under FSMA. In the case of an application by the Secretary of State, the term 'relevant requirement' means any requirement imposed by or under FSMA and whose contravention constitutes an offence which the Secretary of State has power to prosecute under FSMA.

Similar provisions exist for obtaining injunctions in cases of market abuse. FSMA, **24.91** s 381, provides that the FSA may apply for an injunction against market abuse. In order to obtain such an injunction, the FSA must satisfy the court that there is a 'reasonable likelihood' that a person will engage in market abuse or will continue to engage in market abuse or that market abuse will be repeated. Similarly, where the market abuse may be remedied, the FSA may apply for an order requiring the market abuse to be remedied.

Asset protection provisions also exist to bolster the market abuse provisions of **24.92** FSMA. The FSA may apply for a freezing order where the court is satisfied: (1) that any person may be engaged in market abuse; and (2) that he is reasonably likely to dispose of or otherwise deal with his assets.

The FSA or the Secretary of State may apply for a 'restitution order' under **24.93** FSMA, s 381. A restitution order is an order requiring a person to pay a sum of money to the FSA. The court may make such an order if it is satisfied that a person has contravened a relevant requirement, or been knowingly concerned in the contravention of such a requirement, and: (1) that profits have accrued to him as a result of the contravention; or (2) that one or more persons have suffered loss or been otherwise adversely affected as a result of the contravention. The restitution order may be made for 'such sum as appears to the Court to be just' having regard to the profits appearing to the court to have accrued and/or the extent of the loss or other adverse effect (as the case may be). Sums paid to the FSA in respect of losses suffered by others must be distributed to the victims under FSMA, s 381(3).

The court may require the person concerned to supply it with such accounts or **24.94** other information as it may require for any one or more of the following purposes (a) establishing whether any and, if so, what profits have accrued to him, (b) establishing whether any person or persons have suffered any loss or adverse effect and, if so, the extent of that loss or adverse effect, and (c) determining how any amounts are to be paid or distributed by the FSA. The court may require any accounts or other information to be verified in such manner as it may direct.

**24.95** The term 'relevant requirement' in relation to an application by the FSA, means a requirement which is imposed by or under FSMA or by any directly applicable Community regulation made under the Markets in Financial Instruments Directive or which is imposed by or under any other Act and whose contravention constitutes an offence which the FSA has power to prosecute under FSMA. In relation to an application by the Secretary of State, the term 'relevant requirement' means a requirement which is imposed by or under FSMA and whose contravention constitutes an offence which the Secretary of State has power to prosecute under FSMA.

**24.96** Similar provisions exist to deal with cases of market abuse: see FSMA, s 383. Where the court is satisfied that a person has engaged in market abuse or by taking or refraining from taking any action has required or encouraged another person or persons to engage in behaviour which, if engaged in by the person concerned, would amount to market abuse, and profits have accrued to the person concerned as a result of one or more persons have suffered loss or been otherwise adversely affected as a result, the court may make an order requiring the person concerned to pay to the FSA such sum as appears to the court to be just having regard to the profits appearing to the court to have accrued and/or the extent of the loss or other adverse effect. The court may not make such an order if it is satisfied that the person concerned believed, on reasonable grounds, that his behaviour did not constitute market abuse or that he took all reasonable precautions and exercised all due diligence to avoid behaving in a way which amounted to market abuse. Any amount paid to the FSA in pursuance of an order under these provisions must be paid by it to the persons who were deprived of profits, or who suffered loss (qualifying person), or distributed by it among such qualifying persons as the court may direct.

**24.97** The provisions relating to restitution orders in cases of market abuse are supplemented by provisions relating to the provision of information. The court may require the person concerned to supply it with such accounts or other information as it may require for any one or more of the following purposes: (a) establishing whether any and, if so, what profits have accrued to him; (b) establishing whether any person or persons have suffered any loss or adverse effect and, if so, the extent of that loss or adverse effect; and (c) determining how any amounts are to be paid or distributed to qualifying persons. The court may require any such accounts or other information to be verified in such manner as it may direct.

## C. Alteration of Share Capital

A limited company with share capital may not alter its share capital[224] except by: **24.98**
(1) increase of share capital by way of allotment;[225] (2) reduction of capital;[226]
(3) sub-division or reconsolidation of shares;[227] (4) reconversion of stock into
shares;[228] and (5) redenomination of shares.[229] Authorization in the company's
articles is not a prerequisite.[230] A resolution of this nature may be contingent upon
the happening of a future event, such as confirmation of a reduction of capital by
the court.[231] As with all corporate powers, these powers must be exercised bona
fide for the benefit of the company as a whole.[232]

In each case, the directors must ensure that notice is provided to the Registrar in **24.99**
accordance with the statutory rules, together with a statement of capital. Notice
of sub-division or consolidation or reconversion of stock must be sent to the
Registrar within one month[233] and must be accompanied by a statement of
capital.[234] Notice of redenomination or notice of reduction of capital in connection with redenomination must be sent to the Registrar within one month and
must state the date on which the resolution was passed and be accompanied by a

---

[224] 2006 Act, s 617(1) (which comes into force on 1 October 2009, replacing 1985 Act, s 121(1)
with changes). Until 1 October 2009, see 1985 Act, s 121(1).

[225] 2006 Act, s 617(2)(a) (which comes into force on 1 October 2009, replacing 1985 Act,
s 121(2)(a) with changes); see paragraphs 24.03–24.22 above.

[226] 2006 Act, s 617(2)(b) (which comes into force on 1 October 2009, replacing 1985 Act,
s 121(2)(a) with changes); see paragraphs 24.104–24.131 below.

[227] 2006 Act, s 617(3)(a) (which comes into force on 1 October 2009, replacing 1985 Act,
s 121(2) with changes); see also s 618.

[228] 2006 Act, s 617(3)(b) (which comes into force on 1 October 2009, replacing 1985 Act,
s 121(2) with changes); see also s 620 (also coming into force on 1 October 2009). See generally
*Morrice v Aylmer* (1874) 10 Ch App 148 and *Re Home & Foreign Investment & Agency Co* [1912] 1
Ch 72.

[229] 2006 Act, s 617(4), a new provision which comes into force on 1 October 2009; see also
ss 622 and 626 (also new).

[230] *Re Bank of Hindustan* (1873) 9 Ch App 1; *Taylor v Pilsen* (1884) 27 Ch D 268. A company's
undertaking in a shareholders' agreement not to exercise these powers will be unenforceable, but
the shareholders' agreement will be enforceable by the shareholders inter se: *Russell v Northern Bank
Development Corp Ltd* [1992] 1 WLR 588.

[231] *Re Salinas of Mexico* [1919] WN 311; *Re Welsbach Incandescent Gas Light Co* [1904] 1 Ch 87;
*Re Australian Estates & Mortgage Co Ltd* [1910] 1 Ch 414.

[232] *Allen v Gold Reefs of West Africa* [1900] 1 Ch 87.

[233] 2006 Act, ss 618(1) and 621(1); in force on 1 October 2009, replacing 1985 Act, s 121(2)(b)
and (d) and s 122(1)(c) respectively.

[234] 2006 Act, s 618(2) (replacing (with changes) 1985 Act, s 121(3)) and s 621(2) (a new provision); in force on 1 October 2009; see also s 618(3) (replacing 1985 Act, s 121(4) with changes) and
s 621(3) (a new provision).

statement of capital.[235] Default in complying with these requirements is an offence (punishable by fine[236]) committed by every officer in default.[237]

### (1) Class rights

**24.100** Shares are of one class if the rights[238] attached to them are in all respects uniform.[239] However for this purpose the rights attached to shares are not regarded as different from those attached to other shares by reason only that they do not carry the same rights to dividends in the 12 months immediately following their allotment.[240] Any amendment of a provision contained in a company's articles for the variation of the rights attached to a class of shares (or the insertion of any such provision into the articles) is itself to be treated as a variation of those rights.[241] Variation includes abrogation.[242]

**24.101** Rights attached to a class of shares in a company having share capital may only be varied: (1) in accordance with provision in the company's articles for variation; or (2) where the company's articles contain no such provision, if the holders of shares of that class consent to the variation in accordance with the 2006 Act, s 630.[243] That section provides that the consent must be in writing from the holders of at least three-quarters in nominal value of the issued shares of that class (excluding any shares held as treasury shares) or by way of a special resolution passed at a separate general meeting of the holders of that class sanctioning the variation.[244]

---

[235] 2006 Act, s 625(1), (2), (3); s 626(1), (2), (3) (new provisions, all of which are due to come into force on 1 October 2009). A reduction is not effective until the documents are registered: s 627(5). The company must also deliver to the Registrar a statement confirming that the reduction of capital did not exceed 10 per cent of the nominal value of allotted shared immediately after reduction: s 627(6).

[236] 2006 Act, s 619(5); s 621(5); s 625(5); s 627(8) (all of which will come into force on 1 October 2009). Until 1 October 2009, see 1985 Act, s 122.

[237] 2006 Act, s 619(4); s 621(4); s 625(4); s 627(7) (all of which will come into force on 1 October 2009). Until 1 October 2009, see 1985 Act, s 122.

[238] See for example *Eley v Positive Government Security Life Assurance Co* (1875) 1 Ex D 20; *Rayfield v Hands* [1960] Ch 1; *Bushell v Faith* [1970] AC 1099; *Re Blue Arrow plc* [1987] BCLC 585.

[239] 2006 Act, s 629(1). See also *Cumbrian Newspaper Group Ltd v Cumberland & Westmorland Herald & Printing Co Ltd* [1987] Ch 1, 22 (Scott J). A Company's articles usually give it power to issue different classes of share: Table A reg 2; Model Article (pcls) 22; Model Article (plc) 43.

[240] 2006 Act, s 629(2), which comes into force on 1 October 2009, replacing 1985 Act, s 128(2) without changes.

[241] 2006 Act, s 630(5), which comes into force on 1 October 2009, replacing 1985 Act, s 125(7) without changes.

[242] 2006 Act, s 630(6), which comes into force on 1 October 2009, replacing 1985 Act, s 125(8) without changes. See also *White v Bristol Aeroplane Co Ltd* [1935] Ch 65; *Re John Smith's Tadcaster Brewery Co Ltd* [1953] Ch 308; *Greenhalgh v Arderne Cinemas Ltd* [1946] 1 All ER 512, CA.

[243] 2006 Act, s 630(2), which comes into force on 1 October 2009.

[244] 2006 Act, s 630(4), which comes into force on 1 October 2009 replacing 1985 Act, s 125(2) with changes.

The holders of not less in the aggregate than 15 per cent of the issued shares of the **24.102** class in question (being persons who did not consent to or vote in favour of the resolution for the variation) may apply to the court, within 21 days of the consent being given or the resolution passed, to have the variation cancelled.[245] If such an application is made, the variation has no effect unless and until it is confirmed by the court.[246] The court may, if satisfied having regard to all the circumstances of the case that the variation would unfairly prejudice[247] the shareholders of the class represented by the applicant, disallow the variation, and shall if not so satisfied confirm it.[248]

### Functions and liabilities of directors

Where the court makes such an order, the company must within 15 days forward **24.103** a copy of the order to the Registrar of Companies.[249] If this is not done, an offence (punishable by fine and daily default fine for continued contravention) is committed by every officer in default.[250]

A company must give a notice with particulars to the Registrar of Companies **24.104** within one month: (1) if it assigns a name or other description (or new name or new description) to any class or description of shares;[251] (2) if the rights attached to any shares are varied;[252] (3) if, being a company not having a share capital, it creates a new class of members[253] or assigns a name or other designation (or new

---

[245] 2006 Act, s 633(2), which comes into force on 1 October 2009 replacing 1985 Act, s 126 with changes. The applicants must either hold 15 per cent of the shares of the class affected or have been appointed in writing by the holders of 15 per cent at the date of the presentation of the petition and not merely when it comes on for a hearing: *Re Sound City (Films) Ltd* [1947] Ch 169; *Re Suburban & Provincial Stores Ltd* [1943] Ch 156. For this purpose any of the company's share capital held as treasury shares is disregarded.

[246] 2006 Act, s 633(3), which comes into force on 1 October 2009 replacing 1985 Act, s 127(2) without changes. The application must be made within 21 days after the date on which the consent was given or the resolution was passed and may be made on behalf of the shareholders entitled to make the application by such one or more of their number as they may appoint in writing for the purpose: s 633(4). See *Re Suburban & Provincial Stores Ltd* [1943] Ch 156 and *Re Sound City (Films) Ltd* [1947] Ch 169.

[247] See *British America Nickel Corp v O'Brien* [1927] AC 369.

[248] 2006 Act, s 634(5), which comes into force on 1 October 2009. The decision of the court on any such application is final, ie not subject to appeal, unless the reason for dismissing the application is procedural only, in which case an appeal will lie: *Re Suburban & Provincial Stores Ltd* [1943] Ch 156.

[249] 2006 Act, s 635(1) (in force from 1 October 2009; until which date see 1985 Act, s 127(4)).

[250] 2006 Act, s 635(2) and (3) (in force from 1 October 2009, replacing 1985 Act, s 127(5)).

[251] 2006 Act, s 636(1) (in force from 1 October 2009, replacing 1985 Act, s 128(4) with changes).

[252] 2006 Act, s 637(1) (in force from 1 October 2009, replacing 1985 Act, s 128(3) with changes).

[253] 2006 Act, s 638(1) (in force from 1 October 2009, replacing 1985 Act, s 129(1) with changes).

name or new designation) to any class of members[254] or varies the rights of any class of members.[255] Default in complying with any of these requirements is an offence (punishable by fine[256]) committed by every officer in default.[257]

### (2) Reduction of share capital

**24.105** In certain circumstances, the directors of a company may legitimately form the view that the company's capital exceeds its reasonable requirements and that it is desirable to repay a portion of the capital to the company's shareholders.[258] In other cases, the directors may take the view that there has been a loss of capital, eg through unprofitable trading, and that it is necessary to reduce the company's capital in order to restore reality to the company's accounts.[259]

**24.106** A company may reduce its share capital in any way.[260] In particular it may: (1) extinguish or reduce the liability on any of its shares in respect of share capital not paid up;[261] or (2) either with or without extinguishing or reducing liability on any of its shares, cancel any paid up share capital that is lost or unrepresented by its available assets[262] or repay any paid up share capital in excess of the company's wants.[263]

---

[254] 2006 Act, s 639(1) (in force from 1 October 2009, replacing 1985 Act, s 129(3) with changes).

[255] 2006 Act, s 640(1) (in force from 1 October 2009, replacing 1985 Act, s 129(2) with changes).

[256] 2006 Act, s 636(3); s 637(3); s 638(3); s 639(3); s 640(3) (all of which will come into force on 1 October 2009). Until 1 October 2009, see 1985 Act, s 128(5) and Schedule 24.

[257] 2006 Act, s 636(2); s 637(2); s 638(2); s 639(2); s 640(2); in force from 1 October 2009. Until 1 October 2009, see 1985 Act, s 129(4).

[258] *British and American Trustee and Finance Corporation v Couper* [1894] AC 399, 413, *Ex parte Westburn Sugar Refineries Ltd* [1951] AC 625.

[259] *Re Hoare & Co Ltd* [1904] 2 Ch 208; *Re Jupiter House Investments (Cambridge) Ltd* [1985] BCLC 222; *Re Grosvenor Press plc* [1985] BCLC 286; *Re Barrow Haematite Steel Co* [1900] 2 Ch 846.

[260] The provisions in the 2006 Act about reduction of capital, ss 641–657 come into force on 1 October 2009, replacing the corresponding provisions of 1985 Act, ss 135–141, except for the new provisions, contained in ss 641(a), (2)–(6), 642–644, 652(1) and (3) and 654, which came into force on 1 October 2008 (2006 Act Commencement Order No 7, art 2(a)–(c)). These new provisions enable a private company to reduce its capital if supported by a solvency statement and without a court order. The words 'in any way' first appeared in the Companies Act 1908 to confirm that there were no limits on a company's ability to reduce capital by cancelling paid-up capital not lost or unrepresented by available assets; cf *Re Anglo-French Exploration Co* [1902] 2 Ch 845, 854 (Lord Wrenbury); and see *Re Jupiter House Investments (Cambridge) Ltd* [1985] 1 WLR 975.

[261] 2006 Act, s 641(4)(a).

[262] 2006 Act, s 641(4)(b)(i); see also *Re Abstainers' and General Insurance Co* [1891] 2 Ch 124; *Re Barrow Haematite Steel Co* [1900] 2 Ch 846; *Re Hoare & Co Ltd* [1904] 2 Ch 208; *Re Jupiter House Investments (Cambridge) Ltd* [1985] 1 WLR 975.

[263] 2006 Act, s 641(4)(b)(ii); see also *Wilsons & Clyde Coal Co Ltd* [1949] AC 462; *Prudential Assurance Co Ltd v Chatterley Whitfield Collieries Co Ltd* [1949] AC 512; *Ex p Westburn Sugar Refineries Ltd* [1951] AC 625.

*Private companies: reduction of capital supported by solvency statement*

The 1985 Act provides that a reduction of capital cannot be achieved without **24.107** confirmation by the court.[264] However, this procedure has proved to be unduly cumbersome in cases of routine reductions by private companies, and the CLR recommended that private companies should be able to reduce share capital using a new solvency statement procedure for capital reductions.[265] This recommendation was adopted by the legislature, and the new solvency statement procedure for private companies, which permits a reduction of capital without court involvement, appears in ss 641 to 644 of the 2006 Act.

The solvency statement procedure involves three steps over a period of no more **24.108** than 30 days: (1) the making of a solvency statement by all the company's directors; (2) within 15 days, the passing of a special resolution;[266] and (3) within a further 15 days, the registration of the reduction with the Registrar. The reduction takes effect when the third step is completed.[267]

The lack of judicial scrutiny of the process means that the directors' solvency state- **24.109** ment possesses great significance. It is the means by which the process is commenced, and the primary material on which the shareholders of the company will form a view as to whether or not the reduction is viable. For this reason, the 2006 Act creates various offences in connection with the solvency statement.

A company may not reduce its share capital under the solvency statement proced- **24.110** ure if as a result of the reduction there would no longer be any member of the company holding shares other than redeemable shares.[268] The principle behind this requirement is that a private company limited by shares should not be capable of reducing its share capital to zero unless the reduction of capital is sanctioned by the court.[269]

Furthermore, a special resolution for the reduction of a company's capital may not **24.111** provide for a reduction to take effect later than the date on which the resolution

---

[264] 1985 Act, s 135(1). In addition, the 1985 Act provides that a reduction of capital could be achieved only if expressly permitted by the company's articles. The CLR recommended that the need for prior authorization in the articles be removed CLR: *Completing the Structure*, para 2.15. In line with this recommendation, the need for prior authorization in the articles has not been retained, although a company may expressly prohibit or restrict a reduction of capital by making provision to this effect in its articles: see 2006 Act, s 641(6).

[265] CLR: *Final Report*, para 10.6.

[266] Companies Act 2006, s 641(1)(a).

[267] 2006 Act, s 644(4) Accordingly, under the solvency statement procedure, it is not possible to resolve that a reduction will take effect in 16 or more days' time.

[268] 2006 Act, s 641(2).

[269] This replicates the equivalent provision in the 1985 Act, s 162(3), which applied to purchase of own shares.

has effect.[270] This restriction, which would operate to prevent a company passing a resolution on, say, 1 January stating that the reduction is to take effect on 1 October, is necessary to ensure that a reduction authorized at a time of solvency is not effected subsequently when the company's financial position has deteriorated. The 2006 Act, s 644(3) prescribes when the resolution takes effect—that is, when a copy of the resolution, supported by the solvency statement and a statement of capital, has been filed with and registered by the Registrar of Companies.

24.112   The 2006 Act, s 643, provides that a 'solvency statement' for these purposes is a statement that each of the directors: (1) has formed the opinion, as regards the company's situation at the date of the statement, that there is no ground on which the company could then be found to be unable to pay (or otherwise discharge) its debts;[271] and (2) has also formed the opinion (i) if it is intended to commence the winding up of the company within 12 months of that date, that the company will be able to pay (or otherwise discharge) its debts in full within 12 months of the commencement of the winding up or (ii) in any other case, that the company will be able to pay (or otherwise discharge) its debts as they fall due during the year immediately following that date.[272]

24.113   In forming the necessary opinions, the directors must take into account all of the company's liabilities, including any contingent or prospective liabilities.[273]

24.114   The solvency statement must be made by all the directors. If one or more of the directors is unable or unwilling to make this statement, the company will not be able to use the solvency statement procedure to effect a reduction of capital unless the dissenting director or directors resign (in which case the solvency statement must be made by all of the remaining directors).

24.115   Furthermore, the solvency statement must be 'in the prescribed form'.[274] The term 'prescribed' in this context means prescribed by the Secretary of State in regulations or by order made under the Act. The solvency statement must state the date on which it is made and the name of each director of the company but there is no requirement that the directors must all be in the same location when they make this statement.

24.116   If the directors make a solvency statement without having reasonable grounds for the opinions expressed in it, and the statement is delivered to the Registrar, an offence is committed by every officer in default.[275] The penalty on conviction on

---

270  2006 Act, s 641(5).
271  2006 Act, s 643(1)(a).
272  2006 Act, s 643(1)(b).
273  2006 Act, s 643(2).
274  2006 Act, s 643(3).
275  2006 Act, s 643(4).

indictment is imprisonment for a term not exceeding two years or a fine or both;[276] summary conviction may also result in imprisonment, but for a maximum of 12 months, or a fine not exceeding the statutory maximum, or both.[277]

The reduction must be authorized by special resolution which must be passed not **24.117** more than 15 days after the date of the making of the solvency statement.[278] Where the resolution is proposed as a written resolution, the company's directors should ensure that copies of the solvency statement are sent or submitted to every eligible member at or before the time at which the resolution is sent or submitted to him.[279] Where the resolution is proposed at a general meeting, the directors should ensure that a copy of the solvency statement is available for inspection by members at the meeting.[280]

A failure to observe these procedural requirements will not affect the validity of a **24.118** resolution to reduce capital.[281] However, it is an offence committed by every officer in default for a solvency statement which was not provided to the company's members in accordance with these requirements to be filed with the Registrar.[282] Since a reduction of capital by the solvency statement procedure will not become effective unless and until the resolution and the solvency statement are filed with the Registrar,[283] it is important to ensure that the solvency statement is sent to shareholders or made available at the meeting, because failure to comply with these requirements will mean that the reduction is not lawfully capable of taking effect.

Within 15 days after the date on which the resolution for reducing share capital is **24.119** passed, the company must deliver to the Registrar: (1) a copy of the solvency statement; and (2) a statement of capital.[284] The statement of capital must state (with respect to the company's share capital as reduced by the resolution): (1) the total number of shares of the company; (2) the aggregate nominal value of those shares; (3) for each class of share, particulars of the rights attached to the shares, the total number of shares of that class, and the aggregate nominal value of the shares of that class; and (4) the amount paid up and the amount (if any) unpaid on

---

276 2006 Act, s 643(4).
277 2006 Act, s 644(5).
278 2006 Act, s 642(1)(a).
279 2006 Act, s 642(2).
280 2006 Act, s 642(3).
281 2006 Act, s 642(4).
282 2006 Act, s 644(7).
283 2006 Act, s 644(1), (4).
284 2006 Act, s 644(1).

each share.[285] The Registrar must register these documents on receipt.[286] The reduction will take effect upon such registration.[287]

**24.120** In addition, the company must deliver to the Registrar, within 15 days after the resolution is passed, a statement by the directors confirming that the solvency statement was: (1) made not more than 15 days before the date on which the resolution was passed; and (2) provided to the company's members in accordance with the statutory requirements.[288]

**24.121** Although the late delivery of the solvency statement and statement of capital, or the non-delivery of the statement confirming the solvency statement's compliance with the statutory requirements will not affect the validity of the resolution,[289] these defaults will give rise to an offence committed by every officer in default (and by the company itself) punishable by fine.[290] It is therefore important to ensure that the statutory requirements are strictly observed. Furthermore, an offence committed by every officer in default for a solvency statement which was not provided to the company's members in accordance with these requirements to be filed with the Registrar.[291]

*Reduction of capital by order of the court; private and public companies*

**24.122** For public companies, reduction of capital by way of a special resolution confirmed by order of the court remains the only means of lawfully achieving a reduction.[292] This route is also open to private companies, although the solvency statement procedure is likely to be used by private companies in the majority of cases.

**24.123** Section 646 provides that creditors may object to a reduction of capital. This section will always apply where the proposed reduction of capital involves either diminution of liability in respect of unpaid share capital or the payment to a shareholder of any paid up share capital, unless the court orders otherwise.[293]

---

[285] 2006 Act, s 644(2).
[286] 2006 Act, s 644(3).
[287] 2006 Act, s 644(4).
[288] 2006 Act, s 644(5).
[289] 2006 Act, s 644(6).
[290] 2006 Act, s 644(9).
[291] 2006 Act, s 644(7).
[292] 2006 Act, s 641(1)(b) replacing 1985 Act, s 135(1) with changes. The provisions concerning reduction of capital confirmed by the court come into force on 1 October 2009 to replace the corresponding provisions of the 1985 Act.
[293] 2006 Act, s 645(2), which, replaces 1985 Act, s 136(2) and (6) without changes. The disapplication of s 646 is not an 'all or nothing' matter, since the court may, if having regard to any special circumstances of the case it thinks proper to do so, direct that s 646 is not to apply as regards any class or classes of creditors: 2006 Act, s 645(3) (replacing 1985 Act, 136(6) without changes).

In all other cases, s 646 is prima facie inapplicable, although the court has power in any case to direct that it is to apply.[294]

Where the section applies automatically or is applied by the court, every creditor **24.124** of the company who would be entitled to prove in the company's winding up[295] is entitled to object to the reduction of capital.[296] The court is required to settle a list of creditors[297] and for this purpose is required to ascertain the names of the creditors and the nature and amount of their debts or claims.[298] The court may also publish notices fixing a day or days within which creditors must apply to be included on the list or (if they fail to apply) be excluded from the right to object to the reduction of capital.[299]

If a creditor on the list does not consent to the reduction, the court may dispense **24.125** with the consent of that creditor, provided that the company secures payment of his debt or claim.[300] The debt or claim must be secured by appropriating either the full amount of the debt or claim or (if the company does not admit the liability) such amount as may be fixed by the court after an enquiry.[301]

The court has no jurisdiction to confirm a reduction of capital unless it is satisfied **24.126** that every creditor entitled to object has either consented to the reduction or had his debt paid or secured.[302] Where these requirements are satisfied, the court may make an order[303] confirming the reduction on such terms and condition as it thinks fit.[304] Where the court confirms the reduction, it may order the company to publish (1) the reasons for the reduction or such other information in regard to it as the court thinks expedient with a view to giving proper information to the public[305] and (2) the causes that led to the reduction.[306]

---

[294] 2006 Act, s 645(4) (replacing 1985 Act, s 136(2) without changes).
[295] ie including contingent and prospective creditors.
[296] 2006 Act, s 646(1) (replacing 1985 Act, s 136(3) without changes).
[297] 2006 Act, s 646(2) (replacing 1985 Act, s 136(4) without changes).
[298] 2006 Act, s 646(3)(a) (replacing 1985 Act, s 136(4) without changes).
[299] 2006 Act, s 646(3)(b) (replacing 1985 Act, s 136(4) without changes).
[300] 2006 Act, s 646(4) (replacing 1985 Act, s 136(5) without changes).
[301] 2006 Act, s 646(5) (replacing 1985 Act, s 136(5) without changes).
[302] 2006 Act, s 648(2) (replacing 1985 Act, s 137(1) without changes).
[303] As to the scope of the court's jurisdiction, see *British and American Corporation v Couper* [1894] AC 399, *Poole v National Bank of China* [1907] AC 229, and *Re Grosvenor Press Ltd* [1985] 1 WLR 980.
[304] 2006 Act, s 648(1) (replacing s 137(1) of the 1985 Act without changes). The court may, for example, impose a condition that the articles shall be so altered that the shares reduced in amount shall also be reduced in voting power: *Re Pinkey & Sons SS Co* [1892] 3 Ch 125; *Re Continental Union Gas Co* (1891) 7 TLR 47.
[305] See, for example, *Re Truman, Hanbury & Co* [1910] 2 Ch 498.
[306] 2006 Act, s 648(3) (replacing 1985 Act, s 137(2)(b) without changes).

*Statement of capital*

**24.127**   The court must also approve a statement of capital[307] which must state (with respect to the company's capital as altered by the order): (1) the total number of shares of the company; (2) the aggregate nominal value of those shares; (3) for each class of shares, (i) prescribed particulars of the rights attached to the shares, (ii) the total number of shares of that class, and (iii) the aggregate nominal value of shares of that class; and (4) the amount paid up and the amount (if any) unpaid on each share (whether on account of the nominal value of the share or by way of premium).[308]

**24.128**   The court's order and the statement of capital must be registered[309] (subject to special provisions applying where a public company's capital is reduced below the authorized minimum; see below). The reduction of capital takes effect on the registration of the order and statement of capital,[310] unless it is part of a compromise or arrangement sanctioned by the court under Part 26, in which case it takes effect on delivery to the Registrar (rather than actual registration) unless the court orders otherwise.[311]

**24.129**   The Registrar must certify the registration of the order and statement of capital[312] and the certificate must be signed by the Registrar and authenticated by the Registrar's official seal.[313] Such a certificate will be conclusive evidence that the statutory requirements relating to a reduction of capital were satisfied and that the company's share capital is as stated in the statement of capital.[314]

**24.130**   Where by order of the court the nominal value of a public company's allotted capital is reduced below the authorized minimum, the Registrar must not register the order unless: (1) the court so directs;[315] or (2) the company is first re-registered as a private company.[316] Section 651 provides an expedited procedure for re-registration in these circumstances.

**24.131**   Although s 646(2) charges the court with the task of settling a list of creditors, and s 646(3) mandates the court to find out about the company's creditors, the practical reality is that the court will be heavily dependent on information provided by

---

[307]   2006 Act, s 649(1) (replacing 1985 Act, s 138(1) with changes).
[308]   2006 Act, s 649(2) (a new provision).
[309]   2006 Act, s 649(1) (replacing 1985 Act, s 138(1) with changes).
[310]   2006 Act, s 649(3)(b) (replacing 1985 Act, s 138(2) with changes).
[311]   2006 Act, s 649(3)(a) (replacing 1985 Act, s 138(2) with changes).
[312]   2006 Act, s 649(5) (replacing 1985 Act, s 138(4) with changes).
[313]   2006 Act, s 649(6)(a) (replacing 1985 Act, s 138(4) with changes).
[314]   2006 Act, s 649(6)(b) (replacing 1985 Act, s 138(4) with changes).
[315]   See, for example, *Re Minster Assets plc* [1985] BCLC 2000.
[316]   2006 Act, s 650(1), (2) (replacing s 139(1) of 1985 Act without changes).

the company itself. For this reason, the court will expect to be provided with full and accurate information by the company's directors.

To fortify the directors' obligation to provide the court with information, s 647 **24.132** provides that it is an offence for any officer of the company intentionally or recklessly to conceal the name of a creditor entitled to object to a reduction of capital or misrepresent the nature and amount of the debt or claim of a creditor.[317] It is also an offence for any officer of the company to be knowingly concerned in any such concealment or misrepresentations.[318] These offences are punishable on conviction on indictment to a fine or on summary conviction to a fine not exceeding the statutory maximum.[319]

### (3) Public companies: serious loss of capital

Where the net assets of a public company are half or less of its called up share capi- **24.133** tal, the directors are under a statutory obligation to call a general meeting of the company to consider whether any, and if so what, steps should be taken to deal with the situation.[320] The meeting must be called (ie notice given) not later than 28 days from the earliest day on which one or more directors of the company becomes aware of the fact that the net assets are half or less of the called up share capital[321] and must be convened for a date not later than 56 days from that date.[322] In other words, the section begins to operate from the moment a single director becomes aware of the fact. However, it will be difficult in practice to know whether or not the section applies, because difficult questions are likely to arise when making the necessary calculations, particularly having regard to the different methods of valuing assets.

If there is a failure to convene a meeting in accordance with the statutory require- **24.134** ments, an offence (punishable by fine[323]) is committed by each of the directors of the company who knowingly authorizes or permits the failure or (after the period during which the meeting should have been convened) knowingly authorizes or permits the failure to continue.

---

[317] 2006 Act, s 647(1)(a), replacing (with changes) 1985 Act, s 141, which continues to apply until that date.

[318] 2006 Act, s 647(1)(b) (replacing s 141 of 1985 Act with changes).

[319] 2006 Act, s 647(2) (replacing 1985 Act, s 141, Schedule 24).

[320] 2006 Act, s 656(1) (in force from 1 October 2009). This section re-enacts s 142 of the 1985 Act which was itself a re-enactment of s 34 of the Companies Act 1980, which was introduced as a result of the provisions of the Second Directive on Company Law.

[321] 2006 Act, s 656(2) (in force from 1 October 2009, replacing 1985 Act, s 142(1)).

[322] 2006 Act, s 656(3) (in force from 1 October 2009, replacing 1985 Act, s 142(1)). The usual requirements as to notice etc must be complied with in the ordinary way.

[323] 2006 Act, s 656(5) (in force from 1 October 2009, replacing 1985 Act, s 142(1), Schedule 24).

## (4) Acquisition by limited company of its own shares

**24.135**   In *Trevor v Whitworth*,[324] the House of Lords held that a company could not be a member of itself, and that a purchase by a company of its own shares, although expressly authorized by its articles, was *ultra vires* and an unauthorized reduction of capital contrary to the interests of the creditors. A transaction which upon closer examination can be seen to involve an unlawful return of capital to a member, whether directly or indirectly, is void.[325]

**24.136**   The common law position has for many years been replaced by a similar statutory prohibition. After 1 October 2009, the general rule will be contained in s 658 of the Act, which provides that a limited company must not acquire its own shares, whether by purchase, subscription, or otherwise, except in accordance with the provisions of Part 18 of the Act.[326]

**24.137**   If a company purports to acquire its own shares in contravention of this general rule, the purported acquisition is void,[327] and an offence is committed by the company and every officer in default.[328] A person guilty of this offence is liable on conviction on indictment to imprisonment for a term not exceeding two years or a fine or both or on summary conviction to imprisonment for a term not exceeding 12 months or a fine not exceeding the statutory maximum.[329]

**24.138**   The general rule is subject to a number of important exceptions. First, s 658 of the Act does not prohibit a limited company from acquiring any of its own fully paid shares otherwise than for valuation consideration, eg by way of legacy or gift,[330] because such an acquisition does not have the effect of depleting the company's assets.[331] However, since the company cannot be a member of itself, the general rule is that shares must be vested in a nominee to be held on the company's behalf

---

[324]   (1887) 12 App Cas 409.

[325]   *Barclays Bank plc v British & Commonwealth Holdings plc* [1996] 1 BCLC 1; *Aveling Barford Ltd v Perion* [1989] BCLC 626.

[326]   2006 Act, s 658(1) (in force from 1 October 2009, replacing 1985 Act, s 143(1) without changes). It should be noted that this provision does not prohibit Company A from acquiring shares in Company B in circumstances where Company B's sole asset is shares in Company A: *Acatos & Hutcheson plc v Watson* [1995] 1 BCLC 218.

[327]   2006 Act, s 658(2)(b) (in force from 1 October 2009, replacing 1985 Act, s 143(2) without changes). See, for example, *Vision Express (UK) Ltd v Wilson* [1995] 2 BCLC 419 and *Re R W Peak (King's Lynn) Ltd* [1998] 1 BCLC 193.

[328]   2006 Act, s 658(2)(a) (in force from 1 October 2009, replacing 1985 Act, s 143(2) without changes).

[329]   2006 Act, s 658(3) (in force from 1 October 2009, replacing 1985 Act, s 143(3) without changes).

[330]   2006 Act, s 659(1) (in force from 1 October 2009, replacing 1985 Act, s 143(3) without changes); see also *Kirby v Wilkins* [1929] 2 Ch 444 and *Re Castiglione's Will Trusts* [1958] Ch 549.

[331]   However, as a company cannot be a member of itself, the shares must be vested in a nominee to be held on the company's behalf and may be voted as the company directs.

and may be voted as the company directs.[332] Now a company may hold 'qualifying shares' as treasury shares (paragraphs 24.207–24.211 below).

Secondly, the 2006 Act s 658, does not prohibit: (1) the acquisition of shares in a reduction of capital duly made;[333] (2) the purchase of shares in pursuance of an order of the court[334] under s 98 (application to court to cancel resolution for re-registration as a private company), s 721(6) (powers of court on objection to redemption or purchase of shares out of capital), s 759 (remedial order in case of breach of prohibition of public offers by private company), or Part 30 (protection of members against unfair prejudice);[335] or (3) the forfeiture of shares, or the acceptance of shares surrendered in lieu, in pursuance of the company's articles, for failure to pay any sum payable in respect of the shares. In each case, however, failure to comply with the correct procedure will mean that the general rule applies and the purported acquisition will be void.[336] **24.139**

Additionally, a company is not precluded by s 658 from acquiring the shares of another company in circumstances in which the sole asset of the acquired company is shares in the acquiring company.[337] However, in view of the potential for abuse and adverse consequences for shareholders and creditors, the court will look carefully at such transactions to see that the directors of the acquiring company have acted with an eye solely to the interests of the acquiring company (and not eg to the interests of the directors) and have fulfilled their fiduciary duties to safeguard the interests of shareholders and creditors alike. **24.140**

Finally, and most importantly, a company will be able to acquire its own shares in accordance with Chapter 4 of Part 18 of the 2006 Act. The provisions of Chapter 4 of Part 18, which constitute a major exception to the general principle, are considered in detail below. **24.141**

If shares are taken by a subscriber to the memorandum as nominee of the company or are issued to a nominee of the company or are acquired by a nominee of the company, partly paid up, from a third person, then the nominee is treated as holding the shares on his own account, so that the company has no beneficial interest in them.[338] **24.142**

---

[332] *Re Castiglione's Will Trusts* [1958] Ch 549; see also *Kirby v Wilkins* [1929] 2 Ch 444.

[333] 2006 Act, s 659(2)(a) (in force from 1 October 2009, replacing 1985 Act, s 143(3) without changes).

[334] In all of these cases, the court's power to order a company to acquire its own shares is preserved as a means of remedying some other default.

[335] 2006 Act, s 659(2)(b) (in force from 1 October 2009, replacing 1985 Act, s 143(3) without changes).

[336] *Re R W Peak (King's Lynn) Ltd* [1998] 1 BCLC 193.

[337] *Acatos & Hutcheson plc v Watson* [1995] 1 BCLC 218.

[338] 2006 Act, s 660(1), (2) (in force from 1 October 2009, replacing 1985 Act, s 144(1) with changes). This section is not intended to apply to employee share schemes: see 2006 Act, s 660(3) (also in force from 1 October 2009, replacing 1985 Act, s 145(1) and (2)(a) without changes).

**24.143** In addition, if the nominee, having been called on to pay any amount for the purpose of paying up or paying any premium on the shares, fails to pay that amount within 21 days from being called on to do so, then, in the case of shares that he agreed to take as subscriber to the memorandum, the other subscribers are jointly and severally liable with him to pay that amount, and, in any other case, the directors of the company when the shares were issued to or acquired by him are jointly and severally liable with him to pay that amount.[339]

**24.144** However, if the subscriber or director acted honestly and reasonably and having regard to all the circumstances ought fairly to be relieved from liability, the court may relieve him, either wholly or in part, from his liability on such terms as the court thinks fit.[340] Similarly, any subscriber or director who has reason to apprehend that a claim will or might be made for the recovery of any such amount may apply to the court to be relieved from liability.[341]

*Public companies: cancellation, re-registration*

**24.145** Where a public company[342] acquires a beneficial interest in its own shares in the special circumstances described in s 622(1), the company must cancel the shares and diminish the amount of its share capital by the nominal value of the shares cancelled.[343] Where the effect of such cancellation is that the nominal value of the company's allotted share capital is brought below the authorized minimum, the company must apply for re-registration[344] as a private company, stating the effect of the cancellation.[345] Cancellation must occur within a prescribed period from the date of forfeiture or surrender or acquisition (as the case may be).[346] Before such cancellation, neither the company nor its nominee may exercise any

---

[339] 2006 Act, s 661(1), (2) (in force from 1 October 2009, replacing 1985 Act, s 144(2) with changes).

[340] 2006 Act, s 661(3), which comes into force on 1 October 2009 and replaces 1985 Act, s 144(3) without changes.

[341] 2006 Act, s 661(4) (in force from 1 October 2009 to replace 1985 Act, 144(4) without changes).

[342] Or a private company which subsequently re-registers as a public company: see 2006 Act, s 668.

[343] 2006 Act, s 662(1), (2)(a) (in force from 1 October 2009; replacing 146(1), (2) without changes).

[344] Consequential provisions relating to re-registration may be found in ss 664–665; these provisions come into force on 1 October 2009, until which date the matter continues to be governed by 1985 Act, s 147.

[345] 2006 Act, s 662(2)(b) (in force from 1 October 2009, replacing 1985 Act, s 146(2) without changes).

[346] 2006 Act, s 662(3) (in force from 1 October 2009, replacing 1985 Act, s 146(2) and (3) without changes).

voting rights in respect of the shares[347] and any purported exercise of those rights is void.[348]

**24.146** Where a company cancels shares in order to comply with this requirement, it must notify the Registrar of the cancellation within a month of the date of cancellation.[349] The notice must be accompanied by a statement of capital[350] which must state, with respect to the company's share capital immediately following cancellation, (1) the total number of shares of the company, (2) the aggregate nominal value of those shares, (3) for each class of shares, (i) prescribed particulars of the rights attached to the shares, (ii) the total number of shares of that class, and (iii) the aggregate nominal value of the shares of that class, and (d) the amount paid up and the amount (if any) unpaid on each share (whether on account of the nominal value of the share or by way of premium).[351]

*Cancellation, re-registration: criminal liabilities of directors*

**24.147** If a public company required to cancel shares under s 662 fails to do so within the three-year time period, a summary offence punishable by fine[352] is committed by every officer in default.[353] If the company cancels the shares but fails to notify the Registrar within one month of cancellation or fails to provide a statement of capital to the Registrar together with the notice, an offence (punishable on summary conviction by way of fine[354]) is committed by every officer of the company in default.[355] Finally, if a public company cancels shares but fails within the appropriate period to re-register as a private company (in circumstances where its share capital has fallen below the 'authorized minimum' required by s 763), a summary offence punishable by fine[356] is committed by every officer in default.[357]

---

[347] 2006 Act, s 662(5) (in force from 1 October 2009, replacing 1985 Act, s 146(4) without changes).

[348] 2006 Act, s 662(6) (in force from 1 October 2009, replacing 1985 Act, s 146(4) without changes).

[349] 2006 Act, s 663(1) (in force from 1 October 2009, replacing 1985 Act, s 122(1)(f) without changes).

[350] 2006 Act, s 663(2), which comes into force on 1 October 2009; a new provision.

[351] 2006 Act, s 663(3) (in force from 1 October 2009); a further new provision.

[352] 2006 Act, s 667(3) (again from 1 October 2009, replacing 1985 Act, s 149(2), Schedule 24).

[353] 2006 Act, s 667(1)(a), (2) (in force from 1 October 2009, replacing 1985 Act, s 149(2) without changes).

[354] 2006 Act, s 663(5) (in force from 1 October 2009, replacing 1985 Act, s 122(2), Schedule 24, without changes).

[355] 2006 Act, s 663(4) (in force from 1 October 2009, replacing 1985 Act, s 122(2) without changes).

[356] 2006 Act, s 667(3) (in force from 1 October 2009, replacing 1985 Act, s 149(2), Schedule 24).

[357] 2006 Act, s 667(1)(b), (2) (in force from 1 October 2009).

### (5) Financial assistance for purchase of own shares

**24.148** The prohibition on financial assistance arose out of recommendations of the Greene Committee in 1926 to deal with a practice subsequently described by Lord Greene MR in *Re VGM Holdings Ltd*:[358]

> Those whose memories enable them to recall what had been happening after the last war for several years will remember that a very common form of transaction in connection with companies was one by which persons—call them financiers, speculators, or what you will—finding a company with a substantial cash balance or easily realisable assets such as war loan, bought up the whole or the greater part of the shares of the company for cash and so arranged matters that the purchase money which they then became bound to provide was advanced to them by the company whose shares they were acquiring, either out of its cash balance or by realisation of its liquid investments. That type of transaction was a common one, and it gave rise to great dissatisfaction and, in some cases, great scandals.[359]

**24.149** Financial assistance by a company for the purpose of purchasing the company's own shares was first prohibited by the 1929 Act, s 45. Arden LJ summarized the legislative history in *Chaston v SWP Group plc*:[360]

> Section 45 of the Companies Act 1929 . . . was enacted as a result of the previously common practice of purchasing the shares of a company having a substantial cash balance or readily available assets and so arranging matters that the purchase money was lent by the company to the purchaser . . . The general mischief . . . [is] that the resources of the target company and its subsidiaries should not be used directly or indirectly to assist the purchaser financially to make the acquisition. This may prejudice the interests of the creditors of the target or its group, and the interests of any shareholders who do not accept the offer to acquire their shares or to whom the offer is not made.[361]

*No prohibition for assistance by private company*

**24.150** Since 1929, the prohibition on such financial assistance has extended to public and private companies. In 2005, however, the CLR concluded that specific statutory prohibitions were unnecessary in the case of private companies as the mischief in question could be controlled by other means:

> The provisions on financial assistance are designed to protect creditors and shareholders against the misuse and depletion of a company's assets. The CLR concluded that it was inappropriate for private companies to continue to carry the cost of complying with the rules on financial assistance as abusive transactions could be controlled in other ways, e.g. through the provisions on directors duties . . . or through the

---

[358] [1942] Ch 235.
[359] Ibid 239; see also *Selangor United Rubber Estates Ltd v Cradock (No 3)* [1968] 1 WLR 1555; *Wallersteiner v Moir* [1974] 1 WLR 991.
[360] [2003] 1 BCLC 675.
[361] Ibid 686.

wrongful trading and market abuse provisions . . . Private companies will therefore no longer be prevented from providing financial assistance for the purchase of their own shares.[362]

In order to give effect to the reform recommended by the CLR the restrictions in **24.151** the 1985 Act, ss 151–153 and 155–158 on the giving by a private company of financial assistance for the acquisition of its own shares, including the 'whitewash' procedure have been repealed as from 1 October 2008.[363] The relevant provisions of the 2006 Act, which come into force on 1 October 2009 to replace the corresponding provisions of the 1985 Act, will only prohibit the giving of financial assistance in relation to acquisition of shares in public companies.[364] However, private companies will still come within the scope of the legislation where they are subsidiaries of a public company and are providing financial assistance for the purpose of an acquisition of shares in a public company, unless one of the exceptions set out in s 682 is available.[365]

*Meaning of 'financial assistance'*

The term 'financial assistance' is explained by s 677(1): **24.152**

> (1) In this Chapter 'financial assistance' means—
>   (a) financial assistance given by way of gift,
>   (b) financial assistance given—
>     (i) by way of guarantee, security or indemnity (other than an indemnity in respect of the indemnifier's own neglect or default), or
>     (ii) by way of release or waiver,
>   (c) financial assistance given—
>     (i) by way of a loan or any other agreement under which any of the obligations of the person giving the assistance are to be fulfilled at a time when in accordance with the agreement any obligation of another party to the agreement remains unfulfilled, or
>     (ii) by way of the novation of, or the assignment (in Scotland, assignation) of rights arising under, a loan or such other agreement, or

---

[362] White Paper, Company Law Reform, p 41. For the history of this reform, see CLR: *Proposals for Reform of Sections 151–158 of the Companies Act 1985* (October 1993) and CLR: *Financial assistance by a company for the acquisition of its own shares* (November 1996 and April 1997). See also CLR: *The Strategic Framework* at paras 5.4.20–5.4.25; CLR: *Company Formation and Capital Maintenance* (October 1999); CLR: *Completing the Structure* at paras 7.12–7.15; CLR: *Final Report* at para 2.30.

[363] 2006 Act Commencement Order No 5, art 5(2) and 8(b) and Schedule 3.

[364] Attempts to reform the law relating to financial assistance by public companies are hampered by the requirements of the Second Directive on Company Law (EEC 77/91) which provides that a public company may not advance funds, nor make loans, nor provide security, with a view to the acquisition of its shares by a third party: see, specifically, article 23.

[365] See, specifically, s 682(1)(a), (2) (in force from 1 October 2009).

   (d) any other financial assistance given by a company where—

      (i) the net assets of which are reduced to a material extent by the giving of the assistance, or

      (ii) the company has no net assets.

**24.153** Each limb of this definition re-uses the term 'financial assistance' without ever defining it.[366] This omission is particularly important in light of the broad words of paragraph (d), as Ward LJ observed in *Chaston v SWP Group plc*:[367]

> I can understand [a] to [c] and they seem all to be related to direct or indirect assistance given for the actual acquisition of the shares, that is to say help in meeting the consideration for the transaction. But [d] tells one nothing about what comprises financial assistance. The words are as wide as they can be—'any other financial assistance'. Rather it tells you when financial assistance is not financial assistance, namely when it is de minimis.[368]

**24.154** In the absence of a statutory definition, the task of explaining the meaning of the term has been performed by the courts. Perhaps the most commonly cited explanation is that of Hoffmann J in *Charterhouse Investment Trust Ltd v Tempest Diesels Ltd*:[369]

> There is no definition of giving financial assistance in the section, although some examples are given. The words have no technical meaning and their frame of reference is in my judgment the language of ordinary commerce. One must examine the commercial realities of the transaction and decide whether it can properly be described as the giving of financial assistance by the company, bearing in mind that the section is a penal one and should not be strained to cover transactions which are not fairly within it.[370]

**24.155** The meaning of the term 'financial assistance' was also considered in *MT Realisations Ltd v Digital Equipment Co Ltd*,[371] in which Mummery LJ referred to the words of the Federal Court of Australia in *Sterileair Pty Ltd v Papallo*:[372] 'Assistance involves something in the nature of aid or help. It cannot exist in a vacuum; it must be given to someone.' However, it is not enough merely for there to be assistance; the section will not apply unless the assistance is financial.[373]

---

[366] *Charterhouse Investment Trust Ltd v Tempest Diesels Ltd* [1986] BCLC 1, 10; *Chaston v SWP Group plc* [2003] 1 BCLC 675, 687.

[367] [2003] 1 BCLC 675.

[368] Ibid 694.

[369] [1986] BCLC 1.

[370] Ibid 10. This passage was cited with approval by Aldous LJ in *Barclays Bank plc v British & Commonwealth Holdings plc* [1996] 1 WLR 1, 15 and by Arden LJ *in Chaston v SWP Group plc* [2003] 1 BCLC 675, 687.

[371] [2003] 2 BCLC 117, 124.

[372] (1998) 29 ACSR 461.

[373] *Barclays Bank plc v British & Commonwealth Holdings plc* [1996] 1 WLR 1, 15 (Aldous LJ)

In most cases, the financial assistance takes the form of direct contributions **24.156** towards the consideration payable for the shares. Indeed, in *Brady v Brady*,[374] Lord Oliver said that the use of the target company's assets to fund the purchase price is the 'obvious mischief' at which the section is aimed.[375]

However, as the decision of the Court of Appeal in *Chaston v SWP Group plc*[376] **24.157** makes clear, this is not the only prohibited form of financial assistance. In that case, a purchaser (SWP) wished to acquire shares in a company (DCR). SWP wished to carry out a 'due diligence' exercise. DCR paid for a firm of accountants (D&T) to carry out some of the work necessary for the 'due diligence' exercise. As a result, SWP avoided the cost of instructing its own accountants (C&L) to carry out this work. As Buxton LJ held:

> The first obvious conclusion was that if D&T did not do the spadework for the due diligence exercise, then SWP's accountants, C&L, would have had to dig for the information clearly thought to be material to the exercise and C&L would then have charged SWP for doing that work. DCR's incurring those liabilities and discharging part of those debts was, therefore, of financial assistance to SWP. [Therefore] SWP was helped by not having to put its hand in its pocket for part of the fees that would otherwise be incurred in the due diligence exercise.[377]

The payment of D&T's fees by DCR was financial assistance because, as Arden LJ **24.158** observed, 'both the purchaser and the vendors were relieved of any obligation to pay for this service themselves'.[378]

The Court of Appeal's conclusion in the *Chaston* case demonstrates that financial **24.159** assistance is not limited to situations in which the target company actually provides the consideration payable by the purchaser in respect of the shares. It is important to emphasize, however, that each case turns on its own facts. As Arden LJ observed in *Chaston v SWP Group plc*:[379]

> Accordingly, the question whether financial assistance exists in any given case may be fact-sensitive and not one which can be answered simply by applying a legal definition.

Financial assistance will exist where the purchaser obtains a loan to finance the **24.160** acquisition which is then guaranteed by the target company.[380] Similarly, financial assistance will exist where the target company buys an asset from a potential

---

374 [1989] AC 755.
375 Ibid 780.
376 [2003] 1 BCLC 675.
377 Ibid 693.
378 Ibid 698.
379 [2003] 1 BCLC 675, 689.
380 *Arab Bank plc v Mercantile Holdings Ltd* [1994] Ch 71; *Coulthard v Neville Russell* [1998] 1 BCLC 143; *Re Continental Assurance Co of London plc* [1997] 1 BCLC 48.

717

purchaser at an overvalue in order to provide the potential purchaser with funds with which to finance the acquisition of shares in the target company.[381]

*Prohibitions of financial assistance*

**24.161**   There are four separate prohibitions.

**24.162**   First, s 678(1) provides that where a person is proposing to acquire shares in a public company, it is not lawful for that company, or a company that is a subsidiary[382] of that company, to give financial assistance directly or indirectly for the purpose of the acquisition before or at the same time as the acquisition takes place. However, s 678(1) does not prohibit a company from giving financial assistance for the acquisition of shares in it or its holding company if: (a) the company's principal purpose in giving the assistance is not to give it for the purpose of any such acquisition; or (b) the giving of the assistance for that purpose is only an incidental part of some larger purpose of the company; provided that, in either case, the assistance is given in good faith in the interests of the company.[383]

**24.163**   Secondly, s 678(3) provides that where a person has acquired shares in a company and a liability has been incurred (by that or another person) for the purpose of the acquisition, it is not lawful for that company, or a company that is a subsidiary of that company, to give financial assistance directly or indirectly for the purpose of reducing or discharging the liability if, at the time the assistance is given, the company in which the shares were acquired is a public company. However, section 678(3) does not prohibit a company from giving financial assistance if: (a) the company's principal purpose in giving the assistance is not to reduce or discharge any liability incurred by a person for the purpose of the acquisition of shares in the company or its holding company; or (b) the reduction or discharge of any such liability is only an incidental part of some larger purpose of the company; provided that, in either case, the assistance is given in good faith in the interests of the company.[384]

**24.164**   Thirdly, s 679(1) provides that where a person is acquiring or proposing to acquire shares in a private company, it is not lawful for a public company that is a subsidiary of that company to give financial assistance directly or indirectly for the

---

[381] *Belmont Finance Corp v Williams Furniture (No 2)* [1980] 1 All ER 393.

[382] In *Arab Bank plc v Mercantile Holdings Ltd* [1994] Ch 71 the question arose whether it is sufficient if the company providing the assistance is a foreign subsidiary. Millett J held that the phrase 'any of its subsidiaries' had to be construed as being limited to subsidiaries which are companies incorporated under English law, and that a foreign subsidiary was therefore not prohibited from giving financial assistance for the purpose of the acquisition of shares in its English parent company.

[383] 2006 Act, s 678(2) (in force from 1 October 2009, replacing 1985 Act, s 153(1)).

[384] 2006 Act, s 678(4) (in force from 1 October 2009, replacing 1985 Act, s 153(2)).

purpose of the acquisition before or at the same time as the acquisition takes place. However, s 679(1) does not prohibit a company from giving financial assistance for the acquisition of shares in its holding company if: (a) the company's principal purpose in giving the assistance is not to give it for the purpose of any such acquisition; or (b) the giving of the assistance for that purpose is only an incidental part of some larger purpose of the company; provided that, in either case, the assistance is given in good faith in the interests of the company.[385]

Fourthly, s 679(3) provides that where a person has acquired shares in a private **24.165** company and a liability has been incurred by that or another person for the purpose of the acquisition, it is not lawful for a public company that is a subsidiary of that company to give financial assistance directly or indirectly for the purpose of reducing or discharging the liability. However, s 679(3) does not prohibit a company from giving financial assistance if: (a) the company's principal purpose in giving the assistance is not to reduce or discharge any liability incurred by a person for the purpose of the acquisition of its shares in its holding company; or (b) the reduction or discharge of any such liability is only an incidental part of some larger purpose of the company; and, in either case, the assistance is given in good faith in the interests of the company.[386]

*The meaning of 'purpose'*

In each of the four cases identified above, the statutory prohibition will apply if **24.166** the assistance was given either: (a) 'for the purpose' of the acquisition;[387] or (b) for 'for the purpose' of discharging a liability incurred 'for the purpose' of the acquisition.[388] But none of the statutory prohibitions will apply: (a) if the company's 'principal purpose' is not to give assistance 'for the purpose' of the acquisition or to reduce or discharge any liability incurred 'for the purpose' of the acquisition;[389] or (b) if the giving of the assistance for the prohibited purpose 'is only an incidental part of some larger purpose' of the company.[390]

---

[385] 2006 Act, s 679(2) (in force from 1 October 2009, replacing 1985 Act, s 153(1) with changes).

[386] 2006 Act, s 679(4) (in force from 1 October 2009, replacing 1985 Act, s 153(2) with changes).

[387] 2006 Act, ss 678(1) and 679(1) (in force from 1 October 2009, replacing 1985 Act, s 151(1), with changes).

[388] 2006 Act, ss 678(3) and 679(3) (in force from 1 October 2009, replacing 1985 Act, s 151(2) with changes).

[389] 2006 Act, ss 678(2)(a), (4)(a), 679(2)(a), (4)(a) (all of which come into force on 1 October 2009). Until 1 October 2009, the reader is referred to 1985 Act, ss 151, 153.

[390] 2006 Act, ss 678(2)(b), (4)(b), 679(2)(b), (4)(b) (from 1 October 2009). Again, until 1 October 2009, see 1985 Act, ss 151, 153.

**24.167**    The meaning of the word 'purpose' in this context was considered in detail by the House of Lords in *Brady v Brady*.[391] The key passage appears in the speech of Lord Oliver:

> My Lords, 'purpose' is, in some contexts, a word of wide content but in construing it in the context of the fasciculus of sections regulating the provision of finance by a company in connection with the purchase of its own shares there has always to be borne in mind the mischief against which [the statutory prohibition] is aimed. In particular, if the section is not, effectively, to be deprived of any useful application, it is important to distinguish between a purpose and the reason why a purpose is formed. The ultimate reason for forming the purpose of financing an acquisition may, and in most cases probably will, be more important to those making the decision than the immediate transaction itself. But 'larger' is not the same thing as 'more important' nor is 'reason' the same as 'purpose'. If one postulates the case of a bidder for control of a public company financing his bid from the company's own funds—the obvious mischief at which the section is aimed—the immediate purpose which it is sought to achieve is that of completing the purchase and vesting control of the company in the bidder. The reasons why that course is considered desirable may be many and varied. The company may have fallen on hard times so that a change of management is considered necessary to avert disaster. It may merely be thought, and no doubt would be thought by the purchaser and the directors whom he nominates once he has control, that the business of the company will be more profitable under his management than it was heretofore. These may be excellent reasons but they cannot, in my judgment, constitute a 'larger purpose' of which the provision of assistance is merely an incident. The purpose and the only purpose of the financial assistance is and remains that of enabling the shares to be acquired and the financial or commercial advantages flowing from the acquisition, whilst they may form the reason for forming the purpose of providing assistance, are a by-product of it rather than an independent purpose of which the assistance can properly be considered to be an incident.[392]

**24.168**    In other words, the 'purpose' is the outcome sought to be facilitated or enabled by the giving of financial assistance, and the 'reason' is the statement made to explain why that outcome is being pursued. In order to apply Lord Oliver's analysis of the statutory provisions, it is necessary to ask what a company is trying to achieve by giving the financial assistance. If the company is giving the financial assistance in order to promote or enable the acquisition of shares or satisfy a liability incurred as a result of the acquisition of shares, then the financial assistance will prima facie fall within the statutory prohibition. If the company anticipates that the acquisition of shares will produce various benefits, then the company's desire to obtain these benefits is simply the company's reason or motive for seeking to promote the acquisition of shares, and the company's reason or motive is not a 'purpose' in this context. Put another way, a 'purpose' must be some additional objective which the

---

[391] [1989] AC 755.
[392] Ibid 779–80.

company seeks to achieve and which exists alongside the acquisition of shares rather than simply flowing from the acquisition of shares.

In *Plaut v Steiner*,[393] on the basis of Lord Oliver's decision in *Brady*, Morritt J **24.169** dismissed the contention that the principal or larger purpose of the company was to effect the commercial division of the company. The division of the company, he pointed out, could have been effected without the financial assistance, but would never have been proposed without the contemporaneous exchange of shares. Each purpose, he held, was equally large, and neither was incidental to the other, as neither would have existed without the other.

### Unconditional exceptions

The following transactions are permissible as a matter of general company law **24.170** and are expressly excluded by s 681(1) from the prohibitions in ss 678 and 679:

(1) distribution of a company's assets by way of dividend lawfully made or a distribution made in the course of the company's winding up; (2) the allotment of bonus shares; (3) reduction of capital under Chapter 10 of Part 17; (4) a redemption or purchase of shares under Chapter 3 of Part 18 or a purchase of shares under Chapter 4 of Part 18; (5) anything done in pursuance of an order of the court under Part 26 (order sanctioning compromise or arrangement with members or creditors); (6) anything done under an arrangement made in pursuance of the Insolvency Act, s 110 (acceptance of shares by liquidator in winding up as consideration for sale of property); and (7) anything done under an arrangement made between a company and its creditors which is binding on the creditors by virtue of Part 1 of the Insolvency Act.

### Conditional exceptions

The 2006 Act, s 682(2) provides for a number of limited exceptions in cases **24.171** involving: (1) money-lending companies; (2) employees' share schemes; (3) acquisition of shares by employees and the relatives of employees; and (4) the making of loans to employees for the purpose of share acquisitions.

### Criminal liability of directors

If a company contravenes any of the prohibitions on financial assistance, an **24.172** offence is committed by the company and every officer of the company in default.[394] A person guilty of this offence is liable on conviction on indictment to imprisonment for a term not exceeding two years or a fine or both or on summary

---

[393] (1989) 5 BCC 353.
[394] 2006 Act, s 680(1) (in force from 1 October 2009, replacing 1985 Act, s 151(3) without changes).

conviction to imprisonment for a term not exceeding 12 months or a fine not exceeding the statutory maximum or both.[395]

### Civil liability of directors

**24.173**  A director who authorizes the giving of financial assistance in breach of the statutory provisions will be in breach of his duties to the company and liable to make good any loss suffered by the company resulting from the breach.[396]

### Disqualification

**24.174**  Participation by directors in a scheme which contravenes the statutory provisions may be relied on by the Secretary of State in disqualification proceedings as evidence of unfitness.[397]

## (6)  Redemption or purchase of own shares

**24.175**  One of the statutory exceptions to the rule in *Trevor v Whitworth*[398] involves the redemption or purchase by a company of its own shares out of distributable profits or the proceeds of a fresh issue. In the case of redemption, there is in fact no acquisition, because the shares are merely cancelled in accordance with their terms. In either case, however, there is no reduction of capital, because the capital paid out on redemption or by way of consideration for the acquisition is either replaced by the proceeds of the newly issued shares or accounted for by a *pro tanto* reduction in the profits available for dividend. The ability of a company to issue redeemable shares was first introduced by the 1929 Act in respect of 'redeemable preference shares' (although the term 'preference' was not defined) and extended by the Act 1981 Act to enable companies to issue redeemable shares of any class. The related power given to companies to purchase their own shares was first introduced in 1981.

**24.176**  The detailed procedural requirements relating to redemption and purchase are set out below. Non-compliance with these requirements will not be treated as a mere procedural irregularity capable of being waived or dispensed with or validated by unanimous agreement of all members entitled to vote at the meeting because the members are not the sole group for whose benefit the requirements

---

[395]  2006 Act, s 680(2) (in force from 1 October 2009, replacing 1985 Act, s 151(3), Schedule 24, without changes).

[396]  *Selangor United Rubber Estates Ltd v Cradock (No 3)* [1968] 2 All ER 1073; *Steen v Law* [1964] AC 287, *Curtis's Furnishing Store Ltd v Freedman* [1966] 1 WLR 1219; *Karak Rubber v Burden (No 2)* [1972] WLR 602; *Wallersteiner v Moir* [1974] 3 All ER 217; *Belmont Finance Corp Ltd v Williams Furniture Ltd* [1980] 1 All ER 393.

[397]  *Re Dawes & Henderson (Agencies) Ltd (No 2)* [1999] 2 BCLC 317; see also *Re Continental Assurance Co of London plc* [1997] 1 BCLC 48.

[398]  (1887) 12 App Cas 409.

have been imposed.[399] However, informal unanimous consent may be sufficient to cure 'minor' contraventions[400] (such as, perhaps, the accidental omission of one shareholder's name from the memorandum appended to the contract under s 696(4) of the Act) because insignificant errors which prejudice no one ought not to be allowed to invalidate the whole scheme.[401] However, directors should be astute to ensure that the statutory requirements are followed, as numerous offences may be committed in relation to redemption and purchase of a company's own shares by officers in default.

### Redeemable shares

The 2006 Act, s 684(1) expressly provides that a limited company having a share capital may issue shares that are to be redeemed or are liable to be redeemed at the option of the company or the shareholder. A private company's ability to issue redeemable shares does not depend on prior authorization in the company's articles. However, the articles of a private limited company may exclude or restrict the issue of redeemable shares.[402] In the case of a public company, by contrast, prior authorization in the articles is essential, and redeemable shares may not be issued unless so authorized.[403] In the case of any company, no redeemable shares may be issued at a time when there are no issued shares of the company that are not redeemable.[404] The aim of this requirement is to ensure that the company does not find itself entirely without shares, which could occur if the only shares were all redeemable.

**24.177**

### Terms and manner of redemption

The directors of a private or public company have the ability[405] to decide on the terms, conditions, and manner of redemption of shares, provided that the company has authorized them to do so, either in its articles or by way of a resolution.[406] Where the directors are authorized to determine the terms, conditions, and

**24.178**

---

[399] *Re R W Peak (King's Lynn) Ltd* [1998] 1 BCLC 193, *Wright v Atlas Wright (Europe) Ltd* [1999] 2 BCLC 301, *Re Torvale Group Ltd* [1999] 2 BCLC 605.

[400] See, on this issue, *BDG Roof-Bond Ltd v Douglas* [2000] 1 BCC 401, 417.

[401] See *Re Willaire Systems plc* [1987] BCC 67.

[402] 2006 Act, s 684(2) (in force from 1 October 2009; a new provision).

[403] 2006 Act, s 684(3) (in force from 1 October 2009, restating 1985 Act, s 159(2)).

[404] 2006 Act, s 684(4) (in force from 1 October 2009, restating 1985 Act, s 159(2)).

[405] As recommended by the CLR: *Final Report*, para 4.5.

[406] 2006 Act, s 685(1) (in force from 1 October 2009; a new provision). A resolution authorizing the directors in this manner may be an ordinary resolution even though it amends the company's articles: 2006 Act, s 685(2) (in force from 1 October 2009; a new provision). Where the directors are not authorized in the articles or by way of resolution to determine these matters in respect of redeemable shares, the terms, conditions, and manner of redemption must be stated in the company's articles: 2006 Act, s 685(4) (in force from 1 October 2009).

manner of redemption, they must do so before the shares are allotted.[407] It should also be noted that any obligation of the company to state in a statement of capital the rights attached to the shares extends to the terms, conditions, and manner of redemption.[408]

*Payment and financing of redemption*

24.179    Redeemable shares may not be redeemed unless they are fully paid.[409] Under the 1985 Act, it was necessary for payment of the redemption monies to be contemporaneous with redemption. However, s 686 of the 2006 Act provides that the terms of redemption may provide for the amount payable[410] on redemption to be paid on a date later than the redemption date, provided that the holder of the shares is agreeable to this.[411] Where the holder of the shares is not agreeable to deferred payment, then the amount payable on redemption must be paid on redemption.[412]

24.180    Redeemable shares may be redeemed out of capital, provided that the statutory requirements are observed. Redemption out of capital is considered below.[413] Otherwise, redeemable shares may only be redeemed out of distributable profits[414] of the company or the proceeds of a fresh issue of shares made for the purpose of the redemption.[415] Use of such funds ensures that there is no erosion of the capital maintenance doctrine.[416] Further, any premium payable on redemption must be paid out of distributable profits,[417] unless the shares were issued at a premium, in which case the premium payable on redemption may be paid out of the proceeds of a fresh issue of shares made for the purposes of the redemption, up to an amount equal to the lesser of the aggregate of the premiums received by the company on the issue of the shares redeemed or the current amount of the company's share premium account (including any sum transferred to that account

---

[407]  2006 Act, s 685(3)(a) (in force from 1 October 2009; a new provision).

[408]  2006 Act, s 685(3)(b) (in force from 1 October 2009; new).

[409]  2006 Act, s 685(1) (in force from 1 October 2009; also new).

[410]  As to the meaning of payment and the possibility of non-cash consideration, see *BDG Roof-Bond Ltd v Douglas* [2000] 1 BCLC 401.

[411]  2006 Act, s 686(2) (in force from 1 October 2009, replacing 1985 Act, s 159(3) with changes).

[412]  2006 Act, s 686(3) (in force from 1 October 2009, replacing 1985 Act, s 159(3) with changes).

[413]  Paragraphs 24.196–24.205 below.

[414]  As to distributable profits, see paragraphs 24.230–24.238 below.

[415]  2006 Act, s 687(2) (in force from 1 October 2009, replacing 1985 Act, s 160(1)).

[416]  See *Quayle Munro Ltd, Petitioners* [1994] 1 BCLC 410.

[417]  2006 Act, s 689(3) (in force from 1 October 2009; a new provision).

in respect of premiums on the new shares).[418] The amount of the company's share premium account should then be reduced accordingly.[419]

### Notification of redemption; criminal liability of directors

Where shares in a limited company are redeemed, the shares are treated as cancelled, and the amount of the company's issued share capital is diminished accordingly by the nominal value of the shares redeemed.[420] **24.181**

Within one month of redemption, the company must notify the Registrar of the redemption, specifying the shares redeemed.[421] The notice must be accompanied by a statement of capital[422] which must state with respect to the company's share capital immediately following the redemption: (1) the total number of shares of the company; (2) the aggregate nominal value of those shares; (3) for each class of shares, (i) prescribed particulars of the rights attached to the shares, (ii) the total number of shares of that class, and (iii) aggregate nominal value of shares of that class, and (4) the amount paid up and the amount (if any) unpaid on each share (whether on account of the nominal value of the share or by way of premium).[423] **24.182**

If the redemption is not notified to the Registrar as required, an offence is committed by the company and every officer in default.[424] This offence is triable summarily only and punishable by way of a fine not exceeding level 3 on the standard scale and, for continued contravention, a daily default fine not exceeding one-tenth of level 3 on the standard scale.[425] **24.183**

### Purchase of own shares; generally

Under the provisions of the 2006 Act, a limited company will be able purchase its own shares, subject to the provisions of the 2006 Act, without requiring prior authorization in its articles.[426] However, its ability to do so may be fettered by an **24.184**

---

[418] 2006 Act, s 688(4) (in force from 1 October 2009, replacing 1985 Act, s 160(4) with changes).

[419] 2006 Act, s 688(5) (in force from 1 October 2009, replacing 1985 Act, s 160(4) with changes).

[420] 2006 Act, s 688(6) (in force from 1 October 2009, replacing 1985 Act, s 160(4) with changes).

[421] 2006 Act, s 689(1) (in force from 1 October 2009, replacing 1985 Act, s 122(1)(e) without changes).

[422] 2006 Act, s 689(2) (in force from 1 October 2009; a new provision).

[423] 2006 Act, s 689(3) (in force from 1 October 2009; a new provision).

[424] 2006 Act, s 689(4) (in force from 1 October 2009, replacing 1985 Act, s 122(2)).

[425] 2006 Act, s 689(5) (in force from 1 October 2009, replacing 1985 Act, s 122(2), Schedule 24).

[426] Prior authorization in the articles, which is a necessity under the 1985 Act, is being removed in accordance with the recommendations of the CLR: *Completing the Structure*, para 2.15.

express restriction or prohibition in the articles.[427] Further, a limited company may not purchase its own shares if as a result of the purchase there would no longer be any issued shares of the company other than redeemable shares or shares held as treasury shares.[428] It should also be noted that listed companies must also comply with the requirements of the Listing Rules on purchase of own shares (eg in respect of additional disclosure and notification requirements and a prohibition on redemption or purchase of a company's own shares during a 'prohibited period' as defined in the Model Code for dealings by directors set out in the Appendix to Chapter 9 of the Listing Rules). Further, it may be necessary for directors to consult the Takeover Code, which contains additional provisions governing, inter alia, the circumstances where redemption or purchase may result in an obligation to make a mandatory offer, and preventing an offeree company during the course of an offer (or at a time when the board has reason to believe that a bona fide offer might be imminent) from redeeming or purchasing any of its own shares (except in performance of an existing contract) without the approval of shareholders in general meeting.

### Payment and financing of purchase

**24.185** A limited company may not purchase its shares unless they are fully paid.[429] Furthermore, where a limited company purchases its own shares, the shares must be paid for on purchase.[430] In other words, deferred consideration is not permitted, and the terms of the contract must oblige the purchaser to hand over the consideration simultaneously with the transfer of the shares.[431] The scope and rationale of the prohibition of deferred consideration was explained in paragraph 38 of the Department of Trade's consultative document *The Purchase by a Company of its Own Shares*:[432]

> If companies were permitted to buy their own shares it would follow, in the absence of express prohibition, that they could enter into executory contracts, or obtain options, to do so. There seems to be no grounds for prohibition; indeed . . . executory contracts appear to be vital if the aim is to be achieved. Performance of such contracts

---

[427] 2006 Act, s 690(1) (in force from 1 October 2009, replacing 1985 Act, s 162(1) with changes).

[428] 2006 Act, s 690(2) (in force from 1 October 2009, replacing 1985 Act, s 162(3) without changes). As to redeemable shares, see paragraphs 24.176–24.179 above. Treasury shares, ie shares in a listed company which the company itself is permitted to own up to certain levels, are considered in paragraphs 24.206–24.210 below.

[429] 2006 Act, s 691(1) (in force from 1 October 2009, replacing 1985 Act, s 159(3), s 162(2)).

[430] 2006 Act, s 691(2) (in force from 1 October 2009, replacing 1985 Act, s 159(3) and s 163(2)). It has been held that 'payment' in this context is not limited to payment in cash and may include a purchase of shares in return for assets: *BDG Roof-Bond Ltd v Douglas* [2000] 1 BCLC 401

[431] See *Pena v Dale* [2004] 2 BCLC 508; see also *BDG Roof-Bond Ltd v Douglas* [2000] 1 BCLC 401 and *Kinlan v Crimmin* [2006] EWHC 779 (Ch).

[432] Cmnd 7944.

would necessarily be conditional on its being lawful for the company to pay for the shares at the time when the contract is completed, i.e. on the assumption that payment could lawfully be made out of profits only, on the company's having profits available at the time or times of performance. What should happen, however, if the contract had been partly performed? Suppose, for example, that the company has 900 issued shares owned equally by three shareholders. One dies and the company agrees to buy his 300 shares for £30,000 payable by equal instalments out of the profits for the next three years. The first year's payment is made but in the second year insufficient profits are available. If this eventuality has been foreseen and dealt with in the contract all may be well. But what if it has not? It is tempting to say that the purchase of the first 100 shares for £10,000 should be completed but that would be to make a different contract for the parties and, probably, one that would not be satisfactory to either. The estate wants to get out of the company and not to be left with 200 (probably unsaleable) shares. The company has agreed the price on the basis that it is buying a holding which, through the power to block a special resolution, conferred a measure of negative control. An alternative solution (though clearly not one wholly satisfactory to the estate) would be to say that in the absence of agreement to the contrary the whole transaction should be cancelled. This might occasionally present difficulties if the personal representative had distributed the £10,000 or if the 100 shares had already been transferred to the company and cancelled. Neither solution is ideal. But all that seems to be necessary is to provide some rule which, in the absence of express agreement, would provide a workable solution if not a perfect one.

There are two means by which a private company may purchase its own shares. **24.186** The first possibility is a payment out of capital.[433] This possibility is considered below.[434] The second option is a payment out of distributable profits or the proceeds of a fresh issue of shares made for the purpose of financing the transaction.[435] Any premium payable on the purchase must be paid out of distributable profits,[436] unless the shares were issued at a premium, in which case any premium payable on their purchase may be paid out of the proceeds of a fresh issue of shares up to an amount equal to the lesser of the aggregate of the premiums received by the company on issue or the current amount of the company's share premium account (including any sums transferred to that account in respect of premiums on the new shares).[437] The amount of the company's share premium account should then be reduced accordingly.[438]

---

[433] 2006 Act, s 692(1) (in force from 1 October 2009, replacing 1985 Act, s 160(1), s 162(2)).
[434] See paragraphs 24.196–24.205 below.
[435] 2006 Act, s 692(2)(a) (in force from 1 October 2009).
[436] 2006 Act, s 692(2)(b) (in force from 1 October 2009).
[437] 2006 Act, s 693(3) (in force from 1 October 2009, replacing 1985 Act, s 163(2) without changes).
[438] 2006 Act, s 693(4) (in force from 1 October 2009, replacing 1985 Act, s 163(3) without changes).

**24.187**   In addition, it should be noted that any payment apart from the purchase price (eg the price for acquiring an option to buy shares) must be made out of the company's distributable profits.[439] If this requirement is not met, then the relevant contractual right acquired by the company (eg the option) may not be exercised or relied on by the company.[440]

*Authority for purchase of own shares*

**24.188**   The procedure to be applied for the purchase by a company of its own shares will depend on whether the purchase is a 'market purchase' or an 'off-market purchase'. In short, a purchase is a 'market purchase' if it is made on a recognized investment exchange and is subject to a marketing arrangement on the exchange.[441] The term 'recognized investment exchange' is defined in Part 18 of FSMA, but excludes an overseas exchange. A company's shares are subject to a 'marketing arrangement' on a recognized exchange if they are listed under Part 6 of FSMA or the company has been afforded facilities for dealing in the shares to take place on the exchange without prior permission for individual transactions from the authority governing the exchange and without limit as to the time during which those facilities are to be available.[442] A purchase is 'off-market' if the shares are purchased privately, ie otherwise than on a recognized investment exchange (or on a recognized investment exchange but not subject to a marketing arrangement on the exchange).[443] In other words, any private company purchasing its own shares will always make an off-market purchase.

**24.189**   A market purchase must be authorized in accordance with the 2006 Act, s 701.[444] This requires the purchase to be authorized in advance by a resolution.[445] The authorization must specify the maximum number of shares authorized to be acquired and determine both the maximum and minimum prices[446] that may be paid for the shares.[447] The authorization must also specify a date on which it is to

---

[439] 2006 Act, s 705(1) (in force from 1 October 2009).

[440] 2006 Act, s 705(2) (in force from 1 October 2009).

[441] 2006 Act, s 693(2), (3), (4) (in force from 1 October 2009, replacing 1985 Act, s 163).

[442] 2006 Act, s 693(3) (in force from 1 October 2009).

[443] 2006 Act, s 693(2) (in force from 1 October 2009, replacing 1985 Act, s 163(1)).

[444] 2006 Act, s 693(1)(b) (in force from 1 October 2009).

[445] 2006 Act, s 701(1) (in force from 1 October 2009, replacing 1985 Act, s 166(1) without changes). The authority may be general or limited and may be conditional or unconditional: 2006 Act, s 701(2) (in force from 1 October 2009). It may be varied, revoked, or renewed by way of further resolution: 2006 Act, s 701(4) (in force from 1 October 2009).

[446] The authority may specify a particular sum or alternatively provide a basis or formula for calculating the amount of the price, provided that the calculation does not depend on any person's discretion or opinion: 2006 Act, s 701(7) (in force from 1 October 2009, replacing 1985 Act, s 166(6) without changes).

[447] 2006 Act, s 701(3) (in force from 1 October 2009, replacing 1985 Act, s 166(3)(a) and (b) without changes).

expire, which must not be later than 18 months after the date on which the resolution is passed.[448] The purchase must occur during this 'window of opportunity' (although it is possible for the authorization to permit the company to enter into an executory contract during the 'window of opportunity' which falls to be performed after the expiry of the period[449]).

An off-market purchase must be carried out in accordance with the 2006 Act, **24.190** s 694.[450] Either the terms of the contract must be authorized by special resolution prior to execution of the contract, or the contract must contain a condition precedent requiring approval by way of special resolution prior to performance.[451] In the case of a public company, the resolution must specify the date on which the authorization is to expire, which must not be later than 18 months after the date on which the resolution was passed.[452] Special provisions apply in respect of voting for such a resolution. In short, any member who holds shares to which the resolution relates is unable effectively to vote for the resolution.[453]

Where a company seeks a resolution to authorize an off-market purchase, a copy **24.191** of the contract[454] (or a memorandum setting out its terms,[455] if the contract is not a written contract) must be made available to the members,[456] and the resolution is not validly passed if these requirements are not satisfied.[457] Similar provisions

---

[448] 2006 Act, s 701(5) (in force from 1 October 2009, replacing 1985 Act, s 166(3)(c) and (4)).

[449] 2006 Act, s 701(6) (in force from 1 October 2009, replacing 1985 Act, s 166(5)).

[450] 2006 Act, s 693(1)(a); s 694(1); coming into force on 1 October 2009; replacing 1985 Act, s 164(1), s 166(1) without changes.

[451] 2006 Act, s 694(2) (in force from 1 October 2009, replacing 1985 Act, ss 164(2) and 165(2) with changes). The ability to enter into a contract conditional on approval by shareholders is intended to save time by enabling directors to negotiate and agree a contract ahead of shareholder approval.

[452] 2006 Act, s 694(5) (in force from 1 October 2009, replacing 1985 Act, ss 164(4) and 165(2) without changes).

[453] 2006 Act, s 695(2), (3) (in force from 1 October 2009 replacing 1985 Act, ss 164(6), 165(2), Schedule 15A, paras 5(3) and (4)).

[454] If the contract does not contain the names of the members holding shares to which the contract relates, it must be accompanied by a memorandum containing this information: 2006 Act, s 696(3) (in force from 1 October 2009, replacing 1985 Act, ss 164(6) and 165(2) without changes).

[455] Such a memorandum must include the names of the members holding shares to which the contract relates: 2006 Act, s 696(3) (in force from 1 October 2009).

[456] 2006 Act, s 696(2) (in force from 1 October 2009). If the resolution is to be a written resolution, the contract or memorandum must be sent or submitted to every eligible member at or before the time at which the proposed resolution is sent or submitted to him. If the resolution is to be passed at a meeting, the contract or memorandum must be made available for inspection by members of the company both at the company's registered office for not less than 15 days ending with the date of the meeting and at the meeting itself.

[457] 2006 Act, s 696(5) (in force from 1 October 2009).

exist in respect of the variation and release of an authorization to make an off-market purchase.[458]

*Inspection of contract; criminal liability of directors*

**24.192**   Where a company has entered into a contract for a market purchase or an off-market purchase, it is necessary for the company to keep available for inspection at its registered office[459] a copy of the contract (or, if the contract is not in writing, a copy of the memorandum of its terms)[460] for a period of 10 years commencing with the completion of purchase.[461] Every member of the company (and, in the case of a public company, every member of the public) is entitled to inspect the contract without charge.[462]

**24.193**   If the contract (or memorandum of its terms) is not kept available for inspection in accordance with these statutory requirements, or if an inspection requested by a person entitled to do so is refused, an offence (triable summarily and punishable by a level 3 fine with a daily fine for continued contravention[463]) is committed by every officer in default.[464] In addition, in the case of a refusal to permit inspection, the court may make an order compelling immediate inspection.[465]

*Notification to register; criminal liability of directors*

**24.194**   Where the company keeps a copy of the contract or memorandum available for inspection at a place which is not the company's registered office, it must notify the Registrar of the address of the place.[466] If the company fails to give notice to the Registrar within 15 days, an offence (punishable by fine and daily default fine for continued contravention[467]) is committed by every officer in default.[468]

---

[458] See 2006 Act, ss 697, 698, 699, 700, 701 (all of which are due to come into force on 1 October 2009). Until 1 October 2009, see 1985 Act, ss 164, 166.

[459] 2006 Act, s 702(4) (in force from 1 October 2009); or other place specified by regulations made under s 1136, if applicable.

[460] 2006 Act, s 702(2) (in force from 1 October 2009, replacing 1985 Act, s 169(4) with changes).

[461] 2006 Act, s 702(3) (in force from 1 October 2009).

[462] 2006 Act, s 702(6) (in force from 1 October 2009).

[463] 2006 Act, s 702(2) (in force from 1 October 2009).

[464] 2006 Act, s 703(1) (in force from 1 October 2009, replacing 1985 Act, s 169(7) with changes).

[465] 2006 Act, s 703(3) (in force from 1 October 2009, replacing 1985 Act, s 169(8) without changes).

[466] 2006 Act, s 702(5) (in force from 1 October 2009; a new provision).

[467] 2006 Act, s 703(2) (in force from 1 October 2009, replacing 1985 Act, s 169(7), Schedule 24).

[468] 2006 Act, s 703(1) (in force from 1 October 2009, replacing 1985 Act, s 169(7) with changes).

*Return to Registrar; criminal liability of directors*

Where a company has purchased its own shares in accordance with the statutory **24.195** provisions, it must deliver a return to the Registrar within 28 days of the date on which the shares are delivered to it.[469] The return must (inter alia) state, with respect to each class of share purchased, the number and nominal value of the shares and the date on which they were delivered to the company.[470] Additional requirements apply in the case of a public company, which must state in the return the aggregate amount paid for the shares and the maximum and minimum prices paid in respect of shares of each class purchased.[471] If the return is not sent to the Registrar in accordance with these requirements, an offence (punishable by fine[472]) is committed by every officer in default.[473]

*Notice of cancellation; criminal liability of directors*

When a company purchases its own shares, they will be treated as cancelled, unless **24.196** they are held as treasury shares, in which case special provisions apply. Where the shares are treated as cancelled, the company must give notice of cancellation to the Registrar within a period of 28 days commencing with the date of delivery of shares, specifying the shares cancelled.[474] The notice must be accompanied by a statement of capital[475] which must state with respect to the company's share capital immediately following cancellation: (1) the total number of shares of the company; (2) the aggregate nominal value of those shares; (3) for each class of share, (i) prescribed particulars of the rights attached to the shares, (ii) the total number of shares of that class, and (iii) the aggregate nominal value of shares of that class; and (4) the amount paid up and the amount (if any) unpaid on each share (whether on account of the nominal value of the share or by way of premium).[476] If the requirements for notification accompanied by a statement of capital are not observed, an offence (triable summarily and punishable by fine[477]) is committed by every officer in default.[478]

---

[469] 2006 Act, s 707(1) (in force from 1 October 2009, replacing 1985 Act, s 169(1), (1A), (1B), with changes).

[470] 2006 Act, s 707(3) (in force from 1 October 2009, replacing 1985 Act, s 169(1), (1A), (1B), with changes); see also 2006 Act, s 707(2) (in force from 1 October 2009). Particulars of shares delivered to the company on different dates and under different contracts may be included in a single return: 2006 Act, s 707(5) (in force from 1 October 2009).

[471] 2006 Act, s 707(4) (in force from 1 October 2009, replacing 1985 Act, s 169(2)).

[472] 2006 Act, s 707(7) (in force from 1 October 2009, replacing 1985 Act, s 169(6), Schedule 24).

[473] 2006 Act, s 707(6) (in force from 1 October 2009).

[474] 2006 Act, s 708(1) (in force from 1 October 2009, replacing 1985 Act, s 169(1), (1A), (1B), with changes).

[475] 2006 Act, s 708(2) (in force from 1 October 2009; a new provision).

[476] 2006 Act, s 708(3) (in force from 1 October 2009; also new).

[477] 2006 Act, s 708(5) (in force from 1 October 2009, replacing 1985 Act, s 169(6), Schedule 24).

[478] 2006 Act, s 708(4) (in force from 1 October 2009, replacing 1985 Act, s 169(6)).

*Redemption or purchase by private company out of capital*

**24.197**   A private company may redeem redeemable shares, or purchase its own shares, out of capital in accordance with the 2006 Act, ss 709–723.[479] In either case, the profits available for distribution[480] and/or the proceeds of any fresh issue of shares made for the purpose of the redemption or purchase must be applied towards the payment and exhausted before capital may be utilized in this manner.[481] The 'permissible capital payment' (defined by s 710) is essentially such amount of capital as is required to make up the balance of the redemption or purchase payment once these other sources of funds have been exhausted.

**24.198**   In order to make a lawful redemption or purchase of own shares out of capital, four key requirements must be satisfied. First, there must be a directors' statement accompanied by an auditors' report. Secondly, there must be a special resolution approving the payment out of capital. Thirdly, there must be a public notice. Fourthly, the directors' statement and the auditors' report must be available for inspection.

*Directors' statement and auditors' report*

**24.199**   The directors' statement[482] must be made by all the directors (including any de facto directors[483]) and must specify the amount of the permissible capital payment[484] for the shares in question.[485] It must also state that, having made full inquiry into the affairs and prospects of the company, the directors have formed the opinion: (1) as regards its initial situation immediately following the date on which the payment out of capital is proposed to be made, that there will be no grounds on which the company could then be found unable to pay its debts;[486] and (2) as regards its prospects for the year immediately following that date, that (having regard to (i) their intentions with respect to the management of the company's business during that year and (ii) the amount and character of the financial resources that will in their view be available to the company during that year) the

---

[479]   These provisions come into force on 1 October 2009; prior to that date, the provisions of 1985 Act continue to apply: see in particular 1985 Act, s 160, s 171(1).

[480]   Defined by s 711 and calculated in accordance with 2006 Act, s 712.

[481]   2006 Act, s 710(1), s 711, s 712 (coming into force on 1 October 2009 to replace 1985 Act, s 171(3) and s 172).

[482]   It is intended that the Secretary of State will make regulations regarding the precise form and content of the statement in addition to the statutory requirements: see 2006 Act, s 714(5).

[483]   *Re In A Flap Envelope Co Ltd* [2004] 1 BCLC 64.

[484]   The term 'permissible capital payment' is defined by 2006 Act, s 710 (in force from 1 October 2009 to replace 1985 Act, s 171).

[485]   2006 Act, s 714(2) (coming into force on 1 October 2009 to replace 1985 Act, s 173(1) without changes).

[486]   In forming their opinion, the directors must take into account all of the company's liabilities including any contingent or prospective liabilities: see 2006 Act, s 714(4) (coming into force on 1 October 2009).

company will be able to continue to carry on business as a going concern (and will accordingly be able to pay its debts as they fall due) throughout that year.[487] A declaration made without any or sufficient inquiry into the financial affairs of the company is not properly made.[488] The statement must be accompanied by a report addressed to the directors from the company's auditor stating that: (1) he has inquired into the company's state of affairs; (2) the amount specified in the statement as the permissible capital payment for the shares in question has in his view been properly calculated; and (3) he is not aware of anything to indicate that the opinion expressed by the directors in their statement is unreasonable.[489]

*Special resolution*

The payment out of capital must be authorized by a special resolution of the company[490] which must be passed on, or within the week immediately following, the date on which the directors' statement is made.[491] It should be noted that any member who holds shares to which the resolution relates is unable to vote thereon, in the case of a written resolution, and if he votes at a meeting, the resolution (if passed) is not effective if it would not have been passed without his votes.[492] A copy of the directors' statement and auditors' report must be made available to members (either by being sent or submitted with the written resolution or by being made available at the meeting for inspection)[493] and the resolution is ineffective if this requirement is not complied with.[494]  **24.200**

*Public notice*

Within the week immediately following the date of the resolution, the company must cause to be published in the Gazette a notice containing the following particulars: (1) a statement that the company has approved a payment out of capital for the purpose of acquiring its own shares by redemption or purchase or both (as the case may be); (2) particulars of the amount of the permissible capital payment for the shares in question and the date of the resolution; (3) the location of the place where the directors' statement and auditors' report may be inspected; and (4) a statement to the effect that any creditor may within five weeks of the date of  **24.201**

---

[487] 2006 Act, s 714(3) (coming into force on 1 October 2009, replacing 1985 Act, s 173(3) with changes).

[488] *Re In A Flap Envelope Co Ltd* [2004] 1 BCLC 64.

[489] 2006 Act, s 714(6) (coming into force on 1 October 2009, replacing 1985 Act, s 173(5), with changes).

[490] 2006 Act, s 716(1) (coming into force on 1 October 2009, replacing 1985 Act, s 173(2), without changes).

[491] 2006 Act, s 716(1), (2) (replacing 1985 Act, s 173(2) and s 174(1), on 1 October 2009).

[492] 2006 Act, s 717(1), (2), (3), (4) (coming into force on 1 October 2009).

[493] 2006 Act, s 718(2) (coming into force on 1 October 2009).

[494] 2006 Act, s 718(3) (coming into force on 1 October 2009, replacing 1985 Act, s 174(4)).

the resolution apply to the court for an order preventing the payment.[495] The notice must also be published in a national newspaper.[496] But before any such notice is published in the Gazette or a newspaper, the company must provide the Registrar with a copy of the directors' statement and auditors' report.[497]

### Inspection of statement and report

24.202 The directors' statement and auditors' report must be kept available for inspection by members and creditors without charge[498] at the company's registered office (or such other place as may have been specified pursuant to regulations made under s 1136) until a period of five weeks has elapsed since the date of the resolution.[499] If the documents are available somewhere other than the registered office, the location of this place must be notified to the Registrar.[500]

### Right of creditors and members to object

24.203 Any creditor of the company (and any member who did not consent to, or vote in favour of, the resolution) may apply to the court within five weeks of the date of the resolution[501] for the cancellation of the resolution.[502] On being served with the application, the company must immediately notify the Registrar.[503] Similarly, within 15 days of an order by the court in respect of such an application, the company must deliver a copy of the order to the Registrar.[504]

### Payment out of capital

24.204 If there is no application by any creditor or member within the five-week vulnerability period, the company may make the payment out of capital, but it must do so before the expiry of a period of seven weeks commencing with the date of the resolution.[505] In other words, if no creditor objects, the company will have a

---

[495] 2006 Act, s 719(1) (replacing 1985 Act, s 175(1), without changes, on 1 October 2009).

[496] 2006 Act, s 719(2), (3) (coming into force on 1 October 2009, replacing 1985 Act, s 175(2), (3), without changes).

[497] 2006 Act, s 719(4) (replacing 1985 Act, s 175(4) and (5), without changes, on 1 October 2009).

[498] 2006 Act, s 720(4) (coming into force on 1 October 2009, replacing 1985 Act, s 175(6)(b), without changes).

[499] 2006 Act, s 720(1) (coming into force on 1 October 2009, replacing 1985 Act, s 175(4) and (6)(a), without changes).

[500] 2006 Act, s 720(3) (a new provision coming into force on 1 October 2009).

[501] 2006 Act, s 721(2) (coming into force on 1 October 2009, replacing 1985 Act, s 176(1), (2), without changes).

[502] 2006 Act, s 721(1) (replacing 1985 Act, s 176(1), without changes on 1 October 2009).

[503] 2006 Act, s 722(2) (coming into force on 1 October 2009, replacing 1985 Act, s 176(3)(a), without changes).

[504] 2006 Act, s 722(3) (coming into force on 1 October 2009, replacing 1985 Act, s 176(3)(a), without changes).

[505] 2006 Act, s 723(1) (coming into force on 1 October 2009, replacing 1985 Act, s 174(1), without changes).

two-week window in which to make the payment. The tight timetable is designed to ensure that the payment is made before the company's circumstances change in an unexpected adverse manner such as to render the payment imprudent. However, if the company's circumstances do change for the worse in a way which was not foreseen, and the directors consider that it is necessary to renege on the payment, s 735(2) provides that the company will not be liable in damages in respect of its failure to redeem or purchase the shares, and s 735(3) prohibits the court from making an order for specific performance.

*Criminal liabilities of directors*

There are three relevant offences. First, if the directors' statement is made without reasonable grounds for the opinions expressed in it, an offence[506] is committed by every director who is in default.[507] Secondly, if the directors' statement and auditors' report are kept somewhere other than the registered office without notifying the Registrar within 14 days, or if a request for inspection by any member or creditor is refused, an offence[508] is committed by every officer in default.[509] Thirdly, if the company fails to notify the Registrar of an application objecting to the resolution or an order of the court in respect of such an application, an offence[510] is committed by every officer in default.[511]      **24.205**

*Civil liabilities of directors*

A director may find himself under a civil liability pursuant to the Insolvency Act, s 76, which applies where a company is being wound up and has made a payment out of capital in respect of the purchase or redemption of its own shares and the aggregate of its assets and the amounts paid by way of contribution is not sufficient for the payment of its debts and liabilities and the expenses of the winding up. In those circumstances, if the winding up commenced[512] within one year of the date on which the relevant payment out of capital was made, then the person whose shares were redeemed or purchased and the directors who signed the      **24.206**

---

506 Punishable on conviction on indictment to imprisonment for a term not exceeding two years or a fine or both and on summary conviction to imprisonment for a term not exceeding 12 months or a fine not exceeding the statutory maximum or both: 2006 Act, s 715(2) (coming into force on 1 October 2009; until which date see 1985 Act, s 173(6), Schedule 24).

507 2006 Act, s 715(1) (coming into force on 1 October 2009, replacing 1985 Act, s 173(6)).

508 Triable summarily and punishable by fine: 2006 Act, s 720(6) (coming into force on 1 October 2009 to replace s 175(7), Schedule 24 of 1985 Act).

509 2006 Act, s 720(5) (coming into force on 1 October 2009, replacing 1985 Act, s 175(7) with changes).

510 2006 Act, s 722(5) (coming into force on 1 October 2009, replacing 1985 Act, s 176(4) and Schedule 24, without changes).

511 2006 Act, s 722(4) (coming into force on 1 October 2009 to replace 1985 Act, s 176(4), without changes).

512 For the concept of 'commencement' of winding up, see 2006 Act, ss 86 and 129 of the Insolvency Act.

statutory declaration are, so as to enable the insufficiency to be met, liable to contribute to the company's assets.[513] Directors who can discharge the burden of proving that they had reasonable grounds for forming the opinion set out in the declaration are not liable.[514] If the person whose shares were purchased or redeemed complies with his statutory obligation to contribute to the company's assets,[515] he may apply to the court for an order requiring any director who is liable to pay him such amount as the court thinks is just and equitable.[516] Similarly, if a director who is liable and who contributes to the company's assets in accordance with such liability, he may apply to the court for an order that the former shareholder reimburse him to such an extent as the court thinks just and equitable.[517]

*Treasury shares; generally*

24.207    The Second Directive on Company Law required Member States to pass laws permitting listed companies to acquire and hold (without cancellation) a limited proportion of shares in themselves.[518] Accordingly, following a consultation,[519] relevant legislation was introduced in 2003.[520] In the 2006 Act, ss 724 *et seq* (which will come into force on 1 October 2009) provide for the holding of shares purchased by the company as treasury shares, rather than being cancelled. These sections replace provisons in the 1985 Act, ss 162A–162G. This facility is only available where the purchase is of 'qualifying shares'. The term 'qualifying shares' is defined to mean shares that are included in the official list[521] in accordance with the provisions of Part 6 of FMSA, or are otherwise publicly traded on the Alternative Investment Market established under the rules of London Stock Exchange plc, officially listed in an EEA state, or traded on a regulated market.[522] Where a limited company purchases its own shares out of distributable profits and the shares are qualifying shares, then the company may hold the shares[523] or (to

---

[513] Insolvency Act, s 76(2).

[514] Insolvency Act, s 76(2)(b).

[515] Insolvency Act, s 76(2)(a), s 76(3).

[516] Insolvency Act, s 76(4).

[517] Ibid.

[518] 77/91/EEC, Art 19.

[519] See the DTI's consultation paper, *Treasury Shares: A Consultative Document* (September 2001).

[520] See, for historical interest only, the Companies (Acquisition of Own Shares) (Treasury Shares) Regulations 2003 (SI 2003/1116).

[521] The term 'official list' is defined by FSMA, s 103(1).

[522] 2006 Act, s 724(2) (in force from 1 October 2009, replacing 1985 Act, s 162(2B) without changes).

[523] However, the statutory provisions will not override anything in the company's articles to the contrary, such as a requirement to cancel shares immediately upon acquisition.

the extent permitted by the Act) deal with them.[524] Where the shares are held by the company, the company must be entered in its register of members as the member holding the shares.[525] (Private companies and public companies whose shares are not listed or admitted to trading on the identified markets are only able to purchase their own shares for cancellation.)

There are a number of significant restrictions which apply to treasury shares. First, **24.208** a company may not hold more than 10 per cent by nominal value of its issued share capital (or, where the capital is divided into classes, more than 10 per cent of each class).[526] If the company finds that it has acquired more than the permitted maximum, the shares are not cancelled automatically; rather, the company will have 12 months from the date of the contravention in which to dispose of or cancel the excess shares.[527] However, the acquisition of excessive shares is not void.[528] Secondly, a company which holds treasury shares in itself may not exercise any right in respect of the treasury shares, and any purported exercise of such right is void.[529] Therefore, for example, the company is not permitted to vote on the shares. Thirdly, a company which holds treasury shares in itself cannot pay or make any dividend or distribution on those shares, including a distribution of assets to members on winding up.[530] Fourthly, there are restrictions on disposal of treasury shares. Either they must be sold for a cash consideration[531] or they must be transferred for the purposes of an employee share scheme[532] and, whenever a disposal occurs, whether for a cash consideration or for the purposes of an employee share scheme, the disposal must be notified to the Registrar.[533] In addition, the

---

[524] 2006 Act, s 724(3) (in force from 1 October 2009, replacing 1985 Act, s 162A(1) without changes).

[525] 2006 Act, s 724(4) (in force from 1 October 2009, replacing 1985 Act, s 162A(2) without changes).

[526] 2006 Act, s 725(1), (2) (in force from 1 October 2009, replacing 1985 Act, s 162B(1), (2) without changes). The 10 per cent limit on holdings of treasury shares derives from the Second Directive on Company Law (77/91/EEC): see, specifically, Art 19(1)(b). However Directive 2006/68/EC permits domestic legislation to allow for a higher limit.

[527] 2006 Act, s 725(3) (in force from 1 October 2009, replacing 1985 Act, s 162B(3) without changes). However, contravention of the 10 per cent limit will be an offence committed by every officer in default and will result in a daily default fine throughout the period of contravention: see 2006 Act, s 732.

[528] 2006 Act, s 725(4) (in force from 1 October 2009, replacing 1985 Act, s 143(2A) without changes).

[529] 2006 Act, s 726(2) (in force from 1 October 2009).

[530] 2006 Act, s 726(3) (in force from 1 October 2009).

[531] Which includes a cheque received by the company in good faith which the directors have no reason for suspecting will not be honoured: 2006 Act, s 727(2)(b).

[532] 2006 Act, s 727(1), (2) (in force from 1 October 2009, replacing 1985 Act, s 162D(1)(a), (b), 162D(2), with changes).

[533] 2006 Act, s 727(1) (in force from 1 October 2009).

Listing Rules prohibit the sale of treasury shares during a prohibited period,[534] and the Takeover Code treats any sale or transfer of treasury shares as equivalent to a new issue and imposes limits on such sales or transfers during the course of an offer or where the company has reason to believe that a bona fide offer might be imminent without the approval of the shareholders in general meeting. Fifthly, the proceeds of sale must be dealt with in accordance with the 2006 Act, s 731 which provides that such part of the proceeds as amount to a recovery of the amount paid by the company on acquisition must be treated as realized profit of the company, whilst any excess above and beyond mere recoupment of outlay must be transferred to the company's share premium account.

### Treasury shares; criminal liability of directors

**24.209**  Where treasury shares are sold, or transferred for the purposes of an employee share scheme, and the obligation to notify the Registrar of disposal arises, the company must deliver a return to the Registrar within 28 days of the date of disposal.[535] The return must state with respect to shares of each class disposed of (1) the number and nominal value of the shares and (2) the date of disposal.[536] Failure to comply with these requirements gives rise to an offence (punishable by fine and daily default fine for continued contravention[537]) committed by every officer in default.[538]

**24.210**  Treasury shares may be cancelled at any time.[539] There is no obligation on the company to cancel the shares unless they cease to be qualifying shares, in which case they must be cancelled forthwith.[540] Where treasury shares are cancelled, the company must notify the Registrar within 28 days of cancellation[541] and the return must state the number and nominal value of the shares and the date on

---

[534] The Listing Rules also impose additional requirements (eg in respect of notification) designed to maintain investor protection and reduce any perceived scope for market manipulation.

[535] 2006 Act, s 728(1) (in force from 1 October 2009, replacing 1985 Act, s 169A(1)(b)(ii) and (2) without changes).

[536] 2006 Act, s 728(2) (in force from 1 October 2009, replacing 1985 Act, s 169A(2) without changes). Particulars of shares disposed of on different dates may be included in a single return: 2006 Act, s 728(3) (in force from 1 October 2009, replacing 1985 Act, s 169A(3) without changes).

[537] 2006 Act, s 729(5) (in force from 1 October 2009, replacing 1985 Act, s 162D(5) without changes).

[538] 2006 Act, s 728(4) (in force from 1 October 2009, replacing 1985 Act, 169A(4) without changes).

[539] 2006 Act, s 729(1) (in force from 1 October 2009, replacing 1985 Act, s 162D(1)(c) without changes).

[540] 2006 Act, s 729(2) (in force from 1 October 2009, replacing 1985 Act, s 162E(1) without changes). However, if the shares cease to be regarded as qualifying shares merely by reason of a temporary suspension from trading, then there is no obligation to cancel: 2006 Act, s 729(3) (in force from 1 October 2009). The cancellation requirement is aimed at treasury shares which cease to be qualifying shares by reason of loss of listed status or access to the regulated markets.

[541] 2006 Act, s 730(1) (in force from 1 October 2009, replacing 1985 Act, s 169A(1)(b)(i) and (2) without changes).

which they were cancelled.[542] The notice must be accompanied by a statement of capital[543] with must include the particulars specified in the Act.[544] If the company fails to notify the Registrar by way of return accompanied by an appropriate statement of capital, then an offence (punishable by fine and daily default fine for continued contravention[545]) is committed by every officer in default.[546]

In addition to these two specific instances of criminal liability on the part of **24.211** officers in default, the 2006 Act, s 732 contains a 'sweep up' provision in respect of treasury shares by stating that any contravention of the statutory provisions relating to treasury shares is an offence committed by the company and any officer in default punishable by way of fine (either on conviction on indictment or on summary conviction).[547] Possible contraventions would include purchase of treasury shares in excess of the 10 per cent limit, sale of treasury shares for non-cash consideration, and failure to cancel treasury shares upon loss of qualifying status.

# D. Transfer of Shares

*Directors' functions and responsibilities on allotment*

Where shares are allotted by a company, the company must, within two months **24.212** after the allotment, complete (and be ready to deliver) certificates of the shares.[548] The same rule applies to debentures and debenture stock.[549] Default in complying with this requirement, as regards shares, debentures, or debenture stock, is an offence (punishable by fine[550]) committed by every officer in default.[551] Further, a shareholder may serve a notice on the company requiring the company to make good its default; failure by the company to comply within 10 days of the service of the notice will enable the shareholder to apply to court to have the certificates

---

[542] 2006 Act, s 730(2) (in force from 1 October 2009, replacing 1985 Act, 169A(2) without changes). Again, particulars of shares cancelled on different dates may be included in a single return: 2006 Act, s 730(3).

[543] 2006 Act, s 730(4) (in force from 1 October 2009; a new provision).

[544] 2006 Act, s 730(5) (in force from 1 October 2009; also new).

[545] 2006 Act, s 730(7) (in force from 1 October 2009, replacing 1985 Act, s 169A(4), Schedule 24).

[546] 2006 Act, s 730(6) (in force from 1 October 2009, replacing 1985 Act, s 169A(4)).

[547] 2006 Act, s 732(1), (2) (in force from 1 October 2009, replacing 1985 Act, 162G with changes).

[548] 2006 Act, s 769(1). For articles concerning share certificates, see Table A regs 6 and 7; Model Article (pcls) 24 and 25; Model Article (plc) 46 and 47. Model Article (plc) 50 contemplates that a public company may wish to issue uncertificated shares (2006, Act, ss 783–790). The 2006 Act ss 768–790, concerning certification and transfer of securites were brought into force on 6 April 2008 by the 2006 Act Commencement Order No 5, art 3(1)(i).

[549] Ibid.

[550] 2006 Act, s 769(4).

[551] 2006 Act, s 769(3) (in force since 6 April 2008).

delivered to him, and the court may make an order directing the company and any officer to make good the default.[552] Such an application may result in a costs order against the company and/or its officers.[553]

### *Directors' functions and responsibilities on transfer*

**24.213**   A company may not register a transfer of shares or debentures unless: (1) a proper instrument[554] of transfer has been delivered to it; or (2) the transfer is either exempt under the Stock Transfer Act 1982[555] or made in accordance with such regulations as may be made by the Treasury and/or the Secretary of State under Chapter 2 of Part 21 of the Act.[556] Needless to say, this prohibition does not apply to transfers by operation of law,[557] eg to a trustee in bankruptcy pursuant to the Insolvency Act, s 306.

**24.214**   The shares or other interest of any member in a company are transferable in accordance with the company's articles.[558] If there are no restrictions on transfer in a company's articles or elsewhere, the company's shareholders may transfer their shares without constraint or limitation, and the directors will have no discretionary power to refuse to register a transfer made in good faith.[559] However, a company may by its articles restrict its members' right to transfer their shares and may enforce restrictions against its members.[560] Since shares are prima facie transferable, a restriction on the right of transfer must be sufficiently clear and the courts have said that a restriction may not be achieved through uncertain language of doubtful meaning.[561] The directors of a company have no power to authorize registration in circumstances where there has been a breach of the articles.[562]

---

[552] 2006 Act, s 782(1), (2).

[553] 2006 Act, s 782(3).

[554] This provision was first introduced in 1929 to put an end to the practice of avoiding the payment of stamp duty by means of oral transfers. A 'proper instrument' is an instrument which is appropriate or suitable for stamping for stamp duty purposes, and a document may be a 'proper instrument' even if it omits the consideration, since that may be ascertained subsequently for the purpose of stamping: *Nisbet v Shepherd* [1994] 1 BCLC 300. See also *Re Paradise Motor Co Ltd* [1968] 1 WLR 1125 and *Dempsey v Celtic Football & Athletic Co Ltd* [1993] BCC 514.

[555] The Stock Transfer Act 1982 provides that transfers of certain gilt-edged securities are effective without the need for an instrument in writing.

[556] 2006 Act, s 770(1).

[557] 2006 Act, s 770(2).

[558] 2006 Act, s 544(1) (in force since 6 April 2008, pursuant to the 2006 Act Commencement Order No 3, art 3(1)(f)).

[559] *Re Smith, Knight & Co, Weston's Case* (1868) 4 Ch App 20; *Re National Provincial Marine Insurance, Gilbert's Case* (1870) 5 Ch App 559, 565; *Re Cawley & Co* (1889) 42 Ch D 209; *Re Copal Varnish Co Ltd* [1917] 2 Ch 349; *Re Bede Steam Shipping Co Ltd* [1917] 1 Ch 123.

[560] *Borland's Trustee v Steel Bros & Co Ltd* [1901] 1 Ch 279; *Lyle & Scott Ltd v Scott's Trustees* [1959] AC 763.

[561] *Greenhalgh v Mallard* [1943] 2 All ER 234, 237 (Lord Greene).

[562] *Hurst v Crampton Bros (Coopers) Ltd* [2003] 1 BCLC 304; *Tett v Phoenix Property & Investments Co Ltd* [1986] BCLC 149.

Where a company's articles authorize the directors to reject transfers to transferees **24.215**
of whom they disapprove, the directors must, before making any decision, consider the question fairly at a board meeting.[563] Further, their decision must be embodied in a substantive resolution.[564] A power of this kind is a fiduciary power to be exercised bona fide in the best interests of the company.[565]

When a transfer of shares or debentures has been lodged with a company, the **24.216**
company must (as soon as practicable and in any event within two months) either:
(1) register the transfer; or (2) give the transferee notice of refusal to register the transfer, together with reasons for the refusal.[566] A company which refuses to register a transfer must give the transferee such further information about the reasons for the refusal as the transferee may reasonably request.[567] If the company fails to comply with these requirements, an offence (punishable by fine[568]) is committed by the company and every officer in default.[569] Again, this provision does not apply to transfers by operation of law;[570] nor does it apply to transfers if the company has issued a share warrant in respect of the shares.[571]

Also, subject to four statutory exceptions, the company must complete (and be **24.217**
ready to deliver) within two months of the date of receipt of the transfer the appropriate certificates in respect of the shares, debentures, or debenture stock in question.[572] The statutory exceptions, where this rule does not apply, are:
(1) transfers which the company lawfully refuses to register;[573] (2) where the conditions of the issue of the shares, debentures, or debenture stock provide otherwise;[574] (3) transfers to financial institutions;[575] and (4) where, following the transfer, the company has issued a share warrant in respect of the shares.[576]
In a case not falling within one of the statutory exceptions, failure to comply with its

---

[563] *Re Gresham Life Assurance Society, ex p Penney* (1872) 8 Ch App 446.
[564] *Re Hackney Pavilion Ltd* [1924] 1 Ch 276.
[565] *Re Smith & Fawcett Ltd* [1942] Ch 304; *Re Coalport China Co* [1895] 2 Ch 404.
[566] 2006 Act, s 771(1).
[567] 2006 Act, s 771(2).
[568] 2006 Act, s 771(4).
[569] 2006 Act, s 771(3).
[570] 2006 Act, s 771(5)(a).
[571] 2006 Act, s 771(5)(b); see also s 779.
[572] 2006 Act, s 776(1).
[573] 2006 Act, s 776(2).
[574] 2006 Act, s 776(3)(a).
[575] 2006 Act, s 776(3)(b). For these purposes, 'financial institutions' are recognized clearing houses acting in relation to recognized investment exchanges, nominees of recognized clearing houses acting in relation to recognized investment exchanges designated for these purposes by the rules of the recognized investment exchange in question, and nominees of recognized investment exchanges designated for these purposes by the rules of the recognized investment exchange in question: see s 778(2); see also Part 18 of FSMA, which defines the component parts of this definition, eg 'recognized clearing house'.
[576] 2006 Act, s 776(4)(c); see also s 779.

requirements is an offence (punishable by fine[577]) committed by every officer in default.[578] Further, the shareholder may serve a notice on the company requiring the default to be remedied; failure to comply with the notice will entitle the shareholder to bring the matter before the court, and the court may make an order requiring compliance and may also make a costs order against the company and/or its officers.[579]

*Directors' functions and responsibilities in relation to share warrants*

**24.218** A company limited by shares may, if so authorized by its articles, issue, with respect to any fully paid shares, a warrant (known as a 'share warrant') stating that the bearer of the warrant is entitled to the shares specified in it.[580] A share warrant issued under the company's common seal entitles the bearer to the shares specified in it and the shares may be transferred by delivery of the warrant.[581] Unless the company's articles provide otherwise,[582] within two months of the surrender of a share warrant for cancellation, the company must complete (and be ready to deliver) the certificates of the shares specified in the warrant.[583] Default in complying with this requirement where applicable (ie where the company's articles do not provide otherwise) is an offence (punishable by fine[584]) committed by every officer in default.[585] Default will also entitle the person entitled to the certificate to serve a notice on the company requiring compliance within 10 days; non-compliance may result in a court application, and the court is empowered to order the delivery of the appropriate certificate, and costs may be awarded against the company and/or its directors.[586]

**Provisions in the articles**

**24.219** Table A and the Model Articles contain regulations dealing with the transfer of shares and in particular the power of the directors to refuse to register a transfer.

(1) The instrument of transfer should be in any usual form or in any other form approved by the directors and should be executed by the transferor and, if any shares are partly paid, by the transferee (Table A reg 23, Model Article (pcls) 26(1) and Model Article (plc) 63(1)).

---

[577] 2006 Act, s 776(6).
[578] 2006 Act, s 776(5).
[579] 2006 Act, s 782.
[580] 2006 Act, s 779(1).
[581] 2006 Act, s 779(2).
[582] 2006 Act, s 780(2).
[583] 2006 Act, s 780(1).
[584] 2006 Act, s 780(4).
[585] 2006 Act, s 780(3).
[586] 2006 Act, s 782.

(2) No fee is to be charged for registering the transfer and the company may retain any instrument of transfer which is registered (Table A regs 27 and 28, Model Article (pcls) 26(2) and (3) and Model Article (plc) 63(2) and (3)).

(3) The various standard form articles give the directors power to refuse to register the transfer, but they do so in different ways. Table A reg 24 gives the directors a discretionary power to refuse to register the transfer (a) of a share which is not fully paid to a person of whom they do not approve, (b) of a share over which the company has a lien, or (c) which fails to satisfy certain formal requirements (lodged at the correct office, of only one class of share and in favour of not more than four transferees). For public companies Model Article (plc) 63(3) is similar except that (a) there is no need for the directors not to approve of the transferee of a partly paid share (presumably because this was considered unnecessary) and (b) transfer could be refused if the transfer is not accompanied by the share certificates or other evidence of title reasonably required by the directors. For private companies Model Article 26(5) simply gives the directors a discretion to refuse register the transfer.

(4) If the directors refuse to register they must give notice of the refusal to the transferee and return the insrument of transfer (Table A regs 25 and 28, Model Article (pcls) 26(5) and Model Article (plc) 63(6)). The Model Articles entitle the company to retain the instrument where the directors suspect that the proposed transfer may be fraudulent.

(5) Finally Table A reg 26 gives the directors power to suspend the register of transfers of any class of shares for up to 30 days in any year. This power is not included in the Model Articles.

## E. Public Companies: Obtaining Information about Interests in Shares

**24.220** The Act contains provisions designed to enable a public company to discover the identities of its shareholders. There is a two-fold purpose to these provisions: first, to give a public company, and ultimately the public at large, a prima facie unqualified right to know who are the real owners of the company's voting shares;[587] and, secondly, since information notified to listed companies must be

---

[587] *Re Geers Gross plc* [1988] BCLC 140.

publicly announced through a Regulated Information Service, to ensure market transparency.[588]

24.221  A public company may give notice to any person whom the company knows or has reasonable cause to believe to be interested in the company's shares or to have been so interested at any point in the preceding three years.[589] The notice may require the recipient to confirm that fact or (as the case may be) to state: (1) whether or not it is the case; and (2) if he holds, or has during the preceding three years held, any such interest, to give such further information as may be required in accordance with the Act.[590]

24.222  Where the recipient fails to comply with the notice, the company may apply to the court for an order directing that the shares in question be subject to restrictions.[591] The effect of such an order is to ensure that: (1) any transfer of the shares will be void; (2) no voting rights may be exercised in respect of the shares; (3) no further shares may be issued in right of the shares or in pursuance of an offer made to their holder; and (4) except in a liquidation, no payment may be made of sums due from the company on the shares, whether in respect of capital or otherwise.[592] Due to the costs and uncertainties related to the court process, most listed companies take similar powers in their articles, which can be invoked without application to the court, subject to limitations imposed by the FSA's Listing Rules (LR 9.3.9R).

24.223  The members of a company holding at least 10 per cent of such of the paid up capital of the company as carries a right to vote at general meetings of the company (excluding any voting rights attached to any shares in the company held as treasury shares) may require it to issue a notice under s 793 requiring information about interests in shares.[593] If the company fails to comply with such a request, an offence (punishable by fine[594]) is committed by every officer in default.[595]

24.224  Where the company does comply with the request, ie by issuing a notice under s 793, the company must, on the conclusion of its investigation, cause a report to be prepared. The report must be made available for inspection within a reasonable

---

[588] See: EC Directive 88/627/EEC; Directive 2001/34/EC, Article 111; Transparency Directive, Articles 9 to 16.
[589] 2006 Act, s 793(1). The 2006 Act, ss 791–810, 811(1)–(3), 813, and 815–828, concerning information about interests in a company's shares, were brought into force on 20 January 2007 by the 2006 Act Commencement Order No 3, art 3(1)(d).
[590] 2006 Act, s 793(2) (in force since 20 January 2007). Specifically, the notice may require the recipient to give particulars of his own present or past interest in the company's shares: 2006 Act, s 793(3). See also 2006 Act, s 793(4).
[591] 2006 Act, s 794(1).
[592] 2006 Act, s 797(1).
[593] 2006 Act, s 803(1), (2).
[594] 2006 Act, s 804(3).
[595] 2006 Act, s 804(2).

period (not more than 15 days) after the conclusion of the investigation.[596] If the investigations take longer than three months, the company must prepare interim reports every three months, until the investigations are completed.[597] Failure to prepare the necessary reports is an offence punishable by fine committed by every officer in default.[598]

Any such reports must be retained for six years and must be kept available for inspection at the company's registered office or such other place as may be specified in regulations under s 1136. If not kept at the registered officer, the company must notify the Registrar of the place where the reports are kept available for inspection and any change in such place.[599] If default is made for 14 days in complying with this requirement, an offence (punishable by fine) is committed by the company and every officer in default.[600]    **24.225**

Reports must be open to inspection by any person without charge and any person is entitled, on request and on payment of the applicable fee, to be provided with a copy of the report or any part of it within 10 days of making a request for the same.[601] Default in complying with these requirements is an offence punishable by fine committed by the company and every officer in default.[602]    **24.226**

In addition, the company must keep a register of information received by it in pursuance of a requirement imposed under s 793. A company which receives any such information must, within three days of receipt, enter in the register: (1) the fact that the requirement was imposed and the date on which it was imposed; and (2) the information received in pursuance of the requirement.[603] Failure to comply with this requirement is an offence punishable by fine committed by the company and every officer in default.[604]    **24.227**

The register must be kept available for inspection at the company's registered office or at such other place as may be specified in regulations under s 1136. If not kept at the registered office, the company must give notice to the Registrar of the place where the register is kept available for inspection and any change in that place; however, no such notice is required if the register has at all times been kept available at the company's registered office. If default is made in complying with these requirements, an offence (punishable by fine) is committed by the company and every officer in default.[605]    **24.228**

---

[596] 2006 Act, s 805(1).
[597] 2006 Act, s 805(2).
[598] 2006 Act, s 806(3), (4).
[599] 2006 Act, s 805.
[600] 2006 Act, s 806(1), (2).
[601] 2006 Act, s 807(1), (2).
[602] 2006 Act, s 807(3), (4).
[603] 2006 Act, s 808(2). See also 2006 Act, s 808(3), (4).
[604] 2006 Act, s 808(5), (6).
[605] 2006 Act, s 809(4), (5).

**24.229**  Unless the register is kept in such a form as itself to constitute an index, the company must keep an index of the names entered in it. If an alteration is made to the register, a corresponding alteration must be made to the index within 10 days. The index must contain, in respect of each name, a sufficient indication to enable the information entered against it to be readily found. The index must be kept available for inspection at the same place as the register. Default in complying with these requirements is an offence punishable by fine committed by the company and every officer in default.[606]

**24.230**  The register and index must be open to inspection by any person without charge. Any person is entitled, on request and on payment of the relevant fee, to be provided with a copy of any entry in the register. A person seeking to inspect the register or to obtain a copy of an entry must provide a request containing the particulars stipulated by s 811(4) (eg name, address). Where a company receives a request under s 811, it must comply with the request if it is satisfied that it is made for a proper purpose or refuse to comply with the request if it is not so satisfied. A person whose request is refused may apply to the court. If the court is not satisfied that the request was made for a proper purpose, it may dismiss the application. If a request is provided under s 811 which the company considers is made for a proper purpose, but the company wrongly refuses to comply with the request, an offence punishable by fine is committed by the company and every officer in default.[607]

## F. Distributions

**24.231**  Under the 2006 Act, the basic rule will continue to be the same as under the 1985 Act, viz. that a distribution will not be lawful unless there is sufficient distributable profit as shown in the relevant accounts. The relevant provisions are set out below. If the company does not comply with the statutory requirements, the distribution will be unlawful.[608] It cannot therefore be made lawful by ratification. Directors may incur civil liability by reason of an unlawful distribution, and shareholders are also likely to be required to repay.

*Meaning of 'distribution'*

**24.232**  The word 'distribution' is defined by the Act, s 829 to mean every description of distribution of a company's assets to its members, whether in cash or

---

[606]  2006 Act, s 810(5), (6).
[607]  2006 Act, s 813(1), (2).
[608]  See, for example, *Precision Dippings Ltd v Precision Dippings Marketing Ltd* [1986] Ch 447, *Bairstow v Queen's Moat Houses plc* [2001] 2 BCLC 531, CA. If the distribution is in part covered by distributable profits, it may be treated as lawful to that extent: *Re Marini Ltd* [2004] BCC 172.

otherwise.[609] Accordingly, a distribution may include, for example, the gratuitous element in a sale at an undervalue to a member.[610] Benefits in kind to members in their capacity as such may also constitute distributions.[611] The label is not determinative: for example, 'director's remuneration' paid to a director who is also a shareholder may on a closer analysis appear to be a distribution to the director *qua* shareholder.[612]

However, the following are expressly not distributions: an issue of shares as fully **24.233** or partly paid bonus shares; a lawful reduction of capital in accordance with the Act; the lawful redemption or purchase of the company's own shares out of capital or unrealized profits in accordance with the Act; or a distribution of assets to members in a solvent winding up.[613]

### (1) General rules

The basic rule is that a company may only make a distribution out of profits **24.234** available for the purpose.[614] A company's profits available for distribution are its accumulated, realized profits, so far as not previously written off in a reduction or reorganization of capital duly made,[615] less its accumulated, realized losses, so far as not previously written off in a reduction or reorganization of capital. The existence of a profit or loss is determined principally, but not exclusively, by reference to generally accepted accounting principles.[616] Whether a distribution may be made by a company must be determined by reference to the profits, losses, assets, liabilities, provisions, capital, and reserves as stated in the 'relevant accounts'.[617] The 'relevant accounts' may be the last annual accounts, the interim accounts, or the initial accounts.[618] Different requirements must be satisfied in each case.

If the last annual accounts are to be used, s 837 must be consulted. In short, the **24.235** 'last annual accounts' are the individual accounts last circulated to members under s 423 or which formed the basis for a summary statement under s 426. The accounts must have been properly prepared in accordance with the Act or must at the very least be such that any deficiencies are immaterial.[619] In addition, the

---

[609] 2006 Act, s 829(1). The 2006 Act, Part 23, ss 829–853, concerning distributions, came into force on 6 April 2008 pursuant to the 2006 Act Commencement Order No 5, art 3(1)(K).

[610] *Aveling Barford Ltd v Perion Ltd* [1989] BCLC 626.

[611] *Jenkins v Harbour View Courts Ltd* [1966] NZLR 1.

[612] *Re Halt Garage (1964) Ltd* [1982] 3 All ER 1016.

[613] 2006 Act, s 829(2).

[614] 2006 Act, s 830(1).

[615] 2006 Act, s 830(2).

[616] *Gallagher v Jones* [1994] Ch 107.

[617] 2006 Act, s 836(1).

[618] 2006 Act, s 836(2).

[619] 2006 Act, s 837(2). The consequence of the accounts not being properly prepared or not giving a true and fair view is that any distribution in reliance on the accounts will be a breach of the

auditor must have made his report on the accounts and, if the accounts were qualified, the materiality of the matters resulting in the qualification must be addressed
in the context of distributions.[620] The requirement for the auditors to state whether
any qualification in their report is a material one is a mandatory requirement for
the protection of creditors, and so if it is not given before the distribution is made,
then whatever the circumstances the distribution will be unlawful.[621]

**24.236**   Initial accounts may be used, subject to s 839 of the Act, where the company has
only recently commenced trading and the distribution is proposed to be declared
during the company's first accounting reference period, or before any accounts
have been circulated in respect of that period. Initial accounts must enable a
reasonable judgment to be made as to the amounts of the profits, losses, assets,
liabilities, provisions, capital, and reserves.[622] Initial accounts will be insufficient
if they fail to make provision for a tax liability which is likely to be incurred.[623]
Where initial accounts are to be utilized by a public company as the basis for a
distribution, additional requirements will apply.[624]

**24.237**   If a company has previously drawn up and circulated annual accounts, but the
distribution cannot be justified by those accounts, interim accounts must be used
and s 838 must be followed. In short, 'interim accounts' must be accounts which
enable a reasonable judgment to be made as to the amounts of the profits, losses,
assets, liabilities, provisions, capital, and reserves.[625] Where a public company
intends to use interim accounts, additional requirements will apply.[626]

**24.238**   Specific rules apply as to successive distributions by reference to the same
accounts,[627] realized losses and profits and revaluation of fixed assets,[628] realized
profits and losses of long-term insurance business,[629] and the treatment of development costs.[630] Such accountancy matters fall outside the scope of this work.

---

statutory provisions and hence unlawful: see *Bairstow v Queens Moat Houses plc* [2001] 2 BCLC 531;
*Allied Carpets Group plc v Nethercott* [2001] BCC 81.

[620] 2006 Act, s 837(4) (replacing 1985 Act, s 271(3) and (4) without changes).
[621] *Precision Dippings Ltd v Precision Dippings Marketing Ltd* [1986] Ch 447.
[622] 2006 Act, s 839(1).
[623] *Re Loquitur Ltd* [2003] 2 BCLC 442.
[624] 2006 Act, s 839(2)–(7). As with 'interim accounts': the 'initial accounts' must have been
'properly prepared' and must have been subject to an auditor's report (with additional requirements
if that report was qualified) and must have been delivered to the Registrar.
[625] 2006 Act, s 838(1) (replacing 1985 Act, s 270(4) without changes).
[626] 2006 Act, s 838(2) (replacing 1985 Act, s 272(1) without changes). In short, the accounts
must have been 'properly prepared' (that is to say, prepared in accordance with 2006 Act, ss 395 to
397, applying those requirements with such modifications as are necessary because the accounts are
prepared otherwise than in respect of an accounting reference period). In addition, the balance sheet
must have been signed, and a copy of the accounts must have been delivered to the Registrar.
[627] 2006 Act, s 840.
[628] 2006 Act, s 841.
[629] 2006 Act, s 843.
[630] 2006 Act, s 844.

The articles usually provide for the company by ordinary resolution to declare **24.239**
dividends in accordance with members' rights, but that no dividend should exceed
the amount recommended by the directors.[631] The directors have power to decide
to pay interim dividends unless preferential dividends are in arrears. Provided they
act in good faith, directors do not incur liability to preference shareholders for any
loss suffered by the lawful payment of an interim dividend.[632] The directors also
have power to pay dividends at a fixed rate if it appears to them that the profits
available for distribution justify it.[633]

*Civil liability of directors at common law*

A director who causes or permits the payment of an unlawful dividend may be **24.240**
liable to the company at common law for breach of trust or negligence.[634] An early
statement of principle may be found in *Evans v Coventry* per Kindersley V-C:[635]

> It does appear to me that the directors had a duty, not only to the persons who were
> shareholders, but a duty to the persons who effected insurances in this society—a
> duty which imposed on them the necessity of not misapplying the funds of this
> society—that is, applying them in any way not justified by the terms of the deed; still
> more did it impose upon them the duty of not applying those funds in any way, or
> from any motive which was in itself unjustifiable; and I cannot but hold that all those
> who were directors are liable not only to refund those dividends which they them-
> selves received in respect of their shares, but that they are liable to refund all the divi-
> dends, as far as any of them personally were parties to the declaring of dividends or
> concurred in it. I must hold that they are liable to make good to the funds of the
> society the dividends which have thus been declared and paid.[636]

---

[631] Table A regs 102, 104; Model Article (pcls) 30(1)–(4); Model Article (plc) 70(1)–(3). Note
that there are also powers for non-cash distributions and captitalization of profits: Table A regs 105,
110; Model Article (pcls) 34, 36; Model Article (plc) 76, 78.

[632] Tabel A reg 103; Model Article (pcls) 30(1), (5), and (7).

[633] Table A reg 103; Model Article (pcls) 30(6); Model Article (plc) 70(6).

[634] This proposition was established at a very early stage in the development of company law by a
long line of cases including *Evans v Coventry* (1856) 25 LJ Ch 489, 501 (Kindersley V-C) and (1857)
8 De GM & G 835, 616 (Court of Appeal); *In re Mercantile Trading Co, Stringer's Case* (1869) LR 4
Ch App 475, 487 (Selwyn LJ); *In re County Marine Insurance Co, Rance's Case* (1870) LR 6 Ch App
104, 119–20 (James LJ) and 122–4 (Mellish LJ); *Salisbury v Metropolitan Railway Co* (1870) 22 LT
839, 841 (Malins V-C); *In re National Funds Assurance Co* (1878) 10 Ch D 118, 125–9 (Jessel MR);
*In re Exchange Banking Company, Flitcroft's Case* (1882) 21 Ch D 519, 525 (Bacon V-C); *In re Oxford
Benefit Building and Investment Society* (1886) 35 Ch D 502, 509 (Kay J); *Precision Dippings Ltd
v Precision Dippings Marketing Ltd* [1986] Ch 447, CA; *Bairstow v Queens Moat Houses plc*
[2001] 2 BCLC 531, CA at paras 37–48; *Re Paycheck Services 3 Ltd.* [2008] 2 BCLC 613.

[635] (1856) 25 LJ Ch 489, 501, per Kindersley V-C.

[636] Accordingly the Vice-Chancellor declared that 'the respective declarations of dividends from
time to time made out of the funds of the said company or society were breaches of trust' and that the
directors were 'liable to answer and make good to the funds of the said company or society what shall
from time to time have been paid in pursuance thereof from the respective times they were elected
to the office of director or first acted as directors'. This was varied on appeal ((1857) 8 De GM & G
835, 616) to provide: 'Declare that the respective declarations of dividends from time to time made
out of the funds of the said company or society were breaches of trust, and that [the directors] are
respectively liable to answer and make good to the funds of the said company or society what shall

**24.241** The early cases conceptualized the director's liability purely in terms of breach of trust.[637] It was not until 1894 that Lindley and Kay LJJ explained that the trust analysis was not entirely apt, since directors were not actually trustees of the company's assets.[638] However, Lindley and Kay LJJ explained that a director's fiduciary duties provide the basis for liability for wrongful distribution, and this conclusion has been followed consistently ever since.[639]

**24.242** Accordingly the position at common law remains the same today as it was in the late nineteenth century when the position was summarized in the following terms by Kay J in *Re Oxford Benefit Building and Investment Society*:[640]

> It is settled by authorities which I cannot dispute: (1) That directors are quasi-trustees of the capital of the company. (2) Directors who improperly pay dividends out of capital are liable to repay such dividends personally upon the company being wound up. (3) This liability may be enforced by a creditor or by the liquidator . . . or by the incorporated company before a winding-up. (4) The acquiescence of the shareholders does not affect the creditors in such a case. (5) Such an act is a breach of trust, and the remedy is not barred by the Statute of Limitations.

**24.243** It should be noted however that a claim against a director for breach of trust is not the sole means by which a director may be held liable at common law for causing or permitting the payment of an unlawful dividend. A director may also be held liable to pay damages to the company in tort for negligence. This analysis was

---

from time to time have been paid in pursuance thereof from the respective times aforesaid, with interest thereon at the rate of 4 per cent per annum, without prejudice to any right which the said [directors] or any of them may have against the other shareholders of the said company or society who may have received dividends.'

[637] See, for example, in *Salisbury v Metropolitan Railway Co* (1870) 22 LT 839, 841 (Malins V-C); *Wye Valley Railway Co v Hawes* (1880) 16 Ch D 489, 494 (Jessel MR); *Re Exchange Banking Company, Flitcroft's Case* (1882) 21 Ch D 519 (Bacon V-C); and *Leeds Estate Building and Investment Company v Shepherd* (1887) 36 Ch D 787, 797–8 (Stirling J).

[638] In *Re Lands Allotment Company* [1894] 1 Ch 616, Lindley LJ said at 631: 'Although directors are not properly speaking trustees, yet they have always been considered and treated as trustees of money which comes to their hands or which is actually under their control; and ever since joint stock companies were invented directors have been held liable to make good moneys which they have misapplied upon the same footing as if they were trustees.' Kay LJ said at 638: 'Now, case after case has decided that directors of trading companies are not for all purposes trustees or in the position of trustees, or quasi-trustees, or to be treated as trustees in every sense; but if they deal with the funds of a company, although those funds are not absolutely vested in them, but funds which are under their control, and deal with those funds in a manner which is beyond their powers, then as to that dealing they are treated as having committed a breach of trust.'

[639] See, for example *Belmont Finance Corporation Ltd v Williams Furniture Ltd (No 2)* [1980] 1 All ER 393, 405 (Buckley LJ): 'A limited company is of course not a trustee of its own funds: it is their beneficial owner, but in consequence of the fiduciary character of their duties the directors of a limited company are treated as if they were trustees of those funds of the company which are in their hands or under their control, and if they misapply them they commit a breach of trust'.

[640] (1886) 35 Ch D 502, 509.

considered by Stirling J in *Leeds Estate Building and Investment Company v Shepherd*:[641]

> Directors who are proved to have, in fact, paid a dividend out of capital fail to excuse themselves if they have not taken reasonable care to secure the preparation of estimates and statements of account, such as it was their duty to prepare and submit to the shareholders, and have declared the dividends complained of without having exercised thereon their judgment as mercantile men on the estimates and statements submitted to them.[642]

In *Re D'Jan of London Ltd*[643] Hoffmann LJ held that the duty of care owed by a director to a company at common law is accurately stated in the Insolvency Act, s 214:

**24.244**

> [The standard of] a reasonably diligent person having both (a) the general knowledge, skill and experience that may reasonably be expected of a person carrying out the same functions as are carried out by that director in relation to the company and (b) the general knowledge, skill and experience that that director has.[644]

This standard is now part of the statutory code of directors' duties under the 2006 Act.

No repayment of an improperly paid dividend will however be ordered where the payment was made without fault on the part of the directors.[645] This is the case whether the claim is formulated as breach of trust or breach of the directors' contractual duty. The nature and extent of fault which has to be found against a director before he is liable to make repayment of the dividends was considered by Nelson J in *Bairstow v Queens Moat Houses plc*:[646]

**24.245**

> Whilst there are passages in the nineteenth century cases which suggest that the test for judging a director's conduct was at least in part objective, there is no doubt that the standard of care set was undemanding. A 'mere error of judgment' would not permit recovery and 'gross or wilful negligence' had to be established . . . The law has however kept pace with the changing role of directors. An executive director under a

---

[641] (1887) 36 Ch D 787, 801.

[642] Lord Davey cited this statement with approval in *Dovey v Cory* [1901] AC 477 at 490, adding: 'It is by this standard that the conduct of the respondent must be judged in this case.'

[643] [1994] 1 BCLC 561.

[644] See also *Bairstow v Queens Moat Houses plc* [2000] 1 BCLC 549, 559D–E (Nelson J). For an example of a case in which the directors were held liable to pay damages to the company for negligently causing the payment of an unlawful dividend, see *Leeds Estate Building and Investment Company v Shepherd* (1887) 36 Ch D 787, 805 (Stirling J): 'Upon the whole, although the directors were, I believe, ignorant of the true state of the company's affairs, and although I find no trace of their having acted with the view of obtaining any improper benefit for themselves, I feel compelled to hold that they have fallen short of that standard of care which . . . they ought to have applied to the affairs of the company.'

[645] *Bairstow v Queens Moat Houses plc* [2000] 1 BCLC 549, 577 (Nelson J). His judgment on the directors' liability for paying unlawful dividends was upheld by the Court of Appeal: [2001] 2 BCLC 531.

[646] [2000] 1 BCLC 549, 559B–G.

contract of service and paid substantial remuneration must be expected to bring to his work a level of competence commensurate with his responsibilities and his remuneration. As I have found earlier in this judgment in relation to the duty of skill and care generally, an executive director is to be judged at common law by the same test as set under s 214 of the Insolvency Act 1986. Thus he has to have the general knowledge, skill and experience that may reasonably be expected of a person carrying out the same functions as are carried out by that director in relation to the company as well as the general knowledge, skill and experience that that director has . . . This modern objective test requires that a director is judged not merely by that which he knows, but also that which he ought to know as a reasonably diligent person having the knowledge, skill and experience expected of a person carrying out his task. I am satisfied that this is so whether his acts or omissions are being considered in the context of the general duty of skill and care, or his specific duties in relation to the payment of dividends. The test of culpable negligence or carelessness or gross neglect set out in the nineteenth century cases must therefore be considered in the light of the developments in the law relating to the duties of directors, and in so far as they remain extant as tests, must be assessed in relation to the modern role and function of a paid executive director.

**24.246**    Nelson J's conclusions may be found at 559H–560B:

[A] director who authorises the payment of an unlawful dividend in breach of his duty as a quasi-trustee will be liable to repay such dividends:

(1)  if he knows that the dividends were unlawful, whether or not that actual knowledge amounts to fraud; or

(2)  if he knows the facts that established the impropriety of the payments, even though he was unaware that such impropriety rendered the payment unlawful (*Re Kingston Cotton Mill Co (No 2)* [1896] 1 Ch 331 at 347 and *Precision Dippings Ltd v Precision Dippings Marketing Ltd* [1986] Ch 447 at 457);

(3)  if he must be taken in all the circumstances to know all the facts which render the payments unlawful (*Precision Dippings Ltd v Precision Dippings Marketing Ltd* [1986] Ch 447 at 457);

(4)  if he ought to have known, as a reasonably competent and diligent director, that the payments were unlawful (*Norman v Theodore Goddard* [1991] BCLC 1028, *Re D'Jan of London Ltd* [1994] 1 BCLC 561 and s.214 of the Insolvency Act 1986).

**24.247**    In a claim against directors for breach of trust or negligence, the proper claimant before the making of a winding-up order is the company itself. A claim by the company is also possible after the making of a winding-up order. In the alternative the liquidator may bring a claim against a director under the Insolvency Act, s 212, which provides:

(1) This section applies if in the course of the winding up of a company it appears that a person who (a) is or has been an officer of the company . . . or (c) . . . is or has been concerned, or has taken part, in the promotion, formation or management of the company, has misapplied or retained, or become accountable for, any money or other property of the company, or has been guilty of any misfeasance or breach of any fiduciary or other duty in relation to the company . . . (3) The court may, on the application of the official receiver or the liquidator, or of any creditor or contribu-

tory, examine into the conduct of the person falling within subsection (1) and compel him (a) to repay, restore or account for the money or property or any part of it, with interest at such rate as the court thinks just, or (b) to contribute such sum to the company's assets by way of compensation in respect of the misfeasance or breach of fiduciary or other duty as the court thinks just.[647]

A director or former director who faces a claim by the company or the liquidator **24.248** may be able to rely on the 2006 Act, s 1157[648] in defence to such a claim. It is not necessary for a party to plead specially s 1157 and the section may be raised if the parties so wish for the first time at trial.[649] For further discussion of s 1157, see Chapter 16, Section D.

*Civil liability of members at common law*

In many cases, directors are also members. In such cases, the directors may be **24.249** liable at common law, as members, in addition to their liabilities as directors. The common law position as regards members who receive an unlawful dividend is: (1) they may be liable to repay money had and received by reason of a mistake of fact (ie on a restitutionary claim by the company, subject to the defence of change of position); or (2) they may be held liable as constructive trustees on the grounds of knowing receipt of trust property.

The second potential ground of liability was explained in *Belmont Finance* **24.250** *Corporation Ltd v Williams Furniture Ltd (No 2)*:[650]

> If the directors of a company in breach of their fiduciary duties misapply the funds of their company so that they come into the hands of some stranger to the trust who receives them with knowledge (actual or constructive) of the breach, he cannot conscientiously retain those funds against the company unless he has some better equity. He becomes a constructive trustee for the company of the misapplied funds. This is stated very clearly by Jessel MR in *Russell v Wakefield Waterworks Co* (1875) LR 20 Eq 474, 479, where he said: 'In this court the money of the company is a trust fund, because it is applicable only to the special purposes of the company in the hands of the agents of the company, and it is in that sense a trust fund applicable by them to those special purposes; and a person taking it from them with notice that it is being applied to other purposes cannot in this court say that he is not a constructive trustee.'[651]

---

[647] It is well established that this section deals only with procedure and does not create any new rights. It provides a summary mode of enforcing existing rights: *City Equitable Fire Insurance Co* [1925] 1 Ch 407, 507 (Pollock MR).

[648] Which replaced 1985 Act, s 727 on 1 October 2007. In *Bairstow v Queens Moat Houses plc* [2001] 2 BCLC 531 the Court of Appeal refused relief where the directors had been guilty of dishonesty in preparing the relevent accounts. See also *Re Loquitur Ltd* [2003] 2 BCLC 442; *Re Paycheck Services 3 Ltd* [2008] 2 BCLC 613.

[649] *Re Kirbys Coaches Ltd* [1991] BCLC 414 (Hoffmann J).

[650] [1980] 1 All ER 393, 405, per Buckley LJ.

[651] See also *Rolled Steel Products (Holdings) Ltd v British Steel Corporation* [1986] 1 Ch 246, 298 (Slade LJ) and 303–7 (Browne-Wilkinson LJ).

**24.251**  As a statement of law, this passage remains broadly accurate. However, it is submitted that Buckley LJ was wrong if he meant to say that constructive knowledge of a breach of trust would be sufficient. In fact, according to subsequent Court of Appeal authority, it appears that the true position is that a shareholder will not be held liable as a constructive trustee unless his state of knowledge at the time of the receipt of the unlawful dividend was such as to make it unconscionable for him to retain the benefit of the dividend.[652] More recently, a shareholder's liability as a constructive trustee was considered by Colman J in *Allied Carpets Group plc v Nethercott*:[653]

> The constructive trust is imposed on the recipient of the company's property not because he has agreed to hold it as trustee under a bare trust for some special commercial purpose but because the property has been transferred to him and to his knowledge ultra vires the powers of the company. The conjunction of want of power of disposal and knowledge of that deficiency produces the position where no beneficial interest has passed from the company to the transferee. When the company claims repayment of the unlawfully distributed dividends it is simply reclaiming its property from a transferee who, because he acquired it with knowledge that the company has been wrongfully divested of it, is under a duty to restore it.[654]

**24.252**  It is arguable that a shareholder who is also a director may be entitled to be relieved from liability under the 2006 Act, s 1157 although the position is not entirely free from doubt.[655]

*Civil liability of members under statute*

**24.253**  Further, the 2006 Act, s 847 gives companies a statutory means of recouping unlawful dividends from shareholders. It provides:

(1) This section applies where a distribution, or part of one, made by a company to one of its members is made in contravention of this Part.

(2) If at the time of the distribution the member knows or has reasonable grounds for believing that it is so made, he is liable (a) to repay it (or that part of it, as the case may be) to the company, or (b) in the case of a distribution made otherwise than in cash, to pay the company a sum equal to the value of the distribution (or part) at that time.

(3) This is without prejudice to any obligation imposed apart from this section on a member of a company to repay a distribution unlawfully made to him.

---

[652] *Bank of Credit and Commerce International (Overseas) Ltd v Akindele* [2001] Ch 437, CA.

[653] [2001] BCC 81.

[654] See also *Moxham v Grant* [1900] 1 QB 88, 92 (AL Smith LJ) and 94 (Collins LJ), and *Re Cleveland Trust plc* [1991] BCLC 424 (Scott J).

[655] In *Inn Spirit Ltd v Burns* [2003] BPIR 413 the directors of a company had taken large sums of money from the company by way of unlawful dividend. Rimer J dismissed the company's application for summary judgment, holding that the directors had a real prospect of successfully defending the claim under the 1985 Act, s 727.

(4) This section does not apply in relation to (a) financial assistance given by a company in contravention of section 678 or 679, or (b) any payment made by a company in respect of the redemption of purchase by the company of shares in itself.

This section replicates (with immaterial differences) the 1985 Act, s 277, which **24.254** in turn replicated the 1980 Act, s 44. The 1980 Act, s 44, which was enacted to comply with the UK's obligations under Article 16 of the Second Directive on Company Law (79/91/EEC), came into operation on 22 December 1980.[656] There was no corresponding statutory provision in English law before 22 December 1980. Prior to that date a company seeking to recover unlawful dividends was required to rely on its common law remedies, which have been expressly preserved by statute.[657]

The leading case on this provision is *It's A Wrap (UK) Ltd v Gula*,[658] in which the **24.255** Court of Appeal held that for a member to have the knowledge or reasonable grounds for belief required by this provision, he need not know or have reasonable grounds to believe that the distribution will contravene the provisions of the Act, and it will be sufficient if he knows or has reason to believe the relevant facts constituting the contravention.

## (2) Additional provisions for public companies

Additional restrictions apply in respect of public companies. A public company **24.256** may only make a distribution: (1) if the amount of its net assets is not less than the aggregate of its called-up share capital and undistributable reserves; and (2) if, and to the extent that, the distribution does not reduce the amount of those assets to less than that aggregate.[659] For this purpose a company's 'net assets' means the aggregate of the company's assets less the aggregate of its liabilities.[660] The term 'liabilities' here includes: (1) where the relevant accounts are Companies Act accounts, provisions of a kind specified for the purposes of this subsection by regulations under s 396; and (2) where the relevant accounts are IAS accounts, provisions of any kind.[661] A company's undistributable reserves are: (1) its share premium account; (2) its capital redemption reserve; (3) the amount by which its accumulated, unrealized profits (so far as not previously utilized by capitalization) exceed its accumulated, unrealized losses (so far as not previously written off in a reduction or reorganization of capital duly made); (4) any other reserve that the company is prohibited from distributing (i) by any enactment or (ii) by its articles. The reference in this context to capitalization does not include a transfer of profits

---

[656] Companies Act 1980 (Commencement No 2) Order 1980 (SI 1980/1785).
[657] 1980 Act, s 44(2), 1985 Act, s 277(2), and 2006 Act, s 847(3) .
[658] [2006] EWCA Civ 544, [2006] 2 BCLC 634.
[659] 2006 Act, s 831(1).
[660] 2006 Act, s 831(2).
[661] 2006 Act, s 831(3).

of the company to its capital redemption reserve.[662] A public company must not include any uncalled share capital as an asset in any accounts relevant for purposes of this section.[663] Additional requirements apply in the case of investment companies.[664]

## G. Loan Capital

**24.257** Under the Act, the term 'debenture' includes debenture stock, bonds, and any other securities of a company, whether or not constituting a charge on the assets of the company.[665]

*Responsibilities and liabilities of directors in respect of registration*

**24.258** A company must register an allotment of debentures as soon as possible and in any event within two months after the date of allotment.[666] If the company fails to comply with this requirement, an offence (punishable by fine[667]) is committed by the company and every officer in default.[668] A company's register of debenture holders must be kept available for inspection at the company's registered office (or at such other place as may be specified in regulations made under the 2006 Act, s 1136).[669] A company must give notice to the Registrar of the place where the register is kept and any change in that place.[670] If the company makes default for 14 days in complying with this requirement, an offence (punishable by fine[671]) is committed by the company and every officer in default.[672]

*Responsibilities and liabilities of directors in respect of inspection*

**24.259** Every register of debenture holders of a company must be open to inspection free of charge by the registered holder of the debentures or any holder of any shares in the company;[673] in any other case, a fee may be payable.[674] Any person may require a copy of the register, or any part of it, on payment of the relevant fee.[675]

---

[662] 2006 Act, s 831(4).
[663] 2006 Act, s 831(5).
[664] 2006 Act, s 832 *et seq*.
[665] 2006 Act, s 738. The 2006 Act, Part 19, ss 738–754 concerning debentures, came into force on 6 April 2008 pursuant to the 2006 Act Commencement Order No 5, art 3(1)(g).
[666] 2006 Act, s 741(1).
[667] 2006 Act, s 741(3).
[668] 2006 Act, s 741(2).
[669] 2006 Act, s 743(1).
[670] 2006 Act, s 743(4).
[671] 2006 Act, s 743(5).
[672] 2006 Act, s 743(2).
[673] 2006 Act, s 744(1)(a).
[674] 2006 Act, s 744(1)(b).
[675] 2006 Act, s 744(2).

Any request to inspect or copy the register must comply with the Act, s 744(4), which prescribes the necessary contents of such a request. Where a company receives a request, it must within five working days either comply with the request or apply to the court.[676] If on such an application the court is satisfied that the inspection or copy is not sought for a proper purpose, it shall direct the company not to comply with the request and may direct that the company's costs of the application be paid by the person making the request.[677] If the company fails to comply with the request or apply to court before the stipulated deadline, an offence (punishable by fine[678]) is committed by the company and every officer in default.[679]

*Responsibilities and liabilities of directors in respect of copy documents*

Any holder of debentures of a company is entitled, on request and on payment **24.260** of the applicable fee, to be provided with a copy of any trust deed for securing the debentures.[680] Default in complying with any such request is an offence (punishable by fine[681]) committed by the company and every officer in default.[682]

# H. Registration of Charges

A floating charge is a charge over a fluctuating fund, eg a charge over a trading **24.261** company's stock, which covers the company's stock at any one time, but does not prohibit the company from selling such stock in the ordinary course of business.[683] A floating charge is to be contrasted with a fixed charge, which gives the holder of the charge an immediate proprietary interest in the assets subject to the charge which binds all those into whose hands the assets may come with notice of the charge.

The benefit of a floating charge is that it is capable of affording the creditor, by a **24.262** single instrument, an effective and comprehensive security upon the entire undertaking of the debtor company and its assets from time to time, while at the same time leaving the company free to deal with its assets and pay its trade creditors in the ordinary course of business without reference to the holder of the charge.

---

[676] 2006 Act, s 745(1). If the company applies to the court, it must notify the person making the request: 2006 Act, s 745(2).
[677] 2006 Act, s 745(3).
[678] 2006 Act, s 746(2).
[679] 2006 Act, s 746(1).
[680] 2006 Act, s 749(1).
[681] 2006 Act, s 749(3).
[682] 2006 Act, s 749(2).
[683] The floating charge originated in England in a series of cases in the Chancery Division in the 1870s. For a history of the floating charge, see the Opinion of the Privy Council (delivered by Lord Millett) in *Agnew v Commissioners of the Inland Revenue* [2001] 2 AC 710.

**24.263**   Historically, however, floating charges were perceived as a vehicle for fraud, since a company director could advance money to his own company by way of loans rather than by way of capital, grant himself a floating charge over the company's undertaking in respect of the sums owed to him by the company, allow the company to incur credit to third parties despite the existence of the charge, and yet step in at any time, confident of taking priority over the ordinary trade creditors. This was seen by many judges as an injustice and by Lord Macnaghten as a 'great scandal'.[684]

**24.264**   The remedy adopted by Parliament was to require floating charges (and other charges) to be registered so that those proposing to extend credit to a company could discover their existence. The requirement was introduced by the Companies Act 1900, s 14 and (from 1 October 2009) in the 2006 Act, s 860. Registration is to be effected by delivering the prescribed particulars of the charge, together with the instrument (if any) by which the charge is created or evidenced, to the Registrar of Companies.[685]

**24.265**   The registration requirement also applies to charges on land,[686] charges created or evidenced by any instrument which, if executed as an individual, would require registration as a bill of sale,[687] charges created for the purpose of securing debentures,[688] charges on uncalled share capital,[689] charges on calls made but not paid,[690] charges on ships or aircraft or any share in a ship,[691] and charges on goodwill or intellectual property.[692]

**24.266**   If the company fails to register a registrable charge, an offence is committed by the company and every officer who is in default.[693] The penalty on indictment is a fine, and the penalty on summary conviction is a fine not exceeding the statutory maximum.[694]

---

[684]   *Re General South American Co* (1876) 2 Ch D 337, 341 (Malins V-C); *Salomon v A Salomon & Co Ltd* [1897] AC 22, 53 (Lord Macnaghten); *Re London Pressed Hinge Co Ltd* [1905] 1 Ch 576, 581–3 (Buckley J).

[685]   2006 Act, s 860(1). The 2006 Act Commencement Order No 8, art 3(n) brings Part 25, ss 860– 894, concerning company charges into force on 1 October 2009. These provisions replace the 1985 act, ss 395–408.

[686]   2006 Act, s 860(7)(a) (coming into force on 1 October 2009, replacing 1985 Act, s 396(1)).

[687]   2006 Act, s 860(7)(b) (coming into force on 1 October 2009).

[688]   2006 Act, s 860(7)(c) (coming into force on 1 October 2009).

[689]   2006 Act, s 860(7)(d) (coming into force on 1 October 2009).

[690]   2006 Act, s 860(7)(e) (coming into force on 1 October 2009).

[691]   2006 Act, s 860(7)(h) (which comes into force on 1 October 2009).

[692]   2006 Act, s 860(7)(i) (from 1 October 2009).

[693]   2006 Act, s 860(4) (in force on 1 October 2009; to replace 1985 Act, s 399(3), Schedule 24, with changes).

[694]   2006 Act, s 860(5) (in force on 1 October 2009).

The same registration requirements (and the same offences) exist in respect of **24.267** registrable charges over property acquired.[695]

In addition to registering charges with the Registrar of Companies, every limited **24.268** company must keep a register of charges available for inspection. The register must contain details of all fixed and floating charges. There must be a short description of the property charged, the amount of the charge, and the name of the chargeholder.[696] An officer of the company who knowingly and wilfully authorizes or permits the omission of an entry required to be made in the company's register of charges commits an offence[697] punishable on conviction on indictment by way of a fine or on summary conviction by way of a fine not exceeding the statutory maximum.[698]

---

[695] 2006 Act, s 862 (in force on 1 October 2009, replacing 1985 Act, s 400(1), without changes).

[696] 2006 Act, s 876(1) and (2) (in force on 1 October 2009, replacing 1985 Act, s 407(1), (2)).

[697] 2006 Act, s 876(3) (in force on 1 October 2009, replacing 1985 Act, s 407(3), without changes).

[698] 2006 Act, s 876 (in force on 1 October 2009).

# 25

# REORGANIZATIONS AND TAKEOVERS

## A. Introduction

The Companies Act, Part 26, ss 895–901,[1] contain provisions for arrangements **25.01** and reconstructions, which restate, with minor amendments, provisions in the 1985 Act, ss 425–427. Part 27, ss 902–941, contain provisions for mergers and divisions of public companies, which restate provisions in the 1985 Act, s 427A and Schedule 15B with drafting changes. Part 28, ss 942–992, contain provisions about takeovers. Chapters 1 and 2, ss 942–973, concerning the Takeover Panel and impediments to takeovers, are new provisions, while the remaining sections in Part 28 restate with minor amendments provisions contained in the 1985 Act, ss 428–430F. The purpose of this chapter is to discuss the role of directors in relation to these procedures and to identify their duties and liabilities. For this purpose each part of this chapter begins with an introductory description of the provisions and procedures, which is followed by a discussion of the relevant functions and duties of directors.

---

[1] The 2006 Act, ss 895–941 came into force on 6 April 2008: 2006 Commencement Order No 5, art 3(1)(l) and (mm). Sections 942–992 came into force on 6 April 2007: 2006 Commencement Order No 2, art 2(1)(b).

# B. Arrangements and Reconstructions

## (1) The scope of the provisions

**25.02** The Companies Act, Part 26, ss 895–901, preserves the established procedure whereby a company can propose a compromise or arrangement between itself and its creditors (or any class of them) or its members (or any class of them).[2] If a majority in number representing 75% in value of the creditors (or class of creditors) or members (or class of members) as the case may be, vote in favour of a compromise or arrangement then the court may sanction the compromise or arrangement. The compromise or arrangement will then have binding effect on the company and on the creditors (or class of creditors) or members (or class of members).

**25.03** Directors will be concerned with proposals for schemes to effect compromises or arrangements between a company and its members, where it is desired to reorganize the capital of the company or in the context of a takeover or amalgamation.[3] They would only be concerned with schemes to effect compromises or arrangements with creditors if the company is not in administration or liquidation. If the company is or is likely to be unable to pay its debts, a company voluntary arrangement under the Insolvency Act, Part 1 may be a more advantageous procedure and the directors may well be advised to place the company in administration in order to protect its property and enable it to carry on business while the scheme is being promoted.[4] In spite of those considerations, in recent years directors have been

---

[2] These provisions can be traced back to the 1870 Act, when their application was limited to companies being wound up. The 1908 Act brought into force provisions of the 1907 Act, which extended their application to all companies.

[3] *Re Peninsular & Oriental Steam Navigation Company* [2006] EWHC 389 (Ch). In recent times, schemes of arrangement have proved to be increasingly popular as a means of effecting takeovers. The perceived advantages of schemes as a means of effecting takeovers are speed (obtaining 100% control of a company will usually be quicker under a scheme than under a takeover offer) and certainty (since a scheme, if sanctioned, will deliver 100% ownership of the offeree) which may, in particular, give assurance to lenders financing the deal. In addition, a scheme will normally avoid stamp duty (0.5%) on the value of the offeree company's shares acquired by the offeror, as these are typically cancelled and re-issued to the offeror, and no stamp duty is levied on such transaction. A scheme may also prove attractive where the offeree company has a significant number of US shareholders as a court-approved scheme is exempt from the US tender offer requirements under the US Securities Exchange Act 1934. The principal drawback with schemes is that they always require 75% approval by offeree company shareholders present and voting at the relevant shareholders' meetings and are, therefore, to this extent inflexible. They are also more vulnerable to a blocking strategy as a shareholder (for example a competing offeror) with a 25.1% shareholding (or, in practice, significantly lower) can prevent the necessary 75% being achieved. Such a holding would not be sufficient to prevent an offeror achieving 50.1% acceptance under a normal takeover offer (see paragraph 25.84 below).

[4] Once the promotion of the scheme for creditors is underway the court should stay executions against the company's property: *Hudson's Concrete Products Ltd v DB Evans (Bilston) Ltd* (1961) 105

increasingly involved in promoting s 425 schemes between companies and creditors[5] or where a standstill can be agreed with creditors[5] or where a solvent insurance company wishes to compromise policyholders' claims.[6]

*Meaning of 'compromise' and 'arrangement'*

A compromise is an agreement in settlement of a claim which is in doubt, dispute, or difficulty of enforcement.[7] On the other hand, an 'arrangement' has a very wide meaning.[8] The only requirement established by the case law is that an arrangement must involve an element of 'give and take';[9] beyond that, the courts have declined to attempt to define an arrangement. A moratorium on claims may constitute an arrangement.[10] Further, by s 895(2), an 'arrangement' is also specifically defined to include a reorganization of the company's share capital by the consolidation of shares of different classes or by the division of shares into shares of different classes, or by both of these methods.

**25.04**

*Persons with whom they can be made; creditors and members*

Although 'creditor' is not defined in the Companies Act, it has been held that for these purposes (a) a creditor is any person who has a pecuniary claim against the company including those whose claims are future or contingent,[11] and (b) a creditor is not limited to those persons who would have a provable claim in the winding up of the company (though it does include all such persons).[12] However, a bondholder may not be a creditor of a company since the bonds are usually held

**25.05**

---

SJ 281, CA; *D Wilson (Birmingham) Ltd v Metropolitan Property Developments Ltd* [1975] 2 All ER 814, CA; *Rainbow v Moorgate Properties Ltd* [1975] 1 WLR 788, CA; *Roberts Petroleum Ltd v Kenny Ltd* [1983] 2 AC 192, 207–13, HL.

[5] The cases of Marconi (see *Re Marconi plc, Re Marconi Corp plc* [2003] EWHC 1083 (Ch)), Drax (see *Re Drax Holdings Ltd* [2004] 1 WLR 1049), and MyTravel (see *Re MyTravel Group plc* [2005] 2 BCLC 123) are recent examples.

[6] For example *Re Hawk Insurance Co Ltd* [2001] 2 BCLC 480, CA, *Re Pan Atlantic Insurance Co Ltd* [2003] 2 BCLC 678, and *Re Osiris Insurance Ltd* [1999] 1 BCLC 182.

[7] *Mercantile Investment & General Trust Co v International Co of Mexico* [1893] 1 Ch 484n, 491n, CA.

[8] *Re National Bank Ltd* [1966] 1 WLR 819, 829; *Re Calgary and Edmonton Land Co* [1975] 1 WLR 355, 363; *Re Savoy Hotel Ltd* [1981] 1 Ch 351, 359.

[9] *Re NFU Development Trust Ltd* [1972] 1 WLR 1548.

[10] *Inland Revenue Commissioners v Adam & Partners Ltd* [2001] 1 BCLC 222 (CA). It is not a necessary element of an arrangement that it should alter the rights existing between the company and the creditors or members with whom it is made; provided that the context and content of the scheme are such as properly to constitute an arrangement between the company and the members or creditors concerned, it will fall within the section: *Re T&N Ltd (No 3)* [2007] 1 BCLC 563.

[11] *Re Midland Coal, Coke and Iron Co* [1895] 1 Ch 267; *Re Cancol Ltd* [1996] 1 All ER 37.

[12] *Re T&N Ltd* [2006] 1 WLR 1728 at para 40.

by a depositary and it is the depositary rather than the beneficial owner of the bonds who has a claim against the company.[13]

**25.06** The meaning of 'member' does not present any difficulties. The members of a company are the subscribers of the company's memorandum of association once registered and every other person who agrees to become a member of the company and whose name is entered in the register of members.[14]

*Company*

**25.07** A company for the purposes of the Companies Act, Part 26, means any company liable to be wound up under the provisions of the Insolvency Act or the Insolvency (Northern Ireland) Order 1989.[15] Under the provisions of the Insolvency Act both companies incorporated in England and Wales and foreign companies may be wound up.[16]

**25.08** The Court of Appeal has held that there are three conditions which must be satisfied for the making of a winding-up order in respect of a foreign company: (1) there must be a sufficient connection with England (which may, but does not necessarily have to, consist of assets within the jurisdiction); (2) there must be a reasonable possibility, if a winding-up order is made, of benefit to those applying for the winding-up order; and (3) one or more persons interested in the distribution of assets of the company must be persons over whom the court can exercise jurisdiction.[17] In *Re Drax Holdings plc*[18] the court held that the second and third requirements do not need to be satisfied for the court to have jurisdiction to sanction a scheme in respect of a foreign company; it is enough that a sufficient connection with England is shown.

**25.09** In addition to the common law requirements for winding up a foreign company, the EC Insolvency Regulation now restricts the jurisdiction of the English court, in relation to companies with their centre of main interests within the EU, to winding up only such companies as have their COMI or an establishment in England and Wales. The better view is that these rules as to intra-European jurisdiction do not affect the question of whether the company is liable to be wound

---

[13] *Re Dunderland Ltd* [1909] 1 Ch 446. See 'Bondholder Schemes of Arrangement: Playing the Numbers Game' [2003] *Insolvency Intelligence* 73 and 'Issues Arising in Cross-Border Schemes of Arrangements [1994] *International Insolvency Review* 122.

[14] s 112.

[15] s 895(2)(b).

[16] Foreign companies may be wound up as unregistered companies under the Insolvency Act, s 221.

[17] *Stocznia Gdanska SA v Latreefers Inc (No 2)* [2001] 2 BCLC 116, CA.

[18] [2004] 1 WLR 1049. Followed in *Re La Mutuelle du Mans Assurances IARD* [2006] BCC 11; *Re DAP Holdings NV* [2006] BCC 48; *Re Sovereign Marine & General Insurance Co Ltd* [2007] 1 BCLC 228.

up for purposes of the court's jurisdiction to sanction a compromise or arrangement.[19]

## (2) Summary of the procedure

*Court order for holding of meeting*

The procedure for the sanction of a compromise or arrangement is begun by an application being made to the court for an order under s 896 summoning a meeting or meetings of creditors (or class of creditors)[20] or members (or class of members) as the case may be. Under s 896(2) the application may be made by (a) the company, (b) any creditor or member of the company, or (c) if the company is being wound up or an administration order is in force in relation to it, the liquidator or administrator. The application is made by a Part 8 Claim Form and should be supported by evidence in the form of a witness statement which describes the company and the proposed scheme, exhibits a copy of the draft scheme and explanatory statement, and exhibits copies of the forms of the notices of meetings and proxy and voting forms which it is intended to send to the creditors and/or members.[21]

**25.10**

In the case of a compromise or arrangement between a company and its creditors or members, it is the responsibility of the applicant at this stage to determine whether more than one meeting of creditors or members is required to consider the scheme and, if so, to ensure that those meetings are properly constituted by a class of creditors or members.[22] The test to be applied is that each meeting should be constituted by creditors or members whose rights against the company are not so dissimilar as to make it impossible for them to consult together with a view to

**25.11**

---

[19] Whether or not an entity is liable to be wound up depends on its essential nature; it does not depend on what have been described as a company's transient circumstances, amongst which are to be included the location of its centre of main interests or its establishments (*Re DAP Holding NV* [2006] BCC 48, per Lewison J at para 11). Equally, there is nothing in s 895 to suggest that Parliament intended to incorporate international jurisdictional rules such as those contained in the EC Insolvency Regulation. As *Re Drax Holdings* shows, the reference in s 895 to winding up is meant to import the need for a sufficient connection with the English jurisdiction, not to import international jurisdictional choices. Further, since schemes fall outside the scope of the EC Insolvency Regulation, it would be surprising if they fell within its scope indirectly.

[20] A compromise or arrangement may properly be promoted between a company and only some of its creditors. A class of creditors need not be complete in the sense that every creditor with similar rights is included in it. A class of creditors formulated for the purposes of approving a scheme of arrangement does not have to contain all the persons with similar rights who might objectively be said to fall within the class provided that the class is formulated in a commercially rational way or for good commercial reasons. See *Sea Assets Ltd v PT Garuda Indonesia* [2001] EWCA Civ 1696, CA and *Re Telewest Communications plc (No 1)* [2005] 1 BCLC 752 at para 57.

[21] See Practice Direction to CPR Part 49: Applications under the Companies Acts and Related Legislation.

[22] Practice Statement (Companies: Schemes of Arrangement) [2002] 1 WLR 1345 at para 2.

their common interest.[23] The test is to be applied by analysing the rights of creditors or members which are to be released or varied under the scheme and the new rights (if any) which the scheme gives to those whose rights are released or varied.[24] Further, the fact that individuals may hold divergent views based on their private interests not derived from their legal rights against the company is not a ground for calling separate meetings.[25]

**25.12**   At the stage of applying for an order convening a meeting of creditors, it is the responsibility of the applicant by evidence in support of the application or otherwise to draw to the attention of the court as soon as possible any issues which may arise as to the constitution of meetings or creditors or which otherwise affect the conduct of those meetings (referred to as 'creditor issues').[26] For this purpose, unless there are good reasons not to do so, the applicant is required to take all steps reasonably open to it to notify any person affected by the proposed scheme of the purpose which the scheme is designed to achieve, the meetings of creditors which the applicant considers are required, and their composition.[27] Usually, this is done by writing to the affected creditors in advance of the hearing of the application for an order summoning the meeting or meetings of creditors. The purpose of this approach is to enable creditor issues going to the constitution of meetings to be identified and resolved at an early stage in the process.

**25.13**   In making an order for the summoning of a meeting or meetings to consider a compromise or arrangement, the court will invariably give directions as to the means by which the relevant creditors or members (as the case may be) are to be notified of the meeting or meetings and the manner in which the meeting or meetings are to be conducted. In relation to the former, the court will usually give directions for notifying the creditors or members by post and at the same time for the relevant voting and proxy forms to be sent to them. In addition, it is usual for

---

[23]   *Re Hawk Insurance Co Ltd* [2001] 2 BCLC 480, CA at para 30, where Chadwick LJ approved the test stated by Bowen LJ in *Sovereign Assurance Co Ltd v Dodd* [1892] 2 QB 573, CA for identifying a class as being whether the rights of the creditors within the class are not so dissimilar as to make it impossible for them to consult together with a view to their common interest. Among the other cases where this test has been adopted are *Re UDL Argos Engineering & Heavy Industries Co Ltd* [2002] 1 HKC 172, HK CFA, per Lord Millett, *Sea Assets v PT Garuda* [2001] EWCA Civ 1696, CA, and *Re MyTravel Group plc* [2005] 2 BCLC 123, 168f–g, CA. See also Practice Statement (Companies: Schemes of Arrangement) [2002] 1 WLR 1345 at para 2.

[24]   In considering the rights of creditors which are to be affected by the scheme, it is necessary to use the correct comparator. In the case of an insolvent company, where the scheme is proposed as an alternative to an insolvent liquidation, it is their rights as creditors in an insolvent liquidation of the company: *Re Hawk Insurance Co Ltd* above. However, where a company is solvent and will continue in business, it is the creditors' rights against the company as a continuing entity which are the appropriate comparator: *Re British Aviation Insurance Co Ltd* [2006] 1 BCLC 665.

[25]   *Re UDL Argos Engineering & Heavy Industries Co Ltd*, above at para 27(3).

[26]   Practice Statement (Companies: Schemes of Arrangement) [2002] 1 WLR 1345 at para 4.

[27]   Ibid.

the meeting or meetings to be directed to be advertised by means of advertisements inserted in relevant publications which are likely to come to the attention of the relevant creditors or members. In relation to the meetings themselves, the court will usually direct a nominated person to act as chairman of the meetings and to report on the results to the court.

Where a majority in number representing 75% in value of the creditors (or class **25.14** of creditors) or members (or class of members) as the case may be, present and voting (either in person or by proxy) at the meeting or meetings summoned by the court, agree the compromise or arrangement, then the court may, on an application, sanction the compromise or arrangement. It should be noted that the court's jurisdiction to sanction a compromise or arrangement only arises where the compromise or arrangement has been approved by a double majority at each meeting: (1) a simple majority in number of those voting and (2) a 75% majority by value of those voting.

As under s 896(2) for an order convening a meeting or meetings of creditors or **25.15** members, under s 899(2) an application for sanction of a compromise or arrangement may be made by (a) the company, (b) any creditor or member of the company, or (c) if the company is being wound up or an administration order is in force in relation to it, the liquidator or administrator. Accordingly, a compromise or arrangement can be proposed by a creditor or member as well as by the company itself. However, in *Re Savoy Hotel Ltd*[28] the court held that the approval of the company to a compromise or arrangement was essential and, therefore, the court had no jurisdiction to sanction a proposed scheme absent such approval.

The application for sanction is made by way of a Part 8 Claim Form.[29] It should **25.16** be supported by evidence consisting of (a) a witness statement (which will usually be made by a director) verifying the petition, briefly explaining the reasons why it is submitted that the court should sanction the scheme, and drawing any other relevant matters to the court's attention, (b) a witness statement verifying compliance with the court's directions as to the service of the scheme documents and advertisement of the meetings, and (c) a report from the chairman on the meeting or meetings of creditors and/or members verified by a witness statement. The report should have attached to it the printed scheme of arrangement signed by the chairman at the meeting.

The application for sanction of the scheme will then be heard by the court. On an **25.17** application to sanction a scheme, the court must be satisfied that the requirements of the statute (such as the requirement that the scheme has been approved by

---

[28] [1981] Ch 351.
[29] See Practice Direction to CPR Part 49: Applications under the Companies Acts and Related Legislation.

the requisite majorities) have been satisfied so that it has jurisdiction to sanction the scheme.

**25.18** In relation to the exercise of its discretion to sanction a scheme, the court must be satisfied that the arrangement is such as an intelligent, honest man acting in respect of his interest might reasonably approve.[30] But, equally, the court will recognize that creditors (and members) are invariably the best judges of what is in their commercial interest:[31]

> If the creditors are acting on sufficient information and with time to consider what they are about, and are acting honestly, they are, I apprehend, much better judges of what is to their commercial advantage than the Court can be.

Aside from reasonableness, the court may refuse to sanction a scheme where the votes cast at the meeting or meetings do not fairly represent the relevant creditors (for example, because the turnout of those entitled to vote is so low) or because it considers the scheme to be inherently unfair. Other reasons why the court may refuse to sanction a scheme, related to the question of whether the meetings fairly represented the relevant creditors, are if there was some misconduct in the holding of the meetings or defect in the provision of information to the creditors (such as that contained in the explanatory statement).

**25.19** There is also a general principle that where a power is exercisable by a majority of a class then that power must be exercised by the majority in accordance with what is in the interests of the class as a whole.[32] Accordingly, the court may decline to sanction a scheme if the relevant majority creditors voted in favour of the scheme in furtherance of their own individual interests rather than the interests of the class as a whole. However, it is important to note that the requirements of this principle will be satisfied provided that the majority honestly believes that the decision it is taking is in the best interests of the class as a whole. It is therefore in general terms a subjective rather than objective test which is applied, though the lack of reasonable grounds for making a decision may indicate a lack of good faith.[33] It follows that provided that any decision by the majority is taken in good faith as being in the best interests of the class as a whole and there are reasonable grounds to support that view, then the requirements of the principle should be satisfied.

---

[30] *Re National Bank Ltd* [1966] 1 WLR 819 approving a passage from *Buckley on the Companies Acts*.

[31] *Re English, Scottish and Australian Chartered Bank* [1893] 3 Ch 385, 409, CA.

[32] *British America Nickel Corp Ltd v M J O'Brien Ltd* [1927] AC 369, 371, HL; *Redwood Master Fund Ltd v TD Bank Europe Ltd* [2006] 1 BCLC 149.

[33] See *Shuttleworth v Cox Bros & Co (Maidenhead) Ltd* [1927] 2 KB 9, CA; *Citco Banking Corp NV v Pusser's Ltd* [2007] BCC 205, PC.

### The order and its effect

A compromise or arrangement sanctioned by the court is binding on all persons **25.20** subject to the proposed compromise or arrangement, namely, all creditors or the relevant class of creditors or all members or the relevant class of members as the case may be.[34] The court's order takes effect once a copy has been delivered to the Registrar of Companies.[35] Accordingly, it is the Act which gives binding force to a scheme once it has been proposed, approved by the requisite majority of creditors or members, and sanctioned by the court.[36]

Under s 900, the court has certain powers to facilitate a reconstruction of a com- **25.21** pany or amalgamation pursuant to a compromise or arrangement which has been sanctioned. For these purposes, the essence of a 'reconstruction' of a company is that the shareholders in the new company should be the same or substantially the same as those in the old company.[37] In other words, under a 'reconstruction' sub- stantially the same shareholders will continue to carry on the business.[38] An 'amal- gamation' is an amalgamation of two or more companies. The powers under s 900 arise where it is shown that the compromise or arrangement is proposed for the purposes of, or in connection with, a reconstruction or amalgamation and under the scheme the whole or part of the undertaking or the property of any company concerned in the scheme (the transferor company) is to be transferred to another company (the transferee company).[39]

Under s 900(6), every company in relation to which an order is made under s 900 **25.22** must cause a copy of the order to be delivered to the Registrar of Companies within seven days after its making. In the event of default of compliance with this

---

[34] s 899(3).
[35] s 899(4).
[36] *Kempe v Ambassador Insurance Co* [1998] 1 WLR 271, PC.
[37] *Re MyTravel Group plc* [2005] 2 BCLC 123.
[38] *Re South African Supply and Cold Storage Co* [1904] 2 Ch 268; *Brooklands Selangor Holdings Ltd v Inland Revenue Commissioners* [1970] 1 WLR 429; *Fallon v Fellows* [2001] STC 1409.
[39] To this end, the court has power to make provision for any or all of the following matters: (a) the transfer to the transferee company of the whole or any part of the undertaking and of the property or liabilities of any transferor company; (b) the allotting or appropriation by the transferee company of any shares, debentures, policies, or other like interests in that company which under the compromise or arrangement are to be allotted or appropriated by that company to or for any person; (c) the continuation by or against the transferee company of any legal proceedings pending by or against any transferor company; (d) the dissolution, without winding up, of any transferor company; (e) the provision to be made for any persons who, within such time and in such manner as the court directs, dissent from the compromise or arrangement; (f) such incidental, consequential, and supplemental matters as are necessary to secure that the reconstruction or amalgamation is fully and effectively carried out. In s 900 'property' includes property, rights, and powers of any descrip- tion (but will only include property which the company has the right to deal with without obtaining the consent of a third party (*Nokes v Doncaster Amalgamated Collieries Ltd* [1940] AC 1014 (HL)) and 'liabilities' include duties (s 900(5)).

requirement, the company and every officer of the company who is in default will commit an offence.[40]

**25.23** Section 901 provides that if an order under either s 899 sanctioning a scheme or under s 900 facilitating a reconstruction or amalgamation is made which amends the company's articles of association or any resolution or agreement affecting a company's constitution, then a copy of the order must also be delivered to the Registrar of Companies, accompanied by a copy of the articles of association or the relevant resolution or agreement as amended. Further, every copy of the company's articles of association issued after the order has been made must be accompanied by a copy of the order, unless the effect of the order has been incorporated into the articles by amendment. Again, a failure to comply with these requirements will result in the company, and every officer of the company who is in default, committing an offence.

### Recognition abroad

**25.24** One issue which arises following the successful sanction of a scheme concerns its recognition and enforceability in other countries. Where a scheme is sanctioned in the context of insolvency proceedings falling within the scope of the Insolvency Regulation, and such a scheme amounts to a composition between the company and its creditors, then it should automatically be recognized and enforceable in other EU Member States pursuant to Article 25 of the Insolvency Regulation which specifically provides for the recognition of 'compositions approved by the court'. Where the company is not in insolvency proceedings, it may be possible to seek recognition and enforcement of a scheme of arrangement as a judgment under the provisions of the Brussels Regulation.[41] There is some debate as to (a) whether the Brussels Regulation applies at all to schemes and (b) whether an order of the court sanctioning a scheme constitutes a 'judgment' for these purposes. As to (a), Article 1(2)(b) excludes from the Brussels Regulation altogether 'bankruptcy, proceedings relating to the winding-up of insolvent companies or other legal persons, judicial arrangements, compositions and analogous proceedings'. However, it seems unlikely that this was intended to exclude compositions outside insolvency proceedings. First, the Jenard Report and the case law of the European Court of Justice suggest that the exception is limited to insolvency proceedings.[42] Secondly, the Judgments Regulation and the Insolvency Regulation should be construed so as not to give rise to any gaps between them. Given that a scheme outside insolvency proceedings does not fall within the Insolvency

---

[40] s 900(7).

[41] As a regulation, the Judgments Regulation has direct effect in all Member States and, unlike a directive, is not required to be implemented by domestic national legislation. Chapter III of the Judgments Regulation deals with the recognition and enforcement of judgments.

[42] See *Gourdain v Nadler* [1979] ECR 733.

Regulation, this is a further reason why it should fall within the Judgments Regulation. As to (b), judgment' is itself widely defined in the Brussels Regulation to mean 'any judgment given by a court or tribunal of a Member State, whatever the judgment may be called, including a decree, order, decision or writ of execution . . .'.[43] This appears to be conceptually capable of encompassing an order of the court sanctioning a scheme.[44] Further, in the context of recognition of judgments under general principles of private international law, there is some support for the proposition that an order sanctioning a solvent scheme is a judgment for these purposes.[45]

In the United States, recognition of both solvent and insolvent schemes has historically been possible under Section 304 of the United States Bankruptcy Code. Following such recognition, the United States courts may then grant relief in order to give effect to the scheme in the United States.[46] In October 2005 Section 304 was replaced by a new Chapter 15 in the Bankruptcy Code, which implements the UNCITRAL Model Law on Cross-Border Insolvency. Under Chapter 15 the United States courts have continued to recognize both solvent and insolvent schemes of arrangement as 'foreign proceedings' and to grant relief in support of them.[47]    **25.25**

### (3) Directors' particular responsibilities

In view of the complexity, directors should rely on advice from lawyers in relation to the preparation of a scheme of arrangement and it is to be expected that such lawyers will drive the process. Directors' particular functions arise in relation to the recommendation of the scheme, the preparation of the explanatory statement,    **25.26**

---

[43] Art 32. Briggs and Rees, *Civil Jurisdiction and Judgments* (2005), 493 states that '[i]t is not known whether [the Judgments Regulation] would extend to a court order sanctioning a scheme of arrangement under the Companies Act 1985'.

[44] See also Article 25 of the Insolvency Regulation pursuant to which 'compositions approved by [the] court' in the context of insolvency proceedings are to be recognized in other Member States. Pursuant to Article 25.1 of the Insolvency Regulation, the mechanism for the enforcement of such compositions is that contained in the relevant provisions of the Judgments Regulation (as the successor to the Brussels Convention). It appears to follow from this that, at least conceptually, a sanctioned scheme of arrangement is capable of being recognized and enforced under the Judgments Regulation machinery.

[45] *Re Cavell Insurance Company Ltd*, 23 May 2006, Court of Appeal for Ontario on appeal from the Ontario Superior Court of Justice (Farwell J) upholding the decision of the lower court recognizing an order of the English court convening a meeting of creditors for the purposes of considering a scheme proposed pursuant to 1985 Act, s 425.

[46] For the position under s 304, see: *Re Board of Directors of Hopewell International Insurance Ltd* 275 BR 699 (SDNY 2002), where the US District Court affirmed the decision of Tina L Brozman, Chief Judge in the Bankruptcy Court at 238 BR 25 (Bkrtcy SDNY 1999); *Re Kingscroft Insurance Co* 138 BR 121 (Bankr SD Fla 1992).

[47] Effect has been given to the scheme in *Re La Mutuelle du Mans Assurances IARD* [2006] BCC 11 in the USA under Chapter 15.

the preparation of the evidence in support of the applications for an order convening meetings and for sanction, the chairing and conduct of the meeting or meetings, and certain specific statutory duties.

*Recommendation of scheme*

**25.27**  The duties of a director include promoting the success of the company and exercising independent judgment.[48] Accordingly, a director faced with a proposed scheme of arrangement must be satisfied, in exercise of his independent judgment, that the result to be achieved by the scheme is in the company's best interests and will promote its success. This may be because the scheme reduces the company's indebtedness and puts in place a more efficient capital structure or because the scheme facilitates a takeover which the directors consider to be in shareholders' best interests.

**25.28**  Aside from being satisfied as to the desirability of the general result to be achieved by a proposed scheme, a director should also be satisfied that the scheme is a proper one to put to the company's creditors or members (as the case may be) and to seek orders from the court for the convening of a meeting or meetings of creditors or members and, ultimately, in respect of which to seek the sanction of the court. This involves being satisfied that the scheme itself is not inherently unfair to any parties and is such that an intelligent, honest man acting in respect of his interest might reasonably approve it.

*Classes*

**25.29**  A director of a company proposing a scheme should also be satisfied, having taken appropriate advice, that the classes of creditors or members in respect of which the company is proposing to convene meetings to consider the proposed scheme are properly formulated. As noted in paragraph 25.12 above, it is the responsibility of the applicant company to determine whether more than one meeting of creditors or members is required to consider the scheme. The test to be applied is whether the rights of the creditors or members are not so dissimilar as to make it impossible for them to consult together with a view to their common interest. Inevitably, directors will need to take appropriate legal advice on this issue.

**25.30**  A failure to ensure that the correct number of meetings is held may result in the court refusing to sanction the scheme even if approved by the requisite majority of creditors or members. This may result in prejudice to the company in the form of wasted costs and time as well as prejudice in the fact that the scheme will not take effect. However, it does not follow that directors should always err on the side of caution and opt for more rather than less meetings of creditors (or members).

---

[48] ss 172, 173.

Convening too many meetings of creditors may lead to as much prejudice as convening too few meetings because, since a scheme has to be approved by the requisite majority in each meeting, it gives a group of creditors a power to veto the scheme which they would not otherwise have. It is therefore important that the test for deciding how many meetings to convene is always applied in a neutral and balanced way.

*Explanatory statement*

Under s 897, where a meeting has been summoned by the court, every notice   **25.31**
summoning the meeting that is sent to a creditor or member must be accompanied by a statement explaining the effect of the compromise or arrangement. Likewise, any notice summoning a meeting which is given by advertisement must either include such a statement or (as is more likely to be the case in practice) state where and how the creditors or members entitled to attend the meeting can obtain copies of the statement.[49]

In addition to explaining the effect of the compromise or arrangement, the state-   **25.32**
ment must explain any material interests of the directors of the company (whether as directors, members, creditors, or otherwise) and the effect on those interests of the compromise or arrangement in so far as it is different from the effect on the like interests of other persons.[50] It should be noted that where there is a change of the material interests of a director as set out in the explanatory statement which is not disclosed, the court may not sanction the scheme unless satisfied that no reasonable shareholder would alter his decision as to how to act on the scheme if the changes had been disclosed.[51] In relation to the rights of the debenture holders of the company, where the compromise or arrangement affects such rights the explanatory statement must explain the effect on the interests of the trustees of any deed for securing the issue of the debentures of the compromise or arrangement in so far as it is different from the effect on the like interests of other persons.[52] If a company makes a default in complying with these requirements in relation to explanatory statements, then an offence is committed both by the company and by an officer of the company who is in default.[53] However, a person will not be guilty of an offence if he can show that the default was due to the refusal

---

[49] Where a notice given by advertisement states that copies of an explanatory statement can be obtained, then any creditor or member entitled to attend the meeting is entitled to obtain a copy from the company free of charge by making application in the manner indicated by the notice (s 897(4)).

[50] s 897(2).

[51] *Re Minster Assets plc* [1985] BCLC 200.

[52] s 897(3).

[53] An officer of the company for these purposes includes a liquidator or administrator and a trustee of a deed for securing the issue of debentures of the company (s 897(6)).

of a director or trustee for debenture holders to supply the necessary particulars of his interests.[54]

**25.33** Under s 898, it is the duty of any director of the company to give notice to the company of such matters relating to himself as may be necessary for the purposes of the explanatory statement required by s 897. A director who makes default in complying with this section commits an offence and is liable on summary conviction to a fine not exceeding level 3 of the standard scale.[55]

**25.34** As a basic rule the explanatory statement must contain sufficient information to enable the recipient properly to exercise his judgment in respect of the proposed compromise or arrangement. One test of the adequacy of the information in the explanatory statement is whether any missing information would cause a creditor to change his or her view as to whether to consent to the scheme. In this context, it has been said that an explanation of the effects of the scheme requires an explanation of how the scheme will affect a bond holder or creditor commercially and that he needs to be given such up-to-date information as can reasonably be provided on what he can expect if the group were to go into liquidation and as to what he can expect under the scheme.[56] Further, the lack of such information in the explanatory statement may be a ground for the court refusing to sanction the scheme.[57] The explanatory statement will conclude with a recommendation by the directors that the creditors or members, or a class of them, with whom the compromise or arrangement is proposed to be made agree to it by voting in favour of the scheme at the meeting(s) convened for the purpose.[58]

**25.35** One issue in respect of which directors need to exercise particular care relates to side agreements entered into between the company, or a third party acting on the company's behalf, and one or more of its creditors. Any secret deal made in connection with a compromise or arrangement pursuant to which a creditor is to receive more than the other creditors in return for supporting (or not opposing) the compromise or arrangement is illegal and void and the existence of such a deal will render the compromise or arrangement voidable at the instance of an aggrieved creditor.[59] The principles underlying this rule are that creditors of a company must be treated equally[60] and that there should be complete good faith between the debtor and his creditors in connection with a proposed compromise or

---

[54] s 897(7).
[55] s 898(2), (3).
[56] *Re Heron International NV* [1994] 1 BCLC 667.
[57] Ibid.
[58] This is not a requirement under the Act but is a requirement under the Listing Rules in the case of listed companies.
[59] *Cadbury Schweppes plc v Somji* [2001] 1 BCLC 498, CA.
[60] *McKewan v Sanderson* (1875) LR 20 Eq 65.

arrangement.[61] It follows that directors should be careful to ensure that a company, or someone acting for the company, does not enter into such undisclosed agreements which may have the effect of voiding the proposed compromise or arrangement. However, there is nothing inherently objectionable about a company promoting a scheme from reaching agreement with some of its creditors under which they undertake to vote in favour of the scheme.[62]

### Chairing the meeting

Typically, the person nominated by the court to act as the chairman of the convened meetings of creditors or members will be a director of the company. The duties of the chairman are to hold the meeting or meetings in accordance with the directions given by the court. The chairman must ensure that the meeting is held at the correct time and place and that the votes (whether in person or by proxy) are properly admitted and counted. The latter is particularly important since the requirement that a scheme be approved by the relevant majorities goes directly to the court's jurisdiction to sanction the scheme[63] and it is therefore necessary for the court to be satisfied that the majorities have been properly constituted.[64] **25.36**

The chairman should address the meeting and deal with any questions raised by the members or creditors present. The chairman should then put a resolution for approval of the proposed scheme of arrangement to the meeting. Voting at the meeting on the resolution should take place by way of poll and not by way of show of hands since the value of the claims voted is relevant to the calculation of the majorities. The chairman should ensure that all proxies received are in order.[65] If the resolution for approval of the scheme is passed, the chairman should sign a copy of the printed scheme of arrangement which was approved and adopted by the meeting. **25.37**

---

[61] *Dauglish v Tennent* (1866) LR 2 QB 49.

[62] *Re British Aviation Insurance Co Ltd*, n 24 above, para 103.

[63] *Re Dorman Long & Co Ltd* [1934] Ch 635; *Re Savoy Hotel Ltd* [1981] Ch 351.

[64] In many cases the establishment of creditors' claims, which often arise in connection with financing provided to the relevant company, is straightforward. In other cases, the matter can be more complicated and many insurance schemes, in particular, contain provisions providing for the adjudication and determination of creditors' claims at the voting stage, since these claims will often be future or contingent. The provisions in the schemes sanctioned in *Hawk Insurance Co* and in *Re Pan Atlantic Insurance Co Ltd* [2003] 2 BCLC 678 are both examples of this. In the latter case, the court held that such adjudication mechanisms are not inconsistent with the basic right to a court hearing.

[65] It should be noted that directors who receive proxies for and against the proposed scheme have no option whether or not they will use them but are bound to use them to vote; *Re Dorman Long & Co Ltd* [1934] Ch 635.

*Evidence*

**25.38** Finally, as set out above, the directors of a company may have an important role to play in assisting with the preparation of the applications which have to be made to the court in connection with a scheme. Typically, it will be necessary for a director to provide evidence, in the form of a witness statement explaining the relevant background, the proposed scheme, and why the directors consider the scheme to be in the company's best interests. Where a director acts as chairman of the meetings, it will also be necessary for him to prepare a report on the meetings to the court. In practice, such evidence will be prepared in the first instance by the company's lawyers. However, it goes without saying that the relevant director must ensure that all such evidence is completely truthful and gives a full and frank account of the matters which are relevant to the court's consideration of the scheme.

## C. Mergers and Divisions of Public Companies

### (1) Scope of the provisions

**25.39** Where the scheme of arrangement under s 899 concerns a private company which proposes to effect a merger or division (within the meaning of Chapter 2 of Part 27), it can use the court's powers under s 900 to transfer to the transferee company the undertaking, property, and liabilities of the transferor company without the need for further formality. However, where the scheme involves a merger or division and is in relation to a public company the requirements of the Companies Act, Part 27 will need to be met.

**25.40** Part 27 derives from the Third and Sixth EC Company Law Directives and imposes certain specific requirements in the case of mergers and divisions of public companies in addition to those applicable to schemes generally. The aim of these Directives was to harmonize national law in relation to mergers and divisions and, in relation to the former, to introduce the concept in those national law systems which did not already recognize it. Although the Directives were implemented by the previous Companies Act, the provisions contained in Part 27 substantially expand on those contained in the old Act.[66]

**25.41** By s 902(1) Part 27 applies where a compromise or arrangement is proposed between a public company and its creditors (or any class of them) or its members

---

[66] These provisions were inserted in the 1985 Act as s 427A and Schedule 15A by the Companies (Mergers and Divisions) Regulations 1987 (SI 1987/1991) to give effect to the Third EC Directive on Mergers (Dir 78/855/EEC of 25 July 1978) and the Sixth EC Directive on Divisions (Dir 82/891/EEC of 17 December 1982).

(or any class of them) for the purposes of, or in connection with, a scheme for the reconstruction of any company or companies or the amalgamation of any two more companies, the scheme involves a merger or division, and the consideration for the transfer (or each of the transfers) envisaged is to be shares in the transferee company (or one or more of the transferee companies) receivable by members of the transferor company (or transferor companies), without any cash payment to members.

In relation to mergers, the provisions apply to two types of merger:  **25.42**

(1) *merger by absorption*: where the undertaking, property, and liabilities of the relevant public company are to be transferred to another existing public company;

(2) *merger by formation of a new company*: where the undertaking, property, and liabilities of two or more public companies, including the relevant company, are to be transferred to a new company, whether or not a public company.[67]

A division takes place where the undertaking, property, and liabilities of the rele-  **25.43** vant public company are to be divided among and transferred to two or more companies each of which is either an existing public company or a new company, whether or not a public company.[68] In other words, it covers the splitting up of a company and the transfer of its assets to one or more acquiring companies, whether previously existing or newly formed.

The general scheme of the rules relating to mergers and divisions of public com-  **25.44** panies contained in Part 27 is that there must be compliance with both the relevant requirements of Part 26, containing the rules relating to arrangements and reconstructions generally, and with the specific rules relating to mergers and divisions (as the case may be) contained in Part 27. However, certain of the rules contained in both Part 26 and in Part 27 in relation to mergers and divisions are modified or excluded in certain circumstances.

## (2)  Summary of the procedure for mergers

By s 907(1) the central requirement of the procedure for mergers is that, except in  **25.45** certain limited cases relating to mergers by absorption,[69] the scheme by which the merger is to be effected must be approved by a majority in number representing 75% in value of each class of members of each of the merging companies, present and voting either in person or by proxy at a meeting. To this end, s 911(1) and (3) requires that various documents are produced and made available for inspection by the members of each of the merging companies: (a) a draft of the proposed

---

[67] s 904(1).
[68] s 919(1).
[69] See paragraph 25.48 below.

terms for the merger,[70] (b) an explanatory report produced by the directors, (c) an expert's report drawn up on behalf of each of the merging companies,[71] (d) the company's annual accounts and reports for the last three financial years ending on or before the first meeting of the members, or any class of members, summoned for the purposes of approving the scheme; and (e) any supplementary accounting statement required by s 910.

**25.46**  The expert's report which is required is a written report on the draft terms addressed to the members of the relevant company, though the court may on the application of all of the relevant merging companies approve the appointment of a joint expert to produce a single report on behalf of all of the companies.[72] The expert must be a person who is eligible for appointment as a statutory auditor[73] and must meet the independence criterion.[74] Under the requirements of the Act, his report must: (a) indicate the method or methods used to arrive at the share exchange ratio, (b) give an opinion as to whether the method or methods used are reasonable in all the circumstances of the case, indicate the values arrived at using each such method, and (if there is more than one method) give an opinion on the relative importance attributed to such methods in arriving at the value decided on, (c) describe any special valuation difficulties that have arisen, (d) state whether in the expert's opinion the share exchange ratio is reasonable, and (e) in the case of a valuation made by a person other than himself, state that it appeared to him reasonable to arrange for it to be so made or to accept a valuation so made.[75]

**25.47**  In addition to the expert's report, in certain cases a supplementary accounting statement may be required. The requirement to provide such a statement arises where the last annual accounts of any of the merging companies relate to a financial year ending more than seven months before the first meeting of the company summoned for the purposes of approving the scheme.[76] The statement must include, amongst other things, a balance sheet for the company as at a date not more than three months before the draft terms for the merger were adopted.[77]

---

[70]  Directive 2007/63/EC amends the Third and Sixth Directives to dispense with this requirement if all shareholders so agree. This Directive is required to be implemented by 31 December 2008.

[71]  Directive 2007/63/EC amends the Third and Sixth Directives to dispense with this requirement if all shareholders so agree. This Directive is required to be implemented by 31 December 2008.

[72]  s 909(2), (3).

[73]  s 1212.

[74]  s 909(4). In relation to the independence criterion, see ss 936 and 937.

[75]  s 909(5). The obligations of the expert in this regard are further set out in s 935.

[76]  s 910(1).

[77]  s 910(2)(a).

The expert's report, and the directors' explanatory report, are not required in the **25.48** case of a merger by absorption where all of the relevant securities[78] of the transferor company (or, if there is more than one transferor company, of each of them) are held by or on behalf of the transferor company.[79] In addition, in this case, the explanatory statement normally required by s 897 of the Act is not necessary.[80]

The cases where it is not necessary for the scheme to be approved by the requisite **25.49** majorities of members are set out in ss 916, 917, and 918. Section 916 applies in the case of a merger by absorption where 90% or more of the relevant securities of the transferor company or companies are held by or on behalf of the transferee company. In these circumstances, it is not necessary for the scheme to be approved by a meeting of members of the transferee company provided that the court is satisfied that: (a) publication of notice of receipt of the draft terms by the Registrar took place in respect of the transferee company at least one month before the date of the first meeting of members, or any class of members, of the transferor company summoned for the purpose of agreeing to the scheme, (b) the members of the transferee company were able during the period beginning one month before, and ending on, that date to inspect at the registered office of the transferee company copies of the draft terms, the requisite annual accounts and reports, and any supplementary accounting statement required by s 910 and to obtain copies of those documents or any part of them on request free of charge, and (c) one or more members of the transferee company, who together held not less than 5% of the paid-up capital of the company which carried the right to vote at general meetings of the company (excluding any shares in the company held as treasury shares) would have been able, during that period, to require a meeting of each class of members to be called for the purpose of deciding whether or not to agree to the scheme, and no such requirement was made.

Section 916 does not apply where all of the relevant securities of the transferor **25.50** company or companies are held by the transferee, ie where the transferor is a wholly-owned subsidiary of the transferee. In this case, s 917 applies and provides that there is no need for the scheme to be approved by either the members of the transferor company or companies or the members of the transferee company providing that the court is satisfied as to the requirements set out in the preceding paragraph.

Finally, s 918 applies in relation to any merger by absorption, including cases **25.51** where the transferee company does not hold any shares in the transferor company

---

[78] ie shares or other securities carrying the right to vote at general meetings of the company (s 915(6)).

[79] ss 908(3), 909(7), 915(4).

[80] s 915(3).

or companies. Again, in such a case it is not necessary for the scheme to be approved by the members of the transferee company provided that the court is satisfied that the requirements set out in paragraph 25.49 above have been complied with.

**25.52** On the sanction of a scheme involving a merger or division, the court must fix a date on which the transfer or transfers to the transferee company or companies of the undertaking, property, and liabilities of the transferor company is or are to take effect.[81] This may be done either in the order sanctioning the scheme itself or in any order made under s 900 in exercise of the court's powers to facilitate a reconstruction or amalgamation.

### (3) Directors' particular functions and duties in relation to mergers

**25.53** The first functions and duties of the directors of a company which is proposed to be the subject of a merger are to ensure that a draft of the proposed terms of the scheme is first drawn up and is then adopted by the directors.[82] The Act specifies the matters which must be included in the draft terms, namely: (a) the name, address of registered office of the transferor and transferee companies, and whether they are companies limited by shares or a company limited by guarantee and having a share capital, (b) the number of shares in the transferee company to be allotted to members of a transferor company for a given number of their shares (the 'share exchange ratio') and the amount of any cash payment, (c) the terms relating to the allotment of shares in the transferee company, (d) the date from which the holding of shares in the transferee company will entitle the holders to participate in profits, and any special conditions affecting that entitlement, (e) the date from which the transactions of a transferor company are to be treated for accounting purposes as being those of the transferee company, (f) any rights or restrictions attaching to shares or other securities in the transferee company to be allotted under the scheme to the holders of shares or other securities in a transferor company to which any special rights or restrictions attach, or the measures proposed concerning them, (g) any amount of benefit paid or given or intended to be paid or given to any of the experts referred to in s 909 or to any director of a merging company and the consideration for the payment of benefit. The matters set out in subparagraphs (b), (c), and (d) are not required to be stated in the case of a merger by absorption where all of the relevant securities of the transferor company (or, if there is more than one transferor company, of each of them) are held by or on behalf of the transferor company.[83]

---

[81] s 939(1).
[82] s 905(1).
[83] ss 905(3), 915(1), (2).

By s 906(1) the directors are under a duty to ensure a copy of the draft of the pro-  **25.54**
posed terms is delivered to the Registrar of Companies.[84]

In addition to ensuring that the draft terms are prepared and adopted, the direct-  **25.55**
ors of a merging company must draw up and adopt an explanatory report.[85] The
report must contain the explanatory statement which is required under Part 26 in
relation to an arrangement or reconstruction generally and should set out the legal
and economic grounds for the draft terms and, in particular, for the share exchange
ratio and specify any special valuation difficulties. However, again, this requirement does not apply in the case of a merger by absorption where all of the relevant
securities of the transferor company or companies are held by or on behalf of the
transferor company. In addition to the production of the explanatory report, as
noted above, the directors may also be required to prepare a supplementary
accounting statement to bring the last set of accounts up to date.

### (4) Summary of the procedure for divisions

The procedure for divisions essentially follows that for mergers, although the Act  **25.56**
does impose some further disclosure obligations in the case of divisions in order
to provide further protection for shareholders and creditors.

As with mergers, the essential feature of the procedure for divisions is that, except  **25.57**
in certain limited cases, the scheme by which the division is to be effected must be
approved by a majority in number representing 75% in value of each class of
members of each of the merging companies, present and voting either in person
or by proxy at a meeting.[86] Again, this central requirement is given effect to by
obligations to produce and make available for inspection by the relevant members
relevant documents in order that the members may evaluate the division. These
documents are the draft terms (which must also be delivered to the Registrar of
Companies), the directors' explanatory report, an expert's report, the company's
annual accounts and reports for the last three financial years, and any supplementary accounting statement required.[87]

The members of the relevant companies may however agree that the explanatory  **25.58**
report, the expert's report, and the supplementary statement need not be

---

[84] s 906(1).
[85] s 908(1).
[86] s 922(1).
[87] s 926(1), (3). As with mergers, the requirement to provide a supplementary statement arises
where the last annual accounts of any of the companies involved in the division relate to a financial
year ending more than seven months before the first meeting of the company summoned for the
purposes of approving the scheme (s 925(1)). The statement has to include, amongst other things,
a balance sheet for the company as at a date not more than three months before the draft terms for
the merger were adopted (s 925(2)(a)).

produced.[88] In addition, the court has a power to disapply the requirements to deliver the draft terms to the Registrar of Companies under s 921 and to permit inspection of documents in accordance with s 926.[89] In order to exercise this power, the court must be satisfied that three conditions are fulfilled: (a) the members of the company must have received, or been able to obtain free of charge, copies of the documents listed in s 926 in time to examine them prior to the relevant meeting of members,[90] (b) the creditors of that company must have received or been able to obtain free of charge copies of the draft terms in time to examine them before the relevant meeting, and (c) no prejudice would be caused to the members or creditors of the transferor company or any transferee company by making the order in question.

**25.59**  The requirements of the report to be provided by the expert on behalf of each of the relevant companies, or by a joint expert on behalf of all of the companies, are the same as those which apply in the case of a merger.[91] The report must also cover the same matters as are required in the case of a merger.[92]

**25.60**  In certain cases, the requirement for meetings of members may be dispensed with. Pursuant to s 931, where all the shares of the transferor company carrying the right to vote at general meetings are held by or on behalf of one or more existing transferee companies, then it is not necessary for the scheme to be approved by the members of the transferor company if the court is satisfied that the following requirements have been satisfied: (a) publication of notice of receipt of the draft terms by the Registrar took place in respect of all the companies involved in the division at least one month before the date of the court's order, (b) the members of every company involved in the division were able during the period beginning one month before, and ending on, that date to inspect at the registered office of their company copies of the draft terms, the directors' explanatory report, the expert's report, the requisite annual accounts and reports, and any supplementary accounting statement and to obtain copies of those documents or any part of them on request free of charge; and (c) one or more members of the transferor company, who together held not less than 5% of the paid-up capital of the company which carried the right to vote at general meetings of the company (excluding any shares in the company held as treasury shares), would have been able, during that period, to require a meeting of each class of members to be called for

---

[88]  s 933.
[89]  s 934(1).
[90]  Or, in the case of an existing transferee company where no meeting is held pursuant to s 932, in time to require a meeting to be held.
[91]  s 924(1)–(4).
[92]  s 924(5).

the purpose of deciding whether or not to agree to the scheme, and no such requirement was made.

Pursuant to s 932, it is not necessary for a scheme to be approved by members of **25.61** a transferee company if the court is satisfied that the same conditions as set out in the preceding paragraph are satisfied in relation to that company. In addition, the court has the power to disapply the first and second conditions in the circumstances set out in paragraph 25.60 above.[93]

### (5) Directors' particular functions and duties in relation to divisions

As with mergers, the directors of a company which is proposed to be the subject **25.62** of a division are required to adopt a draft of the proposed terms of the scheme.[94] The draft must contain the same matters as are required in the case of a merger (see paragraph 25.53 above) but must also: (a) provide particulars of the property and liabilities to be transferred (to the extent that these are known to the transferor company) and their allocation among the transferee companies, (b) make provision for the allocation among and transfer to the transferee companies of any other property and liabilities that the transferor company has acquired or may subsequently acquire, and (c) specify the allocation to members of the transferor company of shares in the transferee companies and the criteria upon which that allocation is based.

By s 921(1) the directors are further under a duty to ensure a copy of the draft of **25.63** the proposed terms is delivered to the Registrar of Companies. This obligation may, however, be disapplied by order of the court under s 934.

The directors of a company subject to a division must draw up and adopt an **25.64** explanatory report.[95] The report must contain the explanatory statement which is required under Part 26 in relation to an arrangement or reconstruction generally and should set out the legal and economic grounds for the draft terms and, in particular, for the share exchange ratio and for the criteria on which the allocation to the members of the transferor company or shares in the transferee companies was based and specify any special valuation difficulties. It must also state whether a report has been made to any transferee company under s 593 of the Act and, if so, whether that report has been delivered to the Registrar of Companies.[96] This requirement to produce an explanatory report does not, however, apply where all

---

[93] s 932(5).
[94] s 920(1).
[95] s 923(1).
[96] s 923(3).

members holding shares (or other securities giving a right to vote in the companies involved in the division) so agree.[97]

**25.65**  In addition to the production of the explanatory report, as noted above, the directors may also be required to prepare a supplementary accounting statement to bring the last set of accounts up to date. In the case of a division, the directors of the transferor company must also report to every meeting of the members (or class of members) of the transferor company summoned for the purpose of agreeing to the scheme as well as to the directors of each transferee company on any material changes in the property and liabilities of the transferor following the adoption of the draft terms.[98] The directors of the transferee companies must in turn report on these matters to their own members.[99] Again, both the supplementary accounting statement and the report on material changes can be dispensed with where the relevant members so agree.

# D.  Takeovers

## (1)  Scope of the provisions

**25.66**  The provisions of the Companies Act relating to takeovers are contained in Part 28, ss 942 to 991.[100] Amongst other things, these provisions implement the EC Directive on Takeovers (the Takeovers Directive).[101] The Takeovers Directive lays down minimum requirements concerning the regulation of takeovers of companies whose shares are traded on a regulated market.

**25.67**  The Act also places the existing Panel on Takeovers and Mergers (the Panel) on a statutory footing and confers on it various functions set out in Part 28. The Panel was established in 1968 and its main functions are to issue and administer the City Code on Takeovers and Mergers (the Takeover Code or the Code[102]) and to supervise and regulate takeovers and other matters to which the Takeover Code applies. The Code, however, had no statutory force prior to the Act coming into

---

[97] s 933(1).

[98] s 927(1).

[99] s 927(2).

[100] Chapters 1 and 2 implement provisions in the Takeovers Directive (Directive 2004/25/EC). Chapter 3 restates with minor amendments provisions contained in 1985 Act, ss 428–430F. Section 988 includes provisions restating provisions in 1985 Act, s 204.

[101] Directive 2004/25/EC. The Directive was initially implemented by regulations in May 2006 and at that time only applied to companies whose shares were admitted to trading on a regulated market. In effect, therefore, the 2006 Act extends the scope of UK legislation implementing the Directive to cover certain companies to which the Takeover Code applies.

[102] 8th edn, May 2006.

force[103] and one of the main functions of the provisions of the Act dealing with takeovers is now to place the Panel and the Code within a statutory framework. The intention, however, has been to preserve the existing independence and authority of the Panel.[104]

The Panel's existing function is to ensure that shareholders are treated fairly and are not denied an opportunity to decide on the merits of a takeover and that shareholders of the same class are afforded equivalent treatment by an offeror. Likewise, under the Act the central function of the Panel is to regulate takeover bids and merger transactions and other transactions that have or may have an effect on the ownership or control of companies. To this end, the Panel has been given the statutory power to make rules to assist it in the discharge of its functions, including to cover the matters dealt with by the existing Takeover Code, which rules the court is able to enforce on the application of the Panel.[105] The Panel is empowered to give rulings on the interpretation, application, or effect of the rules made by it.[106] The rules which have been made by the Panel are set out in the latest version of the Takeover Code.[107] The Panel is also given other specific statutory powers including the power to require the provision of documents and information.[108]

25.68

The power to require the provision of documents and information extends to any documents and information reasonably required in the exercise by the Panel of its functions.[109] The Panel is entitled to serve a notice on a person setting out the documents or information which it requires and such person is then obliged to comply with the notice at the place specified and within the period of time specified in the notice, provided that this is a reasonable period. Where information is provided to the Panel which relates to the private affairs of an individual or to any particular business, then the general rule is that such information cannot be disclosed without the consent of the individual or the person carrying on the business.[110] However, this rule is subject to a large number of exceptions set out in Schedule 2 to the Act and does not apply to any disclosure that is made for the purpose of facilitating the carrying out by the Panel of any of its functions.[111]

25.69

---

[103] See Sir John Donaldson MR in *R v Panel on Takeovers and Mergers, ex parte Datafin Ltd* [1987] QB 815: the Panel performs its functions 'without visible means of legal support'.

[104] White Paper, 3.6.

[105] s 955.

[106] s 945.

[107] Together with the rules of procedure of the Hearings Committee.

[108] In relation to administrative matters, the Panel is given the power to collect fees and charges for the purpose of meeting its expenses (s 957(1)) and the Secretary of State is empowered to make regulations allowing for a levy to be payable to the Panel (s 958).

[109] s 947(3).

[110] s 948(2).

[111] s 948(3).

**25.70**   Under the provisions of s 951(1)–(3) the rules made by the Panel must make provision for the decisions of the Panel to be subject to review by a committee of the Panel (the Hearings Committee) and for there to be a right of appeal against a decision of the Hearings Committee to an independent tribunal called the Takeover Appeal Board. It seems likely that this will preserve the current position where the courts have held that the Panel is subject to judicial review but have declined to interfere with decisions made by the Panel during the course of takeovers.[112]

**25.71**   The Panel is able to be a party to legal proceedings in its own name[113] and is exempted from liability in damages for anything done or omitted to be done in or in connection with the discharge or purported discharge of its functions, except where such act or omission was in bad faith or where damages would be due under the Human Rights Act 1998, s 6(1).[114]

**25.72**   In addition to requiring bodies (such as the Panel) which regulate takeovers to be placed on a statutory footing, the Takeovers Directive contains substantive provisions which seek to remove impediments to takeovers, in other words, steps that may be taken by companies both prior to and during a takeover bid which have the aim of frustrating a bid. These types of defences broadly consist of 'pre-bid defences' and 'post-bid defences'. Pre-bid defences include differential share structures under which minority shareholders exercise disproportionate voting rights; limitations on share ownership and restrictions on transfer of shares set out in the company's articles or in contractual agreements. Post-bid defences include matters such as seeking to sell key assets of the company without shareholder approval. In relation to the former, Part 28, Chapter 2 sets out rules restricting the use of pre-bid defences. However, these rules are not compulsory but only apply where a company, which has voting shares admitted to trading on a regulated market, has opted in by way of special resolution.[115]

**25.73**   Finally, Part 28, Chapter 3 contains provisions dealing with the problems of, and for, residual minority shareholders following a successful takeover bid by providing for 'squeeze-out' and 'sell-out' rights.[116] Squeeze-out rights enable a successful bidder to purchase compulsorily the shares of remaining minority shareholders who have not accepted the bid. Sell-out rights enable minority shareholders to require the majority shareholder to purchase their shares.

---

[112]   *R v Panel on Takeovers and Mergers, ex parte Datafin Ltd* [1987] QB 815.
[113]   s 960.
[114]   s 961. As to the exemption from liability for acts done in bad faith, see *Three Rivers District Council v The Governor and Company of the Bank of England* [2003] 2 AC 1, HL.
[115]   s 966.
[116]   See 1985 Act, Part 13A.

## (2) Directors' particular functions and duties

The principal responsibility of directors in relation to a takeover bid is to ensure **25.74**
that a company which is either making a takeover bid or is the subject of a bid
complies with the provisions of the Act and with the rules made by the Panel
which will encompass the existing Takeover Code.[117] Under the Act and the Code,
the Panel may give a direction restraining someone from acting in breach of the
Code[118] or may order the payment of compensation for a breach of certain provisions of the Code.[119] The Panel may also apply to the court for an order enforcing
compliance with a requirement under the Code.[120]

The Takeover Code applies to any directors through which a company to which **25.75**
the Code applies acts.[121] All companies to which the Code applies are expected to
ensure that their directors and employees receive appropriate and timely guidance
in respect of the Code and a company will he held responsible for any of its directors' or employees' acts or omissions.

The Takeover Code sets out General Principles which are applicable to all take- **25.76**
overs.[122] Directors of a company which is either the maker or the subject of a
takeover bid are obliged to ensure that they and the company act in accordance
with these principles. The general principles are expressed in broad terms and
companies are required to comply with the spirit of the principles rather than
simply their literal terms. The General Principles[123] are:

(1) All holders of the securities of an offeree company of the same class must be
    afforded equivalent treatment; moreover, if a person acquires control[124] of a
    company, the other holders of securities must be protected.
(2) The holders of the securities of an offeree company must have sufficient time
    and information to enable them to reach a properly informed decision on the
    bid; where it advises the holders of securities, the board of the offeree com-
    pany must give its views on the effects of implementation of the bid on

---

[117] s 943(3). The following paragraphs refer to the 8th edition of the Takeover Code as at 22 May 2006.
[118] s 946.
[119] s 952(1)(a). This applies in relation to a breach of the requirements of Rules 6, 9, 11, 14, 16, or 35.3: see the Takeover Code, A19.
[120] s 955.
[121] Code, A7. For the purposes of the Code, directors include persons in accordance with whose instructions the directors or a director are accustomed to act (Code, C8).
[122] Code, B1.
[123] The General Principles reflect the Takeovers Directive, Art 3.
[124] 'Control' is a key concept in the Takeover Code and is defined as meaning an interest, or interests, in shares carrying in aggregate 30% or more of the voting rights of a company, irrespective of whether such interest or interests give de facto control.

employment, conditions of employment, and the locations of the company's business.

(3) The board of an offeree company must act in the interests of the company as a whole and must not deny the holders of securities the opportunity to decide on the merits of the bid.

(4) False markets must not be created in the securities of the offeree company, of the offeror company, or of any other company concerned by the bid in such a way that the rise or fall of the prices of the securities becomes artificial and the normal functioning of the markets is distorted.

(5) An offeror must announce a bid only after ensuring that he/she can fulfil in full any cash consideration, if such is offered, and after taking all reasonable measures to secure the implementation of any other type of consideration.

(6) An offeree company must not be hindered in the conduct of its affairs for longer than is reasonable by a bid for its securities.

*The approach, announcements, and independent advice*

**25.77** The general rule is that any takeover offer must be made in the first instance to the board of directors of the offeree company or the company's advisers.[125] The identity of the offeror must be disclosed at the outset. Further, the board of the offeree company which is the subject of the approach is entitled to be satisfied that the offeror is, or will be, in a position to implement the offer in full. It follows that the board of a company which is the subject of an approach should request that the offeror provides this information.

**25.78** A key issue prior to and following any approach to the offeree company regarding the making of an offer concerns the need for an announcement. Generally, announcements in relation to a potential takeover are required to be made at an early stage. The circumstances in which an announcement is required are set out in the Takeover Code and include when a firm intention to make an offer which is not subject to any pre-condition has been notified to the offeree company and when, following an approach to the offeree company, it is the subject of rumour or speculation or there is an untoward movement in its share price. Before the board of the offeree company has been approached, the responsibility of making an announcement will rest with the offeror but, following an approach having been made, primary responsibility for making an announcement will rest with the board of the offeree company.[126] Prior to an announcement being made, all price-sensitive information about a contemplated offer must be kept absolutely secret.[127]

---

[125] Takeover Code, rule 1.
[126] Takeover Code, rule 2.3.
[127] Takeover Code, rule 2.1.

The directors of an offeror company are plainly under an important obligation to **25.79** consider carefully whether or not to make a takeover offer. Such a decision clearly falls to be taken consistently with the directors' duty to promote the success of the company. In addition, the Takeover Code specifically provides that an announcement of a firm intention to make an offer should only be made when the offeror has every reason to believe that it can and will continue to be able to implement the offer.[128] Once a firm announcement has been made, an offeror must normally proceed with the offer unless the offeror is entitled to invoke a pre-condition or condition under Rule 13 of the Takeover Code.[129] Rule 13.4 provides that an offeror should not invoke a condition or pre-condition so as to cause the offer not to proceed, to lapse, or to be withdrawn, unless the circumstances which give rise to the right to invoke the condition or pre-condition are of 'material significance' to the offeror in the context of the offer.[130] Where a person makes a statement of an intention not to make an offer then it will not be able to make an offer within six months of the date of the statement.[131]

Having received a takeover offer, the board of the offeree company is obliged to **25.80** obtain competent independent advice on the offer.[132] The substance of the advice must be made available to shareholders. As the Code notes, the requirement for independent advice is of particular importance where the offeror is a management buy-out vehicle or where existing management or controllers are interested in the offeror. The Code advises that the board of an offeree company should appoint an independent adviser as soon as possible after it becomes aware of the possibility that an offer may be made.

*Restrictions on dealings*

During the period between the time when there is reason to suppose an approach **25.81** or an offer is contemplated and the announcement of the approach or offer or of the termination of the discussions, no dealings of any kind can take place in the securities of the offeree company by a person, not being the offeror, who is privy to price-sensitive information.[133] Likewise, during an offer period, the offeror (and any persons acting in concert with it) must not, except with the consent of the Panel, sell any securities in the offeree company.[134]

---

[128] Takeover Code, rule 2.5(a).
[129] Takeover Code, rule 2.7.
[130] By way of example, it was held by the Panel that WPP was not entitled to invoke a condition in its takeover offer for Tempus on the basis that there had been a 'material adverse change' in the prospects for Tempus following the events of 11 September 2001.
[131] Takeover Code, rule 2.8.
[132] Takeover Code, rule 3.1. Such advice will normally be obtained from an investment bank.
[133] Takeover Code, rule 4.1.
[134] Takeover Code, rule 4.2.

*Mandatory offers*

**25.82** In certain circumstances, an obligation under the Takeover Code to make a mandatory offer may be triggered. The purpose of the requirement to make a mandatory offer is to protect the interests of the general body of shareholders when control of a company is acquired. Under Rule 9.1, the obligation to make a mandatory offer arises where:

(1) any person acquires, whether by a series of transactions over a period of time or not, an interest in shares which (taken together with shares in which persons acting in concert with him are interested) carry 30% or more of the voting rights of a company; or

(2) any person (together with persons acting in concert with him) is interested in shares which in aggregate carry not less than 30% of the voting rights but does not hold shares carrying more than 50% of such voting rights and such person (or any persons acting in concert with him) acquires an interest in any other shares which increases the percentage of shares carrying voting rights in which he is interested.

Persons 'acting in concert' comprise persons who, pursuant to an agreement or understanding (whether formal or informal), cooperate to obtain or consolidate control of a company or to frustrate the successful outcome of an offer for a company. Amongst others, a company is presumed to act in concert with its directors (and with any close relatives or related trusts of its directors).

**25.83** A mandatory offer must be made to the holders of all classes of equity share capital (whether voting or non-voting) and to the holders of any other class of transferable securities carrying voting rights to acquire their securities. The consideration offered must be in cash (or be accompanied by a cash alternative) at not less than the highest price paid by the offeror (or any person acting in concert with it) for any interest in shares of that class during the 12 months prior to the announcement of that offer.[135] For directors, it should also be noted that when directors (or their close relatives or related trusts) sell shares to a person as a result of which that person is required to make an offer under Rule 9, then the directors must ensure as a condition of the sale that the person undertakes to fulfil his obligations under Rule 9.[136]

*Voluntary offers*

**25.84** In relation to voluntary offers, the terms of the offer are generally a matter for the offeror company to put forward. However, it is required to be a condition of any

---

[135] Takeover Code, rule 9.5(a).

[136] Takeover Code, rule 9.6. In addition, except with the consent of the Panel, such directors should not resign from the board until the first closing date of the offer or the date when the offer becomes or is declared wholly unconditional, whichever is later.

offer for voting equity share capital (or for any other transferable securities which carry voting rights) which, if it is accepted, would result in the offeror holding shares carrying over 50% of the voting rights of the offeree company, that the offer will not become or be declared unconditional as to acceptances unless the offeror has acquired or agreed to acquire shares carrying over 50% of the voting rights.[137] The purpose of this provision is to ensure that if the offeror does acquire any shares under the offer, it acquires sufficient to give it control of the offeree company.

It is also a requirement under the Code that any offer should not normally be subject to conditions or pre-conditions which depend solely on subjective judgements by the directors of the offeror or offeree company or the fulfilment of which is in their hands.[138] Further, where the offeree company has more than one class of equity share capital a comparable offer must be made for each class of share irrespective of whether they carry voting rights or not.[139]    **25.85**

*Provision of information to shareholders*

A key aspect of directors' duties in relation to takeovers is to keep their shareholders informed since it is the shareholders who will ultimately decide on an offer. The general rule is that shareholders must be given sufficient information and advice to enable them to reach a properly informed decision as to the merits or demerits of an offer.[140] The Code expressly provides that no relevant information should be withheld from shareholders.[141] The information must be made available so that shareholders can make a decision in good time.    **25.86**

Information about companies involved in an offer must be made equally available to all offeree company shareholders, so far as possible, at the same time and in the same manner.[142] In addition, each document or advertisement issued, or statement made, during the course of an offer must be prepared with the highest standards of care and accuracy and the information given must be fairly and adequately presented.[143] A profit forecast in particular may clearly be highly material to a takeover offer. The Code emphasizes that profit forecasts must be compiled with    **25.87**

---

[137] Takeover Code, rule 10.
[138] Takeover Code, rule 13.1.
[139] Takeover Code, rule 14. A comparable offer need not necessarily be an identical offer.
[140] Takeover Code, rule 23.
[141] It also states that the obligation of the offeror in these respects towards the shareholders of the offeree company is no less than the offeror's obligation towards its own shareholders.
[142] Takeover Code, rule 20.1.
[143] Takeover Code, rule 19.1. This applies whether it is issued by the company direct or by an adviser on its behalf.

due care and consideration and such forecasts are the sole responsibility of the directors.[144]

*Board's opinion on the offer*

**25.88** The board of the offeree company must circulate to the company's shareholders its opinion on the offer and must, at the same time, make known to the shareholders the substance of the advice given to the board under Rule 3.1.[145] The opinion must include the views of the board on the effect of implementation of the offer on all the offeree company's interests, including specifically employment, and the offeror's strategic plans for the offeree company and their likely repercussions on employment and the locations of the offeree company's places of business. The opinion must also state the board's reasons for forming its opinion.

**25.89** The requirement for the board to state its opinion on an offer is one of the central obligations upon directors in connection with a takeover.[146] The board's opinion will be based on both the independent advice received and on the board's own commercial judgements and views, in particular, gained from their stewardship of the business. However, it is unlikely that it will be appropriate for a board to recommend an offer unless the advice received is that it is a fair one. If a board is split in its views on an offer, then the minority on the board should also publish their views.

**25.90** In forming its opinion on an offer, the directors must act in accordance with their statutory duties to exercise independent judgement[147] and to promote the success of the company for the benefit of its members as a whole.[148] However, this does not mean that the directors should be solely influenced by what is in the financial best interests of the present members of the company since under s 172 they are also required to have regard to, amongst other things, the likely consequences in the long term, the interests of employees, relationships with suppliers, customers, and others, and environmental issues. These factors should all be reflected in the decision-making process by which the directors form their opinion on a takeover offer.

---

[144] Takeover Code, rule 28.1.

[145] Takeover Code, rule 25.1.

[146] Where a director has a conflict of interest, he should not normally join with the remainder of the board in expressing its views on the offer. A director will normally be regarded as having a conflict of interest where it is intended that he should have any continuing role (whether executive or non-executive) in either the offeror or the offeree company in the event of the offer being successful (see the Codes, note 4 on rule 25.1).

[147] s 173.

[148] s 172.

*Restrictions on frustrating action*

Although the board is required to provide its opinion on an offer, the provisions **25.91** of the Takeover Code reflect the fact that it is ultimately for the shareholders to decide. The Code therefore prohibits action from being taken, once a takeover bid is imminent, in relation to an offeree company which might frustrate that decision. Accordingly, during the course of an offer (or before the date of the offer if the board of the offeree company has reason to believe that a bona fide offer might be imminent) the board must not, without approval of the shareholders in general meeting, take any action which might result in any offer or bona fide possible offer being frustrated or in shareholders being denied the opportunity to decide on its merits.[149] This would, for example, cover the situation where the offeree company proposes to sell a valuable asset. Likewise, the redemption or purchase by the offeree company of its own shares is restricted without approval of the shareholders in general meeting.[150]

It is important to note, however, that there is nothing to prevent directors of an **25.92** offeree company who have received a takeover bid from searching for a competing bidder. Such steps do not frustrate the takeover offer, even though they may make it less likely that the first offer will succeed. Indeed, a competition between bidders may best serve the interests of the shareholders of the offeree company by driving up the final price. In relation to their own shareholdings, directors do not appear to be under a positive duty to accept the highest offer in respect of their own shares, but their recommendation to shareholders given in their capacity as directors should not reflect their own personal interests.[151]

Finally, under the provisions of Part 22 of the Companies Act a public company **25.93** has various powers to obtain information about interests in its shares (see Chapters 24, Section E). These powers may be of use in the context of a takeover offer or rumoured takeover proposal.

*Provision of information and documentation to the Panel*

In relation to the provision of information and documentation, a director may be **25.94** required to comply with a notice served on him by the Panel under s 947. The Code itself requires any person dealing with the Panel to do so in 'an open and co-operative way' and that the Panel expects prompt cooperation and assistance from persons dealing with it.[152] A person who deals with the Panel is obliged to disclose to the Panel any information known to them and relevant to the matter being considered by the Panel (and to correct or update that information if it

---

[149] Takeover Code, rule 25.1.
[150] Takeover Code, rule 37.3.
[151] See *Re a Company* [1986] BCLC 382.
[152] Code, A17.

changes) and to take all reasonable care not to provide incorrect, incomplete, or misleading information to the Panel.[153] A failure to do so may lead to a director being the subject of a direction from the Panel requiring compliance,[154] a sanction being imposed on a director by the Panel,[155] or enforcement by the court.[156]

*Squeeze-out and sell-out rights*

**25.95**   Directors also have particular obligations under the Act in relation to the exercise of squeeze-out or sell-out rights under Chapter 3 of Part 28. Where an offeror serves a notice under Section 979 in relation to the exercise of squeeze-out rights, it must also send a copy of the notice to the company accompanied by a statutory declaration in the prescribed form stating that the conditions for the giving of the notice are satisfied.[157] A failure to do so will be a criminal offence,[158] unless the person can provide that he took reasonable steps for complying with the section.[159] It is also an offence for a person to make the declaration knowing it to be false or without having reasonable grounds for believing it to be true. It should be noted that where the offeror is a company the declaration must be made by a director of the company.[160]

**25.96**   Under s 984, a shareholder can exercise sell-out rights which arise under s 983(2), (3), or (4) by a written communication addressed to the offeror. Further, within one month of the times specified in s 983(2), (3), or (4) (as the case may be) the offeror must give any shareholder who has not accepted the offer notice in the prescribed manner of the rights that are exercisable by that shareholder under s 983(2), (3), or (4) and the period within which the rights are exercisable.[161] An offeror who fails to comply with this requirement commits a criminal offence.[162]

---

[153] Code, A17. In addition, where a matter is determined by the Panel and the person subsequently becomes aware that information they supplied to the Panel was incorrect, incomplete, or misleading then that person must promptly contact the Panel to correct the position (Code, A18). Where a determination of the Panel has continuing effect, the party or parties to that determination must promptly notify the Panel of any new information unless they reasonably consider that it would not be likely to have been relevant to the determination.

[154] s 946.

[155] s 952(1)(b).

[156] s 955(1)(b).

[157] s 980(4).

[158] s 980(6).

[159] s 980(7).

[160] s 980(5).

[161] s 984(3). This does not apply if the offeror has given the shareholder a notice in respect of the shares in question under s 979 (s 984(4)).

[162] s 984(5).

*Implementation—schemes of arrangement*

As noted above, in recent times, schemes of arrangement have proved to be increas-    **25.97**
ingly popular as a means of effecting takeovers. In addition to the provisions of the
Takeover Code, there is a considerable body of law applicable to the promotion of
schemes of arrangement and their consideration by the court. However, in considering the approach to adopt to any scheme of arrangement which implements
a takeover, the court will be heavily influenced by the provisions of the Takeover
Code. In *Expro International Group plc*[163] the court considered an application by
certain shareholders for the adjournment of the sanctioning of a scheme of
arrangement which was to implement a takeover. The purpose of the adjournment would have been to allow the possibility of an improved offer being made.
The court refused the adjournment, on the basis that the shareholders had already
approved the scheme with knowledge of the possibility of a further bid being
made. It was stated that this result was achieved by application of the established
principles applicable to the consideration of schemes of arrangement. However,
the court also expressed the view that there should be a common approach to the
conduct of bids, whether they are structured as an offer or as a scheme, so that the
court procedure inherent in a scheme should not introduce a level of uncertainty
which has otherwise been eliminated by the Takeover Code.

---

[163]  [2008] EWHC 1626 (Ch).

# 26

# PENSION SCHEMES

## A. Overview of Pensions Law

### (1) Surplus to deficit

The first decade of the new millennium has seen a huge increase in the cost to **26.01** companies of providing pensions for their current and former employees. Many defined benefit schemes are in deficit, in the sense that the scheme's liabilities to pay pensions exceed the assets at its disposal. The costs of funding this deficit and the accruing liabilities of the scheme can often be a very significant drain on a company's cash flow and resources.

However, many of the schemes which now face this unpalatable financial outlook **26.02** were in surplus a decade ago. What has happened? Three principal factors have led to this turnaround:

(1) The assumptions used to calculate mortality rates in actuarial valuation of schemes now assume that the members of the scheme will live longer. This means that the members' pensions are more expensive to fund, because the pensions are assumed to be in payment for a longer time.

(2) As yields on gilts and other fixed income instruments fall, the amount which actuaries assume to be required to meet future liabilities is greater than the amount which they had previously assumed to be required when yields were higher.

(3) Many of the surpluses which schemes enjoyed during the 1990s derived from gains made on equities. Similar gains have arisen for investors during the first decade of the new millennium. However, many schemes have been unable to take advantage of these gains because a large proportion of the assets of the scheme have been allocated to fixed income instruments rather than equities.

**26.03** This story illustrates the nature of the liability of employers under a defined benefit contribution scheme. The liability is volatile and dependent on macroeconomic and sociological factors outside the employer's control. The value of the scheme fund is only one of the matters affecting whether or not a scheme is in surplus or in deficit.

### (2) Security of members' benefits and the Pensions Act 2004

**26.04** Equally, however, a deficit in a scheme is not just a problem for the employer. If the employer is unable to meet its liabilities to the scheme, the deficit could mean that the members of the scheme would not have received the benefits to which they are entitled under the scheme.

**26.05** The regime imposed by the Pensions Act 2004 attempts to improve security of members' benefits in the following ways.

(1) By establishing a statutory fund, the Pensions Protection Fund, which (broadly) meets the liabilities for the benefits of members of schemes where (broadly) the sponsoring employer of the scheme is insolvent. The fund is funded from two sources: first, by a statutory levy on schemes which would be eligible for the protection of the fund if their employer were to become insolvent and, secondly, by the assets of the schemes whose members' benefits are met by the fund.

(2) By increasing the costs for employers of withdrawing from a scheme. The liability incurred by an employer on withdrawal from a scheme is now valued on a basis which reflects the cost of purchasing annuities and deferred annuities to meet the pension obligations arising under the scheme. This basis is likely to be more expensive for the employer than the cost of meeting the liabilities of the scheme on an ongoing basis.

(3) By imposing a more demanding statutory regime for the funding of schemes by employers on an ongoing basis. Trustees are therefore better equipped to demand enhanced funding from employers.

**26.06** The duties and obligations of directors of trustee companies and employers to their own companies accord with their general obligations described in more detail in the rest of this book. However, in addition, the pensions legislation confers on the Pensions Regulator power to impose on directors of trustee companies and employers personal liability for civil penalties in certain circumstances where the relevant company is in breach of the provisions of the relevant Act.

The future will disclose whether or not the regime has been effective to enhance **26.07** members' security. However, even now it is clear that the regime will make it harder for employers to withdraw from existing defined benefit schemes and will increase the cost of funding pensions under those schemes. Pensions are likely to continue to cause difficulties for employers and their directors for some time to come.

### (3) Types of pension promise

Companies can make pension provision for their employees in a number of **26.08** different ways.

#### *Funded/unfunded*

It is not necessary for an employer company to set aside a fund separate from the **26.09** assets of the company for the provision of pension benefits. Historically, the principal advantages of setting aside funds in that way have been twofold: first, the assets will be protected from creditors in the event of the company's insolvency and, secondly, the assets set aside receive a more favourable tax treatment in the hands of the scheme trustees than they would receive if they were part of the assets of the company (as to which, see below). However, sometimes one or both of these considerations are not of great importance. In that type of situation, pension benefits may be paid directly by an employer and the rights of the pensioner comprise merely a promise by the employer to pay. This type of arrangement is especially prevalent in the public sector and is sometimes used to provide 'top-up' benefits for highly paid employees.

#### *Registered/unregistered*

Prior to 6 April 2006, pensions were subject to eight different tax regimes.[1] From **26.10** 6 April 2006, the Finance Act 2004, Part 4 imposed a new regime with the intention of simplifying the taxation of pensions. Broadly, all schemes which were eligible for favourable tax treatment under the old regime as exempt approved schemes became eligible for similar treatment under the new regime as registered schemes. In particular, payments to the scheme by the employer remain eligible as a deduction against profit for corporation tax purposes and are not taxable on the employee for the purposes of NIC or income tax as benefits in kind.[2] Equally, the

---

[1] Principally: exempt approved, funded unapproved, unfunded unapproved, personal pension, small self-administered scheme.

[2] Subject to the generous cap imposed by 'the annual allowance'.

assets of the scheme are free from income tax and capital gains tax in the hands of the trustees.

**26.11** However, whereas under the pre-April 2006 regime limits were placed on the amounts which could be paid out of fund to a member from the scheme (expressed, in the case of a defined benefit scheme, as a fraction of final salary), under the new regime the value of the benefits accrued by a member are assessed on 'the benefit crystallization event' (a term of art[3]). If the value of those benefits exceed the lifetime allowance, tax will be charged on the excess at 25% (if the excess is to be paid as a pension) or 55% (if the excess is to be paid as a lump sum).

**26.12** Complex transitional arrangements apply to members with pre-April 2006 benefits not yet in payment. Those provisions are outside the scope of this work.

**26.13** By contrast, the tax treatment of unregistered schemes is unsympathetic.

(1) Payments by employers to unregistered funded schemes are not eligible for upfront corporation tax relief at the time of payment. Rather, the employer must wait for the member to receive payment from the scheme and pay income tax on the payment before receiving a deduction against profits.

(2) Inheritance tax relief is not available on the member's interest in the scheme.[4]

(3) There is no favourable tax treatment for gains arising and income received within the scheme.

**26.14** The change in the tax treatment of unapproved schemes effected by the Finance Act 2004 is likely to make it unattractive in most cases to set up new unregistered schemes, particularly funded unregistered schemes. However, unapproved schemes which have already been set up are unlikely to wind up as a result of the changes, so the distinction is likely still to remain an important one. The provisions of the Pensions Act 1995, s 75, which impose a debt on the employer, do not apply to unregistered schemes.[5]

*Defined benefit/defined contribution*

**26.15** Under a defined benefit scheme, the benefits to be provided by members are set (as the name suggests) with reference to the benefits to be provided to them. So, for example, the scheme might provide that a pension is to be paid to members on their normal retirement date, set at one-eightieth of their final salary for each year of pensionable service undertaken by them.

---

[3] Defined at FA 2004, s 216.

[4] Unregistered schemes are no longer eligible for relief as 'sponsored superannuation schemes' for the purposes of Inheritance Tax Act 1984, s 151(1); Finance Act 2004, s 203(4).

[5] Occupational Pension Schemes (Employer Debt) Regulations 2005 (SI 2005/678), reg 4(1).

The cost of this promise can be unpredictable: the member may live long beyond **26.16** normal retirement date; the member's salary may increase; the yield on the amount put aside to meet the liability may not meet expectations. In a funded defined benefit scheme, this obligation is met from the trust fund and the balance of the cost above any contributions from the employees is funded by a contribution covenant from the employer. The employer therefore takes the burden (and in some cases reaps the benefit) of any fluctuations in the cost of providing the benefits promised to the member.

By contrast, in a defined contribution scheme the employer agrees with the trust- **26.17** ees or the employee to pay an amount into the scheme, often expressed as a percentage of the employee's salary. This amount would be set aside each year as a notional or (in some cases) actual fund for the employee.

When the employee becomes entitled to the benefits (say on retirement), this **26.18** fund is applied to provide whatever benefits can be purchased for the member. There is no additional obligation on the employer. The risk of adverse experience is therefore borne by the member.

Some schemes are hybrid defined contribution and defined benefit schemes. So, **26.19** a scheme may be a defined benefit scheme with a defined contribution section. Equally, the terms of some schemes are written in such a way that issues arise as to whether the scheme is properly analysed as a defined benefit or defined contribu- tion scheme. In *Aon Trust Corporation Limited v KPMG*,[6] the Court of Appeal analysed as defined benefit a scheme with many of the characteristics of a money purchase, or defined contribution, scheme. The effect was that the employer debt provisions of the Pensions Act 1995, s 75 obliged KPMG, the employer, to under- write any shortfall in the scheme, notwithstanding that the scheme did not include a contribution covenant and had been established long before the enactment of any statutory funding requirements.

Unless the text indicates otherwise, the comments and explanations in this chap- **26.20** ter are intended to refer to a funded registered defined benefit scheme, which is the type of scheme most frequently encountered by pensions lawyers in practice.

## (4) The classic defined benefit scheme

*The source of the law*

The core obligation owed by the employer or employers sponsoring the scheme to **26.21** the trustees of the scheme is the employer's contractual obligation to fund the scheme. Equally, the core obligation owed by the trustees of the scheme to the

---

[6] [2006] 1 WLR 97, CA.

members and the other beneficiaries of the scheme is a fiduciary obligation deriving from the trustees' status as trustees.

26.22　However, onto these obligations (which arise as a matter of the general law) has been superimposed a detailed and complex statutory edifice. The two main pillars of that edifice are the Pensions Acts 1995 and 2004. The approach adopted under these Acts is, broadly, to provide an outline scheme of regulation, the details of which are then clarified and particularized in a series of lengthy and (as it has turned out) frequently amended statutory instruments. Not even the most enthusiastic supporter of the current state of the law would argue that the scheme of pensions legislation has progressed in such a way as to make the divination of the law easily approachable by the layman or non-specialist lawyer.

*The cost to the employer*

26.23　The classic defined benefit scheme is contributory, which means that members of the scheme are obliged to make regular contributions to the scheme as a precondition to the provision of benefits for them. The balance of the costs of providing benefits for the members is met by the employer. However, the fact that the scheme is a funded scheme and that the vast majority of the benefits are to be paid in the future means that the assessment of the relevant cost will inevitably amount principally to an assessment of how much is presently required to meet the cost of providing those benefits in the future. This raises the question of how that cost is to be assessed.

26.24　This cost is (and has been) assessed on a number of different bases, of which four are described here. The first is the 'ongoing basis', under which the liabilities and assets of the scheme are valued using assumptions which the scheme actuary believes to be reasonable and appropriate in the circumstances. The factor in the assumptions which has tended to be most influential on the valuation is the difference between the rate of investment return which the actuary uses on the assets of the scheme (which also tends to be used as the discount rate for the valuation of liabilities) and the assumption for salary increases. In practice, however, the fact that the actuary is able to choose his own assumptions has meant that there is considerable scope for variation among actuaries as to the state of funding of the scheme.

26.25　A second basis is 'the buy-out basis'. On this basis, the liabilities of the scheme are valued at the amount it would cost to purchase annuities from an annuity provider adequate to secure those liabilities. In practice, the broad effect of valuation on this basis is that the discount rate applied to the calculation of the liabilities will be equivalent to or very close to the yield on gilts. This will therefore tend to lead to a figure for the cost of the liabilities which is higher than the equivalent figure where the scheme is valued on the ongoing basis.

The Pensions Act 1995, s 75 introduced the 'Minimum Funding Requirement' as **26.26** a statutory basis of valuation. The scheme of the legislation is (and remains) that employers should be obliged to keep schemes funded up to a reasonable level prescribed by statute, which is the Minimum Funding Requirement. The Minimum Funding Requirement was initially intended, broadly, to track the buy-out basis, with a view to eliminating scheme deficits. However, the basis ultimately became considerably 'softer' (or less expensive for the employer) than the buy-out basis. This has to some extent been remedied by the changes effected in 2005 by the introduction of the scheme specific funding requirement under the Pensions Act 2004 (the statutory funding objective), described in the next paragraph, and the amendments to the means of valuation of debts on the employer under the Pensions Act 1995, s 75.

The Pensions Act 2004, ss 221–223 introduced the 'Statutory Funding Objective' **26.27** (SFO). The scheme of the legislation is that the trustees and the employer, with the advice of the scheme actuary, should jointly agree on a statement of funding principles. This in turn leads to a schedule of contributions which the employer must pay. Where the trustees and the employer are unable to agree, the trustees must report the matter to the Regulator, who may intervene by virtue of the Pensions Act 2004, s 229. The Regulator has indicated how he intends to exercise his powers under the Act in a Code of Practice, issued in 2005. In *British Vita Unlimited v British Vita Pension Trustees Ltd*,[7] Warren J considered the extent to which the powers of trustees to set contributions under a contribution rule (where contributions might exceed the amounts payable under the SFO) survived the legislative introduction of the SFO under the Pensions Act 2004, Part 3. The court decided that trustees could claim contributions under the rule at any time before the date on which the first valuation of the scheme was required under the Act. However, the court left open the question as to whether or not the rule could be used by the trustees after that date.

*Liabilities before withdrawal*

While the employer remains liable under the scheme (which is used here as short- **26.28** hand for the state of affairs arising before withdrawal from the scheme for the purposes of the Pensions Act 1995, s 75), the employer is obliged to meet the following ongoing funding requirements.

(1) The employer has contractual liability under the contribution rule in the scheme documentation. In some cases, the trustees will have very wide powers to claim contributions from the employer which exceed the obligations

---

[7] [2008] 1 All ER 37.

imposed on the employer by statute. This power may be curtailed by the Pensions Act 2004, Part 3.[8]

(2) The employer is liable under the Pensions Act 2004, ss 227 and 228 for contributions set out in the schedule of contributions prepared on the basis of the most recent relevant actuarial valuation of the scheme (normally effected every three years).

**26.29** Where the scheme has been valued with an effective date after 22 September 2005, the valuation must include a valuation on the basis of the SFO. The statutory schedule of contributions arising out of the valuation will be fixed on the basis of that SFO valuation. The schedule must be agreed within 15 months of the effective date of the valuation (or 18 months in the case of valuations with an effective date between 22 September and 29 December 2005). Where the contributions payable under the schedule remain unpaid by the employer, they are recoverable as a debt and in certain circumstances the trustees are obliged to report the late payment to the Regulator.[9]

**26.30** Where no such valuation has yet been effected, the MFR regime will continue to apply to the contributions payable under the scheme until the next valuation. The effective date of this valuation (which will trigger the application of the SFO regime to the scheme) must be no later than the third anniversary of the last MFR valuation.[10] This would suggest that all schemes will have been valued on an SFO basis by 22 September 2008. This in turn would suggest that all schemes will have an SFO schedule of contributions in place by 22 December 2009 (15 months later).

*Liabilities on withdrawal*

**26.31** Where a liability is triggered under the Pensions Act 1995, s 75, the employer will prima facie be liable for the full amount of the buy-out debt.[11] Critically, liability under the section is not limited to the cost of providing benefits for members who are or have been employed by the employer, but can relate also to 'orphan' members, ie members who have no employer at the time when the liability is triggered.

---

[8] 'May' is used rather than 'shall' for two reasons: (a) the effect of the rules may be amended by Pensions Act 2004, s 229 and Occupational Pensions (Scheme Funding) Regulations (SI 2005/3377), Schedule 2, and (b) the effect of the contribution rule after the date on which the first valuation of the scheme is required under the Pensions Act 2004 is currently still an open question (see the *British Vita* case [2008] 1 All ER 37).

[9] Pensions Act 2004, s 228(3).

[10] Occupational Pensions (Scheme Funding) Regulations, Schedule 4.

[11] Occupational Pension Schemes (Employer Debt) Regulations (SI 2005/678), reg 3B, as amended by the Occupational Pension Schemes (Employer Debt etc.) (Amendment) Regulations (SI 2005/2224).

Complex additional provisions deal with 'multi-employer' schemes, where more than one employer acts as the sponsoring employer (see below).

The code by which a liability arises under s 75 is complex. However, in outline, a **26.32** liability arises in the following circumstances:

(1) where an 'insolvency event' (in practice administration or winding up) occurs in relation to one or more of the sponsoring employers;

(2) where the trustees or administrators of the scheme notify the Pensions Protection Fund under the Pensions Act 2004, s 129 that the employer is unlikely to continue as a going concern;

(3) when, in the case of a multi-employer scheme, a sponsoring employer ceases to employ active members of the scheme.[12]

The liability under s 75 can be disapplied where a withdrawal arrangement is **26.33** agreed with the Regulator.[13] This provision is of great practical importance where the employer is sold or is restructured, since the payment of a s 75 debt on a buy-out basis would often be an obstacle to the successful completion of the deal.

In some cases, the contractual obligation imposed on the employer in the event of **26.34** the scheme winding up will be an obligation to make provision on a buy-out basis. However, it is difficult to imagine circumstances in which the employer's contractual obligations might exceed the liability imposed on it by statute.

Where a scheme has more than one sponsoring employer, similar considerations **26.35** apply: withdrawal by each employer will trigger liability for each employer on a buy-out basis. However, in some cases there is considerable scope for flexibility in the apportionment of liability between withdrawing employers.

Before 5 April 2008, when the Occupational Pension Schemes (Employer Debt **26.36** and Miscellaneous Amendments) Regulations 2008[14] came into force, the withdrawing employer would in the normal case be liable to pay the proportion of the liability which 'in the opinion of the actuary after consultation with the trustees or managers, the amount of the scheme's liabilities attributable to employment with that employer (*ie the withdrawing employer*) bears to the total amount of the scheme's liabilities attributable to employment with the employers (*ie the current sponsoring employers*)'.[15] It is important to note that (as in the case of the single

---

[12] Occupational Pension Schemes (Employer Debt) Regulations 2005, reg 2(1) (amended by the Occupational Pension Schemes (Emloyer Debt and Miscellaneous Amendments) Regulations 2008 (SI 2008/731).

[13] As described in the Occupational Pension Schemes (Employer Debt) Regulations, Schedule 1A.

[14] SI 2008/731.

[15] Occupational Pension Schemes (Employer Debt) Regulations 2005, reg 6(2)(a).

withdrawing employer) the liability of the employer was not limited to the buy-out cost of the employer's own employees, but also encompassed a proportionate part of the cost of providing benefits for 'orphan' members.

**26.37** However, where the scheme conferred power to apportion contractual liability between different employers, the s 75 debt assessable on the withdrawing employer could be allocated in the same way.[16] Where such a power was available to the trustees, the trustees could therefore prima facie use this power to apportion the s 75 liability between withdrawing employers in such a way as to maximize recovery for the scheme. A notable example of this practice was the case of *Re Phoenix Ventures Holdings Ltd*,[17] relating to the restructuring of the Rover Group, in which the trustees sought to allocate as much as possible of the s 75 liability to the group holding company, which had plenty of assets but had been the employer of only very few members, rather than to the trading companies, which had employed numerous members but had few assets.

**26.38** After 5 April 2008, the effect of the new regulation 6(4) of the Occupational Pension Schemes (Employer Debt) Regulations 2005 (as amended) is that scheme rules allowing trustees to apportion liability between employers in multi-employer schemes are not effective to apportion liability under section 75 if the power to apportion is exercised after that date. Instead employers are only liable for the costs of members' accrual referable to the member's period of employment with that employer, subject to complex provisions in relation to 'orphan' members.

## B. The Position of the Trustee

### (1) Identity and capability of the directors

**26.39** The trustee of the classic scheme will often be a company established for that purpose. Under the Pensions Act 2004, s 242 at least one-third of the directors of the company must be member-nominated directors, appointed in accordance with the requirements at s 242(5). There are detailed exceptions to this rule set out in the Occupational Pension Schemes (Member Nominated Trustees and Directors) Regulations 2006,[18] most notably in cases where the scheme is unapproved or the sole trustee is an 'independent trustee' within the Pensions

---

[16] Occupational Pension Schemes (Employer Debt) Regulations 2005, reg 6(2)(b).
[17] [2005] 38 PBLR, [2005] EWHC 1379 (Ch).
[18] SI 2006/714.

Act 1995, s 23(3).[19] Failure to comply with this requirement will lead to a liability for the trust company to pay civil penalties.[20]

**26.40** The Pensions Act 2004, ss 247–249 imposes an obligation on directors and other officers and employees of corporate trustees to be conversant with the following matters:

(1) the trust deed and rules of the scheme;

(2) any statement of investment principles for the time being maintained under the Pensions Act 1995, s 35;

(3) the most recent statement of funding principles;

(4) any other trustee policy document relating to the administration of the scheme;

(5) the law relating to pensions and trusts;

(6) the principles relating to—(a) the funding of occupational pension schemes, (b) the investment of the assets of such schemes, and (c) such other matters as may be prescribed.

**26.41** Happily for newly appointed trustees or directors of the trustee company, they have six months in which to familiarize themselves with these matters.[21] The scope of the understanding required of trustees by the Regulator is set out in a code prepared by the Regulator and related guidance (called the 'Scope documents'). It is clear from these materials that a relatively high degree of competence and professionalism is expected of trustees. These requirements clearly enhance the standard of care to be expected of a trustee under the Trustee Act 2000, s 1 (ie the standard of care required of a trustee for the purposes of a claim in breach of trust).

## (2) Duties of the trustee

**26.42** As a matter of general trust law, the trustee owes the members of the scheme the fiduciary obligations owed by a trustee to its beneficiaries. This obligation is glossed and amended by the imposition of specific statutory duties.

**26.43** The trustee must administer the trust assets properly and consistently with the standard of care imposed on the trustee by the Trustee Act 2000, s 1 and/or under the general law. The most important practical implications of this obligation for a pension fund trustee are set out below.

---

[19] By virtue of the Pensions Act 2004, s 242(10); Member Nominated Trustee Regulations (SI 2006/714), reg 2(k); Pensions Act 1995, s 23(3).

[20] Pensions Act 2004, s 242(11).

[21] Occupational Pension Scheme (Trustees' Knowledge and Understanding) Regulations (SI 2006/686), reg 3.

*Proper investment*

**26.44** The wide power of investment in the Pensions Act 1995, s 34(1) confers on the trustees power to invest in any asset, subject to the specific terms of the scheme. However, although a particular investment may well be within the trustees' powers (in the sense that the investment will not be *ultra vires)*, the investment decision may well be a breach of trust or in breach of duty as an inappropriate or foolhardy exercise of that power.

**26.45** By the Occupational Schemes (Investment) Regulations 2005,[22] reg 4 (the Investment Regulations), trustees must invest the assets of the fund in the following way:

(1) in the best interests of members and beneficiaries;

(2) in the case of a potential conflict of interest, in the sole interest of members and beneficiaries;

(3) in a manner calculated to ensure the security, quality, liquidity, and profitability of the portfolio as a whole;

(4) in a manner appropriate to the nature and duration of the expected future retirement benefits payable under the scheme (in other words in such a way as to match the projected liabilities of the scheme);

(5) predominantly in investments admitted to trading on regulated markets,[23] so that any investment in assets not traded on regulated markets must be kept to a prudent level (ie in practice the trustees must be cautious about investing in untraded assets or in funds which hold untraded assets (eg some private equity funds));

(6) the assets of the scheme must be properly diversified;

(7) investment in derivative instruments may be made only in so far as they contribute to a reduction of risks or facilitate efficient portfolio management (including the reduction of cost or the generation of additional capital or income with an acceptable level of risk) and must be made and managed so as to avoid excessive risk exposure to a single counterparty and to other derivative operations.

**26.46** In addition, by the Investment Regulations, reg 12 and the Pensions Act 1995, s 40 most large schemes are unable to invest more than 5% of the fund in 'employer-related investments'.[24] These provisions were introduced in order to avoid the

---

[22] SI 2005/3378.

[23] As to the definition of 'regulated market'; see Investment Regulations, reg 4(11). This definition includes collective investment schemes holding investments traded on regulated markets and certain types of insurance policy (see Investment Regulations, reg 4(9)).

[24] Defined by Pensions Act 1995, s 40(2) and Investment Regulations, reg 11.

employer using the capital of the scheme for the business, often to the serious disadvantage of the members of the scheme (eg in the Maxwell debacle).

By the Pensions Act 1995, s 47(2) trustees are obliged to appoint a fund manager. **26.47** The Act makes detailed provision as to the investment management agreement by which the fund manager is to be appointed. In addition, pursuant to the Pensions Act 1995, s 36, the trustees are under an obligation to take 'proper advice' (in practice advice given by a person authorized under the Financial Services and Markets Act 2000 (FSMA)) in relation to the suitability of the investments of the scheme in the light of the investment criteria set out above.

Further, by the Pensions Act 1995, s 35 and the Investment Regulations, reg 2 the **26.48** trustees are obliged to prepare and consult with the employer in relation to the preparation of a statement of investment principles. The trustee must do more by way of consultation than merely giving notice to the employer of its intentions.[25]

The Pensions Act 1995, s 34 confers on the trustees wide power to delegate their **26.49** investment power (which the terms of s 47, requiring appointment of a fund manager, clearly make desirable). However, the section also provides for a limitation of the liability of the trustee in relation to investment decisions once a manager has been appointed. The trustees are not responsible for the act or default of any fund manager in the exercise of any discretion delegated to him if they have taken all such steps as are reasonable to satisfy themselves that (a) the fund manager has the appropriate knowledge and experience for managing the investments of the scheme, and (b) he is carrying out his work competently and complying with the requirements of s 36 (ie in practice complying with the investment criteria set out above).

This is just as well, because the Pensions Act 1995, s 33 curtails the application of **26.50** trustee exoneration clauses in the exercise of investment powers. Trustees cannot be excused for negligence in 'the performance of their investment functions'. In the circumstances, the most likely areas in which the investment activities of trustees are likely to attract the risk of liability are where:

(1) the trustee's power of investment is limited (in such cases it is critical that the scope of the trustees' power is highlighted to the investment manager and the investment manager acts accordingly);

(2) there is a significant mismatch between the liability profile of the scheme and the assets held as investments;

(3) the fund is insufficiently diversified or is held in risky investments;

---

[25] *Pitmans Trustees v The Telecommunications Group plc* [2004] PBLR 32, [2004] EWHC 181 (Ch).

(4) insufficient steps are taken by trustees to oversee the investment managers and to review their performance;

(5) the investment management agreement with the fund manager includes provisions which are unusually onerous for the trustee or unusually lenient for the fund manager.

*Collection*

**26.51** Another critical obligation of the trustee is to recover adequate contributions from the employer. The statutory mechanism for the recovery of contributions is set out in outline above. Although the trustee is clearly under a duty to recover what is properly due from the employer, it is questionable whether trustees are under a duty to use every power at their disposal to maximize the amount which is due. Devices which might be used are the re-allocation of liabilities between employers in multi-employer schemes (as in *Re Phoenix Ventures Holdings Ltd*[26] (considered in paragraph 26.37 above)) and altering the scheme's investment strategy so as to alter the basis of valuation of the scheme's liabilities (as in the *Pitmans* case[27]).

*Payment of benefits*

**26.52** The trustee owes a duty to pay the correct benefits to members and dependants at the right time. A beneficiary is entitled to information from the trustees promptly in relation to the benefits properly payable to him (or her).

**26.53** If the beneficiary has been underpaid, he has a claim against the trustees for his entitlement and against the trustees in breach of trust. If the beneficiary has been overpaid, the trustees may theoretically be able to recover the sums from the beneficiary as money paid under a mistake. However, the beneficiary may have defences based on change of position or estoppel if he has spent the money[28] and it will often be impracticable for trustees to attempt to pursue numerous beneficiaries for small sums. However, the trustees will often be entitled as a matter of law to recoup themselves from the sums payable in the future to the beneficiary. This course in turn may not be free of danger for the trustees, since it may trigger a complaint of maladministration by the beneficiary.

*Making decisions*

**26.54** The obligation of the trustee when exercising a discretionary power is now well-settled: the trustee must 'exercise the power for the purpose for which it is given, giving proper consideration to the matters which are relevant and excluding from

---

[26] [2005] 38 PBLR, [2005] EWHC 137 (Ch).
[27] *Pitmans Trustees v The Telecommunications Group* [2004] EWHC 181.
[28] eg *National Westminster Bank v Somer International* [2002] QB 1286, CA.

consideration matters which are irrelevant'.[29] There is no separate overarching duty for the trustee to act fairly.

Where the trustee of the scheme is a corporate trustee, it may be difficult to piece together the reasoning to be imputed to the company for the purposes of assessing whether or not the trustee has given proper consideration to the matters which are relevant or irrelevant to the decision. Conversely, the fact that the minutes of the board are likely to have been kept and (perhaps) the board's discussion recorded may be helpful.

26.55

In many cases, the directors of the trustee company will be directly interested in the way in which a trustee exercises a discretionary power. If normal principles of fiduciary obligation were to be applied, this interest could vitiate any decision which had the effect of benefiting the director himself.[30] These principles are disapplied by the Pensions Act 1995, s 39 so that a trustee (and by extension the director of a trustee company) is not precluded from exercising trust powers in such a way as to benefit himself.

26.56

However, s 39 does not bar a challenge to a decision made by a trustee under which he in fact benefits himself. The trustee is not entitled to give undue weight to his own personal interests in reaching a decision as to the exercise of trustee powers. The trustee must still exercise the power for its proper purpose, taking into account relevant matters and not taking into account irrelevant matters in reaching his decision, within the formulation in *Edge v Pensions Ombudsman*.[31]

26.57

Further, in making decisions the trustee is not obliged to take into account only the interests of the members and the beneficiaries. The trustee can take into account the interests of the employer as well in the right type of case.[32] Examples might include decisions about the distribution of surplus, amendment, or augmentation of benefits and other matters which might take effect to increase the employer's level of contribution.

26.58

### Whistleblowing

The trustees are under a duty to make a report to the Pensions Protection Fund where they become aware that the sponsoring employer is 'unlikely to continue as a going concern'.[33]

26.59

---

[29] *Edge v Pensions Ombudsman* [2000] Ch 602, 623, CA, per Chadwick LJ.

[30] As in *Re Drexel Burnham Lambert Pension Plan* [1995] 1 WLR 32 and the two cases of Vinelott J on the point: *Re Makin (William) & Sons Ltd* [1993] OPLR 171 and *British Coal Corporation v British Staff Superannuation Scheme Trustees Ltd* [1993] PLR 303.

[31] [2000] Ch 602.

[32] Cf *Thrells v Lomas* [1993] 1 WLR 456 and *Edge v Pensions Ombudsman* [2000] Ch 602 at 626.

[33] Under Pensions Act 2004, s 129.

### (3) Liability of directors of trustee company

**26.60** The nature of the role undertaken by a corporate trustee makes it difficult to think of circumstances in which it will ever be possible for a beneficiary to pierce the trustee company's corporate veil (so as to ascribe the actions of the company to the directors). The directors of the trustee company owe no direct fiduciary duty to the beneficiaries of the scheme.[34]

**26.61** In practice, this leaves only two avenues available to a beneficiary who wishes to make a director personally liable for the actions of a corporate trustee. The first is where the circumstances justify a claim against the director as constructive trustee, most likely for dishonest assistance. In *Barlow Clowes International Ltd v Eurotrust International Ltd*[35] the Privy Council clarified the test for dishonesty in cases of dishonest assistance:

> In summary, [the judge] said that liability for dishonest assistance requires a dishonest state of mind on the part of the person who assists in a breach of trust. Such a state of mind may consist in knowledge that the transaction is one in which he cannot honestly participate (for example, a misappropriation of other people's money), or it may consist in suspicion combined with a conscious decision not to make inquiries which might result in knowledge: see *Manifest Shipping Co Ltd v Uni-Polaris Insurance Co Ltd* [2003] 1 AC 469. Although a dishonest state of mind is a subjective mental state, the standard by which the law determines whether it is dishonest is objective. If by ordinary standards a defendant's mental state would be characterised as dishonest, it is irrelevant the defendant judges by different standards. The Court of Appeal held this to be a correct statement of the law and their Lordships agree.

**26.62** If a director of the trustee company has acted dishonestly in this way, then the scheme exoneration clause will not apply to relieve the trustee from liability for the actions of the dishonest director (assuming the trustee to be vicariously liable for the actions of the dishonest director). Many corporate trustees of pension schemes will now have the benefit of insurance policies against breach of trust claims, so that a claim against the trustee would have some value. The benefit of the claim against the director is therefore likely to be principally tactical (and even then it may be important to check that the necessary allegation of dishonesty does not vitiate the trustee company's insurance policy).

**26.63** However, if the trustee company is not insured in this way, a claim against the company may be valueless, either because the trustee company has no assets or because the principal employer of the scheme is also the scheme trustee (as was often the case before Pensions Act 1995) and the principal employer is insolvent

---

[34] *HR v JAPT* [1997] PLR 97 and *Gregson v HAE Trustees Ltd* [2008] EWHC 1006 (Ch).
[35] [2006] 1 WLR 1476, PC at para 10, per Lord Hoffmann. At paras 14–17 Lord Hoffmann clarified an element of ambiguity in the speech of Lord Hutton in *Twinsectra Ltd v Yardley* [2002] 2 AC 164, HL at paras 35 and 36.

(as may well be the case where the beneficiaries are looking to bring a claim against the trustee). In those circumstances, a claim against the directors of the trustee company personally may be the only way of making recovery.

The second way in which a claim might be brought against the directors of the **26.64** trustee company (at least as a matter of theory) is by a 'dogleg' claim. The reasoning underlying this type of claim is as follows:

(1) The actions of the director would justify a claim against him by the trustee company in breach of fiduciary duty based on standard principles of directors' liability.

(2) The benefit of the trustee company's cause of action is held by the trustee company as an asset of the scheme.

(3) Since the cause of action is a trust asset, a beneficiary is entitled to bring a claim against the trustee company for administration of the cause of action under the principle in *Hayim v Citibank*[36] on the basis that the trustee company is conflicted from bringing the claim.

The claim is brought by the beneficiary joining both the trustee company and the **26.65** director. In *HR v JAPT*,[37] the court refused to strike out a dogleg claim. However, despite this initial (comparative) success, it appears that no claims of this type have been brought successfully. In *Gregson v HAE Trustees Ltd*,[38] Robert Miles QC, sitting as a deputy judge of the Chancery Division, struck out a dogleg claim in circumstances where the trustee company was the trustee of a number of trusts (unlike in *HR v JAPT*). The judgment of the court includes a detailed analysis of the shortcomings of the principle and includes criticism of the decision in *HR v JAPT*. Although the facts of *Gregson* are distinguishable from *HR v JAPT*, it is difficult to avoid the conclusion that *HR v JAPT* would have been decided differently had the ratio of *Gregson* been applied in that case.[39]

The Pensions Acts allow the Regulator to impose civil penalties on trustees for **26.66** breaches of some of the obligations imposed by the act. The specific statutory obligations in relation to which civil penalties may be imposed are too numerous to itemize here. However, they include the following liabilities under the Pensions Acts 1995 and 2004:

(1) failure to prepare and review a statement of funding principles (2004 Act, s 223);

---

[36] [1987] AC 370.
[37] [1997] PLR 99.
[38] [2008] EWHC 1006 (Ch).
[39] See also, in Jersey, *Alhamrani v Alhamrani* [2007] JLR 44.

(2) failure to obtain, receive, and make available to the employer an actuarial valuation of the scheme (2004 Act, s 224);

(3) failure to report to the Regulator an employer's failure to pay contributions where there are reasonable grounds to believe that matter may be of material significance to the Regulator (2004 Act, s 228);

(4) failure to inform the Regulator and members of the Scheme that the employer has not met contributions (1995 Act, s 88).

26.67 Pensions Act 1995, s 10 and Pensions Act 2004, s 314 both provide that these civil penalties may be imposed on a director of the trustee company personally where the act or omission on which the civil penalty is based 'was done with the consent or connivance of, or is attributable to any neglect on the part of' the relevant director. Unsurprisingly, penalties cannot be met from scheme funds (Pensions Act 2004, s 256).

## C. Obligations of the Employer

26.68 The general law imposes on sponsoring employers a duty to its employees 'that the employers will not, without reasonable and proper cause, conduct themselves in a manner calculated or likely to destroy or seriously damage the relationship of confidence and trust between employer and employee'.[40] The obligation applies also in relation to the exercise by the employer of its powers under the scheme, whether or not it holds those powers in a fiduciary capacity. The obligation prima facie applies also in relation to past employees like pensioners and deferred pensioners and might theoretically result in a claim for damages by, for example, trustees against a sponsoring employer.

26.69 In addition to this general obligation at law, statute imposes on employers (and also on the auditor of the employer) a duty to disclose to the actuaries and auditors of the scheme on request any information which is reasonably required for the performance of the duties of the trustees and of the actuaries and auditors. In addition, the employer is obliged to disclose to the trustees without request any event whose occurrence might reasonably be believed to have an impact on the performance of the trustees' duties.[41]

---

[40] *Imperial Group Pension Trust v Imperial Tobacco* [1991] 1 WLR 589, deriving from *Woods v WM Car Services (Peterborough) Limited* [1981] IRLR 347, approved by the Court of Appeal in *Lewis v Motorworld Garages Ltd* [1985] IRLR 465.

[41] Occupational Pension Schemes (Scheme Administration) Regulations 1996, reg 6 and Pensions Act 1995, s 47.

In situations where a company is heading towards financial difficulties, this legislative code has the potential to cause serious difficulties. The employer may be under an obligation to inform the trustees of possible future underperformance by the company under the Occupational Pension Schemes (Scheme Administration) Regulations 1996, reg 6. Once informed, the trustees may be under an obligation to inform the Pensions Protection Fund that the company is 'unlikely to continue as a going concern'.[42] On the worst case scenario, this might in turn trigger a liability under the Pensions Act 1995, s 75, which in many cases would seal the company's fate.

**26.70**

A critical consideration in this type of situation is likely to be the relative size of the pensions liability. In many cases, the trustees of a company's pensions fund will be by far the company's biggest creditors. However, in that type of case the company and the trustees are necessary, if sometimes uneasy, bedfellows.

**26.71**

There is little reason for the trustees to try to wind up the company when the bulk of the scheme's liabilities may well be guaranteed by the PPF. The long-term interests of the members will normally lie with the trustees continuing to collect contributions from the employer and continuing to allow members to accrue service. Nevertheless, the size of the company's liability may often mean that the trustees will feel that this process is precarious.

**26.72**

Conversely, if the company wishes to reduce its exposure to pensions liabilities over time, its interests are likely to lie in limiting future accrual under the scheme (for example by closing the scheme to new members) while meeting its liabilities as they arise. Immediate withdrawal may well currently be unattractively expensive, but there may come a time when financial conditions conspire to make withdrawal affordable. However, until that time, the trustees will continue to insist on (and the company will be obliged to pay) contributions on the basis that the company must over time discharge any deficit in the scheme,[43] with that deficit calculated on a buy-out basis.

**26.73**

The Regulator has power to impose on employers civil penalties for breach of some of the statutory obligations of employers under the pensions legislation. The specific statutory obligations in relation to which civil penalties may be imposed are too numerous to itemize here. However, they include failure of the employer without reasonable excuse to pay contributions under a schedule of contributions (under Pensions Act 2004, section 228(4)(b)).

**26.74**

The Pensions Act 1995, s 10 and Pensions Act 2004, s 314 both provide that these civil penalties may be imposed on a director of the trustee company where the act

**26.75**

---

[42] Under Pensions Act, s 129.
[43] As a 'recovery plan' under Pensions Act 2004, Part 3.

or omission on which the civil penalty is based 'was done with the consent or connivance of, or is attributable to any neglect on the part of' the relevant director.

**26.76**    This raises the prospect of personal liability under the section for a director of a company which fails to meet its liabilities under a schedule of contributions. The extent to which the Regulator will use the power to impose civil penalties in this way remains to be seen.

**26.77**    The obligations of the directors of employer companies to their company otherwise accord with their obligations under the general law.

# PART V

# OTHER LIABILITIES OF DIRECTORS

# 27

# LIABILITIES OF DIRECTORS
# TO THIRD PARTIES

## A. Introduction

A principal purpose of incorporating a company with limited liability is to avoid **27.01** the personal liability that otherwise attaches to an individual if he trades without the protection of the corporate form. Incorporation with limited liability undoubtedly shields a director from the routine liabilities associated with carrying on business when that business is carried on by a company rather than by him as an individual. Legally, the business is then the company's business, not the director's business and therefore any contracts concluded or obligations undertaken in relation to the business are, ordinarily, contracts or obligations of the company.

**27.02**  In *Ferguson v Wilson*[1] Cairns LJ said:

> What is the position of directors of a public company? They are merely agents of a company. The company itself cannot act in its own person, for it has no person; it can only act through directors, and the case is, as regards those directors, merely the ordinary case of principal and agent. Wherever an agent is liable those directors would be liable; where the liability would attach to the principal, and the principal only, the liability is the liability of the company.

Despite this statement of general principle there are a variety of circumstances in which a director may find himself liable to third parties in connection with the business of the company.

**27.03**  This chapter focuses on those circumstances. The liabilities are, for the most part, the creation of the common law. However, statute has an increasing role to play where, for reasons of policy, the imposition of personal liability upon a director to a third party has been deemed appropriate. This chapter also addresses the circumstances in which a director can be held liable for costs incurred by the successful party in litigation where the company has sued or been sued. Finally, the exposure of a director to proceedings for contempt of court is discussed where a company has breached a judgment or order of the court.

## B.  Liabilities of Directors in Relation to Contracts

### (1)  Company contracts

**27.04**  A director, being an agent, is not personally liable to third parties on contracts with third parties purporting to bind his company. This is the position even if the director had no authority to bind the company to the contract although in such circumstances he could be liable for breach of warranty of authority.[2] It is also the position even if the company's failure to perform the contract is due entirely to the fault of the director or if the company could not, at the time of the contract, fulfil it.[3] A director is also not liable in tort at the suit of a third party, if acting in good faith within the scope of his authority, he procures or causes the company to breach a contract with the third party.[4]

---

[1] (1866) LR 2 Ch App 77, 89–90.
[2] *Firbank's Executors v Humphreys & Others* (1886) 18 QBD 54, CA.
[3] *Elkington & Co v Hurter* [1892] 2 Ch 452.
[4] *Said v Butt* [1920] 3 KB 496, 506; see also *G Scammel & Nephew Ltd v Hurley* [1929] KB 419, 443, 449; *DC Thompson & Co Ltd v Deakin* [1952] Ch 646, 680–1, CA; *Welsh Development Agency v Export Finance Co Ltd* [1992] BCLC 148, 171–3, 179–82, 191, CA. This issue is also discussed at paragraph 27.25 below.

The mere fact that a person describes himself as a director does not necessarily **27.05**
lead to the conclusion that a person did not intend to contract personally.[5]
A director may contract so as to make himself personally liable to a third party by,
for example, expressly guaranteeing in his capacity as a director the performance
of a contract between the third party and the company. More difficult are cases
where a director has not expressly guaranteed performance but the question is
whether, having regard to the terms of the contract and the circumstances, the
director must be regarded as having contracted personally. There can be difficulties, in particular, where the contract is an oral one and there has been no express
statement by the director as to the capacity in which he is intending to contract.
It will be necessary, in such event, to consider the surrounding circumstances in
order to determine whether the contract was made with the director personally or
with the company. Where the contract is in writing and it is signed in the direct-
or's own name without any reference to the company of which he is a director,
there is obviously a substantial risk that the director will be found to have contracted personally.[6] By contrast if the company's name appears on the contractual
document and the director signs it 'for and on behalf' of the company, there will
be no doubt that it is the company who is a party to the contract, not the
director.[7]

Until 2006 the Companies Acts had since 1856[8] imposed personal liability on **27.06**
directors for company contracts where the company's name was incorrectly stated
in the contractual document. Historically, great importance was attached to this
statutory liability.[9] It was applied strictly and there were numerous reported cases
where directors were found liable.[10] In 2001 the CLR concluded that the personal
statutory liability attaching to directors was unduly harsh.[11] In particular, concern
was expressed that the civil sanctions could provide a remedy to someone who had
not been misled or suffered loss by the misstatement of the name but through
some other cause such as the insolvency of the company. The CLR recommended

---

[5] *McCollin v Gilpin* (1881) 6 QBD 516, CA.
[6] *Re International Contract Company* (1871) 6 Ch App 525 LJJ; *Gadd v Houghton* (1876) LR 1
Ex D 357; cf *Aggs v Nicholson* (1856) 1 H&N 165.
[7] *Universal Steam Navigation Co v James McKelvie & Co* [1923] AC 492 HL.
[8] 1856 Act, s 31.
[9] In *Atkin v Wardle* (1889) 5 TLR 734 CA Lindley LJ described 1862 Act, ss 41 and 42 as two
of the most important sections and that the court should take care not to relax them.
[10] See eg *Durham Fancy Goods v Michael Jackson (Fancy Goods)* [1968] 2 QB 839; *Lindholst & Co
A/S v Fowler* [1988] BCLC 166; *Blum v OCP Repartition SA* [1988] BCLC 170, CA; *Oshkosh B'gosh
Inc v Dan Marbel Inc Ltd* [1989] BCLC 507, CA; *Novaknit Hellas SA v Kumar Bros International Ltd*
[1998] CLC 971; cf *Banque de L'Indochine et de Suez SA v Euroseas Group Finance Co Ltd* [1981] 3
All ER 198; *Jenice Ltd v Dan* [1993] BCLC 1349.
[11] CLR: *Final Report* at para 11.57.

that civil sanctions should be targeted more closely on those who were really responsible for the breach and on cases where there was a genuine causal link between the misstatement and any loss suffered by the relevant third party.

**27.07** The 2006 Act has removed the personal liability that formerly attached to a director for misstating the name of a company.[12] The Companies (Trading Disclosures) Regulations 2008[13] made under the 2006 Act, s 82 still require the registered name of a company to be stated in a contract and other company documents and communications. However the civil sanction contained in s 83 for failure to make the required disclosure no longer attaches to directors. Section 83, as recommended by the CLR, targets the company in breach of the regulations rather than the individual responsible for the breach. If a company in proceedings seeks to enforce a right arising out of a contract made in the course of a business in respect of which the company was, at the time the contract was made, in breach of the regulations, the proceedings may be dismissed unless the court before which the proceedings are brought is satisfied that it is just and equitable to permit the proceedings to continue. The requirement of justice and equity tends to suggest that proceedings would not be dismissed where the defendant had received a benefit under a contract made in breach of the regulations or there was no suggestion that the defendant had been misled in any way by the breach. Importantly, there is no longer any provision for the imposition of personal liability on a director or any other person who signs or authorizes to be signed an instrument where the company's registered name is not properly stated. However, subs 83(3) preserves any other rights available to a person affected by a failure of company to comply with the regulations. Thus the right of a third party to sue a director personally who signs a cheque as a director without stating the company's name continues unaffected.[14]

**27.08** Although a director no longer incurs personal civil liability for misstating a company's name on a company contract, there may be criminal sanctions. Where a company fails, without reasonable excuse, to comply with any requirement in the Companies (Trading Disclosures) Regulations 2008,[15] the company and every

---

[12] By the repeal of 1985 Act, s 349 on 1 October 2008: 2006 Act Commencement Order No 5, art 8(b) and Schedule 3.

[13] SI 2008/495. The regulations are concerned with disclosure of a company's registered name both at the company's registered office and other locations and in business communications, business letters, order forms, and websites.

[14] Bills of Exchange Act 1882 s 26(2); *Rafsanjan Pistachio Producers Co-operative v Reiss* [1990] BCLC 352.

[15] SI 2008/495.

officer of the company who is in default commits an offence.[16] An officer for the
purposes of the regulation includes a shadow director.[17]

### (2) Pre-incorporation contracts

Until a company has been incorporated it has no legal existence. It cannot make a **27.09**
valid contract, nor can it be bound by contracts purported to have been entered
into on its behalf. However, frequently contracts are entered into by the promoters of a company in anticipation of being able to commence business immediately
upon a company's incorporation. Typically, one or more of the promoters of a
company will become its first directors.

*Common law*

At common law: **27.10**

(1) If the company was not in existence when the contract was signed, there was
    no contract with the company.[18]
(2) There could, however, be a contract with anyone who had made the contract
    purportedly on behalf of the non-existent company.[19]
(3) Whether there was such a contract depended upon the capacity in which the
    maker of the contract was found to have acted.
(4) Where a person was found to have made a contract, solely in his capacity as
    agent, he could not thereafter sue or be sued upon it. However, where a per-
    son was found to have contracted as principal, he could sue or be sued.[20]

In *Kelner v Baxter*[21] the individual defendant promoters of a company which had **27.11**
not yet been incorporated signed a contract for the purchase of a supply of wine
'on behalf of the proposed Gravesend Alexandra Hotel Company (Limited)'.
There, notwithstanding the use of that phrase, the judgment proceeded upon the
basis that the reality of the matter was that the parties signing were acting as principals and that therefore they, not the company, were liable. This was so despite
reference being made to a company which was in contemplation and not incorporated when the contract was signed. It was further held that the contract was not
capable of ratification by the company once it had been incorporated as ratification

---

[16] The Companies (Trading Disclosures) Regulations 2008 (SI 2008/495), reg 10. A person
guilty of an offence is liable on summary conviction to (a) a fine not exceeding level 3 on the standard scale; and (b) for continued contravention, a daily default fine not exceeding one-tenth of level 3
on the standard scale; reg 10(2).
[17] reg 10(3).
[18] *Kelner v Baxter* (1866) LR 2 CP 174.
[19] Ibid.
[20] *Newborne v Sensolid (Great Britain) Ltd* [1954] 1 QB 45, 51, per Lord Goddard CJ.
[21] (1866) LR 2 CP 174.

was not available where the ratifying party was not in existence at the time of the contract.

**27.12**  *Kelner v Baxter* was distinguished in *Newborne v Sensolid (Great Britain) Ltd.*[22] The case concerned a contract for the sale of goods by a company that had not been incorporated at the time of the contract. The company's name was appended to the contract as 'Leopold Newborne (London) Ltd' and underneath the individual promoter, Leopold Newborne, signed his name. The market fell and the purchasers refused to accept delivery. Mr Newborne sought to enforce the contract in his own name on the basis that as the company had not been in existence at the date of the contract, the claim could not be advanced by the company. It was held that Mr Newborne never purported to sell the goods, either as principal or agent. The contract was purportedly made by the, albeit non-existent, company. Mr Newborne had merely added his name to verify that the company was a party. The contract was therefore a nullity and could not be enforced by Mr Newborne.

*Legislation*

**27.13**  The Jenkins Committee considered *Newborne's Case* and recommended that (a) a company should be able to adopt, unilaterally, contracts that purport to be made on the company's behalf prior to incorporation so that it would thereby become a party to the same extent as if the contract had been entered into after incorporation and (b) until the company did adopt such a contract the persons who purported to act for the company should be entitled to sue and be liable to be sued on the contract.[23] Implementation of these recommendations were overtaken by the United Kingdom becoming a member of the European Community. On accession the United Kingdom was obliged to implement the First Company Law Directive,[24] and in particular, Article 7.

**27.14**  Article 7 first found expression in the European Communities Act 1972, s 9(2) and later in the 1985 Act, s 36(4). The 1989 Act[25] amended the 1985 Act, s 36(4) in the form of a new section 36C.[26] This provision is now restated without material change in the 2006 Act, s 51(1) which provides:[27]

---

[22]  [1954] 1 QB 45.

[23]  Report of the Jenkins Committee, paras 44 and 54(b).

[24]  First Council Directive on Harmonisation of Company Law (EC) 68/151/EEC.

[25]  1989 Act, s 130(4).

[26]  The main change was that liability was extended to pre-incorporation deeds and under the law of Scotland the undertaking of an obligation: see s 36C(2)(a) and (b).

[27]  2006 Act, s 51 will not come into force until 1 October 2009: 2006 Act Commencement Order No 8, art 3(d). Until then s 36C remains in force.

A contract that purports to be made by or on behalf of a company at a time when the company has not been formed has effect, subject to any agreement to the contrary, as one made with the person purporting to act for the company or as agent for it, and he is personally liable on the contract accordingly.

The cases on the various statutory formulations of this provision have established **27.15** the following principles.

(1) Even where both parties to the contract know at the date of the contract that the company is not in existence the party who signs 'for and on behalf of' the proposed company is personally liable to repay an advance made pursuant to the contract. The phrase 'any agreement to the contrary' cannot be inferred from the knowledge of the parties. Any agreement must be express.[28]

(2) The provision only applies to companies incorporated under English law, not foreign companies.[29]

(3) The provision does not impose personal liability on a director where the company exists, but is merely misdescribed in the contract.[30]

(4) The provision does not impose personal liability on a director where the company has been incorporated but its change of name has not been registered.[31]

(5) The provision does not permit a director who makes a contract purportedly on behalf of a company that has been dissolved to enforce the contract in his own name or in the name of a new company set up for the purpose.[32]

(6) The provision permits the maker of the contract to enforce it for his benefit as well as be sued on it.[33]

The effect of the 2006 Act, s 51(1) and its predecessors is to protect third parties **27.16** from the consequences of a company that is never incorporated. However this protection does not require that third parties should benefit from an uncovenanted windfall. It follows that where an individual makes a contract as a director on behalf of a company that has not yet been formed, although he will be liable on the contract, he can also enforce it for the benefit of company. The other contracting party will not be able to avoid the consequences of the contract on the basis only of the technicality that the company was not incorporated at the date of the contract.

---

[28] *Phonogram Limited v Lane* [1982] QB 938, CA.
[29] *Rover International Ltd v Cannon Film Sales Ltd* [1987] BCLC 540.
[30] *Badgerhill Properties Ltd v Cottrell* [1991] BCLC 805, CA.
[31] *Oshkosh B'Gosh Inc v Dan Marbel Inc Ltd* [1989] BCLC 507, CA.
[32] *Cotronic (UK) Ltd v Dezonie* [1991] BCLC 721, CA.
[33] *Braymist Ltd v The Wise Finance Co Ltd* [1989] BCLC 507, CA.

### (3) Breach of warranty of authority

**27.17**  A company will itself be liable if a director has actual or implied authority to cause the company to enter into a contract with a third party.[34] Actual authority is given by express words, such as when a board of directors passes a resolution that authorizes two of their number to sign cheques. Authority is implied when it is inferred from the conduct of the parties and the circumstances of the case, such as when the board of directors appoints one of its number to be managing director. The board thereby impliedly authorizes him to do all such things as fall within the usual scope of that office.[35] A company can also be liable if it has been bound by a director's ostensible authority. Ostensible authority is the authority of a director as it appears to others and may in some cases coincide with, and in most cases will, overlap actual or implied authority.[36]

**27.18**  If a director commits his company to a contract with a third party, the director impliedly represents to the third party that he has authority to cause his company to enter into the transaction. At common law a director who committed a company to a contract without any authority to do so was personally liable for breach of warranty of authority.[37] However, the 1985 Act, s 35A, which is now reflected in the 2006 Act, s 40, has reduced the significance of this liability in respect of third parties dealing with a company in good faith.[38] Section 40(1), which is discussed in Chapter 4, Section B(2) of this work, provides that the power of the board of directors to bind the company or to authorize others to do so is deemed to be free of any limitation under the company's constitution. Thus unless the third party is dealing in bad faith,[39] the company will be bound by a transaction which was beyond the power of a director. The scope for a claim against the director by the third party for breach of warranty of authority has therefore been virtually eliminated. A claim against the director by the company would, however, still lie for the director's breach of duty in exceeding his corporate authority.[40]

---

[34] *Hely-Hutchinson v Brayhead Ltd* [1966] 1 QB 549, CA.

[35] Ibid, per Lord Denning MR, 583.

[36] Ibid, per Lord Wilberforce, 588; per Lord Pearson, 593; *Armagas Ltd v Mundogas SA* [1986] 1 AC 717, 777, HL, per Lord Keith of Kinkel.

[37] *Collen v Wright* (1857) 8 E&B 647, 657–8.

[38] Introduced by 1989 Act, s 108. 2006 Act, s 40 which does not apply to companies that are charities, comes into force on 1 October 2009: 2006 Act Commencement Order No 8, art 3(d).

[39] 2006 Act, s 40(2)(b). As to bad faith, see *Barclays Bank Ltd v TOSG Trust Fund Ltd* [1984] BCLC 1, 18.

[40] 2006 Act, s 40(5).

# C. Liability of Directors in Relation to Torts

## (1) Introduction

A director's position in relation to torts is similar to his position in relation to **27.19** contracts. The orthodox position is that the separate legal personality of a limited company means that a director is not liable for the torts of the company of which he is a director.[41] This does not mean, however, that there are no circumstances in which a director could find himself liable for torts committed whilst a director of the company. The issue in such circumstances will be whether the tort was properly one to be attributed to the company alone or whether the tort was also committed by the director personally.

In recent years both in England and in the Commonwealth, courts have seen **27.20** repeated challenges to the boundaries of a director's liability in tort with claims being made against directors for deceit, negligent misstatement, infringement of copyright, and conversion.[42] The cases illustrate a tension between company and common law doctrines. Company law dictates that a non-natural entity should, ordinarily, be responsible for actions committed on its behalf by human actors. The common law focuses on the person who committed the wrongful act.

There is an obvious jurisprudential distinction to be drawn between those who by **27.21** choice enter into contractual arrangements with a corporate entity and should thus be taken to have accepted limited liability and those who have had no dealings with a company and whose only interest is not to be harmed by the conduct of anyone.[43] Perhaps this distinction explains the apparent greater readiness to find a director liable in tort (frequently in conjunction with the company[44]) where there is no pre-existing contractual relationship with the company.

A director will be personally liable in three circumstances where events occur in **27.22** relation to the company. The director is, of course, responsible for his own tortious acts or omissions which are unrelated to the affairs of the company.

(1) A director is personally liable for his own torts committed in relation to the company's affairs, whilst acting as a director or employee of the company. In such circumstances the company will also be vicariously liable for the director's torts.

---

[41] *Williams v Natural Life Health Foods* [1998] 1 WLR 830, 835, HL, per Lord Steyn. See also Grantham and Rickett 'Directors' Tortious Liability: Contract, Tort or Company Law?' (1999) 62 MLR 133, 134.

[42] Armour 'Demystifying the Civil Liability of Corporate Agents' [2003] CLJ 290.

[43] *Johnson Matthey (Aust) Pty Ltd v Dascorp Pty Ltd* [2003] VSC 291, per Redlich J at para 199.

[44] See paragraphs 27.23–27.34 below.

(2) A director can be liable as a joint tortfeasor with the company where he assumes personal responsibility for the acts or omissions of the company which render the company liable in tort.

(3) A director can be liable as a joint tortfeasor with the company where he procures or directs the acts or omissions of the company which render the company liable in tort.

### (2) Liability for the director's own torts

**27.23** If a director commits a tort whilst carrying out duties for his company, the director will, on general principles, be personally liable for his own tort. Whether the director is personally liable depends on whether all the elements of the tort can be established against him. Thus a director will be personally liable in tort if, when driving on company business, he causes personal injury to another person in an accident caused by his negligent or dangerous driving. In such a case all the ingredients of the relevant tort are established against the director and the fact that he was driving on company business is irrelevant to his personal liability. It is, however, relevant to the company's vicarious liability.

**27.24** General principles were momentarily forgotten in *Standard Chartered Bank v Pakistan National Shipping Corporation (No 2)*[45] when the Court of Appeal failed to distinguish the elements of the tort of deceit from those of the tort of negligent misstatement. The Court of Appeal held that a director who made a fraudulent statement whilst acting in the course of the business of his company was not himself liable for deceit unless he had voluntarily assumed personal responsibility for the accuracy of the statement. In reaching this surprising conclusion the Court of Appeal was heavily influenced by the recent decision of the House of Lords in *Williams v Natural Life Health Foods Ltd*,[46] which was concerned with the different tort of negligent misstatement made by a director for which an assumption of responsibility is a necessary element.[47] The House of Lords overturned the judgment in the Court of Appeal and returned to the conventional orthodoxy that a director, just like anyone else, is liable for those torts, including the tort of deceit, that he commits personally.[48] In particular, the House of Lords held that a director cannot avoid liability by claiming that he was acting on behalf of the company.

---

[45] [2001] 1 Lloyd's Rep 218, CA.

[46] [1988] 1 WLR 830 HL, discussed in paragraph 27.29 below.

[47] See paragraphs 27.27–27.30 below.

[48] *Standard Chartered Bank v Pakistan National Shipping (Nos 2 and 4)* [2003] 1 AC 959, HL, in particular paras 21, 22, per Lord Hoffmann, and 39, per Lord Rodger. Cases reflecting the conventional approach, affirmed by the House of Lords are *Barwick v English Joint Stock Bank* (1867) LR 2 Ex 259, 265; *Yuille v B & B Fisheries (Leigh) Ltd* [1958] 2 Lloyd's Rep 596, 619, per Willmer LJ; *Fairline Shipping Corp v Adamson* [1975] QB 180, 190–1; *Noel v Poland* [2001] 2 BCLC 645.

As Lord Hoffmann pointed out: 'No one can escape liability for his fraud by saying: "I wish to make it clear that I am committing this fraud on behalf of someone else and I am not to be personally liable".'[49]

An apparent exception to the conventional orthodoxy is the rule first enunciated **27.25** by McCardie J in *Said v Butt*[50] that a director or other agent is not liable to an action in tort for wrongful interference with contract where, acting bona fide within the scope of his authority, the director procures a breach of contract between his company and a third party.[51] In *Welsh Development Agency v Export Finance Co Ltd*[52] the Court of Appeal expressed considerable doubt about McCardie J's reasoning in *Said v Butt*. In particular, Dillon LJ pointed out that the decision was inconsistent with the principle that an agent or employee is normally personally liable for any tortious acts he does to third parties in the course of that agency or employment. Nevertheless the Court of Appeal was unwilling to interfere with a judgment that had stood for so long and was so widely accepted.

In cases where a director does incur personal liability for his own tort, his company will be liable vicariously for this tort where the director commits the tort whilst acting as a director within the scope of his authority.[53] A company will not be vicariously liable for the torts of its director where: **27.26**

(1) the tort was not committed in the course of the person carrying out his duties as a director;
(2) it is established, rarely, that the company is in fact the agent of the director for the purposes of committing the tort or that the company was merely a 'cloak' or sham under cover of which the tort was committed.[54] In this latter case the company does not escape liability. Its liability, however, is primary, not secondary.

---

[49] Ibid, 968, paras 21 and 22, per Lord Hoffmann.
[50] [1920] 3 KB 497.
[51] McCardie J's conclusion on this point was accepted as correct in *G Scammell & Nephew Ltd v Hurley* [1929] 1 KB 419, 443 and 449, CA. See also *D C Thomson & Co Ltd v Deakin* [1952] Ch 646, 680–1, per Evershed MR; *Telemetrix plc v Modern Engineers of Bristol(Holdings) plc* [1985] BCLC 213, 217.
[52] [1992] BCLC 148, CA, 173, per Dillon LJ; 179, per Ralph Gibson LJ; and 191, per Staughton LJ.
[53] See generally, *Dubai Aluminium Co Ltd v Salaam* [2003] 2 AC 366. See also *Barings Plc v Coopers & Lybrand (No 2)* [2002] 2 BCLC 410, paras 155–7.
[54] *Rainham Chemical Works Ltd v Belvedere Fish Guano Co* [1921] 2 AC 465, 475, HL, per Lord Buckmaster; see also *Townsend v Haworth* (1875) 48 LJ Ch 770 where Sir George Jessel MR described the company in such circumstances as the 'mere tool' or 'cats paw' of the individual director. See also *British Thomson-Houston Company, Limited v Sterling Accessories, Limited* [1924] 2 Ch 33, 37–8.

### (3) Assumption of responsibility for the company's torts

**27.27**  A director may assume personal responsibility for the company's performance by giving a contractual guarantee. It is rare, however, for him to assume personal liability in tort.

**27.28**  In *Fairline Shipping Corpn v Adamson*[55] a director of a company that had contracted to store a customer's goods, wrote to the customer and rendered an invoice in such a way as to create the clear impression that the director was undertaking to be personally answerable for the goods. When the goods were damaged through negligent storage it was held that the director was liable in negligence to the customer.

**27.29**  In *Williams v Natural Life Ltd*[56] an attempt was made to impose liability on a director of a company for inaccurate statements negligently made in the company's promotional literature. The company was insolvent. The claim was rejected by the House of Lords because there had been no exchanges between the director and the claimants or conduct crossing the line which could have conveyed to the claimants that the director was willing to assume personal responsibility to them.[57] From Lord Steyn's speech, with which the other Lords agreed, several principles may be identified.

(1)  In order to render a director of a company liable for a misstatement made by a company, the director, as opposed to the company, must have assumed responsibility so as to create a special relationship. Lord Steyn said that 'the inquiry must be whether the director, or anybody on his behalf, conveyed directly or indirectly to the prospective franchisees that the director assumed personal responsibility towards the prospective franchisees.'[58]

(2)  An objective test is to be applied in deciding whether the director has assumed responsibility and the main enquiry must be into the exchanges between the director and the claimant.[59]

(3)  The assumption of responsibility test is not confined to statements but applies to the provision of services.[60]

---

[55]  [1975] 1 QB 180.

[56]  [1998] 1 WLR 830, HL.

[57]  *Williams v Natural Life Ltd* [1998] 1 WLR 830, 837–8. The position might have been different if the statements had been made by an employed professional who was also a director: see *Merrett v Babb* [2001] QB 1174, CA; *Phelps v Hillingdon LBC* [2001] 2 AC 619.

[58]  *Williams v Natural Life Ltd* [1998] 1 WLR 830 HL, 835H. Direct contact between the director and the claimant will not necessarily be sufficient: see *Trevor Ivory Ltd v Anderson* [1992] 2 NZLR 517 which was approved by the House of Lords in *Williams v Natural Life Ltd* [1998] 1 WLR 830, HL.

[59]  *Williams v Natural Life Ltd* [1998] 1 WLR 830, 835F–G, HL.

[60]  *Williams v Natural Life Ltd* [1998] 1 WLR 830, 834F, HL; *Henderson v Merrett Syndicates Ltd* [1995] AC 145 HL.

(4) The other party must have relied on the assumption of responsibility by the director and the reliance must have been reasonable. Lord Steyn said: 'The test is not simply reliance in fact. The test is whether the plaintiff could reasonably rely on the assumption of personal responsibility by the individual who performed the services on behalf of the company.'[61]

*Williams v Natural Life Ltd* illustrates that it will rarely be possible to impose **27.30** liability on directors at common law for statements made by them whilst they are acting as directors. The fact of the office itself will mean that a statement will seldom be treated as a statement made in a director's personal capacity. Likewise, once the statement is treated as having been made by the company, absent evidence of reliance by the claimant on a personal assurance by a director to be answerable for the statement made by the company, no liability will lie.[62]

### (4) Liability for the company's torts procured or directed by director

The fact that a person is a director of a limited liability company does not, by itself, **27.31** render him liable for torts committed by the company during the period of his directorship.[63] However, a director can be liable as a joint tortfeasor with his company without himself committing the tortious wrong that causes the damage if he procures or directs the company to commit the tort. The court has been careful to control strictly the circumstances in which a director is exposed to personal liability in this way, because of the danger of undermining the principle of the separate corporate personality of the company and prejudicing the benefits of limited liability.

The principles applicable to liability in these circumstances are as follows. **27.32**

(1) A director of a company is not automatically to be identified with the company for the purpose of the law of tort, however small the company may be and however powerful his control over its affairs.[64]

(2) In every case where it is sought to make a director liable for his company's torts it is necessary to examine with care what part he personally played in regard to the act or acts complained of. Mere management of the trade that

---

[61] *Williams v Natural Life Ltd* [1998] 1 WLR 830, 837.

[62] The distinction may be one between mere reliance in fact and reasonable reliance on the director's pocket book: *London Drugs Ltd v Kuehne & Nagel International Ltd* [1992] 3 SCR 299, 387 and *Edgeworth Construction Ltd v N D Lea Associates Ltd* [1993] SCR 206 referred to by Lord Steyn in *Williams v Natural Life Ltd* [1998] 1 WLR 830, 836. See also *Ojjeh v Waller* (14 December 1998, unreported) Buckley J.

[63] *Rainham Chemical Works Ltd v Belvedere Fish Guano Co, Ltd* [1921] 2 AC 465, 488, HL, per Lord Parmoor; *Prichard & Constance (Wholesale) Ltd v Amata Ltd* (1924) 42 RPC 63.

[64] *C Evans Ltd v Spritebrand Ltd* [1985] 1 WLR 317, 329A–B, CA, per Slade LJ.

results in the tortious act is insufficient; the director must procure or direct the commission of the tort by his company.[65]

(3) Further a director will not be made liable where he did no more than carry out his constitutional role in the governance of the company by, for example, voting at board meetings or, if he is a controlling shareholder, exercising his power of control through passing resolutions to appoint directors.[66]

(4) Evidence is not required that the director expressly procured or directed the wrongful act that caused the damage. The director will be liable if he impliedly procured or directed the wrongful act.[67]

(5) Unless knowledge is an essential ingredient of the tort alleged, it is not necessary for the director to know that the acts procured or directed were tortious or that the director was reckless as to whether or not they were likely to be tortious. The focus of the inquiry must be the degree of the director's personal involvement in the tort alleged and each case depends on its own particular facts.[68]

27.33 Thus a director of a company in the business of manufacturing high explosives will not be liable for procuring the tort of nuisance by his company merely because he had control of the business which resulted in the tort.[69] Likewise, a director of a theatre company will not be liable where without his knowledge and in his absence from the theatrical premises works are performed by independent contractors in breach of copyright.[70]

27.34 However, a director might be liable where his company infringes a third party's copyright where the evidence discloses that the director instructed the company's employees to carry out the infringing acts, but the employees themselves did not know that the acts were tortious.[71]

---

[65] *Rainham Chemical Works Ltd v Belvedere Fish Guano Co* [1921] 2 AC 465, 476, HL, per Lord Buckmaster; see also *Performing Right Society Ltd v Ciryl Theatrical Syndicate Ltd* [1924] 1 KB 1, 14, CA, per Atkin LJ.

[66] *MCA Records Inc v Charly Records Ltd* [2003] 1 BCLC 93, 116, 117, CA.

[67] *Performing Right Society v Ciryl Theatrical Syndicate* [1924] 1 KB, 1 CA.

[68] *C Evans Ltd v Spritebrand Ltd* [1985] 1 WLR 317, CA, where the Court of Appeal refused to follow earlier first instance decisions to the effect that knowledge was required: eg *Hoover Plc v George Hulme (Stockport) Ltd* (1982) 8 FSR 565, 596–7, per Whitford J; *White Horse Distillers Ltd v Gregson Associates Ltd* [1984] RPC 61, 91–2, per Nourse J; *Fairfax Dental Ltd v SJ Filhol Ltd* (unreported) 20 July 1984.

[69] *Rainham Chemical Works Ltd v Belvedere Fish Guano Co* [1921] 2 AC 465, HL.

[70] *Performing Right Society v Ciryl Theatrical Syndicate* [1924] 1 KB 1, CA.

[71] *C Evans Ltd v Spritebrand Ltd* [1985] 1 WLR 317, CA.

# D. Liabilities of Directors Created by Statute

There are a variety of miscellaneous statutory provisions that impose personal   **27.35**
liability on directors to third persons. These provisions which are discussed below
are to be found in:

(1) the Companies Acts: breach of pre-emption requirements, public company
allotments, and trading certificates;
(2) FSMA: untrue and misleading statements in prospectuses and listing
particulars;
(3) the Insolvency Act: being concerned in the management of a company with
a prohibited name;
(4) the CDDA: disqualification.

## (1) The Companies Acts

### Pre-emption requirements

The 1985 Act, ss 89–96 contains provisions requiring a company that is propos-   **27.36**
ing to allot equity securities to offer them to existing shareholders and to communicate pre-emption offers to shareholders, unless, in the case of a private
company those provisions are excluded by a provision contained in the company's
memorandum or articles or pre-emption rights are disapplied by special resolution.[72] By the 1985 Act, s 92 where there has been a contravention of the shareholder's right of pre-emption or a failure to communicate a pre-emption offer to
the shareholder, every officer of the company who knowingly authorized or permitted the contravention is jointly and severally liable with the company to compensate any person to whom an offer should have been made or communicated
for any loss, damage, costs, and expenses which the person has sustained by reason
of the contravention.[73] However, there is a two-year time limit for the commencement of any proceedings.[74]

### Public companies: allotment where issue not fully subscribed

The 1985 Act, s 84 provides that a public company may not allot shares for sub-   **27.37**
scription or as wholly or partly payable otherwise than in cash unless the issue is
subscribed for in full or the offer is made on terms that the shares subscribed for
may be allotted in any event or if specified conditions are met and they are met.[75]

---

[72] These provisions will be replaced on 1 October 2009 by provisions in 2006 Act, ss 560–577,
largely without material change: 2006 Act Commencement Order No 8, art 3(k).
[73] 1985 Act, s 92(1) which will be replaced by 2006 Act, s 563(2).
[74] 1985 Act, s 92(2) which will be replaced by 2006 Act, s 563(3).
[75] 1985 Act, subss 84(1) and (4). The provisions of s 84 will be replaced by 2006 Act, s 578
without material change on 1 October 2009: 2006 Act Commencement Order No 8, art 3(k).

If the requirements for an allotment are not fulfilled within 40 days after the first making of the offer all money received from applicants for shares must be repaid to them forthwith without interest.[76] Failure to do so within 48 days after the first making of the offer renders the directors of the company jointly and severally liable to repay the sums with interest, but a director can avoid liability if he proves that the default in the repayment of the money was not due to any misconduct or negligence on his part.[77]

*Public company and trading certificate*

**27.38**   Under the 2006 Act, s 761(1) a company that is a public company, unless it is one that has been re-registered as a public company,[78] must have been issued with a trading certificate by the Registrar of Companies before it does any business or exercises any powers of borrowing.[79] If a trading certificate has not been issued and a company carries on business or borrows money and fails to comply with its obligations in connection with the transaction within 21 days from being called upon to do so, any directors of the company at the time of the relevant transaction are jointly and severally liable to indemnify any other party to the transaction in respect of any loss or damage suffered by him by reason of the company's failure to comply with its obligations.[80]

### (2)   Financial Services and Marketing Act 2000

**27.39**   The FSMA, ss 90 and 90A (introduced by amendments made by the Companies Act, s 1270) contain provisions making directors personally liable for untrue or misleading statements in prospectuses and listing particulars.[81]

**27.40**   Statements made by directors in prospectuses and other fundraising documents are an area deserving of particular attention. In the nineteenth century, when the issue of prospectuses first became a feature of commercial life, the common law allowed an investor who incurred financial loss after investing in reliance on the contents of a false or misleading prospectus to bring a claim in damages but only

---

[76]   1985 Act, s 84(2), which will be replaced by 2006 Act, s 578(2).

[77]   1985 Act, s 84(3), which will be replaced by 2006 Act, s 578(3).

[78]   As defined by Companies Act 2006, s 4(2).

[79]   2006 Act, s 761 which replaces, without substantive change, the 1985 Act provisions in s 117, came into force on 6 April 2008; 2006 Act Commencement Order No 5, art 3(1)(h).

[80]   2006 Act, s 767(3). By subss 767(1) and (2) the company and officers of the company also commit an offence. It was unclear whether the reference to 'obligations' in 1985 Act, s 117(8) referred to the company's obligation to obtain a trading certificate or to its obligations in relation to the transaction. 2006 Act, s 767(3) makes it clear that the requirement to indemnify relates to loss suffered in connection with the transaction.

[81]   By 2006 Act, s 1300(1)(a) these amendments came into force when the Act received the Royal Assent.

if he could establish the tort of deceit. In *Derry v Peek*[82] the House of Lords rejected an attempt to extend liability to negligent statements. The rejection was met with considerable public disquiet and in the following year the Directors' Liability Act 1890[83] was passed.[84] Section 3 of that Act imposed liability for the first time on directors and others for negligent statements in a prospectus. The provisions of the 1890 Act were brought into the mainstream of companies' legislation in 1908 and remained there until 1986 when they were moved to the securities legislation of the Financial Services Act 1986.[85]

**27.41** A prospectus is an invitation issued to the public to subscribe for shares. It is not an invitation to purchase shares in the market.[86] From time to time attempts have been made at common law to extend protection to purchasers in the after-market without much success.[87] In 1990 Mervyn Davies J struck out a claim by purchasers of shares in the after-market against directors for negligent misstatement in a prospectus.[88] More recently the merits of this decision have been doubted. In *Possfund Custodian Trustee Ltd v Diamond*[89] Lightman J accepted that it was arguable that persons responsible for the issue of a modern prospectus owed a duty of care to purchasers in an after-market of unlisted securities. Lightman J was impressed by the fact that modern prospectuses often contain statements that their purpose is to lead to an admission to listing on the Stock Exchange.[90] The prospectus in *Possfund* expressly stated that the shares in question would be traded on the Unlisted Securities Market. This point was sufficiently persuasive to allow the case to go to trial.

**27.42** Current statutory protection is to be found in FSMA, s 90[91] which provides for the payment of statutory compensation where loss is suffered by a person as a result of untrue or misleading statements in either prospectuses or listing particulars where securities are to be offered to the public in the UK or admitted to

---

[82] (1889) 14 App Cas 337, HL.

[83] 53 & 54 Vict c 64.

[84] M Lobban 'Nineteenth Century Frauds in Company Formation: Derry v Peek in Context' (1996) 112 LQR 287, which contains a general discussion of the commercial and legal environment at that time.

[85] The statutory successors to the Directors' Liability Act 1890, s 3 are 1908 Act, s 84; 1927 Act, s 37; 1948 Act, s 45; 1985 Act, s 58; and Financial Services Act 1986, s 166.

[86] See *Peek v Gurney* (1873) LR 6 HL 377.

[87] *Andrews v Mockford* [1896] 1 QB 372; see also *Scott v Dixon* (1859) 29 LJ Ex 62n.

[88] *Al-Nakib Investments (Jersey) Ltd v Longcroft* [1990] 1 WLR 1390 where he applied the principle that had been recently formulated by the House of Lords in *Caparo Industries Plc v Dickman* [1990] 2 AC 605 to restrict liability to persons who knew or ought to have known that the claimant would rely on the statement for a specific purpose.

[89] [1996] 1 WLR 1351.

[90] See *Gower's Modern Company Law*, 5th edn (1992) p 498.

[91] As amended by the Prospectus Regulations 2005 (SI 2005/1433), Schedule 1, para 6.

trading on a regulated market operating in the UK or if the securities are to be admitted to the official list.[92]

**27.43**  Compensation is payable by 'any person responsible' for the relevant document.[93] Unsurprisingly, directors are included within this term.[94] In the case of prospectuses, the FSA applies different rules to (1) equity shares, warrants, or options to subscribe for equity shares which are issued by the issuer of the shares and other securities having similar characteristics to such shares, warrants, and options, and (2) any other securities, including debt and convertible securities. Directors are exposed to liability only in relation to the first classification concerning equity shares unless they expressly accept responsibility for the prospectus in relation to the latter classification.[95] Those who are potentially liable are (i) directors of the issuer at the date of the prospectus, (ii) each person who has authorized himself to be named, and is named as having agreed to become a director of the issuer either immediately or in the future,[96] (iii) directors of the offeror if the company making the offer is a selling shareholder, and (iv) the directors of the company requesting admission, if not the issuer.[97] In the case of listing particulars existing and future directors of the company seeking a listing are potentially liable for statements made in the particulars.[98]

**27.44**  Four features of the statutory liability to pay compensation under s 90 deserve comment.

(1)  First, to be actionable the statement only needs to have been untrue or misleading in fact. Fraud or dishonest intention is not a requirement.

(2)  Secondly, the statutory liability does not appear to require the person who acquired the securities to have relied on the statement or the omission as long as the statement or omission caused the loss. On this basis a claim might lie even if the claimant did not read the prospectus or listing particulars.

(3)  Thirdly, although compensation is payable to the person who acquired the securities there is no reference to the person from whom the securities

---

[92]  The official list as maintained by the FSA: see FSMA, s 103(1).

[93]  FMSA s 91(1).

[94]  See, for listing particulars, Financial Services and Markets Act 2000 (Official Listing of Securities) Regulations 2001 (SI 2001/2956), reg 6(1)(c); for prospectuses, the FSA Handbook Prospectus Rules 5.5.

[95]  FSA Handbook Prospectus Rules 5.5.4R.

[96]  It is common in recommended takeover offers, for example, to state that certain directors of the target company will join the board of the offeror upon the offer becoming unconditional. Those directors will thereby, become responsible for the information concerning the offeror as well as the information concerning their own company.

[97]  FSA Handbook Prospectus Rules 5.5.3R.

[98]  Financial Services and Markets Act 2000 (Official Listing of Securities) Regulations 2001, reg 6.

were acquired. Thus s 90 does not seem to be confined to the original offer but can be used by later market purchasers. This logically flows from the liability extending not just to prospectuses in connection with a public offer but also to an admission to trading without any public offer.[99] It is also a logical consequence of the developing principles of common law illustrated by *Possfund*.[100]

(4) Fourthly, the section provides no guidance as to the appropriate measure of compensation. It is unclear whether the compensation is to be determined on the basis of loss (tort) or expectation (contract). Arguably, the term 'compensation' suggests that the tortious measure of loss should be used. On the other hand since, generally, the object of purchasing shares is to make a profit, it might be said that the expectation measure equates more to a claimant's idea of compensation.

There are a number of important exclusions from or defences to liability of directors in connection with statements made in prospectuses and listing particulars.[101] The most important of these is where the director shows that at the time the document was submitted for publication he reasonably believed, having made all such enquiries as were reasonable, that the statements were true and not misleading or the matter whose omission caused the loss was properly omitted and that: **27.45**

(1) the director continued in that belief until the securities were acquired or the securities were acquired before it was reasonably practicable to bring a correction to the attention of those persons likely to acquire them; or

(2) before the securities were acquired the director had taken all reasonable steps to secure that a correction was brought to the attention of those persons likely to acquire them; or

(3) the directors continued in that belief until after the commencement of dealings in the securities following their admission to the official list or regulated market and the securities were acquired after such a lapse of time that the director ought reasonably to be excused;[102] or

(4) where the person suffering the loss acquired the securities with knowledge that the statement was false or misleading.

Statutory liability for inaccurate statements in listing particulars and prospectuses does not apply to offers that are exempt.[103] Exempt offers are those made to **27.46**

---

[99] FSMA, Schedule 10, para 6.
[100] *Possfund Custodian Trustee Ltd v Diamond* [1996] 1 WLR 1351
[101] See generally FSMA, Schedule 10; Financial Services and Markets Act 2000 (Official Listing of Securities) Regulations 2001, reg 6 in relation to listing particulars; FSA Handbook Prospectus Rules 5.5 R in relation to prospectuses.
[102] FSMA 2000, Schedule 10, para 1.
[103] FSMA, s 86.

qualified investors, those directed at fewer than 100 persons other than qualified investors, where the minimum consideration paid by the person acquiring the securities is at least 50,000 euros or where the total consideration for the securities being offered does not exceed 100,000 euros.[104] It follows that where there is an exempt offer the common law applicable to misstatements will continue to apply.

**27.47**  The 2006 Act, s 1270 amends FSMA by the introduction of a new s 90A which concerns securities that are traded on a regulated market.[105] It imposes liability to pay compensation to any person who has acquired a company's securities and suffered loss in respect of them as a result of any fraudulent statement in or omission from[106] annual financial reports, half-yearly reports, and interim management statements.[107] The statement or omission has to have been known to have been fraudulent by the person discharging managerial responsibilities[108] in relation to the publication within the company. Such a person would include a director or person occupying a position of director.[109] Unlike the position in s 90, s 90A provides that only the company, not the person discharging managerial responsibility with the relevant knowledge, is liable to pay compensation to the person who has acquired the securities.[110] However the director or other person with knowledge that the statement or omission was fraudulent could be liable at common law for the tort of deceit. [111]

### (3)  The Insolvency Act

**27.48**  Under the Insolvency Act there are a variety of claims[112] that can be made by a liquidator, for the benefit of creditors, against former directors of a company. However, such claims are not claims by third parties against directors. They are claims brought by the liquidator of the company to enforce, for the benefit of creditors, the directors' duties owed to the company. These claims are discussed in more detail in Chapter 29, Section I of this work.

---

[104]  Ibid.

[105]  s 90A(2). A regulated market does not include AIM or Plus.

[106]  s 90A(3). The provision broadly replicates the common law tort of deceit save that there is no requirement for the company to have intended that the person acquiring the securities should rely on the statement or omission.

[107]  The relevant publications are those required by Articles 4, 5, or 6 of the Transparency Directive 2004/109/EC—see s 90A(1).

[108]  As defined by s 90A(9).

[109]  s 90A(9)(a)(i).

[110]  In March 2007 the Government published a discussion paper by Professor Paul Davies QC 'Davies Review of Issuer Liability—Liability of misstatements to the market:' see pp 41–2 for a discussion of the extension of section 90A liability to those who make the statements on behalf of the company.

[111]  *Standard Chartered Bank v Pakistan National Shipping (Nos 2 and 4)* [2003] 1 AC 959, HL.

[112]  Claims under Insolvency Act, ss 212, 213, and 214.

Third parties do, however, have direct rights of action under the Insolvency Act, **27.49** s 217 against a director who, in contravention of s 216 of that Act, becomes involved in the management of a new company with a name that is the same as or similar to the name of a company that went into insolvent liquidation at any time in the previous 12 months. In such circumstances the director is personally liable for the debts of the new company. These provisions are discussed in detail in Chapter 29, Section J of this work.

### (4) The Company Directors Disqualification Act 1986

Disqualification of directors is discussed in Chapter 28, Section D of this work. **27.50** The following paragraphs discuss the circumstances in which a person, including a director who is subject to a disqualification order or undertaking, may incur liability to a third party for the debts and liabilities of a company.

The CDDA, subss 15(1)(a) and (2) makes a person responsible for all relevant **27.51** debts of the company, jointly and severally with the company and any other person responsible for those debts, if he is involved in the management of the company in contravention of (a) a disqualification order or disqualification undertaking under the CDDA, ss 1 or 1A or (b) the CDDA, s 11. By the CDDA, s 11 it is an offence for a person to act as a director of a company or directly or indirectly to take part in or be concerned in the promotion, formation, or management of a company without the leave of the court at a time when (a) he is an undischarged bankrupt, (b) a moratorium period under a debt relief order applies in relation to him, or (c) a bankruptcy restrictions order or a debt relief restrictions order is in force in respect of him.[113] Such a person is personally liable for such debts and other liabilities of the company that are incurred at a time when he was involved in the management of the company.[114]

A person is also personally responsible for all relevant debts, jointly and severally **27.52** with the company and any other person responsible for those debts, if he is involved in the management of the company and acts or is willing to act on instructions given, without leave of the court, by a person whom he knows at the time to be the subject of a disqualification order or disqualification undertaking or to be an undischarged bankrupt.[115] Such a person is personally liable for such

---

[113] A bankruptcy restrictions order may be made under the Insolvency Act, Schedule 4A. A debt relief restrictions order may be made under the Insolvency Act, Schedule 4ZB (as inserted by the Tribunals, Courts and Enforcement Act 2007, s 108(2)). The liability continues to attach to a bankrupt even if he subsequently obtains an annulment: *IRC v McEntaggart* [2006] 1 BCLC 476.

[114] CDDA, s 15(3)(a).

[115] CDDA, s 15(1)(b), (2). Interestingly, a person who acts on the instructions given by a person whom he knows is subject to a bankruptcy restrictions order or a bankruptcy restrictions undertaking under the Insolvency Act, Schedule 4A is not included in the class of persons who are personally liable under CDDA, s 15.

debts and liabilities of the company as were incurred when that person was acting or willing to act on the instructions of the person whilst he was disqualified.

**27.53**  A person cannot avoid personal liability for a company's debts under the CDDA, s 15 by seeking to rely on the 2006 Act, s 1157, which gives the court power to grant relief in certain cases (as to which see Chapter 16, Section E of this work) because proceedings under s 15 are not for negligence, default, breach of duty, or breach of trust but merely proceedings to recover a debt.[116]

**27.54**  CDDA, s 15 confers a right only on a creditor of the company to pursue the disqualified director or person who acted on the instructions of the disqualified director. It confers no right on the company or the liquidator of the company to make a claim on behalf of the company's creditors.[117] However, if the company pays the debts to creditors created during the period when the disqualified director was involved in the management of the company or when the person involved in the management of the company acted on the instructions of the disqualified director, the company will have a right of contribution against the disqualified director and the person who acted on his instructions.[118]

## E.  Liabilities of Directors Arising from Legal Proceedings

**27.55**  A director may incur personal liability from legal proceedings relating to the company. First, a director may be personally liable for costs payable to other parties in proceedings where the company, but not the director, is a party. Secondly, a director may be liable to punishment for contempt for breach of an order made by a court, even if he is not a party to the proceedings or even named in the order.

### (1)  Costs

**27.56**  The Supreme Court Act 1981, s 51(3) gives the courts full power to determine by whom and to what extent costs of court proceedings are to be paid. In *Aiden Shipping Co Ltd v Interbulk Ltd*[119] it was held that this provision was not confined to orders against parties to the relevant proceedings but could apply to non-parties. In the last few years the section has often been used against directors where their

---

[116]  *IRC v McEntaggart* [2006] 1 BCLC 476. Section 1157 came into force on 1 October 2008: 2006 Act Commencement Order No 5, art 5(1)(f).

[117]  *Re Prestige Grindings Ltd* [2006] 1 BCLC 440.

[118]  By reason of the joint and several liability created by CDDA, s 15(2): *Re Prestige Grindings Ltd* [2006] 1 BCLC 440, 444–6.

[119]  [1986] AC 965, HL; *Symphony Group plc v Hodgson* [1994] QB 179, CA; *Murphy v Young & Co's Brewery plc* [1997] 1 WLR 1591, CA; *Hamilton v Al Fayed (No 2)* [2003] QB 1175, CA.

company has been the unsuccessful party to proceedings and is then unable to meet an adverse order for costs.

The power to award costs against a non-party has particular relevance where the **27.57** unsuccessful claimant or defendant is a company which is insolvent. Case law has established a number of principles which are relevant for the exercise of the power to award costs against a director of a company which cannot pay costs that it is ordered to pay.

(1) The jurisdiction applies not only for the benefit of those who have been unsuccessfully sued by an insolvent company but also for the benefit of claimants who are successful,[120] although the case of a company which is forced to defend a claim is not necessarily the same as the case of a company that initiates a claim.[121]

(2) The jurisdiction is exceptional.[122]

(3) The ultimate question in the exceptional case is whether in all the circumstances it is just to make the order.[123]

(4) A director's knowledge that his company will not be able to meet an adverse costs order should the company prove to be the unsuccessful party in the litigation is, by itself, insufficient to trigger the exercise of the jurisdiction.[124]

(5) Lack of good faith may be sufficient although it is not a necessary condition to trigger the section.[125]

(6) The question is whether the litigation is being conducted in the interests of the company (its shareholders or, if insolvent, its creditors) or whether the director is the 'real party' for whose benefit the litigation is being conducted.[126]

(7) The conduct of the director must have been the cause of the applicant incurring the costs it seeks to recover.[127]

---

[120] *Taylor v Pace Developments Ltd* [1991] BCC 406, CA.

[121] *Goodwood Recoveries Ltd v Breen* [2006] 1 WLR 2723, CA.

[122] *Metalloy Supplies Ltd v MA (UK) Ltd* [1997] 1 WLR 1613, 1620, CA, per Millett LJ.

[123] *Dymocks Franchise Systems (NSW) Pty Ltd v Todd & Others (Associated Industrial Finance Pty Ltd, Third Party)* [2004] 1 WLR 2807, 2815, PC at para 25.

[124] *Goodwood Recoveries Ltd v Breen* [2006] 1 WLR 2723 CA, per Rix LJ at para 59.

[125] Ibid.

[126] *Dymocks Franchise Systems (NSW) Pty Ltd v Todd (Associated Industrial Finance Pty Ltd, Third Party)* [2004] 1 WLR 2807 PC at para 29; *Sims v Hawkins* [2007] EWCA Civ 1175; *Chantrey Vellacott v Convergence Group plc* [2007] EWHC 1774; *Re North West Holding plc, Secretary of State for Trade and Industry v Backhouse* [2001] 1 BCLC 468; *Metalloy Supplies Ltd v MA (UK) Ltd* [1997] 1 WLR 1613, 1620, CA, per Millett LJ; see also *Re Aurum Marketing Ltd* [2000] 2 BCLC 645 where a director, for his own personal interests, caused the company to contest a winding-up petition; also *Mills v Birchall* [2008] 1 WCR 1829, CA, a case about administrative receivers.

[127] *Goodwood Recoveries Ltd v Breen* [2006] 1 WLR 2723, CA, per Rix LJ at paras 60–66; although *quaere* whether costs have to be caused by all factors which render the case an exception: *Globe Equities Ltd v Globe Legal Services Ltd* [1999] BLR 232, 241, per Morritt LJ.

**27.58**   If a successful party wishes to seek a costs order against a director who was not a party to the proceedings then under CPR 48.2 the director must be added as a party to the proceedings for the purposes of obtaining a costs order against him. The director must also be given a reasonable opportunity to attend a hearing and make representations against an order being made.

### (2)  Civil contempt

**27.59**   A court order binds the person to whom it is addressed, but does not in general compel compliance by other persons.[128] So if an order is made against a company, restraining it from performing an act by itself, its officers, servants, or agents, the effect is not to bind the officers, servants, or agents directly but to make it plain to the company that it will contravene the order if it performs the act through those other persons.[129] The company will be liable for contempt for a breach of the order committed by its officers or servants even if they have been instructed not to contravene the order, provided that the contravention occurs during the course of employment.[130]

**27.60**   A director may however be liable for contempt of court in respect of an order made against a company in two situations: (1) if he knowingly aids and abets a breach of the order by the company, or (2) if with knowledge of the order he does an act which deliberately interferes with the course of justice by frustrating the purpose for which the order was made.[131] The latter contempt is described as criminal contempt and its essential nature is interference with justice. Deliberate interference with the course of proceedings, by destroying disclosable documents or interfering with witnesses is punishable as a contempt, even without a court order.[132]

**27.61**   Where the order is made against the director personally (eg an order for delivery up of company books, papers, and records) the director must, of course, comply with it. A person who alleges that the director is in contempt of court must prove breach of the order beyond reasonable doubt. In *Re Bramblevale Ltd* committal proceedings against a director failed because it was not clear whether the company books were in his possession or control at the time of the order.[133]

---

[128]   *Lord Wellesley v Earl of Mornington* (1848) 11 Beav 180; *Marengo v Daily Sketch* [1948] 1 All ER 406; *A-G v Newspaper Publishing plc* [1988] Ch 333, 366, 367, 377, 384, CA. More recently courts have been prepared to grant injunctions *contra mundum* to protect identity or confidence; *Venables v New Group Newspapers Ltd* [2001] Fam 430.

[129]   *Marengo v Daily Sketch* [1948] 1 All ER 406; *A-G v Newspaper Publishing plc* [1988] Ch 333, 366, CA.

[130]   *Re Supply of Ready Mixed Concrete (No 2)* [1995] 1 AC 456, 465, 481, HL.

[131]   *A-G v Times Newspapers Ltd* [1992] 1 AC 191, 217, 218, 222, HL; *A-G v Punch Ltd* [2003] 1 AC 1046, HL at [39], [66], [87]; *Customs & Excise Commissioners v Barclays Bank plc* [2007] 1 AC 181, HL at [29], [56]–[59]. For freezing orders, see also *Z Ltd v A-Z* [1982] QB 558, 578, CA.

[132]   *British Steel Corporation v Granada Television* [1981] AC 1096, 1127, 1142, CA.

[133]   [1970] Ch 128, CA.

Special factors apply to directors even though they are also agents and often **27.62**
employees as well. This is because CPR Schedule 1, Ord 45.5 provides that where
a body corporate disobeys a judgment or order requiring it to do or abstain from
doing an act the judgment or order may be enforced with permission of the court
by writ of sequestration against the property of any director or by an order of
committal against any director, provided that the order, endorsed with a penal
notice, has been personally served on the director.[134] The purpose of this rule is to
focus the minds of directors on ensuring that the company complies with its
obligations. The rule applies not only where an order has been made against a
company but also where the company has given an undertaking to the court to do
or abstain from doing something on the basis that an undertaking to the court is
equivalent to an injunction.[135] In *Biba Ltd v Stratford Investments Ltd*[136] it was
held that even if a director adopted a purely passive role and did not aid and abet
a contempt in any way, he could be held liable for contempt in consequence of
a breach of an undertaking given by the company of which he was a director.

In *A-G for Tuvalu v Philatelic Distribution Corp*[137] the Court of Appeal explained **27.63**
the position of a director where an order had been made against a company or an
undertaking given by it.

> In our view where a company is ordered not to do certain acts or gives an undertaking
> to like effect and a director of that company is aware of the order or undertaking he
> is under a duty to take reasonable steps to ensure that the order or undertaking is
> obeyed, and if he wilfully fails to take those steps and the order or undertaking is
> breached he can be punished for contempt. We use the word 'wilful' to distinguish
> the situations where the director can reasonably believe some other director is taking
> those steps.

A non-executive director may be justified in believing that the directors respon- **27.64**
sible for managing the company are taking the necessary steps to secure compliance with the order.[138] In the ordinary case the necessary steps will include taking
adequate and continuing steps to ensure that those to whom the director has delegated the handling of matters which fall within the scope of the order or undertaking did not forget, misunderstand, or overlook the obligations imposed by the
order.[139] A director would not be liable if the company was unable to comply with
the order, eg because it lacked the resources to comply. However a court would
undoubtedly subject such a defence to close scrutiny.[140]

---

[134] *Iberian Trust Ltd v Founders Trust and Investment Co Ltd* [1932] 2 KB 87.
[135] CPR Schedule 1, Ord 45.5.3.
[136] [1973] 1 Ch 281.
[137] [1990] 1 WLR 926, 936, CA.
[138] *Director General of Fair Trading v Buckland* [1990] 1 WLR 920, 925.
[139] Ibid, per Woolf LJ at 938F.
[140] *Lewis v Pontypridd Caerphilly and Newport Railway Co* (1895) 11 TLR 203.

# 28

# PUBLIC INTEREST PROCEEDINGS ARISING FROM CONDUCT OF DIRECTORS

## A. Introduction

Serious misconduct or breaches of duty by a company or its directors affecting the **28.01** company's relationships with members of the public may trigger an investigation by the Secretary of State of the manner in which the company's business has been conducted, or even the appointment of inspectors and publication of a formal report. In an appropriate case, the Secretary of State or a regulatory authority may petition the court to wind the company up on the basis that it is 'just and equitable' to do so in the public interest. Such a liquidation need not be predicated on insolvency. A winding-up order terminates the directors' powers of management and is the logical response to misconduct or mismanagement by directors, which is revealed by an inspector's report.

Following an investigation, or where a company has become insolvent, the **28.02** Secretary of State may apply for an order disqualifying the subject from acting as a director of a company or otherwise being concerned in a company's affairs.

A court before whom a person is being tried for a relevant offence may also have jurisdiction to make such an order.

**28.03**   The relevant statutory provisions are not among those consolidated in the 2006 Act, although they have been amended in some respects by that Act. Investigations are conducted under the 1985 Act, Part 14, which continues in force. Public interest winding-up petitions are presented, and the subsequent liquidations are carried out, under the Insolvency Act, with jurisdiction extended by relevant legislation where the company in question or the business it carries out is of a particular type (paragraph 28.53 below). Disqualification proceedings are brought under the Company Directors Disqualification Act 1986 (CDDA). The purpose of this chapter is to consider each regime in turn. Invariably these procedures are invoked because of complaints of breaches of duty or mismanagement by the directors of a company.

## B. Investigations

### (1) Initiating an investigation

**28.04**   The vast majority of investigations will take the form of confidential enquiries utilizing the compulsory powers of the Secretary of State under the 1985 Act, s 447, which provides[1] as follows:

(1) The Secretary of State[2] may act under subsections (2) and (3) in relation to a company.[3]

---

[1]   The present form of 1985 Act, s 447 was substituted by the the the C(AICE) Act, s 21 as from 6 April 2005, subject to the transitional provisions in arts 6–13 of the Companies (Audit, Investigations and Community Enterprise) Act 2004 (Commencement) and Companies Act 1989 (Commencement No 18) Order 2004 (SI 2004/3322). These broadly provide for authorizations and requirements made under the preceding provisions to continue to have effect.

[2]   The legislation refers only to 'the Secretary of State'. From 1983 to 2007, the relevant powers were exercised by the Secretary of State for Trade and Industry. Since 28 June 2007, following a Government reorganization, they have been exercised by the Secretary of State for Business, Enterprise and Regulatory Reform. The Department for Business, Enterprise and Regulatory Reform is known as 'BERR'.

[3]   The section as enacted applies to a company as defined in 1985 Act, s 735(1) (ie a company formed and registered under the 1985 Act, or an existing company when the 1985 Act came into force). Under the 2006 Act, the definition of a 'company' for the purposes of the Companies Acts (a term which, by 2006 Act, s 2(1)(c), includes those provisions of the 1985 Act that remain in force, ie including s 447), is a company formed and registered under the 2006 Act or an existing company (formed under the 1985 Act or earlier legislation). This definition will come into effect when Part 1 of the 2006 Act comes into force (prospectively on 1 October 2009, under 2006 Act Commencement Order No 8, art 3(a), a draft of which was published for consultation in June 2008). 1985 Act, s 453 (which continues in effect, subject to amendments under 2006 Act (deleting subs 453(1A)(b) from 6 April 2007 by s 1176(3), (4) and s 1295, Schedule 16, from 6 April 2007 subject to transitional provisions; deleting subs 453(1A)(d) by s 1295, Schedule 16, from 1 October 2007) extends these provisions so that there is power to investigate overseas companies: bodies

(2) The Secretary of State may give directions to the company requiring it—

    (a) to produce such documents (or documents of such description) as may be specified in the directions;

    (b) to provide such information (or information of such description) as may be specified.

(3) The Secretary of State may authorise a person (an investigator) to require the company (or any other person)—

    (a) to produce such documents[4] (or documents of such description) as the investigator may specify;

    (b) to provide such information (or information of such description) as the investigator may specify.

An investigation will usually commence as a result of a complaint from a member of **28.05** the public or information provided by another regulator or an insolvency practitioner. BERR does not randomly select companies to investigate.[5] In practice, the complaint will be investigated by the CIB.[6] Public statements by CIB indicate that they investigate 'aspects of corporate behaviour which might harm both the business community and the public generally', and make clear that they give higher priority to 'those cases with a higher level of risk to the public'.[7] The results of an investigation are not necessarily made public.

There is a measure of protection under the statutory regime for 'whistle-blowers' **28.06** who make a 'relevant disclosure' to the Secretary of State. Such a disclosure cannot, of and by itself, leave the discloser open to a claim for breach of an obligation of confidence.[8] This would extend to, for example, a director or other insider who wishes to alert CIB to issues of concern. To qualify, the disclosure must be 'of a kind that the person making the disclosure could be required to make' under Part 14 of the 1985 Act.[9] (The conditions which must be satisfied also include that the disclosure is made to the Secretary of State otherwise than in compliance with a

---

corporate incorporated outside Great Britain which are or have at any time carried on business there. The powers under 1985 Act, s 431 to investigate on the application of a company or its members, and under ss 442–445 of that Act to investigate the ownership of a company, do not apply to an overseas company.

[4] The term 'document' is given a wide definition in subs 447(8) for the purposes of these provisions: it 'includes information recorded in any form'.

[5] There was a clear statement of this policy by the DTI, the predecessor of BERR, in the Guidance Document published in January 2005 when the C (AICE) Act 2004 came into force. This publication indicated that only some 5% of complaints and referrals result in an investigation. Of around 5,000 complaints received in 2002/03, around 250 were accepted for investigation.

[6] CIB forms part of the regulatory arm of BERR and is nowadays located within the Insolvency Service, an Executive Agency of BERR, although its remit runs wider than insolvencies. For a general account of how CIB formerly operated and the exercise of powers then contained in the Companies Act 1967, see *In re Golden Chemical Products Ltd* [1976] Ch 300.

[7] These quotations are taken from *About the Companies Investigation Branch* as it appeared on the Insolvency Service website at <http://www.insolvency.gov.uk/cib/index.htm> in February 2008.

[8] subs 448A(1).

[9] subs 448A(2)(b).

requirement under Part 14, but this does not suggest that, where the disclosure is made in compliance with such a requirement, a claim for breach of confidence would arise.) The disclosure must be made in good faith and in the reasonable belief that the disclosure is capable of assisting the Secretary of State for the purpose of exercise of his functions under Part 14,[10] and it must not be more than is reasonably necessary for the purpose of assisting the Secretary of State to exercise those functions.[11] However, there will be no protection if the disclosure is prohibited by an enactment,[12] or if the discloser owes an obligation of confidence in respect of the information in the capacity of banker or lawyer.[13]

**28.07** The relevant statutory provisions refer to things being done and decisions being made by 'the Secretary of State', but in practice the decisions in question are made by a senior official. It is well established as a matter of public law that this is permissible and appropriate.[14]

**28.08** The decision to initiate an investigation or appoint inspectors is merely an administrative decision. There is no requirement for directors and others who may be involved to be given a chance to make representations or offer explanations before such a decision is taken. This does not breach any rules of natural justice, because they should be given an opportunity to do so in the course of the inquiry. However, there must exist at least some reasonable grounds for the decision to investigate, and the decision must be made in good faith.[15] As Lord Denning MR has explained: '... the officers of the Department of Trade are appointed to examine the books, there is no need for the rules of natural justice to be applied. If the company was forewarned and told that the officers were coming, what is to happen to the books? In a wicked world, it is not unknown for books and papers to be destroyed or lost.'[16] The person taking the decision must not exceed or abuse the statutory

---

[10] subs 448A(2)(c).

[11] subs 448A (2)(d).

[12] subs 448A(2)(e) and (3); this includes an Act of the Scottish Parliament and subordinate legislation, and is irrespective of when the enactment was passed or made: subs 448A(5).

[13] subs 448A(2)(e) and (4).

[14] *Carltona Ltd v Commissioners of Works* [1943] 2 All ER 560, 563, CA, per Lord Greene MR; followed by the Court of Appeal in *Lewisham BC v Roberts* [1949] 2 KB 608 and *R v Skinner* [1968] 2 QB 700. In the latter case, Widgery LJ said (at 707): 'if a decision is made on his behalf by one of his officials, then that constitutionally is the Minister's decision. It is not strictly a matter of delegation; it is that the official acts as the Minister himself and the official's decision is the Minister's decision.' This *Carltona* principle was specifically considered and endorsed in the context of CIB investigations by Brightman J in *In re Golden Chemical Products Ltd* (n 6 above), but as Kennedy LJ observed in *R v Secretary of State for Social Services, ex p Sherwin* (1996) 32 BMLR 1, his decision on this point 'really adds nothing to those earlier decisions'.

[15] *Norwest Holst Ltd v Secretary of State for Trade* [1978] Ch 201, CA.

[16] Ibid, 224, CA.

discretion which they are given, and they must not use it for some ulterior purpose.[17]

A flawed decision to initiate an investigation would in principle be open to challenge by judicial review, but in this context the prospects of a successful challenge are unlikely to be high.[18] In *R v Secretary of State for Trade, ex p Perestrello*[19] Woolf J, dismissing an application for judicial review in the context of exercise of powers of inspection of a company's affairs under the 1967 Act, s 109, said that talk of rules of natural justice in this context 'is not really helpful'. Before the Board of Trade exercise their powers, 'they must think there is good reason to do so', so that it is almost inevitable that, before the powers are exercised:

> the officers concerned, and through his officers, the Secretary of State, must regard the situation as one where there are matters to be investigated. They are acting in a policing role. Their function is to see whether their suspicions are justified by what they find, and that being so, it is wholly inappropriate for the case to be approached in the same way as one would approach a person performing a normal judicial role or quasi-judicial role; a situation where the person is making a determination. What is done . . . is to ascertain whether there is evidence to support a prima facie view of a possible undesirable situation in relation to a company, and that being so, the role of the Department is very much the role of the potential prosecutor.

28.09

Apart from the company itself, a present or former director or other officer is within the class of those who may be required to produce documents or provide information to an investigator. A person upon whom a requirement is imposed under subs 447(3) may require the investigator to produce evidence of his authority.[20] A requirement under subss 44 7(2) or (3) must be complied with 'at such time and place as may be specified in the directions or by the investigator (as the case may be)'.[21] This would not give an investigator carte blanche to impose an entirely unreasonable time and place for cooperation, but in a case of urgency, a person could be required to cooperate outside normal office hours.

28.10

---

[17] *R v Secretary of State for Trade, ex p Perestrello* [1981] QB 19, 35, per Woolf J.
[18] In *R v Commission for Racial Equality, ex p Hillingdon London Borough Council* [1982] QB 276, 300, CA, Griffiths LJ considered the *Norwest Holst* decision and said:
> The primary question with which the court was concerned was whether there was an obligation on the Board of Trade to give a hearing to the company before exercising their power to appoint inspectors. The court held there was no such requirement. As to the wide question whether in an appropriate case the court would have power to review the minister's decision if it could be demonstrated that there were no circumstances suggesting misconduct by the company, it is clear from the judgments of Lord Denning M.R. and Geoffrey Lane LJ, 225, 230 respectively, that they considered that the court had such a power, although there were no grounds for exercising it as the affidavit sworn on behalf of the minister in fact revealed circumstances suggesting misconduct. Again I find nothing in this authority to suggest that an administrative power can only be quashed on grounds of bad faith.
[19] [1981] QB 19, 34.
[20] subs 447(4).
[21] subs 447(5).

**28.11**   Documents which are sought in the course of an investigation may be in the hands of a third party such as a lawyer or accountant. Such a professional adviser may have a possessory lien over the documents until their bill is paid. At common law, a possessory lien is lost if the party loses possession of the item over which the lien is claimed.[22] To overcome objection on this score, subs 447(6) provides that the production of a document in pursuance of s 447 does not affect any lien which a person has on the document.

**28.12**   Failure to comply with a requirement under s 447 is not of itself an offence, but the 1985 Act, s 453C[23] provides that the inspector, Secretary of State, or investigator may certify the fact of non-compliance to the court. If, after hearing any witnesses and any statement in defence, the court is satisfied that the offender has failed to comply with the requirement without reasonable excuse, it is punished as if the defaulter was guilty of a contempt of court.[24] It is also one of the factors which the court may take into consideration in deciding whether to make a winding-up order[25] or a disqualification order.

**28.13**   A person who, in purported compliance with a requirement to provide information under s 447, provides information which he knows to be false in a material particular, or who recklessly provides information which is false in a material particular, commits a criminal offence.[26] With effect from 1 October 2007, the penalty is a prison term of up to two years or a fine or both.[27]

**28.14**   It is also an offence for an officer[28] of a company to destroy, mutilate, or falsify a document affecting or relating to the company's property or affairs, to make a false entry in such a document, or to be privy to such a thing being done by another person. If the facts are proved, the officer is guilty 'unless he proves that he had no intention to conceal the state of affairs of the company or to defeat the law'.[29]

---

[22]   Cf *Larner v Fawcett* [1950] 2 All ER 727.

[23]   Inserted by the C(AICE) Act 2004, as from 6 April 2005.

[24]   s 453C.

[25]   Cf *Re Atlantic Property Ltd* [2006] EWHC 610 (Ch), per Lawrence Collins J at [10]–[11].

[26]   s 451(1).

[27]   subs 447(2) as substituted by 2006 Act, s 1124 and Schedule 3, para 5(1).

[28]   1985 Act, s 744 provided that an 'officer' in relation to a body corporate 'includes a director, manager or secretary'. This section is prospectively repealed by 2006 Act, s 1295 and Schedule 16 from a date to be appointed, when for the purposes of the Companies Acts (which by 2006 Act, s 2(1)(c), include provisions of the 1985 Act remaining in force) the definition of 'officer' in relation to a 'body corporate' (defined to include a body incorporated outside the UK) will be replaced by the same definition now contained in 2006 Act, s 1173(1). These changes will prospectively be made from 1 October 2009 under 2006 Act, Commencement Order No 8, art 3(u).

[29]   subs 450(1). The offences under this section are not limited to those which occur or come to light in connection with an investigation. In *R v Chauhan* [2000] 2 CR App R (S) 230, the defendants were accused of a course of conduct which created a false or misleading impression as to the market in or price of investments. The indictment included a charge under 1985 Act, s 450(1) to which the defendant pleaded guilty. He was sentenced to 18 months' imprisonment on each count,

An officer who fraudulently parts with, alters, or makes an omission in any such document,[30] or is privy to someone else doing so, also commits an offence.[31] With effect from 1 October 2007, the penalty for these offences is a prison term of up to seven years or a fine or both.[32]

Where there are reasonable grounds for believing that documents[33] exist which **28.15** have not been produced in compliance with a requirement under Part 14 of the 1985 Act, and that they are thought to be at particular premises, an application may be made to a justice of the peace under the 1985 Act, s 448 for a warrant to enter and search the premises. The information in support of the application must be verified on oath by or on behalf of the Secretary of State or by a person appointed or authorized to exercise powers under Part 14.[34] The application is self-evidently not one which would be made on notice to the company or its directors, because that would defeat its purpose.

A warrant may also be issued if, on information similarly verified on oath, a justice **28.16** of the peace is satisfied that there are reasonable grounds for believing that an offence has been committed for which the penalty on conviction in indictment is imprisonment for a term of not less than two years, that documents relating to whether the offence has been committed exist on any premises, that the Secretary of State, or the person appointed or authorized (ie inspector or investigator) has power to require production, and that there are reasonable grounds for believing that the documents would not be produced if production was required, but instead the documents would be removed from the premises, hidden, tampered with, or destroyed.[35] The warrant can also cover other documents at the premises if the justice of the peace is satisfied on the information on oath that there are reasonable grounds for believing that such other documents are also on the premises.[36]

The warrant will be valid for one month beginning with the day of issue.[37] It must **28.17** name at least one constable, and may name other persons (who would in most

to be served concurrently, and was disqualified from acting as a director for 10 years. The sentence was upheld on appeal. The Court of Appeal considered that it gave a very heavy discount for the assistance which this defendant had given to the prosecuting authorities, and in the circumstances was 'a very lenient sentence indeed'.

[30] This reflects the wording of the Insolvency Act, s 206(10(e) where the conduct has occurred within the 12 months immediately preceding the commencement of the winding up of a company.
[31] subs 450(2).
[32] subs 450(3) as substituted by 2006 Act, s 1124 and Schedule 3, para 4(1).
[33] By subs 448(10) 'document' is again given a wide definition for the purposes of s 448 so that it includes 'information recorded in any form'.
[34] subs 448(1).
[35] subs 448(2).
[36] subs 448(4).
[37] subs 448(5).

cases be the investigator or inspector or members of their staff). Those named in the warrant, and any other constables, are authorized under the warrant to enter the premises specified in the information using such force as is reasonably necessary for the purpose,[38] search them and either take possession of the documents or take any other steps which may appear to be necessary for preserving them or preventing interference with them.[39] They may also take copies of such documents,[40] and under subs 448(3)(d) they may require any person named in the warrant to provide an explanation of the documents or to state where they may be found. It is a criminal offence[41] intentionally to obstruct the exercise of any rights conferred by the warrant, or to fail without reasonable excuse to comply with a requirement under subs 448(3)(d).

**28.18**  Documents seized under s 448 may be retained for three months,[42] unless criminal proceedings to which the documents are relevant are commenced within that period, in which case they may be retained until the conclusion of those proceedings.[43]

## (2) Appointment of inspectors

### *Appointment by the Secretary of State*

**28.19**  In the most serious cases, the Secretary of State will appoint inspectors under the 1985 Act, ss 431 or 432.[44] The Secretary of State is at liberty to appoint anyone he considers suitably qualified, but the usual practice has been to appoint a team comprising a senior accountant and a senior lawyer. According to CIB, inspections are normally carried out 'where the company involved is a major plc and the matters subject to enquiry are of significant public interest'.[45] Appointments of inspectors are comparatively rare.[46]

---

[38] subs 448(3)(a).

[39] subs 448(3)(b).

[40] subs 448(3)(c).

[41] subs 448(7) and (7A). The offence is punishable by a fine.

[42] subs 448(6)(a).

[43] subs 448(6)(b).

[44] Powers to appoint an inspector to examine into the affairs of a company were formerly exercised by the Board of Trade, and can be traced back through the 1948 Act, s 165 and the 1929 Act, s 135 to the 1862 Act, s 56. In an early discussion of the scope of the inspector's function, Lord Esher MR said in *Re Grosvenor and West-End Railway Terminus Hotel Co Ltd* (1897) 76 LT 337, CA: 'The object of the inquiry which the Board of Trade has authority to order under s 56 is to examine into and ascertain facts to enable the inspector to make a report of his opinion to the Board of Trade. That is all.'

[45] Insolvency Service website at <http://www.insolvency.gov.uk/cib/inspectorsreports.htm>, February 2008.

[46] Recent examples have included: Mirror Group Newspapers plc, Sir Roger Thomas and Raymond Turner FCA appointed 1992, report published 2001; Queens Moat Houses plc, Adrian Burn FCA and Patrick Phillips QC appointed 1993, report published 2004; Mr Burn's evidence relied upon in disqualification proceedings (*Secretary of State for Trade and Industry v Bairstow* [2003] 1 BCLC 696, CA, and *Secretary of State for Trade and Industry v Bairstow* [2005] 1 BCLC 136);

*Appointment following application to the Secretary of State*

An appointment under the 1985 Act, s 431 is made following an application to **28.20** the Secretary of State by the company itself,[47] or by a specified proportion of its members. Where the company has share capital, the application must be made by not less than 200 members or members holding not less than one-tenth of the issued shares (not counting treasury shares).[48] In the case of a company not having share capital (such as a company limited by guarantee), the application must be made by not less than one-fifth of the registered members.[49]

An application must be supported by cogent evidence to show that there is 'good **28.21** reason' for requiring the investigation. There is no statutory definition of what will constitute a 'good reason' for these purposes, but to justify an investigation there would need to be prima facie evidence of sufficient weight that at least some serious misconduct involving the public interest may have taken place. The applicants may also be required to give security[50] for the costs of the investigation.

*Appointment of inspectors following court order*

The Secretary of State is required to appoint inspectors if the court declares that the **28.22** company's affairs ought to be investigated.[51] There is no limit on the court's jurisdiction in this respect, so it would appear that this is in principle something which the court could order of its own motion in any case in which it came to the conclusion that such an order is justified on the evidence in proceedings before it.

Where an application has been made to the Secretary of State who has declined to **28.23** appoint inspectors or simply failed to do so, or where it is not possible for the prospective applicant to comply with the requisite conditions described above, a formal application may be made to court for a declaration that the affairs of the company ought to be investigated.[52] As the procedure requires that notice is given

---

Transtec plc (Hugh Aldous FCA and Roger Kaye QC appointed January 2000, report published October 2003); Phoenix Venture Holdings Ltd and MG Rover Group Ltd, Gervase MacGregor FCA and Guy Newey QC appointed May 2005.

[47] subs 431(2)(c): it appears that the directors can resolve to cause the company to apply, without requiring to seek the approval of the shareholders by resolution in general meeting.

[48] subs 431(2)(a).

[49] subs 431(2)(b).

[50] The present limit is £5,000, but a higher amount may be specified by order: subs 431(4).

[51] subs 432(1).

[52] Such applications used to be governed by an old practice direction, reported at [1954] 1 WLR 563, which former editions of the White Book suggested had not been superseded by the introduction of the Civil Procedure Rules (see eg the 2007 White Book at 2G–21). A revised practice direction under Part 49 CPR governing proceedings under the Companies Acts was introduced in the 2008 White Book. Although para 5 of this Practice Direction suggests that this PD applies unless another practice direction provides otherwise, it appears that previous practice directions in this areas are superseded (see note in 2008 White Book at 2G–37). An application should now be commenced by Part 8 Claim Form. Although there is no specific provision in the present practice

to the Secretary of State (by service on his departmental solicitors), the Secretary of State will have an opportunity to consider making an appointment without being directed to do so by the court. Contested applications to court for appointments are understandably rare.

### Discretionary appointment of inspectors by the Secretary of State

**28.24**  The Secretary of State also has a discretionary power to appoint inspectors if it appears to him that there are circumstances suggesting the existence of one or more of the conditions set out in the 1985 Act, subs 432(2). These are:

 (a) that the company's affairs are being or have been conducted with intent to defraud the creditors or the creditors of any other person, or otherwise for a fraudulent or unlawful purpose, or in a manner which is unfairly prejudicial to some part of its members,[53] or
 (b) that any actual or proposed act or omission of the company (including an act or omission on its behalf) is or would be so prejudicial, or that the company was formed for any fraudulent or unlawful purpose, or
 (c) that persons concerned with the company's formation or the management of its affairs have in connection therewith been guilty of fraud, misfeasance or other misconduct towards it or towards its members, or
 (d) that the company's members have not been given all the information with respect to its affairs which they might reasonably expect.

**28.25**  An application which is supported by an insufficient number of members to qualify under the 1985 Act, s 431 may therefore nonetheless be sufficient to trigger an appointment under s 432.

### (3) Investigation by the inspectors and report

### Scope of appointment

**28.26**  An appointment under either ss 431 or 432 is an appointment to investigate 'the affairs of the company'. The term is wide on its face, and there is no statutory definition. The natural meaning connotes the company's 'business affairs', and the expression has been held to include the company's 'goodwill, its profits or losses, its contracts and assets including its shareholding in and ability to control the affairs of a subsidiary . . .' and extended to the activities of a receiver and manager appointed by a debenture-holder who had constituted himself a director of a subsidiary and sold the shareholding in a sub-subsidiary at an undervalue.[54]

---

direction, the application should be supported by full evidence of all facts and matters relied on, and it should be served on the solicitor for BERR. Evidence of such service should be filed with the court.

[53]  subs 432(4) provides that the reference to members in subs 432(2)(a) includes a person who is not a member but to whom shares in the company have been transferred or transmitted by operation of law.

[54]  *R v Board of Trade, ex p St Martin Preserving Co Ltd* [1965] 1 QB 603, 613.

Once inspectors have been appointed, they can extend their investigation to a **28.27** subsidiary or holding company of the company under investigation, or to another member of the same group ('a subsidiary of its holding company or a holding company of its subsidiary') if they think it necessary to do so for the purposes of their investigation. They are required to report also on the affairs of the other body corporate 'so far as they think that the results of their investigation of its affairs are relevant to the investigation of the original subject company'.[55]

Changes introduced under the 2006 Act[56] have made clear that the Secretary of **28.28** State has power to give the inspectors directions, and the 1985 Act, subs 446A(1) provides that an inspector must comply with them. An inspector may also seek directions.[57] The general powers to give directions include:

(1) as to the subject matter of the investigation, by reference to a specified area of the company's operation, a specified transaction, a period of time 'or otherwise';[58]

(2) as to a particular step in the investigation which the inspector is required to take or not to take.[59]

The Secretary of State also now has power to direct that an inspector is to take no **28.29** further steps in his investigation.[60] If the inspector was appointed under the 1985 Act, s 432(1) following a declaration by the court that the affairs of the company ought to be investigated,[61] the Secretary of State may only give a direction bringing an investigation to a premature end on grounds that matters suggesting that a criminal offence has been committed have come to light and been referred to the appropriate prosecuting authority.[62] In such circumstances, any requirement for the inspector to produce an interim report will lapse,[63] and the inspector will only be required to make a final report to the Secretary of State if matters suggesting criminal offences have been committed have been referred to the prosecuting authorities and the Secretary of State requires a report,[64] or the appointment followed an order of the court.[65]

---

[55] 1985 Act, s 433.
[56] ss 446A and 446B, introduced under 2006 Act, s 1035(1) with effect from 1 October 2007 where an inspector is appointed on or after that date.
[57] subs 446A(4)(c).
[58] subs 446A(2)(a).
[59] subs 446A(2)(b).
[60] subs 446B(1).
[61] Or under s 442(3) where inspectors have been appointed to report on the ownership of a company following an application by members.
[62] subs 446B(2).
[63] subs 446B(3).
[64] subs 446B(4)(a).
[65] subs 446B(4)(b).

*Duties towards inspectors*

**28.30**   Under the 1985 Act, s 434(1) it is the duty of all officers and agents of the company or of any related company to which the investigation is extended by inspectors under the 1985 Act, s 433:

(1) to produce to the inspectors all documents of or relating to the company or the body corporate which are in their custody or power,

(2) to attend before the inspectors when required to do so, and

(3) otherwise to give the inspectors all assistance in connection with the investigation which they are reasonably able to give.

**28.31**   Under the 1985 Act, subs 434(2) it is also the duty of an officer or agent of the company or body corporate, or any other person whom the inspectors consider is or may be in possession of information relating to a matter which they believe to be relevant to their investigation to comply with a requirement by them:

(1) to produce to the inspectors any documents in his custody or relating to that matter,

(2) to attend before the directors, and

(3) otherwise to give the inspectors all assistance in connection with the investigation which he is reasonably able to give.

**28.32**   Amendments to the 1985, s 434 made by the 2006 Act have made clear that a 'document' for these purposes includes 'information recorded in any form'.[66] The power to require production of a document includes the power, where the document is not in hard copy form, to require production in hard copy form or from which a hard copy can readily be obtained.[67] The inspectors have power to take copies or extracts from a document produced pursuant to s 434.[68]

**28.33**   Obstruction of inspectors appointed under ss 431 or 432 is treated as a contempt of court and punishable in the same manner.[69] This extends to:

(1) failure to comply with the duties under subs 434(1)(a) and (c) to produce documents, and otherwise give all the assistance the person is reasonably able to give;[70]

(b) failure to comply with the duty under subs 434(1)(b) to attend the inspectors when required to do so or to comply with a requirement of the inspectors under subs 434(2);[71]

---

[66] subs 434(6), amended from 1 October 2007 by 1985 Act, s 1038(1).
[67] subs 434(7), added as above.
[68] subs 434(8), added as above.
[69] s 436.
[70] subs 436(1)(a).
[71] subs 436(1)(b).

(c) refusing to answer any question put to the person by the inspectors for the purposes of the investigation.[72]

These provisions were considered in *Re an Inquiry into Mirror Group Newspapers* **28.34** *plc*[73] when inspectors referred to the court the refusal of an ex-director to answer their questions and his refusal to enter into a confidentiality undertaking not to disclose information which, in the course of their questioning, they put to him. The ex-director's excuse and explanation for his refusal to answer the questions was that the particular circumstances of the case had rendered the questioning of him by the inspectors unfair and oppressive, and he said that the inspectors had no right to require him to give a confidentiality undertaking. Sir Richard Scott V-C said:

> the assistance that those on whom the statutory obligation is placed must give is not unlimited. They must give the assistance that they are 'reasonably able to give.' The word 'reasonably' limits the extent of their obligation. To put the point another way, the inspectors cannot place demands on them that are unreasonable, whether as to the time they must expend or the expense they must incur in preparation for the questions or in any other respect. Inspectors must bear in mind that those summoned before them are not being remunerated for their assistance and will often, perhaps usually, have to take time off their normal business of earning a living in order to provide the requisite assistance. In some cases inspectors will have reason to believe that those they summon to appear before them have committed misfeasances of one sort or another towards the company whose affairs are being investigated.

> That circumstance does not, in my judgment, justify any more onerous demands than would be reasonable to make of a person under no similar cloud. The reasonableness and proportionality of inspectors' demands may depend upon the purpose of the inquiry and the nature of the office in the company held by the particular witness. Inspectors appointed, for example, to inquire into what has become of company assets that have gone missing can reasonably, in my view, place a heavy burden of assistance on directors of the company whose duty it was to manage and preserve those assets. All the circumstances must, in my judgment, be taken into account in deciding whether or not assistance which a person is, in an absolute sense, able to give is also assistance which he is *reasonably* able to give. But, if, in all the circumstances, the demands made on the person go beyond what he is *reasonably* able to give, his failure to comply with the demands will not be a breach of his statutory duty and should not be treated as a contempt of court.

---

[72] subs 436(1)(c).
[73] [2000] 1 Ch 194.

*Procedural fairness and the conduct of investigations by inspectors*

**28.35**  Inspectors who are appointed under the 1985 Act or the FSMA are under a duty to act fairly towards those whose conduct they may criticize in their report.[74] One aspect of this is for such individuals to have the chance to know in advance the criticisms which may be made, and to make representations about them. As Lord Denning MR famously put it:

> The inspectors can obtain information in any way they think best, but before they condemn or criticise a man, they must give him a fair opportunity for correcting or contradicting what is said against him.[75]

**28.36**  The practice is for inspectors to communicate their provisional views once their report is nearing completion, so that they can take account of any responses. It is not necessarily unfair for inspectors to provide a summary of their criticisms, as long as it is sufficient for the subject to understand what they are. It is also not necessarily unfair for the inspectors to proceed to complete their report if the subject of criticisms does not respond.[76]

**28.37**  Where procedural unfairness has denied a party the opportunity to put before the inspectors material which might have made a real difference to their conclusions,[77] it would in principle be possible for the court to grant a declaration to the effect that the inspectors have acted unfairly. However, the courts are reluctant to grant such a declaration which could undermine a report as a whole, and are astute not to allow themselves to be cast in the role of a court of appeal against the findings of inspectors, particularly as Parliament itself has granted no right of appeal against such findings. A declaration would only be granted in exceptional circumstances.[78]

---

[74] *Re Pergamon Press Ltd* [1971] Ch 388, 399, 402, 403, 407, CA.

[75] Ibid, 400A, CA; cited by Chadwick LJ in *R (Clegg) v Secretary of State for Trade* [2003] BCC 128, CA at para 2.

[76] That was the position in *Clegg* [2003] BCC 128, CA. The inspectors were appointed to investigate alleged insider dealing in the shares of Parkway Group Limited which had been the subject of an agreed takeover by Wace Group plc. Mr Clegg had been managing director of Wace Group. The inspectors report was published on 31 August 2000. The inspectors completed their report some five years after provisional criticisms had been put to Mr Clegg. He suggested that he had been led to believe that no report would be completed without a response being received from him. The judge at first instance gave permission to proceed with judicial review, but dismissed the substantive application, and he was upheld by the Court of Appeal.

[77] It is not necessary to show that the outcome would have been different, but it is necessary to show that it might have been different, in other words that he had 'a case of substance to make': per Lord Wilberforce in *Malloch v Aberdeen Corporation* [1971] 1 WLR 1578, 1595; *Clegg* [2003] BCC 128 at para 30.

[78] See comments of Stanley Burnton J quoted with approval by Chadwick LJ in *Clegg* [2003] BCC 128, CA at para 37.

*Confidential nature of an investigation*

The investigation by the inspectors is not a judicial proceeding[79] and ought to be **28.38** held in private.[80] This is in part because it is likely to involve the consideration by the inspectors of information and evidence which is of its nature confidential and in part because the initial report of the inspector to the Secretary of State or prosecuting authorities is a confidential report and there is a risk that it may damage the company or the reputations of individuals if 'unfavourable opinions as to the financial position of the society or company . . . prematurely and wrongly formed in the minds of the public or the policy-holders'.[81] In short, 'irreparable harm might unjustly be done to the reputation of a company . . . by giving publicity to such preliminary investigations'.[82]

In a particular case, the inspectors may need to show a witness confidential infor- **28.39** mation or documents. If they do so, the witness is entitled to use the information to take advice or to prepare for the inspectors' questions, by consulting others who had been involved, in order to check his recollection or remedy his lack of recollection. Using the documents in this way would not be a breach of any duty to those from whom they were obtained or to the inspectors. Disclosure for some other purpose might be a breach of duty to those from whom the documents had been obtained.[83]

An inspector is entitled to the assistance of a person whose assistance is considered **28.40** to be reasonably necessary, which would include a shorthand writer to take a note of proceedings which will assist the inspector when he comes to prepare his report. An officer of the company who is required to answer questions cannot object to doing so because of the presence of such a person.[84] Similarly, parties may attend with counsel to represent them.[85]

---

[79] *In re Grosvenor and West-End Railway Terminus Hotel Co* (1897) 76 LT 337, CA, a case under the 1862 Act. In *Re Pergamon Press Ltd* [1971] Ch 388, Lord Denning MR said at 399 that the 'proceedings are not judicial proceedings . . . They are not even quasi-judicial, for they decide nothing; they determine nothing. They only investigate and report. They sit in private and are not entitled to admit the public to their meetings . . .' The European Court of Human Rights has also held that the functions performed by inspectors are investigative rather than adjudicative, so that Art 6 of the European Convention on Human Rights does not apply: Case No 28/1993/423/502, *Fayed v UK* (1994) 18 EHRR 393.

[80] *Hearts of Oak Assurance Co v Attorney-General* [1932] AC 392, a case concerning examination under the Friendly Societies Act 1896, and the Industrial Assurance Act 1923, but in which the House of Lords considered the closest analogy was the appointment of inspectors under the 1929 Act, s 129; see also *Pergamon* (above) and *Re an Inquiry into Mirror Group Newspapers plc* [2000] Ch 194, 211, 212, per Sir Richard Scott V-C.

[81] *Hearts of Oak Assurance Co v Attorney-General* [1932] AC 392, 397, per Lord Thankerton.

[82] Ibid, 403, per Lord Macmillan.

[83] *Re an Inquiry into Mirror Group Newspapers plc* [2000] 1 Ch 194.

[84] *Re Gaumont-British Picture Corporation* [1940] Ch 506, applying *Hearts of Oak Assurance Co v Attorney-General* [1932] AC 392.

[85] *McLelland, Pope and Langley Ltd v Howard* [1968] 1 All ER 569, HL (Note).

*Use of evidence in other proceedings*

**28.41**    Under the 1985 Act, s 434(3) an inspector may examine a person on oath for the purposes of the investigation, and it is well established that the subject cannot resist answering on the grounds of the usual privilege against self-incrimination.[86] This does not mean that inspectors have unlimited power to pursue investigations, and there may come a point, particularly after a person has been charged with a criminal offence, where further questioning by inspectors on matters relevant to that offence would be regarded as oppressive and unfair.[87]

**28.42**    An answer given by a person to a question put to him in the course of an investigation by inspectors may be used in evidence against him in subsequent proceedings.[88] This formerly included in criminal proceedings,[89] but in 1996 the European Court of Human Rights found that the use of documents obtained by inspectors under compulsion had violated the defendant's right to a fair hearing under Art 6 EHRC in *Saunders v UK*.[90] The position is now governed by subss 434(5A) and (5B)[91] which provide that in criminal proceedings in which the person is charged with an offence other than an offence under the Perjury Act 1911, ss 2 or 5[92] (a) no evidence relating to the answer may be adduced, and (b) no question relating to it may be asked by or on behalf of the prosecution, unless evidence relating to it is adduced, or a question relating to it is asked, in the proceedings by or on behalf of that person. It should be noted that this only affords limited protection, because there is no restriction on the evidence being adduced or a question being asked by a co-defendant (for example, in the course of a 'cut-throat' defence). However, a defendant in a criminal trial cannot compel inspectors to produce witness statements made to the inspector in the course of investigation.[93]

**28.43**    An inspectors' report, certified by the Secretary of State to be a true copy, is admissible in any legal proceedings as evidence of the opinions of the inspectors in relation to

---

[86]   *R v Seelig* [1992] 1 WLR 149, CA; *Re London United Investments plc* [1992] Ch 578, CA; *R v Saunders (No 2)* [1996] 1 Cr App R 463.

[87]   See comments of Dillon LJ in *Re London United Investments plc* [1992] Ch 578, 600.

[88]   subs 434(5).

[89]   *R v Harris* [1970] 1 WLR 1252.

[90]   Case 43/1994/490/572, [1998] BCLC 362. It should however be noted that the European Court of Human Rights did not regard the privilege against self-incrimination as absolute, saying that 'it does not extend to the use in criminal proceedings of material which may be obtained from the accused through the use of compulsory powers but which has an existence independent of the will of the suspect such as, inter alia, documents acquired pursuant to a warrant, breath, blood and urine samples and bodily tissue for the purpose of DNA testing'. The question of whether there had been an infringement of the right had to be examined in the light of all the circumstances of the particular case.

[91]   Inserted by the Youth Justice and Criminal Evidence Act 1999 with effect from 14 April 2000.

[92]   Or the Scottish equivalent.

[93]   *R v Cheltenham JJ, ex parte Secretary of State for Trade* [1977] 1 WLR 95.

any matter contained in the report.[94] It is also evidence of any fact stated therein for the purposes of an application by the Secretary of State for a disqualification order under the CDDA, s 8.[95] A report may also be used to support a winding-up petition by the Secretary of State, or by a contributory if the Secretary of State does not present such a petition.[96] Where the evidence is not challenged, the court may act on the basis of the report supported only by an affidavit of an official,[97] but where it is challenged more direct evidence will be required.[98]

### Publication of a report

The statutory wording previously provided that the inspectors were to report on the affairs of the subject company in such manner as the Secretary of State directs, but a change under the 2006 Act has clarified that the inspectors are to report the result of their investigations to him.[99] This has clarified that, in the first instance, the inspectors are to make an internal report to the Secretary of State. It is then for the Secretary of State (or in practice officials within his department) to decide whether or not to publish a report.[100]    **28.44**

The Secretary of State's powers to give a direction to the appointed inspectors[101] extends to power to direct that a report by the inspector should include or exclude the inspector's views on a specified matter,[102] and also that the report is to be made in a specified form or manner,[103] or by a specified date.[104]    **28.45**

Where inspectors have been appointed pursuant to an order of the court, the Secretary of State is obliged to furnish a copy of any report by them to the court.[105]    **28.46**

If he thinks fit, the Secretary of State may forward a copy of any report of the inspectors to the company's registered office.[106] He may also, if he thinks fit, furnish a copy on request and payment of the prescribed fee to (a) any member of the    **28.47**

---

[94] s 441.

[95] s 441.

[96] *Re St Piran* [1981] 1 WLR 1300.

[97] *Re Travel & Holiday Club* [1967] 1 WLR 711; *Re Allied Produce Co* [1967] 1 WLR 1469.

[98] *Re ABC Coupler Engineering Co* [1962] 1 WLR 1236.

[99] 1985 Act, subss 431(1) and 432(1), amended by 2006 Act, subss 1035(2) and (3) respectively, with effect from 1 October 2007 and applying where an inspector is appointed on or after that date.

[100] 1985 Act, subss 473(3)(c) and 443(1); *R (Clegg) v Secretary of State for Trade and Industry* [2003] BCC 128, CA at para 5.

[101] See paragraph 28.28 above.

[102] subs 446A(3)(a) and (b).

[103] subs 446A(3)(c).

[104] subs 446A(3)(d).

[105] subs 437(2).

[106] subs 437(3)(a).

company or other body corporate which is the subject of the report, (b) the person whose conduct is referred to in the report, (c) the auditors of that company or body corporate, (d) the applicants for the investigation, and (e) any other person whose financial interests appear to the Secretary of State to be affected by the matters dealt with in the report, whether as a creditor of the company or body corporate or otherwise.[107] The Secretary of State may also cause a report to be printed and published,[108] and this is the usual practice.

*Expenses of an investigation*

**28.48**  In the first instance, the expenses of an investigation under Part XIV of the 1985 Act are defrayed by the Secretary of State[109] and met from money provided by Parliament.[110] These expenses will include such reasonable sums as the Secretary of State may determine in respect of general staff costs and overheads.

**28.49**  However, if a person is convicted in proceedings instituted as a result of the investigation, they can be ordered in the criminal proceedings to pay the expenses of the investigation to the extent specified in the order.[111] A change under the 2006 Act means that this no longer only applies where the defendant has been ordered to pay the costs in the criminal proceedings.

**28.50**  If the appointment of inspectors was ordered by the court, the company dealt with by the report is liable for the costs unless it was the applicant, and except to the extent that the Secretary of State directs to the contrary.[112]

**28.51**  The applicants for an investigation under ss 431 or 442(3) are liable to such extent if any as the Secretary of State may direct.[113] Where the Secretary of State has been persuaded to act of his own motion under s 432(2), there is no power to recoup the expenses of the investigation. Where the inspectors were not appointed of the Secretary of State's own motion, they may if they think fit, and must if the Secretary of State so directs them, include in their report recommendations as to how they consider the expenses of the investigation should be directed to be borne.[114]

---

[107]  subs 437(3)(b).
[108]  subs 437(3)(c).
[109]  subs 439(1).
[110]  subs 439(10).
[111]  subs 439(2).
[112]  subs 439(4).
[113]  subs 439(5).
[114]  subs 439(6).

# C. Public Interest Winding-Up Petitions

## (1) Companies that may be wound up in the public interest

Where it appears to the Secretary of State that it is 'expedient in the public interest **28.52** that a company[115] should be wound up', from any of the following reports or information the Secretary of State has power[116] to present a winding-up petition under the Insolvency Act, s 124A. The reports and information specified in subs 124A(1) are:

(1) any report made or information obtained as a result of investigations under Part XIV of the 1985 Act;

(2) any report by inspectors under FSMA, ss 167, 168, 169 or 284, or, in the case of an open-ended investment company, under regulations made as a result of s 262(2)(k) of that Act;

(3) any information or documents obtained by the FSA under FSMA, ss 165, 171–173 and 175, dealing with investigations by the FSA;

(4) any information obtained under Criminal Justice Act 1987, s 2 or the Criminal Justice (Scotland) Act 1987, s 52, dealing with investigations of fraud;

(5) any information obtained under the 1989 Act, s 83, dealing with powers exercisable for the purpose of assisting overseas regulatory authorities.

By the Insolvency Act, s 124B, the Secretary of State also has power to petition for **28.53** the winding up of a Societas Europaea (SE) set up under Art 1 of the EC Statute for a European Company[117] which does not comply with the requirement under Art 7 of that Statute for an SE's registered office to be located in the same Member State as its head office, and it appears to the Secretary of State that it should be wound up.

The FSA has analogous powers to present a petition in respect of a company **28.54** which is authorized under FSMA, s 367,[118] and may also petition for breach of certain obligations by a European Cooperative Society.[119]

---

[115] Including a foreign company: *Re Delfin International (SA) Ltd* [2000] 1 BCLC 71.

[116] Under the Insolvency Act, s 124(4)(b). The Secretary of State may also present a petition under s 124(4)(A) if a company was registered as a public company on original incorporation and more than a year has passed without share capital requirements being satisfied (the Insolvency Act, s 122(1)(b)) or in respect of an 'old public company' under the Companies Consolidation (Consequential Provisions) Act 1985 (ie a company which existed on 22 December 1980 or was incorporated after that date on an earlier application, and was not or would not have been a private company under the repealed 1948 Act, s 28 and has not since re-registered as a public company or become a private company (the Insolvency Act, s 122(1)(c)).

[117] Council Regulation 2157/2001 of 8 October 2001.

[118] Cf *Re Inertia Partnership LLP* [2007] 1 BCLC 738.

[119] Insolvency Act, ss 124(4)(AA), 124C(1) and (2).

**28.55**   In the case of a 'community interest company' established and regulated under Part 2 of the C(AICE) Act 2004, the Regulator of Community Interest Companies may present a winding-up petition.[120]

**28.56**   Such petitions are commonly referred to as 'public interest' petitions. Only the Secretary of State (or by analogy the specified regulator) is entitled to rely solely on the public interest when seeking a winding up on 'just and equitable' grounds.[121] It is open to the Secretary of State also to rely on the insolvency of the company, but it is not necessary for him to do so. Conversely, it has been said that insolvency as such is not sufficient in itself to justify a winding up in the public interest,[122] but the reasons for and circumstances of the insolvency may be highly material.[123]

**28.57**   A public interest petition may be presented in respect of a foreign company.[124] However, the court will only make a winding-up order if it is satisfied that there is sufficient connection with this jurisdiction and/or of prejudice to local public interest.[125] Because it is not necessary for a public interest petition to be founded on insolvency, such proceedings (notwithstanding that the petition and, if an order is made, the liquidation, are conducted under the Insolvency Act) do not constitute *insolvency proceedings* for the purposes of the EC Regulation on Insolvency Proceedings.[126] This means that the court is not concerned to establish that it has sufficient jurisdiction to hear a public interest petition because the *centre of main interest* of the company lies within the UK and not some other EC Member State, but it also means that there is no automatic recognition of a public interest liquidation in other Member States.

## (2)  The Secretary of State's decision

**28.58**   The threshold requirement is that the Secretary of State has formed the opinion that it is 'expedient in the public interest' for the company to be wound up. Forming and holding the relevant opinion give the Secretary of State standing to present his petition.[127] Although the section refers to the decision being made by

---

[120]   Insolvency Act, s 124(4A) and the C(AICE) Act, s 50. Note the former states that the petition may be presented in a case falling within the latter, but the latter merely states that the Regulator may present a petition for a community interest company to be wound up if the court is of the opinion that it is just and equitable that the company should be wound up, not applying if the company is already being wound up by the court.

[121]   *Re Millennium Advanced Technology Ltd* [2004] 1 WLR 2177.

[122]   *Re Senator Hanseatische Verwaltungsgesellschaft mbH* [1997] 1 WLR 515, CA; *Re Marann Brooks CSV Ltd* [2003] BCC 239.

[123]   *Re UK-Europe Group plc* [2007] 1 BCLC 812.

[124]   *Re Delfin International (SA) Ltd* [2000] 1 BCLC 71.

[125]   In *Re a Company (No 007816 of 1994)* [1997] 2 BCLC 685, CA and in *Re Titan International Inc* [1998] 1 BCLC 102, CA public interest petitions failed on these grounds.

[126]   *Re Marann Brooks CSV Ltd* [2003] BCC 239.

[127]   *Re Walter L Jacob & Co Ltd* [1989] BCLC 345, CA.

the Secretary of State, there is no requirement for the decision to be made by the minister personally, and so it may properly be made by the Secretary of State acting through one of his officers.[128]

The decision must be a proper one, as a matter of public law, in that proper **28.59** grounds for it must exist and be relied upon, irrelevant matters must not be taken into account, and the opinion must be one that a reasonable Secretary of State could reach. In theory, formation of that opinion is subject to judicial review. In *Re Walter L Jacob & Co Ltd*,[129] the Court of Appeal said that any challenge to the decision must be brought in judicial review proceedings, if at all, and is not a matter for the court hearing the petition. However, as Nicholls LJ pointed out, such a challenge would normally be pointless in practice, because, if no reasonable Secretary of State could have formed the requisite opinion, the petition will presumably fail on its merits in any event, so that judicial review proceedings would be idle.

The phrase 'expedient in the public interest' is a wide one. As Millett LJ made clear **28.60** in *Re Senator Hanseatische Verwaltungsgesellschaft mbH*,[130] it is not confined to cases of illegality:

> The expression 'expedient in the public interest', is of the widest import; it means what it says. The Secretary of State has a right, and some would say a duty, to apply to the court to protect members of the public who deal with the company from suffering inevitable loss, whether this derives from illegal activity or not. A common case in which he intervenes is where an insolvent company continues to trade by paying its debts as they fall due out of money obtained from new creditors. The insolvency is the cause of the eventual loss, but it is the need to protect the public, not the insolvency, which grounds the Secretary of State's application for a winding up order in such cases.

### (3) The court's discretion

*Where the company is not already in liquidation*

The court has jurisdiction to wind up the company on public interest grounds **28.61** if it thinks it just and equitable to do so. The leading discussion of the principles on which the court exercises its discretion in this regard is to be found in the judgment of Nicholls LJ in the Court of Appeal in *Re Walter L Jacob & Co Ltd*.[131]

---

[128] *Re Golden Chemical Products Ltd* [1976] Ch 300, applying *Carltona Ltd v Commissioners of Works* [1943] 2 All ER 560, *Lewisham BC v Roberts* [1949] 2 KB 608, and *R v Skinner* [1968] 2 QB 700.

[129] [1989] BCLC 345, CA.

[130] [1997] 1 WLR 515, 526, CA.

[131] [1989] BCLC 345. For further discussion of the applicable principles in particular contexts see, among others: *Re Secure and Provide plc* [1992] BCC 405; *Re Market Wizard Systems (UK) Ltd* [1998] 2 BCLC 282; *Re a Company (No 5669 of 1998)* [2000] 1 BCLC 427; *Re Alpha Club (UK)*

In *Re UK-Euro Group plc*,[132] Edward Bartley Jones QC conveniently extrapolated the following summary of the basic principles:

(1) The burden of proof is on the Secretary of State. That burden of proof, on areas of disputed fact, is the normal burden in civil proceedings, namely proof on the balance of probabilities. However, to wind up an active company compulsorily is a serious step, and the Secretary of State who asserts that it is just and equitable for the court to take that step must put forward and establish reasons which have a weight justifying the court taking that step ([1989] BCLC 345).

(2) In considering whether or not to make a winding-up order, the court has to have regard to all the circumstances of the case as established by the material before the court at the hearing. In essence, this is a balancing exercise—taking into account the totality of the material before the court and carefully considering those matters which constitute reasons why the company should be wound up compulsorily, and those which constitute reasons why it should not. But it must be firmly borne in mind that, on a Secretary of State's 'public interest' petition, the reasons being put forward for a compulsory winding up are rooted in considerations of the public interest. The court, if it is to discharge its obligations to carry out the appropriate balancing exercise, must itself evaluate those 'public interest' reasons to the extent necessary for the court to form a view as to whether they do, indeed, afford sufficient reason for the making of a winding-up order (see at [1989] BCLC 351–352, 352–353).

(3) Whilst the court will note that the source for the submissions that the company should be wound up is a government department charged by Parliament with wide-ranging responsibilities in relation to the affairs of companies, indeed a department which has considerable expertise in these matters and which can be expected to act with a proper sense of responsibility when seeking a winding-up order, nevertheless the cogency of the submissions made on behalf of the Secretary of State will fall to be considered and tested in the same way as any other submissions. The Secretary of State's submissions are not, ipso facto, endowed with such weight that those resisting a winding-up petition presented by him will find the scales loaded against them (see at [1989] BCLC 353).

(4) At the end of the day, the court must be able, itself, to identify the aspect or aspects of the public interest which, in the view of the court, would be promoted by making a winding-up order in the particular case (see at [1989] BCLC 353); put another way, the court must be satisfied that a winding-up order is in the public interest and must identify why that is the case (see at [1989] BCLC 354).

(5) For many years Parliament has recognised the need for the general public to be protected against the activities of unscrupulous persons who deal in securities. Whilst the comments of Nicholls LJ (at [1989] BCLC 359) were directed to the activities of the subject company in dealing in third party securities, I see no reason whatsoever why this proposition should not apply, in the present case, to the dealings by the company in its own securities. As I shall indicate, below, the company has been in major breach of various regulatory provisions designed to protect the public against the company's dealings in its own securities (ie its own shares).

---

*Ltd* [2002] 2 BCLC 612; *Re a Company (No 6494 of 2003)* [2004] EWHC 126 (Ch); *Re Supporting Link Alliance Ltd* [2004] 1 WLR 1549; *Re Portfolios of Distinction Ltd* [2006] 2 BCLC 261.

[132] [2007] 1 BCLC 812.

(6) The public interest requires that individuals and companies dealing in securities with the public should maintain at least the generally accepted minimum standards of commercial behaviour and that those who, for whatever reason, fall below those standards should have their activities stopped (see at [1989] BCLC 359).

(7) The more unusual and speculative the investment, the heavier is the burden resting on a vendor of shares to ensure that the contents and get-up of his sales literature are not misleading (see at [1989] BCLC 359).

(8) The fact that the subject company may have ceased its offending activities prior to presentation of the Secretary of State's petition is a factor, and an important factor, to be taken into account (if, indeed, the public is no longer at a risk from the offending activity) but it is by no means a crucial or determinative factor. Balanced against it must be the fact that it would offend ordinary notions of what is just and equitable that, by ceasing its offending activities on becoming aware that the net is closing around it, a company which has misconducted itself can, thereby, enable itself to remain in being despite its previous history. By winding up such a company, the court will be expressing, in a meaningful way, its disapproval of such misconduct. Further, in addition to this being a fitting outcome for the company itself, such a course has the further benefit of spelling out to others that the court will not hesitate to wind up companies whose standards of dealing with the investing public are unacceptable (see at [1989] BCLC 360).

Each case will turn on its own particular facts. In *Re Walter L Jacob & Co Ltd*, **28.62** Nicholls LJ considered that it would not be acceptable on the facts before him to leave in being a company which had raised substantial sums of money on misleading documentation, and then ceased trading, with the consequence that hundreds of investors had been left with shares of questionable value. It would be in the public interest that such a company should be wound up.

One type of business which is considered to put the public particularly at risk is **28.63** the pyramid selling scheme (which may also be impeached as an unlawful lottery[133] or as an unlawful trading scheme[134]). In *Re Senator*, Millett LJ used the phrase 'inherently objectionable' to characterize a 'snowball scheme' called The Titan Business Club under which, upon payment of a fee of £2,500, an individual obtained the right to introduce others to the scheme.[135] If he recruited another member then he earned commission of £450 (thereby recouping part of his outlay). The commission rate rose the more members he introduced: and if the people whom he recruited themselves in turn recruited others, then the commission rate rose again. In his membership application each member explicitly acknowledged that 'my success depends on introducing new members'. Millet LJ described the scheme in these terms:

> The scheme is merely a device for enabling the organisers and a relatively small number of early recruits to make potentially very large profits at the expense of the

---

[133] Contrary to the Lottery and Amusements Act 1976, s 1.
[134] Contrary to the Fair Trading Act 1973, s 120.
[135] [1997] 1 WLR 515, 524, 525.

much larger number of those who are recruited later. Every new participant is in truth gambling on the scheme continuing long enough for him to recover his money and, he hopes, make a profit. But the scheme is not, of course, held out to him on this basis. Schemes of this kind are inherently objectionable and the court has consistently held that it is just and equitable to wind up the companies which operate them. They tend to be sold on a false and deceptive basis, sometimes explicit but usually implicit, that they are a certain source of profit for those who join and are capable of lasting indefinitely. A particular vice of such schemes is that they encourage similar dishonesty on the part of their members, who can recover their money only at the expense of new members whom they induce to enter the scheme . . .

**28.64** In *Secretary of State for Business Enterprise and Regulatory Reform v Amway (UK) Ltd*[136] Norris J set out some particular characteristics of businesses which had been found to be objectionable in previous decisions:

(1) operating a business that mathematically or self-evidently is bound to fail causing loss for the latest participants;[137]

(2) operating a business which consists of nothing beyond the sale of participations in the business itself with the consequence that a relatively small number of early recruits make potentially very large profits at the expense of a much larger number recruited later;[138]

(3) misrepresenting the nature of the business of the company in a serious way;[139]

(4) seriously misrepresenting the product being marketed by the company;[140]

(5) promoting a business on the basis that its participants will earn a reward greater than is commensurate with the effort;[141]

(6) by the nature of the business facilitating wrongdoing by others.[142]

**28.65** A (comparatively rare) example of a case where a public interest petition did not succeed was *Re Portfolios of Distinction Ltd*[143] where the deputy judge, Mr John Jarvis QC, appears to have been satisfied that the company had sufficiently reformed its procedures to render a winding-up order inappropriate.

**28.66** Another example can be found in the decision of Norris J in *Amway*. Norris J considered that the Secretary of State had failed on the balance of probabilities to

---

[136] [2008] BCC 713.

[137] *Re Senator* [1997] 1 WLR 515, CA; *Re Vanilla* (unrep, 1998); *Re Alpha Club* [2002] 2 BCLC 612.

[138] *Re Senator; Re Vanilla; Re Alpha Club; Re Delfin* [2000] 1 BCLC 71.

[139] *Re Walter Jacob* (an apparent adviser in fact operating as a share vendor); *Re Supporting Link Ltd* [2004] 1 WLR 1549 (commercial company holding itself out as a charity fundraiser); *Re UK-Euro Group* [2007] 1BCLC 812 (principal activity of the company the raising of money not the development and sale of a product).

[140] *Re Walter Jacob* (unmarketable shares); *Re Vanilla* (painting 'far too rosy a picture'); *Re Supporting Link* ('local' guide produced nationally and randomly distributed); *Re Equity & Provident* [2002] 2 BCLC 78 (sale of an apparent mechanical warranty in reality no such thing).

[141] *Re Senator*, above.

[142] *Re Senator* where Millett LJ said at [1997] 1 WLR 515, 525: 'a particular vice of such schemes is that they encourage similar dishonesty on the part of their members'.

[143] [2006] 2 BCLC 261.

prove that the company had been carrying on an unlawful lottery or conducting an unlawful trading scheme. He considered it unhelpful to substitute some concept such as 'inherent objectionability' for the 'fundamental question' of whether it was just and equitable to wind up the company.[144] He found that, in the light of a revised business model which the company had put into effect in October 2007, it was not.

*Where the company is already in liquidation*

A public interest petition may not be pursued if the company in question is already **28.67** being wound up by the court.[145] However, voluntary liquidation is no bar to a compulsory winding-up order.[146] It is open to the Secretary of State to pursue a petition, and to the court to make an order, but the fact of voluntary liquidation is one of the circumstances to be taken into account. In *Re Lubin, Rosen and Associates Ltd*,[147] Megarry J said:

> Where the results of that investigation lead the Secretary of State to the conclusion that it is expedient in the public interest that the company should be wound up, and he accordingly presents a petition for a compulsory order, I do not think that the passing of a resolution for a voluntary winding up shortly before the Secretary of State presents his petition, and the subsequent confirmation of that resolution, ought to be allowed to put the voluntary winding up into an entrenched position, as it were, which can be demolished only if the Secretary of State can demonstrate that the process of voluntary winding up will be markedly inferior to a compulsory winding up. The Secretary of State may, of course, reach the conclusion that a voluntary winding up will suffice, and so not proceed with his petition; but if he does proceed, then in my judgment the question is essentially whether, in all the circumstances of the case (including, of course, the existence of a voluntary winding up and the views of the creditors), it is just and equitable for the company to be wound up compulsorily. In addition to the suspicion of offences, the presence of foreign complications such as exist in this case, and the difference between the interests of the disappointed purchasers and those of any other creditors, seem to me to make it both just and equitable that this winding up should be conducted with the full authority and resources of the court.

One particular factor which carried weight with Megarry J in that case was that, although there was provision under the 1948 Act for a voluntary liquidator to report apparent offences, in a compulsory liquidation the official receiver came under a specific duty to submit a report to the court, setting out the state of the

---

144 [2008] EWHC 1054 (Ch).
145 Insolvency Act, s 124A(2).
146 *Re Lubin, Rosen and Associates Ltd* [1975] 1 WLR 122; *Securities and Investments Board v Lancashire and Yorkshire Portfolio Management Ltd* [1992] BCLC 281; *Re Alpha Club (UK) Ltd* [2002] 2 BCLC 612 (resolution for voluntary liquidation had been passed less than a fortnight before the hearing of the petition).
147 A case under the 1967 Act, s 224, the predecessor of Insolvency Act, s 124A.

company and whether further inquiry was desirable. Megarry J went on to conclude that, where there were circumstances of suspicion, as there were in that case, it was highly desirable that the winding up should be by the court, with all the safeguards that this provided, including the investigation of any suspected offences. The desirability of a full and vigorous independent investigation of the company's affairs in a compulsory liquidation was also emphasized more recently by Lightman J in *Re Pinstripe Farming Co Ltd*.[148]

**28.68**   A voluntary liquidator who is in office can properly appear by counsel on the hearing of the petition, and it may be desirable and appropriate for such an office-holder to assist the court with evidence of what he has found and what the present position is, but he should not press a view one way or another.[149] There seems to be no reason in principle why the voluntary liquidator should not in an appropriate case go on to be appointed as liquidator in the compulsory liquidation; in most cases, however, the voluntary liquidator will appear to lack the necessary independence.[150]

## (4)  Provisional liquidator and procedural matters

*Provisional liquidator*

**28.69**   Pending the hearing of a public interest petition, as in the case of any other winding-up petition, in an appropriate case the court will appoint a provisional liquidator.[151] Such an appointment may be justified not only when the company is obviously insolvent or the assets are in jeopardy, but also when 'a good prima facie case'[152] for the company to be wound up on public interest grounds has been made out, even if it appears to be solvent. As Megarry J said in *Re Highfield Commodities*:[153]

> The exercise of that power [to appoint a provisional liquidator] may have serious consequences for the company, and so a need for the exercise of the power must overtop those consequences. In particular, where the winding up petition is presented because the Secretary of State considers that it is expedient in the public interest that the company should be wound up, the public interest must be given full weight, though it is not to be regarded as being conclusive.

> The matter may be tested by considering a well-run and prosperous company thriving on the frauds which it practices on the public. If the Secretary of State presents a

---

[148] [1996] 2 BCLC 295; cf *Re Future Trading Corp* (unrep Robert Walker J, 16 August 1996).
[149] Cf *Re Medisco Equipment Ltd* [1983] BCLC 305.
[150] *Re Pinstripe Farming Co Ltd* [1996] 2 BCLC 295; cf *Re Lowerstoft Traffic Services Ltd* [1986] BCLC 81.
[151] *Re Highfield Commodities Ltd* [1985] 1 WLR 149.
[152] *Re Union Accident Insurance Co Ltd* [1972] 1 All ER 1105, per Plowman J; cited by Megarry J in *Highfield Commodities Ltd* [1985] 1 WLR 149, 158, 159.
[153] [1985] 1 WLR 149, 159.

winding up petition under section 35 of the Act of 1967, I cannot conceive that it would be right to say that as the company is solvent and no assets are in jeopardy, no provisional liquidator should be appointed unless the evidence of fraud is so strong at that stage that it is clear that the company is bound to be wound up. In such a case it might well be highly desirable to put a provisional liquidator in control so that no more money will be taken from the public.

Notwithstanding the possibility that the company may be damaged by the appointment of a provisional liquidator, there is no requirement for a cross-undertaking in damages on an application without notice for the appointment, because the Secretary of State seeks the appointment for the purpose of enforcing the law or in the performance of a public duty: the Secretary of State ought not to be dissuaded from exercising his statutory powers in this behalf by being required to give any undertaking in damages.[154]   **28.70**

In *Re Senator Hanseatische Verwaltungsgesellschaft mbH*, Sir Richard Scott V-C   **28.71** granted injunctions to preserve the position pending the hearing of the winding-up petition. In the Court of Appeal, Millett LJ said of the injunctions and the application for the appointment of provisional liquidators:[155]

> Neither is likely to be completely effective to prevent the organisers [of the scheme] from setting up a similar scheme in the name of another entity and making use of the membership of the existing scheme to continue their activities. In the absence of suitable undertakings from the individuals behind the scheme to refrain from doing this, I would for my part have thought it much the better course to appoint a provisional liquidator. This would have a number of advantages. It would put in place an independent officer of the court to take charge of the company's activities pending the hearing of the petition and to be a focal point for the present members to turn to for advice as to their position. He would also be entitled to obtain possession of the current membership lists and ensure they could not be used, without the approval of the court, to operate similar schemes pending the hearing of the petition.

### *The offer of undertakings*

A company which is the subject of investigation or a public interest petition some-   **28.72** times seeks to protect its position by offering undertakings, to the Secretary of State or to the court, to desist from certain practices or to change its business model. In *Re Supporting Link Ltd* Sir Andrew Morritt V-C referred to the recent cases in which undertakings had been accepted or refused,[156] and accepted that

---

[154] *Re Highfield Commodities* [1985] 1 WLR 149, 156.

[155] [1997] 1 WLR 515, 526, 527.

[156] [2004] 1 WLR 1549. Undertakings satisfactory to the Secretary of State were accepted in *Re Vehicle Options Ltd* [2002] EWHC 3235 (Ch), *Re Easy-Dial Ltd* [2003] EWHC 3508 (Ch), and *Secretary of State for Trade and Industry v KTA Ltd* [2003] EWHC 3512 (Ch). In *Re Equity and Provident Ltd* [2002] 2 BCLC 78 undertakings were refused by Patten J and a winding-up order was made. *Re Derek Colins Associates Ltd* [2002] EWHC 1893 (Ch) is the only case where the judge

the court had power to accept undertakings and to dismiss the petition on that basis.[157] Sir Andrew Morritt V-C went on to conclude:[158]

> In my view unless the Secretary of State is content that the petition is disposed of on undertakings the court should be very slow indeed to accept them in preference to making a winding-up order. All the reasons given by Brightman J in *Re Bamford Publishers* remain as valid now as they were then. If the court is satisfied that the offending business has ceased and it is prepared to trust the existing management then it may be appropriate to dismiss the petition altogether. But if it is not so satisfied or does not trust the existing management then I find it hard to envisage a case in which it would be appropriate to dismiss the petition on undertakings as to the future conduct of the company's business.

**28.73**   In *Secretary of State for Trade and Industry v Bell Davies Trading Ltd*,[159] the Court of Appeal endorsed the Vice-Chancellor's approach in *Re Supporting Link Ltd* and gave the following guidance:

> The judge has a discretion whether or not to make a winding-up order. As for undertakings, the court has a discretion whether or not to accept them if they are proffered and whether or not to make the giving of them a condition of dismissing the petition. In considering the exercise of his discretion the willingness or otherwise of the Secretary of State to accept undertakings, which have to be policed by the Department of Trade and Industry, is an important factor.
>
> Thus, in the exercise of the discretion, the judge is entitled (a) to dismiss the petition on undertakings if, for example, he is satisfied that the offending business has ceased or if the undertakings are acceptable to the Secretary of State; or (b) to dismiss the petition on undertakings, even if that course is opposed by the Secretary of State, although that will be unusual; or (c) to refuse to accept undertakings and to wind the company up, if, for example, he is not satisfied that those giving the undertakings can be trusted.

**28.74**   Following those decisions, in the *Amway* case, Norris J said[160] that the Secretary of State is not a licensor of approved business models or a business design consultant and is under no obligation to approve or to police a scheme of undertakings relating to the conduct of an individual company's business. To be acceptable the revised business model must be 'fully formulated, comprehensive, open and transparent, and capable of effective and ongoing implementation without the supervision of either the Secretary of State or the court'.

---

accepted undertakings and refused to make a winding-up order where that course has been opposed by the Secretary of State.

[157]   At para 55.

[158]   At para 58. In so doing he relied on the decision of Brightman J in *Re Bamford Publishers Ltd*, The Times, 4 June 1977, and observations of the Court of Appeal in *Re Blackspur Group plc* [1998] 1 WLR 422, 433.

[159]   [2005] 1 All ER 324, CA (Note) at paras 110 and 111.

[160]   [2008] EWHC 1054 (Ch) at paras 10–11.

*Procedure*

In general, the procedure for a public interest petition is the same as for any other **28.75** winding-up petition. The petition is verified by witness statement and filed in court under rule 4.7(1) of the Insolvency Rules. The court fixes the venue for the hearing and the petition is then served on the company.

The petition is required to be advertised, unless the court directs otherwise under **28.76** rule 4.11. The onus is on the company to show sufficient cause why the petition should not be advertised. For this purpose the court would have to be satisfied that creditors are not at risk and that advertisement would cause serious damage to the reputation and financial stability of the company.[161]

Different considerations arise where a provisional liquidator is appointed urgently **28.77** at the same time as the petition is presented. These will be cases in which the court has accepted that it is necessary to intervene and take immediate control of the company's assets and business; it may be necessary to announce the appointment to protect the public or enable them to protect themselves, but it is likely that the announcement will have a severe effect on the company's ability to carry on trading. Indeed the likely consequence of the appointment is to bring the company's business to an immediate halt. In *Secretary of State for Trade and Industry v North West Holdings plc*[162] the Court of Appeal reviewed and endorsed BERR's normal practice of issuing a press announcing the provisional liquidator's appointment as soon as he agrees, but observed that in cases of difficulty the directions of the court could be obtained.

*Costs against directors personally*

Although directors are not usually ordered to pay the costs of a company's defence **28.78** against a winding-up petition, the court has jurisdiction to order them to do so which has on occasions been exercised in the context of a public interest petition, particularly where the court considered that the directors had no bona fide belief in the defence advanced.[163]

---

[161] *Re a Company (No 007923 of 1994)* [1995] 1 WLR 953, CA. In that case the Court of Appeal was satisfied that advertisement would do lasting damage, and granted the company's appeal against the judge's refusal to direct that the petitions should not be advertised. In the event the petition was dismissed. Although the companies had technically been guilty of aiding and abetting the carrying on of unauthorized insurance business by foreign companies in the UK, the directors had believed themselves to be acting lawfully and under the circumstances the conduct of the companies had not been intrinsically against the public interest: *Re a Company (No 007293 of 1994) (No 2)* [1995] BCC 641.

[162] [1999] 1 BCLC 425, 430, 431. Publicity protects persons dealing with the company and the provisional liquidator. Chadwick LJ said that it was desirable that the public should be made aware that the Secretary of State has concluded that the company should be wound up in the public interest and the court has been satisfied that a provisional liquidator should be appointed.

[163] eg *Re Aurum Marketing Ltd* [2000] 2 BCLC 645; *Re North West Holdings plc* [2001] 1 BCLC 468, CA; *Secretary of State for Trade and Industry v Liquid Acquisitions Ltd* [2003] 1 BCLC 375.

# D. Disqualification Proceedings

## (1) Disqualification orders

**28.79** The CDDA, subs 1(1) provides that:

> In the circumstances specified below in this Act a court may, and under sections 6 and 9A shall, make against a person a disqualification order, that is to say an order that for a period specified in the order—
>
> (a) he shall not be a director of a company, act as receiver of a company's property or in any way, whether directly or indirectly, be concerned or take part in the promotion, formation or management of a company unless (in each case) he has the leave of the court, and
>
> (b) he shall not act as an insolvency practitioner.

In respect of ss 2 to 5 and 10, any person may be subject to a disqualification order if the conditions of those sections are satisfied and the court sees fit to so order. Under ss 6 and 9A, disqualification is mandatory upon satisfaction of the relevant conditions, but it flows from those conditions that only a director may be disqualified under those sections. For the purpose of ss 6 and 9A, 'director' includes a de facto or shadow director.[164]

**28.80** A disqualification order is not limited in effect to the kind of company in connection with which it was made and the court has no power 'to make a disqualification order in relation to one class of company' only.[165]

**28.81** Section 1(1) does not, however, preclude all activities in connection with a company or its business. The prohibition in the order is necessarily limited and, in the context of s 2(1), the courts have recognized a distinction between 'managing certain specific aspects of the company's activities, such as production, sales, trading and the like, and the central management of the affairs of the company, that is to say the matters normally undertaken by the directors or officers of the company'.[166] This would seem to apply equally to s 1(1), although the line between prohibited and permitted activities is not precisely clear and can be difficult to draw. In circumstances in which it is unclear whether or not an activity falls within the scope of the order, a well-advised former director, or other person, should apply for leave under s 17 to carry on a particular activity, which may readily be obtained in an appropriate case. In *Re TLL Realisations Ltd*, Park J explained that:

> Section 1 of the Act does not impose an absolute prohibition on a disqualified person being concerned in or taking part in the management of a company . . . Indeed applications for leave are common, and an application for leave to undertake a specific job (usually, though not in this case, a directorship of an identified company)

---

[164] CDDA ss 6(3C), 9E(5), 22(4), and 22(5).
[165] *R v Goodman* [1993] 2 All ER 789, 793, CA.
[166] *R v Campbell* [1984] BCLC 83, 85, CA.

is frequently made at the same hearing as that at which the court imposes the general disqualification.[167]

The procedure and requirements for obtaining leave under s 17 are set out at paragraph 28.209 *et seq* below.

**28.82** The period of disqualification will be specified in the order itself, and the order is discharged upon the lapse of that period. In connection with this, subs 1(3) provides:

> Where a disqualification order is made against a person who is already subject to such an order, or to a disqualification undertaking, the periods specified in those orders or, as the case may be, in the order and the undertaking shall run concurrently.

This saving against the accumulation of periods of disqualification is, in practice, not absolute. A breach of a disqualification order, or undertaking, is treated as an aggravating factor in calculating the appropriate period of disqualification on some other ground.[168]

**28.83** The Secretary of State, by the Registrar of Companies, is required under s 18 to maintain a register of disqualification orders and undertakings from prescribed particulars supplied to him by court clerks and managers.[169] The prescribed particulars include all disqualification orders made and undertakings given and any action in consequence of which such an order, or any undertaking, is varied or ceases to be in force. The register is a public register and may currently be accessed in its electronic form without charge.

### (2) Periods of disqualification

**28.84** The period of disqualification, or tariff, is sensitive to the facts of each case and is subject to prescribed minimum and maximum periods which vary according to the grounds upon which disqualification is ordered. In all cases, the period of disqualification begins 21 days from the date of the order.[170]

**28.85** The prescribed minimum and maximum periods are:

(1) *Conviction for an indictable offence:* a maximum of five years where the disqualification order is made by a court of summary jurisdiction, and 15 years in any other case;[171]

(2) *Persistent breaches of companies legislation:* a maximum of five years;[172]

(3) *Disqualification for fraud, etc in winding up:* a maximum of 15 years;[173]

---

[167] [2000] BCC 998, 1003; affd [2000] 2 BCLC 223, CA.
[168] *Re Sevenoaks Stationers (Retail) Ltd* [1991] Ch 164, 174, CA.
[169] Companies (Disqualification Orders) Regulations 2001 (SI 2001/967).
[170] CDDA, s 1(2).
[171] CDDA, s 2(3).
[172] CDDA, s 3(5).
[173] CDDA, s 4(4).

(4) *Disqualification on summary conviction for failing to file returns, etc:* a maximum of five years;[174]

(5) *Disqualification for unfit conduct in connection with an insolvent company:* a minimum of two years and a maximum of 15 years;[175]

(6) *Disqualification for unfit conduct after investigation by the Secretary of State:* a maximum of 15 years;[176]

(7) *Disqualification for unfit conduct in connection with a company in breach of competition law:* a maximum of 15 years.[177]

The Secretary of State, as set out at paragraph 28.197 *et seq* below, may accept a disqualification undertaking if he considers s 6 or s 9A to be satisfied, in which case the maximum and, as the case may be, minimum period that can be specified in the undertaking is the same as that prescribed for the corresponding disqualification order.[178]

**28.86** Within these confines the courts have set out guidelines as to how the appropriate tariff is to be calculated. The leading case is *Re Sevenoaks Stationers (Retail) Ltd*, in which Dillon LJ approved the then practice of the Chancery Division in relation to applications under s 6:

> I would for my part endorse the division of the potential 15-year disqualification period into three brackets . . . viz.:
>
> (i) the top bracket of disqualification for periods over 10 years should be reserved for particularly serious cases. These may include cases where a director who has already had one period of disqualification imposed on him falls to be disqualified yet again.
>
> (ii) The minimum bracket of two to five years' disqualification should be applied where, though disqualification is mandatory, the case is, relatively, not very serious.
>
> (iii) The middle bracket of disqualification for from six to 10 years should apply for serious cases which do not merit the top bracket.[179]

**28.87** In *Re Westmid Packing Services Ltd*[180] Lord Woolf MR further refined the guidelines when he stated that:

(1) The power to grant leave under s 17 is irrelevant to determining the proper period of disqualification.

(2) The period of disqualification must reflect the gravity of the offence and, as such, credit cannot be given for the period of effective disqualification com-

---

[174] CDDA, s 5(5).
[175] CDDA, s 5(5).
[176] CDDA, s 8(4).
[177] CDDA, 9A(9).
[178] CDDA ss 1(A)(2) and 9B(5).
[179] [1991] Ch 164, 174e–g, CA. In *Re Cargo Agency Ltd* [1992] BCLC 686, 689 Harman J observed that Chancery judges were already familiar with this division into three bands.
[180] [1998] 2 All ER 124, 131, 132, CA.

mencing upon the bringing of proceedings and ending with the making of the order.[181]

(3) There is no room for 'plea-bargaining', but there can be negotiation as to the basis upon which an admission might be made, provided the facts are disputed and the starting point correctly reflects the gravity of the conduct.

(4) When it comes to mitigation Lord Woolf MR went on to say that the court is not restricted to the facts supporting the application for disqualification in question: A wide variety of matters—including the former director's age and state of health, the length of time he has been in jeopardy, whether he has admitted the offence, his general conduct before and after the offence, and the periods of disqualification of his co-directors that may have been ordered by other courts—may be relevant and admissible in determining the appropriate period of disqualification.[182]

These include, additionally, the defendant's reliance on professional advice and proper or positive conduct such as cooperation with any office-holder or any attempt to remedy his misconduct or otherwise improve the position of creditors, for example.

The court is also entitled to consider aggravating factors such as the breach of an existing disqualification order or undertaking by the defendant,[183] or, at least in connection with disqualification proceedings under s 6, the defendant's conduct in the proceedings, including his conduct at a witness.[184]   **28.88**

The appropriate tariff is a matter for the trial judge applying these guidelines. The citation of cases as to the period of disqualification is unhelpful,[185] and an appellate court may only review his decision and substitute a different period when the judge has erred in principle.[186] The following provides an indication as to how the guidelines might be applied:   **28.89**

(1) The use of a company as a means of perpetrating a fraud, or a fraud in connection with the management of a company is likely to warrant a tariff in the top bracket. In *Re Vintage Hallmark plc*, the directors were disqualified for 15 years, having fraudulently induced a subscription for shares and the purchase of the company's goods for their own benefit.[187] In *Official Receiver v Doshi*, a

---

[181] Also *Secretary of State for Trade and Industry v Arif* [1997] 1 BCLC 34, 44–5.

[182] [1998] 2 All ER 124, 134, CA.

[183] *Re Sevenoaks Stationers (Retail) Ltd* [1991] Ch 164, 174f, CA.

[184] *Secretary of State v Reynard* [2002] 2 BCLC 625, 629–31, CA; *Re Godwin Warren Control Systems plc* [1993] BCLC 80, 92; *Re Moorgate Metals Ltd* [1995] 1 BCLC 503, 516–17; and *Re Living Images Ltd* [1996] 1 BCLC 349, 377.

[185] *Re Westmid Packing Services Ltd* [1998] 2 All ER 124, 134; and *Re Civica Investments Ltd* [1983] BCLC 456, 457–8.

[186] eg *Re Swift 736 Ltd* [1993] BCLC 896, CA.

[187] [2007] 1 BCLC 788.

director was disqualified for 12 years for carrying out a fraud on the company's debt factor and having 'been shown to be capable of a level of mendacity which is breathtaking in its audacity and remarkable for its fluency'.[188]

(2) The continued trading of a company whilst insolvent coupled with a persistent failure to keep proper accounts and file statutory accounts and returns is more likely to warrant a tariff within the middle bracket, especially where there is some aggravating impropriety, for example, a preferential payment, unfair discrimination against a particular creditor or class of creditor, or the abuse of successive phoenix companies.[189]

(3) The continued trading of a company whilst insolvent or the failure to keep proper accounts and file statutory accounts and returns is, without more, likely to warrant a tariff within the minimum bracket.[190]

**28.90**  These guidelines appear to apply to *all* disqualification proceedings. Indeed, it would be odd were a different approach adopted, given the overlap between the grounds for disqualification under s 6 and ss 2 to 5 and 9 and 10 and the overlapping jurisdiction of the civil and criminal courts. In *Re Land Travel Ltd*, Jacob J considered it 'self-evident' that civil and criminal courts should apply the same standards.[191] In the earlier criminal case of *R v Young*[192] Brooke J had adopted a different approach when he said that the sentencing power under s 2 was 'a completely general and unfettered power given by Parliament to courts on the occasion when a person is convicted of an indictable offence of that type' to which the 'jurisdiction exercised in particular by the judges of the Chancery Division' was irrelevant. A different approach has, however, been taken in other more recent criminal cases[193] and so it would seem that the guidance in *Sevenoaks* is in some way applicable to cases other than those under ss 6, 8, and 9A and which do not require an assessment of unfitness.

### (3)  Grounds for disqualification, other than unfitness

**28.91**  Disqualification for unfitness under s 6(1) is by far the most frequently applied ground for disqualification, but the other statutory grounds fulfil important

---

[188] [2001] 2 BCLC 235 at paras 19 and 118. Tariffs of 12 and 11 years were also imposed in *Re City Truck Group Ltd* [2007] 2 BCLC 649 and *Secretary for State for Trade and Industry v Kappler* [2008] 1 BCLC 120.

[189] *Re Sevenoaks Stationers (Retail) Ltd* [1991] Ch 164, CA; *Re Travel Mondial Ltd* [1991] BCLC 120; *Re Tansoft Ltd* [1991] BCLC 339; *Re City Investment Centres Ltd* [1992] BCLC 956; *Re Godwin Warren Control Systems plc* [1993] BCC 80; *Re Firedart Ltd* [1994] 2 BCLC 340; *Re Britannia Homes Centres Ltd* [2001] 2 BCLC 63; *Re Bunting Electric Manufacturing Co Ltd* [2006] 1 BCLC 550.

[190] *Re New Generation Engineers Ltd* [1993] BCLC 435; *Re Linval Ltd* [1993] BCLC 654; *Re Swift 736 Ltd* [1993] BCLC 896, CA; *Re Continental Assurance Co of London plc* [1997] 1 BCLC 48; *Re Verby Print for Advertising Ltd* [1998] 2 BCLC 23; and *Re Amaron Ltd* [2001] 1 BCLC 562.

[191] [1998] BCC 282, 284.

[192] [1990] BCC 549, 552–3, CA.

[193] *R v Edwards* (1998) 2 Cr App R (S) 213; and *R v Millard* (1994) 15 Cr App R (S) 445.

policy functions both in terms of the jurisdiction exercised by the criminal courts and also in the recent introduction of disqualification for unfitness in connection with a corporate breach of competition law and the management of a company whilst subject of a bankruptcy restriction order.

*Conviction of indictable offence*

The CDDA subs 2(1) provides that:  **28.92**

> The court may make a disqualification order against a person where he is convicted of an indictable offence (whether on indictment or summarily) in connection with the promotion, formation, management, liquidation or striking off of a company, with the receivership of a company's property or with his being an administrative receiver of a company.

An 'indictable offence' means an offence which, if committed by an adult, is triable on indictment, whether it is exclusively so triable or triable either way.[194]

The application of s 2(2) turns on whether the defendant is convicted of an indict-  **28.93** able offence 'in connection with' one or more of the activities specified in s 2(1). In *R v Goodman*,[195] this arose as a result of the defendant's conviction for insider dealing contrary to the Company Securities (Insider Dealing) Act 1985. Staughton LJ explained that 'some relevant factual connection with the management of the company' was required:

> There are three possible ways of looking at the test to be applied. The first might be to say that the indictable offence referred to in the 1986 Act must be an offence of breaking some rule of law as to what must be done in the management of a company or must not be done. Examples might be keeping accounts or filing returns and such matters . . . Another view might be that the indictable offence must be committed in the course of managing the company. That would cover cases such as *Georgiou*, *Corbin*, and *Austen*. What the defendants in all those cases were doing was managing the company so that it carried out unlawful transactions.

> The third view would be that the indictable offence must have some relevant factual connection with the management of the company. That, in our judgment, is the correct answer. It is perhaps wider than the test applied in the three cases we have mentioned, because in those cases there was no need for the court to go wider than in fact it did. But we can see no ground for supposing that Parliament wished to apply any stricter test. Accordingly, we consider that the conduct of Mr Goodman in this case did amount to an indictable offence in connection with the management of the company. Even on a stricter view that might well be the case, because as chairman it was unquestionably his duty not to use confidential information for his own private benefit. It was arguably conduct in the management of the company when he did that.[196]

---

[194] Interpretation Act, s 2(2) and Schedule 1.
[195] [1993] 2 All ER 789, CA.
[196] [1993] 2 All ER 789, 792 CA.

This test is necessarily imprecise, but it has been applied recently in *R v Creddy* to uphold the disqualification of a solicitor who made available his client account 'as a private banking facility' for assets which were, and which he suspected were, the proceeds of crime.[197] This decision is undoubtedly correct, but, in less clear cases, it may be useful, as indicated by Staughton LJ, to apply the narrower tests first developed by the Court of Appeal as a cross-check to the broader test in *R v Goodman*.[198]

*Persistent breaches of companies legislation*

28.94 The CDDA, subs 3(1) provides that:

> The court may make a disqualification order against a person where it appears to it that he has been persistently in default in relation to provisions of the companies legislation requiring any return, account or other document to be filed with, delivered or sent, or notice of any matter to be given, to the registrar of companies.

28.95 The focus of any complaint is likely to be a failure to file accounts and annual returns,[199] but the scope of s 3(1) may properly include *any* return, account, or other document to be filed with the Registrar of Companies under the 2006 Act as well as any such provisions under the Insolvency Act, since the definition of 'companies legislation' for the purpose of s 3 extends to that Act also.[200]

28.96 The 'default' is that of the defendant and not the company. The companies legislation may impose an obligation on the company to file a prescribed return or account, for example, but the focus of s 3(1) is the default of the defendant under the companies legislation. The defendant's default need not be culpable for the defendant to be liable for disqualification under s 3(1), but his culpability is likely to be relevant to the exercise of the court's discretion.[201]

28.97 The expression 'persistently in default' is not defined, but, in *Re Artic Engineering Ltd*, Hoffmann J considered that it connotes 'some degree of continuance or repetition' and an analogy with s 3(2) provided some indication of 'the kind of conduct which the legislature had in mind'.[202] This issue will, however, only arise where s 3(2) is not satisfied. Section 3(2) is a long-stop provision by which persistent default is conclusively proved upon showing that in the five years ending with

---

[197] [2008] 1 BCLC 625, CA, para 14.
[198] *R v Georgiou* [1988] BCC 322, CA; *R v Austen* (1985) 7 Cr App R (S) 214; *R v Corbin* (1984) 6 Cr App R(S) 17.
[199] 2006 Act, ss 441–445 and 1985 Act, s 241 (accounts) and 2006 Act, s 854 and 1985 Act, s 363 (annual return).
[200] CDDA, s 22(7).
[201] *Re Artic Engineering Ltd* [1986] 1 WLR 686, 691, 692.
[202] [1986] 1 WLR 686, 692.

the date of the application the defendant has been 'adjudged guilty' of three or more defaults, whether or not on the same occasion. To be 'adjudged guilty', the defendant must have been—

(1) convicted of an offence consisting in a contravention of, or failure to comply with, a provision of the companies legislation, whether on his own part or on the part of any company, or

(2) subject to a default order in respect of a contravention of, or failure to comply with provisions of the Companies Acts for (a) the delivery of company accounts, (b) the preparation of revised accounts,[203] and (c) the company's duty to make returns;[204]

(3) subject to an order under the Insolvency Act enforcing (a) the duty of a receiver or manager to make returns,[205] and (b) the duty of a provisional liquidator to make returns.[206]

The criminal courts have no jurisdiction under s 3, and an application under s 3 **28.98** can only be made to a court having jurisdiction to wind up a company in relation to which the offence or some other default has been or is alleged to have been committed, s 3(4).

*Fraud in winding up*

The CDDA, subs 4(1) provides that: **28.99**

> The court may make a disqualification order against a person if, in the course of the winding up of a company, it appears that he—
>
> (a) has been guilty of an offence for which he is liable (whether he has been convicted or not) under section 993 of the Companies Act 2006 (fraudulent trading), or
>
> (b) has otherwise been guilty, while an officer or liquidator of the company receiver of the company's property or administrative receiver of the company, of any fraud in relation to the company or of any breach of his duty as such officer, liquidator, receiver or administrative receiver.

The power to make a disqualification order under s 4 is accordingly limited to misconduct discovered 'in the course of the winding up of a company', but the type of winding up, or the solvency or insolvency of the company, is irrelevant.

*Summary conviction*

The CDDA, s 5(2) and (3) entitles a court convicting a defendant of a summary **28.100** offence to make a disqualification order if during the five years ending with the

---

[203] 2006 Act, s 456; 1985 Act, s 245B.
[204] 2006 Act, 1113; 1985 Act, s 713.
[205] Insolvency Act, s 41.
[206] Insolvency Act, s 170.

date of the conviction the defendant has had made against him, or has been convicted of, in total not less than three default orders[207] and offences. The offences include the offence of which he is convicted by that court and any other offence of which he is convicted on the same occasion.

**28.101**   For the purposes of s 5 an 'offence' is one of which the defendant is convicted (either on indictment or summarily) in consequence of a contravention of, or failure to comply with, any provision of the companies legislation requiring a return, account, or other document to be filed with, delivered, or sent, or notice of any matter to be given, to the Registrar of Companies.[208]

**28.102**   The basis for making a disqualification order under s 5 therefore overlaps substantially with that under s 3, but, crucially, only the criminal courts have power to disqualify under this section, and, significantly, only the conviction giving rise to the jurisdiction to disqualify must flow from a summary offence. The defendant's previous convictions may be summary or indictable offences.

*After investigation of company*

**28.103**   The CDDA s 8 provides that:

> (1)  If it appears to the Secretary of State from investigative material that it is expedient in the public interest that a disqualification order should be made against a person who is, or has been, a director or shadow director of a company, he may apply to the court for such an order.
> . . .
> (2)  The court may make a disqualification order against a person where, on an application under this section, it is satisfied that his conduct in relation to the company makes him unfit to be concerned in the management of a company.

This confers a power to disqualify a director who is unfit but imposes no statutory duty to do so. The power is, however, fettered to the extent that the court 'would not, having formed the view that disqualification was necessary in the public interest, be acting judicially if it did not make a disqualification order'.[209] As such, it has been *assumed* that the test of unfitness under s 8(2) is the same as that under s 6(1), although the point remains undecided. In *Secretary of State for Trade and Industry v Hollier*, Etherton J invited counsel to address him on the issue but to his 'surprise' both counsel were agreed that 'the same approach and principles should

---

[207]   By s 5(4) the definition of 'summary offence' in the Interpretation Act, Schedule 1 applies and 'default order' has the same meaning as in s 3(3)(b).
[208]   CDDA, s 5(1).
[209]   Cf *Re Grayan Building Services Ltd* [1995] Ch 241, 253g.

apply as in cases under s 6 in respect of the determination of unfitness and fixing the period of disqualification'.²¹⁰

The approach taken by the court in *Hollier* is adopted here, and cases under s 8²¹¹ have been assimilated with the case law under s 6(1), although specifically referenced as such. A ground sufficient to warrant mandatory disqualification for at least two years should at least be capable of justifying disqualification under s 8(2) and, given the approach currently adopted in practice, there appears to be no discernible difference in the way the courts have approach the issue of unfitness under either section, notwithstanding that the language of s 8(2) focuses more broadly on the defendant's 'conduct in relation to the company' and not merely his 'conduct as a director', which forms part of the test under s 6(1).

**28.104**

*Competition disqualification order*

The CDDA, s 9A provides that:²¹²

**28.105**

   (1) The court must make a disqualification order against a person if the following two conditions are satisfied in relation to him.
   (2) The first condition is that an undertaking which is a company of which he is a director commits a breach of competition law.
   (3) The second condition is that the court considers that his conduct as a director makes him unfit to be concerned in the management of a company.

By s 9A(4) an undertaking commits a breach of competition law if it engages in conduct which infringes (a) the Competition Act 1998, Chapter 1 or Article 81 of the Treaty of the European Union (prohibition on agreements, etc preventing, restricting, or distorting competition),²¹³ or (b) the Competition Act 1998, Chapter 2 or Article 82 of the Treaty of the European Union (prohibition on abuse of a dominant position).

For the purpose of deciding whether a person is unfit to be concerned in the management of a company within the meaning of s 9A(3), the court may have regard to his conduct as a director of a company in connection with any other breach of competition law, but must not have regard to the matters mentioned in Schedule 1.²¹⁴

**28.106**

---

²¹⁰ [2007] BCC 11, paras 45 to 51 and 59. In *Secretary of State for Trade and Industry v Ashman*, Lloyd J, 15 June 1998, (unreported), pp 13–18 of the transcript, Lloyd J recorded that there was 'no great dispute as to the relevant law' and set out the law applicable as it had then developed under s 6.

²¹¹ *Secretary of State for Trade and Industry v Hollier* [2007] BCC 11; *Re JA Chapman & Co Ltd* [2003] 2 BCLC 206; *Secretary of State for Trade and Industry v Ashman*, Lloyd J, 15 June 1998 (unreported); *Re Looe Fish Ltd* [1993] BCC 348; *Re Samuel Sherman plc* [1991] 1 WLR 1070.

²¹² Inserted by the Enterprise Act 2002, s 204 with effect from 20 June 2003.

²¹³ For this purpose references to the conduct of an undertaking are references to its conduct taken with the conduct of one or more other undertakings: CDDA, subs 9A(8).

²¹⁴ CDDA, s 9A(6)(b) and (c).

The test of unfitness turns on the criteria in s 9A(6) (and not the test for unfitness considered below in relation to s 6),[215] specifically:

(1) whether his conduct contributed to the breach of competition law; or

(2) whether, if his conduct did not contribute to that breach, he had reasonable grounds to suspect that the conduct of the undertaking constituted the breach and he took no steps to prevent it; and

(3) he did not know but ought to have known that the conduct of the undertaking constituted the breach.

It is sufficient to bring a defendant within s 9A(6) if his conduct contributed to the breach of competition law because, in such a case, it is immaterial whether the person knew that the conduct of the undertaking constituted the breach.[216]

*Participation in wrongful trading*

**28.107**　The CDDA, subs 10(1) provides that:

> Where the court makes a declaration under section 213 or 214 of the Insolvency Act that a person is liable to make a contribution to a company's assets, then, whether or not an application for such an order is made by any person, the court may, if it thinks fit, also make a disqualification order against the person to whom the declaration relates.

The power to make a declaration under the Insolvency Act, ss 213 or 214 is considered in Chapter 29, Section I(2) and (3).

**28.108**　The jurisdiction to make a disqualification order under s 10 overlaps substantially with the jurisdiction under s 6 and, given the more extensive matters which may be taken into account in assessing unfitness under that section, the majority of applications for disqualification touching on fraudulent or wrongful trading will be brought under s 6. The power to disqualify under s 10 may be used where the liquidator has applied for a contribution order under the Insolvency Act, ss 213 or 214, but no application has been made under the CDDA, s 6.[217]

---

[215] CDDA, s 9A(6)(a).

[216] CDDA, s 9A(7).

[217] In the early case of *Re Bath Glass Ltd* (1988) 4 BCC 130, 133 it was suggested that disqualification under s 10 is most likely to be ordered in a case where a claim for contribution is successfully made for a short period of wrongful trading and, as such, it is felt that a mandatory two-year disqualification is not justified. It is hard to envisage circumstances in which a court would be justified in adopting such a view, given the seriousness with which the courts view a director's failure to have regard to the interests of creditors when the company is in serious financial difficulties (paragraphs 28.132–28.141 below) and a director's responsibility for the company becoming insolvent and failing to provide goods or services (paragraphs 28.166–28.167 below).

*Undischarged bankrupt*

The CDDA, subs 11(1) provides that:　　　　　　　　　　　　　　　　　　**28.109**

It is an offence for a person to act as director of a company or directly or indirectly to take part in or be concerned in the promotion, formation or management of a company, without the leave of the court, at a time when—

(a) he is an undischarged bankrupt,
　　(aa) a moratorium period under a debt relief order applies in relation to him, or
(b) a bankruptcy restrictions order or a debt relief restrictions order is in force in respect of him.

The object of s 11(1)(a), as indicated by the report of the Greene Committee, was to prevent a person obtaining credit and the protection of limited liability for so long as he remained an undischarged bankrupt.[218] The prohibition in s 11(1) is, for this reason, automatic and a breach an 'offence'.

The 'offence' has been construed as a strict liability offence in accordance with the　**28.110** apparent purpose of the legislation. In *R v Brockley*, Henry LJ stated that:

Strict liability will oblige those who have been adjudicated bankrupt to ensure that their bankruptcy has, in fact, been discharged before they engage in any of the forbidden activities in relation to a company. If mens rea were required, then a bankrupt who lay low, buried his head in the sand, and took part in the prohibited activities, would have a defence and an advantage not available to the responsible bankrupt who took steps to establish his position before taking part in such activities.[219]

A careless failure by a bankrupt to enquire as to whether a particular course of activity is prohibited is accordingly irrelevant. The only option is to apply for leave.

Subsections 11(1)(a) and (b) reflect the current bankruptcy regime,[220] in which a　**28.111** person is entitled to automatic discharge from bankruptcy within one year, unless an application is made for an order that the discharge period shall cease to run, but may be subject to specific bankruptcy restrictions upon application of the Secretary of State.[221]

## (4) Disqualification for unfitness

*Duty of court to disqualify*

The CDDA subs 6(1) provides that:　　　　　　　　　　　　　　　　　　**28.112**

The court shall make a disqualification order against a person in any case where, on an application under this section, it is satisfied—

---

[218] Paras 56 and 57.
[219] [1994] 1 BCLC 606, 608, CA.
[220] Introduced by the Enterprise Act 2002, s 257(2) and Schedule 21, para 5, which came into effect on 1 April 2004.
[221] Insolvency Act, ss 279(1), 279(3), 281A, and Schedule 4A.

(a) that he is or has been a director of a company which has at any time become insolvent (whether while he was a director or subsequently), and

(b) that his conduct as a director of that company (either taken alone or taken together with his conduct as a director of any other company or companies) makes him unfit to be concerned in the management of a company.

The court accordingly has a *duty* to disqualify for at least two years anyone whose conduct as a director of a company which has become insolvent makes him unfit to be concerned in the management of a company.

**28.113**  Section 6 specifically applies to directors, including shadow directors.[222] It may also apply to de facto directors. Both types of director are discussed in Chapter 3 Section C(2) and (3).[223]

**28.114**  The first of these conditions, s 6(1)(a), is defined by s 6(2), which emphasizes the entry of the company into formal insolvency proceedings:

For the purposes of this section and the next, a company becomes insolvent if—

(a) the company goes into liquidation at a time when its assets are insufficient for the payment of its debts and other liabilities and the expenses of the winding up,

(b) the company enters administration, or

(c) an administrative receiver of the company is appointed.

The inability of the company to pay its debts is only relevant in the case of liquidation, which must be an insolvent liquidation. The relevant test is balance sheet rather than cash-flow, or commercial, insolvency, as indicated by 'its assets are insufficient for the payment of its debts and other liabilities and the expenses of the winding up'. The validity of the insolvency proceedings is not open to challenge in the disqualification proceedings.[224]

**28.115**  The second condition, s 6(1)(b), is also in part defined by s 6(2), which states that—

references to a person's conduct as a director of any company or companies include, where that company or any of those companies has become insolvent, that person's

---

[222] CDDA, s 6(3C).

[223] In the context of disqualification, see *Re Lo-line Electric Motors Ltd* [1988] Ch 477. The well known statement of Millett J as to the meaning of a de facto director (*Hydrodam (Corby) Ltd* [1994] 2 BCLC 180: 'A *de facto* director is a person who assumes to act as a director. He is held out as a director by the company and claims and purports to be a director, although never actually or validly appointed as such') was applied in *R H Laing Demolition Building Contractors Ltd* [1996] 2 BCLC 324. In *Re Richborough Furniture Ltd* [1996] 1 BCLC 507 Mr Timothy Lloyd QC, sitting as a deputy High Court judge doubted that the *Hydrodam* test was applicable in every case. He suggested that the court would require clear evidence that the person was either the sole person directing the affairs of the company, or on an equal footing with the others directing the company's affairs, and that if the position is unclear the defendant should be given the benefit of the doubt. In *Re Land Travel Ltd, Secretary of State for Trade and Industry v Tjolle* [1998] 1 BCLC 333 Jacob J said that the question was one of degree. Cases in which de facto directors have been disqualified include *Re Moorgate Metals Ltd, Official Receiver v Huhtala* [1995] 1 BCLC 503; *Re Sykes (Butchers) Ltd* [1998] 1 BCLC 110.

[224] *Secretary of State for Trade and Industry v Jabble* [1998] 1 BCLC 598, CA.

conduct in relation to any matter connected with or arising out of the insolvency of that company.

This focus on 'conduct in relation to any matter connected with or arising out of the insolvency of <u>that</u> company' has been articulated in the case law as a focus on conduct in relation to the 'lead' insolvent company to which conduct in relation to any 'collateral' company or companies may be relevant but is not itself sufficient to warrant disqualification under s 6(1) for unfitness. For it to be taken into account, the conduct in relation to any collateral company, or companies, must be relevant as evidence of unfitness but need not be the same as or similar to the conduct in relation to the lead company.[225] The duty to make a disqualification order is accordingly triggered upon satisfaction that the defendant's conduct in relation to the 'lead' company and any relevant conduct in connection with any 'collateral' company or companies 'makes him unfit to be concerned in the management of a company'.

The expression 'makes him unfit to be concerned in the management of a company' does not entitle the court to find a person is not unfit because, at the time of the hearing (a) he has demonstrated in some other way that he is not unfit, or (b) the evidence in that case only proves that his conduct was unfit in connection with the company in issue and not in relation to companies generally. In *Re Grayan Building Services Ltd*,[226] Arden J had held that proceedings under the Insolvency Act, s 239 had brought home to the company's former directors the consequences of granting a preference and that, despite serious shortcomings in their conduct, they were not unfit to be concerned in the management of a company. The Court of Appeal expressly rejected the construction of s 6(1) said to support this conclusion. Hoffmann LJ explained that—

**28.116**

> It is true that the subsection uses the present tense 'makes,' but . . . this means only that the court has to make the decision on the evidence put forward at the hearing . . . The court is concerned solely with the conduct specified by the Secretary of State or official receiver under rule 3(3) of the Insolvent Companies (Disqualification of Unfit Directors) Proceedings Rules 1987. It must decide whether that conduct, viewed cumulatively and taking into account any extenuating circumstances, has fallen below the standards of probity and competence appropriate for persons fit to be directors of companies.
>
> . . . If the court always had to be satisfied at the hearing that the protection of the public required a period of disqualification, there would be no need to make disqualification mandatory . . . The purpose of making disqualification mandatory was to ensure that everyone whose conduct had fallen below the appropriate standard was disqualified for at least two years, whether in the individual case the court

---

[225] *Secretary of State for Trade and Industry v Ivens* [1997] 2 BCLC 334, 338–9; affd [1997] 2 BCLC 359, 346, CA.
[226] [1995] Ch 241, CA.

thought that this was necessary in the public interest or not. Parliament has decided that it is occasionally necessary to disqualify a company director to encourage the others.[227]

**28.117**   A further attempt to construe s 6(1) as conferring some residual discretion was rejected in *Re Barings plc (No 5)*.[228] Jonathan Parker J held that the court is concerned only with the conduct of which complaint is made and not with whether the person is unfit to be concerned in the management of *any* company:

> In the context of an issue as to unfitness it is neither here nor there whether a respondent could have performed some other management role competently. That is not the test of 'unfitness' for the purposes of s 6 . . . Under s 6 the court is concerned only with the conduct in respect of which complaint is made, set in the context of the respondent's actual management role in the company. If in his conduct in that role the respondent was guilty of incompetence to the requisite degree, then a finding of unfitness will be made and (under s 6) a disqualification order must follow.[229]

**28.118**   The court accordingly only has 'discretion' under s 6(1) in deciding whether or not it is 'satisfied' that the defendant's conduct makes him unfit to be concerned in the management of a company. In this respect, a clear thread in the authorities is that 'whatever else is required of a respondent's misconduct if he is to be disqualified, it must at least be "serious".'[230] If it were otherwise, the trigger for mandatory disqualification might be satisfied by a mere breach of duty.

*Matters for determining unfitness*

**28.119**   The courts have not set out precise matters for determining unfitness, but the more recent cases indicate a concern to define more precisely the standard of probity and competence to which directors must adhere.

**28.120**   The case law prior to the introduction of mandatory disqualification under s 6(1) tended to emphasize some breach of the standards of 'commercial morality' as the badge of unfit conduct. In *Re Dawson Print Group Ltd*, in an application under the 1985 Act, s 300, Hoffmann J stated that:[231]

> There must, I think, be something about the case, some conduct which if not dishonest is at any rate in breach of standards of commercial morality, or some really gross incompetence which persuades the court that it would be a danger to the public if he were to be allowed to continue to be involved in the management of companies, before a disqualification order is made.

---

227   [1995] Ch 241, 253.
228   [1999] 1 BCLC 433.
229   [1999] 1 BCLC 433, 485.
230   *Re Polly Peck International plc (No 2)* [1994] 1 BCLC 574, 580.
231   [1987] BCLC 601, 604.

In *Re Lo-Line Electric Motors*, also in an application under the 1985 Act, s 300 Browne-Wilkinson J similarly considered that:

> The primary purpose of the section is not to punish the individual but to protect the public against the future conduct of companies by persons whose past records as directors of insolvent companies have shown them to be a danger to creditors and others. Therefore, the power is not fundamentally penal. But if the power to disqualify is exercised, disqualification does involve a substantial interference with the freedom of the individual. It follows that the rights of the individual must be fully protected. Ordinary commercial misjudgement is in itself not sufficient to justify disqualification. In the normal case, the conduct complained of must display a lack of commercial probity, although I have no doubt that in an extreme case of gross negligence or total incompetence disqualification could be appropriate.

This test may have been more appropriate in the context of the 1985 Act, s 300 and its predecessors, because statute did not then impose an obligation to disqualify a director found to be unfit.

**28.121** Following the enactment of s 6(1), the Court of Appeal, in *Re Sevenoaks Stationers (Retail) Ltd*,[232] however, objected to a gloss being placed upon the actual words of s 6(1). Dillon LJ considered that:

> [T]here seems to have been a tendency, which I deplore, on the part of the Bar, and possibly also on the part of the official receiver's department, to treat the statements as judicial paraphrases of the words of the statute, which fall to be construed as a matter of law in lieu of the words of the statute. The result is to obscure that the true question to be tried is a question of fact—what used to be pejoratively described in the Chancery Division as 'a jury question.'[233]

Descriptions of conduct as being in breach of 'commercial morality', or lacking in 'commercial probity', are accordingly 'helpful in identifying particular circumstances in which a person would clearly be unfit',[234] but are not a substitute for the statutory language, including Schedule 1.

**28.122** The decisions following *Sevenoaks* have not treated the question of unfitness as one of fact, but have instead emphasized the standards of probity and competence appropriate for persons fit to be directors of companies.

(1) In *Re Polly Peck International plc (No 2)*, Lindsay J rejected a submission to the effect that conduct was only relevant to s 6(1) if it breached some privilege of trading through a limited liability company, notwithstanding the previous (and continued) explanation of the purpose of s 6(1) in those terms:

> The Act itself suggests no such qualification and, by making consideration of breach of any duty by a director a matter to which regard is in particular to be

---

[232] [1991] Ch 164, CA.
[233] [1991] Ch 164, 176.
[234] Ibid.

paid by the courts (see s 9(1) of and Sch 1, Pt 1, para 1 to the 1986 Act), would seem to exclude it. There are duties, for example to apply the money of the undertaking only for the purposes of the undertaking, which would seem to me to be as applicable to, say, a partnership as to a limited company and in any event the definition of 'company' in the 1986 Act can include bodies not having limited liability: see s 22(3). I can think of few tasks less profitable in disqualification cases than an examination of whether a given shortcoming of a director could properly be said to be a consequence of or attendant upon the privilege of trading with limited liability.[235]

(2) In *Re Grayan Building Services Ltd*, as noted more fully above, Hoffmann LJ similarly considered that:

> The purpose of making disqualification mandatory was to ensure that everyone whose conduct had fallen below the appropriate standard was disqualified for at least two years, whether in the individual case the court thought that this was necessary in the public interest or not.[236]

(3) In *Secretary of State for Trade and Industry v Goldberg*, Lewison J moreover suggested a principled explanation for this approach:

> [T]he identification of the standard of conduct laid down by the law is important for two reasons. First, because the question of unfitness to do something can, as it seems to me, only be judged against an expectation of what is required of a person doing, or attempting to do, that thing. Secondly, because fairness to a director, or prospective director, requires that he should know what the law expects of him both before accepting his appointment and while carrying out his duties. I am uncomfortable with the notion that an honest director may be held to be unfit on account of conduct that, many years later, a judge may consider was a breach of some indefinable standard of commercial morality.[237]

On this basis, he accepted the submission of counsel that 'commercial morality' was not the relevant test to the extent that:

> [T]he court must be very careful before holding that a director is unfit because of conduct that does not amount to a breach of any duty (contractual, tortious, statutory or equitable) to anyone, and is not dishonest.[238]

**28.123** In this light, it is suggested that it is better to approach the question of unfitness by reference to the general duties imposed on directors as far as possible. Schedule 1 provides a convenient framework in this respect. This is not, of course, to say that matters not specified within Schedule 1 or not amounting to a breach of duty cannot trigger mandatory disqualification under s 6(1) in an appropriate case. Indeed, in *Re Amaron Ltd*, Neuberger J said that:

> [I]n setting out specific grounds in Sch I to the 1986 Act the legislature did not intend other grounds capable, on appropriate facts, of being inherently more culpable

---

[235] [1994] BCLC 574, 579.
[236] [1995] Ch 241, 253.
[237] [2004] 1 BCLC 597, para 42.
[238] Ibid, para 43.

than, on other facts, some of the grounds set out in the schedule, to be of less importance. It seems to me that one takes each allegation of unfitness on its merits and
considers it, irrespective of whether it falls within Sch I or not.[239]

The problem, however, is that, at present, the connection between the law on
disqualification and the general duties imposed on directors is not precisely clear.
As such, it is difficult to advise directors how they should conduct themselves to
discharge their general duties and avoid disqualification should the company
become insolvent.

The approach adopted here is consistent with subsection 9(1), which provides **28.124**
that:

> Where it falls to a court to determine whether a person's conduct as a director . . . of
> any particular company or companies makes him unfit to be concerned in the man-
> agement of a company, the court shall, as respects his conduct as a director of that
> company or, as the case may be, each of those companies, have regard in particular—
>
> (a) to the matters mentioned in Part I of Schedule 1 to this Act, and
> (b) where the company has become insolvent, to the matters mentioned in Part II of
>     that Schedule;
> and references in that Schedule to the director and the company are to be read
> accordingly.

The paragraphs of Schedule 1 are set out under sub-headings (c) to (l) below.

In reviewing this area, it should be kept in mind that the courts have been careful **28.125**
not to adopt too strict an approach to the question of unfitness because of hindsight. In *Re Living Images Ltd*, Laddie J explained that, with the benefit of knowing that the company became insolvent—

> It is very easy therefore to look at the signals available to the directors at the time and
> to assume that they, or any other competent director, would have realised that the
> end was coming. The court must be careful not to fall into the trap of being too wise
> after the event.[240]

This does not mean that latitude is accorded to directors but merely that the court
is likely to approach each charge with caution, especially in cases which involve
assessment of the quality of judgements made in the course of business.

### *Misfeasance, breach of duty*

Schedule 1, Part I, para 1 requires the court to have regard to '[a]ny misfeasance or **28.126**
breach of any fiduciary or other duty by the director in relation to the company'.

---

[239] [2001] 1 BCLC 562, 568; and *Re Migration Services International Ltd* [2000] 1 BCLC 666,
677–8, in which Neuberger J accepted that Schedule 1 may have been intended to draw to the attention of directors their positive duties.
[240] [1996] 1 BCLC 348, 356c.

**28.127**  This matter adopts language used in the Insolvency Act, s 212 (summary remedy against delinquent directors, liquidators, etc) and may overlap with every other matter to which the court is to have regard in Schedule 1. It contains three elements:

(1)  breach of fiduciary duty by the director in relation to the company,

(2)  breach of any other duty by the director in relation to the company, and

(3)  any misfeasance by the director in relation to the company.

This division reflects the generally accepted distinction between the fiduciary and other duties of a director and the fact that 'misfeasance' must mean something other than a breach of duty if it is to have any separate sense. Since the CDDA was enacted the general duties of a director to a company have been codified by the 2006 Act, ss 171–177. The following paragraphs consider the disqualification cases on breach of duty under the headings of the codified general duties.

### (i)  Breach of fiduciary duty

**28.128**  *Failure to act in accordance with the company's constitution, s 171(a).*  A failure to act in accordance with the company's constitution contrary to the 2006 Act, s 171(a) is less likely to be a sufficient basis for disqualification than other matters and is more likely to form part of a charge of incompetence or some other more specific matter which necessarily involves a breach of the company's constitution. The decision in *Re Samuel Sherman plc*[241] is arguably a rare example of a case in which a finding of unfitness under s 8 was justified on the basis of an act falling outside the proper scope of the company's objects. In that case, the director of 'a ladies' garments' company had invested the proceeds of the sale of its stock and premises in a speculative oil and gas venture. The conduct was *ultra vires*, but the true complaint appears to have been the unsuitability of the investment in the circumstances, specifically that it was not readily realizable should its value fall, it carried a liability to put up further funds, and it was effected without recourse to shareholders.[242] To the extent similar facts might now occur,[243] the case might more readily be seen as one of incompetent management, the failure to consult the company in general meeting in relation to an important decision being a particularly serious allegation.

**28.129**  *Failure to exercise powers for the purposes for which they are conferred, s 171(b).*  A failure to exercise a power for its proper purpose is similarly less likely to be a

---

[241]  [1991] 1 WLR 1070.

[242]  Ibid, 1078.

[243]  Under 1985 Act, s 3A (which came into effect on 4 February 1991) a company whose objects are stated to be those of a general trading company has power to carry on any trade or business whatsoever. Under 2006 Act, s 31(1) the objects of a company are now unlimited unless specifically cut-down and, as such, any constitutional limit is likely now to flow from the articles of association only.

sufficient basis for disqualification unless the conduct can be characterized as abusive. The sale of an asset at undervalue, for example, may variously constitute a breach of the duty to promote the success of the company for the benefit of its members, or, where the company is of doubtful solvency, its creditors as well as a failure to properly exercise the power of sale. In such a case, it is the prejudice caused by the transaction and any benefit derived by the director which drives the case for disqualification, but, in an appropriate case, the abuse of a corporate power may itself be sufficient.

In this respect, the decision in *Re Looe Fish Ltd*[244] is significant because it underlines the concern to enforce a particular standard of conduct through disqualification. In that case, the director abused the power to allot shares, so as to defeat attempts by a rival faction among the members to gain control of the board, and caused the company to breach the prohibition on a company acquiring its own shares under the 1985 Act, s 143. Jonathan Parker J did not regard the contravention of s 143 as sufficiently serious to warrant disqualification on the ground of unfitness under s 8 notwithstanding the explanation of that section in terms of providing protection to creditors.[245] He did, however, consider the abuse of the power to allot shares sufficient:

**28.130**

> As to unfitness, I find that in using the power to allot shares in the way he did, Mr Soady displayed a clear lack of commercial probity. He allowed his concern to keep the Cairns group from obtaining control of the company to lead him to abuse his power as a director to allot shares in the company. It is not enough for him to say that he did what he did in the best interests of LFL as he saw them. A director who chooses deliberately to play fast and loose with his powers, as Mr Soady has done in this case, in order to remain in control of the company's affairs, is in my judgment unfit to be concerned in the management of a company, and it is expedient in the public interest that a disqualification order be made against him.[246]

This was so even though there was 'no question of insolvency' and the director 'did not act out of motives of personal gain, nor did he receive any improper benefit'.[247] The reason for disqualification in *Re Looe Fish Ltd* was accordingly the abuse of a corporate power to subvert the ordinary balance of power within the company.[248] Assessed in this light, the abuse of a corporate power may be sufficient to warrant mandatory disqualification whether or not some benefit is derived by the director, or prejudice caused to creditors. As Lord Wilberforce recognized, '[s]elf-interest is only one, though no doubt the commonest, instance of improper motive'.[249]

---

[244] [1993] BCLC 1160.
[245] Cf *Trevor v Whitworth* (1887) 12 App Cas 409, HL.
[246] [1993] BCLC 1160, 1172.
[247] Ibid, 1172f.
[248] Cf *Howard Smith Ltd v Ampol Petroleum Ltd* [1974] AC 821, 837e–838b, HL.
[249] Ibid, 834h.

**28.131** *Failure to act in the way he considers, in good faith, would be most likely to promote the success of the company for the benefit of its members as a whole, s 172.* The set of specific duties flowing from the general duty under s 172 is not closed[250] and, as such, the matters falling within this category of case are numerous; but Schedule 1 separates out more obvious examples such as the misapplication of company property, and these are considered under separate headings. As such, cases in which a disqualification order is made purely on the basis of a breach of the general duty under s 172 alone are likely to be relatively rare. In *Re JA Chapman & Co Ltd*,[251] for example, the director of an insurance brokerage company had caused it to 'gross up' premiums notified to assureds, thereby enabling it to benefit from the difference between the premium received and the true premium paid to the underwriter. This decision resulted in an immediate benefit to the company because it received income in addition to its commission, but, being contrary to accepted market practice, it ultimately resulted in expulsion from Lloyds and insolvency. It was a decision no rational company director could have made in good faith and warranted disqualification under s 8 on the ground of unfitness.

**28.132** *Failure to consider or act in the interests of creditors of the company where the company is in serious financial difficulty.* As set out in Chapter 11, directors owe a duty, where the company is insolvent or of doubtful solvency (a) to take into account the interests of creditors, and (b) to direct the company in a way compatible with the requirements of the Insolvency Act, ss 214, 238, 239, and 423. A failure to comply with these general duties may result in mandatory disqualification under s 6(1) and, in this respect, cases in which disqualification has been justified on the ground of trading while insolvent to the detriment of creditors may be regarded as particular examples of the standard of conduct to which company directors must abide where the company is insolvent or where its solvency is doubtful. The detail of the disqualification case is, however, important because, in the context of disqualification, the courts have identified certain features which aggravate a breach of those general duties and which may constitute grounds for disqualification beyond those general duties.

**28.133** The following three propositions, in particular, emerge from cases in which disqualification has been sought on the basis that the company traded while insolvent to the detriment of creditors:

(1) A director will not normally be at risk of a finding of unfitness, such as to lead automatically to disqualification, merely because he knowingly allows the company to trade while insolvent.[252]

---

[250] *Item Software (UK) Ltd v Fasshi* [2005] 2 BCLC 91, 103–4, CA.

[251] [2003] 2 BCLC 206.

[252] *Re Uno plc* [2006] BCC 725 at para 144; *Secretary of State for Trade and Industry v Creegan* [2002] 1 BCLC 99, 101, CA; *Secretary of State for Trade and Industry v Gash* [1997] 1 BCLC 341.

(2) A director will normally only be at risk of a finding of unfitness sufficient to warrant automation disqualification where, at the time credit is taken by the company, he knows or should know that there is no reasonable prospect of the company avoiding insolvency.[253]

(3) A director will exceptionally be at risk of a finding of unfitness sufficient to warrant automatic disqualification where, notwithstanding that he reasonably believed that the company could avoid insolvency, he is responsible for some other misconduct which, in the circumstances, renders him unfit.[254] That misconduct would ordinarily involve dishonesty, want of commercial probity, or a display of incompetence to a marked degree.[255]

The 'other misconduct' referred to in proposition (3) is typically some form of 'unfair discrimination' against a particular creditor or, more usually, against a particular class of creditors such as the Crown or customers who have made prepayments or deposits for goods or services. In such cases, the company continues to pay its other creditors at the expense of the Crown or its customers and for its own benefit.

**28.134** The above propositions flow from the decision of Blackburne J in *Re Uno plc*,[256] in which the judge considered a charge of unfitness where the directors caused or allowed the companies to continue trading at the risk of customers, who paid deposits against orders for goods, at a time when the companies were insolvent but had a reasonable prospect of avoiding insolvency proceedings.

**28.135** Prior to the decision in *Re Uno plc*, the courts appeared to apply two alternative tests to determine unfitness in cases where a company had traded to the detriment of its creditors. The first test is closely analogous to the test for civil liability for wrongful trading under the Insolvency Act, s 214 in which the court focused on whether (a) the director knew or ought to have concluded that there was no reasonable prospect that the company would avoid becoming insolvent, and (b) he had taken every step with a view to minimizing the potential loss to creditors he ought to have taken.[257] Under the second test the court asked, more broadly, whether the company had taken an unwarranted risk with creditors' money by

---

[253] *Re Uno plc* [2006] BCC 725 at para 144; *Secretary of State for Trade and Industry v Creegan* [2002] 1 BCLC 99, 101, CA; *Re Sevenoaks (Stationers) Ltd* [1991] Ch 164; and *Re Bath Glass Ltd* [1988] 4 BCC 130, 133–4.

[254] *Re Uno plc* [2006] BCC 725 at paras 145–149; *Re Structural Concrete Ltd* [2001] BCC 578; *Secretary of State for Trade and Industry v McTighe* [1997] BCC 224; *Re Sevenoaks (Stationers) Ltd* [1991] Ch 164; and *Re Bath Glass Ltd* [1988] 4 BCC 130, 133–4.

[255] *Re Uno plc* [2006] BCC 725 at para 153, where Blackburne J applied *Re Grayan Building Services Ltd* [1995] Ch 241, 253, CA.

[256] [2006] BCC 725 at para 140.

[257] *Secretary of State for Trade and Industry v Creegan* [2002] 1 BCLC 99, 101, CA; *Re Cubelock Ltd* [2001] BCC 523; and *Secretary of State for Trade and Industry v Gash* [1997] 1 BCLC 341, 348–9.

continuing to trade.[258] The second test is difficult to apply because it leaves at large the question of what makes a risk 'unwarranted'; the answer to which, by definition, has to pick out conduct that cannot be characterized as a failure to take every step a director ought to have taken in circumstances in which he knew or ought to have concluded there was no reasonable prospect that the company could avoid becoming insolvent.

28.136    The value of the decision in *Re Uno plc* is that it focuses on specific features of insolvent trading which put a director at risk of disqualification for unfitness notwithstanding a reasonable belief that the company will not become insolvent. In paragraphs 144 to 149 of his judgment, Blackburne J stated that:

> [144] [A] director will not be at risk of a finding of unfitness, such as to lead automatically to disqualification, merely because he knowingly allows the company to trade while insolvent, ie he allows the company to incur credit (including, I would add, accepting a payment from a customer in advance of the supply of the relevant goods or service) even though, at the time and as he knows, the company is insolvent and later goes into liquidation. It does not add anything to the proposition to say that, in causing the company to incur credit (or accept payment in advance of the supply of the goods or service), the director was 'taking advantage' of the third party in question. In a sense, every company which incurs credit when, as its director knows or ought to know, it is insolvent, is 'taking advantage' of the third party supplier of credit. If the director is to be found unfit there must ordinarily be an additional ingredient. Normally that ingredient is that, at the time that the credit is taken (or the advance payment received, which is in essence the same), the director knows or should know that there is no reasonable prospect of his company avoiding insolvency . . .

> [145] But . . . as the court in *Creegan* recognised, it is not the case that, merely because at the time in question the directors reasonably believed that the company could avoid insolvency, they can escape a finding of unfitness in consequence of having allowed the company to trade while insolvent . . .

> [147] The vice of their conduct was in deliberately allowing the company's liability to the Revenue to mount while using the monies thereby saved (ie the tax deducted from its self-employed operatives) to pay its other creditors . . . without taking any steps to secure the Revenue's agreement to the delayed payment of its mounting debt. They did so in circumstances where, if at any time and as eventually happened, demand was made for payment of the debt, the company had no means of payment, and an insolvent liquidation was bound to ensue. (Emphasis added.)

---

[258] *Re Verby Print for Advertising Ltd* [1998] 2 BCLC 23, 27–8; *Re City Pram and Toy Co Ltd* [1998] BCC 537, 539; *Re Moonlight Foods (UK) Ltd* [1996] BCC 678, 692; *Re Richborough Furniture Ltd* [1996] 1 BCLC 507, 517; *Re Living Images Ltd* [1996] 1 BCLC 348, 359; and *Re Synthetic Technology Ltd* [1993] BCC 549, 562.

It is possible to identify further aggravating features in cases where an insolvent **28.137** company trades to the detriment of its creditors, namely:[259]

(1) unfair treatment of particular creditors;

(2) the abuse of successive 'phoenix' companies, whether or not that abuse also amounts to a breach by the director of the prohibition under the Insolvency Act, s 216;[260] and

(3) the incorporation of an undercapitalized company in circumstances in which insolvent failure is both foreseeable and likely.

The above features might also properly include the accepting of deposits or pre-payments at a time when the company was without a reasonable prospect of avoiding insolvency, or the grant of a preferential payment, or the execution of a transaction at undervalue. These matters are set out at paragraphs 28.168 to 28.174 because Schedule 1 draws specific attention to them.

*Re Synthetic Technology Ltd*,[261] which was the originator of the test of 'the taking of **28.138** unwarranted risks with creditors' money by continuing to trade', is an example of a case where unfair treatment of creditors by an insolvent company with a reasonable prospect of avoiding insolvency proceedings meant that the director responsible was unfit. In that case, the judge could not have held that the company had traded wrongfully in a way analogous to the Insolvency Act, s 214 because the company's business had been purchased from a company in administration whose administrators had produced a favourable report as to 'the rosy prospects' of the business's future success.[262] The deputy judge nevertheless found the director unfit, because he had not merely permitted the company to continue to trade whilst it was insolvent, but had done so unfairly at the expense of the Crown:

> [T]he company under the management of Mr Joiner exploited the Crown together with the company's other creditors by deliberately pursuing a policy of only paying at the last minute those creditors which were pressing, which the Crown together with the bulk of the company's other creditors were not at the material time doing or not with sufficient persistence.[263]

---

[259] *Official Receiver v Stern (No 2)* [2002] 1 BCLC 119; *Re Windows West Ltd* [2002] BCC 760; *Secretary of State for Trade and Industry v Ivens* [1997] 2 BCLC 334, CA; *Re Swift 736 Ltd* [1993] BCLC 896; *Re Linval Ltd* [1993] BCLC 654; *Re Travel Mondial Ltd* [1991] BCC 224; and *Re Ipcon Fashions Ltd* [1989] BCC 773.

[260] A breach of the Insolvency Act, s 216 restricting the use of former company names is a discrete but related ground for disqualification: *Re Skyward Builders plc* [2002] 2 BCLC 750; *Re Migration Services International Ltd* [2000] 1 BCLC 666.

[261] [1993] BCC 549, 562d–e.

[262] Ibid, 563a–c. The judge indicated his 'surprise' at the administrator's report, surmising that they had been 'over-influenced' by the director's prediction that the company would be able to obtain a share of an anticipated increase in the worldwide market for the company's product.

[263] Ibid, 562g–h. The deputy judge followed Dillon LJ in *Re Sevenoaks (Stationers) Ltd* [1991] Ch 164, 183e.

**28.139**  The abuse of successive 'phoenix' companies emerges as a distinct reason for disqualification and not merely as a feature of certain wrongful trading cases. In *Re Windows West Ltd*, Gabriel Moss QC, sitting as a deputy judge of the High Court, explained the problem of phoenix companies in these terms:

> Although 'phoenix' companies are often a menace to the public, I would introduce one note of caution. There are also honest phoenix companies where a failure has occurred through no fault of the management and the business has been rescued into a successor company in the interests of creditors and the public. The 'bad' phoenix company is by contrast characterised by the selfish and dishonest behaviour of the management in looking after their own interests and ignoring those of the creditors and/or the public.[264]

The focus of the court's inquiry is accordingly the abuse by a director of limited liability trading, notwithstanding that the incorporation of a 'phoenix' company is not unlawful.

**28.140**  The incorporation of an undercapitalized company is similarly not necessarily wrongful as there is no general capital adequacy requirement in English law,[265] but it may be improper where failure is likely and any trading can only be at the expense of creditors. In *Re Rolus Properties Ltd*, Harman J considered 'the mere fact that the company had been formed and had embarked with small capital upon a speculative venture would not by itself warrant criticism',[266] but, in the subsequent case of *Re Chartmore Ltd*, he regarded it as significant that the company's 'substantial capital liability was not met with any proper capital provision'.[267] In that case, the company had purchased the assets of the director's father's insolvent company and, in so doing, incurred a liability which could *only* be met by the funds of the company's general creditors because no other capital had been introduced.

**28.141**  *Using the company as a vehicle for fraud.*  There have been many disqualification cases arising out of the use of a company as a vehicle for fraud, or the commission of a fraud in the course of its business.[268] In such a case, the company is itself likely to be liable to the creditors or other persons who have been defrauded, and the directors responsible will have breached their fiduciary duties to the company.

---

[264]  [2002] BCC 760 at para 13.

[265]  A minimum capital requirement exists in relation to a public company, and a failure to comply with this is likely to be regarded as serious: see *Secretary of State for Trade and Industry v Hollier* [2007] BCC 11, a case under s 8 in which the defendant had traded wrongfully and in breach of the minimum capital requirement; *Re Kaytech International plc* [1999] 2 BCLC 351, CA, in which the defendant had falsely stated the paid-up capital of the company.

[266]  [1988] 4 BCC 446, 447.

[267]  [1990] BCLC 673, 675.

[268]  *Secretary for State for Trade and Industry v Kappler* [2008] 1 BCLC 120; *Re City Truck Group Ltd* [2007] 2 BCLC 649; *Re Vintage Hallmark plc* [2007] 1 BCLC 788; *Re Bunting Electric Manufacturing Co Ltd* [2005] EWHC 3345 (Ch); and *Official Receiver v Doshi* [2001] 2 BCLC 235.

But any such breach of fiduciary duty will not be the underlying reason for disqualification: it is the commission of that fraud which renders that person unfit to
be a director.

*Failure to exercise independent judgment, s 173.*   A failure to exercise independent    **28.142**
judgement may warrant mandatory justification under s 6(1), but it is necessary
to examine carefully the circumstances of the failure, in particular, the responsibilities with which the director was tasked in conjunction with the responsibilities
of other directors, individual and collective.[269] The particular problems encountered in the cases are the dominance of the board of directors by an individual
director, the minimum participation required of a company director, and the
failure of a director to take proper responsibility for a duty delegated to another.
The extent of this duty is considered in Chapter 12.

*Failure to avoid a conflict of interest and duty, s 175.*   A failure to avoid a conflict    **28.143**
of interest and duty alone may be sufficient to warrant disqualification under
s 6(1). In *Re Park House Properties Ltd*, Neuberger J explained that 'even on its
own' the conflict of interest and duty in that case warranted mandatory disqualification.[270] The scope of this duty is considered in Chapter 14.

*Failure to refuse a benefit from a third party conferred by reason of his being a director,*    **28.144**
*or his doing (or not doing) anything as director, s 176.*   The receipt of a secret profit
or a bribe is very likely to warrant disqualification under s 6(1) because such a
breach of duty is generally regarded as a more serious breach of duty than a conflict
of interest and duty. The scope of this duty is also considered in Chapter 14.

*Failure to declare an interest in a proposed transaction or arrangement, s 177.*    **28.145**
A failure by a director to declare an interest in a proposed transaction or arrangement may warrant mandatory disqualification under s 6(1).[271] The extent of this
duty is considered in Chapter 15.

### (ii)  Breach of the duty to exercise reasonable care, skill, and diligence, s 174
The one general duty which is not classified as a fiduciary duty is the duty to exer-    **28.146**
cise reasonable care, skill, and diligence. A serious failure by a director to exercise
reasonable care, skill, and diligence contrary to what is now the 2006 Act, s 174
may warrant disqualification under s 6(1). This duty is considered in Chapter 13.

---

[269] *Re AG Manchester Ltd* [2008] BCC 497, in which the judge highlighted the particular
responsibilities of a finance director at para 183 of his judgment; *Re Landhurst Leasing plc* [1999] 1
BCLC 286; *Re Barings plc (No 5)* [1999] 1 BCLC 433; affd [2000] 1 BCLC 523, CA; *Re Westmid
Packing Services Ltd* [1998] 2 All ER 124, CA; *Re Polly Peck International plc (No 2)* [1994] 1
BCLC 574.
[270] [1997] 2 BCLC 530, 551.
[271] *Re Dominion International Group plc (No2)* [1996] 1 BCLC 572; *Re Godwin Warren Control
Systems plc* [1993] BCLC 80; and *Re Tansoft Ltd* [1991] BCLC 339.

**28.147**    The courts have held that unfitness by reason of incompetence may be established even without proof of a breach of duty, but such a finding is unlikely where the application is not supported by some other matter, such as unfair discrimination against a creditor or class of creditor. In *Secretary of State for Trade and Industry v Goldberg*, Lewison J accepted that the general duty as now stated in s 174 represented '[t]he general standard of competence that the law requires of a director'[272] and that '[i]ncompetence in 'a marked degree' is enough to render a person unfit'[273] but he considered himself bound by the decisions in *Re Bath Glass Ltd* and *Re Barings (No 5)* to the extent 'that unfitness by reason of incompetence may be established even without proof of a breach of duty'. [274] Lewison J nonetheless considered that—

> [T]he question of unfitness to do something can . . . only be judged against an expectation of what is required of a person doing, or attempting to do, that thing . . . [T]he court must be very careful before holding that a director is unfit because of conduct that does not amount to a breach of any duty (contractual, tortious, statutory or equitable) to anyone, and is not dishonest.[275]

**28.148**    In this light, disqualification on the basis of incompetence is to be approached by asking (a) whether the director breached his duty of care, skill, and diligence, or, exceptionally, whether some other misconduct is present which justifies a finding of incompetence, and (b) whether, in all the circumstances, that breach of duty or other misconduct is sufficiently serious to warrant a finding of unfitness. The second condition is particularly important because the overriding question is whether incompetence is such that the director should not be concerned in the management of a company.

**28.149**    The cases in which a director has been disqualified for incompetence are accordingly varied and tend to overlap substantially with other, more specific grounds, such as the failure to maintain and file proper accounts and returns, because allegations of failure are often accumulated to support a finding of sufficiently serious incompetence. The more discrete complaints have included complete inactivity amounting to a total abrogation of responsibility,[276] a failure to ensure that the company received a debt due to it from the sale of its assets,[277] a failure to

---

[272] [2004] 1 BCLC 597 at para 19. Lewison J in fact approved the law then stated in *Re D'Jan of London Ltd* [1994] 1 BCLC 561, 563 which phrased the standard of competence in terms equivalent to the Insolvency Act, s 214 and which has since been endorsed by the legislature under 2006 Act, s 174.

[273] Ibid at para 21; and *Re Sevenoaks Stationers (Retail) Ltd* [1991] Ch 164, 184.

[274] *Secretary of State for Trade and Industry v Goldberg* [2004] 1 BCLC 597 at para 28; *Re Barings plc (No 5)* [1999] 1 BCLC 433, 486; affd [2000] 1 BCLC 523, CA; and *Re Bath Glass Ltd* [1988] 4 BCC 130, 133–4.

[275] *Secretary of State for Trade and Industry v Goldberg* [2004] 1 BCLC 597 at para 43.

[276] *Re Kaytech International plc* [1999] 2 BCLC 351, CA; and *Re Westmid Packing Services Ltd* [1998] 2 All ER 124, CA.

[277] *Re Tansoft Ltd* [1991] BCLC 339.

adequately value and capitalize the business of a target company,[278] seriously flawed judgements and valuations in relation to commercial transactions,[279] the advance of a loan to a related company which had no prospect of repayment,[280] the sale of the company's business on deferred terms without security,[281] a failure to introduce and operate appropriate financial and other controls in the management of the company's business,[282] and a failure to properly monitor the carrying on of delegated activities which caused the insolvency of the company.[283]

In assessing the competence of a director, in line with the approach taken to assessing a breach of the general duty of care, higher standards of conduct are expected from more experienced directors and those having or professing competence in a particular area, for example a finance director.[284]     **28.150**

### (iii) Misfeasance

Misfeasance probably has the same meaning as it has in the Insolvency Act, s 212.     **28.151**
It covers breach of trust,[285] but also extends to other acts or omissions which contravene substantive rules of company law or insolvency law. Examples of contraventions of company law that might involve misfeasance on the part of the directors responsible are (a) failure to declare an interest in an existing transaction or arrangement as required by the 2006 Act, s 182, (b) failure to obtain approval of members to transactions with directors as required by the 2006 Act, and (c) making distributions out of capital in contravention of the 2006 Act, Part 23.[286] Making a preference within the Insolvency Act, s 239 is a misfeasance on the part of the director responsible.[287]

*Misapplication of company property*

Schedule 1, Part I, para 2 requires the court to have regard to any misapplication     **28.152**
or retention by the director of, or any conduct by the director giving rise to an

---

[278] *Re City Investment Centres Ltd* [1992] BCLC 956; *Re Austinsuite Furniture Ltd* [1992] BCLC 1047.

[279] *Re Aldermanbury Trust plc* [1993] BCC 598.

[280] *Re Continental Assurance Co of London plc* [1997] 1 BCLC 48.

[281] *Secretary of State v McTighe* [1996] 2 BCLC 477.

[282] *Re Landhurst Leasing plc* [1999] 1 BCLC 286.

[283] *Re Barings plc (No 5)* [1999] 1 BCLC 433; affirmed [2000] 1 BCLC 523, CA.

[284] *Re Barings plc (No 5)* [1999] 1 BCLC 433, 483–4; affirmed [2000] 1 BCLC 523, CA; and *Re Continental Assurance of London plc* [1997] 1 BCLC 48, but cf *Secretary of State for Trade and Industry v Thornbury* [2008] 1 BCLC 139 at para 36 which regarded *Continental Assurance* as merely supporting the more general proposition that a '[l]ack of financial awareness or of a basic obligation to familiarise oneself with the company's financial position is no defence' to a charge of unfitness.

[285] *Coventry and Dixon's Case* (1880) 14 Ch D 660, 670, CA.

[286] *Re National Funds Assurance Co* (1878) 10 Ch D 118, CA; *Re Exchange Banking Co* (1882) 32 Ch D 149, CA; *Re National Bank of Wales* [1899] 2 Ch 629, CA.

[287] *Re Washington Diamond Mining Co* [1893] 3 Ch 95; *Re West Mercia Safetywear Ltd* [1988] BCLC 250, CA.

obligation to account for, any money or other property of the company. This paragraph also adopts language used the Insolvency Act, s 212.

**28.153**  There is an obvious overlap between this matter and a breach of fiduciary duty specified in paragraph 1, but allegations of misappropriation have tended to be framed as a separate matter, reflecting the seriousness of the misconduct.[288] In *Secretary of State for Trade and Industry v Blunt*, the judge explained that:

> Misappropriation by a director is always serious. Creditors would legitimately feel aggrieved at others, particularly those responsible for the management of the company, benefiting at their expense. A deliberate and conscious decision to benefit oneself unlawfully from assets that a person knows do not belong to him is entirely unacceptable. It is a very serious allegation in respect of which disqualification is entirely justified.[289]

**28.154**  This matter would also seem to properly include a payment of excessive remuneration[290] because, although no theft is involved, the payment of excessive remuneration is a 'misapplication' of company money or property and, as such, gives rise to an obligation to account. In *Re Melcast (Wolverhampton) Ltd*, Harman J described the requisite misconduct in the following terms:

> [T]he remuneration . . . cannot be said . . . to amount to conduct which, to put it vulgarly, is often called living 'high on the hog' at the expense of creditors. There is no suggestion . . . that the directors feathered their own nests, ran large and expensive cars, had a great deal of expensive entertaining, or pocketed large salaries on the back of the company. They do not appear to have done any of those things and this is not that sort of case at all. It is a case of gross mismanagement, of complete ignoring of the proper responsibilities of directors, and of shutting their eyes to the proper liabilities attached to the company rather than anything of a dishonest character in the sense of conduct for their own personal financial benefit.[291]

In this way, the test applied by the courts in the disqualification cases is in line with the guidance given as to the appropriate level of remuneration that might be authorized in good faith in the absence of divisible profits.[292]

*Transactions defrauding creditors*

**28.155**  Schedule 1, Part I, paragraph 3 requires the court to have regard to the extent of the director's responsibility for the company entering into any transaction liable

---

[288] *Secretrary of State for Trade and Industry v Blunt* [2005] 2 BCLC 463; *Official Receiver v Stern (No 2)* [2002] 1 BCLC 119, CA; *Re Park House Properties Ltd* [1998] BCC 847; *Re Living Images Ltd* [1996] BCC 112; *Re Continental Assurance Co of London plc* [1997] 1 BCLC 48; *Re Tansoft Ltd* [1991] BCLC 339.

[289] [2005] 2 BCLC 463 at para 23.

[290] *Re A & C Group Services Ltd* [1993] BCLC 1297; *Re Synthetic Technology Ltd* [1993] BCC 549; *Re Cargo Agency Ltd* [1992] BCLC 686; *Re Melcast (Wolverhampton) Ltd* [1991] BCLC 288; *Re McNulty's Interchange Ltd* [1989] BCLC 709; *Re Ipcon Fashions Ltd* [1989] BCC 773.

[291] [1991] BCLC 288, 291.

[292] *Re Halt Garage (1964) Ltd* [1982] 3 All ER 1016, 1038j–1039h.

to be set aside under the Insolvency Act, s 423. What make a transaction contrary to s 423 is considered at Chapter 29, Section K(4).

The courts have not considered this paragraph in any detail, but in *Re Diamond Computer Systems Ltd*, Jules Sher QC, sitting as a deputy judge of the High Court, indicated that a transaction contrary to s 423 would be sufficient to warrant disqualification:  **28.156**

> The official receiver's complaint is that all these transactions took place at a time when Mr Brown and Mr Ballan knew that Diamond was insolvent and that the freehold properties were transferred for the purpose of putting them beyond the reach of Diamond's creditors other than Direction. If these complaints are made out at trial, Mr Brown will be shown to be guilty of misconduct as a director of Diamond.[293]

The question of law the court is most likely to have to resolve in such a case is what is meant by the 'extent of the director's responsibility'. It is suggested that the approach in *Re Living Images Ltd*, discussed below at paragraphs 28.172–28.173, should be followed in such a case, the requirements of s 423 being closely analogous to those of the Insolvency Act, s 238.

*Failure to comply with record keeping and reporting requirements under the Companies Acts*

Schedule 1, Part I, para 4 requires the court to have regard to the extent of the director's responsibility for any failure by the company to comply with provisions of the Companies Acts concerning (a) keeping accounting records,[294] (b) where and for how long accounting records should be kept,[295] (c) the register of directors and secretaries,[296] (d) the obligation to keep up and enter up the register of its members,[297] (e) the location of the register of members,[298] (f) the duty of the company to make annual returns,[299] and (g) the duty of the company to register charges it creates.[300] The case law in relation to this paragraph is set out below. A failure to keep accounting records, maintain registers, and file annual returns and other documents is treated in the same way as a failure to comply with duty  **28.157**

---

[293] [1997] 1 BCLC 174, 178.

[294] As required by 1985 Act, s 221 (replaced by 2006 Act, s 386 with effect from 6 April 2008).

[295] As required by 1985 Act, s 222 (replaced by 2006 Act, s 388 with effect from 6 April 2008).

[296] As required by 1985 Act, s 288 (to be replaced by 2006 Act, ss 162, 167, 275, and 276 with effect from 1 October 2009).

[297] As required by 1985 Act, s 352 (to be replaced by 2006 Act, ss 113, 121, and 128(1) on 1 October 2009).

[298] As required by 1985 Act, s 353 (to be replaced by 2006 Act, s 114 on 1 October 2009).

[299] As required by 1985 Act, s 353 (to be replaced by 2006 Act, ss 854 and 858 on 1 October 2009).

[300] As required by 1985 Act, ss 399 and 415 (to be replaced by 2006 Act, ss 860, 863(5), 878, 882(5) on 1 October 2009).

to prepare, approve, and sign annual accounts under the Companies Act as each impact on the ability of others to protect themselves in their dealings with the company.

*Failure to comply with accounting requirements under the Companies Acts*

**28.158**  Schedule 1 Part I, para 5 requires the court to have regard to the extent of the director's responsibility for any failure by the directors of the company to comply with (a) the duty to prepare annual individual accounts,[301] (b) the duty to prepare annual group accounts,[302] and (c) the duty to have the annual accounts approved and signed.[303]

**28.159**  The failure to maintain accounting records in accordance with the statutory rules is a matter of complaint present in a large number of disqualification cases.[304] It is treated as a serious failure and not a mere 'venial sin'.[305] In *Re Firedart Ltd*, Arden J explained that:

> When directors do not maintain accounting records in accordance with the very specific requirements of s 221 of the Companies Act 1985, they cannot know their company's financial position with accuracy. There is therefore a risk that the situation is much worse than they know and that creditors will suffer in consequence. Directors who permit this situation to arise must expect the conclusion to be drawn in an appropriate case that they are in consequence not fit to be concerned in the management of a company.[306]

Arden J also made clear that a director cannot necessary avoid responsibility for failure to maintain accounting records on the basis that their preparation and filing was delegated to a professional accountant with whom the director must cooperate.[307]

**28.160**  In the case of a small company, the responsibility of a director for a failure to maintain accounting records may be reduced to the extent a professional company secretary is engaged. In *Re Rolus Properties Ltd*, Harman J considered that:

> [A]nyone who obtains a chartered secretary to assist in the administration of the affairs of a company, large or small, would, in my view, have reasonable grounds for saying that he had taken proper steps to provide the company with an officer who

---

[301]  As required by 1985 Act, s 226 (replaced by 2006 Act, s 394 with effect from 6 April 2008).

[302]  As required by 1985 Act, s 227 (replaced by 2006 Act, s 399 with effect from 6 April 2008).

[303]  As required by 1985 Act, s 233 (replaced by 2006 Act, ss 414 and 450 with effect from 6 April 2008).

[304]  *Official Receiver v Stern (No 2)* [2002] 1 BCLC 119, CA; *Re Park House Properties Ltd* [1997] 2 BCLC 530; *Re Firedart Ltd* [1994] 2 BCLC 340; *Re Swift 736 Ltd* [1993] BCLC 896, CA; *Re Linval Ltd* [1993] BCLC 654; *Re New Generation Engineers Ltd* [1993] BCLC 435; *Re Travel Mondial Ltd* [1991] BCC 224; *Re Tansoft Ltd* [1991] BCLC 339; *Re Sevenoaks Stationers (Retail) Ltd* [1991] Ch 164; *Re Chartmore Ltd* [1990] BCLC 673; *Re T&D Services Ltd* [1990] BCC 592; *Re Lo-Line Electric Motors Ltd* [1988] Ch 477; *Re Western Welsh International System Buildings Ltd* [1988] BCC 449.

[305]  *Re Swift 736 Ltd* [1993] BCLC 896, 900, CA.

[306]  [1994] 2 BCLC 340, 352.

[307]  Ibid, 347.

would, by definition above all others, be competent to and should be able to prepare all necessary paperwork.[308]

He accordingly reduced to two years what would otherwise have been a tariff of between four and six years.

A director is, of course, not liable to be disqualified for a professional error by the company's auditor, but a failure to maintain accounting records will be aggravated where those records were deliberately misstated, or otherwise not true and fair.[309] In *Re Austinsuite Furniture Ltd*,[310] Vinelott J disqualified a director for seven years for, amongst other things, procuring the lead company to enter into a transaction with a company whose debt burden it was serving which had no commercial purpose and was intended solely to create a misleading impression as to the true financial position of those companies. The director in that case had insisted it was the responsibility of the lead company's auditors to object to a valuation used in the transaction if they considered it improper, but the judge held that even if true 'it does not absolve him from the charge that his conduct in relation to this transaction was so irresponsible as to evidence a failure to appreciate his duties as a director'.[311] In that case, it was estimated that the lead company would have been compelled to cease trading a year earlier had true accounts been filed.      **28.161**

There may also be special cases in which a failure to maintain proper accounts is inconsequential. In *Re Cargo Agency Ltd*,[312] the company failed to keep and file accounts but had it kept and filed proper accounts only three months' activity would have been recorded and the accounts would have only been available to the public for a very short time before the company in fact went into voluntary liquidation. Harman J accordingly considered that 'there was an undoubted accounting default but one which . . . had almost no practical effect on the particular facts of this case and can therefore be ignored'[313] for the purpose of assessing the appropriate tariff.      **28.162**

*Responsibility for company becoming insolvent*

Schedule 1 Part II, para 6 requires the court to have regard to the extent of the director's responsibility for 'the causes of the company becoming insolvent'. A company may fail for one or many reasons and this paragraph focuses on the      **28.163**

---

308 [1988] 4 BCC 446, 448.

309 *Secretary of State for Trade and Industry v Ashman*, High Court, London, 15 June 1998, a case under s 8 in which the accounts of a public company were grossly misstated. This case arose from the administrative receivership of Blackspur Group plc. For related disqualification proceedings see: [1998] 1 BCLC 676, CA; [2001] 1 BCLC 653; [2002] 2 BCLC 263, CA; [2006] 2 BCLC 489.

310 [1992] BCLC 1047.

311 Ibid, 1059.

312 [1992] BCLC 686.

313 Ibid, 690–1.

responsibility of the director for the circumstances that brought about the particular insolvency. Although the paragraph is expressed in broad general terms and may overlap with other paragraphs, a director would not be disqualified unless his contribution to a cause of the company becoming insolvent was in some way culpable.

**28.164**  The courts appear to have accepted this construction. In *Re Barings plc (No 5)*, Jonathan Parker J explained that:

> [T]he relevant inquiry is not whether the respondent has caused (in any strict legal sense) the insolvency. It raises a different and much broader question, namely: To what extent were the respondent's failings responsible for the causes of the insolvency? In my judgment in addressing that question the court is required to adopt a correspondingly broader approach, eschewing nice legal concepts of causation.[314]

On this basis, he held that one of the directors in that case bore 'a heavy responsibility for the causes of the companies . . . . becoming insolvent' because 'had he performed his management duties properly Leeson's unauthorised activities would almost certainly have come to light and the collapse of the Barings Group might have been avoided.'[315]

**28.165**  The cases within this category include failure to supervise a reckless trader,[316] failure to comply with financial regulations with the consequence that claims against the company precipitated its insolvency,[317] and false representations to obtain financial assistance in the acquisition of a target company which, ultimately, caused the insolvency of both companies.[318]

### Responsibility for failure to supply goods or services

**28.166**  Schedule 1, Part II, paragraph 7 requires the court to have regard to the extent of the director's responsibility for any failure by the company to supply any goods or services which have been paid for (in whole or in part). This matter, like the matter specified in paragraph 6, overlaps with other matters which warrant disqualification, specifically wrongful trading, as it only falls to be considered where a trading company has become insolvent.[319] In *Re City Pram and Toy Company Ltd*, Judge Levy QC allowed the appeal of the Secretary of State against the refusal of Mr Registrar Rawson to disqualify the directors in that case. Having regard to

---

[314] [1999] 1 BCLC 433, 483; and *Re Skyward Builders plc*, High Court, London, 20 December 2002.

[315] Ibid, 575.

[316] *Re Barings plc (No 5)* [1999] 1 BCLC 433.

[317] *Re David M Aaron (Personal Financial Planners) Ltd*, Robin Knowles QC sitting as a deputy judge of the High Court, 7 June 2007 (unreported).

[318] *Re Bunting Electric Manufacturing Co Ltd* [2006] 1 BCLC 550.

[319] *Re City Pram and Toy Company Ltd* [1998] BCC 537; *Secretary of State for Trade and Industry v Lubrani* [1997] 2 BCLC 115.

paragraph 7 and the £31,000 shortfall to unsecured creditors in that case, he explained that—

> I am satisfied, as I have already said, that ground 1 has been made out. In these cir-
> cumstances, in my judgment, it was wrong for the twins to cause or allow the com-
> pany to trade. A fortiori it was wrong for the company to accept deposits from
> customers when they knew or ought to have known that, due to the company's finan-
> cial situation, there was no reasonable prospect of the company being able to pay the
> goods for which the deposits were paid. The Secretary of State therefore succeeds on
> this count.[320]

As noted above, such conduct is likely to be construed as taking an unwarranted risk with creditors' money.

In order to avoid exposing creditors to unwarranted risks, when there is real con-    **28.167**
cern about the company's solvency, deposits for orders for goods and services
should be paid into a trust account.[321]

*Responsibility for transactions within the Insolvency Act, ss 127, 238–240*

Schedule 1 Part II, para 8 requires the court to have regard to the extent of the    **28.168**
director's responsibility for the company entering into any transaction or giving
any preference, being a transaction or preference liable to be set aside under the
Insolvency Act, ss 127 and 238 to 240.[322]

The grant of a preference contrary to s 239,[323] or a transaction at undervalue con-    **28.169**
trary to s 238[324] is likely to be considered as a serious failure and may alone warrant
mandatory disqualification. The courts have not, as yet, considered s 127 in the
context of directors' disqualification, but a well-advised director should seek a
prospective validation order upon the presentation of a winding-up petition
against his company.[325] These sections are considered at Chapter 29, Sections
F(2), and K(1) and (2).

A director may also be disqualified under s 6(1) on the basis of a transaction at    **28.170**
undervalue or preference which does not strictly fall within the scope of ss 238 and

---

[320] [1998] BCC 537, 548.

[321] *Re Kayford Ltd* [1975] 1 WLR 279.

[322] Or in Scotland under the Insolvency Act, ss 242 or 243 or under any rule of law in
Scotland.

[323] *Official Receiver v Stern (No 2)* [2002] 1 BCLC 119, CA; *Re Funtime Ltd* [1999] 1 BCLC 247;
*Re Verby Print for Advertising Ltd* [1998] 2 BCLC 23; *Re Sykes (Butchers) Ltd* [1998] 1 BCLC 110;
*Re Grayan Building Services Ltd* [1995] Ch 241; *Re T&D Services Ltd* [1990] BCC 592.

[324] *Re Genosyis Technology Management Ltd* [2007] 1 BCLC 208; *Re Bradcrown Ltd* [2001] 1
BCLC 547; *Secretary of State for Trade and Industry v Tillman* [2000] 1 BCLC 36; *Secretary of State
for Trade and Industry v Lubrani* [1997] 2 BCLC 115; *Re Keypak Homecase Ltd* (No 2) [1990] BCLC
440.

[325] s 127 has effect from the commencement of the winding up, which is deemed as at the presentation of the winding-up petition, s 129 of the same Act.

In *Re Sykes (Butchers) Ltd*,[326] the defendant director formed a new company which acquired the business and assets of his former company on terms that its indebtedness to its bank, which he had personally guaranteed, would be repaid. In the months prior to that company's winding up, its indebtedness was repaid, but there was a substantial increase in the debt owed to trade creditors. Ferris J upheld the Registrar's finding that the director had caused a preferential payment to be made, saying that:

> [A]lthough responsibility for a statutory preference liable to be set aside under ss 238–240 of the Insolvency Act 1986 is one of the matters to which the court, in determining unfitness, is to have particular regard (see s 9 of and Sch 1, para 8 to the Disqualification Act), it is clear that these matters are not the only ones to which the court may have regard . . .

> [T]he action of a director in causing a company to make a payment in a way which, as he knew and intended, would produce a personal advantage for himself, regardless of the interests of other creditors of the company, would at the time have been regarded as morally reprehensible and indicative of a lack of commercial probity. Given the registrar's conclusion that Mr Richardson was influenced by the fact that his exposure under his guarantee would be eliminated, as well as by other facts, I consider that he was entitled to conclude that charge 3 was established, that it was indicative of Mr Richardson's unfitness to be a director and that it was appropriate to be taken into account together with charge 4 relating to Sykes.[327]

The decision accordingly makes clear that, although the facts in that case would probably have supported a finding of a preference contrary to s 239, a disqualification order can be justified on the basis of a preferential payment which is not strictly within s 239 because, for example, it falls outside the temporal scope of that section.

**28.171** Similarly, in *Re Genosyis Technology Management Ltd*,[328] Lindsay J rejected the submission that a director was not unfit because he had reasonable grounds for believing that the transaction would benefit the company within the Insolvency Act, s 238(5):

> I should add that I am far from sure that s 238(5) would have assisted the appellants in any event. Where it applies, it precludes only an order being made under s 238, but here no-one was seeking an order under s 238. Nothing in s 238(5) would seem to preclude the existence of a transaction at an undervalue being taken into account for purposes, so long as the purposes are not the making of an order under s 238. So much for that first ground.

This statement was strictly *obiter* because there was no evidence that the appellant believed that the company would benefit from the transaction and, anyway, the

---

[326] [1998] 1 BCLC 110.
[327] Ibid, 129–8.
[328] [2007] 1 BCLC 208.

judge considered he 'would have been unable to characterise the belief as reasonable,' but it underlines the fact that an impugned transaction may be relevant for purposes of disqualification though not triggering the statutory provisions listed in para 8.

In cases in which a transaction does fall within para 8, it is important to know **28.172** what is meant by the 'extent of the director's responsibility'. In *Re Living Images Ltd*, Laddie J held that the conduct of the director in question had to be 'blameworthy' in some way and that merely authorizing execution of a transaction at undervalue or a preference was insufficient:

> On the wording of the 1986 Act it would appear that a director could be disqualified for, say, having authorised the offensive transaction even if he was not aware that the company, through other directors, had the desire to benefit the creditor and was influenced by that desire. I do not believe that that is what was intended. Before an order for disqualification is made it must be shown that the director acted in a way which is blameworthy. Therefore it seems to me that before a director can be disqualified on this ground, it must be shown that he was, at the least, aware both of the desire and the fact that that influenced the company to act for the benefit of the creditor.[329]

The justification for this approach flowed from the mechanics of corporate attribution. The relevant desire[330] for the purpose of the Insolvency Act, s 239 is that of the company and might be constituted by attribution of the combined knowledge and intentions of directors, or other persons, other than the director(s) subject of disqualification proceedings.[331]

The courts have not, as yet, determined the requisite 'extent of the director's **28.173** responsibility' for the purpose of transactions liable to be set aside under the Insolvency Act, ss 127 and 238, but it is suggested the approach in *Re Living Images Ltd* should be applied by analogy; ie the director's responsibility for the transaction should only lead to disqualification if he was blameworthy. A transaction may be characterized as either falling within those sections or as a more general breach of duty, and it would be odd if a stricter approach were adopted in the former case. Moreover, in connection with all such transactions, the elements may be made out without the involvement of the directors because a company can only act through its agents, and so something specific must be required to fix a particular director with responsibility for *that* misconduct.[332]

---

[329] [1996] 1 BCLC 348, 357.

[330] *Re MC Bacon Ltd* [1990] BCLC 78.

[331] *Re Fairway Magazines Ltd* [1993] BCLC 643.

[332] In the absence of such evidence, it may be useful to characterize the complaint as a failure to take adequate responsibility, especially in a case in which that transaction is a cause of the company's insolvency.

*Responsibility for failure to comply with the Insolvency Act, s 98*

**28.174**  Schedule 1, Part II, para 9 requires the court to have regard to the extent of the directors' responsibility for any failure by the directors of the company to comply with the Insolvency Act, s 98, being the duty of the company to call a creditors' meeting following a resolution to liquidate the company by a creditors' voluntary winding up.

*Failure to comply with other specified provisions of the Insolvency Act*

**28.175**  Schedule 1 Part II, paragraph 10 requires the court to have regard to a failure—

(1)  to produce a statement of affairs (a) upon the appointment of an administrator,[333] (b) upon the appointment of an administrative receiver,[334] and (c) in a winding up by the court;[335]

(2)  to attend, make out, and cause to be laid before the creditors' meeting a statement of affairs in accordance with s 99 and also to attend the meeting;

(3)  to comply with an order under s 234(2) to deliver up any property, books, papers, or records to which the company appears to be entitled;[336]

(4)  to give the office-holder appointed in relation to the insolvent company such information concerning the company and its promotion, formation, business, dealings, affairs, or property.[337]

A failure to cooperate with an officer-holder is a particularly serious matter which is regarded as sufficient to justify disqualification on its own and, in cases of deliberate concealment, is likely to warrant a high tariff. In *Secretary of State for Trade and Industry v Blunt*, the judge explained that:

> The allegation of concealment is no less serious [than the allegation of misappropriation]. In my view, that allegation would justify disqualification on its own. The failure by a director or any other person involved in the affairs of a company to make a full and frank disclosure to an office-holder about the manner in which such affairs have been conducted may create serious difficulties for the office-holder. He will often have little information about the affairs of the company. He may therefore need to rely entirely upon the information he receives from such persons to re-constitute the affairs of the company. It is not surprising, in the circumstances, that the Insolvency Act 1986 contains numerous provisions specifically requiring directors and others involved in the affairs of a company to co-operate fully with the office-holder and to be truthful about their conduct and involvement in such affairs.

---

[333]  Insolvency Act, Schedule B1, para 47.

[334]  Insolvency Act, s 47 (in Scotland, s 66).

[335]  Insolvency Act, s 131.

[336]  Para 10 is phrased in terms of requiring the court to have regard to a failure to comply with any obligation imposed 'by or under' s 234 and, as such, it appears an order is necessary because s 234 does not otherwise impose any obligation.

[337]  Insolvency Act, s 235.

Any failure by them to co-operate or to be truthful might not only be enforced by court action against them (see for example ss 234 to 236 of the Insolvency Act 1986), but could also result in their incurring criminal liability for their actions (see for example ss 206 to 211 of the Insolvency Act 1986).[338]

This approach is likely to be followed and to apply irrespective of the form of insolvency proceeding in issue. In such cases, it is no defence to assert that the false statements were made on the advice of professional advisers. It is the duty of the director to tell the truth.[339]

## (5) Procedure for obtaining disqualification orders

### Disqualification orders in criminal proceedings

The court's jurisdiction to make a disqualification order where a person has been convicted of an offence is discussed in paragraphs 28.92–28.93 (indictable offence) and 28.100–28.102 (summary offence) above and also in Chapter 30, Section J. The jurisdiction will generally be exercised at the sentencing stage by the court which has made the conviction,[340] although an application may also be made to any court (ie a civil court) having jurisdiction to wind up the company[341] in relation to which the offence was committed.[342] Where the conviction was summary, an application may also be made to any other magistrates' court acting in the same local justice area.[343] The fact that a criminal court has not made a disqualification order when invited to do so at the sentencing stage is not itself a bar to a subsequent civil application by the Secretary of State.[344]

**28.176**

A magistrate's court which has convicted a person of a summary offence in consequence of a contravention of, or failure to comply with, any provision of companies legislation requiring a return, account, or other document to be filed with, delivered, or sent to, or notice of any matter to be given to, the Registrar of Companies (or any other magistrates' court acting in the same local justice area) also has the power to make a disqualification order (of up to five years) if the person has had made against him, or has been convicted of, not less than three relevant default orders and offences in the five years ending with the date of the conviction.[345] For these purposes, the other convictions may be either summary

**28.177**

---

[338] [2005] 2 BCLC 463, para 24.
[339] *Secretary of State for Trade and Industry v Blunt* [2005] 2 BCLC 463 at para 25; *Re Living Images Ltd* [1996] 1 BCLC 348, 376.
[340] CDDA, s 2(2)(b).
[341] Defined in respect of England and Wales in the Insolvency Act, s 117.
[342] CDDA, s 2(2)(a).
[343] Ibid.
[344] *Re Denis Hilton Limited* [2002] 1 BCLC 302.
[345] CDDA, s 5.

or on indictment, and both the immediate conviction before the magistrates' court and any other offence of which he is convicted on the same occasion count towards the three. This enables the magistrates' court to deal summarily with persistent breaches of reporting requirements.

**28.178**   A disqualification order may be made on grounds which include matters other than criminal convictions, notwithstanding that the person in respect of whom it is to be made may be criminally liable in respect of such matters.[346] It follows that disqualification proceedings may be commenced when a criminal prosecution may yet ensue, or may be commenced, stayed pending the criminal proceedings, and then resurrected: even where the trial judge has made a disqualification order, factors which might justify a longer period of disqualification may be raised in the civil proceedings.[347]

*Civil disqualification proceedings: the applicant*

**28.179**   The Secretary of State may apply to the court for a disqualification order to be made if it appears to him:

(1)   that it is expedient in the public interest that a disqualification order under the CDDA, s 6 should be made against any person[348] (in which case the Secretary of State may direct that the application is to be brought by the official receiver[349]); or

(2)   from investigative material[350] that it is expedient in the public interest that a disqualification order should be made against any person who is or has been a director or shadow director of a company.[351]

**28.180**   In respect of applications under the CDDA, ss 2–4, s 16(2) provides that an application may be made to a court having jurisdiction to wind up companies by (a) the Secretary of State, (b) the official receiver, or (c) the liquidator, or any past or present member or creditor of any company in relation to which that person has committed or is alleged to have committed an offence or other default.

---

[346]   CDDA, s 1(4).

[347]   *Re Cedarwood Productions Ltd* [2004] BCC 65, CA.

[348]   CDDA, s 7(1). From the CDDA, subs 6(1)(a) the 'person' must be or have been a director (including a shadow director: CDDA, s 6(3C)) of a company which has at any time become insolvent (whether while he was a director or subsequently).

[349]   CDDA, s 7(1)(b).

[350]   Defined in the CDDA, s 8(1A) as meaning (a) a report by inspectors under (i) 1985 Act, s 437; (ii) FSMA, ss 167, 168, 169, or 284; (iii) where the company is an open-ended investment company, FSMA, s 262(2)(k); and (b) information or documents obtained under (i) 1985 Act, ss 447, 448, 453A; (ii) the Criminal Justice Act 1987, s 2; (iii) the Criminal Law (Consolidation) Scotland Act 1995, s 28; (iv) the 1989 Act, s 83; or FSMA, ss 165, 171, 172, 173, or 175.

[351]   CDDA, s 8(1).

The OFT or a specified regulator[352] may make an application for a competition disqualification order under the CDDA, s 9A.[353]  **28.181**

There are some jurisdictional differences depending on the basis on which the application is brought. Under the CDDA, ss 6 and 9A disqualification for at least a minimum period of two years is mandatory if the court is satisfied on the facts that the requisite conditions are met, while on an application under the CDDA, s 8 the court has discretionary power to make the order.[354] Under the CDDA, ss 8 and 9A it is only conduct as director of the particular company which is relevant, whereas under s 6, conduct in relation to other companies is taken into account. Under s 6, there is a minimum period of disqualification of two years and a maximum of 15.[355] Under ss 8 and 9A, there is no minimum but the same maximum of 15 years.[356]  **28.182**

*Civil disqualification proceedings: the court*

The CDDA prescribes the civil court which has jurisdiction in respect of an application for a disqualification order in particular cases. Where the order is sought for persistent defaults under companies legislation or for fraudulent trading, fraud in relation to the company, or breach of duty as an officer of the company, the relevant court will be any court having jurisdiction to wind up any of the companies in respect of which the relevant offence or other default has been or is alleged to have been committed.[357]  **28.183**

For the purposes of the CDDA, ss 6 and 7 (ie applications based on unfitness), the court with jurisdiction to make a disqualification order is:  **28.184**

(1) where the company in question is being wound up by the court, that court;

(2) where the company is in voluntary liquidation, the court which has or had jurisdiction to wind it up;

---

[352] The 'specified regulators', specified in the CDDA, s 9E(2), are (a) the Office of Communications, (b) the Gas and Electricity Markets Authority, (c) the Director General of Water Services, (d) the Rail Regulator, and (e) the Civil Aviation Authority.

[353] CDDA, s 9A(10).

[354] CDDA, s 1(1).

[355] CDDA, s 6(4).

[356] CDDA, s 8(4).

[357] CDDA, ss 3(4) and s 4(2). The Insolvency Act, s 117 identifies the court with jurisdiction to wind up the company. The general position under the Insolvency Act, s 117 is that the High Court has jurisdiction to wind up any company registered in England and Wales, and the county court for the district where the company has its registered office has concurrent jurisdiction where the share capital of the company does not exceed £120,000. Subsection 117(6) provides that the registered office is the place which has been the company's registered office for the longest period in the six months immediately preceding the presentation for winding up. Subsection 117(7) provides that s 117 is subject to Art 3 of the EC Regulation on Insolvency Proceedings 2000 (which confers exclusive jurisdiction to courts of the EC Member State where a company has its centre of main interest). The CDDA, 6(3A) clarifies that Insolvency Act, s 117 (and s 120 making like provision for Scotland) are to apply for the purposes of s 6(3) as if references to the presentation of the petition for winding up were references to passing the resolution for voluntary winding up, or to the appointment of an administrator or administrative receiver.

(3) where the company is not in liquidation but is in administration or administrative receivership, any court which has jurisdiction to wind it up.[358]

However, proceedings are not invalidated by being commenced in the wrong court, and the court in which they were commenced can retain them.[359] In an appropriate case, they can be transferred to the correct court,[360] although the court has a discretion whether to transfer them or to strike them out.[361]

**28.185** For a competition disqualification order under CDDA s 9A, the relevant court with jurisdiction is the High Court.[362]

**28.186** When a disqualification order is sought as an adjunct to a declaration that a person is liable to contribute to a company's assets under Insolvency Act, ss 213 and 214 (fraudulent and wrongful trading), it is the court making the relevant declaration which also has jurisdiction to order a period of disqualification.[363]

*Civil disqualification proceedings: service outside the jurisdiction*

**28.187** Disqualification proceedings may be commenced against individuals who are outside the jurisdiction, and just as a foreign company may be wound up under the Insolvency Act, a disqualification order may be made against a person of whatever nationality, domicile, or residence. However, where a defendant is outside the jurisdiction, it will be necessary for an application to be made for permission to serve out, and the court has a discretion not to permit service out where it is not satisfied that there is a good arguable case that the requisite conditions for a disqualification order to be made have been satisfied.[364]

*Civil disqualification proceedings: the two-year time limit and delay*

**28.188** There is no time limit imposed under the CDDA on applications under ss 8 or 9. However, for applications under s 7 seeking disqualification under s 6, s 7(2) provides:

> Except with the leave of the court, an application for the making under [section 6] of a disqualification order against any person shall not be made after the end of the period of two years beginning with the day on which the company of which that person is or has been a director became insolvent.

---

[358] CDDA, s 6(3). See preceding footnote for note on the court with jurisdiction to wind up the company.

[359] CDDA, s 6(5).

[360] Between Royal Courts of Justice and a district registry of the High Court and between county courts, under Pt 30 CPR. From High Court to county court, under the County Courts Act 1984, s 40. From county court to High Court, under the County Courts Act 1984, s 42.

[361] Cf *Restrick v Crickmore* [1994] 1 WLR 420; in *Re NP Engineering and Security Products Ltd* [1998] 1 BCLC 208 the Court of Appeal decided that it was appropriate to transfer rather than strike out.

[362] CDDA, s 9E.

[363] CDDA, s 10(1).

[364] *Re Seagull Manufacturing Co Ltd (No 2)* [1994] Ch 91.

The CDDA does not prescribe the factors which are to be taken into account on   **28.189**
an application for permission to issue proceedings or to add a defendant to existing proceedings out of time.[365] Similar issues will arise when, although the proceedings were commenced within the time limit, the evidence was not ready at
that time and permission is sought for an extension of time (until after the two-
year period has expired) in which to serve it.[366] In *Re Probe Data Systems Ltd (No 3)*,[367]
Scott LJ said that the court should take into account: (a) the length of delay,
(b) the reasons for the delay, (c) the strength of the case against the director, and
(d) the degree of prejudice caused to the director by the delay. In *Re Blackspur
Group plc*,[368] Millett LJ said that this was not exhaustive, and the court should take
all relevant circumstances into account.

If an application for permission is required, the Secretary of State is expected to   **28.190**
make it without delay. Applications were refused in *Re Crestjoy Products Ltd*[369]
where the 10-day letters had been sent shortly before the end of the two-year
period but the application was not made until some ten weeks after the end of two
years, there was further delay because of a fault in the form of the application and
Harman J was not satisfied that a good reason for extension of time had been
shown. Similarly, in *Re Cedar Developments Ltd*,[370] permission was refused where
the proceedings had not been commenced in time through an administrative
oversight, although the application for permission was made less than a week after
the two-year period had expired. Delay attributable to the defendant will weigh in
favour of the Secretary of State.[371]

Once disqualification proceedings have been commenced, they must be pro-   **28.191**
gressed with reasonable expedition. The courts will apply (with some adjustment
to take account of the particular nature of the proceedings[372]) the usual principles
applicable in civil litigation to cases where there is unjustifiable and excessive
delay,[373] and in an extreme case have the power under the CPR[374] to strike out

---

[365]   eg *Re Westmid Packaging Services Ltd* [1995] BCC 203.
[366]   The position in *Re Blackspur Group plc, Secretary of State for Trade and Industry v Davies*
[1996] 4 All ER 289, CA.
[367]   [1992] BCLC 405, CA; cf *C M Van Stillevoldt v El Carriers Inc* [1993] 1 WLR 207.
[368]   [1996] 4 All ER 289, CA.
[369]   [1990] BCLC 677.
[370]   [1994] 2 BCLC 714.
[371]   *Re Copecrest Ltd, Secretary of State for Trade and Industry v Tighe* [1993] BCLC 1118; on
appeal [1994] 2 BCLC 284, CA.
[372]   In *Re Manlon Trading Ltd, Official Receiver v Aziz* [1996] Ch 136, CA, Beldam LJ said that,
because disqualification proceedings were brought in the public interest, not to enforce private
rights, they should not be struck out lightly: the public interest nature of the proceedings was to be
balanced against any prejudice suffered by the defendant.
[373]   Cf *Allen v Sir Alfred McAlpine & Sons Ltd* [1968] 2 QB 229, CA; *Birkett v James* [1978] AC
297, HL.
[374]   CPR, rule 3.4(2)(b) and (c).

the proceedings for want of prosecution.[375] In *Re Blackspur Group (No 4),*[376] Arden LJ said:

> Proceedings which, as in this case, are brought at the end of the two-year period are liable to be struck out, if there is inordinate or inexcusable delay: see *Re Manlon Trading Ltd.*[377] Proceedings will be struck out if there is a substantial risk of an unfair trial but they will not be struck out simply because there has been a delay in the course of the preparations for trial or even in the trial itself: see, for example, *Re Manlon Trading Ltd* and *Re Rocksteady Services Ltd, Secretary of State for Trade and Industry v Staton.*[378]

**28.192**  Significant delay may also affect the right of the defendant under Art 6 of the European Court of Human Rights (ECHR) to have civil rights determined within a reasonable time. In *EDC v United Kingdom,*[379] the ECHR held that there had been a breach of such rights where disqualification proceedings had not been brought to trial for some four-and-a-half years pending determination of criminal proceedings. In *Eastaway v UK (App no 1496/01),*[380] the ECHR held that disqualification proceedings arising from the collapse of the Blackspur Group which had been commenced in 1992 and culminated in an undertaking by Mr Eastway in May 2001 had taken too long and so violated Mr Eastway's Article 6 rights. However, in *Re Blackspur Group (No 4),*[381] the Court of Appeal declined to set aside the undertaking the director had given, pointing out that the fact that there has been a violation of Article 6 does not necessarily mean that there cannot be a fair trial or that the proceedings are necessarily to be struck out.[382] While the decision of the ECHR was binding, it had made no finding that there could not be a fair trial because of the delay, and such a finding was not implicit in its judgment.

*Civil disqualification proceeding: before commencement*

**28.193**  The CDDA, s 7(3) requires the office-holder[383] to report the matter to the Secretary of State 'forthwith', if it appears to him that the conditions for making a

---

[375]  eg *Re Noble Trees Ltd* [1993] BCLC 1185; *Official Receiver v B Ltd* [1994] 2 BCLC 1; *Re Manlon Trading Ltd, Official Receiver v Aziz* [1996] Ch 136, CA; *Secretary of State for Trade and Industry v Martin* [1998] BCC 184.

[376]  [2008] 1 BCLC 153 at para 13.

[377]  [1996] Ch 136, CA.

[378]  [2001] 1 BCLC 84; affd [2001] BCC 467, CA.

[379]  [1998] BCC 370.

[380]  [2006] 2 BCLC 361.

[381]  [2008] 1 BCLC 153, CA.

[382]  *A-G's reference (No 2 of 2001)* [2004] 2 AC 72, HL.

[383]  ie the official receiver where a company is being wound up by the court, the liquidator in a voluntary liquidation, an administrator where the company is in administration, or an administrative receiver.

disqualification order set out in s 6(1) are satisfied. In a s 6 case, forming and holding the relevant opinion that it is 'expedient in the public interest'[384] for a disqualification order to be made gives the Secretary of State standing to make the application. Although the section refers to the decision being made by the Secretary of State, there is no requirement for the decision to be made by the minister personally, and so it may properly be made by the Secretary of State acting through one of his officers.[385]

In the case of a prospective competition disqualification order, if the OFT or a specified regulator[386] has reasonable grounds for suspecting that a breach of competition law has occurred, the CDDA, s 9C(1) empowers them to carry out an investigation for the purpose of deciding whether to make an application under s 9A for a disqualification order. If they decide to proceed with such an application, they must first give notice to the person likely to be affected by it, and give that person an opportunity to make representations.   **28.194**

The formation of the requisite opinion and the decision to make an application for a disqualification order must be proper decisions, as a matter of public law, in that proper grounds for them must exist and be relied upon, irrelevant matters must not be taken into account, and the opinion or decision must be one that a reasonable Secretary of State or regulator could reach. In theory, the decision is subject to judicial review. In practice, it has been difficult for prospective defendants to obtain the necessary permission to proceed with an application for judicial review.[387] Similarly, in *R v Secretary of State for Trade and Industry, ex p Lonrho plc*[388] the applicant company failed in an attempt to challenge by judicial review the Secretary of State's decision *not* to pursue disqualification proceedings.   **28.195**

Once the decision to proceed has been taken, CDDA s 16(1), provides:   **28.196**

> A person intending to apply for the making of a disqualification order by the court having jurisdiction to wind up a company shall give not less than 10 days' notice of his intention to the person against whom the order is sought . . .

---

[384] CDDA, s 7(1).

[385] Cf *Re Golden Chemical Products Ltd* [1976] Ch 300, applying *Carltona Ltd v Comrs of Works* [1943] 2 All ER 560, *Lewisham Borough Council v Roberts* [1949] 2 KB 608, and *R v Skinner* [1968] 2 QB 700.

[386] See n 386 above.

[387] eg *R v Secretary of State for Trade and Industry, ex p McCormick* [1998] BCC 379 (refusal by Court of Appeal of permission for judicial review of decision to rely on transcripts of compulsory interviews by inspectors); *R v Secretary of State for Trade and Industry, ex p Eastway* [2000] 1 WLR 2222, in which the House of Lords refused an attempt to appeal from a refusal of leave.

[388] [1992] BCC 325.

This requirement is directory rather than mandatory,[389] so failure to give proper notice is merely a procedural irregularity which does not invalidate the proceedings. The notice does not need to set out in full the grounds on which the application is to be made.[390] However, 10 clear days' notice is required.[391]

*Civil disqualification proceedings: undertakings*

**28.197**   It has been possible since 2 April 2001 for a person to offer and the Secretary of State to accept a disqualification undertaking, as an alternative to an order being made in proceedings.[392] The Secretary of State can accept the undertaking under the CDDA, s 7(2A) if he is satisfied that the conditions in s 6(1) are satisfied, and under s 8(2) where it appears to him from the relevant report, information, or documents that the conduct of the person makes him unfit to be concerned in the management of a company, and in either case, if it also appears to him that it is expedient in the public interest to accept the undertaking instead of applying or proceeding with the application for a disqualification order. The emphasis in the section is on a subject appraisal by the Secretary of State of what is in the public interest, and the Secretary of State is not obliged to accept an undertaking where it is considered that a trial would be preferable.[393]

**28.198**   A disqualification undertaking for purposes of CDDA, ss 7 and 8 is defined in CDDA, s 1A as:

> an undertaking by any person that, for the period specified in the undertaking, the person—
>
> (a) will not be a director of a company, act as receiver of a company's property, or in any way, whether directly or indirectly, be concerned or take part in the promotion, formation or management of a company unless (in each case) he has leave of a court; and
> (b) will not act as an insolvency practitioner.

The maximum period which may be specified in an undertaking is 15 years, as for an order, and the minimum period which may be specified in an undertaking under the CDDA, s 7, is two years.[394]

**28.199**   The OFT or a specified regulator has since 20 June 2003 had a similar power to accept an undertaking as an alternative to a competition disqualification order.[395]

---

389 *Secretary of State for Trade and Industry v Langridge, Re Cedac Ltd* [1991] Ch 402, CA; see also comments of Laddie J in *Re Finelist Ltd, Secretary of State for Trade and Industry v Swan* [2004] BCC 877.
390 *Re Cedac* [1991] Ch 402.
391 *Re Jaymar Management Limited* [1990] BCLC 617.
392 CDDA, ss 7(2A) and 8(2A).
393 *Re Blackspur Group plc (No 3), Secretary of State v Davies (No 2)* [2002] 2 BCLC 363, CA.
394 CDDA, s 1A(2).
395 CDDA, s 9B.

In this case, the wording specified in the CDDA, s 9B(3) is slightly different but to the same effect: that the person will not act as a director of a company or receiver of a company's property, or be concerned or take part in the promotion, formation, or management of a company. There is no automatic provision that the person may act with the leave of the court, but s 9B(4) provides that the undertaking may make such provision.

The usual practice is to provide that a relevant period of disqualification will begin **28.200**
21 days after acceptance by the Secretary of State.[396] This is in part to facilitate any application for leave to act which may be contemplated. Undertakings are registered at Companies House.

The court has power to vary an undertaking to reduce the period or provide for it **28.201**
to cease to be in force, on an application by the person who is subject to it.[397] On such an application, the Secretary of State[398] (or, in a case where the OFT or another regulator accepted the undertaking, that regulator[399]) is to appear and call the attention of court to any matters which seem to him to be relevant.

### Civil disqualification proceedings: procedure

Apart from the specific procedural provisions in the CDDA itself, applications for **28.202**
disqualification orders are governed by the Disqualification Rules[400] and the Disqualification Practice Direction.[401] The Disqualification Rules apply to applications under the CDDA, ss 7, 8, and 9A and the Practice Direction also applies to applications under the CDDA, ss 2–4. The CPR apply to disqualification proceedings except where the Disqualification Rules make provision to inconsistent effect.[402] Disqualification proceedings are allocated to the multi-track[403] and the procedure is close to that under the CPR, Part 8.

Proceedings are commenced by claim form in specified form, including endorse- **28.203**
ments informing the defendant of the maximum period of disqualification that may be imposed, that the application may be determined summarily (with a maximum period of disqualification of five years) or adjourned for substantive hearing, and notifying the defendant of the applicable time limits for evidence.[404]

---

396 By analogy with CDDA, s 1(2); see below.
397 CDDA, s 8A.
398 CDDA, s 8A(2).
399 CDDA, s 8A(2A).
400 Insolvent Companies (Disqualification of Unfit Directors) Proceedings Rules 1987.
401 Civil Procedure 3J-1–3J-77.
402 Rule 2(1).
403 Disqualification PD, para 2.
404 Disqualification Rules, rule 4; Disqualification PD, para 6.1.

28.204　The applicant is required to file evidence in court at the time the application is issued, including a statement of the matters by reference to which the defendant is alleged to be unfit to be concerned in the management of a company.[405] Evidence is to be in the form of affidavits, except that the official receiver may provide a report which is treated as if verified by affidavit.[406] A certified copy of a report by inspectors appointed under Part XIV of the 1985 Act will be admissible in evidence.[407]

28.205　The applicant serves the proceedings on the respondent(s) who then have 28 days to file any evidence on which they wish to rely in opposition to the application.[408] Evidence in reply is to be served within 14 days of receipt of the defendant's evidence[409] although these time periods may be extended prior to the first hearing by written agreement between the parties.[410] The Disqualification Practice Direction provides that '[s]o far as possible all evidence should be filed before the first hearing of the disqualification application'.[411]

28.206　The first hearing takes place before the Registrar,[412] not less than eight weeks after the claim form was issued.[413] At that hearing, the Registrar will either determine the application summarily or adjourn it giving such further directions as may be required.[414]

*Admissibility in evidence of statements*

28.207　Statements made in pursuance of a requirement under specified provisions of the CDDA[415] or under rules made for the purposes of the CDDA are generally admissible in evidence against the maker or a person who concurred in the making of the statement.[416] However, the CDDA, 20(2) provides that in criminal proceedings:[417]

> (a)　no evidence relating to the statement may be adduced, and
> (b)　no question relating to it may be asked,
> by or on behalf of the prosecution, unless evidence relating to it is adduced, or a question relating to it is asked, in the proceedings by or on behalf of that person.

---

[405] Disqualification Rules, rule 3; Disqualification PD, para 9.2.
[406] Disqualification Rules, rule 3(2); Disqualification PD, para 9.1.
[407] 1985 Act, s 441 and Disqualification PD, para 9.1.
[408] Disqualification Rules, rule 6(1); Disqualification PD, para 9.4.
[409] Disqualification Rules, rule 6(2); Disqualification PD, para 9.6.
[410] Disqualification PD, para 9.7.
[411] Disqualification PD, para 9.8.
[412] Disqualification Rules, rule 7(2); Disqualification PD, para 10.2.
[413] Disqualification Rules, rule 7(1); Disqualification PD, para 10.1.
[414] Disqualification Rules, rule 7(3); Disqualification PD, para 10.3.
[415] CDDA, ss 6–10, 15 of 19(c), or Schedule 1.
[416] CDDA, s 20(1).
[417] Other than the limited classes of exceptions listed in CDDA, s 20(3).

In *Secretary of State of Trade and Industry v Crane*,[418] Ferris J discussed the CDDA, **28.208**
s 20, which he regarded as offering an additional and substantial layer of protection in almost all cases in which there are parallel criminal and disqualification
proceedings. This reasoning has been criticized,[419] both on the basis that evidence
a defendant may wish to rely on in disqualification proceedings is not in fact compelled, and it has also been pointed out that the bar in s 20(2) does not prevent a
co-defendant in criminal proceedings from raising material in those proceedings.[420]

## (6) Applications for leave

As set out above, a disqualification order is an order that the person will not act in **28.209**
the prohibited ways unless he has the leave of the court,[421] and there will be similar
provision in an undertaking in the context of proceedings under the CDDA, ss 7
or 8.[422] Equally, the offence under the CDDA, s 11 of acting as a director while an
undischarged bankrupt is committed if the bankrupt does so without the leave of
the court.[423]

Certain procedural aspects for applications for leave are to be found in the CDDA, **28.210**
s 17 and further procedural provision is made by the Disqualification Practice
Direction. It will often be convenient to make an application for leave at the time
the original order is made, an approach which was endorsed by the Court of
Appeal in *Re Dicetrade*[A24] and *Re TLL Realisations Limited, Secretary of State for
Trade and Industry v Collins*.[425] It will usually be in the director's interests because
it avoids delay, and it will enable the judge who is familiar with the case to
deal with the application. However, the fact that the court knows or expects an

---

[418] [2001] 2 BCLC 222.

[419] See Walters and Davis-White QC, *Directors Disqualification and Bankruptcy Restrictions*
(2005) at paras 7-80 to 7-81.

[420] The mere fact that a defendant might give an indication of his likely defence in prospective
criminal proceedings was held not to debar the claimant from nonetheless pursuing civil proceedings by the Court of Appeal in *Jefferson Ltd v Bhetcha* [1979] 1 WLR 898. In *Re TransTec plc,
Secretary of State for Trade and Industry v Carr* [2007] 1 BCLC 93, David Richards J declined to
order a stay of disqualification proceedings because of pending criminal proceedings, considering
that the defendants' position could be suitably protected by directions that the respondents were to
serve their evidence on the Secretary of State before the start of the criminal trial but not to serve it
on each other or file it and that the Secretary of State was to refrain from showing the evidence to
any witness or potential witness in the criminal trial. It has been said that the Secretary of State has
a public duty to apply for the disqualification of unfit directors. He cannot be held up indefinitely
by other proceedings over which he has no control (see *Re Rex Williams Leisure plc* [1994] Ch 350,
368F, CA, per Hoffmann LJ).

[421] CDDA, s 1(1)(a).

[422] CDDA, s 1A(1)(a).

[423] CDDA, s 11(1); cf *Re McQuillan* (1989) 5 BCC 137 and the Australian case *Re Altim Pty Ltd*
[1968] 2 NSWR 762.

[424] [1994] 2 BCLC 113, CA, per Dillon LJ.

[425] [2000] 2 BCLC 223, CA, per Peter Gibson LJ.

application for leave to be made is not a reason for only imposing the minimum period of disqualification: the court starts with what it considers the appropriate period for the gravity of the allegations, and then proceeds to consider whether permission should be granted against that background.[426]

**28.211** Where the disqualification order was made by a court with jurisdiction to wind up companies, the application for permission is to be made to that court.[427] Where the order was made by a court without such jurisdiction (ie under the CDDA, ss 2–5), the application for permission is to be made to the court which would have had jurisdiction to wind up the company (or one of the companies) to which the offence related.[428]

**28.212** Where an undertaking has been accepted by the Secretary of State (ie under the CDDA, ss 7 or 8), application for permission is to be made to a court to which the Secretary of State could have applied for a disqualification order.[429]

**28.213** The Secretary of State is required to appear and call the attention of the court to any matters which seem to him to be relevant,[430] except where the application was for a competition disqualification order under the CDDA, s 9A.[431]

**28.214** Where the undertaking was accepted by the OFT or a specified regulator (ie under the CDDA, s 9B), the application must be made to the High Court[432] and it is the duty of the regulator who originally applied for the order or accepted the undertaking to appear and call the attention of the court to any matters which appear to the regulator to be relevant.[433]

**28.215** In the case of an application for leave to act by an undischarged bankrupt, the court has no power to give leave unless notice of the application has been given to the official receiver, and if the official receiver is of the opinion that it is contrary to public interest for the application to be granted, it is his statutory duty to attend the hearing and oppose the application.[434]

**28.216** Applications for leave are governed by Part IV of the Disqualification Practice Direction. They are made by a Part 8 Claim Form or by an application notice in existing proceedings, supported by affidavit evidence.[435] In the case of a competition

---

[426] *Re Westmid Packing Services Ltd* [1998] 2 All ER 124, CA.
[427] CDDA, s 17(1).
[428] CDDA, s 17(2).
[429] CDDA, s 17(3).
[430] CDDA, s 17(5).
[431] CDDA, s 17(6).
[432] CDDA, s 17(3A).
[433] CDDA, s 17(7).
[434] CDDA, s 11(3).
[435] Disqualification PD paras 20.2 and 22.1.

disqualification order or undertaking, they are to be served on the relevant regulator; in other cases, they are to be served on the Secretary of State.[436]

Although the Secretary of State (or relevant regulator) is required to attend and draw the court's attention to matters considered relevant, the court is not limited to considering those matters.[437] If the Secretary of State does not oppose the application, it will usually be sufficient for a letter to that effect to be provided to the court.[438]

**28.217**

In *Re Westmid Packing Services Ltd*,[439] the Court of Appeal offered guidance on the sort of evidence which would be appropriate on an application for leave, saying that relevant matters might include the director's general reputation and conduct in discharge of the office of director, his age and state of health, the length of time he had been in jeopardy, whether he had admitted the offence, his general conduct before and after the offence, and periods of disqualification of any co-directors that might have been ordered by other courts. But the court should adopt a broad brush approach, so that detailed or repetitive evidence should not be allowed, and the citation of cases would in the great majority of cases be unnecessary and inappropriate. In *Secretary of State for Trade and Industry v Collins*,[440] Peter Gibson LJ said that the application for leave should be supported by clear evidence as to the precise role which the applicant would play in the company or companies in question and up-to-date and adequate information about that company or those companies.

**28.218**

The court will look closely at the conduct which led to disqualification[441] and the applicant will usually need to satisfy the court that the company in respect of which permission to act is sought is solvent and paying its debts as they fall due, and that its trading performance makes it unlikely that there will be any repetition of the misconduct which led to disqualification.[442] The applicant will also usually need to demonstrate that the company is up to date with its accounts and reporting requirements.

**28.219**

---

[436] Disqualification PD paras 23.1 and 23.2.
[437] *Secretary of State for Trade and Industry v Renwick* (unrep) July 1997.
[438] *Re Dicetrade Ltd* [1994] 2 BCLC 113, CA.
[439] [1998] 2 All ER 124, CA.
[440] [2000] 2 BCLC 223, CA.
[441] eg *Re Barings plc (No 5), Secretary of State for Trade and Industry v Baker* [2000] 1 WLR 634; *Re Morija* [2008] 2 BCLC 313, in which the judge set out a short summary of the established principles at paras 32 to 35 of his judgment.
[442] eg *Secretary of State for Trade and Industry v Palfreman* [1995] BCC 193. Contrast with *Re Lombard Shipping & Forwarding Ltd* (unrep) Ch D 22 March 1993, in which an application for permission failed in part because the one of the companies was having difficulties paying its rates bill.

**28.220**  While each case will turn on its own particular facts, the importance of protecting the public from the consequences of possible future defaults will be a significant factor. It will be more likely that permission will be granted where the misconduct resulting in disqualification has been regarded as at the less serious end of the spectrum, particularly those cases where the disqualification period was five years or less.

**28.221**  An order under s 17 gives leave only in respect of one or more specified companies, and may be subject to quite stringent conditions,[443] tailored to the circumstances of the particular case. Examples have included: a requirement that a named person remained a director with voting control;[444] a requirement that a chartered accountant act as co-director;[445] a ban (among other conditions) on signing cheques without a counter-signature;[446] a ban on loans to an associated company;[447] a requirement for prompt settlement of the company's debts and for regular management accounts to be prepared;[448] and restriction to performance in a subordinate capacity.[449]

**28.222**  It appears that the court will not grant permission retrospectively where the applicant is subject to a disqualification order, because to do so might decriminalize past acts which would have been in breach of the restrictions.[450]

### (7) Consequences of breach

**28.223**  A person who acts in breach of a disqualification order or undertaking, or who commits the offence under CDDA, s 11 of acting as a director of a company or involving himself in the management of a company without permission while an undischarged bankrupt[451] faces both a criminal and a civil penalty.

*Criminal liability*

**28.224**  The applicable criminal penalties are (a) on conviction on indictment, imprisonment for not more than two years or a fine or both, and (b) on summary conviction, to imprisonment for not more than six months or a fine not exceeding the statutory maximum, or both.[452]

---

[443]  *Re Westmid Packing Services Ltd* [1998] 2 All ER 124, CA.
[444]  *Re Lo-Line Electric Motors Ltd* [1988] Ch 477.
[445]  *Re Majestic Recording Studios Ltd* 1989 BCLC 1.
[446]  *Re Gibson Davies Chemists Ltd* [1995] BCC 11.
[447]  *Secretary of State for Trade and Industry v Arif* [1997] 1 BCLC 34.
[448]  *Secretary of State for Trade and Industry v Rosenfield* [1999] BCC 413.
[449]  *Re TLL Realisations Ltd* [2000] 2 BCLC 223, CA.
[450]  *Re Brian Sheridan Cars Ltd* [1996] 1 BCLC 327.
[451]  Or who acts in breach of a Northern Irish disqualification order or undertaking (CDDA, ss 12A, 12B).
[452]  CDDA, s 13.

Where the relevant contravention of a disqualification order or undertaking was **28.225** by a body corporate, and 'occurred with the consent or connivance of', or is 'attributable to any neglect on the part of', any director, manager, secretary, or other similar officer of the body corporate, or any person purporting to act in such capacity, that person is guilty of the same offence and liable to be punished accordingly.[453]

There appear to have been relatively few reported prosecutions for outright **28.226** breaches of disqualification orders or undertakings, but some guidance to the approach of the courts can be derived from cases involving acting in the management of a company while an undischarged bankrupt.

In *R v Theivendran*,[454] the Court of Appeal considered a sentence of nine months' **28.227** imprisonment for eight offences of being concerned in management of a company while an undischarged bankrupt to be excessive, and reduced it to a sentence of six months, suspended. Farquharson LJ said:

> If the contravention has been flagrant, that is to say deliberate or reckless, a custodial sentence would in principle be appropriate. If, on the other hand, there are no aggravating features, such as previous offences of the same kind or personal profit gained in fraud of creditors, that may be taken into account as justifying suspension of the sentence in whole or in part.

On the other hand, the defendant had pleaded guilty. There was no dishonesty, the relevant trading activities were genuine, and there was no suggestion of assets being salted away beyond the reach of creditors, which justified the court in suspending the sentence.

In *R v Brockley*,[455] the Court of Appeal confirmed that the offence under CDDA, **28.228** s 13 is one of strict liability, not requiring any *mens rea*, and upheld a sentence of six months' imprisonment suspended for two years for acting as a company director while an undischarged bankrupt.

In *R v Ashby*,[456] the defendant was convicted on four counts of taking part in the **28.229** management of companies while an undischarged bankrupt, one of the companies being Tottenham Hotspur football club. He was sentenced to four concurrent terms of imprisonment. The Court of Appeal considered that this was a case of 'flagrant contravention' and upheld the sentence.

In *R v Pidgeon*,[457] the defendant had been involved in the management of a com- **28.230** pany which designed and installed kitchens, including signing cheques, while an

---

453  CDDA, s 14.
454  (1992) 13 Cr App R (S) 601.
455  [1994] 1 BCLC 606.
456  [1997] EWCA Crim 2890.
457  [1999] EWCA Crim 1522.

undischarged bankrupt. At trial he was sentenced to six months' imprisonment. The Court of Appeal considered that a custodial sentence was justified, but reduced it to two months.

28.231 In *R v Harwood*[458] the defendant pleaded guilty to two counts of being concerned in management of a company while disqualified and one count of acting as an insolvency practitioner while unqualified. He was sentenced to a community service order and to a further period of 10 years' disqualification under CDDA , s 2 and appealed the latter part of the sentence. The Court of Appeal dismissed the appeal, saying:

> This court has said in particular in the guideline case of *Theivendran*[459] that a sentence of imprisonment is not wrong in principle in a case of being concerned in the management of a company when an undischarged bankrupt where no dishonesty had been established. There had been a plain flouting of the order in that case of bankruptcy.

> A fortiori the same applies where there is an express order for disqualification. Compliance with company directors disqualification orders is something which is very difficult to police. It should be understood that in the perhaps comparatively few cases where offenders are caught they are at risk of custodial sentences.

### Civil consequences

28.232 The civil consequences of acting in contravention of a disqualification order or undertaking[460] attach both to the person so acting and to anyone else involved in the management of the company[461] who acts or 'is willing to act' on instructions given without the permission of the court by a person whom he knows at the time to be the subject of a disqualification order or undertaking or an undischarged bankrupt. Either is made personally responsible by the CDDA, s 15(1) for all the relevant debts of the company. Liability is joint and several with the company and any other person who is liable under the CDDA, s 15.[462]

28.233 The person who acts in contravention is liable for 'such debts and other liabilities as are incurred at a time when that person is involved in the management of the company'.[463]

28.234 The person who becomes liable by acting or being willing to act on instructions given without the permission of the court by a person whom he knows at the time

---

[458] [1998] EWCA Crim 3119.
[459] (1992) 13 CAR (S) 601.
[460] Or in contravention of the CDDA, ss 11, 12A, or 12B.
[461] CDDA, s 15(4) provides that a person is 'involved in the management of a company' if he is a director of the company or if he is concerned whether directly or indirectly or takes part in the management of the company.
[462] CDDA, s 15(2).
[463] CDDA, s 15(3)(a).

to be the subject of a disqualification order or undertaking or an undischarged bankrupt is liable for such debts and other liabilities as are incurred at a time when that person was acting or willing to act.[464] There is a statutory presumption that a person who has at any time acted on the instructions of a person whom he knew to be a contravener was willing to act at any time thereafter on the instructions of that person.[465] The onus will therefore be on the defendant to rebut the presumption.

It appears that each relevant creditor can sue a person who is liable for a company's debts under CDDA, s 15 just as they would be able to pursue a director who is jointly and severally liable under the Insolvency Act, s 217 for the debts of a company which has been operating under a name which is prohibited in relation to them.[466]      **28.235**

This remedy will be of particular importance when the company debtor is insolvent and the person liable under s 15 has assets against which a judgment can be enforced. In *Re Prestige Grindings Ltd*,[467] Judge Norris QC held that a creditor who has a relevant debt has an 'immediate and unconditional' claim against a person liable under s 15, which he can pursue for his own benefit, while the company only has a restitutionary right of contribution against that person, arising from the 'joint and several' nature of the liability but only if and when it has paid more than its share. As he put it:      **28.236**

> In my judgment s 15 creates two separate sets of rights. To put the matter shortly and simply, it first makes the disqualified director personally responsible for all the relevant debts; and it secondly provides that the disqualified director is jointly and severally liable with the company for those debts. The first confers on the creditor a separate statutory cause of action against the disqualified director to supplement his contractual right against the company; the second gives the company a right of contribution from someone who by statute has become its co-debtor. The section does not confer on the company (co-debtor A) the right to sue the disqualified director (co-debtor B) for the amount of the debt that is owed to C. That is what para (2) of the originating application seeks when it asks the court to make an order that Mr Yardley pay to the company the value of the relevant debts. But such a right is unknown to the general law and I hold that it cannot be spelled out of the words of the section. The personal responsibility created by the section is to the creditor and with the company. The section does confer on the company (co-debtor A) the right to recover from the disqualified director (co-debtor B) a contribution in circumstances where the general law so allows.

---

[464] CDDA, s 15(3)(b).
[465] CDDA, s 15(5).
[466] ie because of its similarity to the name of a previous company which has gone into liquidation, and they had been a director in the final twelve months; Cf *Thorne v Silverleaf* [1994] 2 BCLC 637, CA.
[467] [2006] 1 BCLC 440.

He therefore held that it was inappropriate for the liquidator to put himself forward as a representative of all the creditors, or for one creditor to be appointed as representative of the creditors as a whole. He could seek a declaration of prospective liability from a co-debtor[468] but the judge considered this premature (apparently because the liquidator had not yet admitted any debts to proof). HM Revenue and Customs were parties to the proceedings and could seek an immediate order to be paid by the defendants the sums due from the company. If other creditors such as the company's landlord wished to pursue claims, they would need to do so separately. In each case it would be necessary to establish: (a) that the conditions in the CDDA, s 15(1) are satisfied,[469] (b) that the company owes a debt or has a liability to the relevant creditor, and (c) that the debt or liability was incurred at the relevant time.

---

[468] By analogy with the sort of declaration which might be granted to a co-surety: cf *Wolmerhausen v Gullick* [1893] 2 Ch 514.

[469] The judge seems to have contemplated that this might need to be established separately in each set of proceedings, but that if it was put in issue the claimant might seek permission to rely on a declaration under s 15 made in previous proceedings.

# 29

# DUTIES AND LIABILITIES OF DIRECTORS IN INSOLVENCY PROCEEDINGS

# A. Introduction

**29.01**  Since the 1844 Winding Up Act, winding-up proceedings have been a means of requiring directors to account for their management of the business of the company, investigating the causes of failure and enabling prosecutions to be brought, and claims made, against delinquent directors.[1] These purposes underline the winding-up provisions that have been incorporated into the successive Companies Acts 1862–1985.[2] The 1862 Act introduced a summary procedure, known as a misfeasance summons, for assessing damages against delinquent directors.[3] Following the report of the Greene Committee, the 1929 Act, s 275 made persons, including directors, responsible for fraudulent trading personally liable without limit for the debts of the company and also liable to criminal prosecution.

**29.02**  The Cork Committee recommended wide-ranging reforms to corporate and individual insolvency law, including the two laws, so far as possible. As a result, provisions about corporate insolvency were removed from the 1985 Act and are now to be found in the Insolvency Act, which adopts many of the Cork Report's recommendations.[4] The reforms made by the Insolvency Act, which are of particular concern to directors are: (a) a new CVA procedure, (b) administration, (c) administrative receivership, (d) power for directors to present a winding-up petition, (e) improved procedures for investigating the company's affairs and getting in its property, (f) personal liability of directors guilty of wrongful trading, (g) personal liability of persons involved in the management of a company that contravenes restrictions on re-use of a company name (the phoenix company syndrome), and (h) improved procedures for adjusting prior transactions.

**29.03**  The Insolvency Act 2000, ss 1–4, reformed the CVA procedure and enabled smaller companies to use a new moratorium provision instead of administration.[5] The Enterprise Act 2002, Part 10, ss 248–255, made major reforms to administration

---

[1] The 1844 Winding Up Act (7&8 Vic, Cap 111), enacted immediately after the Joint Stock Companies Act 1844 (7&8 Vic, Cap 110), was 'An Act for facilitating the winding up the Affairs of Joint Stock Companies unable to meet their pecuniary Engagements'. Directors of companies adjudged bankrupt were required to prepare and file at court a balance sheet and specified accounts (ss 12, 13). As precursors of the provisions in the Insolvency Act, ss 235–237, the court could order the examination of persons, including directors, capable of giving information about the affairs of the company and summary delivery up of company property (ss 15, 16, 18, and 19). There were penalties for concealment of company property and falsification of books (ss 17, 30). A report on the failure was to be produced to the Attorney-General to enable criminal prosecutions to be brought (s 27).

[2] The report of the Cork Committee, paras 74–99, contains a useful summary of the history.

[3] s 165, which is the origin of the provision now in the Insolvency Act, s 212.

[4] The Insolvency Act came into force on 29 December 1986.

[5] These provisions came into force on 1 January 2003.

procedure and prevented holders of floating charges from appointing administrative receivers, except in prescribed circumstances.[6] Further reforms, affecting companies with cross-border affairs, have been made by the EC Regulation (Council Regulation 1346/2000/EC on insolvency proceedings) and the Cross-Border Insolvency Regulation 2006, which brought into force the UNCITRAL Model Law on Cross-Border Insolvency.[7]

The purpose of this chapter is to summarize the provisions of the Insolvency Act **29.04** as amended and associated case law, which particularly affect the powers, duties, and liabilities of directors. This chapter does not attempt to cover the full extent of corporate insolvency law.

Directors of a company which is, or is likely to become, unable to pay its debts, face **29.05** serious consequences, if they do not respond positively to the company's situation. In such a situation the directors owe a general duty to the company to have regard to the interests of its creditors (Chapter 11, Section E), which is reinforced by the risks of being made subject to disqualification proceedings (Chapter 28, Section D) and of potential personal liability for fraudulent or wrongful trading (paragraphs 29.147–29.190 below), as well as criminal prosecution (Chapter 30, Section I). The directors will need to obtain advice from lawyers and an insolvency practitioner. If the directors wish to try to secure the company's survival as a going concern, they may wish to use the CVA procedure in the Insolvency Act, Part I, to deal with the company's debts. Unless they are able to reach a standstill arrangement with the company's major creditors, the directors will need to obtain a moratorium on the payment and enforcement of debts. If the company is eligible, they can do this under the procedure in Schedule A1. If the company is not eligible or Schedule A1 is not considered appropriate, then the company will have to go into administration or liquidation (or administrative receivership if that is an option) and management of the company's affairs will pass from the directors to a qualified insolvency practitioner. This chapter goes on to explore the effect of administration, administrative receivership, and liquidation on directors' powers, duties, and liabilities.

## B. Company Voluntary Arrangement

### (1) Proposal by directors

A voluntary arrangement under Part I made between a company and its creditors **29.06** is 'a composition in satisfaction of its debts or a scheme of arrangement of

---

[6] These provisions came into force on 15 September 2003.

[7] The EC Regulation came into force on 31 May 2002 and the Cross-Border Regulation (SI 2006/1030) came into force on 4 April 2006.

its affairs'.[8] A composition is an agreement to pay a sum in lieu of a larger debt or other obligation, whereas a scheme of arrangement is different from a composition and may involve something less than the release or discharge of creditors' debts, such as a moratorium.[9]

**29.07**   A proposal for a voluntary arrangement may be made by the directors of a company (other than one which is in administration or being wound up).[10] The proposal provides for a nominee, who must be a qualified insolvency practitioner, to act in relation to the voluntary arrangement either as trustee or otherwise for the purpose of supervising its implementation.[11]

**29.08**   The CVA procedure is designed to be simpler, quicker, and cheaper than the long-established power of a company to propose a compromise or arrangement with its creditors if duly approved by the requisite majority of its creditors and sanctioned by the court under what is now the 2006 Act, Part 26 (Chapter 25, Section B of this work), since under the CVA procedure there is no need to consider classes of creditors and there is no court participation (beyond receiving the nominee's report) unless there is a dispute.[12]

**29.09**   The first formal step in the CVA procedure is the preparation of the proposal for the intended nominee to make his report to the court, if he agrees to act.[13] In practice, the directors will have already taken advice from an insolvency practitioner willing to act as nominee and he will assist in the preparation of the proposal. There are several matters that the directors will discuss with the proposed nominee: (a) the terms of the voluntary arrangement, (b) how to persuade creditors to accept it, (c) compliance with disclosure requirements,[14] and (d) how the company will function until the arrangement is approved and becomes binding (ie standstill arrangement or moratorium (paragraphs 29.21–29.26 below)).

**29.10**   The terms of the proposed arrangement must be effective to enable the company to survive. There should be a realistic prospect of the company being able to meet any payment obligations, because default will lead to liquidation. Care must be taken to ensure that contingent and disputed creditors are bound into the CVA, because otherwise such creditors, once their debts are established, will be able to

---

[8]   Insolvency Act, s 1(1).

[9]   *Commissioners of Inland Revenue v Adam & Partners Ltd* [2001] 1 BCLC 222, CA at paras 39, 40, per Mummery LJ. In *Re NFU Development Trust Ltd* [1972] 1 WLR 1548, 1555C–D, Brightman J said that an 'arrangement' in what is now 2006 Act, s 895 involved 'some element of give and take' and if rights are expropriated, there must be some 'compensating advantage'.

[10]   Insolvency Act, s 1(1) and (3).

[11]   Insolvency Act, s 1(2).

[12]   The CVA procedure is contained in the Insolvency Act, Part I, ss 1–7B and the Insolvency Rules, rules 1.1–1.54.

[13]   Insolvency Act, s 2(1)–(3) and Insolvency Rules, rules 1.2 and 1.4.

[14]   Insolvency Act, s 2(3); Insolvency Rules, rules 1.3, 1.5, and 1.6.

insist on payment in full and, if not paid, will petition for winding up.[15] The terms of the proposal should not affect the rights of secured creditors or the priority of preferential creditors unless the consents of the affected secured or preferential creditors can be obtained.[16] Nor should the terms of the voluntary arrangement be unfairly prejudicial to the interests of any creditor, member, or contributory, because otherwise the court may revoke the approval on a challenge under the Insolvency Act, s 6.[17]

The directors' proposal must provide a short explanation why, in their opinion, a **29.11** CVA is desirable, and give reasons why the company's creditors may be expected to concur with such an arrangement.[18]

The Insolvency Rules require the proposal to state or otherwise deal with a large **29.12** number of matters which are listed in rule 1.3(2) and include details of the company's assets and liabilities and prior transactions capable of adjustment under the Insolvency Act, ss 238, 239, 244, and 245. With the agreement in writing of the nominee, the directors' proposal may be amended at any time up to delivery of the former's report to the court.[19] The details required by r 1.3(2) need not include any information the disclosure of which could seriously prejudice the commercial interests of the company.[20]

The Insolvency Rules, rule 1.5 also requires the directors, within seven days after **29.13** their proposal is delivered to the nominee, or within such longer time as he may allow, to deliver to him a statement of the company's affairs, comprising the particulars specified in rule 1.5(2) and supplementing or amplifying, so far as is necessary for clarifying the state of the company's affairs, those already given in the directors' proposal. The statement of affairs shall be made up to a date not earlier than two weeks before the date of the notice to the nominee. However, the nominee may allow an extension of that period to the nearest practicable date (not earlier than two months before the date of the notice); and if he does so, he shall give his reasons in his report to the court on the directors' proposal. The statement shall be

---

[15]  For issues concerning the inclusion of contingent claims, see the schemes of arrangement cases *Re T&N Ltd* [2006] 1 WLR 1728; *Re T&N Ltd (No 3)* [2007] 1 BCLC 563. For issues concerning the inclusion of disputed claims, see *Alman v Approach Housing Ltd* [2001] 1 BCLC 530; *Oakley Smith v Greenberg* [2005] 2 BCLC 74, CA; *El Ajou v Stern* [2007] BPIR 693. These issues are particularly significant in relation to potential costs awards in current proceedings: *Glenister v Rowe* [2000] Ch 76, CA.

[16]  Insolvency Act, s 4(3) and (4); *IRC v Wimbledon Football Club Ltd* [2005] 1 BCLC 66, CA.

[17]  *SISU Capital Fund Ltd v Tucker* [2006] BCC 463 at paras 68–78, per Warren J and *Prudential Assurance Co Ltd v PRG Powerhouse Ltd* [2007] BCC 500 at paras 71–96 where Etherton J revoked approval of a CVA on the ground that a provision for release of guarantees was unfairly prejudicial to the creditors entitled to them.

[18]  Insolvency Rules, rule 1.3(1).

[19]  Insolvency Rules, rules 1.2, 1.3.

[20]  Insolvency Rules, rule 1.3(4).

certified as correct, to the best of their knowledge and belief, by two or more directors of the company, or by the company secretary and at least one director (other than the secretary himself).[21]

29.14    If it appears to the nominee that he cannot properly prepare his report on the basis of information in the directors' proposal and statement of affairs, he may call on the directors to provide him with (a) further and better particulars as to the circumstances in which, and the reasons why, the company is insolvent or (as the case may be) threatened with insolvency, (b) particulars of any previous proposals for a voluntary arrangement which have been made in respect of the company, and (c) any further information with respect to the company's affairs which the nominee thinks necessary for the purposes of his report. The nominee may call on the directors to inform him, with respect to any person who is, or at any time in the two years preceding the notice has been, a director or officer of the company, whether and in what circumstances (in those two years or previously) that person has been concerned in the affairs of any other company which has become insolvent, or has himself been adjudged bankrupt or entered into an arrangement with his creditors. For the purpose of enabling the nominee to consider their proposal and prepare his report on it, the directors must give him access to the company's accounts and records.[22]

29.15    Where the directors do not propose to take steps to obtain a moratorium for the company (under Insolvency Act, s 1A and Schedule A1) the nominee shall, within 28 days after he is given notice of the proposal for a voluntary arrangement, submit a report to the court stating (a) whether, in his opinion, the proposed voluntary arrangement has a reasonable prospect of being approved and implemented, (b) whether, in his opinion, meetings of the company and of its creditors should be summoned to consider the proposal, and (c) if in his opinion such meetings should be summoned, the date on which, and time and place at which, he proposes the meetings should be held.[23] With his report the nominee should deliver to the court a copy of the proposal (with any authorized amendments) and a copy or summary of the statement of affairs.[24]

### (2)  Consideration and implementation of the proposal

29.16    Where the nominee has reported to the court that in his opinion meetings of the company and its creditors should be summoned to consider the directors' proposal, he proceeds to summon those meetings to consider the proposal.[25] Every creditor

---

[21]  Insolvency Rules, rule 1.5.

[22]  Insolvency Rules, rule 1.6.

[23]  Insolvency Act, s 2. Note that there are provisions for the replacement of the nominee: Insolvency Act, s 2(4); Insolvency Rules, rule 1.8. The nominee is expected to satisfy himself that the proposal is serious and viable: *Re a Debtor (No 140 IO of 1995)* [1996] 2 BCLC 429.

[24]  Insolvency Rules, rule 1.7.

[25]  Insolvency Act, s 3(1) and (2); Insolvency Rules, rules 1.9(1) and 1.13.

of the company of whose claim and address the nominee is aware, including those specified in the statement of affairs, should be summoned to the creditors' meeting.[26] The notices summoning the meetings should include (a) a copy of the proposal, (b) a copy of the statement of affairs or a summary of it, and (c) the nominee's comments on the proposal.[27]

**29.17** Notice to attend the meetings should also be given to all directors of the company, and, if the nominee thinks that their presence is required, other officers of the company, or persons who were directors or officers of it at any time in the two years immediately preceding the date of the notice. The nominee, as chairman, may if he thinks fit, exclude any of those persons from attendance at a meeting, either completely or for any part of it.[28]

**29.18** The purpose of the meetings is to decide whether to approve the proposed voluntary arrangement with or without modifications.[29] The decision to approve the proposed voluntary arrangement has effect if it is taken by both meetings or, subject to application to the court, by only the creditors' meeting.[30] At the creditors' meeting for any resolution to pass approving any proposal or modification there must be a majority in excess of three-quarters in value of the creditors present in person or by proxy and voting on the resolution. At a company meeting any resolution is to be regarded as passed if voted for by more than one-half in value of the members present in person or by proxy and voting on the resolution.[31] The nominee, as chairman, reports the result of the meeting to the court.[32]

**29.19** Where a decision to approve the voluntary arrangement has effect, the voluntary arrangement takes effect as if made by the company at the creditors' meeting and binds every person who, in accordance with the Insolvency Rules, was entitled to vote at the meeting (whether or not he was present or represented at it), or would have been entitled if he had had notice of it, as if he were a party to the voluntary arrangement.[33] The decision is, however, subject to challenge on the grounds of unfair prejudice or material irregularity.[34]

---

[26] Insolvency Act, s 3(3); Insolvency Rules, rule 1.9(2).

[27] Insolvency Rules, rule 1.9(3).

[28] Insolvency Rules, rule 1.16.

[29] Insolvency Act, s 4(1)–(4), which restricts modifications prejudicing secured and preferential creditors without their concurrence.

[30] Insolvency Act, s 4A. The circumstances in which a member could successfully challenge a decision by the creditors must be rare.

[31] Insolvency Rules, rule 1.19(1), rule 1.20(1). This is subject to the detailed rules relating to voting rights and majorities set out in Insolvency Rules, rules 1.17–1.21.

[32] Insolvency Act, s 4(6).

[33] Insolvency Act, s 5(1) and (2). As to the legal effect of approval, see *Johnson v Davies* [1999] Ch 117, 138c, CA, per Chadwick LJ; *Raja v Rubin* [2000] Ch 274, 287, per Peter Gibson LJ.

[34] Insolvency Act, s 6. On unfair prejudice, see *SISU Capital Fund Ltd v Tucker* [2006] BCC 463 at paras 68–78, per Warren J and *Prudential Assurance Co Ltd v PRG Powerhouse Ltd* [2007]

**29.20**  The truth and accuracy of the representations made by the directors in the proposal, the statement of affairs, and further information given to the nominee and at the meetings are of critical importance. This is reinforced by the Insolvency Act, s 6A(1) which provides:

> If, for the purpose of obtaining the approval of the members or creditors of a company to a proposal for a voluntary arrangement, a person who is an officer of the company—
>
> (a)  makes any false representation, or
> (b)  fraudulently does, or omits to do, anything, he commits an offence.

A person guilty of an offence under s 6A is liable to imprisonment or a fine.

### (3) Moratorium

**29.21**  Where the directors of an eligible company intend to make a proposal for a CVA, they may take steps to obtain a moratorium in accordance with the Insolvency Act, Schedule A1.[35] Eligible companies are small companies other than companies such as insurance companies and banks[36] which fulfil two of the following three conditions: (a) turnover less than £6.5 million; (b) balance sheet total less than £3.26 million; and (c) having fewer than 50 employees.[37] A company is also ineligible if it is in administration, liquidation, administrative receivership, provisional liquidation, subject to a voluntary arrangement, or has had the benefit of a moratorium within the previous 12 months.[38]

**29.22**  A moratorium, which prohibits most forms of legal process against the company,[39] is only available if (a) the nominee is satisfied that the company is likely to have funds available to it during the proposed moratorium to enable it to carry on business,[40] and (b) the directors are content to carry on managing the business of

---

BCC 500 at paras 71–96. On material irregularity, see *Re Cranley Mansions Ltd* [1994] 1 WLR 1610; *Re Sweatfield Ltd* [1997] BCC 744; *SISU Capital Fund Ltd v Tucker* [2006] BCC 463 at paras 79–81; *Re Newlands (Seaford) Educational Trust* [2006] BCC 195.

[35]  Insolvency Act, s 1A, which, with Schedule A1, was introduced by the Insolvency Act 2000.

[36]  Companies are ineligible if they fall within Insolvency Act, Schedule 1A, paras 2(1)(a) or (b), 4A (the company is party to a capital market arrangement), 4B (the company is a project company or a project which is a public-private partnership project and includes step-in rights), or 4C (the company has incurred a liability under an agreement of £10 million or more). Paras 4D–4K explain paras 4A–4C. By para 5 the Secretary of State may modify the conditions of eligibility.

[37]  Insolvency Act, Schedule 1A, paras 2, 3; 1985 Act, s 247, replaced by 2006 Act, s 382 as amended by the Companies Act 2006 (Amendment)(Accounts and Reports) Regulations 2008 (SI 2008/393), which came into force on 6 April 2008.

[38]  Insolvency Act, Schedule A1, para 4(1).

[39]  Insolvency Act, Schedule A1, paras 12–14.

[40]  Insolvency Act, Schedule A1, para 6(2)(a) and 7(1)(e)(ii).

the company during the moratorium period subject to specified restrictions, enforced by criminal sanction,[41] and monitoring by the nominee.[42] It seems that few, if any, companies are able or willing to meet these requirements, since the provisions of Schedule A1 are rarely used.

If the directors do wish to obtain a moratorium they file at court:  **29.23**

(a) a document setting out the terms of the proposed voluntary arrangement,
(b) a statement of the company's affairs,
(c) a statement that the company is eligible for a moratorium,
(d) a statement from the nominee that he has given his consent to act, and
(e) a statement from the nominee that, in his opinion (i) the proposed voluntary arrangement has a reasonable prospect of being approved and implemented, (ii) the company is likely to have sufficient funds available to it during the proposed moratorium to enable it to carry on its business, and (iii) meetings of the company and its creditors should be summoned to consider the proposed voluntary arrangement.[43]

The moratorium comes into force when these documents are filed with the court  **29.24** and, in broad terms, lasts until the end of the day on which the meetings of members and creditors to consider the proposals are held, which should be within 28 days of the moratorium coming into force.[44]

The procedure for the consideration and implementation of the voluntary  **29.25** arrangement follows the scheme applicable to CVAs under Part 1, as described above, except that there is provision for extending the moratorium and appointing a moratorium committee.[45] There is also provision for a creditor or member to apply to the court to challenge the acts or omissions of the directors during the moratorium period on the ground of unfair prejudice.[46]

Schedule A1, paragraph 41 applies where a moratorium has been obtained for  **29.26** a company and provides for various offences of fraud in anticipation of the moratorium, in terms similar to the Insolvency Act, s 206 in the case of winding up (Chapter 30, paragraph 30.235 and Appendix 2, Table 3).

---

[41] Insolvency Act, Schedule A1, paras 15–23. The restrictions concern publicity of the moratorium, obtaining credit, disposing of company property, paying debts, disposing of charged property, and market contracts.
[42] Insolvency Act, Schedule A1, paras 24–28.
[43] Insolvency Act, Schedule A1, paras 6 and 7.
[44] Insolvency Act, Schedule 1, para 8.
[45] Insolvency Act, Schedule 1, paras 29–39.
[46] Insolvency Act, Schedule 1, para 40.

# C. Administration

### (1) The new administration regime

**29.27**  A new administration regime, contained in the Insolvency Act, Schedule B1 came into effect on 15 September 2003.[47] The original regime, contained in the Insolvency Act, ss 8–27, continues to apply with modifications to certain companies of national significance.[48] The following paragraphs deal only with the position of directors in relation to the administrations under Schedule B1, under which a company,[49] which is not already in administration or liquidation, may enter administration by the appointment of an administrator[50] (a) when the court makes an administration order,[51] or (b) when the appointment is made out of court by the holder of a floating charge,[52] or by the company or directors.[53] The out-of-court procedure is used in the majority of cases because of the saving in time and expense, but there are occasions when an application for an administration order is necessary or desirable.

**29.28**  Whichever procedure is adopted by the directors or the company, there are two conditions for the appointment of an administrator. The first is that 'the company is or is likely to become unable to pay its debts' within the meaning of the Insolvency Act, s 123.[54]

---

[47]  It was introduced by the Enterprise Act 2002, s 248.

[48]  Enterprise Act 2002, s 249. Building society (Building Societies Act 1986, ss 90A and Schedule 15A); water and sewage undertakers (Water Industry Act 1991, ss 23–26 and Schedule 3); protected railway, companies (Railways Act 1993, ss 59–65 and Schedule 6); companies party to a public-private partnership agreement (Greater London Authority Act 1999, ss 220–224 and Schedules 14 and 15); air traffic services companies (Transport Act 2000, ss 26–32 and Schedule 2).

[49]  By Schedule B1, para 111(1A) 'Company' means (a) a company within the meaning of 1985 Act, s 735(1) (to be replaced by 2006 Act, s 1 on 1 October 2009), (b) a company incorporated in an EEA state other than the UK, or (c) a company not incorporated in an EEA state but having its COMI in a Member State other than Denmark. As to companies within (c) of this definition, see *Re BRAC Rent-A-Car International Inc* [2003] 1 WLR 1421; *Re Sendo Ltd* [2006] 1 BCLC 395.

[50]  Insolvency Act, Schedule B1, paras 6–8 contain general restrictions on the appointment of an administrator.

[51]  Insolvency Act, Schedule B1, paras 11–13, 35–39 and Insolvency Rules, rules 2.2–2.14.

[52]  Insolvency Act, Schedule B1, paras 14–21 and Insolvency Rules, rules 2.15–2.19.

[53]  Insolvency Act, Schedule B1, paras 22–34 and Insolvency Rules, rules 2.20–2.27.

[54]  The Insolvency Act, Schedule B1, para 111(1). As to the definition of inability to pay debts in s 123, see *Byblos Bank SAL v Al Khudhairy* [1987] BCLC 232, CA (a pre-Insolvency Act case); *Re Imperial Motors Ltd* [1990] BCLC 29; *Re Dianoor Jewels Ltd* [2001] 1 BCLC 450; *Re Cheyne Finance Ltd (No 2)* 1 BCLC 741 [2008]. Where application is made to the court for an administration order, the court must be satisfied that this is the case on the balance of probabilities: Insolvency Act, Schedule B1, para 11(a): *Re COLT Telecom Group plc* [2003] BPIR 324; *Hammonds v Pro-Fit USA Ltd* [2008] 2 BCLC 159 (both creditors' applications). Where the appointment is made by the company or directors, there must be a statutory declaration made by or on behalf of the person who proposes to make the application to this effect: Insolvency Act, Schedule B1, paras 27(2)(a), 29(2) and 30(a). Where the appointment is made by the holder of a qualifying floating charge, this condition does not have to be satisfied; instead the charge must be enforceable on the date of the appointment: Insolvency Act, Schedule B1, paras 16 and 18(2).

The second is that the purpose of administration is reasonably likely to be achieved.[55]

The redefined purpose of administration, as stated in Schedule B1, para 3, is fundamentally different from the original purposes stated in s 8(3), in that (a) the three objectives are stated in order of priority, designed to encourage rescue, and (b) the objectives contemplate distributions in the administration to secured, preferential, and unsecured creditors, rather than outside the administration, whether on survival of the company, or under a CVA or scheme of arrangement under the 2006 Act, Part 26 or in a winding up.[56] Schedule B1, para 3 provides:    **29.29**

(1) The administrator must perform his functions with the objective of —
   (a) rescuing the company as a going concern, or
   (b) achieving a better result for the company's creditors as a whole than would be likely if the company were wound up (without first being in administration), or
   (c) realising property in order to make a distribution to one or more secured or preferential creditors.
(2) Subject to sub-paragraph (4), the administrator of a company must perform his functions in the interests of the company's creditors as a whole.
(3) The administrator must perform his functions with the objective specified in sub-paragraph (1)(a) unless he thinks either—
   (a) that it is not reasonably practicable to achieve that objective, or
   (b) that the objective specified in sub-paragraph (1)(b) would achieve a better result for the company's creditors as a whole.
(4) The administrator may perform his functions with the objective specified in sub-paragraph (1)(c) only if—
   (a) he thinks it is not reasonably practicable to achieve either of the objectives specified in sub-paragraphs (1)(a) and (b), and
   (b) he does not unnecessarily harm the interests of the company's creditors as a whole.

---

[55] Where application is made to the court for an administration order, the court must consider that there is a real prospect that the statutory purpose might be achieved: Insolvency Act, Schedule B1, para 11(b); Insolvency Rule 2.3(5)(c) and Form 2.2B; *Re Harris Simons Construction Ltd* [1989] 1 WLR 368; *Re Lomax Leisure Ltd* [2000] Ch 502; *Re AA Mutual International Insurance Co Ltd* [2005] 2 BCLC 8; *Re Redman Construction Ltd* [2005] EWHC 1850 (Ch); *Hammonds v Pro-Fit USA Ltd* [2008] 2 BCLC 159. Where the appointment is made by the company or directors (or by the holder of a qualifying floating charge), there must be a statement by the administrator that in his opinion the purpose of administration is reasonably likely to be achieved: Insolvency Act, Schedule B1, paras 18(3)(b), 29(3)(b); Insolvency Rules, rules 2.16(2)(a), 2.23(2)(a) and Form 2.2B.
[56] The potential for distributions to unsecured creditors is implicit in the phrase 'better result' and express provision is made by Schedule B1, para 65, with the permission of the court. The objective of making distributions to secured and preferential creditors follows from administration replacing administrative receivership, which was abolished by the Insolvency Act, s 72A (added by the Enterprise Act 2002, s 250). The new administration regime is to be contrasted with the description of the former regime given by Lord Hoffmann in *Centre Reinsurance International Co v Freakley* [2006] 1 WLR 2863, HL at paras 6 and 7.

### (2) **Appointment of administrator by directors**

**29.30** Where the directors consider that an administrator should be appointed out of court, they may invite the members to make the appointment if that is practicable, but they also have power to make the appointment themselves, acting unanimously or by resolution of the board.[57]

**29.31** The power of the directors or the company to appoint an administrator out of court is restricted in that such an appointment may not be made if:

(1) less than 12 months have elapsed since the date on which (a) the company ceased to be in administration, if an administrator had been appointed by the company or its directors or on an administration application made by the company or its directors,[58] (b) a moratorium ended without a CVA being in force,[59] or (c) a CVA ended if it was made during a moratorium or ended prematurely;

(2) a petition for the winding up of the company has been presented and is not yet disposed of;

(3) an administration application has been made and is not yet disposed of;

(4) an administrative receiver of the company is in office.[60]

**29.32** Where the restrictions apply the company or its directors may apply to the court for an administration order to be made on their application. However, where there is an administrative receiver in office, the court will dismiss the administration application unless the person by or on behalf of whom the receiver was appointed consents to the making of the administration order or the court thinks that, if an administration order were made the security by virtue of which the receiver was appointed would be liable to be released or discharged under the Insolvency Act, ss 238–240 (transactions at undervalue and preference) or avoided under s 245 (avoidance of floating charge).[61]

**29.33** Where the restrictions on appointment do not apply, there are two procedures for the appointment of an administrator, depending on whether it is necessary to give notice of intention to make the appointment. Where there is no need to serve anyone with notice of intention to appoint, an immediate appointment can be made.

**29.34** Where there is a person with a qualifying floating charge, whether or not it is enforceable, the directors must give the holder at least five business days' written

---

[57] Insolvency Act, Schedule B1, paras 22 and 105; *Re Equiticorp International plc* [1989] 1 WLR 1010.

[58] Insolvency Act, Schedule B1, paras 23(2), 1(2)(c).

[59] Insolvency Act, Schedule B1, para 24(1) and (3).

[60] Insolvency Act, Schedule B1, para 25.

[61] Insolvency Act, Schedule B1, para 39.

notice before they can appoint an administrator.[62] The purpose of this is to give the holder an opportunity to (a) appoint an administrative receiver, if he is entitled to, (b) appoint an administrator of his choice, (c) negotiate the identity of the administrator appointed by the directors, or (d) make an administration application. In fact it is pointless for the company or the directors to propose an administrator who is not acceptable to the holder of any qualifying floating charge. Having given notice, the directors must file with the court a copy of the notice, accompanied by specified documents.[63] The filing of these documents brings into force an interim moratorium, which continues until the appointment of the administrator takes effect or ten business days expires without an administrator having been appointed, after which they cannot make an appointment.[64]

The directors must also give notice of intention to appoint an administrator to: **29.35** (a) any enforcement officer, to the knowledge of the person giving the notice, charged with execution or other legal process against the company, (b) any person who, to the knowledge of the person giving the notice, has distrained against the company or its property, (c) any supervisor of a voluntary arrangement, and (d) the company, if the company is not intending to make the appointment.[65] The documents mentioned in the preceding paragraph must be filed with the court, but the directors do not need to wait five days before making the appointment.

The appointment of an administrator by the directors or the company takes effect **29.36** when they file with the court[66] (a) a notice of appointment, which includes a statutory declaration as to prescribed matters and identifies the administrator,[67] (b) a statement by the administrator that he consents to the appointment, and that in his opinion the purpose of the administration is reasonably likely to

---

[62] Insolvency Act, Schedule B1, paras 14, 26(1) and (3) and 28(1) and Insolvency Rules, rule 2.20.

[63] Insolvency Act, Schedule B1, para 27, Insolvency Rules, rules 2.2–2.24; Form 2.8B. The specified documents are a record of their decision to make the appointment, and a statutory declaration (a) that the company is or is likely to become unable to pay its debts, (b) that the company is not in liquidation, (c) that, so far as they are able to ascertain, the appointment is not prevented by the restrictions in paragraph 29.31 above.

[64] Insolvency Act, Schedule B1, paras 28, 42–44.

[65] Insolvency Act, Schedule B1, paras 26(2) and (3); Insolvency Rules, rule 2.20; Form 2.8B. As to the persons in (a) and (b), compare rule 2.9 in relation to an administration application.

[66] Insolvency Act, Schedule B1, paras 29 and 31; Insolvency Rules, rules 2.22–2.26; Forms 2.9B, 2.10B.

[67] The prescribed matters to be included in the statutory declaration are (a) that the person is entitled to make the appointment under para 22; (b) that the appointment is in accordance with Schedule B1; and either (c) where notice of intention to appoint has been given, that, so far as the person making the statement is able to ascertain, the statements made and information given in the statutory declaration filed with the notice of intention to appoint remain accurate, or (d) where no one is entitled to notice of intention to appoint, as to the matters specified in n 63 above; Insolvency Act, Schedule B1, paras 29(2) and 30.

be achieved,[68] and (c) other prescribed documents.[69] The person making the appointment must notify the administrator as soon as is reasonably practicable after these requirements are satisfied.[70] The appointment does not, however, take effect if, before these requirements are satisfied, the holder of a qualifying floating charge has appointed an administrator or an administration order has been made.[71]

**29.37** When the appointment takes effect and the company is in administration, no resolution may be passed, or order made, for the winding up of the company and the moratorium on other legal process applies.[72]

### (3) Directors' application for an administration order

**29.38** An administration order is an order appointing a person as an administrator of a company.[73] The court may make an administration order in relation to a company only if satisfied (a) that the company is or is likely to become unable to pay its debts, within the meaning of the Insolvency Act, s 123, and (b) that the administration order is reasonably likely to achieve the purpose of administration (paragraph 29.29 above).

**29.39** An application to the court for an administration order in respect of a company, known as an 'administration application', may be made only by (a) the company, (b) the directors of the company, (c) one or more creditors of the company, (d) a Magistrates Court officer in respect of fines, or (d) a combination of such persons.[74]

---

[68] The administrator's statement is in Form 2.2B; Insolvency Rules, rule 2.23. He may rely on information supplied by the directors of the company, unless he has reason to doubt its accuracy: Insolvency Act, Schedule B1, para 29(4).

[69] The other prescribed documents are: (a) the written consent of all those persons to whom notice was given in accordance with para 26(1) unless the five-day notice period has expired: Insolvency Rules, rule 2.23(2)(b); (b) where more than one administrator is appointed a statement as to which functions are to be exercised jointly and which by any or all of the administrators: Insolvency Rules, rule 2.23(2)(c) and Schedule B1, para 100(2); and (c) where notice of intention to appoint an administrator has not been given, either a copy of the resolution of the company, or a record of the decision of the directors, to appoint an administrator: Insolvency Rules, rules 2.22 and 2.25.

[70] Insolvency Act, Schedule B1, para 32; Insolvency Rules, rule 2.26. For notice of appointment, see rule 2.27 and Forms 2.11B and 2.12B.

[71] Insolvency Act, Schedule B1, para 33.

[72] Insolvency Act, Schedule B1, paras 42 and 43. Also the administrator may require a receiver of part of the company's property to vacate office: para 41(2).

[73] Insolvency Act, Schedule B1, para 10.

[74] Insolvency Act, Schedule B1, para 12(1)(b). A 'creditor' includes a contingent and a prospective creditor; para 12(4). An administration application may also be made by (a) the liquidator of the company (Schedule B1, para 38), (b) the supervisor of a CVA, which is treated as an application by the company (s 7(4)(b) and Schedule B1, para 12(5), Insolvency Rules, rule 2.2(4)), and (c) the FSA (FSMA, s 359).

Where the directors apply, they may act by a majority and the application is treated for all purposes as the application of the company.[75]

The directors will need to make an administration application where they are **29.40** unable to make an appointment out of court, because of the restrictions mentioned in paragraph 29.31 above. Even where there are no such restrictions it may be desirable to apply for an administration order; eg where an appointment out of court might be challenged by creditors or shareholders, or where court involvement is likely to be required because of a foreign element or the need to obtain directions.

The administration application made by the company or the directors must con- **29.41** tain a statement of the applicant's belief that the company is, or is likely to become, unable to pay its debts.[76] The application must be supported by an affidavit complying with rule 2.4 made by one of the directors, or by the secretary, stating himself to make it on behalf of the company, as to the company's financial position and whether the EC Regulation applies.[77] There must be attached to the application a written statement by each of the persons proposed to be administrator, stating (a) that he consents to accept appointment, (b) details of any prior professional relationship(s) that he has had with the company to which he is to be appointed as administrator, and (c) his opinion that it is reasonably likely that the purpose of the administration will be achieved.[78] Applicants for an administration order owe a duty of candour to the court, which should look critically at the material placed before it.[79]

---

[75] Insolvency Act, Schedule B1, para 105; Insolvency Rules, rule 2.3(2).

[76] Insolvency Rules, rule 2.2(1), by which the administration application must be in Form 2.1B, and rule 2.4(1). By rule 2.3(1), the application must state the name of the company and its address for service, which (in the absence of special reasons to the contrary) is that of the company's registered office. If the application is made by the directors, rule 2.3(2) requires that it is so made under Schedule B1, para 12(1)(b).

[77] Insolvency Rules, rules 2.2(1) and (2). Rule 2.4(2) requires the affidavit in support to contain (a) a statement of the company's financial position, specifying (to the best of the applicant's knowledge and belief) the company's assets and liabilities, including contingent and prospective liabilities, (b) details of any security known or believed to be held by creditors of the company, and whether in any case the security is such as to confer power on the holder to appoint an administrative receiver or to appoint an administrator under para 14, (c) details of any insolvency proceedings in relation to the company including any petition that has been presented for the winding up of the company so far as within the immediate knowledge of the applicant, (d) where it is intended to appoint a number of persons as administrators, details of the matters set out in para 100(2) regarding the exercise of the function of the administrators, and (e) any other matters which, in the opinion of those intending to make the application, will assist the court in deciding whether to make such an order, so far as lying within the knowledge or belief of the applicant. By rule 2.4(4) the affidavit shall also state whether, in the opinion of the person making the application, the EC Regulation will apply and if so, whether the proceedings will be main proceedings or territorial proceedings.

[78] Insolvency Rules, rule 2.3(5). The statement shall be in Form 2.2B.

[79] *Cornhill Insurance plc v Cornhill Financial Services Ltd* [1993] BCLC 914, 956, 957, CA, per Dillon LJ.

**29.42**   The application and all supporting documents are filed with the court, which fixes a venue for the hearing.[80] Where there is no need to serve any of the persons mentioned in the next paragraph or where any such persons consent, the court may hear the application immediately. In other cases the hearing date will be fixed to allow sufficient time for service. The filing of the application brings into force an interim moratorium on insolvency proceedings and other legal process.[81] Once the application has been made it cannot be withdrawn without the permission of the court.[82]

**29.43**   The following must be given not less than five days' notice of the hearing of the application: (a) any administrative receiver of the company, (b) the holder of a qualifying floating charge who may be entitled to appoint an administrative receiver or administrator, (c) the petitioner in respect of any pending winding-up petition (and any provisional liquidator), (d) any Member State liquidator appointed in main proceedings in relation to the company, (e) the person proposed as administrator, (f) the company, if the application is made by anyone other than the company, and (g) the supervisor of a CVA.[83]

**29.44**   In addition notice must be given to any enforcement or other officer, who to the knowledge of the applicant, is charged with an execution or other legal process against the company or its property and any person who, to the applicant's knowledge, has distrained against the company or its property.[84]

**29.45**   The directors and the company may appear or be represented at the hearing of their application, as may the persons served under paragraph 29.43 above.[85] At the hearing the court has wide powers and may (a) make the administration order, (b) dismiss the application, (c) adjourn the hearing conditionally or unconditionally, (d) make an interim order, including one which restricts the exercise of a power of the directors of the company, or makes the management of the company subject to the control of the court or an insolvency practitioner, or (e) treat the application as a winding-up petition and make a winding-up order under the

---

[80]   Insolvency Rules, rule 2.5(1)–(3). By rule 2.5(4), after the application is filed, it is the duty of the applicant to notify the court in writing of the existence of any insolvency proceedings, and any insolvency proceedings under the EC Regulation, in relation to the company, as soon as he becomes aware of them.

[81]   Insolvency Act, Schedule B1, paras 42–44.

[82]   Insolvency Act, Schedule B1, para 12(3).

[83]   Insolvency Act, Schedule B1, para 12(2); Insolvency Rules, rule 2.6(3). As to service, manner of service, and proof of service, see rules 2.6–2.9 and Form 2.3B.

[84]   Insolvency Rules, rule 2.7.

[85]   Insolvency Rules, rule 2.12. With the permission of the court any other person who appears to have an interest justifying his appearance may also appear or be represented: rule 2.12(1)(k). As to appearance by shareholders, see *Re Chelmsford City Football Club (1980) Ltd* [1991] BCC 133; *Re Farnborough-Aircraft.com Ltd* [2002] 2 BCLC 641.

Insolvency Act, s 125.[86] If the court makes an administration order, it takes effect at the time appointed in the order, or if no time is appointed, when the order is made and brings into effect the moratorium on insolvency proceedings and other legal process.[87]

Three particular matters affect the decision of the court on the administration application: the appointment of an administrative receiver, the rights of the holder of a qualifying floating charge, and opposition from creditors.    **29.46**

The issue of an administration application does not prevent the holder of a quali-    **29.47**
fying floating charge appointing an administrative receiver or such receiver carrying out his functions.[88] Where an administrative receiver is in office, whether appointed before or after the making of the administration application, the court must dismiss the application unless the person by or on behalf of whom the receiver was appointed consents to the making of the administration order or the court thinks that the security by virtue of which the receiver was appointed would be liable to be released or discharged under the Insolvency Act, ss 238–240 (transaction at undervalue or preference) or avoided under s 245 (avoidance of floating charge) if an administration order were made.[89] If the holder of the qualifying floating charge does consent to the making of an administration order, the administrative receiver vacates office, so that there is only an administrator in office.[90]

The issue of an administration application does not prevent the holder of a quali-    **29.48**
fying floating charge from appointing an administrator under paragraph 14.[91] The effect of such an appointment is that the court cannot make an administration order on the application of the company or the directors, which must therefore be dismissed.[92] Instead of appointing its own administrator out of court, the holder of a qualifying floating charge may intervene in the administration application and apply to the court to appoint a specified person as administrator instead of the person nominated by the applicant. The court must grant that application

---

[86] Insolvency Act, Schedule B1, para 13, which is subject to para 39; see paragraph 29.46 below. For an interim order, see *Re Galidoro Trawlers Ltd* [1991] BCLC 411. In *Re Ci4net.com Inc* [2005] BCC 277 a winding-up order was made on an administration application made by a creditor.

[87] Insolvency Act, Schedule B1, paras 13(2), 42, 43. The administration order is in Form 2.4B. See Insolvency Rules, rule 2.12 and rule 2.14 for notice of the order, and rule 2.27 for notice of appointment of administrator and Forms 2.11B and 2.12B.

[88] Insolvency Act, Schedule B1, para 44(7)(c) and (d).

[89] Insolvency Act, Schedule B1, para 39; *Chesterton International Group plc v Deka Immobilien Inv GmbH* [2005] BPIR 1103.

[90] Insolvency Act, Schedule B1, para 41(1) and (3).

[91] Insolvency Act, Schedule B1, para 44(7) (b).

[92] Insolvency Act, Schedule B1, para 7, which is subject to paras 90–97 and 100–103 about replacement and additional administrators.

unless, because of the particular circumstances of the case, the court thinks it right to refuse it.[93]

**29.49** The administration application made by the company or the directors may be opposed by creditors, who may have presented a winding-up petition. Provided that the court is satisfied that there is a real prospect that the purpose of administration may be achieved the court will be disposed to make an administration order and dismiss any winding-up petition.[94] Where there is a dispute as to the identity of the administrator, the relevant factors are usually independence and cost saving.[95] Even if the directors' or company's administration application is unsuccessful, the directors will not be ordered to pay costs if they have acted in good faith in performance of their duties to the company.[96]

### (4) Effect of appointment of administrator on directors' powers

**29.50** An administrator is a person appointed under the Insolvency Act, Schedule B1 to manage the company's affairs, business, and property.[97] He is an officer of the court, even if appointed out of court, and must perform his functions as quickly and efficiently as reasonably practicable.[98] The administrator is empowered to do anything necessary or expedient for the management of the affairs, business, and property of the company;[99] and he is given a number of specific powers.[100] The administrator on his appointment takes custody or control of all the property to which he thinks the company is entitled.[101]

**29.51** The administrator's powers include the power to remove or appoint a director (whether or not to fill a vacancy).[102] It follows that the appointment of an administrator does not, without more, terminate the office of a director. However,

---

[93] Insolvency Act, Schedule B1, para 36; Insolvency Rules, rule 2.10.

[94] On the making of an administration order, a petition for the winding up of the company shall be dismissed: Insolvency Act, Schedule B1, para 40(1)(a), unless the petition is under s 124A (public interest), s 124B (SEs), or by the FSA under FSMA, s 367. For cases, under the original administration regime of petitions opposed by creditors, see *Re Consumer and Industrial Press Ltd* [1988] BCLC 177; *Re Land and Property Trust Co plc (No 2)* [1991] BCLC 849; *Re Arrows Ltd (No 3)* [1992] BCLC 555; *Re Structures & Computers Ltd* [1998] 1 BCLC 292; *Re Stallton Distribution Ltd* [2002] BCC 486. For such a case under the new regime, see *El Ajou v Dollarland (Manhattan) Ltd* [2007] BCC 953.

[95] *Re Maxwell Communication Corp Plc* [1992] BCLC 465; *Re World Class Homes Ltd* [2005] 2 BCLC 1.

[96] *Re Land and Property Trust Co plc (No 4)* [1994] 1 BCLC 232, CA; *Re Tajik Air Ltd* [1996] 1 BCLC 317.

[97] Insolvency Act, Schedule B1, para 1(1).

[98] Insolvency Act, Schedule B1, paras 4 and 5.

[99] Insolvency Act, Schedule B1, para 59(1).

[100] Insolvency Act, Schedule B1, para 60, Schedule 1.

[101] Insolvency Act, Schedule B1, para 67.

[102] Insolvency Act, Schedule B1, para 61. Even though it is in administration a company must have the minimum number of directors required by the Companies Act, s 154.

a director may not exercise a management power—which means a power which could be exercised so as to interfere with the exercise of the administrator's powers—without the consent of the administrator.[103] It follows that the administrator is at liberty to give a director an active role in the management of the company.

The board of directors retains its role as an organ of the company notwithstanding **29.52** the appointment of an administrator, and the directors continue to be subject to statutory and common law duties. But the directors may not interfere with the management by the administrator of the company's affairs, business, and property. If they do they risk being in contempt of court, since an administrator is an officer of the court.[104]

## D. Administrative Receivership

An administrative receiver can only be appointed pursuant to a qualifying floating **29.53** charge which was created before 15 September 2003, unless one of the exceptions applies.[105] In practice banks and other holders of qualifying floating charges created before 15 September 2003 are usually content to appoint an administrator or to concur in such an appointment by the company or the directors. Accordingly, appointments of administrative receivers are becoming increasingly rare.

An administrative receiver is the receiver and manager of the whole or substan- **29.54** tially the whole of the company's property, which property is charged in law or equity to the holders of charges, which include a floating charge.[106] The administrative receiver's function is to get in the company's property in order to discharge, so far as possible, the secured debts. For this purpose the administrative receiver has all the powers in the debenture by which he is appointed as well as the powers contained in the Insolvency Act, Schedule 1.[107] The administrative receiver is, or

---

[103] Insolvency Act, Schedule B1, para 64.

[104] Insolvency Act, Schedule B1, para 5.

[105] Insolvency Act, s 72A; Insolvency Act 1986, Section 72A (Appointed Day) Order 2003 (SI 2003/2095). The exceptions, provided for by ss 72B–72H are (i) capital market arrangements, (ii) public-private partnerships with step-in rights, (iii) utility and urban regeneration projects with step-in rights, (iv) project finance with step-in rights (*Feetum v Levy* [2006] Ch 585, CA), (v) financial market charge under the 1989 Act, s 173, a system-charge within the meaning of the Financial Markets and Insolvency Regulations 1996 (SI 1996/1469), or a collateral security charge within the meaning of the Financial Markets and Insolvency (Settlement Finality) Regulations 1999 (SI 1999/2979), and (vi) a company holding an appointment under the Water Industry Act 1991, Part II, Ch 1, a protected railway company within the meaning of the Railways Act 1993, s 59 (including that section as it has effect by virtue of the Channel Tunnel Rail Link Act, 1996, s 19), and a licence company within the meaning of the Transport Act 2000, s 26.

[106] Insolvency Act, s 29(2).

[107] Insolvency Act, s 42. The powers in Schedule 1 apply to both administrators and administrative receivers.

is deemed to be, the company's agent unless and until the company goes into administration, but liquidation does not prevent the administrative receiver from exercising his powers to manage and get in the company's property in the name of the company.[108]

29.55 The appointment of an administrative receiver has no effect on the office of the directors, but the receiver replaces the board as the person having authority to exercise the company's powers, so that the board's powers are suspended and it can no longer dispose of the company's property without the consent of the debenture holder or receiver.[109]

29.56 The position is different where the receiver has no interest in taking into his possession or control a particular asset, such as a claim against the debenture holder. This was the position in *Newhart Developments Ltd v Co-operative Commercial Bank Ltd* where the Court of Appeal held that the power to bring proceedings in the name of the company conferred on receivers (in that case, by the terms of the debenture) was an enabling power; and the provision conferring that power did not 'divest the directors of their power, as the governing body of the company, of instituting proceedings in a situation where so doing did not in any way impinge prejudicially upon the position of the debenture holders by threatening or imperilling the assets subject to the charge'.[110] In *Newhart* the Court of Appeal held that the directors, who provided the company with a full indemnity for costs, were entitled to cause the company to bring proceedings against the debenture holder without having to obtain the receiver's consent. In *Tudor Grange Holdings v Citibank* Sir Nicholas Browne-Wilkinson V-C distinguished the *Newhart* case on the ground that the proceedings against the debenture holder could impinge on the property subject to the receivers' powers, since there was no indemnity against adverse costs in place, and also expressed reservations whether *Newhart* was correctly decided.[111]

29.57 The board may also be able demonstrate a need for information from the receivers, beyond what is contained in the receiver's statutory accounts, in order to

---

[108] Insolvency Act, s 44; *Re Henry Pound Son v Hutchins* (1889) 42 Ch D 402, CA; *Gosling v Gaskell* [1897] AC 595, HL; *Goughs Garages Ltd v Pugsley* [1930] 1 KB 615, CA; *Sowman v David Samuel Trust Ltd* [1978] 1 WLR 22; *Re Beck Foods Ltd* [2002] 1 WLR 1304, CA.

[109] *Moss Steamship Co Ltd v Whinney* [1912] AC 254, 263, HL, per Lord Atkinson; *Newhart Developments Ltd v Co-operative Commercial Bank Ltd* [1978] QB 814, 819, 821, CA, per Shaw LJ; *Re Emmadart Ltd* [1979] Ch 540, 547, per Brightman J; *Gomba Holdings UK Ltd v Homan* [1986] 1 WLR 1301, 1306, per Hoffmann J; *Village Cay Marina Ltd v Acland* [1998] 2 BCLC 327, 333, PC, per Lord Hoffmann.

[110] [1978] QB 814, 819, 821, per Shaw LJ; followed in *Watts v Midland Bank plc* [1986] BCLC 15; *Sutton v GE Capital Commercial Finance Ltd* [2004] 2 BCLC 662, CA at [45]. Note the explanation of *Newhart* given by Hoffmann J in *Gomba Holdings UK Ltd v Homan* [1986] 1 WLR 1301, 1307.

[111] [1992] Ch 53, 63.

comply with its statutory obligation to render accounts or to exercise the company's right to redeem. But even then the board's interest in obtaining the information is subordinated to the receiver's primary duty not to do anything which may prejudice the interests of the debenture holder.[112]

# E. Voluntary Winding Up

## (1) Voluntary winding up: general

Where the directors of a company that is, or is about to become, unable to pay its debts find that a CVA, administration, or administrative receivership are not available options, they will have to consider liquidation. A company may be wound up voluntarily as an alternative to being wound up by the court, but unregistered companies cannot be wound up voluntarily except in accordance with the EC Regulation.[113] The overwhelming majority of windings up are voluntary and the directors would only resort to winding up by the court in rare cases where the necessary resolution of the members could not be obtained or where it is desirable to obtain the immediate appointment of a provisional liquidator.

**29.58**

A voluntary winding up is a process initiated by a resolution of shareholders (for the procedures, see Chapter 22 above). A company may be wound up voluntarily in two circumstances: (a) when the period (if any) fixed for the duration of the company by the articles expires, or the event (if any) occurs, on the occurrence of which the articles provide that the company is to be dissolved, and the company in general meeting has passed an ordinary resolution requiring it to be wound up voluntarily, or (b) if the company resolves by special resolution that it be wound up voluntarily.[114] Where there is a holder of a qualifying floating charge, the holder must be given five days' written notice of the resolution before it is passed, unless the holder gives his written consent. This is to give the holder an opportunity to appoint an administrator. After the company has entered administration or an administration application has been made, no resolution may be passed for the winding up of the company.[115]

**29.59**

Companies frequently go into voluntary liquidation after a winding-up petition has been presented or threatened, usually for the legitimate reasons of expedition

**29.60**

---

[112] *Gomba Holdings UK Ltd v Homan* [1986] 1 WLR 1301, 1307, 1308.

[113] Insolvency Act, ss 73 and 221(4). For the meaning of company, see 1985 Act, s 735 (Insolvency Act, s 251), which will be replaced by 2006 Act, s 1(1) on 1 October 2009.

[114] Insolvency Act, s 84(1). Section 84(1)(c), providing for voluntary winding up pursuant to an extraordinary resolution, was repealed with effect from 1 October 2007; 2006 Act Commencement Order No 3, Schedule 4, para 39 and Schedule 5.

[115] Insolvency Act, Schedule B1, paras 42 and 44.

and saving costs, but occasionally because the directors hope that the liquidator appointed in the voluntary winding up will be more favourably disposed towards them. Voluntary winding up does not bar the right of a creditor (or contributory) to have the company wound up by the court and creditors who have concerns about the voluntary winding up may press for a winding-up order.[116] In exercising its discretion in such a case, the court takes account of the views of the majority of independent creditors, but it will also consider the reasons for creditors' views.[117]

**29.61** When a company has passed a resolution for voluntary winding up, the directors must ensure that (a) within 15 days after the passing of the resolution a copy of it is forwarded to the Registrar, and (b) within 14 days after the passing of the resolution notice of the resolution is advertised in the Gazette. If default is made in complying with these obligations, the company and every officer of it who is in default is liable to a fine and, for continued contravention, to a daily default fine.[118]

**29.62** A voluntary winding up is deemed to commence at the time of the passing of the resolution for voluntary winding up.[119] From the commencement of the winding up the company shall cease to carry on its business, except so far as may be required for its beneficial winding up, but the company's corporate state and powers continue until it is dissolved.[120] Also, after the commencement of the winding up any transfer of shares, not being to or with the sanction of the liquidator, or alteration in the status of members is void.[121] The resolution for voluntary winding up brings into effect the statutory scheme for distributing the company's property in satisfaction of its liabilities and, subject to that and the payment of the expenses of the voluntary winding up, among the members according to their rights and interests.[122] The court is not involved in the process of the winding up unless a question is referred to it.[123]

---

[116] Insolvency Act, s 116 (and also s 124(5)).

[117] Insolvency Act, s 195; *Re JD Swain Ltd* [1965] 1 WLR 909, CA; *Re Southard & Co Ltd* [1979] 1 WLR 1198, CA; *Re Lowerstoft Traffic Services Ltd* [1986] BCLC 81; *Re Palmer Marine Surveys Ltd* [1986] 1 WLR 573; *Re Falcon RJ Developments Ltd* [1987] BCLC 437; *Re MCH Services Ltd* [1987] BCLC 535; *Re Gordon & Breach Science Publishers Ltd* [1995] 2 BCLC 189; *Re Inside Sport Ltd* [2000] 1 BCLC 302; *Re Zirceram Ltd* [2000] 1 BCLC 751. The case for a compulsory order is stronger where the petition is presented in the public interest: *Re Lubin, Rosen Ltd* [1975] 1 WLR 122.

[118] Insolvency Act, ss 84(3) and 85; 1985 Act, s 380 (to be replaced by 2006 Act, ss 29 and 30 on 1 October 2009).

[119] Insolvency Act, s 86.

[120] Insolvency Act, s 87.

[121] Insolvency Act, s 88.

[122] Insolvency Act, ss 107 and 115; Insolvency Rules, rule 4.218. As an alternative an arrangement under s 110 could be sanctioned or distributions could be made under a CVA or scheme under 2006 Act, Part 26.

[123] Insolvency Act, s 112.

Before the resolution for voluntary winding up is passed the directors should **29.63** consider whether they are able to make a statutory declaration as regards the company's solvency. If they do make such a declaration, the winding up will be a 'members' voluntary winding up' under the control of members, appoint the liquidator; if they do not, the winding up will be a 'creditors' voluntary winding up' under the control of creditors whose nomination of liquidator prevails over the members' choice.[124] If a members' voluntary winding up becomes insolvent it converts into a creditors' voluntary winding up.[125]

## (2) Members' voluntary winding up

The statutory declaration of solvency may be made by the directors (or, in the case **29.64** of a company having more than two directors, the majority of them) at a directors' meeting to the effect that they have made a full inquiry into the company's affairs and that, having done so, they have formed the opinion that the company will be able to pay its debts in full, together with interest at the official rate (as defined in s 251), within such period, not exceeding 12 months from the commencement of the winding up, as may be specified in the declaration. Such a declaration by the directors has no effect unless (a) it is made within the five weeks immediately preceding the date of the passing of the resolution for winding up, or on that date but before the passing of the resolution, and (b) it embodies a statement of the company's assets and liabilities as at the latest practicable date before the making of the declaration. The declaration shall be delivered to the Registrar of Companies before the expiration of 15 days immediately following the date on which the resolution for winding up is passed.[126]

A declaration of solvency is not invalidated because of minor inaccuracies in the **29.65** statement of assets and liabilities, provided there is something which can reasonably and fairly be described as 'a statement of the company's assets and liabilities'.[127]

The penalties imposed on directors who fail to comply with these obligations are **29.66** stringent. A director making a declaration without having reasonable grounds for the opinion that the company will be able to pay its debts in full, together with interest at the official rate, within the period specified is liable to up to two years' imprisonment or an unlimited fine, or both. If the company is wound up in pursuance of a resolution passed within five weeks after the making of the declaration,

---

[124] Insolvency Act, ss 90, 91, 100.
[125] Insolvency Act, ss 95, 96.
[126] Insolvency Act, s 89(1)–(3). By s 251 the official rate of interest is the rate payable under s 189(4).
[127] *De Courcy v Clements* [1971] Ch 693; *Re New Millennium Experience Co Ltd* [2004] 1 All ER 687 at paras 107–115.

and its debts (together with interest at the official rate) are not paid or provided for in full within the period specified, it is to be presumed (unless the contrary is shown) that the director did not have reasonable grounds for his opinion. If a declaration required to be delivered to the Registrar is not so delivered within the time prescribed, the company and every officer in default is liable to a fine and, for continued contravention, to a daily default fine.[128]

### (3) Creditors' voluntary winding up

**29.67**   Where there is no declaration of solvency the Insolvency Act, s 98(1) applies. It provides:

> The company shall—
> (a) cause a meeting of its creditors to be summoned for a day not later than the 14th day after the day on which there is to be held the company meeting at which the resolution for voluntary winding up is to be proposed;
> (b) cause the notices of the creditors' meeting to be sent by post to the creditors not less than 7 days before the day on which that meeting is to be held; and
> (c) cause notice of the creditors' meeting to be advertised once in the Gazette and once at least in two newspapers circulating in the locality (that is to say the locality in which the company's principal place of business in Great Britain was situated during the relevant period).

Subsection 98(2) provides that the notice must identify an insolvency practitioner to provide information to creditors and the place where a list of the company's creditors may be inspected.[129] The company (but not its officers) commits an offence if, without reasonable excuse, it fails to comply with subss 98(1) and (2).[130]

**29.68**   By the Insolvency Act, s 99(1) the directors are under obligations to:

(a) make out a statement in the prescribed form as to the affairs of the company;
(b) cause that statement to be laid before the creditors' meeting under section 98; and
(c) appoint one of their number to preside at that meeting; and it is the duty of the director so appointed to attend the meeting and preside over it.

By subs 99(2) the statement of affairs, which must be in Form 4.19,[131] must be verified by affidavit by some or all of the directors and show:

> (a) particulars of the company's assets, debts and liabilities; (b) the names and addresses of the company's creditors; (c) the securities held by them respectively; (d) the dates when the securities were respectively given; and (e) such further or other information as may be prescribed.

---

[128] Insolvency Act, s 89(4)–(6), s 430, Schedule 10.
[129] Insolvency Act, s 98(2), which with subss 98(3)–(5) and Insolvency Rules, rule 4.51 contain further provisions about the notice and place of the meeting.
[130] Insolvency Act, subs 98(6).
[131] Insolvency Rules, rule 4.34.

The reasonable and necessary expenses of preparing the statement of affairs are an expense of the liquidation.[132] If the directors without reasonable excuse fail to comply with subss 99(1) and (2), they are liable to a fine.[133]

If a director does not attend the meeting, the creditors may appoint their own **29.69** nominee to preside over the meeting, and the absence of the director will not invalidate the meeting.[134] If the statement of affairs does not state the company's position at the date of the meeting, the directors must give a written or oral report on any material transactions between the date of the statement and the date of the meeting.[135]

The business at the meeting under s 98 is limited to resolutions (a) for the appoint- **29.70** ment of a liquidator or liquidators (and if more than one, whether acts are to be done by both or all of them, or by only one), (b) for the establishment of a liquid- ation committee, (c) dealing with remuneration of the liquidators (unless a liqui- dation committee is established), (d) for adjournment for not more than three weeks, and (e) on other matters which the chairman thinks it right to allow for special reasons.[136] The creditors' nomination of liquidator prevails over any appointment by the members.[137]

If a liquidator appointed by the members has been in office before the s 98 meet- **29.71** ing, during that period he may not exercise his powers under the Insolvency Act, s 165, except for the purpose of taking the company's property into his custody or under his control, disposing of perishable goods and goods the value of which is likely to diminish if not immediately disposed of, and taking other steps to protect the company's assets. Such a liquidator must account for his dealings at the s 98 meeting and apply to the court for directions if the company or the directors fail to comply with their obligations under ss 98 and 99. If the liquidator fails to com- ply with these obligations he is liable to a fine.[138]

If there is a liquidation committee, the liquidator must give it notice of the dis- **29.72** posal by him of any company property to a director or other person connected with the company.[139]

---

[132] Insolvency Rules, rule 4.38(1).
[133] Insolvency Act, s 99(3).
[134] *Re Salcombe Hotel Development Co Ltd* [1991] BCLC 44.
[135] Insolvency Rules, rule 4.53B.
[136] Insolvency Rules, rule 4.52.
[137] Insolvency Act, s 100.
[138] Insolvency Act, s 166. These provisions were introduced to control the abuse associated with the procedure adopted from the case of *Re Centrebind Ltd* [1967] 1 WLR 377.
[139] Insolvency Act, s 165(6). Section 249 gives the meaning of 'connected' with the company.

### (4) Effect of voluntary winding up on directors' powers

**29.73** A voluntary winding up does not bring a director's office to an end; although it may well be that his employment is terminated.[140] In the rare case where no liquidator has been appointed or nominated by the company, the powers of the directors are severely limited. Those powers may not be exercised, except with the sanction of the court (or in the case of a creditors' voluntary winding up) so far as may be necessary to ensure compliance with s 98 (creditors' meeting) and s 99 (statement of affairs). This is subject to an exception allowing the directors to dispose of goods the value of which is likely to diminish if they are not immediately disposed of, and to do other things necessary for the protection of the company's assets. It is an offence for a director to fail to comply with these obligations without reasonable excuse.[141]

**29.74** On the appointment of a liquidator in a members' voluntary winding up, all the powers of the directors cease, except so far as the company in general meeting or the liquidator sanctions their continuance.[142] Upon the appointment of a creditors' voluntary liquidator, all the powers of the directors cease, except so far as the liquidation committee (or, if there is no such committee, the creditors) sanction their continuance.[143] A transaction purportedly made by directors on behalf of a company without authority is not binding on the company.[144]

## F. Winding Up by the Court

### (1) Power of directors to present petition

**29.75** A petition to wind up a company may be presented by the company or its directors.[145] It is highly unusual for a company to petition, since the members may resolve to wind up voluntarily, but, as mentioned in paragraph 29.58 above, there may be rare cases where the directors, in discharge of their duties, need to petition. If so, they must either act unanimously or by a duly passed resolution at a board meeting.[146] It is, of course, more common for winding-up petitions to be presented

---

[140] For effect on office, see Insolvency Act, s 114; *Midland Counties District Bank Ltd v Attwood* [1905] 1 Ch 357. For effect on employment, see *Fowler v Commercial Timber Co Ltd* [1930] 2 KB 1, 6, CA.

[141] Insolvency Act, s 114.

[142] Insolvency Act, s 91(2).

[143] Insolvency Act, s 103.

[144] *Re London and Mediterranean Bank* (1870) 5 Ch App 567.

[145] Insolvency Act, s 124. The power for directors to petition was introduced by the Insolvency Act to reverse *Re Emmadart Ltd* [1979] Ch 540. For the meaning of 'company', see n 113 above.

[146] *Re Instrumentation Electrical Services Ltd* [1988] BCLC 550; *Re Equiticorp International plc* [1989] 1 WLR 1010.

by creditors, contributories, or the Secretary of State in the public interest. It is beyond the scope of this work to deal with the extensive law relating to winding-up petitions.[147] Instead the following paragraphs consider the effect of the presentation of a winding-up petition on the directors' powers of management, and the effect on the directors of the appointment of a provisional liquidator or a winding-up order.

## (2) Effect of petition on directors' powers of management

The Insolvency Act, s 127 provides: **29.76**

> In a winding up by the court, any disposition of the company's property, and any transfer of shares, or alteration in the status of the company's members, made after the commencement of the winding up is, unless the court otherwise orders, void.[148]

The winding up of a company is deemed to commence at the time of the presentation of the petition for winding up, unless before the presentation of a winding-up petition, a resolution has been passed by the company for voluntary winding up, in which case the winding up is deemed to have commenced at the time of the passing of the resolution.[149]

The purposes of s 127 are to prevent the directors from disposing of company **29.77** property to the prejudice of creditors, and to secure the rateable distribution of the company's property, as it existed at the commencement of the winding up, among its creditors.[150]

It follows that any disposition of the company's property, whether in the course of **29.78** carrying on business or otherwise, is void if a winding-up order is made on the petition unless the court orders otherwise. Payments and transfers to the company are not affected and are a good discharge of obligations owed to the company.[151] A payment out of the company's bank account, whether in credit or overdrawn, is

---

[147] Insolvency Act, ss 117–130; Insolvency Rules, rules 4.4–4.31.

[148] The Insolvency Act, s 436 gives 'property' a wide definition, but it does not apply to property which, before the presentation of the petition, the company has charged or to real property which the company has agreed to sell: *Sowman v David Samuel Trust Ltd* [1978] 1 WLR 22, 30; *Re Margart Pty Ltd* [1985] BCLC 314, NSW SC; *Re French's Wine Bar Ltd* [1987] BCLC 499; *Re Branston & Gothard Ltd* [1999] BPIR 466.

[149] Insolvency Act, s 129.

[150] *Re Wiltshire Iron Co* (1868) 3 Ch App 443, 447; *Re Liverpool Civil Service Association Ltd* (1874) 9 Ch App 511; *Re Civil Service and General Store Ltd* (1887) 57 LJ Ch 119; *Re Leslie Enginers Co Ltd* [1976] 1 WLR 292, 304; *Re Gray's Inn Construction Ltd* [1980] 1 WLR 711, 717, CA, per Buckley LJ; *Denney v John Hudson & Co Ltd* [1992] BCLC 901, 904, CA, per Fox LJ; *Hollicourt (Contracts) Ltd v Bank of Ireland* [2001] Ch 555, CA at paras 20–23, per Mummery LJ.

[151] *Re Barned's Banking Co* (1867) 3 Ch App 105; *Mersey Steel and Iron Co v Naylor, Benzon & Co* (1884) 9 App Cas 434, 440, HL.

a disposition in favour of the payee, but is not a disposition to the bank rendering the bank liable in restitution.[152] Payments into an overdrawn bank account are dispositions in favour of the bank.[153]

**29.79** The court may make a validation order either in advance or after the winding-up order.[154] There are two reasons why the directors should apply for a validation in advance. The first is self-protection. If a winding-up order is made and a disposition effected by them is not validated and the property recovered, the directors may be personally liable for breach of their duties to compensate the company for loss to its estate.[155] The second reason is that, once the company's bank is on notice of the presentation of the petition, it will close the company's account unless a validation order is obtained.[156]

**29.80** Where the directors consider it to be in the interests of the company and its creditors that it should carry on business pending the hearing of the petition, they may apply for a validating order. In *Denney v John Hudson & Co Ltd*, a case of post-winding-up order validation, Fox LJ summarized the relevant principles:[157]

(1) The discretion vested in the court by [s 127] is entirely at large, subject to the general principles which apply to any kind of discretion, and subject also to limitation that the discretion must be exercised in the context of the liquidation provisions of the statute.

(2) The basic principle of law governing the liquidation of insolvent estates, whether in bankruptcy or under the companies legislation, is that the assets of the insolvent at the time of the commencement of the liquidation will be distributed pari passu among the insolvent's unsecured creditors as at the date of the bankruptcy. In a company's compulsory liquidation this is now achieved by . . . s 127 of the Insolvency Act . . .

(3) There are occasions, however, when it may be beneficial not only for the company but also for the unsecured creditors, that the company should be able to dispose of some of its property during the period after the petition has been presented, but

---

[152] *Hollicourt (Contracts) Ltd v Bank of Ireland* [2001] Ch 555, CA at paras 31, 32.

[153] *Rose v AIB Group (UK) plc* [2003] 1 WLR 2791 at para 11.

[154] *Re AI Levy (Holdings) Ltd* [1964] Ch 19; *Re Sugar Properties (Derisley Wood) Ltd* [1988] BCLC 146; *Practice Direction (Companies Court: Contributory's Petition)* [1990] 1 WLR 490.

[155] *Re Neath Harbour Smelting and Rolling Works* [1887] WN 87, 121; *Re Civil Service and General Stores* (1887) 57 LJ Ch 119.

[156] *Re Gray's Inn Construction Co Ltd* [1980] 1 WLR 711, 720, CA, per Buckley LJ; *Hollicourt (Contracts) Ltd v Bank of Ireland* [2001] Ch 555, CA at para 7, per Mummery LJ.

[157] [1992] BCLC 901, 904, 905, CA. Russell and Staughton LLJ agreed with the judgment of Fox LJ. The principles were derived from the judgment of Buckley LJ in *Re Gray's Inn Construction Co Ltd* [1980] 1 WLR 711, 717–19, CA and were applied in *Rose v AIB Group (UK) plc* [2003] 1 WLR 2791 at paras 13–16. In *Re Argentum Reductions (UK) Ltd* [1975] 1 WLR 186 an order was made to validate transactions in the ordinary course of business. An order will be refused if the company is trading at a loss; *Re a Company (No 007523 of 1986)* [1987] BCLC 200. Examples of orders being refused under the 4th and 6th paragraphs of Fox LJ's principles are: *Re Webb Electrical Ltd* [1988] BCLC 382; *Re Fairway Graphics Ltd* [1991] BCLC 468; *Re Rafidain Bank Ltd* [1992] BCLC 301.

before the winding-up order has been made. Thus, it may sometimes be beneficial to the company and its creditors that the company should be able to continue the business in its ordinary course.

(4) In considering whether to make a validating order, the court must always do its best to ensure that the interests of the unsecured creditors will not be prejudiced.

(5) The desirability of the company being enabled to carry on business was often speculative. In each case the court must carry out a balancing exercise.

(6) The court should not validate any transaction or series of transactions which might result in one or more pre-liquidation creditors being paid in full at the expense of other creditors, who will only receive a dividend, in the absence of special circumstances making such a course desirable in the interests of creditors generally. If, for example, it were in the interests of the creditors generally that the company's business should be carried on, and this could only be achieved by paying for goods already supplied to the company when the petition is presented (but not yet paid for) the court might exercise its discretion to validate payment for those goods.

(7) A disposition carried out in good faith in the ordinary course of business at a time when the parties were unaware that a petition had been presented would usually be validated by the court unless there is ground for thinking that the transaction may involve an attempt to prefer the disponee—in which case the transaction would not be validated.

If the directors apply for an order validating a proposed sale of company property, the court will grant the order if satisfied that the sale is at a proper market price and is advantageous to the company and its creditors. In such a case the price replaces the property sold and there is no infringement of the *pari passu* principle.[158] The court may also make a validating order in respect of the costs of defending the petition[159] or in respect of an arrangement for funding to support litigation being pursued by the company.[160]      **29.81**

Where the company is solvent, the court will validate dispositions made under transactions which the directors consider necessary or expedient in the company's interest, provided that the reasons given by the directors for their opinion are ones that an intelligent and honest man could reasonably hold. In such a case, it is for those opposing ratification to satisfy the court that the proposed transactions are harmful to the company.[161]      **29.82**

---

[158] *Denney v John Hudson & Co Ltd* [1992] BCLC 901, 905, CA. Examples of the court making orders validating sales are: *Re AI Levy (Holdings) Ltd* [1964] Ch 19; *Re French's Wine Bar Ltd* [1987] BCLC 499; *Re Tramway Building & Construction Co Ltd* [1988] Ch 293; *Re Sugar Properties (Derisley Wood) Ltd* [1988] BCLC 146; *Re Rescupine Ltd* [2003] 1 BCLC 661.

[159] *Re Crossmore Electrical and Civil Engineering Ltd* [1989] BCLC 137.

[160] *Richbell Information Services Inc v Atlantic General Investments Trust Ltd* [1999] BCC 871.

[161] *Re Burton & Deakin Ltd* [1977] 1 WLR 390. But an order may be refused in the case of an allegedly solvent company where the petition is presented by the Secretary of State in the public interest: *Re a Company (No 007130 of 1998)* [2000] 1 BCLC 582.

**(3) Effect of appointment of provisional liquidator and winding-up order on directors' powers**

29.83   The court may at any time after the presentation of a winding-up petition appoint a provisional liquidator, who carries out such functions as the court confers on him.[162] It is common practice for a provisional liquidator to be appointed in respect of an insurance company to promote a scheme of arrangement under the 2006 Act, Part 30.[163] The provisional liquidator is usually appointed to investigate, get in, and safeguard the company's assets pending the hearing of the petition, but he would not take any major step without obtaining directions from the court and he is not responsible for making distributions. Notwithstanding the appointment, the directors remain in office and may instruct solicitors on behalf of the company to oppose the petition or the appointment of the provisional liquidator.[164] The appointment, so long as it subsists, determines the power of the directors to manage the company or deal with its property.[165] In *Pacific and General Insurance Co Ltd v Hazell* Moore-Bick J held that the appointment of a provisional liquidator automatically revokes the authority of agents appointed to act on behalf of the company by or under the authority of the directors.[166]

29.84   A compulsory winding-up order has the effect of terminating the powers of the directors, so that in the words of Lord Esher MR the position of the directors is that 'they have ceased to exist'.[167] In *Measures Brothers Ltd v Measures* the Court of Appeal held that the winding-up order terminated the director's appointment and discharged him from further performance of his obligations to the company.[168]

## G. Directors' Duties in Relation to Investigation Procedures

29.85   The following paragraphs consider directors' obligations to provide information to administrators, administrative receivers, liquidators, and provisional liquidators (office-holders). The information is required not merely for the purpose of enabling the office-holder to fulfil his function of getting in and realizing assets in

---

[162] Insolvency Act, s 135.

[163] *New Cap Reinsurance Corp Ltd v HIH Casualty & General Insurance Ltd* [2002] 2 BCLC 228, CA at para 11, per Jonathan Parker LJ.

[164] *Re Union Accident Insurance Co Ltd* [1972] 1 All ER 1105, 1113.

[165] *Re Oriental Bank Corporation* (1884) 28 Ch D 634, 640; *Re Mawcon Ltd* [1969] 1 WLR 78, 82; *Re Union Accident Insurance Co Ltd* [1972] 1 All ER 1105, 1113.

[166] [1997] BCC 400, 408.

[167] *Re Ebsworth & Tidy's Contract* (1889) 42 Ch D 23, 43, CA; also *Re Oriental Inland Steam Co* (1874) 9 Ch App 557, 560; *Re Farrow's Bank* [1921] 2 Ch 164, 173, CA.

[168] [1910] 2 Ch 248, 254, 256, 259, CA. In contrast in the early case of *Madrid Bank Ltd v Bayley* (1866) LR 2 QB 37, Blackburn J held that directors remained officers of a company after it had been ordered to be wound up for the purposes of answering interrogatories.

the estate and identifying liabilities. Investigations by office-holders and the official receiver are also concerned with accounting for the reasons for any failure of the company and reporting on the conduct of the directors and others involved in the management. Those reports and evidence obtained may be passed on to the Secretary of State or prosecuting authorities with a view to disqualification or criminal proceedings being taken.

### (1) Directors' duty to provide statement of affairs and accounts

Where the company proposes a CVA or goes into a voluntary liquidation the **29.86** provision by the directors of a statement of affairs is an integral part of the process. When an administrator, administrative receiver, or provisional liquidator is appointed or when a winding-up order is made certain specified persons, including the directors, are under a duty on notice to provide a statement of affairs.[169] Those specified persons are (a) officers or former officers of the company, (b) certain promoters or employees of the company, and (c) certain officers or employees of a company which is an officer of the company.[170]

In each case the statement of affairs, which is to be in a prescribed form, verified **29.87** and filed, must include (a) particulars of the company's assets, debts, and liabilities, (b) the names and addresses of the company's creditors, (c) the securities held by each creditor, and (d) the dates when the securities were given.[171] The statement of affairs must be provided within 11 days in the case of administration and 21 days in the other cases, but the relevant office-holder or the court may revoke the requirement or extend the time for providing it.[172] The expenses of preparing

---

[169] For administration the notice is to be sent as soon as reasonably practicable: Insolvency Act, Schedule B1, para 47(1); Insolvency Rules, rule 2.28 and Form 2.13B. For administrative receivership the notice must be sent forthwith: Insolvency Act, s 47(1); Insolvency Rules, rule 3.3 and Form 3.1B. For winding up by the court or on appointment of provisional liquidator the official receiver may give notice: Insolvency Act, s 131(1); Insolvency Rules, rule 4.32 and Form 4.16.

[170] For administration: Insolvency Act, Schedule B1, para 47(3). For administrative receivership: Insolvency Act, s 47(3). For provisional liquidation and winding up by the court: Insolvency Act, s 131(3). By the Insolvency Act, s 235 broadly the same persons are under a duty to cooperate with the office-holder.

[171] For administration the statement of affairs is to be verified by a statement of truth in accordance with the CPR and the administrator may apply to the court for a limited disclosure order in relation to delivery to the Registrar and filing at court: Insolvency Act, Schedule B1, para 47(2); Insolvency Rules, rules 2.29, 2.30 and Forms 2.14B–2.16B. For administrative receivership the statement of affairs is to be verified by affidavit and the administrative receiver may apply to the court for a limited disclosure order in relation to inspection of the statement: Insolvency Act, Schedule B1, para 47(2); Insolvency Rules, rules 3.4, 3.5, and Form 3.2. For winding up by the court or on appointment of provisional liquidator the statement of affairs is to be verified by affidavit and the official receiver may apply for a limited disclosure order in relation to inspection of the statement: Insolvency Act, s 131(2); Insolvency Rules, rules 4.33, 4.35, and Form 4.17.

[172] For administration: Insolvency Act, Schedule B1, para 48(1)–(3); Insolvency Rules, rule 2.31. For administrative receivership: Insolvency Act, s 47(4) and (5); Insolvency Rules, rule 3.6.

the statement of affairs may be paid as an expense of the administration, administrative receivership, or liquidation.[173]

**29.88** There are civil and criminal consequences for default. The court may make such orders as it thinks necessary to enforce the obligations to provide the statement of affairs.[174] A person commits an offence if he fails without reasonable excuse to comply with a requirement to provide a statement of affairs.[175]

**29.89** The directors and other persons identified in paragraph 29.86 above may come under a duty, at the request of the official receiver in a winding up by the court and by the liquidator in a voluntary winding up, to furnish accounts of the company of such nature, as at such date, and for such period as may be specified.[176] The specified period may begin from a date up to three years preceding the date of presentation of the winding-up petition or resolution for winding up (as the case may be), or from such earlier date to which audited accounts of the company were last prepared, but in a compulsory winding up, the court may, on the official receiver's application, require accounts for any earlier period.[177] The expenses of preparing these accounts may be paid as an expense of the liquidation.[178] The official receiver or voluntary liquidator may require the accounts to be verified and they must be delivered within 21 days of the request, unless a longer period is allowed.[179]

**29.90** In a winding up by the court, the official receiver may also require the deponents of the statement of affairs or accounts, or any one or more of them, to submit (in writing) further information amplifying, modifying, or explaining any matter contained in the statement of affairs or in accounts. Again the official receiver may require the further information to be verified and they must be delivered within 21 days of the request, unless a longer period is allowed.[180]

---

For winding up by the court or on appointment of provisional liquidator: Insolvency Act, s 131(4) and (5); Insolvency Rules, rule 4.36.

[173] For administration: Insolvency Rules, rule 2.32. For administrative receivership: Insolvency Rules, rule 3.7. For winding up by the court or on appointment of provisional liquidator: Insolvency Rules, rule 4.37.

[174] Insolvency Rules, rule 7.20(1)(a).

[175] For administration: Insolvency Act, Schedule B1, para 48(4). For administrative receivership: Insolvency Act, s 47(6). For winding up by the court or on appointment of provisional liquidator: Insolvency Act, s 131(7).

[176] Insolvency Rules, rules 4.39(1) and 4.40(1).

[177] Insolvency Rules, rules 4.39(2) and (3) and 4.40(2). Note that small companies and dormant companies are exempt from audit (2006 Act, ss 477–481) and that accounts and reports of private and public companies must be filed within nine and six months of the end of the relevant accounting reference period (2006 Act, ss 441, 442).

[178] Insolvency Rules, rules 4.37, 4.39(4), and 4.41.

[179] Insolvency Rules, rules 4.39(5) and 4.40(3).

[180] Insolvency Rules, rule 4.42.

**(2) Directors' duties in investigation procedures in winding up by the court: public examination**

Under the Insolvency Act, s 132(1) the official receiver has a duty to investigate, if **29.91** the company has failed, the causes of the company's failure; and generally its promotion, formation, business, dealings, and affairs and to make such report, if any, to the court as he thinks fit. The report is prima facie evidence of the facts stated in it.[181] The statement of affairs made and submitted by directors or others, with any accounts, should be a significant contribution to the investigation. The official receiver also has power under s 135 to require those persons, among others, to give such information concerning the company and its promotion, formation, dealings, affairs, and property as he may reasonably require (paragraphs 29.101–29.104 below).

The public examination of the company's officers under the Insolvency Act, s 133 **29.92** is a valuable weapon to compel the officers of the company to comply with their duties in relation to the statement of affairs and the official receiver's investigation. It applies in all cases and not merely cases where there is a report alleging fraud.[182] A public examination may form the basis of the official receiver's report concerning the affairs of the company. It is also a means of obtaining material information for the administration of the estate which cannot as well be obtained privately and giving publicity, for the information of creditors and the community at large, to the salient facts and unusual features connected with the company's failure.[183] Thus the purpose of a public examination is not merely to obtain a full and complete disclosure of the company's assets and the affairs relating to its insolvency, but to protect the public by (a) exposing serious misconduct, (b) promoting higher standards of commercial and business morality, and (c) serving as a sanction against former officers who have not adequately assisted the official receiver or liquidator in their investigations.[184]

The official receiver may at any time before the dissolution of the company apply **29.93** to the court for the public examination of, among others, any person who is or has been an officer of the company; and he must make such an application, unless the court otherwise orders, if requested to do so by one-half in value of the company's

---

[181] Insolvency Act, s 132(2). As to provision of the report to creditors and contributories, see Insolvency Rules, rules 4.43–4.48.

[182] This is one of the significant changes between the terms of the Insolvency Act, s 133 and its predecessors, 1948 Act, s 270(1) and 1985 Act, s 563: *Re Casterbridge Properties Ltd* [2004] 1 BCLC 96, CA at para 49, per Chadwick LJ.

[183] Report of the Cork Committee at para 655; *Re Seagull Engineering Ltd* [1993] Ch 345, 355, CA; *Re Richbell Strategic Holdings Ltd (No 2)* [2000] 2 BCLC 794, 800; *Re Casterbridge Properties Ltd* [2004] 1 BCLC 96, CA at para 48.

[184] *Re Pantmaenog Timber Co Ltd* [2004] 1 AC 158, HL at [47], [48], per Lord Millett, and also paras 77–87, per Lord Walker.

creditors or three-quarters in value of the company's contributories.[185] An application for a public examination may also be made where the company is in voluntary liquidation pursuant to the Insolvency Act, s 112.[186]

**29.94**  On such an application, the court will direct that a public examination of the officer shall be held on a day appointed by the court; and the officer must attend on that day and be publicly examined as to the promotion, formation, or management of the company or as to the conduct of its business and affairs, or his conduct or dealings in relation to the company.[187] The court is thus directed to make an order for public examination, although it would not do so in the rare case where no question could properly be put to the witness.[188] These provisions for public examination are intended to ensure that those responsible for the formation and running of an English company are liable to examination in public whether or not they are within the jurisdiction of the English courts. They therefore apply to directors residing abroad.[189]

**29.95**  At the public examination the official receiver, liquidator, special manager, any creditor who has tendered a proof, and any contributory may take part and question the examinee.[190] The conduct of the examination is under the control of the court and the examinee must answer all such questions as the court may put, or allow to be put, to him.[191] The examinee is to give the best answers that he can and it is no objection to questions that they extend to other members of the company's group.[192] (For self-incriminatory answers, see paragraph 29.113 below.)

**29.96**  If a person without reasonable excuse fails to attend his public examination, he is guilty of a contempt of court and liable to be punished accordingly.[193]

### (3)  Directors' liability to deliver up the company's property, books, papers, and records

**29.97**  When the company enters administration, an administrative receiver is appointed, the company goes into liquidation, or a provisional liquidator is appointed, the relevant office-holder is entitled and bound to take the company's property into

---

[185]  Insolvency Act, s 133(1), (2).
[186]  *Re Pantmaenog Timber Co Ltd* [2004] 1 AC 158, HL at para 56, per Lord Millett.
[187]  Insolvency Act, s 133(3). For procedure in relation to the public examination, see Insolvency Rules, rules 4.211–4.217.
[188]  *Re Casterbridge Properties Ltd* [2004] 1 BCLC 96, CA at paras 44, 49, and 52, per Chadwick LJ. The change from 'may' in 1948 Act, s 270(1) and 1985 Act, s 563 to 'shall' in s 133(3) represents another significant change in the law.
[189]  *Re Seagull Manufacturing Co Ltd* [1993] Ch 345, CA.
[190]  Insolvency Act, s 133(4).
[191]  Insolvency Rules, rule 4.215(1).
[192]  *Re Richbell Strategic Holdings Ltd (No 2)* [2000] 2 BCLC 794.
[193]  Insolvency Act, s 134(1).

his possession or control and the directors' functions with respect to it are displaced.[194] The directors are therefore not entitled to retain any of the company's property or its books, papers, and records.

If the directors, or anyone else, wrongly retain company property or records, the    **29.98**
Insolvency Act, s 234(2) provides the office-holder with a summary remedy. It provides:

> Where any person has in his possession or control any property, books, papers or records to which the company appears to be entitled, the court may require that person forthwith (or within such period as the court may direct) to pay, deliver, convey, surrender or transfer the property, books, papers or records to the office-holder.

The section should only be used for the legitimate purposes of the relevant insolvency proceeding, which may include getting in and realizing the company's property for the benefit of its creditors, achieving the purpose of administration or, in the case of books, papers and records, furthering the public interest in investigating and reporting on the company's affairs, with a view to disqualification proceedings or prosecution.[195]

The application should be made in the name of the relevant office-holder.[196] It    **29.99**
should be made on notice to the respondent, unless giving notice would cause injustice because of delay or risk of dissipation or destruction of the relevant property or records.[197] The section can be used to determine disputes as to ownership or possession of property.[198] But the section does not apply where the company's right of possession depends on establishing its title in foreign proceedings.[199]

It should be noted that s 234(3) and (4) provide a measure of protection for the    **29.100**
office-holder when he seizes or disposes of property which he wrongly believes belongs to the company:

> (3) Where the office-holder—
> (a) seizes or disposes of any property which is not property of the company, and

---

[194] For administration: Insolvency Act, Schedule B1, paras 1(2), 59, 60–69, 111(1) and Schedule 1 and paragraphs 29.50–29.52 above. For administrative receivership: Insolvency Act, s 42 and Schedule 1 and paragraphs 29.55–29.57 above. For liquidation and provisional liquidation: Insolvency Act, ss 143(1), 144(1), 247(2), and paras 29.73, 29.74, 29.83, and 29.84 above.

[195] *Re Pantmaenog Timber Co Ltd* [2004] 1 AC 158, HL at paras 5, 6, per Lord Hope, paras 51–58, per Lord Millett, paras 79–87, per Lord Walker; *Sutton v GE Capital Commercial Finance Ltd* [2004] 2 BCLC 662, CA at paras 33–42.

[196] *Smith v Bridgend BC* [2002] 1 AC 336, HL at para 32, per Lord Hoffmann. The application would be made under the following provisions of the Insolvency Act: Schedule B1, para 63 (administration), s 35 receivership), s 112 (voluntary winding up), s 168(3) (winding up by the court).

[197] *Re First Express Ltd* [1992] BCLC 824.

[198] *Euro Commercial Leasing Ltd v Cartwright & Lewis* [1995] 2 BCLC 618; *Re Cosslett (Contractors) Ltd* [1998] Ch 495, CA.

[199] *Re Leyland Daf Ltd* [1994] 2 BCLC 106, CA.

      (b) at the time of seizure or disposal believes, and has reasonable grounds for believing, that he is entitled (whether in pursuance of an order of the court or otherwise) to seize or dispose of that property, the next subsection has effect.

   (4) In that case the office-holder—

      (a) is not liable to any person in respect of any loss or damage resulting from the seizure or disposal except in so far as that loss or damage is caused by the office-holder's own negligence, and

      (b) has a lien on the property, or the proceeds of its sale, for such expenses as were incurred in connection with the seizure or disposal.

Although 'property' is given an extremely wide meaning by the Insolvency Act, s 426, the protection given to office-holders by this provision applies to tangible property and not to choses in action.[200]

### (4) Directors' duty to cooperate with office-holder

**29.101**    Section 235, which applies in the same circumstances as s 234, provides that certain specified persons, including the directors, are under a duty to cooperate with the relevant office-holder. Where a winding-up order has been made in respect of the company, the official receiver is an office-holder for the purpose of the section, whether or not he is the liquidator. Those specified persons are (a) officers or former officers of the company, (b) certain promoters or employees of the company, and (c) certain officers or employees of a company which is an officer of the company.[201] Subsection 235(2) provides that each of those persons shall:

      (a) give to the office-holder such information concerning the company and its promotion, formation, business, dealings, affairs or property as the office-holder may at any time after the effective date reasonably require, and

      (b) attend on the office-holder at such times as the latter may reasonably require.[202]

**29.102**    In practice enforcement of the duty to provide information under s 235 is the way in which office-holders obtain information about the company from the directors and others. In *Re Arrows Ltd (No 4)* Lord Browne-Wilkinson recorded that leading insolvency practitioners attach much greater importance to the confidentiality of information obtained under s 235 than they do to information obtained under formal examination under s 236, because s 235 is the means for obtaining

---

[200] *Welsh Development Agency v Export Finance Co Ltd* [1992] BCLC 148, CA. There are no such protective provisions in relation to anything other than chattels because it would never have occurred to Parliament that strict liability for conversion could exist for anything other than chattels: *OBG Ltd v Allan* [2008] AC 1, HL.

[201] Insolvency Act, subss 235(1) and (3).

[202] By s 235(4) the 'effective date' is 'whichever is applicable of the following dates – (a) the date on which the company entered administration, (b) the date on which the administrative receiver was appointed or, if he was appointed in succession to another administrative receiver, the date on which the first of his predecessors was appointed, (c) the date on which the provisional liquidator was appointed, and (d) the date on which the company went into liquidation'.

speedy and reliable information from those concerned with the company, whether or not they are involved in any wrongdoing.[203] In complex cases a director may be required to submit to questioning over many days.[204] The privilege against self-incrimination is not a reasonable excuse for refusing to answer a question.[205] Nor may a director required to provide information under s 235 insist on the office-holder keeping it confidential or only using it for the purposes of the insolvency proceedings, because the duty of confidence cannot operate so as to prevent the office-holder from disclosing it to persons to whom he is required or authorized by statute to make disclosure.[206]

Section 235 should be read with s 236, but whereas s 235 contains a mandatory obligation on the director or other officer to give information reasonably required, under s 236 the court has a discretion whether to order a private examination.    **29.103**

There are civil and criminal consequences for default in complying with obligations under s 235. The office-holder may apply for an order enforcing those obligations[207] or he may apply for an order for a private examination under s 236. By subs 235(5), if a person without reasonable excuse fails to comply with any obligation imposed by the section, he is liable to a fine and, for continued contravention, to a daily default fine.    **29.104**

### (5) Private examination

Section 236, which applies in the same circumstances as s 234, gives the court power to compel directors to appear before it for private examination and to produce documents. Where a winding-up order has been made in respect of the company, the official receiver is included as an office-holder.[208] The court's powers under s 236 are:    **29.105**

> (2) The court may, on the application of the office-holder, summon to appear before it—
>   (a) any officer of the company,
>   (b) any person known or suspected to have in his possession any property of the company or supposed to be indebted to the company, or
>   (c) any person whom the court thinks capable of giving information concerning the promotion, formation, business, dealings, affairs or property of the company.

---

[203] [1995] 2 AC 75, 101, HL.

[204] In *Re an inquiry into Mirror Group Newspapers plc* [1999] 2 All ER 641, 645, Sir Richard Scott V-C recorded that office-holders had interrogated Kevin Maxwell over 28 days in relation to the insolvencies of the Maxwell Group companies.

[205] *Bishopsgate Investments Ltd* [1993] Ch 1, CA.

[206] *Re Arrows Ltd (No 4)* [1995] 2 AC 75, 102, HL, per Lord Browne-Wilkinson, commenting that the dicta of Millett J, to a contrary effect, in *Re Barlow Clowes Gilt Managers Ltd* [1992] Ch 208, 217, were too wide.

[207] Insolvency Rules, rule 7.20(1)(c).

[208] Insolvency Act, s 236(1).

(3) The court may require any such person as is mentioned in subsection (2)(a) to (c) to submit an affidavit to the court containing an account of his dealings with the company or to produce any books, papers or other records in his possession or under his control relating to the company or the matters mentioned in paragraph (c) of the subsection.

The procedure for an examination under s 236 is set out in the Insolvency Rules, Part 9.

### Application for order

**29.106**   The application under s 236 may be made without notice and is supported by a confidential statement of the grounds for the application.[209] An application without notice should be justified on the ground of urgency or because notice could frustrate the examination by leading to the disappearance of the witness or the destruction of documents.[210] The application is supported by a confidential statement, which the examinee cannot inspect unless on a disputed application the court is of the opinion that it will or may be unable fairly and properly to dispose of the application, but even then the office-holder may satisfy the court that confidentiality in whole or in part is nevertheless appropriate.[211]

**29.107**   The examination may be used for the purpose of getting 'sufficient information to reconstitute the state of knowledge that the company should possess', so as to enable the office-holder to identify, get in, and realize its assets and identify its liabilities.[212] But this is not the limit of the examination. It may be used to enable claims to be investigated or to enable the official receiver to report on conduct with a view to disqualification proceedings or criminal prosecution.[213] In *Re British & Commonwealth plc (Nos 1 and 2)* Lord Slynn said that the court's discretion under s 236:

> must be exercised after a balancing of the factors involved—on the one hand the reasonable requirements of the [office-holder] to carry out his task, on the other the need to avoid making an order which is wholly unreasonable, unnecessary, or 'oppressive' to the person concerned . . . The protection for the person called upon to produce documents lies, thus, not in a limitation by category of documents ('reconstituting the company's state of knowledge') but in the fact that the applicant must satisfy the court that, after balancing all relevant factors, there is a proper case for

---

[209] Insolvency Rules, rule 9.2.

[210] *Re PFTZM Ltd* [1995] 2 BCLC 354; *Re Murjani* [1996] 1 WLR 1498, 1509, 1510, a case on s 366 (the bankruptcy equivalent), where Lightman J disagreed with the judgment of Vinelott J in *Re Maxwell Communications Corporation plc (No 3)* [1995] 1 BCLC 521, 528.

[211] Insolvency Rules, rule 9.5; *Re British & Commonwealth Holdings plc (Nos 1 and 2)* [1992] Ch 342, 355, CA, per Nourse LJ.

[212] *Cloverbay Ltd v Bank of Credit and Commerce SA* [1991] Ch 90, 102, CA, per Sir Nicholas Browne-Wilkinson V-C.

[213] *Re British & Commonwealth Holdings plc* [1993] AC 426, 439, HL, per Lord Slynn; *Re Pantmaenog Timber Co Ltd* [2004] 1 AC 158, HL.

such an order to be made. The proper case is one where the [office-holder] reasonably requires to see documents to carry out his functions and the production does not impose an unnecessary and unreasonable burden on the person required to produce them in the light of the [office-holder's] requirements. An application is not necessarily unreasonable because it is inconvenient for the addressee of the application or causes him a lot of work or may make him vulnerable to future claims, or is addressed to a person who is not an officer or employee of or contractor with the company . . . but all these will be relevant factors, together no doubt with many others.[214]

Where the examinee is a director or former director, the case for making an order under s 236 will be stronger than it would be against a third party, since a director owes fiduciary duties and his knowledge ought to made available to the company, but even in the case of a director the balancing exercise should be undertaken.[215] The court will usually give great weight to views of the office-holder, given his knowledge of the problems that exist in relation to the company's affairs and the information required.[216] The court may regard an order for oral examination as more oppressive than an order for production of documents.[217]   **29.108**

Orders are frequently made to enable the office-holder to investigate possible claims against a director or others. Although an examination is not to be used to obtain an unfair advantage in litigation, an examination may be ordered while proceedings are on foot against the examinee to enable the office-holders to carry out their functions. The existence of the proceedings, even if containing serious allegations, will not bar an order for examination, provided that the examination is not conducted in a way designed to give the office-holders an advantage in litigation against the examinee.[218] The court will always be alive to the dangers of the examination providing an unfair advantage in litigation.[219]   **29.109**

There is an unresolved issue whether an order for a private examination under s 236 may be served outside the jurisdiction. The problem stems from the decision   **29.110**

---

[214] *Re British & Commonwealth Holdings plc (Nos 1 and 2)* [1993] AC 426, 439, 440, HL, per Lord Slynn. In the quotation 'office-holder' has been substituted for 'administrator'.

[215] *Cloverbay Ltd v Bank of Credit and Commerce SA* [1991] Ch 90, 102, CA, per Sir Nicholas Browne-Wilkinson V-C; *Re British and Commonwealth Holdings plc (Nos 1 and 2)* [1992] Ch 342, 372, CA, per Ralph Gibson LJ; *Bishopsgate Investment Management Ltd v Maxwell* [1992] BCLC 470 (not appealed on this point); *Shierson v Rastoggi* [2003] 1 WLR 586, CA at paras 28–39, per Peter Gibson LJ and paras 53–63, per Mance LJ.

[216] *Re British and Commonwealth Holdings plc (Nos 1 and 2)* [1992] Ch 342, 371, 372 CA, per Ralph Gibson LJ.

[217] *Re British and Commonwealth Holdings plc (Nos 1 and 2)* [1992] Ch 342, 371, 372 CA, per Ralph Gibson LJ. In an appropriate case an order may be made for disclosure of redacted documents: *Re Galileo Group Ltd* [1999] Ch 100.

[218] *Shierson v Rastoggi* [2003] 1 WLR 586, CA; *Daltel Europe Ltd v Makki* [2005] 1 BCLC 594; but see *Re Atlantic Computers plc* [1998] BCC 200.

[219] *Re John T Rhodes Ltd* [1987] BCLC 77; *Re Bank of Credit and Commerce International SA* [1997] 1 BCLC 526; *Re Atlantic Computers plc* [1998] BCC 200, 208–9; *Sasea Finance Ltd v KPMG* [1998] BCC 216; *Re Sasea Finance Ltd* [1998] 1 BCLC 559.

of the Court of Appeal in *Re Tucker*, a decision on the Bankruptcy Act 1914, s 25.[220] Although the Court of Appeal has held that an order for a public examination may be served outside the jurisdiction,[221] there has been no decision on s 236 determining the issue. In *Re Casterbridge Properties Ltd*, Burton J summarized the issue and the authorities, but did not have to decide the point.[222] This uncertainty as to the reach of s 236 does not seem to have caused practical problems. One reason is that the court can restrain the examinee from leaving the jurisdiction until after the examination.[223] Another reason is that the court may be able to rely on assistance from foreign courts. Section 237(4) gives the court power to order an examination of a person who is not in England and Wales outside the jurisdiction, either elsewhere in the United Kingdom or in a place outside the United Kingdom. An order made under this provision would be given effect to elsewhere in the United Kingdom.[224] If the court made an order for examination at a place outside the jurisdiction, it would rely on the assistance and cooperation of the foreign court to give effect to the order.[225]

**29.111**   If an order is made for a person to attend for examination, he should be tendered a reasonable sum in respect of travelling expenses incurred in connection with his attendance.[226]

### The examination

**29.112**   As to the examination itself, s 237(4) provides that any person who appears or is brought before the court may be examined on oath, either orally or by interrogatories. Insolvency Rules, rule 9.3 provides for the order to require the submission of affidavits and the production of books, papers, and records. In *Shierson v Rastoggi* Peter Gibson LJ said: [227]

> The court in ordering an examination does not give carte blanche to the questions which may be asked of the witness at the examination, and if a particular line of

---

[220]   [1990] Ch 148, CA.
[221]   *Re Seagull Manufacturing Co Ltd* [1992] Ch 128, CA.
[222]   [2002] BCC 453 at [37]–[45], [48]. The issue was not raised before the Court of Appeal [2004] 1 BCLC 96.
[223]   *Re Oriental Credit Ltd* [1988] Ch 204.
[224]   Insolvency Act, s 426.
[225]   This could be under a provision equivalent to the Insolvency Act, s 426 applicable in the foreign court, under Article 21 of UNCITRAL, or by recognition under the European Insolvency Regulation. In *Re Anglo-American Insurance Co Ltd* [2002] BCC 715 provisional liquidators applied under the inherent jurisdiction for the English court to issue letters of request to the New York and Bermuda courts for the examination of individuals in their jurisdictions. In *Re Impex Services Worldwide Ltd* [2004] BPIR 564 the Isle of Man court as a matter of comity exercised its common law jurisdiction to order an examination as if under s 236 in response to a request from the English court.
[226]   Insolvency Rules, rule 9.6(4).
[227]   [2003] 1 WLR 586, CA at para 43.

inquiry is oppressive or if there are good reasons why particular questions should not be answered it is the right and duty of the court to limit the enquiry. The procedure is governed by the Insolvency Rules 1986. By rule 9.4(1) the liquidator may put such questions to the examinee as the court may allow and by r 9.4(5) the examinee may be represented by a legal representative who may put to him such questions as the court may allow for the purpose of enabling him to explain or qualify any answers given by him and may make representations on his behalf. The court therefore has control and if it thought that a line of questioning was unfair, for example if there had been no prior notice of it and the court thought such notice appropriate, it could stop such questions until the examinee was in a proper position to answer them.

The director may not refuse to answer questions on the ground that he may **29.113** incriminate himself.[228] In any case, evidence obtained on the examination cannot be used against a director in criminal proceedings unless he relies on it.[229] The director cannot refuse to answer questions or withhold documents on the ground of legal professional privilege, where the privilege is the right of the company, but the personal privilege of the director or a third party will be protected.[230] The director should bear in mind that the office-holder may be able to obtain evidence against him from other sources, such as regulatory or prosecuting bodies, inspectors, or other office-holders.[231]

The written record of the examination, which should be signed by the witness, **29.114** may, in any proceedings, whether under the Insolvency Act or otherwise, be used as evidence against the witness of any statement made by him in the course of his examination.[232]

Section 237(1) and (2) gives the court power, on the application of the office- **29.115** holder and on consideration of the evidence, to make orders for delivery up of property and payment of debts, but these provisions would only be used in clear cases or where admissions are made.[233]

If the examination is made necessary because the director has unreasonably failed **29.116** to cooperate with the office-holder, the director may be ordered to pay the costs of the examination.[234] Subject to that, unless the court otherwise orders, the

---

[228] *Bishopsgate Investment Management Ltd v Maxwell* [1993] Ch 1, CA.

[229] Insolvency Act, s 433(2). See further, paragraph 29.118 below.

[230] *Re Brook Martin & Co (Nominees) Ltd* [1993] BCLC 328; *Re Murjani* [1996] 1 WLR 1498, 1505, 1506; *Re Ouvaroff* [1997] BPIR 712. The director may not be able to rely on his own legal advice or litigation privilege if a prima facie case of fraud is shown: *Barclays Bank plc v Eustice* [1995] 1 WLR 1238, CA; *Kuwait Airways Corp v Iraqi Airways Co* [2005] 1 WLR 2734, CA.

[231] *Morris v Director of the SFO* [1993] Ch 373; *Soden v Burns* [1996] 1 WLR 1513; *Secretary of State for Trade and Industry v Baker* [1998] Ch 356; *Re Trading Partners Ltd* [2002] 1 BCLC 655.

[232] Insolvency Rules, rule 9.4(6) and (7).

[233] If the court makes an order under s 237(1) and (2), it may also order the person against whom the order is made to pay the costs of the application for the order: Insolvency Rules, rule 6(2).

[234] Insolvency Rules, rule 9.6(1); *Miller v Bain* [2002] BCC 899.

applicant's costs are paid out of the insolvent estate.[235] Where the applicant is the official receiver acting otherwise than as liquidator and therefore solely in the public interest, no order for costs may be made against him.[236]

**29.117**  Where (a) a person without reasonable excuse fails to appear before the court when he is summoned to do so under s 236, or (b) there are reasonable grounds for believing that a person has absconded, or is about to abscond, with a view to avoiding his appearance before the court under s 236, the court may, for the purpose of bringing that person and anything in his possession before the court, cause a warrant to be issued for the arrest of that person, and for the seizure of any books, papers, records, money, or goods in that person's possession.[237]

### (6) Use of evidence obtained from directors

**29.118**  The evidence obtained under the above provisions may be used to support a claim by the company or the office-holder. The record of an examination conducted under s 236 for the purpose of determining whether to institute proceedings is protected by legal professional privilege.[238] The office-holder may disclose documents to creditors to obtain their approval of proceedings.[239] But it is not a legitimate use of the office-holder's information gathering powers to pass the company's confidential documents to the debenture holder or another creditor for the purpose of their proceedings in which the company is not interested.[240] By s 433(1) in any proceedings any statement of affairs or other statement made pursuant to a requirement under ss 235 and 236 is admissible as evidence against any person who made or concurred in making the statement (but see paragraph 29.120 below for criminal proceedings).[241]

**29.119**  The office-holder may disclose to the Secretary of State for the purpose of director disqualification proceedings the transcripts of interviews conducted and documents provided pursuant to the powers in s 236, because such disclosure would be for the purpose of the administration.[242] By the CDDA, s 7(4) such disclosure may be required in addition to the report made to the Secretary of State under s 7(3).[243] The transcripts of evidence obtained from a director under ss 235 or 236

---

[235]  Insolvency Rules, rule 9.6(3).
[236]  Insolvency Rules, rule 9.6(5).
[237]  Insolvency Act, s 236(4)–(5).
[238]  *Dubai Bank Ltd v Galadari* [1990] BCLC 90.
[239]  *Re ACLI Metals (London) Ltd* [1989] BCLC 749. See also *Walker Morris v Khalastchi* [2001] 1 BCLC 1.
[240]  *Sutton v GE Capital Commercial Finance Ltd* [2004] 2 BCLC 662.
[241]  *R v Kansal* [1993] QB 244; *Re Arrows Ltd (No 4)* [1995] 2 AC 75; *R v Sawtell* [2001] BPIR 381.
[242]  *Re Polly Peck International plc* [1994] BCC 15.
[243]  CDDA, s 7(3) and (4) and Insolvent Companies (Reports on Conduct of Directors) Rules 1996.

may be used against him in disqualification proceedings.[244] The admission in evidence at the hearing of disqualification proceedings of statements obtained under s 235 does not necessarily involve a breach of the right to a fair trial under Article 6(1) of the Human Rights Convention since the issue of fair trial is one which must be considered in the round having regard to all the relevant factors. These factors include the fact that disqualification proceedings are not criminal proceedings and are primarily for the protection of the public and that there are degrees of coercion involved in different investigative procedures available in corporate insolvency and these differences might be reflected in different degrees of prejudice involved in the admission, in disqualification proceedings, of statements obtained by such procedures. Issues of fairness should therefore generally be decided by the trial judge.[245]

Where the official receiver is satisfied that material obtained pursuant to s 235 (or **29.120** s 236) is required by another prosecuting authority for the purpose of investigating crime, he is free to disclose that material to that prosecuting authority without an order of the court or notice to the person who had provided it. The purpose of the powers under ss 235 and 236 includes the identification of potential criminal or other misconduct and the taking of appropriate steps in relation to it.[246] However, by the Insolvency Act, s 433(2) in criminal proceedings in which any person who made or concurred in the making of a statement of affairs or other statement pursuant to a requirement imposed under ss 235 and 236 is charged with an offence (other than specified offences), no evidence relating to the statement may be adduced, and no question relating to it may be asked, by or on behalf of the prosecution, unless evidence relating to it is adduced, or a question relating to it is asked, by or on behalf of that person.[247]

## H. Claims against Directors Brought in the Name of the Company

### (1) Power of office-holder to bring proceedings in the name of the company

Administrators, administrative receivers, and liquidators all have power to bring **29.121** claims in the name of the company against directors to obtain relief for breach of

---

[244] Insolvency Act, s 433(1).

[245] *Re Westminster Property Management Ltd, Official Receiver v Stern* [2000] 1 WLR 2230, CA.

[246] *R v Brady* [2004] 1 WLR 3240, CA.

[247] Insolvency Act, s 433(2)–(4) was inserted by the Youth Justice and Criminal Evidence Act 1999, ss 59, 68(3) and Schedule 3, para 7(2) and (3) with effect from 14 April 2000. These subsections were inserted to meet the difficulties exposed by *Saunders v UK* (1997) 23 EHRR 313. By subs 433(3) the offences to which subs 433(2) does not apply include various offences under the Insolvency Act and under the Perjury Act 1911, ss 1, 2, and 5.

fiduciary and other duties, to recover company property in their possession or control, or to recover debts owed to the company. The proceedings are brought in the name of the company because the cause of action is vested in it and the office-holders are merely agents.[248] A provisional liquidator may be given the same litigation powers as a liquidator by the terms of the order appointing him. Whether the supervisor of a CVA has these powers depends on the terms of the CVA.[249]

29.122   Among the powers of an administrator or administrative receiver are powers (a) to take such proceedings as may seem to him expedient in order to take possession of, collect, and get in the property of the company, (b) to appoint a solicitor to assist him in the performance of his functions, (c) to bring or defend any action or other legal proceedings in the name and on behalf of the company, and (d) to refer to arbitration any question affecting the company.[250]

29.123   Liquidators have power to bring or defend any action or legal proceeding in the name and on behalf of the company, but where the company is being wound up by the court the exercise of this power requires the sanction of the court or the liquidation committee.[251] Any such sanction shall not be a general permission but shall relate to the particular proposed exercise of the liquidator's power in question.[252]

29.124   The Insolvency Act, s 234 gives an office-holder the option of applying in his own name for an order for delivery up of property and this section can be invoked even in cases of dispute.[253] Also a liquidator has the option of applying for a summary order under s 212 (paragraphs 29.138–29.146 below). If the case is fit for summary determination there is little to choose between the alternative procedures.[254] If the claim is likely to be contested on substantial grounds, the treatment of costs may be an important consideration in choosing the mode of proceeding. If the proceedings are brought in the name of the company, the defendant may apply for security for costs under CPR Part 25, rules 25.12–25.14 on the ground that there is reason to believe that it will be unable to pay the defendant's costs if ordered to

---

[248]   Insolvency Act, Schedule B1, para 69 (administrator); Insolvency Act, s 44(1) (administrative receiver). The terms of the debenture may extend or restrict the receiver's powers. After the company has gone into liquidation an administrative receiver ceases to be agent, but may continue to use the company's name, including in litigation: *Goughs Garages v Pugsley* [1930] 1 KB 615, CA. A liquidator is agent of the company and so is not personally liable for engagements made on its behalf: *Re Anglo-Moravian Railway Co* (1875) 1 Ch D 130; *Knowles v Scott* [1891] 1 Ch 717; *Stead Hazel & Co v Cooper* [1933] 1 KB 840, 843; *Butler v Broadhead* [1975] Ch 97, 108. By the Insolvency Act, s 145 the claim could be vested in the liquidator, but this section is rarely used.

[249]   The CVA may appoint the supervisor trustee or give him other powers for the purpose of implementing the CVA: Insolvency Act, s 1(2).

[250]   Insolvency Act, s 42, Schedule B1, para 60 and Schedule 1, paras 1, 4–6.

[251]   Insolvency Act, ss 165, 167 and Schedule 4, para 4.

[252]   Insolvency Rules, rule 4.184.

[253]   *Re London Iron & Steel Co Ltd* [1990] BCLC 372.

[254]   In proceedings outside the Insolvency Act, the court has ample powers to summarily determine the claim under CPR Parts 8 and 24.

do so.[255] But, if there are funds in the estate, such an application is usually answered by satisfying the defendant or the court that any costs that the company is ordered to pay can be paid as a priority expense.[256] If the proceedings are brought in name of the office-holder he will be personally liable for costs if he loses and an order for costs is made in favour of the successful party, but the office-holder is indemnified out of the company's assets.[257]

## (2) Defence of set-off

Where the director has made loans to the company or has a claim against it for wrongful or unfair dismissal, the possible availability of a defence of set-off needs to be considered. It will be advantageous to the estate if the company can recover its claims against the director clear of set-off, so that the director is limited to a right of proof in the administration or liquidation. If the director is limited to a right of proof, he will not be entitled to receive a dividend until he has paid his debt to the company.[258] In consequence the liquidator may recover the debt from the director by deducting it from any dividend otherwise payable to the director.[259]

**29.125**

### *Administrative receivership*

Before turning to administration, it is convenient to consider set-off where an administrative receiver is appointed. Under the floating charge contained in the debenture, the debenture holder takes the benefit of debts owed to the company and the company's claims subject to equities affecting the debts and claims at the date of the appointment of the administrative receiver. The only rights of set-off that may be relied on as a defence to a claim by a company in administrative receivership are in respect of (a) debts that accrued due before the appointment, whether or not they were payable before that date, and (b) debts which arise out of the same contract as that which gave rise to the assigned debt or are closely connected with that contract.[260]

**29.126**

---

[255] 1985 Act, s 726 is repealed with effect from 1 October 2009.

[256] For liquidations, see Insolvency Rules, rule 4.220(2); *Norglen Ltd v Reeds Rains Prudential Ltd* [1999] 2 AC 1, 20, HL, per Lord Hoffmann; *Smith v UIC Insurance Co Ltd* [2001] BCC 11.

[257] Insolvency Rules, rule 2.67(1)(a) for administration. Insolvency Rules, rule 4.218(1)(a)(i) for liquidation, which effectively reverses *Re MC Bacon Ltd (No 2)* [1991] Ch 127 and *Lewis v IRC* [2001] 3 All ER 499, CA. See also *Re Wilson Lovatt & Sons Ltd* [1977] 1 All ER 274; *Re MT Realisations Ltd* [2004] 1 WLR 1678 (but note that the judgment does not refer to the new form of rule 4.218(1)(a)(i), which came into effect on 1 January 2003 (SI 2002/2712)).

[258] This follows from the rule in *Cherry v Boultbee* (1839) 4 My & Cr 442, which applies to company liquidations; *Re SSSL Realisations (2002) Ltd* [2006] Ch 610, CA.

[259] *Re Davies Chemists Ltd* [1993] BCLC 544. Hoffmann LJ achieved the same result in *Re D'Jan of London Ltd* [1994] 1 BCLC 561, 564.

[260] *Business Computers Ltd v Anglo-African Leasing Ltd* [1977] 1 WLR 578, which contains a review by Templeman J of the earlier authorities; *Marathon Electrical Manufacturing Corp v Mashreqbank PSC* [1997] 2 BCLC 460.

*Administration*

**29.127** The position of set-off in administration is more complex, having regard to the new purpose of administration with its three distinct objectives (paragraph 29.29 above), which came into effect on 15 September 2003, and the new set-off rule (rule 2.85), which was substituted with effect from 1 April 2005.

**29.128** There is one reported case under the original administration regime where insolvency set-off was unsuccessfully relied on as a ground for a staying execution of a judgment awarded to a company in administration: *Isovel Contracts Ltd v ABB Building Technologies Ltd.*[261] The case arose out of a building sub-contract under which the contractor tendered a cheque to the sub-contractor to make an interim payment. The sub-contractor left the works, the contractor countermanded the cheque, and an administration order was made in respect of the sub-contractor. The court gave the sub-contractor judgment on the dishonoured cheque and refused the contractor's application for a stay of execution on the ground that it had a Part 20 counterclaim for damages for breach of contract exceeding the amount of the cheque, which it wished to pursue with leave under the Insolvency Act, s 11. This was because (a) the contractor should not be in a better position than it would have been if it had paid the cheque before the administration, (b) a stay would not further the purpose of administration (more advantageous realization of assets), and (c) set-off under Insolvency Rules, rule 4.90 should not be extended to administration. It is respectfully suggested that the dishonoured cheque was the critical factor in the case. The original administration regime was not used by administrators as a means of depriving debtors with cross-claims of the benefit of set-off under rule 4.90 that would be available when the company moved from administration to winding up.

**29.129** It is suggested that issues of set-off under the new administration regime should be considered having regard to which of the objectives forming the purpose of administration are realistically achievable. If it is reasonably practicable for the administrator to achieve the first objective, rescuing the company as a going concern (without a CVA or 2006 Act, Part 26 scheme), then there is no need to consider insolvency set-off under Insolvency Rules, rules 2.85 and 4.90 at all. The defendant's position in relation to set-off should be the same as it would have been if he was sued by a solvent company (Chapter 16, Section E(2) above). If the only objective of administration that is reasonably practicable is the third one, realizing property in order to make a distribution to one or more secured or preferential creditors, the set-off issue may appear rather different. There is no reason to think that the new administration regime and the abolition of administrative receivership was intended either to prejudice or enhance the security of debenture holders

---

[261] [2002] 1 BCLC 390.

in respect of a company's debts and claims. If that is right then the principles summarized in paragraph 29.126 above should apply.

The second objective of administration is achieving a better result for the company's **29.130** creditors as a whole than would be likely if the company were wound up (without first being in administration). If it is reasonably practicable to achieve this, then it is necessary to consider insolvency set-off. This is because the realizations will be distributed in the administration under Schedule B1, paragraphs 65 and 66, in a subsequent voluntary or compulsory winding up, or under a CVA or in a scheme under 2006 Act, Part 26 replicating the rights that creditors would have in a winding up.[262]

If the administrator is authorized to make distributions in the administration, **29.131** Insolvency Rules, rule 2.85 provides for set-off. Unlike rule 4.90 it does not apply automatically when the company enters administration, but like rule 4.90 it contains provisions excluding from set-off debts arising out of obligations incurred, or acquired by assignment or otherwise, after the company had entered administration or liquidation or certain steps had been taken to those ends.[263] Subject to those exceptions it applies to all mutual dealings between the company and a creditor in substantially the same way as rule 4.90 applies in a winding up.

*Winding up*

In the form that has been in effect since 1 April 2005[264] Insolvency Rules, rule **29.132** 4.90 provides for mutual credits and set-off, subject to the exclusion of debts arising out of obligations incurred, or acquired by assignment or otherwise, after the company had entered administration or liquidation or certain steps had been taken to those ends.[265] The substantive provisions of rule 4.90 are:

> 4.90(1) This Rule applies where, before the company goes into liquidation there have been mutual credits, mutual debts or other mutual dealings between the company and any creditor of the company proving or claiming to prove for a debt in the liquidation.
>
> 4.90(3) An account shall be taken of what is due from each party to the other in respect of the mutual dealings, and the sums due from one party shall be set off against the sums due from the other.
>
> 4.90(8) Only the balance (if any) of the account owed to the creditor is provable in the liquidation. Alternatively the balance (if any) owed to the company shall be paid to the liquidator as part of the assets except where all or part of the balance results from a contingent or prospective debt owed by the creditor and in such a case the balance (or part of it which results from the contingent or prospective debt) shall be paid if and when that debt becomes due and payable.

---

[262] *Re Hawk Insurance Co Ltd* [2001] 2 BCLC 480, CA; *Prudential Assurance Co Ltd v PRG Powerhouse Ltd* [2008] 1BCLC 289.

[263] Insolvency Rules, rule 2.85(2)(a)–(e).

[264] Insolvency (Amendment) Rules (SI 2005/527).

[265] Insolvency Rules, rule 4.90(2).

Those provisions are supplemented by rule 4.90(4)–(7) and (9), which makes it clear that the set-off rule applies to future and contingent liabilities owed by or to the company, whether the liabilities are contractual, statutory, or tortious.[266]

**29.133** Set-off under rule 4.90 is mandatory and cannot be contracted out of.[267] It is automatic and self-executing on the company going into liquidation, so as to discharge the mutual credits and debts to the extent of the set-off, and it applies both to proof in the liquidation and to claims brought by the liquidator.[268]

**29.134** There is no reason to doubt that set-off applies as between ordinary debts owed between a director and the company.[269] Authorities on misfeasance applications under the Insolvency Act, s 212 and its predecessors show that set-off is denied where the company's claim is in respect of a breach of duty, but the precise extent of this principle may need re-examination in light of the recent developments (paragraph 29.145 below, and Chapter 16, Section E(2) above).

**29.135** There are a number of clear cases where the director cannot assert a set-off: (a) where the company's claim against him is to recover money taken without authority ie conversion and a void payment;[270] (b) where the company makes a proprietary claim to recover its own money or property; (c) where the director has agreed to subordinate his loan to the company until after all other debts have been paid, so that he cannot prove in respect of it; (d) where the director has guaranteed, but not discharged, a debt of the company (eg to its bank) and the rule against double proof prevents him from claiming set-off in respect of his guarantee liability.[271]

### (3) Other defences

**29.136** Where the office-holder brings proceedings in the name of the company, the director may rely on the same defences as would have been available to him if the company had brought the proceedings while the directors were managing its affairs. The defences of relief from liability under the 2006 Act, s 1157 and limitation are discussed in Chapter 16, Sections D and E(1).

---

[266] These provisions confirm *Secretary of State for Trade and Industry v Frid* [2004] 2 AC 506, HL.

[267] *National Westminster Bank Ltd v Halesowen Presswork and Assemblies Ltd* [1972] AC 785, HL.

[268] *Stein v Blake* [1996] AC 243, 252–5, HL, per Lord Hoffmann (a case on the Insolvency Act, s 323, the bankruptcy equivalent of rule 4.90); *Re Bank of Credit and Commerce International SA (No 10)* [1997] Ch 213, 248, per Sir Richard Scott V-C; *Secretary of State for Trade and Industry v Frid* [2004] 2 AC 506, HL at para 6, per Lord Hoffmann.

[269] *Re Etic Ltd* [1928] Ch 861.

[270] *Smith v Bridgend CBC* [2002] 1 AC 336, HL at para 35 where Lord Hoffmann approved the judgment of Millett LJ in *Manson v Smith* [1997] 2 BCLC 161, 164. *Re Reliance Wholesale (Toys, Fancy Goods and Sports) Ltd* (1979) 76 LS Gaz 731 is an example of set-off being denied as a defence to a claim to recover an unauthorized payment.

[271] *Secretary of State for Trade and Industry v Frid* [2004] 2 AC 506, HL at para 13, per Lord Hoffmann.

The director may defend the proceedings on the ground that the conduct complained of was authorized or ratified by the members, either acting unanimously and informally or by duly passed resolution, so that neither the company nor the liquidator has a claim against him. The means of passing resolutions are discussed in Chapter 22 and paragraphs 22.16–22.23 deal with informal unanimous consent. Chapter 19, Section D(4) discuss the limits on the power to ratify.  **29.137**

## I. Claims against Directors Brought on the Liquidator's Application

### (1) Summary remedy against delinquent directors

The Insolvency Act, s 212 provides a summary remedy against delinquent directors and others where a company has gone into liquidation and without the need for an action in the name of the company. In origin this provision can be traced back to the 1862 Act, s 165. So far as relevant to directors, s 212 provides:  **29.138**

(1) This section applies if in the course of the winding up of a company it appears that a person who—
   (a) is or has been an officer of the company, . . .
   (c) not being a person falling within paragraph (a) . . . , is or has been concerned, or has taken part, in the promotion, formation or management of the company, has misapplied or retained, or become accountable for, any money or other property of the company, or been guilty of any misfeasance or breach of any fiduciary or other duty in relation to the company.

(3) The court may, on the application of the official receiver or the liquidator, or of any creditor or contributory, examine into the conduct of the person falling within subsection (1) and compel him—
   (a) to repay, restore or account for the money or property or any part of it, with interest at such rate as the court thinks just, or
   (b) to contribute such sum to the company's assets by way of compensation in respect of the misfeasance or breach of fiduciary or other duty as the court thinks just.

(5) The power of a contributory to make an application under subsection (3) is not exercisable except with the leave of the court, but is exercisable notwithstanding that he will not benefit from any order the court may make on the application.

The section is a procedural section which provides a summary means of enforcing, by application in the liquidation, rights and obligations that could have been enforced by the company itself by ordinary action.[272] It may also be used to enforce  **29.139**

---

[272] *Coventry and Dixon's Case* (1880) 14 Ch D 660, 670, CA, per James LJ; *Cavendish Bentinck v Fenn* (1887) 12 AC 652, 669, HL, per Lord Macnaghton; *Re City Equitable Fire Insurance Co* [1925] Ch 407, 507, 527, CA, per Pollock MR and Sargant LJ; *Re Windsor Steam Coal Company (1901) Ltd* [1929] 1 Ch 151, 160, CA; *Cohen v Selby* [2001] 1 BCLC 176, CA at para 20, per Chadwick LJ.

new rights acquired in the winding up.[273] Thus the liquidator may use the section to recover compensation to recover from a director in respect of a preference within the Insolvency Act, s 239, which the payee was unable to repay.[274] Before the winding up the company would not have had a claim against the director. The reach of subs 212(1) has been extended so that it applies to the duty to exercise reasonable skill, care, and diligence under the 2006 Act, s 174.[275] The section therefore extends to all the general duties of a director stated in the 2006 Act, Part 10, Chapter 2, ss 170–179, as well as specific duties under that Act.[276] It does not, however, cover a simple claim to recover a debt owed by a director, which involved no breach of duty.[277]

29.140 Although the section is described as providing a summary remedy its use is not confined to uncomplicated cases or ones where there is no defence.[278] The section may be invoked whenever there has been misconduct within subs 212(1). The remedies in subs 212(3) appear to be complementary. Thus, where a director has misapplied or retained or become accountable for any money or other property of the company, the court may order him to repay, restore, or account for the money or other property, with interest. Where the director has been guilty of any misfeasance or any breach of his duties owed to the company the court may order him to contribute to the company's assets by paying compensation.[279]

29.141 The section may be invoked by the official receiver, the liquidator, or any creditor or contributory. By subs 212(5) a contributory can only apply with the permission of the court, but he does not have to establish a tangible interest in the outcome; ie that if the claim succeeded he would receive a distribution.[280] Any recoveries are for the benefit of the liquidation, not the individual creditor or

---

[273] *Re National Funds Assurance Co* (1878) 10 Ch D 118, 125; *Flitcroft's Case* (1882) 21 Ch D 519, 530, CA.

[274] *West Mercia Safetywear Ltd v Dodd* [1988] BCLC 250, CA.

[275] *Re D'Jan of London Ltd* [1994] 1 BCLC 561. The liquidator must prove that the negligence complained of caused the alleged loss: *Cohen v Selby* [2001] 1 BCLC 176, CA at [20]. The 1986 Act adds the words 'or other duty in relation to the company', without which it had been held that the predecessor provision did not apply to negligence claims: *Re B Johnson & Co Builders Ltd* [1955] Ch 634, CA.

[276] *Re Westlowe Storage and Distribution Ltd* [2000] 2 BCLC 590, 611 where Hart J accepted the submission that s 212 covered the whole spectrum of directors' duties.

[277] *Re Etic Ltd* [1928] Ch 861; *Ciro Citterio Menswear plc v Thakrar* [2002] 1 WLR 2217 at para 32.

[278] *Stringer's Case* (1869) 4 Ch App 475, 493; *Rance's Case* (1870) 6 Ch App 104; *Re Kingston Cotton Mill Co (No 2)* [1896] 2 Ch 283, 288, CA.

[279] 'Misfeasance' means 'misfeasance in the nature of a breach of trust': *Coventry and Dixon's Case* (1880) 14 Ch D 660, 670, CA, per James LJ.

[280] This change in the law reverses *Cavendish Bentinck v Fenn* (1887) 12 App Cas 652, in recognition of the fact that a contributory, even if he will not benefit personally, may be the only person able and willing to pursue a proper claim that the company may have against a director.

contributory that pursued the claim.[281] Recoveries in respect of a claim that the company had when it went into liquidation may be caught by charges contained in a debenture. Rather than pursuing the claim himself, the liquidator may therefore exercise his power to sell the claim to anyone who is willing to pursue it.[282]

**29.142** For discussion about directors' duties, the breach of which give rise to a misfeasance application, reference should be made to Chapters 9–15 above. The duty to the company to have regard to the interests of creditors is of particular relevance to misfeasance applications and this is discussed in Chapter 11, Section E above. Chapter 16 above discusses remedies for breach of duty and also the defences of relief from liability under the 2006 Act, s 1157, limitation, set-off, and contributory negligence. Paragraph 29.137 above refers to the defence of authorization or ratification and identifies the other paragraphs in this work where those matters are addressed. The following paragraphs draw attention to particular issues that have arisen in the context of misfeasance applications in relation to (a) relief from liability under the 2006 Act, s 1157, (b) limitation, (c) set-off, and (d) the problem that arises where the director is concurrently liable to compensate the company for misfeasance and also for wrongful or fraudulent trading.

**29.143** The director may ask for relief from liability under the 2006 Act, s 1157, on the ground that he acted honestly and reasonably and that, having regard to all the circumstances, he ought fairly to be excused. This provision may overlap with the court's discretion under s 212 itself, by which the court may limit the amount of compensation to the amount required to pay creditors in full, or otherwise as may seem just.[283]

**29.144** The director may raise a limitation defence. The same limitation rules apply to an application under s 212 as they would to proceedings by the company.[284] In most cases the limitation period is six years from the date when the cause of action for breach of duty accrued, but the Limitation Act, s 21 will apply if the claim is an action in respect of trust property and time may be extended by acknowledgement or part payment or for fraud, mistake, or concealment under the Limitation Act, ss 29–32.

---

[281] *Oldham v Kyrris* [2004] 1 BCLC 305, CA, where a claim by an unsecured creditor, alleging breach of duty owed to him by an administrator, was struck out.

[282] *Re Oasis Merchandising Services Ltd* [1998] Ch 170, 181, CA, per Peter Gibson LJ, contrasting the power to assign a claim under s 212 with claims under ss 213 and 214, which may not be assigned.

[283] *Re Home and Colonial Insurance Co Ltd* [1930] 1 Ch 102; *Re VGM Holdings Ltd* [1942] Ch 235. In exercising his discretion under 1985 Act, s 727 in *Re D'Jan of London Ltd* [1994] 1 BCLC 561 Hoffmann LJ took into account the position of the director and his wife as creditors. Also see *Re Loquitur Ltd* [2003] 2 BCLC 442 at paras 138–141, 247.

[284] *Re Eurocruit Europe Ltd* [2007] 2 BCLC 598.

**29.145** Paragraphs 29.125–29.135 above discuss set-off after the company has entered administration, administrative receivership, or liquidation. The question arises whether there is a special rule that prevents a director from relying on set-off as a defence to a claim under s 212 (eg for repayment of a loan or damages for wrongful dismissal). Old authority indicates that set-off is not available as a defence to a claim under s 212.[285] In *Re Etic Ltd* Maugham J said that this was settled law.[286] Millett LJ endorsed this view when refusing leave to appeal in *Manson v Smith*.[287] In *Smith v Bridgend BC* Lord Hoffmann approved Millett LJ's conclusion that a director could not raise a defence of set-off against a claim that he had taken company money without authority (ie the transfer of property was void), but did not express a view on the other justifications for the rule relied on by Millett LJ.[288] The question whether set-off can be raised as a defence to a claim under s 212 may merit further consideration given that (a) the scope of s 212 is extended to include claims for negligence, (b) Insolvency Rules, rule 4.90 has been amended so as to make it clear that contingent liabilities owed to and by the company are subject to its provisions, and (c) recent authority of the House of Lords has established that set-off under the Insolvency Rules, rule 4.90 operates automatically and is not a procedural provision, applies to ordinary actions and applications in the liquidation, and applies to claims under statute and in tort.[289] There is a useful discussion of these issues in *Derham, The Law of Set-Off* (3rd edn) at [8.64]–[8.71].

**29.146** Where a director is found liable for misfeasance, he may also find himself liable to pay sums to the company for wrongful or fraudulent trading (Insolvency Act, ss 213, 214). The issue then arises whether such liability is concurrent. If the misfeasance occurred after the start of the director's duty under s 214 to take steps to minimize loss, it will usually constitute a breach of that duty, so that the claims will be duplicated and any recovery under s 212 will reduce the director's liability under s 214. Thus in *Re DKG Contractors Ltd* it was ordered that liability should not be cumulative, but that payments under ss 212 and 239 were to be taken as satisfying an order made under s 214.[290] If the misfeasance occurred before the start of the director's duty under s 214, no duplication will be involved if there is

---

[285] *Pelly's Case* (1882) 21 Ch D 492, 498, 503, 507, 508, CA; *Flitcroft's Case* (1882) 21 Ch D 519, CA; *Re Carriage Co-operative Supply Association* (1884) 27 Ch D 322.

[286] [1928] Ch 861, 870, 873. In this case the secretary wished to set off a claim for salary in lieu of notice against a claim by the liquidator for sums overdrawn against future remuneration. Maugham J took into account the exclusion of set-off as a reason for limiting the scope of the misfeasance section to cases of breach of trust and true cases of misapplication or retention of company money or property (p 875).

[287] [1997] 2 BCLC 161.

[288] [2002] 1 AC 336, HL at para 35.

[289] *Stein v Blake* [1996] AC 243, HL; *Secretary of State for Trade and Industry v Frid* [2004] 2 AC 506, HL.

[290] [1990] BCC 903.

full recovery under both sections. In *Re Purpoint Ltd*, an order was made for separate payments under ss 212 and 214, subject to the proviso that the director was not required under s 212 to recoup more than was needed to meet the company's liabilities at the date on which it should have been plain to him that the company could not avoid going into insolvent liquidation.[291]

### (2) Fraudulent trading

Since 1929 the Companies Acts have contained provisions dealing with 'fraudulent trading', making this a criminal offence and a ground for imposing personal liability.[292] The civil sanction may only be invoked in a winding up, whereas the criminal sanction (now provided for in the 2006 Act, s 993) has for some time applied whether or not the company has been or is being wound up.[293] The criminal aspects of fraudulent trading are discussed in Chapter 30, paragraphs 30.218–30.228 below. **29.147**

Following recommendations of the Cork Committee, as discussed in paragraph 29.163 below, a new liability for wrongful trading was introduced by the Insolvency Act, s 214. Whilst the pre-existing civil liability for fraudulent trading has been retained with minor amendment in s 213, recourse to this provision is now relatively rare, since all cases of fraudulent trading by a director which fall within s 213 are likely to fall within the wrongful trading provisions of s 214, and the burden of establishing the claim is less onerous in relation to wrongful trading. Fraudulent trading retains its utility, because its scope also extends to conduct by third parties.[294] **29.148**

Sections 213 and 214 have effect notwithstanding that the person concerned may be criminally liable in respect of matters on the ground of which the declaration is to be made.[295] **29.149**

Section 213 provides: **29.150**

   (1) If in the course of the winding up of a company it appears that any business of the company has been carried out with intent to defraud creditors of the company or creditors of any other person, or for any fraudulent purpose the following has effect.

---

[291] [1991] BCLC 491.

[292] 1929 Act, s 275.

[293] This was first provided by the 1981 Act, s 96, which reversed the decision of the House of Lords in *Director of Public Prosecutions v Schildkamp* [1971] AC 1.

[294] The liquidators of BCCI companies brought several fraudulent trading claims against other banks and outsiders: *Re BCCI (No 9)* [1994] 2 BCLC 636, CA; *Re BCCI (No 13), Banque Arabe International d'Investissement SA v Morris* [2001] 1 BCLC 263; *Morris v Bank of America National Trust* [2001] BCLC 771, CA; *Re BCCI (No 14), Morris v State Bank of India* [2004] 2 BCLC 236; *Re BCCI (No 15), Morris v Bank of India* [2004] 2 BCLC 279, [2005] 2 BCLC 328, CA.

[295] Insolvency Act, s 215(5).

(2) The court, on the application of the liquidator, may declare than any persons who were knowingly parties to the carrying on of the business in the manner above-mentioned are to be liable to make such contributions (if any) to the company's assets as the court thinks proper.

### Carrying on business

**29.151**  A company is to be considered to be carrying on business for the purposes of the section even though its only activity is the collection of assets and payment of debts.[296]

**29.152**  The carrying on of business is to be distinguished from the carrying out of business, so that it is not sufficient, for the purposes of s 213, to show that while the company was carrying on business it entered into fraudulent transactions. For example, the director of a company dealing in second-hand cars who knowingly misrepresents the age and capabilities of a vehicle is not carrying on the company's business for a fraudulent purpose, although he carries out a particular business transaction in a fraudulent manner. He does not intend to defraud a creditor for the purposes of the section, because he does nothing to make it impossible for the customer, once he becomes a creditor to recover the sum due to him as a creditor.[297]

**29.153**  It is, however, possible to carry on business with intent to defraud creditors where only one creditor is defrauded and by a single transaction.[298]

### Intent to defraud

**29.154**  The phrases 'with intent to defraud creditors' and 'for any fraudulent purpose' require a finding of actual dishonesty, which Maugham J characterized as 'involving, according to current notions of fair trading among commercial men, real moral blame'.[299]

**29.155**  In the first case on 'fraudulent trading', *Re William C Leitch Bros Ltd*, Maugham J directed himself that 'if a company continues to carry on business and to incur debts at a time when there is to the knowledge of the directors no reasonable prospect of the creditors ever receiving payment of those debts, it is, in general, a proper inference that the company is carrying on business with intent to defraud'.[300]

---

[296]  *Morphitis v Bernasconi* [2003] Ch 552 CA at para 41, per Chadwick LJ. In *Carman v The Cronos Group SA* [2006] BCC 451 at para 37 it was held that a company cannot be regarded as carrying on business for the purposes of s 213 after a winding-up petition has been presented and its dispositions are void under the Insolvency Act, s 127.

[297]  *Re Gerald Cooper Chemicals Ltd* [1978] Ch 262.

[298]  *Morphitis v Bernasconi* [2003] Ch 552, CA at paras 43–46, where Chadwick LJ discusses and explains *Re Gerald Cooper Chemicals Ltd* [1978] Ch 262, 267, 268.

[299]  *Re Patrick and Lyon Ltd* [1933] Ch 786, 790.

[300]  [1932] 2 Ch 71, 77.

In *R v Grantham* the Court of Appeal did not dissent from that statement, but held that a company also carried on business with intent to defraud creditors if it incurs credit when there is no good reason for thinking that funds will become available to pay the debts when they become due or shortly thereafter.[301] To act in this way was to expose the creditors to the risk of loss which the company had no right to take. It is not necessary to prove that the director or other person alleged to have been responsible for fraudulent trading knew at the time the debts were incurred that there was no reasonable prospect of the creditors *ever* receiving payment of their debts. Further, it is not sufficient for the directors to assert that they believed that the company would be able to pay its debts; there must be a good reason for their belief.[302] Applying this approach, it has been held that deliberately setting out to cheat Her Majesty's Commissioners of Excise of large sums of VAT and failing to make any provision for PAYE on wages falls within s 213.[303]

The required intent to defraud is subjective rather than objective and it is necessary to show either deliberate intention or a reckless indifference whether creditors are defrauded.[304] It is not enough to show that the company is currently insolvent, because continuing to incur credit may be justifiable in reliance on a comfort letter of the parent company which is ultimately not honoured.[305] Nor is it enough to show that an insolvent company preferred to pay some creditors over others.[306]    **29.156**

The words 'or for any fraudulent purpose' could not be wider, and include frauds against potential creditors.[307]    **29.157**

*Attribution of knowledge to outsider companies*

Where it is alleged that an outside company was 'knowingly party' to fraudulent trading by the company, the question arises as to through whom the requisite knowledge may be attributed to the outside company. The Court of Appeal addressed this issue in *Re Bank of Credit and Commerce SA (No 15), Morris v Bank of India*.[308] The liquidators brought a claim under s 213 against the defendant bank. The relevant knowledge was 'blind-eye' knowledge, which required a suspicion that the relevant facts existed and a deliberate decision to avoid confirming    **29.158**

---

[301] [1984] QB 675, 681–4.
[302] The Court of Appeal disapproved the statement by Buckley J to a contrary effect in *Re White and Osmond (Parkstone) Ltd* (30 June 1960, unreported), which became known as the 'sunshine test' and is quoted at [1984] QB 675, 682.
[303] *Re L Todd (Swanscombe) Ltd* [1990] BCLC 454.
[304] *Bernasconi v Nicholas Bennett & Co* [2000] BCC 921.
[305] *Re Augustus Barnett & Sons Ltd* [1986] BCLC 170.
[306] *Re Sarflax Ltd* [1979] Ch 529.
[307] *R v Kemp* [1988] QB 645, CA.
[308] [2005] 2 BCLC 328, CA.

that they existed.[309] The bank contended that knowledge could only be attributed to it through its directors and that no such knowledge was established against them. The Court of Appeal rejected this argument and upheld the liquidators' claim. It reasoned as follows:[310]

(1) The policy of imposing civil liability for fraudulent trading should be considered separately from the policy of imposing criminal liability. Section 213 was not a penal provision.

(2) The proper approach to the question of attribution for the purposes of s 213 turns on the construction and purpose of that section, which was to enable the liquidator to recover compensation for the benefit of those who had suffered as a result of the fraud from those who had knowingly assisted the fraudulent conduct of the business of the company in liquidation.

(3) It would be inappropriate to limit attribution for the purposes of s 213 to the board or those specifically authorized by a resolution of the board. It would ignore the reality that the relevant transactions often take place below board level and risk emasculating the policy behind s 213 if an outsider company could shelter behind an argument that the only relevant knowledge was that of its board and that it could escape liability if the board delegated decisions to senior managers and accepted their recommendations.

(4) Accordingly there was to be attributed to the outsider company the knowledge of a person within its organization who was authorized by it to deal with the company in liquidation in respect of the relevant transactions. That person was to be regarded as 'the directing mind and will' of the outsider company.

(5) But such an attribution was not to be made irrespective of the facts of the case, because otherwise an outsider company could be made liable even though it had acted in good faith and with scrupulous care. The more senior and important within the hierarchy the agent and the greater his freedom to act, the more readily the attribution will be made. Also attribution will be made if communications from the agent put the board on inquiry.

(6) For the purpose of s 213 there was a special rule of attribution under which the knowledge of an employee or officer of an outsider company was to be attributed to it, even though that employee or officer acted dishonestly and in

---

[309] The test for 'blind eye' knowledge is set out at [2005] 2 BCLC 328 at para 14.

[310] [2005] 2 BCLC 328 at paras 99, 107, 108, 111, 112, 116, 118, 120, 129, 130. For the rules of attribution on knowledge to a company, see *Meridian Global Funds Management Asia Ltd v Securities Commission* [1995] 2 AC 500, 507, PC, per Lord Hoffmann. Note that it may be possible to allege that a company is vicariously liable to contribute under s 213 where its employee is knowingly party to fraudulent trading: para 113.

breach of his duties to the outsider company and in circumstances in which he would not have passed on his knowledge to the outsider company.

### Remedies

There has to be some nexus between the loss which has been caused to the company's creditors generally by the carrying on of the business in the manner falling within s 213 and the contribution which those knowingly party to the carrying on of the business in that manner should be ordered to make to the assets. There is no power to include a punitive element in the amount of any contribution which a person should be declared liable to make to the assets of the company. The principle on which the power should be exercised is that the contribution to the assets in which the company's creditors share in the liquidation should reflect and compensate for the loss caused to those creditors by carrying on the business in the manner which gives rise to the exercise of the power.[311] **29.159**

The declaration of liability ought to state the amount for which the director is liable.[312] The order may declare that a director is liable for such amount as will suffice to repay all creditors whose debts arose during the period of trading while insolvent and direct an inquiry as to what debts did so arise.[313] **29.160**

The court is empowered to order that the liability of the person declared liable for fraudulent trading should be charged on any debt or security due to him or that the whole or part of a debt owed by the company to the director should be subordinated to the other debts owed by the company and interest on those debts.[314] **29.161**

A person guilty of fraudulent trading may be made the subject of a disqualification order.[315] **29.162**

### (3) Wrongful trading

The report of the Cork Committee considered that the fraudulent trading provision, then found in the 1948 Act, s 332, was inadequate to deal with irresponsible trading for which directors and others should be held personally accountable, mainly because of the strict standards of pleading and proof required in fraud cases. The Committee recommended that civil liability to pay compensation could arise where loss was suffered as a result of 'unreasonable' conduct, which they proposed should be called 'wrongful trading', and that this should include **29.163**

---

[311] *Morphitis v Bernasconi* [2003] Ch 552, CA at paras 53 and 55, per Chadwick LJ.
[312] *Re William C Leitch Bros Ltd* [1932] 2 Ch 71.
[313] *Re L Todd (Swanscombe) Ltd* [1990] BCLC 454.
[314] Insolvency Act, s 215(2) and (4). The reason for the statutory power to impose a charge on security is explained in the report of the Cork Committee at para 92.
[315] CDDA, ss 4, 10.

the provision for civil liability for fraudulent trading.[316] The Government accepted the broad thrust of the Cork Committee's recommendation when enacting the wrongful trading provisions contained in the Insolvency Act, s 214, which complement, but do not replace, s 213.[317]

**29.164**  Section 214 provides:

(1) Subject to subsection (3) below, if in the course of the winding up of a company it appears that subsection (2) of this section applies in relation to a person who is or has been a director of the company, the court may declare that that person is liable to make such contribution (if any) to the company's assets as the court thinks proper.

(2) This subsection applies in relation to a person if—
(a) the company has gone into insolvent liquidation,
(b) at some time before the commencement of the winding up of the company, that person knew or ought to have concluded that there was no reasonable prospect that the company would avoid going into insolvent liquidation, and
(c) that person was a director of the company at that time; . . .

(3) The court shall not make a declaration under this section with respect to any person if it is satisfied that after the condition specified in subsection (2)(b) was first satisfied in relation to him that person took every step with a view to minimising the potential loss to the company's creditors as (assuming him to have known that there was no reasonable prospect that the company would avoid going into insolvent liquidation) he ought to have taken.

(4) For the purposes of subsections (2) and (3), the facts which a director of a company ought to know or ascertain, the conclusions which he ought to reach and the steps which he ought to take are those which would be known or ascertained, or reached or taken, by a reasonably diligent person having both—
(a) the general knowledge, skill and experience that may reasonably be expected of a person carrying out the same functions as are carried out by that director in relation to the company, and
(b) the general knowledge, skill and experience that that director has.

(5) The reference in subsection (4) to the functions carried out in relation to a company by a director of the company includes any functions which he does not carry out but which have been entrusted to him.

(6) For the purposes of this section, a company goes into insolvent liquidation if it goes into liquidation at a time when its assets are insufficient for the payment of its debts and other liabilities and the expenses of the winding up.

(7) In this section 'director' includes a shadow director.

(8) This section is without prejudice to section 213.

---

[316]  The report of the Cork Committee at Chapter 44, paras 1775–1806. It should be noted that the Cork Committee reported in 1982, before the decision in *R v Grantham* [1984] QB 675, and at a time when it appeared to be necessary to show that it was 'clear that the company will *never* be able to satisfy its creditors' and that directors would have a good defence if they 'genuinely believe that the clouds will roll away and the sunshine of prosperity will shine upon them again and disperse the fog of their depression'. This was 'the sunshine test' as formulated by Buckley J in the well-known but unreported case of *Re White and Osmond (Parkstone) Ltd*, 30 June 1960, which made fraudulent trading claims particularly difficult to sustain.

[317]  Insolvency Act, s 214(8).

Although the marginal note indicates that s 214 is concerned with 'wrongful trad- **29.165** ing', the expression does not appear in the section, and it may be objected that the section is vague as to what conduct falls within its scope. Instead, the court is given power to order a person to make a contribution to the company's assets if (a) the company has gone into insolvent liquidation,[318] (b) at some time the person knew or ought to have known that insolvent liquidation could not reasonably be avoided, (c) at that time the person was a director of the company, and (d) the court is not satisfied that after that time the person failed to take every step to minimize creditors' losses. Although it should be easier for a liquidator to establish those matters than dishonesty or reckless disregard under s 213, there appear to have been relatively few wrongful trading cases since the Insolvency Act came into force.

*Insolvent liquidation*

As with fraudulent trading this provision is not available if the company goes into **29.166** administration. The application can only be made by the liquidator. This means that directors of a company in financial difficulties can avoid exposure to a wrongful trading claim if creditors can be persuaded to accept a CVA scheme under the 2006 Act, Part 26 or some other consensual restructuring.

A right of action against directors for wrongful trading and the fruits of such an **29.167** action cannot be charged by a debenture, nor can they be assigned.[319] This is because a distinction is to be drawn between assets which are the property of the company at the time of the commencement of the liquidation and property representing it, including rights of action which arose and might have been pursued by the company itself prior to the liquidation, and assets which only arise after the liquidation of the company and are recoverable only by the liquidator pursuant to statutory powers conferred on him. The fruits of a claim for wrongful trading are not the property of the company at the commencement of the liquidation but are subsequently acquired by him through the exercise of his statutory rights and are not therefore 'the company's property' within paragraph 6 of Schedule 4 to the Act of 1986 and may not therefore be assigned by him.

Subsection 214(6) provides that a company is in insolvent liquidation if its assets **29.168** are insufficient to pay its debts and liabilities, taking into account the expenses of the liquidation.[320] The contribution that the court may order may make good that deficiency.

---

[318] s 247(2) identifies when a company goes into liquidation.
[319] *Re Oasis Merchandising Services Ltd* [1998] Ch 170, CA.
[320] A similar definition appears in the CDDA, s 6(2)(a).

*Appreciation of unavoidable insolvent liquidation*

**29.169**   There are three aspects of this critical element of many wrongful trading claims: (a) identifying the time from which the company is alleged to have been wrongfully trading, (b) what the director knew or ought to have been known of the company's financial circumstances at that time, and (c) whether at that time the director knew or ought to have concluded that there was no reasonable prospect that the company would avoid going into insolvent liquidation.

**29.170**   The liquidator must allege a particular time from which wrongful trading occurred and prove his case by reference to that time. The court will not permit the liquidator to amend his case at a late stage or at trial to allege that wrongful trading occurred from some later date where that would be unjust to the respondents.[321] Although the liquidator's case will often be based on hindsight, the court has warned that 'there is always the danger of hindsight, the danger of assuming that what has in fact happened was always bound to happen and was apparent'.[322]

**29.171**   In assessing the knowledge that the directors had or ought to have had and the conclusions reached or which ought to have been reached, the court is directed to apply the standards of knowledge, skill, and experience set out in subs 214(4). These standards reflect the common law duty of care, now set out in the 2006 Act, s 174 (Chapter 13 above).[323] The standard set by subs 214(4)(a) is an objective minimum, and the general knowledge, skill, and experience postulated will be much less extensive in a small company in a modest way of business, with simple accounting procedures and equipment, than it will be in a large company with sophisticated procedures.[324] Likewise, the standard may be raised by subs 214(4)(b) on account of the particular attributes of the director in question.

**29.172**   One cannot be a 'sleeping' director; so a wife whose function in the company's affairs was limited, but who was nonetheless a director and received benefits as a director, was subject to the test under s 214(4) of a reasonably diligent person who has taken on the office of director. The Insolvency Act, s 214(4)(a) relates only to where a director performed a special function, such as finance or marketing director, and cannot be used to reduce the basic standard on the grounds that the director in question exercised no particular functions in the company's management.[325]

---

[321] *Re Sherborne Associates Ltd* [1995] BCC 40, 42; *Re Continental Insurance Co of London plc (No 4)* [2007] 2 BCLC 287 at para 99.
[322] *Re Sherborne Associates Ltd* [1995] BCC 40, 54.
[323] *Norman v Theodore Goddard* [1991] BCLC 1028, 1030, 1031; *Re D'Jan of London Ltd* [1994] 1 BCLC 561, 563.
[324] *Re Produce Marketing Consortium Ltd (No 2)* [1989] BCLC 520, 550.
[325] *Re Brian D Pierson (Contractors) Ltd* [2001] 1 BCLC 275, 310.

Section 214(5) provides that 'the reference in subsection (4) to the functions    **29.173**
carried out in relation to a company by a director of a company includes any functions which he does not carry out by which have been entrusted to him'. The effect
of this subsection is that omissions by a director are treated in the same way as
commissions.

In relation to the knowledge that the directors had or ought to have had as to the    **29.174**
company's financial position at the relevant time, the cases in which directors have
been held liable are typically cases in which the directors closed their eyes to the
reality of the company's position, or failed to ensure that accounting records
compliant with what is now the 2006 Act, Part 15, Chapters 2–4 were kept.[326]
This was the case in *Re Produce Marketing Consortium Ltd (No 2)*, where the company had kept inadequate accounting and the court proceeded on the basis that it
should assume, for the purposes of applying the test in s 214(2), that the financial
results for the year in question were known at least to the extent of the size of the
deficiency of the assets over liabilities.[327]

In *Re DKG Contractors Ltd* a declaration was made against the directors under    **29.175**
s 214 because they had failed to meet the standard required by subs 214(4)(a). The
court said that 'Patently, [the directors]' own knowledge, skill and experience were
hopelessly inadequate for the task they undertook. That is not sufficient to protect
them.'[328]

On the other hand, in *Re Continental Assurance Co of London plc* an application    **29.176**
under s 214 was dismissed.[329] The judge held that the directors took a responsible
and conscientious attitude at all times from the first board meeting when major
and unexpected losses were reported to them. A director expressly raised the question of whether the company could properly continue to trade; the directors considered the question directly, closely and frequently. At every board meeting,
and at times in between board meetings, they sought assurance from the finance
director and others that the company was still solvent. As the financial position
looked bleaker, they reduced the scale of trading to minimal and cautious levels.
When it was reported to the directors that the company had become insolvent
they gave instructions that it should not do any more business, and took advice
from insolvency practitioners. The commencement of a formal liquidation did
not happen for some time, but that was in order to keep open as long as possible
the chance of selling the company. The insolvency practitioners were aware of that
at the time and raised no objections.

---

[326] *Re Continental Insurance Co of London plc (No 4)* [2007] 2 BCLC 287 at para 106; *Re The Rod Gunner Organisation Ltd* [2004] 2 BCLC 110.
[327] [1989] BCLC 520, 550, 551.
[328] [1990] BCC 903, 912.
[329] [2007] 2 BCLC 287 at paras 106, 109, 281, 378.

**29.177** Turning to the prospects of avoiding insolvent liquidation, the cases where wrongful trading has been established are those where the company carried on trading long after it should have been obvious to the directors that the company was insolvent and that there was no way out for it. In those cases, the directors had been irresponsible and had not made any genuine attempt to grapple with the company's real position.[330] In *Re Sherborne Associates Ltd* the court found that the directors were aware of the company's financial difficulties and responded positively and responsibly to it. The court was not prepared to find that their belief that the company could trade out of its difficulties was unreasonable or fanciful.[331]

### A director at the time

**29.178** Subsection 214(7) explicitly applies the wrongful trading provisions to shadow directors as well as appointed directors. In *Re a Company (No 005009 of 1987)*[332] the court refused to strike out a claim that the bank was liable for wrongful trading, made on the basis that the directors were accustomed to act in accordance with the bank's directions and instructions. Section 214 also applies to de facto directors, but the liquidator must plead and prove his case that the director was either an appointed director, or a shadow or de facto director.[333]

**29.179** An application may be made against the foreign directors of a foreign company which is being wound up in this jurisdiction as an unregistered company.[334] The court also has jurisdiction to make an order under Insolvency Act, s 426 in response to a request by a foreign court for assistance in enforcing a corresponding insolvency jurisdiction.[335]

**29.180** The fact that a director has died before the application is heard does not deprive the liquidator of the right to seek relief against him.[336]

### Limit on declaration

**29.181** The standards in subs 214(4) apply to the defence under subs 214(3). Where the directors appreciate the grave financial position of the company they invariably consult an insolvency practitioner and either put the company into an insolvency proceeding or manage the company in accordance with his advice. In those circumstances no question of wrongful trading should arise. Where the directors do not appreciate the gravity of the company's situation and carry on trading in

---

[330] *Re Continental Insurance Co of London plc (No 4)* [2007] 2 BCLC 287 at para 106.
[331] [1995] BCC 40, 54, 55.
[332] [1989] BCLC 13.
[333] *Re Hydrodam (Corby) Ltd* [1994] 2 BCLC 180.
[334] *Re Howard Holdings Ltd* [1998] BCC 549.
[335] *Re Bank of Credit and Commerce International SA (No 9); Re Bank of Credit and Commerce International (Overseas) Ltd* [1994] 3 All ER 764, Rattee J and CA.
[336] *Re Sherborne Associates Ltd* [1995] BCC 40.

disregard of creditors' interests they cannot expect to bring themselves within subs 214(3). Thus it has been said that the defence is intended to apply to cases where a director takes specific steps with a view to preserving or realizing assets or claims for the benefit of creditors, even if he fails to achieve that result, and does not cover the very act of wrongful trading itself, even if it was done with the intention of trying to make a profit.[337]

### No defence of acting honestly and reasonably

The Companies Act, s 1157 does not apply to claims made under s 214.[338] **29.182**
Parliament did not intend the essentially subjective test under s 1157 to be operated at the same time as the objective tests within s 214. In any case the court has a discretion under subs 214(1) whether to order payment of a contribution and if so as to the amount.

### Limitation

A wrongful trading application must be commenced within six years from the **29.183**
time when the company goes into insolvent liquidation.[339]

### Remedies

Where the court's discretion to make a declaration arises, the amount of the con- **29.184**
tribution is also in the court's discretion: the amount is described in s 214(1) as 'such contribution (if any) to the company's assets as the court thinks proper'.
In the first reported case, *Re Produce Marketing Consortium Ltd (No 2)*[340] Knox J recorded argument of counsel for the liquidator, Mary Arden QC that the extent of liability is analogous to the assessment of damages in tort, being a matter of causation not culpability, and that the discretion is intended to enable allowance to be made for questions of causation and to avoid unjust results and held that:

(1) the jurisdiction was primarily compensatory rather than penal;

(2) prima facie the appropriate amount that a director is declared to be liable to contribute is the amount by which the company's assets can be discerned to have been depleted by the director's conduct which caused the discretion under subs 214(1) to arise;

(3) without limiting the factors to be taken into account for reducing the prima facie amount, it may be appropriate to consider whether the director was guilty of deliberate wrongdoing or a failure to appreciate the situation;

---

[337] *Re Brian D Pierson (Contractors) Ltd* [2001] 1 BCLC 275.
[338] *Re Produce Marketing Consortium Ltd* [1989] 1 WLR 745.
[339] *Re Farmizer (Products) Ltd* [1997] 1 BCLC 589, CA.
[340] [1989] BCLC 520, 553, 554.

(4) the jurisdiction was to be exercised in a way that will benefit unsecured creditors.

**29.185** In *Re Purpoint Ltd* Vinelott J followed Knox J's approach to the prima facie amount and observed that purpose of s 214 is to recoup loss to creditors as a whole, so that creditors whose debts were incurred after the company stopped trading did not have a stronger claim than creditors with existing debts. But where it was impossible, because of the director's failure to ensure that proper records were kept, to ascertain the precise extent to which the company's net liabilities were increased by the continuance of the company's trading, the loss was to be quantified as the aggregate of the debts incurred after the date when it should have been plain to the director that the company could not avoid going into insolvent liquidation.[341]

**29.186** The conclusion that the jurisdiction is compensatory not penal and that there should be some connection between the loss caused by the wrongful trading and amount of the contribution ordered to be made is supported by subsequent decisions of the Court of Appeal.[342] In *Re Continental Assurance Co of London plc* Park J expressed the view that there must be some connection between the director's wrongful conduct and the losses that the liquidator wishes to recover from him. This connection would be satisfied in the case of normal trading losses, but not for losses caused by unforeseen events not attributable to the impugned conduct, such as unexpected weather conditions or costly litigation conducted by the liquidator.[343]

**29.187** The court has the same ancillary powers to impose charges and direct subordination as it has on a fraudulent trading claim (paragraph 29.161 above).

**29.188** Where wrongful trading is alleged against a number of directors, the starting point is that liability will not be joint and several, because there is no single claim against the board collectively, but rather as many claims as there are respondent directors.[344] The court has a discretion to order two or more directors to be jointly and severally liable, but this will only arise where the court positively exercises its discretion to impose it.

---

[341] *Re Purpoint Ltd* [1991] BCLC 491, 498, 499. In *Re DKG Contractors Ltd* [1990] BCC 903, 912 the judge ordered the directors to contribute an amount equal the debts incurred after trading should have ceased.

[342] *Cohen v Selby* [2001] 1 BCLC 176 at para 21; *Morphitis v Bernasconi* [2003] Ch 552 at para 53 (a fraudulent trading case).

[343] [2007] 2 BCLC 287 at paras 376–381. His judgment, delivered in 2000, was adopted in *Re Marini Ltd* [2004] BCC 172 at para 68. For reducing the prima facie amount on account of unexpected events, see *Re Brian D Pierson (Contractors) Ltd* [2001] 1 BCLC 275, 311.

[344] *Re Continental Insurance Company of London plc* [2007] 2 BCLC 287 at paras 383–387.

A person guilty of wrongful trading may be made the subject of a disqualification    **29.189**
order.[345] An application for a declaration under s 214 may be consolidated with
disqualification proceedings.[346] In *Brian D Pierson (Contractors) Ltd* the court
found the directors liable for wrongful trading and drew attention to its powers
under CDDA, s 10. Following post-judgment discussion between the judge,
counsel for the liquidator, and counsel for the directors, and in light of written
comments from the Secretary of State for Trade and Industry, the judge made an
order disqualifying the directors under CDDA, s 10.[347]

## J. Liability on Contravention of Restriction on Re-use of Company Name

### (1) The restriction

In the report of the Cork Committee attention was drawn to the widespread dis-    **29.190**
satisfaction at the ease with which a person trading through the medium of one or
more companies with limited liability can allow such a company to become insolvent, form a new company, and then carry on trading much as before, leaving
behind him a trail of unpaid creditors. It was pointed out that the dissatisfaction
was greatest where the director of an insolvent company has set up business again
using a similar name for the new company, and trades with assets purchased at
a discount from the liquidator of the old company.[348] It appears that the Insolvency
Act, ss 216 and 217 are provisions which are designed to eradicate this 'phoenix
syndrome'.

However, these provisions as enacted apply to a wider set of circumstances than    **29.191**
the case of a person attempting to exploit the goodwill of a previous insolvent
company. In the absence of an application under s 216(3) for leave, the court is
left with no discretion on the application of the sections, and a creditor of a company is entitled to take advantage of the statutory provisions, if they can be shown
to be applicable.[349]

The provisions are an example of a limited, though significant, departure from the    **29.192**
general principle of corporate law that a company is a legal entity separate from its
directors and members, so that only the company is liable for its debts and the

---

[345] CDDA, s 10.
[346] *Official Receiver v Doshi* [2001] 2 BCLC 235.
[347] [2001] 1 BCLC 275.
[348] Paras 1813, 1826–1837.
[349] *Thorne v Silverleaf* [1994] 1 BCLC 637, 642, 643, CA, per Peter Gibson LJ.

creditors of the company do not have a right of recourse to the assets of the directors and members for payment of the company's debts.

29.193 It appeared to Parliament that the mischief at which the Insolvency Act s 216 is directed was of such gravity that a person acting in contravention of that section should not only be subjected to criminal sanctions by s 216(3), of which the severity would depend upon the discretion of the court, but that such person should also thereby be made personally responsible by s 217(1)(a) for all debts of the company incurred at a time when that person was involved in the management of the company. It must have been supposed that such a person would, in the ordinary course of things, learn of this provision of the law or that directors of companies which go into insolvent liquidation should be left to inform themselves of the consequences in law of acting in contravention of s 216. That burden of responsibility for the debts was also imposed upon a further category of persons by s 217(1)(b), namely any person who is involved in the management of the company and who acts or is willing to act on instructions given (without the leave of the court) by a person whom he knows to be in contravention in relation to the company of s 216; but such a person is not by the words of s 216 himself caused to be in contravention of s 216 and therefore guilty of the offence created by s 216(3).[350]

29.194 By subs 216(1), s 216 applies 'to a person where a company ("the liquidating company") has gone into insolvent liquidation on or after the appointed day and he was a director or shadow director of the company at any time in the period of 12 months ending with the day before it went into liquidation'.[351] For the purposes of s 216 a company goes into insolvent liquidation if it goes into liquidation at a time when its assets are insufficient for the payment of its debts and other liabilities and the expenses of the winding up.[352]

29.195 Subsection 216(2) explains what is meant by a prohibited name. It provides:

(2) For the purposes of this section, a name is a prohibited name in relation to such a person if—

(a) it is a name by which the liquidating company was known at any time in that period of 12 months, or

(b) it is a name which is so similar to a name falling within paragraph (a) as to suggest an association with that company.

References in s 216, in relation to any time, to a name by which a company is known are to the name of the company at that time or to any name under which the company carries on business at that time.[353]

---

[350] *Thorne v Silverleaf* [1994] 1 BCLC 637, 646, CA, per Ralph Gibson LJ.

[351] The appointed day is 29 December 1986: Insolvency Act, ss 436, 443. In s 216, 'company' includes a company which may be wound up under Part V of the Insolvency Act: subs 216(8).

[352] Insolvency Act, s 216(7).

[353] Insolvency Act, s 216(6).

In deciding whether a company name is so similar to another as to suggest an **29.196** association with it, it is necessary to make a comparison of the names in the context of all the circumstances in which they are actually used or likely to be used: the types of product dealt in, the locations of the business, the types of customers dealing with the companies and those involved in the operation of the two companies.[354] Having regard to the civil and criminal consequences of breaching the restriction on re-use of a prohibited name, the similarity between the two names must be such as to give rise to a probability that members of the public, comparing the names in the relevant context, will associate the two names with each other, whether as successor companies or as part of the same group.[355] On this basis, the court held that the name 'Air Equipment Co Ltd' was a name so similar to 'The Air Component Co Ltd' as to suggest an association with that company.[356]

Section 216(3) states the restriction which renders a person who contravenes it **29.197** liable to criminal punishment under subs 216(4) and civil liability under s 217. It provides:

Except with leave of the court[357] or in such circumstances as may be prescribed, a person to whom this section applies shall not at any time in the period of 5 years beginning with the day on which the liquidating company went into liquidation—
(a)  be a director of any other company that is known by a prohibited name, or
(b)  in any way, whether directly or indirectly, be concerned or take part in the promotion, formation or management of any such company, or
(c)  in any way, whether directly or indirectly, be concerned or take part in the carrying on of a business carried on (otherwise than by a company) under a prohibited name.

It is not therefore necessary that the person concerned should hold the position of director in the second company, only that he should be a director or shadow director of the liquidating company.[358]

References, in relation to any time, to a name by which a company is known are **29.198** to the name of the company at that time or to any name under which the company carries on business at any time.[359]

---

[354] *Ad Valorem Factors Ltd v Ricketts* [2004] 1 All ER 894, CA at para 22, per Mummery LJ (applied in *Revenue and Customs Commissioners v Benton-Diggins* [2006] 2 BCLC 255).
[355] *Ad Valorem Factors Ltd v Ricketts* [2004] 1 All ER 894, CA at para 30, per Simon Brown LJ. Applied in *Revenue and Customs Commissioners v Walsh* [2005] 2 BCLC 455.
[356] *Ad Valorem Factors Ltd v Ricketts* [2004] 1 All ER 894, CA. Differences in the way the names are presented on the company's documents are irrelevant: *Archer Structures Ltd v Griffiths* [2004] 1 BCLC 201 at para 19. Also see *R(Griffin) v Richmond Magistrates Court* [2008] BCC 575; *First Independent Factors Ltd v Mountford* [2008] 2 BCLC 297.
[357] 'Court' means any court having jurisdiction to wind up companies; and on any application for leave under subs 216(3), the Secretary of State or the official receiver may appear and call the attention of the court to any matters which seem to him to be relevant: subs 216(5).
[358] *R v Doring* [2002] BCC 838, CA.
[359] Insolvency Act, s 216(6).

**29.199** A director is therefore able to protect himself from the risk of committing criminal offences and from the burden of personal liability for the debts of the successor company in two ways: he can resign his directorship and take no further part in the management of the successor company; or he can make an immediate application to the court for leave under s 216 to act in relation to a company with a prohibited name.[360]

### (2) Application for leave

**29.200** When considering an application for leave under s 216, the court may call on the liquidator, or any former liquidator, of the liquidating company for a report of the circumstances in which that company became insolvent, and the extent (if any) of the applicant's apparent responsibility for its doing so.[361]

**29.201** In *Penrose v Secretary of State for Trade and Industry* Chadwick J stated the following principles in relation to an application for leave.[362]

(1) It is wrong to treat an applicant who seeks leave under s 216 as if he were a person who had been disqualified for any of the reasons under the CDDA unless there is evidence which shows that he ought to be disqualified for one or more of those reasons.

(2) In particular, it is wrong to treat him, without evidence of misconduct, as if he were unfit to be a company director. The fact that the applicant intends to continue to trade through a company with a prohibited name does not entitle the court, without more, to impose restrictions upon him as if he were a person who had been disqualified for some form of misconduct.

(3) Unless the court is satisfied that the applicant is a person whose conduct in relation to the liquidating company makes him unfit to be concerned in the management of a company, it should exercise its discretion under s 216(3) with regard only to the purposes for which s 216 was enacted and not on the more general basis that the public requires some protection from the applicant's activities as a company director.

**29.202** So, as a matter of principle, where an application is made for leave, the court should exercise its discretion to allow the director to act in relation to a company using a prohibited name, if it is satisfied that there is no risk to the creditors of the old company and no risk to the creditors of the new company beyond that which was permitted under the law relating to the incorporation of limited liability companies—that is to say, no risk beyond that which the legislature, in permitting

---

[360] *Ad Valorem Factors Ltd v Ricketts* [2004] 1 All ER 894, CA at para 19, per Mummery LJ.
[361] Insolvency Rules, rule 4.227.
[362] [1996] 1 WLR 482, 489.

those who are inexperienced to trade through companies which are undercapitalized, must be taken to have regarded as acceptable.[363]

In the earlier case *Re Bonus Breaks Ltd* leave was given where the director gave an **29.203** undertaking that the company would not redeem any redeemable shares nor purchase its own shares out of distributable profits for a period of two years unless that was approved by an unconnected director.[364] However, the judge did not have to decide in that case whether leave would be given if the undertakings were not given. Following *Penrose*, the practice is not to require such undertakings.

### (3) Excepted cases

As contemplated by s 216(3), circumstances have been prescribed which consti- **29.204** tute exceptions to the prohibition. These exceptions are contained in the Insolvency Rules, rules 4.228–4.230. There are three excepted cases.

*First excepted case*

The first excepted case, rule 4.228(1), applies where the insolvency practitioner **29.205** sells the business of the insolvent company to the successor company and notice is given to the creditors of the liquidating company. This fulfils two purposes: preventing the assets of the liquidating company from being acquired at an undervalue or otherwise expropriated and preventing creditors of the liquidating company from being misled as to the identity of the new company.[365]

In its original form it was held in *First Independent Factors and Finance Ltd v* **29.206** *Churchill* that the first excepted case is unavailable if the director is already working with the management of the successor company.[366] The decision gave rise to a number of difficulties. For example, it made the rule inapplicable in management buy-outs. A new rule 4.228 has therefore been substituted in place of the former one. The new rule only applies where arrangements for the acquisition of the business from the insolvent company are entered into on or after 6 August 2007.[367]

As before, the new rule makes provision for a director of a company which goes **29.207** into insolvent liquidation to act as a director of a company with a prohibited name where that company acquires the whole or substantially the whole of the business of the insolvent company, provided certain notice requirements are complied with. Unlike the previous rule, it also provides for such a person to carry on

---

[363] *Penrose v Secretary of State for Trade and Industry* [1996] 1 WLR 482, 490. This was followed in *Re Lightning Electrical Contractors Ltd* [1996] 2 BCLC 302, where leave was granted in respect of certain named but then dormant companies.
[364] [1991] BCC 546.
[365] *Penrose v Secretary of State for Trade and Industry* [1996] 1 WLR 482, 489.
[366] [2007] 1 BCLC 293, CA.
[367] Insolvency (Amendment) Rules 2007 (SI 2007/1974).

business under a prohibited name other than by way of a company, subject to the same requirements. In the new rule the notice requirements have also been expanded. Notice must be published in the Gazette and given to all creditors whose name and address is known to the director or could be ascertained by him on making reasonable enquiries. The prescribed notice may be given before the company enters into insolvent liquidation, for example where it is in administration or administrative receivership and may go into liquidation later. In cases where the company is not in insolvent liquidation, notice can be given where the director of the insolvent company is already a director of the acquiring company. However, notice must always be given before a director acts in a way that would be prohibited by s 216.

**29.208**    The notice to creditors must be in Form 4.73 (which is a new form). In all cases the notice must state the name and registered number of the insolvent company; the name of the director or shadow director; that it is his intention to act (or, where the company has not entered liquidation, to act or continue to act) in any or all of the ways specified in s 216(3) in connection with the carrying on of the business of the insolvent company; and the prohibited name, or where the company has not entered liquidation, the name under which the business is being or will be carried on which would be prohibited in the event that the company goes into liquidation.

**29.209**    In *Re Bonus Breaks Ltd* the applicant referred to a widely held understanding that 'the business of the company' for the purpose of rule 4.228 must be the business comprising both assets and liabilities.[368] Morritt J, without hearing full argument, said that it seemed to him at least arguable that the purchase of a business or part of a business from an insolvency practitioner acting as liquidator of the company did not have to include the purchase of all or any of the liabilities of the company.

*Second excepted case*

**29.210**    The second excepted case is provided for by rule 4.229. This provides that where a person to whom s 216 applies as having been a director or shadow director of the liquidating company applies for leave of the court under that section not later than seven days from the date on which the company went into liquidation, he may, during the period specified in rule 4.229(2), act in any of the ways mentioned in s 216(3), notwithstanding that he has not obtained the leave of the court under that section. The period specified in rule 4.229(2) begins with the day on which the company goes into liquidation and ends either on the day falling

---

[368] [1991] BCC 546.

six weeks after that date or on the day on which the court disposes of the application for leave under s 216, whichever of those days occurs first.

This second excepted case therefore enables a person seeking leave to act as a director, or in the other ways mentioned in s 216(3), pending the hearing of the application and so avoid disruption to the management of the business of the new company. **29.211**

### Third excepted case

The third excepted case, set out in rule 4.230, indicates that the mischief addressed by s 216 is not thought to exist where a company having the prohibited name has been established and trading for not less than 12 months before the liquidating company went into liquidation.[369] Rule 4.230 provides: **29.212**

> The court's leave under section 216(3) is not required where the company referred to, though known by a prohibited name within the meaning of the section—
> (a) has been known by that name for the whole of the period of 12 months ending with the day before the liquidating company went into liquidation, and
> (b) has not at any time in those 12 months been dormant within the meaning of section 252(5) of the Companies Act.

The expression 'known by' in rule 4.230 has the same meaning as in s 216(6). So rule 4.230 is capable of application where a name change has taken place in the relevant period.[370] **29.213**

The object of rule 4.230 is to take outside ss 216 and 217 companies which were not phoenix companies, and since companies within the same group (formal or informal) often share a common word or acronym in their names, it may be inferred that the third excepted case should cover group companies, whether the group is formal or informal.[371] **29.214**

### (4) Personal liability and penalty

If a person acts in contravention of s 216, he is liable to imprisonment or a fine, or both.[372] The offence is one of strict liability and *mens rea* is not necessary for reasons of social policy and prudence;[373] it is irrelevant that there has been no express misrepresentation or that anyone has actually been deceived or confused into thinking that there was an association. **29.215**

---

[369] *Penrose v Secretary of State for Trade and Industry* [1996] 1 WLR 482, 490.
[370] *ESS Production Ltd v Sully* [2005] 2 BCLC 547, CA at paras 62, 81, per Arden LJ and at paras 92, 95, per Chadwick LJ.
[371] *ESS Production Ltd v Sully* [2005] 2 BCLC 547, CA at paras 8, 60.
[372] Insolvency Act, s 216(4).
[373] *R v Doring* [2002] BCC 838, CA.

**29.216**  Notwithstanding that the legislative purpose of ss 216 and 217 is to curb the 'phoenix syndrome', if a name is a prohibited name within the natural and ordinary meaning of the language of s 216(2), the case is caught by the restrictions, even if it is not a 'phoenix syndrome' case.[374]

**29.217**  Section 217 provides for civil liability:

(1)  A person is personally responsible for all the relevant debts of a company[375] if at any time—
   (a)  in contravention of section 216, he is involved in the management of the company, or
   (b)  as a person who is involved in the management of the company, he acts or is willing to act on instructions given (without the leave of the court) by a person whom he knows at that time to be in contravention in relation to the company of section 216.

(2)  Where a person is personally responsible under this section for the relevant debts of a company, he is jointly and severally liable in respect of those debts with the company and any other person who, whether under s 217 or otherwise, is so liable.

(3)  For the purposes of this section the relevant debts of a company are—
   (a)  in relation to a person who is personally responsible under paragraph (a) of subsection (1), such debts and other liabilities of the company as are incurred at a time when that person was involved in the management of the company, and
   (b)  in relation to a person who is personally responsible under paragraph (b) of that subsection, such debts and other liabilities of the company as are incurred at a time when that person was acting or was willing to act on instructions given as mentioned therein.

(4)  For the purposes of this section, a person is involved in the management of a company if he is a director of the company or if he is concerned, whether directly or indirectly, or takes part, in the management of the company.

(5)  For the purposes of this section a person who, as a person involved in the management of a company, has at any time acted on instructions given (without the leave of the court) by a person whom he knew at that time to be in contravention in relation to the company of section 216 is presumed, unless the contrary is shown, to have been willing at any time thereafter to act on any instructions given by that person.

**29.218**  There has been a steady flow of cases in which persons have been held to be personally liable for the debts of the successor company where there has been a contravention of s 216.[376] It has also been held that a person's liability to a creditor of the successor company under s 217 is not reduced on account of a set-off under

---

[374] *Ricketts v Ad Valorem Factors Ltd* [2004] 1 All ER 894, CA; *First Independent Factors Ltd v Mountford* [2008] 2 BCLC 297.

[375] In s 217 'Company' includes a company which may be wound up under the Insolvency Act, Part V (unregistered companies): subs 217(6).

[376] *Thorne v Silverleaf* [1994] 1 BCLC 637, CA; *Inland Revenue Commissioners v Nash* [2004] BCC 150; *Archer Structures Ltd v Griffiths* [2004] 1 BCLC 201; *Revenue and Customs Commissioners v Walsh* [2005] 2 BCLC 455; *Revenue and Customs Commissioners v Benton-Diggins* [2006] 2 BCLC

Insolvency Rules, rule 4.90 of a debt owed by the creditor to the successor company.[377]

## K. Liabilities of Directors in Relation to the Adjustment of Prior Transactions

The final section of this chapter deals with the provisions in the Insolvency Act for adjusting prior transactions (a) under ss 238–241 where the company enters administration or goes into liquidation and the transaction is at an undervalue or a preference, (b) under s 245 where the company enters administration or goes into liquidation and the company has created a floating charge on its undertaking or property, and (c) under s 423 where the transaction is a fraud on creditors. Remedies for transactions within ss 238–241 and 245 are directed towards achieving a *pari passu* distribution of the insolvent company's estate or furthering the purpose of administration.[378] None of the provisions in terms provides remedies for misconduct or breach of duties by directors, but they are relevant to the duties and liabilities of directors in four respects. First, the directors, or some of them, will have caused the company to enter into the impugned transaction and their conduct in doing so may expose them to personal liability to compensate the company for any loss which is not restored by an order made under these provisions of the Insolvency Act. Secondly, if the transaction is within these provisions, the director may not be protected from liability by having obtained the consent, approval, authorization, or ratification of the members. Thirdly, under ss 238–241 and 245 there are different rules for directors and other connected persons, which make transactions with them particularly vulnerable. Fourthly, transactions at undervalue and preferences within ss 238–240 are matters to be taken into account for the purposes of disqualification for unfitness under the CDDA.[379]

**29.219**

### (1) Transactions at undervalue

Section 238 of the Insolvency Act applies in the case of a company only where the company enters administration or goes into liquidation.[380] The administrator or liquidator may apply to the court for an order under s 238 'where the company has at a relevant time (defined in section 240) entered into a transaction with any

**29.220**

---

255; *First Independent Factors and Finance Ltd v Churchill* [2007] 1 BCLC 293, CA. *First Independent Factors Ltd v Mountford* [2008] 2 BCLC 297.

[377] *Archer Structures Ltd v Griffiths* [2004] 1 BCLC 201. If this decision is correct a person may face a larger liability under s 217 than if he had been a guarantor: Derham, *The Law of Set-Off* (3rd edn) at [18.30].

[378] Report of the Cork Committee at para 1209, discussing the earlier law.

[379] CDDA, s 9, Schedule 1, Part II, para 8.

[380] Insolvency Act, s 238(1). Section 339 is the equivalent provision for personal bankruptcy.

person at an undervalue'.[381] The reasoning that prevents a liquidator from assigning a wrongful trading claim or its fruits applies equally to a transaction at undervalue claim (paragraph 29.167 above).

29.221 Subsection 238(3) provides that, subject to the further provisions of s 238, 'the court shall, on such an application, make such order as it thinks fit for restoring the position to what it would have been if the company had not entered into that transaction'. There are therefore four matters to be considered: (a) whether the transaction took place at a relevant time, (b) whether the transaction was at an undervalue, (c) whether the court is prevented from making an order, because the transaction was entered into in good faith and for the purpose of carrying on the company's business and there were reasonable grounds for believing that the transaction would benefit the company, and (d) the relief, if any, to be granted.

*Relevant time*

29.222 Whether or not a transaction takes place at a 'relevant time' depends on two matters. The first is purely chronological. Section 240(1) provides that, subject to s 240(2), the time at which a company enters into a transaction at an undervalue is a relevant time if the transaction is entered into at a time (a) in the period of two years ending with the onset of insolvency, (b) between the making of an administration application in respect of the company and the making of an administration order on that application, or (c) between the filing with the court of a copy of notice of intention to appoint an administrator under paragraphs 14 or 22 of Schedule B1 and the making of an appointment under that paragraph.

29.223 Section 240(3) provides a definition of 'the onset of insolvency', for the purposes of calculating the two-year period in s 240(1) and also the periods for preference claims under s 239 which is, misleadingly, not defined by reference to when the company is first unable to pay its debts. The onset of insolvency is:

(a) in a case where section 238 or 239 applies by reason of an administrator of a company being appointed by administration order, the date on which the administration application is made,

(b) in a case where section 238 or 239 applies by reason of an administrator of a company being appointed under paragraph 14 or 22 of Schedule B1 following filing with the court of a copy of a notice of intention to appoint under that paragraph, the date on which the copy of the notice is filed,

(c) in a case where section 238 or 239 applies by reason of an administrator being appointed otherwise than as mentioned in paragraph (a) or (b), the date on which the appointment takes effect,

---

[381] Insolvency Act, s 238(2). A liquidator should obtain sanction in accordance with the Insolvency Act, ss 165 or 167, so that the costs are recoverable as an expense under Insolvency Rules, rule 4.218(1)(a)(i).

(d) in a case where section 238 or 239 applies by reason of a company going into liquidation either following conversion of administration into winding up by virtue of Article 37 of the EC Regulation or at the time when the appointment of an administrator ceases to have effect, the date on which the company entered administration (or, if relevant, the date on which the application for the administration order was made or a copy of the notice of intention to appoint was filed), and

(e) in a case where section 238 or 239 applies by reason of a company going into liquidation at any other time, the date of the commencement of the winding up.

A voluntary winding up is deemed to commence at the time of the passing of the resolution for voluntary winding up and that remains the time of commencement even if the voluntary winding up is superseded by a winding up by the court.[382] If the winding-up order is made under Schedule B1, paragraph 13(1)(e), the winding up commences on the making of the order and in any other case, it commences at the time of the presentation of the winding-up petition.[383]

**29.224**  The second matter which determines whether or not a transaction takes place at a 'relevant time' relates to the company's financial position. Section 240(2) provides that where a company enters into a transaction at an undervalue in the period of two years ending with the onset of insolvency, that time is not a relevant time for the purposes of s 238 unless the company—

(a) is at that time unable to pay its debts within the meaning of section 123 in Chapter VI of Part IV, or

(b) becomes unable to pay its debts within the meaning of that section in consequence of the transaction . . .;

but the requirements of this subsection are presumed to be satisfied, unless the contrary is shown, in relation to any transaction at an undervalue which is entered into by a company with a person who is connected with the company.

In deciding whether a company is unable to pay its debts, it is not correct to take into account any hope or expectation that the company will obtain assets in the future where there was no right to these assets.[384]

**29.225**  A person is connected with a company if he is a director or shadow director of the company or an associate of such a director or shadow director; or an associate of the company.[385] Whether or not a person is an associate of the company is determined in accordance with the provisions of Insolvency Act, s 435. It follows that, where a company enters into a transaction at an undervalue with a director, the burden of proving the company's inability to pay its debts shifts from the office-holder to the director. This is logical, because a director should at all times

---

[382] Insolvency Act, ss 86, 129(1).
[383] Insolvency Act, s 129(2) and (3).
[384] *Byblos Bank SAL v Al-Khudhairy* [1987] BCLC 232, 247, CA (a pre-Insolvency Act case); *Re Cheyne Finance plc* (No 2) 1 BCLC 741 [2008].
[385] Insolvency Act, s 249.

be aware of the company's financial position and therefore able to determine whether it can enter into the transaction without prejudicing the interests of creditors.[386]

*Transaction at undervalue*

**29.226**    Subsection 238(4) provides for the interpretation of 'transaction at undervalue':

> For the purposes of this section and section 241, a company enters into a transaction with a person at an undervalue if—
> (a)  the company makes a gift to that person or otherwise enters into a transaction with that person on terms that provide for the company to receive no consideration, or
> (b)  the company enters into a transaction with that person for a consideration the value of which, in money or money's worth, is significantly less than the value, in money or money's worth, of the consideration provided by the company.

Substantially the same language is used in s 423, concerning transactions defrauding creditors (paragraph 29.266 below).

**29.227**    There are therefore three elements, the first of which is that there must be a transaction entered into by the company. In all cases the first question is to identify the transaction which is under attack.[387] The word 'transaction' includes a gift, agreement, or arrangement, and references to entering into a transaction are to be construed accordingly.[388] Apart from a gift, s 238 envisages that a transaction is something which involves some element of dealing between the parties. This is implicit in the word 'transaction', and is reinforced by the references in s 238 to the 'entry into' the transaction, 'with a person', and 'on terms that provide'.[389] An arrangement is, on its natural meaning and in the context of the Insolvency Act, apt to include an agreement or understanding between parties, whether formal or informal, oral, or in writing.[390] Further, it must be the company itself that enters into the transaction. The requirements of the section are not satisfied if the mortgagee of company property enters into the transaction.[391] But the transaction for the purposes of the section may be a wider arrangement of which a sale of property by a mortgagee forms a vital part.[392]

---

[386]  *Re Ciro Citterio Menswear plc* [2002] 1 WLR 2217 at paras 42–47 is an example of a case where a person connected with the company discharged the burden of proving solvency.

[387]  *National Bank of Kuwait v Menzies* [1994] 2 BCLC 306, 313, CA (a s 423 case); *National Westminster Bank plc v Jones* [2002] 1 BCLC 55, CA at para 26.

[388]  Insolvency Act, s 436.

[389]  *Re Taylor Sinclair (Capital) Ltd* [2001] 2 BCLC 176 at paras 20, 21.

[390]  *Feakins v Department for Environment Food and Rural Affairs* [2007] BCC 54, CA at para 76, per Jonathan Parker LJ (a s 423 case).

[391]  *Re Brabon* [2001] 1 BCLC 11, 43 (a personal insolvency and s 423 case).

[392]  *Feakins v Department for Environment Food and Rural Affairs* [2007] BCC 54, CA at para 77.

The second element is that the transaction must be with a person, but that person **29.228** need not be the provider of all or any consideration to the company, since subs 234(4) does not stipulate by what person or persons the consideration is to be provided.[393]

The third element is undervalue. Section 238 is concerned with the depletion of **29.229** a company's assets by transactions at an undervalue. The purpose of the section is to restore to a company for the benefit of its creditors money or other assets which ought not to have left the company. Gifts and transactions for no consideration within subs 238(4)(a) do not call for further comment.[394] For the purposes of the comparison under subs 238(4)(b), it is necessary to compare the value obtained by the company for the transaction and the value of consideration provided by the company. Both values must be measurable in money or money's worth and both must be considered from the company's point of view.[395]

In *Phillips v Brewin Dolphin Bell Lawrie Ltd* Lord Scott said of subs 238(4): **29.230**

> It simply directs attention to the consideration for which the company has entered into the transaction. The identification of this 'consideration' is in my opinion, a question of fact. It may also involve an issue of law, for example, as to the construction of some document. But if a company agrees to sell an asset to A on terms that B agrees to enter into some collateral agreement with the company, the consideration for the asset will, in my opinion, be the combination of the consideration, if any, expressed in the agreement with A and the value of the agreement with B. In short, the issue in the present case the issue is not, in my opinion, to identify the section 238(4) 'transaction'; the issue is to identify the section 238(4) 'consideration'.[396]

In *Re M C Bacon Ltd* Millett J held that the granting of a debenture was not a **29.231** transaction at an undervalue; the mere creation of a security over a company's assets did not deplete them and did not come within s 238. By charging its assets the company appropriates them to meet the liabilities due to the secured creditor and adversely affects the rights of other creditors in the event of insolvency, but it does not deplete its assets or diminish their value. It retains the right to redeem and the right to sell or remortgage the charged assets. All it loses is the ability to apply the proceeds otherwise than in satisfaction of the secured debt. That is not something capable of valuation in monetary terms and it is not customarily

---

[393] *Phillips v Brewin Dolphin Bell Lawrie Ltd* [2001] 1 WLR 143, HL at para 20, per Lord Scott.

[394] In *Re Barton Manufacturing Co Ltd* [1999] 1 BCLC 740 a company transferred money to a director's wife, with no intention that she should repay it. She lent the money so received to the company's parent to reduce the companies' overdraft. It was held that the transactions between the company and the wife were gifts within subs 238(4)(a).

[395] *Re M C Bacon Ltd* [1990] BCLC 324, 340.

[396] [2001] 1 WLR 143, HL at para 20 .

disposed of for value.[397] Similarly a company does not enter into a transaction at an undervalue when it establishes a trust account to pay creditors.[398]

29.232　When the court is considering the value of the consideration passing between the company and the other party, the following principles may be derived from the speech of Lord Scott in *Phillips v Brewin Dolphin Bell Lawrie Ltd*:[399]

(1) The value of the consideration in money or money's worth is to be assessed at the date of the transaction.

(2) If at that date value is dependent on the occurrence or non-occurrence of some event and that event occurs before the assessment of value has been completed then the valuer may have regard to it. Lord Scott said that it was unsatisfactory and unnecessary for the court to pretend that it did not know what had happened.

(3) The valuer is entitled, indeed bound, to take account of all other matters relevant to the determination of value as at the date of the transaction.

(4) Where the value of the consideration provided to the company is speculative at the time of the transaction, it is for the party who relies on the consideration to establish its value. So, if part of the consideration is the taking of a sublease under which no payments are in fact made to the company, its value as consideration to the company is nil.

(5) The value of an asset that is being offered for sale is, prima facie, not less than the amount that a reasonably well-informed purchaser is prepared, in arm's length negotiations, to pay for it.

29.233　Whilst it is preferable for a court to arrive at a precise figure for the incoming and outgoing values where it is possible to do so, the court is not required to ascribe a precise figure; all that is required is that the court has to be satisfied that, whatever the precise values, the incoming value is significantly less than the outgoing value. If the court considers it appropriate to do so, it may address the issue of undervalue by taking from a range of possible values those which are most favourable to the party seeking to uphold the transaction.[400]

---

[397] *Re M C Bacon Ltd* [1990] BCLC 324, 340. In *Hill v Spread Trustee Co Ltd* [2007] 1 WLR 2404, CA at [93] the Court of Appeal cautioned that Millett J did not say that the grant of security could never amount to a transaction at undervalue, but did not comment on the difficulty of valuing the consideration passing between the parties. *Re MC Bacon Ltd* was followed in *Re Mistral Finance Ltd* [2001] BCC 27.

[398] *Re Lewis's of Leicester Ltd* [1995] 1 BCLC 428, 438, 439.

[399] *Phillips v Brewin Dolphin Bell Lawrie Ltd* [2001] 1 WLR 143, HL at paras 26, 27, and 30; *Re Thoars* [2003] 1 BCLC 499 at [17], per Sir Andrew Morritt V-C.

[400] *Re Thoars, Reid v Ramlort (No 2)* [2005] 1 BCLC 331, CA at paras 102–105, per Jonathan Parker LJ (a personal insolvency case), who referred to *National Westminster Bank plc v Jones* [2002] 1 BCLC 55, CA at paras 28, 29, per Mummery LJ (a s 423 case).

In all cases the court is concerned with the commercial reality of the consideration **29.234**
given and received; with the real economic benefits of the transaction and with
real value, not book value or mere 'hope' value.[401] The courts have found there to
have been a transaction at an undervalue:

(1) where a finance leasing company transferred its lease agreements, with the
    benefit of the income stream, in return for quarterly-in-arrears payments;[402]

(2) where property subject to mortgage, but with a substantial equity of redemp-
    tion, was transferred in consideration of the transferee merely undertaking to
    discharge the mortgage repayments;[403]

(3) where a mortgagor of agricultural property granted a tenancy at a proper
    market rent, because the tenant thereby acquired additional benefits of value
    (surrender value, which could be claimed as a ransom from the mortgagee)
    which corresponded to the diminution in the value of the mortgagor's
    property;[404]

(4) where the company agreed to pay interest retrospectively;[405]

(5) where a Cuban company sold its shares in an English company at par in ster-
    ling, but to be paid in Cuban pesos, the exchange calculated at the artificial
    official rate, when the commercial rate was much lower;[406]

(6) where the company received £1 million for a going concern business that was
    worth £2.41 million, even though the company could not afford to carry on
    trading and the transferee was the only potential purchaser.[407]

*Restriction on remedies*

By subs 238(5) the court may not make an order under s 238 if it is satisfied: **29.235**

(a) that the company which entered into the transaction did so in good faith and for
    the purpose of carrying on its business, and

---

[401] *Agricultural Mortgage Corporation v Woodward* [1995] 1 BCLC 1, 10–12, CA, per Slade LJ;
*Pinewood Joinery v Starelm Properties Ltd* [1994] 2 BCLC 412, 417 (a s 423 case); *Pena v Coyne
(No 1)* [2004] 2 BCLC 703 at para 114.
[402] *Arbuthnot Leasing International Ltd v Havelet Leasing Ltd (No 2)* [1990] BCC 636, 644
(a s 423 case).
[403] *Re Kumar* [1993] 1 WLR 224 (a personal insolvency case). *Chohan v Saggar* [1992] BCC
306, 321 is a similar case.
[404] *Agricultural Mortgage Corporation v Woodward* [1995] 1 BCLC 1, 10, 11, CA (followed in
*Barclays Bank plc v Eustice* [1995] 1 WLR 1238, 1244–6, CA.) This was a case under the Insolvency
Act, s 423, but the issue considered by the Court of Appeal was whether the transaction was at an
undervalue.
[405] *Re Shapland* [2000] BCC 106.
[406] *Banco Nacional de Cuba v Cosmos Trading Corp* [2001] 1 BCLC 813, 815, 819, CA.
[407] *Re MDA Investment Ltd* [2004] 1 BCLC 217 at paras 73, 114–123.

(b) that at the time it did so there were reasonable grounds for believing that the transaction would benefit the company.

**29.236**  The first of those requirements involves both subjective and objective elements. The second is entirely objective.[408] It follows that the directors may cause a company to enter into a transaction at an undervalue provided that to do so is consistent with both their fiduciary duties and their duty of care, skill, and diligence, except that any authorization or ratification by shareholders would be irrelevant to the issue under subs 238(5).[409] Thus, the subsection may protect a sale of an asset by a company in financial difficulties for a price which the directors consider to be an undervalue in order to raise cash to enable the company to carry on trading.

*Limitation*

**29.237**  Applications to set aside transactions under Insolvency Act, s 238 are generally actions on a specialty within the meaning of the Limitation Act 1980, s 8(1) and subject to a 12-year limitation period accordingly. However, where the substance of the claim is not to set aside a transaction but 'to recover a sum recoverable by virtue of' s 238, such applications will be governed by the Limitation Act 1980, s 9(1) and are subject to a six-year limitation period accordingly.[410]

*Remedies*

**29.238**  Section 238(3) provides that the court 'shall, on such an application [under s 238], make such order as it thinks fit for restoring the position to what it would have been if the company had not entered into' the transaction.

**29.239**  Despite the use of the verb 'shall', the phrase 'such order as it thinks fit' confers on the court a broad discretion as to whether it makes an order and its terms.[411] Section 241 provides a list of possible types of orders which indicate that the applicant is not entitled to any particular form of order as of right. The burden of showing that the court should not make an order under s 238 in respect of a transaction at an undervalue is on the respondent, not the office-holder.[412] The fact that a secured creditor may benefit from order is not a reason for not making it.[413]

---

[408] *Lord v Sinai Securities Ltd* [2005] 1 BCLC 295 at para 21.

[409] 2006 Act, ss 170–181.

[410] *Re Priory Garage (Walthamstow) Ltd* [2001] BPIR 144. See paragraph 29.271 below for the limitation rule in relation to s 423 claims.

[411] *Re Paramount Airways Ltd (No 2)* [1993] Ch 223, 239, CA; *Phillips v Brewin Dolphin Bell Lawrie Ltd* [2001] 1 WLR 143, HL at para 34. In *Re MDA Investment Management Ltd* [2004] 1 BCLC 217 at paras 122–124, the court refused to make an order restoring the position, because if the transaction had not occurred the company would have been in a worse position. In the bankruptcy case *Singla v Brown* [2008] 2 WLR 283 the court exercised its discretion to make no order.

[412] *Re Barton Manufacturing Ltd* [1999] 1 BCLC 740.

[413] *Re Shapland Inc* [2000] BCC 106 (but note that *Re Oasis Merchandising Services Ltd* [1998] Ch 170, CA, was not cited).

The order may be made against persons who were not party to the transaction  **29.240**
with the company, but s 241 contains provisions protecting persons who acquired
an interest in the relevant property in good faith and for value, but directors and
other persons connected with the company are presumed, unless the contrary is
shown, to have received the property otherwise than in good faith.[414] An order
may be made in relation to a transaction into which the company had no power
to enter.[415] A person against whom a claim is brought under s 238 is not under a
common liability with someone against whom a claim had not been made for the
purposes of the Civil Liability (Contribution) Act 1978.[416]

The court does not start, so far as remedy is concerned, with a presumption in  **29.241**
favour of monetary compensation as opposed to setting aside the transaction; the
court starts from no a priori position but fashions the most appropriate remedy
with a view to restoring so far as practicable and just to do so the position the parties would have been in if the company had not entered into the transaction. In
deciding how to exercise its discretion in respect of the most appropriate remedy,
the court must have regard to subsequent events.[417] The court's primary, and possibly only, concern under s 238(3) is the restoration of the company's position.
The position of a counter-party is a matter to be considered by the court as a general matter of discretion but the court is not obliged to ensure that such a person
is restored in every particular to the status quo before the transaction, since there
are many cases where that will be impossible.[418]

The scope of application of s 238 is not limited territorially. If a foreign element is  **29.242**
involved, the court has to be satisfied that, in respect of the relief sought against
the defendant, the defendant is sufficiently connected with England for it to be
just and proper to make the order. A person who wishes to serve proceedings
abroad has to obtain leave under the Insolvency Rules, rule 12.12.[419]

*Summary in relation to directors*

Where a company enters into a transaction with a director or person connected  **29.243**
with him in the two-year period, the question whether the transaction was at an
undervalue will be assessed on an objective basis, without regard to any weakness
in the company's bargaining position. The burden is on the director or connected
party to prove solvency and justify the transaction as being in the interests of
the company within subs 238(5). If a director uses an intermediary to acquire

---

[414] Insolvency Act, ss 241(2), (2A), 249.
[415] Insolvency Act, s 241(4).
[416] *Re International Championship Management Ltd* [2007] 2 BCLC 274.
[417] *Re Thoars, Reid v Ramlort Ltd (No 2)* [2005] 1 BCLC 331, CA (a personal insolvency case).
[418] *Lord v Sinai Securities Ltd* [2005] 1 BCLC 295.
[419] *Re Paramount Airways Ltd (No 2)* [1993] Ch 223, CA.

the property his title will be vulnerable, because it is assumed the director acted in bad faith.

### (2) Preferences

**29.244**  Section 239 of the Insolvency Act applies in the case of a company only where the company enters administration or goes into liquidation.[420] The administrator or liquidator may apply to the court for an order under s 239 'where the company has at the relevant time (defined in [section 240]) given a preference to any person'.[421] The reasoning that prevents a liquidator from assigning a wrongful trading claim or its fruits applies equally to a transaction at undervalue claim (paragraph 29.166 above).

**29.245**  Subsection 239(3) provides that subject to the further provisions of s 239 'the court shall, on such an application, make such order as it thinks fit for restoring the position to what it would have been if the company had not given the preference'. There are therefore four matters to be considered: (a) whether the preference was given at a relevant time, (b) whether a preference was given to a person, (c) whether the company which gave the preference was influenced in deciding to give it by a desire to prefer, and (d) the relief, if any, to be granted.

*Relevant time*

**29.246**  Relevant time is defined in substantially the same way for a preference within s 239 as it is for a transaction within s 238 (paragraphs 29.222–29.225 above). There are however the following differences:

(1)  The two-year period in subs 240(1)(a) only applies where the preference is given to a director, shadow director, or other person who is connected with the company.[422]

(2)  In any other case of preference the period is six months ending with the onset of insolvency.

**29.247**  Identifying the time at which a preference may be said to have been given can be difficult. Where the preference is the grant of security, the relevant date is when the decision to grant it was made, not the time when the debenture was created.[423] On the other hand, where the preference is repayment of a loan, the relevant date for the purposes of considering the debtor company's mental state is when

---

[420]  Insolvency Act, s 239(1). Section 340 is the comparable provision for personal bankruptcy.
[421]  Insolvency Act, s 239(2).
[422]  Insolvency Act, s 239 identifies other persons connected with a company.
[423]  *Re MC Bacon Ltd* [1990] BCLC 324, 336.

repayment was effected, not some earlier date, when the creditor had agreed with the company to defer calling in the loan for a fixed period.[424]

### Preference

Subsection 239(4) provides for the interpretation of 'gives a preference':   **29.248**

> For the purposes of this section and section 241, a company gives a preference to a person if—
> (a) that person is one of the company's creditors or a surety or guarantor for any of the company's debts or other liabilities, and
> (b) the company does anything or suffers anything to be done which (in either case) has the effect of putting that person into a position which, in the event of the company going into insolvent liquidation, will be better than the position he would have been in if that thing had not been done.

The first element of the definition is the identification of persons who may be   **29.249** preferred: a creditor, surety, or guarantor of any of the company's debts or liabilities.[425] The second element is that the company does something or suffers something to be done which produces the effect of a preference. The fact that something has been done in pursuance of the order of a court does not, without more, prevent the doing or suffering of that thing from constituting the giving of a preference.[426] The third element is the preference effect, which is improving the person's position in the event of the company going into insolvent liquidation. The question is whether the person's position will be better in the assumed liquidation, not that it may be better.[427]

### Desire to prefer

Issues invariably arise in respect of the restriction on the court's power to make an   **29.250** order under s 239, which is contained in subs 239(5):

> The court shall not make an order under this section in respect of a preference given to any person unless the company which gave the preference was influenced in deciding to give it by a desire to produce in relation to that person the effect mentioned in subsection (4)(b).

In *Re MC Bacon Ltd* Millett J provided an authoritative explanation of the new   **29.251** provision, which has been followed in subsequent cases:[428]

---

[424] *Wills v Corfe Joinery* [1998] 2 BCLC 75, 77, 78.
[425] In *Re Thirty-Eight Building Ltd* [1999] 1 BCLC 416, it was held that the reference is to creditor in the legal sense.
[426] Insolvency Act, s 239(7).
[427] *Re Ledingham-Smith* [1993] BCLC 635, 641 (a bankruptcy case). In *Re Hawkes Hill Publishing Co Ltd* [2007] BCC 937 there was no preference in fact.
[428] [1990] BCLC 324, 335, 336.

(1) As to the contrast between 'desire' under sub-s 239(5) and 'intention' which had been a feature of the previous preference provisions:

> Intention is objective, desire is subjective. A man can choose the lesser of two evils without desiring either of them. It is not however sufficient to establish a desire to make the payment or grant the security which it is sought to avoid. There must have been a desire to produce the effect mentioned in the subsection, that is to say, to improve the creditor's position in the event of an insolvent liquidation. A man is not to be taken as *desiring* all the necessary consequences of his actions.

(2) As to commercial transactions with a company in financial difficulties:

> It will still be possible to provide assistance to a company in financial difficulties provided that the company is actuated only by proper commercial considerations. Under the new regime a transaction will not be set aside as a voidable preference unless the company positively wished to improve the creditor's position in the event of its own insolvency.

(3) As to proving the presence of the desire:

> There is of course, no need for there to be direct evidence of the requisite desire. Its existence may be inferred from the circumstances of the case just as the dominant intention could be inferred under the old law.[429]

(4) As to the influence of the desire on the transaction: subs 239(5):

> requires only that the desire should have influenced the decision. That requirement is satisfied if it was one of the factors which operated on the minds of those who made the decision. It need not have been the only factor or even the decisive one. In my judgment, it is not necessary to prove that, if the requisite desire had not been present, the company would not have entered into the transaction. That would be too high a test.

29.252 It is not necessary to establish that the directors knew or believed that the company was insolvent at the relevant time.[430] A finding that a company desired to put a particular creditor in a position of advantage in the event of that company's liquidation is not a finding of moral turpitude on the part of the directors of either that company or the creditor company.[431]

29.253 There is a distinction between cases where the person preferred is a director, shadow director, or other person connected with the company and cases where the person preferred is not so connected.[432] In the former cases, subs 239(6) has

---

[429] In *Re Transworld Trading Ltd* [1999] BPIR 628, 634 it was said that events subsequent to the grant of a preference will sometimes throw light upon what was the desire of the company when it granted the preference, and upon whether that desire influenced the company in making the grant, but it is ordinarily the evidence of events leading up to the grant which is the most relevant.

[430] *Katz v McNally* [1999] BCC 291, 296, CA.

[431] *Re Transworld Trading* [1999] BPIR 628, 635.

[432] Insolvency Act, s 249, read with s 435, explains who are connected with a company. A repayment of a loan made by a directors' pension scheme was not a payment to a person connected with the company, because of the provisions of the exclusion of pension scheme trustees from being associates for the purposes of the Insolvency Act, ss 249 and 435, which is made by subs

the effect of reversing the burden of proving the influence of the requisite desire:

> A company which has given a preference to a person connected with the company (otherwise than by reason only of being its employee) at the time the preference was given is presumed, unless the contrary is shown, to have been influenced in deciding to give it by such a desire as is mentioned in subsection (5).

Where the preferred person is connected with the company it is in practice diffi-    **29.254**
cult for that person to show that the decision to repay or secure a debt owed to him was actuated only by commercial considerations and entirely uninfluenced by the requisite desire.[433] The burden of proof had been discharged where the company made an early rental payment to the landlord in respect of premises occupied by the company and let to its directors;[434] where the company created a floating charge to secure fresh advances from a director;[435] where the director received a redundancy payment in common with other employees.[436] But the fact that at the time of the giving of the alleged preference the directors were optimistic about the prospects for rescuing the company will not be sufficient to rebut the presumption of a preference.[437]

In contrast it is very unusual for an office-holder to bring a preference claim against    **29.255**
a person who is not connected with the company. In *Re MC Bacon Ltd* the liquidators claim to set aside as a preference a debenture given to the bank failed.[438] The company had no choice but to grant the security insisted on by the bank as a condition of the bank continuing to provide banking facilities so that the company could continue to trade. There was no desire to prefer and, in acceding to the bank's terms, the company was actuated only by commercial considerations.

---

435(5): *Re Thirty-Eight Building Ltd* [1999] 1 BCLC 416; *Re Thirty-Eight Building Ltd (No 2)* [2000] 1 BCLC 201.

[433] The office-holder's claim succeeded in recovering payments to directors as preferences in the following cases: *Re DKG Contractors Ltd* [1990] BCC 903; *Re Exchange Travel (Holdings) Ltd (No 3)* [1996] 2 BCLC 524, [1997] 2 BCLC 579, CA (payments to directors had been made by the finance director, who had no desire to prefer, but on the instructions of directors who did not discharge the burden of proving that they were not influenced by a desire to prefer); *Wills v Corfe Joinery Ltd* [1998] 2 BCLC 75; *Re Brian D Pierson Ltd* [2001] 1 BCLC 275 (but not in respect of redundancy payments); *Re MDA Investment Management Ltd* [2004] 1 BCLC 217 at paras 136–161; *Re Sonatacus Ltd* [2007] 2 BCLC 627, CA. In *Weisgard v Pilkington* [1995] BCC 108 leases granted to directors were set aside as a preference in reduction of debts owed to the directors. In *Re Shapland Inc* [2000] BCC 106 a charge granted to a director was set aside as a preference. In *Re Conegrade Ltd* [2003] BPIR 358 a transfer of property to a director was set aside as a preference since the sale price had been applied in reduction of the debt owed to the director.

[434] *Re Beacon Leisure Ltd* [1992] BCLC 565.

[435] *Re Fairway Magazines Ltd* [1993] BCLC 643.

[436] *Re Brian D Pierson Ltd* [2001] 1 BCLC 275, 298.

[437] *Re Conegrade Ltd* [2003] BPIR 358, 372–4.

[438] [1990] BCLC 324.

*Remedies*

**29.256** Section 239(3) provides that the court 'shall, on such an application [under s 239], make such order as it thinks fit for restoring the position to what it would have been if the company had not given the preference'. This provision corresponds to s 238(3) in the case of transactions at an undervalue, and the principles explained in paragraphs 29.239–29.242 above apply to preference claims.

*Summary in relation to directors*

**29.257** A director or shadow director is particularly exposed to a claim under s 239 in that claims can be made in respect of preferences given within two years of the onset of insolvency (not six months) and the burden is on him to prove that (a) the company was solvent for the purposes of s 240 at the time the preference was given, and (b) the preference was not at all influenced by a desire to prefer.

**29.258** If the court cannot make an effective order against someone other than the director restoring the position to what it would have been had the preference not occurred, the director may be liable to make good the loss on the ground that he was in breach of his general duties in causing or procuring the preference to be given.[439] In *Re Brian D Pierson Ltd* Hazel Williamson QC held that misfeasance or breach of duty must be positively proved and could not be established from the mere fact a preference claim had succeeded by virtue of the statutory presumption under subs 239(6).[440]

## (3) Avoidance of certain floating charges

**29.259** Even though a floating charge created by a company in favour of a director, shadow director, or other person connected with the company within two years of the onset of insolvency may not be set aside as a preference under s 239, it may be invalid under the Insolvency Act, s 245, which avoids certain floating charges created by a company that enters administration or goes into liquidation. [441]

**29.260** The condition for invalidity under s 245 is simply that the floating charge was created at a relevant time. In the case of a floating charge created in favour of a director, shadow director, or other person connected with the company, the time is a relevant time if the charge is created within two years of the onset of insolvency, whether or not the company was unable to pay its debts at the time the charge was created. In the case of a floating charge created in favour of any other person, the time is reduced to 12 months before the onset of insolvency, but the

---

[439] *Re Washington Diamond Mining Co* [1893] 3 Ch 95, 115, CA; *West Mercia Safetywear Ltd v Dodd* [1988] BCLC 250, 252, CA.

[440] [2001] 1 BCLC 275, 299.

[441] 'Floating charge' is defined by the Insolvency Act, s 251. For 'connected with the company', see s 249, read with s 435; *Re Kilnoore Ltd* [2006] Ch 489.

time is only a relevant time if the company is then unable to pay its debts within the meaning of the Insolvency Act, s 123 or becomes unable to pay its debts within that meaning in consequence of the transaction under which the charge is created.[442]

By subs 245(2) a floating charge created at a relevant time is invalid except to the extent of:　　　　**29.261**

(a) the value of so much of the consideration for the creation of the charge as consists of money paid, or goods or services supplied, to the company at the same time as, or after, the creation of the charge,

(b) the value of so much of that consideration as consists of the discharge or reduction, at the same time as, or after, the creation of the charge, of any debt of the company, and

(c) the amount of such interest (if any) as is payable on the amount falling within paragraph (a) or (b) in pursuance of any agreement under which the money was so paid, the goods or services were so supplied or the debt was so discharged or reduced.

The paragraphs of subs 245(2) have been drafted to ensure that a floating charge within the reach of the section is only valid to the extent of new consideration which is of real value to the company. To the extent that such a charge merely secures existing liabilities, it will be invalid.[443]

### (4) Transactions defrauding creditors

The Insolvency Act, s 423 replaced the Law of Property Act 1925, s 172 (which in　**29.262** turn replaced the Fraudulent Conveyances Act 1571), which avoided conveyances of property made with intent to defeat and delay creditors. Unlike the provisions of the Insolvency Act, ss 238–241, whose purpose is to assist the *pari passu* distribution of the company's property, the purpose of s 423, like its predecessors, is to protect creditors from fraud.[444] In fact, there is little evidence of the Law of Property Act, s 172 or its predecessors being used in the company context.[445] The new s 423 seems to have attracted rather more use in that context, although most of the reported cases concern individual debtors.

The court is given power to make an order under s 423 in relation to a company,　**29.263** if (a) the application is made by a person qualified to make it under s 424, (b) the

---

[442] Insolvency Act, s 245(3) and (4). The time is also relevant if it is in the periods specified in subs 245(3)(c) and (d), which are in the same terms as subs 240(1)(c) and (d) (paragraph 29.222 above). 'Onset of insolvency' is defined by subs 245(5) in substantially the same terms as subs 240(3) (paragraph 29.223 above).

[443] *Re Fairway Magazines Ltd* [1993] BCLC 643; *Re Shoe Lace Ltd, Power v Sharp Investments Ltd* [1994] 1 BCLC 111, CA.

[444] Report of the Cork Committee at para 1209.

[445] The only reported cases appear to be *Re Lloyd's Furniture Palace Ltd* [1925] Ch 853 and *Re Shilena Hosiery Ltd* [1980] Ch 219.

company has entered into a transaction at undervalue within subs 423(1), and (c) the conditions for making an order under subs 423(3) are satisfied.[446]

### The applicant

**29.264** Section 424(1) prevents an application for an order under s 423 from being made unless the applicant is qualified to make it. If the company is being wound up or is in administration, the application may be made by the liquidator or administrator or, with the leave of the court, by a victim of the transaction.[447] In a case where a victim is bound by a CVA the application may be made by the supervisor of the CVA or by any person who (whether or not so bound) is a victim of the transaction. In any other case concerning a company the application may be made by a victim of the transaction.

**29.265** For the purposes of ss 423–425, subs 423(5) provides that a victim of a transaction is a person who is, or is capable of being, prejudiced by it. The definition is not restricted to creditors with present or actual debts. The definition of 'victim' is employed in relation to the criteria for relief in s 423(2), but it is not used in s 423(3), which defines the necessary purpose. The person or persons who fulfil the conditions in s 423(3) may thus be a narrower class of persons than those who at the date of the transaction are victims for the purpose of s 423(5). For a person to be a 'victim' there is no need to show that the person who effected the transaction intended to put assets beyond his reach or prejudice his interests. Put another way, a person may be a victim, and thus a person whose interests the court thinks fit to protect by making an order under s 423, but he may not have been the person within the purpose of the person entering into the transaction. Prejudice or potential prejudice is a condition for obtaining relief, but that prejudice does not have to be achieved by the purpose with which the transaction was entered into, nor does the purpose have to be one which by itself is capable of achieving prejudice.[448]

### Transaction at undervalue

**29.266** In relation to a company subs 423(1) gives substantially the same meaning of 'transaction at undervalue' as is given by subs 238(4), which is discussed at

---

[446] In the case of a company, the court is the High Court or any other court having jurisdiction to wind it up: Insolvency Act, s 423(4).

[447] *Re Ayala Holdings Ltd* [1993] BCLC 256 (leave given to victim to apply where there was an arguable case and no application by liquidator) and on appeal as *National Bank of Kuwait v Menzies* [1994] 2 BCLC 306, CA. As to whether leave may be granted retrospectively, see the discussion in *Dora v Simper* [2000] 2 BCLC 561, 572.

[448] *Hill v Spread Trustee Co Ltd* [2007] 1 WLR 2404, CA at para 101, per Arden LJ.

paragraphs 29.226–29.234 above, to which further reference should be made. It provides, so far as relevant to a company:

> This section relates to transactions entered into at an undervalue; and a person enters into such a transaction with another person if—
> (a) he makes a gift to the other person or he otherwise enters into a transaction with the other on terms that provide for him to receive no consideration; . . . or
> (c) he enters into a transaction with the other for a consideration the value of which, in money or money's worth, is significantly less than the value, in money or money's worth, of the consideration provided by himself.

### Condition for making an order under s 423

**29.267** Whereas under s 238 the power of the court to make an order in respect of a transaction at undervalue is limited by the restriction that it must have been entered into at a relevant time, under s 423 there is no restriction in terms of time. Instead the restriction is that the court may only make an order if satisfied that the purpose for entering into the transaction is within subs 423(3), which provides:

> In the case of a person entering into such a transaction, an order shall only be made if the court is satisfied that it was entered into by him for the purpose—
> (a) of putting assets beyond the reach of a person who is making, or may at some time make, a claim against him, or
> (b) of otherwise prejudicing the interests of such a person in relation to the claim which he is making or may make.

**29.268** After some uncertainty, the question whether the purpose specified by subs 423(3) must be the dominant purpose or whether it is sufficient for it to be a substantial purpose has now been resolved by the Court of Appeal in *Inland Revenue Commissioners v Hashmi*.[449] It is now clear that putting assets beyond the reach of a potential claimant does not have to be the dominant purpose of a transaction. It is sufficient if the purpose specified in subs 423(3) is a real substantial purpose and not merely a consequence or by-product of the transaction under consideration. This may be done by showing that the company or other debtor was substantially motivated by one or other of the aims in subs 423(3).[450] There is however a distinction to be drawn between settled aims, which are required for the purposes of subs 423(3) and mere hopes.[451]

---

[449] [2002] 2 BCLC 489. The earlier cases are *Chohan v Saggar* [1992] BCC 306, 323; *Pinewood Joinery v Starelm Properties Ltd* [1994] 2 BCLC 412, 418; *Royscot Spa Leasing Ltd v Lovett* [1995] BCC 502, 507, CA; *Jyske Bank (Gibraltar) Ltd v Spjeldnaes* [1999] 2 BCLC 101, 120; *Law Society v Southall* [2001] BPIR 301; *Re Brabon* [2001] 1 BCLC 11, 44.

[450] *Inland Revenue Commissioners v Hashmi* [2002] 2 BCLC 489, CA at paras 21–25, per Arden LJ, paras 32, 33, per Laws LJ, para 39, per Simon Brown LJ. This case was followed in *Kubiangha v Ekpenyong* [2002] 2 BCLC 597 at para 12, *Beckenham MC Ltd v Centralex Ltd* [2004] 2 BCLC 764 at para 32, *Gil v Baygreen Properties Ltd* [2005] BPIR 95 at para 24; *Hill v Spread Trustee Ltd* [2007] 1 WLR 2404, CA at paras 131–133.

[451] *Hill v Spread Trustee Ltd* [2007] 1 WLR 2404, CA at para 132.

**29.269**  It follows that the purpose of the company or other debtor in effecting the transaction does not have to be dishonest. Nor is the presence of a purpose within subs 423(3) displaced by the fact that lawyers had advised that the transaction is proper and can be carried into effect.[452] Nevertheless in most cases a transaction within s 423 will be dishonest, because if a man 'disposes of an asset which would be available to his creditors with the intention of prejudicing them by putting it, or its worth, beyond their reach, he is in the ordinary case acting in a fashion not honest in the context of the relationship of debtor and creditor'.[453] If the circumstances in relation to setting up the transaction are shown to be sufficiently iniquitous the court may order that communications between the debtor and his legal advisers relating to the setting up of the transaction are not privileged and should be disclosed.[454]

**29.270**  The entry into the transaction must have the necessary purpose, but not necessarily the transaction itself. The reference in subs 423(3)(b) to 'interests' shows that the statutory purpose is concerned with the wider interests of the claimant or prospective claimant, not merely with his rights.[455] If the company or other debtor has the statutory purpose, the recipient's belief that he is receiving benefits of value is irrelevant.[456]

*Limitation*

**29.271**  Unlike the Insolvency Act s 238, ss 423–425 do not limit the time for applying for relief by identifying a relevant time when the impugned transaction must have been entered into. In *Hill v Spread Trustee Co Ltd* the Court of Appeal held that (a) a claim under s 423 was subject to a limitation period under the Limitation Act 1980, (b) if the claim is to set aside a transfer of property it is a claim on a specialty within s 8(1) of the Limitation Act 1980 to which a 12-year limitation period applies, (c) if the claim is to recover a sum the limitation period is six years under s 9(1), and (d) time starts to run against a trustee in bankruptcy from the date of the bankruptcy order.[457] It follows that time will start to run against a liquidator from the date when the company goes into liquidation and against an

---

[452] *Arbuthnot Leasing International Ltd v Havelet Leasing Ltd (No 2)* [1990] BCC 636, 644.

[453] *Lloyds Bank Ltd v Marcan* [1973] 1 WLR 1387, 1390, CA, per Russell LJ (a case on the Law of Property Act 1925, s 172).

[454] *Barclays Bank plc v Eustice* [1995] 1 WLR 1238, CA. In *Royscot Spa Leasing Ltd v Lovett* [1995] BCC 502, CA, a prima facie case of substantial purpose within subs 423(3) was not shown and the court refused an order for disclosure of privileged documents.

[455] *Hill v Spread Trustee Co Ltd* [2007] 1 WLR 2404, CA at paras 101, 102, per Arden LJ.

[456] *Moon v Franklin* [1996] BPIR 196.

[457] [2007] 1 WLR 2404 at paras 106–118, per Arden LJ, paras 140–151, per Sir Martin Nourse, and para 152, per Waller LJ. A claim remains a claim on a specialty even though the property whose transfer is challenged has been sold and the claim is converted into a money claim: *Giles v Rhind (No 3)* [2007] 2 BCLC 531 at para 33, affirmed [2008] 2 BCLC 1, CA.

administrator from the date when the company enters administration. Time starts to run against a victim from the time when he qualifies as a person capable of being prejudiced by the transaction.[458] The running of time for bringing a claim under s 423 may be postponed on the ground of concealment under the Limitation Act 1980, s 32.[459]

*Remedies*

Subsection 423(2) corresponds with subss 238(3) and 239(3), but any order made must also protect victims. It provides: **29.272**

> Where a person has entered into such a transaction, the court may, if satisfied under [subsection (5)], make such order as it thinks fit for—
> (a) restoring the position to what it would have been if the transaction had not been entered into, and
> (b) protecting the interests of persons who are victims of the transaction.

Although the power to grant relief is discretionary 'the courts must set their faces against transactions which are designed to prevent plaintiffs in proceedings, creditors with unimpeachable debts, from obtaining the remedies by way of execution that the law would normally allow them'.[460] Accordingly in a s 423 case it is much less likely that a court would exercise its discretion to make no order than might be the case with an application under s 238 or s 239. **29.273**

> The object of ss 423 and 425 being to remedy the avoidance of debts, the 'and' between paras (a) and (b) of s 423(2) must be read conjunctively and not disjunctively. Any order made under that subsection must seek, so far as practicable, both to restore the position to what it would have been if the transaction had not been entered into and to protect the interests of the victims of it. It is not a power to restore the position generally, but in such a way as to protect the victims' interests; in other words, by restoring assets to the debtor to make them available for execution by victims.[461]

The reference to execution in that passage may be extended to collective execution in a winding up and to alternative modes of distribution to creditors through a CVA or 2006 Act, Part 26 scheme.[462]

Without prejudice to the generality of this provision, s 425(1) provides examples of the sorts of orders which made by made. These are in substantially the same terms as s 241 (paragraphs 29.239–29.240 above), but taking into account the **29.274**

---

[458] *Giles v Rhind (No 3)* [2007] 2 BCLC 531 at paras 27–31, affirmed [2008] 2 BCLC 1, CA.
[459] Ibid, at para 41, affirmed [2008] 2 BCLC 1, CA.
[460] *Arbuthnot Leasing International Ltd v Havelet Leasing Ltd (No 2)* [1990] BCC 636, 645.
[461] *Chohan v Saggar* [1994] 1 BCLC 706, 714, CA, per Nourse LJ.
[462] For winding up as a mode of collective execution: *Wight v Eckhardt Marine GmbH* [2004] 1 AC 147, PC at [26], per Lord Hoffmann; *Buchler v Talbot* [2004] 2 AC 298, HL at [28], per Lord Hoffmann.

fact that s 423 may be applied outside insolvency proceedings and at a time when the claimant's debt is not established.[463]

**29.275** An order may affect the property of, or impose any obligation on, any person whether or not he is the person with whom the debtor entered into the transaction; but such an order (a) shall not prejudice any interest in property which was acquired from a person other than the debtor and was acquired in good faith, for value, and without notice of the relevant circumstances, or prejudice any interest deriving from such an interest, and (b) shall not require a person who received a benefit from the transaction in good faith, for value, and without notice of the relevant circumstances to pay any sum unless he was a party to the transaction. For these purposes the relevant circumstances in relation to a transaction are the circumstances by virtue of which an order under s 423 may be made in respect of the transaction.[464]

---

[463] In *Moon v Franklin* [1996] BPIR 196 a declaration was made under s 423 and a freezing order was made to preserve the property pending litigation on the claimant's claim.

[464] Insolvency Act, s 425(2)–(3). In *Arbuthnot Leasing International Ltd v Havelet Leasing Ltd (No 2)* [1990] BCC 636, 645 the court ordered that the transferee hold the relevant leasing contracts on trust for the transferor, without prejudice to the claims of the transferee's creditors who had become creditors since the date of the transfer. In *Chohan v Saggar* [1994] 1 BCLC 706, CA, the position of a secured creditor restricted the orders that might be made.

# 30

# CRIMINAL LIABILITY OF DIRECTORS

## A. Introduction

### (1) Scope of the chapter

Shortly put, the criminal liability of company directors is as wide as the criminal **30.01** law. Company directors appear before the criminal courts in connection with the conduct of their working lives on charges as varied as false accounting, harassment, corruption, and assault.

30.02 Rather than attempt an overview of the entire body of the criminal law, this chapter will focus on those offences for which directors are especially vulnerable to attract liability when carrying out their ordinary financial and fiduciary obligations.

30.03 It should be noted that cartel offences under the Enterprise Act 2002 and money laundering are specifically excluded from this work. In addition, this work will not consider the power of the courts to confiscate a convicted defendant's assets representing the value of his benefit from criminal conduct under the Proceeds of Crime Act 2002. As for the Corporate Manslaughter and Corporate Homicide Act 2007, other than a brief discussion of the new form of corporate liability contained in s 1 of that Act (as to which see paragraph 30.21 below), these new provisions will not be considered: in its final form, the Act did not create any new forms of criminal liability against individual company directors, either as primary or secondary parties.

### (2) Basic principles of criminal liability

30.04 Establishing whether an individual is exposed to the risk of criminal charge and conviction is not as simple as identifying the physical and mental elements of the offence in question and determining whether these elements may be proved against the individual concerned. Outside the terms of individual statutory offences, and beyond the definition of offences proscribed by the common law, there exists a collection of principles which enlarge the ambit of liability for all crime. Before an individual may be reassured that his proposed course of conduct does not disclose a crime or that, in respect of historical behaviour, he is not at risk of criminal conviction, the effect of these principles upon the reach of the relevant offence must be considered with care. A brief statement of these principles is set out below.

*Principals, secondary parties, and joint enterprise*

30.05 An individual becomes liable to criminal conviction if he acts as the principal party to an offence, a secondary party to an offence, or if he participates in a criminal 'joint enterprise'. A principal party is liable to conviction because he himself has carried out the act or acts constituting the physical elements of the offence with the relevant guilty state of mind. In other words, a principal is a party liable to conviction because each element of the offence can be proved against him personally.

30.06 A secondary party is a person who does not carry out the offence himself but is nevertheless liable to conviction on the basis that he 'aids, abets, counsels or procures'[1] or—broadly speaking—wilfully assists or encourages a principal party to

---

[1] Accessories and Abettors Act 1861, s 8.

commit a crime. The assistance or encouragement may be given during the commission of the offence or prior to it, for example where equipment or information is made available to another to enable him to commit a crime at a later date.[2] Under the law as it currently stands, unlike liability for an inchoate offence (as to which, see below) secondary liability of this sort depends upon proof that the principal offender in fact went on to carry out the physical elements of the offence charged.[3]

Lastly, a person is liable to criminal conviction if he participates in a joint enterprise in which a group of persons acting together commits an offence.[4] Even if, when viewed as individuals, each participant has not committed all or any of the physical acts necessary to constitute the offence, each is liable for the acts done in pursuance of the common design. Therefore, once the crime has been committed, each participant is liable for the full offence. **30.07**

Whether responsibility for a crime is established as a straightforward principal, as a secondary party, or as a participant in a joint enterprise, the individual concerned is liable to be prosecuted and convicted for the full offence in the ordinary way. The maximum sentence available on conviction of any secondary party is exactly the same as is available in respect of a principal offender. **30.08**

Secondary party liability and the doctrine of joint enterprise substantially increase the vulnerability of an individual to charge for criminal offences, particularly offences which are tightly drawn and difficult to prove. **30.09**

For example, an individual purchases a large number of shares in a company shortly before the board makes a positive announcement about recently secured, lucrative contracts. Insider dealing is suspected. In order to establish that the individual who purchased the shares was a principal offender, the prosecution would have to prove (among other things) that he possessed specific and precise inside information at the time he dealt.[5] This may be impossible to prove. However, if the prosecution can assert on the basis of circumstantial evidence that the dealer was acting in concert with a director of the company, knowing that he was in **30.10**

---

[2] *Blakely v DPP* [1991] RTR 405, DC.

[3] This, however, will change subsequent to the coming into force of Part 2 of the Serious Crime Act 2007 (to be appointed). Part 2 of the 2007 Act creates a new statutory offence of encouraging or assisting crime, which will substantially widen the law relating to accessories to crime generally. Note in particular that, in order to establish a charge of encouragement or assistance under the new provisions, it will not be necessary for the prosecution to prove that the primary offence in fact took place (see s 49(1)).

[4] This principle is so fundamental to the operation of the criminal law in practice that no authority needs to be cited in support of it. However, for a discussion of the ambit and application of the principle see eg: *R v Anderson and Morris* [1966] 1 QB 110, CA, *R v Powell, R v English* [1999] AC 1, HL, and *R v Gilmour* [2000] 2 Cr App R 407, CA NI.

[5] Criminal Justice Act 1993, ss 52, 57, 56(1).

possession of price-sensitive inside information, both the dealer and the director may be liable to conviction on the basis of joint enterprise: the director despite the fact he has not dealt in shares;[6] the dealer despite the fact he was not put in possession of the inside information itself. The prosecutor would be likely to assert that, because of their joint enterprise or common purpose, the director and the share dealer were liable for each other's conduct in relation to the offence.

*Directors' liability beyond joint enterprise*

30.11   In relation to certain statutory offences, individual directors may be criminally liable for the acts or omissions of other directors or officers outside the context of joint enterprise. For example, the Insolvency Act, s 432 provides:

   (1)  This section applies to offences under this Act other than those excepted by subsection (4).
   (2)  Where a body corporate is guilty of an offence to which this section applies and the offence is proved to have been committed with the consent or connivance of, or to be attributable to any neglect on the part of, any director, manager, secretary or other similar officer[7] of the body corporate, or a person who was purporting to act in any such capacity, he, as well as the body corporate, is guilty of the offence and liable to be proceeded against and punished accordingly.

30.12   A director who consents to or connives in the commission of an offence would be likely to be party to a joint enterprise to commit the offence in any event. But the words 'attributable to any neglect' in this section, and in others like it, expand the liability of an individual director beyond the scope of the doctrine of joint enterprise very considerably.

30.13   This does not represent a general principle of the criminal law and applies only where statute specifically provides it. Other examples of similar statutory provisions include the Companies Act 2006, ss 1121 and 1255, the Theft Act 1968, s 18, and the Fraud Act 2006, s 12 (although note in respect of the latter two that the words 'attributable to any neglect' do not appear). Note, in contrast, that the Corporate Manslaughter and Homicide Act 2007, s 18 specifically excludes the possibility of individual directors' liability as secondary parties to the new offence of statutory corporate manslaughter, which may only be committed by a company.

*Substantive and inchoate offences*

30.14   The doctrines of secondary and joint enterprise liability apply to substantive criminal offences only. Historically it has been (and until Part 2 of the Serious

---

   [6]  This would be the case, via the doctrine of joint enterprise, even if it were not for the operation of the Criminal Justice Act 1993, s 55(1)(b).
   [7]  See *R v Boal* [1992] QB 591, CA as to the necessary position which an officer of the corporation must have before fulfilling this description.

Crime Act 2007 is brought into force it remains[8]) necessary first to prove that the physical elements of the offence in question were carried through to completion before establishing guilt against a secondary party or against a participant in a joint enterprise. Liability for a separate group of offences exists in certain circumstances where an intention to bring about an offence is formed, but the physical elements of the offence are never carried out. Offences of the latter sort are inchoate.

Inchoate offences are committed where a person attempts to commit a crime,[9] incites another to commit a crime (even where that incitement has no effect),[10] or conspires with at least one other person to commit a crime.[11]     **30.15**

So far as the liability of directors is concerned, the most significant of the inchoate     **30.16** offences is conspiracy and in particular conspiracy to commit an offence contrary to the Fraud Act 2006 and the residual, common law offence of conspiracy to defraud. For reasons discussed in Section C of this chapter, any agreement between two directors to carry out conduct which might be said to prejudice or risk prejudice to the interests of the company, which is formed in circumstances of secrecy and therefore could be described as dishonest, might expose those directors to criminal liability for conspiracy to defraud. As with all criminal conspiracies, liability for conspiracy to defraud arises immediately upon entering into the agreement: it does not depend upon any subsequent act done in furtherance of the conspirators' plans.

*Corporate criminal liability for the acts of directors: the doctrine of identification*

Although vicarious liability may exist in relation to some summary offences of a     **30.17** regulatory or quasi-regulatory nature, there is no general doctrine of vicarious liability in the criminal law.[12] However, the acts or omissions of a director may expose the company which he represents to criminal liability by reason of the doctrine of identification.

The doctrine of identification operates to recognize the embodiment of the com-     **30.18** pany in those individuals who represent the company's directing will and mind. Whether a particular individual will be identified as the company in any given situation will be a matter of fact and degree, depending on the nature of the offence charged (in particular, within which area of the company's business the conduct said to amount to an offence falls), the relative seniority and ambit of

---

[8] See n 3 above.

[9] Criminal Attempts Act 1981, s 1.

[10] *DPP v Armstrong* [2000] Crim LR 379, DC. Note however that the common law offence of incitement will be repealed when Part 2 of the Serious Crime Act 2007 comes into force (to be appointed): see s 59.

[11] Criminal Law Act 1977, s 1 and preservation of certain common law conspiracies in s 5.

[12] See eg *Tesco Supermarkets Ltd v Natrass* [1972] AC 153, 179F, HL, per Lord Reid.

responsibility of the officer or employee concerned, and all the other circumstances of the case.[13] (An example of a circumstance which might be argued to be relevant to the issue of identification is the state of mind of the individual concerned vis-à-vis the company itself: was the individual acting in the interests of the company; was he acting honestly towards the company?) Normally—although not always—the directing will and mind of a company will be identified as the board of directors, the managing director, and perhaps other superior officers of a company who carry out the function of management.[14]

**30.19** In practical terms, the doctrine of identification differs from the vicarious liability of the civil law by requiring guilty participation in the criminal activity by a much more senior officer or employee within the defendant company.

**30.20** Generally speaking, the doctrine of identification operates to create corporate criminal liability only when at least one individual representing the directing will and mind of the company is demonstrably guilty of the offence himself. Individual directors of the company may of course be guilty when their conduct is viewed together on a joint enterprise basis; in these circumstances, the company itself is at risk of conviction. That aside, under the common law there is no generally applicable[15] means of aggregating the acts or omissions of different individuals, none of whom are individually guilty of an offence, in order to produce corporate liability for an offence.[16]

**30.21** There is now, however, an important statutory exception to the common law position of 'no aggregation' of the faults of individual directors when determining corporate criminal liability. It is provided by the Corporate Manslaughter and Corporate Homicide Act 2007. Section 1 of the Act[17] creates a new offence in circumstances where the way in which the company's activities are 'managed or organised by its senior management' forms a 'substantial element' in a 'gross breach of a relevant duty of care' which is itself a cause of a person's death. This statutory means of fixing the company with criminal responsibility for death produces a much broader form of liability than the common law process of proving that any one individual director is guilty of manslaughter, and then attributing this guilt to the body corporate via the doctrine of identification.

---

[13] *R v ICR Haulage Co Ltd* [1944] KB 551, 559 per Stable J.

[14] *Tesco Supermarkets Ltd v Natrass* [1972] AC 153, 171, HL, per Lord Reid.

[15] In relation to certain offences, it is sometimes possible to combine the *actus reus* carried out by an ordinary employee with the *mens rea* of recklessness on the part of the directing will and mind of the company in order to produce corporate liability for an offence: *Information Commissioner v Islington LBC* [2003] LGR 38, DC.

[16] The Corporate Manslaughter and Corporate Homicide Act 2007 alters this position in respect of homicide offences only.

[17] Which came into force 6 April 2008 (except in relation to anything done or omitted before that date): see s 27(3) and SI 2008/401, art 2(1).

## B. Production of Information for Criminal Investigations

There are two principal methods via which a criminal investigator may compel   **30.22**
the production of information from a company.

### (1) PACE search warrants

The first is where police execute a warrant to enter premises in order to search for   **30.23**
and seize material. The powers are governed primarily—although not exclusively—by PACE, s 8. Under this section, a justice of the peace is empowered to issue
a search warrant to a police constable where there are reasonable grounds to suspect (inter alia) that: (i) an indictable offence has been committed;[18] and (ii) there
is material on the specified premises which is likely to constitute relevant evidence
of substantial value to the investigation of the offence.[19]

Section 8 warrants are issued and executed without notice. Therefore, in order to   **30.24**
obtain such a warrant, the police must demonstrate that it would either be impractical or pointless to gain entry to the premises with the cooperation of the occu-
piers of the premises.[20] This will occur, for example, where the person or persons
suspected of involvement in the offence have access to the premises and might
interfere with or destroy evidence if granted notice of the police's intention to
conduct a search.

Once issued, a section 8 PACE warrant empowers the police to force entry to the   **30.25**
premises in question, to search for and to seize material of the type described in
the warrant. Material subject to legal professional privilege, 'excluded material',[21]
and 'special procedure material'[22] is always outside the remit of a section 8
warrant.[23]

---

[18] s 8(1)(a).
[19] s 8(1)(b) and (c).
[20] s 8(1)(e) and (3).
[21] Excluded material is confidential medical or quasi-medical documents, human tissue taken
for diagnosis or treatment purposes, and journalistic material. See further PACE, s 11.
[22] Special procedure material is defined by PACE, s 14 as material (other than legally privileged
or excluded material) which is in the possession of a person who acquired or created the material in
the course of his/her occupation and who holds the material subject either to an express or implied
undertaking to hold it in confidence, or to an obligation of secrecy/restriction on disclosure imposed
by any enactment. This material enjoys an enhanced degree of protection under PACE. In particular, no search warrant may be granted in relation to it. Instead, a constable must make an on-notice
application for a production order. If the order is made, the subject of the order will be given at least
seven days in which to comply with it.
[23] s 8(1)(d).

## (2) Compelled information

**30.26** The second method is where a criminal investigator is empowered to compel an individual either to attend for interview at a specified time and place in order to answer questions, or to produce certain documentation.

**30.27** Many investigative agencies,[24] as well as some individuals (including an office-holder in corporate insolvency,[25] a trustee in bankruptcy,[26] or an investigator appointed by the Secretary of State under the Companies Act 2006, s 457(1)[27]) possess compulsory powers of this kind.[28] However, in the context of criminal investigations and for the purposes of illustration it is sufficient to consider: (i) the CJA 1987, s 2, under which the Director of the SFO may require attendance at a compulsory interview or compel the production of documents, and (ii) the FSMA, Part XI, under which an investigator appointed by the FSA may likewise compel attendance at an interview or the production of information including documents.

**30.28** The compulsory powers of both the SFO and the FSA may be exercised against the person under investigation (the suspect) and/or against any other person for the purpose of the investigation (ie potential witnesses).

**30.29** An important difference between these compulsory powers and PACE powers of search and seizure is that, prima facie, both the CJA 1987, s 2 powers and FSMA, Part XI powers are exercised on notice in writing. There is no element of surprise to their execution. However, in a situation where it would be either impractical to serve notice in writing, or where it would frustrate the purpose of the investigation to give notice of a production requirement (or where a production requirement has already been issued but has not been complied with), both the SFO[29] and the FSA[30] are entitled to seek a search warrant from a justice of the peace. Such a warrant must be executed by a police constable.

---

[24] Other examples include financial investigators under the Proceeds of Crime Act 2002, the Serious and Organised Crime Agency, and certain environmental agencies.

[25] Insolvency Act, s 235.

[26] Insolvency Act, s 333.

[27] In relation to the authorized investigators' powers to require explanations, note the wide remit of this power as previously interpreted under the Companies Act 1985, s 447 (which remains in force); *Attorney-General's Reference (No 2 of 1998)* [2000] QB 412, CA.

[28] See also Fraud Act 2006, s 13(1) which removes the privilege against self-incrimination in all civil proceedings relating to property. This has the effect of extending the entirely compulsory nature of, for example, search orders in civil proceedings from limited types of actions—such as intellectual property cases—to all actions concerning property of any kind. It will therefore no longer be possible for litigants in civil fraud cases to avoid answering questions or complying with court orders on the basis of self-incrimination.

[29] CJA 1987, s 2(4).

[30] FSMA, s 176.

*Legal professional privilege*

In relation to the production of documents, as with the execution of section 8 **30.30**
PACE warrants, neither the SFO nor the FSA may require the production of
material which is subject to legal professional privilege.[31] Where the privilege is
that of the company, an individual director will not be able to resist production if
the organ of the company (for example a new board or a liquidator) does not resist.
A director will however be protected in respect of legal advice given to him.[32]

*Failure to comply*

Failure to comply with the SFO's or FSA's exercise of compulsory powers without **30.31**
reasonable excuse is punishable by imprisonment.[33] In respect of the FSA's powers,
a company director may be punished for the non-compliance of the company.[34]

In addition, there are specific offences of intentionally or recklessly providing false **30.32**
or misleading information in response to a compulsory information requirement,
the maximum penalty for which (on conviction on indictment) is two years.[35]

Further, any person who knows or suspects that an investigation is being con- **30.33**
ducted or is likely to be conducted by the SFO (or by the FSA under FSMA, Part
XI) and who falsifies, conceals, or destroys a document which he know or suspects
to be relevant to the investigation (or who causes or permits another to do the
same) is guilty of an offence unless he proves (on a balance of probabilities) that
he had no intention of concealing the facts disclosed by the documents from persons carrying out such an investigation.[36] In respect of an FSA investigation, such
an offence (on conviction on indictment), carries a maximum of two years' imprisonment.[37] In respect of an SFO investigation, the offence carries a maximum of a
massive seven years.[38]

Finally, any act intended to destroy or alter evidence of a crime is likely to give rise **30.34**
to liability for a charge of perverting the course of justice, an offence against the
common law for which there is no maximum penalty.[39]

---

[31] CJA 1987, s 2(9); FSMA, s 413.
[32] *Re Ouveroff* [1997] BPIR 712; *R (Morgan Grenfell) v Special Commissioners* [2003] 1 AC
563, HL.
[33] In relation to the SFO, a specific, summary only offence is created by CJA 1987, s 2(13) the
maximum penalty for which is a level 5 fine or six months' imprisonment. In relation to the FSA,
failure to comply may be treated as a contempt of court, punishable by way of fine or imprisonment
of up to two years. (See further FSMA, s 177.)
[34] FSMA, s 177(2).
[35] CJA 1987, s 2(14); FSMA, s 177(4) and (5).
[36] CJA 1987, s 2(16); FSMA, s 177(3).
[37] FSMA, s 177(5).
[38] CJA 1987, s 2(17).
[39] *R v Vreones* [1891] 1 QB 360; *R v Andrews* [1973] QB 422.

*Privilege against self-incrimination*

**30.35**   It is the essence of the compulsory powers granted to investigators such as the SFO and the FSA that a person subject to their exercise must produce the information or document required, or must answer questions put to him in interview, even if in so doing he will or may incriminate himself. Without more, a desire not to incriminate oneself does not amount to a reasonable excuse for failing to produce information or to answer a question.[40]

**30.36**   In respect of evidential, pre-existing documents produced in response to an information or production requirement (such as company accounting documents or email correspondence) there is no restriction on the use to which that evidence may be put: it may subsequently be used against the producer in criminal proceedings. However, a restriction on evidential use is imposed upon statements actually made by a person while under compulsion. (This applies to statements made—orally or via a prepared written statement—in interview under compulsion with investigators.)

**30.37**   A person who is subject to compulsory interview by the SFO or FSA, for example, enjoys statutory protection from the prospect of his answers being used against him by the prosecution in a criminal trial for any offence other than an offence directly connected with the making of the statement itself (such as making a misleading statement under compulsion, contrary to the CJA 1987, s 2(14)).

**30.38**   For example, under the CJA 1987, s 2:[41]

   (8)   A statement by a person in response to a requirement imposed by virtue of this section may only be used in evidence against him—
      (a)   on a prosecution for an offence under subsection (14)[42] below; or
      (b)   on a prosecution for some other offence where in giving evidence he makes a statement inconsistent with it.
   (8AA)   However, the statement may not be used against that person by virtue of paragraph (b) of subsection (8) unless evidence relating to it is adduced, or a question relating to it is asked, by or on behalf of that person in the proceedings arising out of the prosecution.

**30.39**   Similar provisions restrict the use in evidence of compulsory statements made under the Insolvency Act, s 433 and the 2006 Act, s 459(6)).[43] Even where no such protection exists in statutory form, it is almost inevitable that the prosecution will be prevented from using a statement made under compulsion in evidence

---

[40]   *R v Hertfordshire County Council, ex parte Green Environment Industries Ltd* [2000] 2 AC 412, HL; *Saunders v United Kingdom* (1997) 23 EHRR 313; *IJL and others v UK*, (2000) 33 EHHR 11.
[41]   In respect of an FSA investigation, see FSMA, s 174(2).
[42]   ie making a false or misleading statement in purported compliance with a requirement under the section.
[43]   See also Fraud Act 2006, s 13(2). For the effect of s 13(1), see n 28 above.

against the maker of the statement (otherwise than on a charge under the CJA 1987, s 2(14) or equivalent) by an exercise of the judicial discretion to exclude evidence under PACE, s 78.

### European Court of Human Rights

Domestic jurisprudence in respect of compulsory powers to require answers in interview has always been that no violation of a suspect's fundamental rights could occur unless and until any statement made by him under compulsion is used against him in criminal proceedings.[44] According to this reasoning, a defendant's privilege against self-incrimination is adequately protected by statutory (or even judicial[45]) restriction on the subsequent use of statements made under compulsion. **30.40**

Recent authority from the European Court of Human Rights has (again) cast doubt upon this position. In *Shannon v UK*,[46] the Court held that a suspect's Article 6 rights (specifically, his right not to incriminate himself) may be violated by a compulsory requirement that he answer questions itself, regardless of whether his answers are subsequently used against him or not. *Shannon* concerned a piece of legislation in which the protection against subsequent use by the prosecution was not as comprehensive as is the case under both the CJA 1987, s 2 and FSMA, Part XI. (The relevant piece of legislation allowed the prosecution to use the statement made under compulsion as evidence of a previous inconsistent statement in a subsequent trial.) In addition, in *Shannon* the suspect had already been charged with a criminal offence when the exercise of compulsory powers occurred. However, the decision of the court was not necessarily dependent on either of these facts. In particular, the court stressed that information provided by a suspect may assist investigators even if it is not admitted into evidence against him.[47] If this is right (and it is submitted that it is right), then it may well be a basis for alleging a violation of Article 6 even where compulsory powers are exercised before charge and even where the prohibition on subsequent use in proceedings is absolute.[48] **30.41**

---

[44] *Ex parte Green Environment Industries Ltd,* n 40 above.

[45] *Ibid*; also, *IJL and others v UK* (2000) 33 EHHR 11.

[46] (6563/03) (2006) 42 EHRR 265.

[47] It is not difficult to imagine how: the statement may lead to other lines of fruitful enquiry, disclose the suspect's case at an early stage, or reveal that he has no answer to the potential charge, thereby encouraging the investigators to proceed against him.

[48] The prohibition is never absolute. For example, nothing in FSMA prevents the use of statements made under compulsion against the maker of the statement at the behest of a co-defendant. It is far from fanciful to imagine a situation in which an investigator, in possession of a significant confession obtained under compulsion, would have a real forensic advantage in contemplating the use of that confession against the maker at the behest of a co-defendant in a cut-throat situation.

**30.42**  Frequently, compulsory powers of interview are exercised against individuals whom the investigator currently views as a potential witness. In such a situation, *Shannon* will not provide a basis to argue that the privilege against self-incrimination is or should be a reasonable excuse for failure to comply. Likewise, where an investigator genuinely has an open mind—is the individual a suspect or a witness?—it might be difficult to object to the use of compulsion. However, the FSA in particular reserves the right to exercise compulsory powers against people who are definitely under investigation as suspects for criminal offences.[49] In practice, the FSA has sought to exercise this power in circumstances where the suspect has previously undergone a PACE interview and has exercised his right to silence.[50] To date, the lawfulness of this approach has not been litigated. However, if the policy is maintained, it is inevitable that at some point, in light of *Shannon*, it will be subject to challenge by way of judicial review.

# C. Fraud

## 1. Introduction

*Width and evolution of criminal fraud law*

**30.43**  The long-standing common law offence of conspiracy to defraud criminalizes the act of agreeing to carry out conduct which would not in itself, if pursued by an individual protagonist, amount to a criminal offence (at least, not if committed prior to the coming into force of the Fraud Act 2006 on 15 January 2007). Successive reports of the Law Commission have criticized the offence as too wide;[51] successive governments have remained committed to the preservation of the offence.[52]

**30.44**  The offence of conspiracy to defraud is dependent, inter alia, upon proof of prejudice to the rights of another and dishonesty. Over the centuries, the standards of honesty in business have changed, as has the scope of recognized rights which may be affected by fraud. As these standards evolve, so too does the common law offence.

*New substantive offences*

**30.45**  Criminal fraud law is additionally subject to evolution thanks to the recent creation of new substantive offences of fraud.

---

[49]  See para 4.23 of the FSA's *Enforcement Guide*.

[50]  In almost all circumstances, the impression created is that the investigator is motivated by a specific intention to circumvent a suspect's PACE and Article 6 ECHR rights.

[51]  Law Com 276, July 2002.

[52]  Fraud Act 2006, which—contrary to the recommendation of the Law Commission—does not repeal the common law offence of conspiracy to defraud.

The Fraud Act 2006, which came into force (in so far as it had not already done **30.46** so) on 15 January 2007,[53] for the first time creates substantive offences of fraud which are not dependent on proof of an agreement by two or more people to carry out the conduct concerned. This enlarges the reach of the criminal liability in respect of fraud by criminalizing dishonest conduct pursued by one person acting alone, which previously was only subject to criminal sanction when pursed by more than one person, following the formation of a conspiracy.

However, the Fraud Act does not abolish the common law offence of conspiracy **30.47** to defraud. Therefore, there will be a residual area of conduct which falls outside the statutory definition of substantive fraud, but which will nevertheless be criminal if it is pursued by more than one person acting in agreement. In short, the Fraud Act expands the reach of the substantive criminal law and the liability of individuals acting alone, but it does not restrict the scope of the corresponding inchoate offence of conspiracy or the liability of groups acting in concert.[54]

The Fraud Act will be considered in detail under Section (3) of this part of this **30.48** chapter and under Section D, which relates to theft and deception: the Fraud Act repeals the old deception offences under the Theft Acts.

## (2) Common law conspiracy to defraud

It is no easy thing to give a definition of the common law offence of conspiracy to **30.49** defraud. Historically, different formulations have been used in different authorities[55] and there has been a tendency among practitioners to blend different aspects of the various definitions, without sufficient reference to the facts underlying the decided cases. However, it is submitted that 'to defraud' is best defined as dishonestly to prejudice or take the risk of prejudicing another's rights or interests, having no right to do so.[56] Conspiracy to defraud is agreeing with another or others to act in a way which may be described in these terms.

---

[53] Fraud Act 2006 (Commencement) Order 2006 (SI 2006/3200).

[54] This observation is subject to one caveat. Now that the Fraud Act is in force, two or more people conspire to commit a statutory offence of fraud, then prosecutors might be called upon to justify a charge of common law fraud rather than the alternative statutory conspiracy or a substantive statutory offence as provided by Parliament. (See *R v Rimmington* [2006] 1 AC 459, HL, and *Deutsche Morgan Grenfell Group plc v IRC* [2007] 1 AC 558, HL.)

[55] *Welham v DPP* [1961] AC 103, HL; *Scott v Metropolitan Police Commissioner* [1975] AC 819, HL; *Wai Yu Tsang v R* [1992] 1 AC 269, PC.

[56] Note that the offence is sometimes defined more widely, in particular by omitting the 'having no right to do so' element. It is submitted that such omission is unjustified and would, if it truly represented the law, produce absurd results, criminalizing many instances of conduct which are plainly not unlawful. Further, it is submitted that there is no decided case in which criminal liability for fraud has been found in a situation in which the defendant had a right to act as he did.

**30.50** The elements of the common law offence of conspiracy to defraud may therefore be isolated as: the act of entering an agreement; the terms of the agreement involving the prejudice or risk of prejudice to another's rights/interests; circumstances in which the parties to the agreement have no right to cause such prejudice/take such risk; the state of mind of dishonesty.

*The agreement*

**30.51** The essence of any criminal conspiracy is the act of agreement itself. The offence is complete once the agreement is formed: even if no act is done in pursuance of it; even if one or all of the parties to the agreement experience a change of heart and communicate their withdrawal from the scheme. The principle was made plain by Brett JA in *R v Aspinall*:[57]

> Now, first, the crime of conspiracy is completely committed, if it is committed at all, the moment two or more have agreed that they will do, at once or at some future time, certain things. It is not necessary in order to complete the offence that any one thing should be done beyond the agreement. The conspirators may repent and stop, or may have no opportunity, or may be prevented, or may fail. Nevertheless the crime is complete; it was completed when they agreed.

**30.52** Beyond this, the term 'agreement' itself should be given its ordinary and natural meaning. Proof of an agreement does not depend upon establishing elements of offer and acceptance, consideration, or any other feature of contractual liability as recognized by the civil law.[58]

**30.53** The existence of the conspiracy will continue for as long as it remains unfulfilled, and there are at least two people party to it. Therefore, a person may join the conspiracy, and become criminally liable for it, at a time after the conspiracy was formed by others.

**30.54** It is relatively rare for a prosecutor to have access to direct evidence of the formation of the criminal agreement.[59] More usually, the prosecution must invite the tribunal of fact to infer the existence of the agreement from evidence of the subsequent conduct of the participants, apparently working pursuant to a common design. Therefore, although in law a criminal conspiracy to defraud is complete once the agreement is entered into, in practice, a successful prosecution for the offence will often depend upon evidence of the fulfilment, or the partial or attempted fulfilment, of the agreement in question.

---

[57] (1876) 2 QBD 48, 58, CA.

[58] *R v Anderson* [1986] AC 27, HL.

[59] Such evidence does sometimes exist, for example where one conspirator gives evidence for the prosecution against his co-conspirators, where the conversations and/or correspondence in which the agreement was formed have been intercepted by the authorities, or where the terms of the agreement have been reduced into writing by the participants. The later scenario is extremely rare but not unprecedented.

*Risk of prejudice to another's rights or interests*

In order to amount to the common law offence of conspiracy to defraud, the **30.55** agreement in question—if it were to be fulfilled—must involve the prejudice, or risk of prejudice, to the rights or interests of another person or body.

Although there is some controversy on this point within the decided cases, it is **30.56** generally considered that the range of rights and interests protected by the law against conspiracies to defraud are not limited to economic rights or interests; proof of conspiracy to defraud is not dependent on proof of actual or threatened economic loss.[60]

The best means of illustrating the breadth of the range of rights and interests rec- **30.57** ognized by the criminal law for these purposes is by way of example. Conspiracy to defraud may be alleged in law in circumstances where the terms of an agreement involve injury, or the risk of injury, to:

(1) The right of the state, or the person or body performing a duty on behalf of the state, to have public duties properly fulfilled.

To induce dishonestly any such person or body to act in a way which would be contrary to his/its duty were he/it in possession of the true facts is to act fraudulently.[61] In practice, therefore, any dishonest agreement to conceal certain behaviour from the public authority charged with the duty of supervizing such conduct, in order to prevent the authority from fulfilling its public duty to investigate or scrutinize the conduct, will amount to a fraud on that authority. For example, an agreement to conceal dishonestly the identity of a director trading in company shares in order to prevent the FSA from investigating the possibility of insider dealing or market abuse, may amount to a conspiracy to defraud the Authority, quite apart from any proof that insider dealing has in fact occurred.

(2) The right of a principal to disclosure of the profits obtained by an agent in connection with the performance of his fiduciary duty.[62]

(3) Any right or interest vested in a principal which is capable of being protected by an action for breach of trust if compromised by one fiduciary acting alone. Such an interest will inevitably enjoy the protection of the criminal law in circumstances where the fiduciary agrees with another person dishonestly to carry out the breach of trust concerned, even if no economic loss is involved.

---

[60] *Welham v DPP* [1961] AC 103, HL; *Wai Yu Tsang v R* [1992] 1 AC 269, PC. Cf the opinion of Lord Diplock in *Scott v Metropolitan Police Commissioner* [1975] AC 819, 840, 841, HL.
[61] *Welham v DPP* [1961] AC 103, HL.
[62] *Adams v R* [1995] 1 WLR 63, PC.

For example, a principal's right to disclosure of a conflict of interests is a right prejudice to which may found an allegation of conspiracy to defraud.[63]

**30.58** These examples have obvious implications for the criminal liability of company directors. Whenever a director agrees with another to take any action which will injure or risk injury to the interests of the company, in circumstances which might be described as dishonest, the director is at risk of attracting criminal liability. In addition, whenever a director agrees with another dishonestly to conceal a significant situation or fact from a body such as Companies House, Her Majesty's Customs and Excise, the FSA, the Health and Safety Executive, or an officer appointed by the court in connection with the company's affairs, it is highly likely that the director will be at risk of criminal charge.

### Dishonesty

**30.59** Dishonesty is an essential element of the offence of conspiracy to defraud. There is leading authority on the offence of conspiracy to defraud which fails to mention the issue of dishonesty.[64] However, it is beyond argument that dishonesty must be proved to the satisfaction of the jury in order to support a conviction[65] and all criminal trials proceed on this basis.

**30.60** For the purposes of the criminal law, the test of dishonesty was described by Lord Lane CJ in *R v Ghosh*[66] in this way:

> In determining whether the prosecution has proved that the defendant was acting dishonestly, a jury must first of all decide whether according to the ordinary standards of reasonable and honest people what was done was dishonest. If it was not dishonest by those standards, that is the end of the matter and the prosecution fails. If it was dishonest by those standards, the jury must consider whether the defendant himself must have realised that what he was doing was by those standards dishonest.

**30.61** The test of criminal dishonesty is therefore twofold, containing an objective and a subjective element. The conduct must be dishonest by ordinary, objective standards. Subjectively, the defendant must have realized that the conduct was (by those objective standards) dishonest. Therefore a defendant who personally

---

[63] In January 2005, at Southampton Crown Court, the trial of *R v Stovold* was heard. The case concerned the role of the directors of a brokerage company within the local authority operational lease market. The SFO had indicted the defendant with conspiracy to defraud on the basis of an alleged agreement dishonestly to conceal the existence of a conflict of interests and secret profits from his principals. The trial concluded at the close of the Crown's case with the acquittal of the defendant on the direction of the judge because, taking the Crown's case at its highest, the facts of the allegation had not been made out. However, the defence conceded that the allegation, if proved, would be capable of amounting to a criminal conspiracy.

[64] *Welham v DPP* [1961] AC 103, HL.

[65] *Landy and Kaye* [1981] 1 WLR 355, CA; *Wai Yu Tsang v R* [1992] 1 AC 269, PC.

[66] [1982] QB 1053, 1064, CA.

(perhaps for peculiar ideological reasons) believes his conduct to be morally justified and honest, nevertheless has a dishonest state of mind according to the criminal law if he realizes that his conduct would be judged to be dishonest by the objective standards of the reasonable man. The question of dishonesty is quintessentially a matter for the determination of a jury. Generally speaking, in a criminal trial the judge will not specifically direct a jury on the meaning of dishonesty unless there is a real issue as to the second limb of the *Ghosh* test, ie the defendant has raised the possibility that he did not know that the conduct in question was dishonest by ordinary standards.[67]

In order to make out the element of dishonesty, it is unnecessary for the prosecution to establish that any lie was told, misrepresentation was made, or act of deceit took place.[68] The content of the agreement itself may be described as dishonest, even if the suspects did not intend to deceive their victim by telling lies or actively concealing their conduct. **30.62**

On the other hand, the presence or absence of attendant circumstances of lies, misrepresentation, concealment, and secrecy, may amount to powerful evidence in support of an allegation of dishonesty. As a matter of common sense, a jury will be invited to consider that such attendant lies or secrecy prove that the defendant must have known that his primary conduct was dishonest: otherwise, why would he have hidden it? **30.63**

### Defences

On a charge of common law conspiracy to defraud, assuming that the elements of the offence are made out, there are three principal defences which may be raised: (i) no conspiracy between husband and wife, (ii) no intention to fulfil plan, and (iii) impossibility. **30.64**

First, a charge of conspiracy is not made out when the agreement alleged was formed between a husband and wife and involved no other person.[69] This may be of relevance to family-run companies. However, if a third party joins the agreement, then a conspiracy exists and all parties to it, including the married couple, are criminally liable. **30.65**

As to the second defence, under the common law, there is a defence to a charge of conspiracy in circumstances where, although the defendant expressed his agreement to the criminal plan, his mind did not go with his expression and he had no **30.66**

---

[67] *R v Roberts (W)* 84 Cr App R 117, CA.
[68] *Scott v Metropolitan Police Commissioner* [1975] AC 819, HL.
[69] *Mawji v R* [1957] AC 126, PC. The effect of the law of statutory conspiracy is the same; Criminal Law Act 1977, s 2(2).

intention that the plan be carried out.[70] This may be described as the 'fingers crossed behind the back' defence. Once it is raised, the prosecution must disprove it to the criminal standard. This the prosecution might readily accomplish by adducing evidence that the defendant did some act in furtherance of the conspiracy.

30.67 Thirdly, there is a defence to a charge of common law conspiracy[71] in circumstances where the agreement in question was incapable of fulfilment. Again, once the defence of impossibility is raised, it is for the prosecution to disprove it to the criminal standard. The leading authority on impossibility is *DPP v Nock*.[72] The case concerned an agreement to carry out a specific chemical procedure with the intention of producing cocaine. In fact, the procedure was incapable of producing the chemical: the Privy Council held that no criminal conspiracy was disclosed on the facts.

30.68 The principle of impossibility obviously has a very limited application where the agreement in question is not an agreement to achieve a highly specific goal, such as the production of cocaine, but an agreement which has the more nebulous effect of risking injury to another's rights. It is difficult to think of many situations in which an agreement to defraud might be saved from criminal liability by reason of the impossibility of fulfilment. However, the defence will apply, for example, where the agreement is to defraud a company which (unbeknownst to would-be conspirators) no longer exists, or a person who has already died at the time the agreement is formed.

*Penalty*

30.69 Conspiracy to defraud (which is an offence which may only be tried on indictment) carries an unlimited fine, or a maximum of ten years' imprisonment, or both.[73]

### (3) Fraud Act substantive fraud

*Three new substantive acts of fraud*

30.70 The Fraud Act,[74] s 1 has changed the landscape of criminal fraud by creating three new substantive offences of fraud. Subsections (1) and (2) provide:

> (1) A person is guilty of fraud if he is in breach of any of the sections listed in subsection (2) (which provide for different ways of committing the offence).

---

[70] *R v Thomas* (1965) 50 Cr App R 1. Under a charge of statutory conspiracy (ie a charge of conspiring to commit a statutory offence, contrary to the Criminal Law Act 1977, s 1(1)) the law is slightly different; *R v Anderson* [1986] AC 27, HL.

[71] But not to statutory conspiracy; Criminal Law Act 1977, s 1(2).

[72] [1978] AC 979, PC.

[73] CJA, 12(3).

[74] It came into force on 15 January 2007; Fraud Act 2006 (Commencement) Order (SO 2006/3200).

(2) The sections are—
  (a) section 2 (fraud by false representation),
  (b) section 3 (fraud by failing to disclose information), and
  (c) section 4 (fraud by abuse of position).

Each substantive offence set out in ss 2, 3, and 4 proscribes a different physical act: **30.71** false representation; failing to disclose information which one has a legal duty to disclose; abusing one's position as a fiduciary.[75] In addition, each offence shares the requirement of proving:

(1) dishonesty;[76] and
(2) an intent to (a) make gain for oneself or another, or (b) cause loss to another or to expose another to the risk of loss.

The relevant sections read: **30.72**

**2 Fraud by false representation**
  (1) A person is in breach of this section if he—
    (a) dishonestly makes a false representation, and
    (b) intends, by making the representation—
      (i) to make a gain for himself or another, or
      (ii) to cause loss to another or to expose another to a risk of loss.
  (2) A representation is false if—
    (a) it is untrue or misleading, and
    (b) the person making it knows that it is, or might be, untrue or misleading.
  (3) 'Representation' means any representation as to fact or law, including a representation as to the state of mind of—
    (a) the person making the representation, or
    (b) any other person.
  (4) A representation may be express or implied.
  (5) For the purposes of this section a representation may be regarded as made if it (or anything implying it) is submitted in any form to any system or device designed to receive, convey or respond to communications (with or without human intervention).

**3 Fraud by failing to disclose information**
A person is in breach of this section if he—
  (a) dishonestly fails to disclose to another person information which he is under a legal duty to disclose, and
  (b) intends, by failing to disclose the information—
    (i) to make a gain for himself or another, or
    (ii) to cause loss to another or to expose another to a risk of loss.

---

[75] In order to commit this type of fraud, the defendant must 'occupy a position in which he is expected to safeguard, or not to act against, the financial interests of another person': s 4(1)(a).
[76] Dishonesty for these purposes will be *Ghosh* dishonesty, as to which see paragraphs 30.55–30.59 above.

**4 Fraud by abuse of position**

(1) A person is in breach of this section if he—

   (a) occupies a position in which he is expected to safeguard, or not to act against, the financial interests of another person,

   (b) dishonestly abuses that position, and

   (c) intends, by means of the abuse of that position—

      (i) to make a gain for himself or another, or

      (ii) to cause loss to another or to expose another to a risk of loss.

(2) A person may be regarded as having abused his position even though his conduct consisted of an omission rather than an act.

**30.73** There is one major difference between the type of fraud proscribed as substantive offences under the Fraud Act, and the type of fraud which may be the subject of a common law conspiracy to defraud. As was discussed above, the common law is not restricted to prejudice to proprietary rights or economic interests; the Fraud Act is.

**30.74** Under the Fraud Act, s 5(2) the terms 'gain' and 'loss' used in the definition of the offences extend only to gains or losses of money or other property (which includes things in action and other intangibles). The Fraud Act, s 5 reads:

**5 'Gain' and 'loss'**

(1) The references to gain and loss in sections 2 to 4 are to be read in accordance with this section.

(2) 'Gain' and 'loss'—

   (a) extend only to gain or loss in money or other property;

   (b) include any such gain or loss whether temporary or permanent; and 'property' means any property whether real or personal (including things in action and other intangible property).

(3) 'Gain' includes a gain by keeping what one has, as well as a gain by getting what one does not have.

(4) 'Loss' includes a loss by not getting what one might get, as well as a loss by parting with what one has.

**30.75** This definition is identical in its effect as the definition of 'gain' and 'loss' for the purposes of the Theft Act 1968. Therefore, case law upon gain and loss for the purpose of false accounting under that statute (as to which see Section E below) provides a useful aid to interpreting this provision of the new Fraud Act.

*Two types of conspiracy to defraud*

**30.76** Now that the Fraud Act 2006 is in force, there are two different types of conspiracy to defraud: conspiracy to commit one of the statutory forms of fraud proscribed by the Act, which would necessarily be charged under the Criminal Law Act 1977, s 1(1); conspiracy to defraud charged under the common law. The latter will not be rendered obsolete by the advent of the new statute, particularly because of the wider definition of rights and interests which are recognized for the purpose of the common law offence.

By the Fraud Act 2006, s 1(3) a person who is guilty of fraud is liable: on summary **30.77** conviction, to imprisonment for a term not exceeding 12 months or to a fine not exceeding the statutory maximum (or to both); on conviction on indictment, to imprisonment for a term not exceeding 10 years or to a fine (or to both).

# D. Theft and Deception

As stated in the introduction to this chapter, an overview of the entire criminal law **30.78** is beyond the scope of this work and this comment may be repeated with specific application to the law of theft and deception. There are many specific offences under the Theft Acts, only the principal of which will be discussed here. Particular emphasis will be placed on the way in which the law has developed in relation to the liabilities of company directors.

## (1) Theft

Theft is defined by the Theft Act 1968, s 1(1): **30.79**

> A person is guilty of theft if he dishonestly appropriates property belonging to another with the intention of permanently depriving the other of it; and 'thief' and 'steal' shall be construed accordingly.

Later sections of the Act elaborate on the definition of each of the constituent elements of the offence.

### Appropriation

Under the 1968 Act, s 3: **30.80**

> (1) Any assumption by a person of the rights of an owner amounts to an appropriation, and this includes, where he has come by the property (innocently or not) without stealing it, any later assumption of a right to it by keeping or dealing with it as owner.
> (2) Where property or a right or interest in property is or purports to be transferred for value to a person acting in good faith, no later assumption by him of rights which he believed himself to be acquiring shall, by reason of any defect in the transferor's title, amount to theft of the property.

Thus the concept of appropriation is wide. Crudely speaking, theft is not limited **30.81** to the act of picking something up and walking off with it, but extends to a much wider range of conduct in which the thief acts as if the property in question was his own. 'Any assumption . . . of the rights of an owner' has effectively been interpreted by the criminal courts to mean 'the assumption of *any* of the rights of an owner'. For example, the act of showing a prospective purchaser of furniture around someone else's unoccupied house for the purpose of allowing the purchaser to select items to buy will amount to an appropriation of the furniture for the purposes of theft.[77] In practice, the act of appropriation is so wide that it is rarely necessary for a prosecutor to charge an offence of attempted theft. It also ensures that there is a very considerable overlap between the offence of theft and the offence of handling stolen goods (which will not specifically be addressed in this work).

**30.82**  Further, an act of appropriation may be made out even where the owner of the property in question consents to the act. The words 'without the consent of the owner' are not to be read into the statutory definition of the theft.[78] Therefore, a taxi driver who takes bank notes many times in excess of the value of his rightful fare from an open wallet offered to him by a tourist who speaks no English appropriates the money, despite the fact that (on one view[79]) he takes the money with the consent of the owner. Likewise, the acceptance of a gift will amount to an act of appropriation and may found an allegation of theft if it is dishonest and accompanied by the requisite intention permanently to deprive.[80] This feature of the law of theft is responsible for a large degree of overlap between offences of theft and offences of obtaining property or services by deception.

**30.83**  The width of the definition of appropriation, together with the absence of a requirement to prove a lack of consent, has particular ramifications for the liability of company directors for acts of theft.

**30.84**  Where a company is wholly owned by its two directors, the fact that each consents to the other's act of pocketing company funds will not prevent either director from being guilty of theft. It is possible to construct an argument that this should not be so: the company directors, according to the doctrine of identification, *are* the company for the purpose of the criminal law; they consent to the act, the company consents to the act; how can they be said to have dishonestly appropriated the company's money? In *Attorney-General's Reference (No 2 of 1982)*,[81] the Court of Appeal dealt with the effect of the doctrine of identification in this way:

> The speeches in the House of Lords in *Tesco Supermarkets Ltd. v. Nattrass*,[82] merely illustrate that in situations like the present the defendants 'are' the company in the sense that any offences committed by them in relation to the affairs of the company would be capable of being treated as offences committed by the company itself. The decision has no bearing on offences committed against the company.

---

[77]  *R v Pitham and Hehl* (1976) 65 Cr App R 45, CA.

[78]  *Lawrence v Metropolitan Police Commissioner* [1972] AC 626, HL; *R v Gomez* [1993] AC 320, HL.

[79]  A dissenting view would be that lack of consent is an essential part of dishonesty, and that the material point on these facts is that no *true* consent is present.

[80]  *R v Hinks* [2001] 2 AC 241, HL.

[81]  [1984] QB 624, 640 per Kerr LJ, CA.

[82]  [1972] AC 153, HL.

Therefore, where shareholders or directors act illegally or dishonestly against the **30.85** company itself, knowledge of that dishonesty was not to be imputed to the company. So in this case, the company could not said to have consented or to have been party to the acts of appropriation by the directors. On this basis, the victimization of the company by the directors appeared to be what was critical in order to establish that an appropriation or—at least—that a dishonest appropriation had occurred.

However, an alternative basis on which to rationalize the court's decision that the **30.86** directors' conduct was capable of amounting to theft is to return to the more basic proposition that lack of consent on the part of the company and/or its directors and officers is not a requirement of the offence of theft. The practical distinction between the two rationales is illustrated on the following theoretical facts. [83]

A company has two directors, one of whom is approached by an important cus- **30.87** tomer who makes plain that the company will only win the renewal of a supply contract—critical to the company's profitability and survival—if a large bribe is paid; the director consults with his co-director, who consents to the course of using company monies to pay the bribe. Thereafter the first director approves the transfer of the monies in order to pay the bribe. Has he appropriated the company funds? Putting aside any liability for an act of corruption, is he guilty of theft? It is difficult to see how the directors' conduct can form an act against the company so as to prevent knowledge and/or consent to the act to be imputed to the company in accordance with the rationale of *Attorney-General's Reference (No 2 of 1982)*.[84]

The question has been tested in the Administrative Court, which upheld the first **30.88** instance decision that such facts would disclose an act of appropriation, it being a question for a jury whether the appropriation was dishonest.[85] The defence argued the contrary position, attempting to distinguish the case from classic instances of directors' theft on the basis that there was no victimization of the company here: the director acted for the company's benefit; there was therefore no basis on which to depart from the normal effect of the doctrine of identification; the director's act was the act of the company itself; the director could not be said to have appropriated the company's funds. These arguments were roundly rejected. The court was loyal to the classic position in which 'appropriation' is a neutral term, involving no

---

[83] In the SFO prosecution from which this example is drawn, the facts were hotly contested, and the scenario as posited here, although considered by the trial judge and the Administrative Court for the purpose of identifying the correct terms in which to the direct the jury, did not reflect the case for the prosecution, or for the defence. The defendant director asserted that he was not party to corruption. The prosecution maintained that he was, but that he did not inform or obtain the consent of any other director. The company director was ultimately acquitted.

[84] [1984] QB 624, CA.

[85] *AFP Regan*, CO/1019/2001, 17/5/2001, QBD, *coram* Lord Woolf CJ and Bell J.

trace of the concept of 'misappropriation' and entirely silent as the honesty of the perpetrator or the 'victimization' of the owner of the property.[86]

30.89   Is it then the case that every time a director uses company property for a corrupt or dishonest purpose, the director is guilty of stealing the property from the company? The answer is no. In the case discussed immediately above, although the Administrative Court kept the definition of 'appropriation' wide, it reintroduced the concept of 'victimisation' by stressing that the prosecution was obliged to prove that the defendant was dishonest *towards* the victim of the theft, ie that the director was dishonest *towards* the company. However, the court declined to stipulate that the jury should be directed that such dishonesty could not be made out where the director has obtained the consent of his only co-director. Dishonesty was a question for the jury, and in addition to the question whether the other director had consented, the following factors might influence their deliberations: whether the company's parent company was fully informed of events; whether it could be said that the director acted in the interests of the company; whether the long-term interests of the company were jeopardized by potential civil and criminal liabilities arising from the director's alleged corruption.

*Dishonesty*

30.90   In order to make out an offence of theft, the prosecution must not only prove an appropriation, but also that the appropriation was a dishonest one. As discussed above, a charge of theft requires dishonesty to be directed towards the victim of the theft. Further than that, the definition of dishonesty for these purposes is as set out in the case of *Ghosh*.[87]

30.91   Finally, the 1968 Act, s 2 sets out three specific instances of states of mind which do not amount to dishonesty for the purposes of theft, and one instance of a circumstance which will not necessarily prevent a finding of dishonesty. It provides:

> (1) A person's appropriation of property belonging to another is not to be regarded as dishonest—
>   (a) if he appropriates the property in the belief that he has in law the right to deprive the other of it, on behalf of himself or of a third person;
>   (b) if he appropriates the property in the belief that he would have the other's consent if the other knew of the appropriation and the circumstances of it; or
>   (c) (except where the property came to him as trustee or personal representative) if he appropriates the property in the belief that the person to whom the property belongs cannot be discovered by taking reasonable steps.
> (2) A person's appropriation of property belonging to another may be dishonest notwithstanding that he is willing to pay for the property.

---

[86]   See further *R v Gomez* [1993] AC 320, HL.
[87]   [1982] QB 1053, CA. See above Section C of this chapter.

*Property*

By the Theft Act 1968, s 4, property includes money, things in action (including **30.92** debts), and other intangible property (such as export quotas[88]) but excludes land.

Importantly, property does not include information. Confidential information **30.93** cannot be the object of theft.[89]

*Belonging to another*

'Another' for the purposes of the Theft Act includes a company, a company being a **30.94** legal person for the purpose of the criminal law.[90] The concept of 'belonging to another' is widened by the Theft Act 1986, s 5(1) to include any person having possession or control of the property, or having any proprietary right or interest in it.

Where property is subject to trust, the person to whom it belongs is regarded as **30.95** the person who has the right to enforce the trust.[91] Note however that secret profits obtained by a trustee will be regarded as his own property and not property belonging to the beneficiary of the trust for the purposes of the law of theft.[92] The trustee will have a civil obligation to disgorge himself of the secret profits (and in some circumstances he will be guilty of an offence of fraud and perhaps false accounting[93]) but he will not be guilty of stealing from the trust or his principal.

In addition, where a person receives property from or on account of and is under **30.96** an obligation to another to retain and deal with that property or its proceeds in a particular way, the property or proceeds shall be regarded (as against him) as belonging to the other.[94] Note however, that the obligation must be a legal one, rather than a purely social or moral one.[95] The effect of this provision is to enable a suspect to be charged with theft for the act of mixing with his own money (or the money of his own business) the money received by him from his client or principal which ought to have been kept in a separate account.

Likewise, where a person receives property by another's mistake, and is under an **30.97** obligation to make complete or partial restoration of the property or its proceeds, then the property or its proceeds are to be regarded (as against him) as belonging

---

[88] *AG of Hong Kong v Nai-Keung* [1987] 1 WLR 1339, PC.
[89] *Oxford v Moss* (1978) 68 Cr App R 183, DC.
[90] *Attorney-General's Reference (No 2 of 1982)* [1984] 1 QB 624, CA.
[91] Theft Act 1968, s 5(2).
[92] *Attorney-General's Reference (No 1 of 1985)* [1986] QB 491, CA.
[93] In particular note how the concept of 'gain' and 'loss' for the purposes of false accounting and—it must be assumed—the new Fraud Act offences includes avoiding an obligation to account to one's principal in respect of a secret profit: *Lee Cheung Wing v R* (1991) 94 Cr App R 355, CA. See further under Section C above.
[94] Theft Act 1968, s 5(3).
[95] *R v Hall* [1973] QB 126.

to the other to the extent of that obligation.[96] Again, the obligation must be a legal, rather than a moral or social obligation.[97] This provision is apt to cover situations in which a director receives an overpayment from his company by way of remuneration.

*Intention permanently to deprive*

**30.98** It has been said that there is no offence of 'dishonest borrowing' in English law. Strictly speaking this is true. However, on a charge of theft, it is in some circumstances possible to secure a conviction despite the fact that the defendant meant ultimately to restore the property to its rightful owner.

**30.99** The Theft Act 1968, s 6 reads:

(1) A person appropriating property belonging to another without meaning the other permanently to lose the thing itself is nevertheless to be regarded as having the intention of permanently depriving the other of it if his intention is to treat the thing as his own to dispose of regardless of the other's rights; and a borrowing or lending of it may amount to so treating it if, but only if, the borrowing or lending is for a period and in circumstances making is equivalent to an outright taking or disposal.

(2) Without prejudice to the generality of subsection (1) above, where a person, having possession or control (lawfully or not) of property belonging to another, parts with the property under a condition as to its return which he may not be able to perform, this (if done for the purposes of his own and without the other's authority) amounts to treating the property as his own to dispose of regardless of the other's rights.

**30.100** This provision will apply, and should be left to the consideration of the jury, in circumstances where a director 'borrows' money from a company meaning one day to repay it, but intending to deal with it in the meantime in such a manner that he knows he is risking its loss. The 'critical notion' in this provision is whether the defendant intended to treat the property as his own to dispose of, regardless of the other's rights.[98]

*Penalty*

**30.101** The maximum sentence for theft on conviction on indictment is seven years' imprisonment.[99]

### (2) Offences of deception

*Pre-Fraud Act 2006*

**30.102** For the period prior to the coming into force of the Fraud Act 2006 on 15 January 2007 there remain five principal deception offences under the Theft Acts of 1968

---

[96] Theft Act 1986, s 5(4).
[97] *R v Hall* [1973] QB 126.
[98] *R v Fernandez* [1996] 1 Cr App R 175, 188, CA, per Auld LJ.
[99] Theft Act 1986, s 7.

and 1978: (i) obtaining property,[100] (ii) obtaining a money transfer,[101] (iii) obtaining a pecuniary advantage,[102] (iv) obtaining services,[103] and (v) evading a liability[104] by deception. Each of these offences is repealed by the 2006 Act.[105] However, the old offences of deception will continue to have effect in relation to any conduct committed, or partly committed, before the commencement date.[106] For the purpose of this work, only the first of the old deception offences will be examined. The principles discussed are of general application, regardless of the particular provision which applies to the object of the offence.

The Theft Act 1968, s 15 provides:                                                                       **30.103**

(1) A person who by any deception dishonestly obtains property belonging to another, with the intention of permanently depriving the other of it, shall on conviction on indictment be liable to imprisonment for a term not exceeding ten years.

(2) For the purposes of this section a person is to be treated as obtaining property if he obtains ownership, possession or control of it, and 'obtain' includes obtaining for another or enabling another to obtain or retain.

(3) Section 6 above [relating to intention permanently to deprive] shall apply for the purposes of this section with the necessary adaptation of the reference to appropriating, as it applies for purposes of section 1.

(4) For the purposes of this section 'deception' means any deception (whether deliberate or reckless) by words or conduct as to fact or as to law, including a deception as to the present intention of the person using the deception or any other person.

The leading authority on the meaning of deception is *DPP v Ray*.[107] Note that    **30.104**
deception is not restricted to deliberate deception, but includes reckless deception, that is, deception caused with indifference or disregard as to whether the statement is true or false.[108] In order to make out any offence of obtaining by deception, the deception in question must be effective, ie it must operate on the mind of the person deceived so as to constitute the effective cause by which the property is obtained.[109] It follows that the deception must precede the obtaining of the property in order to make out the offence.

---

[100] Theft Act 1968, s 15.

[101] Theft Act 1968, s 15A. The need to enact this separate offence was highlighted by the decision of the House of Lords in *R v Preddy* [1996] AC 815, HL in which it was decided that inducing a financial institution to advance mortgage monies did not involve obtaining 'property belonging to another' within the meaning of the Theft Act 1968. Rather than obtain a chose in action which belonged to someone else, the defendant had induced the bank to create a new thing in action in the form of the enlarged credit balance in his own account. Absent s 15A, the same problem would exist in relation to cheques: *R v Clark* [2001] Crim LR 572, CA.

[102] Theft Act 1968, s 16.

[103] Theft Act 1978, s 1.

[104] Theft Act 1978, s 2.

[105] Fraud Act 2006, s 14(3) and Sch 1, para 1.

[106] Fraud Act 2006 Sch 2, para 3(1).

[107] [1974] AC 370, HL.

[108] *R v Staines* (1970) 60 Cr App R 160, CA.

[109] *R v Clucas* [1949] 2 KB 226; *R v King and Stockwell* [1987] QB 547.

**30.105**  As to 'dishonesty', see generally paragraphs 30.90 and 30.91 above. Note that dishonesty is completely separate to the element of deception in an offence under s 15. There may be circumstances in which deception is proved, but a jury is nevertheless unsure as to whether the defendant acted dishonestly (for example where the deception occurred through negligence rather than as a result of a deliberate act).

**30.106**  As to the requirements to prove that the object of the offence was 'property', 'belonging to another', and that the suspect acted with an 'intention permanently to deprive', see the discussion at paragraphs 30.92–30.100 above.

**30.107**  The maximum sentence for an offence of obtaining property by deception contrary to the 1968 Theft, s 15 Act is 10 years' imprisonment (ie longer than for theft).

*Post-Fraud Act 2006*

**30.108**  In respect of conduct which takes place wholly after the coming into force of the relevant section of the Fraud Act 2006,[110] the old offences of obtaining by deception are replaced by the three new substantive fraud offences (as to which see above) and one offence of obtaining services *dishonestly*.

**30.109**  By the Fraud Act 2006, s 11:

(1)  A person is guilty of an offence under this section if he obtains services for himself or another—
    (a)  by a dishonest act, and
    (b)  in breach of subsection (2).
(2)  A person obtains services in breach of this subsection if—
    (a)  they are made available on the basis that payment has been, is being or will be made for or in respect of them,
    (b)  he obtains them without any payment having been made for or in respect of them or without payment having been made in full, and
    (c)  when he obtains them, he knows—
        (i)  that they are being made available on the basis described in paragraph (a), or
        (ii)  that they might be, but intends that payment will not be made, or will not be made in full.

**30.110**  It is probable that many instances of deceit which previously would have been charged as obtaining property by deception will in future be charged under the Fraud Act 2006, s 2 as fraud by false representation.

**30.111**  An important contrast between the old offences of deception and the new substantive fraud offences is that the latter do not depend upon proof that any property was in fact obtained as a result of the deceit. Thus the new fraud offences set out in the 2006 Act, ss 2–4 overlap significantly with the inchoate versions of the

---

[110]  ie 15 January 2007.

old deception offences (such as attempts to obtain property by deception) as well as the old deception offences themselves.

**30.112**  In addition, the restriction of the new fraud offences to conduct tending to prejudice only the financial interests of the victim of the fraud by effecting a loss to him of money or other property, represents a change in the law. Under the old law, the object of most of the deception offences was some form of property, or a pecuniary interest. But in the case of obtaining *services* by deception, the loss caused to the victim did not need to be financial in order to make out the offence. The definition of the old statutory offence required the service in question to be a service rendered on the understanding that it had or would be paid for,[111] but it did not require the operative deception to be that the service provider would be paid when this was not in fact the case. In contrast, the new offence of obtaining services dishonestly is dependent on proof that the defendant did not intend to pay for the services, at all or in full, at the time he obtained them.[112]

**30.113**  As with other fraud offences under the new Act, an offence contrary to s 11 carries a maximum of 12 months' imprisonment (and/or a fine) on summary conviction and ten years' imprisonment (and/or a fine) on conviction on indictment.

# E. False Accounting and Forgery

## (1) Introduction

**30.114**  Directors' liabilities for accounting and forgery offences arise by reason of the general offence of false accounting, proscribed by the Theft Act 1968, the general forgery offences of the Forgery and Counterfeiting Act 1981, and also by reason of specific liabilities imposed upon directors under both the Theft Act 1968 and under Company Act legislation.

## (2) False accounting under the Theft Act 1968

**30.115**  The Theft 1968, s 17(1) provides:

(1) Where a person dishonestly, with a view to gain for himself or another or with intent to cause loss to another—
   (a) destroys, defaces, conceals or falsifies any account or any record or document made or required for any accounting purpose; or
   (b) in furnishing information for any purpose, produces or makes use of any account, or any such record or document as aforesaid, which to his knowledge is or may be misleading, false or deceptive in a material particular;

---

[111]  Theft Act 1978, s 1(2).
[112]  Fraud Act 2006, s 11(2)(c).

> he shall, on conviction on indictment, be liable to imprisonment for a term not exceeding seven years.

**30.116** This offence is of obvious application to any act committed by a director in relation to his own company's accounts. However, the offence of false accounting is wider than may appear at first glance.

*Made or required for an accounting purpose*

**30.117** The words 'made or required' together cover any document or record which is meant for, or subsequently used for, an accounting purpose. A document specifically made for an accounting purpose is obviously covered, and will remain covered even if the document is never in fact used.[113] The offence also applies to documents made for an entirely different purpose (for example, an application form for a loan from a bank) which is subsequently used for an accounting purpose by another person (eg when the bank uses the form to input data into its own account of the transaction).[114]

**30.118** In addition, it should be noted that the requirement 'for an accounting purpose' is a requirement which attaches to the nature of the document itself. Where the prosecution rely upon a false statement contained in the document, it is not necessary for the prosecution to prove that false statement in question was material to the accounting purpose.[115]

**30.119** Therefore, if a company director were to insert a false particular about the company upon an application form seeking a corporate loan from a bank, so long as he had the requisite state of mind,[116] he is liable for an offence of false accounting if that application form is subsequently used by the bank to enter the details of the loan into its own internal accounts, even though the falsehood in question has no effect on the accuracy of the bank's ledger.

*Gain and loss*

**30.120** Gain and loss are defined by the Theft Act 1968, s 34(2) in these terms:

> For the purposes of this Act—
> (a) 'gain' and 'loss' are to be construed as extending only to gain and loss in money or other property, but as extending to any such gain or loss whether temporary or permanent; and—
>   (i) 'gain' includes a gain by keeping what one has, as well as a gain by getting what one does not; and

---

[113] *R v Sharma* [1990] 1 WLR 661.
[114] *Attorney-General's Reference (No 1 of 1980)* [1981] 1 WLR 84, CA.
[115] *R v Mallet* [1978] 1 WLR 820, CA.
[116] ie dishonesty and a view to cause gain for himself or another (including the company) or with intent to cause loss to another (including the company).

> (ii) 'loss' includes a loss by not getting what one might get, as well as a loss by part-
> ing with what one has . . .

In order to establish that the defendant acted with a view to gain for himself or **30.121**
another, it is not necessary for the prosecution to exclude the possibility that the
defendant was lawfully entitled to the property he sought to acquire. A person
who furnishes false information in order to obtain money acts with a view to gain
for himself, even if the money is undoubtedly owing to him, since by his actions
he converts a mere right of action in respect of the debt into obtained cash, and
thereby gains more than he already had; *Attorney-General's Reference (No 1 of
2001).*[117] This case confirmed pre-existing first instance authority to the effect
that the term 'gain' is not restricted to the idea of making a profit.[118]

Whether inducing a creditor to forbear suing on a debt may amount to a 'gain' on **30.122**
the part of the debtor is less clear. In *R v Goleccha*[119] the court held that a debtor
acting with such a purpose did not act with a view to gain for himself. This authority was not specifically considered by the Court of Appeal in *Attorney-General's
Reference (No 1 of 2001)* (above), but it must be doubted whether the earlier
decision survives the later. If inducing the payment of a lawful debt may amount
to a 'gain' of the subsequent cash payment, it must follow that inducing a creditor
not to sue on a debt amounts to a 'loss' of cash on his part, albeit potentially
only temporary loss. *Goleccha* was a curious case because the prosecution put its
allegation on the somewhat artificial basis that the defendant, by inducing the
forbearance of his creditor, 'gained' the continued existence of the provision of
the credit facility. The Court of Appeal rejected that as a proper basis for a conviction, but neither the prosecution nor the court appear to have considered that,
regardless of what the defendant could be said to have 'gained'[120] from deceitfully
inducing forbearance of his default, he undoubtedly caused a loss to the bank.
Argument before the court does not appear to have focused on those parts
of s 34(2) which provide that loss need not be permanent and that loss can include
not getting what one might get (such as money in repayment of a debt), as well
as parting with what one already has. In a subsequent, unreported decision of
the Court of Appeal,[121] *Goleccha* was described as a decision 'turning very much
on its own facts'. It is submitted that *Goleccha* should not be treated as
good law.

---

[117] *Attorney-General's Reference (No 1 of 2001)* [2003] 1 WLR 395.
[118] *R v Parkes* [1973] Crim LR 358, Crown Court.
[119] [1989] 1 WLR 1050, CA.
[120] See further *R v Eden* (1971) 55 Cr App R 193, CA in which a defendant who was proved to
have acted to 'put off the evil day of having to sort out the muddle and pay up' was held by the Court
of Appeal to have acted with a view to temporary gain.
[121] *R v Masterson*, unreported, 30 April 1996, CA (94/02221/X5).

**30.123**    A company director who falsifies a document with a view to avoiding an obligation to account to his principal company in respect of personal profits obtained by
him in the course of his activities on behalf of the company acts with a view to gain
for himself, even if he has caused no loss to his principal by his activities.[122] 'Gain'
of course, is defined by s 34(2) to include keeping what one has, as well as gaining
what one has not.

**30.124**    A company director who creates false invoices purportedly issued by recently acquired
companies with a view to mollifying his co-directors as to the wisdom of those acquisitions does not act with a view to gain for himself. It is artificial for the Crown to seek
to demonstrate the contrary by speculating that the director, if his attempts at mol-
lification failed, might have had to placate his co-directors using his own financial
resources, in circumstances where he was under no legal obligation so to do.[123]

*Falsifying*

**30.125**    The term 'falsifies' is not defined by the 1968 Act, but s 17 does contain a deeming
provision which applies to accounts and documents (but not to other, mechanical
forms of record). Subsection 17(2) provides:

> For the purposes of this section a person who makes or concurs in the making in an
> account or ot particular, or who omits or concurs in omitting a material particular
> from an account or other document, is to be treated as falsifying the account or
> document.

*Dishonesty*

**30.126**    See generally paragraphs 30.59–30.63 above.

*Penalty*

**30.127**    The maximum penalty for an offence contrary to s 17 is a term of imprisonment
of seven years.

### (3) Forgery

**30.128**    The principal forgery offence—the offence of making a false instrument—is set
out in the Forgery and Counterfeiting Act 1981 (the 1981 Act), s 1. Other offences
under the same Act include copying,[124] using,[125] and possessing[126] a false instrument. Only the principal forgery offence will be discussed in this work.

---

[122] *Lee Cheung Wing v R* (1992) 94 Cr App R 355, PC.
[123] *R v Masterson*, unreported, 30 April 1996, CA (94/02221/X5).
[124] 1981 Act, s 2.
[125] 1981 Act, s 3.
[126] 1981 Act, s 5.

The 1981 Act, s 1 provides: **30.129**

> A person is guilty of forgery if he makes a false instrument with the intention that he or another shall use it to induce somebody to accept it as genuine, and by reason of so accepting it, to do or not to do some act to his own of any other person's prejudice.

*Instrument*

The offence of making a false instrument applies to a wider range of documents **30.130** than the offence of false accounting (which is restricted to documents and records made or required for an accounting purpose). The anti-forgery legislation applies to all documents, be they formal or informal, and to all disks, tapes, soundtracks, and other devices used to store information.[127]

*False*

However, the offence of forgery is in other ways narrower than the offence of false **30.131** accounting. In essence, the terms of the 1981 Act require the document in question to bear false information *about itself* (for example, that it was made by a person who did not in fact make it, or that it was made on a date on which it was not in fact made), as opposed to merely bearing false information about the person who made it (for example, that person's—or his company's—assets, liabilities, credit status, or history).[128]

Under the 1981 Act, a person is to be deemed to have 'made' a false instrument if **30.132** he alters a document so as to make it tell a lie about itself in any way which would qualify to trigger the offence under the Act.[129]

*Prejudice*

The term 'prejudice' is given special definition under the 1981 Act. Under s 10(1), **30.133** an act or omission intended to be induced is to a person's prejudice only if it is one which, if it occurs, will result: in his loss of property or of opportunity to gain a financial advantage, or in his becoming liable to someone else gaining a financial advantage from him; or if it is the result of a person having accepted the false instrument as genuine in connection with his performance of a duty.

As in relation to the offence of false accounting, loss in this context embraces (under **30.134** the terms of s 10) permanent and temporary loss, and includes loss by not getting what one might have gained, as well as parting with what one already has.

---

[127] 1981 Act, s 8(1).
[128] 1981 Act, s 9(1) and *R v More* [1987] 1 WLR 1578, HL.
[129] 1981 Act, s 9(2).

*Penalty*

**30.135**   A person convicted of forgery is liable summarily to 12 months' imprisonment or a fine (or both) and on indictment to 10 years' imprisonment.[130]

### (4)  Directors' accounting liabilities

**30.136**   The Theft Act 1968, s 19(1) provides:

> (1) Where an officer of a body corporate or unincorporated association (or a person purporting to act as such), with intent to deceive members or creditors of the body corporate or association about its affairs, publishes or concurs in publishing a written statement which to his knowledge is or may be misleading, false or deceptive in a material particular, he shall on conviction on indictment be liable to a term of imprisonment not exceeding seven years.

**30.137**   This liability is in addition to specific liabilities contained in the Companies Act 2006 (as to which see Section H below). For discussion of the concept of knowledge, see paragraph 30.191 below. Note that the words 'is or may be' in s 19 mean that the offence can be committed with a reckless state of mind in respect of the accuracy of the written statement.

**30.138**   In relation to deceit and deception, see paragraph 30.104 above. Note, however, that in contrast to some other statutory offences of deception, an offence under s 19 requires a specific intention to deceive.

# F.  Corruption

## (1)  Introduction

**30.139**   The law of corruption has been criticized by the Law Commission for its width, its uncertainty, and its inconsistency.[131] It is also remarkable for its antiquity.

**30.140**   When first introduced under the common law, the offence of corruption was relatively restricted in its terms, pertaining only to acts of bribery committed in relation to persons performing some form of public duty[132] (although the law criminalized both parties to the bribe).[133] Even more narrow in its application was the first statutory offence of corruption (under the Public Bodies Corrupt Practices Act 1889), which related to bribes made or offered to members, officers or servants of a 'public body', which was defined under the Act to mean some form of

---

[130]   1981 Act, s 6.
[131]   per Law Commission (1998).
[132]   *R v Whitaker* [1914] 3 KB 1283.
[133]   In 2002, the common law offence was extended to cover foreign officials whose functions are carried out overseas, with no connection to the United Kingdom: Anti-Terrorism Crime and Security Act 2001, s 108(1), which came into effect on 14 February 2002.

local government.[134] Both the ancient common law offence and the earliest statutory offence of corrupting public servants have never been repealed and remain extant today.

However, there is third form of corruption,[135] only slightly younger but much wider than either of its older counterparts. It is this third form of the offence, under the Prevention of Corruption Act 1906, which is most likely to be associated with the performance of a director's duties. It is this form of statutory corruption which will be considered in this part. The specific offence of making a corrupt inducement to affect the appointment of a liquidator will not be considered.[136]     **30.141**

### (2) Prevention of Corruption Act 1906

Under the Prevention of Corruption Act 1906, s 1(1):     **30.142**

> If any agent[137] corruptly accepts or obtains, or agrees to accept or attempts to obtain, from any person, for himself or for any other person, any gift or consideration as an inducement or reward for doing or forbearing to do, or for having after the passing of this Act done or forborne to do, any act in relation to his principal's affairs or business, or for showing or forbearing to show favour or disfavour to any person in relation to his principal's affairs or business; or

> If a person corruptly gives or agrees to give or offers any gift or consideration to any agent as an inducement or reward for doing or forbearing to do, or for having after the passing of this Act done or forborne to do, any act in relation to his principal's affairs or business, or for showing or forbearing to show favour or disfavour to any person in relation to his principal's affairs or business; or

> If any person knowingly gives to any agent, or if any agent knowingly uses with intent to deceive his principal, any receipt, account or other document in respect of which the principal is interested, and which contains any statement which is false or erroneous or defective in any material particular, and which to his knowledge is intended to mislead the principal;

> he shall be guilty [of an offence]. . .

---

[134] The scope of this offence was also extended in 2002 to cover equivalent public bodies situated outside the United Kingdom: Anti-Terrorism Crime and Security Act 2001, s 108(3), which came into effect on 14 February 2002.

[135] Indeed, there is a fourth form under the Honours (Prevention of Abuses) Act 1925, which applies only to the grant of honours and will not be considered in this work.

[136] See Insolvency Act, s 164.

[137] By subs 1(4) (inserted by the Anti-Terrorism Crime and Security Act 2001, s 108) it is immaterial whether the agent, his functions, the principal, or his business are within or without the territory of the United Kingdom.

*'Corruptly' otiose*

**30.143** It is well established law that the word 'corruptly' does not mean 'dishonestly' and that dishonesty is not an element of the offence of corruption.[138] Moreover, the word 'corruptly' in the first two paragraphs of s 1 imposes no obligation of proof upon the prosecution over and above the obligation to prove conduct fulfilling the description which follows. Properly viewed, s 1 does no more than to deem three different types of conduct as corrupt; the fact that the first two paragraphs contain the word 'corruptly' and the third does not, does not mean that there is a significant distinction between the three different modes of committing the offence.

**30.144** The otiose nature of the word 'corruptly' within s 1 is well demonstrated by *R v Smith*.[139] The defendant had been charged with an offence of corruption for offering a gift to a local mayor in order to induce him to use his influence with the borough council in the defendant's favour.[140] The defendant's case was that he had made the offer of the gift, but only with the intention to expose the mayor's corruption, not for the purpose of corrupting the mayor or obtaining his influence. The trial judge directed the jury that this did not amount to a defence to the charge:

> What does the word 'corruptly' mean? . . . [It] means with the intention to corrupt. In other words, if I offer you a reward in order that you should do something which may help me, or if I am offering and hoping that the offer will induce you to act in the way in which I want you to act, I am doing it corruptly. Motive does not matter; it may be that I do it because I am anxious to help myself; it may be that I am anxious to help a widow, who, perhaps, is starving and whom I think I can help by getting a public official, a person in public life, to do something which would help her. In one sense I suppose it could be said that any such act sprang from the best possible motive, the endeavour to help. It does not matter; when I offer you that gift I do it with the intention that you should so receive a reward for doing something in connection with your public duties. This is the meaning of the word 'corrupt'—intent to corrupt, the intention to corrupt the person to whom the offer is made.[141]

It is submitted that the logical implication of this direction is that the word 'corruptly' does indeed add nothing to the description of conduct proscribed by the statute. Indeed, this implication was expressly considered by the Court of Appeal,[142] which nevertheless accepted it and approved the terms of the trial judge's summing-up to the jury.

**30.145** One of the boundaries between acts of corruption as defined in *Smith* and acts which a jury may conclude were not corrupt was drawn by Lord Goddard CJ

---

[138] *R v Godden-Wood* (2001) Crim LR 810, CA.

[139] [1960] 2 QB 423.

[140] The charge was laid under the Pubic Bodies Corrupt Practices Act 1889, but the authority is of equal relevance to a charge brought under the 1906 Act.

[141] As quoted by Lord Parker CJ in the Court of Appeal, at 427.

[142] At 429.

when refusing leave to pursue an appeal against conviction in the case of *R v Carr*.[143] Although, under *Smith*, a person who offers a bribe to an agent in order to illustrate and expose his corruption may be guilty of an offence, under *Carr* an agent who accepts a bribe with the intention only of giving it immediately to the authorities in order to expose the crime of the giver is not guilty of corruption.

An intention to accept a bribe but then to show no favour to the giver, ie an intention to double-cross the person who seeks to bribe, will not, however, entitle a defendant to a not-guilty verdict.[144]      **30.146**

### Ex post facto *gifts*

It should also be noted that, where a gift or reward is given *ex post facto*, it is not necessary for the gift to have been part of an agreement formed before the agent carried out the conduct which is rewarded, or for the gift in any other way to have formed part of an operative inducement causing or influencing the agent to act in the desired way. This is clear from the terms of the statute itself, and was confirmed by the Court of Appeal in *R v Parker*,[145] in which the following direction to the jury was approved:      **30.147**

> You will see . . . that this wording does not only catch the ordinary bribe, where someone agrees to do something in return for a sum of money; corruption for this purpose includes receipt of money for a past favour without there having been any agreement beforehand, so that really the position for practical purposes is that a councillor must not accept a reward for having done something in the course of his public duty. This is a very severe view of course for the law to take, but the reason it takes that severe view is in order to protect the public [servant] from being put in a position of temptation.

This case was decided in relation to the Public Bodies Corrupt Practices Act 1889, but it is submitted that the *ratio* applies equally to the Prevention of Corruption Act 1906. Indeed, in the earlier authority of *R v Andrew-Weatherfoil Ltd*,[146] a case also decided in relation to the 1889 Act, the court specifically considered the terms of the 1906 Act and indicated that the same interpretation would apply: the word 'reward' should be given the natural meaning of an *ex post facto* gift without any antecedent agreement, and without any notion of inducement. In addition, subsequent case law upon the 1906 Act has stressed that there is no difference between the test for corruption in relation to public (the 1889 Act) and private (the 1906 Act) domains.[147]      **30.148**

---

[143] [1957] 1 WLR 165, C-MAC.
[144] Ibid.
[145] (1985) 82 Cr App R 69, CA.
[146] [1972] 1 WLR 118, CA.
[147] *R v Godden-Wood* (2001) Crim LR 810, CA.

**30.149**   It is therefore submitted that authorities which stress the need for the prosecution to prove that the defendant intended the gift to operate on the mind of the recipient[148] must be confined in their effect to cases where the prosecution on the facts allege acceptance/offering of 'any gift or consideration *as an inducement*' rather than 'any gift or consideration *as a reward*'.

### *'In relation to his principal's affairs'*

**30.150**   These words have been construed widely by the criminal courts. A person who receives corrupt payment in respect of work which he carries out in connection with his duties to a professional body, club, or trade union as well as in connection with his principal's affairs, will nevertheless be liable under s 1.[149] Corrupt commission payments which an agent receives through his position vis-à-vis his principal are inevitably caught by the Act, even if the work for which the commission is to be paid is not work related to a duty owed by him to his principal.[150]

### *Presumption of corruption in respect of contracts obtained from public bodies*

**30.151**   By the Prevention of Corruption Act 1916, s 2:

> Where in any proceedings against a person for an offence under the *Prevention of Corruption Act* 1906, or the Public Bodies Corrupt Practices Act 1889, it is proved that any money, gift, or other consideration has been paid or given to or received by a person in the employment of Her Majesty or any Government Department or a public body[151] by or from a person, or agent of a person, holding or seeking to obtain a contract from Her Majesty or any Government Department or public body, the money gift, or consideration shall be deemed to have been paid or given or received corruptly as such inducement or reward as is mentioned in such Act unless the contrary is proved.

**30.152**   The effect of this provision is to reverse the burden of proof on a charge of corruption whenever a payment or gift is made to a public servant by an individual or company which holds or is seeking to obtain a contract from that servant's body or department. The onus will then be on the defendant to prove, on the balance of probabilities, that he did not act corruptly.

---

[148]  *R v Smith* [1960] 2 QB 423, CA; *R v Harvey* [1999] Crim LR 70, CA.

[149]  *Morgan v DPP* [1970] 3 All ER 1053, CA.

[150]  *R v Dickinson and De Rable* (1949) 33 Cr App R 5, CA.

[151]  'Public body' now includes foreign public bodies: Anti-Terrorism Crime and Security Act 2001, s 108(4). However, s 110 of the 2001 Act prevents s 2 of the 1916 Act from applying to conduct which is only justiciable in the UK by reason of Part 12 of the 2001 Act. Thus, in the event of a prosecution for an extra-territorial offence of corruption of a public official, the presumption of corruption will not apply.

### (3) Extra-territorial effect for UK nationals and UK incorporated bodies

More generally, Part 12 of the Anti-Terrorism Crime and Security Act 2001[152] **30.153**
extends jurisdiction in respect of the offence of corruption to cover the conduct of
all nationals of the United Kingdom and bodies incorporated under the law of any
part of the United Kingdom, wherever in the world the conduct takes place. This
extension applies to all conduct which would amount to an offence of corruption
if it had been committed within the United Kingdom, whether under the common law, the 1889, or 1906 Act. The effect of these provisions is to make it an
offence for a British director resident overseas to bribe a foreign agent in respect of
a business transaction no part of which is to take place within this jurisdiction,
and which is wholly unconnected with the interests of any person situated within
the United Kingdom.

This obviously has very serious implications for company directors working **30.154**
abroad in very different business environments from our own, where 'commission
payments' and small bribes may be an accepted, or indeed the only way of conducting business. Since jurisdiction over the offence was extended in 2001, reports
have circulated of SFO investigations into several different cases of suspected corruption overseas, including in Iraq, but no charges have been brought. In practice,
prosecutions in respect of conduct which takes place wholly outside the United
Kingdom are likely to be rare. As Robert Wardle, Director of the SFO said in
2005, 'It is of course one thing to pass an Act criminalising a type of conduct. It is
another thing to detect, investigate and finally prosecute the case.'[153] It is highly
unlikely that the SFO, or any other domestic authority would consider devoting
the resources necessary to lead an investigation into events overseas unless a significant sum of money was involved[154] and/or the national interest was in some
way affected.[155] The SFO has, however, expressed its commitment to make the
prevention of international corruption a priority and has formed a small specialist
team for this purpose.[156] It has also stressed its ability and willingness to provide

---

[152] See in particular s 109.
[153] Robert Wardle at the Risk Advisory Group Conference on Tuesday 3 May 2005 at 3.00 pm,
The Lincoln Centre, 8 Lincoln's Inn Fields, WC2A 3ED.
[154] The SFO do not generally accept cases for investigation unless the sum of money involved is
at least £1 million.
[155] The 2001 Act is the UK equivalent of the much older US Foreign Corrupt Practices Act
(FCPA). The FCPA has historically been pursued by US prosecutors with a degree of vigour not yet
demonstrated on this side of the Atlantic. It may be that, as with other forms of financial and commercial crime, a UK national facing an international anti-corruption investigation engaging both
the British and the American national interest will in practice have more reason to fear the prospect
of extradition to face trial in the USA, than the more remote possibility of indictment in the UK.
[156] See the SFO's Annual Report of 2004–05 and of 2005–06.

mutual legal assistance to any foreign state seeking to prosecute such offences within its own jurisdiction.[157]

## (4) Penalties

**30.155** For an offence of corruption contrary to common law, sentence is at large and there is no maximum penalty. For an offence contrary to the Prevention of Corruption Act 1906, s 1 the maximum penalty on summary conviction is 12 months' imprisonment and/or a fine; on indictment, the maximum penalty is seven years' imprisonment and/or a fine.

## G. Insider Dealing and Market Rigging

**30.156** This chapter will not be concerned with the civil or regulatory liabilities which may arise under FSMA. In particular, the FSA's powers to levy financial penalties against regulated and non-regulated persons for conduct amounting to market abuse will not be considered. However, the regulatory offence of market abuse has equivalent offences under the criminal law. Regulatory market abuse translates into the criminal offences of insider dealing and market rigging, which are discussed below.

## (1) Insider dealing

*Introduction*

**30.157** Insider dealing is currently proscribed as an offence by the Criminal Justice Act 1993 (the 1993 Act), Part V. The statutory provisions are, like their predecessors were,[158] technical and complicated. Prosecutions for the offence are relatively rare. For this reason there is no extensive body of case law upon the subject. However, what case law there is makes plain that the legislation should not be further complicated by an unduly technical or elaborate interpretation of its terms.[159] Instead, a purposive approach should be adopted, bearing in mind the mischief at which the legislation is aimed.[160]

---

[157] See Robert Wardle at the Risk Advisory Group Conference on Tuesday 3 May 2005 at 3.00 pm, The Lincoln Centre, 8 Lincoln's Inn Fields, WC2A 3ED; SFO's Annual Report 2005–06.

[158] ie the Company Securities (Insider Dealing) Act 1985 and the Companies Act 1980, ss 68–73. The latter was based upon the White Paper, The Conduct of Company Directors, Cmnd. 7037 (1977).

[159] *Attorney-General's Reference (No 1 of 1988)* [1989] AC 971, HL; *R v Staines and Morrisey* [1997] 2 Cr App R 426, 438, CA. Both cases were decided in relation to the 1985 Act. It is submitted that they apply equally to the modern statute.

[160] *Attorney-General's Reference (No 1 of 1988)* [1989] AC 971, HL; *R v Staines and Morrisey* [1997] 2 Cr App R 426, CA.

The mischief at which the legislation is aimed may at least be simply stated. **30.158**
A 1977 White Paper, *The Conduct of Company Directors*,[161] commented that there
was a need for laws which would prevent situations in which a person bought and
sold securities when he, but not the other party to the transaction, was in possession of confidential information which affected the value of to be placed upon
them. Lord Lowry, in *Attorney-General's Reference (No 1 of 1988)*,[162] put the matter even more succinctly: 'The mischief [at which the legislation is aimed] consists
of dealing in securities while in possession of the confidential information.'[163]
This purpose must be borne in mind when reading the provisions of the current
statute.[164]

*Offence creating provision*

The main offence-creating provision of Part V of the 1993 Act is s 52. It proscribes **30.159**
three forms of insider dealing: (i) where a person who has information as an insider
himself deals in securities; (ii) where he encourages another to deal; and (iii) where
he discloses inside information to another (other than in the proper course of his
employment).

Under the Criminal Justice Act 1993, Part V, s 52: **30.160**

 (1) An individual who has information as an insider is guilty of insider dealing if, in the
    circumstances mentioned in subsection (3), he deals in securities that are price-
    affected securities in relation to the information.
 (2) An individual who has information as an insider is also guilty of insider dealing if—
    (a) he encourages another person to deal in securities that are (whether or not that
       other knows it) price-affected securities in relation to the information, know-
       ing or having reasonable cause to believe that the dealing would take place in
       the circumstances mentioned in subsection (3); or
    (b) he discloses the information, otherwise than in the proper performance of the
       functions of his employment, office or profession to another person.
 (3) The circumstances referred to above are that the acquisition or disposal in question
    occurs on a regulated market, or that the person dealing relies on a professional
    intermediary or is himself acting as a professional intermediary.
 (4) This section has effect subject to section 53.[165]

Whichever of the three forms is charged, it is the definition of 'a person who has **30.161**
information as an insider' which is the first, essential element of the offence.

---

[161] Cmnd. 7037 (1977).
[162] [1989] AC 971, HL.
[163] At 735.
[164] For a further statement of the purpose of the legislation, see *R v Staines and Morrisey* [1997]
2 Cr App R 426, 430, CA, per Lord Bingham CJ.
[165] See below. Section 53 sets out defences to the charge.

*Person who has information as an insider*

**30.162** The definition of 'a person who has information as an insider' is provided by the 1993 Act, s 57. Within the definition, reference is made to another term of art used within Part 5 of the Act: 'inside information'. The term is itself defined in s 56 of the Act. Putting the effect of ss 56 and 57 of the Act together, a person has information as an insider if and only if:

(1) He possesses—and knows that he possesses—inside information, that is information which—

(a) relates[166] to particular securities or to a particular issuer or to particular issuers of securities and not to securities generally or to issuers of securities generally;

(b) is specific or precise;

(c) has not been made public;[167] and

(d) is price-sensitive, ie would be likely to have significant effect on the price of any securities if it were made public.[168]

(2) He has, and knows that he has, the inside information from an inside source, that is—

(a) he has it—(i) through being a director, employee or shareholder of an issuer of securities,[169] or (ii) by virtue of his employment, office or profession;[170] or

(b) the direct or indirect source of the information is a person within (a) above.[171]

**30.163** 'A person who has information as an insider' is therefore a person who possesses what he knows to be inside information, from what he knows to be an inside source. Any person who fulfils this definition is subject to the s 52 prohibition against dealing, encouraging others to deal in the securities in question, or disclosing the inside information to any other person otherwise than in the proper performance of his functions of his employment, office, or profession. Whether each

---

[166] Under s 60(4) of the 1993 Act, where an issuer of securities is a company, information shall be treated as 'relating' to the issuer not only where it is about the company, but also where it may affect the company's business.

[167] A non-exhaustive lists of instances in which information is to be treated as made public, and of matters which need not prevent information being treated as made public, are contained in s 58. The issue will be a question of fact for the jury. It is submitted that the thrust of s 58 is that whether information is made public is a function of the extent to which it is generally available.

[168] ss 57(1)(a) and 56(1) and (2).

[169] This reflects s 57(2)(a)(i) and covers people connected directly with the company—the people most literally 'inside' it.

[170] This reflects s 57(2)(a)(ii) and is apt to cover people employed outside the company itself but brought inside as professional advisors. A company's bankers, business consultants, public relations agents, accountants, and legal advisors will frequently move into the category of insiders.

[171] s 57(2)(b).

part of the definition of 'a person who has information as an insider' is fulfilled will be a matter of fact for the jury,[172] underlining again that the provisions of the Act should not be read in a technical or over-elaborate manner.

The purposive approach of the criminal courts in respect of this offence is well demonstrated by judicial interpretation of the statutory definition of 'inside information' in particular.    **30.164**

By the terms of s 56, inside information must relate to particular securities (or to a particular issuer or to particular issuers), must be specific or precise, must not have been made public and must be price-sensitive. However, the Court of Appeal has specifically declined to read into the definition of inside information the additional requirement that the information disclosed from the inside source must, in and of itself, enable the person to whom it is disclosed to identify the securities to which it relates.[173] Therefore if an accountant tells a friend socially that he is working on a bid which one of his firm's clients is proposing to make for the publicly quoted capital of a target company and his friend subsequently uses the information provided and some further research in order to discover the name target, the friend has 'information as an insider'[174] and is subject to s 52. In reaching this conclusion, the court expressly noted that the effect of the appellant's dealing fell squarely within the type of mischief the Act was intended to prohibit and interpreted the provisions of the Act accordingly.[175]    **30.165**

At first glance, it might be asked what the requirement that the defendant had the inside information from an 'inside source' adds to the elements of the offence, other than an extra level of complexity. If the information in question fulfils all the necessary requirements to constitute 'inside information'—particularly the requirement that it not be public information—is it not inevitable that it will have emanated, directly or indirectly, from an inside source? The answer is no; the requirement that the defendant must have the inside information from an inside source serves an important purpose in distinguishing between legitimate and illegitimate instances of acting on non-public, price sensitive information.    **30.166**

For example, a shareholder of a company is returning from holiday by train. He passes by the company's largest factory and sees that it is on fire.[176] The shareholder possesses inside information within the meaning of s 56. However, he does not possess the inside information from an inside source within the meaning of    **30.167**

---

[172]  *R v Staines and Morrisey* [1997] 2 Cr App R 426, 438.

[173]  *R v Staines and Morrisey* [1997] 2 Cr App R 426.

[174]  What was called 'unpublished price sensitive information' at the time of the decision in *Staines and Morrisey*.

[175]  *Staines and Morrisey* at 438.

[176]  This example is taken from the Market Conduct Manual of the FSA's Handbook (reference code MAR 1.4.8) as it was as of 1 January 2004. It does not appear in the current Handbook.

s 57: he does not have it by reason of his status as a shareholder, but by reason of his observation from the train. He is therefore not a 'person who has information as an insider' for the purpose of s 52 of the Act and he is perfectly entitled to call his broker and instruct him to sell his stock. This position can be contrasted with the position of the chief executive of the company, who is informed of the fire by an employee. The chief executive has the inside information by virtue of his directorship, and therefore from an inside source: he is subject to the prohibition of s 52 until the information is made public. The same must be said for the shareholder's broker. If the shareholder informs the broker why he wishes to sell his shares, the broker comes by the inside information by virtue of his employment, and therefore from an inside source by reason s 57(2)(a)(ii). He is therefore a person who has information as an insider and he too is subject to s 52.

*Dealing*

30.168    By s 55(1) of the 1993 Act, a person deals in securities within the terms of s 52 of the Act if he himself acquires[177] or disposes[178] of them (whether on his own behalf or as the agent of another) or if he directly or indirectly procures an acquisition or disposal of the securities by any other person.[179]

30.169    So far as the first two forms of the offence created by s 52 are concerned (dealing and encouraging another to deal), the dealing in question must take place: on a regulated market; relying on a professional intermediary; or where the offender is himself acting as a professional intermediary.[180] Private, off-market transactions fall outside the scope of the Act and may not form an allegation of insider dealing.

30.170    'Regulated market' is defined by articles 9 and 10 of the Insider Dealing (Securities and Regulated Markets) Order 1994 (SI 1994/187) to be any market which is established under the rules of an investment exchange specified in the Schedule to the Order. The list has been expanded by subsequent amendment.[181] The list of UK markets currently covered are OFEX and those markets established under the rules of: the London Stock Exchange; LIFFE Administration & Management; OMLX, the London Securities and Derivatives Exchange Limited; virt-x Exchange Limited; and CoredealMTS.

---

[177] This includes agreeing to acquire and entering into a contract which creates the security: s 55(2).

[178] This includes agreeing to dispose and bringing an end to the contract which created the security: s 55(3).

[179] The latter alternative provides for a large margin of overlap between the first two forms of the offence of insider dealing (dealing and encouraging another to deal) by making a person guilty of the first, perhaps as well as the second, whenever he 'procures' another to deal in the securities.

[180] s 52(3).

[181] ie the Insider Dealing (Securities and Regulated Markets) (Amendment) Order 1996 (SI 1996/1561); the Insider Dealing (Securities and Regulated Markets) (Amendment) Order 2000 (SI 2000/1923); the Insider Dealing (Securities and Regulated Markets) (Amendment) Order 2002 (SI 2002/1874).

'Professional intermediary' is defined by s 59 of the Act. It is apt to cover profes-  **30.171**
sional share traders and stock brokers.

*Securities to which the Act applies*

The 1993 Act, Part V applies to any security which is listed within Schedule 2 and  **30.172**
which satisfies any order made by the Treasury under s 54(1)(b). The only order
currently issued is the Insider Dealing (Securities and Regulated Markets) Order
1994 (SI 1994/187) as amended.[182] Under the terms of the Order, Part V of the
Act applies only to securities which fall within Schedule 2 if they are officially
listed in a State within the European Economic Area, or are dealt with or quoted
on a regulated market.[183]

*Defences*

The scope of the offence is undoubtedly broad but it is narrowed in its effect by  **30.173**
the availability of four general and several special defences.

The general defences to a charge of insider dealing are set out in s 53 of the Act.  **30.174**
The effect of the section is as follows.

Where a person is accused of one of the first two forms of the offence (dealing or  **30.175**
encouraging another to deal) he is not guilty if he shows that:

(1) he did not at the time expect the dealing to result in a profit attributable to the
    fact that the information in question was price sensitive information in rela-
    tion to the securities; or
(2) at the time he believed on reasonable grounds that the information had been
    disclosed widely enough to ensure that none of those taking part in the deal-
    ing would be prejudiced by not having the information; or
(3) he would have done what he did even if he did not have the information.[184]

The second of these general defences allows for a not-guilty verdict where the  **30.176**
inside information, although not public, was nevertheless reasonably believed by
the defendant to have been sufficiently widely known to prevent that particular
deal being conducted on an unfair basis. The question of drawing the line between
cases which fall inside and outside this defence will be an issue of fact for the jury
(except, perhaps, in an extreme case, for example where on the Crown's own evidence, the defendant trader was dealing on his own account with a professional
colleague whom he reasonably believed to possess the same information as
himself).

---

[182] See immediately preceding footnote.
[183] See paragraph 30.170 above.
[184] See subss 53(1) and (2).

**30.177**   The third of the general defences represents a significant narrowing of the offence. In previous statutory incarnations of insider dealing, as now, there was also no requirement for the Crown to prove causation as part of its case, but unlike the present position, it was no defence to prove that a defendant would have done exactly as he did even had he not had the information.[185]

**30.178**   Where a person is accused of the third type of insider dealing (committed by disclosure of information held as an insider), he is not guilty if he shows that:

(1)   he did not at the time expect any person, because of the disclosure, to deal in securities on a regulated market or relying on or as a professional intermediary;

(2)   as per the first general defence set out in paragraph 30.175 above, although he did have such an expectation, he did not at the time expect the dealing to result in a profit attributable to the fact that the information in question was price-sensitive information in relation to the securities.

**30.179**   The special defences available on a charge of insider dealing are contained in Schedule 1 of the 1993 Act and are subject to amendment by order of the Treasury.[186] At present, the special defences designated by Schedule 1 of the Act provide that an individual is not guilty of an offence of insider dealing if he shows that:

(1)   he acted in good faith in the course of his business as a market maker or his employment in the business of a market maker;[187] or

(2)   the information which he had was market information[188] and either—

    (a)   it was reasonable for an individual in his position to have acted as he did despite having that information as an insider at the time;[189] or

    (b)   that he acted in connection with and with a view to accomplishing an acquisition or disposal (or a series of such) which was under consideration or subject to negotiation, and the market information in question arose directly out of his involvement in the acquisition or disposal (or series of such);[190] or

---

[185]   *Attorney-General's Reference (No 1 of 1988)* [1989] AC 971, HL.

[186]   subss 53(4) and (5). Sch 1 has to date been amended by the Financial Services and Markets Act 2000 (Consequential Amendments and Repeals) Order 2001 (SI 2001/3649), art 341, and by the Financial Services and Markets Act 2000 (Market Abuse) Regulations 2005 (SI 2005/381), reg 3.

[187]   Sch 1, art 1. Simply put, a market maker is a person who holds himself as willing to buy and sell shares and is recognized as doing so under the rules of the market.

[188]   Broadly speaking, market information is information about share trading (rather than information about the company which issued its shares or its business). Market information is defined in Sch 1, art 4 as information consisting of one or more facts such as: particular securities have been or are to be acquired; the price (or range of prices) at which they have been or are to be acquired; the identity of any person involved or likely to be involved in the acquisition.

[189]   Sch 1, art 2.

[190]   Sch 1, art 3.

(3) he acted in conformity with the price stabilization rules[191] or with the relevant provisions of Commission Regulation (EC) No 2273/2003.

There is no decided case upon whether the general or special defences provided by the Act are for the defendant to prove on a balance of probabilities, or for the prosecution to disprove (if raised by the defence) to the usual criminal standard. However, similar, previous statutory provisions[192] have been held to reverse the burden, requiring the defendant to prove his defence to the civil standard.[193] This obviously provides the prosecutor with a good starting point from which to argue that, under the 1993 Act, the burden must likewise lie with the defence. However, this will not automatically follow. Previous statutory provisions were interpreted before the enactment of the Human Rights Act 1998, which requires statutes wherever possible to be interpreted compatibly with the European Convention on Human Rights Article 6(2) presumption of innocence.[194] The arguments against construing a reversed burden in relation to defences under the 1993 Act would include the fact that the defences in question are not limited to straightforward, technical questions of status, exemption, or licence, but include concepts such as good faith and reasonableness. Ordinarily, where good faith is relevant, if there is a possibility that the defendant did possess it, he ought to be entitled to be acquitted on that basis (especially where the offence is a serious one, carrying a maximum penalty of a lengthy prison sentence). **30.180**

A further limitation on the application of s 52 is provided by s 63 of the 1993 Act. Section 52 does not apply to anything done by an individual acting on behalf of a public sector body in pursuit of monetary policies or policies in respect to exchange rates or the management of public debt or foreign exchange reserves. Unlike the general and special defences mentioned above, if this issue is raised by the defence, the prosecution will bear the burden of disproving the suggestion to the criminal standard. **30.181**

### Jurisdiction

The territorial scope of the offence is clearly set out in s 62. Broadly, it is confined to dealing which is conducted within the United Kingdom or in relation to a market regulated in the United Kingdom, and to disclosure of information which is made or received within the United Kingdom. **30.182**

---

[191] Made under FSMA, s 144(1).
[192] ie Company Securities (Insider Dealing) Act 1985, s 3(1).
[193] *R v Cross* (1990) 91 Cr App R 115, CA.
[194] For an example of a case in which, post-Human Rights Act 1998, a statutory provision has been held *not* to reverse the burden of proof (despite the use of the words, 'It is a defence for a person charged to prove that . . .') see *R v Carass* [2002] 1 WLR 1714, CA.

*Penalties*

**30.183** By s 61(1) the maximum penalty for insider dealing on summary conviction at the magistrates' court is a fine not exceeding the statutory maximum, or imprisonment for a term of six months, or both. On conviction on indictment before the Crown Court, a defendant is liable to an unlimited fine or imprisonment for a term not exceeding seven years, or both.

**30.184** An offence of insider dealing committed by a market professional, or involving profit or loss on any sort of scale, is likely to be met by a substantial term of immediate imprisonment.[195]

### (2) Market rigging

*Introduction*

**30.185** Market rigging is currently prohibited by FSMA, s 397, which replaced the provisions formally found in the Financial Services Act 1986, ss 47 and 133, and the Banking Act 1987, s 35. The earliest incarnation of similar offences was contained in the Prevention of Fraud (Investments) Act 1953.

*Offence-creating provision*

**30.186** Section 397 creates two different offences with a degree of overlap. The first type of offence, contained in subss (1) and (2), covers misleading *statements* and dishonest concealments in relation to investments. Conduct which may be charged under this part of the section includes a situation in which a director makes an unduly favourable profit forecast, realizing that this may prevent existing shareholders from disposing of their stock in the company, or where an investor lies about the cash balance of a company at a time when he is seeking to dispose of his shares. The second type of offence, contained in subs 397(3), covers misleading *practices*, such as market manipulation by the conduct of artificial trades, designed to create the impression that there is more interest in a particular stock than there truly is.

*Misleading statements*

**30.187** There are three elements which the prosecution must prove to make out an offence of making a misleading statement in relation to an investment. The prosecution must prove that the defendant:

(1) made a misleading statement or concealed any material facts;

---

[195] *R v Butt* [2006] EWCA 137 (Crim); *R v Spearman*, unreported, Southwark CC, 4 June 2004. Spearman received 30 months' imprisonment for insider dealing. He and his wife had received inside information from a man who worked as a proof-reader for a company which printed confidential documentation in relation to company mergers and acquisitions. He had invested over £2 million in various different stocks and had made an illicit profit in excess of £200,000.

(2) with the requisite state of mind in relation to either the accuracy of the statement or the fact of the concealment respectively;

(3) intended, or was reckless as to whether, the statement/concealment would have the effect of inducing any person to act or refrain from acting in a way specified in subs (2).

Subsection 397(1) applies to any person who makes 'a statement, promise or **30.188** forecast'.[196] These terms clearly cover all formal announcements made about a company or its business by its officers. For example, public profit warnings, company reports and accounts, as well as statements made by directors in meetings with individuals or groups of investors will all fall well within the terms of the offence. However, the subsection is wide enough to embrace in addition all private remarks made about a particular investment by individual shareholders, investors, traders, or any other person.

The statement, promise of forecast must be 'misleading, false or deceptive in a **30.189** material particular' in order to be caught by subs (1). Where a series of statements are made, it would be contrary to common sense to examine each in isolation to establish whether it is misleading. It is perfectly permissible to view all of the statements together in order to determine the overall effect.[197]

Subsection (1) also applies to a person who conceals any material facts,[198] whether **30.190** in connection with a statement promise of forecast or not.[199] It is submitted that this part of the subsection is just as wide in its reach as the remainder of the provision; it is not restricted in its scope to directors who have positive duties in relation to the disclosure of matters concerning a company's business.

Where the prosecution relies upon a positive statement, promise, or forecast, it **30.191** must prove that the defendant, at the time he made the statement, knew that it was misleading, false, or deceptive in a material particular,[200] or that he was reckless to the same.[201] Knowledge means actual knowledge, as opposed to suspicion or even belief, but evidence that a person 'wilfully shut his eyes to the truth' may be treated as evidence that in fact he knew what he was attempting to

---

[196] subs (1)(a) and (b).

[197] *Aaron's Reefs Ltd v Twiss* [1986] AC 273, HL.

[198] 'Facts' includes a person's present intention: *R v Central Criminal Court, ex p Young* [2002] 2 Cr App R 12, DC, decided in relation to the 1986 Act, s 47. Therefore a person who dishonestly conceals his own plan to take a particular position in relation to a stock falls within the terms of subs (1), creating a significant degree of overlap between this offence and the offence under subs (3), as to which see below from paragraph 30.198.

[199] subs (1)(c).

[200] subs (1)(a).

[201] subs (1)(c).

ignore.[202] Recklessness in this context has been held to mean a 'rash statement . . . with no real basis of fact to support it and not caring whether it was true or false': *R v Page*.[203] This case was decided in relation to the Financial Services Act 1986, and before the decision of the House of Lords in *R v G*,[204] in which various definitions of recklessness persisting in the criminal law were considered and standardized. *Page* was not considered in the opinions of their Lordships, neither was it cited in argument. An application of *R v G* to FSMA, s 397 would result in the test for recklessness in this part of the section being 'that the defendant knew of the risk that the statement was misleading (false or deceptive)'. However, since this decision of the House of Lords there has been first instance precedent of the application of *Page* to s 397.[205] It is submitted that *Page* provides a peculiarly culpable form of recklessness, and therefore a greater hurdle to the prosecution in proving the elements of its case.

30.192  Dishonesty is not an essential element of this form of the offence, although of course it may be present, particularly where the statement is made with knowledge as to its false nature. However, even a person who recklessly makes a false statement might in some circumstances also act dishonestly,[206] for example if he deliberately gives the impression that he has carefully verified the accuracy of what he says.

30.193  Where the prosecution relies on the concealment of material facts in order to prove the charge, then it is obliged to prove that the defendant acted dishonestly.[207] Dishonesty is an issue of fact upon which no specific direction is usually given by a trial judge; where direction is required, it is the *Ghosh* test which applies.[208]

30.194  By subs 397(2), a person who makes the misleading statement or dishonestly conceals the material fact is guilty of an offence only if he thereby intends to induce, or is reckless as to whether he may induce, another person to:

(1)  enter into, offer to enter into, or refrain from entering or offering to enter into a relevant agreement,[209] (eg an agreement to buy or sell shares or stock, or any derivative product, in the share capital of a company[210]); or

---

[202]  *Warner v Metropolitan Police Commissioner* [1969] 2 AC 256, 279, HL, per Lord Reid. See also re 'knowingly' (in the context of fraudulent trading) *Re Bank of Credit and Commerce International SA (No 15)* [2004] 2 BCLC 479, [2005] 2 BCLC 328, CA.

[203]  [1996] Crim LR 821, CA.

[204]  [2004] 1 AC 1034, HL.

[205]  *R v Rigby, Bailey and another,* Southwark Crown Court, 2005.

[206]  subs (1)(b) specifically applies to a person who recklessly makes a misleading etc statement, promise, or forecast 'dishonestly or otherwise'.

[207]  subs (1)(b).

[208]  *R v Ghosh* [1982] QB 1053, CA; *R v Roberts (W)* (1985) 84 Cr App R 117, CA.

[209]  subs (2)(a).

[210]  subss (9) to (12) and Sch 2.

(2) exercise, or refrain from exercising, any rights conferred by a relevant investment[211] (eg shares or stock held in the share capital of a company[212]).

The person whom it is intended to induce or who may be induced by the statement/concealment need not be the same person to whom the misleading statement was made, or from whom the material fact was concealed.[213] Further, it is not necessary for the inducement to be effective in order for the offence to be made out. **30.195**

In relation to the possibility of inducement, it is submitted that the test of recklessness which should be applied is that contained in *R v G*.[214] A person is reckless for the purpose of subs (2) if he is aware of a risk of inducement and unreasonably goes on to take that risk by making the misleading statement/concealing the material facts. **30.196**

Where a person is charged with having made a statement, promise, or forecast which he knew to be misleading, false, or deceptive in a material particular (but not where the charge is one of recklessly making a statement or dishonestly concealing material facts), subs 397(4) provides three specific defences. It is a defence for the accused to show that the defendant acted in conformity with: price stabilizing rules; control of information rules; or the relevant provisions of Commission Regulation (EC) No 2273/2003. These defences are similar in their effect to one of the special defences to a charge of insider dealing provided by the Criminal Justice Act 2003, Schedule 1.[215] **30.197**

*Misleading practices*

The second offence created by s 397[216] applies to a person who does any act, or engages in any course of conduct, which creates a false or misleading impression as to the market in or the price of value of any relevant investments.[217] Conduct falling within the terms of this offence would include a major shareholder of a company who wishes to sell his entire holding, but who first contrives a number of small transactions between himself and an anonymous associate, in order to give the impression that there is interest in the stock, thereby raising its value before disposing of the bulk of his shares. **30.198**

---

[211] subs (2)(b).
[212] subss (10) to (12) and Sch 2.
[213] subs (2).
[214] [2004] 1 AC 1034, HL.
[215] Paragraph 30.179 above.
[216] subs (3).
[217] As to the meaning of 'relevant investment', see paragraph 30.194 above and the footnotes to that paragraph.

**30.199**  Unlike the offence of making a misleading statement, this offence may not be committed recklessly. It is incumbent on the prosecution to prove that the defendant intended to:

(1) create the false or misleading impression; and

(2) thereby induce another person to acquire, dispose of, subscribe for, or underwrite the relevant investments, or from exercising any rights conferred by those investments, or to refrain from doing any of the above.

**30.200**  Subsection 397(5) purports to create four defences to a charge under subs 397(3). However, it is submitted that only three of these operate as effective defences to the charge. The first paragraph of subs (5) provides that it is a defence for a person to show that he reasonably believed his conduct would not create an impression that was false or misleading. Since the elements of the offence under subs (3) require the defendant to have acted for the purpose of giving this very impression, this defence is counter-intuitive, if not entirely otiose. The only way to reconcile the two provisions would be to hold that a person who acts with the intention of misleading is not guilty of an offence if he nevertheless believes on reasonable grounds that he will be frustrated in his attempt. Such a direction would however be absurd and would confuse the concept of intention with the ideas of wish and desire, in a manner expressly prohibited by long-established principles of the criminal law.[218] It is submitted that the correct view is: evidence that a person reasonably believed that his conduct would be not misleading is evidence that he had no intention to mislead; intention remains an element of the offence which must be proved to the criminal standard by the prosecution, with no burden on the defence to disprove this allegation.

**30.201**  The three effective paragraphs of subs (5) provide defences that are similar in terms to the defences to an offence under subss 397(1) and (2) provided by subs (4):[219] they concern price stabilization, the control of information rules, and the provisions of Commission Regulation (EC) No 2273/2003.

*Jurisdiction*

**30.202**  The jurisdictional extent of offences under subss 397(1) and (2) and offences under subs 397(3) is governed by subss (6) and (7) respectively. Under the former, the statement or concealment in question, or the person whom it is intended to induce or may be induced, or the formation of the relevant agreement, must take place/be in the United Kingdom. For the false practices offence, either the defendant's conduct or the false or misleading impression created must take place in the United Kingdom.

---

[218] *R v Woollin* [1999] 1 AC 82, HL.

[219] Paragraph 30.197 above.

*Penalties*

The maximum penalty for market rigging is the same as for insider dealing. By **30.203** subs 397(8), a person convicted of any offence under that section is liable on summary conviction in the magistrates' court to a fine not exceeding the statutory maximum or imprisonment for a term not exceeding six months, or to both. On conviction on indictment before the Crown Court, he is liable to a fine or imprisonment for a term not exceeding seven years or both. For discussion of the appropriate penalty in a case where a company directors had recklessly made misleading statements see paragraph 30.191 above.[220]

## H. Companies Act Offences

### (1) Introduction

Like its predecessors, the 2006 Act contains a raft of criminal sanctions in respect **30.204** of misconduct of diverse kinds and orders of seriousness. The 2006 Act contains provisions which enact (or re-enact) criminal liabilities for company directors in respect of: (i) record keeping, (ii) accounting and auditors, (iii) disclosure of interests, (iv) wrongful disclosure of information, (v) issuing of shares, (vi) the company's acquisition of its own shares, and (vii) removal from the register.[221]

The 2006 Act also contains the principal provision in English law against fraudu- **30.205** lent trading. This offence will be discussed separately below.

### (2) Classification

*Three classes*

The wide variety of criminal provisions contained in the 2006 Act may be clas- **30.206** sified into three groups: those which create serious offences, which are triable on indictment; those which create intermediate offences, which are triable only summarily but which carry a maximum penalty of a level 5 fine;[222] and quasi-regulatory offences, which are triable only summarily and which carry a maximum penalty of a level 2 or 3 fine only.

In addition to the offences created by the Act itself, the Act contains provision for **30.207** the creation of Corporate Governance Regulations by the Secretary of State.[223]

---

[220] *R v Rigby and another* [2005] EWCA 3487 (Crim).
[221] Note that loans to directors and connected persons ceased to be criminal offences on 1 October 2007, when ss 330–347 of the 1985 Act were repealed by the Companies Act 2006 Commencement Order No 3, art 8 and Schedule 2.
[222] ie level 5 on the standard scale under the Criminal Justice Act 1982.
[223] s 1273.

These regulations may create offences, including criminal offences, but these may only be tried summarily and the maximum penalty may not exceed the statutory maximum fine.[224]

**30.208** By the Criminal Justice Act 1982, s 37, the standard scale of maximum fines for summary offences is:

| Level on the scale | Amount of fine |
| --- | --- |
| 1 | £200 |
| 2 | £500 |
| 3 | £1,000 |
| 4 | £2,500 |
| 5 | £5,000 |

**30.209** Each class of offence contained within the 2006 Act is distinguished not only by the maximum sentence in terms of imprisonment or fine, but by the consequences which flow with regard to the Company Directors Disqualification Act 1986 (CDDA) (as to which see Section J below). Only offences in the first class of serious offences will give rise on conviction to the broad discretion to disqualify an individual from acting as a director (for up to 15 years if on indictment, five years summarily) under the CDDA, s 2. However, conviction of more than three intermediate or quasi-regulatory offences in a five-year period may also give the Magistrates' Court power to disqualify under the CDDA, s 5.[225]

**30.210** A final distinction between the quasi-regulatory offences and the more serious offences contained in the Act is that it may be open to a prosecutor to argue that quasi-regulatory offences (punishable with a maximum of a £1,000 fine) are not criminal offences within the meaning of Article 6 of the European Convention on Human Rights. If such an argument were upheld in respect of any offence, the primary effect would be that statements made under compulsion (further to the exercise of a compulsory information requirement under this Act or any other statute) prima facie would be admissible in order to prove that offence against the maker of the statement.[226]

### (3) Serious offences under the Companies Act 2006

**30.211** The serious offences contained in the 2006 Act, together with the serious offences under the 1985 Act that remain in force until 1 October 2009 (*excluding* offences which can be committed only by individuals other than directors, eg auditors) are

---

[224] s 1273(4).
[225] Section J below.
[226] On this topic, see further paragraph 25.35 *et seq* above.

summarized in Table 1 in Appendix 2 below. Although all of the offences are triable on indictment, the vast majority do not carry a sentence of imprisonment and may only be dealt with by way of fine.

### Knowledge and recklessness

Some of the serious offences under the 2006 Act refer to concepts of knowledge **30.212** or recklessness. For a discussion of these concepts, see paragraph 30.191 above.

### Misleading, false, or deceptive

Comment on these matters is at paragraph 30.189 above. **30.213**

### Financial assistance to acquire public company's own shares

It is an offence contrary to the 1985 Act, s 151 to contravene the prohibition **30.214** against a company (or its subsidiary) giving financial assistance directly or indirectly to a person who is acquiring or proposing to acquire shares in that company, for the purpose of the acquisition before or at the same time the acquisition takes place. On 1 October 2009 these provisions are to be replaced by the 2006 Act, ss 678–680, which only apply to public companies. Note that the 2006 Act, s 680 (like the 1985 Act, s 151(3)) has the effect of making individual directors criminally liable for a default of these provisions, on pain of imprisonment.

The phrase 'financial assistance' in the 1985 Act, ss 151 and 152 (and also the **30.215** 2006 Act, ss 677–680) does not have a technical meaning; instead the court identifies the commercial realities of the transaction, bearing in mind that the purpose of the prohibition is to prevent the resources of the target company and its subsidiaries being used directly or indirectly to assist the purchaser to make the acquisition to the possible prejudice of the creditors of the target or its group or the remaining shareholders.[227] It is not however necessarily detrimental to the target or its group.[228] Thus there is financial assistance where the target company pays an excessive price for an asset and the money is used to buy shares in the target;[229] where a company agrees to pay consultancy services to its shareholder directors to induce two of them to sell their shares to the third for nominal amounts;[230] or where a subsidiary pays for accountants' due diligence fees in connection with the acquisition of its parent's shares.[231] On the other hand, assistance must amount

---

[227] *Chaston v SWP Group Ltd* [2003] 1 BCLC 675, CA at paras 31, 32 per Arden LJ; *MT Realisations Ltd v Digital Equipment Co Ltd* [2003] 2 BCLC 117, CA, at para 28.

[228] *Chaston v SWP Group Ltd* [2003] 1 BCLC 675, CA at paras 38–40 per Arden LJ; *MT Realisations Ltd v Digital Equipment Co Ltd* [2003] 2 BCLC 117, CA, at para 32 per Mummery LJ.

[229] *Belmont Finance Corporation Ltd v Williams Furniture Ltd (No 2)* [1980] 1 All ER 393, CA, a case on the 1948 Act, s 54.

[230] *Macpherson v European Strategic Bureau Ltd* [2000] 2 BCLC 683, CA.

[231] *Chaston v SWP Group Ltd* [2003] 1 BCLC 675, CA.

to financial help of some kind, not simply the short circuiting of process for the sake of convenience.[232] There is further discussion of these issues in Chapter 24, Section C(5).

**30.216**  Note that it is not *in itself* a defence to a charge under s 680 for a director to have acted in the best interests of the company. Motive (to benefit the company) must always be distinguished from purpose (acquisition of company shares): see *Chaston* above. However, the 2006 Act, subss 678(4) and 679(4) (and the 1985 Act, s 151) provide a defence to a charge under these provisions where the assistance is given in good faith in the interests of the company and the company's principal purpose in giving assistance was not to reduce or discharge any liability incurred by a person for the purpose of the acquisition of shares; or the reduction or discharge of any such liability was only an incidental part of some larger purpose of the company.

**30.217**  Note also that the 2006 Act, ss 681 and 682 (and under the 1985 Act, subss 153(3)–(5) and 154(1) and (2)) contain a number of unconditional and conditional exceptions to the prohibition on financial assistance. The unconditional exceptions include: dividends lawfully made; distribution in the course of winding up; allotment of bonus shares; a reduction of capital under Chapter 10 of Part 17; a redemption of shares under Chapter 3 or a purchase of shares under Chapter 3 of Part 18. The conditional exceptions include transactions where: the company lends money as part of its ordinary business; the company provides financial assistance for the purposes of an employees' share scheme, in good faith in the interests of the company or its holding company.

### (4) Fraudulent trading

**30.218**  By far the most serious offence under the 2006 Act is fraudulent trading. It is the only offence under the Act which carries a sentence of imprisonment of more than two years, the maximum penalty being 10 years' imprisonment. This is an increase from seven years' imprisonment, which was the maximum penalty for the equivalent offence under the 1985 Act, s 458. For the civil aspects of fraudulent trading under the Insolvency Act, s 213, see Chapter 29, Section I(2).

**30.219**  The 2006 Act, subss 993(1) and (2) of the 2006 Act provide:

(1)  If any business of a company is carried on with intent to defraud creditors of the company or creditors of any other person, or for any fraudulent purpose, every person who is knowingly a party to the carrying on of the business in that manner commits an offence.

---

[232]  *M T Realisations Ltd v Digital Equipment Co Ltd* [2003] 2 BCLC 117, CA.

(2) This applies whether or not the company has been, or is in the course of being, wound up.

This provision is identical to the 1985 Act, s 458. Therefore, although the cases **30.220** cited below pertain to the old s 458, they are equally relevant to the offence in its new statutory form. The section creates two different offences: carrying on a business with intent to defraud creditors; carrying on a business for any other fraudulent purpose.[233]

### Business carried on

Business may be 'carried on' even where it has ceased all trading activities, with the **30.221** debt collection and the payment of creditors.[234] In addition, one large transaction may constitute the carrying on of business,[235] although the section is not aimed at individual transactions.

### Knowingly party to the carrying on of the business

It was said by Lord Lane CJ in *R v Grantham*[236] that the section is intended to **30.222** cover those who are 'running the business', and that 'party to the carrying on of the business' must therefore be interpreted to mean those people exercising control or management. It is submitted that the effect of this is to place a different meaning on the word 'party' in this section than is to be found elsewhere in the criminal law (where party means nothing more than an active participant, rather than someone in control).[237]

A financial adviser does not become party to the carrying on of the business by **30.223** failing to advise the directors that the company is insolvent and should cease trading.[238] (It is submitted that he would be unlikely to become a party, even if the word was interpreted as it normally is in the context of the criminal law.)[239]

A problem with Lord Lane CJ's interpretation of the provision may arise when **30.224** one considers the position of a person who is not responsible for or in any way involved in the management or running of the company or its business but who nevertheless knowingly participates in the fraudulent acts themselves. The view has been expressed that such a person should be, and is, covered by the terms of the section.[240]

---

[233] *R v Inman* [1967] 1 QB 140.
[234] *Re Sarflax Ltd* [1979] Ch 140.
[235] *Re Gerald Cooper Chemicals* [1978] Ch 262.
[236] [1984] QB 675, CA. His words were later approved in *R v Miles* [1992] Crim L R 657, CA.
[237] Section A of this chapter.
[238] *Re Maidstone Building Provisions Ltd* [1971] 1 WLR 1085.
[239] Section A of this chapter.
[240] *Re Augustus Barnett & Sons Ltd* [1986] BCLC 170 per Hoffmann J.

*With intent to defraud creditors*

**30.225**  Where the prosecution relies on proving an intention to defraud creditors (as opposed to some other fraudulent purpose) it is necessary to prove intent to defraud creditors in general. Therefore evidence that, for a short period, one creditor was in fact defrauded may be insufficient to make out the offence.[241] In addition, the fraud must be aimed at actual, rather than potential creditors.[242] (In contrast, where the prosecution alleges 'any other fraudulent purpose', potential creditors may suffice.[243])

**30.226**  The offence requires proof of dishonesty[244] in the *Ghosh* sense.[245] Where the prosecution alleges an intention to defraud creditors, the dishonesty must have been directed towards the creditors.[246]

**30.227**  In relation to 'intent to defraud' and in relation to fraudulent purpose in general, see Section C of this chapter.

*Sentencing*

**30.228**  Doubtless because fraudulent trading always involves some form of breach of trust, under the 1985 Act, quite naturally many practitioners and judges took the view that *R v Clark*[247] (which sets tariff sentences for offences of theft committed in breach of trust, according to the value of the theft) was an appropriate guide to sentencing in fraudulent trading cases (substituting the value of the theft with the outstanding amount owed to creditors). However, there then came clear guidance from the Court of Appeal that this was not the correct approach: offences of fraudulent trading should be seen as less serious than offences of theft; the tariff figures contained in *Clark* should not be applied to fraudulent trading without adjustment downwards.[248] It is submitted that this guidance will need to be reviewed in light of the increase in the maximum penalty for fraudulent trading from seven years (which was in line with the maximum penalty for theft) to one of 10 years (in line with the maximum penalty for conspiracy to defraud and the new substantive fraud offences under the Fraud Act 2006).

### (5)  Intermediate and quasi-regulatory offences

**30.229**  The summary only offences contained in the Act (other than those which can be committed only by individuals other than directors, eg auditors) are set out in

---

[241]  *Morphitis v Bercansoni* [2003] Ch 552.
[242]  *R v Inman* [1967] 1 QB 140
[243]  *R v Kemp* [1988] 1 QB 645
[244]  *R v Cox and Hodges* (1982) 75 Cr App R 291.
[245]  Paragraph 30.60 above.
[246]  *R v Smith* [1996] 2 Cr App R 1.
[247]  [1998] Cr App R 137, CA.
[248]  *R v Gibson* [1999] 2 Cr App R(S) 52.

Table 2 of Appendix 2, along with the intermediate and quasi-regulatory offences under the 1985 Act that remain in force until 1 October 2009.

# I. Insolvency Act Offences

## (1) Introduction

There is a multiplicity of offences under the Insolvency Act 1986. This section will focus on the principal criminal offences which may be committed by company directors specifically (as opposed to bankrupts).[249]

**30.230**

## (2) Directors' liabilities

Under the Insolvency Act, company directors may attract criminal liability for a very wide variety of misconduct: (i) when making a statutory declaration of a company's insolvency; (ii) in relation to a company's creditors; (iii) in relation to a moratorium; (iv) in relation to winding up and liquidation; (v) in relation to the company's administrator; (vi) in relation to record keeping.

**30.231**

Most of these offences may be committed by the company and by its officers. In relation to some offences, the Insolvency Act, s 432[250] makes special provision for the liability of company directors which is wider in ambit than the general doctrine of joint enterprise under the criminal law.

**30.232**

A helpful summary of all punishable offences under the Insolvency Act 1986, together with the mode of trial and maximum penalty attaching to each offence, can be found in Schedule 10 to the Act itself. (In addition, a summary of offences under the Insolvency Rules 1986 can be found in Schedule 5 to the Rules.)

**30.233**

## (3) Principal offences under Insolvency Act, Part IV

The Insolvency Act, Part IV contains the principal offences which may be committed by company directors before and during the liquidation of the company. The offences that relate to conduct before the winding up are: fraud in anticipation of winding up and transactions in fraud of creditors.[251] The offences that relate to conduct during the winding up are: misconduct in course of winding up, falsification of company's books, material omissions from statement relating to company's affairs, and false representations to creditors.[252] Finally s 216 makes it an offence of strict liability[253] to re-use the company's name after it has gone into

**30.234**

---

[249] Insolvency Act, Part IX deals with offences which may be committed by bankrupts.
[250] Paragraph 30.11 above.
[251] Insolvency Act, ss 206 and 207.
[252] Insolvency Act, ss 208–211.
[253] *R v Cole* [1998] 2 BCLC 234.

liquidation, except in prescribed circumstances.[254] Table 3 of Appendix 2 sets out, in more detail than the Insolvency Act, Schedule 10, the substance of the principal offences under Part IV of the Act.

**30.235** In relation to the offence of fraud in anticipation of winding up (s 206), note that where the prosecution rely on subs 1(b) (fraudulently removing company property to the value of £500 or more), 'removing' includes diverting. Therefore, where an officer of the company transfers company money to a third party for the purpose of honest transaction, but the transaction does not go ahead and the money is returned to the officer, the officer is liable under s 206(1)(b) if, at that point, he fraudulently fails to return to money to the company: see *R v Robinson*.[255] Note further that company property includes the fruit of company property, at least where that fruit is compiled by an officer of the company: *R v McCredie, R v French*.[256]

**30.236** Where misconduct in the course of winding up is charged (s 208), note that an officer of the company has a duty actively to disclose to the liquidator the company's property, books, and papers, and therefore may be criminally liable for failure to meet that obligation even where no prior request for delivery has been made: *R v McCredie, R v French*.[257]

**30.237** Several of the offences contained in Part IV of the Act are subject to provision that it is a defence for an accused 'to prove' that he had no intent to defraud. Note that these provisions do not have the effect of reversing the burden of proof; the defendant is subject only to an evidential burden to raise its lack of intent as an issue. See further: *R v Carass*.[258]

### (4) Sentence

**30.238** All of the offences set out in Table 3 are triable either way (that is, before the magistrates or before the Crown Court). With the exception of an offence under s 116 (for which the maximum penalty on indictment is two years' imprisonment, or a fine, or both) the maximum penalty for each offence on indictment is seven years' imprisonment, or a fine, or both.

**30.239** A conviction for any offence which involves fraud by a director against the company or its creditors is very likely to result in the imposition of a period of immediate custody. For example, a conviction for failing to make full and true disclosure of a company's property to the liquidator during winding up contrary to the 1986

---

[254] See Chapter 29, Section J for civil implications.
[255] [1990] BCC 656
[256] [2000] 2 BCLC 438, CA
[257] Ibid.
[258] [2002] 1 WLR 1714, CA.

Act, s 208(1)(a) has been held to warrant a sentence of nine months' imprisonment (together with an order under the Company Directors Disqualification Act 1986 of two years' disqualification).[259]

## J. The Company Directors Disqualification Act 1986

### (1) Introduction

The CDDA has three significant effects so far as the criminal law is concerned. **30.240** First, it provides for the penalty of disqualification to be imposed against individuals (whether they are currently company directors or not) on conviction of criminal offences. Secondly it enacts a further criminal offence of contravening a director's disqualification order. Thirdly, it prohibits (on pain of criminal conviction) undischarged bankrupts from acting as directors. The civil aspects of the disqualification of directors are considered in Chapter 28, Section D.

### (2) The penalty of disqualification

The CDDA, subs 1(1) provides: **30.241**

   (1) In the circumstances specified below in this Act a court may, and under section 6 shall, make against a person a disqualification order, that is to say an order that for a period specified in the order—

     (a) he shall not be a director of a company, act as a receiver of a company's property, or in any way, whether directly or indirectly, be concerned or take part in the promotion, formation or management of a company unless (in each case) he has the leave of the court, and

     (b) he shall not act as an insolvency practitioner.

A disqualification order under the CDDA prohibits the subject of the order from **30.242** acting as a director in fact. The effect of the order cannot be circumvented by the subject's acting unofficially or informally, or by acting as a director in fact but under a different title. This is ensured by the wide terms of subs 1(1)(a) itself and by the interpretation section of the statute, which defines 'director' to include anyone who occupies the position of a director, by whatever name.[260]

*Discretionary disqualification on conviction of indictable offence*

The circumstances in which a court may make a disqualification order (ie an order **30.243** described in the CDDA, s 1(1)) are defined by the CDDA, s 2. They exist where a person is convicted of an indictable offence (on indictment or summarily) in connection with the promotion, formation, management, or liquidation of

---

[259] *R v Bevis*, The Times, 8 February 2001, CA.
[260] CDDA, s 22(4).

a company, with the receivership of a company's property or with his being an administrative receiver of a company.[261]

**30.244** The following courts are empowered to make a discretionary disqualification order of this kind: any court having jurisdiction to wind up the company in relation to which the offence was committed; the court before which the person is convicted of the offence, or (in the case of summary conviction) any other magistrates' court in the same local justice area.[262]

**30.245** The maximum period of a discretionary disqualification of this kind is, before a magistrates' court, five years and in any other case, 15 years.[263]

**30.246** 'In connection with the promotion, formation, management' of a company has been given a wide interpretation by the courts. For example, 'management' is not limited to the internal supervision of the ordinary and legitimate affairs of a company. The correct test is whether the offence had some relevant factual connection with the company.[264] A disqualification order may therefore be made in respect of a crime committed in the course of the trading activities of a company (for example, insider trading[265] or the former offence of obtaining by deception[266]).

**30.247** The discretion given to the courts by the CDDA, s 2 is unlike the mandatory power exercised by judges of the Chancery Division (which requires an express finding that the person concerned is guilty of conduct which makes him unfit to be concerned in the management of a company). Section 2 gives the sentencing court a completely general discretion to impose an additional sanction in respect of criminal offences connected with the running of companies and no other condition precedent must be established in order to justify the exercise of the power.[267]

**30.248** The primary purpose of a disqualification order is to protect the public and therefore a period of disqualification may be appropriate in respect of accounting offences where there is no suggestion of dishonesty, but where there is a degree of carelessness or incompetence from which the public require protection.[268] However, disqualification also forms part of the punishment for a criminal offence and therefore its imposition and length must bear some correlation to the gravity of the offence in respect of which the defendant has been convicted. It is not

---

[261] CDDA, s 2(1).
[262] CDDA, s 2(2).
[263] CDDA, s 2(3).
[264] *R v Goodman* [1993] 2 All ER 789, CA.
[265] Ibid.
[266] *R v Corbin* (1984) 6 Cr App R (S) 17.
[267] *R v Young* (1990) 12 Cr App R (S) 262.
[268] *R v Victor* [1999] 2 Cr App R (S) 102.

appropriate, for example, to combine a disqualification order with a conditional discharge.[269] In addition, long disqualification orders (above 10 years) should be reserved for particularly serious cases (including cases where the director has previously been disqualified).[270]

*Disqualification for three default notices/failure to file returns etc*

Under the CDDA, s 5, on summary conviction for an offence of contravening **30.249** companies legislation requiring a return, account, or other document to be filed with the Registrar of Companies, a person who has been convicted (on indictment or summarily) within a five-year period (ending on the date of this summary conviction but including any other qualifying offences of which he is convicted on that day) of at least three default orders and offences of the same kind may be disqualified by the magistrates' court for a period of up to five years.

### (3) Contravention of a disqualification order

The CDDA, s 13 provides that it is a criminal offence (inter alia) to act in contra- **30.250** vention of a disqualification order or a disqualification undertaking.[271] The offence is punishable, on summary conviction, by imprisonment of six months, a fine up to the statutory maximum, or both. On indictment, the offence carries a maximum of two years' imprisonment, or a fine, or both.

A company is itself capable of being disqualified from acting as a director of **30.251** another company. Where such an offence is committed by a company with the consent or connivance of, or was attributable to any neglect on the part of any director, manager, etc, or any person who was purporting to act in any such capacity, he as well as the company is guilty of the offence under s 13 and is liable to be punished accordingly.[272]

Flagrant and persistent breaches of a disqualification order are likely to result in a **30.252** term of immediate imprisonment. In *R v Ashby*[273] the Court of Appeal upheld a sentence of four months' imprisonment for violating a disqualification order over the course of 3½ years and in respect of four different companies. No fraudulent enrichment could be shown, but the defendant nevertheless demonstrated a 'serious disregard of the law'.

---

[269] *R v Young*, n 267 above.
[270] *R v Millard* (1993) 15 Cr App R (S) 445. For examples of facts justifying disqualification for between eight and 10 years, see *R v Devol* (1992) 14 Cr App R (S) 407; *R v Ahmed* [1997] 2 Cr App R (S) 8. For an example of facts justifying a three-year disqualification order, see *R v Thobani* [1998] 1 Cr App R 227.
[271] As to which, see CCDA, s 1A.
[272] CDDA, s 14.
[273] [1998] 2 Cr App R (S) 37, CA.

### (4) Undischarged bankrupts

**30.253**  By section 11 of the CCDA 1986, it is a criminal offence for a person to act as a director of a company or indirectly or directly take part in or be concerned in the promotion, formation, or management of a company, without leave of the court, at a time when: (i) he is un undischarged bankrupt; or (ii) a bankruptcy restrictions order is in force in respect of him.

**30.254**  The offence is one of strict liability.[274]

---

[274]  *R v Brockley* (1993) 99 Cr App R 385, CA; *R v Doring* [2003] 1 Cr App R 9, CA.

# PART VI

# DIRECTORS OF FOREIGN COMPANIES

# 31

# DUTIES AND LIABILITIES OF DIRECTORS OF FOREIGN COMPANIES

## A. Introduction

One of the features of the increased globalization of the world economy is that **31.01** many of the companies which carry on business in England and Wales are companies incorporated abroad. Many of these companies may carry out a substantial part, or even all of their activities in England. The question which arises for the directors of such companies is to what extent they are subject to the provisions of the Companies Act 2006 and to the other aspects of English company law.

In general terms, the question raised by foreign companies is of identifying the **31.02** system of law which is to govern the company's affairs, including the duties and obligations of its directors. In the case of individuals, it is relatively straightforward to identify the country with which that individual is connected, for example, by residence. The position in relation to companies is less straightforward since companies are of course legal rather than physical persons and thus must be linked with a particular jurisdiction by legal rather than physical concepts.[1] The treatment

---

[1] For a discussion of the differing approaches to jurisdiction over companies in civil litigation, see Fawcett, 'A New Approach to Jurisdiction over Companies in Private International Law' (1988) 37 ICLQ 645.

of companies in international law is characterized by the use of a number of different concepts to identify a company with a particular legal system. These concepts include: place of incorporation, place of registered office, seat, and centre of main interests. However, there are two main ways by which a company may be tied to a particular legal system: by its place of incorporation or by the place where its seat is located.[2]

**31.03** According to the incorporation theory[3], a foreign company created in accordance with a foreign legal system and having its statutory seat (ie registered office) in a foreign state is recognized as such by the host state in which such company operates. In other words, the company is governed by the law according to which it was duly established. The rationale for the incorporation theory is the need for certainty and maximum uniformity in the choice of law.[4]

**31.04** By contrast, under the real seat (or *siège réel*) theory,[5] it is the law where the company has its 'real' seat (ie its centre of management and control) which governs the company. The advantages of the real seat theory are said to be that it enables the authorities of the country where the company is in reality based to control the company efficiently and to safeguard the protection of the company's creditors and other interested parties. Furthermore, the theory is said to secure proper regard for the economic reality and prevent fraud on, or abuse of, the law. This is because the real seat theory 'recognises the actual facts of the company's corporate life and therefore reduces the opportunity for the evasion of regulations under the law of the state where the corporate life of the company is actually centred and upon which state the company's activities might well have the greatest impact'.[6]

**31.05** English law, however, has long preferred the certainty and uniformity offered by the use of a company's place of incorporation as the decisive factor in identifying a company with a legal system and therefore follows the incorporation theory.[7]

---

[2] See generally Rameloo, *Corporations in Private International Law* (2001).

[3] Countries that apply the incorporation theory include the UK, The Netherlands, Ireland, Denmark, Switzerland, the United States, and Japan.

[4] Dr Torsten Koller, 'The English Limited Company—Ready to Invade Germany?' [2004] 11 ICCLR 334, 335.

[5] Countries that apply the real seat theory include Austria, Belgium, France, Greece, Italy, Luxembourg, Portugal, and Spain. However, within the European Union the principle of freedom of establishment has made inroads on the real seat theory. Thus, a Member State must recognize a company formed in accordance with the law of another Member State even if it would not be recognized under its own domestic conflicts of law rules: Case C-208/00 *Überseering BV v Nordic Construction Company Baumanagement GmbH (NCC)* [2002] ECR I-9919.

[6] Matthew G Clarke, 'The Conflict of Law Dimension' in *Corporate Law, The European Dimensions* (1991), 162.

[7] Cath notes that the incorporation theory is especially popular in countries with a long-standing commercial maritime tradition and where an open attitude to trade is expected to be met with reciprocity as opposed to the more mercantilist attitude adopted in other countries: Inne G F Cath,

In other words, under English choice of law rules, a company will be governed by the law of its place of incorporation. Under English law, the concepts of domicile and nationality of a company stem from the place of incorporation. Thus, a company is domiciled in England if it is incorporated in England.[8] Further, neither the nationality nor the domicile of a company depends on the nationality or domicile of its members.[9]

This approach is reflected in the definition of 'company' contained in the 2006 Act, s 1, which replaces the definition in the 1985 Act, s 735(1)(a) and (b) and (4) without material change on 1 October 2009.[10] A 'company' for the purposes of the 2006 Act is defined as a company formed and registered under the Act. This includes both companies formed and registered after the commencement of Part 1 of the 2006 Act and companies that immediately before the commencement of Part 1 of the 2006 Act were formed and registered under the Companies Act 1985 or the Companies (Northern Ireland) Order 1986 or were existing companies for the purposes of the 1985 Act or the 1986 Order.

**31.06**

Accordingly, the general rule is that the provisions of the Companies Act 2006 apply only to companies incorporated in England and Wales. Under English rules, foreign incorporation companies are regarded as being governed by the laws of their places of incorporation, irrespective of where the company's operations are in fact based. The 2006 Act, subs 1(3) states that for provisions of that Act applying to companies incorporated outside the United Kingdom, reference should be made to Part 34, ss 1044–1059, which is discussed in Section B below. In contrast the 1985 Act, subs 745(1) provides that the 1985 Act, to the extent that it remains in force, does not apply to or in relation to companies registered or incorporated in Northern Ireland or outside Great Britain, except where otherwise expressly provided.[11]

**31.07**

---

'Freedom of Establishment of Companies: a New Step Towards Completion of the Internal Market' (1986) 6 *Yearbook of European Law* 247.

[8] *Gasque v Inland Revenue Commissioners* [1940] KB 80 and *The Eksbridge* [1931] P 51.

[9] *R v Arnaud* [1946] 9 QB 806; *Jansen v Drieftein Consolidated Mines Ltd* [1902] AC 484, 497, 501, 505, HL; *Continental Tyre and Rubber Co (Great Britain) Ltd v Daimler Co Ltd* [1915] 1 KB 893, 904, CA, per Lord Reading CJ; on appeal sub nom *Daimler Co Ltd v Continental Tyre and Rubber Co (Great Britain) Ltd* [1916] 2 AC 307, 349, HL, per Lord Parmoor. Exceptionally, in times of war, an English company assumes an enemy character if it is controlled by persons resident in the enemy country or adhering to that enemy, see *Daimler Co Ltd v Continental Tyre and Rubber Co (Great Britain) Ltd* [1916] 2 AC 307, 345, HL.

[10] 2006 Act Commencement Order No 8, art 3(a).

[11] The 2006 Act applies to the whole of the United Kingdom, including Northern Ireland: Part 45 and s 1299.

## B. Directors' Functions and Responsibilities in Relation to Registration Requirements

### (1) The 1985 Act

**31.08** Section 744 defines an 'oversea company' as a company incorporated elsewhere than in Great Britain with an established place of business in Great Britain. Part XXIII, ss 690A–703R applies to oversea companies until the 2006 Act, Part 34 comes into force on 1 October 2009.[12] Part XXIII deals with registration requirements (including provisions about trading disclosure, company name, and service), delivery of accounts and reports, and winding up. For the purposes of the registration requirements in Chapter 1, ss 690A–699, 'director' includes shadow director and 'secretary' includes any person occupying the position of secretary by whatever name called.[13]

**31.09** Part XXIII establishes two distinct regimes. One regime applies to any limited company which '(a) is incorporated outside the United Kingdom and Gibraltar, and (b) has a branch in Great Britain' and gives effect to the Eleventh Company Law Directive (89/666/EEC).[14] The other regime applies to a company incorporated outside Great Britain which establishes 'a place of business in Great Britain', but is outside the former regime.[15]

**31.10** For the Eleventh Company Law Directive regime, a critical question is whether the company has a branch in Great Britain. Section 698(2)(b) provides that (except for the purposes of s 699A and Schedule 21C) 'branch' means a branch within the meaning of the Eleventh Company Law Directive, as discussed in paragraph 31.15 below. The application of the other regime turns on whether the company has established a place of business in Great Britain. In *Re Oriel Ltd*[16] Oliver LJ said that establishing a place of business

> connotes not only setting up a place of business at a specific location, but a degree of permanence or recognisability as being a location of the company's business. The concept, as it seems to me, is of some more or less permanent location, not necessarily

---

[12] The 2006 Act Commencement No 8 Order, art 3(q) brings Part 34 into force on 1 October 2009.

[13] 1985 Act, s 698(1).

[14] 1985 Act, ss 690A, 690B.

[15] 1985 Act, s 691. Section 692A and Schedule 21B contain provisions about change in the registration regime.

[16] [1985] BCLC 343, 347, CA. See also *South India Shipping Corporation Ltd v The Export-Import Bank of Korea* [1985] BCLC 163; *Cleveland Museum v Capricorn Art International SA* [1990] BCLC 546, 550; *Rakusens Ltd v Baser Ambalaj Plastick Sanayi Ticaret AC* [2002] 1 BCLC 104, CA.

owned or leased by the company, but at least associated with the company and from which habitually or with some degree of regularity its business is conducted.

A company subject to the Eleventh Company Law Directive regime must comply **31.11** with the following requirements.

(1) Schedule 21A provides that within one month of opening a branch in a part of Great Britain the company must deliver to the Registrar for registration a return in the prescribed form containing specified particulars about the company and the branch, including prescribed details of its directors and secretary and the powers of the directors to represent the company in dealings with third parties and in legal proceedings.[17] If an oversea company fails to comply with s 695A or Schedule 21, the company and every officer or agent of the company who knowingly or wilfully authorizes or permits commits an offence and is liable to be fined.[18]

(2) It must deliver accounts and reports to the Registrar under Schedule 21C, if it is a credit or financial institution to which s 699A applies, or under Schedule 21D, if it is not.[19] If the institution or company fails to comply with the relevant requirement within the time allowed it, and every person who was a director (or in the case of a credit or financial institution, a person occupying an equivalent office) at the relevant time is guilty of an offence and liable to a fine, but it is a defence for a person charged with such an offence to prove that he took all reasonable steps for securing that the requirements in question would be complied with.[20]

(3) If it is wound up or becomes subject to specified insolvency proceedings, particulars of the proceedings must be delivered to the Registrar.[21] If the company fails to comply within the time allowed, it and every person who immediately before the end of the period allowed for compliance was a director of it is guilty of an offence and liable to be fined, subject to the defence of taking all reasonable steps to secure compliance.[22]

---

[17] 1985 Act, Schedule 21A, in particular paras 1–4A. The requirement to disclose directors' residential addresses is subject to any confidentiality order made under s 723B.

[18] 1985 Act, subs 697(3).

[19] 1985 Act, ss 699A, 699AA, and 699B.

[20] 1985 Act, Schedule 21C, para 7 (for institutions required to prepare accounts under parent law) and para 15 (for institutions not required to prepare accounts under parent law) and Schedule 21D, para 5 (for companies required to make disclosure under parent law) and para 13 (for companies not required to make disclosure under parent law). For the purposes of Schedule 21C, para 15, and Schedule 21D, para 13, it is not a defence in relation to failure to deliver copies to the Registrar to prove that the documents in question were not in fact prepared as required by the relevant Schedule (paras 15(3) and 13(3)).

[21] 1985 Act, ss 703O–703Q.

[22] 1985 Act, s 703R(1) and (3).

**31.12**   Under the other regime, to which s 691 applies, the company must deliver to the Registrar within one month of establishing its place of business in Great Britain certified copies of its constitutional documents and a return including prescribed particulars of its directors and secretary and a statutory declaration as to the date when the place of business in Great Britain was established.[23] Section 692 provides for registration of altered particulars. If there is a failure to comply with ss 691, 692, or 696, the company and every officer or agent of the company who knowingly and wilfully authorized or permitted the default commits an offence and is liable to a fine.[24]

**31.13**   Whichever regime applies, the company must comply with the trading disclosure requirements of s 693 and the company is subject to regulation with respect to its name under s 694. If the company fails to comply with s 693 or contravenes a notice under subs 694(6) requiring it to cease carrying on business in Great Britain under its corporate name, it and every officer or agent of the company who knowingly authorized or permitted the default or contravention commits an offence and is liable to a fine.[25]

### (2)  The 2006 Act

**31.14**   Part 34 of the 2006 Act applies to 'overseas companies', that is companies incorporated outside the United Kingdom. Under the provisions of this Part an overseas company with a branch in the United Kingdom must register with the Registrar of Companies. The provisions of Part 34 largely implement the Eleventh Company Law Directive (89/666/EEC) and therefore those provisions and the regulations to be made under them correspond with the regime under the 1985 Act discussed in paragraph 31.10 above.[26] The Regulations may specify the persons responsible for complying with any specified requirements of the Regulations and provide for any specified contravention to be an offence, punishable by imprisonment or a fine.[27]

**31.15**   Under the provisions of Part 34, the Secretary of State is given the power to make provision by regulations requiring an overseas company to deliver to the Registrar of Companies a return in a specified form together with specified documents.[28]

---

[23] The statement as to the date of establishing the place of business in Great Britain may be given by electronic means: subss 691(3A) and (4A). Section 692 provides for registration of altered particulars.

[24] 1985 Act, subs 697(1).

[25] 1985 Act, subss 697(1) and (2).

[26] Explanatory Notes to the Companies Act 2006, paras 1326–1364.

[27] 2006 Act, s 1054.

[28] 2006 Act, s 1046(1).

The regulations must require an overseas company[29] to register the particulars if the company opens a branch in the United Kingdom.[30]

In accordance with these powers, the Secretary of State intends to promulgate **31.16** regulations and has produced draft Overseas Companies Regulations 2008. References in this text are to the draft regulations. Under Part 2 of the Regulations, an overseas company must register prescribed particulars each time it opens an establishment in the United Kingdom.[31] The prescribed particulars include particulars of the company and particulars of the establishment.

For these purposes 'establishment' means a branch within the meaning of the **31.17** Eleventh Company Law Directive (89/666/EEC) or a place of business which is not such a branch.[32] There is no definition of 'branch' in this Directive but in relation to credit institutions branch has been defined as 'a place of business which forms a legally dependent part of a credit institution and which conducts directly all or some of the operations inherent in the business of credit institutions' (Directive 77/780/EEC, Directive 89/117/EEC). In *Somafer v Saar-Ferngas* Case 33/78 [1978] ECR 2183 the ECJ ruled that:

> the concept of branch, agency or other establishment implies a place of business which has the appearance of permanency, such as the extension of a public body, has a management and is materially equipped to negotiate business with third parties so that the latter, although knowing that there will if necessary be a legal link with the parent body, the head office of which is abroad, do not have to deal directly with such parent body but may transact business at the place of business constituting the extension.[33]

The Regulations require an overseas company to register its name.[34] The name **31.18** may be either the company's corporate name (its name under the law of the country or territory in which it is incorporated) or an alternative name under which the overseas company proposes to carry on the business in the United Kingdom.[35] However, an EEA company (being a company governed by the law of an EEA state[36]) must always register its corporate name.[37] The registration of the name of

---

[29] Except in the case of a Gibraltar company in which case the Regulations may make such provision (s 1046(2)(b)).

[30] 2006 Act, s 1046(2)(a). Regulations may also require an overseas company to give notice to the Registrar if it closes its branch and ceases to have a registrable presence: s 1058.

[31] reg 3.

[32] reg 2(1).

[33] For a case on the meaning of 'operations of a branch, agency or other establishment', see *SAR Schotte GmbH v Parfums Rothschild SAR* [1992] BCLC 235.

[34] 2006 Act, s 1047(1); Regulations, reg 5(1)(a).

[35] 2006 Act, ss 1047(2), 1048.

[36] 2006 Act, s 1170.

[37] 2006 Act, ss 1047(3).

a non-EEA company is subject to various of the restrictions which apply to the names of companies formed and registered under the Companies Acts.[38]

**31.19** The other particulars of the company which are required to be registered are its legal form, the identity of any register on which the company is registered in the country of its incorporation, a list of its directors and secretary (containing specified particulars of the directors and secretary, including their names, any former names, their service address and, in the case of directors, their usual residential address, nationality, country of residence, business occupation, and date of birth) and the extent of the powers of the directors or secretary to represent the company in dealings with third parties and in legal proceedings.[39] Further particulars are also required in the case of a company in an EEA state.[40]

**31.20** The particulars of an establishment which are required to be registered are the address of the establishment, the date on which it was opened, the business carried on at it, the name of the establishment (if different from the name of the company), the name and service address of every person resident in the United Kingdom authorized to accept service on behalf of the company in respect of the establishment or a statement that there is no such person,[41] a list of every person authorized to represent the company as a permanent representative of the company in respect of the establishment, the extent of the authority of any such person, and the name of any person with whom any such person is authorized to act jointly.[42]

**31.21** An overseas company which is obliged to register particulars is also obliged to register details of any alternations in the company's constitution or of the particulars of the company or the establishment which have been registered.[43]

**31.22** In relation to the registration by an overseas company of the particulars of an individual's usual residential address, the Regulations contain provision corresponding to the 2006 Act, Part 10, Chapter 8 concerning the circumstances in which a director's residential address is protected from disclosure (Chapter 6, paras 6.96–6.105 of this work).[44]

---

[38] 2006 Act, s 1047(4). The provisions which apply are s 53 (prohibited names), ss 54–56 (sensitive words and expressions), s 65 (inappropriate use of indications of company type or legal form), ss 66–74 (similarity to other names), s 75 (provision of misleading information), and s 76 (misleading indication of activities). The provisions of s 57 (permitted characters etc) apply in every case (s 1047(5)).

[39] Regulations, reg 5(1), (3), (4).

[40] Regulations, reg 5(2).

[41] 2006 Act, s 1056.

[42] Regulations, reg 6(1).

[43] Regulations, reg 12(1).

[44] Regulations, Part 8, regs 61–71.

The Regulations also make provision for an overseas company that has an establishment in the United Kingdom to prepare accounts and reports from the directors and auditors. If the overseas company is required by its parent law to prepare, have audited, or disclose accounts or is an EEA company and is required by its parent to prepare and disclose accounts, then the company is required to deliver to the Registrar of Companies a copy of all of the accounting documents disclosed in accordance with the parent law.[45] In the case of other overseas companies, provisions of Parts 15 (accounts and report) and 16 (audit) of the 2006 Act are applied to such companies.[46] Such companies are therefore required to prepare and deliver accounts in accordance with these provisions of the Act.

31.23

The Regulations further make provision for the registration of specified charges over property in the United Kingdom of an overseas company that has a UK establishment.[47] Charges which require registration are those listed in the 2006 Act, s 860(7) which are created by an overseas company that has a UK establishment at the time it is created, and on the date the charge was created the property subject to the charge was located in the UK.[48] In relation to such charges, particulars of the charges are required to be registered and, for these purposes, certain provisions of the 2006 Act, Part 25 relating to company charges, are applied.[49]

31.24

In addition to the provision of particulars and the filing of accounts and reports, the Regulations also require overseas companies carrying on business in the United Kingdom to provide certain information in the course of trading.[50] Specifically, an overseas company carrying on business in the United Kingdom is required to display its name and country of incorporation at the service address of every person authorized to accept service of documents and at every other location in the United Kingdom where it carries on business.[51] The company's name must also be stated on all business correspondence and websites.[52]

31.25

## C. Capacity and Internal Management

The general rule of English private international law is that all matters concerning the constitution of a company are governed by the law of the place of incorporation.[53] This rule is one aspect of the general principle of English rules of conflicts

31.26

---

[45] Regulations, regs 17(1), 18(1).

[46] 2006 Act, s 1049(1), (2), (3). Regulations, regs 25–30.

[47] 2006 Act, s 1052(1); Regulations, reg 45.

[48] Regulations, reg 46.

[49] 2006 Act, s 1052(3); Regulations, reg 47.

[50] 2006 Act, s 1051(1); Regulations, part 10, regs 78–86.

[51] Regulations, reg 80.

[52] Regulations, reg 82.

[53] Dicey, Morris & Collins, *The Conflict of Laws* (14th edn), rule 162(2).

of law that the law of the place of incorporation governs matters of substantive company law. This principle has been increasingly recognized and given effect to in recent authorities.[54]

*Capacity*

31.27   The capacity of a company refers to the legal power of the company to do certain acts. So far as directors are concerned, it is obviously a matter of good governance to ensure that a company acts within its capacity at all times.

31.28   As *Dicey, Morris and Collins* points out, the capacity of a company may be limited in two ways.[55] First, the company's capacity may be limited by the terms of its own constitution. The source of the constitution will be the company's own constitutive documents (for example, its memorandum and articles of association) together with relevant provisions of statutory and other law which apply to the company. The terms and effect of a company's constitution is governed by the law of the place of incorporation. If, under its constitution, a company lacks capacity to do a certain act then any such act which the company purports to do may be invalid and ineffective.

31.29   Secondly, the capacity of a company may be limited under the law of the country which governs the relevant transaction. In other words, the law of the country which is applicable to the transaction under the usual principles of private international law may limit the ability of the company to enter into the transaction. Under English law, such restrictions are rare. However, this issue needs to be borne in mind where a company is entering into a transaction governed by foreign law, particularly where the transaction involves the purchase of real property abroad.

*Internal management*

31.30   The law of the place of incorporation determines the composition and powers of the organs of the company and the formalities and procedures laid down for them.[56] This means that the law of the place of incorporation will determine, amongst other things, whether the directors have been validly appointed. In *Speed Investments Ltd v Formula One Holdings Ltd*[57] the Court of Appeal accepted that this was the position.[58] This position complements the position in relation to the jurisdiction of the courts. The EC Regulation on Civil Jurisdiction

---

[54] See eg *Base Metal Trading Ltd v Shamurin* [2005] 1 WLR 1157, CA.
[55] 14th edn at para 30-021.
[56] *Grupo Torras SA v Al-Sabah* [1996] 1 Lloyd's Rep 7, 15.
[57] [2005] 1 BCLC 455.
[58] See also *Sierra Leone Telecommunications Co Ltd v Barclays Bank plc* [1998] 2 All ER 821.

and Judgments,[59] which sets out the rules for the allocation of jurisdiction in proceedings against persons domiciled in the European Union,[60] gives exclusive jurisdiction to the courts in which a company has its seat in relation to proceedings which have as their object the validity of decisions of a company's organs.[61]

*Financial assistance*

The 2006 Act contains provisions dealing with financial assistance (Part 18, Chapter 2) which replace those which were found in the 1985 Act, ss 151–158.[62] These provisions illustrate how the English Companies Acts do not legislate in respect of the constitutional affairs of a foreign company. The consequence is that a director of a foreign company is not obliged to secure compliance by the company with provisions of the 2006 Act concerning maintenance of a company's capital.   **31.31**

By its terms, the 2006 Act, s 678 applies in relation to the acquisition of shares in a public company and the provision of assistance by that company or a subsidiary of that company for the purpose of the acquisition. 'Public company' is defined in the 2006 Act, s 4 and incorporates the definition of 'company' in s 1. Accordingly, the financial assistance provisions do not apply in relation to the acquisition of shares in a foreign public company.   **31.32**

In relation to the provision of assistance, it is possible that an English public company may have a foreign subsidiary and the question is therefore whether s 678 would prohibit the giving of assistance by that company. In *Arab Bank v Mercantile Holdings*[63] it was held that the equivalent provision in the 1985 Act did not extend to the foreign subsidiaries of English public companies. This provision referred to the public company and 'any of its subsidiaries'. The presumption was that in the absence of a contrary intention, the provision was not intended to have an extra-territorial effect and that the term 'any of its subsidiaries' was to be construed accordingly. The 2006 Act, s 678 now makes this clear beyond doubt by specifically referring to 'a company that is a subsidiary' thereby incorporating the definition of 'company' in s 1.   **31.33**

---

[59] Council Regulation (EC) No 44/2001 of 22 December 2000 on jurisdiction and the recognition and enforcement of judgments in civil and commercial matters

[60] Except Denmark.

[61] Article 22(2).

[62] The provisions of the 2006 Act come into force and replace the 1985 Act provisions on 1 October 2009 (the 2006 Act Commencement Order No 8, art 3(l)), but private companies became exempt from these provisions on 1 October 2008 (2006 Act Commencement Order No 5, arts 5(2) and 8(b) and Schedule 3).

[63] [1994] Ch 71.

## D. Execution of Documents on Behalf
## of a Foreign Company

**31.34**   As with the 1985 Act, the 2006 Act contains provisions concerning the manner in which documents are executed by companies formed and registered under the 2006 Act and previous Companies Acts. The 2006 Act, s 43, which re-enacts the 1985 Act, s 36 without change, provides that a company may make a contract by writing under its common seal or a contract may be made on behalf of a company by a person acting under its authority, express or implied.[64] Section 44 provides that a document is executed by a company by the affixing of its common seal or if it is signed on behalf of the company by two authorized signatories or by a director of the company in the presence of a witness who attests to the signature.[65] Sections 46 and 47 deal with the execution of deeds and other documents.

**31.35**   Under the 1985 Act, the equivalent provisions were extended to apply to foreign companies with modifications by the Foreign Companies (Execution of Documents) Regulations 1994.[66] The effect of these Regulations was that the execution of documents by and on behalf of a foreign company was governed by the law of the company's place of incorporation. A foreign company could there-fore make a contract in any manner permitted by the law of the place of incorporation and by any person who under that law was acting under the authority (express or implied) of the company.[67]

**31.36**   Accordingly, a contract could be executed in any manner permitted by the law of the place of incorporation and would have the same effect as a document executed by an English company. If a contract was signed by persons having express or implied authority under the law of the place of incorporation of the company and the contract was expressed to be executed by the company, the contract would be deemed to be duly executed by the foreign company.

**31.37**   Under the 2006 Act, the Secretary of State is given power to make provision by regulations applying ss 43 to 52 to overseas companies subject to necessary exceptions, adaptations, or modifications.[68] Such regulations are contained in the draft Overseas Companies Regulations 2008, Part 9, Chapter 5 and apply

---

[64] 2006 Act, ss 43, 46, and 47 comes into force on 1 October 2009: 2006 Act Commencement Order No 8, art 3(d). Section 46 replaces 1985 Act, s 36AA without change and s 47 replaces 1985 Act, s 38 with changes.

[65] 1985 Act, s 44 came into force on 6 April 2008: 2006 Act Commencement Order No 5, art 3(1) and replaced 1985 Act, s 36A without change, except that subs (20(b) is new.

[66] SI 1994/950; amended by SI 1995/1729.

[67] See also *Azov Shipping Co v Baltic Shipping Co* [1999] 2 Lloyd's Rep 159.

[68] 2006 Act, s 1045.

ss 43 to 52 to overseas companies (with relevant modifications) in the same way the 1994 Regulations applied the equivalent provisions of the 1985 Act to such companies.

## E. Duties Owed by Directors of a
## Foreign Company

The duties owed by a director of a company under English law have historically **31.38** arisen both at common law and in equity. A director owed a duty of care to the company at both common law and in equity.[69] In addition, a director may have owed duties under his contract of employment with the company.

The duties of directors have now been codified in Part 10 of the Companies Act **31.39** 2006, as discussed in Chapters 9–15 of this work.[70] These provisions apply in relation to a company as defined in the 2006 Act, s 1, namely, a company formed or registered under the Companies Acts. The new statutory duties therefore do not apply to directors of a foreign incorporated company.

In relation to foreign companies, as noted above, the general rule of English pri- **31.40** vate international law is that all matters concerning the constitution of a corporation are governed by the law of the place of incorporation.[71] As a result, it has been held that the law of the place of incorporation will govern the nature and extent of the duties owed by directors to the corporation.[72] The position underlying this general proposition is, however, somewhat more complex since under English rules of private international law different rules may apply depending on whether the relevant duties of a director are said to arise at common law, in equity, or as a matter of contract.

### Equitable duties

Under English law (until the 2006 Act, Part 10 came into force), a director's equit- **31.41** able duties included the equitable duty of care which he owed to exercise skill and care in relation to the company's affairs and the fiduciary duties of fidelity and loyalty imposed on a director (now the 2006 Act, ss 171–173 and 175–177).

---

[69] *Bristol & West Building Society v Mothew* [1998] Ch 1, CA.

[70] As of 1 October 2008 all the duties codified by the 2006 Act, ss 170–181 are in force: 2006 Act Commencement Orders No 3, art 2(1) and No 5, art 5(1).

[71] *Dicey, Morris & Collins* (14th edn) rule 162(2).

[72] *Dicey, Morris & Collins* (14th edn) para 30-024; *Pergamon Press Ltd v Maxwell* [1970] 1 WLR 1167; *Konamaneni v Rolls-Royce Industrial Power (India) Ltd* [2002] 1 WLR 1269; *Shaker v Al-Bedrawi* [2003] Ch 350, CA; *Base Metal Trading Ltd v Shamurin* [2002] CLC 3221 [2005] 1 WLR 1157, CA.

**31.42**    The law applicable to a director's equitable duties was considered by the Court of Appeal in the case of *Base Metal Trading Ltd v Shamurin*.[73] The Court of Appeal held that a director's equitable duty arises from and only from the director's relationship with the company and that, if it does not relate to the constitution of the company, then it relates to its internal management. Since the duty is inextricably bound up with those matters than it must be governed by the place of the company's incorporation.[74]

**31.43**    This conclusion is supported by other authorities. In *Pergamon Press Ltd v Maxwell*[75] the court held that it was not open to the English court to control the exercise of a fiduciary power arising in the internal management of a foreign company. In *Konamaneni v Rolls-Royce Industrial Power (India) Ltd*[76] the court held that the extent of the duties of the director of a foreign company was governed by the law of that country's place of incorporation and that the point was 'unexceptional and indeed obvious'. In *Shaker v Al Bedrawi*[77] the court proceeded on the basis that the law of Pennsylvania was the applicable law to the duties of directors of a company incorporated there.

**31.44**    This conclusion also achieves the most practically desirable result. It means that it is possible to identify with certainty the system of law which will govern a director's equitable duties without having to undertake a factual inquiry. As the Court of Appeal pointed out in *Base Metal*, any other result would have created huge uncertainty and hampered the requirement for good corporate governance and proper regulatory control.[78] In practice, however, it may be difficult for the directors of a foreign company to persuade an English court that they do not owe the company fiduciary duties under the company's law of incorporation.[79]

*Common law duties*

**31.45**    In addition to equitable duties, a director owed duties at common law to the company. Under English law, such duties include the common law duty to act with reasonable care and skill in relation to the affairs of the company which is the common law counterpart of the equitable duty of care. This duty is now embodied in

---

[73] [2005] 1 WLR 1157, CA.
[74] [2005] 1 WLR 1157, paras 56, 69.
[75] [1970] 1 WLR 1167.
[76] [2002] 1 WLR 1269.
[77] [2003] Ch 350, CA.
[78] [2005] 1 WLR 1157, CA, para 56.
[79] See for example Chadwick J in *Re Howard Holdings Inc* [1998] BCC 549 in relation to the duties of directors where the company is insolvent: 'I find it difficult to envisage that any developed system of corporate law which does not impose some obligation on those charged with responsibility of the management of a company's affairs to pay regard to the question whether or not it is, from time to time, solvent and, if insolvent, to consider what should be done about it.'

the duty under the Act 2006 on a director to exercise reasonable care, skill, and diligence.[80]

Under the English system, a breach of the common law duty of care is actionable **31.46** by a claim in tort against the director for damages for breach of duty. The law applicable to a claim in tort is in general determined by the provisions of the Private International Law (Miscellaneous Provisions) Act 1995.[81] The general rule is that the applicable law is the law of the country in which the events constituting the tort occur.[82] However, importantly, this general rule may be displaced if it appears that, in all the circumstances, from a comparison of (a) the significance of the factors which connect a tort with the country whose law would be applicable under the general rule and (b) the significance of any factors connecting the tort with another country, that it is substantially more appropriate for the applicable law to be the law of the other country.[83]

In the case of duties owed by directors, it may be strongly arguable that the most **31.47** significant factor is the relationship between the director and the company. The essential characteristic of a claim for breach of duty is that there has been a breach by the director of the obligations which lie upon him by virtue of his office as a director. Given that the general principle of English private international law is that the law of the place of incorporation will govern matters of substantive company law, this strongly suggests that it would be substantially more appropriate for the law of the place of incorporation to apply to a tort founded on a director's breach of duty.

In *Base Metal* it was held that the tort claim for breach of duty was governed by the **31.48** Russian law, rather than by the law of the place of incorporation (Guernsey), on the basis that Russia was the place where in substance the tort had been committed since this was where, amongst other things, the directors were based. This applied the old common law test as the relevant events had occurred prior to the enactment of the 1995 Act.[84] Following the enactment of the 1995 Act, it may well be that the law of the place of incorporation will apply for the reasons discussed above.

---

[80] Companies Act 2006, s 174(1).
[81] *Dicey, Morris & Collins* (14th edn) rule 231.
[82] Private International Law (Miscellaneous Provisions) Act 1995, s 11(1).
[83] Private International Law (Miscellaneous Provisions) Act 1995, s 12(1). For recent discussion of choice of law in relation to tort claims and assessment of damages: *Harding v Wealands* [2007] 2 AC 1, HL; *Re T&N Ltd (No 2)* [2006] 1 WLR 1792; *Trafigura Beheer BV v Kookmin Bank Co* [2006] 2 Lloyd's Rep 455.
[84] *Metall und Rohstoff v Donaldson Lufkin and Jenrette Inc* [1990] 1 QB 391, CA.

*Contractual duties*

**31.49**   A director may also owe duties to the company under a contract between himself and the company. The rules of the Rome Convention[85] do not apply to determine the law applicable to such duties since this falls within the exception for company law issues contained in Article 1(2)(e) of the Convention.[86] Accordingly, the law applicable to such duties falls to be determined in accordance with English common law rules of private international law. The general rule at common law is that the law applicable to a contract is governed by the express or inferred intention of the parties or, in the absence of such intention, by the system of law with which the contract has the closest and most real connection.[87]

**31.50**   It follows that duties owed by a director to the company under a contract with the company will be governed by the law intended by the parties to govern such duties or, failing any such intention, the law with which such duties are most closely connected. Where there is an express choice of law provision in the contract this system of law is therefore likely to apply. However, in any case, it appears that these general choice of law rules are, in relation to the duties owed by a director to a company, subject to a further rule that a company and a director cannot by the terms of a contract vary the duties which the director would otherwise owe to the company under the law of the place of incorporation unless that law permits such variation.[88] Accordingly, a director can by a contract assume additional or further duties to those which he would owe under the law of the place of incorporation generally, but he cannot by a contract exclude or limit those duties.

**31.51**   The law applicable to the duties of a director as an *employee* of the company, as opposed to those owed by him by virtue of his office as a director of the company, will be governed by the provisions of the Rome Convention. In the absence of an express choice of law provision in the contract of employment, Article 6(2) of the Rome Convention provides that the contract is to be governed by the law of the country in which the employee habitually carries out his work in performance of the contract.

**31.52**   Overall, it is possible that a director's different duties in equity, at common law, and under contract may be governed by different systems of law. This may be regrettable but is a consequence of the recognition in English law of the possibility of concurrent causes of action in equity, tort, and contract.[89] However, in practice,

---

[85]   The Rome Convention on the Law Applicable to Contractual Obligations 1980, enacted into English law by the Contracts (Applicable Law) Act 1990, Schedule 1.

[86]   *Base Metals Ltd v Shamurin* [2005] 1 WLR 1157, CA, para 65.

[87]   *Dicey, Morris & Collins*, (14th edn) para 32-005; *Bonython v Commonwealth of Australia* [1951] AC 201, PC.

[88]   *Base Metals Ltd v Shamurin* [2005] 1 WLR 1157, CA, para 69.

[89]   *Henderson v Merrett Syndicates Ltd* [1995] 2 AC 145, HL.

it is likely that the law of the place of incorporation will play an increasingly important role in determining all of the duties owed by a director to a company.

*Effect of insolvency*

Once a company is insolvent, the interests of creditors (including future creditors) **31.53** displace the interests of the company itself since the creditors become prospectively entitled to displace the power of the directors and the shareholders to deal with the company's assets.[90] Accordingly, upon insolvency the directors of a company may be required to preserve the company's assets for the benefit of all creditors.[91] These issues are discussed in Chapter 11, Section E and Chapter 19, Section D. However, the directors do not owe a legal duty to creditors, in the sense that they do to the company prior to the insolvency, which the creditors might enforce by bringing an action against the directors. Rather, the obligation on directors upon the insolvency of a company to act in the interests of creditors is enforceable by the office-holder in any subsequent insolvency using the tools available to him under the insolvency legislation or by bringing an action in the name of the company.

It follows from this that the nature and extent of the duties of directors where a **31.54** company enters the zone of insolvency may in practice be influenced by the law applicable to any subsequent insolvency proceedings. Thus where insolvency proceedings are commenced in England in relation to the company, it will be English law and, in particular, the provisions of the Insolvency Act, which will determine the nature and extent of the remedies available to the insolvency office-holder, for example, in relation to setting aside transactions or for fraudulent or wrongful trading.[92] Accordingly, English law will determine the liability of a director in relation to such matters. In this way, English law will influence the duties of the directors prior to the insolvency in the sense that if a director acts in a way which triggers the remedies available to an English insolvency office-holder, he may then face liability under English law in respect of such matters.

# F. Civil Litigation

One of the issues of which a director of a foreign company needs to be aware is the **31.55** risk of the company being subject to civil litigation in England. If the company is unsuccessful, the director may be exposed to liability for costs, as discussed in

---

[90] *Kinsela v Russell Kinsela Pty Ltd (in liq)* (1986) 4 NSWLR 722, 730; *West Mercia Safetywear Ltd v Dodd* [1988] BCLC 250, CA.
[91] See 2006 Act, s 172(3).
[92] See further Section H below.

Chapter 27, Section E. A director of a company which unsuccessfully defends a claim may also be susceptible to the machinery which the English court makes available to a successful litigation in order to assist with the enforcement of his judgment.

**31.56** The rules for jurisdiction in civil proceedings involving persons domiciled in the European Union (except Denmark) are contained in the EC Regulation on Civil Jurisdiction and Judgments[93] (the Judgments Regulation). Under the Judgments Regulation, the general rule, subject to exceptions, is that a person domiciled in the EU may be sued in the courts of the state where he is domiciled.[94] The place of incorporation is one of the tests for determining the domicile of a company (the others being place of central administration and principal place of business).[95] Accordingly, a company incorporated in a Member State may be sued in its country of incorporation under the Judgments Regulation.

**31.57** The Judgments Regulation also specifically provides that proceedings which have as their object the validity of the constitution, the nullity or the dissolution of companies or other legal persons, or the validity of the decisions of their organs are to be dealt with exclusively by the courts of the Member State in which the company or other legal person has its seat.[96] The seat for these purposes is to be determined in accordance with domestic rules of private international law. In the case of England, a company will be treated as having its seat in England if it was incorporated in England.[97]

**31.58** Civil jurisdiction over companies domiciled in Denmark and in EEA states (which are, principally, Norway and Switzerland) are dealt with by the Brussels and Lugano Conventions respectively.[98] Under these Conventions the seat of a company is to be treated as its domicile with the seat to be determined in accordance with domestic rules of private international law.[99] Under English rules, a company is to be treated as having its seat in the United Kingdom if it was incorporated or formed under the law of part of the United Kingdom and has its registered office or some other official address in the United Kingdom or if its central management and control is exercised in the United Kingdom.[100] The Brussels and Lugano Conventions also contained similar provisions to those contained in the Judgments Regulation reserving jurisdiction over proceedings which have as their object the

---

[93] Council Regulation (EC) No 44/2001 of 22 December 2000 on jurisdiction and the recognition and enforcement of judgments in civil and commercial matters
[94] Art 2.
[95] Art 60(1), (2).
[96] Arts 22(2).
[97] Civil Jurisdiction and Judgments Order 2001 (SI 2001/3929), Schedule 1 para 10.
[98] Civil Jurisdiction and Judgments Act 1982, ss 2(1), 3A(1); Schedule 1, Schedule 3C.
[99] Brussels Convention, Art 53; Lugano Convention, Art 53.
[100] Civil Jurisdiction and Judgments Act 1982, s 42(3).

validity of the constitution, the nullity or the dissolution of companies or other legal persons, or the validity of the decisions of their organs exclusively to the courts where the company has its seat.[101]

The Judgments Regulation and the Brussels and Lugano Conventions do not apply to bankruptcy, proceedings relating to the winding up of insolvent companies or other legal persons, judicial arrangements, compositions, and other analogous proceedings.[102] Insolvency proceedings are subject to the EC Regulation on insolvency proceedings.[103]  **31.59**

In relation to companies domiciled outside the EU and EEA, the usual English rules of jurisdiction apply. Proceedings may be served on a company in the jurisdiction by leaving them at, or sending by post to, the registered address of any person resident in the United Kingdom who is authorized to accept service of documents on the company's behalf or by sending by post to any place of business of the company in the United Kingdom.[104] In addition, the proceedings may be sent or left at any place within England and Wales where the company carries on its activities.[105] It also seems that proceedings may be personally served on a company by leaving the proceedings with a person holding a senior position within the company.[106]  **31.60**

Further, in certain circumstances, it may be possible to obtain permission from the English court to serve proceedings on a foreign company, not domiciled in the EU or EEA, outside the jurisdiction.[107]  **31.61**

Finally, it appears that the English court has jurisdiction to make an order under CPR Part 71 to obtain information from a judgment debtor resident outside the jurisdiction. It is clear that the court may make an order requiring a judgment debtor within the jurisdiction to answer questions about assets outside the jurisdiction.[108] There was some doubt as to whether the court also had jurisdiction to make an order against a judgment debtor or officers of a judgment debtor who are  **31.62**

---

[101] Brussels Convention, Art 16(2); Lugano Convention, Art 16(2); Civil Jurisdiction and Judgments Act 1982, s 43.

[102] Judgments Regulation, Art 1(2)(b); Brussels Convention, Art 1; Lugano Convention, Art 1.

[103] See paragraph 31.80 below.

[104] 2006 Act, s 1139(2).

[105] CPR rule 6.9(2). This method of service is in addition to those specified in the Companies Act: *Sea Assets Ltd v PT Garuda Indonesia* [2000] 4 All ER 371.

[106] CPR rule 6.5(3)(b). It is not entirely clear whether CPR rule 6.5(3)(b) was intended to apply to a foreign company. However, CPR rule 6.3(2) suggests that the term 'company' in this context can include a foreign company and in *Lakah Group v al-Jazeera Satellite Channel* [2003] EWHC 1231 it appeared to be assumed that service could be effected on a foreign company under rule 6.5(3)(b) though the point was not argued.

[107] CPR rule 6.36.

[108] *Interpool Ltd v Galani* [1988] QB 738.

outside the jurisdiction. In *Vitol SA v Capri Marine Ltd*[109] it was held that the court did not have jurisdiction to grant permission for service out of the jurisdiction of orders made under CPR rule 71.2 requiring officers of a judgment debtor company who were resident abroad to attend court for questioning and to produce documents. However, in *Masri v Consolidated Contractors*[110] the Court of Appeal held that CPR rule 71.2 is not restricted to persons in the UK as it would defeat its object if it were and that service out of the jurisdiction may be permitted under CPR rule 6.38(1).

## G. Remedies of Shareholders in a Foreign Company in England

**31.63** The principal right and remedy of a shareholder in a company, where there has been breach of directors' duties or the company is being managed in a manner prejudicial to his interests, is to exercise his rights under the constitution of the company. However, where these rights and remedies are ineffective, a shareholder may be able to commence legal proceedings. The principal forms of action available to a shareholder under English law in this regard are the commencement of derivative proceedings by the shareholder (for example, against a director of the company) or the presentation of a petition to wind up the company on just and equitable grounds, as discussed in Chapter 21, Sections C and F.

**31.64** The further remedy which is available to a shareholder in a company formed and registered under the Companies Acts is to apply to the court for an order under Part 30 of the 2006 Act on the grounds that the company's affairs are being or have been conducted in a manner that is unfairly prejudicial to the interests of members generally or of some part of its members (discussed in Chapter 21, Section E of this work).[111] However, this remedy is only available to a company within the meaning of the 2006 Act, which does not include a foreign company.[112]

*Derivative proceedings*

**31.65** The general rule is that a company is the proper claimant in an action to redress harm done to the company or to prosecute a cause of action vested in the company. However, in certain circumstances established by the case law, the courts held that a shareholder in a company could be permitted to bring proceedings by way of derivative action. The action is brought in representative form by the

---

[109] [2008] EWHC 378 (Comm).
[110] [2008] EWCA Civ 876.
[111] 2006 Act, s 994(1).
[112] 2006 Act, s 994(3), s 1.

shareholder and the company is joined as a defendant in order for it to be bound by any judgment.

The question is whether the English court has jurisdiction to hear a derivative **31.66** claim in relation to a foreign company. In *Konamaneni v Rolls-Royce Industrial Power (India) Ltd*,[113] the claimants, minority shareholders in an Indian company, sought to bring a derivative action on its behalf against two English companies who were alleged to have paid bribes to the managing director of the Indian company. The court held that the English court had jurisdiction to hear the claim since it had jurisdiction over two of the defendants and the Indian company could be joined to the proceedings as a necessary or proper party to the proceedings.[114] However, the court also held that service of the proceedings would be set aside on the grounds that the place of incorporation of a foreign company would almost invariably be the most appropriate forum for the resolution of issues relating to the existence of the right of shareholders to sue on behalf of the company.

The law and procedure in relation to derivative claims is now codified the 2006 **31.67** Act, Part 11, ss 260 to 264. However, these provisions only apply to a claim by a member of a company which, as defined in the 2006 Act, s 1 is a company formed and registered under the Companies Acts. Sections 260 to 264 therefore do not apply in respect of derivative claims in relation to a foreign company.

The position in relation to the jurisdiction of the English court over such claims **31.68** will therefore remain as the court held in *Konamaneni* at least so far as companies outside the European Union are concerned. In other words, the English court will have jurisdiction over such claims provided that it has jurisdiction over one or more of the defendants in accordance with its usual rules; the foreign company may then be joined to the proceedings as a necessary or proper party.[115] The claim will thereafter be subject to the procedural filter provided for by CPR rule 19.9 (which requires the claimant to seek the permission of the court to continue the claim).

However, aside from the question of jurisdiction, where permission is sought to **31.69** serve out of the jurisdiction on the foreign company as a necessary or proper party to the proceedings, the English court will have a discretion as to whether or not to permit such service. It will only give permission where it is satisfied that England is the proper place in which to bring the claim.[116] In this respect, it is very likely that the English court would refuse as a matter of discretion to permit service out of the jurisdiction where it was sought to bring a derivative action in relation to

---

[113] [2002] 1 WLR 1269.
[114] CPR Part 6, Practice Direction B, para 3.1(3).
[115] Pursuant to CPR Part 6, Practice Direction B, para 3.1(3).
[116] CPR rule 6.37(3).

a foreign company. This is because the place of incorporation of the company will almost invariably be the appropriate forum for the determination of the proceedings.[117]

**31.70**  In particular, as the court pointed out in *Konamaneni*, the law of the place of the incorporation of a company governs the right of a shareholder to bring a derivative action in England. Although a matter of English domestic law, the exceptions to the rule have been regarded as a matter of procedure, their real nature is not procedural in the international context. They confer a right on the shareholders to protect the value of their shares by giving them a right to sue and recover on behalf of the company. The court pointed out that it would be odd if that right could be conferred under English law on the shareholders of a company incorporated in a jurisdiction which has no such rule.

**31.71**  The position is more complicated where the foreign company is domiciled within the EU or EEA and one or more of the other defendants is domiciled in England. In these circumstances, the provisions of the Judgments Regulation and the Lugano Convention apply. Under the provisions of the Judgments Regulation and the Lugano Convention, it is arguable that the foreign company could be joined to the claim under the provisions of the Regulation and the Convention which permit the joinder of co-defendants to proceedings.[118]

**31.72**  However, it is doubtful whether this provision can be invoked to permit the English court to take jurisdiction over a derivative claim in respect of a company domiciled elsewhere in the EU or EEA. The language of the provisions, which envisage distinct claims against each of the defendants which might result in irreconcilable judgments if not heard together, is inapt to apply to a derivative claim. It must also be extremely doubtful whether it was ever the intention behind these provisions to confer jurisdiction on the courts of one Member State to hear a derivative claim in relation to a company based in another Member State. This is particularly so given that the Regulation and the Convention specifically refer matters relating to the validity of the constitution of a company to the Member State where it has its seat.[119]

**31.73**  Furthermore, if the provisions of the Regulation and the Convention did confer jurisdiction to determine derivative claims in relation to a company incorporated in another Member State, then it is doubtful whether the courts would have a

---

[117] See also *SMAY Investments Limited v Sachdev* [2003] 1 WLR 1973, para 49.
[118] Article 6(1) of the Judgments Regulation (where the party is domiciled in the EU excluding Denmark) or Art 6(1) of the Lugano Convention, as enacted by the Civil Jurisdiction and Judgments Act 1982, Schedule 3C (where the party is domiciled in an EEA state outside the EU).
[119] Judgments Regulation, Art 22(2); Lugano Convention, Art 16(2).

discretion to decline to hear such proceedings.[120] Thus the route taken in *Konamaneni* would probably not be open to the court. This itself is a further indication that the provisions of the Regulation and the Convention do not confer jurisdiction to hear derivative proceedings in relation to companies in other Member States.

*Just and equitable winding up*

The further remedy potentially available to a shareholder is to present a petition for the winding up of the company on the grounds that it is just and equitable that the company should be wound up. Under the provisions of the Insolvency Act, a petition may be presented for the winding up of a foreign company on such grounds.[121]     **31.74**

In relation to foreign companies, it is necessary to consider the position separately in relation to companies whose seat is not in a Member State of the European Union or EEA and companies whose seat is in such a country. So far as companies with their seat in the EU or EEA are concerned, as noted above, the Judgments Regulation and the Brussels and Lugano Conventions specifically confer jurisdiction over proceedings which have as their object the dissolution of a company on the state where the company has its seat.[122] It is considered that a petition for the winding up of a company on just and equitable grounds would fall within this provision.[123] Accordingly, the English court will not have a jurisdiction to wind up on just and equitable grounds a company which has its seat in another EU or EEA Member State.     **31.75**

In relation to foreign companies whose seats are outside the EU and EEA, there is no fetter on the English court's jurisdiction to make a winding-up order on just and equitable grounds. However, in such cases, it is likely that the court would accede to an application to stay the petition on grounds of *forum non conveniens* or would refuse to permit service of the petition out of the jurisdiction on the basis that the proper forum was the place of the company's incorporation.[124]     **31.76**

---

[120] Briggs & Rees, *Civil Jurisdiction and Judgments*, 4th edn (2005), 2.176.

[121] Insolvency Act, s 221(5)(c).

[122] Judgments Regulation, Art 22(2); Brussels Convention, Art 16(2); Lugano Convention, Art 16(2). As to the meaning of seat for these purposes, see the Civil Jurisdiction and Judgments Act 1982, s 43 and the Civil Jurisdiction and Judgments Order 2001 (SI 2001/3929), Schedule 1 para 10.

[123] See *Re Senator Hanseatische Verwaltungsgeschellschaft* [1996] 2 BCLC 563.

[124] See *Re Harrods (Buenos Aires) Ltd* [1992] Ch 72, CA. Other aspects of the decision in *Re Harrods* have been overruled by the decision of the ECJ in *Owusu v Jackson* [2005] QB 801.

# H. Insolvency Proceedings

31.77 A director of a foreign company may have to consider English insolvency proceedings either where the company is insolvent and requires protection from its creditors or where it is necessary to place the company into insolvency proceedings as part of a consensual restructuring. In the former context, the director may have to consider whether insolvency proceedings represent the best way of obtaining the necessary protection or, alternatively, the director may have to consider whether the company should resist an application for English insolvency proceedings brought by a creditor. In the latter context, the question may be whether English insolvency proceedings represent the most effective route of achieving the desired restructuring. In practice, the views of the company's creditors on this question will also be critical. Also a creditor may take insolvency proceedings in England against a foreign company with a view to proceedings being taken by the office-holder or the company against the director.

*Availability of English insolvency proceedings for foreign companies*

31.78 The principal insolvency procedures available in relation to companies under the Insolvency Act, as discussed in Chapter 29, are: administration, creditors' voluntary liquidation, compulsory liquidation, and members' voluntary liquidation. The Enterprise Act 2002 reformed the administration procedure and effectively abolished administrative receivership in relation to floating charges created on or after 15 September 2003.

31.79 International insolvency proceedings are principally governed by the European Council Regulation on Insolvency Proceedings and the UNCITRAL Model Law on Cross-Border Insolvency. In addition, the English court has the power to grant assistance in relation to insolvency matters to foreign courts in certain specified states pursuant to the Insolvency Act, s 426. The EC Regulation, the Model Law, the Insolvency Act, s 426 together with the powers of the courts under common law,[125] essentially form a suite of measures by which the English courts can grant assistance to and cooperate with foreign insolvency proceedings.

*EC Regulation on Insolvency Proceedings*

31.80 The European Council Regulation on Insolvency Proceedings (the EC Regulation), which came into force in 2001, is of central importance to

---

[125] *Cambridge Gas Transport Corporation v The Official Committee of Unsecured Creditors of Navigator Holdings plc* [2007] 1 AC 508, PC.

insolvency proceedings with a foreign element.[126] The EC Regulation governs, in relation to all Member States of the European Union (except Denmark), the jurisdiction to commence insolvency proceedings and the recognition and enforcement of judgments arising from such proceedings.

The general scheme of the EC Regulation is that the jurisdiction to open insolvency proceedings in respect of a company with its centre of main interests within the European Union is conferred on the courts of the Member State where the debtor's COMI is situated.[127] These proceedings are known as 'main proceedings'. In the case of companies and legal persons, it is presumed, in the absence of evidence to the contrary, that the place of the registered office is the centre of main interests.[128] Where a debtor's centre of main interests is located in a Member State, the courts of other Member States only have jurisdiction to open insolvency proceedings in relation to the debtor if he has an 'establishment' in that Member State;[129] the effects of such proceedings (known as 'secondary proceedings') are restricted to the assets situated in that Member State.[130]     **31.81**

Accordingly, for directors faced with the need to reorganize a company through insolvency proceedings the location of the company's centre of main interests will be of critical importance. If the centre of main interests is located in another EU state, then it will not be possible to open main proceedings in England. On the other hand, if the centre of main interests is located in England it will be possible to place the company into main insolvency proceedings in England, including administration, notwithstanding that the company is incorporated elsewhere (whether in another EU state or outside the EU).[131] In appropriate circumstances,     **31.82**

---

[126] Council Regulation (EC) No 1346/2000 of 29 May 2000 on insolvency proceedings. See further Moss, Fletcher, Isaacs, *The EC Regulation on Insolvency Proceedings* (2002).

[127] Art 3.1. The term 'centre of main interests' is not defined in the EC Regulation though Recital 13 suggests that it should correspond to the place where the debtor conducts the administration of his interests on a regular basis and is therefore ascertainable by third parties.

[128] Art 3.1. In *Re Eurofood IFSC Ltd* [2006] Ch 508, the European Court of Justice held that where a debtor is a subsidiary company whose registered office and that of its parent company are situated in two different Member States, the presumption can be rebutted only if factors which are both objective and ascertainable by third parties enable it to be established that an actual situation exists which is different from that which location at that registered office is deemed to reflect. That could be so in particular in the case of a company not carrying out any business in the territory of the Member State in which its registered office is situated but where a company carries on its business in the territory of the Member State where its registered office is situated, the mere fact that its economic choices are or can be controlled by a parent company in another Member State is not enough to rebut the presumption.

[129] Art 3.2. An 'establishment' is defined as any place of operations where the debtor carries out a non-transitory economic activity with human means and goods: Art 2(h).

[130] Art 3.2.

[131] See *Re BRAC Rent-A-Car International Inc* [2003] 1 WLR 1421; *Re Daisytek-ISA Limited* [2004] BPIR 30. The location of a debtor's centre of main interests has been equated, in the case

it may be possible to move a company's centre of main interests to England in order to open main insolvency proceedings in England.

### Section 426

**31.83** Under the Insolvency Act, s 426 the English court has the obligation to grant assistance in relation to insolvency matters to foreign courts in certain specified states (essentially Commonwealth states).[132] Section 426 provides that the English court 'shall assist' the requesting state and, in order to do so, it is given the authority to apply either English insolvency law or the corresponding insolvency law of the requesting state. The overriding consideration is to assist the foreign court unless there is a compelling reason why such assistance cannot be granted.[133] Section 426 is frequently invoked for the purpose of investigating or pursuing claims against directors.

### Administration

**31.84** In relation to companies with their centres of main interests outside the European Union, the English court may make an administration order in respect of a company incorporated overseas pursuant to a request for assistance from a foreign court in one of the specified states pursuant to s 426.

**31.85** In *Re Dallhold Estates (UK) Pty Ltd*[134] an administration order was made in England over an Australian company pursuant to a request from the Australian court made under s 426.[135] The administration order in *Dallhold Estates* was made despite

---

of companies, with the place where the 'head office functions' of the debtor are carried out. This approach has been followed in various other cases both in England (*Re Ci4net.com Inc* [2005] BCC 277; *Re TXU German Finance BV* [2005] BPIR 209; *Re Collins & Aikman* [2007] 1 BCLC 182), and in other EU states (in particular, France: see *Re MPOTEC GmbH*, Tribunal de Commerce de Nanterre, [2006] BCC 681; *Re ISA Daisytek SAS*, Cour de Cassation, [2006] BCC 841; *Re Eurotunnel Finance Ltd*, Paris Commercial Court, 2 August 2006) and was endorsed by the Advocate-General in *Re Eurofood* [2006] Ch 508 (at paras 111–112).

[132] The relevant territories are the Channel Islands and the Isle of Man, Anguilla, Australia, the Bahamas, Bermuda, Botswana, Canada, Cayman Islands, Falkland Islands, Gibraltar, Hong Kong, Republic of Ireland, Montserrat, New Zealand, St Helena, Turks and Caicos Islands, Tuvalu, Virgin Islands, Malaysia, Republic of South Africa, and Brunei Darussalam: Insolvency Act, s 426(11) and Co-operation of Insolvency Courts (Designation of Relevant Countries and Territories) Order 1986 (SI 1986/2123); Co-operation of Insolvency Courts (Designation of Relevant Countries and Territories) Order 1996 (SI 1996/253); Co-operation of Insolvency Courts (Designation of Relevant Countries and Territories) Order 1998 (SI 1998/2766).

[133] The principles underlying the application of s 426 are set out in the decisions of the Court of Appeal in *Hughes v Hannover Rückversicherungs-Aktiengesellschaft* [1997] 1 BCLC 497, CA; *Smith v England* [2001] Ch 419, CA; and by the House of Lords in *Re HIH Casualty and General Insurance Ltd* [2008] 1 WLR 852.

[134] [1992] BCLC 621.

[135] In *O.T. Computers Limited* [2002 JLR Note 10] the Jersey Royal Court held that it was within its inherent jurisdiction to issue a letter of request authorizing an English court to place an

the fact that in Australia there was no jurisdiction to make an equivalent order. Having identified the matters specified in the request from the Australian court, the English court identified the relevant insolvency law applicable to comparable matters falling within its jurisdiction and applied those laws to the matters falling within the request, disregarding the fact that the company which was the subject matter of the request was foreign. The court therefore treated the Australian company as if it was an English company.

However, outside s 426, it is doubtful whether the English court has jurisdiction **31.86** to make an administration order in relation to a foreign company with its centre of main interests outside of the EU. In *Re International Bulk Commodities Ltd*[136] Mummery J held that a company incorporated overseas was a 'company' for the purposes of the provisions in the Insolvency Act relating to administrative receivership. By virtue of the Insolvency Act, s 251, the relevant definition of a 'company' was that contained in the 1985 Act, s 735 (now contained in the 2006 Act, s 1), namely, unless the contrary intention appeared, a company formed and registered under the 1985 Act. However, Mummery J held that it appeared from the provisions relating to administrative receivership that there had been a contrary intention that these provisions should apply to foreign companies.

In *Re Dallhold* Chadwick J held that it would not have been open to the court, **31.87** absent the request made under s 426, to have made an administration order in relation to the Australian company. The reason was that the 1986 Act, s 8 only enabled the English court to make an administration order in relation to a 'company' as defined by the 1985 Act, s 735. Unlike Mummery J, Chadwick J found no contrary intention in the administration provisions to displace this definition. Although contrary views have been expressed,[137] it is suggested that Chadwick J's view was correct.

Although the 1986 Act, s 8 has now been replaced by the administration proced- **31.88** ure in Schedule B1, the definition of company remains the same.[138] Further, the definition in the 2006 Act, s 1 is essentially the same as that which was contained in the 1985 Act, s 735. It follows that the position will remain that, absent a request being made under the Insolvency Act, s 426, the English court will

---

insolvent Jersey company into administration. An administration order was subsequently made by the English court.

[136] [1993] Ch 77. This decision was not followed in *Re Devon and Somerset Farmers Ltd* [1994] Ch 57.

[137] For example, by Moss in Lightman & Moss, *The Law of Administrators and Receivers of Companies*, 4th edn, pp 805–7.

[138] Insolvency Act, Schedule B1, para 111.

not have jurisdiction to make an administration order in relation to a foreign company with its centre of main interests outside the EU.

### Winding up

**31.89** Under the provisions of the Insolvency Act both companies incorporated in England and Wales and, subject to the provisions of the EC Regulation, foreign companies may be wound up. In particular, foreign companies may be wound up as unregistered companies under the Insolvency Act, s 221. It follows that a foreign company with its centre of main interests outside the EU may be wound up by the English court. There are numerous cases in which the English court has in fact made a winding-up order in relation to such companies.

**31.90** In *Re Latreefers Inc*[139] the Court of Appeal held that there are three conditions which must be satisfied for the making of a winding-up order in respect of a foreign company: (1) there must be a sufficient connection with England (which may, but does not necessarily have to, consist of assets within the jurisdiction); (2) there must be a reasonable possibility, if a winding-up order is made, of benefit to those applying for the winding-up order; and (3) one or more persons interested in the distribution of assets of the company must be persons over whom the court can exercise jurisdiction.

**31.91** Under the Insolvency Act, s 221, a foreign company can be wound up on grounds other than insolvency, for example, if the court is of the opinion that it is just and equitable to do so. However, in relation to European companies, Article 22(2) of the Judgments Regulation[140] applies in relation to solvent liquidations and provides that the courts of the Member State in which the company, legal person, or association has its seat shall have exclusive jurisdiction in proceedings which have as their object the validity of the constitution, the nullity or the dissolution of companies or other legal persons or associations of natural or legal persons, or of the validity of the decisions of their organs.[141]

### Company voluntary arrangements

**31.92** As with the provisions relating to administration, the provisions of the Insolvency Act relating to voluntary arrangements apply to companies within the meaning of the 1985 Act, s 735(1) (to be replaced by the 2006 Act, s 1).[142] For the same reasons as discussed above in relation to administration, it is doubtful that company voluntary arrangements are therefore available to a foreign company with its

---

[139] *Stocznia Gdanska SA v Latreefers Inc (No 2)* [2001] 2 BCLC 116, CA.
[140] Council Regulation (EC) No 44/2001 of 22 December 2000 on jurisdiction and the recognition and enforcement of judgments in civil and commercial matters.
[141] *Re Senator Hanseatische Verwaltungsgeschellschaft* [1996] 2 BCLC 563.
[142] Insolvency Act 1986, s 1(4).

centre of main interests outside the EU. However, as with administration, the provisions relating to voluntary arrangements may be applied to a foreign company pursuant to a request made under the Insolvency Act, s 426.[143]

### Schemes of arrangement

Finally, although not strictly an insolvency proceeding, schemes of arrangement **31.93** under the Companies Act 2006 Act, Part 26, ss 895–901, as discussed in Chapter 25, may be sanctioned in relation to a foreign company. A company for the purposes of the Companies Act, Part 26, means any company liable to be wound up under the provisions of the Insolvency Act or the Insolvency (Northern Ireland) Order 1989.[144] In *Re Drax Holdings plc*[145] the court held that the second and third requirements of the test set out in *Latreefers*[146] for winding up a foreign company do not need to be satisfied for the court to have jurisdiction to sanction a scheme in respect of a foreign company since they go to discretion rather than to jurisdiction; it is enough that a sufficient connection with England is shown.

### Obligations of directors in insolvency proceedings

The provisions of the Insolvency Act which require the director of an insolvent **31.94** company to cooperate with office-holders apply where a foreign company is in insolvency proceedings in England. In the case of a foreign company being wound up as an unregistered company the provisions of the Insolvency Act are specifically applied to such companies.[147] In the case of foreign companies placed into liquidation or administration in England on the grounds that their centres of main interests are here, then the relevant provisions of the Insolvency Act must be taken to apply as they would to an English company.[148] The following paragraphs deal with a director's obligations under the Insolvency Act, ss 234–236. These provisions are discussed in more detail in Chapter 29, Section G.

Under the Insolvency Act, s 234 the office-holder is entitled to get in the com- **31.95** pany's property including its books, papers, and records and the court may order any person, including a director, to deliver such property to the office-holder.

---

[143] *Re Television Trade Rentals Ltd* [2002] BPIR 859.

[144] s 895(2)(b).

[145] [2004] 1 WLR 1049. Followed in *Re La Mutuelle du Mans Assurances IARD* [2006] BCC 11; *Re DAP Holdings NV* [2006] BCC 48; *Re Sovereign Marine & General Insurance Co Ltd* [2007] 1 BCLC 228.

[146] Paragraph 23.70 above.

[147] Insolvency Act, ss 221(1), 229(1).

[148] Definitions for the first group of parts of the Insolvency Act relating to corporate insolvency are contained in s 251. This applies the definitions in the Companies 1985, Part XXVI, which include the definition of 'company', *'except in so far as the context otherwise requires'*. Where a foreign company is in liquidation or administration in England because its centre of main interests is in England then the reference to 'company' in Part VI must be read as including such a company.

Under s 235 various persons, including officers of the company, are under a duty to cooperate with the office-holder and to give to the office-holder such information concerning the company and its promotion, formation, business, dealings, affairs, or property as the office-holder may reasonably require.

**31.96** In addition to these provisions, s 236 contains important powers which enable the office-holder to seek orders from the court requiring various persons, including any officer of the company, to submit an affidavit to the court containing an account of his dealings with the company or to produce any books, papers, or other records in his possession or under his control relating to the company or the promotion, formation, business, dealings, affairs, or property of the company. Any person who is brought before the court pursuant to s 236 may also be examined orally on oath.[149]

**31.97** As well as applying where a foreign company is in insolvency proceedings in England, these provisions will apply where the relevant property or documents which the office-holders seeks to obtain are located abroad. The court has jurisdiction under s 236 to make an order requiring the production of documents located abroad where the liquidator reasonably required to see those documents in order to carry out his statutory functions and production of them does not impose an unnecessary or unreasonable burden on the person required to produce them in the light of those requirements.[150]

**31.98** The more difficult question is whether an application under s 236 can be made against a person who it outside the jurisdiction. In *Re Tucker*[151] the Court of Appeal decided that the equivalent provision of the Bankruptcy Act 1914[152] in relation to personal insolvency was confined to persons in England at the relevant time who could be served with a summons of the English court in England. The language of s 236 is similar to that of the Bankruptcy Act 1914 and it might therefore be arguable that the same reasoning should apply. However, under rule 12.12 of the Insolvency Rules 1986 the court is given power to order the service of process outside the jurisdiction and there is no suggestion that this does not include an application under s 236. Accordingly, it is suggested that an application under s 236 can be made against a person outside the jurisdiction.[153]

---

[149] s 237(4).
[150] *Re Mid East Trading Ltd* [1998] 1 All ER 577, CA.
[151] [1990] Ch 148, CA. See also *Re Seagull Manufacturing Co Ltd* [1992] Ch 128.
[152] Bankruptcy Act 1914, s 25.
[153] This was the result in *McIsaac and Wilson, Petitioners* [1995] SLT 498 cited in *Dicey, Morris & Collins*, para 30-085 fn 79, though some aspects of that decision are difficult to support.

The court also has jurisdiction under the Insolvency Act, s 133 to order the public **31.99** examination of a director irrespective of the nationality of the director or whether he is resident or present in England.[154]

*Liabilities of directors arising from insolvency proceedings*

Where a foreign company is subject to insolvency proceedings in England, then it **31.100** will be subject to the same provisions regarding the setting aside of antecedent transactions and the liabilities of directors as if the company was English.[155] Directors' liabilities in these respects are discussed in Chapter 29, Sections I and K.

Accordingly, it has been held that the provisions of the Insolvency Act 1986 which **31.101** impose liability on directors for wrongful trading may apply to the directors of a foreign company in liquidation in England.[156] This was so despite the fact that the directors were resident and abroad and there was no similar liability under the law of the country in which the company was incorporated. Indeed, it is important to note that the possibility of bringing claims against the directors of a foreign company under the Insolvency Act, ss 213 and 214 (fraudulent trading and wrongful trading) may itself be a reason why it is appropriate for the English court to make a winding-up order in respect of a foreign company.[157] In addition, claims may be made against directors of a foreign company in the English court under ss 213 and 214 pursuant to s 426 where a request has been received from the courts of a relevant country or territory even though the company is not in fact in insolvency proceedings in England.[158]

The provisions relating to the setting aside of antecedent transactions on grounds **31.102** that they were at an undervalue or were preferences contained in the Insolvency Act, ss 238, 239, and 423 will also apply in relation to a foreign company in insolvency proceedings in England so as to enable the court to grant relief against any person whether or not they are resident in England.[159] There is no territorial limitation on the application of these provisions. However, the relief under these provisions is discretionary and, if a foreign element is involved, the court will need to be satisfied that in respect of the relief sought against him the defendant is sufficiently connected with England for it to be just and proper to make the order against him despite the foreign element.

---

[154] *Re Seagull Manufacturing Co Ltd* [1992] Ch 128.

[155] See in relation to the winding up of a foreign company, Insolvency Act 1986, ss 221(1), 229(1).

[156] *Re Howard Holdings Inc* [1998] BCC 549.

[157] *International Westminster Bank plc v Okeanos Maritime Corp* [1988] Ch 210; *Stocznia Gdanska SA v Latreefers Inc (No 2)* [2001] 2 BCLC 116, Lloyd J and CA.

[158] *Re Bank of Credit and Commerce International SA (No 9)* [1994] 2 BCLC 636.

[159] *Re Paramount Airways Ltd* [1993] Ch 223, CA. See also *Jyske Bank (Gibraltar) Ltd v Spjeldnaes* [1999] 2 BCLC 101; *Banco Nacional de Cuba v Cosmos Trading Corp* [2000] 1 BCLC 813, CA.

**31.103**   The EC Regulation on Insolvency Proceedings also envisages that avoidance actions such as those available under ss 238, 239, and 423 are governed by the law of the state in which the proceedings are opened.[160] The position would be more complex where there two sets of insolvency proceedings in different countries and the matter falls outside the scope of the EC Regulation. In those circumstances, it is to be expected that the courts and the laws of the country in which the principal insolvency proceedings are based would be permitted to take the lead.[161]

**31.104**   In addition, where a proposed respondent to an application is located abroad it is necessary for the applicant to seek the leave of the court for service out of the jurisdiction. The Insolvency Rules 1986 disapply the usual rules contained in the Civil Procedure Rules and make specific provision for service out of the jurisdiction of any proceedings arising in the course of insolvency proceedings with the permission of the court (rule 12.12).[162] The court will make an order under this rule where it is satisfied that there is a real issue between the claimant and the defendant which the claimant can reasonably ask the court to try.[163] Where a foreign element is involved one of the factors which the court will consider is whether the defendant has a sufficient connection with England in connection with the relief sought.[164]

**31.105**   In relation to the disqualification of directors under the CDDA, the provisions apply to any company wherever incorporated which could be wound up under the Insolvency Act[165] and anyone, of whatever nationality, can be disqualified for conduct rendering him unfit to be a director of a company.[166] This is irrespective of where the conduct complained of occurred. Disqualification under the CDDA is discussed in Chapter 28.

---

[160] Article 4(2)(m).

[161] *In re Maxwell Communication Corporation* 170 BR 800 (US Bankruptcy Court for the Southern District of New York) presented an analogous problem, in relation to the question of which system of law should govern the avoidability of pre-insolvency transactions, which the US bankruptcy and district courts resolved by deferring to English law and the English courts based on the finding that England was the centre of the case. This was despite the fact that US creditors would have done better if US rather than English law been applied to the preference issue.

[162] Rule 12.12 does not apply to claims made under the Insolvency Act, s 324 and permission for service out of the jurisdiction has to be sought under CPR rule 6.20: *Re Banco Nacional de Cuba* [2001] 1 WLR 2039.

[163] *Re Paramount Airways Ltd* [1993] Ch 223, CA; *Re Howard Holdings Inc* [1998] BCC 549.

[164] *Re Paramount Airways Ltd* [1993] Ch 223, CA.

[165] See CDDA, ss 6(1), 22(2).

[166] *Re Seagull Manufacturing Co Ltd (No 2)* [1994] Ch 91.

## I. Foreign Disqualification

The 2006 Act, Part 40, ss 1182–1191, come into force on 1 October 2009[167] and **31.106** give the Secretary of State power to make regulations for the disqualification of persons who are subject to foreign restrictions.

These provisions close a gap in the previous law. Previously, a person who was **31.107** disqualified from acting as a director, or subject to a similar restriction, in another country was able to act as a director of a company in the UK. Part 40 of the 2006 Act closes this gap by empowering the Secretary of State to make regulations to disqualify persons who have been disqualified in another country from acting as directors of a UK company.

For these purposes, a person is subject to 'foreign restrictions' if under the law of **31.108** another country or territory he is, by reason of misconduct or unfitness, disqualified to any extent from acting in connection with the affairs of a company or he is, by reason of misconduct or unfitness, required to obtain permission or meet any other condition before acting in connection with the affairs of a company or he has, by reason of misconduct or unfitness, given relevant undertakings.[168] This is intended to encompass those persons who have been disqualified under, or fallen foul of, foreign laws equivalent to the Company Directors Disqualification Act 1986.[169]

The regulations may make any provision for any such person being disqualified **31.109** from being a director of a UK company, acting as receiver of a UK company's property or, in any way, whether directly or indirectly, being concerned or taking part in the promotion, formation, or management of a UK company.[170]

---

[167] 2006 Act Commencement Order No 8, art 3(w).
[168] 2006 Act, s 1182(2).
[169] See the Explanatory Notes to the 2006 Act.
[170] 2006 Act, s 1184(1).

# Implementation of the Companies Act 2006

Provisions of the Companies Act 2006 in force as at 1 October 2008, either on the Royal Assent pursuant to s 1300(1) or pursuant to the following Commencement Orders:

The Companies Act 2006 (Commencement No 1, Transitional Provisions and Savings) Order 2006, made 20 December 2006 (SI 2006/3428)

The Companies Act 2006 (Commencement No 2, Consequential Amendments, Transitional Provisions and Savings) Order 2007, made 29 March 2007 (SI 2007/1093)

The Companies Act 2006 (Commencement No 3, Consequential Amendments, Transitional Provisions and Savings) Order 2007, made 25 July 2007 (SI 2007/2194)

The Companies Act 2006 (Commencement No 4 and Commencement No 3 (Amendment)) Order 2007, made 6 September 2007 (SI 2007/2607)

The Companies Act 2006 (Commencement No 5, Transitional Provisions and Savings) Order 2007, made 17 December 2007 (SI 2007/3495)

The Companies Act 2006 (Commencement No 6, Savings and Commencement Nos 3 and 5 (Amendment) Order 2008, made 7 March 2008 (SI 2008/674)

The Companies Act 2006 (Commencement No 7 and Transitional Provisions) Order 2008, made 16 July 2008 (SI 2008/1886)

The Companies Act 2006 (Commencement No 8, Transitional Provisions and Savings) Order 2008 (SI 2008/2860).

Those regulations and orders which have been published in draft are shown in italics.

| Part or Sections | Subject of Part or Sections | 2006 Act Comm. Order | In force | Supporting Regulations | Under sections of the 2006 Act[1] | In force |
|---|---|---|---|---|---|---|
| Part 1 | General Introductory Provisions | | | | | |
| 1 | Companies | 8, art 3(a) | 1.10.09 | | | |
| 2 | The Companies Acts | 2, art 2(1)(a) | 6.4.07 | | | |
| 3–6 | *Types of company* | *8, art 3(a)* | *1.10.09* | | | |

[1] In addition to ss 1288–1292, 1294 and any provisions in Part 38 (Companies: Interpretation) and Part 39 (Companies: Minor Amendments).

| Part or Sections | Subject of Part or Sections | 2006 Act Comm. Order | In force | Supporting Regulations | Under sections of the 2006 Act | In force |
|---|---|---|---|---|---|---|
| **Part 2** | **Company Formation** | | | | | |
| 7–16 | General: method of forming a company, memorandum of association; requirements for registration; registration and effect | 8, art 3(b) | 1.10.09 | The Companies (Registration) Regs (SI 2008/3014) | 8(2), 10(3), 11(2) | 1.10.09 |
| | | | | *The Companies (Shares, Share Capital and Authorised Minimum) Regs (SI 2008/*)* | 10(2) | 1.1 0.09 |
| **Part 3** | **A Company's Constitution** | | | | | |
| 17-28 | Introductory, articles of association | 8, art 3(c) | 1.10.09 | The Companies (Model Articles) Regs (SI 2008/3229) | 19 | 1.10.09 |
| 29, 30 | Resolutions and agreements affecting a company's constitution to be forwarded to the Registrar | 3, art 2(1)(a) | 1.10.07 | | | |
| 31–38 | Statement of company's objects; supplementary provisions | 8, art 3(c) | 1.10.09 | *The Companies (Shares, Share Capital and Authorised Minimum) Regs (SI 2008/*)* | 32(2) | 1.10.09 |
| **Part 4** | **A Company's Capacity and Related Matters** | | | | | |
| 39–43, 45–52 | Capacity of company and power of directors to bind it, formalities of doing business and other matters concerning official seal, pre-incorporation contracts, bills of exchange, and promissory notes | 8, art 3(d) | 1.10.09 | | | |

| Part or Sections | Subject of Part or Sections | 2006 Act Comm. Order | In force | Supporting Regulations | Under sections of the 2006 Act | In force |
|---|---|---|---|---|---|---|
| **Part 4** | **A Company's Capacity and Related Matters** | | | | | |
| 44 | Execution of documents | 5, art 3(1)(a) | 6.4.08 | | | |
| **Part 5** | **A Company's Name** | | | | | |
| 53-68 | Prohibited names, sensitive words and expressions, permitted characters; indications of company type or legal form; similarity to other name on Registrar's index | 8, art 3(e) | 1.10.09 | The Company and Business Names (Miscellaneous Provisions) Regs (SI 2008/*) | 57, 60, 65, 66[2] | 1.10.09 |
| | | | | *The Non-Companies Acts Companies Authorised to Register Regs (SI 2008/*)* | *54(1)(c), 55, 56(1), 65(1) and (2), 66(2), 67(2)* | *1.10.09* |
| 69–74 | Similarity to other name in which person has goodwill | 5, art 5(1)(a) | 1.10.08 | The Company Names Adjudicator Rules (SI 2008/1738) | 71 | 1.10.08 |
| | | | | *The Non-Companies Acts Companies Authorised to Register Regs (SI 2008/*)* | *71* | *1.10.09* |
| 75–81 | Powers of Secretary of State in relation to misleading information and indication of activities; change of name | 8, art 3(e) | 1.10.09 | | | |

---

[2] Also under Part 41 (Business Names), s 1197.

| Part or Sections | Subject of Part or Sections | 2006 Act Comm. Order | In force | Supporting Regulations | Under sections of the 2006 Act | In force |
|---|---|---|---|---|---|---|
| **Part 5** | **A Company's Name** | | | | | |
| 82–85 | Trading disclosures | 5, art 5(1)(b) | 1.10.08 | The Companies (Trading Disclosures) Regs (SI 2008/495) | 82, 84 | 1.10.08 |
| | | | | *The Non-Companies Acts Companies Authorised to Register Regs (SI 2008/\*)* | *82, 84* | *1.10.09* |
| | | | | *The Companies (Unregistered Companies) Regs (SI 2008/\*)* | *82, 84* | *1.10.09* |
| | | | | *The Companies (Trading Disclosures) (Amendment) Regs (SI 2008/\*)* | *82* | *1.10.09* |
| **Part 6** | **A Company's Registered Office** | | | | | |
| 86–88 | General, Welsh companies | 8, art 3(f) | 1.10.09 | | | |
| **Part 7** | **Re-Registration as a Means of Altering a Company's Status** | | | | | |
| 89–111 | Introductory, private company becoming public, public company becoming private, private limited company becoming unlimited, unlimited private company becoming limited, and public company becoming private and unlimited | 8, art 3(g) | 1.10.09 | The Companies (Registration) Regs (SI 2008/3014) | 103(2)(a), 110(2)(a) | 1.10.09 |

| Part or Sections | Subject of Part or Sections | 2006 Act Comm. Order | In force | Supporting Regulations | Under sections of the 2006 Act | In force |
|---|---|---|---|---|---|---|
| Part 7 | Re-Registration as a Means of Altering a Company's Status | | | | | |
| | | | | *The Companies (Shares, Share Capital and Authorised Minimum) Regs (SI 2008/\*)* | 108(3) | 1.10.09 |
| Part 8 | A Company's Members | | | | | |
| 112–115, 120, 122–127, 129–144 | Members of a company; the register of members other than provisions in ss 116–119, 121 and 128; overseas branch registers; prohibition of subsidiary company being a member of its holding company | 8, art 3(h) | 1.10.09 | | | |
| 116–119 | Right to inspect or require copy of register of members[3] | 3, art 2(1)(b) | 1.10.07 | The Companies (Fees for Inspection and Copying of Company Records) Regs (SI 2007/2612) | 116(1)(b), (2) | 1.10.07 |
| 121, 128 | Removal of entries relating to former members; time limit for claims arising from entry in register | 5, art 3(1)(b) | 6.4.08 | | | |

---

[3] These sections introduce safeguards so that public right of access to a company's register is not abused. The Companies Act 2006 (Annual Return and Service Address) Regs 2008 (SI 2008/3000) replace the requirement for every company limited by share capital to provide the names and addresses of all its members with effect from 1 October 2009, so that after that members' addresses need not be shown. Until then the Companies Act

| Part or Sections | Subject of Part or Sections | 2006 Act Comm. Order | In force | Supporting Regulations | Under sections of the 2006 Act | In force |
|---|---|---|---|---|---|---|
| **Part 9** | **Exercise of Members' Rights** | | | | | |
| 145–153 | Effect of provisions in company's articles, information rights, exercise of rights where shares are held on behalf of others | 3, art 2(1)(c) | 1.10.07 | | | |
| **Part 10** | **A Company's Directors** | | | | | |
| 154 | Companies required to have directors | 3, art 2(1)(d) | 1.10.07 | | | |
| 155–159 | Requirement to have at least one director who is a natural person;[4] under-age directors | 5, art 5(1)(c) | 1.10.08 | | | |
| 160, 161 | Appointment of directors of public company to be void unless voted on individually; validity of acts of directors; | 3, art 2(1)(d) | 1.10.07 | | | |
| 162–167 | Register of directors | 8, art 3(i) | 1.10.09 | The Companies (Fees for Inspection of Company Records) Regs (SI 2008/3007) | 162(5)(b) | 1.10.09 |
| 168, 169 | Resolution to remove a director; director's right to protest against removal | 3, art 2(1)(d) | 1.10.07 | | | |

1985 (Annual Return) and Companies (Principal Business Activities) (Amendment) Regs 2008 (SI 2008/1659) contains similar provisions which applies from 1 October 2008 to 1 October 2009.

[4] para 46 of Schedule 4 to Commencement Order No 5 gives a grace period until 1 October 2010 if on 6 November 2006 none of the company's directors was a natural person and the 1985 Act, s 282 was complied with in relation to the company.

| Part or Sections | Subject of Part or Sections | 2006 Act Comm. Order | In force | Supporting Regulations | Under sections of the 2006 Act | In force |
|---|---|---|---|---|---|---|
| Part 10 | A Company's Directors | | | | | |
| 170–174 | General duties of directors: scope and nature; duties to act within powers, to promote the success of the company, to exercise independent judgment, and to exercise reasonable skill, care, and diligence; consent approval or authorization of members; modifications for charitable companies | 3, art 2(1)(d) | 1.10.07 | | | |
| 175–177 | General duties of directors: duties to avoid conflict of interest,[5] not to accept benefits from third parties and to declare interest in proposed transaction or arrangement | 5, art 5(1)(d) | 1.10.08 | | | |
| 178–181 | Civil consequences of breach; cases within more than one of the general duties; consent, approval, or authorization by members; modification in relation to charitable companies of provisions relating to those duties | 3, art 2(1)(d) | 1.10.07 | | | |

[5]  para 47 of Schedule 4 to Commencement Order No 5 makes the option in the 2006 Act, s 175, whereby disinterested directors can authorize a conflict, available to private companies if the members agree by ordinary resolution.

| Part or Sections | Subject of Part or Sections | 2006 Act Comm. Order | In force | Supporting Regulations | Under sections of the 2006 Act | In force |
|---|---|---|---|---|---|---|
| **Part 10** | **A Company's Directors** | | | | | |
| 182–187 | Duty of directors to declare of interest in existing transaction or arrangement | 5, art 5(1)(e) | 1.10.08 | | | |
| 188–226 | Transactions with directors requiring approval of members | 3, art 2(1)(d) | 1.10.07 | | | |
| 227–230 | Directors' service contracts | 3, art 2(1)(d) | 1.10.07 | The Companies (Fees for Inspection and Copying of Company Records) Regs (SI 2007/2612) | 229(2) | 1.10.07 |
| 231 | Contracts with sole members who are directors | 3, art 2(1)(d) | 1.10.07 | | | |
| 232–239 | Directors' liabilities: provisions protecting directors from liability; ratification of acts giving rise to liability | 3, art 2(1)(d) | 1.10.07 | The Companies (Fees for Inspection and Copying of Company Records) Regs (SI 2007/2612) | 238(2) | |
| 240–246 | Directors' residential addresses, protection from disclosure | 8, art 3(i) | 1.10.09 | The Companies (Disclosure of Address) Regs (SI 2008/*) | 243(3)–(6) | 1.10.09 |
| *247* | *Provision for employees on cessation of business* | *8, art 3(i)* | 1.10.09 | | | |
| | | | | *The Non-Companies Acts Companies Authorised to Register Regs (SI 2008/*)* | *243(3)–(6)* | *1.10.09* |
| | | | | *The Companies (Unregistered Companies) Regs (SI 2008/*)* | *243(3)–(6)* | *1.10.09* |

| Part or Sections | Subject of Part or Sections | 2006 Act Comm. Order | In force | Supporting Regulations | Under sections of the 2006 Act | In force |
|---|---|---|---|---|---|---|
| **Part 10** | **A Company's Directors** | | | | | |
| 248–259 and Schedule 1 | Supplementary provisions: records of meeting of directors; meaning of director and shadow director; other definitions | 3, art 2(1)⁶ | 1.10.07 | | | |
| **Part 11** | **Derivative Claims and Proceedings by Members** | | | | | |
| 260–269 | Derivative claims in England and Wales and Northern Ireland; derivative proceedings in Scotland | 3, art 2(1)(e) | 1.10.07 | | | |
| **Part 12** | **Company Secretaries** | | | | | |
| 270–274, 280 | Private company not required to have secretary; secretaries of public companies; discharge of functions where office vacant or secretary unable to act; acts done by person in dual capacity | 5, art 3(1)(c) | 6.4.08 | | | |
| 275–279 | Register of secretaries to be kept by private companies with a secretary and by public companies | 8, art 3(j) | 1.10.09 | The Companies (Fees for Inspection of Company Records) Regs (SI 2008/3007) | 275(5)(b) | 1.10.09 |

⁶ 2006 Act Commencement Order No 4, art 4(1) substitutes '248' for '247', in order to postpone the coming into force of s 247 (provision for employees on cessation or transfer of business) until 2006 Act, s 31 is also in force.

| Part or Sections | Subject of Part or Sections | 2006 Act Comm. Order | In force | Supporting Regulations | Under sections of the 2006 Act | In force |
|---|---|---|---|---|---|---|
| **Part 13** | **Resolutions and Meetings** | | | | | |
| 308, 309, 333 | Notice of meetings to be given in hard copy form, in electronic form or by means of a website or partly by one such means and partly by another | 1, art 3(1)(a) and (b) | 20.1.07 | | | |
| 281–307, 310–327(2)(b), 327(3)–330(6)(b), 330(7)–332, 334–361 | The remaining provisions about resolutions and meetings, except for ss 327(2)(c) and 330(6)(c) relating to polls | 3, art 2(1)(f) | 1.10.07 | The Companies (Fees for Inspection and Copying of Company Records) Regs (SI 2007/2612) | 358(4) | 1.10.07 |
| **Part 14** | **Control of Political Donations and Expenditure** | | | | | |
| 362–379 | All provisions except those relating to independent election candidates | 3, arts 2(2) | 1.10.07 | The Companies (Political Expenditure Exemption) Order (SI 2007/2081) | 377 | 1.10.07 |
| | | | | The Companies (Interest Rate for Unauthorised Political Donation or Expenditure) Regs (SI 2008/2242) | 369(5)(b) | 1.10.07 |
| 362–379 | Provisions relating to independent election candidates | 3, art 5(1) | 1.10.08 | *The Non-Companies Acts Companies Authorised to Register Regs (SI 2008/\*)* | 377 | *1.10.09* |
| | | | | *The Companies (Unregistered Companies) Regs (SI 2008/\*)* | 377 | *1.10.09* |

| Part or Sections | Subject of Part or Sections | 2006 Act Comm. Order | In force | Supporting Regulations | Under sections of the 2006 Act | In force |
|---|---|---|---|---|---|---|
| **Part 15** | **Accounts and Reports** | | | | | |
| 417 | Contents of directors' report: business report (no application to a company subject to the small companies regime) | 3, art 2(1)(g) | 1.10.07 | | | |
| 463 | Liability for false and misleading statements in directors' report, directors' remuneration report, and summary financial statement so far as derived from either of those reports | 1, art 3(1)(c) | 20.1.07 | | | |
| 380–416, 418–462, 464–474 | The remaining provisions about accounts and reports | 5, art 3(1)(d) | 6.4.08 | The Companies (Revision of Defective Accounts and Reports) Regs (SI 2008/373) | 454(3) | 6.4.08 |
| | | | | The Companies (Summary Financial Statement) Regs (SI 2008/374) | 426(1), 427(2)–(5), 428(2)–(5) | 6.4.08 |
| | | | | The Companies Act 2006 (Amendment) (Accounts and Reports) Regs (SI 2008/393) | 468(1) and (2), 473(2) | 6.4.08 |
| | | | | The Small Companies and Groups (Accounts and Directors' Report) Regs (SI 2008/409) | 396(3), 404(3), 409(1)–(3), 412(1)–(3), 416(4), 443(3) (a) and (b) | 6.4.08 |

| Part or Sections | Subject of Part or Sections | 2006 Act Comm. Order | In force | Supporting Regulations | Under sections of the 2006 Act | In force |
|---|---|---|---|---|---|---|
| Part 15 | Accounts and Reports | | | | | |
| | | | | The Large and Medium-Sized Companies and Groups (Accounts and Reports) Regs (SI 2008/410) | 396(3), 404(3), 409(1)–(3), 412(1)–(3), 416(4), 421(1) and (2), 445(3)(a) | 6.4.08 |
| | | | | The Companies (Late Filing Penalties) and Limited Liability Partnerships (Filing Periods and Late Filing Penalties) Regs (SI 2008/497) | 453 | 6.4.08 |
| | | | | The Companies (Defective Accounts and Directors' Reports) (Authorised Person) and Supervision of Accounts and Reports (Prescribed Body) Order (SI 2008/623) | 457 | 6.4.08 |
| | | | | *The Companies Act 2006 (Accounts, Reports, and Audit) Regs (SI 2009/*)* | *468(1), (2)* | *6.4.09* |
| | | | | *The Non-Companies Acts Companies Authorised to Register Regs (SI 2008/*)* | *409, 412, 416(4)* | *1.10.09* |
| | | | | *The Companies (Unregistered Companies) Regs (SI 2008/*)* | *409, 412, 416(4)* | *1.10.09* |
| Part 16 | Audit | | | | | |
| 485–488 | Appointment of auditors of a private company | 3, art 2(1)(h) | 1.10.07 | | | |

| Part or Sections | Subject of Part or Sections | 2006 Act Comm. Order | In force | Supporting Regulations | Under sections of the 2006 Act | In force |
|---|---|---|---|---|---|---|
| **Part 16** | **Audit** | | | | | |
| 475–484, 489–539 | The remaining provisions about audit | 5, art 3(1)(e) | 6.4.08 | The Companies Act 2006 (Amendment) (Accounts and Reports) Regs (SI 2008/393) | 484 | 6.4.08 |
| | | | | The Companies (Disclosure of Auditor Remuneration and Liability Limitation Agreements) Regs (SI 2008/489) | 494, 538 | 6.4.08 |
| | | | | The Statutory Auditors (Delegation of Functions etc) Order (SI 2008/496) | 504(1)(b)(ii) | 6.4.08[7] |
| | | | | *The Non-Companies Acts Companies Authorised to Register Regs (SI 2008/\*)* | 494 | 1.10.09 |
| | | | | *The Companies (Unregistered Companies) Regs (SI 2008/\*)* | 494 | 1.10.09 |
| **Part 17** | **A Company's Share Capital** | | | | | |
| 544 | Shares and interests in shares are transferable in accordance with a company's articles, but subject to Part 21 (title may be transferred or evidenced without written instrument) | 5, art 3(1)(f) | 6.4.08 | | | |

---

[7] Except that arts 1 and 2 came into force on 1 March 2008, arts 3, 6, and 8 came into force on 1 March 2008 for the purposes of functions in relation to appointments of auditors for financial years beginning on or after 6 April 2008, and arts 4 and 9 came into force on 29 June 2008 for the purpose of transferring the functions under ss 1242–1244 and Schedule 12 in relation to appointments of registered third country auditors for financial years beginning on or after 29 June 2008.

| Part or Sections | Subject of Part or Sections | 2006 Act Comm. Order | In force | Supporting Regulations | Under sections of the 2006 Act | In force |
|---|---|---|---|---|---|---|
| **Part 17** | **A Company's Share Capital** | | | | | |
| 641(1)(a), (2)–(6), 642–644, 652(1) and (3), 654 | Reduction of capital of private company; treatment of reserve arising from reduction of capital | 7, art 2(a)–(c) | 1.10.08 | The Companies (Reduction of Share Capital) Order (SI 2008/1915) | 643 | 1.10.08 |
| 540–543, 545–640, 641(b), 645–651, 652(2), 653, 655–657 | The remaining provisions about share capital: allotment of shares, share premiums, alteration of share capital, classes of shares and class rights, reduction of capital | 8, art 3(k) | 1.10.09 | *The Companies (Shares, Share Capital and Authorised Minimum) Regs (SI 2008/\*)* | 555(3) and (4), 556(3), 583(4), 619(3), 621(3), 625(3), 627(3), 649(2) | 1.10.09 |
| **Part 18** | **Acquisition by Limited Company of its own Shares** | | | | | |
| 658–737 | General provisions, financial assistance for purchase of own shares,[8] | 8, art 3(l) | 1.10.09 | The Companies (Shares, Share Capital and Authorised Minimum) Regs (SI 2008/\*) | 663(3), 689(3), 708(3), 730(5) | 1.10.09 |
| **Part 19** | **Debentures** | | | | | |
| 738–754 | All the provisions about debentures | 5, art 3(1)(g) | 6.4.08 | The Companies (Fees for Inspecting and Copying of Company Records) (No 2) Regs (SI 2007/3535) | 744(1)(b), 744(2), 749(1) | 6.4.08 |

---

[8] 2006 Act Commencement Order No 5, arts 5(2) and 8(b) and Schedule 3 repealed the restrictions under 1985 Act, ss 151–153 and 155–158 on the giving by a private company of financial assistance for the acquisition of its own shares, including the 'whitewash' procedure with effect from 1 October 2008.

| Part or Sections | Subject of Part or Sections | 2006 Act Comm. Order | In force | Supporting Regulations | Under sections of the 2006 Act | In force |
|---|---|---|---|---|---|---|
| **Part 20** | **Private and Public Companies** | | | | | |
| 755–767 | Prohibition of public offers by private companies; minimum share capital requirement for public companies | 5, art 3(1)(h) | 6.4.08 | The Companies (Authorised Minimum) Regs (SI 2008/729) | 763, 766(1)(a) and (2) | 6.4.08 |
| | | | | The Companies (Shares, Share Capital and Authorised Minimum) Regs (SI 2008/*) | 763(2), 766 | 1.10.09 |
| **Part 21** | **Certification and Transfer of Securities** | | | | | |
| 768–790 | All the provisions about certification of transfer of securities | 5, art 3(1)(i) | 6.4.08 | | | |
| **Part 22** | **Information about Interests in a Company's Shares** | | | | | |
| 791–810, 811(1)–(3), 813, 815–828 | All the provisions about information about interests in a company's shares, except the provisions about inspecting the register of disclosed interests | 1, art 3(1)(d) | 20.1.07 | The Companies (Fees for Inspection and Copying of Company Records) Regs (SI 2007/2612) | 807(2), 811(2) | 1.10.07 |
| 811(4), 812, 814 | Exercise of right to inspect register of disclosed interests in company shares | 5, art 3(1)(j) | 6.4.08 | | | |
| **Part 23** | **Distributions** | | | | | |
| 829–853 | All the provisions about distributions | 5, art 3(1)(k) | 6.4.08 | | | |

| Part or Sections | Subject of Part or Sections | 2006 Act Comm. Order | In force | Supporting Regulations | Under sections of the 2006 Act | In force |
|---|---|---|---|---|---|---|
| **Part 24** | **A Company's Annual Return** | | | | | |
| 854–859 | Delivery and contents | 8, art 3(m) | 1.10.09 | The Companies Act 2006 (Annual Return and Service Addresses) Regs (SI 2008/*)[9] | 855, 856, 857 | 1.10.09 |
| | | | | *The Non-Companies Acts Companies Authorised to Register Regs (SI 2008/*)* | *857* | 1.10.09 |
| | | | | *The Companies (Unregistered Companies) Regs (SI 2008/*)* | *857* | *1.10.09* |
| **Part 25** | **Company Charges** | | | | | |
| 860–894 | All the provisions about registration of charges | 8, art 3(n) | 1.10.09 | The Companies (Particulars of Company Charges) Regs (SI 2008/2996) | 860, 862, 878, 880 | 1.10.09 |
| | | | | The Companies (Fees for Inspection of Company Records) Regs (SI 2008/3007) | 877, 892 | 1.10.09 |
| **Part 26** | **Arrangements and Reconstructions** | | | | | |
| 895–901 | All the provisions about arrangements and reconstructions | 5, art 3(1)(l) | 6.4.08 | | | |
| **Part 27** | **Mergers and Divisions of Public Companies** | | | | | |
| 902–941 | All the provisions about mergers and divisions of public companies | 5, art 3(1)(m) | 6.4.08 | | | |

---

[9] The Companies Act 1985 (Annual Return) and Companies (Principal Business Activities) (Amendment) Regs (SI 2008/1659) came into force on 1 October 2008. See footnote 3 above.

| Part or Sections | Subject of Part or Sections | 2006 Act Comm. Order | In force | Supporting Regulations | Under sections of the 2006 Act | In force |
|---|---|---|---|---|---|---|
| **Part 28** | **Takeovers etc** | | | | | |
| 942–992 and Schedule 2 | All the provisions about takeovers: takeover panel; impediments to takeovers; squeeze-out and squeeze-in | 2, art 2(1)(b) | 6.4.07 | | | |
| **Part 29** | **Fraudulent Trading** | | | | | |
| 993 | The offence of fraudulent trading | 3, art 2(1)(i) | 1.10.07 | | | |
| **Part 30** | **Protection of Members against Unfair Prejudice** | | | | | |
| 994–999 | All the provisions about protection of members from unfair prejudice | 3, art 2(1)(j) | 1.10.07 | [Rules are made under the Insolvency Act, s 411] | | |
| **Part 31** | **Dissolution and Restoration to the Register** | | | | | |
| 1000–1034 | Striking off; property of a dissolved company; restoration to the register | 8, art 3(o) | 1.10.09 | *The Companies (Registrar of Companies and Applications for Striking Off) Regs (SI 2008/*)*[10] | *1003(2)* | *1.10.09* |
| **Part 32** | **Company Investigations: Amendments** | | | | | |
| 1035–1039[11] | All the provisions amending the 1985 Act, Part XIV about investigations | 3, art 2(1)(k) | 1.10.07 | | | |

---

[10] This version will be withdrawn and an amended version laid in draft in early 2009.

[11] Also s 1124 and Schedule 3.

| Part or Sections | Subject of Part or Sections | 2006 Act Comm. Order | In force | Supporting Regulations | Under sections of the 2006 Act | In force |
|---|---|---|---|---|---|---|
| Part 33 | UK Companies not Formed under Companies Legislation | | | | | |
| 1040–1042 | Companies not formed under companies legislation but authorized to register | 8, art 3(p) | 1.10.09 | *The Non-Companies Acts Companies Authorised to Register Regs (SI 2008/\*)* | 1042 | 1.10.09 |
| 1043 | Unregistered companies | 2, art 2(1)(c) | 6.4.07 | The Companies Acts (Unregistered Companies) Regs (SI 2007/318) | 1043 | 6.4.07 |
| | | | | *The Companies (Unregistered Companies) Regs (SI 2008/\*)* | *1043* | *1.10.09* |
| Part 34 | Overseas Companies | | | | | |
| 1044–1059 | All the provisions about overseas companies | 8, art 3(q) | 1.10.09 | *Overseas Companies Regs (SI 2008/\*)* | 1045(1), 1046(1), (2), (4) and (6), 1047(1), 1049(1)–(3), 1050(3)–(5), 1051(1)–(3), 1052(1)–(4), 1053(2)–(5), 1054(1) and (2), 1055, 1056, 1057(2), 1058(1)–(3) | 1.10.09 |
| Part 35 | The Registrar of Companies | | | | | |
| 1063 | Fees payable to Registrar | 1, art 4(1)(a) | 6.4.07 | | | |
| 1068(1) – (4), (6) and (7) | Registrar's duty to accept delivery by electronic means of documents so far as necessary for documents subject to Directive disclosure requirements | 3, art 4(1) | 15.12.07 | | | |

| Part or Sections | Subject of Part or Sections | 2006 Act Comm. Order | In force | Supporting Regulations | Under sections of the 2006 Act | In force |
|---|---|---|---|---|---|---|
| **Part 35** | **The Registrar of Companies** | | | | | |
| 1068(5) | Registrar's duty to accept delivery by electronic means of documents subject to Directive disclosure requirements | 1, art 2(1)(a) | 1.1.07 | | | |
| 1077–1080 | Public notice by the Registrar of receipt of certain documents subject to Directive disclosure requirements (constitutional documents, particulars of directors, accounts, reports and returns, registered office, winding up, and in the case of a public company: particulars of share capital, mergers, and divisions); record-keeping by Registrar | 1, art 2(1)(b)–(e) | 1.1.07 | | | |
| 1085–1092 | Inspection of the register and right to take copies | 1, art 2(1)(f) | 1.1.07 | The Companies (Registrar, Languages and Trading Disclosures) Regs (SI 2006/3429) | 1091(4) | 1.1.07 |
| | | | | *The Companies (Disclosure of Address) Regs (SI 2008/\*)* | 1088(1)–(3) and (5) | 1.10.09 |
| 1102–1107 | Language requirements and translation | 1, art 2(1)(g) | 1.1.07 | The Companies (Registrar, Languages and Trading Disclosures) Regs (SI 2006/3429) | 1105(2)(d), 1106(2) | 1.1.07 |

| Part or Sections | Subject of Part or Sections | 2006 Act Comm. Order | In force | Supporting Regulations | Under sections of the 2006 Act | In force |
|---|---|---|---|---|---|---|
| Part 35 | The Registrar of Companies | | | | | |
| 1111 | Certification and verification of documents delivered to Registrar | 1, art 2(1)(h) | 1.1.07 | | | |
| 1060– 1062, 1063,[12] 1064– 1067, 1068(1)– (4), (6) and (7), 1069– 1076, 1081– 1084, 1093– 1101, 1112–1120 | The Registrar, registered numbers, delivery of documents to the Registrar, requirements for proper delivery, the register, correction or removal of material on the register, the Registrar's index of names, language requirements and transliteration, supplementary provisions[13] | 8, art 3(r) | 1.10.09 | *The Companies (Disclosure of Address) Regs (SI 2008/*)* | *1081(2)* | *1.10.09* |
| Part 36 | Offences under the Companies Acts | | | | | |
| 1120–1123 | Liability of officer in default | | With relevant provisions[14] | | | |
| 1124 and Schedule 3 | Amendments to offences under the 1985 Act | 3, art 2(1)(k) | 1.10.07 | | | |
| 1125 | Meaning of 'daily default fine' | | With relevant provisions | | | |

[12] So far as not already in force.

[13] 2006 Act Commencement Order No 5, art 3(2) brought into force s 1117(1)–(3) to enable the Registrar to make and publicize rules on 6 April 2008.

[14] These sections and ss 1125, 1127–1133 are fully brought into force on 1 October 2009 by 2006 Act Commencement Order No 8, art 3(s).

| Part or Sections | Subject of Part or Sections | 2006 Act Comm. Order | In force | Supporting Regulations | Under sections of the 2006 Act | In force |
|---|---|---|---|---|---|---|
| **Part 36** | **Offences under the Companies Acts** | | | | | |
| 1126 | Consents required for prosecutions under the 2006 Act, ss 458, 460, or 949 (offences of unauthorized disclosure of information), the 2006 Act, s 953 (failure to comply with rules about takeover bids), the 1985 Act, ss 448–451, or 453A (offences in connection with company investigations), and the 2006 Act, s 798 or the 1985 Act, s 455 (offence of attempting to evade restrictions on shares) | 5, art 3(1)(n) | 6.4.08 | | | |
| 1127–1133 | General provisions, production and inspection of documents, transitional provision | | With relevant provisions | | | |
| **Part 37** | **Companies: Supplementary Provisions** | | | | | |
| 1137(1), (4), (5)(b), and (6) | Regulations about inspection of records and provision of copies | 4, art 2(1) | 30.9.07 | The Companies (Fees for Inspection and Copying of Company Records) Regs (SI 2007/2612) | 1137(1) and (4) | 1.10.07 |

| Part or Sections | Subject of Part or Sections | 2006 Act Comm. Order | In force | Supporting Regulations | Under sections of the 2006 Act | In force |
|---|---|---|---|---|---|---|
| Part 37 | Companies: Supplementary Provisions | | | | | |
| | | | | The Companies (Fees for Inspection and Copying of Company Records) (No 2) Regs (SI 2007/3535 | 1137(1) and (4) | 6.4.08 |
| 1134–1142 | Other provisions about company records and service addresses | | With relevant provisions[15] | *The Companies (Fees for Inspection of Company Records Regs (SI 2008/\*)* | *1137* | *1.10.09* |
| | | | | The Companies (Company Records) Regs (SI 2008/\*) | 1136, 1137 | 1.10.09 |
| | | | | *The Companies Act 2006 (Annual Return and Service Addresses) Regs (SI 2008/\*)* | *1141* | *1.10.09* |
| 1143–1148 and Schedules 4 and 5 | The company communications provisions, sending, or supplying documents or information by or to a company | 1, art 3(1)(e) | 20.1.07 | | | |
| 1149–1156 | Requirements as to independent valuation, notice of appointment of certain officers | | With relevant provisions | | | |
| 1157 | Power of court to grant relief in certain cases | 5, art 5(1)(f) | 1.10.08 | | | |

---

[15] These sections and ss 1149–1156 are fully brought into force on 1 October 2009 by 2006 Act Commencement Order No 8, art 3(t).

| Part or Sections | Subject of Part or Sections | 2006 Act Comm. Order | In force | Supporting Regulations | Under sections of the 2006 Act | In force |
|---|---|---|---|---|---|---|
| **Part 38** | **Companies: Interpretation** | | | | | |
| 1158–1160 | Meaning of 'UK-registered company', 'subsidiary' | | With relevant provision[16] | | | |
| 1161, 1162, Schedule 7 | Meaning of 'undertaking' and related expressions, parent and subsidiary undertakings; | 5, art 3(1)(o) | 6.4.08 | | | |
| 1163 | Meaning of 'non-cash asset' | | With relevant provisions | | | |
| 1164, 1165 | Meaning of 'banking company' and 'banking group', 'insurance company' and related expressions | 5, art 3(1)(p) and (q) | 6.4.08 | | | |
| 1166–1168 | Meaning of "employees' share scheme", "prescribed", hard copy and electronic form and related expressions | | With relevant provisions | | | |
| 1169 | Dormant companies | 5, art 3(1)(r) | 6.4.08 | | | |
| 1170 | Meaning of 'EEA State' and related expressions[17] | 2, art 2(1) | 6.4.07 | | | |
| 1171, 1174 | The former Companies Acts; index of defined expressions | | With relevant provisions | | | |

[16] These sections and ss 1163, 1166, 1168, 1171, 1173, and 1174 are fully brought into force on 1 October 2009 by 2006 Act Commencement Order No 8, art 3(u).

[17] Pursuant to European Communities Act 1972, s 2, the definition of 'EEA State' in s 1170 was substituted by the Companies (EEA State) Regs (SI 2007/732).

| Part or Sections | Subject of Part or Sections | 2006 Act Comm. Order | In force | Supporting Regulations | Under sections of the 2006 Act | In force |
|---|---|---|---|---|---|---|
| **Part 38** | **Companies: Interpretation** | | | | | |
| 1172, 1173 | References to requirements of the Act, minor definitions: 'credit institution', 'working day' | 5, art 3(1)(s) and (t) | 6.4.08 | | | |
| **Part 39** | **Companies: Minor Amendments** | | | | | |
| 1175 (only for Part 1 of Schedule 9) | Removal of special provisions about accounts and audit of charitable companies | 6, art 3(1)(a) and (b) | 1.4.08 | | | |
| 1176 | Repeal of the 1985 Act, 438 which gave power to the Secretary of State to bring civil proceedings on company's behalf | 1, art 4(1)(b) | 6.4.07 | | | |
| 1177 | Repeal of the 1985 Act, Part 10, s 311 (prohibition of tax-free payments to directors), ss 323–327 (prohibition on directors dealing in share options), ss 324–326, 328–329 and Parts 2 and 4 of Schedule 13 (register of directors' interests), ss 343 and 344 (special procedure for disclosure by banks) | 1, art 4(1)(c) | 6.4.07 | | | |

| Part or Sections | Subject of Part or Sections | 2006 Act Comm. Order | In force | Supporting Regulations | Under sections of the 2006 Act | In force |
|---|---|---|---|---|---|---|
| **Part 39** | **Companies: Minor Amendments** | | | | | |
| 1178 | Repeal of the 1985 Act, s 720 and Schedule 23 (certain companies to publish periodical statement) | 1, art 4(1)(d) | 6.4.07 | | | |
| 1179 | Repeal of the 1985 Act, s 729 (annual report to Parliament by Secretary of State on matters within the Companies Acts)[18] | 1, art 4(1)(e) | 6.4.07 | | | |
| 1180 | Repeal of certain provisions about company charges | 8, art 3(v) | 1.10.09 | | | |
| 1181 | Access to constitutional documents of RTE and RTM companies | 8, art 3(v) | 1.10.09 | | | |
| **Part 40** | **Company Directors: Foreign Disqualification etc** | | | | | |
| 1182–1191 | Persons subject to foreign restrictions, meaning of 'the court' and 'UK company'; power to disqualify; power to make persons liable for company's debts; power to require statement to be sent to the Registrar | 8, art 3 | 1.10.09 | | | |

[18] As a result the report for the year ended 31 March 2006, presented pursuant to 1985 Act, s 729 is the last such report.

| Part or Sections | Subject of Part or Sections | 2006 Act Comm. Order | In force | Supporting Regulations | Under sections of the 2006 Act | In force |
|---|---|---|---|---|---|---|
| **Part 41** | **Business Names** | | | | | |
| 1192–1208 | Restricted or prohibited names; disclosure required in case of individual or partnership; offences and interpretation | 8, art 3(x) | 1.10.09 | *The Non-Companies Acts Companies Authorised to Register Regs (SI 2008/\*)* | *1193(1)(c), 1194(1), 1195(1), 1197(1) and (2)* | *1.10.09* |
| | | | | *The Company and Business Names (Miscellaneous Provisions) Regs (SI 2008/\*)* | *1197* | *1.10.09* |
| **Part 42** | **Statutory Auditors** | | | | | |
| 1209–1241, 1245–1264, Schedules 10, 11, 13, and 14 | Meaning of 'statutory auditor', eligibility for appointment; individuals and firms; auditors general; register of auditors; supplementary and general | 5, art 2(1)(u) | 6.4.08 | The Statutory Auditors and Third Country Auditors Regs (SI 2007/3494), apart from regs 32, 33, and 40(2) (b)–(d)[19] | 1239, 1241(2) (c), 1246 | 6.4.08 |
| | | | | The Independent Supervisor Appointment Order (SI 2007/3534) | 1228 | 6.4.08 |
| | | | | The Statutory Auditors (Delegation of Functions etc) Order (SI 2008/496) | 1252(1), (4) (a), (5) and (8), and 1253(4) | 6.4.08[20] |

---

[19] Apart from regs 32, 33, and 40(2)(b)–(d) following amendment by Statutory Auditors and Third Country Auditors (Amendment) Regs (SI 2008/499).

[20] Except that arts 1 and 2 came into force on 1 March 2008, arts 3, 6, and 8 came into force on 1 March 2008 for the purposes of functions in relation to appointments of auditors for financial years beginning on or after 6 April 2008, and arts 4 and 9 came into force on 29 June 2008 for the purpose of transferring the functions under ss 1242–1244 and Schedule 12 in relation to appointments of registered third country auditors for financial years beginning on or after 29 June 2008.

| Part or Sections | Subject of Part or Sections | 2006 Act Comm. Order | In force | Supporting Regulations | Under sections of the 2006 Act | In force |
|---|---|---|---|---|---|---|
| **Part 42** | **Statutory Auditors** | | | | | |
| | | | | The Statutory Auditors and Third Country Auditors (Amendment) Regs (SI 2008/499) | 1239 | 5.4.08 |
| 1242–1244, Schedule 12 | Registered third country auditors | 5, art 4 | 29.6.08 | The Statutory Auditors and Third Country Auditors Regs (SI 2007/3494) Regs 32, 33, and 40(2) (b)–(d)[21] | | 29.6.08 |
| | | | | The Statutory Auditors and Third Country Auditors (Amendment) (No 2) Regs (SI 2008/2639) | 1239, 1246 | 31.10.08 |
| **Part 43** | **Transparency Obligations and Related Matters** | | | | | |
| 1265–1273 | Provisions giving effect to the Transparency Directive[22] | s 1300 | 8.11.06 | | | |
| **Part 44** | **Miscellaneous Provisions** | | | | | |
| 1274, 1276 | Regulation of actuaries | s 1300 | 8.11.06 | | | |
| 1275 | Levy to pay expenses of bodies concerned with actuarial standards | 8, art 3(y) | 1.10.09 | | | |

[21]  Except that arts 1 and 2 came into force on 1 March 2008, arts 3, 6, and 8 came into force on 1 March 2008 for the purposes of functions in relation to appointments of auditors for financial years beginning on or after 6 April 2008, and arts 4 and 9 came into force on 29 June 2008 for the purpose of transferring the functions under ss 1242–1244 and Schedule 12 in relation to appointments of registered third country auditors for financial years beginning on or after 29 June 2008.

[22]  Except amendment in Schedule 15, para 11(2) of the definition of 'regulated market' in FSMA, Part 6.

| Part or Sections | Subject of Part or Sections | 2006 Act Comm. Order | In force | Supporting Regulations | Under sections of the 2006 Act | In force |
|---|---|---|---|---|---|---|
| **Part 44** | **Miscellaneous Provisions** | | | | | |
| 1277–1280 | Information as to exercise of voting rights by institutional investors | 5, art 5(1)(g) | 1.10.08 | | | |
| 1281 | Disclosure of information under the Enterprise Act 2002 | 1, art 4(1)(f) | 6.4.07 | | | |
| 1282 | Payment of expenses of winding up | 5, art 2(1)(v) | 6.4.08 | | | |
| *1283* | *Commonhold associations* | *8, art 3(y)* | *1.10.09* | | | |
| **Part 45** | **Northern Ireland** | | | | | |
| 1284–1287 | Extension to Northern Ireland | | With relevant provisions[23] | | | |
| **Part 46** | **General Supplementary Provisions** | | | | | |
| 1288–1294, 1296, 1297 | Regulations and Orders; meaning of 'enactment'; consequential amendments etc, transitional provisions and savings, continuity of law | s 1300 | 8.11.06 | | | |
| 1295, Schedule 16 | Repeals | | With relevant provisions[24] | | | |
| **Part 47** | **Final Provisions** | | | | | |
| 1298–1300 | Short title, extent, commencement | s 1300 | 8.11.06 | | | |

[23] These sections are fully brought into force on 1 October 2009 by 2006 Act Commencement Order No 8, art 3(z).

[24] 2006 Act Commencement Order No 5, art 5(2) repealed 1985 Act, ss 151–153 and 155–158 as they apply to private companies with effect from 1 October 2008.

# APPENDIX 2

# Serious Offences under the Companies Act 2006

Note that offences under the Companies Act, Parts 17, 18, 25, 31, 35 and 40 will not come into force until 1 October 2009 and Part 37, s 1153 comes into force with the provisions of the 2006 Act to which it relates. Except for ss 542, 627, 643 and 644, which are new, the offences in Parts 17, 18, 25 and 31 replace provisions in the 1985 Act, without material change, and the offences in Parts 35 and 40 are new.

| 2006 Act | Offence | Max penalty on indictment |
|---|---|---|
| *Part 10* | *A company's directors* | |
| 183 | Failure to comply with requirements of s 182 to declare interest in existing transaction or arrangement | Fine |
| *Part 13* | *Resolutions and meetings* | |
| 291 | Failure to comply with s 291 as to circulation of written resolution proposed by directors | Fine |
| 293 | Failure to comply with s 293 as to circulation of written resolution proposed by members, which company is required to circulate | Fine |
| 315 | Failure to circulate member's statement as required by s 314 | Fine |
| 336 | Failure by public company to hold AGM | Fine |
| 339 | Failure to circulate members' resolutions for public company AGM | Fine |
| 350(3) | Knowingly/recklessly providing misleading information to independent assessor of poll, re quoted company | 2 years |
| *Part 15* | *Accounts and reports* | |
| 387 | Failure to keep accounting records in accordance with s 386 | 2 years |
| 389 | Failure to keep accounting records at registered office for inspection by company's officers | 2 years |
| 414 | Approving and signing accounts, knowing they are non-compliant etc | Fine |
| 415 | Failure to prepare directors' report | Fine |
| 418 | False statement in directors' report | 2 years |
| 419 | Approving and signing directors' report knowing it is non-compliant etc | Fine |
| 420 | Failure to prepare quoted company directors' report | Fine |
| 422 | Approving and signing quoted company directors' remuneration report, knowing it is non-compliant etc | Fine |
| 425 | Default in sending out copies of accounts and reports in accordance with ss 423, 424 | Fine |
| 450 | Approval and signing of non-compliant abbreviated accounts | Fine |

| 2006 Act | Offence | Max Penalty on indictment |
|---|---|---|
| *Part 16* | *Audit* | |
| 501(1) | Misleading information to auditors | 2 years |
| 507 | Knowingly or recklessly causing auditor's report to include misleading, false, or deceptive material | Fine |
| 517 | Failure to send notice of auditor's resignation to Registrar | Fine |
| 518 | Failure to convene meeting of company on requisition of resigning auditor | Fine |
| 520 | Failure to comply with duties in relation to resigning auditor's statement | Fine |
| 523 | Failure to notify appropriate audit office of auditor ceasing to hold office before the end of his term of office | Fine |
| 530 | Default in relation to quoted company website publication requirements | Fine |
| *Part 17*[1] | *A company's share capital* | |
| 542 | Allotment of shares in contravention of s 542 | Fine |
| 549 | Knowing contravention of s 549 relating to directors' power to allot shares | Fine |
| 557 | Failure to make returns of allotment in accordance with ss 555 or 556 | Fine |
| 572 | Knowingly or recklessly authorizing or permitting the inclusion of misleading, false, or deceptive material in directors' statement under s 571 | 2 years |
| 590 | Contravention of ch 5 concerning payment for shares | Fine |
| 597 | Failure to deliver to Registrar copy of report on valuation on non-cash consideration for shares in case of public company | Fine |
| 607 | Contravention of ch 6 concerning public company allotting shares for non-cash consideration or entering into agreement for transfer of non-cash asset | Fine |
| 627 | Failure to give notice to Registrar of reduction of capital in connection with redenomination | Fine |
| 643 | Making solvency statement in relation to reduction of capital without reasonable grounds | 2 years |
| 644 | Default in registering resolution and supporting documents in relation to reduction of capital | Fine |
| 647 | Concealment or misrepresentation in relation to list of creditors for reduction of capital | Fine |
| 656 | Failure by directors of public company to call meeting on serious loss of capital | Fine |

[1] Part 17 comes into force on 1 October 2009. Sections 542, 627, 643, and 644 are new. The other sections will replace the corresponding sections of 1985 Act: ss 80, 88, 95, 111, 114, 141, and 142.

| 2006 Act | Offence | Max Penalty on indictment |
|---|---|---|
| *Part 18[2]* | *Acquisition by limited company of its own shares* | |
| 658 | Contravention of general rule against limited company acquiring its own shares | 2 years |
| 680 | Contravention of prohibition of financial assistance for purchase of own shares | 2 years |
| 707 | Failure to deliver to Registrar a return of purchase of own shares | Fine |
| 715 | Making s 714 statement without reasonable grounds | 2 years |
| 728 | Failure to give notice to Registrar of disposal of treasury shares | Fine |
| 732 | Contravention of ch 6 re treasury shares (except s 730) | Fine |
| *Part 19* | *Debentures* | |
| 747 | Knowingly/recklessly making a statement that is misleading, false, or deceptive in relation to a request under s 744 (register of debenture holders) | 2 years |
| *Part 20* | *Private and public companies* | |
| 767 | Public company doing business or exercising borrowing powers in contravention of s 761 | Fine |
| *Part 22* | *Information about interests in a company's shares* | |
| 795 | Failure to comply with a s 793 notice requiring information re interests in a company's shares, or making a misleading statement in respect of the same | Fine |
| 798 | Issue of shares in contravention of restriction | Fine |
| 804 | Failure to comply with requirement of members to exercise powers under s 803 | Fine |
| 814 | Making a false statement in a request under s 811 (register of interests/right to inspect) | 2 years |
| *Part 25[3]* | *Company charges* | |
| 860 | Failure to register charge created by company | Fine |
| 862 | Failure to register charge on existing property acquired | Fine |
| 876 | Knowingly or wilfully authorizing etc the omission of entry on register of charges | Fine |
| *Part 26* | *Arrangements and reconstructions* | |
| 897 | Failure to circulate and make available explanatory statement | Fine |
| *Part 28* | *Takeovers etc* | |
| 949 | Disclosure of information in contravention of s 948 | 2 years |
| 953 | Offer document published otherwise than in compliance with offer document rules | 2 years |
| 980 | Failure to give notice or statutory declaration as required by s 980(4) or makes false declaration | Fine |
| 984 | Failure to give notice under s 984(3) | Fine |

[2] Part 18 comes into force on 1 October 2009. These sections will replace the corresponding sections of 1985 Act: ss 143, 151, 162C, 162G, 169, and 173.

[3] Part 25 comes into force on 1 October 2009. These sections will replace the corresponding sections of 1985 Act: ss 399, 400, and 407.

| 2006 Act | Offence | Max Penalty on indictment |
|---|---|---|
| *Part 29* | *Fraudulent trading* | |
| 993 | Fraudulent trading | 10 years |
| *Part 31*[4] | *Dissolution and restoration to the register* | |
| 1004 | Application to strike off in contravention of s 1004 | Fine |
| 1005 | Application to strike off in contravention of s 1005 | Fine |
| 1006 | Failure to give copies of application to specified persons | Fine |
| 1007 | Failure to give notice of application to specified persons | Fine |
| 1009 | Failure to comply with duties under s 1009 | Fine |
| *Part 35* | *The Registrar of Companies* | |
| 1112 | Knowingly or recklessly to deliver to Registrar a document or to make a statement to the Registrar that is misleading, false, or deceptive | 2 years |
| *Part 37* | *Companies: supplementary provisions* | |
| 1153 | Knowingly or recklessly giving misleading etc information to valuer | 2 years |
| *Part 40* | *Company directors: foreign disqualification etc* | |
| 1186 | Breach of regulations made under s 1184 (disqualification of persons subject to foreign restrictions) | 2 years |
| 1191 | Failure to comply with regulations made under s 1188 / 1189 | 2 years |

# Intermediate and Quasi-regulatory Offences under the Companies Act 2006

Note that offences under the Companies Act, Parts 3–5, 7, 8, 17, 18, 24, 25, 31, 34, 35, and 41 will not come into force until 1 October 2009 and Part 37. Sections 1135, 1138, and 1145 come into force with the provisions of the 2006 Act to which they relate. Except for ss 35, 108, 120, 272, 554, and 625, which are new, the offences in Parts 3–5, 7, 8, 17, 18, 24, and 25 replace provisions in the 1985 Act, without material change. The offences in Parts 31, 34, and 35 are new. The offences in Part 41 will replace provisions in the Business Names Act 1985 and the 1985 Act, section 34A.

---

[4] Part 31 comes into force on 1 October 2009. These sections will replace the corresponding sections of 1985 Act: ss 652B–652E.

| 2006 Act | Offence | Level of fine (SSL[5]) |
|---|---|---|
| *Part 3*[6] | *A company's constitution* | |
| 26 | Failure to comply with duty to send to the Registrar a copy amended articles | 3 |
| 30 | Failure to comply with duty to forward to the Registrar a copy of every resolution or agreement to which Part 3, Chapter 3 applies | 3 |
| 32 | Failure to comply with duty to send to any member, on request, copies of the constitutional documents specified in s 32 | 3 |
| 34 | Failure to comply with duty to give notice to the Registrar of the alteration of the company's constitution by an enactment, other than an enactment amending the general law | 3 |
| 35 | Failure to comply with duty to give notice to the Registrar of the alteration of the company's constitution by an order of a court or other authority | 3 |
| 36 | Failure to comply with duty to incorporate in or accompany copies of articles issued by the company the documents specified in s 36 | 3 |
| *Part 4*[7] | *A company's capacity and related matters* | |
| 45 | Failure to comply with duty to have the company's name engraved in legible characters on its seal | 3 |
| *Part 5*[8] | *A company's name* | |
| 63 | Failure to comply with duty an exempt company amending its articles so that it ceases to comply with the conditions for exemption under ss 61 or 62 | 5 |
| 64 | Failure to comply with a direction from the Secretary of State under s 64 to the company to change its name so that it ends with 'limited' or one of the permitted alternatives | 5 |
| 68 | Failure to comply with a direction from the Secretary of State under s 67 to the company to change its name in case of similarity to an existing name | 3 |
| 75 | Failure to comply with a direction from the Secretary of State under s 75 to the company to change its name where misleading information has been provided etc | 3 |
| 76 | Failure to comply with a direction from the Secretary of State under s 76 to the company to change its name where it gives a misleading indication of its activities | 3 |
| 84 | Failure without reasonable excuse to comply with any specified requirement of regulations under s 82 to disclose name etc | 3 |

---

[5]  ie standard scale level.

[6]  Part 3 comes into force on 1 October 2009. Section 35 is new. The other sections will replace the corresponding sections of 1985 Act: ss 18, 19, and 380.

[7]  Part 4 comes into force on 1 October 2009. This section will replace the corresponding section of 1985 Act: s 350.

[8]  Part 5 comes into force on 1 October 2009. These sections will replace the corresponding sections of 1985 Act: 28, 31, 32C, 348, 349, 351, and the Business Names Act 1985, s 4.

| 2006 Act | Offence | Level of fine (SSL) |
|---|---|---|
| *Part 7*[9] | *Re-registration as a means of altering a company's status* | |
| 99 | Failure to give notice to the Registrar of the making of an application under s 98 (application to court to cancel resolution by a public company to re-register as a private limited company) and of the making of the court's order | 3 |
| 108 | Failure to deliver to the Registrar a statement of capital on re-registration of an unlimited company as a limited company | 3 |
| *Part 8*[10] | *A company's members* | |
| 113 | Failure to keep a register of the company's members complying with s 113 | 3 |
| 114 | Failure to give notice to the Registrar of the place where the register of members is kept available for inspection and of any change in that place | 3 |
| 115 | Failure, where the company has more than 50 members, to keep an index of the names of the members of the company, unless the register of members is in such a form as to constitute in itself an index | 3 |
| 118 | Refusal of inspection, or provision of a copy, of the register of members required under s 116 | 3 |
| 120 | Failure to inform person inspecting register of members of the most recent date (if any) on which alterations were made to the register or to inform person inspecting the index whether there is any alteration to the register that is not reflected in the index | 3 |
| 123 | Failure, where the company is formed as, or becomes, a single member company, to enter in the company's register of members a statement that the company has only one member | 3 |
| 130 | Failure to give notice to the Registrar that the company has begun to keep an overseas branch register, stating the country or territory in which the register is kept | 3 |
| 132 | Failure, where the company keeps an overseas branch register, to keep available for inspection the register or a duplicate of it at the place in the UK where the company's main register is kept available for inspection | 3 |
| 135 | Failure to give notice to the Registrar of discontinuance of overseas branch register | 3 |
| *Part 10* | *A company's directors* | |
| 156 | Failure to comply with direction of the Secretary of State under s 156 to make the necessary appointment(s) of directors and to give notice to the Registrar under s 167 | 5 |
| 162 | Failure to keep a register of directors, containing the required particulars, and keep it available for inspection | 5 |
| 165 | Failure to keep a register of directors' residential addresses | 5 |

[9] Part 7 comes into force on 1 October 2009. Section 108 is new. Section 99 will replace the corresponding section of 1985 Act: s 54.

[10] Part 8 comes into force on 1 October 2009. Section 120 is new. The other sections will replace the corresponding sections of 1985 Act: ss 352, 352C, 353, 354, 356, and 362.

| 2006 Act | Offence | Level of fine (SSL) |
|---|---|---|
| *Part 10* | *A company's directors* | |
| 167 | Failure to notify Registrar of changes of directors | 5 |
| 228 | Failure to keep available for inspection a copy of every director's service contract, or, if not in writing, a memorandum of it | 3 |
| 229 | Failure to provide a member with a copy of the contract or memorandum on request | 3 |
| 231 | Failure to ensure that a contract with a sole member who is also a director, if not in writing, is set out in a written memorandum or recorded in the minutes of the first meeting of directors following its making | 5 |
| 237 | Failure to comply with requirement re keeping copy/memo of provision of qualifying indemnity | 3 |
| 238 | Failure to comply with request of member to inspect copy/memo of provision of qualifying indemnity | 3 |
| 246 | On Registrar giving notice of decision that a director's usual residential address is to be put on the public record, failure to enter it in its register of directors and if notified of a more recent address to give notice to the Registrar of the change | 5 |
| 248 | Failure to cause minutes of all proceedings at meetings of directors to be recorded | 3 |
| *Part 12* | *Company secretaries* | |
| 272 | Failure to comply with direction requiring a public company to appoint a secretary | 5 |
| 275 | Failure to keep a register of secretaries, containing the required particulars, and to keep it available for inspection | 5 |
| 276 | Failure to notify Registrar of changes of secretary | 5 |
| *Part 13* | *Resolutions and meetings* | |
| 325 | Failure to contain statement of rights in notice convening meeting of company | 3 |
| 326 | If company-sponsored invitations to appoint proxies are issued, failure to issue invitations to all members | 3 |
| 341 | Failure to make result of quoted company poll on website | 3 |
| 343 | Failure to appoint independent assessor of poll | 5 |
| 350(1) | Failure to provide information to independent assessor of poll, re quoted company | 3 |
| 351 | Failure to make information about appointment of independent assessor available on quoted company website | 3 |
| 355 | Failure to keep record of company resolutions and meetings | 3 |
| 357 | Failure of sole member to provide company with copy of decision taken in general meeting | 2 |
| 358 | Failure to give notice to Registrar of place where records of resolutions and meetings are available for inspection and to permit inspection by member | 3 |

| 2006 Act | Offence | Level of fine (SSL) |
|---|---|---|
| *Part 15* | *Accounts and reports* | |
| 410 | Failure to give information about related undertakings in next annual return | 3 |
| 412 | Failure to give information about directors' benefits | 3 |
| 421 | Failure to give information for quoted company directors' remuneration report | 3 |
| 429 | Failure to comply with ss 426–428 concerning summary financial statements | 3 |
| 430 | Failure to make quoted company annual accounts and reports available on website | 3 |
| 431 | Failure to comply with demand of member or debenture holder for copies of unquoted company accounts and reports | 3 |
| 432 | Failure to comply with demand of member or debenture holder for quoted company accounts and reports | 3 |
| 433 | Failure to have name of signatory on balance sheet, directors' report and, for quoted company, directors' remuneration report | 3 |
| 434 | Publishing accounts without audit report | 3 |
| 435 | Publication of non-statutory requirements without required statement | 3 |
| 438 | Failure to lay public company accounts and reports | 5 |
| 440 | Failure to comply with quoted company approval procedure | 3 |
| 451 | Default in filing accounts and reports, subject to reasonable steps defence | 5 |
| *Part 16* | *Audit* | |
| 486 | Failure to give notice to the Secretary of State that his power to appoint auditors in respect of private company has become exercisable | 3 |
| 490 | Failure to give notice to the Secretary of State that his power to appoint auditors in respect of public company has become exercisable | 3 |
| 501 | Failure of parent company to comply with ss 499 or 500 in relation to general information or information from overseas subsidiaries | 3 |
| 505 | Publishing auditor's report without s 505 statement | 3 |
| 512 | Failure to give notice to Registrar of passing of resolution removing auditor from office | 3 |
| *Part 17[11]* | *A company's share capital* | |
| 554 | Failure to register allotment | 3 |
| 602 | Failure to deliver to Registrar copy of resolution and valuer's report on non-cash asset | 3 |
| 619 | Failure to give notice to Registrar of sub-division or consolidation | 3 |

[11] Part 17 comes into force on 1 October 2009. Sections 554 and 625 are new. The other sections will replace the corresponding sections of 1985 Act: ss 111, 122, 127–129.

| 2006 Act | Offence | Level of fine (SSL) |
|---|---|---|
| *Part 17* | *A company's share capital* | |
| 621 | Failure to give notice to Registrar of reconversion of stock into shares | 3 |
| 625 | Failure to give notice to Registrar of redenomination | 3 |
| 635 | Failure to forward to Registrar court order on application under ss 633 or 634 | 3 |
| 636 | Failure to give notice to Registrar of particulars of name or other designation of class of shares | 3 |
| 637 | Failure to give notice to Registrar of particulars of variation of rights attached to shares | 3 |
| 638 | Failure to give notice to Registrar of particulars of rights attaching to a new class of members in case of company not having a share capital | 3 |
| 639 | Failure to give notice to Registrar of name or other designation of class of members in case of company not having a share capital | 3 |
| 640 | Failure to give notice to Registrar of particulars of variation of class rights in case of company not having a share capital | 3 |
| *Part 18[12]* | *Acquisition by limited company of its own shares* | |
| 663 | Failure to give notice to Registrar of cancellation of shares | 3 |
| 667 | Failure to cancel shares or re-register | 3 |
| 689 | Failure to give to Registrar of redemption | 3 |
| 703 | Failure to comply with right to inspect copy or memorandum | 3 |
| 708 | Failure to give notice to Registrar of cancellation of shares | 3 |
| 720 | Failure to give notice to Registrar of place where directors' statement and auditor's report are available for inspection | 3 |
| 722 | Failure to give notice to Registrar of court application under s 721 or order | 3 |
| 730 | Failure to give notice to Registrar of cancellation of treasury shares | 3 |
| *Part 19* | *Debentures* | |
| 741 | Failure to register allotment of debentures | 3 |
| 743 | Failure to keep register of debenture holders available for inspection | 3 |
| 746 | Refusal of inspection | 3 |
| 749 | Failure to provide holder of debenture with trust deed | 3 |
| *Part 21* | *Certification and transfer of securities* | |
| 769 | Failure to issue certificates etc on allotment of shares etc | 3 |
| 771 | Failure to register transfer of shares or debentures | 3 |
| 776 | Failure to issue certificates etc on transfer of shares etc | 3 |
| 780 | Failure to issue certificates on surrender of share warrant | 3 |

---

[12] Part 18 comes into force on 1 October 2009. These sections will replace the corresponding sections of 1985 Act: ss 122, 149, 169, 169A, 175, and 176.

| 2006 Act | Offence | Level of fine (SSL) |
|---|---|---|
| *Part 22* | *Information about interests in a company's shares* | |
| 806 | Failure to give notice to Registrar of place where report on outcome of investigation is available for inspection | 3 |
| 807 | Refusal of inspection | 3 |
| 808 | Failure to keep register of information | 3 |
| 809 | Failure to keep register available for inspection | 3 |
| 810 | Failure to keep associated index | 3 |
| 813 | Refusal of inspection | 3 |
| 815 | Deletion of entry from register | 3 |
| 819 | Failure to keep register on ceasing to be a public company | 3 |
| *Part 24*[13] | *Annual return* | |
| 858 | Failure to deliver annual return | 5 |
| *Part 25*[14] | *Company charges* | |
| 865 | Failure to cause copy of certificate of registration to be endorsed on debenture | 3 |
| 877 | Failure to keep register of charges available for inspection | 3 |
| *Part 26* | *Arrangements and reconstructions* | |
| 898 | Failure to provide information for explanatory statement | 3 |
| 900 | Failure to deliver order to Registrar | 3 |
| 901 | Failure cause order to be accompanied by any resolution or agreement to amend articles | 3 |
| *Part 30* | *Protection of members against unfair prejudice* | |
| 998 | Failure to deliver to Registrar copy of order altering constitution | 3 |
| 999 | Failure to accompany order with any amendment to articles | 3 |
| *Part 31*[15] | *Dissolution and restoration to register* | |
| 1033 | Failure on restoration to change name and give notice to Registrar of change | 5 |
| *Part 34*[16] | *Overseas companies* | |
| 1054 | Offences under regulations | 5 |
| *Part 35*[17] | *The Registrar of Companies* | |
| 1093 | Failure to deliver documents in response to notice from Registrar | 5 |

[13] Part 24 comes into force on 1 October 2009. This section will replace the corresponding section of 1985 Act: s 363.

[14] Part 25 comes into force on 1 October 2009. These sections will replace the corresponding sections of 1985 Act: ss 402 and 408.

[15] Part 31 comes into force on 1 October 2009. This section is new.

[16] Part 34 comes into force on 1 October 2009. This section is new

[17] Part 35 comes into force on 1 October 2009. This section is new.

| 2006 Act | Offence | Level of fine (SSL) |
|---|---|---|
| *Part 37* | *Companies: supplementary provisions* | |
| 1135 | Failure to comply with section as to form of company records | 3 |
| 1138 | Failure to guard against falsification of records not kept in bound books | 3 |
| 1145 | Failure to provide documents in hard copy form | 3 |
| *Part 41*[18] | *Business names* | |
| 1193 | Name suggesting connection with government or public authority | 3 |
| 1194 | Name including sensitive words or expression | 3 |
| 1197 | Name containing inappropriate indication of company type or legal form | 3 |
| 1198 | Name giving misleading indication of activities | 3 |

# Insolvency Act Offences

| Section | Offence | Defence (where applicable) | s 432 applies |
|---|---|---|---|
| 206(1) | *Fraud in anticipation of winding up* | It is a defence— | No |
| | Where a company officer, within the 12 months immediately prior to the commencement of the winding up: | for a person charged under paragraph (a) or (f) to prove that he had no intent to defraud | |
| | (a) concealed any part of the company's property to the value of [£500] or more, or concealed any debt due to or from the company, or | for a person charged under paragraph (c) or (d) to prove that he had no intent to conceal the state of affairs of the company or to defeat the law. | |
| | (b) fraudulently removed any part of the company's property to the value of [£500] or more, or | | |
| | (c) concealed, destroyed, mutilated, or falsified any book or paper affecting or relating to the company's property or affairs, or | | |

1159

| Section | Offence | Defence (where applicable) | s 432 applies |
|---|---|---|---|
| | (d) made any false entry in any book or paper affecting or relating to the company's property or affairs, or | | |
| | (e) fraudulently parted with, altered or made any omission in any document affecting or relating to the company's property or affairs, or | | |
| | (f) pawned, pledged, or disposed of any property of the company which has been obtained on credit and has not been paid for (unless the pawning, pledging, or disposal was in the ordinary way of the company's business). | | |
| 206(2) | *Fraud in anticipation of winding up*<br><br>A company officer is deemed to have committed an offence if within prior to the commencement of winding up he has been privy to the doing by others of any of the things mentioned in paragraphs (c), (d), and (e) of section 206(1); and he commits an offence if, at any time after the commencement of the winding up, he does any of the things mentioned in paragraphs (a) to (f) of that subsection, or is privy to the doing by others of any of the things mentioned in paragraphs (c) to (e) of it. | It is a defence—<br><br>for a person charged under section 206(2) but in respect of matters mentioned in section 206(1) paragraphs (a) or (f) to prove that he had no intent to defraud, and<br><br>for a person charged under section 206(2) but in respect of matters mentioned in section 206(1) paragraphs (c) or (d) to prove that he had no intent to conceal the state of affairs of the company or to defeat the law. | No |
| 207 | *Transactions in fraud of creditors*<br><br>When a company is ordered to be wound up or passes a resolution for voluntary winding up, an officer of the company is deemed to have committed an offence if he<br><br>(a) has made or caused to be made any gift or transfer of, or charge on, or has caused or connived at the levying of any execution against, the company's property, or<br><br>(b) has concealed or removed any part of the company's property since, or within 2 months before, the date of any unsatisfied judgment or order for the payment of money obtained against the company. | *A person is not guilty of an offence under section 207 — by reason of conduct constituting an offence under subsection (a) which occurred more than 5 years before the commencement of the winding up,*[19]<br>or<br><br>if he proves that, at the time of the conduct constituting the offence, he had no intent to defraud the company's creditors. | No |

---

[19] The burden of proof remains on the prosecution in respect of this

| Section | Offence | Defence (where applicable) | s 432 applies |
|---------|---------|---------------------------|---------------|
| 208(1) | *Misconduct in course of winding up* <br><br> When a company is being wound up, whether by the court or voluntarily, any person, being a past or present officer (or shadow director) of the company, commits an offence if he— <br><br> (a) does not to the best of his knowledge and belief fully and truly discover to the liquidator all the company's property, and how and to whom and for what consideration and when the company disposed of any part of that property (except such part as has been disposed of in the ordinary way of the company's business), or <br><br> (b) does not deliver up to the liquidator (or as he directs) all such part of the company's property as is in his custody or under his control, and which he is required by law to deliver up, or <br><br> (c) does not deliver up to the liquidator (or as he directs) all books and papers in his custody or under his control belonging to the company and which he is required by law to deliver up, or <br><br> (d) knowing or believing that a false debt has been proved by any person in the winding up, fails to inform the liquidator as soon as practicable, or <br><br> (e) after the commencement of the winding up, prevents the production of any book or paper affecting or relating to the company's property or affairs. | It is a defence— <br><br> for a person charged under paragraph (a), (b), or (c) to prove that he had no intent to defraud, <br> and <br><br> for a person charged under paragraph (e) to prove that he had no intent to conceal the state of affairs of the company or to defeat the law. | No |
| 208(2) | *Misconduct in course of winding up* <br><br> A person described in section 208(1) commits an offence if after the commencement of the winding up he attempts to account for any part of the company's property by fictitious losses or expenses; and he is deemed to have committed that offence if he has so attempted at any meeting of the company's creditors within the 12 months immediately preceding the commencement of the winding up. | | No |

| Section | Offence | Defence (where applicable) | s 432 applies |
|---|---|---|---|
| 209 | *Falsification of company's books*<br>When a company is being wound up, an officer or contributory of the company commits an offence if he destroys, mutilates, alters or falsifies any books, papers or securities, or makes or is privy to the making of any false or fraudulent entry in any register, book of account or document belonging to the company with intent to defraud or deceive any person. | | No |
| 210(1) | *Material omissions from statement relating to company's affairs*<br>When a company is being wound up, whether by the court or voluntarily, any person, being a past or present officer (or shadow director) of the company, commits an offence if he makes any material omission in any statement relating to the company's affairs. | It is a defence for a person charged under this section to prove that he had no intent to defraud. | No |
| 211 | *False representations to creditors*<br>When a company is being wound up, whether by the court or voluntarily, any person, being a past or present officer (including a shadow director) of the company—<br>(a) commits an offence if he makes any false representation or commits any other fraud for the purpose of obtaining the consent of the company's creditors or any of them to an agreement with reference to the company's affairs or to the winding up, and<br>(b) is deemed to have committed that offence if, prior to the winding up, he has made any false representation, or committed any other fraud, for that purpose. | | No |
| 216 | *Re-use of company name*<br>For 5 years, beginning with the day on which a company goes into insolvent liquidation, except with leave of the court, it is an offence for a person who was a director or shadow director of the company at any time in the period of 12 months ending with the day before it went into liquidation to be a director | | Yes |

| Section | Offence | Defence (where applicable) | s 432 applies |
|---------|---------|---------------------------|---------------|
| | of (or in any direct of indirect way be concerned with the promotion, management or formation of) any company which is known by:<br>– the same name as a name which was used by the liquidating company in that period of 12 months, or<br>– by a name which is so similar to a such a name as to suggest an association with that company.[20] | | |

---

[20] The factors which might be relevant to determination of this issue were considered in *Ricketts v Ad Valorem Factors Ltd* [2004] 1 All ER 894, CA.

FINANCIAL REPORTING COUNCIL

THE COMBINED CODE ON CORPORATE GOVERNANCE

JUNE 2008

# THE COMBINED CODE ON CORPORATE GOVERNANCE

## June 2008

# Contents

## The Combined Code on Corporate Governance

# CODE ON CORPORATE GOVERNANCE

## PREAMBLE

1. Good corporate governance should contribute to better company performance by helping a board discharge its duties in the best interests of shareholders; if it is ignored, the consequence may well be vulnerability or poor performance. Good governance should facilitate efficient, effective and entrepreneurial management that can deliver shareholder value over the longer term. The Combined Code on Corporate Governance ('the Code') is published by the FRC to support these outcomes and promote confidence in corporate reporting and governance.

2. The Code is not a rigid set of rules. Rather, it is a guide to the components of good board practice distilled from consultation and widespread experience over many years. While it is expected that companies will comply wholly or substantially with its provisions, it is recognised that non-compliance may be justified in particular circumstances if good governance can be achieved by other means. A condition of non-compliance is that the reasons for it should be explained to shareholders, who may wish to discuss the position with the company and whose voting intentions may be influenced as a result. This 'comply or explain' approach has been in operation since the Code's beginnings in 1992 and the flexibility it offers is valued by company boards and by investors in pursuing better corporate governance.

3. The Listing Rules require UK companies listed on the Main Market of the London Stock Exchange to describe in the annual report and accounts their corporate governance from two points of view, the first dealing generally with their adherence to the Code's main principles, and the second dealing specifically with non-compliance with any of the Code's provisions. The descriptions together should give shareholders a clear and comprehensive picture of a company's governance arrangements in relation to the Code as a criterion of good practice.

4. In relation to the requirement to state how it has applied the Code's main principles, where a company has done so by complying with the associated provisions it should be sufficient simply to report that this is the case; copying out the principles in the annual report adds to its length without adding to its value. But where a company has taken additional actions to apply the principles or otherwise improve its governance, it would be helpful to shareholders to describe these in the annual report.

5.   If a company chooses not to comply with one or more provisions of the Code, it must give shareholders a careful and clear explanation which shareholders should evaluate on its merits. In providing an explanation, the company should aim to illustrate how its actual practices are consistent with the principle to which the particular provision relates and contribute to good governance.

6.   Smaller listed companies, in particular those new to listing, may judge that some of the provisions are disproportionate or less relevant in their case. Some of the provisions do not apply to companies below the FTSE 350. Such companies may nonetheless consider that it would be appropriate to adopt the approach in the Code and they are encouraged to do so. Externally managed investment companies typically have a different board structure, which may affect the relevance of particular provisions; the Association of Investment Companies's Corporate Governance Code and Guide can assist them in meeting their obligations under the Code.

7.   In their turn, shareholders should pay due regard to companies' individual circumstances and bear in mind in particular the size and complexity of the company and the nature of the risks and challenges it faces. Whilst shareholders have every right to challenge companies' explanations if they are unconvincing, they should not be evaluated in a mechanistic way and departures from the Code should not be automatically treated as breaches. Institutional shareholders should be careful to respond to the statements from companies in a manner that supports the 'comply or explain' principle and bearing in mind the purpose of good corporate governance. They should put their views to the company and be prepared to enter a dialogue if they do not accept the company's position. Institutional shareholders should be prepared to put such views in writing where appropriate.

8.   Companies and shareholders have a shared responsibility for ensuring that 'comply or explain' remains an effective alternative to a rules-based system. Satisfactory engagement between company boards and investors is therefore crucial to the health of the UK's corporate governance regime. Although engagement has been improving slowly but steadily for many years, practical obstacles necessitate a constant effort to keep the improvement going.

9.   Companies can make a major contribution by spreading governance discussion with shareholders outside the two peak annual reporting periods around 31$^{st}$ December and 31$^{st}$ March and by raising further the general standard of their explanations justifying non-compliance. Shareholders for their part can still do more to satisfy companies that they devote adequate resources and scrutiny to engagement.

10. References to shareholders in this Preamble also apply to intermediaries and agents employed to assist shareholders in scrutinising governance arrangements.

11. This edition of the Code applies to accounting periods beginning on or after 29 June 2008, and takes effect at the same time as new FSA Corporate Governance Rules implementing European requirements relating to audit committees and corporate governance statements. The relevant sections of these Rules are summarised in Schedule C. There is some overlap between the content of the Code and the Rules, and the Rules state that in these areas compliance with the Code will be deemed sufficient also to comply with the Rules. However, where a company chooses to explain rather than comply with the Code it will need to demonstrate that it nonetheless meets the minimum requirements set out in the Rules.

12. The Code itself is subject to periodic reviews by the FRC, the latest of which was conducted in 2007 and was generally reassuring about the Code's content and impact. In the normal course of events the next review will take place in 2010.

Financial Reporting Council
June 2008

# CODE OF BEST PRACTICE

## SECTION 1   COMPANIES

### A.   DIRECTORS

### A.1   The Board

**Main Principle**

**Every company should be headed by an effective board, which is collectively responsible for the success of the company.**

**Supporting Principles**

The board's role is to provide entrepreneurial leadership of the company within a framework of prudent and effective controls which enables risk to be assessed and managed. The board should set the company's strategic aims, ensure that the necessary financial and human resources are in place for the company to meet its objectives and review management performance. The board should set the company's values and standards and ensure that its obligations to its shareholders and others are understood and met.

All directors must take decisions objectively in the interests of the company.

As part of their role as members of a unitary board, non-executive directors should constructively challenge and help develop proposals on strategy. Non-executive directors should scrutinise the performance of management in meeting agreed goals and objectives and monitor the reporting of performance. They should satisfy themselves on the integrity of financial information and that financial controls and systems of risk management are robust and defensible. They are responsible for determining appropriate levels of remuneration of executive directors and have a prime role in appointing, and where necessary removing, executive directors, and in succession planning.

## Code Provisions

A.1.1 The board should meet sufficiently regularly to discharge its duties effectively. There should be a formal schedule of matters specifically reserved for its decision. The annual report should include a statement of how the board operates, including a high level statement of which types of decisions are to be taken by the board and which are to be delegated to management.

A.1.2 The annual report should identify the chairman, the deputy chairman (where there is one), the chief executive, the senior independent director and the chairmen and members of the nomination, audit and remuneration committees. It should also set out the number of meetings of the board and those committees and individual attendance by directors[1].

A.1.3 The chairman should hold meetings with the non-executive directors without the executives present. Led by the senior independent director, the non-executive directors should meet without the chairman present at least annually to appraise the chairman's performance (as described in A.6.1) and on such other occasions as are deemed appropriate.

A.1.4 Where directors have concerns which cannot be resolved about the running of the company or a proposed action, they should ensure that their concerns are recorded in the board minutes. On resignation, a non-executive director should provide a written statement to the chairman, for circulation to the board, if they have any such concerns.

A.1.5 The company should arrange appropriate insurance cover in respect of legal action against its directors.

## A.2   Chairman and chief executive

### Main Principle

**There should be a clear division of responsibilities at the head of the company between the running of the board and the executive responsibility for the running of the company's business. No one individual should have unfettered powers of decision.**

### Supporting Principle

The chairman is responsible for leadership of the board, ensuring its effectiveness on all aspects of its role and setting its agenda. The

---

[1] Provisions A.1.1 and A.1.2 overlap with FSA Rule DTR 7.2.7 R; Provision A.1.2 also overlaps with DTR 7.1.5 R (see Schedule C).

chairman is also responsible for ensuring that the directors receive accurate, timely and clear information. The chairman should ensure effective communication with shareholders. The chairman should also facilitate the effective contribution of non-executive directors in particular and ensure constructive relations between executive and non-executive directors.

## Code Provisions

A.2.1 The roles of chairman and chief executive should not be exercised by the same individual. The division of responsibilities between the chairman and chief executive should be clearly established, set out in writing and agreed by the board.

A.2.2 The chairman should on appointment meet the independence criteria set out in A.3.1 below. A chief executive should not go on to be chairman of the same company. If exceptionally a board decides that a chief executive should become chairman, the board should consult major shareholders in advance and should set out its reasons to shareholders at the time of the appointment and in the next annual report[2].

## A.3 Board balance and independence

### Main Principle

**The board should include a balance of executive and non-executive directors (and in particular independent non-executive directors) such that no individual or small group of individuals can dominate the board's decision taking.**

### Supporting Principles

The board should not be so large as to be unwieldy. The board should be of sufficient size that the balance of skills and experience is appropriate for the requirements of the business and that changes to the board's composition can be managed without undue disruption.

To ensure that power and information are not concentrated in one or two individuals, there should be a strong presence on the board of both executive and non-executive directors.

The value of ensuring that committee membership is refreshed and that undue reliance is not placed on particular individuals should be taken into account in deciding chairmanship and membership of committees.

---

[2] Compliance or otherwise with this provision need only be reported for the year in which the appointment is made

No one other than the committee chairman and members is entitled to be present at a meeting of the nomination, audit or remuneration committee, but others may attend at the invitation of the committee.

**Code provisions**

A.3.1 The board should identify in the annual report each non-executive director it considers to be independent[3]. The board should determine whether the director is independent in character and judgement and whether there are relationships or circumstances which are likely to affect, or could appear to affect, the director's judgement. The board should state its reasons if it determines that a director is independent notwithstanding the existence of relationships or circumstances which may appear relevant to its determination, including if the director:

- has been an employee of the company or group within the last five years;

- has, or has had within the last three years, a material business relationship with the company either directly, or as a partner, shareholder, director or senior employee of a body that has such a relationship with the company;

- has received or receives additional remuneration from the company apart from a director's fee, participates in the company's share option or a performance-related pay scheme, or is a member of the company's pension scheme;

- has close family ties with any of the company's advisers, directors or senior employees;

- holds cross-directorships or has significant links with other directors through involvement in other companies or bodies;

- represents a significant shareholder; or

- has served on the board for more than nine years from the date of their first election.

A.3.2 Except for smaller companies[4], at least half the board, excluding the chairman, should comprise non-executive directors determined by the board to be independent. A smaller company should have at least two independent non-executive directors.

A.3.3 The board should appoint one of the independent non-executive directors to be the senior independent director. The senior independent director should be available to shareholders if they have

---

[3] A.2.2 states that the chairman should, on appointment, meet the independence criteria set out in this provision, but thereafter the test of independence is not appropriate in relation to the chairman.
[4] A smaller company is one that is below the FTSE 350 throughout the year immediately prior to the reporting year.

concerns which contact through the normal channels of chairman, chief executive or finance director has failed to resolve or for which such contact is inappropriate.

## A.4 Appointments to the Board

### Main Principle

**There should be a formal, rigorous and transparent procedure for the appointment of new directors to the board.**

### Supporting Principles

Appointments to the board should be made on merit and against objective criteria. Care should be taken to ensure that appointees have enough time available to devote to the job. This is particularly important in the case of chairmanships.

The board should satisfy itself that plans are in place for orderly succession for appointments to the board and to senior management, so as to maintain an appropriate balance of skills and experience within the company and on the board.

### Code Provisions

A.4.1 There should be a nomination committee which should lead the process for board appointments and make recommendations to the board. A majority of members of the nomination committee should be independent non-executive directors. The chairman or an independent non-executive director should chair the committee, but the chairman should not chair the nomination committee when it is dealing with the appointment of a successor to the chairmanship. The nomination committee should make available[5] its terms of reference, explaining its role and the authority delegated to it by the board.

A.4.2 The nomination committee should evaluate the balance of skills, knowledge and experience on the board and, in the light of this evaluation, prepare a description of the role and capabilities required for a particular appointment.

A.4.3 For the appointment of a chairman, the nomination committee should prepare a job specification, including an assessment of the time commitment expected, recognising the need for availability in the event of crises. A chairman's other significant commitments should be

---

[5] The requirement to make the information available would be met by including the information on a website that is maintained by or on behalf of the company.

disclosed to the board before appointment and included in the annual report. Changes to such commitments should be reported to the board as they arise, and their impact explained in the next annual report.

A.4.4 The terms and conditions of appointment of non-executive directors should be made available for inspection[6]. The letter of appointment should set out the expected time commitment. Non-executive directors should undertake that they will have sufficient time to meet what is expected of them. Their other significant commitments should be disclosed to the board before appointment, with a broad indication of the time involved and the board should be informed of subsequent changes.

A.4.5 The board should not agree to a full time executive director taking on more than one non-executive directorship in a FTSE 100 company nor the chairmanship of such a company.

A.4.6 A separate section of the annual report should describe the work of the nomination committee, including the process it has used in relation to board appointments[7]. An explanation should be given if neither an external search consultancy nor open advertising has been used in the appointment of a chairman or a non-executive director.

## A.5 Information and professional development

**Main Principle**

> **The board should be supplied in a timely manner with information in a form and of a quality appropriate to enable it to discharge its duties. All directors should receive induction on joining the board and should regularly update and refresh their skills and knowledge.**

**Supporting Principles**

The chairman is responsible for ensuring that the directors receive accurate, timely and clear information. Management has an obligation to provide such information but directors should seek clarification or amplification where necessary.

The chairman should ensure that the directors continually update their skills and the knowledge and familiarity with the company required to fulfil their role both on the board and on board committees. The company

---

[6] The terms and conditions of appointment of non-executive directors should be made available for inspection by any person at the company's registered office during normal business hours and at the AGM (for 15 minutes prior to the meeting and during the meeting).
[7] This provision overlaps with FSA Rule DTR 7.2.7 R (see Schedule C).

should provide the necessary resources for developing and updating its directors' knowledge and capabilities.

Under the direction of the chairman, the company secretary's responsibilities include ensuring good information flows within the board and its committees and between senior management and non-executive directors, as well as facilitating induction and assisting with professional development as required.

The company secretary should be responsible for advising the board through the chairman on all governance matters.

## Code Provisions

A.5.1 The chairman should ensure that new directors receive a full, formal and tailored induction on joining the board. As part of this, the company should offer to major shareholders the opportunity to meet a new non-executive director.

A.5.2 The board should ensure that directors, especially non-executive directors, have access to independent professional advice at the company's expense where they judge it necessary to discharge their responsibilities as directors. Committees should be provided with sufficient resources to undertake their duties.

A.5.3 All directors should have access to the advice and services of the company secretary, who is responsible to the board for ensuring that board procedures are complied with. Both the appointment and removal of the company secretary should be a matter for the board as a whole.

## A.6  Performance evaluation

### Main Principle

**The board should undertake a formal and rigorous annual evaluation of its own performance and that of its committees and individual directors.**

### Supporting Principle

Individual evaluation should aim to show whether each director continues to contribute effectively and to demonstrate commitment to the role (including commitment of time for board and committee meetings and any other duties). The chairman should act on the results of the performance evaluation by recognising the strengths and addressing the weaknesses of the board and, where appropriate, proposing new members be appointed to the board or seeking the resignation of directors.

**Code Provision**

A.6.1 The board should state in the annual report how performance evaluation of the board, its committees and its individual directors has been conducted. The non-executive directors, led by the senior independent director, should be responsible for performance evaluation of the chairman, taking into account the views of executive directors.

**A.7    Re-election**

**Main Principle**

**All directors should be submitted for re-election at regular intervals, subject to continued satisfactory performance. The board should ensure planned and progressive refreshing of the board.**

**Code Provisions**

A.7.1 All directors should be subject to election by shareholders at the first annual general meeting after their appointment, and to re-election thereafter at intervals of no more than three years. The names of directors submitted for election or re-election should be accompanied by sufficient biographical details and any other relevant information to enable shareholders to take an informed decision on their election.

A.7.2 Non-executive directors should be appointed for specified terms subject to re-election and to Companies Acts provisions relating to the removal of a director. The board should set out to shareholders in the papers accompanying a resolution to elect a non-executive director why they believe an individual should be elected. The chairman should confirm to shareholders when proposing re-election that, following formal performance evaluation, the individual's performance continues to be effective and to demonstrate commitment to the role. Any term beyond six years (e.g. two three-year terms) for a non-executive director should be subject to particularly rigorous review, and should take into account the need for progressive refreshing of the board. Non-executive directors may serve longer than nine years (e.g. three three-year terms), subject to annual re-election. Serving more than nine years could be relevant to the determination of a non-executive director's independence (as set out in provision A.3.1).

## B.    REMUNERATION

### B.1    The Level and Make-up of Remuneration

**Main Principles**

> Levels of remuneration should be sufficient to attract, retain and motivate directors of the quality required to run the company successfully, but a company should avoid paying more than is necessary for this purpose. A significant proportion of executive directors' remuneration should be structured so as to link rewards to corporate and individual performance.

**Supporting Principle**

> The remuneration committee should judge where to position their company relative to other companies. But they should use such comparisons with caution, in view of the risk of an upward ratchet of remuneration levels with no corresponding improvement in performance. They should also be sensitive to pay and employment conditions elsewhere in the group, especially when determining annual salary increases.

**Code Provisions**

**Remuneration policy**

B.1.1   The performance-related elements of remuneration should form a significant proportion of the total remuneration package of executive directors and should be designed to align their interests with those of shareholders and to give these directors keen incentives to perform at the highest levels. In designing schemes of performance-related remuneration, the remuneration committee should follow the provisions in Schedule A to this Code.

B.1.2   Executive share options should not be offered at a discount save as permitted by the relevant provisions of the Listing Rules.

B.1.3   Levels of remuneration for non-executive directors should reflect the time commitment and responsibilities of the role. Remuneration for non-executive directors should not include share options. If, exceptionally, options are granted, shareholder approval should be sought in advance and any shares acquired by exercise of the options should be held until at least one year after the non-executive director leaves the board. Holding of share options could be relevant to the determination of a non-executive director's independence (as set out in provision A.3.1).

B.1.4 Where a company releases an executive director to serve as a non-executive director elsewhere, the remuneration report[8] should include a statement as to whether or not the director will retain such earnings and, if so, what the remuneration is.

## Service Contracts and Compensation

B.1.5 The remuneration committee should carefully consider what compensation commitments (including pension contributions and all other elements) their directors' terms of appointment would entail in the event of early termination. The aim should be to avoid rewarding poor performance. They should take a robust line on reducing compensation to reflect departing directors' obligations to mitigate loss.

B.1.6 Notice or contract periods should be set at one year or less. If it is necessary to offer longer notice or contract periods to new directors recruited from outside, such periods should reduce to one year or less after the initial period.

## B.2 Procedure

### Main Principle

**There should be a formal and transparent procedure for developing policy on executive remuneration and for fixing the remuneration packages of individual directors. No director should be involved in deciding his or her own remuneration.**

### Supporting Principles

The remuneration committee should consult the chairman and/or chief executive about their proposals relating to the remuneration of other executive directors. The remuneration committee should also be responsible for appointing any consultants in respect of executive director remuneration. Where executive directors or senior management are involved in advising or supporting the remuneration committee, care should be taken to recognise and avoid conflicts of interest.

The chairman of the board should ensure that the company maintains contact as required with its principal shareholders about remuneration in the same way as for other matters.

---

[8] As required under the Directors' Remuneration Report Regulations 2002.

**Code Provisions**

B.2.1 The board should establish a remuneration committee of at least three, or in the case of smaller companies[9] two, independent non-executive directors. In addition the company chairman may also be a member of, but not chair, the committee if he or she was considered independent on appointment as chairman. The remuneration committee should make available[10] its terms of reference, explaining its role and the authority delegated to it by the board. Where remuneration consultants are appointed, a statement should be made available[11] of whether they have any other connection with the company.

B.2.2 The remuneration committee should have delegated responsibility for setting remuneration for all executive directors and the chairman, including pension rights and any compensation payments. The committee should also recommend and monitor the level and structure of remuneration for senior management. The definition of 'senior management' for this purpose should be determined by the board but should normally include the first layer of management below board level.

B.2.3 The board itself or, where required by the Articles of Association, the shareholders should determine the remuneration of the non-executive directors within the limits set in the Articles of Association. Where permitted by the Articles, the board may however delegate this responsibility to a committee, which might include the chief executive.

B.2.4 Shareholders should be invited specifically to approve all new long-term incentive schemes (as defined in the Listing Rules) and significant changes to existing schemes, save in the circumstances permitted by the Listing Rules.

---

[9] See footnote 4.
[10] This provision overlaps with FSA Rule DTR 7.2.7 R (see Schedule C).
[11] See footnote 5.

## C. ACCOUNTABILITY AND AUDIT

### C.1 Financial Reporting

**Main Principle**

**The board should present a balanced and understandable assessment of the company's position and prospects.**

**Supporting Principle**

The board's responsibility to present a balanced and understandable assessment extends to interim and other price-sensitive public reports and reports to regulators as well as to information required to be presented by statutory requirements.

**Code Provisions**

C.1.1 The directors should explain in the annual report their responsibility for preparing the accounts and there should be a statement by the auditors about their reporting responsibilities.

C.1.2 The directors should report that the business is a going concern, with supporting assumptions or qualifications as necessary.

### C.2 Internal Control[12]

**Main Principle**

**The board should maintain a sound system of internal control to safeguard shareholders' investment and the company's assets.**

**Code Provision**

C.2.1 The board should, at least annually, conduct a review of the effectiveness of the group's system of internal controls and should report to shareholders that they have done so[13]. The review should cover all material controls, including financial, operational and compliance controls and risk management systems.

---

[12] The Turnbull guidance suggests means of applying this part of the Code. Copies are available at www.frc.org.uk/corporate/internalcontrol.cfm

[13] In addition FSA Rule DTR 7.2.5 R requires companies to describe the main features of the internal control and risk management systems in relation to the financial reporting process (see Schedule C).

## C.3    Audit Committee and Auditors[14]

### Main Principle

**The board should establish formal and transparent arrangements for considering how they should apply the financial reporting and internal control principles and for maintaining an appropriate relationship with the company's auditors.**

### Code provisions

C.3.1    The board should establish an audit committee of at least three, or in the case of smaller companies[15] two, independent non-executive directors. In smaller companies the company chairman may be a member of, but not chair, the committee in addition to the independent non-executive directors, provided he or she was considered independent on appointment as chairman. The board should satisfy itself that at least one member of the audit committee has recent and relevant financial experience[16].

C.3.2    The main role and responsibilities of the audit committee should be set out in written terms of reference and should include[17]:

- to monitor the integrity of the financial statements of the company, and any formal announcements relating to the company's financial performance, reviewing significant financial reporting judgements contained in them;

- to review the company's internal financial controls and, unless expressly addressed by a separate board risk committee composed of independent directors, or by the board itself, to review the company's internal control and risk management systems;

- to monitor and review the effectiveness of the company's internal audit function;

- to make recommendations to the board, for it to put to the shareholders for their approval in general meeting, in relation to the appointment, re-appointment and removal of the external auditor and to approve the remuneration and terms of engagement of the external auditor;

- to review and monitor the external auditor's independence and objectivity and the effectiveness of the audit process, taking into consideration relevant UK professional and regulatory requirements;

---

[14] The Smith guidance suggests means of applying this part of the Code. Copies are available at www.frc.org.uk/corporate/auditcommittees.cfm

[15] See footnote 4.

[16] This provision overlaps with FSA Rule DTR 7.1.1 R (see Schedule C).

[17] This provision overlaps with FSA Rules DTR 7.1.3 R (see Schedule C).

- to develop and implement policy on the engagement of the external auditor to supply non-audit services, taking into account relevant ethical guidance regarding the provision of non-audit services by the external audit firm; and to report to the board, identifying any matters in respect of which it considers that action or improvement is needed and making recommendations as to the steps to be taken.

C.3.3 The terms of reference of the audit committee, including its role and the authority delegated to it by the board, should be made available[18]. A separate section of the annual report should describe the work of the committee in discharging those responsibilities[19].

C.3.4 The audit committee should review arrangements by which staff of the company may, in confidence, raise concerns about possible improprieties in matters of financial reporting or other matters. The audit committee's objective should be to ensure that arrangements are in place for the proportionate and independent investigation of such matters and for appropriate follow-up action.

C.3.5 The audit committee should monitor and review the effectiveness of the internal audit activities. Where there is no internal audit function, the audit committee should consider annually whether there is a need for an internal audit function and make a recommendation to the board, and the reasons for the absence of such a function should be explained in the relevant section of the annual report.

C.3.6 The audit committee should have primary responsibility for making a recommendation on the appointment, reappointment and removal of the external auditors. If the board does not accept the audit committee's recommendation, it should include in the annual report, and in any papers recommending appointment or re-appointment, a statement from the audit committee explaining the recommendation and should set out reasons why the board has taken a different position.

C.3.7 The annual report should explain to shareholders how, if the auditor provides non-audit services, auditor objectivity and independence is safeguarded.

---

[18] See footnote 5.
[19] This provision overlaps with FSA Rules DTR 7.1.5 R and 7.2.7 R (see Schedule C).

## D.    RELATIONS WITH SHAREHOLDERS

## D.1    Dialogue with Institutional Shareholders

### Main Principle

**There should be a dialogue with shareholders based on the mutual understanding of objectives. The board as a whole has responsibility for ensuring that a satisfactory dialogue with shareholders takes place[20].**

### Supporting Principles

Whilst recognising that most shareholder contact is with the chief executive and finance director, the chairman (and the senior independent director and other directors as appropriate) should maintain sufficient contact with major shareholders to understand their issues and concerns.

The board should keep in touch with shareholder opinion in whatever ways are most practical and efficient.

### Code Provisions

D.1.1 The chairman should ensure that the views of shareholders are communicated to the board as a whole. The chairman should discuss governance and strategy with major shareholders. Non-executive directors should be offered the opportunity to attend meetings with major shareholders and should expect to attend them if requested by major shareholders. The senior independent director should attend sufficient meetings with a range of major shareholders to listen to their views in order to help develop a balanced understanding of the issues and concerns of major shareholders.

D.1.2 The board should state in the annual report the steps they have taken to ensure that the members of the board, and in particular the non-executive directors, develop an understanding of the views of major shareholders about their company, for example through direct face-to-face contact, analysts' or brokers' briefings and surveys of shareholder opinion.

---

[20] Nothing in these principles or provisions should be taken to override the general requirements of law to treat shareholders equally in access to information.

### D.2    Constructive Use of the AGM

**Main Principle**

**The board should use the AGM to communicate with investors and to encourage their participation.**

**Code Provisions**

D.2.1 At any general meeting, the company should propose a separate resolution on each substantially separate issue, and should in particular propose a resolution at the AGM relating to the report and accounts. For each resolution, proxy appointment forms should provide shareholders with the option to direct their proxy to vote either for or against the resolution or to withhold their vote. The proxy form and any announcement of the results of a vote should make it clear that a 'vote withheld' is not a vote in law and will not be counted in the calculation of the proportion of the votes for and against the resolution.

D.2.2 The company should ensure that all valid proxy appointments received for general meetings are properly recorded and counted. For each resolution, after a vote has been taken, except where taken on a poll, the company should ensure that the following information is given at the meeting and made available as soon as reasonably practicable on a website which is maintained by or on behalf of the company:

- the number of shares in respect of which proxy appointments have been validly made;
- the number of votes for the resolution;
- the number of votes against the resolution; and
- the number of shares in respect of which the vote was directed to be withheld.

D.2.3 The chairman should arrange for the chairmen of the audit, remuneration and nomination committees to be available to answer questions at the AGM and for all directors to attend.

D.2.4 The company should arrange for the Notice of the AGM and related papers to be sent to shareholders at least 20 working days before the meeting.

# SECTION 2   INSTITUTIONAL SHAREHOLDERS

## E.   INSTITUTIONAL SHAREHOLDERS[21]

### E.1   Dialogue with companies

**Main Principle**

**Institutional shareholders should enter into a dialogue with companies based on the mutual understanding of objectives.**

**Supporting Principles**

Institutional shareholders should apply the principles set out in the Institutional Shareholders' Committee's "The Responsibilities of Institutional Shareholders and Agents – Statement of Principles"[22], which should be reflected in fund manager contracts.

### E.2   Evaluation of Governance Disclosures

**Main Principle**

When evaluating companies' governance arrangements, particularly those relating to board structure and composition, institutional shareholders should give due weight to all relevant factors drawn to their attention.

**Supporting Principle**

Institutional shareholders should consider carefully explanations given for departure from this Code and make reasoned judgements in each case. They should give an explanation to the company, in writing where appropriate, and be prepared to enter a dialogue if they do not accept the company's position. They should avoid a box-ticking approach to assessing a company's corporate governance. They should bear in mind in particular the size and complexity of the company and the nature of the risks and challenges it faces.

---

[21] Agents such as investment managers, or voting services, are frequently appointed by institutional shareholders to act on their behalf and these principles should accordingly be read as applying where appropriate to the agents of institutional shareholders.

[22] Available at www.institutionalshareholderscommittee.co.uk.

### E.3    Shareholder Voting

### Main Principle

**Institutional shareholders have a responsibility to make considered use of their votes.**

### Supporting Principles

Institutional shareholders should take steps to ensure their voting intentions are being translated into practice.

Institutional shareholders should, on request, make available to their clients information on the proportion of resolutions on which votes were cast and non-discretionary proxies lodged.

Major shareholders should attend AGMs where appropriate and practicable. Companies and registrars should facilitate this.

## Schedule A: Provisions on the design of performance related remuneration

1.  The remuneration committee should consider whether the directors should be eligible for annual bonuses. If so, performance conditions should be relevant, stretching and designed to enhance shareholder value. Upper limits should be set and disclosed. There may be a case for part payment in shares to be held for a significant period.

2.  The remuneration committee should consider whether the directors should be eligible for benefits under long-term incentive schemes. Traditional share option schemes should be weighed against other kinds of long-term incentive scheme. In normal circumstances, shares granted or other forms of deferred remuneration should not vest, and options should not be exercisable, in less than three years. Directors should be encouraged to hold their shares for a further period after vesting or exercise, subject to the need to finance any costs of acquisition and associated tax liabilities.

3.  Any new long-term incentive schemes which are proposed should be approved by shareholders and should preferably replace any existing schemes or at least form part of a well considered overall plan, incorporating existing schemes. The total rewards potentially available should not be excessive.

4.  Payouts or grants under all incentive schemes, including new grants under existing share option schemes, should be subject to challenging performance criteria reflecting the company's objectives. Consideration should be given to criteria which reflect the company's performance relative to a group of comparator companies in some key variables such as total shareholder return.

5.  Grants under executive share option and other long-term incentive schemes should normally be phased rather than awarded in one large block.

6.  In general, only basic salary should be pensionable.

7.  The remuneration committee should consider the pension consequences and associated costs to the company of basic salary increases and any other changes in pensionable remuneration, especially for directors close to retirement.

## Schedule B: Guidance on liability of non-executive directors: care, skill and diligence

1. Although non-executive directors and executive directors have as board members the same legal duties and objectives, the time devoted to the company's affairs is likely to be significantly less for a non-executive director than for an executive director and the detailed knowledge and experience of a company's affairs that could reasonably be expected of a non-executive director will generally be less than for an executive director. These matters may be relevant in assessing the knowledge, skill and experience which may reasonably be expected of a non-executive director and therefore the care, skill and diligence that a non-executive director may be expected to exercise.

2. In this context, the following elements of the Code may also be particularly relevant.

   (i) In order to enable directors to fulfil their duties, the Code states that:

   - The letter of appointment of the director should set out the expected time commitment (Code provision A.4.4); and

   - The board should be supplied in a timely manner with information in a form and of a quality appropriate to enable it to discharge its duties. The chairman is responsible for ensuring that the directors are provided by management with accurate, timely and clear information. (Code principle A.5).

   (ii) Non-executive directors should themselves:

   - Undertake appropriate induction and regularly update and refresh their skills, knowledge and familiarity with the company (Code principle A.5 and provision A.5.1)

   - Seek appropriate clarification or amplification of information and, where necessary, take and follow appropriate professional advice. (Code principle A.5 and provision A.5.2)

   - Where they have concerns about the running of the company or a proposed action, ensure that these are addressed by the board and, to the extent that they are not resolved, ensure that they are recorded in the board minutes (Code provision A.1.4).

   - Give a statement to the board if they have such unresolved concerns on resignation (Code provision A.1.4)

3. It is up to each non-executive director to reach a view as to what is necessary in particular circumstances to comply with the duty of care, skill and diligence they owe as a director to the company. In considering whether or not a person is in breach of that duty, a court would take into account all relevant circumstances. These may include having regard to the above where relevant to the issue of liability of a non-executive director.

## Schedule C: Disclosure of Corporate Governance Arrangements

Corporate governance disclosure requirements are set out in three places:

- FSA Listing Rule 9.8.6 (which includes the 'comply or explain' requirement);

- FSA Disclosure and Transparency Rules Sections 7.1 and 7.2 (which set out certain mandatory disclosures); and

- The Combined Code (in addition to providing an explanation where they choose not to comply with a provision, companies must disclose specified information in order to comply with certain provisions).

These requirements are summarised below. The full text of Listing Rule 9.8.6 and Disclosure and Transparency Rules 7.1 and 7.2 are contained in the Listing, Prospectus and Disclosure section of the FSA Handbook, which can be found at http://fsahandbook.info/FSA/html/handbook/.

There is some overlap between the mandatory disclosures required under the Disclosure and Transparency Rules and those expected under the Combined Code. Areas of overlap are summarised in the Appendix to this Schedule. In respect of disclosures relating to the audit committee and the composition and operation of the board and its committees, compliance with the relevant provisions of the Code will result in compliance with the relevant Rules.

**Listing Rules**

Paragraph 9.8.6 R of the Listing Rules states that in the case of a listed company incorporated in the United Kingdom, the following items must be included in its annual report and accounts:

- a statement of how the listed company has applied the Main Principles set out in Section 1 of the Combined Code, in a manner that would enable shareholders to evaluate how the principles have been applied;

- a statement as to whether the listed company has:

  - complied throughout the accounting period with all relevant provisions set out in Section 1 of the Combined Code; or

  - not complied throughout the accounting period with all relevant provisions set out in Section 1 of the Combined Code and if so, setting out:

    (i) those provisions, if any, it has not complied with;

(ii) in the case of provisions whose requirements are of a continuing nature, the period within which, if any, it did not comply with some or all of those provisions; and

(iii) the company's reasons for non-compliance.

**Disclosure and Transparency Rules**

Section 7.1 of the Disclosure and Transparency Rules concerns <u>audit committees or bodies carrying out equivalent functions</u>.

DTR 7.1.1 R to 7.1.3 R sets out requirements relating to the composition and functions of the committee or equivalent body:

- DTR 7.1.1 R states that an issuer must have a body which is responsible for performing the functions set out in DTR 7.1.3 R, and that at least one member of that body must be independent and at least one member must have competence in accounting and/or auditing.

- DTR 7.1.2 G states that the requirements for independence and competence in accounting and/or auditing may be satisfied by the same member or by different members of the relevant body.

- DTR 7.1.3 R states that an issuer must ensure that, as a minimum, the relevant body must:

  (1) monitor the financial reporting process;

  (2) monitor the effectiveness of the issuer's internal control, internal audit where applicable, and risk management systems;

  (3) monitor the statutory audit of the annual and consolidated accounts;

  (4) review and monitor the independence of the statutory auditor, and in particular the provision of additional services to the issuer.

DTR 7.1.5 R to 7.1.7 R explain what disclosure is required:

- DTR 7.1.5 R states that the issuer must make a statement available to the public disclosing which body carries out the functions required by DTR 7.1.3 R and how it is composed.

- DTR 7.1.6 G states that this can be included in the corporate governance statement required under DTR 7.2 (see below).

- DTR 7.1.7 R states that compliance with the relevant provisions of the Combined Code (as set out in the Appendix to this Schedule) will result in compliance with DTR 7.1.1 R to 7.1.5 R.

Section 7.2 concerns <u>corporate governance statements</u>. Issuers are required to produce a corporate governance statement that must be either included in the directors' report (DTR 7.2.1 R); or in a separate report published together with the annual report; or on the issuer's website, in which case there must be a cross-reference in the directors' report (DTR 7.2.9 R).

DTR 7.2.2 R requires that the corporate governance statements must contain a reference to the corporate governance code to which the company is subject (for listed companies incorporated in the UK this is the Combined Code). DTR 7.2.3 R requires that, to the extent that it departs from that code, the company must explain which parts of the code it departs from and the reasons for doing so. DTR 7.2.4 G states that compliance with LR 9.8.6R (6) (the 'comply or explain' rule in relation to the Combined Code) will also satisfy these requirements.

DTR 7.2.5 R to 7.2.7 R and DTR 7.2.10 R set out certain information that must be disclosed in the corporate governance statement:

- DTR 7.2.5 R states that the corporate governance statement must contain a description of the main features of the company's internal control and risk management systems in relation to the financial reporting process. DTR 7.2.10 R states that an issuer which is required to prepare a group directors' report within the meaning of Section 415(2) of the Companies Act 2006 must include in that report a description of the main features of the group's internal control and risk management systems in relation to the process for preparing consolidated accounts.

- DTR 7.2.6 R states that the corporate governance statement must contain the information required by paragraph 13(2)(c), (d), (f), (h) and (i) of Schedule 7 to the Large and Medium-sized Companies and Groups (Accounts and Reports) Regulations 2008 (SI 2008/410) where the issuer is subject to the requirements of that paragraph.

- DTR 7.2.7 R states that the corporate governance statement must contain a description of the composition and operation of the issuer's administrative, management and supervisory bodies and their committees. DTR 7.2.8 G states that compliance with the relevant provisions of the Combined Code (as set out in the Appendix to this Schedule) will satisfy the requirements of DTR 7.2.7 R.

**The Combined Code**

In addition the Code includes specific requirements for disclosure which are set out below:

The <u>annual report should record</u>:

- a statement of how the board operates, including a high level statement of which types of decisions are to be taken by the board and which are to be delegated to management (A.1.1);

- the names of the chairman, the deputy chairman (where there is one), the chief executive, the senior independent director and the chairmen and members of the nomination, audit and remuneration committees (A.1.2);

- the number of meetings of the board and those committees and individual attendance by directors (A.1.2);

- the names of the non-executive directors whom the board determines to be independent, with reasons where necessary (A.3.1);

- the other significant commitments of the chairman and any changes to them during the year (A.4.3);

- how performance evaluation of the board, its committees and its directors has been conducted (A.6.1);

- the steps the board has taken to ensure that members of the board, and in particular the non-executive directors, develop an understanding of the views of major shareholders about their company (D.1.2).

The <u>annual report should also include</u>:

- a separate section describing the work of the nomination committee, including the process it has used in relation to board appointments and an explanation if neither external search consultancy nor open advertising has been used in the appointment of a chairman or a non-executive director (A.4.6);

- a description of the work of the remuneration committee as required under the Directors' Remuneration Report Regulations 2002, and including, where an executive director serves as a non-executive director elsewhere, whether or not the director will retain such earnings and, if so, what the remuneration is (B.1.4);

- an explanation from the directors of their responsibility for preparing the accounts and a statement by the auditors about their reporting responsibilities (C.1.1);

- a statement from the directors that the business is a going concern, with supporting assumptions or qualifications as necessary (C.1.2);

- a report that the board has conducted a review of the effectiveness of the group's system of internal controls (C.2.1);

- a separate section describing the work of the audit committee in discharging its responsibilities (C.3.3);

- where there is no internal audit function, the reasons for the absence of such a function (C.3.5);

- where the board does not accept the audit committee's recommendation on the appointment, reappointment or removal of an external auditor, a statement from the audit committee explaining the recommendation and the reasons why the board has taken a different position (C.3.6); and

- an explanation of how, if the auditor provides non-audit services, auditor objectivity and independence is safeguarded (C.3.7).

The following information should be made available (which may be met by placing the information on a website that is maintained by or on behalf of the company):

- the terms of reference of the nomination, remuneration and audit committees, explaining their role and the authority delegated to them by the board (A.4.1, B.2.1 and C.3.3);

- the terms and conditions of appointment of non-executive directors (A.4.4) (see footnote 8 on page 10); and

- where remuneration consultants are appointed, a statement of whether they have any other connection with the company (B.2.1).

The board should set out to shareholders in the papers accompanying a resolution to elect or re-elect directors:

- sufficient biographical details to enable shareholders to take an informed decision on their election or re-election (A.7.1);

- why they believe an individual should be elected to a non-executive role (A.7.2); and

- on re-election of a non-executive director, confirmation from the chairman that, following formal performance evaluation, the individual's performance continues to be effective and to demonstrate commitment to the role, including commitment of time for board and committee meetings and any other duties (A.7.2).

The board should <u>set out to shareholders in the papers recommending appointment or reappointment of an external auditor:</u>

- if the board does not accept the audit committee's recommendation, a statement from the audit committee explaining the recommendation and from the board setting out reasons why they have taken a different position (C.3.6).

**Additional guidance**

The Turnbull Guidance and Smith Guidance contain further suggestions as to information that might usefully be disclosed in the internal control statement and the report of the audit committee respectively. Both sets of guidance are available on the FRC website at http://www.frc.org.uk/corporate/.

## OVERLAP BETWEEN THE DISCLOSURE AND TRANSPARENCY RULES AND THE COMBINED CODE

| DISCLOSURE AND TRANSPARENCY RULES | COMBINED CODE |
|---|---|
| **D.T.R 7.1.1 R**<br><br>Sets out minimum requirements on composition of the audit committee or equivalent body. | **Provision C.3.1**<br><br>Sets out recommended composition of the audit committee. |
| **D.T.R 7.1.3 R**<br><br>Sets out minimum functions of the audit committee or equivalent body. | **Provision C.3.2**<br><br>Sets out the recommended minimum terms of reference for the committee. |
| **D.T.R 7.1.5 R**<br><br>The composition and function of the audit committee or equivalent body must be disclosed in the annual report<br><br>*DTR 7.1.7 R states that compliance with Code provisions A.1.2, C.3.1, C.3.2 and C.3.3 will result in compliance with DTR 7.1.1 R to DTR 7.1.5 R.* | **Provision A.1.2:**<br><br>The annual report should identify members of the board committees.<br><br>**Provision C.3.3**<br><br>The annual report should describe the work of the audit committee. Further recommendations on the content of the audit committee report are set out in the Smith Guidance |
| **D.T.R 7.2.5 R**<br><br>The corporate governance statement must include a description of the main features of the company's internal control and risk management systems in relation to the financial reporting process.<br><br>*While this requirement differs from the requirement in the Combined Code, it is envisaged that both could be met by a single internal control statement.* | **Provision C.2.1**<br><br>The Board must report that a review of the effectiveness of the internal control system has been carried out. Further recommendations on the content of the internal control statement are set out in the Turnbull Guidance. |

**DTR 7.2.7 R**

The corporate governance statement must include a description of the composition and operation of the administrative, management and supervisory bodies and their committees.

*DTR 7.2.8 R states that compliance with Code provisions A.1.1, A.1.2, A.4.6, B.2.1 and C.3.3 with result in compliance with DTR 7.2.7 R.*

This requirement overlaps with a number of different provisions of the Code:

**A.1.1**: the annual report should include a statement of how the board operates.

**A.1.2**: the annual report should identify members of the board and board committees.

**A.4.6**: the annual report should describe the work of the nomination committee.

**B.2.1**: a description of the work of the remuneration committee should be made available. [Note: in order to comply with DTR 7.2.7 R this information will need to be included in the corporate governance statement].

**C.3.3**: the annual report should describe the work of the audit committee.

FINANCIAL REPORTING COUNCIL
5TH FLOOR
ALDWYCH HOUSE
71-91 ALDWYCH
LONDON WC2B 4HN
TEL: +44 (0)20 7492 2300
FAX: +44 (0)20 7492 2301
WEBSITE: www.frc.org.uk

ISBN 978-1-84798-077-9

9 781847 980779

UP/FRC-B18016

# INDEX

# Index